STO

S0-BWT-585

Your Source for Business Information that Works

Millions of businesspeople use Hoover's Online every day for research, analysis, and prospecting. Hoover's updates information daily on thousands of companies and hundreds of industries worldwide.

USE HOOVER'S ONLINE FOR:

- **COMPANY RESEARCH**
  Overview
  History
  Competitors
  News
  Products
  Location(s)
  Financials
  Stock data

- **INDUSTRY RESEARCH**
  Quick synopsis
  Leading companies
  Analysis of trends
  Associations
  Glossary of terms
  Research reports

- **PROSPECTING**
  Search by industry,
  location, sales, keyword
  Full officer lists
  Company history
  Financials

You simply can't find more information on corporate America in any other single source." —*Business Week*

For accurate online business information, visit us at www.hoovers.com

Hoover's Handbook of Private Companies

2003

BUSINESS PRESS

Austin, Texas

Hoover's Handbook of Private Companies 2003 is intended to provide readers with accurate and authoritative information about the enterprises covered in it. Hoover's asked all companies and organizations profiled to provide information. Many did so; some did not. The information contained herein is as accurate as we could reasonably make it. In many cases we have relied on third-party material that we believe to be trustworthy, but were unable to independently verify. We do not warrant that the book is absolutely accurate or without error. Readers should not rely on any information contained herein in instances where such reliance might cause loss or damage. The publisher, the editors, and their data suppliers specifically disclaim all warranties, including the implied warranties of merchantability and fitness for a specific purpose. This book is sold with the understanding that neither the publisher, the editors, nor any content contributors are engaged in providing investment, financial, accounting, legal, or other professional advice.

The financial data in this book are from the companies profiled or from trade sources deemed to be reliable. Hoover's, Inc., is solely responsible for the presentation of all data.

Many of the names of products and services mentioned in this book are the trademarks or service marks of the companies manufacturing or selling them and are subject to protection under US law. Space has not permitted us to indicate which names are subject to such protection, and readers are advised to consult with the owners of such marks regarding their use. Hoover's is a trademark of Hoover's, Inc.

BUSINESS PRESS

10 9 8 7 6 5 4 3 2 1

Publishers Cataloging-in-Publication Data

Hoover's Handbook of Private Companies 2003

Includes indexes.

1. Business enterprises — Directories. 2. Corporations — Directories.

HF3010 338.7

Hoover's Company Information is also available on America Online, Bloomberg Financial Network, Factiva, LexisNexis, and on the Internet at Hoover's Online (www.hoovers.com), FORTUNE (www.fortune.com), MSN Money (www.moneycentral.com), NewsEdge (www.newsedge.com), ProQuest (www.proquest.com), The Washington Post (www.washingtonpost.com), Yahoo! (www.yahoo.com), and other Web sites.

A catalog of Hoover's products is available on the World Wide Web at www.hooversbooks.com.

ISBN 1-57311-084-1

ISSN 1073-6433

The Hoover's Handbook series is edited by George Sutton and produced for Hoover's Business Press by Sycamore Productions, Inc., Austin, Texas, using Quark, Inc.'s QuarkXPress 4.04; EM Software, Inc.'s Xtags 4.1; and fonts from Adobe's Clearface and Myriad families. Cover design is by Shawn Harrington. Electronic prepress and printing were done by Edwards Brothers Incorporated, Ann Arbor, Michigan. Text paper is 50# Arbor.

US AND WORLD DIRECT SALES
Hoover's, Inc.
5800 Airport Blvd.
Austin, TX 78752
Phone: 512-374-4500
Fax: 512-374-4538
e-mail: orders@hoovers.com

EUROPE
William Snyder Publishing Associates
5 Five Mile Drive
Oxford OX2 8HT
England
Phone & fax: +44-186-551-3186
e-mail: snyderpub@aol.com

HOOVER'S, INC.

Founder: Gary Hoover
Chairman, President and CEO: Jeffrey R. Tarr
EVP, Corporate Strategy and Development: Carl G. Shepherd
EVP, Marketing: Russell Secker
SVP and CFO: Lynn Atchison

EDITORIAL

VP and Managing Editor: Nancy Regent
Assistant Managing Editor: Valerie Pearcy
Senior Editors: Rachel Brush, Margaret Claughton, Paul Geary
Kathleen Kelly, Dennis Sutton, Tom Ziegler
Senior Editor, Financials: Dennis Sutton
Research Manager: Amy Degner
Editors: Joy Aiken, Sally Alt, Linnea Anderson, Alex Biesada, Larry Bills, Angela Boeckman,
Joe Bramhall, Travis Brown, James Bryant, Ryan Caione, Jason Cella, Elizabeth Cornell,
Jason Cother, Danny Cummings, Lesley Dings, Michaela Drapes, Bobby Duncan, Alison Ehlig,
Carrie Geis, Allan Gill, Joe Grey, David Hamerly, Stuart Hampton, Jeanette Herman, Guy Holland,
Andreas Knutsen, Jay Koenig, Julie Krippel, Anne Law, Diane Lee, Josh Lower, John MacAyeal,
Michael McLellan, Barbara Murray, Nell Newton, Anna Porlas, Jennifer Powers, David Ramirez,
Rob Reynolds, Kcevin Rob, Melanie Robertson, Matt Saucedo, Amy Schein, Seth Shafer,
Joe Simonetta, Daysha Taylor, Vanita Trippe, Tim Walker, Josh Wardrip, Randy Williams,
David Woodruff
Financial Editors: Adi Anand, Troy Bryant, John Flynn, Chris Huston, Joel Sensat, Matthew Taylor
Editorial Projects Manager: Audra Martin
QC Editors: Anthony Staats, John Willis
Chief Copyeditor: Emily Domaschk
Research Coordinator: Jim Harris
Library Coordinator: Kris Stephenson
Library Assistant: Makiko Schwartz

HOOVER'S BUSINESS PRESS

Director, Hoover's Business Press: Dana Smith
Distribution Manager: Rhonda Mitchell
Fulfillment and Shipping Manager: Michael Febonio
Order Processing Clerk: James H. Taylor IV
Shipping Clerk: Paul Olvera

ABOUT HOOVER'S, INC. – THE BUSINESS INFORMATION AUTHORITY™

Hoover's, Inc. (NASDAQ: HOOV) is a leading provider of business information. Hoover's publishes authoritative information on public and private companies worldwide, and provides industry and market intelligence that helps sales, marketing, and business development professionals and senior-level executives get the global intelligence they need to grow their businesses. This information, along with advanced searching tools, is available through Hoover's Online (www.hoovers.com), the company's premier online service. Hoover's business information is also available through corporate intranets and distribution agreements with licensees, as well as via print and CD-ROM products from Hoover's Business Press.

Abbreviations

AFL-CIO – American Federation of Labor and Congress of Industrial Organizations
AMA – American Medical Association
AMEX – American Stock Exchange
ARM – adjustable-rate mortgage
ASP – application services provider
ATM – asynchronous transfer mode
ATM – automated teller machine
CAD/CAM – computer-aided design/ computer-aided manufacturing
CD-ROM – compact disc – read-only memory
CD-R – CD-recordable
CEO – chief executive officer
CFO – chief financial officer
CMOS – complementary metal-oxide semiconductor
COO – chief operating officer
DAT – digital audiotape
DOD – Department of Defense
DOE – Department of Energy
DOS – disc operating system
DOT – Department of Transportation
DRAM – dynamic random access memory
DVD – digital versatile disk/digital videodisk
DVD-R – DVD-recordable
EPA – Environmental Protection Agency
EPROM – erasable programmable read-only memory
EPS – earnings per share
ESOP – employee stock ownership plan
EU – European Union
EVP – executive vice president
FCC – Federal Communications Commission
FDA – Food and Drug Administration
FDIC – Federal Deposit Insurance Corporation
FTC – Federal Trade Commission
FTP – file transfer protocol
GATT – General Agreement on Tariffs and Trade
GDP – gross domestic product
HMO – health maintenance organization
HR – human resources
HTML – hypertext markup language
ICC – Interstate Commerce Commission
IPO – initial public offering
IRS – Internal Revenue Service
ISP – Internet service provider
kWh – kilowatt-hour
LAN – local-area network
LBO – leveraged buyout

LCD – liquid crystal display
LNG – liquefied natural gas
LP – limited partnership
Ltd. – limited
mips – millions of instructions per second
MW – megawatt
NAFTA – North American Free Trade Agreement
NASA – National Aeronautics and Space Administration
NASDAQ – National Association of Securities Dealers Automated Quotations
NATO – North Atlantic Treaty Organization
NYSE – New York Stock Exchange
OCR – optical character recognition
OECD – Organization for Economic Cooperation and Development
OEM – original equipment manufacturer
OPEC – Organization of Petroleum Exporting Countries
OS – operating system
OSHA – Occupational Safety and Health Administration
OTC – over-the-counter
PBX – private branch exchange
PCMCIA – Personal Computer Memory Card International Association
P/E – price-to-earnings ratio
RAM – random access memory
R&D – research and development
RBOC – regional Bell operating company
RISC – reduced instruction set computer
REIT – real estate investment trust
ROA – return on assets
ROE – return on equity
ROI – return on investment
ROM – read-only memory
S&L – savings and loan
SEC – Securities and Exchange Commission
SEVP – senior executive vice president
SIC – Standard Industrial Classification
SOC – system on a chip
SVP – senior vice president
USB – universal serial bus
VAR – value-added reseller
VAT – value-added tax
VC – venture capitalist
VoIP – Voice over Internet Protocol
VP – vice president
WAN – wide-area network
WWW – World Wide Web

Contents

ABOUT *HOOVER'S HANDBOOK* OF *PRIVATE COMPANIES 2003*

Privately held enterprises are major players in the US economy (giant food processor Cargill or insurer State Farm, for example), and because our mission with this volume is to fill the information gap that exists around some private enterprises, we have increased our coverage significantly this year — from a total of 750 companies to 900 companies.

Publishing current, relevant information about these companies can be a challenge, as many of them see secrecy as a competitive strategy, but in this eighth edition of *Hoover's Handbook of Private Companies*, we have compiled the hard-to-find facts on 900 of the largest and most influential enterprises in the US.

This book contains two-page, in-depth profiles on 200 of these enterprises, mostly larger companies, but we've included several smaller but equally interesting ones as well. In addition, we provide basic information, including officers, sales, and top competitors for 700 other major private enterprises with revenue of $590 million or more. We believe no other guide provides the comprehensive information contained in *Hoover's Handbook of Private Companies 2003*.

If you are interested in finding out more about other companies, we encourage you to visit Hoover's Online (www.hoovers.com), which provides coverage of some 12 million business enterprises. Our goal with our Web site is to provide one location that addresses all the needs of business professionals. Hoover's has partnered with other prestigious business information and service providers to bring you all the right business information, services, and links in one place. Additionally, Hoover's Company Information is available on other sites on the Internet, including The Washington Post, LexisNexis, and online services Bloomberg Financial Network, Factiva, and America Online.

Hoover's Handbook of Private Companies is one of a four-title series that is available as an indexed set. The other three titles are *Hoover's Handbook of American Business* (in two volumes), *Hoover's Handbook of World Business,* and *Hoover's Handbook of Emerging Companies*.

We believe anyone who buys from, sells to, invests in, lends to, competes with, interviews with, or works for a company should know about that enterprise. This book and our other Hoover's products and resources represent the most complete source of basic corporate information readily available to the general public.

This book consists of five sections:

1. Using the Profiles describes the contents of our profiles and explains the ways in which we gather and compile our data.

2. A List-Lover's Compendium contains lists of the largest private companies. The lists are based on the information in our profiles, or compiled from well-known sources.

3. Profiles of 200 major private enterprises, arranged alphabetically, make up the major portion of the book.

4. Capsule summaries of 700 other major private companies, arranged alphabetically, follow the profiles.

5. Four indexes complete the book. The companies are indexed by company name, industry group, and headquarters location, and there is a main index of all the brand names, companies, and people mentioned in the book.

We hope you find our books useful. We invite your comments by phone (512-374-4500), fax (512-374-4538), mail (5800 Airport Blvd., Austin, TX 78752), or e-mail (comments@hoovers.com).

The Editors
Austin, Texas
January 2003

USING THE PROFILES

COMPANIES PROFILED

The 200 enterprises profiled in this book include the largest and most influential private enterprises in America. Among them are:

- private companies, from the giants (Cargill and Koch) to the colorful and prominent (King Ranch and Calvin Klein)
- mutuals and cooperative organizations owned by their customers (State Farm Insurance, Ace Hardware, Ocean Spray Cranberries)
- not-for-profits (American Red Cross, Kaiser Foundation Health Plan, Smithsonian Institution)
- joint ventures (Motiva Enterprises, Dow Corning)
- partnerships (Baker & McKenzie, Kohlberg Kravis Roberts & Co.)
- universities (Columbia, Harvard, University of California)
- government-owned corporations (US Postal Service, New York City's Metropolitan Transportation Authority)
- and a selection of other enterprises (National Basketball Association, AFL-CIO, Texas Lottery Commission).

ORGANIZATION

The profiles are presented in alphabetical order. We have shown the full legal name of the enterprise at the top of the page, unless it is too long, in which case you will find it above the address in the Where section of the profile. If a company name is also a person's name, such as Edward J. DeBartolo or Mary Kay, it will be alphabetized under the first name; if the company name starts with initials, for example, L.L. Bean or S.C. Johnson, look for it under the combined initials (in the above examples, LL and SC, respectively). All company names (past and present) used in the profiles are indexed in the main index in the book. Basic financial data are listed under the heading Historical Financials & Employees.

The annual financial information contained in the profiles is as current as possible through fiscal year-ends as late as October 2002. We have included certain nonfinancial developments, such as officer changes, through December 2002.

OVERVIEW

In the first section of the profile, we have tried to give a thumbnail description of the company and what it does. The description will usually include information on the company's strategy, reputation, and ownership. We recommend that you read this section first.

HISTORY

This extended section reflects our belief that every enterprise is the sum of its history, and that you have to know where you came from in order to know where you are going. While some companies have limited historical awareness and were unable to help us much and other companies are just plain boring, we think the vast majority of the enterprises in this book have colorful backgrounds. We have tried to focus on the people who made the enterprises what they are today. We have found these histories to be full of twists and ironies; they make fascinating reading.

OFFICERS

Here we list the names of the people who run the company, insofar as space allows.

While companies are free to structure their management titles any way they please, most modern corporations follow standard practices. The chief officer, the person on whose desk the buck stops, is usually called the chief executive officer (CEO). Often, he or she is also the chairman of the board.

Because corporate management has become more complex, it is common for the CEO to have a right-hand person who oversees the day-to-day operations of the company, allowing the CEO plenty of time to focus on strategy and long-term issues. This right-hand person is usually designated the chief operating officer (COO) and is often the president of the company. In other cases one person is both chairman and president.

A multitude of other titles exists, including chief financial officer (CFO), chief administrative officer, and vice chairman. We have always tried to include the CFO, the chief legal officer, and the chief human resources or personnel officer (HR). The Officers section also includes the name of the company's auditing (accounting) firm, where available.

The people named in the profiles are also included in the main index.

LOCATIONS

Here we include the company's headquarters, street address, telephone and fax numbers, and Web site, as available. An index of companies listed by headquarters location is located in the back of the book.

In some cases we have also included information on the geographical distribution of the company's business, including sales and profit data. Note that these profit numbers, like those in the Products/Operations section below, are usually operating or pretax profits rather than net profits. Operating profits are generally those before financing costs (interest income and payments) and before taxes, which are considered costs attributable to the whole company rather than to one division or part of the world. For this reason the net income figures (in the Historical Financials & Employees section) are usually much lower, since they are after interest and taxes. Pretax profits are after interest but before taxes.

PRODUCTS/OPERATIONS

This section lists as many of the company's products, services, brand names, divisions, subsidiaries, and joint ventures as we could fit. We have tried to include all its major lines and all familiar brand names. The nature of this section varies by company and amount of information available. If the company publishes sales and profit information by type of business, we have included it. The brand, division, and subsidiary names are listed in the main index in the book.

COMPETITORS

In this section we have listed companies that compete with the profiled company. This feature is included as a quick way to locate similar companies and compare them.

HISTORICAL FINANCIALS & EMPLOYEES

Here we have tried to present as much data about each enterprise's financial performance as we could compile. Many private companies don't readily give out information about themselves, but we have tried to provide annual sales and employment figures (although in some cases they are estimates based on statistics from numerous sources). The following information is generally present:

A 10-year table, with relevant annualized compound growth rates, covering:
- **Sales** — fiscal year sales (year-end assets for most financial companies)

- **Net Income** (where available) — fiscal year net income (before accounting changes)
- **Income as a Percent of Sales** (where available) — fiscal year net income as a percent of sales (as a percent of assets for most financial firms)
- **Employees** — fiscal year-end or average number of employees

The information on employees is intended to aid the reader interested in knowing whether a company has a long-term trend of increasing or decreasing employment. As far as we know, we are the only company that publishes this information in print form.

The year at the top of each column in the Historical Financials & Employees section is the year in which the company's fiscal year actually ends. Thus a company with a September 30, 2002, year-end is shown as "9/02." Generally, for private companies, we have graphed net income or, where that is unavailable, sales.

Key year-end statistics are included in this section for insurance companies and companies required to file reports with the SEC. They generally show the financial strength of the enterprise, including:
- Debt ratio (total debt as a percent of combined total debt and shareholders' equity)
- Return on equity (net income divided by the average of beginning and ending common shareholders' equity)
- Cash, marketable securities, and short-term investments on hand
- Current ratio (ratio of current assets to current liabilities)
- Total long-term debt (including capital lease obligations)
- Fiscal year sales for financial institutions.

OTHER MAJOR COMPANIES

Each of the 700 shorter capsule summaries contains the company's name, headquarters address, phone and fax numbers, and Web address (where available); the names of the chief executive officer (CEO), chief financial officer (CFO), and chief human resources officer (HR); the company's fiscal year-end; the most recent annual sales figure available; the sales change over the prior year; and the number of employees. It also includes an overview of the company's operations and ownership and a list of key competitors. Since some entities (associations, foundations, universities) do not compete against one another in the traditional sense, for them we have omitted the list of key competitors.

Hoover's Handbook of Private Companies

A LIST-LOVER'S COMPENDIUM

The 300 Largest Companies by Sales in
Hoover's Handbook of Private Companies 2003

Rank	Company	Sales ($ mil.)	Rank	Company	Sales ($ mil.)
1	Blue Cross and Blue Shield	143,200	51	Farmland Industries, Inc.	6,574
2	United States Postal Service	65,834	52	Enterprise Rent-A-Car	6,500
3	Cargill, Incorporated	50,826	53	The University of Texas System	6,461
4	State Farm Insurance Companies	47,900	54	The Marmon Group, Inc.	6,414
5	Koch Industries, Inc.	40,000	55	Health Care Service Corporation	6,198
6	Federal Reserve System	31,068	56	Science Applications International	6,095
7	Nationwide	29,538	57	Seagate Technology Holdings	6,087
8	Marathon Ashland Petroleum	27,348	58	Chevron Phillips Chemical	6,010
9	TIAA-CREF	23,411	59	Rosenbluth International	6,000
10	New York Life Insurance Company	22,514	60	DHL Worldwide Express, Inc.	6,000
11	IGA, INC.	21,000	61	Land O'Lakes, Inc.	5,973
12	Kaiser Foundation Health		62	Equistar Chemicals, LP	5,909
	Plan, Inc.	19,700	63	Wakefern Food Corporation	5,900
13	Motiva Enterprises LLC	19,446	64	Catholic Health Initiatives	5,742
14	Verizon Wireless Inc.	17,393	65	MacAndrews & Forbes Holdings	5,700
15	Mars, Incorporated	17,000	66	MidAmerican Energy Holdings	5,337
16	Massachusetts Mutual Life	15,980	67	Menard, Inc.	5,300
17	University of California	15,887	68	VT Inc.	5,299
18	Publix Super Markets, Inc.	15,370	69	State University of New York	5,211
19	Northwestern Mutual	15,345	70	Doctor's Associates Inc.	5,170
20	Time Warner Entertainment	15,302	71	Kemper Insurance Companies	5,026
21	Cingular Wireless	14,300	72	S.C. Johnson & Son, Inc.	5,000
22	PricewaterhouseCoopers	13,800	73	Graybar Electric Company, Inc.	4,815
23	Bechtel Group, Inc.	13,400	74	Catholic Healthcare West	4,800
24	Deloitte Touche Tohmatsu	12,500	75	Trinity Health	4,800
25	Blue Cross Blue Shield		76	American Family Insurance Group	4,714
	of Michigan	11,883	77	Alticor Inc.	4,500
26	KPMG International	11,700	78	Giant Eagle Inc.	4,415
27	Liberty Mutual Insurance	11,037	79	Catholic Health East	4,300
28	Penske Corporation	11,000	80	New York City Health and Hospitals	
29	Carlson Wagonlit Travel	11,000		Corporation	4,300
30	Meijer, Inc.	10,600	81	Bonneville Power Administration	4,279
31	Ernst & Young International	10,124	82	Levi Strauss & Co.	4,259
32	H. E. Butt Grocery Company	9,900	83	MBM Corporation	4,236
33	FMR Corp.	9,800	84	National Football League	4,200
34	Carlson Companies, Inc.	9,800	85	Advance Publications, Inc.	4,200
35	C&S Wholesale Grocers, Inc.	9,700	86	New York State Lottery	4,185
36	Duke Energy Field Services	9,598	87	Mayo Foundation	4,135
37	USAA	8,970	88	Hy-Vee, Inc.	4,100
38	Cox Enterprises, Inc.	8,693	89	Metropolitan Transportation	
39	The Trump Organization	8,500		Authority	4,052
40	Huntsman Corporation	8,500	90	California State University	4,050
41	Dairy Farmers of America	7,902	91	YMCA of the USA	4,000
42	Cenex Harvest States Cooperatives	7,845	92	CCA Global Partners	4,000
43	JM Family Enterprises, Inc.	7,800	93	Hallmark Cards, Inc.	4,000
44	Swift & Company	7,733	94	United Way of America	4,000
45	Army and Air Force Exchange	7,133	95	Guardian Industries Corp.	4,000
46	Tennessee Valley Authority	6,999	96	Hyatt Corporation	3,950
47	Guardian Life Insurance	6,947	97	Massachusetts State Lottery	3,936
48	Ascension Health	6,853	98	Reyes Holdings LLC	3,900
49	Highmark Inc.	6,799	99	Peter Kiewit Sons', Inc.	3,871
50	CFM International, Inc.	6,700	100	WorldTravel BTI	3,800

Source: Hoover's, Inc., Database, December 2002

Rank	Company	Sales ($ mil.)	Rank	Company	Sales ($ mil.)
101	The Lefrak Organization	3,800	151	The American Red Cross	2,743
102	Gulf States Toyota, Inc.	3,800	152	The Port Authority of New York and New Jersey	2,715
103	TAP Pharmaceutical Products Inc.	3,787	153	Allegis Group, Inc.	2,700
104	Southern Wine & Spirits	3,750	154	Perdue Farms Incorporated	2,700
105	Blue Cross and Blue Shield of Massachusetts, Inc.	3,725	155	Keystone Foods LLC	2,700
106	Eby-Brown Company	3,670	156	Gilbane, Inc.	2,658
107	Pacific Mutual Holding Company	3,653	157	Intermountain Health Care, Inc.	2,652
108	Milliken & Company Inc.	3,600	158	University of Washington	2,647
109	Visa International	3,600	159	JohnsonDiversey, Inc.	2,641
110	Sutter Health	3,500	160	Hendrick Automotive Group	2,639
111	Major League Baseball	3,500	161	TruServ Corporation	2,619
112	Roundy's, Inc.	3,449	162	Catholic Healthcare Partners	2,602
113	Penske Truck Leasing	3,400	163	Consolidated Electrical Distributors Inc.	2,600
114	McKinsey & Company	3,400	164	Clark Retail Group, Inc.	2,600
115	SYNNEX Information Technologies	3,340	165	Bill Heard Enterprises	2,600
116	The Hearst Corporation	3,300	166	Bloomberg L.P.	2,600
117	Delta Dental Plan of California	3,300	167	International Data Group	2,580
118	ContiGroup Companies, Inc.	3,300	168	Stater Bros. Holdings Inc.	2,574
119	Topco Associates LLC	3,300	169	University System of Maryland	2,565
120	Pension Benefit Guaranty Corporation	3,298	170	The Connell Company	2,525
121	Providence Health System	3,274	171	H.T. Hackney Co.	2,500
122	Raley's Inc.	3,200	172	Quality Chekd Dairies, Inc.	2,500
123	North Shore-Long Island Jewish Health System	3,200	173	Clark Enterprises, Inc.	2,500
124	The University of Pennsylvania	3,191	174	Dow Corning Corporation	2,438
125	The University of Wisconsin System	3,160	175	Transammonia, Inc.	2,434
126	NRT Incorporated	3,159	176	The Ford Foundation	2,432
127	Flying J Inc.	3,150	177	Health Insurance Plan of Greater New York	2,410
128	Associated Wholesale Grocers, Inc.	3,097	178	Whiting-Turner Contracting	2,400
129	Sammons Enterprises, Inc.	3,085	179	Quality King Distributors Inc.	2,400
130	QuikTrip Corporation	3,050	180	Springs Industries, Inc.	2,400
131	J.R. Simplot Company	3,000	181	Do it Best Corp.	2,390
132	Schwan's Sales Enterprises, Inc.	3,000	182	Schneider National, Inc.	2,388
133	Chemoil Corporation	. 3,000	183	State of Florida Lottery	2,330
134	Alliance Capital Management L.P.	2,993	184	Salvation Army USA	2,313
135	The University of Michigan	2,944	185	Aid Association for Lutherans/ Lutheran Brotherhood	2,308
136	RaceTrac Petroleum, Inc.	2,942	186	University of Minnesota	2,301
137	Stanford University	2,940	187	Sinclair Oil Corporation	2,300
138	Unified Western Grocers, Inc.	2,929	188	Bon Secours Health System, Inc.	2,300
139	Wegmans Food Markets, Inc.	2,920	189	A-Mark Financial Corporation	2,300
140	California State Lottery	2,895	190	SIRVA	2,249
141	Ace Hardware Corporation	2,894	191	Belk, Inc.	2,243
142	Adventist Health	2,869	192	Harvard University	2,228
143	Texas Lottery Commission	2,826	193	Black & Veatch	2,224
144	Harbour Group Industries, Inc.	2,800	194	DreamWorks SKG	2,219
145	The Martin-Brower Company	2,800	195	SRP	2,214
146	Kohler Co.	2,800	196	BJC Health System	2,200
147	Los Angeles Department of Water and Power	2,784	197	Micro Warehouse, Inc.	2,200
148	University of Florida	2,782	198	CHRISTUS Health	2,200
149	Brown Automotive Group Ltd.	2,750	199	Renco Group Inc.	2,175
150	Gordon Food Service	2,750	200	National Basketball Association	2,164

The 300 Largest Companies by Sales in
Hoover's Handbook of Private Companies 2003 (continued)

Rank	Company	Sales ($ mil.)	Rank	Company	Sales ($ mil.)
201	The Pennsylvania State University	2,150	251	UniGroup, Inc.	1,896
202	The Jones Financial Companies	2,142	252	Sentry Insurance	1,880
203	Metaldyne Corporation	2,128	253	Gold Kist Inc.	1,864
204	Schnuck Markets, Inc.	2,107	254	Venture Industries	1,860
205	Holman Enterprises	2,105	255	Emory University	1,860
206	The Structure Tone Organization	2,100	256	The University of Alabama System	1,848
207	The Johns Hopkins University	2,100	257	EPIX Holdings Corporation	1,842
208	The Golub Corporation	2,100	258	Dr Pepper/Seven Up Bottling Group, Inc.	1,820
209	The Scoular Company	2,100	259	Hunt Construction Group	1,811
210	Amtrak	2,100	260	Minnesota Mutual Companies, Inc.	1,801
211	Kinko's, Inc.	2,100	261	Software House International, Inc.	1,800
212	Booz Allen Hamilton Inc.	2,100	262	Golden State Foods	1,800
213	CALPERS	2,095	263	Tauber Oil Company	1,800
214	The Mutual of Omaha Companies	2,053	264	Discovery Communications, Inc.	1,800
215	CUNA Mutual Group	2,030	265	DPR Construction, Inc.	1,800
216	Power Authority of the State of New York	2,016	266	Ag Processing Inc	1,789
217	Wawa, Inc.	2,010	267	Indiana University	1,782
218	KB Toys	2,000	268	MasterCard Incorporated	1,774
219	Quexco Incorporated	2,000	269	Hensel Phelps Construction Co.	1,771
220	Demoulas Super Markets Inc.	2,000	270	Vision Service Plan	1,770
221	Tufts Associated Health Plans, Inc.	2,000	271	Lincoln Property Company	1,766
222	Henry Ford Health System	2,000	272	Leprino Foods Company	1,750
223	JELD-WEN, inc.	2,000	273	Southern States Cooperative	1,739
224	Kinray Inc.	2,000	274	Follett Corporation	1,733
225	Ohio National Financial Services	2,000	275	Houchens Industries Inc.	1,727
226	California Dairies Inc.	2,000	276	The University of Iowa	1,721
227	CARQUEST Corporation	2,000	277	University of Missouri System	1,720
228	Gores Technology Group	2,000	278	Haworth Inc.	1,710
229	The Jordan Automotive Group	2,000	279	Rich Products Corporation	1,702
230	NASCAR	2,000	280	Brookshire Grocery Company	1,700
231	OhioHealth	2,000	281	Harvard Pilgrim Health Care, Inc.	1,700
232	MedStar Health	1,990	282	J. M. Huber Corporation	1,700
233	Ohio Lottery Commission	1,983	283	Cumberland Farms, Inc.	1,700
234	Alex Lee, Inc.	1,980	284	Lumbermens Merchandising	1,700
235	J.F. Shea Co., Inc.	1,968	285	The Vanguard Group, Inc.	1,700
236	DynCorp	1,960	286	Grant Thornton International	1,700
237	The Pennsylvania Lottery	1,947	287	Southwire Company	1,700
238	CH2M HILL Companies, Ltd.	1,941	288	Quad/Graphics, Inc.	1,700
239	Zachry Construction Corporation	1,940	289	E. & J. Gallo Winery	1,700
240	Goodwill Industries International	1,940	290	Crown Central Petroleum	1,700
241	TravelCenters of America, Inc.	1,935	291	AECOM Technology Corporation	1,700
242	Ingram Industries Inc.	1,929	292	Andersen Corporation	1,700
243	The Texas A&M University System	1,928	293	National Distributing Company	1,700
244	The City University of New York	1,927	294	Central National-Gottesman Inc.	1,700
245	Sheetz, Inc.	1,920	295	Columbia University	1,700
246	Navy Exchange Service Command	1,916	296	Allina Health System	1,700
247	84 Lumber Company	1,904	297	Pilot Corporation	1,700
248	Trader Joe's Company	1,900	298	National Hockey League	1,697
249	Fry's Electronics, Inc.	1,900	299	Gulf Oil Limited Partnership	1,680
250	Vertis Inc.	1,900	300	Advocate Health Care	1,675

The 300 Largest Companies by Employees in
Hoover's Handbook of Private Companies 2003

Rank	Company	Number of Employees	Rank	Company	Number of Employees
1	United States Postal Service	797,795	51	New York City Health and Hospitals Corporation	33,600
2	Express Personnel Services	224,000	52	Providence Health System	32,929
3	Carlson Companies, Inc.	192,000	53	The Ohio State University	32,000
4	Blue Cross and Blue Shield	150,000	54	FMR Corp.	31,033
5	Publix Super Markets, Inc.	126,000	55	University System of Maryland	30,901
6	PricewaterhouseCoopers	124,563	56	University of Minnesota	30,823
7	Kaiser Foundation Health Plan	111,000	57	Catholic Healthcare Partners	30,000
8	Ernst & Young International	110,000	58	The City University of New York	30,000
9	University of California	108,827	59	Mars, Incorporated	30,000
10	KPMG International	103,000	60	North Shore-Long Island Jewish Health System	30,000
11	Deloitte Touche Tohmatsu	98,000	61	Life Care Centers of America	29,350
12	Cargill, Incorporated	97,000	62	Wegmans Food Markets, Inc.	29,072
13	IGA, INC.	92,000	63	Metromedia Company	28,500
14	Ascension Health	83,412	64	The Johns Hopkins University	28,000
15	Meijer, Inc.	83,402	65	Marathon Ashland Petroleum	27,462
16	The University of Texas System	80,000	66	The Pennsylvania State University	27,112
17	Hyatt Corporation	80,000	67	KinderCare Learning Centers, Inc.	27,000
18	State Farm Insurance Companies	79,400	68	24 Hour Fitness Worldwide Inc.	27,000
19	Cox Enterprises, Inc.	76,000	69	Bon Secours Health System, Inc.	27,000
20	DHL Worldwide Express, Inc.	71,480	70	The Jones Financial Companies	26,460
21	Catholic Health Initiatives	66,000	71	University of Missouri System	26,316
22	Metropolitan Transportation Authority	64,169	72	Giant Eagle Inc.	26,000
23	Goodwill Industries International	61,766	73	BJC Health System	25,801
24	H. E. Butt Grocery Company	60,000	74	YMCA of the USA	25,000
25	Army and Air Force Exchange	52,400	75	KB Toys	25,000
26	NRT Incorporated	51,000	76	Delaware North Companies Inc.	25,000
27	Bechtel Group, Inc.	50,000	77	Buffets, Inc.	25,000
28	Enterprise Rent-A-Car	50,000	78	RTM Restaurant Group	25,000
29	Seagate Technology Holdings	46,000	79	Amtrak	24,600
30	Hy-Vee, Inc.	46,000	80	Advocate Health Care	24,500
31	Mayo Foundation	45,536	81	Texas A&M University System	24,000
32	Salvation Army USA	45,000	82	University of Wisconsin System	24,000
33	Trinity Health	44,500	83	Asplundh Tree Expert Co.	24,000
34	Catholic Health East	43,000	84	University of Florida	23,500
35	Science Applications International Corporation	40,400	85	University of Washington	23,462
36	RGIS Inventory Specialists	40,000	86	DynCorp	23,300
37	California State University	40,000	87	Intermountain Health Care, Inc.	23,000
38	Verizon Wireless Inc.	40,000	88	ClubCorp, Inc.	23,000
39	Chick-fil-A Inc.	40,000	89	Advance Publications, Inc.	22,785
40	Alcoa Fujikura Ltd.	40,000	90	Allina Health System	22,102
41	Catholic Healthcare West	36,000	91	The Schwan Food Company	22,000
42	Penske Corporation	36,000	92	USAA	22,000
43	CARQUEST Corporation	36,000	93	The Trump Organization	22,000
44	Time Warner Entertainment	35,300	94	SSM Health Care System Inc.	22,000
45	The Marmon Group, Inc.	35,000	95	Grant Thornton International	21,879
46	The American Red Cross	35,000	96	MedStar Health	21,700
47	Sutter Health	35,000	97	Banner Health System	21,500
48	Liberty Mutual Insurance	35,000	98	Swift & Company	21,400
49	Nationwide	35,000	99	Penske Truck Leasing	21,000
50	The Freeman Companies	34,000	100	UNICCO Service Company	20,500

Source: Hoover's, Inc., Database, December 2002

The 300 Largest Companies by Employees in
Hoover's Handbook of Private Companies 2003 (continued)

Rank	Company	Number of Employees	Rank	Company	Number of Employees
101	The Day & Zimmermann Group	20,000	151	Renco Group Inc.	13,500
102	Kohler Co.	20,000	152	Roundy's, Inc.	13,451
103	Hallmark Cards, Inc.	20,000	153	Cornell University	13,319
104	Perdue Farms Incorporated	20,000	154	International Data Group	13,050
105	Kinko's, Inc.	20,000	155	McKinsey & Company	13,000
106	American Golf Corporation	20,000	156	Tennessee Valley Authority	13,000
107	University of Alabama System	20,000	157	Methodist Healthcare	13,000
108	JELD-WEN, inc.	20,000	158	Inova Health System	13,000
109	MacAndrews & Forbes Holdings	19,800	159	J.R. Simplot Company	13,000
110	The Golub Corporation	19,700	160	General Parts, Inc.	13,000
111	Schneider National, Inc.	19,349	161	Wawa, Inc.	13,000
112	Emory University	19,288	162	Demoulas Super Markets Inc.	12,700
113	Guardian Industries Corp.	19,000	163	Stater Bros. Holdings Inc.	12,600
114	Belk, Inc.	18,500	164	Domino's, Inc.	12,600
115	Schnuck Markets, Inc.	18,000	165	Metaldyne Corporation	12,500
116	Venture Industries	18,000	166	The University of Pennsylvania	12,290
117	Gold Kist Inc.	18,000	167	Princeton University	12,238
118	The Hearst Corporation	17,170	168	Health Midwest	12,000
119	University of Southern California	17,000	169	The University of Chicago	12,000
120	Springs Industries, Inc.	17,000	170	The University of Iowa	12,000
121	Lifetouch Inc.	17,000	171	Boscov's Department Stores	12,000
122	Raley's Inc.	17,000	172	Novant Health, Inc.	12,000
123	Levi Strauss & Co.	16,700	173	Turner Industries, Ltd.	12,000
124	Vanderbilt University	16,679	174	New York Life Insurance Company	11,800
125	Investors Management Corp.	16,500	175	Booz Allen Hamilton Inc.	11,510
126	Detroit Medical Center	16,500	176	Flying J Inc.	11,500
127	Loews Cineplex Entertainment	16,500	177	Brookshire Grocery Company	11,500
128	Adventist Health	16,500	178	William Beaumont Hospital	11,500
129	The Lefrak Organization	16,200	179	Provena Health	11,400
130	Carrols Corporation	16,100	180	University of Rochester	11,200
131	Indiana University	16,070	181	MediaNews Group, Inc.	11,200
132	BREED Technologies, Inc.	16,000	182	Knowledge Universe, Inc.	11,000
133	Navy Exchange Service Command	16,000	183	Cushman & Wakefield Inc.	11,000
134	Carondelet Health System	16,000	184	Foster Poultry Farms	11,000
135	Texas Health Resources Inc.	16,000	185	Koch Industries, Inc.	11,000
136	Peter Kiewit Sons', Inc.	16,000	186	The Vanguard Group, Inc.	11,000
137	AECOM Technology Corporation	15,500	187	American Retail Group Inc.	11,000
138	OhioHealth	15,340	188	Montefiore Medical Center	11,000
139	Hobby Lobby Stores, Inc.	15,000	189	Highmark Inc.	11,000
140	Shoney's, Inc.	15,000	190	Bashas' Inc.	10,800
141	Henry Ford Health System	15,000	191	CH2M HILL Companies, Ltd.	10,500
142	Harvard University	15,000	192	Quad/Graphics, Inc.	10,500
143	Platinum Equity Holdings	15,000	193	Alticor Inc.	10,500
144	ContiGroup Companies, Inc.	14,500	194	Group Health Cooperative of Puget Sound	10,500
145	JohnsonDiversey, Inc.	14,500	195	Concentra Inc.	10,276
146	Huntsman Corporation	14,000	196	TravelCenters of America, Inc.	10,255
147	Taylor Corporation	14,000	197	NESCO, Inc.	10,250
148	Zachry Construction Corporation	14,000	198	Carilion Health System	10,200
149	Milliken & Company Inc.	14,000	199	MSX International, Inc.	10,142
150	Farmland Industries, Inc.	13,800	200	New York University	10,136

The 300 Largest Companies by Employees in
Hoover's Handbook of Private Companies 2003 (continued)

Rank	Company	Number of Employees	Rank	Company	Number of Employees
201	University of North Carolina at Chapel Hill	10,111	251	Methodist Health Care System	8,100
202	DHL Airways, Inc.	10,087	252	Carlson Wagonlit Travel	8,083
203	Retail Brand Alliance, Inc.	10,036	253	Motiva Enterprises LLC	8,000
204	Gores Technology Group	10,000	254	Cinemark, Inc.	8,000
205	Scripps	10,000	255	Vanguard Health Systems, Inc.	8,000
206	Haworth Inc.	10,000	256	Allegis Group, Inc.	8,000
207	Follett Corporation	10,000	257	Washington University in St. Louis	8,000
208	Watkins Associated Industries	10,000	258	NCH Corporation	8,000
209	Stevedoring Services of America	10,000	259	Baker & McKenzie	8,000
210	United Space Alliance	10,000	260	Mark IV Industries, Inc.	8,000
211	TRT Holdings	10,000	261	IASIS Healthcare Corporation	8,000
212	Beaulieu of America, LLC	10,000	262	CHRISTUS Health	8,000
213	University of Pittsburgh	10,000	263	Big Y Foods, Inc.	7,850
214	Steiner Corporation	10,000	264	Horseshoe Gaming Holding Corp.	7,843
215	Vertis Inc.	10,000	265	Geisinger Health System	7,817
216	Graybar Electric Company, Inc.	9,800	266	J. Crew Group, Inc.	7,800
217	MidAmerican Energy Holdings	9,780	267	Memorial Sloan-Kettering Cancer Center	7,609
218	CBRE Holding, Inc.	9,700	268	Fiesta Mart, Inc.	7,600
219	Puerto Rico Electric Power	9,550	269	Mohegan Tribal Gaming Authority	7,583
220	Parsons Corporation	9,500	270	The Holmes Group, Inc.	7,500
221	S.C. Johnson & Son, Inc.	9,500	271	Holiday Retirement Corp.	7,500
222	Barnes & Noble College Bookstores	9,500	272	C&S Wholesale Grocers, Inc.	7,500
223	Parsons Brinckerhoff Inc.	9,294	273	Timex Corporation	7,500
224	Menard, Inc.	9,200	274	Berwind Group	7,500
225	HBE Corporation	9,100	275	Dow Corning Corporation	7,500
226	Towers Perrin	9,009	276	Trader Joe's Company	7,488
227	Outsourcing Solutions Inc.	9,000	277	American Family Insurance Group	7,431
228	AMSTED Industries Incorporated	9,000	278	Delco Remy International, Inc.	7,422
229	Kemper Insurance Companies	9,000	279	Clark Retail Group, Inc.	7,400
230	Massachusetts Mutual Life	9,000	280	Yale University	7,398
231	Nypro Inc.	9,000	281	Contran Corporation	7,300
232	Alex Lee, Inc.	9,000	282	Save Mart Supermarkets	7,300
233	UIS, Inc.	8,900	283	Presbyterian Healthcare Services	7,253
234	Boston University	8,900	284	Bloomberg L.P.	7,200
235	BE&K Inc.	8,822	285	Pilot Corporation	7,200
236	Dr Pepper/Seven Up Bottling	8,800	286	Columbia University	7,072
237	Bass Pro Shops, Inc.	8,800	287	Cabela's Inc.	7,041
238	MIT	8,700	288	The Longaberger Company	7,000
239	K-VA-T Food Stores, Inc.	8,700	289	Quexco Incorporated	7,000
240	Battelle Memorial Institute	8,700	290	Ritz Camera Centers, Inc.	7,000
241	SAS Institute Inc.	8,636	291	Crown Equipment Corporation	7,000
242	DFS Group Limited	8,600	292	Bose Corporation	7,000
243	Land O'Lakes, Inc.	8,600	293	VT Inc.	7,000
244	Estes Express Lines	8,531	294	Andersen Corporation	7,000
245	Black & Veatch	8,500	295	EnerSys Inc.	7,000
246	Sheetz, Inc.	8,500	296	Colson & Colson Construction	7,000
247	Dresser, Inc.	8,500	297	Oxford Automotive, Inc.	7,000
248	R. B. Pamplin Corp.	8,500	298	Anderson News Company	7,000
249	Discount Tire Co.	8,415	299	Cumberland Farms, Inc.	6,976
250	Variety Wholesalers, Inc.	8,300	300	Sinclair Oil Corporation	6,900

The *Inc.* 500 Fastest-Growing Private Companies in America

Rank	Company	Headquarters	1997–2001 Sales Growth Increase (%)
1	Outsource Group	Walnut Creek, CA	54,330
2	Integrity Staffing Solutions	Newark, DE	11,373
3	Prometheus Laboratories	San Diego, CA	11,243
4	Turner Professional Services	Baton Rouge, LA	11,123
5	Blue Pumpkin Software	Sunnyvale, CA	10,945
6	Larkin Enterprises	Bangor, ME	10,192
7	Tastefully Simple	Alexandria, MN	7,627
8	Sterling Financial Group of Companies	Boca Raton, FL	7,409
9	Greenwich Technology Partners	White Plains, NY	7,082
10	Orange Glo International	Greenwood Village, CO	6,714
11	Technology and Management Associates	Galloway, NJ	6,289
12	Summit Energy	Heber City, UT	5,785
13	Coadvantage Resources	Orlando, FL	5,677
14	Staff One	Woodridge, IL	5,597
15	Visionary Systems	Atlanta, GA	5,526
16	Atlantic Credit & Finance	Roanoke, VA	5,362
17	SupplyCore.com	Rockford, IL	5,152
18	Taycor Financial	Culver City, CA	4,854
19	Computer Source	Lenexa, KS	4,843
20	Tripwire	Portland, OR	4,808
21	Digital Visual Display Technologies	Atlanta, GA	4,780
22	Adea Solutions	Dallas, TX	4,678
23	Consultants' Choice	Houston, TX	4,536
24	United Asset Coverage	Naperville, IL	4,367
25	TeleSynthesis	Greenwood Village, CO	4,323
26	Scooter Store	New Braunfels, TX	4,192
27	National Bankcard Systems	Austin, TX	4,186
28	Universal Solutions	Ridgeland, MS	4,181
29	Partnership in Building	Austin, TX	4,045
30	Oakleaf Waste Management	East Hartford, CT	3,910
31	In Zone	Atlanta, GA	3,906
32	CHIPS Solutions	Lake Success, NY	3,664
33	Cima Consulting Group	Coral Gables, FL	3,656
34	ScripNet	Las Vegas, NV	3,536
35	Advanced Internet Technologies	Fayetteville, NC	3,514
36	Freedom Medical	Exton, PA	3,501
37	Global Domains International	Carlsbad, CA	3,479
38	PowerLight	Berkeley, CA	3,417
39	Floorgraphics	Princeton, NJ	3,410
40	CapTech Ventures	Richmond, VA	3,408
41	Questar Capital	Ann Arbor, MI	3,377
42	Y2Marketing	De Soto, TX	3,300
43	Intrasphere Technologies	New York, NY	3,232
44	Commercial Energy of Montana	Cut Bank, MT	3,214
45	Connected	Framingham, MA	3,198
46	Key Information Systems	Woodland Hills, CA	3,182
47	Speakeasy	Seattle, WA	3,177
48	Tilson HR	Greenwood, IN	3,092
49	Synhrgy HR Technologies	Houston, TX	3,078
50	Hat World	Indianapolis, IN	3,031
51	HealthCare Financial Group	Aurora, CO	2,960
52	esoftsolutions	Plano, TX	2,908
53	Navarro Research and Engineering	Oak Ridge, TN	2,840
54	York Enterprise Solutions	Westchester, IL	2,828
55	Magnet Communications	Atlanta, GA	2,800

Source: *Inc.* 500; October 15, 2002

Rank	Company	Headquarters	1997–2001 Sales Growth Increase (%)
56	Z Corporation	Burlington, MA	2,786
57	Heartland Payment Systems	Princeton, NJ	2,771
58	ComGlobal Systems	San Diego, CA	2,720
59	ProClarity	Boise, ID	2,641
60	Micro Solutions Enterprises	Chatsworth, CA	2,533
61	Carteret Mortgage	Centreville, VA	2,516
62	Enterprise Computing Solutions	Mission Viejo, CA	2,487
63	MRE Consulting	Houston, TX	2,472
64	NLX	Sterling, VA	2,402
65	Automated License Systems	Nashville, TN	2,400
66	Cardtronics	Houston, TX	2,386
67	Strategic Data Systems	San Diego, CA	2,356
68	Phoenix Rehabilitation and Health Services	Indiana, PA	2,350
69	Unica	Lincoln, MA	2,322
70	ProSys Information Systems	Norcross, GA	2,300
71	CyberThink	Bridgewater, NJ	2,274
72	Democracy Data & Communications	Alexandria, VA	2,270
73	Lydian Trust	Palm Beach Gardens, FL	2,243
74	Sweet Productions	Amityville, NY	2,152
75	Arkidata	Downers Grove, IL	2,127
76	Bigdough.com	Bethesda, MD	2,116
77	VoiceLog	Gaithersburg, MD	2,108
78	Market First	Kennesaw, GA	2,077
79	Flow Management Technologies	Saratoga Springs, NY	2,073
80	Vesta	Portland, OR	2,065
81	Eze Castle Software	Boston, MA	2,020
82	Refinery	Huntingdon Valley, PA	2,020
83	Think Tank Systems	Cerritos, CA	1,987
84	3t Systems	Greenwood Village, CO	1,975
85	Blue Ocean Software	Tampa, FL	1,948
86	DataTrend Information Systems	Denver, CO	1,926
87	Integrated Decisions and Systems	Eagan, MN	1,904
88	PharmaFab	Grand Prairie, TX	1,900
89	Virtual Meeting Strategies	Indianapolis, IN	1,892
90	Spotfire Holdings	Somerville, MA	1,890
91	Teamstudio	Beverly, MA	1,888
92	Omega Insurance Services	St. Petersburg, FL	1,883
93	Granite Systems	Manchester, NH	1,868
94	Clover Technologies Group	Ottawa, IL	1,839
95	Investment Scorecard	Nashville, TN	1,824
96	Virtual Financial Services	Indianapolis, IN	1,823
97	Invision.com	Commack, NY	1,821
98	Miracle Software Systems	Southfield, MI	1,789
99	Texas Residential Mortgage	Dallas, TX	1,775
100	Auction Systems Auctioneers & Appraisers	Phoenix, AZ	1,766
101	Analytical Management Services	Encinitas, CA	1,745
102	Service Source	Adrian, MI	1,738
103	Fetch Logistics	Amherst, NY	1,726
104	First American Equipment Finance	Chicago, IL	1,725
105	Noodles & Co.	Boulder, CO	1,707
106	HealthScribe	Sterling, VA	1,702
107	Envision Telephony	Seattle, WA	1,693
108	Capstone	Dallas, TX	1,683
109	Boldtech Systems	Denver, CO	1,667
110	ScriptSave	Tucson, AZ	1,653

The *Inc.* 500 Fastest-Growing Private Companies in America (continued)

Rank	Company	Headquarters	1997–2001 Sales Growth Increase (%)
111	Innovate E-Commerce	Pittsburgh, PA	1,647
112	Direct Data	Horsham, PA	1,645
113	Extra Mile Transportation	Buffalo, NY	1,644
114	Portosan	El Monte, CA	1,641
115	Signature Consultants	Fort Lauderdale, FL	1,632
116	GCI	Parsippany, NJ	1,632
117	TechBooks	Fairfax, VA	1,631
118	Networking Technologies and Support	Richmond, VA	1,612
119	Trek Equipment	Sausalito, CA	1,602
120	Quantum Loyalty Systems	Incline Village, NV	1,587
121	Alden Systems	Birmingham, AL	1,578
122	C & A Industries	Omaha, NE	1,575
123	Grant Harrison Advertising	Houston, TX	1,569
124	Northwoods Software Development	Brown Deer, WI	1,556
125	First Revenue Assurance	Denver, CO	1,554
126	Third Millennium Telecommunications	Piscataway, NJ	1,552
127	Caliber Collision Centers	Irvine, CA	1,548
128	Technica	Dulles, VA	1,541
129	Conquest Systems	Washington, DC	1,522
130	Computer World Services	Washington, DC	1,504
131	New Horizons Computer Learning Center of Miami	Miami, FL	1,502
132	E Commerce Group Products	New York, NY	1,491
133	Denali Ventures	Cheyenne, WY	1,486
134	Associated Business Systems	Portland, OR	1,484
135	Portage Environmental	Idaho Falls, ID	1,481
136	Network Management Resources	Severna Park, MD	1,481
137	WCI	Seattle, WA	1,474
138	Liners Direct	Itasca, IL	1,466
139	StoneTech Professional	Union City, CA	1,453
140	Call Henry	Cocoa, FL	1,451
141	Genghis Grill	Dallas, TX	1,450
142	Integra Telecom	Beaverton, OR	1,446
143	Mindworks	Santa Clara, CA	1,444
144	Professional Placement Resources	Jacksonville Beach, FL	1,442
145	eCopy	Nashua, NH	1,436
146	Cura Group	Ft. Lauderdale, FL	1,403
147	Restaurant Partners	Orlando, FL	1,402
148	IVCi	Hauppauge, NY	1,390
149	Conquest	Annapolis Junction, MD	1,381
150	MQ Software	Minneapolis, MN	1,374
151	Marlabs	Edison, NJ	1,351
152	Data Company	Memphis, TN	1,351
153	Cherokee Information Services	Arlington, VA	1,349
154	AccuCode	Denver, CO	1,346
155	Dataprise	Rockville, MD	1,340
156	SourceGear	Champaign, IL	1,328
157	Hencie	Dallas, TX	1,319
158	Axis Consulting	Short Hills, NJ	1,318
159	National Heritage Academies	Grand Rapids, MI	1,311
160	Pacific Data Designs	San Francisco, CA	1,308
161	Scott Pipitone Design	Pittsburgh, PA	1,294
162	Jolly Enterprises	Gardendale, AL	1,270
163	Prosum	El Segundo, CA	1,261
164	Access Systems	Fairfax, VA	1,251
165	TimeVision	Irving, TX	1,250

The *Inc.* 500 Fastest-Growing Private Companies in America (continued)

Rank	Company	Headquarters	1997–2001 Sales Growth Increase (%)
166	Astute	Columbus, OH	1,247
167	SimStar Internet Solutions	Princeton, NJ	1,238
168	Gold Crest Distributing	Mexico, MO	1,232
169	North American Theatrix	Waterbury, CT	1,230
170	Strategic Management Initiatives	Gaithersburg, MD	1,229
171	New Media Communications	Richfield, OH	1,219
172	Formatech	Andover, MA	1,216
173	AXSA Document Solutions	Tampa, FL	1,197
174	White Wave	Boulder, CO	1,191
175	Zaiq Technologies	Woburn, MA	1,185
176	RS Information Systems	McLean, VA	1,182
177	NoBrainerBlinds.com	Houston, TX	1,177
178	Nexxtworks	Clearwater, FL	1,171
179	Socket Internet	Columbia, MO	1,168
180	ATA Services	Salt Lake City, UT	1,167
181	ACS International Resources	Newark, DE	1,166
182	netNumina	Cambridge, MA	1,155
183	U.S. Energy Services	Wayzata, MN	1,150
184	Global Wireless Data	Norcross, GA	1,149
185	Diamond Technologies	New Castle, DE	1,147
186	Homebuilders Financial Network	Miami Lakes, FL	1,139
187	Baesch Computer Consulting	Glen Burnie, MD	1,138
188	Gillani	Richardson, TX	1,125
189	Web Group	Troy, MI	1,125
190	EPAM Systems	Princeton, NJ	1,109
191	Vertex Solutions	Falls Church, VA	1,106
192	Benecon Group	Leola, PA	1,100
193	WestNet Learning Technologies	Arvada, CO	1,097
194	Yash Technologies	East Moline, IL	1,097
195	Telwares Communications	Destin, FL	1,095
196	Security Check	Oxford, MS	1,089
197	Extreme Pizza	San Francisco, CA	1,080
198	GTS Refreshment Services	Kingsport, TN	1,077
199	Capella Education	Minneapolis, MN	1,070
200	Viacell	Boston, MA	1,070
201	Portfolio Recovery Associates	Norfolk, VA	1,068
202	Ultimus	Cary, NC	1,059
203	Shirt Factory	Derry, NH	1,059
204	USA Instruments	Aurora, OH	1,057
205	DB Professionals	Portland, OR	1,057
206	Service Link	Aliquippa, PA	1,053
207	Tropical Oasis	McKinney, TX	1,040
208	Quality Assured Services	Orlando, FL	1,036
209	Telepoint Communications	Somerdale, NJ	1,034
210	Pearl Law Group	San Francisco, CA	1,031
211	Employer Services	Amherst, NY	1,029
212	Keller Williams Realty Ahwatukee Foothills	Phoenix, AZ	1,027
213	Business Plus Corporation	Hampton, VA	1,024
214	Staff Force	Schaumburg, IL	1,020
215	Ivory Systems	Parsippany, NJ	1,017
216	Interface Software	Oak Brook, IL	1,012
217	Vitacost.com	Boynton Beach, FL	1,011
218	Elite Medical	Tucker, GA	1,009
219	Staff Force	Houston, TX	1,004
220	Ositis Software	Pleasanton, CA	1,001

The *Inc.* 500 Fastest-Growing Private Companies in America (continued)

Rank	Company	Headquarters	1997–2001 Sales Growth Increase (%)
221	Tigris Consulting	New York, NY	1,000
222	Heartlab	Westerly, RI	1,000
223	Aloha NY Systems	Orangeburg, NY	991
224	Advanced Technologies Group	West Des Moines, IA	986
225	Serentec	Raleigh, NC	981
226	Linksys	Irvine, CA	981
227	Maverick Construction	Boston, MA	979
228	Trinity HomeCare	College Point, NY	976
229	Midwest Media Group	Milwaukee, WI	975
230	Pioneer Data Systems	Edison, NJ	969
231	Cardinal Cartridge	Elmhurst, IL	968
232	McKee Wallwork Henderson	Albuquerque, NM	967
233	Dancor	Columbus, OH	964
234	Advantage Credit International	Pensacola, FL	961
235	Catamount Constructors	Evergreen, CO	952
236	IPS Advisory	Knoxville, TN	946
237	Diamond Group	Dallas, TX	945
238	Sammy's Woodfired Pizza	La Jolla, CA	942
239	Bluff City Steel	Memphis, TN	940
240	Pinnacle Staffing	Greenville, SC	939
241	TechRX	Coraopolis, PA	927
242	Dankoff Solar Products	Santa Fe, NM	927
243	Printcafe Software	Pittsburgh, PA	927
244	Terra Firma	Denver, CO	927
245	America's Choice Healthplans	King of Prussia, PA	924
246	Great Lakes Technologies Group	Southfield, MI	916
247	Montpelier Plastics	Montpelier, OH	914
248	Mission Controls Automation	Irvine, CA	910
249	GRT	Stamford, CT	903
250	GHR Systems	Wayne, PA	902
251	Security Mortgage Group	Fort Lauderdale, FL	899
252	Unicru	Beaverton, OR	898
253	Veri-Tek International	Wixom, MI	898
254	Paisley Consulting	Cokato, MN	897
255	Exinom Technologies	Iselin, NJ	895
256	Travizon	Boston, MA	893
257	Genex Technologies	Kensington, MD	889
258	Venoco	Carpinteria, CA	886
259	Linac Systems	Lakewood, NJ	884
260	Kitba Consulting Services	Houston, TX	884
261	V-Span	King of Prussia, PA	882
262	Nature's Cure	Oakland, CA	882
263	Priority Leasing	Malden, MA	877
264	Providence Service	Tucson, AZ	876
265	Arrow Financial Services	Lincolnwood, IL	868
266	Morgan Research	Huntsville, AL	868
267	Bestever	Rancho Dominguez, CA	866
268	Authoria	Waltham, MA	865
269	Atlantic.Net	Gainesville, FL	860
270	CookTek	Chicago, IL	860
271	Digital Motorworks	Austin, TX	857
272	Cold Stone Creamery	Scottsdale, AZ	852
273	Progressive Designs	Des Moines, IA	850
274	Access US	St. Louis, MO	846
275	Smartronix	California, MD	845

The *Inc.* 500 Fastest-Growing Private Companies in America (continued)

Rank	Company	Headquarters	1997–2001 Sales Growth Increase (%)
276	Joe Lombardo Plumbing + Heating of Rockland	Suffern, NY	836
277	httprint	San Francisco, CA	829
278	Comm-Works	Plymouth, MN	829
279	Stone Brewing	San Marcos, CA	826
280	Megha Systems	Dallas, TX	816
281	MicroTek	Oakbrook Terrace, IL	816
282	American Pan & Engineering	Palmetto, GA	815
283	Hardwood Wholesalers	Norwalk, CT	813
284	GDA Technologies	San Jose, CA	811
285	PrintingForLess.com	Livingston, MT	810
286	Joseph Sheairs Associates	Shamong, NJ	805
287	Laboratory Management Systems	New Castle, DE	805
288	Apex Systems	Richmond, VA	804
289	Iris Software	Metuchen, NJ	802
290	Spenser Communications	Irwindale, CA	802
291	Tilia	San Francisco, CA	802
292	Sequoia System International	Naperville, IL	799
293	Savela & Associates	Birmingham, AL	793
294	Diversitech	Cincinnati, OH	789
295	FlavorX	Bethesda, MD	786
296	Advanced Vending Systems	Ringgold, GA	780
297	Swiss Watch International	Hollywood, FL	776
298	Career Control Group	Dallas, TX	775
299	Solipsys	Laurel, MD	773
300	Parker Compound Bows	Staunton, VA	772
301	SALT Group	Kerrville, TX	770
302	Data Warehouse	Boca Raton, FL	769
303	Meritage Technologies	Columbus, OH	765
304	Heritage Microfilm	Cedar Rapids, IA	760
305	SEI/Aaron's	Atlanta, GA	758
306	Timberlane Woodcrafters	North Wales, PA	758
307	ZonePerfect Nutrition Company	Boston, MA	757
308	Sea Fox Boat	Charleston, SC	754
309	SYS-CON Media	Montvale, NJ	752
310	Inspiration Software	Portland, OR	745
311	LogistiCare	Atlanta, GA	743
312	Horizon Consulting	Falls Church, VA	741
313	QSS Group	Lanham, MD	740
314	AQuickDelivery	Atlanta, GA	737
315	Lloyd Group	New York, NY	735
316	EagleOne	Fort Smith, AR	732
317	Knightsbridge Solutions	Chicago, IL	724
318	SSCI	West Lafayette, IN	723
319	KSJ & Associates	Falls Church, VA	718
320	Entelligence	Houston, TX	716
321	North Highland	Atlanta, GA	713
322	Solution Builders	Atlanta, GA	713
323	Spectrum Communications Cabling Services	Corona, CA	712
324	Qestrel Cos.	Pasadena, CA	710
325	DrinkMore Water	Gaithersburg, MD	706
326	Traffic Management	Minneapolis, MN	706
327	MedSource Consulting	Houston, TX	704
328	Pyramid Digital Solutions	Birmingham, AL	704
329	Progressive Medical	Westerville, OH	702
330	TRX	Atlanta, GA	698

The *Inc.* 500 Fastest-Growing Private Companies in America (continued)

Rank	Company	Headquarters	1997–2001 Sales Growth Increase (%)
331	SCI	Depew, NY	697
332	Fiber Network Solutions	Columbus, OH	693
333	Multimedia Live	Petaluma, CA	693
334	Kelmoore Investment	Palo Alto, CA	693
335	Open Software Solutions	Greensboro, NC	692
336	OnStaff	Burbank, CA	689
337	CIW Services	Phoenix, AZ	689
338	Lindin Consulting	New York, NY	689
339	PSC Info Group	Valley Forge, PA	688
340	SafeHome Security	Provo, UT	686
341	Infinity Contractors	Haltom City, TX	685
342	Imports By Four Hands	Austin, TX	682
343	John Keeler & Co.	Miami, FL	680
344	Active Services	Birmingham, AL	674
345	Pioneer Mortgage	Novi, MI	674
346	Flake-Wilkerson Market Insights	Little Rock, AR	674
347	Harrison & Shriftman	New York, NY	672
348	I.T.S.	Oxnard, CA	669
349	Marathon Heater	Del Rio, TX	667
350	Procurement Centre	Houston, TX	661
351	ProfitLine	San Diego, CA	660
352	Maverick Technologies	Fairview Heights, IL	660
353	Big Yank Sports	San Francisco, CA	659
354	Blue Angel Technologies	Valley Forge, PA	659
355	Tracer Technologies	New York, NY	658
356	Advanced Vision Research	Woburn, MA	657
357	Accredited Home Lenders	San Diego, CA	656
358	Print-Tech	Madison, WI	653
359	School Technology Management	Clarksville, MD	652
360	Alogent	Alpharetta, GA	651
361	Comnet International	Lisle, IL	641
362	MoneyLine Lending Services	Lake Forest, CA	641
363	And 1	Paoli, PA	640
364	Calence	Tempe, AZ	638
365	Monitronics International	Dallas, TX	637
366	One Source Printing	Franklin, TN	636
367	Custom Solutions International	Boca Raton, FL	635
368	Random Walk Computing	New York, NY	635
369	Global Science and Technology	Greenbelt, MD	627
370	Cody-Kramer Imports	Blauvelt, NY	626
371	SM Consulting	Linthicum, MD	625
372	Contract Counsel	Madison Heights, MI	622
373	MHF Logistical Solutions	Cranberry Twp, PA	621
374	TMA Resources	McLean, VA	619
375	Prosoft Technology Group	Downers Grove, IL	618
376	BASE Consulting Group	Oakland, CA	618
377	Mathis, Earnest & Vandeventer	Cedar Falls, IA	617
378	Franklin American Mortgage	Franklin, TN	617
379	Doral Dental USA	Mequon, WI	616
380	Advertising Ventures	Providence, RI	615
381	Alternative Technology	Denver, CO	615
382	Pragmatech Software	Amherst, NH	614
383	J.C. Malone Associates	Louisville, KY	614
384	Bowman Consulting Group	Chantilly, VA	613
385	Creditors Interchange	Buffalo, NY	612

The *Inc.* 500 Fastest-Growing Private Companies in America (continued)

Rank	Company	Headquarters	1997–2001 Sales Growth Increase (%)
386	Navigator Systems	Dallas, TX	610
387	Myricom	Arcadia, CA	609
388	American Service Systems	Dallas, TX	609
389	Execuscribe	Rochester, NY	608
390	Sunstream	Kent, WA	608
391	Strategic Products and Services	Cedar Knolls, NJ	607
392	Parksite	Batavia, IL	604
393	Simply Certificates	Guilderland, NY	602
394	USA Environmental Management	Upper Darby, PA	601
395	G.A. Beck Artistic Services	Lawrenceville, GA	601
396	Loss Mitigation Services	Paris, TX	600
397	Learning Voyage	Cincinnati, OH	600
398	Valley Oak Systems	Alamo, CA	599
399	Evinco	Alcoa, TN	598
400	Hospital Solutions	Houston, TX	597
401	InfoVision Consultants	Richardson, TX	597
402	L.E.M. Products	Miamitown, OH	595
403	Diamond Pharmacy Services	Indiana, PA	594
404	Market-Based Solutions	Los Angeles, CA	593
405	Sensor Technologies	Tinton Falls, NJ	585
406	KeyMark	Greenville, SC	584
407	Technology Resource Center	West Dundee, IL	582
408	Electrical Solutions	Cottage Grove, WI	582
409	Network Hardware Resale	Santa Barbara, CA	582
410	Coridian Technologies	Chanhassen, MN	581
411	TEOCO	Fairfax, VA	581
412	STI Knowledge	Atlanta, GA	581
413	Operational Technologies	San Antonio, TX	581
414	Aquascape Designs	Batavia, IL	579
415	Uniserve Facilities Services	Los Angeles, CA	577
416	ASAP Staffing	Norcross, GA	576
417	Typhoon	Portland, OR	572
418	Perfect Order	Mechanicsburg, PA	572
419	Topics Entertainment	Renton, WA	570
420	Studio B Productions	Indianapolis, IN	562
421	Miller Systems	Boston, MA	562
422	Process Plus	Cincinnati, OH	562
423	ID Label	Lake Villa, IL	558
424	Innovative Lighting	Roland, IA	552
425	Bashen Consulting	Houston, TX	552
426	Client Network Services	Rockville, MD	552
427	Tilson Landscape	Vienna, VA	552
428	Gray Hawk Systems	Alexandria, VA	551
429	All Star Consulting	San Francisco, CA	549
430	Gagwear	Norcross, GA	547
431	SPS Commerce	St. Paul, MN	546
432	Labrada Nutrition	Houston, TX	546
433	Street Glow	Wayne, NJ	545
434	Alternative Business Systems	Lincoln, NE	545
435	Amerisource Funding	Houston, TX	545
436	Club One	San Francisco, CA	542
437	Legacy Financial Group	Arlington, TX	542
438	Trainersoft	Raleigh, NC	541
439	Great Lakes Media Technology	Mequon, WI	537
440	New View Gifts & Accessories	Media, PA	535

The *Inc.* 500 Fastest-Growing Private Companies in America (continued)

Rank	Company	Headquarters	1997–2001 Sales Growth Increase (%)
441	Outta the Box Dispensers	Dayton, OH	532
442	Component Graphics	Roseville, CA	532
443	Angie's List	Indianapolis, IN	528
444	Alliance of Professionals & Consultants	Raleigh, NC	527
445	DC Group	Minneapolis, MN	522
446	MindIQ	Norcross, GA	519
447	Black Mountain Management	New York, NY	518
448	Momentum Marketing Services	Washington, DC	515
449	Herbeau Creations of America	Naples, FL	514
450	TLS Service Bureau	Altlanta, GA	513
451	Cynergy Data	College Point, NY	510
452	Network Display	Passaic, NJ	507
453	Palm Beach Tan	Carrollton, TX	503
454	Kingston	Columbus, OH	497
455	AC Technologies	Fairfax, VA	496
456	Accuship	Germantown, TN	493
457	Telechem International	Sunnyvale, CA	492
458	Computer Engineering Organization	Boca Raton, FL	491
459	Nu Info Systems	Jacksonville, FL	490
460	Elite Computers & Software	Santa Clara, CA	490
461	Lynk Systems	Atlanta, GA	488
462	TruSecure	Herndon, VA	486
463	Priority Express Courier	Boothwyn, PA	480
464	Unger Technologies	The Woodlands, TX	480
465	Newton Interactive	Pennington, NJ	479
466	ORI Services	San Diego, CA	478
467	WRG Services	Willoughby, OH	478
468	Southern Homes and Remodeling	Central, SC	475
469	E Group	Minneapolis, MN	475
470	Signal Perfection	Columbia, MD	474
471	Fiberlink Communications	Blue Bell, PA	473
472	Gorman Richardson Architects	Hopkinton, MA	473
473	Ogio International	Bluffdale, UT	473
474	WAV	West Chicago, IL	471
475	Acsis	Marlton, NJ	471
476	Banfe Products	Barrington, NJ	470
477	Mosaic	Renton, WA	467
478	SHOT, Inc.	Greenville, IN	467
479	Primus Software	Duluth, GA	467
480	Cambridge Home Health Care	Akron, OH	466
481	Brandt Information Services	Tallahassee, FL	466
482	CLT Meetings International	Orlando, FL	465
483	SmartDraw.com	San Diego, CA	464
484	Accurate Autobody	Tulsa, OK	464
485	MidAmerica Auto Glass	Bloomington, MN	462
486	Infinity Software Development	Tallahassee, FL	459
487	Imaging Business Machines	Birmingham, AL	459
488	ELMCO	Huntsville, AL	459
489	InsurMark	Houston, TX	458
490	Softworld	Waltham, MA	457
491	Greyhawk North America	Woodbury, NY	457
492	Kingland Companies	Clear Lake, IA	456
493	Abdon Callais Offshore	Golden Meadow, LA	456
494	American Megacom	Livonia, MI	455
495	InfoPros	Citrus Heights, CA	453
496	Analytics Operations Engineering	Boston, MA	449
497	ATX Forms	Caribou, ME	446
498	Gentra Systems	Minneapolis, MN	446
499	Painted Word	Cambridge, MA	443
500	Appriss	Louisville, KY	440

The *Forbes* Largest Private Companies in the US

Rank	Company	Industry	Revenue ($ mil.)
1	Cargill	Agricultural Services	50,826
2	Koch Industries	Conglomerates	40,000
3	Mars	Sugar & Confectionery	17,500
4	PricewaterhouseCoopers	Accounting Services	16,100
5	Publix Super Markets	Grocery Retailing	15,370
6	Bechtel	Heavy Construction	13,400
7	Meijer	Grocery Retailing	10,600
8	Ernst & Young	Accounting Services	10,100
9	H.E. Butt Grocery	Grocery Retailing	9,900
10	Fidelity Investments	Asset Management	9,807
11	C&S Wholesale Grocers	Food Wholesale — to Grocers	9,700
12	Huntsman	Diversified	8,000
13	JM Family Enterprises	Auto Dealers & Distributors	7,800
14	Swift & Co.	Meat Products	7,733
15	Enterprise Rent-A-Car	Car & Truck Rental	6,500
16	Marmon Group	Conglomerates	6,414
17	Science Applications Intl.	Information Technology Consulting Services	6,095
18	Seagate Technology	Data Storage Devices	6,087
19	Menard	Building Materials	5,200
20	S.C. Johnson & Son	Cleaning Products	5,000
21	Graybar Electric	Industrial Equipment & Products Distribution	4,815
22	Giant Eagle	Grocery Retailing	4,415
23	Levi Strauss & Co.	Apparel	4,259
24	MBM	Food Wholesale — to Restaurants	4,236
25	Cox Enterprises	Media	4,230
26	Advance Publications	Publishing	4,185
27	Alticor	Drug, Health & Beauty Product Retailing	4,185
28	Hy-Vee	Grocery Retailing	4,100
29	Guardian Industries	Glass & Clay Products	4,000
30	Gulf States Toyota	Auto Dealers & Distributors	3,900
31	Reyes Holdings	Food Wholesale — to Restaurants	3,900
32	Hallmark Cards	Publishing	3,890
33	Peter Kiewit Sons'	Heavy Construction	3,871
34	InterTech Group	Specialty Chemicals	3,750
35	Southern Wine & Spirits	Bottlers & Wholesale Distributors	3,750
36	Eby-Brown	Food Wholesale — to Grocers	3,670
37	Roundy's	Food Wholesale — to Grocers	3,619
38	Milliken & Co.	Textile Manufacturing	3,600
39	McKinsey & Co.	Management Consulting Services	3,336
40	ContiGroup Cos.	Agricultural Operations & Products	3,300
41	Raley's	Grocery Retailing	3,300
42	Hearst	Media	3,270
43	Capital Group of Cos.	Asset Management	3,200
44	Platinum Equity	Investment Firms	3,200
45	Flying J	Convenience Stores & Gas Stations	3,150
46	Sammons Enterprises	Conglomerates	3,085
47	QuikTrip	Convenience Stores & Gas Stations	3,050
48	Bloomberg	Information Collection & Delivery Services	3,000
49	Kohler	Plumbing & HVAC Equipment	3,000
50	Schwan's Sales Enterprises	Canned & Frozen Foods	3,000
51	J.R. Simplot	Agricultural Operations & Products	3,000
52	RaceTrac Petroleum	Convenience Stores & Gas Stations	2,942
53	Wegmans Food Markets	Grocery Retailing	2,920
54	Gordon Food Service	Food Wholesale — to Restaurants	2,750

Source: *Forbes*; November 7, 2002

The *Forbes* Largest Private Companies in the US (continued)

Rank	Company	Industry	Revenue ($ mil.)
55	Keystone Foods	Food Wholesale — to Restaurants	2,716
56	Perdue Farms	Meat Products	2,700
57	Tenaska Energy	Independent Power Producers & Marketers	2,665
58	Gilbane	Heavy Construction	2,658
59	Stater Bros. Markets	Grocery Retailing	2,653
60	Allegis Group	Staffing, Outsourcing & Other Human Resources	2,610
61	JohnsonDiversey	Specialty Chemicals	2,600
62	International Data Group	Publishing	2,580
63	Connell	Agricultural Services	2,525
64	Clark Enterprises	Heavy Construction	2,500
65	Clark Retail Enterprises	Convenience Stores & Gas Stations	2,500
66	H.T. Hackney	Food Wholesale — to Grocers	2,500
67	Quality King Distributors	Drugs & Sundries — Wholesale	2,450
68	Transammonia	Petroleum Product Distribution	2,434
69	Consolidated Electrical Distributors	Industrial Equipment & Products Distribution	2,400
70	Springs Industries	Home Furnishings	2,400
71	Whiting-Turner Contracting	Heavy Construction	2,400
72	Schneider National	Trucking	2,388
73	Kinray	Drugs & Sundries — Wholesale	2,310
74	A-Mark Financial	Miscellaneous Financial Services	2,300
75	Sinclair Oil	Oil & Gas Refining & Marketing	2,300
76	Sirva	Trucking	2,249
77	Belk	Department Stores	2,243
78	Black & Veatch	Engineering & Architectural Services	2,224
79	DreamWorks SKG	Motion Picture & Video Production & Distribution	2,219
80	Renco Group	Steel Production	2,175
81	Edward Jones	Investment Banking & Brokerage	2,142
82	Golub	Grocery Retailing	2,125
83	Schnuck Markets	Grocery Retailing	2,107
84	Booz Allen Hamilton	Management Consulting Services	2,100
85	Structure Tone	Heavy Construction	2,100
86	Tishman Realty & Construction	Real Estate Development	2,080
87	Jeld-Wen Holding	Miscellaneous Building Materials	2,040
88	Wawa	Convenience Stores & Gas Stations	2,010
89	H Group Holding	Property Investment & Management	2,000
90	KB Toys	Toy & Hobby Retailing & Wholesale	2,000
91	Kinko's	Printing, Photocopying & Graphic Design	2,000
92	Micro Warehouse	Computer & Software Retailing	2,000
93	Alex Lee	Food Wholesale — to Grocers	1,980
94	J.F. Shea	Heavy Construction	1,968
95	DynCorp	Information Technology Consulting Services	1,960
96	CH2M Hill Companies	Engineering & Architectural Services	1,941
97	HB Zachry	Heavy Construction	1,940
98	TravelCenters of America	Convenience Stores & Gas Stations	1,935
99	Ingram Industries	Music, Video, Book & Entertainment	1,929
100	Sheetz	Convenience Stores & Gas Stations	1,920
101	84 Lumber	Building Materials	1,904
102	DeMoulas Super Markets	Grocery Retailing	1,900
103	Vertis	Marketing & Public Relations Services	1,900
104	Scoular	Agricultural Services	1,898
105	UniGroup	Trucking	1,896
106	Carlson Cos.	Travel Services	1,885
107	Fry's Electronics	Computer & Software Retailing	1,850
108	Epix Holdings	Staffing, Outsourcing & Other Human Resources	1,842
109	Dr Pepper/7 Up Bottling Group	Bottlers & Wholesale Distributors	1,820

The *Forbes* Largest Private Companies in the US (continued)

Rank	Company	Industry	Revenue ($ mil.)
110	VarTec Telecom	Miscellaneous End-User Communications Services	1,820
111	Hunt Construction Group	Heavy Construction	1,811
112	Andersen Windows	Miscellaneous Building Materials	1,800
113	Grant Thornton International	Accounting Services	1,800
114	Leprino Foods	Dairy Products	1,800
115	Software House International	Computer Products Distribution & Support	1,800
116	Venture Industries	Automotive & Transport — Auto Parts	1,800
117	E&J Gallo Winery	Wineries	1,780
118	Hensel Phelps Construction	Heavy Construction	1,771
119	DPR Construction	Heavy Construction	1,748
120	Brookshire Grocery	Grocery Retailing	1,740
121	Follett	Music, Video, Book & Entertainment	1,733
122	Houchens Industries	Grocery Retailing	1,727
123	National Distributing	Bottlers & Wholesale Distributors	1,725
124	Haworth	Office & Business Furniture & Fixtures	1,710
125	Rich Products	Diversified Foods — Other	1,702
126	Aecom Technology	Engineering & Architectural Services	1,700
127	Crown Central Petroleum	Oil & Gas Refining & Marketing	1,700
128	Cumberland Farms	Convenience Stores & Gas Stations	1,700
129	Hunt Consolidated/Hunt Oil	Oil & Gas Exploration & Production	1,700
130	Quad/Graphics	Printing, Photocopying & Graphic Design	1,700
131	Gulf Oil	Petroleum Product Distribution	1,680
132	Purdue Pharma	Drug Manufacturers	1,660
133	Golden State Foods	Food Wholesale — to Restaurants	1,659
134	Services Group of America	Food Wholesale — to Restaurants	1,650
135	Central National-Gottesman	Paper & Paper Products	1,628
136	Glazer's Wholesale Drug	Bottlers & Wholesale Distributors	1,600
137	Purity Wholesale Grocers	Food Wholesale — to Grocers	1,600
138	Save Mart Supermarkets	Grocery Retailing	1,600
139	General Parts	Auto Parts Retailing & Wholesale	1,562
140	Builders FirstSource	Building Materials	1,561
141	Asplundh Tree Expert	Building Maintenance & Related Services	1,557
142	Swinerton	Heavy Construction	1,549
143	Dresser	Fluid Control Equipment, Pumps, Seals & Valves	1,546
144	WinCo Foods	Grocery Retailing	1,540
145	DiGiorgio	Food Wholesale — to Grocers	1,539
146	Dunn Industries	Heavy Construction	1,533
147	Dot Foods	Food Wholesale — to Restaurants	1,500
148	Frank Consolidated Enterprises	Car & Truck Rental	1,500
149	Grocers Supply	Food Wholesale — to Grocers	1,500
150	Maritz	Travel Services	1,500
151	Parsons	Heavy Construction	1,500
152	Schreiber Foods	Dairy Products	1,500
153	Southwire	Wire & Cable	1,500
154	Young's Market	Bottlers & Wholesale Distributors	1,485
155	BE&K	Engineering & Architectural Services	1,478
156	Towers Perrin	Management Consulting Services	1,469
157	DHL Airways	Air Delivery, Freight & Parcel Services	1,462
158	Ergon	Conglomerates	1,460
159	Flint Ink	Specialty Chemicals	1,450
160	Walsh Group	Heavy Construction	1,443
161	Horizon Natural Resources	Coal	1,413
162	Apex Oil	Petroleum Product Distribution	1,400
163	Bose	Consumer Electronics	1,400
164	Delaware North Cos.	Specialty Eateries & Catering Services	1,400

The *Forbes* Largest Private Companies in the US (continued)

Rank	Company	Industry	Revenue ($ mil.)
165	Heico Cos.	Investment Firms	1,400
166	Mary Kay	Personal Care Products	1,400
167	Metaldyne	Automotive & Transport — Auto Parts	1,400
168	AG Spanos Cos.	Residential Construction	1,400
169	Vought Aircraft Industries	Aerospace/Defense	1,400
170	Metromedia	Restaurants	1,397
171	ABC Supply	Building Materials	1,382
172	EBSCO Industries	Conglomerates	1,380
173	DeBruce Grain	Agricultural Services	1,378
174	Borden Chemical	Specialty Chemicals	1,372
175	Amsted Industries	Diversified Machinery	1,360
176	Bashas'	Grocery Retailing	1,359
177	Parsons Brinckerhoff	Engineering & Architectural Services	1,350
178	Lanoga	Building Materials	1,344
179	Life Care Centers of America	Long-Term Care Facilities	1,340
180	Ritz Camera Centers	Miscellaneous Retail	1,340
181	Discount Tire	Auto Parts Retailing & Wholesale	1,320
182	Sierra Pacific Industries	Lumber, Wood Production & Timber Operations	1,315
183	Day & Zimmermann	Engineering & Architectural Services	1,300
184	National Gypsum	Miscellaneous Building Materials	1,300
185	Polaroid	Photographic Equipment & Supplies	1,300
186	G-I Holdings	Miscellaneous Building Materials	1,293
187	SF Holdings	Packaging & Containers	1,277
188	Foster Farms	Meat Products	1,269
189	IMG	Miscellaneous Business Services	1,260
190	Rooms to Go	Home Furnishings & Housewares Retailing	1,260
191	Domino's Pizza	Restaurants	1,258
192	Austin Industries	Heavy Construction	1,257
193	Barton Malow	Engineering & Architectural Services	1,251
194	Medline Industries	Medical Instruments & Supplies	1,251
195	Riverwood International	Paper & Paper Products	1,250
196	ICC Industries	Diversified	1,249
197	Taylor	Printing, Photocopying & Graphic Design	1,248
198	Barnes & Noble College Bookstores	Music, Video, Book & Entertainment	1,240
199	WL Gore & Associates	Textile Manufacturing	1,230
200	Skadden, Arps	Legal Services	1,225
201	Rooney Brothers	Heavy Construction	1,201
202	Genmar Holdings	Automotive & Transport — Pleasure Boats	1,200
203	Sealy	Home Furnishings	1,197
204	Ben E. Keith	Food Wholesale — to Restaurants	1,185
205	Wilbur-Ellis	Agricultural Services	1,185
206	Battelle Memorial Institute	Technical & Scientific Research Services	1,176
207	Big Y Foods	Grocery Retailing	1,170
208	Hoffman	Heavy Construction	1,165
209	Michael Foods	Agricultural Operations & Products	1,161
210	Conair	Appliances	1,151
211	SAS Institute	Corporate, Professional & Financial Software	1,130
212	FHC Health Systems	Specialized Health Services	1,128
213	M.A. Mortenson	Heavy Construction	1,128
214	Goodman Manufacturing	Appliances	1,125
215	TIC-The Industrial Co.	Heavy Construction	1,123
216	Baker & Taylor	Music, Video, Book & Entertainment	1,122
217	J.M. Huber	Specialty Chemicals	1,122
218	Modern Continental Cos.	Heavy Construction	1,117
219	American Tire Distributors	Auto Parts Retailing & Wholesale	1,108

The *Forbes* Largest Private Companies in the US (continued)

Rank	Company	Industry	Revenue ($ mil.)
220	Ashley Furniture Industries	Home Furnishings	1,100
221	L.L. Bean	Clothing, Shoes & Accessories	1,100
222	Breed Technologies	Automotive & Transport — Auto Parts	1,100
223	Columbia House	Music, Video, Book & Entertainment	1,100
224	Dart Container	Packaging & Containers	1,100
225	Dick Corp.	Heavy Construction	1,100
226	Shamrock Foods	Food Wholesale — to Grocers	1,093
227	Bass Pro	Sporting Goods Retailing	1,090
228	Love's Travel Stops	Convenience Stores & Gas Stations	1,086
229	Honickman Affiliates	Bottlers & Wholesale Distributors	1,076
230	Nesco	Diversified Machinery	1,065
231	Noveon	Diversified	1,063
232	Arctic Slope Regional	Oil & Gas Services	1,062
233	Baker & McKenzie	Legal Services	1,060
234	North Pacific Group	Building Materials	1,060
235	UIS	Automotive & Transport — Auto Parts	1,056
236	Anderson News	Music, Video, Book & Entertainment	1,054
237	Delco Remy International	Automotive & Transport — Auto Parts	1,053
238	Boston Consulting Group	Management Consulting Services	1,050
239	Stevedoring Services of America	Logistics & Other Transportation Services	1,046
240	Buffets	Restaurants	1,045
241	JD Heiskell & Co.	Agricultural Operations & Products	1,036
242	McCarthy Building Cos.	Heavy Construction	1,036
243	Carpenter	Plastics & Fibers	1,035
244	24 Hour Fitness Worldwide	Sporting Activities	1,029
245	Herbalife International	Vitamins & Health-Related Products	1,020
246	Menasha	Paper & Paper Products	1,018
247	Yates Cos.	Heavy Construction	1,016
248	ClubCorp	Sporting Activities	1,015
249	Hobby Lobby Stores	Toy & Hobby Retailing & Wholesale	1,015
250	Printpack	Packaging & Containers	1,015
251	Agrilink Foods	Canned & Frozen Foods	1,011
252	Boscov's	Department Stores	1,010
253	Rudolph and Sletten	Heavy Construction	1,002
254	Crowley Maritime	Shipping	1,001
255	Primus	Building Materials	1,001
256	Connell Limited Partnership	Diversified Machinery	1,000
257	Swagelok	Fluid Control Equipment, Pumps, Seals & Valves	1,000

American Lawyer's Top 25 US Law Firms

Rank	Firm	Number of Lawyers	Gross Revenue ($ mil.)
1	Skadden, Arps, Slate, Meagher & Flom	1,602	1,225.0
2	Baker & McKenzie	3,031	1,000.0
3	Jones, Day, Reavis & Pogue	1,481	790.0
4	Latham & Watkins	1,165	769.5
5	Sidley Austin Brown & Wood	1,276	715.0
6	Shearman & Sterling	1,039	619.5
7	White & Case	1,315	603.0
8	Weil, Gotshal & Manges	845	581.0
9	Morgan, Lewis & Bockius	1,083	574.5
10	Mayer, Brown & Platt	893	573.0
11	Davis Polk & Wardwell	594	570.0
12	Sullivan & Cromwell	596	568.0
13	McDermott, Will & Emery	874	562.5
14	Akin, Gump, Strauss, Hauer & Feld	949	553.0
15	Gibson, Dunn & Crutcher	709	537.0
16	Kirkland & Ellis	725	530.0
17	Simpson Thacher & Bartlett	588	516.0
18	Cleary, Gottlieb, Steen & Hamilton	610	492.0
19	Morrison & Foerster	889	490.0
19	O'Melveny & Myers	738	490.0
21	Holland & Knight	1,094	466.5
22	Paul, Hastings, Janofsky & Walker	722	455.5
22	Vinson & Elkins	777	455.5
24	Foley & Lardner	907	452.5
25	Brobeck, Phleger & Harrison	792	447.0

Source: *American Lawyer;* July 2002

America's Top 25 Tax & Accounting Firms Ranked by US Revenue

Rank	Firm	Headquarters	2001 US Revenue ($ mil.)
1	PricewaterhouseCoopers	New York	8,057.0
2	Deloitte & Touche	New York	6,130.0
3	Ernst & Young	New York	4,485.0
4	Andersen	Chicago	4,300.0
5	KPMG	New York	3,400.0
6	H&R Block	Kansas City, MO	3,001.6
7	RSM McGladrey/McGladrey & Pullen	Bloomington, MN	507.4
8	BDO Seidman	Chicago	420.0
9	Century Business Services Inc.	Cleveland	388.6
10	Grant Thornton	Chicago	380.0
11	American Express Tax & Business Services Inc.	New York	350.0
12	Jackson Hewitt Tax Service	Parsippany, NJ	253.1
13	BKD	Springfield, MO	197.6
14	Crowe, Chizek and Co.	Indianapolis	182.6
15	Moss Adams	Seattle	167.0
16	Centerprise Advisors Inc.	Chicago	162.3
17	Plante & Moran	Southfield, MI	153.0
18	Clifton Gunderson	Peoria, IL	123.2
19	Fiducial	New York	118.3
20	Gilman & Ciocia Inc.	White Plains, NY	106.5
21	Virchow, Krause & Co.	Madison, WI	88.7
22	Constantin Associates	New York	87.9
23	Larson, Allen, Weishair & Co.	Minneapolis	78.9
24	Eisner	New York	77.0
25	Reznick Fedder & Silverman	Bethesda, MD	63.9

Source: *Accounting Today;* March 18–April 7, 2002

Top 50 Universities

Rank	School	Rank	School
1	Princeton University	25	University of Michigan – Ann Arbor*
2	Harvard University	25	Wake Forest University
2	Yale University	28	Tufts University
4	California Institute of Technology	28	University of North Carolina – Chapel Hill*
4	Duke University	30	College of William and Mary*
4	Massachusetts Institute of Technology	31	Brandeis University
4	Stanford University	31	University of California – San Diego*
4	University of Pennsylvania	31	University of Southern California
9	Dartmouth College	31	University of Wisconsin – Madison*
10	Columbia University	35	New York University
10	Northwestern University	36	University of Rochester
12	University of Chicago	37	Case Western Reserve University
12	Washington University in St. Louis	38	Georgia Institute of Technology*
14	Cornell University	38	University of Illinois – Urbana-Champaign*
15	Johns Hopkins University	40	Boston College
15	Rice University	40	Lehigh University
17	Brown University	40	Yeshiva University
18	Emory University	43	Tulane University
18	University of Notre Dame	43	University of California – Davis*
20	University of California – Berkeley*	45	Pennsylvania State University – University Park*
21	Carnegie Mellon University		
21	Vanderbilt University	45	University of California – Irvine*
23	University of Virginia*	47	Pepperdine University
24	Georgetown University	47	Rensselaer Polytechnic Institute
25	University of California – Los Angeles*	47	University of California – Santa Barbara*
		47	University of Texas – Austin*

*Denotes a public school
Ranked by composite score, including such factors as graduation and retention rates, faculty resources, and student-to-faculty ratio.

Source: *U.S. News and World Report;* September 23, 2002

Top 10 Health Care Systems by Net Patient Revenue

Rank	System	2001 Revenue ($ mil.)
1	U.S. Department of Veterans Affairs	24,366.0
2	HCA	17,953.0
3	Tenet Healthcare Corp.	11,542.0
4	Ascension Health	6,452.5
5	Catholic Health Initiatives	5,300.0
6	New York-Presbyterian Healthcare System	4,993.2
7	Catholic Healthcare West	4,618.5
8	Mayo Foundation	3,406.8
9	Catholic Health East	3,386.0
10	Trinity Health	3,378.8

Source: *Modern Healthcare;* June 3, 2002

Top 25 US Foundations

Rank	Name	State	Assets ($ mil.)
1	Bill & Melinda Gates Foundation	WA	21,149.1
2	Lilly Endowment Inc.	IN	12,814.4
3	The Ford Foundation	NY	10,814.7
4	The Robert Wood Johnson Foundation	NJ	9,044.5
5	J. Paul Getty Trust	CA	8,793.5
6	The David and Lucile Packard Foundation	CA	6,196.5
7	W. K. Kellogg Foundation	MI	5,719.7
8	The Starr Foundation	NY	4,781.1
9	John D. and Catherine T. MacArthur Foundation	IL	4,479.2
10	The Pew Charitable Trusts	PA	4,338.6
11	The Andrew W. Mellon Foundation	NY	4,135.6
12	The William and Flora Hewlett Foundation	CA	3,930.4
13	The California Endowment	CA	3,366.3
14	The Rockefeller Foundation	NY	3,211.1
15	The Annenberg Foundation	PA	2,932.2
16	Charles Stewart Mott Foundation	MI	2,881.8
17	Casey Family Programs	WA	2,811.0
18	The Annie E. Casey Foundation	MD	2,592.4
19	The Duke Endowment	NC	2,489.2
20	Robert W. Woodruff Foundation, Inc.	GA	2,422.6
21	The Kresge Foundation	MI	2,416.0
22	John S. and James L. Knight Foundation	FL	2,199.0
23	Ewing Marion Kauffman Foundation	MO	2,022.3
24	The McKnight Foundation	MN	2,006.4
25	The Harry and Jeanette Weinberg Foundation, Inc.	MD	1,936.3

Source: The Foundation Center; http://www.fdncenter.org; December 9, 2002

Hoover's Handbook of Private Companies

COMPANIES COVERED

Companies Covered in *Hoover's Handbook of Private Companies 2003*

Hoover's Handbook of Private Companies 2003 contains two-page, in-depth profiles on 200 key US non-public enterprises (mostly larger companies, but we've included several smaller but equally interesting ones as well). In addition, we provide basic information, including officers, sales, and top competitors, for 700 other major enterprises with revenues of $625 million or more.

Companies Covered in *Hoover's Handbook of Private Companies 2003*

Companies Covered in *Hoover's Handbook of Private Companies 2003*

Companies Covered in *Hoover's Handbook of Private Companies 2003*

Companies Covered in *Hoover's Handbook of Private Companies 2003*

Companies Covered in *Hoover's Handbook of Private Companies 2003*

Companies Covered in *Hoover's Handbook of Private Companies 2003*

Companies Covered in *Hoover's Handbook* of *Private Companies 2003*

Hoover's Handbook of Private Companies

IN-DEPTH PROFILES
OF KEY COMPANIES

AARP

AARP is gearing up for the geezer boom. Open to anyone age 50 or older (dues are $12.50 per year), the not-for-profit organization is the largest organization of older adults in the US with more than 35 million members and is also the largest lobbyist for the elderly (it spends about $57 million on lobbying and related activities). On a mission to enhance the quality of life for older Americans, AARP is active in four areas: information and education, community service, advocacy, and member services. It also publishes the monthly *AARP Bulletin* and the bimonthly *Modern Maturity* magazine.

AARP disseminates information in a variety of formats (a Web site, public policy agendas, and radio and TV spots) and pursues educational and research efforts through the AARP Andrus Foundation, the Research Information Center, and the Public Policy Institute.

AARP may not be the most exclusive club around, but it is one of the most powerful. AARP is attempting to transform itself by adapting to its changing demographics. The organization has initiated a $100 million, five-year marketing plan to attract aging baby boomers who are becoming eligible for membership, including the launch of a new magazine called *My Generation.*

AARP members are eligible for services, including savings on prescription drugs, travel, investment opportunities, and health, life, and auto insurance. Retired educators who join the National Retired Teachers Association (a division of AARP) can receive both AARP services and other benefits designed specifically for them.

HISTORY

Ethel Andrus, a retired Los Angeles high school principal who founded the National Retired Teachers Association (NRTA) in 1947, founded the American Association of Retired Persons (AARP) in 1958 with the help of Leonard Davis, a New York insurance salesman who had helped her find an underwriter for the NRTA. The new organization's goal: to "enhance the quality of life" for older Americans and "improve the image of aging."

Andrus offered members the same low rates for health and accident insurance provided to NRTA members. She also started publishing AARP's bimonthly magazine, *Modern Maturity,* in 1958. The organization's first local chapter opened in Youngstown, Arizona, in 1960. Still an insurance man, Davis formed Colonial Penn Insurance in 1963 to take over the AARP account. Andrus led the AARP and its increasingly powerful lobby for the elderly until her death in 1967.

With criticism of Colonial Penn mounting in the 1970s (critics charged the organization was little more than a front for the insurance company), Prudential won AARP's insurance business in 1979. The NRTA merged with AARP in 1982, and the following year it lowered the membership eligibility age from 55 to 50. The organization continued to expand its offerings, adding an auto club and financial products such as mutual funds and expanded insurance policies. The organization also started a federal credit union for members in 1988, but despite rosy projections, it ceased operations two years later.

AARP forked over $135 million to the IRS in 1993 as part of a settlement regarding the tax status of profits from some of its activities, but the dispute remained unresolved. AARP switched insurance providers again in 1996 (to New York Life) and started offering discounted legal services. Also that year, AARP said it would let HMOs offer managed-care services to members. The plan drew objections over its potential violation of Medicare anti-kickback laws, and AARP developed a revised payment plan in 1997.

AARP's image was bruised in 1998 when Dale Van Atta wrote a scathing account of the organization, *Trust Betrayed: Inside the AARP.* The book accused the organization of operating out of lavish accommodations, acting as a shill for businesses to hawk their wares, and concealing a drop in membership. Also in 1998, recognizing that nearly a third of its members were working, the organization dropped the American Association of Retired Persons moniker and began to refer to itself by the AARP abbreviation.

To end the long-running dispute with the IRS, AARP reached a settlement over its alleged profit-making enterprises by creating a new taxable subsidiary called AARP Services in 1999. The following year AARP initiated a five-year plan to attract aging baby boomers. AARP launched its new *My Generation* magazine 2001.

OFFICERS

Executive Director and CEO: William D. Novelli, age 60
President: James G. Parkel
CFO: Robert Hagans
VP Membership and Member Services:
Charles J. Mendoza
VP, Secretary, and Treasurer: Charles Leven
Associate Executive Director, Operations:
Richard Henry
Associate Executive Director, Field Operations:
Thomas C. Nelson
Associate Executive Director, Membership:
Dawn Sweeney
Director of Human Resources: Russ Consaul
General Counsel: Joan Wise

LOCATIONS

HQ: 601 E St. NW, Washington, DC 20049
Phone: 202-434-2277   **Fax:** 202-434-6548
Web: www.aarp.org

AARP has offices in all 50 states, the District of
Columbia, Puerto Rico, and the Virgin Islands.

PRODUCTS/OPERATIONS

2001 Sales

	$ mil.	% of total
Membership dues	164	28
Health care options	101	17
Royalties	81	14
Advertising	80	13
Federal grant & other program income	74	12
Investment & other income	64	11
Member service & programs	31	5
Total	**595**	**100**

Selected Operations and Programs
55 ALIVE/Mature Driving
AARP Andrus Foundation (gerontology research)
AARP Bulletin (monthly news update)
AARP Legal Services Network
AARP Services (taxable product management,
marketing, and e-commerce subsidiary)
Financial Planning
Mature Focus Radio (daily news program)
Modern Maturity (bimonthly magazine)
National Retired Teachers Association
Public Policy Institute
Research Information Center
Senior Community Service Employment Program
Tax-Aide

HISTORICAL FINANCIALS & EMPLOYEES

Association FYE: December 31	Annual Growth	12/92	12/93	12/94	12/95	12/96	12/97	12/98	12/99	12/00	12/01
Sales ($ mil.)	7.7%	305	369	469	506	475	529	541	486	580	595
Employees	0.5%	1,718	1,793	1,752	1,800	1,850	1,900	2,000	2,000	2,000	1,800

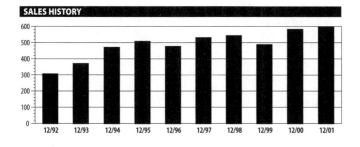

SALES HISTORY

ACE HARDWARE CORPORATION

Luckily, Ace has John Madden up its sleeve. Despite the growth of warehouse-style competitors, Ace Hardware has remained a household name, thanks to ads featuring Madden, a former Oakland Raiders football coach and TV commentator. The Oak Brook, Illinois-based company is the #2 hardware cooperative in the US, behind TruServ (operator of True Value and several other hardware chains). Ace dealer-owners operate about 5,000 Ace Hardware stores throughout the US and in about 70 other countries. The co-op distributes to its retailers from more than 20 wholesale warehouses.

Ace distributes products such as electrical and plumbing supplies, garden equipment, hand tools, housewares, and power tools. It also makes its own brand of paint and offers thousands of other Ace-brand products. Subsidiary Ace Insurance Agency offers dealers insurance for their stores and employees. Ace also provides training programs and advertising campaigns.

Challenged by big-box chains such as The Home Depot and Lowe's, Ace has unveiled its Next Generation store concept, which calls for signage with detailed product descriptions and different flooring to set off departments, among other features. Ace dealers own the company and receive dividends from Ace's profits.

Sodisco-Howden is buying all the shares of Ace Hardware Canada.

HISTORY

A group of Chicago-area hardware dealers — William Stauber, Richard Hesse, Gern Lindquist, and Oscar Fisher — decided in 1924 to pool their hardware buying and promotional costs. In 1928 the group incorporated as Ace Stores, named in honor of the superior WWI fliers dubbed aces. Hesse became president the following year, retaining that position for the next 44 years. The company also opened its first warehouse in 1929, and by 1933 it had 38 dealers.

The organization had 133 dealers in seven states by 1949. In 1953 Ace began to allow dealers to buy stock in the company through the Ace Perpetuation Plan. During the 1960s Ace expanded into the South and West, and by 1969 it had opened distribution centers in Georgia and California — its first such facilities outside Chicago. In 1968 it opened its first international store in Guam.

By the early 1970s the do-it-yourself market began to surge as inflation pushed up plumber and electrician fees. As the market grew, large home center chains gobbled up market share from independent dealers such as those franchised through Ace. In response, Ace and its dealers became a part of a growing trend in the hardware industry — cooperatives.

Hesse sold the company to its dealers in 1973 for $6 million (less than half its book value), and the following year Ace began operating as a cooperative. Hesse stepped down in 1973. In 1976 the dealers took full control when the company's first Board of Dealer-Directors was elected.

After signing up a number of dealers in the eastern US, Ace had dealers in all 50 states by 1979. The co-op opened a plant to make paint in Matteson, Illinois, in 1984. By 1985 Ace had reached $1 billion in sales and had initiated its Store of the Future Program, allowing dealers to borrow up to $200,000 to upgrade their stores and conduct market analyses. Former head coach John Madden of the National Football League's Oakland Raiders signed on as Ace's mouthpiece in 1988.

A year later the co-op began to test ACENET, a computer network that allowed Ace dealers to check inventory, send and receive e-mail, make special purchase requests, and keep up with prices on commodity items such as lumber. In 1990 Ace established an International Division to handle its overseas stores. (It had been exporting products since 1975.) EVP and COO David Hodnik became president in 1995. That year the co-op added a net of 67 stores, including a three-store chain in Russia. Expanding further internationally, Ace signed a five-year joint-supply agreement in 1996 with Canadian lumber and hardware retailer Beaver Lumber. Hodnik added CEO to his title in 1996.

Ace fell further behind its old rival, True Value, in 1997 when ServiStar Coast to Coast and True Value merged to form TruServ, a hardware giant that operated more than 10,000 outlets at the completion of the merger.

Late in 1997 Ace launched an expansion program in Canada. (The co-op already operated distribution centers in Ontario and Calgary.) In 1999 Ace merged its lumber and building materials division with Builder Marts of America to form a dealer-owned buying group to supply about 2,700 retailers. In 2000, Ace gained 208 member outlet stores, but saw 279 member outlets terminated. The next year it gained 220, but lost 255. Also in 2001 more than 160 stores operating under TruServ, which acknowledged financial irregularities in 2000, applied to join Ace.

OFFICERS

President and CEO: David F. Hodnik, age 54, $752,840 pay
EVP, Strategic Planning: Rita D. Kahle, age 45, $434,280 pay
EVP, Retail: Ray A. Griffith, age 48
SVP, International and Technology: Paul M. Ingevaldson, age 56, $377,800 pay
SVP, Retail Support and Logistics: David F. Myer, age 56, $380,980 pay
VP, Human Resources: Jimmy Alexander, age 45
VP, Marketing, Advertising, Retail Development, and Company Stores: Michael C. Bodzewski, age 52, $367,380 pay
VP, Merchandising: Lori L. Bossmann, age 41
VP, Retail Operations: Ken L. Nichols, age 53
Treasurer: Sandy Brandt
Controller: Ron Knutson
Director, Application Development: Jay Heubner
Director, International Licensees: Maurice Ademe
Director, People Development and Learning Systems: Ron Wagner
Director, Retail Operations for the Midwest Division: Bob Guido
Manager, Advertising: Frank Rothing
Manager, Corporate Communications and Public Relations: Paula Erickson
Manager, General Merchandise: Gary Paulson
Manager, Marketing: John Venhvizen
Manager, New Business: Bill Jablonowski
Manager, Retail Program Execution: Art Freedman
Manager, Retail Technology Products: Frank Murphy
Department Manager, Inventory: Scott Smith
General Counsel: Donna Flenard
Customer Service: Tim Schubert
Auditors: KPMG LLP

LOCATIONS

HQ: 2200 Kensington Ct., Oak Brook, IL 60523
Phone: 630-990-6600   **Fax:** 630-990-6838
Web: www.acehardware.com

Ace Hardware wholesales products to dealers with retail operations in the US and about 70 other countries.

PRODUCTS/OPERATIONS

2001 Sales

	% of total
Paint, cleaning and related supplies	21
Plumbing and heating supplies	15
Garden, rural equipment and related supplies	14
Hand and power tools	14
Electrical supplies	12
General hardware	11
Sundry	8
Housewares and appliances	5
Total	**100**

Subsidiaries
Ace Corporate Stores, Inc. (operation of company-owned stores)
Ace Hardware Canada, Limited (hardware wholesaler)
Ace Hardware de México, S.A. de C.V. (hardware wholesaler)
Ace Insurance Agency, Inc. (dealer insurance program)
A.H.C. Store Development Corp. (operation of company-owned stores)
Loss Prevention Services, Inc. (security training and loss prevention services for dealers)
National Hardlines Supply, Inc. (sells to retailers outside the Ace dealer network)

COMPETITORS

84 Lumber	Lowe's
Akzo Nobel	McCoy
Benjamin Moore	Menard
Building Materials	Northern Tool
Holding	Reno-Depot
Carolina Holdings	Sears
Costco Wholesale	Sherwin-Williams
Do it Best	Sutherland Lumber
Fastenal	TruServ
Grossman's	United Hardware
Home Depot	Distributing Co.
ICI American Holdings	Wal-Mart
Kmart	Wickes
Lanoga	Wolohan Lumber

HISTORICAL FINANCIALS & EMPLOYEES

Cooperative FYE: December 31	Annual Growth	12/92	12/93	12/94	12/95	12/96	12/97	12/98	12/99	12/00	12/01
Sales ($ mil.)	5.0%	1,871	2,018	2,326	2,436	2,742	2,907	3,120	3,182	2,945	2,894
Net income ($ mil.)	2.1%	61	57	65	64	72	76	88	93	80	73
Income as % of sales	—	3.2%	2.8%	2.8%	2.6%	2.6%	2.6%	2.8%	2.9%	2.7%	2.5%
Employees	5.4%	3,256	3,405	3,664	3,917	4,352	4,685	4,672	5,180	5,513	5,229

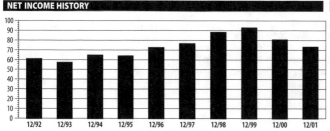

NET INCOME HISTORY

2001 FISCAL YEAR-END
Debt ratio: 37.8%
Return on equity: 25.9%
Cash ($ mil.): 25
Current ratio: 1.37
Long-term debt ($ mil.): 170

ADVANCE PUBLICATIONS, INC.

Advance Publications gets its marching orders from the printed page. One of the top US periodical publishers, Advance owns 22 daily newspapers around the country, including *The Star-Ledger* (New Jersey), *The Cleveland Plain Dealer*, and its namesake *Staten Island Advance*. It also owns American City Business Journals (41 weekly papers) and Parade Publications (*Parade Magazine* Sunday insert). Advance is the #2 magazine publisher in the US (behind Time, Inc.) through units Condé Nast Publications, with its popular titles such as *Allure, Glamour*, and *Vanity Fair*, and trade journal publisher Fairchild Publications (*Women's Wear Daily*). Samuel "Si" Newhouse Jr. and his brother Donald own the company.

Aside from publishing, Advance is a major online publisher with nearly a dozen regional news Web sites. Its CondéNet unit runs Web versions of Condé Nast's magazines and other Internet properties, including Epicurious (food and dining) and Concierge (travel). The company also has stakes in cable TV systems (33%, with AOL Time Warner), broadband ISP Road Runner (9%), and cable broadcaster Discovery Communications (25%).

Advance took steps to increase its magazine portfolio by acquiring The New York Times Company's Golf Properties unit (*Golf Digest)* for about $430 million and Miami-based Ideas Publishing Group, which produces Spanish language versions of US magazines.

HISTORY

Solomon Neuhaus (later Samuel I. Newhouse) got started in the newspaper business after dropping out of school at age 13. He went to work at the *Bayonne Times* in New Jersey and was put in charge of the failing newspaper in 1911; he managed to turn the paper around within a year. In 1922 he bought the *Staten Island Advance* and formed the Staten Island Advance Company in 1924. After buying up more papers, he changed the name of the company to Advance Publications in 1949. By the 1950s the company had local papers in New York, New Jersey, and Alabama.

In 1959 Newhouse bought magazine publisher Condé Nast as an anniversary gift for his wife. (He joked that she had asked for a fashion magazine, so he bought her *Vogue*.) His publishing empire continued to grow with the addition of the *Times-Picayune* (New Orleans) in 1962 and *The Cleveland Plain Dealer* in 1967. In 1976 the company paid more than $300 million for Booth Newspapers, publisher of eight Michigan papers and *Parade Magazine*.

Newhouse died in 1979, leaving his sons Si and Donald to run the company, which encompassed more than 30 newspapers, a half-dozen magazines, and 15 cable systems. The next year Advance bought book publishing giant Random House from RCA. Si resurrected the Roaring Twenties standard *Vanity Fair* in 1983 and added *The New Yorker* under the Condé Nast banner in 1985. The Newhouses scored a victory over the IRS in 1990 after a long-running court battle involving inheritance taxes. Condé Nast bought Knapp Publications (*Architectural Digest*) in 1993 and Advance later acquired American City Business Journals in 1995.

In 1998 the company sold the increasingly unprofitable Random House to Bertelsmann for about $1.2 billion. It later bought hallmark Internet magazine *Wired* (though it passed on Wired Ventures' Internet operations). That year revered *New Yorker* editor Tina Brown, credited with jazzing up the publication's content and increasing its circulation, left the magazine; staff writer and Pulitzer Prize winner David Remnick was named as Brown's replacement.

In 1999 Advance joined with Donrey Media Group (now called Stephens Media Group), E.W. Scripps, Hearst Corporation, and MediaNews Group to purchase the online classified advertising network AdOne (later named PowerOne Media). It also bought Walt Disney's trade publishing unit, Fairchild Publications, for $650 million. In 2000 the company shifted *Details* from Condé Nast to Fairchild and relaunched the magazine as a fashion publication. Later that year the company announced it would begin creating Web versions of its popular magazine titles.

In 2001 Condé Nast bought a majority stake in Miami-based Ideas Publishing Group (Spanish language versions of US magazines). Also that year Advance bought four golf magazines, including *Golf Digest*, from the New York Times Company for $430 million. Condé Nast picked up *Modern Bride* magazine from PRIMEDIA in early 2002 for $52 million.

OFFICERS

Chairman and CEO; Chairman, Condé Nast Publications: Samuel I. Newhouse Jr.
President: Donald E. Newhouse
COO, Advance Magazine Publishers; COO, Condé Nast: Charles H. Townsend
VP Data Processing: Nick Guido
VP Finance and Human Resources; Comptroller, Staten Island Advance: Arthur Silverstein
VP Investor Services: George Fries
VP Marketing: Jack Furnari
VP Sales: Gary Cognetta

Chairman, CEO, and Publisher, Parade Publications:
Walter Anderson
Chairman and Editorial Director, Golf Digest Companies: Jerry Tarde
Chairman, American City Business Journals: Ray Shaw
President and CEO, Condé Nast Publications:
Steven T. Florio
Executive Director of Human Resources Recruiting:
Pammy Brooks

LOCATIONS

HQ: 950 Fingerboard Rd., Staten Island, NY 10305
Phone: 718-981-1234 **Fax:** 718-981-1456
Web: www.advance.net

Advance Publications publishes 22 newspapers in more than 20 cities and 41 business weeklies in 22 states.

PRODUCTS/OPERATIONS

Selected Operations

Broadcasting and Communications
Cartoonbank.com (database of cartoons from *The New Yorker*)
Discovery Communications (25%, cable TV channel)
Newhouse Broadcasting (33%, cable TV joint venture with AOL Time Warner)
Newhouse News Service
Religion News Service
Road Runner (9%, broadband Internet service)

Magazine Publishing
Condé Nast Publications

Allure	*House & Garden*
Architectural Digest	*Modern Bride*
Bon Appetit	*The New Yorker*
Bride's	*Self*
Condé Nast Traveler	*Vanity Fair*
Glamour	*Vogue*
Gourmet	*Wired*
GQ	

Fairchild Publications

Details	*W*
Jane	*Women's Wear Daily*
Supermarket News	

The Golf Digest Companies

Golf Digest	*Golf World*
Golf for Women	*Golf World Business*

Newspaper Publishing
American City Business Journals (41 weekly titles in 22 states)
Street & Smith's Sports Business Group (*SportsBusiness Journal*)
Newhouse Newspapers (22 papers in more than 20 cities)
Parade Publications

Online Publishing
Advance Internet
CondéNet
Concierge (travel information)
Epicurious (recipes and fine dining)
Style.com (fashion and beauty)

Selected Newspapers
The Birmingham News (Alabama)
The Oregonian (Portland)
The Plain Dealer (Cleveland)
The Star-Ledger (Newark, NJ)
Staten Island Advance (New York)
The Times-Picayune (New Orleans)

COMPETITORS

American Express
Crain Communications
Dow Jones
E. W. Scripps
Freedom Communications
Gannett
Gruner + Jahr
Hachette Filipacchi Médias
Hearst
Knight Ridder
MSO
McClatchy Company
Meredith
New York Times
North Jersey Media
PRIMEDIA
Reader's Digest
Reed Elsevier Group
Time
Tribune
Washington Post

HISTORICAL FINANCIALS & EMPLOYEES

Private FYE: December 31	Annual Growth	12/92	12/93	12/94	12/95	12/96	12/97	12/98	12/99	12/00	12/01
Sales ($ mil.)	(0.6%)	4,416	4,690	4,855	5,349	4,250	3,669	3,859	4,228	4,542	4,200
Employees	2.0%	19,000	19,000	19,000	24,000	24,000	24,000	24,000	26,300	23,000	22,785

SALES HISTORY

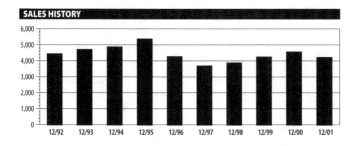

AFL-CIO

Talk about spending a long time in labor: The AFL-CIO (American Federation of Labor and Congress of Industrial Organizations) has been at it for more than a century. Based in Washington, DC, the AFL-CIO is an umbrella organization for 66 autonomous national and international unions representing more than 13 million workers — ranging from actors and airline pilots to teachers and Teamsters — and works to improve wages and working conditions. The organization charters 51 state federations and nearly 580 central labor councils. Union members generally receive about 33% higher pay and more benefits than do nonmembers.

The organization's membership has been decreasing because of the decline in manufacturing jobs and the increased use of temporary workers and automation. However, the AFL-CIO is reviving under the leadership of John Sweeney, primarily because of his aggressive emphasis on recruiting. It also is restructuring for the first time in about 45 years; the plan calls for consolidating some of the AFL-CIO's nearly 600 local labor councils and giving the national office greater power to set the agenda for the more autonomous state affiliates.

HISTORY

The American Federation of Labor (AFL) was formed in 1886 in Columbus, Ohio, by the merger of six craft unions and a renegade craft section of the Marxist-oriented Knights of Labor. Samuel Gompers, a New York cigar factory worker who headed the AFL until his death in 1924, initiated the AFL's pragmatic focus: to work within the economic system to increase wages, improve working conditions, and abolish child labor.

Gompers' successes incensed employers, whose arsenal, supported by the US courts and public opinion, included government-backed police forces to crush strikes, injunctions, and the Sherman Anti-Trust Act (used to assail union monopoly powers).

WWI's production needs boosted AFL membership to 4 million by 1919. Labor clashes with management were widespread in the 1920s amid the fear of Bolsheviks. As part of open-shop drives, employers replaced strikers with southern African-Americans and Mexican workers.

The Great Depression brought more supportive public and pro-labor laws, including the National Industrial Recovery Act (NIRA, 1933), which allowed union organizing and collective bargaining. After NIRA was declared unconstitutional, the Wagner Act (1936) restated many of NIRA's provisions and established the legal basis for unions.

Union power split in 1935 when AFL coal miner John L. Lewis began organizing unskilled workers. Lewis and his allies, expelled from the AFL, formed the Congress of Industrial Organizations (CIO, 1938) and enjoyed success in unionizing the auto, steel, textile, and other industries. By 1946 the AFL and CIO had 9 million and 5 million members, respectively.

Amid postwar concern over rising prices, communist infiltration, and union corruption, Congress passed the Taft-Hartley Act in 1947 (which outlawed closed shops). The new climate of hostility led the AFL (headed by plumber George Meany) and the CIO (headed by autoworker Walter Reuther) to merge in 1955. The AFL-CIO soon expelled the Teamsters and other unions on charges of corruption. (The Teamsters reaffiliated in 1987.)

AFL-CIO membership jumped after President Kennedy gave federal employees the right to unionize (1962); state, county, and municipal workers soon followed.

Union membership, which peaked in the mid-1940s with more than a third of the US labor force, was particularly hurt by a jump in imported goods in the 1970s and automation's triumph over manual labor in the 1980s. Legislation supported by the AFL-CIO included a law requiring 60 days' notice for plant closings (1988) and the Family Leave Act (1993). But labor lost its battle against NAFTA (North American Free Trade Agreement), which it feared would export jobs to Mexico.

In 1995 John Sweeney, former head of the Service Employees International Union, became president of the AFL-CIO in its first contested election. Under Sweeney the union spent $35 million in advertising in 1996 to draw attention to issues. After years with little focus on organizing, in 1997 the AFL-CIO launched a massive campaign to organize construction, hospital, and hotel workers in Las Vegas, and committed a third of its budget to recruiting and reorganizing. It supported the Teamsters' successful strike against UPS in 1997 and in 1998 threw its weight behind the Air Line Pilots Association's walkout on Northwest Airlines. It approved a restructuring plan in 1999 and the next year spent significant time and money rallying members all across the US in support of losing presidential candidate Al Gore. In early 2002 AFL-CIO announced its pledge of $750 million to create affordable housing in New York City.

OFFICERS

President: John J. Sweeney, age 68
EVP: Linda Chavez-Thompson, age 58
Secretary and Treasurer: Richard L. Trumka, age 53
VP; President, American Federation of State, County, and Municipal Employees: Gerald W. McEntee
VP; President, American Federation of Teachers: Sandra Feldman
VP; President, International Association of Machinists and Aerospace Workers: R. Thomas Buffenbarger
VP; President, International Brotherhood of Teamsters: James P. Hoffa
VP; President, International Brotherhood of Electrical Workers: Edwin D. Hill
VP; President, Sheet Metal Workers Union: Mike Sullivan
VP; President, U.A.W.: Stephen P. Yokich
Director Corporate Affairs: Ron Blackwell
Director International Affairs: Barbara Shailor
Director Human Resources: Karla Garland
Director Legislative: Peggy Taylor
Director Office of Investment: Bill Patterson
General Counsel: Jonathan Hiatt

LOCATIONS

HQ: 815 16th St. NW, Washington, DC 20006
Phone: 202-637-5000   **Fax:** 202-637-5058
Web: www.aflcio.org

The AFL-CIO encompasses 66 national and international unions.

PRODUCTS/OPERATIONS

Selected Trades and Workers Represented
Acting
Airline pilots
Broadcasting
Building trades
Education
Electrical trades
Engineering
Farmworkers
Firefighters
Flight attendants
Food trades
Government workers
Hotel employees
Industrial trades
Maritime trades
Metal trades
Mining
Music
Office employees
Police
Postal employees
Restaurant employees
Teachers
Transportation trades
Utility workers
Writers

AG PROCESSING INC

Soy far, soy good for Ag Processing (AGP), one of the largest soybean processors in the US. AGP's chief soybean products include vegetable oil and commercial animal feeds. The cooperative is also promoting its corn-based ethanol and soybean oil-based bio-fuels, fuel additives, and solvents. AGP processes some 15,000 acres of soybeans a day from its members' farms. Its grain division has the capacity to store more than 50 million bushels. The co-op's owners include 300,000 members from 16 states and Canada. The members, mostly in the Midwest, are represented through nearly 300 local co-ops and 10 regional co-ops.

AGP also turns its products into food ingredients, such as lethicin and meat extenders for ground beef. Its Consolidated Nutrition joint venture with Archer Daniels Midland makes commercial feeds. Internationally, AGP is involved in feed manufacturing through joint ventures in Hungary and Venezuela.

To capitalize on new EPA emission limits and mandates, the co-op is lobbying to increase retail demand for ethanol. Additionally, AGP is promoting methyl ester, a by-product of soy oil refining, for use as a clean fuel and fuel additive, agricultural spray, and non-toxic solvent to replace petroleum-based products.

HISTORY

Seeking strength in numbers, Ag Processing (AGP) was formed in 1983 when agricultural cooperatives Land O' Lakes and Farmland Industries merged their money-losing soybean operations into similarly struggling Boone Valley Cooperative.

Separately, AGP's six soybean mills had been unable to compete successfully against each other and larger corporations. The entire industry had been hampered by the Soviet grain embargoes imposed by the US in 1973 and 1979, and US government policies had contributed to increased competition from heavily subsidized soy producers in Argentina and Brazil. Soy exports from the US had fallen dramatically, leading to a production capacity surplus.

Collectively, AGP was able to attract a stronger management staff than its predecessors had; it hired 21-year Archer Daniels Midland (ADM) veteran James Lindsay as CEO and general manager. With operations scattered over four states, AGP placed its headquarters in Omaha, Nebraska — chosen for its central location and close proximity to the co-op's main bank.

In its first two years, AGP cut employee rolls by 20% and scaled back production, thus trimming costs and squeezing higher prices for finished products. A turnaround came quickly, and in 1985 members received a dividend from the co-op's $8 million pretax profit. That year AGP purchased two Iowa plants from AGRI Industries.

AGP dismantled two plants in 1987. By the next year the co-op witnessed an increase in domestic demand and had resumed selling to the Soviet Union. It generated additional sales by further processing soybean oil into food-grade products like hydrogenated oil and lecithin.

With an eye on diversification and value-added products, by 1991 AGP had expanded to eight soybean plants and two vegetable oil refineries; it also acquired the feed and grain business of International Multifoods that year through an 80%-owned joint venture with ADM. The acquisition included 29 feed plants in the US and Canada, 26 retail centers, 18 grain elevators, and the brands Supersweet and Masterfeeds. In 1994 AGP formed feed manufacturer Consolidated Nutrition, a 50-50 joint-venture with ADM.

Consolidated Nutrition introduced a Swine Operations program in 1996. The program grew quickly through the development of PORK PACT, a partnership to serve pork producers. The next year AGP's grain division sold nine grain elevators in Ohio and Indiana to Cargill. That year the co-op gained control of Venezuelan feed manufacturer Proagro.

By 1998 passage of the Freedom to Farm Act and growing demand had spurred soybean planting. The co-op in 1998 opened an additional processing plant in Emmetsburg, Iowa, followed by another in Eagle Grove, Iowa. AGP sold off its pet food operations in 1998 to Windy Hill, which was later acquired by Doane Pet Care Enterprises. Also that year Consolidated Nutrition combined its Master Mix and Supersweet feed brands into the Consolidated Nutrition label.

In 1999 the company added the Garner-Klemme-Meservey cooperative to its grain operations. It opened a new plant late that year in St. Joseph, Missouri, to make value-added products such as hardfat (used in emulsifiers).

Fire shut down the co-op's soybean crusher in Mason City, Iowa, in February 2001. Customers were routed to crushing facilities in Eagle Grove, Iowa, and Emmetsburg, Iowa, while repairs were made. (As of the end of 2002, the soybean crusher was still undergoing repair and upgrading.)

In June 2001 AGP sold its 50% share of Consolidated Nutrition to ADM. In 2002 the co-op's Masterfeeds business acquired four feed mills and a merchandising operation from Saskatchewan Wheat Pool.

OFFICERS

Chairman: Denis E. Leiting
CEO: Martin P. Reagan
CFO: Keith Spackler
SVP Food Group: George L. Hoover
SVP Human Resources: Judy Ford
SVP Member Relations: Mike Maranell
SVP Transportation: Terry J. Voss
VP Animal Nutrition: Rob Flack
VP Government Relations: John B. Campbell
VP Grain Operations and Marketing: Michael J. Knobbe
VP Hedging: Daryl D. Dahl
VP Marketing and Sales, Intellectual Property Holdings LLC: Blake Hendrix
VP Research and Technology: Wayne L. Stockland
VP Soybean/Corn Operations: Gary L. Olsen
VP Technical Operations: Richard P. Copeland
VP and Corporate Controller: Tim E. Witty

LOCATIONS

HQ: 12700 W. Dodge Rd., Omaha, NE 68103
Phone: 402-496-7809   **Fax:** 402-498-5548
Web: www.agp.com

Ag Processing has operations in 16 states in the US and Canada, as well as subsidiary ventures in Hungary and Venezuela.

PRODUCTS/OPERATIONS

Selected Brands
Consolidated Nutrition (feeds, US)
Masterfeeds (feeds, Canada)
SOYGOLD (bio-diesel, solvents, fuel additives)
Tindle Mills (feeds)

Selected Operations
Commercial feeds
Food (lecithin, soybean oil, vegetable oil)
Grain
Industrial products (ethanol, methyl ester)
Soybean processing
Transportation (barge, rail, truck)

Selected Subsidiaries
Ag Environmental Products (soybean methyl ester products)
AGP Grain Cooperative
AGP Grain, Ltd.
Consolidated Nutrition (50%, commercial feed)
Intellectual Property Holdings LLC

COMPETITORS

Agway
Andersons
ADM
Bunge Limited
Cargill
Cenex Harvest States
ConAgra
Corn Products International
DeBruce Grain
Farmland Industries
Griffin Industries
High Plains
MFA
Riceland Foods
Southern States
Stake Technology

HISTORICAL FINANCIALS & EMPLOYEES

Cooperative FYE: August 31	Annual Growth	8/92	8/93	8/94	8/95	8/96	8/97	8/98	8/99	8/00	8/01
Sales ($ mil.)	5.3%	1,127	1,219	1,377	2,132	2,765	2,948	2,615	2,095	1,962	1,789
Employees	(5.5%)	—	—	—	—	3,050	3,000	2,550	2,500	2,500	2,300

SALES HISTORY

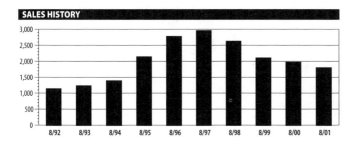

AMERICAN CANCER SOCIETY, INC.

The American Cancer Society (ACS) works as a firefighter for your lungs. Dedicated to the elimination of cancer, the not-for-profit organization is staffed by professionals and more than 2 million volunteers at some 3,400 local units across the country. ACS is the largest source of private cancer research funds in the US. Recipients of the society's funding include 32 Nobel Prize laureates. In addition to research, the ACS supports detection, treatment, and education programs. The organization encourages prevention efforts with programs such as the Great American Smokeout. Patient services include moral support, transportation to and from treatment, and camps for children who have cancer.

The ACS has generated considerable income by marketing its name for antismoking nicotine patches and orange juice, and is contemplating even more lucrative deals. Programs account for about 73% of expenses; 27% goes to administration and fund-raising.

HISTORY

Concerned over the lack of progress in detecting and treating cancer, a group of 10 physicians and five laymen met in New York City in 1913 to form the American Society for the Control of Cancer (ASCC). Because public discussion of cancer was taboo, the group struggled with how to educate people without raising unnecessary fears. Some physicians even preferred keeping knowledge of the disease from the public. In the 1920s the ASCC began sponsoring cancer clinics and collecting statistics on the disease. By 1923 some states reported improvements in early diagnosis and treatment. In 1937 the ASCC started its first nationwide public education program, with the help of volunteers known as the Women's Field Army. President Franklin Roosevelt named April National Cancer Control Month, a practice since followed by every president.

By 1944 some cancer rates were rising but the word "cancer" still couldn't be mentioned on radio. Mary Lasker, wife of prominent ad executive Albert Lasker, was instrumental in getting information about cancer broadcast. At her insistence, in 1945 the newly renamed American Cancer Society began donating at least 25% of its budget to research. The society raised $4 million in its first major national fund-raising campaign.

The link between smoking and lung cancer became known after a study in the early 1950s by ACS medical director Charles Cameron. That information became part of the Surgeon General's Report of 1964. In 1973 an ACS branch in Minnesota held the first Great American Smokeout to encourage people to quit smoking.

The ACS backed the 1971 congressional bill that inaugurated the War on Cancer. The society was attacked in the 1970s for emphasizing cures rather than prevention because, critics claimed, research would reveal environmental causes from industrial products made by companies with connections to ACS directors. In the 1970s and 1980s, the ACS backed tougher restrictions on tobacco and, in response to earlier criticism, directed research toward prevention as well as treatment. The society played a major role in the 1989 airline smoking ban.

John Seffrin, a former Indiana University professor, was named CEO of ACS in 1992. The first of several genetic breakthroughs came in the 1990s when ACS grantees isolated genes believed to be responsible for triggering various types of cancer. In 1995 the ACS accused the tobacco industry of infiltrating its offices in the 1970s and using its papers to aid in the early marketing of low-tar cigarettes.

In 1996 the ACS announced that new data showed a drop in the US cancer death rate for the first time ever. The ACS entered agreements with SmithKline Beecham (NicoDerm antismoking patches) and the Florida Department of Citrus in 1996 to allow the use of the American Cancer Society name in marketing.

The proposed $369 billion settlement between the attorneys general of 40 states and the tobacco industry was big news in 1997. The ACS had wanted more concessions, such as a $2-per-pack tax increase, more power for industry regulation by the FDA, and underage use rate-reduction targets for smokeless tobacco products as stringent as those for cigarettes.

In 1998 the ACS launched a $5 million national advertising campaign to combat what it sees as "misleading" information spread by the tobacco industry. It argued in Supreme Court in 1999 to help the FDA gain control over cigarette production and distribution. In 2000 ACS restructured its $50-million-a-year research program to increase the size of individual grants; it also awarded its largest-ever award, $1.7 million, to study the side effects of cancer treatment. In 2001 ACS filed petitions to the FDA urging them to regulate new tobacco products marketed as being safer than traditional cigarettes.

OFFICERS

Chairman: H. Fred Mickelson
Chairman-Elect: David M. Zacks
Vice Chairman: Gary J. Streit
CEO: John R. Seffrin
President: Robert C. Young
CFO: Peter Tartikoff
First VP: Mary Simmonds
Second VP: Ralph B. Vance
National VP Corporate Communications:
A. Gregory Donaldson
National VP Federal and State Governmental Affairs:
Daniel E. Smith
National VP Human Resources: Aurelia C. Stanley
CIO: Vic Ayers

LOCATIONS

HQ: 1599 Clifton Rd. NE, Atlanta, GA 30329
Phone: 404-320-3333   **Fax:** 404-329-7791
Web: www.cancer.org

PRODUCTS/OPERATIONS

Selected Patient Services Programs
Children's Camps (for children and teens with cancer; some for siblings)
Hope Lodge (housing assistance)
I Can Cope (education and support classes on living with cancer)
Look Good ... Feel Better (cosmetics and beauty techniques for women experiencing side effects of cancer treatment)
Man To Man Prostate Cancer Support
Pamphlets and brochures for cancer patients and their families
Reach to Recovery (support for women with breast cancer and their families)
Road to Recovery (transportation services)

Selected Public Education Programs and Publications
Great American Smokeout (national stop-smoking-for-a-day event)
Making Strides Against Breast Cancer (fund-raiser)
Relay for Life (fund-raiser)

Selected Research Grants and Awards
Clinical Research Professorships
Clinical Research Training Grants
Institutional research grants
Postdoctoral fellowships
Research Opportunity Grants
Research Professorships

HISTORICAL FINANCIALS & EMPLOYEES

Not-for-profit FYE: August 31	Annual Growth	8/92	8/93	8/94	8/95	8/96	8/97	8/98	8/99	8/00	8/01
Sales ($ mil.)	9.7%	358	388	392	420	458	602	677	672	812	821
Employees	3.8%	4,650	4,200	4,100	4,656	4,500	4,418	4,500	4,500	6,000	6,500

SALES HISTORY

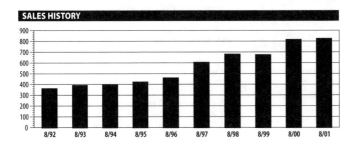

AMERICAN FAMILY INSURANCE

Even singles can get insured through American Family Insurance Group. The company specializes in property/casualty insurance, but also offers life, health, and homeowners coverage, as well as investment and retirement-planning products. It is among the largest US mutual companies that concentrate on auto insurance (State Farm is the biggest). American Family also provides coverage for apartment owners, restaurants, contractors, and other businesses. Through the company's consumer finance division, agents can also offer their customers home equity and personal lines of credit.

The company has around 4,000 agents operating primarily in the Midwest. Unlike many of its competitors, American Family has said it has no plans to demutualize.

HISTORY

In 1927 Herman Wittwer founded Farmers Mutual Automobile Insurance to sell coverage to Wisconsin farmers. As farms became mechanized in the 1920s, the insurance market grew. Low-density rural traffic reduced the potential for accidents, a fact that attracted Wittwer and others, such as State Farm (founded in 1922) to serve the similar markets. Wittwer also noted that rural Wisconsin's severe winters made cars unusable for a good part of the year, further reducing risk.

Farmers Mutual grew despite the Depression and WWII, spreading to Minnesota (1933); Missouri (1939); Nebraska and the Dakotas (1940); and Indiana, Iowa, and Kansas (1943). The war years were generous to insurers: Rising incomes allowed people to insure their cars, but rationing programs limited use of the cars. The postwar suburban boom — when cars became a necessity rather than a luxury — also helped auto insurers.

Growing prosperity for single-earner households in the 1950s helped boost the demand for life insurance. In 1958 Farmers Mutual formed American Family Life Insurance. The company wrote $1.6 million in insurance on its first day in the life insurance business. During that decade, Farmers Mutual moved into Illinois.

The 1960s brought growth and change. To capture more auto business, it founded American Standard Insurance to write nonstandard auto insurance. The firm also launched consumer finance operations for insurance customers and noncustomers alike, departing from standard industry practice by selling through agents rather than offices. In 1963, in recognition of its growing diversification, Farmers Mutual changed its name to American Family Mutual Insurance.

During the 1970s and 1980s, the company strengthened its infrastructure and added regional offices. It moved into Arizona and later formed American Family Brokerage to fill in gaps in its own coverage by obtaining insurance for clients through other insurers.

During this period American Family suffered cultural pains. It moved beyond its traditional rural clientele and into the urban unknown as it sought to increase its market share. In 1981 community groups questioned whether the company was adequately serving racially mixed neighborhoods. In 1988 the US Justice Department began investigating allegations that the firm engaged in redlining (offering inferior or no service for minority neighborhoods); a class-action suit based on similar claims was filed in 1990. The suit went all the way to the Supreme Court, which ruled that insurance sales must comply with the Fair Housing Act.

The company had begun rectifying its practices before the case was decided. Nevertheless, when American Family settled the case in 1995, it agreed to pay a $14.5 million settlement plus about $2 million in court costs. Part of the settlement was to compensate people who had suffered from the company's discrimination. But most of the money went to fund community programs begun in 1996 to promote home ownership among minorities. In 1997 trouble came from within and without: One lawsuit claimed the company falsely promised to shrink premiums as policies earned dividends, and two dissident agents filed a civil complaint for wrongful termination (the latter case was settled the next year).

The company's profits tumbled in 1998 due to severe storms in Minnesota and Wisconsin. The next year American Family expanded its operations in Colorado and moved into Cleveland.

In 2000 Wisconsin was again pounded by hail, high winds, and floods. American Family Insurance announced $100 million in expected losses from the event. Streamlining claims processing, the company closed nine of its offices in 2001.

OFFICERS

Chairman and CEO: Harvey R. Pierce
President, COO, and Director: David R. Anderson
EVP, Administration: Darnell Moore
EVP, Corporate Legal, and Secretary: James F. Eldridge
EVP, Finance and Treasurer: J. Brent Johnson
EVP, Sales: Daniel R. DeSalvo
VP and Controller: Daniel R. Schultz
VP, Actuarial: Bradley J. Gleason
VP, Claims: Terese A. Taarud
VP, Commercial, Farm/Ranch: Jerry G. Rekowski
VP, Education: Nancy M. Johnson
VP, Government Affairs and Compliance: Mark V. Afable

VP, Human Resources: Vicki L. Chvala
VP, Information Services: Byrne W. Chapman
VP, Investments: Thomas S. King
VP, Legal: Christopher S. Spencer
VP, Marketing: Alan E. Meyer
VP, Office Administration: Richard J. Haas
VP, Personal Lines: Jack C. Salzwedel
VP, Public Relations: Richard A. Fetherston
VP, Sales, Great Lakes Region: David N. Krueger
VP, Sales, Midland Region: Michael G. Duran
VP, Sales, Mountain Region: Donald D. Alfermann
VP, Sales, Valley Region: Ralph E. Kaye
VP, American Family Life Insurance:
Joseph W. Tisserand
Auditors: PricewaterhouseCoopers LLP

LOCATIONS

HQ: American Family Insurance Group
6000 American Pkwy., Madison, WI 53783
Phone: 608-249-2111   Fax: 608-243-4921
Web: www.amfam.com

American Family Insurance Group operates in Arizona,
Colorado, Illinois, Indiana, Iowa, Kansas, Minnesota,
Missouri, Nebraska, Nevada, North Dakota, Ohio,
Oregon, South Dakota, and Wisconsin.

PRODUCTS/OPERATIONS

2001 Assets

	$ mil.	% of total
Cash	34	—
Bonds	5,408	53
Stocks	1,952	19
Mortgage loans	187	2
Real estate	257	2
Policy loans	160	2
Receivables	708	7
Other	1,569	15
Total	**10,275**	**100**

Selected Subsidiaries
American Family Mutual Insurance Co.
American Family Financial Services, Inc.
American Family Insurance Co.
American Family Life Insurance Co.
American Standard Insurance Company of Ohio
American Standard Insurance Company of Wisconsin

COMPETITORS

21st Century
Allstate
American Financial
American General
AIG
Berkshire Hathaway
Chubb
CIGNA
Cincinnati Financial
Citigroup
CNA Financial
GeneralCologne Re
The Hartford
Kemper Insurance
Liberty Mutual
Lincoln National
Loews
Mutual of Omaha
Nationwide
Ohio Casualty
Old Republic
Progressive Corporation
Prudential
SAFECO
St. Paul Companies
State Farm
USAA

HISTORICAL FINANCIALS & EMPLOYEES

Mutual company FYE: December 31	Annual Growth	12/92	12/93	12/94	12/95	12/96	12/97	12/98	12/99	12/00	12/01
Assets ($ mil.)	9.1%	4,698	5,228	5,706	6,256	6,836	8,348	8,949	9,569	9,970	10,275
Net income ($ mil.)	(3.9%)	144	159	163	218	55	252	40	282	237	100
Income as % of assets	—	3.1%	3.0%	2.9%	3.5%	0.8%	3.0%	0.4%	2.9%	2.4%	1.0%
Employees	1.6%	6,436	6,373	6,365	6,411	6,506	6,800	6,940	7,247	7,300	7,431

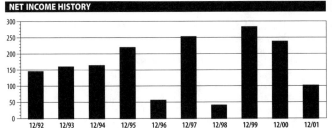

NET INCOME HISTORY	2001 FISCAL YEAR-END

2001 FISCAL YEAR-END
Equity as % of assets: 32.1%
Return on assets: 1.0%
Return on equity: 3.0%
Long-term debt ($ mil.): —
Sales ($ mil.): 4,714

THE AMERICAN RED CROSS

When it comes to disaster, the Red Cross is the master. The American Red Cross is a member of the International Red Cross and Red Crescent Movement, a not-for-profit organization that helps victims, especially after disasters. Chartered by Congress in 1905, the American Red Cross isn't a government agency. Its staff is largely volunteer — more than 1 million of them. Aside from helping victims of more than 73,000 disasters each year, the Red Cross teaches CPR, first aid, and AIDS awareness courses; provides counseling for US military personnel; and maintains some of the nation's largest blood, plasma, and tissue banks.

The mission of the American Red Cross was highlighted after the 2001 terrorist attacks on New York City and Washington, DC. As the Red Cross gained praise immediately after the attacks, it soon drew fire from critics. Dr. Bernadine Healy, who was appointed as president and CEO of the organization in 1999 to succeed Elizabeth Dole, was pushed out after many board members disagreed with a plan to use some proceeds from donations made in light of the September 11 attacks for a blood bank reserve. A public outcry resulted, as some felt the donations should only be used to benefit the families of the terrorist attack victims. The American Red Cross named Marsha Johnson Evans as its new president and CEO in 2002.

HISTORY

The Red Cross traces its start to a trip made in 1859 by Jean-Henri Dunant, a Swiss businessman. Dunant was traveling in northern Italy when he saw the aftermath of the Battle of Solferino — 40,000 dead or wounded troops, left without help. He published a pamphlet three years later calling for the formation of international volunteer societies to aid wounded soldiers.

In 1863 a five-member committee (including Dunant) formed the International Committee of the Red Cross in Geneva. Delegates of 16 countries attended the first conference, which resulted in the formation of national Red Cross societies across Europe. A red cross on a white background (the reverse of the Swiss flag) was chosen as the organization's symbol; the Red Crescent symbol was added in 1876 by Muslim relief workers during the Russo-Turkish War. In 1864 the group's principles were codified into international law — initially signed by 12 nations — through the Geneva Convention.

Clara Barton, famous for her aid to soldiers during the US Civil War, learned about the Red Cross when she assisted with relief efforts during the Franco-Prussian War (1870-71). After

the war, Barton returned home and persuaded Congress to support the Geneva Convention. In 1881 she and some friends founded the American Association of the Red Cross, with the first chapter in Dansville, New York. The US signed the Geneva Convention in 1882.

Barton soon expanded the Red Cross' mission to include aiding victims of natural disasters. The group received a congressional charter in 1905, making it responsible for providing assistance to the US military and disaster relief in the US and overseas.

Membership soared during WWI as the number of chapters jumped from 107 to 3,864, and volunteers from the US and other nations served with the armed forces in Europe. After the war, the American Red Cross helped refugees in Europe, recruited thousands of nurses to improve the health and hygiene of rural Americans, and provided food and shelter to millions during the Depression. The Red Cross established its first blood center, in New York's Presbyterian Hospital, in 1941. During WWII the American Red Cross again mobilized massive relief efforts. At home, volunteers taught nutrition courses, served in hospitals, and collected blood.

In 1956 the Red Cross began research to increase the safety of its blood supply. It also continued to provide assistance during natural disasters, as well as during the Korean and Vietnam Wars and other US military conflicts.

During the 1980s the Red Cross was criticized for moving too slowly to improve testing of its blood supply for the HIV virus. Elizabeth Dole, named the organization's president in 1991, reorganized the blood collection program. (Dole took a leave of absence in 1996 to help her husband, Bob Dole, in his unsuccessful bid for the US presidency.)

In 1996 *Money* magazine reported that the Red Cross spent more than 91 cents of every dollar on programs, the best ratio of any major charity. The next year HemaCare settled a bloodproduct-pricing lawsuit against the Red Cross without disclosing terms, and Ellis & Associates challenged the organization's hold on lifeguard training (certifying about 32,000 guards versus 185,000 for the Red Cross).

In 1998 the organization ran up against its costliest year ever, spending more than $162 million to fight some 240 disasters across the US. The next year Dole resigned from the Red Cross and followed in her husband's footsteps by making her own bid for the US presidency in 2000 (she later dropped out of the race). Dole was succeeded by Dr. Bernadine Healy, a former dean of the Ohio State University College of Medicine and the first physician to head the association. In

2001 the mission of the American Red Cross was spotlighted following the terrorist attacks on New York City and Washington, DC. Healy was given her walking papers less than two months after the September 11 attacks amid disagreements with the Red Cross board and ire from critics. General Counsel Harold Decker was tapped to replace Healy at the end of 2001. That same year the FDA announced that the Red Cross had failed to be in compliance with safety laws in its blood collection program, despite being under a consent decree since 1993. The American Red Cross appointed Marsha Johnson Evans as president and CEO in 2002.

OFFICERS

Chairman: David T. McLaughlin
President and CEO: Marsha Johnson Evans
EVP and CEO, Biomedical Services: Ramesh Thadani
EVP Chapter Services Network: James Krueger
EVP Human Resources: Stan Davis
VP Finance and CFO: John D. Campbell
Interim VP Disaster Services: John McDivitt
Chief Diversity Officer: Anthony J. Polk
CIO: Tom Schwaninger
Interim Corporate Secretary: Andrea Morici

LOCATIONS

HQ: 430 17th St. NW, Washington, DC 20006
Phone: 202-737-8300   **Fax:** 202-639-3141
Web: www.redcross.org

The American Red Cross has 1,100 chapters worldwide.

PRODUCTS/OPERATIONS

2001 Sales

	$ mil.	% of total
Contributions	763	28
Investment income & other	172	6
Products & services	1,808	66
Total	**2,743**	**100**

Selected Activities

Armed Forces Emergency Services
Counseling
Emergency assistance
Veterans assistance

Biomedical Services
Blood
Dental programs
Plasma operations
Research and development
Stem cell
Tissue

Disaster Services
Disaster mitigation
Emergency assistance
Long-term assistance
Mass care

Health and Safety Education
Babysitting courses
CPR courses
First aid courses
HIV/AIDS education
Nurse assistant training

COMPETITORS

America's Blood Centers
Daxor
HemaCare
Tissue Banks

HISTORICAL FINANCIALS & EMPLOYEES

Not-for-profit FYE: June 30	Annual Growth	6/92	6/93	6/94	6/95	6/96	6/97	6/98	6/99	6/00	6/01
Sales ($ mil.)	6.4%	1,568	1,796	1,740	1,724	1,814	1,940	2,080	2,421	2,529	2,743
Employees	3.8%	25,000	25,000	32,169	31,000	30,021	29,850	30,000	35,000	35,000	35,000

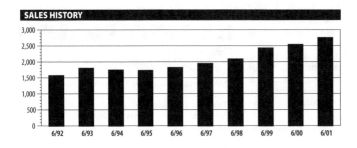

SALES HISTORY

ANDERSEN CORPORATION

Windows of opportunity open and shut daily for Andersen, a leading maker of wood-clad windows and patio doors in the US. With one of the most-recognized brands in the industry, Andersen offers a wide array of window designs from hinged, bay, and double-hung to skylight, gliding, and picture windows. The company also makes patio doors (sold under the Frenchwood brand) and, through its EMCO subsidiary, storm and screen doors. The company sells its products through independent and company-owned distributorships to architects, general contractors, and building owners throughout the world. The Andersen family owns the majority of the company.

Andersen competes in the marketplace by building strong brand recognition for its products. Acquisitions play an important role in the company's growth strategy, and Andersen has been buying many of the independent distributorships that carry its products, including Morgan Products, the largest US distributor of its products.

HISTORY

Danish immigrant Hans Andersen and his two sons, Fred and Herbert, founded Andersen in 1903. Andersen's first words in English, "All together, boys," became the company motto. Andersen had arrived in Portland, Maine, in 1870 and worked as a lumber dealer and manufacturer. In the 1880s he bought a sawmill in St. Cloud, Minnesota, and later managed one in Hudson, Wisconsin. When the Hudson mill owners asked him to let workers go during the off season, Andersen refused and then resigned. He subsequently launched his own lumber business — Andersen Lumber Company — and hired some of the men who were laid off. He opened a second lumberyard, in Afton, Minnesota, in 1904. Andersen and his sons revolutionized the window industry in the early 1900s by introducing a standardized window frame with interchangeable parts. Buoyed by success, the Andersens sold their lumberyards in 1908 in order to focus on the window-frame business. (Andersen purchased lumberyards again in 1916 before exiting the lumberyard business for good in the 1930s.)

Thrifty Hans launched the company's first (and the US's third) profit-sharing plan shortly before his death in 1914. Herbert became VP, secretary, treasurer, and factory manager, and Fred became president. Herbert died in 1921 (at age 36), but Fred proved to be a versatile and capable successor. Among his accomplishments, Fred came up with the tag line "Only the rich can afford poor windows."

In 1929 the company changed its name to Andersen Frame Corporation. In the following decade Andersen introduced a number of innovations, including Master Frame (a frame with a locked sill joint, 1930); a casement window, the industry's first complete factory-made window unit (1932); and a basement window (1934). The company adopted its current name in 1937.

Andersen introduced the gliding window concept in the early 1940s. It also launched the Home Planners Scrap Book consumer ad campaign in 1943. During the 1950s Andersen's new products included the Flexivent awning window, which featured welded insulating glass that served as an alternative to traditional storm windows. In the 1960s the company produced a gliding door and introduced the Perma-Shield system. The system featured easy-to-maintain vinyl cladding to protect wood frames from weathering. By 1978 Perma-Shield products accounted for three-quarters of sales. Fred, who had run the company as president until 1960 and had subsequently held the positions of chairman and chairman emeritus, died in 1979 at age 92.

Between 1984 and 1994 the company increased its sales threefold by introducing additional customized and state-of-the-art products, including patio doors. In 1995 it launched Renewal by Andersen, a retail window-replacement business that has expanded to about 40 US locations.

In 1997 Andersen acquired former long-term strategic partner Aspen Research (materials testing, research, and product development). Among its jointly developed products is Fibrex, a composite material used in replacement windows. Also in 1997 the company moved its international division office from Bayport, Minnesota, to the Minnesota World Trade Center in St. Paul to help boost its export drive.

In 1998 company veteran Donald Garofalo succeeded Andersen's president and CEO Jerold Wulf, who retired after 39 years with the company. Andersen reinforced its company-owned distributorships in 1999 when it bought millwork distributors Morgan Products and Independent Millwork.

Expanding its product offerings, Andersen purchased EMCO Enterprises, a private manufacturer of storm doors and accessories, in 2001.

OFFICERS

Chairwoman: Sarah J. Andersen
President and CEO: Donald L. Garofalo
EVP and CFO: Michael O. Johnson
SVP, Human Resources and Communications:
 Mary D. Carter
COO: James E. Humphrey
Director of Corporate Communications:
 Maureen McDonough

General Manager, International Division, Andersen
Windows, Inc.: Ross A. Dahlin
Assistant to General Manager, International Division,
Andersen Windows, Inc.: Teri Merrigan
Manager Administrative Services, International
Division, Andersen Windows, Inc.: Nancy Hamble
Manager Technical Marketing, International Division,
Andersen Windows, Inc.: Curt Nordahl
International Coordinator, International Division,
Andersen Windows, Inc.: Lori Kamps
Area Manager, Asia, International Division, Andersen
Windows, Inc.: Russ Johnson
Area Manager, Europe/Mid East, International Division,
Andersen Windows, Inc.: Paul Linduska
Area Manager, Japan, International Division, Andersen
Windows, Inc.: Glenn Tanimoto
Area Manager, Mexico and Latin America, International
Division, Andersen Windows, Inc.: Pete Curcio
Sales Representative, Asia, International Division,
Andersen Windows, Inc.: Michael J. Brown
Sales Representative, Caribbean and Puerto Rico,
International Division, Andersen Windows, Inc.:
Ferdinand Muniz
Sales Representative, Europe/Mid East, International
Division, Andersen Windows, Inc.: John Fowler
Sales Representative, Latin America, International
Division, Andersen Windows, Inc.: Tom Danisch
President, EMCO Enterprises, Inc.: J. Glasnapp

LOCATIONS

HQ: 100 4th Ave. North, Bayport, MN 55003
Phone: 651-264-5150   **Fax:** 651-264-5107
Web: www.andersencorp.com

Andersen markets its products throughout the Americas,
Asia, Europe, and the Middle East.

PRODUCTS/OPERATIONS

Selected Products and Brands

Doors
Patio doors
    Art glass (Frank Lloyd Wright designs)
    Frenchwood Collection (gliding, hinged, and
        outswing)
    Narroline gliding patio doors
    Perma-Shield gliding patio doors
Screen doors
Storm doors

Windows
Art glass
Awning
Basement
Bay and bow
Casement
Double-hung
Fixed
Gliding
Horizontal sliding
Picture
Skylights and roof windows
Transom
Utility

COMPETITORS

Bocenor
JELD-WEN
Overhead Door
Pella
Royal Group Technologies
Sierra Pacific Industries
Thermal Industries
Weru

HISTORICAL FINANCIALS & EMPLOYEES

Private FYE: December 31	Annual Growth	12/92	12/93	12/94	12/95	12/96	12/97	12/98	12/99	12/00	12/01
Estimated sales ($ mil.)	6.1%	1,000	1,000	1,100	1,200	1,250	1,300	1,400	1,500	1,700	1,700
Employees	9.5%	—	—	3,700	3,700	3,700	3,700	3,700	6,000	6,000	7,000

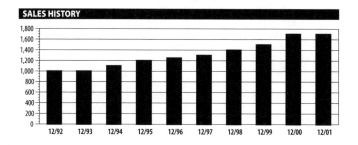

SALES HISTORY

ARMY AND AIR FORCE EXCHANGE

Be all that you can be and buy all that you can buy at the PX (Post Exchange). The Army and Air Force Exchange Service (AAFES) runs more than 10,000 facilities — including PXs and BXs (Base Exchanges) — at US Army and Air Force bases worldwide. Its outlets range from tents to shopping centers that have retail stores, fast-food outlets, movie theaters, beauty shops, and gas stations. AAFES serves active-duty military personnel, reservists, retirees, and their family members. A government agency under the Department of Defense (DoD), it receives no funding from the DoD.

While the AAFES receives no federal money, it pays neither taxes nor rent to occupy US government property. More than 70% of AAFES's profits go into Morale, Welfare, and Recreation Programs for amenities such as libraries and youth centers. Other profits are used to renovate or build stores. Active military personnel head AAFES, but its staff consists mostly of military family members and other civilians.

HISTORY

During the American Revolution, peddlers known as sutlers followed the Army, selling items such as soap, razors, and tobacco. The practice lasted until after the Civil War, when post traders replaced sutlers. This system was replaced in 1889 when the War Department authorized canteens at military bases.

The first US military exchanges were established in 1895, creating a system to supply military personnel with personal items on US Army bases around the world. The exchanges were run independently, with each division creating a Post Exchange (PX) to serve its unit. The post commander would assign an officer to run the PX (usually along with other duties) and would decide how profits were spent.

In 1941 the Army Exchange Service was created, and the system was reorganized. A five-member advisory committee made up of civilian merchandisers was created to provide recommendations for the reorganization. The restructuring made the system more like a chain store business. The independent PXs were bought by the War Department from the individual military organizations that ran them. Civilian personnel were brought in to staff the PXs, and a brigadier general was named to head an executive staff made up of Army officers and civilians that provided centralized control of the system. The Army also created a special school to train officers to run the PXs.

Sales at the PXs skyrocketed during WWII; a catalog business was added so soldiers could order gifts to send home to their families. The Department of the Air Force was established in 1947, and the exchange system organization was renamed the Army and Air Force Exchange Service (AAFES) the next year.

In 1960 the government allowed the overseas exchanges to provide more luxury items in an effort to keep soldiers from buying foreign-made goods. By the time the military had been cranked up again for the Vietnam War, big-ticket items such as TVs, cameras, and tape recorders were among the exchanges' best-sellers. In 1967 AAFES moved its headquarters from New York City to Dallas.

By 1991 the exchanges were open to the National Guard and the Reserve; AAFES's customer base had grown to 14 million. When the military began downsizing during the 1990s following the end of the Cold War, AAFES's customer base shrank by 35%.

AAFES stores sold more than $12 million of pornographic materials in 1995. The House of Representatives passed the Military Honor and Decency Act the next year prohibiting the sale of pornography on US military property, including AAFES stores; this ban was struck down as unconstitutional in 1997. That year AAFES was approved as a provider of medical equipment covered by federal CHAMPUS/TRICARE insurance. It also created a Web site to offer online shopping in 1997.

The Supreme Court upheld the 1996 porn ban in 1998; the Pentagon banned the sale of more than 150 sexually explicit magazines (such as *Penthouse*), while a military board permitted the continued sale of certain publications (including *Playboy*). Maj. Gen. Barry Bates took over as AAFES's Commander and CEO in 1998. To better battle other retailers, that year AAFES announced its stores would offer best-price guarantees, matching prices of local stores and refunding price differences if customers found lower prices within 30 days of buying products.

In 1999 AAFES expanded to Macedonia and Kosovo, providing its services to military personnel in Operation Joint Guardian. In 2000 Bates was replaced as AAFES commander and CEO by Maj. Gen. Charles J. Wax.

Wax stepped down as commander and CEO in August 2002 and was replaced by Maj. Gen. Katherine Frost of the US Army.

OFFICERS

Chairman: Lt. Gen. Michael E. Zettler, USAF
Commander and CEO: Maj. Gen. Katherine Frost, USA
Deputy Commander and Director, Equal Opportunity:
Brig. Gen. Toreaser A. Steele, USAF
COO: W. Michael Beverly
CFO: Terry B. Corley
SVP Human Resources Directorate: James K. Winters
SVP Sales Directorate: Robert D. Bohn
General Counsel: Col. Athena Jones, USAF
Auditors: Ernst & Young LLP

LOCATIONS

HQ: Army and Air Force Exchange Service
3911 S. Walton Walker Blvd., Dallas, TX 75236
Phone: 214-312-2011   **Fax:** 214-312-3000
Web: www.aafes.com

The Army and Air Force Exchange Service has
operations in all 50 states and in 25 countries and
overseas areas.

PRODUCTS/OPERATIONS

Selected Merchandise and Services
Barber and beauty shops
Books, newspapers, and magazines
Catalog services
Class Six stores
Concessions
Food facilities (mobile units, snack bars, name-brand
fast-food franchises, and concession operations)
Gas stations and auto repair
Military clothing stores
Movie theaters
Retail stores
Vending centers

COMPETITORS

7-Eleven
Best Buy
Circuit City
Costco Wholesale
J. C. Penney
Kmart
Kroger
METRO AG
Sears
Target
Wal-Mart

HISTORICAL FINANCIALS & EMPLOYEES

Government agency FYE: January 31	Annual Growth	1/93	1/94	1/95	1/96	1/97	1/98	1/99	1/00	1/01	1/02
Sales ($ mil.)	0.6%	6,763	7,276	6,746	6,710	6,874	6,620	6,783	6,992	7,369	7,133
Net income ($ mil.)	2.4%	301	315	269	228	348	337	343	361	381	373
Income as % of sales	—	4.5%	4.3%	4.0%	3.4%	5.1%	5.1%	5.1%	5.2%	5.2%	5.2%
Employees	(3.6%)	72,562	60,000	58,556	56,495	57,583	53,946	54,000	54,000	52,400	52,400

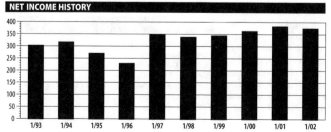

NET INCOME HISTORY

2002 FISCAL YEAR-END
Debt ratio: 0.0%
Return on equity: 12.3%
Cash ($ mil.): 147
Current ratio: 2.27
Long-term debt ($ mil.): 0

ASCENSION HEALTH

Things are looking up for Ascension Health. Formed in the 1999 merger of the Daughters of Charity National Health System and the Sisters of St. Joseph Health System, Ascension Health's network consists of some 60 Roman Catholic hospitals, as well as nursing homes, psychiatric wards, long-term care centers, and other health care facilities in about 15 states and the District of Columbia. Ascension Health is the largest Catholic hospital system the United States. Ascension Health is also the largest not-for-profit health care provider in the United States.

Ascension's facilities are primarily located in the southern, midwestern, and northeastern areas of the US.

The system takes to heart the words of St. Vincent de Paul, co-founder of the Daughters of Charity, who advised the order to serve "the poor sick bodily, ministering to them in all their needs, and spiritually also so that they will live and die well."

As such, Nuns from Ascension's sponsoring religious orders sit on its governing board, which is led by non-clergy CEO Douglas French.

In this age of high-cost health care, Ascension realizes the need for fiscal health. In addition to selling money-losing hospitals, Ascension has reorganized its facilities by geographic regions, with each region headed by a VP who controls costs and speeds decision making.

In response to rising health care costs, Ascension is merging with national Catholic health care provider Carondelet Health System.

HISTORY

The Daughters of Charity order was formed in France in 1633 when St. Vincent de Paul recruited a rich widow (St. Louise de Marillac) to care for the sick on battlefields and in their homes.

Elizabeth Ann Seton, America's first saint (canonized 1974), brought the order to the US. In 1809 Seton earned the title of Mother and started the Sisters of Charity. The Sisters adopted the vows of the Daughters of Charity, adding "service" to them in 1812.

The Sisters officially became part of the Daughters of Charity in 1850. The Daughters cared for soldiers during the Civil War and were responsible for training Florence Nightingale. In the late 1800s the Daughters pioneered exclusive provider arrangements (similar to today's managed care contracts) with railroads, lumber camps, and the like. During the next 100 years, the order furthered its mission of caring for the sick and the poor. To support their efforts, the nuns founded hospitals (44 by 1911), schools, and other charity centers.

In 1969 the charity association formed a health care services cooperative, which became the Daughters of Charity National Health System (DCNHS).

DCNHS operated as two regional institutions (one based in Maryland, the other in Missouri) until 1986, when the systems merged. The first task was to balance their holy mission with the need to make money. With competition from managed care companies increasing, DCNHS responded by cutting staff and diversifying into nursing homes and retirement centers.

The Daughters of Charity's western unit combined its six hospitals in California with Mullikin Centers (a physician-owned medical group) in 1993 to form one of the largest health care associations in the state.

DCNHS expanded its network in 1995 by merging its hospitals with and becoming a co-sponsor of San Francisco-based Catholic Healthcare West. That year it joined with Catholic Relief Services to operate a hospital in war-torn Angola.

In 1996 DCNHS dropped a proposed merger of its struggling 221-bed Carney Hospital in Boston with Quincy Hospital because the municipally owned Quincy facility was required by law to provide abortions. Instead, DCNHS sold Carney Hospital to Caritas Christi Health Care System (owned by the Boston Roman Catholic archdiocese), one of about a dozen hospital sales by DCNHS in the mid-1990s.

DCNHS reorganized its leadership in 1997, creating SVP positions for system direction and policy and for program development to strengthen and update its programs. In 1998 Sister Irene Kraus, who had founded DCNHS and led it through its expansion, died.

In 1999 DCNHS merged with fellow Catholic caregiver Sisters of St. Joseph Health System, then Michigan's largest health care system.

In 2000 Ascension saw the collapse of a five-hospital merger in Florida between subsidiary St. Vincent's Health System and Baptist Health System. The organization also launched the Voice for the Voiceless initiative, which combines private monies and federal grants to fund programs for the uninsured in Detroit, New Orleans, and Austin, Texas.

OFFICERS

Chairperson: Sister Joyce DeShano
President and CEO: Douglas D. French, age 48
EVP and COO: Anthony R. Tersigni
SVP and CFO: Anthony Speranzo
SVP Central and Southern States Operating Group: Charles J. Barnett
SVP Strategic Business Development and Innovation; President, Ascension Health Ventures: John D. Doyle

SVP Great Lakes and Mid-Atlantic States Operating
Group: Robert J. Henkel
SVP Legal Services and General Counsel: Rex P. Killian
Human Resources Manager: Kate Brandt
Auditors: Ernst & Young LLP

LOCATIONS

HQ: 4600 Edmundson Rd., St. Louis, MO 63134
Phone: 314-253-6700   Fax: 314-253-6807
Web: www.ascensionhealth.org

Selected Facilities

Alabama
Providence Hospital (Mobile)

Arkansas
DePaul Health Center (Dumas)
St. Elizabeth Health Center (Gould)

Connecticut
Hall-Brooke Hospital (Westport)
St. Joseph Family Life Center (Stamford)
St. Vincent's Medical Center (Bridgeport)

District of Columbia
Carroll Manor Nursing and Rehabilitation Center
Providence Hospital

Florida
Haven of Our Lady of Peace (Pensacola)
Sacred Heart Hospital (Pensacola)
St. Catherine Labouré Manor (Jacksonville)

Indiana
St. Elizabeth Ann Seton Hospital (Boonville)
Welborn Hospital (Evansville)

Louisiana
Daughters of Charity Health Center (New Orleans)
Vincentian Ministries (New Orleans)

Maryland
St. Catherine Nursing Center (Emmitsburg)

Michigan
Father Murray Nursing Home (Detroit)
Genesys Regional Medical Center at East Flint Campus
St. John Gratiot Center (Detroit)
St. John Hospital and Medical Center (Detroit)
St. John Northeast Community Hospital (Detroit)

Missouri
Seton Center Family and Health Services (Kansas City)

New York
Mount St. Mary's Hospital of Niagara Falls (Lewiston)
Our Lady of Lourdes Memorial Hospital (Binghamton)
Schuler Ridge-Seton Ridge Nursing Home (Clifton Park)
St. Mary's Hospital (Troy)

Pennsylvania
Good Samaritan Regional Medical Center (Pottsville)

Tennessee
Middle Tennessee Medical Center (Murfreesboro)
Saint Thomas Health Services (Nashville)

Texas
Brackenridge Hospital (Austin)
Children's Hospital of Austin
DePaul Family Center (San Antonio)
El Carmen Center (San Antonio)
Seton Edgar B. Davis Memorial Hospital (Luling)
Seton Medical Center (Austin)
Seton Northwest Hospital (Austin)
Seton South Community Health Center (Austin)

Wisconsin
Sacred Heart Rehabilitation Institute (Milwaukee)
St. Mary's Hospice (Milwaukee)
St. Mary's Hospital of Milwaukee

PRODUCTS/OPERATIONS

Facilities
Acute care hospitals
Adult residential facilities
Community health centers
Long-term acute care
Long-term care
Psychiatric hospitals
Rehabilitation facilities

COMPETITORS

Beverly Enterprises	HEALTHSOUTH
Catholic Health East	Kindred
Catholic Health Initiatives	Life Care Centers
Catholic Healthcare	Tenet Healthcare
Partners	Triad Hospitals
HCA	Trinity Health
HMA	Universal Health Services

HISTORICAL FINANCIALS & EMPLOYEES

Not-for-profit FYE: June 30	Annual Growth	6/92	6/93	6/94	6/95	6/96	6/97	6/98	6/99	6/00	6/01
Sales ($ mil.)	1.7%	5,900	6,500	7,000	6,200	5,700	5,700	6,170	6,400	6,400	6,853
Employees	3.1%	—	—	67,400	62,300	61,100	60,000	65,000	67,000	67,000	83,412

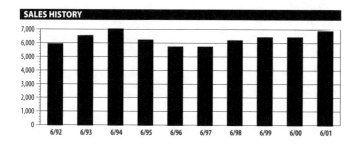

SALES HISTORY

THE ASSOCIATED PRESS

This just in: The Associated Press (AP) is reporting tonight and every night wherever news is breaking. AP is the world's largest newsgathering organization, with about 240 news bureaus serving more than 120 countries. It provides news, photos, graphics, and audiovisual services that reach people daily through print, radio, and television. In addition to its traditional news services, the not-for-profit cooperative, which is owned by its 1,550 member newspapers, runs an international television division (APTN), a digital ad delivery service (AP AdSEND), an ad processing and billing service, photo archives, and a continuous online news service (The WIRE).

AP's news reports are translated into five languages (Dutch, English, French, German, and Spanish) and reach more than 1 billion people daily. The cooperative has been in operation for more than 150 years. Its AP Digital division sells news to the Internet and wireless markets.

HISTORY

The Associated Press was formed in 1848 when six New York City newspapers joined to share news that arrived by telegraph wire. A year later the organization established its first foreign bureau in Halifax, Nova Scotia. Halifax was the first North American port of call for Cunard's ocean liners coming from Europe, and when each ship arrived, the latest news from Europe was telegraphed to AP's New York office. In 1850 the AP began selling wire reports to other papers and before long started creating regional associations.

By the turn of the century, the AP began to expand its services internationally. In 1902 the company created a cable service to serve Cuba, the Philippines, and Central America, and in 1919 it began service to 22 newspapers in South America. In 1933 the AP began service to Japan's Ringgo news agency.

In 1927 the company began offering news pictures along with its stories. Originally, the photos were delivered by an air, sea, and rail system, but in 1935 the company introduced the AP WirePhoto network, transmitting pictures to all AP affiliates simultaneously via telephone wires. Meanwhile the AP was adapting to changing tastes and interests, by expanding its offerings. It began covering sports, financial, and public interest stories in the 1920s. The company also adapted to new technologies, adding a service to create news reports for radio stations in 1941.

In the late 1960s AP and Dow Jones introduced services to improve business and financial reporting. AP improved photo delivery, reception, and storage in the 1970s with the advent of Laserphoto and the Electronic Darkroom. In 1974 the company launched the AP Radio Network to provide hourly newscasts, sportscasts, and business programs to member radio stations.

The company began transmitting news by satellite and offering color photographs to newspapers in the 1980s. In 1985 Louis Boccardi took over the job as president and CEO of the company.

AP adjusted to the media-heavy culture of the 1990s by launching the APTV international news video service and the All News Radio network in 1994. In 1996 the company formed a joint venture with Trans World International (TWI) to launch sports news video service SNTV. Also in 1996 the AP moved onto the Internet when it launched The WIRE. The next year it began offering online access to its Photo Archive. The group bought Worldwide Television News in 1998, combining it with APTV to form APTN (Associated Press Television News). The following year it purchased the radio news contracts of UPI after the rival organization announced it was getting out of broadcast news.

In 2000 AP created an Internet division, AP Digital, to focus on marketing news to online providers. The cooperative continued its Internet focus the following year, launching AP Online en Español (news for Spanish-language Web sites) and AP Entertainment Online (multimedia entertainment news for Web sites). Also that year AP bought the Newspaper Industry Communication Center from the Newspaper Association of America.

In 2002 the company launched an expanded editorial partnership with Dow Jones Newswires, increasing the amount of financial news distributed on AP wires.

OFFICERS

Chairman: Donald E. Newhouse
Vice Chairman: Robert Osborne
President and CEO: Louis D. Boccardi
SVP: Jonathan P. Wolman
SVP and CFO: Patrick T. O'Brien
VP and Director, Business Development:
Tom Brettingen
VP and Director, Corporate Communications:
Kelly Smith Tunney
VP, Secretary, and Director Human Resources:
James M. Donna
Executive Editor: Kathleen Carroll, age 46
Director, Business Operations and Development:
Greg Groce
Director, Networks and Syndication: Dave Gwizdowski
Director, Television Groups and Stations: Larry Price
Sales Manager, Cable/TV Syndication: Wayne Ludkey
Manager, Hispanic Broadcast Markets and TV Groups:
Roy Blom
Treasurer: Daniel M. Boruch
Assistant Secretary: Lilo Jedelhauser
Assistant Treasurer: Ann Randolph

LOCATIONS

HQ: 50 Rockefeller Plaza, New York, NY 10020
Phone: 212-621-1500   **Fax:** 212-621-5447
Web: www.ap.org

The Associated Press has about 240 news bureaus
serving 121 countries.

PRODUCTS/OPERATIONS

Selected Products and Services
AP AdSEND (digital transmission of advertisements)
AP Digital (news for Internet and wireless markets)
AP Information Services (news products for
corporations, government, and online distributors)
AP Photo Archive (more than 750,000 online photos)
AP Telecommunications (land-based and satellite
information networks)
AP Wide World Photos (20th-century historical photos
for professional photographers)
APTN (Associated Press Television Network,
international television news service)
ENPS (electronic news production system)
NICC (Newpaper Industry Communication Center; ad
placement, billing and tear sheet processing)
The WIRE (24-hour news service for the Internet)

COMPETITORS

Agence France-Presse
Bloomberg
Business Wire
COMTEX
Corbis
Dow Jones
Gannett
Getty Images
Knight Ridder
New York Times
PR Newswire
Reuters
Tribune
UPI

HISTORICAL FINANCIALS & EMPLOYEES

Cooperative FYE: December 31	Annual Growth	12/91	12/92	12/93	12/94	12/95	12/96	12/97	12/98	12/99	12/00
Sales ($ mil.)	5.8%	—	365	382	406	390	418	441	495	572	574
Employees	2.2%	—	3,100	3,150	3,150	3,150	3,000	3,500	3,500	3,500	3,700

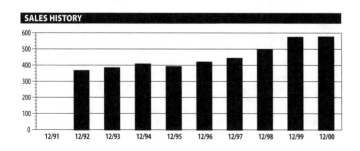

SALES HISTORY

ASSOCIATED WHOLESALE GROCERS

Associated Wholesale Grocers (AWG) knows its customers can't live by bread and milk alone. The AWG cooperative supplies more than 850 member-stores with wholesale grocery sales, advertising and market support, store decorating and design, and selecting appropriate technology. The co-op's territory covers primarily Arkansas, Kansas, Missouri, and Oklahoma, but also six other midwestern and southern states. The co-op offers its members the use of such banners as Country Mart, Thriftway, Price Chopper, and Sun Fresh. AWG also operates more than 30 of its own Falley's and Food 4 Less stores in Kansas and Missouri, as well as 43 Homeland stores throughout Oklahoma.

AWG acquired Homeland Stores in September 2002 and formed a new subsidiary, Associated Retail Grocers, to oversee Homeland and its Falley's chain. (Wholesaler AWG moved into food retailing in 1998 with its acquisition of Falley's.)

AWG supplies members with brand-name and private-label food (Always Save and Best Choice) and nonfood items; other services the co-op provides include property and casualty insurance, employee benefits packages, loan programs, and real estate lease assistance. It also helps its members appeal to Hispanic customers with its "Authentic Hispanic" product line of more than 300 items.

Other AWG banners include Apple Market, Cash Saver, and Price Mart (a food warehouse format).

HISTORY

About 20 Kansas City, Kansas-area grocers met in a local grocery in 1924 and organized the Associated Grocers Company to get better deals on purchases and advertising. They elected J. C. Harline president, and each chipped in a few hundred dollars to make their first purchases. It took a while to find a manufacturer who would sell directly to them; a local soap maker was finally convinced, and others gradually followed.

In 1926 the group was incorporated as Associated Wholesale Grocers (AWG). It outgrew two warehouses in four years, finally moving to a 16,000-sq.-ft. facility big enough to add new lines and more products. Membership doubled between 1930 and 1932 as grocers moved from ordering products a year ahead to the new wholesale concept, and members took seriously the slogan: "Buy, Sell, Buy Some More." They met every week to plan how to sell their products, and buyer and advertising manager Harry Small gave sales presentations and advertising ideas (his trade-in plan for old brooms sold more than two train-carloads of brooms in two weeks). Heavy newspaper advertising also paid off; AWG topped $1 million in sales in 1933.

The cooperative made its first acquisition in 1936, buying Progressive Grocers, a warehouse in Joplin, Missouri; a second warehouse named Associated Grocers was acquired the next year in Springfield, Missouri. AWG continued building and expanding warehouses, and annual sales were at $11 million by 1951.

Louis Fox became CEO in 1956. Fox maximized year-end rebates for members, led several acquisitions, and formed a new subsidiary for financing stores and small shopping centers where AWG members had a presence (Supermarket Developers). Sales increased nearly fifteenfold to over $200 million in his first 15 years.

James Basha, who succeeded Fox when he retired in 1984, saw sales reach $2.4 billion by his own retirement in 1992.

Basha was followed by former COO Mike DeFabis, who was once a deputy mayor of Indianapolis. DeFabis orchestrated several acquisitions, including 41 Kansas City-area stores — most of which were quickly bought by members — from bankrupt Food Barn Stores in 1994 and 29 Oklahoma stores and a warehouse from Safeway spinoff Homeland Stores in 1995 (members bought all the stores).

AWG's nonfood subsidiary, Valu Merchandisers Co., was established in 1995; its new Kansas warehouse began shipping health and beauty aids and housewares the following year to help members battle big discounters. Members narrowly defeated a proposal in late 1996 to convert the cooperative into a public company. Proponents promptly petitioned for a second vote, which was defeated early the next year.

AWG veteran Doug Carolan succeeded DeFabis in 1998, becoming only the fifth CEO in the cooperative's history. The company bought five Falley's and 33 Food 4 Less stores in Kansas and Missouri from Fred Meyer in 1998 for $300 million. In a break with tradition, AWG is operating the stores rather than selling them to members.

In 2000, after a months-long labor dispute with the Teamsters was resolved, Carolan left AWG. The company's CFO, Gary Phillips, was named president and CEO later that year. In 2001 the company debuted a new format, ALPS (Always Low Price Stores) — small stores that carry a limited selection of grocery top-sellers. Also that year AWG's Kansas City division began distributing to more than 10 new stores that had formerly been served by Fleming, the #2 US wholesale food distributor after SUPERVALU.

In 2002 supermarket operator Homeland Stores, which operates 43 stores throughout Oklahoma, emerged from bankruptcy as a fully owned subsidiary of AWG.

OFFICERS

Chairman: J. Fred Ball
President and CEO: Gary Phillips
EVP and CFO: Robert C. Walker
EVP, Marketing: Jerry Garland
SVP and General Manager, KC Division: Mike Rand
SVP, Real Estate: Scott Wilmoski
VP and General Counsel: Chi Chi Puhl
VP, Secretary, and Treasurer: Joe Campbell
VP, Corporate Sales: Bill Lancaster
VP, Human Resources: Frank Tricamo
VP, Procurement: Dennis Kinser

LOCATIONS

HQ: Associated Wholesale Grocers, Inc.
5000 Kansas Ave., Kansas City, KS 66106
Phone: 913-288-1000 **Fax:** 913-288-1508
Web: www.awginc.com

Associated Wholesale Grocers serves grocers in
Arkansas, Illinois, Iowa, Kansas, Kentucky, Missouri,
Nebraska, Oklahoma, Tennessee, and Texas. The
cooperative has four distribution centers in Kansas,
Missouri, and Oklahoma.

PRODUCTS/OPERATIONS

Selected Private-Label Brands
Always Save
Best Choice

Selected Services
Advertising
Employee training
Financial planning
In-store marketing
Insurance
Market research and analysis
Private-label products
Product positioning
Real estate lease assistance
Site acquisition
Store engineering and construction
Store financing
Store remodeling

Selected Store Formats
Apple Market (15,000-25,000-sq.-ft. grocery stores
designed for neighborhood locations in both rural and
metropolitan areas)
Cash Saver (designed with fewer perishables to serve
rural areas)
Country Mart (25,000-45,000-sq.-ft. value-priced stores
designed for county-seat and medium-sized towns)
Falley's (conventional supermarkets)
Food 4 Less (warehouse stores)
Price Chopper and Price Mart (50,000-92,000-sq.-ft.
value-priced warehouse stores designed for high-
volume areas)
Sun Fresh (40,000-63,000-sq.-ft. stores designed to serve
medium- to upper-income customers)
Thriftway (neighborhood locations)

Selected Operations/Subsidiaries
Benchmark Insurance Co.
Supermarket Developers, Inc. (financing for stores and
supermarkets)
Supermarket Insurance Agency Inc.
Valu Merchandisers Company (health and beauty
supplies, general merchandise, and pharmacy
products)

COMPETITORS

Affiliated Foods
Albertson's
Delhaize America
Fleming Companies
GSC Enterprises
H.T. Hackney
Hy-Vee
IGA
Kroger
Nash Finch
Roundy's
S. Abraham & Sons
Schnuck Markets
Shurfine International
Spartan Stores
SUPERVALU
Topco Associates
Wal-Mart

HISTORICAL FINANCIALS & EMPLOYEES

Cooperative FYE: December 31	Annual Growth	12/92	12/93	12/94	12/95	12/96	12/97	12/98	12/99	12/00	12/01
Sales ($ mil.)	2.9%	2,404	2,540	2,600	2,970	3,096	3,129	3,180	3,370	3,267	3,097
Net income ($ mil.)	(4.5%)	—	—	—	—	—	64	66	65	46	53
Income as % of sales	—	—	—	—	—	—	2.0%	2.1%	1.9%	1.4%	1.7%
Employees	3.4%	—	—	—	2,797	3,000	3,100	3,300	3,300	3,300	

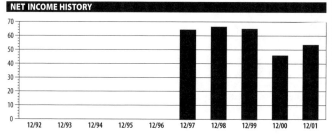

NET INCOME HISTORY

2001 FISCAL YEAR-END
Debt ratio: 25.4%
Return on equity: 32.4%
Cash ($ mil.): 12
Current ratio: 1.05
Long-term debt ($ mil.): 55

BAKER & MCKENZIE

Baker & McKenzie knows that size has its advantages (and disadvantages). Chicago-based Baker is one of the world's largest law firms with more than 3,000 lawyers serving in more than 60 offices across some 35 countries. Although Baker's size helps attract attorneys as well as clients, the firm also has had to fight the image that it is focused more on franchising than quality legal work. Russell Baker and John McKenzie founded the firm in 1949 with a focus on building an international practice.

Baker has become one of the first major practices to appoint a woman as its top partner. Christine Lagarde was chosen in 1999 to replace outgoing chairman John Klotsche. In addition to closing the gender gap, Lagarde is also one of the youngest partners, age 43 when she was elected, to lead the firm.

Baker is a full-service firm offering legal advice in areas such as banking, securities, labor, international trade, and tax. The half-century-old firm has handled the legal affairs of such heavy-duty clients as Chase Manhattan (now J.P. Morgan Chase), Honeywell, and Ingersoll-Rand.

The firm is known for the global scale of its practice, with some 80% of Baker attorneys practicing outside the US. However, it is beginning to face new competition on the global scene from firms such as Clifford Chance (which merged with two other practices in 2000 to create a network larger than Baker's).

HISTORY

Russell Baker traveled from his native New Mexico to Chicago on a railroad freight car to attend law school. Upon graduation in 1925 he started practicing law with his classmate Dana Simpson under the name Simpson & Baker. Inspired by Chicago's role as a manufacturing and agricultural center for the world and influenced by the international focus of his alma mater, the University of Chicago, Baker dreamed of creating an international law practice. He began developing an expertise in international law, and in 1934 Abbott Laboratories retained him to handle its worldwide legal affairs. Baker was on his way to fulfilling his dream.

Baker joined forces with Chicago litigator John McKenzie in 1949, forming Baker & McKenzie. In 1955 the firm opened its first foreign office in Caracas, Venezuela, to meet the needs of its expanding US client base. Over the next 10 years it branched out into Asia, Australia, and Europe, with offices in London, Manila, Paris, and Tokyo. Baker's death in 1979 neither slowed the firm's growth nor changed its international character. The next year it expanded into the Middle East and opened its 30th office in 1982 (Melbourne). To manage the sprawling law firm, Baker & McKenzie created the position of chairman of the executive committee in 1984.

In late 1991 the firm dropped the Church of Scientology as a client, losing an estimated $2 million in business. It was speculated that pressure from client Eli Lilly (maker of the drug Prozac, which Scientologists actively oppose) influenced the decision. In 1992 Baker & McKenzie was ordered to pay $1 million for wrongfully firing an employee who later died of AIDS. (The case became the basis for the 1993 film *Philadelphia*.) The firm fought the verdict but eventually settled for an undisclosed amount in 1995.

In 1994 Baker & McKenzie closed its Los Angeles office (the former MacDonald, Halsted & Laybourne; acquired 1988) amid considerable rancor. Also that year a former secretary at the firm received a $7.1 million judgment for sexual harassment by a partner. (A San Francisco Superior Court judge later reduced the award to $3.5 million.)

John Klotsche, a senior partner from the firm's Palo Alto, California, office was appointed chairman in 1995. The following year the firm began a major expansion into California's Silicon Valley as part of an initiative to serve technology companies around the world. It also expanded its Warsaw, Poland, office through a merger with the Warsaw office of Dickinson, Wright, Moon, Van Dusen & Freman.

In 1998 Baker & McKenzie formed a special unit in Singapore to deal with business generated by the financial troubles in Asia. The opening of offices in Taiwan and Azerbaijan in 1998 brought the firm's total number of offices to 59. Klotsche stepped down in 1999 as the firm celebrated its 50th anniversary; Christine Lagarde replaced him. In early 2001 Baker & McKenzie created a joint venture practice with Singapore-based associate firm Wong & Leow. Also that year it merged with Madrid-based Briones Alonso y Martin to create the largest independent law firm in Spain.

OFFICERS

Chairman Executive Committee: Christine Lagarde, age 45
COO: Peter Smith
CFO: Robert S. Spencer
CTO: Craig Courter
General Counsel: Edward J. Zulkey
Director, Professional Development: Anne Waldron
Global Director Marketing: Roberta Montafia

LOCATIONS

HQ: 1 Prudential Plaza, 130 E. Randolph Dr., Ste. 2500, Chicago, IL 60601
Phone: 312-861-8800   **Fax:** 312-861-8823
Web: www.bakernet.com

Baker & McKenzie has more than 60 offices throughout Asia, Australia, Europe, Latin America, the Middle East, and North America.

PRODUCTS/OPERATIONS

Selected Practice Areas
Banking and finance
Corporate and securities
E-commerce
International commercial arbitration
International trade
IP, IT, and Communications
Labor and employment
Tax
US Litigation

COMPETITORS

Clifford Chance
Deloitte Touche Tohmatsu
Ernst & Young
Jones, Day
Kirkland & Ellis
KPMG
Mayer, Brown, Rowe & Maw
McDermott, Will
PricewaterhouseCoopers
Sidley Austin Brown & Wood
Skadden, Arps

HISTORICAL FINANCIALS & EMPLOYEES

Partnership FYE: June 30	Annual Growth	6/93	6/94	6/95	6/96	6/97	6/98	6/99	6/00	6/01	6/02
Sales ($ mil.)	7.7%	512	546	594	646	697	785	818	940	1,000	1,000
Employees	5.2%	5,054	5,114	5,248	5,680	6,100	6,700	6,900	8,000	8,000	8,000

SALES HISTORY

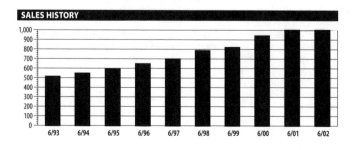

BATTELLE MEMORIAL INSTITUTE

When you use a copier, hit a golf ball, or listen to a CD, you're using technologies developed by Battelle Memorial Institute. The nonprofit trust operates one of the world's largest research enterprises. Originally formed to promote metallurgy and related industries, the institute has diversified into research and development for agriculture, automobiles, chemicals, energy, software, and medicine. Battelle is also a major source of research and development expertise for the US government. It serves the departments of Energy, Defense, and Health and Human Services; the Environmental Protection Agency; and nearly 800 other government organizations.

The institute, which works with corporations and governments in nearly 30 countries, was instrumental in developing the photocopy machine, optical digital recording (used with compact discs), and bar codes. Primarily a contract research provider, the institute continues to explore next-generation technologies including advanced medical products, alternative fuels, and recycling processes.

Battelle is spinning off for-profit companies to benefit its nonprofit cause; it has shed its medical, flat-panel display, and software units as subsidiaries. Current development projects include cancer prevention, crude oil extraction, and paper mill waste recycling.

HISTORY

Battelle Memorial Institute was founded with a $1.5 million trust willed by Gordon Battelle, who died in 1923. Battelle was a champion of research for the advancement of humankind, and before taking his father's place as president of several Ohio steel mills, he had funded a former university professor's successful work to extract useful chemicals from mine waste. Battelle's mother, upon her death in 1925, left the institute an additional $2.1 million. The institute opened in 1929.

The institute took on perhaps the most important project in its history in 1944 when it helped an electronics company's patent lawyer, Chester Carlson, find practical uses for his invention, called xerography. Eventually Battelle developed the first photocopy machine, and in 1955 it sold the patent rights for the machine to Haloid (now Xerox) in exchange for royalties.

During WWII Battelle worked on uranium refining for the Manhattan Project, and in the early 1950s it established the world's first private nuclear research facility. The company also set up operations in Germany and Switzerland.

The tax man came knocking in 1961, questioning the tax-free status of some of Battelle's activities. The organization eventually had to pay $47 million. In 1965 Battelle developed a coin with a copper core and a copper-and-nickel-alloy cladding for the US Treasury.

As the result of a ruling that reinterpreted a clause in Gordon Battelle's will, in 1975 the institute gave $80 million to philanthropic enterprises. This ruling, coupled with the taxes that the organization was still unaccustomed to paying, forced Battelle to reexamine its strategy.

Battelle co-developed the Universal Product Code (the bar code symbol found today on nearly all consumer goods packaging) in the 1970s. The institute also landed a lucrative contract from the US Department of Energy (DOE) to manage its commercial nuclear waste isolation program.

In 1987 Battelle chose Douglas Olesen — a 20-year veteran of the institute — to replace retiring CEO Ronald Paul. The company signed an extension with the DOE in 1992 to run its Pacific Northwest Laboratory (which it has operated since 1965).

An Ohio court in 1997 approved a seven-page agreement with the institute outlining the key principles that must be followed according to Gordon Battelle's will. This agreement replaced the 1975 decree and ended more than 20 years of scrutiny by the state Attorney General's Office.

In 1998 the DOE contracted Brookhaven Science Associates — a partnership between State University of New York and Battelle — to operate Brookhaven National Laboratory. That year a Battelle contract to dispose of Vietnam War-era napalm drew national attention when subcontractor Pollution Control Industries backed out of the project, citing safety concerns. Under Battelle's direction, Houston-based GNI Group took the 3.4 million gallons of napalm off the US Navy's hands.

Battelle and the University of Tennessee in 1999 won a five-year contract to operate the US government's Oak Ridge National Laboratory. That year the institute made several breakthroughs in cancer research, including FDA approval to test an inhalation delivery system for treating lung cancer.

In 2000 the company spun off OmniViz (data mining software) and Battelle Pulmonary Therapeutics (pulmonary and drug delivery technology) as wholly owned subsidiaries. In 2001 Battelle chose former Kodak EVP and chief technology officer Carl Kohrt to replace Olesen.

OFFICERS

Chairman: John B. McCoy Jr.
First Vice Chairman: John J. Hopfield
Second Vice Chairman: W. George Meredith
President and CEO: Carl F. Kohrt, age 57
EVP, Department of Energy Market Sector; Director, Oak Ridge National Laboratory: William J. Madia
EVP, Government Market Sectors: Merwyn R. VanderLind
SVP and CTO, Core Technology Development: Richard C. Adams
SVP, CFO, and Treasurer: Mark W. Kontos
SVP; Director, Pacific Northwest Laboratory: Lura J. Powell
SVP; General Manager, Automotive Technology Market Sector: Donald P. McConnell
SVP; General Manager, Chemical Products Market Sector: Benjamin G. Maiden
SVP; General Manager, Energy Products Market Sector: Henry J. Cialone
SVP; General Manager, Pharmaceutical and Medical Products Market Sector: Richard D. Rosen
SVP, Administration, General Counsel, and Secretary: Jerome R. Bahlmann
SVP, Organizational Development: Robert W. Smith Jr.
President and CEO, Battelle Pulmonary Therapeutics: Dennis Cearlock
VP, Government Market Sectors: Gregory L. Frank
Director, Human Resources: Bob Lincoln

LOCATIONS

HQ: 505 King Ave., Columbus, OH 43201
Phone: 614-424-6424   **Fax:** 614-424-5263
Web: www.battelle.org

Battelle Memorial Institute manages programs in nearly 30 countries.

PRODUCTS/OPERATIONS

Selected Inventions
Automobile cruise control (1960s)
Exploded-tip paintbrush (nylon brush for Wooster Brush Co., 1950)
Golf ball coatings (1965)
Heat Seat (microwaveable heated stadium cushion, 1990s)
Holograms (work began in the 1970s)
Insulin injection pen (for Eli Lilly, 1990s)
Oil spill outline monitor (1992)
PCB-cleaning chemical process (1992)
Photocopy machine (with Haloid, 1940s)
Plastic breakdown process (1990s)
"Sandwich" coins (copper/copper and nickel alloy cladding design for US Treasury, 1965)
SenSonic toothbrush (with Teledyne/WaterPik, 1990s)
Smart cards (cards embedded with tiny computer chips that store information, 1980s)
SnoPake (correction fluid, 1955)
Universal Product Code (co-creator; bar code, 1970s)

Subsidiaries
Battelle Pulmonary Therapeutics, Inc.
Geosafe Corporation
Global Transaction Company, Inc.
OmniViz, Inc.
Research Insurance Company Ltd.
Scientific Advances, Inc.
State Science and Technology Institute
Vitex Systems, Inc.

COMPETITORS

Altran Technologies
The Charles Stark Draper Laboratory
Kendle
MIT
MITRE
PAREXEL
Quintiles Transnational
Research Triangle Institute
SAIC
Southwest Research Institute
SRI International
University of California

HISTORICAL FINANCIALS & EMPLOYEES

Not-for-profit FYE: September 30	Annual Growth	9/93	9/94	9/95	9/96	9/97	9/98	9/99	9/00	9/01	9/02
Sales ($ mil.)	3.4%	869	958	974	945	946	710	901	950	1,029	1,176
Employees	0.4%	8,400	8,583	7,500	7,163	7,060	7,250	7,060	7,100	7,607	8,700

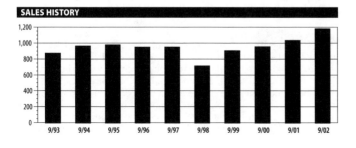

SALES HISTORY

BECHTEL GROUP, INC.

Whether it's raising an entire city or razing a nuclear power plant, you can bet the Bechtel Group will be there to bid on the business. The firm is the US's #1 contractor (ahead of Fluor). The engineering, construction, and project management firm operates worldwide, participating in such notable projects as the construction of Hoover Dam and the cleanup of the Chernobyl nuclear plant. Subsidiary Bechtel Enterprises invests in infrastructure projects and arranges financing for its clients. The group is in its fourth generation of leadership by the Bechtel family, with chairman and CEO Riley Bechtel at the helm. The billionaire Bechtel family owns a controlling stake in the firm.

Bechtel has made a name for itself by participating in mega-projects. It completes more than 1,000 projects a year. The services Bechtel offers are as broad as the industries it serves. Besides project management and design, the company offers such services as environmental restoration and remediation, telecommunications infrastructure (installing cable-optic networks and constructing data centers), and e-business infrastructure (including design, systems integration, and commissioning).

Among Bechtel's major projects is its expansion of AT&T Wireless Services' US network. With a downturn in the telecommunications industry, however, Bechtel has looked to other areas of infrastructure. In Europe it is expanding its rail business by participating in the construction of the Channel Tunnel Rail Link, the UK's first major new railroad project in a century. Bechtel is also managing the upgrade of the UK's West Coast main line and has joined a consortium to renovate part of London's 139-year-old subway.

Bechtel has been finding the environmental market to be another source of steady income. The group's Bechtel National, Inc. (BNI) subsidiary has been selected by the US Department of Energy to be the prime contractor for design and construction of the Hanford Waste Treatment Plant in Washington State, one of the DOE's most complex cleanup projects. The project's aim is to treat 53 million gallons of high-level radioactive waste stored at the Hanford site.

In 1898 25-year-old Warren Bechtel left his Kansas farm to grade railroads in the Oklahoma Indian territories, then followed the rails west. Settling in Oakland, California, he founded his own contracting firm. Foreseeing the importance of roads, oil, and power, he won big projects such as the Northern California Highway

and the Bowman Dam. By 1925, when he incorporated his company as W.A. Bechtel & Co., it ranked as the West's largest construction company. In 1931 Bechtel helped found the consortium that built Hoover Dam.

Under the leadership of Steve Bechtel (president after his father's death in 1933), the company obtained contracts for large infrastructure projects such as the San Francisco-Oakland Bay Bridge. Noted for his friendships with influential people, including Dwight Eisenhower, Adlai Stevenson, and Saudi Arabia's King Faisal, Steve developed projects that spanned nations and industries, such as pipelines in Saudi Arabia and numerous power projects. By 1960, when Steve Bechtel Jr. took over, the company was operating on six continents.

In the next two decades, Bechtel worked on transportation projects — such as San Francisco's Bay Area Rapid Transit (BART) system and the Washington, DC, subway system — and power projects, including nuclear plants. After the 1979 Three Mile Island accident, Bechtel tried its hand at nuclear cleanup. With nuclear power no longer in vogue, it focused on other markets, such as mining in New Guinea (gold and copper, 1981-84) and China (coal, 1984). Bechtel's Jubail project in Saudi Arabia, begun in 1976, raised an entire industrial port city on the Persian Gulf.

The US recession and rising developing-world debt of the early 1980s sent Bechtel reeling. It cut its workforce by 22,000 and stemmed losses by piling up small projects.

Riley Bechtel, great-grandson of Warren, became CEO in 1990. After the 1991 Gulf War, Bechtel extinguished Kuwait's flaming oil wells and worked on the oil-spill cleanup. During the decade it also worked on such projects as the Channel tunnel (Chunnel) between England and France, the new airport in Hong Kong, and pipelines in the former Soviet Union.

In 1996 Bechtel bought PG&E's share of InterGen, then sold a 50% stake in InterGen to a unit of Royal Dutch/Shell in early 1997. In 1998 it joined Battelle and Electricité de France in project management of a long-term plan to stabilize the damaged reactor of the Chernobyl nuclear plant in Ukraine.

In 1999 Bechtel was hired to decommission the Connecticut Yankee nuclear plant. It also won contracts with Internet companies, including failed online grocer Webvan, to build a series of 26 automated grocery warehouses in the US in a deal worth nearly $1 billion. However, only four were completed before Webvan fizzled in mid-2001. The next year Bechtel teamed up with Shell Oil to build a $400 million power plant in

Baja California to meet the high demands of the US-Mexico border region. It also formed Nexant, an energy consulting service for the oil and gas industry and utilities.

Bechtel expanded its telecommunications operations in 2001 to provide turnkey network implementation services in Europe, the Middle East, and Asia. In 2002 Bechtel was once again called on to work on the UK's rail system, taking over management of the upgrade of the West Coast main line from financially troubled Railtrack. The company also joined UK facilities management giants Jarvis and Amey to bid on modernizing part of London's aging subway system, although Amey later relinquished its stake in the consortium.

OFFICERS

Chairman Emeritus: Steve Bechtel Jr.
Chairman and CEO: Riley P. Bechtel, age 50
Vice Chairman: Paul Unruh
Vice Chairman, President, and COO: Adrian Zaccaria
SVP, CFO, and Director: Georganne Proctor
EVP and Director; President, Bechtel Enterprises: Tim Statton
EVP and Director; President, Bechtel Systems and Infrastructure: Jude Laspa
EVP and Director; President, Civil Engineering and Construction Business Unit: Lee McIntire
EVP and Director; President, Pipeline Engineering and Construction Business Unit: Mike Thiele
SVP and Director; President, Petroleum and Chemical Engineering and Construction Business Unit: Bill Dudley
SVP and Director; President, Bechtel National: Thomas Hash
SVP and Manager of Procurement and Contracts: Jack Futcher
President, Bechtel Infrastructure: John McDonald
President, Mining and Metals Engineering and Construction Business Unit: Andy Greig
President, Power Engineering and Construction Business Unit: Scott Ogilvie
President, Telecommunications and Industrial Engineering and Construction Business Unit: George Conniff

Manager Human Resources: Jim Illich
Manager Information Systems and Technology: Geir Ramleth
Public Communications Manager: Jeff H. Berger
Auditors: PricewaterhouseCoopers LLP

LOCATIONS

HQ: 50 Beale St., San Francisco, CA 94105
Phone: 415-768-1234   **Fax:** 415-768-9038
Web: www.bechtel.com

PRODUCTS/OPERATIONS

Selected Services
Automation technology
Community relations
Environmental health and safety
Equipment operations
International consulting
Labor relations
Project management, engineering, and financing
Worldwide procurement

COMPETITORS

ABB	HOCHTIEF	Philipp
AMEC	Hyundai	Holzmann
Black & Veatch	Engineering	Powergen
Bouygues	and	RWE
CH2M HILL	Construction	Safety-Kleen
Chicago Bridge	ITOCHU	Samsung
and Iron	J.A. Jones	Schneider
Chiyoda Corp.	Jacobs	Shaw Group
Duke/Fluor	Engineering	Siemens
Daniel	Kvaerner	Skanska
Eiffage	Marubeni	Technip-Coflexip
EllisDon	NKK	URS
Construction	Parsons	VINCI
Enron	Perini	Washington
Fluor	Peter Kiewit	Group
Foster Wheeler	Sons'	WESTON
Halliburton		

HISTORICAL FINANCIALS & EMPLOYEES

Private FYE: December 31	Annual Growth	12/92	12/93	12/94	12/95	12/96	12/97	12/98	12/99	12/00	12/01
Sales ($ mil.)	6.2%	7,774	7,337	7,885	8,504	8,157	11,329	12,645	12,600	15,108	13,400
Employees	5.5%	30,900	29,400	29,200	29,400	30,000	30,000	30,000	40,000	40,000	50,000

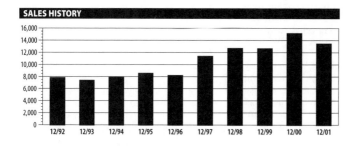

SALES HISTORY

BELK, INC.

Belk has shed a lot of bulk. Now a relatively svelte 207-store retailer operating in 13 states, the chain was a confederation of 112 separate companies, formed over the past century, before its 1998 reorganization. Belk stores, located in the Southeast and Mid-Atlantic (primarily in the Carolinas and Georgia), offer mid-priced brand-name and private-label apparel, shoes, cosmetics, gifts, and home furnishings. Its stores usually anchor malls or shopping centers in small to medium-sized markets. The Belk family runs the show and owns most of the company, which is the largest privately owned department store chain in the US.

Larger Belk stores may also have hair salons, restaurants, and optical centers.

While some might say a public offering is the logical next step, chairman John Belk has vowed that will not happen while he is alive. The Belk brood has not always brimmed with brotherly love, but there is no need to call in Richard Dawson to settle the Belk family feud.

HISTORY

William Henry Belk didn't mind being known as a cheapskate. At 26 he opened his first store, New York Racket, in 1888 in Monroe, North Carolina. He nicknamed the tiny shop "The Cheapest Store on Earth" and created the slogan "Cheap Goods Sell Themselves." In 1891 Belk convinced his brother John to give up a career as a doctor and join him in the retail business.

The new company, Belk Brothers, opened stores in North and South Carolina, often with partners who were family members or former employees, resulting in many two-family store names such as Belk-Harry and Hudson-Belk.

The Belks formed a partnership with the Leggett family (John's in-laws) in 1920. But feuding between the two families led to a split in 1927. The Leggetts agreed that the Belk family could keep a 20% share of the Leggett stores. John died the next year.

A strict no-credit policy worked in William's favor during the Depression, when he was able to buy out his more lenient competitors for rock-bottom prices. The shrewd businessman grew the chain from 29 stores in 1929 to about 220 stores by 1945, employing concepts such as a no-haggling policy and easy returns. William died in 1952.

That year one of his six children, William Henry Jr., opened a Belk-Lindsey store in Florida using a new format that featured, among other things, an Oriental design. Most of his siblings balked at the store's new look, but William Jr. opened another store in 1953 following the same format.

Two years later four of William Jr.'s siblings — John, Irwin, Tom, and Sarah — cut ties with the Florida stores and formed Belk Stores Services to organize their other stores. Angry at the rebuke, William Jr. and another brother, Henderson, sued the rest of the family, but they later dropped the lawsuit. In 1956 Belk Stores, with John at the helm, bought out 50-store rival chain Effird.

John had political ambitions and was elected mayor of Charlotte, North Carolina, in 1969, despite attempts by his brother William Jr. to foil the campaign. He remained mayor until 1977. Tom became the company's president in 1980.

Belk Stores continued to hold its own in the 1980s against larger department store chains on the prowl for acquisitions, but the company was stung by family discord and a loose ownership structure. Some relatives sold Belk stores to competitors such as Proffitt's (now Saks Inc.) and Dillard's. Irwin and his family, discouraged about the company's direction, sold their stock to John. In 1996 the Leggetts came back into the fold when Belk Stores bought out their 30-store chain.

Tom died in 1997 after complications from gall bladder surgery. His three sons, Johnny, McKay, and Tim, stepped up as co-presidents but continued to answer to their uncle John, the CEO. Also in 1997 Belk Stores closed its struggling 13 Tags off-price outlets.

A year later the firm reorganized and brought all 112 separate corporations under one company, streamlining the company's accounting (previously it had to fill out tax forms for all 112 businesses) and other operations. Soon after, Belk consolidated its 13 divisional offices into four regional units. Also in 1998 it traded several store locations with Dillard's.

In 1999 Belk formed Belk National Bank in Georgia to manage its credit card operations. In 2001 the company closed four of its distribution centers, consolidating their operations into its new Blythewood, South Carolina, center.

Chairman and CEO: John M. Belk, age 82,
$1,134,667 pay
Vice Chairman: B. Frank Matthews II, age 74
President, Finance Systems and Operations, and
Director: John R. Belk, age 43, $778,391 pay
President, Merchandising, Marketing, and Merchandise
Planning, and Director: H. W. McKay Belk, age 45,
$778,391 pay
President, Store Divisions and Real Estate, and
Director: Thomas M. Belk Jr., age 47, $778,391 pay
EVP, Finance: Brian T. Marley, age 45
EVP, Human Resources: Stephen J. Pernotto
EVP, Real Estate and Store Planning:
William L. Wilson, age 54
EVP, Secretary, and General Counsel: Ralph A. Pitts,
age 48, $579,782 pay
EVP, Systems: Robert K. Kerr Jr., age 53
SVP and Controller: Edward J. Record
Auditors: KPMG LLP

LOCATIONS

HQ: 2801 W. Tyvola Rd., Charlotte, NC 28217
Phone: 704-357-1000   Fax: 704-357-1876
Web: www.belk.com

2002 Stores

	No.
North Carolina	73
Georgia	38
South Carolina	38
Florida	19
Virginia	19
Kentucky	4
Alabama	3
Tennessee	3
Texas	3
Arkansas	2
Maryland	2
West Virginia	2
Mississippi	1
Total	**207**

PRODUCTS/OPERATIONS

Private Labels
Home Accents
J.Khaki
Kim Rogers
Madison Studio
Meeting Street
Saddlebred

COMPETITORS

Dillard's
Elder-Beerman Stores
Federated
J. C. Penney
Kohl's
May
Saks Inc.
Sears
Stein Mart
Target
TJX
Wal-Mart

HISTORICAL FINANCIALS & EMPLOYEES

Private FYE: January 31	Annual Growth	1/93	1/94	1/95	1/96	1/97	1/98	1/99	1/00	1/01	1/02
Sales ($ mil.)	3.4%	1,662	1,674	1,694	1,685	1,773	1,974	2,091	2,145	2,270	2,243
Net income ($ mil.)	1.4%	56	54	49	44	101	54	57	71	57	63
Income as % of sales	—	3.4%	3.2%	2.9%	2.6%	5.7%	2.8%	2.7%	3.3%	2.5%	2.8%
Employees	(5.8%)	—	—	—	—	25,000	29,000	22,000	21,000	21,000	18,500

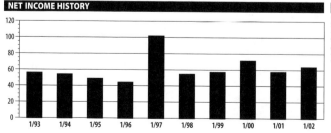

NET INCOME HISTORY

2002 FISCAL YEAR-END

Debt ratio: 30.8%
Return on equity: 7.2%
Cash ($ mil.): 22
Current ratio: 3.28
Long-term debt ($ mil.): 399

BILL & MELINDA GATES FOUNDATION

You don't have to be one of the richest men in the world to attract attention to your charitable foundation, but it doesn't hurt. Established in 1994, The William H. Gates Foundation was thrust into the spotlight in 1999 after receiving more than $2 billion from Microsoft chairman and foundation namesake Bill Gates. Later that year it combined with the Gates Learning Foundation to form the Bill & Melinda Gates Foundation. Its contributions fund work in the areas of world health (vaccine research) and education; it also supports library computer programs and community service initiatives in the Pacific Northwest. William Gates Sr. is CEO of the foundation, which is the largest in the US, with an endowment of about $24 billion.

Some of the foundation's beneficiaries have included the Global Health Council, Helen Keller International, International Planned Parenthood, the International Vaccine Institute, the National Institute of Child Health and Human Development, the Pacific Institute for Women's Health, and the United Negro College Fund. The foundation also has the Gates Millennium Scholars Program, which plans to provide scholarships to 20,000 minority students over the next 20 years. Gates has said he would like to give away most of his fortune while he is still living.

HISTORY

Bill Gates created the William H. Gates Foundation in 1994 with $106 million. During the next four years, he added about $2 billion to the charity. He appointed his father the head of the foundation, which at first was housed in Bill Gates Sr.'s basement.

In 1997 Gates established the Gates Learning Foundation (originally the Gates Library Foundation), a philanthropic effort to improve technology and Internet access at libraries. Some of Gates' critics saw the effort as a way for him to plant Microsoft software at libraries nationwide. Patty Stonesifer, a former executive at Microsoft, ran the organization from an office above a pizza parlor.

During 1998 the Gates Learning Foundation provided funding and computers for approximately 1,000 libraries. Also that year the Gateses donated $20 million to Duke University, Melinda Gates' alma mater. At the end of 1998 the couple established the Bill and Melinda Gates Children's Vaccine program with an initial grant of $100 million.

In 1999 Gates decided to merge his two charity programs into one entity: the Bill & Melinda Gates Foundation, to be run by the elder Gates

and Stonesifer. Bill and his wife Melinda contributed some $16 billion to the foundation that year, making it the largest philanthropic foundation in the world.

In early 2000 Gates made another $5 billion gift of stock to the foundation. That year a federal judge ordered that Microsoft be split up. That ruling was eventually struck down, and Microsoft reached a settlement with the US Justice Department. What effect, if any, Microsoft's legal wranglings will have on the foundation is unclear. (Most of its donations come in the form of stock that is then converted to cash.) In 2000 the foundation pledged $10 million toward construction of an underground visitors center at Capitol Hill in Washington, DC.

The Bill & Melinda Gates Foundation donated another $10 million in 2001 to be awarded over three years to the Hope for African Children Initiative, which will help African children affected by AIDS. Also in 2001 the foundation gave a five-year, $1 million grant to Smith College to support a residency program for five African scholars. The program will provide fellowships for faculty members from universities in Africa at Amherst, Hampshire, Mount Holyoke, and Smith, and the University of Massachusetts. Also that year Bill and Melinda Gates donated another $2 billion to the foundation, boosting its endowment to nearly $24 billion.

In 2002 the foundation gave a grant of $7.5 million to The Alan Guttmacher Institute to develop a five-year research program to study youth attitudes toward sex and to improve programs designed to prevent HIV/AIDS in Sub-Saharan Africa as well as worldwide.

OFFICERS

Co-Founder and Trustee: William H. Gates III, age 46
Co-Founder: Melinda French Gates, age 37
Co-Chairman and CEO: William H. Gates Sr.
Co-Chairman and President: Patricia "Patty" Q. Stonesifer, age 45
CFO and Administrative Officer: Allan C. Golston
EVP: Sylvia Mathews
Executive Director, Education: Tom Vander Ark
Executive Director, Libraries Program: Richard Akeroyd
Director, Global Health Program: Gordon W. Perkin
Director, Human Resources: Julie Olson

LOCATIONS

HQ: 1551 Eastlake Ave. East, Seattle, WA 98102
Phone: 206-709-3100   **Fax:** 206-709-3180
Web: www.gatesfoundation.org

PRODUCTS/OPERATIONS

2001 Grant Distribution

	% of total
Global health	75
Education	15
Libraries	4
Pacific Northwest & other	3
Special projects	3
Total	**100**

Selected Beneficiaries

Alliance for Cervical Cancer Prevention ($3.9 million over two years)
Gay City Health Project ($30,000 over three years)
Global Health Council ($4.8 million over three years)
Helen Keller International ($5 million over five years)
International Planned Parenthood Federation ($8.8 million over five years)
International Tuberculosis Foundation ($1.9 million over five years)
International Vaccine Institute ($40 million over five years)
Library and Information Commission ($4.2 million over one year)
National Institute of Child Health and Human Development ($15 million over five years)
Oxfam ($2.9 million over four years)
Pacific Institute for Women's Health ($1 million over three years)
Population Council ($4 million over two years)
Portland Children's Museum ($600,000 over three years)
United Negro College Fund ($1 billion over 20 years)
US Fund for UNICEF ($15 million over five years)

HISTORICAL FINANCIALS & EMPLOYEES

Foundation FYE: December 31	Annual Growth	3/92	3/93	3/94	3/95	3/96	3/97	3/98	*12/99	12/00	12/01
Sales ($ mil.)	110.0%	—	—	—	—	—	—	128	276	304	1,182
Employees	73.2%	—	—	—	—	—	—	2	4	6	—

* Fiscal year change

SALES HISTORY

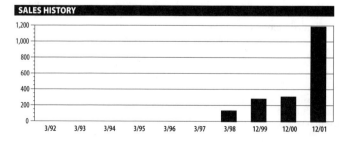

BLOOMBERG L.P.

What do you do when you've conquered Wall Street? You become mayor of the city the famous financial district calls home. After leading his financial news and information company to success, founder Michael Bloomberg left his corporate empire in 2001 to lead the Big Apple.

The Bloomberg Professional Service consists of proprietary terminals that provide real-time, around-the-clock financial news, market data, and analysis. With more than 160,000 terminals installed, Bloomberg ranks among the world's largest providers of such devices. The company also has a syndicated news service; publishes books and magazines; and disseminates business information via TV, radio, and the Web.

Bloomberg serves more than 200,000 customers in 120 countries. Although terminals generate most of the company's sales (Bloomberg charges a monthly fee of $1,285 per terminal), the company distributes financial news and information through many other channels in an effort to build its brand and keep up with the intense competition. In addition to the company's media products, Bloomberg also offers an order-matching system, the Bloomberg Tradebook. In 2001 the company established Bloomberg Index License, which creates and licenses indices to fund managers, stock exchanges, and other clients.

Bloomberg still controls the company; Merrill Lynch also has an ownership stake.

HISTORY

By the mid-1970s Michael Bloomberg had worked his way up to head of equity trading and sales at New York investment powerhouse Salomon Brothers. He left Salomon in 1981, just after the firm went private, cashing out with $10 million for his partnership interest.

Bloomberg founded Innovative Marketing Systems and spent the next year developing the Bloomberg terminal, which allowed users to manipulate bond data. In 1982 he pitched it to Merrill Lynch, which bought 20 machines. Regular production of the terminals began in 1984, and in 1985, Merrill Lynch invested $39 million in the company to gain a 30% stake. The company prospered during the 1980s boom, and over time the data, not the machines, became the heart of the business, which was renamed Bloomberg L.P. in 1986.

The company weathered the stock market crash of 1987, opening offices in London and Tokyo. Bloomberg made its entry into newsgathering and delivery in 1990 when Bloomberg News began broadcasting on its terminals. The firm built its news organization from scratch, hiring away reporters from such publications as *The Wall Street Journal* and *Forbes*. Bloomberg bought a New York radio station in 1992 and converted it to an all-news format. The next year it built an in-house TV studio and created a business news show for PBS. A satellite TV station followed in 1994, along with the *Bloomberg Personal Finance* magazine.

In 1995 Bloomberg began offering business information via its Web site. The company also introduced the Bloomberg Tradebook, an electronic securities-trading venue designed to compete with Reuters' Instinet. (In 1997 Tradebook was approved by the SEC for use in connection with some NASDAQ-listed stocks.) Bloomberg also started offering its services to subscribers in a PC-compatible format and selling its data to other news purveyors, such as LexisNexis (an online information service).

In 1996 the company went further into financial publishing, issuing *Swap Literacy: A Comprehensive Guide* and *A Common Sense Guide to Mutual Funds*. That year Michael Bloomberg bought back 10% of the company from Merrill Lynch for $200 million, giving Bloomberg L.P. an estimated market value of $2 billion. The company agreed in 1997 to supply the daytime programming for Paxson Communications' New York TV station WPXN.

When Bridge Information Systems bought Dow Jones Markets from Dow Jones in 1998, Bridge surpassed Bloomberg in number of financial information terminals installed, bumping Bloomberg from the #2 spot into third place. But Bloomberg continued expanding its offerings through strategic agreements with Internet companies such as America Online (now AOL Time Warner) and CNET Networks, and through the introduction of new magazines such as *Bloomberg Money* in 1998 as well as *On Investing* and *Bloomberg Wealth Manager* in 1999.

In 1999 Bloomberg secured a deal with the Australian stock exchange that would allow its terminals to facilitate international order routing into the Australian market. The company also expanded its presence in the Spanish-language market through its agreement with CBS Telenoticias to produce a TV news program (*Noticiero Financiero*). In 2000 Bloomberg joined with Merrill Lynch to make Merrill Lynch's institutional e-commerce portal available to Bloomberg customers.

OFFICERS

Founder: Michael R. Bloomberg, age 60
Chairman: Peter T. Grauer
CEO: Lex Fenwick
Director of Public Relations: Chris Taylor
Head of Affiliate Relations & Marketing: David Wachtel
Human Resources: Linda Norris

LOCATIONS

HQ: 499 Park Ave., New York, NY 10022
Phone: 212-318-2000   **Fax:** 212-980-4585
Web: www.bloomberg.com

Bloomberg has offices in New York City; Princeton, New Jersey; and San Francisco; as well as Frankfurt; Hong Kong; London; Sao Paulo; Singapore; Sydney; and Tokyo.

PRODUCTS/OPERATIONS

Selected Products and Services
Bloomberg Data License (financial database service)
Bloomberg Energy (Web site focusing on energy)
Bloomberg Index License (indices creation and licensing)
Bloomberg Investimenti (financial publication focusing on Italian finance)
Bloomberg Magazine (financial magazine)
Bloomberg Money (financial magazine for European investors)
Bloomberg News (syndicated news service)
Bloomberg Personal Finance (personal finance magazine)
Bloomberg Portfolio Trading System (asset management tool)
Bloomberg Press (book publishing)
Bloomberg Pro (wireless access to news and information)
Bloomberg Professional Service (24-hour, real-time financial information system)
Bloomberg Radio (syndicated radio news service)
Bloomberg Television (24-hour news channel and syndicated reports)
Bloomberg Tradebook (equities trading technology)
Bloomberg Trading System (Bloomberg information combined with trading technology)
Bloomberg Wealth Manager (magazine for financial planners and investment advisers)
Bloomberg.com (Web site)

COMPETITORS

Agence France-Presse
Associated Press
Dow Jones
FactSet
Forbes
Interactive Data
Intuit
MarketWatch.com
Media General
Multex.com
Reuters
TheStreet.com
Thomson Corporation

HISTORICAL FINANCIALS & EMPLOYEES

Private FYE: December 31	Annual Growth	12/92	12/93	12/94	12/95	12/96	12/97	12/98	12/99	12/00	12/01
Estimated sales ($ mil.)	27.6%	290	370	550	650	760	1,300	1,500	2,300	2,800	2,600
Employees	23.2%	1,100	1,800	2,000	2,500	3,000	4,000	4,900	5,150	7,200	7,200

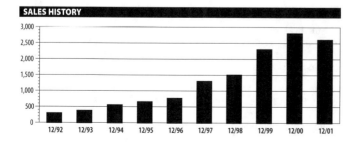

SALES HISTORY

BLUE CROSS AND BLUE SHIELD

The rise of managed health care has had some of its members singing the blues, but the Blue Cross and Blue Shield Association still has major market power. The Blue Cross and Blue Shield Association coordinates about 45 chapters that provide health care coverage to more than 80 million Americans through indemnity insurance, Health Maintenance Organizations (HMOs), preferred provider organizations (PPOs), point-of-service (POS) plans, and fee-for-service plans. Blue Cross and Blue Shield chapters also administer Medicare plans for the federal government.

While some Blues always faced competition head-on, most received tax benefits for taking all comers. But as lower-cost plans attracted the hale and hearty, the Blues' customers became older, sicker, and more expensive. With their quasi-charitable status and outdated rate structures, many Blues lost market share.

They have fought back by merging among themselves, creating for-profit subsidiaries, forming alliances with for-profit enterprises, or dropping their not-for-profit status and going public — while still using the Blue Cross Blue Shield name. A history of tax breaks complicates these efforts and usually requires the creation of charitable foundations. As a result, the umbrella association is becoming a licensing and brand-marketing entity. The conversion of the Blues to for-profit status is sparking a backlash by consumer organizations.

HISTORY

Blue Cross was born in 1929, when Baylor University official Justin Kimball offered schoolteachers 21 days of hospital care for $6 a year. A major plan feature was a community rating system that based premiums on the community claims experience rather than members' conditions.

The Blue Cross symbol was devised in 1933 by Minnesota plan executive E. A. van Steenwyck. By 1935 many of the 15 plans in 11 states used the symbol. Many states gave the plans nonprofit status, and in 1936 the American Hospital Association formed the Committee on Hospital Service (renamed the Blue Cross Association in 1948) to coordinate them.

As Blue Cross grew, state medical societies sponsored prepaid plans to cover doctors' fees. In 1946 they united under the aegis of the American Medical Association (AMA) as the Associated Medical Care Plans (later the Association of Blue Shield Plans).

In 1948 the AMA thwarted a Blue Cross attempt to merge with Blue Shield. But the Blues increasingly cooperated on public policy matters

while competing for members, and each Blue formed a not-for-profit corporation to coordinate its plans' activities.

By 1960 Blue Cross insured about a third of the US. Over the next decade the Blues started administering Medicare and other government health plans, and by 1970 half of Blue Cross' premiums came from government entities.

In the 1970s the Blues adopted cost-control measures such as review of hospital admissions; many plans even abandoned the community rating system. Most began emphasizing preventive care in HMOs or PPOs. The two Blues finally merged in 1982, but this had little effect on the associations' bottom lines as losses grew.

By the 1990s the Blues were big business. Some of the state associations offered officers high salaries and perks but still insisted on special regulatory treatment.

Blue Cross of California became the first chapter to give up its tax-free status when it was bought by WellPoint Health Networks, a managed care subsidiary it had founded in 1992. In a 1996 deal, WellPoint became the chapter's parent and converted it to for-profit status, assigning all of the stock to a public charitable foundation that received the proceeds of its subsequent IPO. WellPoint also bought the group life and health division of Massachusetts Mutual Life Insurance.

The for-profit switches picked up in 1997. Blue Cross of Connecticut merged with insurance provider Anthem, and other mergers followed. Half the nation's Blues formed an alliance called BluesCONNECT, competing with national health plans by offering employers one nationwide benefits organization. The association also pursued overseas licensing agreements in Europe, South America, and Asia, assembling a network of Blue Cross-friendly caregivers aiming for worldwide coverage.

In 1998 Blues in more than 35 states sued the nation's big cigarette companies to recoup the costs of treating smoking-related illnesses. In a separate lawsuit, Blue Cross and Blue Shield of Minnesota received nearly $300 million from the tobacco industry. In 1999, Anthem moved to acquire or affiliate with Blues in Colorado, Maine, and New Hampshire.

In 2000, after years of discussions, the New York Attorney General permitted Empire Blue Cross and Blue Shield to convert to for-profit status.

Chairman: Michael B. Unhjem
President and CEO: Scott P. Serota
SVP, Corporate Secretary, and General Counsel:
  Roger G. Wilson
SVP, Strategic Services: Maureen Sullivan
SVP and Chief Medical Officer: Allan M. Korn
VP, Finance and Administration: Ralph Rambach
VP, Human Resources: Bill Colbourne
Auditors: PricewaterhouseCoopers LLP

LOCATIONS

HQ: Blue Cross and Blue Shield Association
  225 N. Michigan Ave., Chicago, IL 60601
Phone: 312-297-6000   **Fax:** 312-297-6609
Web: www.bcbs.com

The Blue Cross and Blue Shield Association has offices in Chicago and Washington, DC, with licensees operating throughout the US as well as in Africa, Australia, Asia, Canada, Latin America, the Middle East, and western Europe.

PRODUCTS/OPERATIONS

2001 Health Care Members

	Members (mil.)	% of total
PPO	38	45
Traditional Indemnity	22	26
HMO	17	20
Point-of-service (POS)	7	9
Total	**84**	**100**

Selected Operations

BlueCard Worldwide (care of US members in foreign countries)
BluesCONNECT (nationwide alliance)
Federal Employee Health Benefits Program (federal employees and retirees)
Health maintenance organizations
Medicare management
Point-of-service programs
Preferred provider organizations

COMPETITORS

Aetna
CIGNA
Health Net
Humana
Kaiser Foundation
Oxford Health Plans
PacifiCare
Prudential
UniHealth
UnitedHealth Group

HISTORICAL FINANCIALS & EMPLOYEES

Association FYE: December 31	Annual Growth	12/92	12/93	12/94	12/95	12/96	12/97	12/98	12/99	12/00	12/01
Sales ($ mil.)	8.1%	70,913	71,161	71,414	74,400	75,200	76,500	94,700	93,700	126,000	143,200
Employees	0.5%	143,000	135,883	146,352	146,000	150,000	150,000	150,000	150,000	150,000	150,000

SALES HISTORY

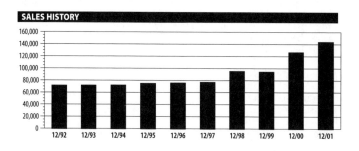

BLUE CROSS OF MASSACHUSETTS

Hobbled by its past, Blue Cross and Blue Shield of Massachusetts (BCBSMA) has worked its way back into the race. Serving more than 2.4 million members, it offers indemnity insurance, HMOs, preferred provider organizations, and Medicare extension programs. The not-for-profit organization runs HMO Blue, HMO Blue New England, and Blue Choice New England, as well as Medex, a Medicare supplemental plan. BCBSMA also teams up with other regional Blues to offer plans HMO Blue New England and Blue Choice New England, which feature discounts at some health clubs.

BCBSMA has battled its way back to financial health by selling noncore businesses and reducing staff after spending recent years in the red.

Like Blues nationwide, it has been hit hard by competition. The company is now refocusing on its core business (health insurance) through divestitures and new products. BCBSMA also entered the risky business of reinsurance.

HISTORY

The predecessor of the Blue Cross Association was founded in Dallas in 1929 to allow teachers to prepay for hospitalization. The idea spread quickly during the Depression. By 1937, when its 26th affiliate was founded in Massachusetts, the organization had become associated with the Blue Cross logo. Fairly priced by Depression standards, Blue Cross pegged its premiums to care costs in each region rather than underwriting each policyholder or group individually.

Seeing the success of Blue Cross, doctors joined up to offer similar prepayment plans known together as the Blue Shield Association. Doctor participation in Massachusetts was so widespread that members had a nearly unlimited choice of physicians.

Blue Cross and Blue Shield worked almost as one unit in Massachusetts but remained legally separate. At first they limited memberships to groups, but during the 1940s they began accepting individuals. In the 1960s the groups became co-administrators of the state's Medicare program. The Medex program was started in 1966 to supplement Medicare, but later evolved to encompass a state-mandated program for the medically indigent elderly. During the 1970s the companies began creating HMOs, but mostly for rural areas.

The groups continued to dominate Massachusetts health care in the 1980s. By the decade's end, however, the Massachusetts Blues had hit hard times, suffering lost market share, bloated management, and antiquated systems. As Blues in other states merged, competitors repeatedly blocked efforts to join the two Massachusetts organizations. Both Blues lost money from 1986 to 1988.

Efforts to help the situation only made matters worse (a failed upgrade of Blue Cross' information systems was abandoned in 1992 after six years and $100 million). The groups' efforts to drive harder bargains with hospitals led to cries that the plans were trying to force rejected hospitals out of business.

In 1988 the organizations were at last allowed to merge. William Van Faasen became CEO in 1990, charged with reengineering BCBSMA. For five years his efforts seemed to work. But the Medex segment was an earnings vacuum, and the new management drew criticism for hefty pay raises.

Blaming Medex, BCBSMA lost $90 million in 1996, which led the state insurance commissioner to step in and oversee its operations. To make money like a regular health care company, BCBSMA started acting like a regular health care company — it slashed 16% of its workforce, enforced 10% pay cuts for those executives who survived a year-long purge, sold 10 clinics (to what is now Caremark Rx), and attempted to cancel 7,000 policies.

In 1998 BCBSMA agreed to pay $9.5 million to settle lawsuits that it overcharged Massachusetts subscribers for medical care. It also agreed in 1999 to pay $4.75 million to reimburse the US government for claims paid on people who were actually covered by BCBSMA. In the meantime, it created a new health insurance plan, Access Blue (launched in 2000), that lets patients see specialists without referrals. The plan has met resistance from hospitals and doctors, who consider its premiums too low to be financially viable.

BCBSMA filed to divide its operations into three companies, a move shot down by state legislators in 1998. Meanwhile, for-profit Blues licensees, such as Anthem, continue to buy Blues (including those in Connecticut and New Hampshire). BCBSMA is pursuing affiliation with other not-for-profit regional Blues, although its attempt to do so in Rhode Island was rejected by the state's attorney general. In 2000 BCBSMA put its dental insurance product up for sale and got state permission to enter the reinsurance business.

OFFICERS

Chairman Emeritus: Milton L. Glass
Chairman, President, and CEO: William C. Van Faasen
Vice Chairman: Robert J. Haynes
COO: Arthur E. Banks
CFO: Allen P. Maltz
EVP and Chief Legal Officer: Sandra L. Jesse
EVP, Healthcare Services: Sharon L. Smith
EVP, Sales, Marketing, and Services: Stephen R. Booma
EVP, Corporate Affairs: Peter G. Meade
SVP, Corporate Relations: Fredi Shonkoff
SVP, Corporate Planning and Development:
  Phyllis L. Baron
SVP, Human Resources: Robert Martin
SVP and CIO: Carl J. Ascenzo
Chief Actuary: Bruce W. Butler
Auditors: Ernst & Young LLP

LOCATIONS

HQ: Blue Cross and Blue Shield of Massachusetts
  LandMark Center 401 Park Dr., Boston, MA 02215
Phone: 617-246-5000   **Fax:** 617-246-4832
Web: www.bcbsma.com

PRODUCTS/OPERATIONS

Selected Services
Blue Care Elect Preferred (managed care plan)
Blue Choice (managed care plan)
Blue Choice New England (regional managed care)
Comprehensive Major Medical (traditional plan)
Dental Blue
Dental Blue PPO
Direct Blue (nongroup plans)
HMO Blue (statewide managed care)
HMO Blue New England (regional managed care)
Medex (Medicare supplement)

COMPETITORS

Aetna
Anthem
CIGNA
Harvard Pilgrim
Prudential
Tufts Health Plan

HISTORICAL FINANCIALS & EMPLOYEES

Not-for-profit FYE: December 31	Annual Growth	12/92	12/93	12/94	12/95	12/96	12/97	12/98	12/99	12/00	12/01
Sales ($ mil.)	1.0%	3,397	3,792	3,595	3,575	3,504	2,123	2,041	2,120	2,883	3,725
Net income ($ mil.)	18.3%	29	54	43	11	(90)	13	64	110	132
Income as % of sales	—	0.9%	1.4%	1.2%	0.3%	—	0.6%	3.1%	2.9%	3.8%	3.5%
Employees	(7.1%)	6,559	6,171	5,865	5,630	5,500	2,756	2,579	2,601	2,601	3,396

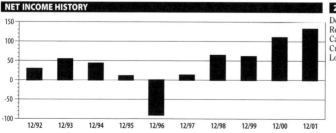

NET INCOME HISTORY

2001 FISCAL YEAR-END
Debt ratio: —
Return on equity: 25.0%
Cash ($ mil.): 1,471
Current ratio: —
Long-term debt ($ mil.): —

BLUE CROSS OF MICHIGAN

Blue Cross Blue Shield of Michigan (BCBSM) is one of the nation's top Blue Cross Blue Shield health insurance associations, serving more than 4.8 million members, including autoworkers for GM and Ford. The company's insurance plans include traditional indemnity, Blue Preferred (PPO), and Blue Care Network (HMO). BCBSM also offers dental, vision, and Medicare supplement coverage, as well as workers' compensation insurance, health assessment, and health care management services. The firm's for-profit subsidiary, Preferred Provider Organization of Michigan, offers private health care management services.

For BCBSM operating a "profitable" not-for-profit is a constant struggle.

While other Blues have converted to for-profit status or have teamed up with for-profit companies to become more competitive, BCBSM is committed to remaining not-for-profit. Rate hikes have helped get the company's insurance operations back into the black, and it plans to continue raising rates to keep up with the skyrocketing costs of health care.

HISTORY

The history of prepaid medical care began in 1929, when Baylor University Hospital administrator Justin Kimball developed a plan to offer schoolteachers 21 days of hospital care for $6 a year. Fundamental to the plan was a community rating system, which based premiums on the community's claims experience rather than subscribers' conditions.

A similar program was started in Michigan in 1938 when a group of hospitals formed the Michigan Society for Group Hospitalization, which became the Michigan Hospital Service and later became a chapter of the national Blue Cross association. The health care plan was funded by local hospitals and private grants. (A group of private donors, including Oldsmobile automotive founder Ransom Olds, loaned the group $5,000.)

The state insurance commission approved tax-exempt status for the Michigan Blue Cross in 1939. Nine days after opening a three-person office in Detroit, Blue Cross landed its first customer, insurance company John Hancock Mutual Life. John Hancock's Detroit branch manager became the first subscriber, paying $1.90 per month for 21 days of hospitalization coverage for his family of eight.

Due in part to the addition of Chrysler, Ford, and GM to its health plans, Blue Cross grew from less than 1 million members in the 1940s to more than 3 million in the 1950s. In 1945 it

began to offer coverage for individuals; 14 years later the association started to offer policies to seniors who were ineligible for group coverage. Blue Cross took over operation of Michigan's Medicare program in 1966.

Michigan's Blue Cross merged with longtime partner Blue Shield in 1975 to create Blue Cross Blue Shield of Michigan, with a total of 5 million subscribers. Blue Shield, a prepayment plan that covered doctors' services, had been started in 1939 by the Michigan State Medical Society (a group of Michigan physicians).

As overseas competition forced automakers to cut their employment rolls, BCBSM's membership contracted. BCBSM chairman John McCabe, realizing the need to generate additional revenue, pushed for an end to the company's not-for-profit status in the 1980s but was rejected by the Michigan legislature. This failure was at least partially behind McCabe's resignation in 1987.

The struggling Michigan Blues moved towards profitability in 1994 when the state legislature specially authorized its $291 million purchase of the for-profit State Accident Fund, the state's workers' compensation program. It also lost its large, but hard-to-manage, state Medicare contract to Blue Cross Blue Shield of Illinois (now Health Care Service Corporation). In 1996 the company reorganized, with a division for Michigan residents and one for nationwide accounts. In 1997 BCBSM continued its efforts to increase revenue by acquiring private health management company Preferred Provider Organization of Michigan, which operates in Michigan and nearby states. BCBSM president and CEO Richard Whitmer then announced that he was willing to compete with other Blues in bordering states.

In 1998 BCBSM consolidated four regional HMOs into a single statewide HMO, the Blue Care Network. Costs of the merger and growing losses in drug coverage constrained earnings, but were counterweighted by returns on assets invested in the stock market. In 1999 and 2000 the company rankled Detroit's small business owners with double-digit premium hikes.

OFFICERS

Chairman: Charles L. Burkett
President and CEO: Richard E. Whitmer
SVP and CFO: Mark R. Bartlett
SVP and CIO: Raymond R. Khan
SVP, General Counsel, and Secretary: Steven C. Hess
SVP, Auto/National Business Unit: Leslie A. Viegas
SVP, Health Care Products and Provider Services: Marianne Udow
SVP, Human Resources, and Chief Administration Officer: George F. Francis III
SVP, Michigan Sales and Services: J. Paul Austin
SVP, Corporate Communications: Richard T. Cole
Auditors: Deloitte & Touche LLP

LOCATIONS

HQ: Blue Cross Blue Shield of Michigan
600 E. Lafayette Blvd., Detroit, MI 48226
Phone: 313-225-9000   **Fax:** 313-225-5629
Web: www.bcbsm.com

PRODUCTS/OPERATIONS

Selected Health Care Plans
Blue Care Network (health maintenance)
Blue Choice (point of service)
Blue MedSave (prescription plan)
Blue Preferred PPO (preferred provider for auto industry workers)
Blue Traditional (prepayment)
Blue Vision PPO
Community Blue PPO
Community Dental
Medicare Blue HMO
Personal Plus HMO
Preferred Rx (prescription plan)
Traditional Dental
Traditional Rx (prescription plan)
Traditional Vision Coverage

COMPETITORS

Aetna
Anthem
CIGNA
Henry Ford Health System
Humana
United American Healthcare
UnitedHealth Group

HISTORICAL FINANCIALS & EMPLOYEES

Not-for-profit FYE: December 31	Annual Growth	12/92	12/93	12/94	12/95	12/96	12/97	12/98	12/99	12/00	12/01
Sales ($ mil.)	7.5%	6,177	6,193	6,411	6,926	7,001	7,731	8,432	9,487	10,506	11,883
Net income ($ mil.)	(9.1%)	—	120	71	154	101	43	83	89	65	56
Income as % of sales	—	—	1.9%	1.1%	2.2%	1.4%	0.6%	1.0%	0.9%	0.6%	0.5%
Employees	1.2%	—	8,417	8,415	6,500	7,980	8,827	—	—	—	—

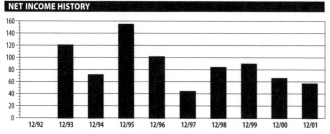

NET INCOME HISTORY

(chart, values 0–160)

12/92 12/93 12/94 12/95 12/96 12/97 12/98 12/99 12/00 12/01

2001 FISCAL YEAR-END

Debt ratio: —
Return on equity: —
Cash ($ mil.): 346
Current ratio: —
Long-term debt ($ mil.): —

BOOZ ALLEN HAMILTON INC.

Booz Allen Hamilton has been on a big consulting bender for more than 80 years. Founded in 1914, the consultancy provides government agencies and FORTUNE 500 companies with international management and technology expertise. The firm's technology business unit covers such areas as defense and national security, the environment, transportation, and space. Its commercial unit includes consumer and engineered products; communications, media, and technology; energy; and financial services.

Booz Allen's enormous staff of more than 11,000 covers the US and more than 30 other countries through more than 100 offices. The rising tide of privatization in many foreign governments has provided an increasing source of consulting work for the company, and Booz has plenty of experience working with governments: the US government is the company's largest customer. Booz Allen is also leveraging its government work in the commercial sector, specifically in such areas as strategic and information security as well as its experience in transportation and food and drug safety.

HISTORY

Edwin Booz graduated from Northwestern University in 1914 with degrees in economics and psychology and started a statistical analysis firm in Chicago. After serving in the army during WWI, he returned to his firm, renamed Edwin Booz Surveys. In 1925 Booz hired his first full-time assistant, George Fry, and in 1929 he hired a second, James Allen. By then the company had a long list of clients, including U.S. Gypsum, the *Chicago Tribune,* and Montgomery Ward, which was losing a retail battle with Sears, Roebuck and Co.

In 1935 Carl Hamilton joined the partnership, and a year later it was renamed Booz, Fry, Allen & Hamilton. The firm prospered well into the next decade by providing advice based on "independence that enables us to say plainly from the outside what cannot always be said safely from within," according to a company brochure.

During WWII the firm worked increasingly on government and military contracts. Fry opposed the pursuit of such work for consultants and left in 1942. The firm was renamed Booz, Allen & Hamilton. Hamilton died in 1946, and the following year Booz retired (he died in 1951), leaving Allen as chairman. Allen successfully steered the firm into lucrative postwar work for clients such as Johnson Wax, RCA, and the US Air Force.

A separate company, Booz, Allen Applied Research, Inc. (BAARINC), was formed in 1955 for technical and government consulting, including missile and weaponry work, as well as consulting with NASA. By the end of the decade, *Time* had dubbed Booz Allen "the world's largest, most prestigious management consultant firm." The partnership was incorporated as a private company in 1962, and in 1967 Commissioner Pete Rozelle requested its services for the merger of the National Football League and American Football League.

When Allen retired in 1970, Charlie Bowen became the new chairman, and the company went public. However, as the economy stalled during the energy crisis, spending for consultants plunged. Jim Farley replaced Bowen in 1975, and the company was taken private again in 1976. A turnaround was engineered, and the firm was soon helping Chrysler through its historic bailout and developing strategies for the breakup of AT&T.

Booz Allen again experienced troubles in the 1980s as Farley set up a competition to select his successor. In 1984 Michael McCullough was chosen, but the selection process had taken a toll on morale. McCullough began restructuring the firm along industry lines, creating a department store of services in an industry characterized by boutique houses. The turmoil was too much, and by 1988 nearly a third of the partners had quit.

William Stasior became chairman in 1991 and reorganized Booz Allen yet again, splitting it down public and private sector lines. James Allen died in 1992, the same year the firm moved to McLean, Virginia. The company began privatization work in the former Soviet Union and in Eastern Europe in 1992 and continued to emphasize government business, including contracts with the IRS (1995) for technology modernization and with the General Services Administration (1996) to provide technical and management support for all federal telecommunications users.

In 1998 the company won a 10-year, $200 million contract with the US Defense Department to establish a scientific and technical data warehouse. Ralph Shrader was appointed CEO in early 1999; Stasior retired as chairman later that year. Booz Allen acquired Scandinavian consulting firm Carta in 1999 and formed a venture capital firm for startups with Lehman Brothers in 2000. The company announced in late 2000 that it would spin off Aestix, its e-commerce business, but reconsidered amid a general economic slowdown and hostile IPO market.

OFFICERS

Chairman and CEO: Ralph W. Shrader
CFO: Doug Swenson
President, Worldwide Commercial Business:
Daniel C. Lewis
Chief Personnel Officer: DeeAnne Aguirre
Senior Director Public Relations: Marie Lerch

LOCATIONS

HQ: 8283 Greensboro Dr., McLean, VA 22102
Phone: 703-902-5000   **Fax:** 703-902-3333
Web: www.boozallen.com

Booz Allen Hamilton has more than 100 offices in the
US and more than 30 other countries.

Foreign Offices

Abu Dhabi, United Arab	Malmo, Sweden
Emirates	Melbourne
Amsterdam	Mexico City
Bangkok	Milan, Italy
Beirut	Moscow
Bogotá, Colombia	Munich, Germany
Brisbane, Australia	Oslo
Buenos Aires	Paris
Caracas, Venezuela	Rio de Janeiro
Copenhagen	Rome
Düsseldorf, Germany	Santiago, Chile
Frankfurt	São Paulo
Gothenburg, Sweden	Seoul
Helsinki, Finland	Stockholm
Hong Kong	Sydney
Jakarta, Indonesia	Tokyo
London	Wellington, New Zealand
Madrid	Zurich

PRODUCTS/OPERATIONS

Selected Consulting Services

Commercial Services
Corporate strategy
E-business strategy
Innovation
Knowledge management
Productivity improvement
Strategic security

Technology Business Services
Engineering
Information technology
Management consulting (systems development/systems
integration)

COMPETITORS

Accenture
American Management
A.T. Kearney
Bain & Company
BearingPoint
Boston Consulting
Cap Gemini
Computer Sciences
Day & Zimmermann
Deloitte Consulting
IBM
MAXIMUS
McKinsey & Company
SRI International
Towers Perrin

HISTORICAL FINANCIALS & EMPLOYEES

Private FYE: March 31	Annual Growth	3/93	3/94	3/95	3/96	3/97	3/98	3/99	3/00	3/01	3/02
Sales ($ mil.)	13.0%	700	804	989	1,100	1,300	1,400	1,600	1,800	2,100	2,100
Employees	9.7%	5,000	5,481	6,000	6,700	7,500	8,000	9,000	9,800	11,045	11,510

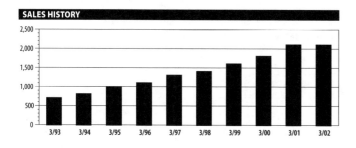

SALES HISTORY

BOSE CORPORATION

Bose doesn't subscribe to the theory that bigger is better. One of the world's leading speaker makers, the company has been concentrating on making its speakers smaller to better blend in to home and office décors. Bose makes a variety of audio products, including auto sound systems and speakers, home stereo speakers, music systems, PC sound systems, aviation headsets, and professional loudspeakers. Its critically acclaimed Wave radio (compact in size but not in sound) has been a success despite its $350 price tag. Bose makes its goods in North America and Ireland and sells them through retailers and about 100 of its own stores worldwide. Founder Amar Bose, an MIT professor, is the company's largest shareholder.

Bose keeps his company sharp with unconventional products and methods. The firm stands out by offering tiny, yet technologically advanced, products such as palm-sized cube speakers and compact radios with rich sound. To stay on the cutting edge, Bose invests much of its profits in research and development. The company has operations in Australia, Canada, Europe, Japan, and the US and is entering markets in Russia, China, and India.

HISTORY

Music and electronics struck a chord in Amar Bose, the son of an Indian emigrant from Calcutta. As a youngster he studied violin and liked fixing electronic gadgets. A teenaged Bose started a radio repair shop in his basement during WWII that turned out to be the family's main source of income when his father's import business faltered during the war. Bose's interest in electronics led him to college at MIT in 1947.

His quest to develop a better sound system began nearly a decade later when the hi-fi stereo he bought as a reward for doing well in his graduate studies made his violin record sound shrill. MIT allowed Bose to research the topic while he taught there. He formed his namesake company in 1964 and hired as its first employee Sherwin Greenblatt, a former student who later became company president.

Bose discovered that most speaker systems funneled sound directly at the listener, while live concerts sent sound directly and indirectly by bouncing it off walls, floors, and ceilings. He designed a system in which only some speakers are aimed at the listener while others reflect the sounds around the room. Calling the concept "reflected sound," Bose began selling his 901 stereo speakers in 1968.

A feud with *Consumer Reports* showed the arrogant side of the self-made entrepreneur.

After the magazine concluded in a 1970 review that Bose speakers created a sound that tended to "wander around the room," Bose sued, claiming product disparagement. (The lawsuit was settled 13 years later when the Supreme Court ruled in favor of *Consumer Reports*.) Bose began making professional loudspeakers in 1972.

After trying and failing to gain market share in Japan throughout the 1970s, in 1978 Bose hired sales executive Sumi Sakura, who convinced 400 Japanese dealers to find space in their jam-packed stores for Bose products. Sales jumped within months. Bose also turned his attention to car stereos in the 1970s. After promising talks with General Motors in 1979, he risked $13 million and four years developing a stereo that could be custom-designed for cars. The first one was offered in 1983 in a Cadillac Seville. Contracts with other major carmakers followed, usually for their top-of-the-line models.

In the 1980s the company took its technology to TV sets. With an agreeable guinea pig in Zenith, Bose developed a speaker tube that could coil inside the set without adding much bulk. The set was a hit, even with a price tag of more than $1,400 (in 1987). The firm's speakers were also used in several space shuttle flights, beginning in 1992 with *Endeavour*.

The critically acclaimed Wave radio was introduced in 1993 and has been a huge success, even though it is primarily offered through direct mail. A year later Bose acquired professional loudspeaker maker US Sound from Carver. In 1996 it teamed up with satellite TV firm PRIMESTAR to offer the home theater Companion systems. (The systems were discontinued in 1999, dissolving the partnership.) The next year Bose and IBM paired up to upgrade the quality of PC sound systems.

Bose upped the ante on its retail operations in 1997 when it began opening more upscale showcase stores where audiophiles can test sound systems at in-store music theaters. The company began making its sound systems for more mainstream cars, such as the Chevrolet Blazer, the following year. In 1999 Bose began selling its products online and introduced a new version of its popular Wave radio (with a CD player). In 2001 Bose introduced the Bose Wave/PC interactive system that provides one-touch access to Internet radio, digital audio files, AM/FM radio, and CDs through a PC.

OFFICERS

Chairman and CEO: Amar G. Bose, age 72
President: John Coleman
VP of Finance and CFO: Daniel A. Grady, age 65
VP of Engineering: Joseph Veranth
VP of Europe: Nic A. Merks
VP of Human Resources: John Ferrie
VP of Manufacturing: Thomas Beeson
VP of Research: Thomas Froeschle
VP of Sales: David Wood
VP: Sumiyoshi Sakura
Secretary: Alexander Bernhard
Treasurer: William R. Swanson
Assistant Secretary: Mark E. Sullivan
Director of Public Relations: Dena Knop
Auditors: PricewaterhouseCoopers LLP

LOCATIONS

HQ: The Mountain, Framingham, MA 01701
Phone: 508-766-1099   **Fax:** 508-766-7543
Web: www.bose.com

Bose has plants in Canada, Ireland, Mexico, and the US.

PRODUCTS/OPERATIONS

Selected Brands
131 (marine speakers)
141 (speakers)
151 (environmental speakers)
201, 301, 501, 701, 901 Series (direct/reflecting
  speakers)
Acoustic Wave (music systems)
Acoustimass (speaker systems)
Auditioner (computer system used to analyze building
  acoustics based on architectural blueprints)
Jewel Cube (speakers)
Lifestyle (music systems)
Wave radio (compact radio with full stereo sound)
Wave radio (with CD player)

Selected Products
Aircraft entertainment systems
Auto sound systems and speakers
Aviation headsets
Custom home audio systems
Home stereo speakers
Marine speakers
Multimedia speakers
Music systems
Outdoor audio systems
PC sound systems
Professional loudspeakers
Radios
Speaker accessories

COMPETITORS

Aiwa
Allen Organ Company
Bang & Olufsen
Boston Acoustics
Cambridge SoundWorks
Cerwin-Vega
Creative Technology
Emerson Radio
Harman International
Jamo
Kenwood
Koss
Matsushita
Mitek Corp.
Paradigm Electronics
Philips Electronics
Phoenix Gold
Pioneer
Polk Audio
QSC
Recoton
Rockford
Ruark Acoustics
Sharp
Snell Acoustics
Sony
Telex Communications
Victor Company of Japan
Yamaha

HISTORICAL FINANCIALS & EMPLOYEES

Private FYE: March 31	Annual Growth	3/93	3/94	3/95	3/96	3/97	3/98	3/99	3/00	3/01	3/02
Sales ($ mil.)	12.5%	450	500	600	700	750	850	950	1,100	1,250	1,300
Employees	9.9%	3,000	3,100	3,100	3,500	4,000	4,000	4,000	6,000	7,000	7,000

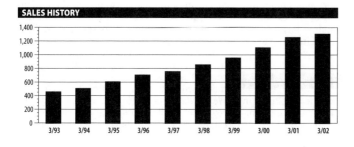

SALES HISTORY

CALPERS

California's public-sector retirees already have a place in the sun; CalPERS gives them the money to enjoy it. CalPERS is the California Public Employees' Retirement System, one of the largest public pension systems in the US. It manages retirement and health plans for approximately 1.3 million beneficiaries (employees, retirees, and their dependents) from nearly 2,500 government agencies and school districts. Even though all of the system's beneficiaries are from the Golden State, CalPERS brings its influence to bear in all 50 states and beyond.

With nearly $145 billion in assets, CalPERS uses its clout to sway such corporate governance issues as company performance, executive compensation, and even social policy. It is also a powerful negotiator for such services as insurance; rates established by the system serve as benchmarks for employers throughout the nation.

Most of CalPERS' revenue comes from its enormous investment program: It has interests in US and foreign securities, real estate development and investment, and even hedge funds and venture capital activities. CalPERS has steadily increased its investments in private equity, looking to take ownership stakes in more firms (it already owns 10% of investment bank Thomas Weisel).

The system has invested $485 million in LBO firm Texas Pacific Group and $425 million in investment firm The Carlyle Group (netting a stake of just more than 5%, with an option to double it). In addition, the system spent about $2 billion to acquire Cabot Industrial Trust and its approximately 350 industrial properties in 20 states.

Over the next few years CalPERS may be forced to sell assets, as it is expected to be hit with a wave of early retirements by middle-aged workers. In the meantime it is eyeing more short-term investments with higher returns.

CalPERS' board (consisting of six elected members, three appointed, and four designated state officials) has seen its share of disputes, on issues ranging from staff salaries to how to invest assets. An abysmal performance in 2001 (the fund's worst in nearly two decades) hasn't helped matters. The public and sometimes nasty donnybrooks have led to the exodus of several key personnel, including former CEO James Burton and former chief investment officer Daniel Szente.

HISTORY

The state of California founded CalPERS in 1931 to administer a pension fund for state employees. By the 1940s the system was serving other public agencies and educational institutions on a contract basis. When the Public Employees' Medical and Hospital Care Act was passed in 1962, CalPERS added health coverage. The fund was conservatively managed in-house, with little exposure to stocks. Despite slow growth, the state used the system's funds to meet its own cash shortfalls.

CalPERS became involved in corporate governance issues in the mid-1980s, when California treasurer Jesse Unruh became outraged by corporate greenmail schemes. In 1987 he hired as CEO Wisconsin pension board veteran Dale Hanson, who led the movement for corporate accountability to institutional investors.

In the late 1980s CalPERS moved into real estate and Japanese stocks. When both crashed around 1990, Hanson came under pressure. CalPERS was twice forced to take major writedowns for its real estate holdings and turned to expensive outside fund managers, but its investment performance deteriorated and member services suffered.

Legislation in 1990 enabled CalPERS to offer long-term health insurance. Governor Pete Wilson's 1991 attempt to use $1.6 billion from CalPERS to help meet a state budget shortfall resulted in legislation banning future raids. CalPERS made its first direct investment in 1993, an energy-related infrastructure partnership with Enron.

CalPERS suffered in the 1994 bond crash. That year Hanson resigned amid criticism that his focus on corporate governance had depressed fund performance. The system moved to an indexing strategy.

CalPERS eased its corporate relations stance, creating a separate office to handle investor issues and launching an International Corporate Governance Program. However, the next year CalPERS was uninvited from a Kohlberg Kravis Roberts & Co. investment pool because of criticism of its fund management and fee structure.

In 1996 the system teamed with the Asian Development Bank to invest in the Asia/Pacific region; it took a major hit in the Asian financial crisis the next year, but used the downturn as an opportunity to expand its position there in undervalued stocks. In 1998 CalPERS pressured foreign firms to adopt more transparent financial reporting methods.

In 2000 the system raised health care premiums almost 10% to keep up with rising care costs. It widened the scope of its direct investments with stakes in investment bank Thomas Weisel Partners (10%) and asset manager Arrowstreet Capital (15%); it also moved into real estate development, buying Genstar Land Co.

with Newland Communities, and announcing plans to invest in high-tech firms focused on B2B online real estate services. CalPERS said that year it would sell off more than $500 million in tobacco holdings; it then invested the same amount in five biotech funds (including one from what is now GlaxoSmithKline), its first foray into the sector.

In 2001 Kathleen Connell, California state controller and CalPERS board member, successfully sued the system for not following state-sanctioned rules regarding pay increases. CalPERS was forced to cut salaries for investment managers, a move that prompted chief investment officer Daniel Szente to resign.

OFFICERS

CEO: Fred R. Buenrostro Jr.
Deputy Executive Officer: James H. Gomez
Assistant Executive Officer, Financial and Administration Services: Vincent P. Brown
Assistant Executive Officer, Governmental Affairs, Planning, and Research: Robert D. Walton
Assistant Executive Officer, Health Benefit Services: Allen D. Feezor
Assistant Executive Officer, Investment Operations: Robert Aguallo
Assistant Executive Officer, Member and Benefit Services: Barbara D. Hegdal
Chief, Human Resources: Tom Pettey
Chief, Information Technology Services Division: Jack Corrie
Chief Investment Officer: Mark J. P. Anson
Chief, Office of Public Affairs: Patricia K. Macht
Chief Actuary: Ronald L. Seeling
General Counsel: Peter H. Mixon
Auditors: PricewaterhouseCoopers LLP

LOCATIONS

HQ: California Public Employees' Retirement System
Lincoln Plaza, 400 P St., Sacramento, CA 95814
Phone: 916-326-3000   **Fax:** 916-558-4001
Web: www.calpers.ca.gov

PRODUCTS/OPERATIONS

Selected Retirement Plans
Defined Benefit Plans
  Judges' Retirement Fund
  Judges' Retirement Fund II
  Legislators' Retirement System
  Public Employees' Retirement Fund
  Volunteer Firefighters' Length of Service Award
    System
Defined Contribution Plans
  State Peace Officers' and Firefighters' Defined
    Contribution Plan Fund
Health Care Plans
  Public Employees' Health Care Fund
  Public Employees' Contingency Reserve Fund
Others
  Replacement Benefit Fund
  Public Employees Long-Term Care Fund
  Public Employees' Deferred Compensation Fund
  Old Age & Survivors' Insurance Revolving Fund

COMPETITORS

A.G. Edwards	Nationwide Financial
Alliance Capital	Principal Financial
Management	Putnam Investments
AXA Financial	Raymond James Financial
Charles Schwab	Salomon Smith Barney
FMR	Holdings
Franklin Resources	State Street
Janus	SunAmerica Inc.
Legg Mason	T. Rowe Price
Mellon Financial	TIAA-CREF
Merrill Lynch	UBS PaineWebber
MFS	USAA
Morgan Stanley	Vanguard Group

HISTORICAL FINANCIALS & EMPLOYEES

Government-owned FYE: June 30	Annual Growth	6/92	6/93	6/94	6/95	6/96	6/97	6/98	6/99	6/00	6/01
Sales ($ mil.)	(20.4%)	—	13,027	4,986	16,174	17,179	23,918	27,514	20,889	18,845	2,095
Employees	8.7%	—	—	900	1,000	1,037	1,089	1,247	1,500	1,594	1,614

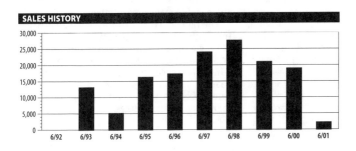

SALES HISTORY

(Bar chart showing sales from 6/92 to 6/01, with y-axis from 0 to 30,000)

CALIFORNIA STATE UNIVERSITY

California State University (CSU) turns students into teachers. The university traces its roots to the state's teaching colleges and trains some 60% of California's teachers. CSU is also neck and neck with the State University of New York (SUNY) as the nation's largest university system. With the baby boomers' children reaching college age and college participation increasing, CSU's student body has grown to around 400,000. The system has campuses in 23 cities, including Bakersfield, Los Angeles, San Francisco, and San Jose. The university primarily awards bachelor's and master's degrees in about 240 subject areas, leaving higher levels of study to the University of California (UC) system.

CSU is developing strategies to cope with an expected enrollment increase of about 40% through 2010 — what it calls Tidal Wave II. The first waves have started already, with more than 20,000 additional students flooding the system in the fall of 2001. To battle the crippling influx of new students, CSU has begun offering distance-education programs in which students are taught via teleconferencing and the Internet. Other strategies involve adding a summer semester to create year-long schooling and expanding the use of off-campus centers.

HISTORY

In 1862 San Francisco's Normal School, a training center for elementary teachers, became California's first state-founded school for higher education. Six students attended its first classes, but there were 384 by 1866. It later moved to San Jose to escape the bustle of San Francisco.

In the late 1880s State Normal Schools opened in Chico, San Diego, and San Francisco, followed in 1901 by California State Polytechnic Institute, which offered studies in agriculture, business, and engineering. Other new colleges included Fresno State (1911) and Humboldt State (1913). Most of the schools offered four-year programs and admitted any student with eight years of grammar school education.

The Normal Schools were renamed Teachers Colleges in 1921 to reflect their role in teacher education. Two years later the colleges began awarding bachelor of arts degrees in education.

In 1935 the schools were renamed State Colleges and expanded into liberal arts. In 1947 they were authorized to confer master's degrees in education.

After WWII, students on the GI Bill boosted enrollment, and campuses opened in Los Angeles, Sacramento, and Long Beach. The prospect of the first baby boomers reaching college age prompted the founding of more campuses in the late 1950s. Russia's 1957 launch of *Sputnik* spurred additional focus on science and math at all education levels. The next year the colleges began awarding master's degrees in subjects unrelated to teacher education.

During the Red Scare, the system's first chancellor, Buell Gallagher, was accused by the press of being soft on communism. Other faculty were subpoenaed to appear before the House Committee on Un-American Activities.

In 1961 the system became the California State Colleges (CSC) and the board of trustees was created, giving the schools more independence from state government. In 1969 student and faculty groups seeking ethnic studies departments went on strike in San Francisco; the unrest closed the campus.

In 1972 CSC became known as the California State University and Colleges. Ten years later it adopted California State University as its name.

Barry Munitz became chancellor in 1991, taking over a system that had become oppressive due to a heavy-handed administration. Munitz, who came from corporate America, brought his business sense to the university and increased private fund-raising, among other activities. He used words like "consumer" and "product" to describe his job. Munitz also increased tuition, which caused enrollments to drop from 1991-1995.

CSU added two new campuses in 1995, including CSU Monterey Bay, the first military base to be converted into a university since the end of the Cold War.

In 1997 Charles Reed was named to replace Munitz as chancellor. That year CSU proposed the California Educational Technology Initiative (CETI), a plan to build high-speed computer and telephone networks linking its campuses. CETI failed in 1998 after Microsoft and other investors pulled out. In 1999, after lengthy contract negotiations between Reed and faculty members failed to produce accord over teacher salaries and employment conditions, Reed imposed his own merit-based plan. The faculty responded with official rebukes and a vote of no confidence in Reed. The two sides eventually settled on a new three-year contract with provisions that salary and benefits may be negotiated annually.

The rancor over pay continued in 2000 when the California Faculty Association issued a report claiming women were discriminated against and the merit system was inherently unfair. CSU issued its own report denying the charges. In 2001 Reed, stirring up more controversy, began a new quest that will allow CSU to offer doctorate degrees.

LOCATIONS

HQ: Trustees of the California State University
401 Golden Shore, Long Beach, CA 90802
Phone: 562-951-4000 **Fax:** 562-951-4949
Web: www.calstate.edu

California State University has campuses in 23 cities.

California State University Campuses
California Maritime Academy
California Polytechnic State University, San Luis Obispo
California State Polytechnic University, Pomona
California State University
Bakersfield
Channel Islands
Chico
Dominguez Hills
Fresno
Fullerton
Hayward
Long Beach
Los Angeles
Monterey Bay
Northridge
Sacramento
San Bernardino
San Marcos
Stanislaus
Humboldt State University
San Diego State University
San Francisco State University
San Jose State University
Sonoma State University

PRODUCTS/OPERATIONS

Selected Majors
Agriculture
Anthropology
Asian studies
Business administration
Chemistry
Communications
Computer science
Economics
Education
History
Latin American studies
Mathematics
Nursing
Philosophy
Physics
Psychology
Public administration
Theater arts

HISTORICAL FINANCIALS & EMPLOYEES

School FYE: June 30	Annual Growth	6/92	6/93	6/94	6/95	6/96	6/97	6/98	6/99	6/00	6/01
Sales ($ mil.)	7.4%	2,131	2,085	2,121	3,121	3,889	2,522	2,612	3,272	3,803	4,050
Employees	2.1%	—	33,859	34,779	33,000	37,360	38,512	39,000	40,323	40,000	40,000

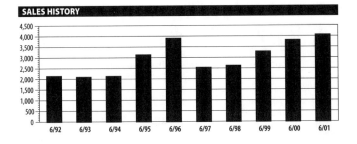

SALES HISTORY

CALVIN KLEIN, INC.

Mark Wahlberg's underwear and Brooke Shields' implied lack thereof made everyone aware of their Calvins. From its tighty-whitey briefs to the *haute couture* of runway fashion, Calvin Klein is known for simply elegant and plainly pricey clothes for men, women, and children; fragrances; and accessories. The company makes its flagship ready-to-wear collection of women's clothing, but gets most of its revenue from licensing its name to makers of shoes, coats, fragrances, handbags, coats, jeans, underwear, men's clothing, women's clothing, furnishings, hosiery, watches, eyewear, socks, bedding, and tabletop products. The firm was founded in 1968 by CEO Barry Schwartz and VC Calvin Klein, who are its sole owners. Clothing maker Philips-Van Heusen is buying most of the company.

The deal will not include Calvin Klein's underwear or the license for Calvin Klein jeans (both controlled by licensee Warnaco). Calvin Klein is expected to remain at the helm of the company.

The company's other licensees include Warnaco (underwear and jeans), Unilever (fragrances, including Obsession and cK One), and Jones Apparel (shoes and handbags). Altogether, Calvin Klein-licensed products generate more than $5 billion a year in retail sales.

Almost as well known as the clothes are Calvin Klein's sometimes controversial advertisements, created in-house by CRK Advertising. Calvin Klein has slimmed down, cutting jobs from its headquarters and shutting down its mid-priced sportswear division in the US (the company's last self-manufacturing division).

HISTORY

After five years designing for other Seventh Avenue fashion houses, Calvin Klein went out on his own in 1968, bankrolled with $10,000 from childhood friend Barry Schwartz, who handled the business. That year a Bonwit Teller executive stumbled into Klein's small showroom, leading to a $50,000 order. Klein expanded from coats into sportswear in 1970. Schwartz, realizing that coats only sold during one season, helped the company expand into the more lucrative sportswear market by only selling coats to buyers who also bought the other line.

Nurturing the aura of exclusivity, Calvin Klein kept his outlets few. The designer's look became so influential by 1975 that *Vogue* was calling it "a definitive picture of the American look." Klein introduced his designer jeans in a self-directed commercial in 1980. He paid 15-year-old Brooke Shields $500,000 to suggest that she was pantiless beneath her Calvins. Sales of designer jeans peaked in 1982. In the early 1980s the company introduced gender-bending boxer shorts for women, complete with a fly. In an effort to increase profits, Calvin Klein purchased its jeanswear licensee, Puritan Fashions, for $60 million in 1983. Two years later Klein touted his first fragrance, Obsession, with a slew of ads featuring nude models.

The company signed a pact with Marchon Eyewear in 1991 to make Calvin Klein eyewear (introduced in 1992). Pal David Geffen bailed the company out of $62 million in junk bond debt (stemming from the Puritan purchase) in 1992 and helped Klein license his underwear business to Warnaco. The company also licensed apparel manufacturer Designer Holdings for jeans. In the early 1990s Klein benefited when the youth market suddenly turned on to his clothes. The youthful resurgence also led the designer to shift down from the kind of exclusive fashions sold at Bergdorf Goodman to a more casual, universal look.

Calvin Klein hired Armani veteran Gabriella Forte as president and COO in 1994; she was instrumental in giving the Calvin Klein name a strong global licensing presence. Also in 1994 the company opened its first retail store in Tokyo. The next year Calvin Klein introduced its home collection (including blankets, pillows, towels, and rugs) in department stores. In 1997 Warnaco bought Designer Holdings.

In the mid-1990s Calvin Klein drew criticism for using models who looked anorexic, underaged, and drugged. New advertising in 1998 focused on a more wholesome lifestyle, with healthier looking models in outdoor settings. But it didn't take the firm long to wind up back in the hot seat when it used children in an underwear campaign, which was withdrawn in 1999.

Also in 1999, after Forte announced she was leaving, Calvin Klein began shopping for a merger or buyout. The company took itself off the market in 2000. Calvin Klein later filed suit against Warnaco, accusing it of selling full-price merchandise in discount outlets. Warnaco fired back with a lawsuit of its own. The companies announced a settlement moments before their trial was due to begin in 2001.

In 2001 Calvin Klein cut 10% of its headquarters staff and shut down its CK mid-priced sportswear division in the US (the last business manufactured by the company itself). In 2002 the company said it might buy back its CK Calvin Klein Jeans license and Calvin Klein Underwear business from bankrupt Warnaco.

OFFICERS

Chairman and CEO: Barry Schwartz
Vice Chairman: Calvin Klein
President and COO: Tom Murry
CFO: Len LaSalandra
President, Calvin Klein Cosmetics: Hilary Dart

LOCATIONS

HQ: 205 W. 39th St., New York, NY 10018
Phone: 212-719-2600   **Fax:** 212-221-4541

Calvin Klein has offices in Asia, Europe, and the US.

PRODUCTS/OPERATIONS·

Brands
Calvin Klein Collections (upscale women's and men's
  apparel and home furnishings)
Calvin Klein Cosmetics (CK One, Eternity, Obsession)
Calvin Klein Tabletop
Calvin Klein Underwear
CK Calvin Klein Jeans (jeans for women, men, juniors,
  and kids)

Licensed Products
Accessories
Apparel
Bedding
Coats
Eyewear
Fragrances
Home furnishings
Hosiery
Shoes
Sleepwear
Socks
Swimwear
Tabletop products
Underwear
Watches

COMPETITORS

Armani
Benetton
Burberry
Christian Dior
Diesel
Donna Karan
Ellen Tracy
Estée Lauder
The Gap
Gianni Versace
Gucci
Hugo Boss
Jil Sander
Joe Boxer
Jones Apparel
Kenneth Cole
Levi Strauss
Liz Claiborne
LVMH
Nautica Enterprises
Perry Ellis International
Polo
Prada
Tommy Hilfiger

HISTORICAL FINANCIALS & EMPLOYEES

Private FYE: December 31	Annual Growth	12/92	12/93	12/94	12/95	12/96	12/97	12/98	12/99	12/00	12/01
Estimated sales ($ mil.)	(2.8%)	220	280	177	127	141	150	160	175	170	170
Employees	(2.6%)	—	—	—	—	900	900	1,000	900	810	—

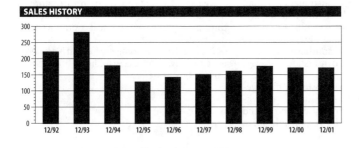

SALES HISTORY

C&S WHOLESALE GROCERS, INC.

C&S Wholesale Grocers is at the bottom of the food chain — and likes it that way. The company is New England's largest food wholesaler and one of the biggest in the US, delivering groceries to some 4,000 independent supermarkets, major supermarket chains, mass marketers (including Wal-Mart), and wholesale clubs from Maine to Maryland. The company sells more than 53,000 items, including groceries, produce, and non-food items. It runs facilities in Connecticut, Maryland, Massachusetts, New Jersey, New York, Pennsylvania, and Vermont. Chairman and CEO Richard Cohen owns the company, which his grandfather started in 1918.

Under pressure from the rapid growth of self-distributing grocery chains (most notably Wal-Mart Supercenters), C&S Wholesale has grown its business by providing outsourced distribution and logistics services to its retailer customers. The wholesaler has taken over the facilities and runs distribution and logistics for customers including the Stop & Shop, Pathmark, Safeway's Eastern Division, and Tops Markets supermarket chains.

To avoid losing one of its top customers, the company, through affiliate GU Markets, bought bankrupt supermarket chain The Grand Union Company's assets in March 2001, expanding C&S Wholesale into retailing. However, C&S Wholesale has since closed or sold off most of Grand Union's 170 stores.

C&S Wholesale is moving its headquarters and 400 jobs from Brattleboro, Vermont, to Keene, New Hampshire. The wholesaler will build new offices in Keene and keep its warehouse operations and about 800 workers in Brattleboro.

HISTORY

Israel Cohen and Abraham Siegel began C&S Wholesale Grocers in 1918 in Worcester, Massachusetts. Cohen ran the company for more than 50 years after buying out Siegel in 1921. It became a family concern in 1972 when Cohen turned the company over to his son Lester, who soon brought in his sons, Jim and Rick.

C&S Wholesale expanded over the years, growing along with its customers. It had $98 million in sales in 1981, the year its skyrocketing growth began. Also in 1981 Rick, now the company's chairman, and CEO, engineered a move to Brattleboro, in southern Vermont, where it had better access to interstate highways and a larger workforce.

After attending a seminar hosted by management whiz Tom Peters, in 1987 Rick set up self-managed teams of 3-8 employees who would act as small business units responsible for a

customer's order from the time it was received to when it was delivered. Team members were paid for the amount of time they worked and were given bonuses for error-free operations and penalties for errors or damaged goods. His plan saw an immediate response in terms of increased sales, and by 1992 C&S Wholesale had more than $1 billion in sales. Rick bought out his father in 1989 and the next year became the company's single shareholder when he bought out his brother.

C&S Wholesale started its produce business in 1990 (by 1994 it was the major purchaser of locally grown fruits and vegetables) and began making plans to build an 800,000-sq.-ft. refrigerated warehouse near a scenic highway in Brattleboro. However, it ran up against environmentalists and Vermont's Act 250 environmental impact law, and eventually dropped its original plan, opting instead to expand at its headquarters.

In 1992 the wholesaler offered plans for a smaller, revised warehouse, but again met opposition. After a two-year battle, C&S Wholesale gave up and said it would build elsewhere. (Most of its employees and warehouses are now in Massachusetts and New Jersey.)

The following year C&S Wholesale welcomed 127 Grand Union stores and several East Coast Wal-Mart stores as customers. The next year the company picked up another 103 Grand Union stores; The Grand Union Company said it was closing two distribution centers and shifting distribution to C&S Wholesale in a deal worth $500 million a year. A $650 million-per-year contract with Edwards stores was inked in 1996, the year C&S Wholesale's sales topped $3 billion.

The company acquired ice-cream distributor New England Frozen Foods in 1997. Continuing its move toward the Mid-Atlantic, C&S Wholesale took over the distribution and supply operations of New Jersey-based grocery chain Pathmark Stores in 1998 for $60 million. In 1999 C&S Wholesale purchased Shaw's Supermarkets' Star Markets' wholesale division and moved into Pennsylvania with a facility in York.

In 2001 the company, through affiliate GU Markets, bought most of the assets of one of its biggest customers, the bankrupt Grand Union. C&S acquired about 170 of Grand Union's 197 stores in the purchase. It transferred most of the stores to third-party purchasers, but will continue operating about 20 of them.

In June 2002 the company formed a new holding company, called C&S Holdings, to oversee its various businesses.

Chairman and CEO: Richard B. "Rick" Cohen
President: Edward Albertian
EVP, CFO, and General Counsel: Mark Gross
SVP Human Resources: Charlotte Edwards
SVP Strategic Planning: William Hamlin
President, C&S Holdings; Acting President, ES3:
Ron Wright

LOCATIONS

HQ: Old Ferry Rd. P.O. Box 821, Brattleboro, VT 05301
Phone: 802-257-4371   **Fax:** 802-257-6727
Web: www.cswg.com

C&S Wholesale Grocers has warehouses and distribution
facilities in Aberdeen and Collingwood, Maryland;
Brattleboro, Vermont; Hatfield and Westfield,
Massachusetts; Montgomery and Newburgh, New York;
Windsor Locks, Connecticut; Woodbridge, New
Brunswick, North Brunswick, and Dayton, New Jersey;
and York, Pennsylvania.

PRODUCTS/OPERATIONS

Selected Customers
A&P
Big Y Foods
BJ's Wholesale Club
Foodtown
Giant-Carlisle (owned by Royal Ahold)
Giant-Landover (owned by Royal Ahold)
Pathmark
Safeway
Shaw's
Stop and Shop
Wal-Mart

COMPETITORS

Associated Wholesalers
Bozzuto's
Di Giorgio
Fleming Companies
IGA
Krasdale Foods
McLane
Nash Finch
Richfood
SUPERVALU
Wakefern Food

HISTORICAL FINANCIALS & EMPLOYEES

Private FYE: September 30	Annual Growth	9/93	9/94	9/95	9/96	9/97	9/98	9/99	9/00	9/01	9/02
Sales ($ mil.)	20.1%	1,867	1,837	2,650	3,348	3,665	5,120	6,050	7,000	8,500	9,700
Employees	21.5%	1,300	1,500	2,000	2,850	3,000	3,800	4,000	5,000	7,000	7,500

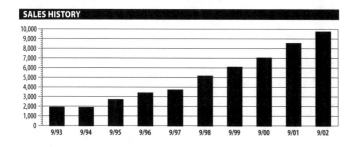

SALES HISTORY

CARGILL, INCORPORATED

Cargill may be private, but all of its parts are highly visible. The US's largest private corporation, Cargill's diversified operations include grain, cotton, sugar, and petroleum trading; financial trading; food processing; futures brokering; feed and fertilizer production; and steelmaking. The company is the leading grain producer in the US, and its Excel unit is the #2 US meatpacker (behind Tyson Foods). Cargill's brands include Diamond Crystal (salt), Gerkens (cocoa), Honeysuckle White (poultry), and Sterling Silver (fresh meats). Descendants of the founding Cargill and MacMillan families own about 85% of Cargill.

Being private doesn't mean Cargill is cut off from the world. The agribusiness giant has operations in 59 countries throughout the world. Along with its grain and meatpacking businesses, Cargill is a commodity trader and a producer of animal feed and crop fertilizers. It is also a global supplier of oils, syrups, flour, and other products used in food processing.

Cargill also is involved in petroleum trading, financial trading, futures brokering, and shipping. Its North Star subsidiary is a major minimill steelmaker in the US. To focus on processing, Cargill sold its seed operations and coffee trading business and is selling part of its steel business. It is forming a joint venture with Hormel Foods to market fresh beef, along with pork, under the brand name Always Tender.

HISTORY

William W. Cargill founded Cargill in 1865 when he bought his first grain elevator in Conover, Iowa. He and his brother Sam bought grain elevators all along the Southern Minnesota Railroad in 1870, just as Minnesota was becoming an important shipping route. Sam and a third brother, James, expanded the elevator operations while William worked with the railroads to monopolize transport of grain to markets and coal to farmers.

Around the turn of the century, William's son William S. invested in a number of ill-fated projects. William W. found that his name had been used to finance the projects; shortly afterward, he died of pneumonia. Cargill's creditors pressed for repayment, which threatened to bankrupt the company. John MacMillan, William W.'s son-in-law, took control and rebuilt Cargill. It had recovered by 1916 but lost its holdings in Mexico and Canada. MacMillan opened offices in New York (1922) and Argentina (1929), expanding grain trading and transport operations.

In 1945 Cargill bought Nutrena Mills (animal feed) and entered soybean processing; corn processing began soon after and grew with the demand for corn sweeteners. In 1954 Cargill benefited when the US began making loans to help developing countries buy American grain. Subsidiary Tradax, established in 1955, became one of the largest grain traders in Europe. A decade later Cargill began trading sugar by purchasing sugar and molasses in the Philippines and selling them abroad.

Cargill made its finances public in 1973 (as a requirement for its unsuccessful takeover bid of Missouri Portland Cement), revealing it to be one of the US's largest companies, with $5.2 billion in sales. In the 1970s it expanded into coal, steel, and waste disposal, and became a major force in metals processing, beef, and salt production.

In the early 1990s Cargill began selling branded meats and packaged foods directly to supermarkets. To placate family heirs who wanted to take Cargill public, CEO Whitney MacMillan, grandson of John, created an employee stock plan in 1991 that allowed shareholders to cash in their shares. He also boosted dividends and reorganized the board, reducing the family's control. MacMillan retired in 1995 and non-family member Ernest Micek became CEO and chairman.

The firm bought Akzo Nobel's North American salt operations in 1997, becoming the #2 US salt company. In 1999 Micek resigned as CEO and was replaced by Warren Staley. Also in 1999 Cargill fessed up to misappropriating some genetic seed material from rival Pioneer Hi-Bred, killing the $650 million sale of its North American seed assets to Germany's AgrEvo.

Cargill sold its coffee trading unit in 2000 and bought Agribrands International (Purina and Checkerboard animal feeds sold outside the US). In 2001 the company bought family-held turkey and chicken processor Rocco Enterprises.

In 2002 Cargill Health & Food Technologies introduced trehalose, a naturally occuring type of sugar made from cornstarch. Trehalose has a blunted insulin response relative to other sugars and helps preserve food flavor, color, and texture. Cargill also launched OliggooFiber, a line of natural soluble fiber ingredients that increases calcium absorption as well as the number of beneficial bacteria in the body. Both are marketed to the food industry for use in nutrition bars, sports drinks, bakery products, ice cream, and confections. That same year Cargill purchased a 97% stake in Cerestar (starches, syrups, feeds).

While its Wilbur Chocolate subsidiary is generally quiet, Cargill plumped it up by acquiring Peter's Chocolate from Nestlé USA in late 2002.

OFFICERS

Chairman and CEO: Warren R. Staley, age 60
Vice Chairman and CFO: Robert L. Lumpkins, age 59
Vice Chairman: F. Guillaume Bastiaens, age 59
Vice Chairman: David W. Raisbeck, age 54
President, COO, and Director: Gregory R. Page
EVP: Fredric W. Corrigan
EVP: David M. Larson
EVP: Hubertus P. Spierings
SVP, Director of Corporate Affairs: Robbin S. Johnson
Corporate VP, Human Resources: Nancy P. Siska
Auditors: KPMG LLP

LOCATIONS

HQ: 15407 McGinty Rd. West, Wayzata, MN 55391
Phone: 952-742-7575   **Fax:** 952-742-7393
Web: www.cargill.com

PRODUCTS/OPERATIONS

Selected Products

Agriculture
Animal feed
Aquaculture feed

Feed phosphates
Fertilizer
Pet food

Food Processing
Apples
Bulk and packaged oils
Chicken products
Citric acid
Cocoa and cocoa products
Copra (dried coconut meat)
Corn (including dextrose and starch production)
Cottonseed
Egg products
Erythritol
Ethanol
Hazelnuts
High fructose corn syrups
Lactic acid polymers
Nutraceuticals

Oranges
Palm oil
Peanuts
Poultry (production, processing, marketing)
Protein products (flavored soy protein, soy flour, and textured vegetable protein)
Rapeseed
Salt
Sodium citrate
Soybeans
Sunflower seeds
Trehalose (cornstarch sugar)
Turkey products

Industrial
Industrial-grade starches
Industrial oils and lubricants
Phosphate mining and fertilizer manufacturing
Salt process evaporated, rock, and solar
Steel and wire products
Steel minimills

Trading
Cargill Investor Services (CIS, futures/futures options broker and risk management consultant)
Cargill Marine and Terminal
Cargo Carriers (operates jumbo dry and liquid cargo barges)
G&M Stevedoring
Greenwich Marine (ocean shipping)
Hohenberg Bros (cotton trading)
Rogers Terminal & Shipping (stevedoring services)

COMPETITORS

ADM
Ag Processing
BASF AG
Bethlehem Steel
Bunge Limited
Cenex Harvest States
Cereol
COFCO
ConAgra
ContiGroup
Corn Products International
Dow Chemical
DuPont
Farmland Industries
General Mills

Hormel
IBP
King Arthur Flour
Koch
Land O' Lakes Farmland Feed
Morton Salt
Nippon Steel
Nucor
Perdue
Rohm and Haas
Saskatchewan Wheat Pool
Smithfield Foods
Tate & Lyle
Tyson Foods
United States Steel

HISTORICAL FINANCIALS & EMPLOYEES

Private FYE: May 31	Annual Growth	5/93	5/94	5/95	5/96	5/97	5/98	5/99	5/00	5/01	5/02
Sales ($ mil.)	0.8%	47,100	47,135	51,000	56,000	56,000	51,418	45,697	47,602	49,204	50,826
Net income ($ mil.)	9.7%	358	571	671	902	814	468	597	480	358	827
Income as % of sales	—	0.8%	1.2%	1.3%	1.6%	1.5%	0.9%	1.3%	1.0%	0.7%	1.6%
Employees	3.7%	70,000	70,700	73,300	76,000	79,000	80,600	84,000	84,000	90,000	97,000

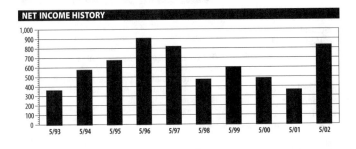

NET INCOME HISTORY

CARLSON COMPANIES, INC.

Carlson Companies began in 1938 as the Gold Bond Stamp Company but has evolved into a leisure services juggernaut. The company owns 50% of travel giant Carlson Wagonlit Travel (French hotelier Accor owns the rest). It also owns more than 800 hotels under brands such as Radisson, Country Inns & Suites By Carlson, Park Inn, and Park Plaza. Carlson's restaurant empire includes the 700-unit T.G.I. Friday's chain. A specialist in relationship marketing, Carlson Marketing Group offers services such as sales promotion and customer loyalty programs. CEO Marilyn Carlson Nelson and director Barbara Carlson Gage, the daughters of late founder Curtis Carlson, each own half of the company.

One of the largest business travel firms in the world, Carlson Wagonlit has more than 3,000 locations worldwide and counts AT&T, General Electric, and IBM among its clients.

Carlson's lodging empire includes the 430-unit Radisson chain, as well as the Country Inns & Suites By Carlson (300 hotels), Park Inn and Park Plaza Hotels (100), and Regent International (about a dozen). In 2002 the company announced it was building about 20 new hotels, largely Radisson and Country Inns & Suites, in India. Carlson also is active in cruise operations through its Radisson Seven Seas Cruises, which offers one all-suite and five deluxe ships sailing to about 485 destinations.

The company's Carlson Restaurants Worldwide subsidiary also operates eateries under the Fishbowl, Italianni's, Mignon, Samba Room, Star Canyon, Taqueria Canonita, Pick Up Stix, and Timpano Italian Chophouse names.

In 2002 CEO Nelson was appointed by President Bush to chair the National Women's Business Council.

HISTORY

Curtis Carlson, the son of Swedish immigrants, graduated from the University of Minnesota in 1937 and went to work selling soap for Procter & Gamble in the Minneapolis area. In 1938 he borrowed $55 and formed Gold Bond Stamp Company to sell trading stamps. His wife, Arleen, dressed as a drum majorette and twirled a baton to promote the concept. By 1941 the company had 200 accounts. Business was slowed by WWII but took off in the 1950s. During the 1960s the company began diversifying into other enterprises such as travel, marketing, hotels, and real estate.

In 1962 Gold Bond Stamp bought the Radisson Hotel in Minneapolis and began expanding the chain. The company adopted the Carlson Companies name in 1973. Carlson Companies continued expanding its holdings during the 1970s, buying the 11-unit T.G.I. Friday's chain, as well as Country Kitchen International, a string of family restaurants.

In 1979 Carlson bought First Travel Corp., which owned travel agency Ask Mr. Foster and Colony Hotels. Carlson Companies slowed the pace of its acquisitions in the 1980s. Hired in 1984, Juergen Bartels changed the hospitality division's strategy from building and owning hotels to franchising and managing them. This enabled Carlson to weather the crash that followed the 1980s hotel building boom.

The company took T.G.I. Friday's public to fund expansion in 1983, but it reacquired all outstanding shares in 1989. Carlson launched its cruise ship business in 1992, when the luxury liner SSC *Radisson Diamond* set sail.

The company made a major international advance in 1994 when it formed joint venture Carlson Wagonlit Travel, with France's Accor. In 1997 Carlson expanded into the luxury hotel business when it bought Regent International from Four Seasons. In a nod to its roots, the company also unveiled the Gold Points Reward guest loyalty system to reward customers who frequent its hotels and restaurants.

In 1998 Curtis appointed his daughter, Marilyn Carlson Nelson, as the company's CEO (he remained chairman). The following year Carlson Companies merged its UK leisure travel business with UK-based travel and financial services firm Thomas Cook. Founder Curtis died that year and Nelson added chairman to her title. The company later filed to spin off its T.G.I. Friday's unit as Carlson Restaurants Worldwide, but decided to put that offering on hold until market conditions improved.

In 2001 Carlson Companies sold its 22% stake in Thomas Cook Holdings to German tour company C&N (which then changed its name to Thomas Cook AG). In mid-2001 the company bought 52-unit Asian restaurant chain Pick Up Stix. That year it also added a sixth ship to its cruise line.

OFFICERS

Chairman and CEO: Marilyn Carlson Nelson, age 63
EVP and CFO: Martyn R. Redgrave, age 50
SVP and CIO: Stephen S. Brown
SVP and General Counsel: William A. Van Brunt
SVP Human Resources: Rosalyn Mallet
VP and Treasurer: John M. Diracles Jr.
VP Corporate Audit and Consulting: Vicki Rasmusen
VP Corporate Financial Services and Business Risk Management: Anita Phillips
VP Corporate Human Resources: Charles Montreuil

VP Corporate Public Relations and Communications: Douglas R. Cody
VP Legal and Corporate Secretary: Ralph Beha
VP Tax: Darrel M. Hamann
President and CEO, Carlson Leisure Group: Michael Batt
President, Carlson Shared Services: Walter W. Erickson
President and CEO, Carlson Wagonlit Travel: Hervé Gourio
COO, Carlson Consumer Group: Curtis C. Nelson
COO, Carlson Corporate Solutions: James J. Ryan
EVP and General Manager, Gold Points Rewards: Harold Schrum
VP Finance, Carlson Shared Services: Frank Peskar
VP Financial Shared Services, Carlson Shared Services: Jim Hotze
Director of Public Relations: Sam Macalus

LOCATIONS

HQ: P.O. Box 59159, Minneapolis, MN 55459
Phone: 763-212-5000   Fax: 763-212-2219
Web: www.carlson.com

Carlson Companies has operations in more than 140 countries.

PRODUCTS/OPERATIONS

Selected Operations
Cruises
  Radisson Seven Seas Cruises
Hotels
  Country Inns & Suites By Carlson
  Park Inn and Park Plaza hotels
  Radisson Hotels & Resorts
  Regent International Hotels
Marketing
  Carlson Employee Marketing
  Carlson Marketing Group
Restaurants

Fishbowl	Samba Room	T.G.I. Friday's
Italianni's	Star Canyon	Timpano
Mignon	Taqueria	Italian
Pick Up Stix	Canonita	Chophouse

Travel
  Carlson Destination Marketing Services
  Carlson Leisure Fulfillment Services
  Carlson Wagonlit Travel (50%)
  CarlsonTravel.com
  Neiman Marcus Travel Services
  Travel Agents International
Other
  Carlson Leasing Group (equipment lease financing)
  Carlson Vacation Ownership (vacation ownership properties)
  Gold Points Rewards (consumer loyalty program)
  Provisions (food and beverage distribution)

COMPETITORS

American Express	Metromedia
Applebee's	O'Charley's
Brinker	Omnicom
Carnival	Outback Steakhouse
Darden Restaurants	Ritz-Carlton
Denny's	Rosenbluth International
Fairmont Hotels	Royal Caribbean Cruises
Four Seasons Hotels	Six Continents
Gage Marketing	Starwood Hotels & Resorts
Hilton	Sunterra
Hyatt	TRT Holdings
Interpublic Group	WorldTravel
Maritz	WPP Group
Marriott International	Wyndham International

HISTORICAL FINANCIALS & EMPLOYEES

Private FYE: December 31	Annual Growth	12/91	12/92	12/93	12/94	12/95	12/96	12/97	12/98	12/99	12/00
Estimated sales ($ mil.)	15.0%	—	3,200	3,500	3,900	4,500	4,900	6,600	7,800	9,800	9,800
Employees	18.5%	—	49,350	41,000	65,000	69,000	65,462	68,530	147,000	188,000	192,000

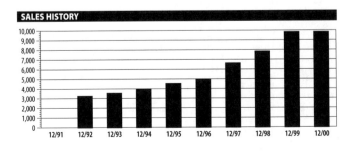

SALES HISTORY

CARLSON WAGONLIT TRAVEL

No, Carlson Wagonlit Travel did not get its middle name from Indians trying to explain to pioneers that their covered wagons were on fire. The company is descended from both the creator of the Orient Express (Wagons-Lits) and the oldest US travel agency chain (Ask Mr. Foster). It manages business travel from more than 3,000 travel offices in more than 140 countries. The company is the #2 travel firm in the world, behind American Express. It is co-owned by the US firm Carlson Companies (whose US leisure and franchise operations also fall under the Carlson Wagonlit brand) and France's Accor Group.

Carlson Companies is a service conglomerate with non-business travel operations such as hospitality (it franchises Radisson Hotels, T.G.I. Friday's and Italianni's restaurants, and luxury cruise lines) and marketing services (motivational and incentive programs for businesses).

The company's two parents have invested €100 million to get Carlson Wagonlit (pronounced Vah-gon-LEE) online with business-to-consumer and business-to-business sites. Accor also is reaping the benefits of training the company's travel agents in booking Accor hotel rooms.

HISTORY

Belgian inventor Georges Nagelmackers' first enterprise was adding sleeping compartments to European trains in 1872. Nagelmackers later created the Orient Express. Over the years his Wagons-Lits company expanded its mission to become Wagonlit Travel.

While Nagelmackers was establishing his business in Europe, Ward G. Foster was giving out steamship and train schedules from his gift shop facing the stately Ponce de Leon Hotel in St. Augustine, Florida. As legend has it, hotel patrons with travel questions were directed to Foster's shop with: "Ask Mr. Foster. He'll know." In 1888 he founded Ask Mr. Foster Travel (it became the oldest travel agency in the US). By 1913 the company had offices located in pricey department stores and in the lobbies of upscale hotels and resorts throughout the country. After 50 years at the helm, Foster sold his business in 1937, three years before his death.

After suffering hard times during WWII and into the 1950s, the company changed hands again in 1957 when Donald Fisher and Thomas Orr, two Ask Mr. Foster shareholders, bought controlling interests for $157,000. In 1972 Peter Ueberroth (Major League Baseball commissioner and Los Angeles Olympic Organizing Committee president) bought the company, then sold it in 1979 to Carlson Companies, Carlson Wagonlit's parent. In 1990 Ask Mr. Foster became Carlson

Travel Network. Also that year Carlson Companies acquired the UK's A.T. Mays, the Travel Agents — a leading UK seller of vacation and tour packages. By 1992 Carlson Companies, besides adding a travel agency a day to the 2,000-plus it already owned, was adding a new hotel every 10 days.

Europe's Wagonlit Travel and the US's Carlson Travel Network joined forces in 1994 to pursue expansion efforts. Under a dual-president ownership, the parent companies owned operations in specific world regions. The two companies began developing new business technology and expanded into new global business markets. In 1994 the venture acquired Germany's Brune Reiseburo travel agency and opened a branch office in Moscow. Acquisitions in 1995 and 1996 targeted the Asia/Pacific region, including Hong Kong's and Japan's Dodwell Travel and the corporate travel business of Singapore's Jetset Travel. The venture also formed a partnership with Traveland, an Australian travel agency.

In 1997 Wagonlit Travel and Carlson Travel Network finalized the merger of their business activities operations, renamed Carlson Wagonlit Travel. The following year the new company acquired Florida's Travel Agents International, with more than 300 franchised operations and $600 million in annual sales. In 1999 three travel agencies in eastern Canada consolidated under the Carlson Wagonlit Travel brand, creating the largest travel network in that region. Also, Carlson Companies' founder and Carlson Wagonlit Travel chairman Curtis Carlson died. In 2000 the company agreed to form a Japan-based joint venture with Japan Travel Bureau (now JTB Corp.). The arrangement will increase Carlson Wagonlit's presence in Asia while increasing the number of JTB locations in North America.

In 2001 Carlson Wagonlit cut jobs because of a slowdown in business travel.

OFFICERS

CEO and President; President, Europe, Middle East, and Africa: Hervé Gourio
President, Asia Pacific: Geoffrey Marshall
President, North America: Robin Schleien
CFO: Tim Hennessy
EVP Associate Division: Roger E. Block
EVP Business Development and Marketing, North America: Bob Briggs
EVP Business Travel: Dan Miles
EVP Europe, Middle East, and Africa: Richard Lovell
EVP Global Sales and Account Management: Liliana Frigerio
EVP Supplier Relations: Robert Deliberto
EVP Vacation and Business Travel: Thomas Baumann
CIO: Loren Brown

CFO, Europe, Middle East, and Africa:
  Nicholas Francou
VP Account Management Business Travel Services,
  North America: Michael Woodward
VP Human Resources, North America: Cindy Rodahl
VP Information Technology, Europe, Middle East, and
  Africa: Len Blackwood
VP Finance, Americas: Nick Bluhm
Corporate Communications: Steve Loucks
Public Relations: Mollie Quinn

COMPETITORS

American Express
JTB
Kuoni Travel
Maritz
Rosenbluth International
Thomas Cook AG
TUI
WorldTravel

LOCATIONS

HQ: 1405 Xenium Ln., Plymouth, MN 55441
Phone: 763-212-4000   **Fax:** 763-212-2219
Web: www.carlsonwagonlit.com

HISTORICAL FINANCIALS & EMPLOYEES

Joint venture FYE: December 31	Annual Growth	12/92	12/93	12/94	12/95	12/96	12/97	12/98	12/99	12/00	12/01
Sales ($ mil.)	3.0%	—	—	—	—	9,500	10,600	11,000	11,000	12,000	11,000
Employees	(16.6%)	—	—	—	—	20,000	20,000	20,100	7,015	7,702	8,083

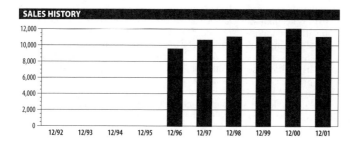

SALES HISTORY

THE CARLYLE GROUP

Can you say military-industrial complex? The Carlyle Group can. With former Defense Secretary Frank Carlucci leading the charge, the firm takes part in management-led buyouts (MBOs), acquires minority stakes, and provides other investment capital for companies in aerospace and defense, consumer products, energy, health care, information technology, real estate, bottling companies, and telecommunications. Defense and aerospace firms make up a significant share of the world's largest private equity firm's portfolio. MBOs make up the bulk of Carlyle's investments.

Carlyle's directorship reads like George W. Bush's inaugural ball invite list. Reagan Secretary of the Treasury James Baker serves as a senior counselor, and Richard Darman, former director of the Office of Management and Budget under George Bush (the elder), is a managing director. Former President George Bush has served with Carlyle, and Colin Powell, before becoming Secretary of State, made an appearance on behalf of the firm.

The company has more than $13 billion in assets under management, and its part in MBOs has provided investment capital for companies such as United Defense Industries, of Crusader artillery fame; Dr Pepper/Seven Up Bottling Group, Inc.; and MedPointe Inc.

Although the majority of the firm's money is in North America, it is also pushing more intensely overseas, launching funds aimed at Asia, Europe, Latin America, and Russia. The firm (along with Apax Partners and UK-based cinven) is taking a 28% share of France-based health care and business publisher Vivendi Universal Publishing. It's also buying the US-based power transmission unit, Rexnord, of UK-based Invensys. One of the company's larger moves overseas is its planned purchase of the transportation business of The Daiei, Japan's #2 retailer. But its moves overseas haven't all been lucrative. Carlyle has returned portions of its European venture capital group funds to investors after the values of its investments lessened and the availability of target acquisitions decreased.

The Carlyle Group, along with investment firm Welsh, Carson, Anderson & Stowe, is buying the yellow pages business of the financially strapped Qwest Communications. The firm is keeping an eye on the transportation and health care industries as possible candidates for deal-making. But the maturing buy-out market creates fewer prize deals and more competitors. Carlyle has also moved into the resale market on private equity.

The firm has about 20 offices in more than a dozen countries. California Public Employees' Retirement System, or CalPERS, owns more than 5% of Carlyle.

HISTORY

In 1987 T. Rowe Price director Edward Mathias brought together David Rubenstein, a former President Carter aide; Stephen Norris and Daniel D'Aniello, both executives with Marriott Corp.; William Conway Jr., the CFO of MCI; and Greg Rosenbaum, a VP with a New York investment firm. They pooled their experience along with a load of money from T. Rowe Price Associates, Alex. Brown & Sons (now Deutsche Banc Alex. Brown), First Interstate (now part of Wells Fargo), and Pittsburgh's Mellon family to form a buyout firm.

Named after the Carlyle Hotel in New York, the firm opted to make Washington, DC, its headquarters so it wouldn't get lost in the crowd of New York investment firms. The company spent its first years investing in a mish-mash of companies, using Norris' and D'Aniello's Marriott experience to focus primarily on restaurant and food service companies (including Mexican restaurant chain Chi-Chi's).

In 1989 it wooed the well-connected Frank Carlucci, who had served as President Reagan's Secretary of Defense, to join the group. Soon thereafter, Carlyle began making more high-profile deals. That year it acquired Coldwell Banker's commercial real estate operations (sold 1996) and Caterair International, Marriott's airline food services (sold 1995).

Carlucci helped redirect the firm's focus to the downsizing defense industry. Among its targets were Harsco Corp. (1990), BDM International (1991), and LTV Corp.'s missile and aircraft units (1992). Carlyle helped overhaul their operations and make them attractive (for the right price) to the industry's elite, including Boeing and Lockheed Martin.

As the company's reputation grew, so did its cast of players. Among its new backers were James Baker and Richard Darman (both Reagan and Bush administration alums) and investor George Soros, who chipped in some $100 million into the Carlyle Partners L.P. buyout fund. With the help of its "access capitalists," such as Baker and Saudi Prince al-Waleed bin Talal (whose fortune the firm helped add to in a 1991 Citicorp stock transaction), Carlyle made deals in the Middle East and Western Europe (including a bailout of Euro Disney) in the mid-1990s.

While the firm continued to be a side in the iron triangle, acquiring such defense companies as aircraft castings maker Howmet in 1995, it picked up a grab bag of holdings, such as natural food grocer Fresh Fields Markets (1994; sold 1996); the quick turnaround helped build Carlyle's war chest. The firm also began investing in industrial-cleanup companies, seeing increased government spending as a major opportunity for profit.

As Carlyle's esteem rose, so did the number of its investors. In the late 1990s the firm launched buyout funds targeting Asia (closed 1999), Europe (closed 1998), Russia, and Latin America. At home, it faced a dwindling number of opportunities as the long-running bull market drove up prices and more investors chased fewer deals. Among those was its partnership with Cadbury Schweppes to buy the Dr Pepper Bottling Co. of Texas and merge it with its own American Bottling Co.

In 2000 the company inked a deal for Ssangyong Information & Communications Corp., a computer network integration firm in South Korea, but the deal was called off the next year. Also in 2001 Carlyle launched Carlyle Asset Management Group. The events of September 11th, 2001, brought Carlyle to the general public's attention when it was revealed that both the Bush family and the bin Laden family had made profits from transactions related to the firm.

OFFICERS

Chairman and Managing Director: Frank C. Carlucci, age 71
Chairman: Louis V. Gerstner Jr., age 60
Senior Counselor: James A. Baker III, age 71
Managing Director, Carlyle Management Group: B. Edward Ewing
Chairman of Carlyle Europe: John Major, age 58
Founder and Managing Director: William E. Conway Jr., age 52
Founder and Managing Director: Daniel A. D'Aniello
Founder and Managing Director: David M. Rubenstein
Senior Advisor: Arthur Levitt Jr., age 71
Managing Director and CFO: John F. Harris
Manager, Human Resources: Lori Sabet
VP Corporate Communications: Chris Ullman
Principal: Ted Hobart
Managing Director: Richard G. Darman, age 59

LOCATIONS

HQ: 1001 Pennsylvania Ave. NW, Ste. 220 South, Washington, DC 20004
Phone: 202-347-2626   **Fax:** 202-347-1818
Web: www.thecarlylegroup.com

Offices

Bangalore, India	Munich
Barcelona, Spain	New York
Bellevue, Washington	Newport Beach, CA
Charlotte, North Carolina	Paris
Dallas	Riyadh, Saudi Arabia
Frankfurt	San Francisco
Greenwich, Connecticut	Seoul
Hong Kong	Singapore
London	Tokyo
Milan	Tysons Corner, Virginia
Moscow	Washington, DC

COMPETITORS

ABN AMRO
Bain Capital
Blackstone Group
Credit Suisse First Boston (USA), Inc.
Forstmann Little
Goldman Sachs
Hicks, Muse
Investcorp
J.P. Morgan Partners
KKR
Lehman Brothers
Texas Pacific Group
Thomas Lee
UBS Warburg

CATHOLIC HEALTH EAST

Catholic Health East doesn't believe prayers to St. Jude are necessary to continue providing health care to any person in need. Catholic Health East is one of the top religious health systems in the US. The company carries out its mission of serving the poor and the old by offering health care through more than 30 hospitals, about 40 nursing homes, and some 20 independent- and assisted-living facilities, primarily on the East Coast. The network also operates behavioral health facilities and offers adult day care, home health services, and hospice care.

Catholic Health East is governed by a board composed of 10 sisters, eight secular health care professionals, and one reverend.

Like many religious health care systems, Catholic Health East continues to struggle with the problem of keeping both the faith and the bottom line intact. Providing indigent care is becoming increasingly difficult thanks to the ever-rising costs of health care coupled with cuts in reimbursements that have hurt not only the system's hospital services but its nursing home and outpatient services as well.

HISTORY

It was three easy pieces that made up Catholic Health East in 1997. Allegany Health System, Eastern Mercy Health System, and Sisters of Providence Health System operated almost entirely in separate, but adjacent, geographic areas on the East Coast, overlapping only in Florida.

Catholic Health East's history goes as far back as 1831, when the Sisters of Mercy was founded in Dublin, Ireland, by Catherine McAuley, who established a poorhouse using her inheritance. Some of the sisters hopped the Pond in 1843, establishing the first Catholic hospital in the US, the Mercy Hospital of Pittsburgh, four years later. Over the years the Sisters of Mercy expanded throughout the US. By 1991 there were 25 Sisters of Mercy congregations; they united that year under the newly formed Institute of the Sisters of Mercy of the Americas.

The Sisters of Providence came from Kingston, Ontario, to found the first hospital in Holyoke, Massachusetts. Having established their own ministry, the sisters in Holyoke became a separate congregation in 1892. The congregation expanded slowly, moving into North Carolina in 1956, eventually forming the Sisters of Providence Health System.

A Polish nun, Mother Colette Hilbert, formed a new congregation in Pittsburgh in 1897 after the other members of her former parish were recalled to Poland. The new congregation entered health care in 1926, establishing a home for the elderly in New York. In honor of Hilbert's favorite saint, the order became the Franciscan Sisters of St. Joseph in 1934.

The Franciscan Sisters of St. Joseph and the Sisters of Mercy united to form the ministry that became Pittsburgh Mercy Health System in 1983. In 1986 the congregations formed Eastern Mercy Health System as a holding company for the health concern. The consolidation served to cut costs, as well as to preserve the organization's religious mission.

The Franciscan Sisters of Allegany congregation got its start in 1859 teaching children in Buffalo, New York. In 1883 the order took over St. Elizabeth Hospital in Boston, expanding its health care services ministry throughout New York, New Jersey, and Florida by the 1930s. In 1986 the sisters organized the operations as Allegany Health System.

In the early 1990s Catholic health care systems underwent a round of consolidation. Allegany Health Systems and Eastern Mercy Health Systems combined services, aiming to lower costs through economies of scale.

The mid-1990s also brought consolidation, but this time operational costs weren't the major problem; Catholic health systems across the nation were facing a shortage of sisters. To have a sufficient number of sisters to keep the "Catholic" in Catholic health care, the three health systems merged in 1997, becoming Catholic Health East.

After the merger, the company continued to build its network through acquisitions, including Mercy Health in Miami (1998) and a suffering, secular Cooper Health System in Camden, New Jersey (1999). In 2000 it gained control of two troubled hospitals in Palm Beach, Florida, only to sell them the following year. Catholic Health East remains focused on reducing costs as it expands.

OFFICERS

President and CEO: Daniel F. Russell
EVP and COO: Robert V. Stanek
EVP and CFO: C. Kent Russell
EVP, Continuing Care: Robert H. Morrow
EVP, Mission Integration: Sister Juliana Casey
EVP and Chief Administration Officer: Stanley T. Urban
EVP and Chief Medical Officer: Richard F. Afable
EVP, Mid-Atlantic Division: Mark O'Neil
EVP, Northeast Division: Sister Kathleen Popko
EVP, Southeast Division: Howard Watts
VP, Advocacy and Government Relations:
Kenneth A. Becker
VP, Communications: Salvatore C. Foti
VP, Corporate Compliance and Legal Services:
Michael C. Hemsley
VP, Financial Services: Patricia Gathers
VP, Financial Services: Randal Schultz
VP, Information Technology and CIO: Jack Hueter

VP, Leadership Formation and Human Resources:
George F. Longshore
VP, Mission Services: Mary Ann Carter
VP, Quality and Patient Safety: Diane S. Denny
VP, Risk Management Services and Chief Risk Officer:
Theodore Schlert
VP, Strategy Development: Elaine Bauer
VP, Materiels Management: Thomas Gruber
VP, Treasury Services: Paul Klinck
VP, Claims Services: Kathleen Murphy
VP, Financial Services, Mid-Atlantic Division:
Raymond Bartosh
VP, Financial Services, Northeast Division: Arun R. Adya
VP, Financial Services, Southeast Division: Ronald Kroll

LOCATIONS

HQ: 14 Campus Blvd., Ste. 300,
Newtown Square, PA 19073
Phone: 610-355-2000   **Fax:** 610-355-2050
Web: www.che.org

PRODUCTS/OPERATIONS

Divisions

Long Term Care
Mercy Community Health (West Hartford, CT)
Mercy Medical (Daphne, AL)
Mercy Uihlein Health Corporation (Lake Placid, NY)
St. Joseph of the Pines (Pinehurst, NC)

Mid-Atlantic
Lourdes Health System (Camden, NJ)
Mercy Health System (Conshohocken, PA)
Pittsburgh Mercy Health System

Northeast
Catholic Health System (Buffalo, NY)
Mercy Health System of Maine (Portland)
Mercycare Corporation (Albany, NY)
Sisters of Providence Health System (Springfield, MA)
St. James Mercy Health System (Hornell, NY)

Southeast
BayCare Health Systems (Clearwater, FL)
Holy Cross Health Ministries (Fort Lauderdale, FL)
Intracoastal Health System (West Palm Beach, FL)
Mercy Hospital (Miami)
Saint Joseph's Health System (Atlanta)
St. Mary's Health Care System, Inc. (Athens, GA)

Other
Catholic Health Association (St. Louis)
Catholic Managed Care Consortium (St. Louis)
Children's Health Matters (Alexandria, VA)
Franciscan Health Foundation (Tampa, FL)
Mercy Resource Management, Inc. (Naperville, IL)
NewCap Insurance Company, Limited (Cayman
Islands)
Premier (California, Illinois, and North Carolina)

Supporting Congregations

Franciscan Sisters of Allegany (St. Bonaventure, NY)
Franciscan Sisters of St. Joseph (Hamburg, NY)
Hope Ministries (Newtown Square, PA)
Sisters of Mercy (Albany, NY)
Sisters of Mercy (Baltimore)
Sisters of Mercy (Buffalo, NY)
Sisters of Mercy (Hartsdale, NY)
Sisters of Mercy (Merion, PA)
Sisters of Mercy (Pittsburgh)
Sisters of Mercy (Portland, ME)
Sisters of Mercy (Rochester, NY)
Sisters of Mercy (West Hartford, CT)
Sisters of Providence (Holyoke, MA)
Sisters of St. Joseph (St. Augustine, FL)

COMPETITORS

Ascension
Bon Secours Health
Catholic Health Initiatives
HCA
Triad Hospitals

HISTORICAL FINANCIALS & EMPLOYEES

Not-for-profit FYE: December 31	Annual Growth	12/92	12/93	12/94	12/95	12/96	12/97	12/98	12/99	12/00	12/01
Sales ($ mil.)	9.8%	—	—	—	—	2,700	3,000	3,800	4,300	4,300	4,300
Employees	7.8%	—	—	—	—	—	31,838	45,000	45,000	44,000	43,000

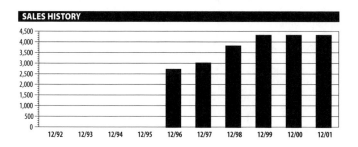

SALES HISTORY

| | 12/92 | 12/93 | 12/94 | 12/95 | 12/96 | 12/97 | 12/98 | 12/99 | 12/00 | 12/01 |

CATHOLIC HEALTH INITIATIVES

Giant not-for-profit Catholic Health Initiatives is an amalgamation of four Roman Catholic health care systems (Catholic Health Corporation of Omaha, Nebraska; Franciscan Health System of Aston, Pennsylvania; Sisters of Charity Health Care Systems of Cincinnati; and Sisters of Charity of Nazareth Health Care System of Bardstown, Kentucky). A leading Roman Catholic health system, Catholic Health Initiatives (CHI) operates more than 60 hospitals and more than 40 long-term care, assisted-living, and residential facilities. The organization is sponsored by 12 different congregations and serves communities in some 20 states.

"And he sent them out to preach the Kingdom of God and to heal the sick" (Luke 9:2). CHI hopes to make those words the driving force behind its initiative.

As a reflection of its divine purpose in a mundane health care market, the company's governing board is made up of both religious and lay officers.

CHI has to deal with the conundrum facing many Catholic health systems: Their religious mission — to care for the "unserved and underserved" (and underinsured) members of its communities — is financially uncompetitive. CHI offsets the expense of its mission by also providing health care to the general public and by making business decisions more often associated with secular business (cutting staff, centralizing functions, and joining with other Catholic health care institutions to drive harder bargains with medical suppliers).

HISTORY

In 1860 the Sisters of St. Francis established a hospital in Philadelphia, laying the foundation for a larger health care organization. In 1981 Franciscan Health System was formally established to be a national holding company for Catholic hospitals and related organizations. By the mid-1990s the system consisted of 12 member and two affiliate hospitals and 11 long-term-care facilities located in the mid-Atlantic states and the Pacific Northwest.

Sisters of Charity of Cincinnati and the Sisters of St. Francis Perpetual Adoration of Colorado Springs co-sponsored The Sisters of Charity Health Care Systems, incorporated in 1979 as a multi-institutional health care network. By the mid-1990s the system included 20 hospitals in Colorado, Kentucky, Nebraska, New Mexico, and Ohio.

Three congregations collaborated to form Catholic Health Corporation in 1980, one of the first such health care partnerships between religious communities within the Roman Catholic Church in the US. By 1996 this coalition operated 100 health care facilities in 12 states.

The development of modern managed care health care systems put pressure on the smaller Catholic hospital operations, so the three systems established CHI in 1996 as a national entity serving five geographic regions. Patricia Cahill, a lay health care veteran who previously served the Archdiocese of New York, was appointed president and CEO of CHI. The following year CHI absorbed the 10-hospital Sisters of Charity of Nazareth Health Care System, based in Bardstown, Kentucky (founded in a log cabin in 1812).

That year CHI continued to seek new partnerships to improve efficiency. With Alegent Health it formed provider network Midwest Select with nearly 200 hospitals, marketing discounted rates to businesses. CHI allied with the Daughters of Charity to form for-profit joint venture Catholic Healthcare Audit Network to provide operational, financial, compliance, and information systems audits, as well as due diligence reviews. CHI also joined insurance joint venture NewCap Insurance with the Daughters of Charity and Catholic Health East; the firm allowed CHI to operate independently of commercial insurers.

CHI made a secular tie-in with the University of Pennsylvania Health System in 1998, whereby the university's system would offer care through five Catholic hospitals (CHI made plans to transfer these hospitals to Catholic Health East in 2001). The next year CHI announced its first loss, due to lackluster performance in the Midwest. During 2000 the company responded by streamlining operations and changing management, resulting in a positive bottom line. In 2001 it sold three hospitals in Pennsylvania and one in Delaware to Catholic Health East; it also made plans to sell facilities in New Jersey.

OFFICERS

Chairman: Maryanna Coyle
President and CEO: Patricia A. Cahill
EVP and COO: Kevin Lofton
SVP, Finance and Treasury: Sister Geraldine Hoyler
SVP and Chief Medical Officer: Harold E. Ray
SVP, Human Resources, and Chief Administrative Officer: Michael Fordyce
Auditors: Ernst & Young LLP

LOCATIONS

HQ: 1999 Broadway, Ste. 2605, Denver, CO 80202
Phone: 303-298-9100   **Fax:** 303-298-9690
Web: www.catholichealthinit.org

2002 Facilities

	No.
Colorado	18
Nebraska	11
Oregon	11
Kentucky	9
Minnesota	9
Iowa	8
North Dakota	8
South Dakota	6
Washington	6
Arkansas	5
Ohio	5
New Mexico	4
Pennsylvania	4
Kansas	3
Missouri	3
Tennessee	2
Wisconsin	2
California	1
Idaho	1
Maryland	1
New Jersey	1
Total	**118**

PRODUCTS/OPERATIONS

Sponsoring Congregations
Benedictine Sisters of Mother of God Monastery
 (Watertown, SD)
Congregation of the Dominican Sisters of St. Catherine
 of Siena (Kenosha, WI)
Franciscan Sisters of Little Falls (Little Falls, MN)
Nuns of the Third Order of St. Dominic (Great Bend,
 KS)
Sisters of Charity of Cincinnati
Sisters of Charity of Nazareth (Bardstown, KY)
Sisters of the Holy Family of Nazareth (Philadelphia, PA)
Sisters of Mercy of the Americas, Regional Community
 of Omaha (Omaha, NE)
Sisters of the Presentation of the Blessed Virgin Mary
 (Fargo, ND)
Sisters of St. Francis of Colorado Springs
Sisters of St. Francis of the Immaculate Heart of Mary
 (Hankinson, ND)
Sisters of St. Francis of Philadelphia

COMPETITORS

Allina Health
Ascension
Beverly Enterprises
BJC Health
Catholic Healthcare Partners
HCA
Health Midwest
HMA
Life Care Centers
Mayo Foundation
OhioHealth
Presbyterian Healthcare Services
Tenet Healthcare

HISTORICAL FINANCIALS & EMPLOYEES

Not-for-profit FYE: June 30	Annual Growth	6/92	6/93	6/94	6/95	6/96	6/97	6/98	6/99	6/00	6/01
Sales ($ mil.)	24.7%	—	985	1,116	3,800	3,755	4,002	4,500	5,000	5,551	5,742
Net income ($ mil.)	73.2%	—	—	—	—	—	—	—	—	97	167
Income as % of sales	—	—	—	—	—	—	—	—	—	1.7%	2.9%
Employees	14.5%	—	—	—	—	—	—	44,000	—	56,100	66,000

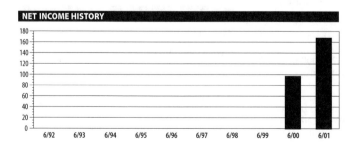

NET INCOME HISTORY

CATHOLIC HEALTHCARE WEST

Catholic Healthcare West (CHW) has found it takes a lot of nunsense to become one of the largest private, not-for-profit health care providers in the state of California. CHW has a network of more than 40 facilities in California, Arizona, and Nevada. CHW's health care system consists of acute care hospitals, skilled nursing facilities, and medical centers. CHW also has an alliance with Scripps, a major San Diego-based health care provider. The organization was formed when the hospital operations of several Roman Catholic women's religious orders consolidated, along with some non-Catholic community hospitals.

With both clergy and laity on its governing board, CHW has grown by consolidating hospitals owned by Roman Catholic women's religious orders. Additional affiliations with non-Catholic institutions have raised some hackles because Catholic doctrine opposes abortion, most forms of birth control, and in vitro fertilization.

The rapid expansion that made CHW a name in the California health care industry also left it bloated. Rising health care costs and trouble with its physician management groups cut deeply into earnings. Management casualties occurred as CHW reorganized.

HISTORY

CHW traces its roots to 1857, when the Sisters of Mercy founded St. Mary's Hospital in San Francisco. The order expanded in that area, and in 1986 two different communities of the Sisters of Mercy merged their hospitals into an organization with one retirement home and 10 hospitals from the Bay Area to San Diego. Declining membership in Roman Catholic religious orders, combined with consolidation in the field, led the orders to see merger as their only route to survival.

Rising medical costs, slow payers, and merger expenses dropped the organization's combined net income to $20 million in 1988 (from nearly $58 million in 1986). One of the hardest-hit CHW affiliates was Mercy Healthcare Sacramento, which lost $4.2 million between 1986 and 1987. In 1988 Mercy Healthcare restructured along regional lines.

The next year the Sisters of St. Dominic brought two hospitals into the alliance. CHW launched the Community Economic Assistance program, which provided $220,000 in grants to 16 human service and health care agencies in its first year.

CHW continued to add facilities, including AMI Community Hospital in Santa Cruz, California, in 1990. Since CHW already owned the area's only other acute care hospital, Dominican

Santa Cruz Hospital, CHW in 1993 was ordered not to acquire any more acute care hospitals in Santa Cruz County without FTC approval.

As the trend to managed care became a stampede in the 1990s, CHW moved more into preventive care and began reining in costs through productivity improvement plans. It continued to add hospitals, including tax-supported institutions trying to compete with national for-profit systems.

The network increased its medical clout in 1994 by allying with San Diego-based Scripps Health, one of the state's largest HMO systems. In 1995 the Daughters of Charity Province of the West realigned its six-hospital operation with CHW. The next year the Dominican Sisters (California), the Dominican Sisters of St. Catherine of Siena (Wisconsin), and the Sisters of Charity of the Incarnate Word allied their California hospitals with CHW.

Charity and cost-consciousness clashed in 1996 when union members staged a walkout to protest non-union outsourcing of vocational nursing, housekeeping, and kitchen jobs. This dispute was settled, but CHW continued to be a target for union organizers, with a bitter battle against the Service Employees International Union (SEIU) starting in 1998.

CHW agreed in 1996 to merge with Samaritan Health Systems (now Banner Health System) in a move that would have made CHW one of the US's top five providers, but the deal fell apart in 1997. In 1998 CHW merged with UniHealth, a group with eight facilities in Los Angeles and Orange counties. Mounting costs forced CHW to post a loss, and in 1999 it cut some managerial positions and reorganized to recover.

The year 2000 brought CHW more problems with labor relations: SEIU argued that the organization was resistant to unionization. Continued losses led the organization to implement a major restructuring the following year, as its 10 regional divisions were consolidated into four.

In 2001 CHW stepped up donations, grants, and other sponsorship efforts designed to benefit areas served by its hospitals and clinics.

OFFICERS

Chairperson: Diane Grassilli
President and CEO: Lloyd H. Dean
EVP and CFO: Michael Blaszyk
SVP and Chief Medical Officer: George Bo-Linn
SVP Legal Services and General Counsel:
Robert Johnson
SVP Mission Services: Bernita McTernan
VP Finance: Mary Connick
VP Human Resources: Ernie Urquhart
Chief Administrative Officer: Elizabeth Shih

LOCATIONS

HQ: 1700 Montgomery St., Ste. 300,
San Francisco, CA 94111
Phone: 415-438-5500   **Fax:** 415-438-5724
Web: www.chw.edu

Catholic Healthcare West operates hospitals in Arizona, California, and Nevada.

PRODUCTS/OPERATIONS

Selected CHW Network Facilities

Arizona
Barrow Neurological Institute, Phoenix
Chandler Regional Hospital, Phoenix
Chandler Regional Medical Center, Phoenix
CHW Business Services Center, Phoenix
St. Joseph's Hospital and Medical Center, Phoenix

California
Bakersfield Memorial Hospital, Bakersfield
California Hospital Medical Center, Los Angeles
Community Hospital of San Bernardino, San Bernardino
Dominican Hospital, Santa Cruz
Glendale Memorial Hospital & Health Center, Glendale
Mercy General Hospital, Sacramento
Mercy Hospital, Bakersfield
Mercy Hospital of Folsom, Folsom
Mercy Medical Center Merced, Merced
Mercy Medical Center Mt. Shasta, Mt. Shasta
Mercy San Juan Medical Center, Carmichael
Mercy Southwest Hospital, Bakersfield
Methodist Hospital of Sacramento, Sacramento
Northridge Hospital - Sherman Way Campus, Van Nuys
Northridge Hospital Medical Center, Northridge
Roscoe Boulevard Campus, Northridge
Sequoia Hospital, Redwood City
St. Bernardino Medical Center, San Bernardino
St. Francis Medical Center, Santa Barbara
St. Francis Memorial Hospital, San Francisco
St. John's Regional Medical Center, Oxnard
St. Joseph's Behavioral Health Center, Stockton
St. Joseph's Medical Center, Stockton
St. Mary Medical Center, Long Beach
St. Mary's Medical Center, San Francisco
Woodland Healthcare, Woodland

Nevada
St. Rose Dominican Hospital, Henderson

Sponsoring Organizations
Daughters of Charity, Province of the West
Dominican Sisters of San Rafael
Franciscan Sisters of the Sacred Heart of Frankfort, Illinois
Sisters of Charity of the Incarnate Word of Houston, Texas
Sisters of Mercy, Auburn and Burlingame Regional Communities
Sisters of St. Catherine of Siena of Kenosha, Wisconsin
Sisters of St. Dominic of Adrian, Michigan
Sisters of St. Francis of Penance and Christian Charity of Redwood City, California

COMPETITORS

Adventist Health
Carondelet Health
Catholic Health Initiatives
HCA
Los Angeles County Department of Health
Memorial Health Services
Sutter Health
Tenet Healthcare
Triad Hospitals

HISTORICAL FINANCIALS & EMPLOYEES

Not-for-profit FYE: June 30	Annual Growth	6/93	6/94	6/95	6/96	6/97	6/98	6/99	6/00	6/01	6/02
Sales ($ mil.)	12.7%	1,633	2,584	2,674	2,688	2,749	3,301	4,200	4,513	4,807	4,800
Net income ($ mil.)	—	45	91	99	160	36	73	82	(47)	(87)	(47)
Income as % of sales	—	2.8%	3.5%	3.7%	6.0%	1.3%	2.2%	2.0%	—	—	—
Employees	8.4%	17,451	17,618	20,000	21,495	17,451	20,000	38,000	40,000	36,000	36,000

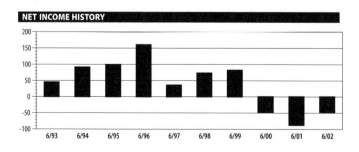

NET INCOME HISTORY

CENEX HARVEST STATES

Cenex Harvest States Cooperatives (CHS) goes with the grain. As the largest US cooperative marketer of grain and oilseed, CHS represents some 325,000 farmers, primarily in the Midwest and Northwest. CHS trades grain and sells supplies to members through its stores. It also processes soybeans for use in salad dressings, margarines, and animal feeds and markets petroleum. In addition, CHS grinds wheat into flour used in pastas and bread; subsidiary Sparta Foods makes tortillas. The co-op's joint ventures sell crop nutrient and protection products and market grain.

CHS's grain trading activities include buying, selling, and arranging for transport. The co-op operates wheat mills to produce flour for pasta and bread, and it provides farm supplies at more than 300 stores; CHS also processes soybeans for use in margarine, salad dressings, and animal feed. The energy division operates oil refineries, and the Country Energy subsidiary sells wholesale propane and other petroleum products and operates more than 800 convenience stores. Joint ventures with Farmland and Land O'Lakes (Agriliance), Mitsui (United Harvest), and Cargill supply farmers with crop products, market grain, and produce and export feed.

HISTORY

To help farmers through the Great Depression, the Farmers Union Terminal Association (a grain marketing association formed in 1926) created the Farmers Union Grain Terminal Association (GTA) in 1938. With loans from the Farmers Union Central Exchange (later known as CENEX) and the Farm Credit Association, the organization operated a grain elevator in St. Paul, Minnesota. By 1939 GTA had 250 grain-producing associations as members.

GTA leased terminals in Minneapolis and Washington and built others in Montana and Wisconsin in the early 1940s. It then took over a Minnesota flour mill and created Amber Milling. GTA also began managing farming insurance provider Terminal Agency. In 1958 the association bought 57 elevators and feed plants from the McCabe Company.

Adding to its operations in 1960, GTA bought the Honeymead soybean plant. The next year the co-op acquired Minnesota Linseed Oil. In 1977 it acquired Jewett & Sherman (later Holsum Foods), which helped transform the company into a provider of jams, jellies, salad dressings, and syrups.

In 1983 GTA combined with North Pacific Grain Growers, a Pacific Northwest co-op incorporated in 1929, to form Harvest States Cooperatives. Harvest States grew in the early and

mid-1990s by acquiring salad dressing makers Albert's Foods, Great American Foods, and Saffola Quality Foods; soup stock producer Private Brands; and margarine and dressings manufacturer and distributor Gregg Foods.

The company started a joint venture to operate the Ag States Agency agricultural insurance company in 1995. The next year the co-op's Holsum Foods division and Mitsui & Co.'s edible oils unit, Wilsey Foods, merged to form Ventura Foods, a distributor of margarines, oils, spreads, and other food products.

Harvest States merged in 1998 with CENEX, a Minnesota-based 16-state agricultural supply co-op that had been founded in 1931 as Farmers Union Central Exchange. (Among CENEX's major operations was a farm inputs, services, marketing, and processing joint venture with dairy cooperative Land O'Lakes formed in 1987.) CENEX CEO Noel Estenson took the helm of the resulting co-op, CHS, which soon formed a petroleum joint venture called Country Energy with Farmland Industries.

CHS members rejected a proposed merger with Farmland Industries in 1999. Also that year Cenex/Land O'Lakes Agronomy (it became Agriliance in 2000 when Farmland Industries joined the joint venture) bought Terra Industries' $1.7 billion distribution business (400 farm supply stores, seed and chemical distribution operations, partial ownership of two chemical plants).

CHS bought the wholesale propane marketing operations of Williams Companies in 2000, and the co-op paid $14 million for tortilla and tortilla-chip maker Sparta Foods. Additionally Estenson retired that year and company president John Johnson took over as CEO. CHS launched an agricultural e-commerce site (Rooster.com) in conjunction with Cargill and DuPont in 2000. The site was shut down the next year, however, because of a lack of funds. Also in 2001 the cooperative became the full owner of Country Energy by purchasing Farmland Industries' share.

In 2002 CHS acquired Agway's Grandin, North Dakota-based sunflower business and formed a wheat-milling joint venture (Horizon Milling) with Cargill.

President and CEO: John D. Johnson, age 54,
$1,631,750 pay
EVP and CFO: John Schmitz, age 52, $561,800 pay
EVP and COO, Energy and Crop Inputs:
Leon E. Westbrock, age 55, $795,400 pay
EVP and COO, Grains and Foods: Mark Palmquist,
age 44, $795,400 pay
EVP, Corporate Planning: Patrick Kluempke, age 54,
$389,875 pay
EVP, Public Affairs: Tom Larson, age 54, $401,300 pay
SVP, Foods: James D. Tibbetts, age 50
VP, Food Service Sales: Tim Cauley
VP, Human Resources: Dick Baldwin
VP, Retail: Steven Jennings
Director, Corporate Communications: Lani Jordan
Auditors: PricewaterhouseCoopers LLP

LOCATIONS

HQ: Cenex Harvest States Cooperatives
5500 Cenex Dr., Inver Grove Heights, MN 55077
Phone: 651-451-5151   **Fax:** 651-451-5073
Web: www.chsco-ops.com

Cenex Harvest States Cooperatives has operations in
Arizona, Colorado, Idaho, Iowa, Kansas, Louisiana,
Minnesota, Missouri, Montana, Nebraska, North Dakota,
Oklahoma, Oregon, Pennsylvania, South Dakota, Texas,
Utah, Washington, Wisconsin, and Wyoming.

PRODUCTS/OPERATIONS

Selected Joint Ventures
Agriliance, LLC (with Land O'Lakes and Farmland
Industries to supply crop nutrients and protection
products to farmers)
Horizon Milling, LLC (with Cargill, wheat milling)
Rocky Mountain Milling, LLC (with Farmland
Industries, Bay State Milling, and other local co-ops)
TEMCO (with Cargill to produce and export feed grains
for overseas customers)
Ventura Foods, LLC (with the Wilsey Foods subsidiary of
Mitsui & Co. to produce vegetable-oil based products
for consumers)

Selected Operations
Farm financing (Fin-Ag, Inc.)
Farm supplies (Agri-Service Centers)
Crop-protection products
Fertilizer
Grain purchasing
Seeds
Feed manufacturing
Futures and option services (Country Hedging, Inc.)
Grain merchandising (grain purchasing, transportation,
and sales)
Petroleum marketing (Country Energy, LLC)
Soybean crushing (soybean conversion into animal feed
and crude soybean oil)
Soybean refining (soybean oil conversion into
margarine, salad dressings, and baked goods)
Wheat milling (semolina and durum wheat milling for
flour)

COMPETITORS

7-Eleven
ADM
Ag Processing
Agway
Andersons
Barilla
Bartlett and Company
Bunge Limited
Cargill
Central Soya
ConAgra
ContiGroup
Dakota Growers
Farmland Industries
Ferrellgas Partners
Frito-Lay
George Warren
GROWMARK
King Arthur Flour
Louis Dreyfus
Riceland Foods
Scoular
Shell Oil Products
Wilbur-Ellis

HISTORICAL FINANCIALS & EMPLOYEES

Cooperative FYE: August 31	Annual Growth	8/93	8/94	8/95	8/96	8/97	8/98	8/99	8/00	8/01	8/02
Sales ($ mil.)	9.4%	3,482	3,898	5,121	8,236	7,109	5,607	6,435	8,571	7,875	7,845
Net income ($ mil.)	16.5%	32	35	45	51	53	57	86	87	179	126
Income as % of sales	—	0.9%	0.9%	0.9%	0.6%	0.7%	1.0%	1.3%	1.0%	2.3%	1.6%
Employees	18.6%	—	—	—	2,428	2,178	2,404	2,576	5,308	5,897	6,750

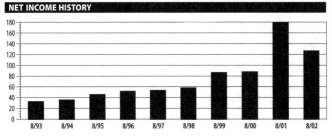

NET INCOME HISTORY

2002 FISCAL YEAR-END
Debt ratio: 25.9%
Return on equity: 9.2%
Cash ($ mil.): 108
Current ratio: 1.17
Long-term debt ($ mil.): 483

THE CITY UNIVERSITY OF NEW YORK

CUNY is the big "U" in the Big Apple. The City University of New York has 20 campuses in the five boroughs of New York City and is the US's largest urban university system. About 200,000 undergraduate and graduate students are enrolled at CUNY. The university also teaches some 204,000 students in adult and continuing education programs. CUNY has 10 senior colleges, six community colleges, a doctoral-granting graduate school, a four-year technical school, and medical and law schools. Its 1,230 programs range from specialized, career-oriented courses to traditional liberal arts curricula. CUNY's 12,000-person faculty is split almost evenly between full- and part-time members and its student body includes students from 145 countries.

CUNY has made some big changes, including tougher admission standards that critics feared would hurt the university's ethnic diversity, a hallmark of the school (enrollment numbers have proven otherwise). Notable CUNY alumni include novelist Oscar Hijuelos, Secretary of State Colin Powell, comedian Jerry Seinfeld, and 11 Nobel laureates.

As with many public universities throughout the US, CUNY is enduring tough times economically. In order to free up the money to hire more full-time professors, the university has had to end a 10-year tradition: not charging four-year students for the last semester of their senior year. Tuition and fees account for about 30% of funds for the university.

HISTORY

The New York State Legislature first created a municipal college system in New York City in 1926, when it formed the New York City Board of Higher Education to manage the operations of the City College of New York and Hunter College. City College's roots were established in 1847 when New York passed a referendum creating the Free Academy, a tuition-free school. Hunter College was founded in 1870 as a women's college, and it was the first free teacher's college in the US.

The Board of Higher Education authorized City College to create the Brooklyn Collegiate Center (a two-year men's college) in 1926; Hunter established a similar two-year women's branch in Brooklyn. Four years later the schools merged to create the Brooklyn College of the City of New York, the city's first public, co-ed liberal arts college. Other schools added to the municipal system included Queens College (1937), New York City Community College (1947), Staten Island Community College (1955), Bronx Community College (1957), and Queensborough Community College (1958).

The state legislature renamed New York City's municipal college system The City University of New York (CUNY) in 1961 and ordered its board of trustees to expand the system's facilities and scope. One of the first actions was to create a graduate school. CUNY chartered a number of new schools during the 1960s, including Richmond College (1965), York College (1966), Medgar Evers College (1968), and several community colleges. CUNY took over management of the New York State Institute of Applied Arts and Sciences (renamed New York City Technical College) in 1964 and established the John Jay College of Criminal Justice. CUNY became affiliated with Mount Sinai School of Medicine in 1967.

Despite its expansion, the university system had difficulty keeping up with demand, particularly after 1970, when it established an open admissions policy for all New York City high school graduates. Richmond College and Staten Island Community College became the College of Staten Island in 1976. Both CUNY and the City of New York ran into serious financial problems in the mid-1970s, spelling the end of CUNY's tradition of free undergrad tuition for New York City residents. To increase state financial support for CUNY, the legislature signed the City University Governance and Financing Act in 1979.

The City University School of Law held its first classes in 1983. The following year the state Board of Regents authorized CUNY to offer a doctor of medicine degree. CUNY's law school received accreditation from the American Bar Association in 1992. Since abandoning the free enrollment policy in the 1970s, the university's tuition continued to increase. In 1992, after presenting a nearly $600 increase in tuition, CUNY initiated its "last semester free" program, whereby four-year students did not have to pay tuition for the last semester of their senior year.

After several years of budget cuts and steadily increasing enrollment, CUNY declared a state of financial emergency in 1995. The following year New York's Governor George Pataki proposed new budget cuts, and in 1997 he called for tuition hikes. CUNY's board of trustees introduced a resolution calling for the elimination of remedial education programs at the senior college level in 1998. The state Board of Regents approved the plan in 1999. Matthew Goldstein was appointed chancellor in 1999 and has worked to increase CUNY's budget to hire more full-time faculty.

Belt-tightening continued in 2002. The university was forced to begin charging four-year students for the last semester of their senior year in order to earn more money.

OFFICERS

Chancellor: Matthew Goldstein
Executive Vice Chancellor for Academic Affairs:
Louise Mirrer
Vice Chancellor for Facilities Planning, Construction, and Management: Emma Espino Macari
Vice Chancellor for Faculty and Staff Relations:
Brenda Richardson Malone
Vice Chancellor for University Relations:
Jay Hershenson
Interim Vice Chancellor for Budget and Finance:
Ernesto Malave
General Counsel and Vice Chancellor for Legal Affairs:
Frederick P. Schaffer
University Dean for Instructional Technology and Information Services: Michael Ribaudo
University Dean for Student Services and Enrollment Management: Otis Hill
University Dean for The Executive Office:
Robert Ptachik
University Dean for Research: Spiro D. Alexandratos
University Dean for Academic Affairs and Deputy to the Executive Vice Chancellor: John Mogulescu
Special Counsel to the Chancellor: Dave Fields
Auditors: KPMG LLP

LOCATIONS

HQ: 535 E. 80th St., New York, NY 10021
Phone: 212-794-5555   **Fax:** 212-209-5600
Web: www.cuny.edu

The City University of New York has schools serving the Bronx, Brooklyn, Manhattan, Queens, and Staten Island boroughs of New York City.

PRODUCTS/OPERATIONS

2001 Sales

	$ mil.	% of total
Government appropriations	830	43
Tuition & fees	597	31
Government grants & contracts	332	17
Private gifts & grants	71	4
Investment income	36	2
Sales & services	17	1
Student activity fees	15	—
Other	29	2
Total	**1,927**	**100**

Senior Colleges
Bernard M. Baruch College
Brooklyn College
City College
City University School of Law at Queens College
The College of Staten Island
The Graduate School and University Center
Herbert H. Lehman College
Hunter College
John Jay College of Criminal Justice
Medgar Evers College
New York City College of Technology
Queens College
York College

Community Colleges
Borough of Manhattan Community College
Bronx Community College
Hostos Community College
Kingsborough Community College
LaGuardia Community College
Queensborough Community College

HISTORICAL FINANCIALS & EMPLOYEES

School FYE: June 30	Annual Growth	6/92	6/93	6/94	6/95	6/96	6/97	6/98	6/99	6/00	6/01
Sales ($ mil.)	2.2%	—	—	1,655	1,722	1,756	1,729	1,784	1,873	1,900	1,927
Employees	2.5%	—	—	—	25,800	25,800	27,900	28,000	28,000	30,000	30,000

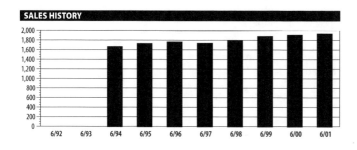

SALES HISTORY

CLUBCORP, INC.

ClubCorp makes its green from the green — the golf green, that is. The world's largest operator of golf courses, country clubs, private business clubs, and resorts, the company owns and operates more than 200 properties in nearly a dozen countries. Its holdings include Mission Hills Country Club near Palm Springs, California, and North Carolina's Pinehurst Resort and Country Club (site of the 1999 US Open). The company has sold its interests in ClubLink, a leading Canadian developer and operator of golf courses, and PGA European Tour Courses, an operator of tournament golf courses across Europe. The family of late founder Robert Dedman owns 75% of ClubCorp.

Striving to stay on top of the game, the company has been acquiring new properties and is building new ones in a joint venture with golf legend Jack Nicklaus. Dedman, who was named by *Forbes* magazine as one of the 400 wealthiest Americans, died in 2002. His son, Robert Jr., took over as CEO. ClubCorp's other shareholders include The Cypress Group, which owns about 16%.

HISTORY

Though his childhood in Depression-era Arkansas was dominated by intense poverty, ClubCorp founder Robert Dedman knew how to dream big. At a young age he vowed to become "very, very rich," and the scrappy Dedman embarked on achieving that goal by earning a college scholarship, obtaining a law degree, and eventually launching a flourishing Dallas law practice.

Dedman's law firm was successful, but he realized that it wouldn't bring him the $50 million he wanted to earn by age 50. In 1957 he formed Country Clubs, Inc., to venture into the country club business. At that time, doctors and lawyers working on a volunteer basis were managing most clubs, and Dedman believed his new company could bring professional management expertise to these facilities. The company opened its first country club, Dallas' Brookhaven Country Club, in 1957. Through the subsequent purchase of 20 more clubs, Country Clubs refined its management style, implementing unique practices such as reducing playing time on the golf course and developing specialized training for club staff.

In 1965 the company expanded into city and athletic clubs and assumed the Club Corporation of America name. The expansion drive that followed fueled a 30% growth rate that the company maintained from the 1960s through the 1980s. In 1985 the company was restructured and divided into a handful of separate companies owned by the newly formed Club Corporation International holding company.

In 1988 the company bought an 80% interest in Franklin Federal Bancorp. The bank's club properties had initially caught his eye, but Dedman also believed that the 400,000 members of his clubs might prove fertile ground for the marketing of financial services. In 1996, however, Club Corporation International sold the financial institution to Norwest. Although Franklin Federal was turning a profit, losses from investments in derivatives, coupled with the bank's inability to compete with larger competitors, prompted the company to sell the bank and refocus on its core club and resort business.

In 1996 Japanese cookie-maker Tohato sued the company, claiming that it intentionally mismanaged the Pinewild Country Club. Pinewild was owned by Tohato, managed by Club Corporation International, and located next door to Club Corporation International's Pinehurst Resort and Country Club. Tohato alleged that the company's mismanagement was part of a scheme to eventually buy Pinewild at a reduced price. The case was eventually settled, but the nasty legal wrangling that ensued cast a pall over the impending 1999 US Open at Pinehurst.

In 1998 the company was reincorporated as ClubCorp International, Inc. It expanded its international base that year by purchasing nearly 30% of PGA European Tour Courses. The company also entered into a joint venture with Jack Nicklaus to develop three dozen new golf courses.

The company shortened its moniker to Club-Corp in 1999. Among the additions ClubCorp made to its holdings that year were 22 properties acquired from The Meditrust Companies. The company also increased its ownership of Canadian club developer ClubLink to 25%. An influx of funds for further expansion came in 1999 after investment firm The Cypress Group took a 15% stake. In 2001 the company sold its interests in ClubLink and PGA European Tour Courses.

In 2002 Dedman passed away. He was succeeded as CEO by his son, Robert Jr.

OFFICERS

Chairman and CEO; Chairman, ClubCorp USA:
Robert H. Dedman Jr., age 44, $750,828 pay
President, COO, and Director: John A. Beckert, age 49
CFO: Jeffrey P. Mayer, age 45, $442,000 pay
EVP: Mark W. Dietz, age 48
EVP: James E. Maser, age 64
EVP Strategic Operations: Murray S. Siegel, age 56
EVP, Secretary and General Counsel: Terry A. Taylor, age 46
SVP Food and Beverage: John Hornsby
VP and Chief Accounting Officer: John D. Bailey, age 44
CIO: Colby H. Springer, age 54
President, The Pinehurst Company: Patrick A. Corso, age 51, $310,700 pay
Managing Director, Asia/Pacific: David McMann
EVP Domestic Club Operations, ClubCorp USA Inc.:
Douglas T. Howe, age 44
EVP Sales, ClubCorp USA, Inc: Frank C. Gore, age 52
Director, Human Resources: Lori Park
Auditors: KPMG LLP

LOCATIONS

HQ: 3030 LBJ Fwy., Ste. 700, Dallas, TX 75234
Phone: 972-243-6191   **Fax:** 972-888-7338
Web: www.clubcorp.com

ClubCorp has operations worldwide.

PRODUCTS/OPERATIONS

2001 Sales

	% of total
Country club & golf facilities	49
Business & sports clubs	24
Resorts	21
Real estate & international operations	6
Total	**100**

Selected Clubs

The Athletic and Swim Club at Equitable Center (New York)
Barton Creek Resort and Country Club (Texas)
Columbia Tower Club (Washington)
Drift Golf Club (UK)
Firestone Country Club (Ohio)
Golden Bear Golf Club (South Carolina)
Inverrary Country Club (Florida)
Kingwood Cove Golf Club (Texas)
Lakelands Gold Club (Australia)
Metropolitan Club (Illinois)
Mission Hills Country Club (California)
Pinehurst Resort and Country Club (North Carolina)
Teal Bend Golf Club (California)

COMPETITORS

American Golf
Club Med
Four Seasons Hotels
Golf Trust of America
Hillman
Hilton
Hyatt
Marriott International
National Golf Properties
ResortQuest International
Sandals Resorts
Silverleaf Resorts
Starwood Hotels & Resorts

HISTORICAL FINANCIALS & EMPLOYEES

Private FYE: December 25	Annual Growth	12/92	12/93	12/94	12/95	12/96	12/97	12/98	12/99	12/00	12/01
Sales ($ mil.)	1.5%	884	1,200	773	761	784	840	851	1,028	1,069	1,015
Net income ($ mil.)	—	19	41	15	(11)	29	122	38	12	(16)	(106)
Income as % of sales	—	2.1%	3.4%	1.9%	—	3.7%	14.5%	4.5%	1.1%	—	—
Employees	7.5%	12,000	13,000	19,200	19,800	19,000	20,000	21,000	23,000	24,000	23,000

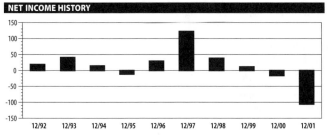

NET INCOME HISTORY

2001 FISCAL YEAR-END

Debt ratio: 57.9%
Return on equity: —
Cash ($ mil.): 3
Current ratio: 0.59
Long-term debt ($ mil.): 595

COLT'S MANUFACTURING COMPANY

The Colt .45 may have won the West, but it took a New York investment firm to save Colt's Manufacturing from a post-Cold War decline in weapons sales and tough foreign competition. Through its subsidiaries, Colt's makes handguns (Cowboy, Defender) and semiautomatic rifles for civilian use. It also makes military weapons (M-16, M-4 Carbine) for the US and other governments. Colt's also licenses its name to a variety of other companies, such as Encore Software (for Encore's *Wild West Shootout* game). Founded in 1836 by Samuel Colt, the company is about 83%-owned by investment firm Zilkha & Co.

With the firearms industry taking cover from safety and health care expense-related lawsuits filed by cities and counties across the US, Colt's is discontinuing a number of handguns it makes for the consumer market. The company spun off its "smart gun" division as iColt but the division soon closed. Colt's sold military weapons manufacturer Saco Defense to General Dynamics.

Zilkha & Co. has been reviving Colt since 1994 when it bought the firm out of bankruptcy.

HISTORY

After waiting four years for a patent, Samuel Colt started the Patent Arms Manufacturing Company in 1836 to make his revolutionary handgun, a revolver. The newfangled gun was slow to catch on (the company went bankrupt in 1842), but it gained fame after being adopted by the Texas Rangers. The US Army delegated Capt. Samuel Walker to work with Colt to improve the design, and sales of the resulting "Walker Colt" enabled Colt to set up a factory in Hartford, Connecticut.

In 1851 the company was the first American manufacturer to open a plant in England. Four years later Patent Arms Manufacturing was renamed Colt's Patent Fire Arms Manufacturing Co. Colt was a millionaire when he died in 1862 at age 47.

Colt's introduced the six-shot Colt .45 Army Model, "the gun that won the West," in 1873. More products followed, including machine guns and automatic pistols designed by inventor John Browning. Colt's widow sold the firm to an investor group in 1901.

Business boomed during both World Wars, but by the 1940s labor strife and outmoded equipment began to take a toll, and Colt's lost money during the last years of WWII. In 1955 the struggling firm was acquired by conglomerate Penn-Texas. In 1959 Colt's patented the M-16 rifle; in 10 years it sold a million units to the US military. During the Vietnam War the company flourished, but the 1980s brought low-end competition and shrinking defense orders. Colt's sales were

hurt when the US government replaced the Colt .45 as the standard-issue sidearm for the armed forces. A three-year strike prompted the Army to shift its M-16 contract to Belgium's FN Herstal in 1988.

Two years later Colt's was acquired by private investors and a Connecticut state pension fund and was renamed Colt's Manufacturing. Sales remained flat, however, forcing the company to seek bankruptcy protection in 1992. There Colt's remained until New York investment firm Zilkha & Co. bailed it out in 1994, reorganizing the company. The new management made an offer for rival FN Herstal in 1997, but the deal was blocked by the Belgian government and fell through. Late that year the company won a contract to supply M-4 rifles to the Army.

Colt's bought military weapons specialist Saco Defense, maker of MK 19 and Striker grenade launchers, in 1998. Also that year Steven Sliwa succeeded retiring CEO Ronald Stewart.

As US cities began suing Colt's and other makers of firearms in attempts to recover safety and health expenses attributed to gun violence, the company stepped up lobbying in 1999 and said it would increase gun safety efforts, including development of its "smart gun" technology.

A restructuring in 1999 ended most of Colt's consumer handgun business. It also spun off its smart gun technology as a separate company, iColt. Sliwa left to head iColt, and retired US Marine Lieutenant General William Keys was named president and CEO of Colt's. Also in 1999 Colt's bought Ultra-Light Arms, a maker of upscale hunting rifles, and said it would buy Heckler & Koch, a small arms manufacturer based in Germany. By 2000 the company had withdrawn iColt (investors didn't seem interested in a lawsuit laden industry) and stepped away from the Heckler & Koch deal. The company continues to focus on weapons for the military and police, but in 2001 it lost out to CAPCO Inc. in a bid for a contract to upgrade M-16 rifles used by the Air Force.

Chairman: Donald Zilkha
President and CEO: William M. Keys
Human Resources Manager: Mike Magouirk

HQ: Colt's Manufacturing Company, Inc.
545 New Park Ave., West Hartford, CT 06110
Phone: 860-236-6311   Fax: 860-244-1442
Web: www.colt.com

Selected Products and Brands
Commercial rifles
  Colt accurized rifles
  Match target rifles
Law enforcement
  AR15
  Carbine
  Colt accurized rifles
  Commando
  M-16
  M203 Grenade Launchers
  M-4 Carbine
  Match target rifles
  Submachine guns
Performance products
  Colt XS Series
  Gold Cup Trophy
  Special Combat Government Competition
Personal protection
  Colt Defender
  M1991A1
Western
  Colt Cowboy
  Model Ps

Action Arms
BAE SYSTEMS
Beretta
Browning
Crosman
FN Manufacturing
Glock
Magnum Research
Mauser-Werke
Navegar
Remington Arms
Ruger
Saf T Lok
SIG
Smith & Wesson Holding
Springfield Inc.
U.S. Repeating Arms

Private FYE: December 31	Annual Growth	12/91	12/92	12/93	12/94	12/95	12/96	12/97	12/98	12/99	12/00
Estimated sales ($ mil.)	2.8%	—	—	—	—	—	—	92	96	100	100
Employees	0.0%	—	—	—	—	—	—	700	700	700	700

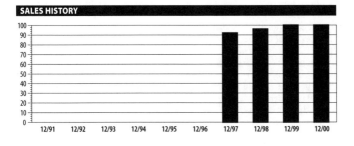

COLUMBIA UNIVERSITY

Predating the American Revolution, Columbia University (founded as King's College in 1754) is the fifth-oldest institution of higher learning in the US. With a student population of almost 23,000 students and a campus spread across 36 acres in Manhattan, Columbia's 16 schools and colleges grant undergraduate and graduate degrees in about 100 disciplines, including its well-known programs in journalism, law, and medicine. The Ivy League university's 7,700-member faculty has included 64 Nobel laureates and former Vice President Al Gore. Columbia also has a strong reputation for research and ranks #1 among universities earning funds through patents and royalties.

Columbia has forged affiliations with nearby institutions such as Barnard College, Teachers College, and Union Theological Seminary. The Columbia-Presbyterian Medical Center, the result of more than 70 years of partnership between Columbia and The Presbyterian Hospital, helped pioneer the concept of academic medical centers.

Columbia's list of alumni includes such luminaries as Yankee great Lou Gehrig, Supreme Court Justice Ruth Bader Ginsberg, and President Franklin Roosevelt. Columbia has gone to its alumni well (and others sources) often over the past 10 years, collecting a record $4.3 billion in fund-raising.

HISTORY

Created by royal charter of King George II of England, the university was founded in 1754 as King's College. Its first class of eight students met in a schoolhouse adjacent to Trinity Church (in what is now Manhattan). Some of the university's earliest students included Alexander Hamilton and John Jay. King's College was renamed Columbia College in 1784, a name that symbolized the patriotic mind-set of the age.

The college moved to 49th Street and Madison Avenue in 1849. The School of Law was founded in 1858, followed by the predecessor to the School of Engineering and Applied Science in 1864. The Graduate School of Arts and Sciences was established in 1880, and Columbia became affiliated with Barnard College in 1889.

Columbia College became Columbia University in 1896, and the following year it moved to its present location, the former site of the Bloomingdale Insane Asylum. (Columbia retained its original site, on which Rockefeller Center was built, until selling it in 1985.) Columbia continued to expand during the early 20th century. It added the School of Journalism in 1912 with funding from publishing magnate Joseph Pulitzer. Other additions included the

School of Business (1916), the School of Public Health (1921), and the School of International and Public Affairs (1946).

Dwight Eisenhower became president of Columbia in 1948, retaining the position until becoming President of the United States in 1953. During the late 1960s Columbia gained a reputation for student political action, and in 1968 students closed down the university for several days in protest of the Vietnam War.

Facing financial woes, an escalating New York City crime rate, and contention among its faculty, Columbia struggled to maintain its reputation during the 1970s and 1980s. With this challenge as a backdrop, the university continued to evolve, welcoming its first co-ed freshman class in 1983.

Still facing economic pressures and reductions in government research spending, Columbia was forced to cut costs, eliminating its linguistics and geography departments in 1991. George Rupp became Columbia's president in 1993. Columbia took over operation of the controversial Biosphere 2 laboratory in Arizona in 1996 (the university had been associated with the lab since 1994, when it formed a consortium with other universities to overhaul the ailing science experiment).

By the late 1990s Columbia had begun to recover from its financial and academic decline. Under the leadership of president Rupp, the university improved its fund-raising efforts and became more selective in student admissions. Microsoft founder Bill Gates donated $150 million to Columbia's School of Public Health in 1999 for research into the prevention of death and disability from childbirth in developing countries. That year Columbia created Morningside Ventures, a for-profit company focused on producing educational materials.

The university partnered with the British Library, Cambridge University Press, the London School of Economics, the New York Public Library, and the Smithsonian to form Fathom.com in 2000, another for-profit venture that provides online access to various scholarly resources from each institution. The next year the National Science Foundation awarded Columbia a $90,000 grant to gather personal accounts and create an oral history piece on the World Trade Center attacks of September 11. In 2002 Columbia received a pledge of $8 million from Bernard Spitzer for stem cell research to develop new treatments for Parkinson's disease and other neurological disorders.

OFFICERS

Chairman: David J. Stern, age 58
President: Lee C. Bollinger
Provost and Dean of Faculties: Jonathan R. Cole
Executive Vice Provost: Michael M. Crow
EVP Administration: Emily Lloyd
EVP Finance: John Masten
VP and Dean of Arts and Sciences: David Cohen
VP Human Resources: Colleen M. Crooker
Secretary: R. Keith Walton
Treasurer and Controller: Patricia L. Francy
Vice Provost for Academic Administration:
Stephen Rittenberg
Auditors: Deloitte & Touche LLP

LOCATIONS

HQ: 2690 Broadway, New York, NY 10027
Phone: 212-854-1754   **Fax:** 212-749-0397
Web: www.columbia.edu

Columbia University in the City of New York is located
in the Morningside Heights section of Manhattan.

PRODUCTS/OPERATIONS

Selected Schools, Colleges, and Programs
Continuing Education
Graduate and Professional Schools
 College of Physicians and Surgeons
  Human Nutrition
  Occupational Therapy
  Physical Therapy
 The Fu Foundation School of Engineering & Applied
  Science
 Mailman School of Public Health
 School of Architecture, Planning & Preservation
 School of the Arts
 School of Arts and Sciences
 School of Business
  Executive Education Program
  Executive MBA Program
 School of Dental & Oral Surgery
 School of International and Public Affairs
 School of Journalism
 School of Law
 School of Nursing
 School of Social Work
Undergraduate Schools
 Columbia College
 The Fu Foundation School of Engineering and Applied
  Science
 School of General Studies

HISTORICAL FINANCIALS & EMPLOYEES

School FYE: June 30	Annual Growth	6/92	6/93	6/94	6/95	6/96	6/97	6/98	6/99	6/00	6/01
Sales ($ mil.)	6.6%	953	1,032	1,103	1,160	1,234	1,339	1,448	1,574	1,789	1,700
Employees	(9.9%)	—	—	14,639	16,565	16,300	17,930	15,300	—	—	7,072

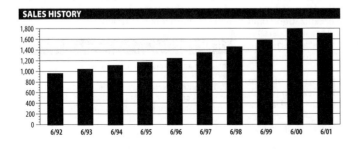

SALES HISTORY

CONSUMERS UNION

Consumers Union of United States (CU) inspires both trust and fear. Best known for publishing *Consumer Reports* magazine (4 million subscribers), the not-for-profit organization also serves as a consumer watchdog through newsletters, books, TV and radio programming, and the *Consumer Reports for Kids Online* site. Its subscriber Web site (1 million paid subscribers) rates products ranging from candy bars to cars. The company tests and rates thousands of products annually. Its Consumer Policy Institute conducts research and education projects on issues such as air pollution, biotechnology, food safety, and right-to-know laws.

It maintains 50 laboratories within its National Testing and Research Center in Yonkers, New York. In addition to conducting its own product testing, CU gathers product information by surveying the readers of its publications.

CU derives revenue from sales of its publications, from car and insurance pricing services, and from contributions, grants, and fees. It also has an online licensing deal with Yahoo!

The organization testifies before legislative and regulatory entities and files lawsuits on behalf of consumers. CU is governed by an 18-member board. To preserve its independence, CU accepts no advertising and does not permit its ratings or comments to be used commercially.

HISTORY

In 1926 engineer Frederick Schlink organized a "consumer club" (in White Plains, New York), which distributed lists of recommended and non-recommended products. The lists led to the founding of Consumers' Research and a magazine devoted to testing products.

Schlink moved the group to Washington, New Jersey, in 1933. In 1935 three employees formed a union. Schlink fired them. Faced with another strike that year, Schlink accused the strikers of being "Red" and responded with strikebreakers and armed detectives. The next year the strikers set up their own organization, the Consumers Union of United States (CU).

CU's first magazine, *Consumers Union Reports*, came out three months later and rated products that the fledgling organization could afford to test, such as soap and breakfast cereals. Subsequent issues focused on food and drug regulation and working conditions for women in textile mills.

The organization drew the wrath of both *Reader's Digest* and *Good Housekeeping* (which accused it in 1939 of prolonging the Depression). The next year the House Un-American Activities Committee put CU on its list of suspect organizations. CU cut staff and dropped "Union" from its magazine title, but circulation remained low until after WWII.

By 1950, however, Americans began consuming again, helping to boost circulation to almost 400,000. During the 1950s CU published a series of reports on the health hazards of smoking.

In 1960 CU helped found the International Organization of Consumers Unions (now Consumers International) to foster the consumer movement worldwide. Rhoda Karpatkin was hired as publisher in 1974. During the 1970s CU established consumer advocacy offices in California, Texas, and Washington, DC.

Recession and an increase in not-for-profit mailing rates caused the organization to lose money in the early 1980s. CU looked to its readers, who donated more than $3 million. The organization was hit by a 13-week strike in 1984 by union members calling for more say in management decisions.

In 1996 CU slapped "not acceptable" ratings on the Isuzu Trooper and the Acura SLX. The next year the National Highway Traffic Safety Administration declared that CU's testing procedure of the Trooper was flawed, but CU stood by its tests of the vehicle.

CU hit another bump in 1998 when it was compelled to retract a story on the nutritional value of Iams and Eukanuba pet food. Admitting its test results were incorrect, CU's retraction of the story was something of a rarity — its last retraction had occurred almost 20 years earlier when the organization retracted a story on condoms.

In 1999 the company defended itself in court against allegations by Isuzu and Suzuki that their companies were defamed through negative reviews by Consumer Reports. The following year a jury found CU guilty of falsely reporting on the Isuzu but declined to impose fines on the publisher. Also in 2000 a district court upheld the dismissal of Suzuki's suit against CU (based on CU's 1988 rating of the Suzuki Samurai as "not acceptable" due to rollover risks); Suzuki is appealing.

Karpatkin stepped down as president in 2001; James Guest, CU's chairman since 1980, took over. Later that year CU agreed to license its content to Internet portal Yahoo!

OFFICERS

Chairman and President: James Guest
CFO: Conrad Harris
VP, Technical Director: David Pittle
Director, Consumer Policy Institute: Jean Halloran
Director, Washington, DC Office: Gene Kimmelman
Director, Southwest Regional Office: Reggie James

Media Director, Washington, DC Office: David Butler
Project Director, Eco-labeling Project: Urvashi Rangan
Research Associate, Consumer Policy Institute:
Michael K. Hansen
Human Resources: Rick Lustig
Auditors: KPMG LLP

LOCATIONS

HQ: Consumers Union of United States, Inc.
101 Truman Ave., Yonkers, NY 10703
Phone: 914-378-2000   **Fax:** 914-378-2900
Web: www.consumersunion.org

Consumers Union of United States performs most
product tests at a renovated warehouse in Yonkers, New
York. It tests cars and trucks in East Haddam,
Connecticut, and has consumer advocacy offices in
Austin, Texas; San Francisco; and Washington, DC.

PRODUCTS/OPERATIONS

Selected Products and Services

Auto Services
CR New Car Price Service
CR Used Car Price Service

Books and Buying Guides
Auto Books
  New Car Buying Guide 2002
  New Car Preview 2002
  Used Car Buying Guide 2002
  Used Car Yearbook
House and Home
  Best Buys for Your Home 2002
  Buying Guide 2002
  Home Computer Buying Guide 2002
Money
  Consumer Reports Money Book
  How to Plan for a Secure Retirement
Personal and Leisure
  Consumer Drug Reference 2002
  Guide to Baby Products
  Guide to Health Care for Seniors
  Home Computer Buying Guide 2002
  Travel Well for Less 2002

Educational Videos
  The 30-Second Seduction
  America At Risk: A History Of Consumer Protest
  Buy Me That! A Kid's Survival Guide To TV Advertising
  *Buy Me That Too! A Kid's Survival Guide To TV
    Advertising*
  Buy Me That 3! A Kid's Guide To Food Advertising
  Earth To Kids: A Guide to Parents for a Healthy Planet
  *Kids and Lead Hazards: What Every Family Should
    Know*
  Smoke Alarm: The Unfiltered Truth About Cigarettes
  Staying Alive: A Consumer Reports Car Safety Special
  To Care: A Portrait of Three Older Caregivers
  Warning: Dieting May Be Hazardous To Your Health
  Zillions TV: A Kid's Guide to the Best Toys and Games

Magazines and Newsletters
  Consumer Reports Magazine
  Consumer Reports on Health
  Consumer Reports Travel Letter

TV and Radio
  Consumer Reports TV News
  Report to Consumers (radio feature)

Web Sites
  ConsumerReports.org
  Consumer Reports for Kids Online (zillions.org)

COMPETITORS

Consumers' Research
Epinions
Hearst
International Data Group
J.D. Power
National Technical Systems
PRIMEDIA
Reader's Digest
Reed Elsevier Group
Underwriters Labs

HISTORICAL FINANCIALS & EMPLOYEES

Not-for-profit FYE: May 31	Annual Growth	5/91	5/92	5/93	5/94	5/95	5/96	5/97	5/98	5/99	5/00
Sales ($ mil.)	2.1%	—	—	—	124	129	136	135	140	140	140
Employees	(0.0%)	—	—	—	451	453	451	461	475	482	450

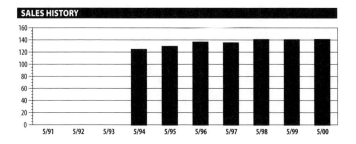

SALES HISTORY

CONTIGROUP COMPANIES, INC.

It's farther up the food chain now, but ContiGroup Companies (CGC, formerly Continental Grain) is still a big name in agribusiness. CGC has exited the grain export business and now operates through ContiBeef (the #2 cattle feedlot operator, behind Cactus Feeders), Premium Standard Farms (#2 US fresh pork producer, after Smithfield Foods), and Wayne Farms, a major poultry processor. Overseas the company has interests in feed milling, aquaculture, shipping, and energy trading. Chairman Paul Fribourg (the founder's great-great-great-grandson) and his family own CGC.

In China, the Caribbean, and Latin America, CGC has interests in flour milling, animal feed, poultry processing, and aquaculture. In the Far East, ContiChem-LPG handles about 12% of the world's trade in liquid petroleum gas (LPG) and charters shipping. CGC's investment arm, ContiInvestments, maintains interest in real estate and other investments.

Despite its size and scope, the company remains genteelly private about its business.

HISTORY

Simon Fribourg founded a commodity trading business in Belgium in 1813. It operated domestically until 1848, when a drought in Belgium caused it to buy large stocks in Russian wheat.

As the Industrial Revolution swept across Europe and populations shifted to cities, people consumed more traded grain. In the midst of such rapid changes, the company prospered. After WWI, Russia, which had been Europe's primary grain supplier, ceased to be a major player in the trading game, and Western countries picked up the slack. Sensing the shift, Jules and Rene Fribourg reorganized the business as Continental Grain and opened its first US office in Chicago in 1921.

Throughout the Depression the company bought US grain elevators, often at low prices. Through its purchases, Continental Grain built a North American grain network that included major locations like Kansas City, Missouri; Nashville, Tennessee; and Toledo, Ohio.

In Europe, meanwhile, the Fribourgs were forced to endure constant political and economic upheaval, often profiting from it (they supplied food to Republican forces during the Spanish Civil War). When Nazis invaded Belgium in 1940, the Fribourgs were forced to flee, but they reorganized the business in New York City after the war.

Following the war, Continental Grain pioneered US grain trade with the Soviets. The company went on a buying spree in the 1960s and 1970s, acquiring Allied Mills (feed milling, 1965)

and absorbing many agricultural and transport businesses, including Texas feedlots, a bakery, and the Quaker Oats agricultural products unit.

During the 1980s Continental Grain sold its baking units (Oroweat and Arnold) and its commodities brokerage house. Amid an agricultural bust, it formed ContiFinancial and other financial units.

Michel Fribourg the founder's great-great-grandson, stepped down as CEO in 1988 and was succeeded by Donald Staheli, the first nonfamily-member CEO. The company entered a grain-handling and selling joint venture with Scoular in 1991. Three years later Staheli added the title of chairman, and Michel's son Paul became president. Continental Grain sold a stake in ContiFinancial (home equity loans and investment banking) to the public in 1996. Also in 1996 the firm formed ContiInvestments, an investment arm geared toward the parent company's areas of expertise.

That year Continental Grain and an overseas affiliate (Arab Finagrain) agreed to pay the US government $35 million, which included a $10 million fine against Arab Finagrain, to settle a fraud case involving commodity sales to Iraq.

Paul succeeded Staheli as CEO in 1997. The company bought Campbell Soup's poultry processing units that year, and in 1998 it bought a 51% stake in pork producer/processor Premium Standard Farms. Meanwhile, ContiFinancial diversified into retail home mortgage and home equity lending. Continental Grain sold its commodities marketing business in July 1999 to #1 grain exporter Cargill. With its grain operations gone, in 1999 the company renamed itself ContiGroup Companies.

During 2000 ContiFinancial declared bankruptcy, and ContiGroup sold its Animal Nutrition Division (Wayne Foods) to feed manufacturer Ridley Inc for $37 million. In mid-2000, Premium Standard Farms doubled its processing capacity with the purchase of Lundy Packing Company. Chairman emeritus Michel Fribourg died in 2001. That same year ContiSea, the salmon and seafood processing joint venture between ContiGroup and Seaboard, was sold to Norway's Fjord Seafood, giving ContiGroup a significant share of Fjord.

OFFICERS

Chairman, President, and CEO: Paul J. Fribourg
EVP and COO: Vart K. Adjemian
EVP, Investments and Strategy and CFO; President, ContiInvestments: Michael J. Zimmerman, age 51
EVP, Human Resources and Information Systems: Teresa E. McCaslin
CEO, ContiBeef: John Rakestraw
CEO, Premium Standard Farms: John M. Meyer
CEO, Wayne Farms: Elton Maddox
SVP and Managing Director, Asian Industries Division: Michael A. Hoer
VP and General Manager, ContiLatin: Brian Anderson

LOCATIONS

HQ: 277 Park Ave., New York, NY 10172
Phone: 212-207-5100   **Fax:** 212-207-2910
Web: www.contigroup.com

ContiGroup Companies operates in the Caribbean, China, Latin America, and the US.

PRODUCTS/OPERATIONS

Major Business Units

Asian Industries
Feed milling (China)
Pork production (China)
Poultry production (China)

ContiBeef, LLC
Cattle feedlots

ContiInvestments, LLC
Investment management

ContiLatin
Feed and flour milling
Poultry operations
Salmon farming
Seafood processing
Shrimp farming

Premium Standard Farms (51%)
Pork production

Wayne Farms, LLC
Poultry production

COMPETITORS

Cactus Feeders
Cargill
Cenex Harvest States
ConAgra
Farmland Industries
Smithfield Foods
Tyson Foods

HISTORICAL FINANCIALS & EMPLOYEES

Private FYE: March 31	Annual Growth	3/93	3/94	3/95	3/96	3/97	3/98	3/99	3/00	3/01	3/02
Estimated sales ($ mil.)	(15.5%)	15,000	15,000	14,000	15,000	16,000	15,000	10,500	10,000	4,000	3,300
Employees	(0.2%)	14,700	15,500	16,000	16,000	16,800	17,500	14,000	13,500	14,500	14,500

SALES HISTORY

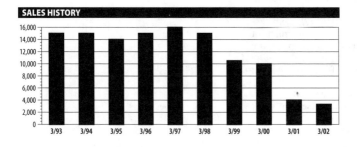

CONVERSE INC.

As Converse has shown, even teams full of All Stars can find themselves in a slump. The North Reading, Massachusetts-based maker of athletic and leisure footwear — including the classic Chuck Taylor All Star canvas basketball sneaker — has struggled with an industrywide downturn in demand for traditional athletic shoes. Converse is now trying to rebound. It has sold nearly 575 million pairs of its Chuck Taylor sneaker, which has appealed to everyone from school kids to clothing designers. Converse also licenses sports apparel from head to toe. Its products are sold in 110 countries through about 5,500 sporting goods, department, and shoe stores.

Following years of declining sales, the company filed for Chapter 11 bankruptcy protection in 2001. Footwear Acquisition soon bought the company and has mapped a strategy (including new lines of high performance and designer athletic footwear) it hopes will revitalize the firm. It closed the company's remaining US and Mexican plants and turned over all production to Far East and Indonesian manufacturers.

HISTORY

With a capital investment of $250,000, in 1908 Marquis Converse established the Converse Rubber Co. in Malden, Massachusetts, with 15 employees. The company got its big break shortly after its Converse canvas All Star shoe was launched in 1917. The shoe was chosen by young basketball star Chuck Taylor as his favorite basketball sneaker. Taylor joined the Converse sales team in 1921 and — in one of the first examples of sports endorsement — peddled the shoes at basketball clinics he hosted at schools and colleges. In 1923 Taylor's signature was added to the brand.

Converse fell into bankruptcy in 1929 and was acquired by Hodgman Rubber. The Depression and reduced profits led to another takeover in 1933, when the Stone family of Boston began its lucrative 39-year period of ownership. WWII provided a boost to the firm as it supplied the US military with protective footwear, parkas and other equipment.

The company expanded after WWII, establishing plants in New Hampshire (1946) and a subsidiary in Puerto Rico (1953). It then acquired Tyler Rubber Co. (1961) and the Hodgman line of sporting goods (1964). Taylor retired from Converse in 1968.

In 1972 Converse was acquired by Eltra, which made electrical and typesetting equipment. Within a year Converse expanded with the purchase of B.F. Goodrich's footwear division.

Eltra was acquired by conglomerate Allied Corp. in 1979. Converse executives led a buyout of the division in 1982 before taking it public in 1983. The rise of the retro look in fashion starting in the mid-1980s made the old Chuck Taylor sneaker hot with models, film stars, and the fashion-conscious.

INTERCO (furniture, footwear, and apparel) bought Converse in 1986. After a costly defense in an 1988 hostile takeover attempt by the Rales brothers of Washington, DC, INTERCO filed for bankruptcy in 1991 — then one of the largest such cases in US history.

As part of INTERCO's reorganization, Converse in 1994 was a public company controlled by financial adviser Leon Black. The next year it dumped its outdoor, running, walking, tennis and football lines. Converse, hurt particularly by weak sales of basketball sneakers and restructuring charges, posted losses and saw revenue fall in 1995 and 1996.

Sporting goods veteran Glenn Rupp was hired as chairman and CEO in 1996. Converse had record sales in 1997, but still finished in the red, due in part to a slowdown in retail demand in the last half of the year. The company laid off 5% of its workforce in 1998 and another 20% in 1999.

In 2000 Converse slipped close to NYSE delisting due to low stock price and market cap. The company filed for Chapter 11 bankruptcy protection in January 2001.

A firm backed by Chairman Marsden Cason and private investor William Simon stepped in that spring, however, and bought the rights to the names and property of Converse. Former Converse employee Jack Boys was named CEO. The company closed its factories in North America (two in the US and one in Mexico) and sent all production to its suppliers in the Far East and Indonesia. Menswear designer John Varvatos signed an agreement in late 2001 to design a series of Chuck Taylor All Star and Jack Purcell products for fall 2002.

Co-Chairman: Marsden Cason
Co-Chairman: William Simon
CEO: Jack Boys
VP Distribution: Lloyd Wallsten
VP Finance: Lisa Kempa
VP Legal: Laura Kelley
VP Licensing: Tim Ouellette
VP Marketing and Product Development:
  David Maddocks
VP Sales: Jim Stroesser
Managing Director, Far East Operations: Jerry Lan
Director of Information Technology: Ellen Garvey
Human Resources Manager: Susan Rogato
Auditors: PricewaterhouseCoopers LLP

LOCATIONS

HQ: One Fordham Rd., North Reading, MA 01864
Phone: 978-664-1100   Fax: 978-664-7472
Web: www.converse.com

Converse distributes its products in 110 countries
through 5,500 athletic specialty, sporting goods,
department, and shoe stores.

COMPETITORS

adidas-Salomon
ASICS
Deckers Outdoor
Fila
K-Swiss
New Balance
NIKE
PUMA
R. Griggs
Reebok
Saucony
Skechers U.S.A.
Stride Rite
Timberland
Vans

HISTORICAL FINANCIALS & EMPLOYEES

Private FYE: December 31	Annual Growth	12/92	12/93	12/94	12/95	12/96	12/97	12/98	12/99	12/00	12/01
Sales ($ mil.)	(6.7%)	316	380	437	408	349	450	308	232	209	170
Net income ($ mil.)	—	(11)	12	18	(72)	(18)	(5)	(23)	(44)	(27)	51
Income as % of sales	—	—	3.2%	4.0%	—	—	—	—	—	—	30.3%
Employees	(26.4%)	—	3,042	3,053	2,459	2,249	2,956	2,658	2,024	1,510	261

NET INCOME HISTORY

2001 FISCAL YEAR-END

Debt ratio: 0.0%
Return on equity: —
Cash ($ mil.): 7
Current ratio: 2.81
Long-term debt ($ mil.): 0

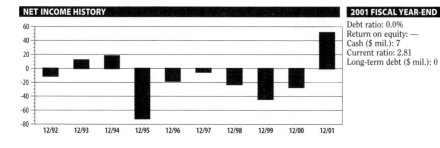

CPB

This organization is made possible by a grant from the federal government and by support from viewers like you. The Washington, DC-based Corporation for Public Broadcasting (CPB) is an independent, not-for-profit government organization (not a government agency) that receives appropriations from Congress to help fund programming for more than 1,000 member-owned stations of the Public Broadcasting Service, National Public Radio, Public Radio International, and other organizations. The organization's funding is often a political hot potato (often a target of Republicans who are opposed to government funding of educational, informational, and cultural programming).

Funding has been approved through 2003, despite a 1999 investigation that revealed some PBS stations had given their mailing lists to the Democratic party for fundraising purposes. CPB's funding was approved at $350 million for 2002 and $365 million for 2003.

HISTORY

As commercial radio began to fill the radio dial, the FCC in 1945 reserved 20 channels from 88 FM to 92 FM for noncommercial, educational broadcasts. The FCC reserved television channels for similar purposes in 1952, and the first public television station started broadcasting in Houston in 1953. In 1962 the Federal government began funding public broadcasting through passage of the Education Television Facilities Act. By 1965 there were 124 public TV stations across the country. To help allocate government funds to these public TV and radio stations, Congress created the Corporation for Public Broadcasting (CPB) in 1967.

CPB was officially formed in 1968. That same year one of public television's most popular programs, *Mister Rogers' Neighborhood*, debuted. *Sesame Street* debuted the following year. Also in 1969 CPB formed the Public Broadcasting Service (PBS) to handle its television operations. PBS began distributing television programming five nights a week that year.

CPB formed National Public Radio (NPR) in 1970, with 90 public radio member stations. A year later NPR debuted its long-running news program *All Things Considered*. PBS's popular nightly news program, the *Robert MacNeil Report* (later the *MacNeil/Lehrer NewsHour*) made its debut in 1975. PBS began distributing its programming by satellite in 1978. In 1980 NPR also began distributing programming via satellite. That same year author Garrison Keillor's *A Prairie Home Companion* debuted on public radio.

In 1981 Walter Annenberg, a publisher who made his fortune with *TV Guide* and the *Daily Racing Form*, teamed with CPB to create the Annenberg/CPB Project to provide educational videos and other materials to public schools. PBS began to look to "event programming" as a way to attract more viewers with big hits including *Eyes on the Prize* (1987) and Ken Burns' *Civil War* documentary (1990).

CPB has always been politically controversial; critics have often charged it with elitism, cultural bias, and liberalism. When Republicans gained control of Congress in 1994, their laundry list of grievances included government cultural spending. They were foiled in their effort to eliminate funding for CPB, however, in part because of public support for public television. Congress still cut funding by $100 million, forcing CPB to reduce its staff by almost 25% and introduce performance criteria for stations seeking grant money, including listenership and community financial support minimums.

To help make up the loss in funding, in 1995 the CPB introduced its Future Funds program, which provides financial incentives to television and radio stations that find innovative ways to raise money or to streamline their operations. Those ideas are then passed on to other member stations.

In 1996 the Annenberg/CPB Project launched a satellite TV channel providing schools, public libraries, and other community agencies with teacher development and instructional programming free of charge.

Robert Coonrod was promoted to CEO in 1997. The following year Congress approved additional funding to help public television's transition from analog to digital broadcasting. Frank Cruz was appointed chairman of CPB in 1999. In 2000 the Annenberg/CPB channel expanded to 24 hour-a-day, seven day-a-week programming.

Increased funding for 2003 (funding is approved two years in advance) was threatened when it was discovered that some PBS stations were giving their mailing lists to the Democratic party for fundraising purposes. Nevertheless, funding for CPB was increased in the 2001 budget. In late 2001 businesswoman Katherine Milner Anderson was voted in as chairman, taking over for Cruz. (Cruz remained on the board.)

HISTORICAL FINANCIALS & EMPLOYEES

Not-for-profit FYE: September 30	Annual Growth	9/92	9/93	9/94	9/95	9/96	9/97	9/98	9/99	9/00	9/01
Sales ($ mil.)	1.7%	341	339	275	286	296	282	285	283	383	398
Employees	1.0%	101	900	100	95	85	90	90	90	100	110

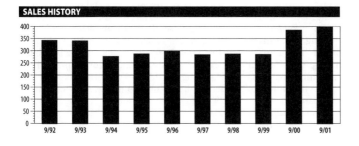

SALES HISTORY

COX ENTERPRISES, INC.

The Cox family has been working at this enterprise for more than 100 years. One of the largest media conglomerates in the US, family-owned Cox Enterprises publishes 17 daily newspapers (including *The Atlanta Journal-Constitution*) and about 30 weeklies and shoppers and owns 15 TV stations through Cox Television. It also owns about 62% of Cox Radio (more than 80 radio stations) and controls 76% of Cox Communications, one of the US's largest cable systems with more than 6 million subscribers in 23 states. Cox's Manheim Auctions runs 115 automobile auctions worldwide and owns a majority-stake in AutoTrader.com. Cox Interactive Media operates about 20 city-specific Web sites.

While Cox Communications is the company's biggest revenue generator, Cox Enterprises has been spending a lot of money and time, like many other media conglomerates, on the Internet. AutoTrader.com is one of the few profitable Internet companies. Manheim is the world's largest used-car auctioneer, with about 115 automobile auctions worldwide, and the combination of the businesses has proved lucrative for Cox. Manheim spent $1 billion in acquiring ADT Automotive from Tyco International in 2000 and plans on spending another $1 billion over the next five years improving and expanding its operations.

However, Cox has also learned the hard lesson that numerous media companies have been taught as they try to be successful on the Internet. Cox scrapped a plan for an AutoTrader.com IPO in 2000 when the market soured. And in 2002 the company cut about 75 jobs from its Cox Interactive unit and dropped a plan to develop a nationwide network of local city Web sites.

Barbara Cox Anthony (mother of chairman and CEO James Kennedy) and Anne Cox Chambers, daughters of founder James Cox, own the company. The sisters were recently ranked in *Forbes'* list of the richest Americans.

HISTORY

James Middleton Cox, who dropped out of school in 1886 at 16, had worked as a teacher, reporter, and congressional secretary before buying the *Dayton Daily News* in 1898. After acquiring the nearby *Springfield Press-Republican* in 1905, he took up politics, serving two terms in the US Congress (1909-1913) and three terms as Ohio governor (1913-1915; 1917-1921). He even ran for president in 1920 (his running mate was future President Franklin Roosevelt) but lost to rival Ohio publisher Warren G. Harding.

Once out of politics, Cox began building his media empire. He bought the *Miami Daily News*

in 1923 and founded WHIO (Dayton, Ohio's first radio station). He bought Atlanta's WSB ("Welcome South, Brother"), the South's first radio station, in 1939 and added WSB-FM and WSB-TV, the South's first FM and TV stations, in 1948. Cox founded Dayton's first FM and TV stations (WHIO-FM and WHIO-TV) the next year, and *The Atlanta Constitution* joined his collection in 1950. Cox died in 1957.

The company continued to expand its broadcasting interests in the late 1950s and early 1960s. It was one of the first major broadcasting companies to expand into cable TV when it purchased a system in Lewistown, Pennsylvania, in 1962. The Cox family's broadcast properties were placed in publicly held Cox Broadcasting in 1964. Two years later its newspapers were placed into privately held Cox Enterprises, and the cable holdings became publicly held Cox Cable Communications. The broadcasting arm diversified, buying Manheim Services (auto auctions, 1968), Kansas City Automobile Auction (1969), and TeleRep (TV ad sales, 1972).

Cox Cable had 500,000 subscribers in nine states when it rejoined Cox Broadcasting in 1977. Cox Broadcasting was renamed Cox Communications in 1982, and the Cox family took the company private again in 1985, combining it with Cox Enterprises. James Kennedy, grandson of founder James Cox, became chairman and CEO in 1987.

Expansion was the keyword for Cox in the 1990s. The company merged its Manheim unit with the auto auction business of Ford Motor Credit and GE Capital in 1991. It also formed Sprint Spectrum, a partnership with Sprint, TCI (now part of AT&T), and Comcast in 1994 to bundle telephone, cable TV, and other communications services (Sprint bought out Cox in 1999). Then, in one of its biggest transactions, Cox bought Times Mirror's cable TV operations for $2.3 billion in 1995 and combined them with its own cable system into a new, publicly traded company called Cox Communications. The following year it spun off its radio holdings into a public company called Cox Radio.

To expand its online presence, the company formed Cox Interactive Media in 1996, establishing a series of city Web sites and making a host of investments in various Internet companies, including CareerPath, Excite@Home, iVillage, MP3.com, and Tickets.com. Cox also applied the online strategy to its automobile auction businesses, establishing AutoTrader.com in 1998 and placing the Internet operations of Manheim Auctions into a new company, Manheim Interactive, in 2000.

OFFICERS

Chairman and CEO: James Cox Kennedy, age 54
President and COO: G. Dennis Berry, age 58
EVP and CFO: Robert C. O'Leary, age 63
SVP Administration: Timothy W. Hughes
SVP Public Policy: Alexander V. Netchvolodoff, age 65
VP and CIO: Gregory B. Morrison, age 43
VP and General Tax Counsel: Preston B. Barnett
VP Human Resources: Marybeth H. Leamer, age 45
VP Legal Affairs and Secretary: Andrew A. Merdek
President and CEO, Cox Communications, Inc.:
James O. Robbins, age 59
President, Cox Newspapers Inc.: Jay R. Smith, age 52
President and CEO, Cox Radio: Robert F. Neil, age 43
President, Cox Television: Andrew S. Fisher, age 54

LOCATIONS

HQ: 6500 Peachtree Dunwoody Rd., Atlanta, GA 30328
Phone: 678-645-0000 **Fax:** 678-645-1079
Web: www.coxenterprises.com

PRODUCTS/OPERATIONS

2001 Sales

	$ mil.	% of total
Cable TV	4,071	47
Auctions	2,260	26
Newspapers	1,350	15
TV stations	617	7
Radio stations	395	5
Total	**8,693**	**100**

Selected Operations
Cox Communications (76%, cable system)
Cox Interactive Media (city sites)
Cox Newspapers
  Daily Newspapers
    The Atlanta Journal-Constitution
    Austin American-Statesman (Texas)
    Dayton Daily News (Ohio)
    The Daily Reflector (Greenville, NC)
    The Daily Sentinel (Nacogdoches, TX)
    Longview News-Journal (Texas)
    The Lufkin Daily News (Texas)
    Palm Beach Daily News (Florida)
    The Palm Beach Post (Florida)
    Springfield News Sun (Ohio)

Cox Custom Media
SP Newsprint (33%)
Trader Publishing (50%, classified advertising)
Valpack (direct mail advertisements)
Cox Radio (62%)
  Atlanta (WBTS-FM, WSB-AM, WSB-FM)
  Birmingham, AL (WBHJ-FM, WBHK-FM, WZZK-FM)
  Honolulu (KRTR-FM, KXME-FM)
  Houston (KLDE-FM)
  Jacksonville, FL (WAPE-FM, WFYV-FM, WKQL-FM)
  Long Island, NY (WBAB-FM, WBLI-FM)
  Miami (WEDR-FM, WHQT-FM)
  San Antonio (KCYY-FM, KISS-FM, KONO-FM)
  Tampa, FL (WDUV-FM, WWRM-FM)
  Tulsa, OK (KRAV-FM, KRMG-AM, KWEN-FM)
Cox Television
  TV stations
    KICU (San Francisco/San Jose, CA)
    KIRO (Seattle)
    KTVU (Oakland/San Francisco, CA)
    WAXN (Charlotte, NC)
    WFTV (Orlando, FL)
    WPXI (Pittsburgh)
    WRDQ (Orlando, FL)
    WSB-TV (Atlanta)
    WSOC (Charlotte, NC)
  Harrington, Righter & Parsons (sales)
  TeleRep (TV ad sales)
Manheim Auctions
  Manheim Interactive (online auto auctions)
    AutoTrader.com (majority owned, online auto sales)
Sports teams
  Atlanta Beat (women's professional soccer)
  San Diego Spirit (women's professional soccer)

COMPETITORS

Advance	Hearst	Time Warner
Publications	Knight Ridder	Cable
Belo	Media General	Tribune
Clear Channel	Morris Com-	Viacom
Comcast	munications	Walt Disney
Dow Jones	New York Times	Washington Post
E. W. Scripps	News Corp.	
Gannett	Ticketmaster	

HISTORICAL FINANCIALS & EMPLOYEES

Private FYE: December 31	Annual Growth	12/92	12/93	12/94	12/95	12/96	12/97	12/98	12/99	12/00	12/01
Sales ($ mil.)	14.9%	2,495	2,675	2,939	3,806	4,591	4,936	5,355	6,097	7,824	8,693
Employees	10.5%	30,865	31,000	37,000	38,000	43,000	50,000	55,500	61,000	74,000	76,000

SALES HISTORY

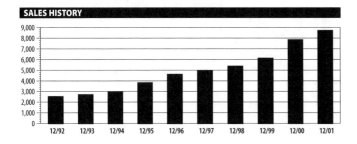

DAIRY FARMERS OF AMERICA

Dairy Farmers of America (DFA) are partners in cream and ready to curdle their competitors. DFA is now the world's largest dairy cooperative, with more than 25,000 members in 45 states. The co-op produces more than a quarter of the US milk supply with an annual pool of over 45 billion pounds of milk. Along with fresh and shelf-stable fluid milk, the co-op also produces cheese, butter, and other products for wholesale and retail customers worldwide. DFA is seeking strength in value-added products and joint ventures to distribute its milk and milk-based food ingredients to wider regions.

DFA is a major supplier to Dean Foods, holds the license to produce Borden cheeses, and bottles up Starbucks' Frappuccino coffee drink. In addition, the co-op provides marketing, research and development, and legislative lobbying on behalf of its members.

American dairy farmers have had to come to terms with consolidation in the retail industry, dissolving government milk price supports, and increased foreign competition. DFA itself was formed by the 1997 merger of four large regional co-ops. To better compete with other dairy processors, DFA has invested heavily in facilities and joint ventures to process its fluid milk into value-added products and high-end ingredients.

HISTORY

Mid-America Dairymen (Mid-Am), the largest of the cooperatives that merged to form Dairy Farmers of America (DFA), was born in 1968. At that time, several midwestern dairy co-ops banded together to attack common economic problems, such as reduced government subsidies, price drops resulting from a rising milk surplus, dealer consolidation, and improvements in production, processing, and packaging. The merging organizations — representing 15,000 dairy farmers — were Producers Creamery Company (Springfield, Missouri), Sanitary Milk Producers (St. Louis), Square Deal Milk Producers (Highland, Illinois), Mid-Am (Kansas City, Missouri), and Producers Creamery Company of Chillicothe (north central Missouri).

During the early 1970s Mid-Am struggled with internal restructuring. Most dairy farmers and co-ops were hit hard by the energy crisis and the government's decision to allow increased dairy imports in 1973, the same year the US Justice Department filed an antitrust suit against Mid-Am. (A judge cleared the co-op 12 years later.)

In 1974 Mid-Am lost almost $8 million on revenues of $625 million, chalked up to record-high feed prices, a weakened economy, a milk surplus, and a massive inventory loss. Co-op veteran Gary

Hanman was named CEO that year. Over the next two years, Mid-Am cut costs, sold corporate frills, downsized management, and began marketing more of its own products under the Mid-America Farms label, thus reducing dependency on commodity sales.

Mid-Am expanded its research and development efforts throughout the 1980s. The co-op opened its services to farmers in California and New Mexico in 1993, and a series of mergers in 1994 and 1995 nearly doubled its size. In 1997 it purchased some of Borden's dairy operations, including rights to the valuable Elsie the Cow and Borden's trademarks.

Wary of falling milk prices, Mid-Am merged with Western Dairymen Cooperative, Milk Marketing, and the Southern Region of Associated Milk Producers at the end of 1997 to form DFA. Hanman moved into the seat of CEO at the new co-op. DFA began a series of joint ventures with the #1 US dairy processor, Suiza Foods.

DFA added California Gold (more than 330 farmers, 1998) and Independent Cooperative Milk Producers Association (730 dairy farmer members in Michigan and parts of Ohio and Indiana, 1999). In another joint venture with Suiza, in early 2000 DFA sold its 50% stake in the US's #3 fluid milk processor, Southern Foods, in exchange for 34% of a new company named Suiza Dairy Group.

After mollifying the government's antitrust fears, DFA acquired the butter operations of Sodial North America in mid-2000. It then molded all its butter businesses into a new entity, Keller's Creamery, LLC.

During 2001 the cooperative went in with Land O'Lakes 50-50 to purchase a cheese plant from Kraft. Later in the year as Suiza Foods acquired Dean Foods (and took on its name), DFA sold back its stake in Suiza Dairy Group to the new Dean Foods. DFA then teamed up with a group of dairy investors to form a new 50-50 joint venture, National Dairy Holdings, which received 11 processing plants from Dean Foods as part of the exchange for Suiza Dairy.

OFFICERS

President and CEO: Gary E. Hanman
EVP: Don H. Schriver
CFO: Gerald Bos
Corporate VP, Human Resources & Administration: Harold Papen
Corporate VP, Legal Counsel: David A. Geisler
Corporate VP, Marketing and Economic Analysis: John J. Wilson
SVP; COO, Southwest Area, Mountain Area: David C. Jones
SVP, Finance: Rick J. Hoffman

SVP, Southeast Area, Mideast Area, and Central Area;
  COO, Southeast Area: John I. Collins
VP; COO, Mideast Area: James F. Carroll
VP; COO, Western Area: David L. Parrish
VP; COO, Central Area: Randall S. McGinnis
CEO, Dairylea; COO, Northeast Area: Rick Smith
President, Dairy Food Products: Sam E. McCroskey
Auditors: Deloitte & Touche LLP

LOCATIONS

HQ: 10220 N. Ambassador Dr., Kansas City, MO 64153
Phone: 816-801-6455   Fax: 816-801-6456
Web: www2.dfamilk.com

Dairy Farmers of America includes more than 25,000
members from 45 states.

PRODUCTS/OPERATIONS

Selected Products
Butter (Breakstone's, Hotel Bar, Keller's, Plugra)
Cheese dips
Cheeses (Borden)
Coffee creamer
Condensed milk
Cream
Dehydrated dairy products
Infant formula
Nonfat dry milk powder
Shelf-stable nutritional beverages (Sport Shake)
Whey products

COMPETITORS

AMPI
California Dairies Inc.
Dairylea
Dean Foods
Fonterra
Foremost Farms
Galaxy Nutritional Foods
Kraft Foods North America
Lactalis
Land O'Lakes
Leprino Foods
Northwest Dairy
Parmalat Finanziaria
Prairie Farms Dairy
Quality Chekd
Saputo
Schreiber Foods
Suprema Specialties
Unilever
WestFarm Foods

HISTORICAL FINANCIALS & EMPLOYEES

Cooperative FYE: December 31	Annual Growth	12/92	12/93	12/94	12/95	12/96	12/97	12/98	12/99	12/00	12/01
Sales ($ mil.)	17.4%	1,868	1,826	2,491	3,681	4,085	3,818	7,284	7,483	6,586	7,902
Net income ($ mil.)	39.9%	3	1	12	14	17	26	70	43	39	62
Income as % of sales	—	0.2%	0.1%	0.5%	0.4%	0.4%	0.7%	1.0%	0.6%	0.6%	0.8%
Employees	1.2%	3,600	3,500	3,000	3,100	3,200	5,300	5,300	5,000	4,000	4,000

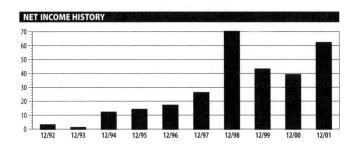

NET INCOME HISTORY

DART CONTAINER CORPORATION

Dart Container is a world cup winner — maybe not in soccer, but it is the world's top maker of foam cups and containers, with about half of the global market in cups. The company uses a secret method of molding expandable polystyrene to make its products, which include cups, lids, dinnerware, and cutlery for customers like hospitals, schools, and restaurants. To cut costs, Dart Container makes its own feedstocks, builds its own molding machinery, and operates its own distribution trucks. The firm sells its recycled polystyrene to companies that make such items as insulation material and egg cartons. Although often embroiled in litigation, the Dart family continues to own the company.

The king of cups has a simple strategy — secrecy. The cup-making machine developed by the Darts was never patented to avoid revealing how it works. Most of its factory workers have never seen the machines, and the firm's salespeople are not allowed inside the plants. After years of legal battles, the Darts have reached an agreement regarding alleged discrepancies in the family inheritance. The terms of the settlement are, naturally, secret.

In terms of Dart's products, the company is moving into foam lid and plastic containers for industrial or retail use.

The company runs four polystyrene-recycling plants and operates in the US and through subsidiaries in Argentina, Australia, Canada, Mexico, and the UK.

HISTORY

William F. Dart founded a Michigan firm to make steel tape measures in 1937. Dart's son William A. started experimenting with plastics in 1953, and in the late 1950s the two devised a cheap way to mold expandable polystyrene and built a cup-making machine. Dart Container was incorporated in Mason, Michigan, in 1960 and shipped its first cups that year. By the late 1960s the rising demand for plastic-foam products sparked an increase in R&D. In 1970 the company built a plant in Corona, California.

It was a family feud in the making in 1974, as William F. divided the business among his grandsons — Tom, Ken, and Robert — in separate trusts that named William A. trustee for all. Tom branched out in 1975 and founded oil and gas company Dart Energy, which was later absorbed into Dart Container. William F. died the next year. Following the oil market crash of the early 1980s, Tom went through a sticky divorce and admitted to cocaine abuse. His father temporarily removed him as head of Dart Energy in 1982,

and the next year the entire family underwent group psychiatric counseling.

The family reorganized its assets in 1986, giving Ken and Robert the cup business and Tom the energy business plus $58 million in cash. In 1987 Ken began to swell the family fortune with a series of successful investments. Better tax rates motivated Dart family members to move to Sarasota, Florida, in 1989. They set up shop in an unmarked building behind a sporting-goods store. By the late 1980s Dart Container commanded more than 50% of the worldwide market for foam cups.

In 1990 the company paid $250,000 to settle a factory worker's minority discrimination lawsuit. The next year Ken bought 11% of the Federal Home Loan Mortgage Corp. (Freddie Mac), as well as portions of Salomon and Brazil's foreign debt. According to Tom, that year Ken also financed brain research in hopes of finding a way to keep his brain alive after the death of his body in an attempt to avoid future estate taxes.

Tom sued his brothers and father in 1992 for allegedly cheating him out of millions in trust money in the 1986 reorganization. Ken turned a $300 million investment into $1 billion by selling the Freddie Mac shares. The next year he and Robert renounced their US citizenship to avoid paying taxes. Ken also made a failed attempt to block the restructuring of Brazil's debt (of which Dart owned 4%). That year Ken's new $1 million Sarasota home was firebombed (the case remains unsolved), and Robert moved to Britain, where he soon filed for divorce.

Ken began hiring bodyguards, and he moved his family to the Cayman Islands in 1994. Dart shelled out $230,000 to settle yet another discrimination case. In 1995 Tom was fired from Dart Energy, and Ken tried — and failed — to return to the US as a diplomat of Belize. In 1996 Tom accused Judge Donald Owens of being biased in favor of William A. The judge succumbed to the pressure in 1997 and removed himself from the proceedings, only to be ordered back on the case by Michigan's Court of Appeals. The lawsuit was settled in 1998 before going to trial, but the terms were kept secret.

The following year saw yet another series of lawsuits for the container company. In 1999 Dart Container filed an appeal to an IRS demand to pay $31 million in back taxes and late penalties. The legal wrangling continued through 2001, but in 2002 the company agreed to pay $26 million to settle the issue. Meanwhile, the company has expanded their foam lid and container products for wholesale industrial or retail use.

President: Kenneth B. Dart
VP: Robert C. Dart
CFO and Treasurer: William Myer
VP, Administration: Jim Lammers
Director, Human Resources: Mark Franks

LOCATIONS

HQ: 500 Hogsback Rd., Mason, MI 48854
Phone: 517-676-3800   Fax: 517-676-3883
Web: www.dartcontainer.com

Dart Container has four recycling centers in Canada and the US, and manufacturing operations in Argentina, Australia, Canada, Mexico, the UK, and the US.

PRODUCTS/OPERATIONS

Selected Products
Clear containers
Container lids
Deli containers and lids
Dinnerware
Foam cups
Hinged containers
Paper cups and lids
Plastic cups and lids
Plastic cutlery

Selected Services
CARE (Cups Are REcyclable) Program (provides
    densifier to larger customers to compact their
    polystyrene, which Dart then picks up)
Foam-Recycling (four plants in Canada, Florida,
    Michigan, and Pennsylvania and a drop-off site in
    Georgia)
Recycla-Pak (provides small-volume businesses with
    cup-shipping containers that double as recycling bins)

COMPETITORS

Berry Plastics
Huhtamäki
NOVA Chemicals
Radnor Holdings
sf holdings
Smurfit-Stone Container
Sonoco Products
Temple-Inland

HISTORICAL FINANCIALS & EMPLOYEES

Private FYE: December 31	Annual Growth	12/92	12/93	12/94	12/95	12/96	12/97	12/98	12/99	12/00	12/01
Estimated sales ($ mil.)	10.8%	475	600	800	1,000	1,000	1,000	1,150	1,100	1,200	1,200
Employees	5.8%	3,000	3,750	3,600	4,300	4,300	5,000	5,000	5,000	5,000	5,000

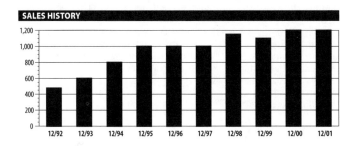

SALES HISTORY

THE DEBARTOLO CORPORATION

Real estate holdings, gambling, horse racing, a felony conviction, and warring siblings surrounded by a storied NFL franchise — sounds like an old episode of *Dallas*. But the story of The DeBartolo Corporation takes place in Youngstown, Ohio (where the company is based), via San Francisco (where the company owns the 49ers football team). The company also provides management services to the Louisiana Downs racetrack in Bossier City. The firm's other interests include a software firm in Tennessee and a few health care companies in Oklahoma and Pennsylvania. DeBartolo Corp. is also trying to bring an Arena Football League team to San Francisco.

The saga of the DeBartolo family concerns chairman and CEO Denise DeBartolo York and her brother, former CEO Eddie DeBartolo Jr., children of the company's founder. Eddie's guilty plea to charges of failing to report a felony led to his ouster and a lawsuit from his sister to recover a $94 million debt he owed the company. Eddie countersued, and after much wrangling, the siblings reached an agreement whereby Denise DeBartolo York took the company name, the 49ers, and the racetrack (which it then later sold but still operates), and Eddie DeBartolo received real estate and the firm's 11% of Simon Property Group (SPG), one of North America's largest public real estate companies.

HISTORY

Edward J. DeBartolo left his stepfather's paving business in 1944 and established the eponymous Edward J. DeBartolo Corporation. DeBartolo's foresight about the growth of the suburbs led him to build one of the first strip-style malls outside California, the Belmont Plaza near Youngstown, Ohio, in 1949. Over the next 15 years, the company built 45 more strip centers throughout the US. In the 1960s DeBartolo became one of the first to develop large, covered regional malls in many parts of the nation. DeBartolo opened the Louisiana Downs racetrack in 1974 and moved the company into the sports business in 1977 when he helped his son, Edward Jr. (Eddie), buy the San Francisco 49ers.

When the management of Allied Stores asked DeBartolo to help fend off a bid by real estate developer Robert Campeau, DeBartolo thought that control of Allied's department store chains would provide anchor stores for his mall developments and loaned Campeau $150 million for the takeover instead. Two years later DeBartolo borrowed $480 million and lent it to Campeau for his acquisition of Federated Department Stores.

The company reached its zenith in the late 1980s (opening the Rivercenter in San Antonio and Lakeland Square in Florida), but Campeau was in trouble — the highly leveraged Allied and Federated went bankrupt and threatened to take DeBartolo with them. As part of the bankruptcy settlement, DeBartolo took a 60% interest in California-based Ralphs supermarket (since sold) and started selling off assets in 1991 to cover the loan he made to Campeau and the company's own $4 billion debt. The fire sale included his private jet, three malls, two office buildings, a 50% stake in Higbee's department stores, and the Rivercenter.

Edward DeBartolo died in 1994. His daughter, Denise DeBartolo York, became chairman, and his son, Eddie (who was also chairman and CEO of the 49ers) became president and CEO. Eddie reshuffled the company's assets with most of its real estate holdings turned into DeBartolo Realty, a real estate investment trust that went public that year, raising $575 million. Mounting tensions between the siblings intensified in 1995 when Eddie formed DeBartolo Entertainment, his own separate company in the gaming business (Denise tried to distance the family business from Eddie's new company in a press release). DeBartolo Realty merged with Simon Property Group the following year.

Eddie ran into trouble in 1997 when an investigation revealed that he had paid former Louisiana governor Edwin Edwards $400,000 in an effort to obtain a riverboat gambling license for DeBartolo Entertainment. (Before the gambling fraud probe became public, San Francisco voters approved a $100 million bond issue to help finance a $525 million stadium/shopping mall for the 49ers. Those plans were put on ice.) Eddie pleaded guilty to felony charges of concealing wrongdoing the next year, was fined $2 million, and stepped down from DeBartolo Corp. (His later testimony against Louisiana Gov. Edwin Edwards helped lead to the government official's conviction on extortion charges.) The NFL then fined Eddie another $1 million and banned him from the 49ers in 1999. Later that year Denise sued Eddie for debt owed to the company, and he countersued. DeBartolo Corp. also sold two of its racetracks (Thistledown and Remington Park).

In 2001 the DeBartolos completed the division of the company's assets between them. DeBartolo York also shortened the company's name to The DeBartolo Corporation.

Chairman and CEO: Marie Denise DeBartolo York, age 51
EVP; VP, San Francisco 49ers: John C. York II
CFO: Tim Ciple
VP: Anthony Nasrallah
President and CEO, 49ers: Peter Harris
General Manager, 49ers: Terry Donahue, age 58
Head Coach, San Francisco 49ers: Steve Mariucci

LOCATIONS

HQ: 7620 Market St., Youngstown, OH 44512
Phone: 330-965-2000   **Fax:** 330-965-2077
Web: http://www.49ers.com

The DeBartolo Corporation has operations in California, Louisiana, Ohio, Oklahoma, Pennsylvania, and Tennessee.

COMPETITORS

Atlanta Falcons
Carolina Panthers
Fair Grounds
Harrah's Entertainment
New Orleans Saints
St. Louis Rams

HISTORICAL FINANCIALS & EMPLOYEES

Private FYE: June 30	Annual Growth	6/92	6/93	6/94	6/95	6/96	6/97	6/98	6/99	6/00	6/01
Estimated sales ($ mil.)	(7.4%)	500	525	550	230	220	250	250	254	250	250
Employees	0.7%	—	—	3,800	3,000	3,000	3,000	4,000	4,000	4,000	4,000

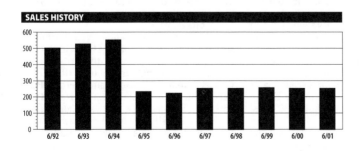

SALES HISTORY

DELOITTE TOUCHE TOHMATSU

This company is "deloitted" to make your acquaintance, particularly if you're a big business in need of accounting services. Deloitte Touche Tohmatsu (DTT; in the US it does business as Deloitte & Touche) is one of accounting's Big Four, along with KPMG, PricewaterhouseCoopers, and Ernst & Young. The firm offers traditional audit and fiscal oversight services to a multinational clientele. It also provides human resources and tax consulting services, as well as services to governments and international lending agencies working in emerging markets.

In the wake of Enron's collapse (which capsized Andersen and put the entire accounting industry under scrutiny), DTT announced in 2002 it would separate its accounting and consulting businesses, shelving the Deloitte Consulting name in favor of new moniker Braxton. Deloitte Consulting, which has been the firm's fastest-growing line, offers strategic and management consulting, in addition to information technology and human resources consulting services.

DTT spent the 1980s and 1990s pursuing a strategy of using accountants and consultants in concert to provide seamless service in auditing, accounting, strategic planning, information technology, financial management, and productivity. DTT and the rest of the industry, however, found that these combined operations were increasingly coming under fire as regulators and observers questioned whether accountants could maintain objectivity when auditing clients for whom they also provided consulting services.

DTT picked up new business and members in the collapse of former Big Five rival Andersen, but learned in 2002 that James Copeland had decided not to stand for re-election as global and US CEO at the end of his term in May 2003.

HISTORY

In 1845 William Deloitte opened an accounting office in London, at first soliciting business from bankrupts. The growth of joint stock companies and the development of stock markets in the mid-19th century created a need for standardized financial reporting and fueled the rise of auditing, and Deloitte moved into the new field. The Great Western Railway appointed him as its independent auditor (the first anywhere) in 1849.

In 1890 John Griffiths, who had become a partner in 1869, opened the company's first US office in New York City. Four decades later branches had opened throughout the US. In 1952 the firm partnered with Haskins & Sells, which operated 34 US offices.

Deloitte aimed to be "the Cadillac, not the Ford" of accounting. The firm, which became Deloitte Haskins & Sells in 1978, began shedding its conservatism as competition heated up; it was the first of the major accountancy firms to use aggressive ads.

In 1984 Deloitte Haskins & Sells tried to merge with Price Waterhouse, but the deal was dropped after Price Waterhouse's UK partners objected.

In 1989 Deloitte Haskins & Sells joined the flamboyant Touche Ross (founded in 1899) to become Deloitte & Touche. Touche Ross's Japanese affiliate, Ross Tohmatsu (founded in 1968) rounded out the current name. The merger was engineered by Deloitte's Michael Cook and Touche's Edward Kangas, in part to unite the former firm's US and European strengths with the latter's Asian presence. Cook continued to oversee US operations, with Kangas presiding over international operations. Many affiliates, particularly in the UK, rejected the merger and defected to competing firms.

As auditors were increasingly held accountable for the financial results of their clients, legal action soared. In the 1990s Deloitte was sued because of its actions relating to Drexel Burnham Lambert junk bond king Michael Milken, the failure of several savings and loans, and clients' bankruptcies.

Nevertheless, in 1995 the SEC chose Michael Sutton, the firm's national director of auditing and accounting practice, as its chief accountant. That year DTT formed Deloitte & Touche Consulting to consolidate its US and UK consulting operations; its Asian consulting operations were later added to facilitate regional expansion.

In 1996 the firm formed a corporate fraud unit (with special emphasis on the Internet) and bought PHH Fantus, the leading corporate relocation consulting company. The next year DTT and Thurston Group (a Chicago-based merchant bank) teamed up to form NetDox, a system for delivering legal, financial, and insurance documents via the Internet. In 1997, amid a new round of industry mergers, rumors swirled that a DTT and Ernst & Young union had been scrapped because the firms could not agree on ownership issues. DTT disavowed plans to merge and launched an ad campaign directly targeted against its rivals.

In 1998 the Asian economic crisis hurt overseas expansion, but provided a boost in restructuring consulting. In 1999 the firm sold its accounting staffing service unit (Resources Connection) to its managers and Evercore Partners, citing possible conflicts of interest with its core audit business. Also that year Kangas (now chairman emeritus) stepped down as CEO to be succeeded by James Copeland, and Deloitte

Consulting decided to sell its computer programming subsidiary to CGI Group.

In 2001 the SEC forced Deloitte & Touche to restate the financial results of Pre-Paid Legal Services. In an unusual move, Deloitte & Touche publicly disagreed with the SEC's findings.

OFFICERS

Chairman Emeritus: Edward A. Kangas
Chairman: Piet Hoogendoorn
CEO: James E. Copeland Jr.
CFO: William A. Fowler
CEO, Deloitte Consulting: Douglas M. McCracken
Managing Partner, Assurance, Accounting and Advisory Services; Chief Executive and Senior Partner, Deloitte & Touche (UK): John P. Connolly
Global Managing Partner, Tax and Legal: Jerry Leamon
Managing Partner, Human Resources: Libero Milone
Managing Director, Finance and Administration: S. Ashish Bali
Managing Director, Marketing and Communications: Adrian Smith
National Director, Human Capital and Actuary Practice: Ainar D. Aijala Jr.
National Director, Marketing, Communications, and Public Relations: Paul Marinaccio
National Director, U. S. International Operations: Tom Schiro
National Director, Operations: William H. Stanton
International Counsel: Joseph J. Lambert
Director, Human Resources: Martyn Fisher
Director, Communications: David Read

LOCATIONS

HQ: 1633 Broadway, New York, NY 10019
Phone: 212-492-4000   **Fax:** 212-492-4001
Web: www.deloitte.com

Deloitte Touche Tohmatsu operates through about 700 offices in about 140 countries.

PRODUCTS/OPERATIONS

Selected Services
Accounting and auditing
Corporate finance
Emerging markets consulting
Forensic services
Human resources, actuarial, insurance, and managed care consulting
Information technology consulting
Management consulting
Reorganization services
Tax advice and planning
Transaction services

Selected Industry Specializations
Aerospace
Agribusiness
Automotive
Banking
Biotechnological, pharmaceutical, and medical products
Chemicals
Higher education
Insurance
Investment management
Manufacturing
Mining
Mortgage banking and finance companies
Not-for-profit entities
Real estate and construction
Retail/consumer products
Securities
Technology, media, and telecommunications
Transportation
Travel/leisure
Utilities
Wholesale/distribution

COMPETITORS

Accenture
BDO International
Booz Allen
Boston Consulting
Cap Gemini
Cap Gemini Ernst & Young U.K.
EDS
Ernst & Young
Grant Thornton International
H&R Block
KPMG
Marsh & McLennan
McKinsey & Company
PricewaterhouseCoopers
Towers Perrin
Watson Wyatt

HISTORICAL FINANCIALS & EMPLOYEES

Partnership FYE: May 31	Annual Growth	8/93	8/94	8/95	8/96	8/97	8/98	8/99	*5/00	5/01	5/02
Sales ($ mil.)	10.7%	5,000	5,200	5,950	6,500	7,400	9,000	10,600	11,200	12,400	12,500
Employees	6.4%	56,000	56,600	59,000	63,440	65,000	82,000	90,000	90,000	95,000	98,000

* Fiscal year change

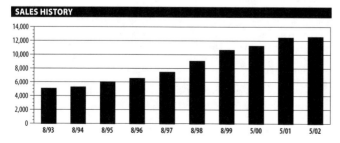

SALES HISTORY

DISCOVERY COMMUNICATIONS, INC.

Discover science and nature in the comfort of your living room with Discovery Communications (DCI). Reaching more than 85 million households, its Discovery Channel is one of the top-rated cable networks in the US. DCI owns other cable networks as well, including The Learning Channel, Travel Channel, and Animal Planet. DCI also operates Discovery Channel retail stores, and its Internet unit, Discovery.com, houses various nature and science Web sites. Liberty Media Corp. (49%), Cox Communications (25%), and Advance/Newhouse Communications (25%) own DCI.

The company also operates six digital Discovery cable channels focused on specific topics such as science and home and health. The company is also launching a new digital cable network called Discovery HD Theater, which would feature high-definition quality television.

Building on its name brand, DCI creates original programming, games, and activities for a series of science and nature Web sites under the Discovery.com name, and publishes videos, books, and CD-ROMs. It also operates about 170 Discovery Channel retail stores.

Speculation about whether DCI would be acquired has made headlines in recent times, but CEO and founder John Hendricks has denied all reports of a sale.

HISTORY

John Hendricks, a history graduate who wanted to expand the presence of educational programming on TV, founded Cable Educational Network in 1982. Three years later he introduced the Discovery Channel. Devoted entirely to documentaries and nature shows, the channel premiered in 156,000 US homes. After dodging bankruptcy (it had $5,000 cash and $1 million in debt to the BBC), within a year the Discovery Channel had 7 million subscribers and a host of new investors, including Cox Cable Communications and TCI (now AT&T Broadband). It expanded its programming from 12 hours to 18 hours a day in 1987.

Discovery continued to attract subscribers, reaching more than 32 million by 1988. The next year it launched Discovery Channel Europe to more than 200,000 homes in the UK and Scandinavia. The company began selling home videos in 1990 and entered the Israeli market. The following year Discovery Communications, Inc. (DCI) was formed to house the company's operations, and it bought The Learning Channel (TLC, founded in 1980). The company revamped TLC's programming, and in 1992 introduced a daily, six-hour, commercial-free block of children's

programs. The next year it introduced its first CD-ROM title, *In the Company of Whales,* based on the Discovery Channel documentary.

DCI increased its focus on international expansion in 1994, moving into Asia, Latin America, the Middle East, North Africa, Portugal, and Spain. The next year the company introduced its Web site, and began selling company merchandise such as CD-ROMs and videos. DCI solidified its move into the retail sector in 1996 with the acquisition of The Nature Company and Scientific Revolution chains (renamed Discovery Channel Store). Also that year it launched its third major cable channel, Animal Planet.

The company continued expanding internationally throughout the mid-1990s, establishing operations in Australia, Canada, India, New Zealand, and South Korea (1995); Africa, Brazil, Germany, and Italy (1996); and Japan and Turkey (1997). DCI also added to its stable of cable channels with the purchase of 70% of Paxson Communications' Travel Channel in 1997 (it acquired the rest in 1999). The company's 1997 original production "Titanic: Anatomy of a Disaster" attracted 3.2 million US households, setting a network ratings record.

The following year DCI and the British Broadcasting Corporation launched Animal Planet in Asia through a joint venture and agreed to market and distribute new cable channel BBC America. It also bought CBS's Eye on People, renaming the channel Discovery People (DCI shut the channel down in 2000). DCI spent $330 million launching its new health and fitness channel, Discovery Health, in 1999 and formed partnerships with high-speed online service Road Runner (to provide interactive information and services to Road Runner customers) and Rosenbluth Travel (to provide vacation packages based on DCI programming).

DCI reorganized its Internet activities into one unit called Discovery.com in 2000 with plans to eventually take it public. Later that year the Discovery Channel set back-to-back records with the two highest rated documentaries ever on cable, "Raising the Mammoth" (10.1 million people) and "Walking With Dinosaurs" (10.7 million people). In 2001 the company cut about 50 jobs as part of a restructuring. Later that year Discovery Communications struck a three-year deal to lease time from NBC on Saturday mornings (paying $6 million per season) to show its Discovery Kids programs.

In 2002 the company launched a 24-hour high-definition television network called Discovery HD Theater.

OFFICERS

Chairman and CEO, Discovery Communications and Discovery.com: John S. Hendricks, age 50
President and COO: Judith A. McHale, age 55
EVP and CFO: Gregory B. Durig
EVP Corporate Operations and General Counsel: Mark Hollinger
EVP Human Resources and Administration: Pandit Wright
EVP Strategy & Development: Donald A. Baer
EVP Advertising Sales: Scott McGraw
VP Government Relations and Public Policy: Alexa Verveer
President of Discovery Networks, US: Billy Campbell
President, Discovery Consumer Products: Michela English
President, Ad Sales: Joe Abruzzese
President, Content Group: John Ford
President, Discovery Networks International: Dawn McCall
SVP and General Manager, Discovery Digital Networks: David Karp
VP, National Advertising Sales: John Carrozza
VP, Ad Sales, Eastern Region, Discovery Networks: Lisa Fischer
VP, Strategic Marketing, Affiliate Sales and Marketing, Discovery Networks: Anne Murphy
VP, Program Planning, Discovery Networks, US: Dan Salerno

LOCATIONS

HQ: 7700 Wisconsin Ave., Bethesda, MD 20814
Phone: 301-986-0444   **Fax:** 301-771-4064
Web: www.discovery.com

Selected International Networks
Discovery Asia
Discovery Australia/New Zealand
Discovery Canada
Discovery Channel Middle East
Discovery Español
Discovery Europe
Discovery Germany
Discovery India
Discovery Japan
Discovery Portugués
Discovery Southeast Asia

PRODUCTS/OPERATIONS

Selected Operations
Discovery Consumer Products
  Discovery Channel Catalog (product catalog)
  Discovery Channel School (educational programs)
  Discovery Channel Stores (approximately 170 Discovery Channel retail outlets)
  DisoveryStore.com (online store)
Discovery HD Theater (digital channel featuring high-definition TV programming)
Discovery Networks International (33 languages, 155 countries)
Discovery Networks US
  Animal Planet (74 million households)
  BBC America (markets and distributes for the BBC)
  Discovery Channel (85 million)
  Discovery Civilization Channel (digital)
  Discovery en Español (digital)
  Discovery Health Channel (28 million)
  Discovery Home & Leisure Channel (digital)
  Discovery Kids Channel (digital)
  Discovery Science Channel (digital)
  Discovery Wings Channel (digital)
  The Learning Channel (81 million)
  Travel Channel (59 million)

COMPETITORS

A&E Networks
AOL Time Warner
CPB
Crown Media
E. W. Scripps
F.A.O.
Lifetime
National Geographic
NBC
News Corp.
Viacom
Walt Disney

HISTORICAL FINANCIALS & EMPLOYEES

Joint venture FYE: December 31	Annual Growth	12/92	12/93	12/94	12/95	12/96	12/97	12/98	12/99	12/00	12/01
Sales ($ mil.)	55.7%	—	52	200	452	662	860	1,100	1,400	1,730	1,800
Employees	38.9%	—	—	400	500	1,900	3,000	3,000	3,500	4,000	4,000

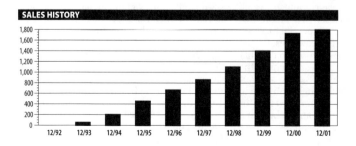

SALES HISTORY

DOCTOR'S ASSOCIATES INC.

You don't have to go underground to catch this Subway. The sandwich chain, owned by Doctor's Associates, has more than 16,500 restaurants in nearly 75 countries — second only to McDonald's in number of units. (However, Subway actually surpasses McDonald's in the US.) Virtually all Subway restaurants are franchises and offer such fare as hot and cold sandwiches, turkey wraps, and salads. Subways are located in freestanding buildings, as well as in airports, convenience stores, sports facilities, and other locations. President and CEO Fred DeLuca and former chairman Peter Buck own the company they founded in 1965.

With a low initial franchise cost and simple operations (minimum space requirements and little on-premises cooking), Subway has been one of the fastest-growing franchises in the world. But the company's heavy reliance on franchising hasn't been without controversy. Disgruntled franchisees have involved Subway in a number of legal skirmishes. However, the company continues to expand and is placing emphasis on growth in international markets. In 2002 it announced plans to expand in the UK, where it hopes to add 2,000 restaurants over 10 years. The UK sandwich market has been growing by about 8%, and DeLuca readily admits the company takes its cues from McDonald's, which took a 33% stake in UK sandwich maker Pret A Manger in 2001.

A successful ad campaign featuring Jared Fogle, a customer who claims to have lost 245 pounds on a diet of Subway sandwiches, has helped the company move from controlling 27% to nearly 31% of the nation's sandwich market in four years.

HISTORY

In 1965 17-year-old Fred DeLuca dreamed of becoming a doctor and worked as a stockboy in a Bridgeport, Connecticut, hardware store to earn college tuition. It wasn't enough, so he cornered family friend Peter Buck at a backyard barbecue and asked for advice. Buck, a nuclear physicist, suggested DeLuca open a submarine sandwich shop and put up $1,000 to get him started.

As the summer of 1965 was coming to an end, DeLuca rented a small location in a remote area of Bridgeport, opened Pete's Super Submarines, and began selling foot-long sandwiches. On the first day the sandwiches were so popular that DeLuca hired customers to work behind the counter; by the end of the day, he had sold out of all his supplies. The sandwiches continued to be popular for a while, but within a few months the shop started losing money, and DeLuca and Buck found that selling submarine sandwiches

was a seasonal business. They decided they could create an illusion of success by opening a second location and then a third. The third store was finally successful, partly because of its more visible location and increased marketing and partly because of a new name — Subway.

DeLuca and Buck had set a goal of 32 shops open by 1975, but they had only 16 by 1974. They realized that the only way they could reach their goal in one year was to license the Subway name. The first franchise opened that year, in Wallingford, Connecticut, and there were 32 by the end of 1975. The partners hit 100 by 1978 and 200 by 1983, and DeLuca set a new goal: 5,000 Subway shops by 1994. The first international Subway opened in Bahrain in 1984, and DeLuca hit his goal of 5,000 shops by 1990.

During the 1990s, DeLuca experimented with several other franchise concepts, including Care Hair (budget styling salons), Cajun Joe's (spicy fried chicken), and Q Burgers. But none of these ventures fared as well as his sandwich empire. As Subway grew, however, controversy surrounding its treatment of franchisees began to surface. A Federal Trade Commission investigation of the company was dropped in 1993, but Subway continued to battle franchisees complaining about broken contracts, market over-saturation (and, therefore, too much competition), and what the franchisees viewed as unreasonably high royalty fees.

In spite of its franchising troubles, Subway kept growing. It expanded into Russia and China in the mid-1990s, and opened its 11,000th restaurant in 1995. In 1997 Subway inked deals with the Army, Navy, and Air Force exchange services to bring Subway units to military bases. Two years later the company opened its 14,000th restaurant in Mount Gambier, Australia, an event that coincided with Subway's renewed push to expand internationally.

The company got some unexpected publicity in 1999 when 22-year-old Jared Fogle claimed that he dropped 245 pounds from his 425-pound frame by subsisting on a diet of Subway turkey sandwiches. Subway helped Fogle extend his 15 minutes of fame by featuring him and his oversized pants in a TV commercial. (The company has since built an entire campaign around Fogle which features other weight watchers attributing their success to Jared and Subway.) Subway introduced its largest menu initiative ever in 2000 when it unveiled its Subway Selects Gourmet Sandwiches, adding 13 items to the menu. In April of 2001 the company opened its 15,000th store. Also that year, Buck retired as chairman, but stayed on as a member of the board of directors.

OFFICERS

President and Director: Frederick A. DeLuca
Chief Marketing Officer: Bill Schettini
Controller: David Worroll
Director, Development and Franchise Sales:
Don Fertman
Director, Corporate Communications: Michele Klotzer
Director, Human Resources: Wendy Kopazna
Public Relations Manager: Annie Smith

LOCATIONS

HQ: 325 Bic Dr., Milford, CT 06460
Phone: 203-877-4281   **Fax:** 203-876-6695
Web: www.subway.com

Doctor's Associates has Subway restaurants in about 75
countries.

PRODUCTS/OPERATIONS

Selected Menu Items
Breakfast sandwiches
  Bacon and egg
  Cheese and egg
  Ham and egg
  Western egg
Chips
Cookies
Salads
  Tuna
  Turkey breast
  Veggie
Sandwiches
  Club
  Cold cut trio
  Italian B.M.T.
  Meatball
  Roast beef
  Roasted chicken breast
  Seafood and crab
  Steak and cheese
  Tuna
  Turkey breast
  Veggie
Wraps
  Chicken parmesan
  Steak and cheese
  Turkey breast and bacon

COMPETITORS

7-Eleven	Miami Subs
Blimpie	Papa John's
Burger King	Pret A Manger
Chick-fil-A	Quizno's
CKE Restaurants	Schlotzsky's
Dairy Queen	Triarc
Domino's Pizza	Wall Street Deli
Jack in the Box	Wawa
Little Caesar	Wendy's
McDonald's	Yum!

HISTORICAL FINANCIALS & EMPLOYEES

Private FYE: December 31	Annual Growth	12/92	12/93	12/94	12/95	12/96	12/97	12/98	12/99	12/00	12/01
Estimated sales ($ mil.)	11.3%	—	2,200	2,400	2,600	2,700	3,300	3,100	3,200	4,720	5,170
Employees	0.0%	—	—	—	—	—	—	—	—	730	730

SALES HISTORY

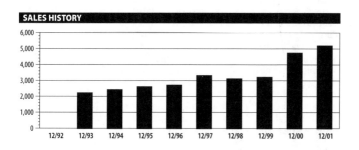

DOMINO'S, INC.

No pawn in the pizza wars, Domino's is scrabbling away to ensure that success is in the cards. The world's #1 pizza delivery company and the #2 pizza chain overall (behind Yum! Brands' Pizza Hut), Domino's Pizza has nearly 7,100 stores (most are franchised) in about 65 countries. While the company built its reputation with speedy delivery, it also has begun to emphasize quality with its Italian Originals line of Italian-spiced pizzas. Domino's founder Thomas Monaghan retired in 1998, selling his 93% stake to Boston-based investment firm Bain Capital.

More than two-thirds of the company's locations are in the US. Internationally, toppings vary from place to place — refried beans are popular in Mexico, while pie-lovers elsewhere favor pickled ginger (India), green peas (Brazil), canned tuna and corn (UK), and squid (Japan). The company also owns 18 regional distribution centers in Canada, France, the Netherlands, and the US.

In the hard-fought war for pizza market share, the company restructured and closed some underperforming units and has moved aggressively into e-commerce territory by offering online ordering at many locations. It's even testing a $1 delivery charge in certain markets. Domino's founder Thomas Monaghan, a devout Catholic, retired from the company in 1998 to concentrate on his religious activities.

Domino's is expanding in Europe through its 2001 majority stake in Dutch Pizza Beheer B.V. The Netherlands franchise operation is Domino's first new office in Europe in almost 20 years.

HISTORY

Thomas Monaghan's early life was one of hardship. After growing up in an orphanage and numerous foster homes, Monaghan spent his young adult life experimenting, trying everything from a Catholic seminary to a stint in the Marine Corps.

In 1960 Monaghan borrowed $500 and bought DomiNick's, a failed pizza parlor in Ypsilanti, Michigan, which he operated with the help of his brother James. In 1961 James traded his share in the restaurant to his brother for a Volkswagen Beetle, but Thomas pressed on, learning the pizza business largely by trial and error. After a brief partnership with an experienced restaurateur with whom he later had a falling out, Monaghan developed a strategy to sell only pizza and to locate stores near colleges and military bases. In 1965 the company changed its name to Domino's.

In the 1960s and 1970s, Monaghan endured setbacks that brought the company to the brink of bankruptcy. Among these were a 1968 fire that destroyed the Domino's headquarters and a 1975 lawsuit from Domino Sugar maker Amstar (now

Tate & Lyle) for trademark infringement. But the company won the ensuing legal battles, and by 1978 it was operating 200 stores.

In the 1980s Domino's grew phenomenally. Between 1981 and 1983 the company doubled its number of US stores to 1,000; it went international in 1983, opening a store in Canada. The company's growth brought Monaghan a personal fortune. In 1983 he bought the Detroit Tigers baseball team and amassed one of the world's largest collections of Frank Lloyd Wright objects.

Domino's expansion continued in the mid-1980s. With sales figures mounting, the company introduced pan pizza (its first new product) in 1989. That year Monaghan put Domino's up for sale, but his practice of linking his personal and professional finances had gotten both the founder and company into such dire fiscal straits that no one wanted to buy the chain. Monaghan removed himself from direct management in 1989 and installed a new management group.

When company performance began to slide, Monaghan returned in 1991, having experienced a religious rebirth. He sold off many of his private holdings (including his resort island and his baseball team, which went to cross-town pizza rival Michael Ilitch of Little Caesar) to reinvigorate the company and reorganize company management.

In 1989 a Domino's driver, trying to fulfill the company's 30-minute delivery guarantee, ran a red light and collided with another car. The $79 million judgment against the company in 1993 prompted Domino's to drop its famous 30-minute policy and replace it with a satisfaction guarantee.

The company revamped its logo and store interiors with a new look in 1997. The following year it introduced a patented delivery bag designed to keep pies hot and crispy. Also in 1998, prompted by his decision to devote more time to religious pursuits, Monaghan retired from the business he had guided for nearly 40 years. He sold 93% of his company to investment firm Bain Capital. David Brandon, former CEO of sales promotion company Valassis Communications, replaced Monaghan as chairman and CEO in 1999. That same year the company initiated a restructuring that involved eliminating 100 managers; it closed or sold 142 stores to franchisees. The company also introduced the first in its line of Italian Originals — specialty pizzas featuring Italian spices. It also began selling pizza online through a number of franchisees.

In 2001 Domino's bought a majority stake in Dutch Pizza Beheer B.V., an operator of 52 Domino's restaurants in the Netherlands. With the buy, the company is establishing a base to manage future expansion in Europe.

OFFICERS

Chairman and CEO: David A. Brandon, age 49, $1,700,000 pay
EVP, Finance and CFO: Harry J. Silverman, age 43, $860,000 pay
EVP, Build the Brand: Ken C. Calwell
EVP, Communications and Investor Relations: Lynn M. Liddle
EVP, Distribution: Michael D. Soignet, age 42, $790,000 pay
EVP, Flawless Execution: Patrick W. Knotts, age 47, $768,558 pay
EVP, General Counsel, and Secretary: Elisa D. Garcia, age 44
EVP, International: J. Patrick Doyle, age 38, $715,000 pay
EVP, PeopleFirst: Patricia A. Wilmot, age 53
EVP and Special Assistant to Chairman and CEO: James G. Stansik, age 46
CIO: Timothy Monteith, age 49
VP, Brand Growth: Terri Snyder
VP, Corporate Communications: Tim McIntyre
VP, Purchasing: Jim Caldwell
VP and Corporate Controller: Jeffrey D. Lawrence, age 28
VP and Associate General Counsel: Edwina W. Divins
VP and Treasurer: Joseph Donovan
Manager, Public Relations: Holly Ryan
Auditors: PricewaterhouseCoopers LLP

LOCATIONS

HQ: 30 Frank Lloyd Wright Dr., Ann Arbor, MI 48106
Phone: 734-930-3030   **Fax:** 734-747-6210
Web: www.dominos.com

Domino's Pizza has operations in about 65 countries.

2001 Sales

	$ mil.	% of total
US distribution	692	55
US company-owned restaurants	362	28
US franchised restaurants	134	11
International	70	6
Total	**1,258**	**100**

PRODUCTS/OPERATIONS

2001 Sales

	$ mil.	% of total
Domestic distribution	797	58
Domestic sales	496	36
International sales	70	6
Adjustments	(105)	—
Total	**1,258**	**100**

Menu Items
Pizzas
  Classic Hand Tossed
  Crunchy Thin Crust
  Italian Originals
  Ultimate Deep Dish
Sides
  Breadsticks
  Buffalo wings
  Cheesy bread

COMPETITORS

Bertucci's
Burger King
CEC Entertainment
CKE Restaurants
Godfather's Pizza
KFC
LDB Corp
Little Caesar
McDonald's
Papa John's
Pizza Hut
Pizza Inn
Round Table
Sbarro
Subway
Uno Restaurant
Wendy's
Whataburger

HISTORICAL FINANCIALS & EMPLOYEES

Private FYE: December 31	Annual Growth	12/92	12/93	12/94	12/95	12/96	12/97	12/98	12/99	12/00	12/01
Sales ($ mil.)	5.3%	—	—	875	905	970	1,045	1,177	1,157	1,166	1,258
Net income ($ mil.)	121.2%	—	—	0	25	20	61	77	2	25	37
Income as % of sales	—	—	—	0.0%	2.8%	2.0%	5.8%	6.5%	0.2%	2.2%	2.9%
Employees	(3.9%)	—	—	—	—	—	—	14,200	14,400	14,600	12,600

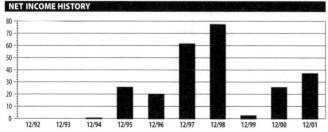

NET INCOME HISTORY

2001 FISCAL YEAR-END

Debt ratio: 100.0%
Return on equity: —
Cash ($ mil.): 35
Current ratio: 0.85
Long-term debt ($ mil.): 612

DOW CORNING CORPORATION

Cosmetic surgery has caused major health problems at Dow Corning. A 50-50 joint venture of chemical titan Dow Chemical and glass giant Corning, Dow Corning is operating under bankruptcy protection as a result of thousands of claims by women alleging the company's silicone-gel breast implants harmed them. Dow Corning produces about 7,000 silicone-based products such as adhesives, insulating materials, and lubricants for aerospace, automotive, and electrical uses. Because silicone does not conduct electricity, it is also used in its hard polycrystalline form (silicon) as the material on which semiconductors are built. With manufacturing plants worldwide, the company sells about 55% of its products outside the US.

Although the breast-implant case has dragged on for nearly a decade, Dow Corning appeared close to a settlement that would help it emerge from bankruptcy protection. The deal was stymied, however, when the bankruptcy judge ruled that women who did not agree to the settlement could still sue Dow Corning's corporate parents. Dow Corning and about 94% of the women who have sued it appealed the judge's ruling.

HISTORY

Dow Corning was founded in 1943 as a joint venture between Dow Chemical and Corning Glass Works. Corning, founded by Amory Houghton in 1875, provided Thomas Edison with glass for the first lightbulbs. It developed Pyrex heat-resistant glass in 1915.

Corning made its first silicone resin samples in 1938. It teamed with a group of Dow Chemical scientists who were also working on silicone products in 1940. Dow Chemical president Willard Dow and Corning Glass Works president Glen Cole shook hands on the idea of a joint venture in 1942, and 10 months later Dow Corning was formed. Its first product, the engine grease DOW CORNING 4, enabled B-17s to fly at 35,000 feet (a major contribution to the Allied war effort). In 1945 DOW CORNING 35 (an emulsifier used in tire molds) and Pan Glaze (which made baking pans stick-proof and easier to clean) were instant successes on the home front.

Dow Corning expanded rapidly in international markets and in 1960 set up Dow Corning International to handle sales and technical service in markets outside North America. By 1969 the company had operations worldwide.

Dow Corning's first breast implants went on the market in 1964. Since then Dow Corning and other silicone makers have sold silicone breast implants to more than a million women in the US. In the early 1980s breast-implant recipients began suing Dow Corning and other implant makers, claiming that the silicone gel in the implants leaked and caused health problems. Dow Corning, the leading implant maker, defended the devices as safe. Dow Corning stopped making implants in 1992, after the Food and Drug Administration called for a moratorium on silicone-gel implants.

In 1993 Baxter International, Bristol-Myers Squibb, and Dow Corning offered $4.2 billion to settle thousands of claims. The corporation declared bankruptcy in 1995 to buy time for financial reorganization. A federal judge stripped Dow Chemical of its protection from direct liability, and the company was later ordered to pay a Nevada couple $4.1 million in damages (other jurisdictions did not follow suit). Dow Corning sold its Polytrap polymer technology to Advanced Polymer, maker of polymer-based pharmaceutical delivery systems, in 1996. The following year the company sold Bisco Products, its silicone-foam business, to Rogers Corporation for $12 million.

Dow Corning's $3.7 billion bankruptcy reorganization plan, offered in 1997, allowed for $2.4 billion to be set aside to settle most implant lawsuits against the corporation. However, a federal bankruptcy judge found legal flaws in the proposal and refused to allow claimants to vote on it. In 1998 Dow Corning upped the ante to $4.4 billion — $3 billion to the silicone claimants and the rest to creditors.

Both sides later agreed to a $3.2 billion compensation package, and in 1999 the plan received approval from a bankruptcy judge and creditors. However, the settlement stalled when the judge ruled that women who disagreed with the settlement could sue Dow Corporation and Corning (Dow Corning is appealing). Despite its court battles, in 2000 the company acquired the 51% of Universal Silicones & Lubricants (high-tech lubricants and silicone sealants) it did not own and renamed the company Dow Corning India.

OFFICERS

Chairman, President, and CEO: Gary E. Anderson
EVP: Stephanie A. Burns
SVP; General Manager, Geographic Development Business Unit: Richard Hoover
SVP; General Manager, Paper and Process Industries and Specialty Chemicals Industry Business Unit (IBU): Jere Marciniak
SVP, Mergers and Acquisitions and Special Projects: John W. Churchfield
VP and Chief Human Resources Officer: Burnett S. Kelly

VP, Communications and Chief Communications Officer: Barbara S. Carmichael
VP, General Counsel, and Secretary: Sue K. McDonnell
VP; General Manager, Construction Industry and Core Products Business Unit: Chris Bowyer
VP; General Manager, Electronics Industry and Advanced Materials Business IBU: Ian Thackwray
VP; General Manager, Life Sciences Industry and Life Sciences Product Business IBU: Endvar Rossi
VP; General Manager, New Ventures Business Unit: Jean-Marc Gilson
VP; General Manager, Service Enterprise Unit: Alan Ludgate
VP; General Manager, Transportation, Energy and Fabrication Industries and Engineered Elastomers and Lubricants Business IBU: Bruno Sulmon
VP; General Manager, Web Business: J. Donald Sheets
VP, Planning and Finance and CFO: Gifford E. Brown
VP and Executive Director, Supply Chains: Alex Royez
CIO and Executive Director, Information Technology/Knowledge Management: Abbe Mulders
President, Hemlock Semiconductor Corporation: Donald Pfuehler
President, Multibase: Andy Tometich
Auditors: PricewaterhouseCoopers LLP

LOCATIONS

HQ: 2200 W. Salzburg Rd., Midland, MI 48686
Phone: 989-496-4000   Fax: 989-496-4393
Web: www.dowcorning.com

Dow Corning has about 25 manufacturing sites worldwide. Its principal manufacturing facilities in the US are located in Kentucky and Michigan. Its principal non-US manufacturing facilities are located in Belgium, Germany, Japan, and the UK.

2001 Sales

	$ mil.	% of total
US	1,046	43
Japan	323	13
Germany	143	6
UK	114	5
South Korea	112	4
Other countries	700	29
Total	**2,438**	**100**

PRODUCTS/OPERATIONS

Selected Products and Applications

Aerospace
  Adhesives
  Encapsulants
  Exotic composite
    materials
  Greases
  High-purity fluids
  Protective coatings
  Sealants
Automotive
  Body components
  Brake systems
  Chassis
  Electrical component
  Electronic components
  Engine/drivetrain
  Exterior lighting
  Fuel systems
Chem. and Mat. Mfg.
  Agrochemicals
  Auto appearance
    chemicals
  Industrial release agents
  Materials treatment
  Oil and gas
  Process aid antifoams
  Pulp manufacturing
Cleaning Products
  Hand cleaners
  Janitorial floor waxes
  Laundry detergents
Coatings and Plastics

Electrical/Electronics
  Adhesives and sealants
  Conformal coatings
  Dielectric gels
  High-voltage insulators
  Hyperpure
    polycrystalline silicon
  Interlayer dielectric and
    passivation materials
  Liquid transformer fluid
  Silicone encapsulants
  Silicone grease for
    insulators
  Silicone RTV coating for
    insulators
  Silicone rubber
    insulators
  Thermally conductive
    adhesives
Food and Beverage
  Packaging
Healthcare
  Industrial Assembly &
    Maintenance
  Moldmaking
  Paper Manufacturing &
    Finishing
Personal Care
Plastics
Rubber Fabrication
Textiles

COMPETITORS

3M
Aventis
BASF AG
Baxter
Bristol-Myers Squibb
Crompton
Degussa

Exxon Mobil
Imperial Chemical
Lexington Precision
Shin-Etsu Chemical
Th. Goldschmidt
Wacker-Chemie
Witco Corporation

HISTORICAL FINANCIALS & EMPLOYEES

Joint venture FYE: December 31	Annual Growth	12/92	12/93	12/94	12/95	12/96	12/97	12/98	12/99	12/00	12/01
Sales ($ mil.)	2.5%	1,956	2,044	2,205	2,493	2,532	2,644	2,568	2,603	2,751	2,438
Net income ($ mil.)	—	(72)	(287)	(7)	(31)	222	238	207	110	105	(23)
Income as % of sales	—	—	—	—	—	8.8%	9.0%	8.0%	4.2%	3.8%	—
Employees	(1.5%)	8,600	8,000	8,300	8,500	8,900	9,100	9,000	9,000	9,000	7,500

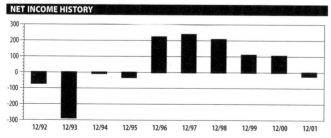

NET INCOME HISTORY

2001 FISCAL YEAR-END

Debt ratio: 6.1%
Return on equity: —
Cash ($ mil.): 583
Current ratio: 2.30
Long-term debt ($ mil.): 39

DREAMWORKS SKG

DreamWorks SKG has moguls times three. Created in 1994 by Steven Spielberg (famed film director/producer), Jeffrey Katzenberg (former Disney film executive and animation guru), and David Geffen (recording industry maven), Dream-Works has established itself in the entertainment industry after a rocky start.

The company produces films (Best Picture winner *Gladiator*), TV shows (*Undeclared*), and music, including the soundtracks to Dream-Works films and record deals with artists such as Toby Keith. DreamWorks has pulled out of the GameWorks video arcade business it started with SEGA and Universal Pictures. The three founders collectively own 66% of DreamWorks; Microsoft co-founder Paul Allen owns about 26%.

The division of labor is spread out among DreamWorks founders. Spielberg oversees the live-action movies, which include the box-office hit *A Beautiful Mind* (co-produced by Universal Pictures, the film went on to win the Best Picture Oscar in 2001). Former Disney head of production Katzenberg leads the animation division, responsible for such films as *Chicken Run* and *Shrek* (one of 2001's highest grossing films), while Geffen runs DreamWorks Records, producing the soundtracks to all DreamWorks films and albums for popular artists.

The company's progress has been marked by a few obstacles: its television division has produced only one notable hit (*Spin City*), its first animated feature (*Prince of Egypt*) and early live-action films (*Amistad, Almost Famous*) flopped at the box office, and DreamWorks scuttled plans for a Web entertainment division. In addition, the company's bid to build a new film studio in LA failed, and DreamWorks' current offices remain located at Universal Pictures, where Spielberg hangs his hat. DreamWorks has since cut about 150 jobs, and in 2002 the company received a cash infusion through refinancing from J.P. Morgan Chase and FleetBoston Financial Corp, which it is using to expand its animation facilities as well as its live-action film production.

HISTORY

Before pooling their collective talents in 1994, Steven Spielberg, Jeffrey Katzenberg, and David Geffen had each established an impressive track record. Spielberg had spawned such blockbusters as *Jaws, The Indiana Jones Trilogy,* and *Jurassic Park.* Katzenberg had guided Walt Disney's return to animation (*The Lion King, Aladdin*) before a falling out with Disney CEO Michael Eisner. Music guru Geffen had helped make superstars of the Eagles and Nirvana.

A high-tech who's who embraced the SKG dream. Microsoft invested around $30 million to develop video games, while Microsoft co-founder Paul Allen shelled out nearly $500 million for a stake in the new company. Soon DreamWorks had arranged a $100 million programming deal with ABC, a 10-year HBO licensing agreement worth an estimated $1 billion, and co-founded a $50 million animation studio with Silicon Graphics. DreamWorks then announced plans in 1995 to build the first new studio since the 1930s, just outside of Los Angeles in Playa Vista.

DreamWorks produced a string of TV flops before finding success in 1996 with the Michael J. Fox comedy *Spin City.* Later that year the company released the first record under its new label, a dud from pop star George Michael, and it announced a partnership with SEGA and MCA (now Universal Studios) to develop SEGA GameWorks (video arcade super-centers featuring SEGA titles and games designed by Spielberg).

The company finally released its first three movies in 1997 (*The Peacemaker, Amistad,* and *Mouse Hunt*) to mixed critical reviews and mediocre box office performance. Combined with DreamWorks' less-than-stellar offerings in TV and music, buzz circulated that the meeting of the minds at DreamWorks wasn't all it was cracked up to be.

But DreamWorks started showing signs of life in 1998 with the comet disaster film *Deep Impact* and Spielberg's Oscar-winning *Saving Private Ryan,* the highest grossing film of the year. It also introduced its first animated films that year, which included the successful *Antz.* DreamWorks finished the year with the highest average gross per film of all the major studios.

After facing a multitude of environmental protests, cost overruns, and construction delays, DreamWorks scrapped its Playa Vista studio plans in 1999. Later that year DreamWorks joined with Imagine Entertainment and Paul Allen's Vulcan Ventures to create POP.com, a Web site offering digital short films and streaming video features. It also announced a five-picture deal with Academy Award-winning animation firm Aardman Animations, with which it co-produced *Chicken Run* (released in 2000).

DreamWorks and Microsoft sold DreamWorks Interactive, their video game joint venture, to Electronic Arts in 2000. Later that year *American Beauty* took home the Oscar for Best Picture of 1999, and the studio continued its successful box-office run with three films that grossed more than $100 million (*Gladiator,* which scored the studio its second Best Picture Oscar, *Chicken Run,* and *What Lies Beneath*). After Allen failed to merge the struggling, unlaunched POP.com with iFilm.com (in which he is also a major investor), DreamWorks and Imagine shut down the netcaster.

The studio scored an early summer hit in 2001 with *Shrek,* which became one of that year's highest grossing films with more than $265 million at the box office. *A Beautiful Mind,* its co-production with Universal Pictures won one of the company's films yet another Best Picture Oscar. Also that year the company exited the GameWorks venture when the arcades failed to catch on quickly. In 2002 another round of financing injected DreamWorks with a cash infusion that the company is using to increase its live-action film production and expand its animation production facilities.

OFFICERS

Principal: David Geffen, age 59
Principal: Jeffrey Katzenberg, age 51
Principal: Steven Spielberg, age 55
CFO: Ronald L. Nelson, age 49
COO: Helene Hahn
Head of Consumer Products: Brad Globe
Head of DreamWorks Records: Mo Ostin
Head of DreamWorks Records: Michael Ostin
Head of DreamWorks Records: Lenny Waronker
Head of DreamWorks Television: Justin Falvey
Head of DreamWorks Television: Darryl Frank
Head of Feature Animation: Ann Daly
Head of Marketing and Public Relations: Terry Press
Head of Motion Picture Division: Laurie MacDonald
Head of Motion Picture Division: Walter Parkes
Head of Technology: Andy Hendrickson
Director, Human Resources: Heidi Gonggryp

LOCATIONS

HQ: 1000 Flower St., Glendale, CA 91201
Phone: 818-733-7000   **Fax:** 818-695-7574
Web: www.dreamworks.com

DreamWorks SKG has offices in Glendale, Los Angeles, and Universal City, California.

PRODUCTS/OPERATIONS

Selected Films, Recording Artists, and Television Shows

DreamWorks Pictures
A Beautiful Mind (2001, co-produced with Universal Studios)
Almost Famous (2000)
American Beauty (1999)
Amistad (1997)
Antz (1998)
Chicken Run (2000, co-produced with Aardman Animation)
Deep Impact (1998, co-produced with Paramount Pictures)
Galaxy Quest (1999)
Gladiator (2000, co-produced with Universal Studios)
The Legend of Bagger Vance (2000)
Mouse Hunt (1997)
The Peacemaker (1997)
The Prince of Egypt (1998)
Road Trip (2000)
Saving Private Ryan (1998, co-produced with Paramount Pictures)
Shrek (2001)
Small Time Crooks (2000)
What Lies Beneath (2000, co-produced with 20th Century Fox)

DreamWorks Records	DreamWorks Television
Buckcherry	*The Job*
Toby Keith	*Spin City*
Randy Newman	*Undeclared*
Papa Roach	
Chris Rock	
Henry Rollins	
Elliott Smith	

COMPETITORS

Alliance Atlantis Communications
Artisan Entertainment
Carsey-Werner-Mandabach
Fox Entertainment
Lions Gate Entertainment
Lucasfilm
MGM
Miramax
Paramount Pictures
Pixar
Sony Pictures Entertainment
Universal Studios
Warner Bros.

HISTORICAL FINANCIALS & EMPLOYEES

Private FYE: December 31	Annual Growth	12/92	12/93	12/94	12/95	12/96	12/97	12/98	12/99	12/00	12/01
Sales ($ mil.)	30.4%	—	—	—	—	—	—	1,000	1,242	1,873	2,219
Employees	(2.1%)	—	—	—	—	—	—	1,600	1,500	1,500	1,500

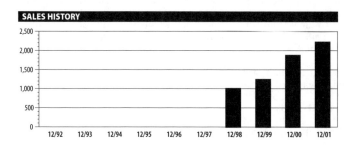

SALES HISTORY

E. & J. GALLO WINERY

Let them drink wine! E. & J. Gallo Winery brings merlot to the masses. The world's largest wine maker makes about 25% of the wine sold in the US, thanks in part to its inexpensive jug brands Carlo Rossi and Gallo. It also makes the fortified Thunderbird brand. The vintner cultivates more than 3,000 acres in Sonoma County, California. Gallo also makes its own labels and bottles and is the leading US wine exporter. It also produces premium wines, imports and sells Italian wine Ecco Domani, and is a leading brandy producer. The Gallo family owns the vintner.

Gallo sells nearly 35 brands over a wide price range, from alcohol-added wines and wine coolers to upscale varietals that fetch more than $50 a bottle. Gallo once only sold wine in the low-to-moderate price range, but has successfully expanded into premium wines such as Turning Leaf and Gossamer Bay, which don't have the Gallo name on the label. The vintner's strong affiliation with Wal-Mart has boosted wine sales in new Wal-Mart markets such as Germany and the UK.

Gallo also buys grapes from other Sonoma County growers.

HISTORY

Giuseppe Gallo, the father of Ernest and Julio Gallo, was born in 1882 in the wine country of northwest Italy. Around 1900 he and his brother, Michelo (they called themselves Joe and Mike), traveled to America seeking their fame and fortune in the San Francisco area. Both brothers became wealthy by growing grapes and anticipating the growth of the market during Prohibition. (Home winemaking was legal and popular.)

Giuseppe's eldest sons, Ernest and Julio, worked with their father from the beginning. Their relationship was strained, and the father was reluctant to help his sons, particularly Ernest, in business. However, the mysterious murder-suicide that ended the lives of Giuseppe and his wife in 1933 eliminated that problem: The sons inherited the business their father had been unwilling to share.

From then on Ernest ran the business end, assembling a large distribution network and building a national brand, while Julio made the wine and Joe Jr., the third, much younger, brother, worked for them. In the early 1940s Gallo opened bottling plants in Los Angeles and New Orleans, using screw-cap bottles, which then seemed more hygienic and modern than corks. Gallo lagged during WWII, when alcohol was diverted for the military. Under Julio's supervision, it upgraded its planting stock and refined its technology.

In an attempt to capitalize on the sweet wines popular in the 1950s, Gallo introduced Thunderbird, a fortified wine (its alcohol content boosted to 20%), in 1957. In the 1960s Gallo spurred its growth by advertising heavily and keeping prices low. It introduced Hearty Burgundy, a jug wine, in 1964, along with Ripple. Gallo introduced the carbonated, fruit-flavored Boone's Farm Apple Wine in 1969, creating an interest in "pop" wines that lasted for a few years.

The company introduced its first varietal wines in 1974. In the 1970s Gallo field workers switched unions, from the United Farm Workers to the Teamsters. Repercussions included protests and boycotts, but sales were largely unaffected. From 1976 to 1982 Gallo operated under an FTC order limiting its control over wholesalers. The order was lifted after the industry's competitive balance changed.

Through the 1970s and 1980s, Gallo expanded its production of varietals; in 1988 it began adding vintage dates to the wines' labels. But it also kept a hand in the lower levels of the market, introducing Bartles & Jaymes wine coolers.

Gallo began a legal battle in 1986 with Joe, who had been eased out of the business, over the use of the Gallo name. In 1992 Joe lost the use of his name for commercial purposes. Julio died the next year when his jeep overturned on a family ranch.

In 1996 rival Kendall-Jackson sued Gallo for trademark infringement over Gallo's new wine brand, Turning Leaf, claiming Gallo copied its Vintner's Reserve bottle and label. A jury ruled in Gallo's favor in 1997; a federal appeals court supported that decision in 1998.

In May 2000 Gallo announced plans to promote wine-cooler market leader Bartles & Jaymes with a new advertising campaign, although the category continues to wane.

In 2001 Gallo's reseach team patented a number of diagnostic tools that can be licensed to winemakers around the world; one tool, for example, can spot an infected vine in a matter of hours, rather than years.

In 2002 Gallo bought the Louis M. Martini Winery in Napa Valley, furthering its expansion into the premium wine business. It also bought the brand name and stocks of San Jose-based wine producer Mirassou Vineyards, one of the oldest wineries in California.

Chairman: Ernest Gallo
Co-President: James E. Coleman
Co-President: Joseph E. Gallo
Co-President: Robert J. Gallo
EVP and General Counsel: Jack B. Owens
EVP, Marketing: Albion Fenderson
VP, Controller, and Assistant Treasurer: Tony Youga
VP, Human Resources: Mike Chase
VP, Information Systems: Kent Kushar
VP, Media: Sue McClelland
VP, National Sales: Gary Ippolito

LOCATIONS

HQ: 600 Yosemite Blvd., Modesto, CA 95354
Phone: 209-341-3111   **Fax:** 209-341-3569
Web: www.gallo.com

E. & J. Gallo Winery has four wineries in the California counties of Fresno, Livingston, Modesto, and Sonoma, and vineyards throughout the region. Its wine is sold throughout the US and in more than 85 countries.

PRODUCTS/OPERATIONS

Selected Products and Labels

Bargain generic and varietals (Carlo Rossi, Livingston Cellars, Peter Vella, Wild Vines)
Brandy (E & J Brandy, E&J Cask & Cream, E&J VSOP)
Dessert (Fairbanks, Gallo, Sheffield Cellars)
Flagship (Ernest & Julio Gallo Vineyards, Gallo of Sonoma)
Fortified and jug (Gallo, Hearty Burgundy, Night Train, Ripple, Thunderbird)
Hospitality industry (Burlwood, Copperidge by E&J Gallo, William Wycliff Vineyards)
Imported varietals (Ecco Domani)
Mid-priced varietals (Garnet Point, Gossamer Bay, Turning Leaf)
Sparkling (André, Ballatore, Indigo Hills, Tott's)
Ultra-premium (Anapamu, Indigo Hills, Marcelina, Rancho Zabaco)
Wine-based and other beverages (Bartles & Jaymes, Boone's Farm, Hornsby's Pub Draft Cider)

COMPETITORS

Allied Domecq	LVMH
Asahi Breweries	Pernod Ricard
Bacardi USA	Ravenswood Winery
Beringer Blass	R.H. Phillips
Brown-Forman	Robert Mondavi
Chalone Wine	Sebastiani Vineyards
Concha y Toro	Taittinger
Constellation Brands	Terlato Wine
Foster's	Trinchero Family Estates
GIV	UST
Heaven Hill Distilleries	Vincor
Jim Beam Brands	Wine Group
Kendall-Jackson	

HISTORICAL FINANCIALS & EMPLOYEES

Private FYE: December 31	Annual Growth	12/92	12/93	12/94	12/95	12/96	12/97	12/98	12/99	12/00	12/01
Estimated sales ($ mil.)	6.1%	1,000	1,100	980	1,100	1,200	1,300	1,500	1,520	1,610	1,700
Employees	1.7%	3,000	4,000	4,000	4,000	5,000	5,000	5,000	5,250	3,600	3,500

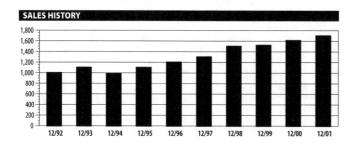

SALES HISTORY

ENCYCLOPAEDIA BRITANNICA, INC.

Encyclopaedia Britannica thinks it knows everything, and it probably does. The company publishes reference works including its flagship 32-volume *Encyclopaedia Britannica* (first published in 1768), *The Annals of America,* and *Great Books of the Western World.* It also publishes a variety of dictionaries (*Merriam Webster's Collegiate Dictionary, Merriam Webster's Biographical Dictionary*) through its Merriam-Webster subsidiary. Most of the company's products are available online, as well as on CD-ROM and DVD. Swiss financier Jacob Safra (a nephew of the late banking king Edmond Safra) owns the company.

Its Britannica.com Web site offers access for a fee to its entire collection of encyclopedia articles, an editorially reviewed Web site directory, and third-party content from *The New York Times* and other providers. Britannica's site also features an online store where users can buy its print and interactive products.

After initially being late to the CD-ROM and dot-com party, Encyclopaedia Britannica decided to commit to Britannica.com, a sister firm devoted to electronic content which was to be spun off in an IPO. But the idea turned out to be disastrous (in part because of bad publicity over traffic jams at the site and a downturn in online advertising), and the company has since focused back on its core business with a renewed interest in print products under new CEO Ilan Yeshua. The company is considering selling its Merriam-Webster subsidiary to raise capital.

HISTORY

Engraver Andrew Bell and printer and bookseller Colin Macfarquhar created the first edition of the *Encyclopaedia Britannica* in Scotland, releasing the three-volume set in weekly installments between 1768 and 1771. Benjamin Franklin and John Locke were among early contributors. The second edition, completed in 1784, expanded to 10 volumes; the fourth (1809) contained 20. The ninth edition (1889) captured the scientific spirit of the age with articles by Thomas Henry Huxley and James Clerk Maxwell.

American businessmen Horace Hooper and Walter Jackson purchased the *Encyclopaedia* in 1901 and established the Encyclopaedia Britannica Company in the US. It published the first *Britannica Book of the Year* in 1913. Sears chairman Julius Rosenwald bought the company in 1920 and tried to market *Britannica* through Sears' retail operations, as well as with door-to-door sales. William Benton (of Benton & Bowles Advertising) bought the business from Sears in 1941 and built a nationwide sales force with a hard-sell reputation. Britannica released its first

foreign-language encyclopedia, *Enciclopedia Barsa,* in 1957 and acquired dictionary publisher G. & C. Merriam in 1964.

When Benton died in 1974, he bequeathed the operation to the non-profit William Benton Foundation, the sole beneficiary of which was the University of Chicago. Britannica later bought out rival Compton's Encyclopedia in the mid-1970s. The 1989 CD-ROM release of *Compton's MultiMedia Encyclopedia* was a first for the industry, but Britannica sold Compton's NewMedia division to Chicago's Tribune Company in 1993 just before the CD-ROM market exploded. The company also promised not to release a competing multimedia version of *Encyclopaedia Britannica* for two years. Not realizing that the electronic revolution was upon them and reluctant to change its established and profitable door-to-door sales techniques, the conservative company fell behind challengers who offered CD-ROMs, including Microsoft and its *Funk & Wagnalls* product (later relaunched as *Encarta*).

Jacob Safra, a *Britannica* lover since childhood, led a group that paid $135 million for the struggling company in 1996. With book sales dwindling and heavy competition, Britannica cut its prices and ceased its door-to-door marketing that year. It agreed to sell both its CD-ROM and print encyclopedias in retail stores in 1997, and lured publisher Paul Hoffman away from Walt Disney's successful *Discover* magazine. Britannica Internet Guide (BIG), a free Internet search engine, launched that year. Britannica added guest columns and other features to BIG in 1998 and renamed it eBlast (it changed the site's name again to Britannica the following year).

Encyclopaedia Britannica Holdings (Safra's umbrella firm for the publisher) launched a sister firm, Britannica.com, in 1999 to oversee the company's electronic and Internet products and services. CEO Don Yannias resigned his post with the print company and took the reins of the new digital firm, allowing Hoffman to take over as the publisher's president. Britannica.com struggled with the rest of the Internet industry in 2000, laying off almost 25% of its staff.

In 2001 Yannias left the company entirely and was replaced by Ilan Yeshua, an executive from an Israeli educational technology firm. Later that year, the company integrated Britannica.com back into the encyclopedia unit of Encyclopaedia Britannica, a move that involved severely downsizing the Web staff.

OFFICERS

Chairman: Jacob E. Safra
CEO: Ilan Yeshua
EVP, Secretary, and General Counsel: William J. Bowe
VP Operations and Finance: Richard Anderson
VP and Editor: Dale Hoiberg
President and Publisher, Merriam-Webster: John Morse
Director Strategic Marketing and Planning:
Diana Simeon Spadoni
Auditors: PricewaterhouseCoopers

LOCATIONS

HQ: 310 S. Michigan Ave., Chicago, IL 60604
Phone: 312-347-7000 **Fax:** 312-347-7399
Web: corporate.britannica.com

PRODUCTS/OPERATIONS

Selected Products
Dictionaries
Merriam Webster's Biographical Dictionary
Merriam Webster's Collegiate Dictionary
Merriam Webster's Collegiate Thesaurus
Merriam Webster's Dictionary of Law
Encyclopedias
Britannica First Edition Replica Set
Encyclopaedia Britannica
The Encyclopedia of Popular Music
Other Reference Works
The Annals of America
Gray's Anatomy
Great Books of the Western World

COMPETITORS

Berkshire Hathaway
Dow Jones
Franklin Electronic Publishers
Grolier
Harcourt General
LexisNexis
McGraw-Hill
Microsoft
Pearson
Random House
Thomson Corporation
Time
Vivendi Universal Publishing

HISTORICAL FINANCIALS & EMPLOYEES

Private FYE: December 31	Annual Growth	9/92	9/93	9/94	9/95	9/96	9/97	9/98	*12/99	12/00	12/01
Sales ($ mil.)	(10.1%)	586	540	453	400	375	325	300	279	275	225
Employees	(14.8%)	1,100	1,000	900	800	700	400	400	350	300	260

* Fiscal year change

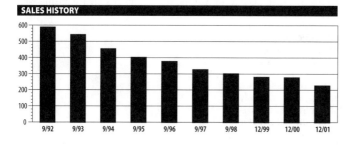

SALES HISTORY

ENTERPRISE RENT-A-CAR

This Enterprise is boldly going where it hasn't gone before — the airport. The company, which offers to ferry customers to the rental office, is the largest car rental firm in the US. With about 525,000 cars in its fleet, Enterprise operates in the US, Canada, Germany, Ireland, and the UK. The company targets customers whose own cars are in the shop or who need a rental for short trips; it has also begun serving the airport market. Controlled by founder Jack Taylor and his family, Enterprise has spun off its non-automotive operations (balloons, footwear, a golf course, hotel amenities, and prison supplies, formerly known as Enterprise Capital Group) as Centric Group.

Enterprise Rent-A-Car operates through more than 5,000 offices in North America and Europe. The company's sites in and near the nation's top 100 airports offer rates that are up to 20% lower than those of most major competitors.

Enterprise also leases vehicles and manages fleets for other companies (Enterprise Fleet Services), and it sells cars (Enterprise Car Sales).

Founder Taylor's son Andrew is Enterprise's chairman and CEO.

HISTORY

In 1957 Jack Taylor, the sales manager for a Cadillac dealership in St. Louis, hit on the idea that leasing cars might be an easier way to make money than selling them. Taylor's idea sounded good to his boss, Arthur Lindburg, who agreed to set Taylor up in the leasing business. In return for a 50% pay cut, Taylor received 25% of the new enterprise, called Executive Leasing, which began in the walled-off body shop of a car dealership.

In the early 1960s Taylor started renting cars for short periods as well as leasing them. When his leasing agents expressed annoyance with the rental operation, Taylor turned that business over to Don Holtzman. Holtzman realized that his 17-car rental operation was too little to take on industry giants like Hertz and Avis; instead, he concentrated on the "home city" or replacement market. He offered competitive rates to insurance adjusters who needed to find cars for policyholders whose cars were damaged or stolen. Propelled by court decisions that required casualty companies to pay for loss of transportation, Taylor expanded from his St. Louis base in 1969 with a branch office in Atlanta. Since another car leasing outfit in Georgia was already named Executive, Taylor changed the name of his company to Enterprise Rent-A-Car.

The company expanded into Florida and Texas in the early 1970s, targeting garages and body shops that performed repairs for insured drivers. Oil price shocks of that period compelled Taylor to diversify his operations. In 1974 Enterprise acquired Keefe Coffee and Supply, a supplier of coffee, packaged foods, and beverages to prison commissaries. To service *FORTUNE* 1000 companies wanting to lease or buy more than 50 vehicles, the company started Enterprise Fleet Services in 1976.

Enterprise acquired Courtesy Products (coffee and tea for hotel guests) in 1980, and the following year sales reached the $100 million mark. It acquired ELCO Chevrolet in 1986, the same year it formed Crawford Supply (hygiene products for prisons). Taylor bought out the Lindburg family's interest in Enterprise the next year. In 1989 Enterprise raised its brand recognition with a national TV campaign that focused on an older and higher-income audience by showing its commercials exclusively on CBS. Also in the late 1980s, the company began targeting "discretionary rentals" to families with visiting relatives or with children home for the holidays.

Taylor's son, Andrew, became CEO of Enterprise in 1991, and sales topped $1 billion for the first time. By 1994 sales had passed $2 billion, and the company had expanded into Canada and the UK. By 1996 Enterprise had a fleet of more than 300,000 vehicles. That year it opened several locations in the UK. In 1997 the company opened locations in Ireland, Munich, Scotland, and Wales.

In 1998 Enterprise battled other rental firms over use of the advertising tagline, "We'll pick you up," which it had trademarked. Rent-A-Wreck lost a court case over the matter; Hertz settled with Enterprise over use of the phrase.

In 1999 the company more than doubled the number of its airport locations in an attempt to woo occasional travelers (rather than hard-core corporate fliers). That year the Taylor family split off their non-automotive operations (including companies involved in prison supplies, hotel amenities, a golf course, mylar balloons, and athletic shoes) as Centric Group.

In 2001 the company's COO, Donald Ross, became the first non-Taylor to be promoted to president after Jack Taylor was named chairman emeritus and Andrew gave up the president title to assume the company's chairmanship while remaining as CEO.

Chairman and CEO: Andrew C. Taylor
President and COO: Donald L. Ross
SVP and CFO: William W. Snyder
SVP of Corporate Strategy: M.W. Rogers
SVP of North American Operations: Pam Nicholson
VP of Corporate Communications: Patrick Farrell
VP of ELCO Chevrolet: Mark S. Hadfield
VP of Fleet Services: Steven E. Bloom
VP of Human Resources: Ed Adams
VP of International Operations: Mike Robertson
VP of Marketing Communications: Steve Smith
VP of Rental: Jim Runnels
Assistant VP of Corporate Communications:
  Christy Conrad
Auditors: Ernst & Young LLP

LOCATIONS

HQ: 600 Corporate Park Dr., St. Louis, MO 63105
Phone: 314-512-5000   **Fax:** 314-512-4706
Web: www.enterprise.com

Enterprise Rent-A-Car has more than 5,000 offices in
the US, Canada, Germany, Ireland, and the UK.

PRODUCTS/OPERATIONS

Operations
ELCO Chevrolet Inc. (car dealership, St. Louis)
Enterprise Car Sales (used car sales)
Enterprise Fleet Services (vehicle leasing)
Enterprise Rent-A-Car

COMPETITORS

Airways Transportation Group
AMERCO
AutoNation
Budget Group
Cendant
Dollar Thrifty Automotive Group
Hertz
Penske
Rent-A-Wreck
Ryder
Sixt

HISTORICAL FINANCIALS & EMPLOYEES

Private FYE: July 31	Annual Growth	7/93	7/94	7/95	7/96	7/97	7/98	7/99	7/00	7/01	7/02
Sales ($ mil.)	16.4%	1,659	2,108	2,464	3,127	3,680	4,180	4,730	5,600	6,300	6,500
Employees	15.2%	14,000	18,500	21,703	28,806	35,182	37,000	40,000	45,000	50,000	50,000

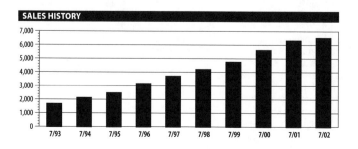

SALES HISTORY

EQUITY GROUP INVESTMENTS

Equity Group Investments is the apex of financier Sam Zell's pyramid of business holdings. The Chicago-based private investment group controls a multi-billion dollar mix of businesses, including real estate investment trusts (REITs), restaurants, and cruise ships. Zell's REIT portfolio makes him the US's largest owner of property leased by manufactured homeowners (Manufactured Home Communities), office buildings (Equity Office Properties Trust is ranked # 1 in the nation), and apartments (Equity Residential Properties Trust). Sam Zell has a controlling interest in Equity Group Investments.

Equity Office Properties is one of the largest landlords in San Francisco and Seattle. Zell has made his niche — and a lot of money — by purchasing distressed properties and turning them into profitable investments (for which he earned the nickname "Grave Dancer").

Equity Group Investments has rescued many companies floundering in bankruptcy and often buys during downturns. Many acquisitions are made through the Zell/Chilmark Fund. Zell's Equity Residential Properties continues to build its portfolio through acquisitions.

Zell has made forays into other investments with mixed success. He bought into sugar mills in Mexico that were nationalized by the government. Another holding, American Classic Voyages, suffered a combo of misfortune with the soft Hawaiian cruise industry on one side and the aftermath of September 11 on travel on the other. It has filed for Chapter 11 reorganization. As bargains dry up in the US, Zell is rediscovering a junk-bond investing strategy.

HISTORY

Sam Zell's first business endeavor was photographing his eighth-grade prom. In 1953 he graduated to reselling 50-cent *Playboy* magazines to schoolmates at a 200% markup.

While at the University of Michigan in the 1960s, Zell teamed with fraternity brother Robert Lurie to manage off-campus student housing. In graduate school, they invested in residential properties and formed Equity Financial and Management Co. after graduation. Their collection of distressed properties grew in the 1970s as Zell made the deals and Lurie made them work. Zell's hands-off management style had its drawbacks, however: In 1976 Zell and three others (including his brother-in-law) were indicted on federal tax-related charges after selling a Reno, Nevada, hotel and apartment complex. The charges were later dropped against Zell and another defendant (only the brother-in-law was convicted).

In the 1980s tax-law changes led the team to begin buying troubled companies. They started in 1983 with Great American Management and Investment, a foundering real estate manager they turned into an investment vehicle. Other targets included Itel (1984, now Anixter International) and oil and gas company Nucorp (1988, now part of insurer CNA Surety). The true attraction in many of these acquisitions, however, lay in tax-loss carryforwards that could be applied against future earnings.

Lurie died in 1990, after which Zell began to consolidate his power and ease out old friends. (Lurie's estate still owns shares of many Zell enterprises.) That year Zell and David Schulte formed the Zell/Chilmark Fund, which soon owned or controlled such companies as Schwinn (sold 1997), Sealy (sold 1997), and Revco (sold 1997). Among the fund's failures was West Coast retailer Broadway Stores, which Zell bought out of bankruptcy in 1992; when California's slumping economy prevented a rapid turnaround, Zell sold it (once again near bankruptcy) in 1995.

Starting in 1987, Zell formed four real estate funds with Merrill Lynch; six years later, both Equity Residential Properties Trust and Manufactured Home Communities went public. As REITs became popular with investors, more trusts began vying for distressed assets — Zell's traditional lifeblood. In 1997 Zell melded four of his commercial real estate funds into another REIT, Equity Office Properties Trust, and took it public.

In 1998, as investors and financiers looked for fresh opportunities, Zell launched Equity International Properties, a fund targeting acquisitions in Latin America and elsewhere. That year a civil racketeering suit brought against Zell by former executive Richard Perlman shed light on "handshake" loans to top executives and other informal business deals. In 1999 Zell sold Jacor Communications to radio industry consolidator Clear Channel Communications. Equity Group Investments remains diversified, however: That year Equity Office Properties teamed with venture capital firm Kleiner Perkins Caufield & Byers to form Broadband Office to offer Internet and phone services to Zell's tenants and those of other property owners.

Equity Office Properties Trust continued its buying into the 21st century, claiming New York-based Cornerstone Properties (2000) and California's Spieker Properties (2001).

Chairman: Samuel Zell, age 60
Co-Chairman: Sheli Z. Rosenberg, age 60
President: Donald J. Liebentritt, age 51

LOCATIONS

HQ: Equity Group Investments, L.L.C.
    2 N. Riverside Plaza, Ste. 600, Chicago, IL 60606
Phone: 312-454-1800   **Fax:** 312-454-0610

PRODUCTS/OPERATIONS

Selected Affiliates
American Classic Voyages Co. (36%, cruises)
Angelo & Maxie's, Inc. (38%, restaurants)
Anixter International, Inc. (14%, communications
    network equipment)
Capital Trust, Inc. (commercial real estate finance)
Davel Communications, Inc. (14%, pay-telephone
    operator)
Equity International Properties (overseas buyout fund)
Equity Office Properties Trust (4%, office property REIT)
Equity Residential Properties Trust (3%, apartments
    REIT)
Manufactured Home Communities, Inc. (15%, mobile
    home communities REIT)
Transmedia Network (40%, consumer savings programs)
Zell/Chilmark Fund L.P. (investment vulture fund)

COMPETITORS

Apollo Advisors
Blackstone Group
Carlyle Group
Clayton, Dubilier
Goldman Sachs
JMB Realty
KKR
Thomas Lee
Trump

ERNST & YOUNG INTERNATIONAL

Accounting may actually be the *second*-oldest profession, and Ernst & Young is one of the oldest practitioners. Ernst & Young is also one of the world's largest accounting firms, offering auditing and accounting services around the globe. The firm also provides legal services and services relating to emerging growth companies, human resources issues, online security, risk management, and transactions (mergers and acquisitions, IPOs, and the like).

Ernst & Young has one of the world's largest tax practices, serving multinational clients that have to comply with multiple local tax laws.

After spending decades building them, the big accountancies have all moved toward shedding their consultancies, because of internal and regulatory pressures, as well as the perceived conflict of interest in providing auditing and consulting services to the same clients. Ernst & Young was the first to split off its consultancy, selling it in 2000 to what is now Cap Gemini Ernst & Young.

Ernst & Young, which gained an impressive amount of weight in former rival Andersen's diaspora, has also boosted its legal services, assembling some 2,000 lawyers in more than 60 countries.

In 2002 Ernst & Young ran into Andersen-style trouble of its own, when federal regulators sued the firm for its alleged role in the failure of Superior Bank FSB, and threatened civil charges for purported fraud relating to Cendant.

Ernst & Young that year also formed an alliance with former New York City mayor Rudy Giuliani to help launch a business consultancy and an investment firm bearing the Giuliani name.

HISTORY

In 1494 Luca Pacioli's *Summa di Arithmetica* became the first published text on double-entry bookkeeping, but it was almost 400 years before accounting became a profession.

In 1849 Frederick Whinney joined the UK firm of Harding & Pullein. His ledgers were so clear that he was advised to take up accounting, which was a growth field as stock companies proliferated. Whinney became a name partner in 1859 and his sons followed him into the business. The firm became Whinney, Smith & Whinney (WS&W) in 1894. After WWII, WS&W formed an alliance with Ernst & Ernst (founded in Cleveland in 1903 by brothers Alwin and Theodore Ernst), with each firm operating on the other's behalf across the Atlantic.

Whinney merged with Brown, Fleming & Murray in 1965 to become Whinney Murray. In 1979 Whinney Murray, Turquands Barton Mayhew

(also a UK firm), and Ernst & Ernst merged to form Ernst & Whinney.

But Ernst & Whinney wasn't done merging. Ten years later, when it was the fourth-largest accounting firm, it merged with #5 Arthur Young, which had been founded by Scotsman Arthur Young in 1895 in Kansas City. Long known as "old reliable," Arthur Young fell on hard times in the 1980s because its audit relationships with failed S&Ls led to expensive litigation (settled in 1992 for $400 million).

Thus the new firm of Ernst & Young faced a rocky start. In 1990 it fended off rumors of collapse. The next year it slashed payroll, even thinning its partner roster. Exhausted by the S&L wars, in 1994 the firm replaced its pugnacious general counsel, Carl Riggio, with the more cost-conscious Kathryn Oberly.

In the mid-1990s Ernst & Young concentrated on consulting, particularly in software applications, and grew through acquisitions. In 1996 the firm bought Houston-based Wright Killen & Co., a petroleum and petrochemicals consulting firm, to form Ernst & Young Wright Killen. It also entered new alliances that year, including ones with Washington-based ISD/Shaw, which provided banking industry consulting, and India's Tata Consulting.

In 1997 Ernst & Young was sued for a record $4 billion for its alleged failure to effectively handle the 1993 restructuring of the defunct Merry-Go-Round Enterprises retail chain (it settled for $185 million in 1999.) On the heels of a merger deal between Coopers & Lybrand and Price Waterhouse, Ernst & Young agreed in 1997 to merge with KPMG International. But Ernst & Young called off the negotiations in 1998, citing the uncertain regulatory process they faced.

In 1999 the firm reached a settlement in lawsuits regarding accounting errors at Informix and Cendant and sold its UK and Southern African trust and fiduciary businesses to Royal Bank of Canada (now RBC Financial Group).

In 2000 Ernst & Young became the first of the (then) Big Five firms to sell its consultancy, dealing it to France's Cap Gemini Group for about $11 billion. The following year the UK accountancy watchdog group announced it would investigate Ernst & Young for its handling of the accounts of UK-based The Equitable Life Assurance Society. The insurer was forced to close to new business in 2000 because of massive financial difficulties.

Global Chairman; Chairman and CEO, Ernst & Young LLP: James S. Turley
CEO, Ernst & Young Global Practice: Richard S. Bobrow
Global Managing Partner - Markets: Mike Cullen
CFO and Global Managing Partner - Finance and Infrastrucure: Norbert R. Becker
Global Managing Partner - Practice Integration: Jean-Charles Raufast
Global Managing Partner - People: Timothy T. Griffy
Global Executive Partner: Paul J. Ostling
Deputy Global Managing Partner - Infrastructure; VC of Knowledge & Technology, Ernst & Young LLP: John G. Peetz Jr.
Vice Chairman - Strategy: Beth A. Brooke
Vice Chairman - Tax: Karl Johansson
Vice Chairman - Law: Patrick Bignon
Vice Chairman - Sales: Patrick J.P. Flochel

LOCATIONS

HQ: 5 Times Square, New York, NY 10036
Phone: 212-773-3000   **Fax:** 212-773-6350
Web: www.eyi.com

PRODUCTS/OPERATIONS

2002 Sales

	$ mil.	% of total
Assurance & advisory business services	5,752	57
Tax & law	3,418	34
Corporate finance	732	7
Other	222	2
Total	**10,124**	**100**

Selected Services

Assurance and Advisory
Accounting advisory
Actuarial services
Audits
Business risk services
Internal audit
Real estate advisory services
Technology and security risk services
Transaction support services

Emerging Growth Companies
Corporate finance services
IPO services
Mergers and acquisitions advisory
Operational consulting
Strategic advisory

Global Employment Solutions
Compensation and benefits consulting
Cost optimization and risk management
Global workforce management advisory
Transaction support services

Law
Anti-trust, competition, and regulated marks advisory
Banking and securities advisory
Bankruptcy and insolvency assistance and advisory
Commercial and trade advisory and compliance
Corporate mergers and acquisitions advisory and compliance
E-commerce advisory and compliance
Employment advisory and compliance
Environmental advisory and compliance
Intellectual property advisory, protection, and compliance
Real estate/commercial property advisory and compliance

Tax
Customs and international trade
Electronic VAT assurance
International tax
Partial exemption evaluation process
Tax outsourcing

Transactions
Capital management
Due diligence and transaction support
Financial and business modeling
M&A advisory
Strategic finance
Valuation

COMPETITORS

American Management   Grant Thornton
Bain & Company   International
BDO International   IBM
Deloitte Touche Tohmatsu   KPMG
                                        PricewaterhouseCoopers

HISTORICAL FINANCIALS & EMPLOYEES

Partnership FYE: June 30	Annual Growth	9/93	9/94	9/95	9/96	9/97	9/98	9/99	*6/00	6/01	6/02
Sales ($ mil.)	6.3%	5,839	6,020	6,867	7,800	9,100	10,900	12,500	9,500	9,900	10,124
Employees	7.3%	58,377	61,287	68,452	72,000	79,750	85,000	97,800	88,625	82,000	110,000

* Fiscal year change

SALES HISTORY

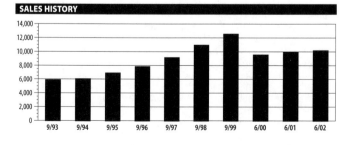

FARMLAND INDUSTRIES, INC.

Farmland Industries helps its members farm land industriously. Farmland is the #1 agricultural cooperative in the US and is a competitor in agribusiness worldwide, exporting products (mainly grain) to about 60 countries. It is a major beef packer in the US and also a top producer of pork products. Farmland Industries owned by about 1,700 local co-ops that are made up of about 600,000 farmers in the US, Canada, and Mexico. The co-op provides farmers with feed, fertilizer, and pesticides; it also processes, stores, and markets their crops and livestock. Farmland lost $90 million in 2001 and filed for Chapter 11 bankruptcy in 2002.

As a major US meat company, the company makes and markets fresh and processed beef, catfish, and pork through its Farmland National Beef, Southern Farm Fish Processors, and Farmland Foods subsidiaries. It also has more than 60 joint ventures and alliances, including WILFARM (with Wilbur-Ellis Company, chemical products).

After declaring bankruptcy Farmland sought court approval to pay approximately $8 million to 96 employees so that they would stay with the company through its reorganization.

HISTORY

In 1929 President Herbert Hoover pushed passage of the Agricultural Marketing Act (AMA) to encourage cooperatives as one means to remedy the hard times facing the US agriculture industry in the 1920s. However record grain harvests in 1928 and 1929 foiled its intent; a glut ground down prices, and later the Depression (and drought) dried up markets.

By the time of the AMA, Union Oil Company, Farmland Industries' predecessor, was already in the works. Union Oil was formed in 1929 to provide petroleum supplies to farmers in a period of rapid agricultural mechanization. In the early 1930s, as the government sought to regulate supply by introducing payments for taking land out of production, Union Oil increased the range of its co-op activities. It changed its name to Consumers Cooperative Association in 1935.

Farming did not revive until WWII, though price controls and supports remained an important feature of agricultural policy. Throughout this period the performance of Consumers Cooperative's growing membership of primary producers and local co-ops remained tied to raw commodity prices. In 1959, however, to decrease its reliance on commodity prices, Consumers Cooperative bought a pork processing plant in Denison, Iowa, and began making Farmbest meat products. It was a success, and four years later the co-op opened another plant in Iowa Falls. In 1966

Consumers Cooperative became Farmland Industries, and in the 1970s it expanded into beef production. However, when prices and consumption declined, it exited the field.

Overzealous expansion by American farmers in the 1970s was followed in the 1980s by an industrywide crisis. When the farm economy went down, it hurt the co-op's sales of inputs such as fertilizers. Cheap fertilizer imports, low crude oil prices, and high natural gas prices also took their toll, and the co-op lost more than $210 million in 1985 and 1986. James Rainey took over as CEO in 1986 and turned the operation around. Farmland began placing a greater emphasis on food processing and marketing, otherwise known as outputs.

Harry Cleberg succeeded Rainey in 1991. The co-op had stopped handling grains in 1985, after a period of volatile prices, but it profitably re-entered the market in 1992. The next year it bought the Tradigrain unit of British Petroleum (now BP plc). The purchase led Farmland into markets outside the US. Also in 1993 the co-op resumed beef processing and expanded its pork processing facilities.

During the late 1990s, the co-op formed joint ventures and partnerships spanning its range of activities; feeds, grain marketing, energy products and in 1998 absorbed SF Services, an agricultural cooperative.

In 1999 Farmland and Cenex Harvest States voted to merge their entire operations; although Farmland members approved the deal, Cenex members voted it down. Instead Farmland partnered with Land O'Lakes and Cenex to form Agriliance to supply farm products to members. In 2000 Farmland combined its feed business with Land O' Lakes in a joint venture forming North America's top feed company. In the fall of 2000 company veteran Robert Honse was named CEO as Cleberg retired.

Skyrocketing natural gas prices during 2000 hit the co-op's fertilizer business hard, prompting it to shut down one facility. Laden with debt, in mid-2001 the co-op handed the operation of its 24 grain elevators over to Archer Daniels Midland as part of a new grain-marketing venture with the agribusiness giant. In November 2001 the co-op sold its interest in Country Energy to CHS Cooperatives. Farmland lost $90 million in 2001, but the co-op also reduced its debt that year by $268 million and administrative costs by nearly $40 million.

In 2002 Smithfield Foods offered to buy out troubled Farmland; however, Farmland chose to file for bankruptcy instead.

OFFICERS

Chairman: Harry Fehrenbacher, age 54
Vice Chairman and VP: Jody Bezner, age 61
President and CEO: Robert B. Terry, age 46
EVP and CFO: Steve Rhodes, age 48
EVP; President, Crop Production: Stanley A. Riemann, age 51, $298,782 pay
EVP; President, Refrigerated Foods:
William G. Fielding, age 55, $350,000 pay
EVP; President, World Grain: Tim R. Daugherty, age 49
VP, Human Resources: Holly D. McCoy
VP, Strategic Sourcing: Michael T. Sweat, age 56
Auditors: KPMG LLP

LOCATIONS

HQ: 12200 N. Ambassador Dr., Kansas City, MO 64163
Phone: 816-713-7000   **Fax:** 816-713-6323
Web: www.farmland.com

More than 600,000 farmers and their cooperatives, located in the US, Canada, and Mexico, form Farmland Industries, which conducts business in nearly 60 countries.

PRODUCTS/OPERATIONS

Selected Subsidiaries and Joint Ventures
Agriliance, LLC (with Land O'Lakes and Cenex Harvest
    States to supply fertilizer, pesticides, herbicides, and
    seed to farmers)
Farmland Foods (99%, 11 food processing plants)
Farmland Hydro, LP (50%, with Norsk Hydro; phosphate
    fertilizer manufacturing)
Farmland MissChem Limited (50%, anhydrous ammonia
    manufacturing)
Farmland National Beef Packing Co., LP (71%)
Land O'Lakes Farmland Feed
SF Phosphates, Limited Liability Company (50%,
    fertilizer manufacturing)
Southern Farm Fish Processors
Tradigrain SA (international grain trading)
WILFARM, LLC (50%, with Wilbur-Ellis Co.; pesticides)

Consumer Product Brands
Black Angus Beef
Carando (bread, specialty meats)
Farmland (processed pork products)
Farmstead
Maple River
OhSe
Regal
Roegelein (processed pork products)
Springwater Farms

COMPETITORS

ADM
Ag Processing
Agway
American Foods
Cargill
Cenex Harvest States
CF Industries
ConAgra
ContiGroup
DeBruce Grain
Exxon Mobil
Gold Kist
GROWMARK
Hormel
IBP
IMC Global
JR Simplot
Rose Packing
Royal Dutch/Shell Group
Scoular
Smithfield Foods
Southern States
Transammonia

HISTORICAL FINANCIALS & EMPLOYEES

Cooperative FYE: August 31	Annual Growth	8/93	8/94	8/95	8/96	8/97	8/98	8/99	8/00	8/01	8/02
Sales ($ mil.)	3.7%	4,723	6,678	7,257	9,789	9,148	8,775	10,709	12,239	11,763	6,574
Net income ($ mil.)	—	(30)	74	163	126	135	59	14	(29)	(90)	(347)
Income as % of sales	—	—	1.1%	2.2%	1.3%	1.5%	0.7%	0.1%	—	—	—
Employees	6.0%	8,155	12,000	12,700	14,700	14,600	16,100	17,700	15,000	14,500	13,800

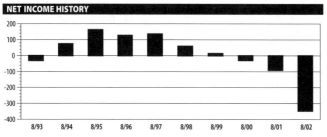

NET INCOME HISTORY

2002 FISCAL YEAR-END
Debt ratio: 24.6%
Return on equity: —
Cash ($ mil.): 0
Current ratio: 1.40
Long-term debt ($ mil.): 140

FEDERAL RESERVE SYSTEM

Where do banks go when they need a loan? To the Federal Reserve System, which sets the discount interest rate (or prime rate), the base rate at which its member banks may borrow. Known as the Fed, the system oversees a network of 12 Federal Reserve Banks located in major US cities; these in turn regulate banks in their districts and ensure they maintain adequate reserves. The Fed also clears money transfers, issues currency, and buys or sells government securities to regulate the money supply. Through its powerful New York bank, the Fed conducts foreign currency transactions, trades on the world market to support the US dollar's value, and stores gold for foreign governments and international agencies.

A seven-member Board of Governors, chaired by former Ayn Rand compadre Alan Greenspan, oversees the Fed's activities. As chairman under four different presidents, Greenspan has wielded more power than perhaps any Fed chief in history and securities markets virtually dangle on his every word.

Fed Members are appointed by the US President and confirmed by the Senate for one-time 14-year terms, staggered at two-year intervals to prevent political stacking. The seven governors compose the majority of the 12-person Federal Open Market Committee, which determines monetary policy. The five remaining members are reserve bank presidents who rotate in one-year terms, with New York always holding a place. Although the Fed enjoys significant political and financial freedom (it even operates at a profit), the chairman is required to testify before Congress twice a year. National member banks must own stock in their Federal Reserve Bank, though it is optional for state-chartered banks.

HISTORY

When New York's Knickerbocker Trust Company failed in 1907, it brought on a panic that was stemmed by J. P. Morgan, who strong-armed his fellow bankers into supporting shaky New York banks. The incident showed the need for a central bank.

Morgan's actions sparked fears of his economic power and spurred congressional efforts to establish a central bank. After a six-year struggle between eastern money interests and populist monetary reformers, the 1913 Federal Reserve Act was passed. Twelve Federal Reserve districts were created, but New York's economic might ensured it would be the most powerful.

New York bank head Benjamin Strong dominated the Fed in the 1920s, countering the glut of European gold flooding the US in 1923 by selling securities from the Fed's portfolio. After

he died in 1928, the Fed couldn't stabilize prices. Such difficulty, along with low rates encouraging members to use Fed loans for stock speculation, helped set the stage for 1929's crash.

During the Depression and WWII, the Fed yielded to the demands of the Treasury to buy bonds. But after WWII it sought independence, cultivating Congress to help free it from Treasury demands. This effort was led by chairman William McChesney Martin, with the assistance of New York bank president Alan Sproul (also a rival for the chairmanship). Martin diluted Sproul's influence by governing by consensus with the other bank leaders.

The Fed managed the economy successfully in the postwar boom, but it was stymied by inflation in the late 1960s. In the early 1970s the New York bank also faced the collapse of the fixed currency exchange-rate system and the growth of currency trading. Its role as foreign currency trader became even more crucial as the dollar's value eroded amid rising oil prices and a slowing economy.

The US suffered from double-digit inflation in 1979 as President Jimmy Carter appointed New York Fed president Paul Volcker as chairman. Volcker, believing that raising interest rates a few points would not suffice, allowed the banks to raise their discount rates and increased bank reserve requirements to reduce the money supply. By the time inflation eased, Ronald Reagan was president.

During the 1980s and 1990s, US budget fights limited options for controlling the economy through spending decisions, so the Fed's actions became more important. Its higher profile brought calls for more access to its decision-making processes. Alan Greenspan took over as chairman in 1987 (and has since been reappointed by Presidents Bush and Clinton).

The US economy seemed immune to the Asian currency crisis of 1997 and 1998, so the Federal Reserve remained relatively quiescent. But when Russia defaulted on some of its bonds in 1998, leading to the near-collapse of hedge fund Long-Term Capital Management, the New York Federal Reserve Bank brokered a bailout by the fund's lenders and investors.

This led in 1999 to new guidelines for banks' risk management. The next year, the Fed faced up to the Internet age, taking a look at e-banking supervision. After raising interest rates to stave off inflation during the go-go late 1990s, the Fed cut rates an unprecedented 11 times in 2001 (to a 40-year low of 1.75%) to help spur the flagging post-boom economy.

Chairman of the Board of Governors: Alan Greenspan, age 76
Vice Chairman of the Board of Governors: Roger W. Ferguson Jr., age 50
Member of the Board of Governors: Edward M. Gramlich, age 63
Member of the Board of Governors: Susan Schmidt Bies, age 55
Member of the Board of Governors: Mark W. Olson
Member of the Board of Governors: Ben S. Bernanke, age 48
Member of the Board of Governors: Donald L. Kohn, age 59
President, Federal Reserve Bank of Boston: Cathy E. Minehan, age 55
President, Federal Reserve Bank of New York: William J. McDonough, age 68
President, Federal Reserve Bank of Philadelphia: Anthony M. Santomero, age 56
President, Federal Reserve Bank of Cleveland: Jerry L. Jordan, age 60
President, Federal Reserve Bank of Richmond: J. Alfred Broaddus, age 63
President, Federal Reserve Bank of Atlanta: Jack Guynn, age 59
President, Federal Reserve Bank of Chicago: Michael H. Moskow
President, Federal Reserve Bank of St. Louis: William Poole, age 65
President, Federal Reserve Bank of Minneapolis: Gary H. Stern, age 57
President, Federal Reserve Bank of Kansas City: Thomas N. Hoenig, age 56
President, Federal Reserve Bank of Dallas: Robert D. McTeer, age 59
President, Federal Reserve Bank of San Francisco: Robert T. Parry, age 63

HQ: 20th Street and Constitution Avenue NW, Washington, DC 20551
Phone: 202-452-3000
Web: www.federalreserve.gov

Federal Reserve Banks
Atlanta
Boston
Chicago
Cleveland
Dallas
Kansas City, Missouri
Minneapolis
New York
Philadelphia
Richmond, Virginia
St. Louis
San Francisco

HISTORICAL FINANCIALS & EMPLOYEES

Government agency FYE: December 31	Annual Growth	12/92	12/93	12/94	12/95	12/96	12/97	12/98	12/99	12/00	12/01
Assets ($ mil.)	(1.5%)	—	—	—	—	—	—	—	674,460	609,877	654,949
Net income ($ mil.)	3.3%	—	—	—	—	—	—	—	26,262	29,868	28,035
Income as % of assets	—	—	—	—	—	—	—	—	3.9%	4.9%	4.3%
Employees	—	—	—	—	—	—	—	—	—	23,056	—

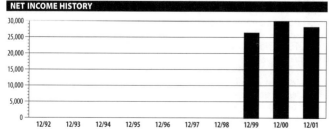

NET INCOME HISTORY

2001 FISCAL YEAR-END
Equity as % of assets: 2.2%
Return on assets: 4.4%
Return on equity: 196.9%
Long-term debt ($ mil.): 611,757
Sales ($ mil.): 31,068

FELD ENTERTAINMENT, INC.

A lot of clowning around has helped Feld Entertainment become one of the largest live entertainment producers in the world. The company entertains some 10 million people each year through its centerpiece, Ringling Bros. and Barnum & Bailey Circus, which visits about 90 locations. It also produces the upscale Barnum's Kaleidoscope, which features acrobats and aerialists instead of elephants and clowns. In addition, Feld produces several touring ice shows, including Disney On Ice shows such as *Beauty and the Beast* and *Toy Story,* and it owns the Siegfried & Roy show in Las Vegas.

Chairman and CEO Kenneth Feld, whose father Irving began managing the circus in 1956, owns the company and personally oversees many of its productions.

HISTORY

When five-year-old Irving Feld found a $1 bill in 1923, he told his mother, "I'm going to buy a circus." He started by working the sideshows of traveling circuses before settling in Washington, DC, in 1940. Feld, who was white, opened the Super Cut-Rate Drugstore in a black section of the segregated city with the backing of the NAACP. In 1944 he opened the Super Music City record store and started his own record company, Super Disc. Feld and his brother Israel also began promoting outdoor concerts. When rock and roll became popular in the 1950s, Feld promoted Chubby Checker and Fats Domino, among others.

Feld came a step closer to his dream in 1956 when he began managing the Ringling Bros. and Barnum & Bailey Circus for majority owner John Ringling North. North's circus traced its roots back to 1871 and P. T. Barnum's Grand Traveling Museum, Menagerie, Caravan, and Circus. Barnum's circus merged with James Bailey's circus in 1881, creating Barnum & Bailey. In 1907 Bailey's widow sold Barnum & Bailey to North's uncles, the Ringling brothers, who had started their circus in 1884.

Among Feld's suggestions to North was moving the circus into air-conditioned arenas, saving $50,000 a week, because 1,800 roustabouts were no longer needed to set up tents. Feld continued to promote music acts, but he suffered a serious blow in 1959 when three of his stars — Buddy Holly, Ritchie Valens, and J. P. Richardson (the Big Bopper) — died in a plane crash.

Feld's dream of owning a circus finally was realized in 1967 when he and investors paid $8 million for Ringling Brothers. He fired most of the circus' performers and opened a Clown College to train new ones. Feld bought a German circus

the following year to obtain animal trainer Gunther Gebel-Williams (who then spent the next 30 years with Ringling Brothers). Feld split the circus into two units in 1969, so he could book it in two parts of the country at the same time and double his profits. Feld took the company public that year.

Feld and the other stockholders sold the circus to Mattel in 1971 for $47 million in stock; Feld stayed on as manager and held on to the lucrative concession business, Sells-Floto. He persuaded Mattel to buy the Ice Follies, Holiday on Ice, and the Siegfried & Roy magic show in 1979. Mattel sold the circus back to Feld in 1982 for $22.5 million, along with the ice shows and the magic show. Feld died two years later, and his son Kenneth became head of the company. A chip off the old block, Kenneth fired almost all the circus performers when he took over.

In an attempt to leverage the Barnum & Bailey brand, the company opened four retail store locations in 1990, but the venture failed and the stores were closed two years later. A constant target of animal rights activists, Feld began backing conservation efforts on behalf of the endangered Asian elephant, and established the Center for Elephant Conservation in Florida in 1995. The next year the company changed its name to Feld Entertainment.

Under increasing pressure as the company's creative guru and managerial boss, Feld hired Turner Home Entertainment executive Stuart Snyder as president and COO in 1997, so he could focus on the creative side of the business. That focus produced Barnum's Kaleidoscape in 1999, an upscale version of the original circus, featuring specialty acts, gourmet food, plush seats, and audience interaction. (Plus, for the first time since 1956, a Feld circus was performed under a tent.) Snyder resigned later that year.

In an effort to inject new life into the 130-year-old Ringling Bros. and Barnum & Bailey Circus, Feld Entertainment launched two new marketing campaigns (one aimed at adults, the other aimed at children) in 2001. Also that year, a district court judge dismissed a complaint filed against the company by several animal activist groups who claimed that Feld Entertainment didn't comply with federal regulations regarding the care of Asian elephants.

Chairman and CEO: Kenneth Feld, age 53
CFO: Mike Ruch
SVP Marketing: Julie Robertson
VP Human Resources: Kirk McCoy
VP International Sales and Business Development:
  Robert McHugh

LOCATIONS

HQ: 8607 Westwood Center Dr., Vienna, VA 22182
Phone: 703-448-4000   **Fax:** 703-448-4100
Web: www.feldentertainment.com

Feld Entertainment produces shows in 45 countries on
six continents.

PRODUCTS/OPERATIONS

Selected Attractions
Barnum's Kaleidoscape
Disney On Ice
  Beauty and the Beast
  Disney Classics Come to Life on Ice!
  The Jungle Book
  The Lion King! Live on Ice!
  Tarzan
  Toy Story
Ringling Bros. and Barnum & Bailey Circus
Siegfried & Roy

COMPETITORS

Cirque du Soleil
Clear Channel Entertainment
Clyde Beatty-Cole Brothers Circus
Corporación Interamericana de Entretenimiento
Great American Circus
Hannaford Family Circus
On Stage Entertainment
Pickle Family Circus
Renaissance Entertainment
Six Flags
TBA
Tom Collins
Walt Disney

HISTORICAL FINANCIALS & EMPLOYEES

Private FYE: January 31	Annual Growth	1/92	1/93	1/94	1/95	1/96	1/97	1/98	1/99	1/00	1/01
Estimated sales ($ mil.)	5.6%	—	500	570	600	625	550	630	645	675	776
Employees	0.0%	—	2,500	2,500	2,500	2,500	2,500	2,500	2,500	2,500	2,500

SALES HISTORY

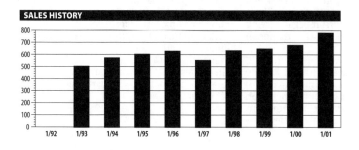

FMR CORP.

FMR Corp. is *semper fidelis* (ever faithful) to its core business. The financial services conglomerate, better known as Fidelity Investments, is the world's #1 mutual fund company. Serving some 17 million individual and institutional clients, Fidelity manages more than 300 funds and has more than $800 billion of assets under management. Its Magellan fund was for many years the US's largest, but it now jockeys with the Vanguard 500 Index Fund for the top spot. The founding Johnson family controls most of FMR; Abigail Johnson, CEO Ned's daughter and heir apparent, is the largest single shareholder with about 25%.

Fidelity's nonfund offerings include life insurance, trust services, securities clearing, retirement services, and a leading online discount brokerage; it is one of the largest administrators of 401(k) plans, a segment the firm continues to grow.

FMR has major holdings in telecommunications (COLT Telecom Group) and transportation (BostonCoach). Like many institutional investors, Fidelity uses its clout to sway the boards of companies in which it has significant holdings.

HISTORY

Boston money management firm Anderson & Cromwell formed Fidelity Fund in 1930. Edward Johnson became president of the fund in 1943, when it had $3 million invested in Treasury bills. Johnson diversified into stocks, and by 1945 the fund had grown to $10 million. In 1946 he established Fidelity Management and Research to act as its investment adviser.

In the early 1950s Johnson hired Gerry Tsai, a young immigrant from Shanghai, to analyze stocks. He put Tsai in charge of Fidelity Capital Fund in 1957. Tsai's brash, go-go investment strategy in such speculative stocks as Xerox and Polaroid paid off; by the time he left to form his own fund in 1965, he was managing more than $1 billion.

The Magellan Fund started in 1962. The company entered the corporate pension plans market (FMR Investment Management) in 1964, and retirement plans for self-employed individuals (Fidelity Keogh Plan) in 1967. It began serving investors outside the US (Fidelity International) in 1968.

Holding company FMR was formed in 1972, and that year Johnson gave control of Fidelity to his son Ned, who vertically integrated FMR by selling directly to customers rather than through brokers. The next year he formed Fidelity Daily Income Trust, the first money market fund to offer check writing.

Peter Lynch was hired as manager of the Magellan Fund in 1977. During his 13-year tenure, Magellan grew from $20 million to $12 billion in assets and outperformed all other mutual funds. Fidelity started Fidelity Brokerage Services in 1978, becoming the first mutual fund company to offer discount brokerage.

In 1980 the company launched a nationwide branch network and in 1986 entered the credit card business. The Wall Street crash of 1987 forced its Magellan Fund to liquidate almost $1 billion in stock in a single day. That year FMR moved into insurance by offering variable life, single premium, and deferred annuity policies. In 1989 the company introduced the low-expense Spartan Fund, targeted toward large, less-active investors.

Magellan's performance faded in the early 1990s, dropping from #1 performer to #3. Most of Fidelity's best performers were from its 36 select funds, which focus on narrow industry segments. FMR founded London-based COLT Telecom in 1993. In 1994 Ned Johnson gave his daughter Abigail a 25% stake in FMR.

Jeffrey Vinik resigned as manager of Magellan in 1996, one of more than a dozen fund managers to leave the firm that year and the next. Robert Stansky took the helm of the $56 billion fund, which FMR decided to close to new investors in 1997. Fidelity had a first that year when it went with an outside fund manager, hiring Bankers Trust (now part of Deutsche Bank) to manage its index funds.

FMR did some housecleaning in the late 1990s. It sold its Wentworth art galleries (1997) and *Worth* magazine (1998). Despite continued management turnover, it entered Japan and expanded its presence in Canada.

In 1999 the firm formed a joint venture with Charles Schwab; Donaldson, Lufkin & Jenrette, known now as Credit Suisse First Boston (USA); and Spear, Leeds & Kellogg to form an electronic communications network (ECN) to trade NASDAQ stocks online. That year Fidelity teamed with Internet portal Lycos (now part of Terra Lycos) to develop its online brokerage.

FMR opened savings and loan Fidelity Personal Trust Co. in 2000. That year the Magellan Fund for a time lost its longtime title as the US's largest mutual fund to the Vanguard Index 500 Fund. In 2001 the company teamed up with Frank Russell to offer a new fund for wealthy clients. Also that year the company announced it would cut about 2% of its workforce in the face of economic woes.

Chairman and CEO: Edward C. Johnson III, age 71
Vice Chairman and COO; President, Fidelity Investments Institutional Retirement Group: Robert L. Reynolds
President, Fidelity Management and Research: Abigail P. Johnson, age 40
EVP and CFO: Stephen P. Jonas
SVP and Chief of Administration: David C. Weinstein
VP and General Counsel: Lena G. Goldberg
President, Fidelity Capital: Steven P. Akin
President, Fidelity Corporate Real Estate: Ronald C. Duff
President, Fidelity Corporate Systems and Services: Mark A. Peterson
President, Fidelity International Limited: Barry R.J. Bateman, age 56
President, Fidelity Investments Canada: Jeffrey R. Carney
President, Fidelity Investments European Mutual Funds: Thomas Balk
President, Fidelity Investments Institutional Brokerage Group: David F. Denison
President, Fidelity Investments Institutional Services: Kevin J. Kelly
CIO, Fidelity Investments; President, Fidelity Investments Systems: Donald A. Haile
President, Fidelity Security Services: George K. Campbell
President, Fidelity Ventures: Timothy T. Hilton
VP, Human Resources: Ilene B. Jacobs
VP, Marketing and Corporate Communications: Betsy Pohl
Auditors: PricewaterhouseCoopers LLP

LOCATIONS

HQ: 82 Devonshire St., Boston, MA 02109
Phone: 617-563-7000   **Fax:** 617-476-6150
Web: www.fidelity.com

FMR has offices in about 70 US cities, as well as in Australia, Austria, Bermuda, Canada, France, Germany, Hong Kong, India, Ireland, Japan, Luxembourg, the Netherlands, South Korea, Spain, Sweden, Switzerland, Taiwan, the UK, and United Arab Emirates.

PRODUCTS/OPERATIONS

Selected Subsidiaries
Fidelity Capital
Fidelity Financial Intermediary Services
 Fidelity Investments Canada Limited
 Fidelity Investments Institutional Services Company, Inc.
Fidelity International Limited (Bermuda)
Fidelity Investments Institutional Retirement Group
 Fidelity Benefits Center
 Fidelity Group Pensions International
 Fidelity Institutional Retirement Services Company
 Fidelity Investments Public Sector Services Company
 Fidelity Investments Tax-Exempt Services Company
 Fidelity Management Trust Company
Fidelity Investments Life Insurance Company
Fidelity Personal Investments and Brokerage Group
 Fidelity Brokerage Technology Group
 Fidelity Capital Markets
 Fidelity Investment Advisor Group
 National Financial Correspondent Services
Fidelity Technology & Processing Group
Strategic Advisers, Inc.

COMPETITORS

Alliance Capital	MassMutual
American Century	Merrill Lynch
Ameritrade	MetLife
AXA Financial	Morgan Stanley
Barclays	Northwestern Mutual
Charles Schwab	Prudential
Citigroup	Putnam Investments
Datek Online	Quick & Reilly/Fleet
Dow Jones	Raymond James Financial
E*TRADE	T. Rowe Price
Goldman Sachs	TD Waterhouse
John Hancock Financial	TIAA-CREF
Services	UBS PaineWebber
Lehman Brothers	Vanguard Group
Marsh & McLennan	

HISTORICAL FINANCIALS & EMPLOYEES

Private FYE: December 31	Annual Growth	12/92	12/93	12/94	12/95	12/96	12/97	12/98	12/99	12/00	12/01
Sales ($ mil.)	20.5%	1,824	2,570	3,530	4,277	5,080	5,878	6,776	8,845	11,096	9,800
Net income ($ mil.)	29.9%	125	225	315	431	423	536	446	1,008	2,170	1,320
Income as % of sales	—	6.9%	8.8%	8.9%	10.1%	8.3%	9.1%	6.6%	11.4%	19.6%	13.5%
Employees	14.7%	9,000	12,900	14,600	18,000	23,300	25,000	28,000	30,000	33,186	31,033

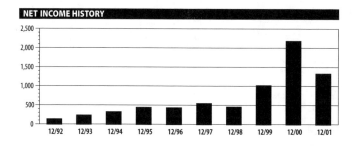

NET INCOME HISTORY

THE FORD FOUNDATION

As one of the US's largest philanthropic organizations (with a nearly $11 billion diversified investment portfolio), The Ford Foundation can afford to be generous. The not-for-profit foundation offers grants to individuals and institutions in the US and abroad that meet its stated goals of strengthening democratic values, reducing poverty and injustice, promoting international cooperation, and advancing human achievement. The Ford Foundation's charitable giving covers a wide spectrum, from A (Association for Asian Studies) to Z (Zanzibar International Film Festival).

The Ford Foundation gives to a variety of causes in one of three areas: Asset Building and Community Development (designed to help expand opportunities for the poor and reduce hardship); Peace and Social Justice (promotes peace, the rule of law, human rights, and freedom); and Education, Media, Arts, and Culture (aimed at strengthening education and the arts and at building identity and community). Following the September 11 terrorist attacks in 2001, The Ford Foundation joined other philanthropic organizations in providing disaster relief.

The foundation is governed by an international board of trustees and no longer has stock in Ford Motor Company or ties to the Ford family. Funds are derived from a diversified investment portfolio that includes publicly traded equity and fixed-income securities.

HISTORY

Henry Ford and his son Edsel gave $25,000 to establish The Ford Foundation in Michigan in 1936, followed the next year by 250,000 shares of nonvoting stock in the Ford Motor Company. The foundation's activities were limited mainly to Michigan until the deaths of Edsel (1943) and Henry (1947) made the foundation the owner of 90% of the automaker's nonvoting stock (catapulting the endowment to $474 million, the US's largest).

In 1951, under a new mandate and president (Paul Hoffman, former head of the Marshall Plan), Ford made broad commitments to the promotion of world peace, the strengthening of democracy, and the improvement of education. Early education program grants overseen by University of Chicago chancellor Robert Maynard Hutchins ($100 million between 1951 and 1953) helped establish major international programs (e.g., Harvard's Center for International Legal Studies) and the National Merit Scholarships.

Under McCarthyite criticism for its experimental education grants, the foundation in 1956 granted $550 million (after selling 22% of its

Ford shares) to noncontroversial recipients such as liberal arts colleges and not-for-profit hospitals. The organization's money set up the Radio and Television Workshop (1951); public TV support became a foundation trademark.

International work, begun in Asia and the Middle East (1950) and extended to Africa (1958) and Latin America (1959), focused on rural development and education. The foundation also supported the Population Council and research in high-yield agriculture with The Rockefeller Foundation.

In the early 1960s Ford targeted innovative approaches to employment and race relations. McGeorge Bundy (former national security adviser to President John F. Kennedy), named president of the foundation in 1966, increased the activist trend with grants for direct voter registration; the NAACP; public-interest law centers serving consumer, environmental, and minority causes; and housing for the poor.

The early 1970s saw support for black colleges and scholarships, child care, and job training for women; however, inflation, weak stock prices, and overspending had eroded assets by 1974. Programs were cut, but continued support for social justice issues led Henry Ford II to quit the board in 1976.

Under lawyer Franklin Thomas (named president in 1979), Ford established the nation's largest community development support organization, Local Initiatives Support. Thomas, the first African-American to lead the foundation, was a catalyst in a series of meetings between white and black South Africans in the mid-1980s.

Thomas stepped down in 1996, and new president Susan Berresford, formerly EVP, consolidated the foundation's grant programs into three areas: Asset Building and Community Development; Peace and Social Justice; and Education, Media, Arts, and Culture. In the late 1990s Ford was surpassed by various other foundations and had to relinquish its 30-year title as the biggest charitable organization in the US.

In 2000 the foundation announced its largest grant ever, the 10-year, $330 million International Fellowship Program to support graduate students studying in 20 countries. The Ford Foundation provided aid to people affected by the September 11 attacks in 2001, committing grants of $10 million in New York City and more than $1 million in Washington, DC.

Chairman: Paul A. Allaire
President: Susan V. Berresford
EVP, Secretary, and General Counsel: Barron M. Tenny
SVP: Barry D. Gaberman
VP and Chief Investment Officer: Linda B. Strumpf
VP Asset Building and Community Development:
Melvin L. Oliver
VP Communications: Alexander Wilde
VP Education, Media, Arts, and Culture:
Alison R. Bernstein
VP Peace and Social Justice: Bradford K. Smith
Controller, Treasurer, and Director Financial Services:
Nicholas M. Gabriel
Senior Director Office Management Services:
Natalia Kanem
Director Community and Resource Development:
Cynthia Duncan
Director Economic Development: Frank F. DeGiovanni
Director Education, Knowledge, and Religion:
Janice Petrovich
Director Governance and Civil Society:
Michael A. Edwards
**Director Human Development and Reproductive
Health:** Virginia Davis Floyd
Director Human Resources: Bruce D. Stuckey
Director Human Rights and International Cooperation:
Alan Jenkins
Assistant Secretary and Associate General Counsel:
Nancy P. Feller
Auditors: PricewaterhouseCoopers LLP

LOCATIONS

HQ: 320 E. 43rd St., New York, NY 10017
Phone: 212-573-5000   **Fax:** 212-599-4184
Web: www.fordfound.org

The Ford Foundation has representatives in New York City, as well as Beijing; Cairo; Hanoi, Vietnam; Jakarta, Indonesia; Johannesburg; Lagos, Nigeria; Manila, Philippines; Mexico City; Nairobi, Kenya; New Delhi; Rio de Janeiro; Moscow; and Santiago, Chile.

PRODUCTS/OPERATIONS

Program Area Grants
Asset Building and Community Development
    Community and Resource Development
    Economic Development
    Human Development and Reproductive Health
Education, Media, Arts, and Culture
    Education, Knowledge, and Religion
    Media, Arts, and Culture
Peace and Social Justice
    Governance and Civil Society
    Human Rights and International Cooperation

HISTORICAL FINANCIALS & EMPLOYEES

Foundation FYE: September 30	Annual Growth	9/91	9/92	9/93	9/94	9/95	9/96	9/97	9/98	9/99	9/00
Sales ($ mil.)	22.1%	—	493	797	489	586	899	1,005	1,087	1,785	2,432
Employees	0.2%	—	590	590	597	587	570	574	580	576	600

SALES HISTORY

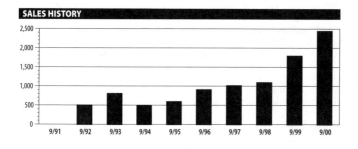

FRY'S ELECTRONICS, INC.

Service may be heavy-handed, but where else can you buy appliances, build a computer, grab some Ho-Ho's or Maalox, and find the latest *Playboy* or *Byte*? The 20-store Fry's Electronics chain offers all that plus low prices, extensive inventory (including Crock-Pots, vacuums, stereos, TVs, and computer software and hardware), and whimsically themed displays (such as Wild West motifs). The technogeek's superstore — whose notoriously bad service is chronicled on unaffiliated Web pages — began in 1985 as the brainchild of CEO John Fry (with brothers Randy and Dave) and EVP Kathryn Kolder. The Fry brothers, who got their start at Fry's Food Stores, still own the company.

Its mammoth stores, some swallowing almost 200,000 sq. ft., cater to the intensely technical shopper. Fry's outlets (a regular stop on bus tours) stock more than 50,000 low-priced electronic items and are known for their decor and displays. Each follows a theme, from *Alice in Wonderland* to a UFO crash site. The geek-gaws range from silicon chips to potato chips, from *Byte* to *Playboy,* and high-speed PCs (plus software and peripherals) to No-Doz (and other over-the-counter drugs).

But Fry's unfriendly reputation has left it a target of gripe-filled Web sites. Employees are searched at the end of each day as an antitheft measure (a concern that also keeps Fry's products stacked on the sales floor because of the elimination of stock rooms). Customers hoping to return items must abide by a process known internally as the "double H," for hoops and hurdles. One manager of an anti-Fry's Web site has likened the experience to a bizarre game of S&M.

Fry's also owns tech products e-tailer Cyberian Outpost. CEO John Fry, a mathematician who collects the writings of Nobel Prize winners for fun, is known for hiring computer-illiterate sales clerks for a pittance.

HISTORY

The Fry brothers — David, John, and Randy — wear genes stitched of retailing. Their father, Charles, started Fry's Food Stores supermarket chain in the 1950s in South Bay, California. The 40-store chain was sold for $14 million in 1972 before Charles' progeny heard the retail calling.

Charles gave each of his sons $1 million from the sale of the supermarkets. His oldest, John, who had gained technical expertise while running the supermarket's computer system, convinced his siblings of the viability of a hard-core computer retail store. The brothers pooled their funds and in 1985 started the first in Sunnyvale, California, along with Kathryn Kolder (EVP).

They added a store in Fremont in 1988; the Palo Alto store was completed two years later with an adjacent corporate headquarters.

John mixed his supermarket sales experience with a sharp marketing acumen, selling prime shelf space at smart prices to suppliers. He stocked the stores with everything for a computer user's survival and slashed prices. The first Los Angeles-area store opened in 1992; a second one opened the following year.

Hiring an ex-Lucasfilm designer, John spent $1 million on each location, decorating stores like medieval castles, Mayan temples, Wild West saloons, and other individual fantasy themes.

In 1994 the Los Angeles computer retail market began to see increased competition from nationwide discount computer superstores. The next year Fry's responded by opening a new store in Woodland Hills with an *Alice in Wonderland* motif. It was the first Southern California Fry's Electronics store to offer appliances and an expanded music department.

The chain continued to gain notoriety for the contempt it seemed to show its customers. Local Better Business Bureaus started ranking Fry's "unsatisfactory" because the stores would not respond to complaints. Visitors were usually met by security guards, scores of hidden surveillance cameras, and employees who were promised bonuses for talking customers out of cash returns.

Still the company thrived, turning over its inventories twice as fast as competitors. One customer who sued Fry's for injuries allegedly received at the hands of store security guards went back for deals soon thereafter. Fry's went on an expansion frenzy in 1996, opening new California stores in Burbank, San Jose, and Anaheim. Moving beyond its Pacific roots, the company in 1997 spent $118 million to buy six of Tandy's failed Incredible Universe retail megaoutlets in Arizona, Oregon, and Texas. The company also won a legal battle with Frenchy Frys, a Seattle vending machine maker, for the right to own and use the frys.com URL. The company in 1998 continued to restructure its new stores into Fry's outlets.

Fry's opened a new store in Houston in 2001 and announced plans to open several stores in the Chicago area. That year the company also acquired e-tailer Cyberian Outpost. Fry's agreed to acquire all of technology products marketer Egghead.com's assets, but the deal fell through.

CEO and Director: John Fry
President and Director: William R. (Randy) Fry
CFO, CIO, and Director: David (Dave) Fry
EVP Business Development and Director:
Kathryn Kolder

LOCATIONS

HQ: 600 E. Brokaw Rd., San Jose, CA 95112
Phone: 408-487-4500   **Fax:** 408-487-4700
Web: www.frys.com

Fry's Electronics has stores in Arizona, California,
Oregon, and Texas.

PRODUCTS/OPERATIONS

Selected Computer Products
Computer chips
Motherboards
PCs
Peripherals
Software

Other Products
Audio CDs
Beer
Coffeemakers
Digital mixers
Fax machines
Magazines
Over-the-counter medicines
Potato chips
Razors
Soda
Stereos
Telephones
Telescopes
Televisions
Video systems

COMPETITORS

Best Buy	Insight Enterprises
Beyond	Micro Electronics
BUY.COM	Micro Warehouse
CDW Computer Centers	Office Depot
Circuit City	PC Connection
CompUSA	PC Mall
Cyberian Outpost	RadioShack
Dell Computer	Staples
Gateway	Systemax
Good Guys	Zones

HISTORICAL FINANCIALS & EMPLOYEES

Private FYE: December 31	Annual Growth	12/92	12/93	12/94	12/95	12/96	12/97	12/98	12/99	12/00	12/01
Estimated sales ($ mil.)	28.9%	—	250	327	414	535	950	1,250	1,420	1,500	1,900
Employees	18.0%	—	1,300	1,500	1,500	2,000	4,000	4,000	4,100	4,450	4,900

SALES HISTORY

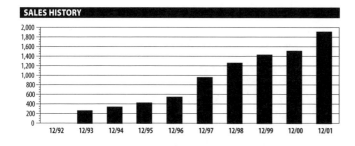

GIANT EAGLE INC.

With its talons firmly wrapped around western Pennsylvania, Giant Eagle is eyeing new territory. The #1 food retailer in Pittsburgh, it operates more than 150 supermarkets (about 60,000 sq. ft. in size) and has 60-plus franchisees in Maryland, Ohio, western Pennsylvania, and northern West Virginia. In addition to food, many Giant Eagle stores feature video rental, banking, photo processing, and ready-to-eat meals. Chairman and CEO David Shapira is the grandson of one of the five men who founded the company in 1931. The founders' families own Giant Eagle.

As with other birds of the retailing feather, Giant Eagle's supermarkets carry private-label merchandise (Eagle Valley and Giant Eagle brands) and nonfood items; many have pharmacies.

Giant Eagle became the #1 food seller in eastern Ohio through a 1997 acquisition, and the supermarket chain has expanded to Cleveland, Toledo, and Columbus. The company's goal is to grow Giant Eagle food and drug sales through a combination of acquisitions and organic growth to $9 billion by 2006. To that end in 2002 Giant Eagle launched a successful bid for the remaining assets of bankrupt discount drugstore chain Phar-Mor.

HISTORY

When Joe Porter, Ben Chait, and Joe Goldstein sold their chain of 125 Eagle grocery stores in Pittsburgh to Kroger in 1928, the agreement stated that the men would have to leave the grocery business for three years. In retrospect, Kroger should have made the term last for the length of their lives, because in 1931 the three men joined the owners of OK Grocery — Hyman Moravitz and Morris Weizenbaum — and launched a new chain of grocery stores called Giant Eagle. Eventually, the chain would knock Kroger out of the Pittsburgh market.

Although slowed by the Great Depression, the chain expanded, fighting such large rivals as Acme, A&P, and Kroger for Pittsburgh's food shoppers. The stores were mom-and-pop operations with over-the-counter service until they began converting to self-service during the 1940s. Store sizes expanded to nearly 15,000 sq. ft. in the 1950s. During that time Giant Eagle, with about 30 stores, launched Blue Stamps in answer to Green Stamps and other loyalty programs.

It phased out trading stamps in the 1960s in lieu of everyday low prices. To accommodate its growth, in 1968 Giant Eagle acquired a warehouse in Lawrenceville, Pennsylvania, that more than doubled its storage area. Also that year the firm opened its first 20,000-sq.-ft. Giant Eagle store.

During the inflationary 1970s Giant Eagle introduced generic items and began offering the Food Club line, a private-label brand, in conjunction with wholesaler Topco. It continued its expansion, and by 1979 it had become Pittsburgh's #1 supermarket chain, as chains such as Kroger, Acme, and A&P were leaving the city. In 1981 Giant Eagle, with 52 stores, acquired Tamarkin, a wholesale and retail chain in Youngstown, Ohio, part-owned by the Monus family. The purchase moved it into the franchise business, and later that year the first independent Giant Eagle store opened in Monaca (outside Pittsburgh).

The Tamarkin purchase brought together Mickey Monus and Giant Eagle CEO David Shapira, grandson of founder Goldstein. In 1982 they created Phar-Mor, a deep-discount drugstore chain (Wal-Mart's Sam Walton once said it was the only competitor he truly feared). From a single store in Niles, Ohio, Phar-Mor grew rapidly to 310 outlets in 32 states in the early 1990s.

Phar-Mor president Monus helped found the World Basketball League (WBL) in 1987 and became the owner of three teams. In 1992 an auditor discovered two unexplainable Phar-Mor checks to the WBL totaling about $100,000. Investigators soon uncovered three years of overstated inventories and a false set of books; Shapira (who was also CEO of Phar-Mor), Giant Eagle owners (which held a 50% stake in Phar-Mor until 1992), and other investors had been duped out of more than $1 billion. Shapira fired Monus and his cronies on July 31, 1992. The next day the WBL folded; about two weeks after that Phar-Mor filed for Chapter 11 bankruptcy. A mistrial in 1994 couldn't save Monus from prison; he was reindicted in 1995 and sentenced to 20 years (later reduced to 12). Giant Eagle made its largest acquisition in 1997, paying $403 million for Riser Foods, a wholesaler (American Seaway Foods) with 35 company-owned stores under the Rini-Rego Stop-n-Shop banner.

In 2000 Giant Eagle opened several stores in Columbus, Ohio. The grocer moved into Maryland in 2001 when it acquired six Country Market stores in Maryland and Pennsylvania. Also in 2001, the grocer founded ECHO Real Estate Services Co. to develop retail, housing, and golf course projects.

In 2002 Giant Eagle was among the winning bidders for the remaining assets of bankrupt Phar-Mor. The firm acquired leases to 10 Phar-Mor stores and the inventory and prescription lists for 27 stores.

OFFICERS

Chairman and CEO: David S. Shapira, age 60
Vice Chairman: Anthony Rego
President and COO: Raymond Burgo
SVP and CFO: Mark Minnaugh
SVP, Information Services: Robert P. Garrity
SVP, Marketing: Laura Karet
VP, Logistics: Bill Parry
VP, Personnel: Raymond A. Huber

LOCATIONS

HQ: 101 Kappa Dr., Pittsburgh, PA 15238
Phone: 412-963-6200   **Fax:** 412-968-1561
Web: www.gianteagle.com

2002 Stores

	No.
Ohio	
Cleveland	46
Youngstown	29
Akron/Canton	26
Columbus	5
Toledo	1
Pennsylvania	
Pittsburgh	72
Johnstown	11
Erie	9
Lake	5
West Virginia	6
Maryland	4
Total	**214**

PRODUCTS/OPERATIONS

Private Labels
Eagle Valley
Giant Eagle

Selected Services
Bakery
Banking services
Childcare
Deli department
Dry cleaning
Fresh seafood
Greeting cards
Pharmacy
Photo developing
Ready-to-eat meals
Ticketmaster outlet
Video rental

COMPETITORS

A&P
Ahold USA
Giant Food
Heinen's
IGA
Kroger
SUPERVALU
Wal-Mart
Wegmans
Weis Markets

HISTORICAL FINANCIALS & EMPLOYEES

Private FYE: June 30	Annual Growth	6/93	6/94	6/95	6/96	6/97	6/98	6/99	6/00	6/01	6/02
Estimated sales ($ mil.)	9.2%	2,000	2,000	2,100	2,200	3,800	4,050	4,360	4,221	4,435	4,415
Employees	9.2%	11,800	7,200	7,200	12,000	19,200	25,000	25,600	25,600	25,600	26,000

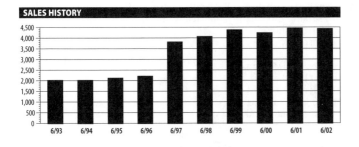

SALES HISTORY

GOLDEN STATE FOODS

Did somebody say McDonald's? Food processor and distributor Golden State Foods is listening. The company is one of the fast-food giant's major suppliers, providing its restaurants with more than 130 products. These include beef patties, the Big Mac sauce (which it formulated), buns, ketchup, mayonnaise, and salad dressing. Golden State Foods has 12 distribution centers in the US and overseas (Australia, Egypt, and Mexico) and operates two food processing plants in the US. The company was founded in 1947 by the late William Moore. Investment firm Yucaipa owns a majority of Golden State, while CEO Mark Wetterau's family-owned management company Wetterau Associates owns most of the rest.

Yucaipa and Wetterau Associates bought Golden State in 1998 from its management, which kept a small stake in the company.

Golden State Foods supplies more than 10,000 individual McDonald's restaurants throughout the US and worldwide. McDonald's and its suppliers have established a symbiotic relationship. Golden State Foods adheres to McDonald's standards and gears its operations toward furthering the restaurant chain's interests. The company serves McDonald's without the benefit of a long-term, written contract, but McDonald's is known for its loyalty to its suppliers.

HISTORY

In 1947 William Moore founded Golden State Meat, a small meat-supply business that served restaurants and hotels in the Los Angeles area. In 1954 he added several new clients to his business — franchises of a new chain of hamburger stands called McDonald's that was founded in San Bernardino, California in 1948. In 1961 Ray Kroc, a franchisee from Illinois, bought out the founding McDonald brothers, and the next year he moved to California to oversee a massive expansion in that state.

Moore and Kroc met, were mutually impressed, and became friends. Moore at first tried to get Kroc to buy him out, but Kroc's view of McDonald's did not include micromanaging its supply operations. He wanted to find suppliers the company could trust, and preferred smaller ones that weren't intent on breaking into the retail market. Golden State's relationship with McDonald's was sealed by a handshake between Kroc and Moore.

Moore and a partner bought a McDonald's franchise in 1965; two years later they had five. When Moore's partner died, McDonald's bought the units back for stock. Moore later sold the stock to finance a meat processing plant and warehouse. In 1969 Golden State Meat incorporated as Golden State Foods.

In 1972, after the new facilities were completed, Moore introduced the idea of total distribution. In addition to processing and distributing meat (by now delivered as frozen patties rather than fresh meat, which had limited delivery ranges in the 1950s and 1960s), Moore began supplying most of the needs of the McDonald's stores, making and delivering ketchup, mayonnaise, packaging, and syrup base for soft drinks. This allowed clients to reduce the number of weekly deliveries they received from as many as 30 to about three. The company went public in 1972, and two years later it dropped all of its other clients to cater exclusively to McDonald's.

Golden State grew in the 1970s, supplying a large share of the millions of McDonald's hamburgers sold every day. Moore died in 1978. Soon thereafter, a group of executives led by newly appointed CEO James Williams began exploring the possibility of taking the company private. In 1980, with backing from Butler Capital, they paid $29 million for the company, which then had sales of $330 million.

During the next decade Golden State expanded its relationship with McDonald's (and with the buying co-ops that supply stores operated by franchisees), opening facilities in other parts of the country. In 1990 the owners of Golden State tried to cash out by putting the company up for sale, but they withdrew it from the market within two years.

Golden State moved its headquarters from Pasadena to Irvine in 1992. In 1996 the company opened a distribution center in Portland, Oregon, and international expansion followed.

Yucaipa and Wetterau Associates, whose management hails from a major midwestern food wholesaler sold to SUPERVALU in 1992, bought Golden State in 1998 for about $400 million. The purchase represented Yucaipa's first significant acquisition outside the supermarket arena. James Williams, who had been with Golden State Foods for 38 years and served as its CEO for more than two decades, resigned in 1999. He was replaced by Mark Wetterau, who is a partner in Wetterau Associates with his brother Conrad and father Ted Wetterau.

Chairman and CEO: Mark S. Wetterau
EVP and CFO: Mike Waitukaitis
SVP, Liquid Products Group: Frank Listi
VP, Accounting and Information Services:
Richard D. Moretti
VP, Beef Processing Group: David H. Gilbert
VP, Distribution Group: Robert Jorge
VP, Human Resources: Steve Becker
VP, International: Phillip Crane
**VP, Legal Affairs, General Counsel, and Assistant
Secretary:** Michael J. Hoppe Jr.
Assistant VP, Technical Services: T. Webber Neal
Director of Development: John Walter

LOCATIONS

HQ: 18301 Von Karman Ave., Ste. 1100,
Irvine, CA 92612
Phone: 949-252-2000   **Fax:** 949-252-2080
Web: www.goldenstatefoods.com

Golden State Foods has distribution and processing
facilities in Arizona, California, Georgia, Hawaii, New
York, North Carolina, Oregon, South Carolina, Virginia,
and Washington as well as Australia, Egypt, and Mexico.

PRODUCTS/OPERATIONS

Selected Products
Beef patties
Buns
Ketchup
Jelly
Lettuce
Mayonnaise
Onions
Salad dressing
Sundae toppings

COMPETITORS

Foodbrands America
JR Simplot
Keystone Foods
Martin-Brower
MBM
McLane Foodservice
Reyes Holdings
Services Group
Shamrock Foods
SYSCO
U.S. Foodservice

HISTORICAL FINANCIALS & EMPLOYEES

Private FYE: December 31	Annual Growth	12/92	12/93	12/94	12/95	12/96	12/97	12/98	12/99	12/00	12/01
Estimated sales ($ mil.)	6.4%	1,032	1,160	1,260	1,340	1,450	1,500	1,600	1,750	1,764	1,800
Employees	1.8%	1,700	1,700	1,700	1,700	2,000	2,000	1,800	2,000	2,000	2,000

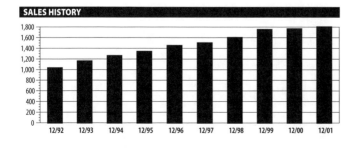

SALES HISTORY

GOYA FOODS, INC.

Called frijoles or hibicuelas, beans are beans, and Goya's got 'em. Goya produces about 1,000 Hispanic and Caribbean grocery items, including canned and dried beans, canned meats, olives, rice, seasonings, plantain and yuca chips, and frozen entrees. It sells more than 20 rice products and 30 types of beans and peas. Brands include Goya and Canilla. It also sells beverages such as tropical fruit nectars and juices, tropical sodas, and coffee. Goya is owned by one of the richest Hispanic *familias* in the US, the Unanues, who founded the company in 1936.

Goya has historically served the Hispanic communities in the Northeast and Florida with mostly Cuban, Dominican, and Puerto Rican customers. The company now has products geared toward the tastes of Hispanics in California and the Southwest with roots in Mexico and Central and South America. A growing taste for ethnic foods across the US has fueled Goya's growth beyond its Hispanic roots. In addition, its "all-in-one-aisle" product placement in food stores has proven very successful.

Yet it faces competition from food giants such as Kraft Foods, which have lines of Hispanic specialty products. It's also challenged by food manufacturers from Mexico who are turning north to tap the pocketbooks of US consumers.

Goya is one of the largest Hispanic-owned companies in the US.

HISTORY

Immigrants from Spain by way of Puerto Rico, husband and wife Prudencio Unanue and Carolina Casal founded Unanue & Sons in New York City in 1936. The couple imported sardines, olives, and olive oil from Spain, but when the Spanish Civil War (1936-1939) interrupted supply lines, they began importing from Morocco.

In 1949 the company established a cannery in Puerto Rico; the Puerto Rican imports were distributed to local immigrants from the West Indies. Each of the couple's four sons eventually joined the family business, and in 1958 the firm relocated to Brooklyn. The company took its current name, Goya Foods, in 1962 when the family bought the Goya name — originally a brand of sardines — for $1.

The oldest Unanue son, CEO Charles, was fired from Goya in 1969 — and subsequently cut out of Prudencio's will — when he spoke out about an alleged tax evasion scheme. (Legal wrangling between Charles and the rest of the family continued into the late 1990s.) Goya moved to its present New Jersey headquarters in 1974.

Another son, Anthony, died in 1976, as did Prudencio. That year Joseph, another sibling, was named president and CEO. Along with his brother Frank, president of Goya Foods de Puerto Rico, he began a cautious expansion campaign by adding traditional products to the company's existing line of Latin Caribbean and Spanish favorites.

Buoyed by the growing popularity of Mexican food, in 1982 Goya began distributing its products in Texas, targeting the region's sizable Mexican and Central American population. At first, the move proved a disaster. Goya's products were not suited to the Mexican palate, which generally preferred spicier food. Likewise, a similar strategy to capture a portion of Florida's huge Cuban market share initially met with only moderate success, but Goya persevered, eventually turning the tables in its favor.

During the 1980s the company also attempted to woo the non-Hispanic market. While Goya's cream of coconut — a key ingredient in piña coladas — found a broader market, its ad campaign featuring obscure actress Zohra Lampert did little to attract a large following of non-Hispanic customers.

Success in that market came in the 1990s. America's interest in the reportedly healthier "Mediterranean diet" boosted sales of Goya's extra-virgin olive oil. Recommendations for low-fat, high-fiber diets prompted the company's launch of the "For Better Meals, Turn to Goya" advertising campaign — its first in English — in 1992. Three years later the company released a line of juice-based beverages. In 1996 Goya sponsored an exhibition of the works of the Spanish master Goya at the New York Metropolitan Museum of Art. Continuing its efforts to reach out to non-Hispanics and English-dominant Hispanics, in 1997 the company began including both English and Spanish on the front of its packaging.

To lure more snackers, the next year Goya added yuca (a.k.a. cassava) chips to its line. In 1999 Goya began packaging its frozen entrees in microwaveable trays. In 2001 it bought a new factory in Spain.

In 2002 Goya added 12 flavors (including guava, mandarin orange, and tamarind) to its line of Refresco Goya Fruit Sodas, thus joining the beverage industry trend toward offering more diverse flavors.

OFFICERS

President and CEO: Joseph A. Unanue
EVP and COO: Andrew Unanue
VP, Computer Information Services: David Kinkela
VP, Purchasing: Joseph Perez
VP, Sales & Marketing: Conrad O. Colon
President, Goya Foods de Puerto Rico:
Francisco J. Unanue
Controller: Tony Diaz
Director, Finance: Miguel Lugo
Director, Public Relations: Rafael Toro
Director, Human Resources: Johana Soco
Director, Marketing: Esperanza Carrion
Director, Sales: Richard Gonzales
General Manager, West Coast Operations:
Francisco Javier Ahumada
General Counsel: Carlos Ortiz
Deputy Counsel: Ira Matestsky
Assistant, Public Relations: Evanessa Mangual
Corporate Secretary: Maribel Alvarez

LOCATIONS

HQ: 100 Seaview Dr., Secaucus, NJ 07096
Phone: 201-348-4900   **Fax:** 201-348-6609
Web: www.goya.com

Goya Foods has 13 facilities located in the Caribbean, Europe, and the US.

PRODUCTS/OPERATIONS

Selected Products

Beverages
Café Goya
Coconut Water
Malta (malt beverage)
Nectars and juices (apple, apricot, banana, guanabana, guava, mango, passion fruit, papaya, peach, pear, pear/passion, pineapple, pineapple/guava, pineapple/passion, strawberry, strawberry/banana, tamarind, tropical fruit punch)
Tropical sodas (apple, coconut, cola champagne, fruit punch, ginger beer, grape, guaraná, guava, lemon lime, mandarin orange, pineapple, strawberry, tamarind)

Foods and Other Products
Beans (black-eyed peas, chick peas, lentils, refried)
Bouillon
Cooking sauces
Cooking wine
Cornmeal
Devotional candles
Flour
Frozen foods
Marinades
Meat (chorizo, corned beef, potted, vienna sausage)
Olive oil
Olives
Pasta
Plantain chips
Rice
Seafood
Seasonings
Spices
Yuca chips

COMPETITORS

American Rice
Authentic Specialty Foods
Bimbo
Chiquita Brands
ConAgra
Del Monte Foods
Dole
Frito-Lay
Herdez
Hormel
Kraft Foods
McCormick
Nestlé
Pinnacle Foods Corporation
Pro-Fac
Riceland Foods
Riviana Foods
Seneca Foods
Unilever

HISTORICAL FINANCIALS & EMPLOYEES

Private FYE: May 31	Annual Growth	5/92	5/93	5/94	5/95	5/96	5/97	5/98	5/99	5/00	5/01
Sales ($ mil.)	6.4%	410	453	480	528	560	600	620	653	695	715
Employees	5.8%	1,500	1,800	2,000	2,000	2,200	3,000	3,000	2,200	2,500	2,500

SALES HISTORY

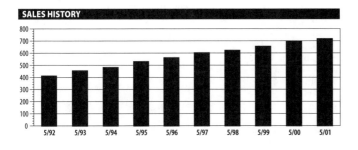

GRANT THORNTON

Grant Thornton International is a kid brother to the Big Four. The umbrella organization of accounting and management consulting firms operates from more than 650 offices around the world, making it one of the top second-tier companies that trail around behind the biggest of the big guys (Deloitte Touche Tohmatsu, Ernst & Young International, KPMG International, and PricewaterhouseCoopers). Grant Thornton's member firms elect representatives to an international policy board that runs the day-to-day operations of the accounting company.

Industry consolidation prompted Grant Thornton and other second-tier firms to enter such niche areas as information technology and corporate finance. And while the Big Four focus on large corporations, Grant Thornton locks in on midsized companies, helping them with accounting, audit, and tax issues, as well as growth strategies. It is facing new competitors for its target market; such firms as H&R Block and American Express have been adding accounting, tax planning, and consulting services.

With the lowering of trade barriers in Latin America and Europe, Grant Thornton has been focusing on developing business in emerging markets. Member firms have been working to increase cross-border cooperation by pooling resources and cutting costs. The organization also helped pick up the pieces as Andersen crumbled, acquiring clients and offices from the felled giant.

HISTORY

Cameron, Missouri accountant Alexander Grant founded Alexander Grant & Co. in 1924 with William O'Brien. They built their firm in Chicago and concentrated on providing services to midwestern clients.

In the 1950s and 1960s, the firm began expanding both domestically and internationally. Alexander Grant & Co. continued to focus on manufacturing and distribution companies.

In 1973 O'Brien died. In 1979 the company began publishing its well-known (and sometimes controversial) index of state business climates. An attempt to merge with fellow second-tier accounting firm Laventhol & Horwath failed that year. The next year Grant Thornton International was formed when Alexander Grant & Co. and its British affiliate, Thornton Baker, combined their offices around the world to form a network. The UK and US branches, however, kept their respective names.

The 1980s brought turmoil and change for the firm. Financial scandals led investors and the government to hold accounting firms liable for their audits. Along with the (then) Big Six, Alexander

Grant & Co. was hit with several lawsuits alleging fraud and cover-ups. One case marred the firm's squeaky-clean image and caused dozens of clients to jump ship: Just days after Alexander Grant issued it a clean audit, a Florida trading firm was shut down by the SEC. Jilted investors sued to reclaim lost money; Alexander Grant settled for $160 million. Chairman Herbert Dooskin and other leaders also left the company; although they denied it was because of the scandal, their departures left Alexander Grant rudderless during a critical time.

Meanwhile, the company merged with Fox & Co. to create the US's #9 accounting firm. With scandal-scared partners leaving (and taking clients), Fox looked to the merger to shore up its reputation. But Alexander Grant's auditing troubles led some Fox partners and clients to flee from the merged company.

After the fallout from the lawsuits and the merger, the company began rebuilding, taking on new clients, reclaiming lost ones, and refocusing on midsized companies. In 1986 both Alexander Grant & Co. and Thornton Baker took the Grant Thornton name.

The early 1990s recession reduced accounting revenues but increased demand for management consulting. As political and economic barriers fell during the decade, Grant Thornton grew. The firm entered emerging markets in Africa, Asia, Europe, and Latin America. In 1998 the Big Six became the Big Five; Grant Thornton added refugee firms and partners to its global network. In 1999 the firm's US branch entertained merger offers from H&R Block and PricewaterhouseCoopers, but instead announced plans to reposition itself as a corporate services firm to better compete.

In 2000 the company pulled out of its advisory position to companies involved in controversial diamond mining in war-torn portions of Africa. It also agreed to merge its UK operations with those of HLB Kidsons; the merged firm retained the Grant Thornton name.

The following year, after disagreements about strategy, US CEO Dom Esposito resigned. UK partner David McDonnell was named the global CEO. In 2002, Grant Thornton grew by picking up pieces of Andersen that fell away as a result of the Enron scandal.

Chairman: Leonard Brehm
Global CEO: David C. McDonnell
Divisional Director, Asia Pacific: Gabriel Azedo
Divisional Director, Europe, Middle East, and Africa:
  Clive Bennett
Divisional Director, The Americas: Shelley Stein
Worldwide Director, Audit and Quality Control:
  Barry Barber
Worldwide Director, Client Services: Soren Carlsson
International Director, Marketing Communication:
  Sue Palmer
Treasurer and Director of Administration:
  Louis A. Fanchi
Director of Administration: Ricky Lawrence

COMPETITORS

American Express Tax and Business Services
Andersen
Baker Tilly International
BDO International
Deloitte Touche Tohmatsu
Ernst & Young
H&R Block
KPMG
McGladrey & Pullen
McKinsey & Company
Moores Rowland
PricewaterhouseCoopers
RSM McGladrey, Inc.

LOCATIONS

HQ: Grant Thornton International
  1 Prudential Plaza, Ste. 800 130 E. Randolph Dr.,
  Chicago, IL 60601
Phone: 312-856-0001   **Fax:** 312-616-7142
Web: www.gti.org

Grant Thornton International has offices in 109
countries in Africa, Asia, Europe, North America, and
South America.

PRODUCTS/OPERATIONS

Selected Services
Assurance
Corporate finance
Corporate recovery and business reorganization
Family businesses
International tax

HISTORICAL FINANCIALS & EMPLOYEES

Not-for-profit FYE: December 31	Annual Growth	12/92	12/93	12/94	12/95	12/96	12/97	12/98	12/99	12/00	12/01
Sales ($ mil.)	5.8%	—	—	—	—	1,285	1,405	1,600	1,800	1,690	1,700
Employees	3.6%	—	—	—	—	18,300	18,562	20,160	20,000	20,300	21,879

SALES HISTORY

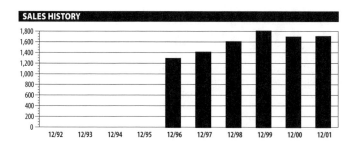

GRAYBAR ELECTRIC COMPANY, INC.

Keeping connected is no problem for Graybar Electric, one of the largest distributors of electrical products in the US. Purchasing from thousands of manufacturers, the company distributes nearly one million electrical and communications components, including wire, cable, and lighting products. Its customers include electrical contractors, industrial plants, power utilities, and telecommunications providers. Subsidiary Graybar Financial Services offers equipment leasing and financing. Employee-owned Graybar Electric has nearly 300 offices and distribution facilities in Canada, Mexico, Puerto Rico, Singapore, and the US.

The construction industry has been the company's traditional market, but rapid changes in telecommunications have prompted it to solidify relationships with major vendors such as Lucent and GE.

Graybar has reorganized its sales force, setting up districts throughout the US. To help bring supply, distribution, and inventory costs down, the company uses electronic data interchange and supplier-assisted inventory management, and urges its suppliers to have bar codes on all products. Graybar Electric has grown by targeting both national and international accounts. The *FORTUNE* 500 company is owned by its nearly 10,000 employees.

HISTORY

After serving as a telegrapher during the Civil War, Enos Barton borrowed $400 from his widowed mother in 1869 and started an electrical equipment shop in Cleveland with George Shawk. Later that year Elisha Gray, a professor of physics at Oberlin College who had several inventions (including a printing telegraph) to his credit, bought Shawk's interest in the shop, and the firm moved to Chicago, where a third partner joined. The company incorporated as the Western Electric Manufacturing Co. in 1872, with two-thirds of the company's stock held by two Western Union executives. As the telegraph industry took off, the enterprise grew rapidly, providing equipment to towns and railroads in the western US.

Gray and his company missed receiving credit for inventing the telephone in 1875 when Gray's patent application for a "harmonic telegraph" reached the US Patent Office a few hours after Bell's application for his telephone. However, the telephone and the invention of the lightbulb in 1879 opened new doors for Western Electric. The company began to grow into a major corporation, selling and distributing a variety of electrical equipment, including batteries, telegraph keys, and fire-alarm boxes. By 1900 the firm was the world's #1 maker of telephone equipment.

Western Electric formed a new distribution business in 1926; Graybar Electric Co. (from "Gray" and "Barton") became the world's largest electrical supply merchandiser. In 1929 employees bought the company from Western Electric for $3 million in cash and $6 million in preferred stock. During the 1930s it marketed a line of appliances and sewing machines under the Graybar name.

In 1941 the company bought the outstanding shares of stock from Western Electric for $1 million. Graybar Electric was a vital link between manufacturers and US defense needs during WWII. Graybar's men and equipment wired the Panama Canal with telephone cable; it also helped the US military during the Korean War and the Vietnam War.

By 1980 Graybar Electric had reached nearly $1.5 billion in sales. Business was hurt when construction slowed in the late 1980s and the early 1990s, and the company reorganized in 1991, closing regional offices and cutting jobs. Rebounding in 1992 as the US economy improved, Graybar acquired New Jersey-based Square Electric Co.

The company acquired a minority interest in R.E.D. Electronics, a Canadian data communications and computer networking company, and realigned its operations into two business segments: electrical products and communications and data products in 1994.

In 1995 Graybar Electric formed the Solutions Providers Alliance with wholesale distributors Kaman Industrial Technologies, VWR Scientific Products, and Vallen Corporation. The national and international network provides products and services to the companies' maintenance, repair, and operations customers. In 1996 AT&T's Global Procurement Group named the company as one of only three suppliers for its electrical products.

Graybar Electric in 1998 opened a subsidiary in Chile and formed a joint venture, Graybar Financial Services, with Newcourt Financial (formerly AT&T Capital). The next year Graybar Electric bought the Connecticut-based electrical wholesaler Frank A. Blesso, Inc., and it expanded its distribution partnership with wire and cable manufacturer Belden Electronics, in 2000.

In 2001 Graybar opened a new distribution location in northeastern Pennsylvania. In that same year the company reorganized its sales force, creating new districts to improve customer focus and enhance sales specialization.

President, CEO, and Chairman: Robert A. Reynolds
Group VP and Director: John C. Loff
SVP and CFO: Juanita H. Hinshaw, age 57
Director and VP, Human Resources: Jack F. Van Pelt
VP, Operations: Lawrence R. Giglio
VP, Government Sales: Jeffrey M. Cook
VP, Electrical Sales (Dallas District):
Lindsey G. Darnell
VP, SBC: James M. Ertle
VP, Service (Eastern Districts): T. N. Fleming
VP: James A. Grimshaw
VP, Electrical Sales (Houston District):
John H. Hawfield
VP, Electrical Sales (Cincinnati District):
Joseph F. LaMotte
VP, Electrical Sales (Cincinnati District):
Kenneth L. Netherton
VP, Electrical Sales (Minneapolis District):
Robert L. Nowak
VP, Service (Central Districts): John T. Roney
VP, Electrical Sales (Chicago District): Michael N. Wall
VP, Electrical Sales (St. Louis District):
Thomas F. Williams
Director, Accounting and Finance:
Timothy E. Carpenter
Operating Manager (Cincinnati District):
J. William Grindle
Operating Manager (Chicago District): Martin A. Aske
Operating Manager (Houston District): Dennis Brown
Operating Manager (St. Louis District):
Cindy J. Johnson
Operating Manager (Dallas District): Scott B. Neubauer
Operating Manager (Minneapolis District): Paul D. Wise
Financial Manager (St. Louis District): Reiders L. Abel
Financial Manager (Dallas District): Darryl B. Bain
Financial Manager (Houston District):
Timothy D. Birky
Financial Manager (Chicago District): Steven Bourbeau
Financial Manager (Cincinnati District):
Thomas G. Karrenbauer
Auditors: Ernst & Young LLP

HQ: 34 N. Meramec Ave., Clayton, MO 63105
Phone: 314-512-9200   **Fax:** 314-512-9453
Web: www.graybar.com

Graybar Electric Company has nearly 300 offices and distribution facilities in Canada, Mexico, Puerto Rico, Singapore, and the US.

Selected Products and Services

Ballasts	Industrial fans
Batteries	Lighting
Cable	Lubricants
Conduit	Paints
Connectors	Smoke detectors
Emergency lighting	Testing and measuring
Fiber optic cable	instruments
Fittings	Timers
Fluorescent lighting	Transfer switches
Fuses	Transformers
Hand tools	Utility products
Hangers/fasteners	Wire
Heating and ventilating	

Anixter International	Molex
Arrow Electronics	Pioneer-Standard
Avnet	Electronics
Communications Supply	Premier Farnell
Consolidated Electrical	Rexel, Inc.
Cooper Industries	Siemens
Eaton	SPX
Emerson Electric	Tech Data
GE	Tyco International
Hagemeyer	WESCO International
Matsushita	W.W. Grainger

Private FYE: December 31	Annual Growth	12/92	12/93	12/94	12/95	12/96	12/97	12/98	12/99	12/00	12/01
Sales ($ mil.)	10.9%	1,894	2,033	2,356	2,765	2,991	3,338	3,744	4,300	5,214	4,815
Net income ($ mil.)	13.4%	10	15	19	37	45	53	60	65	66	32
Income as % of sales	—	0.5%	0.7%	0.8%	1.3%	1.5%	1.6%	1.6%	1.5%	1.3%	0.7%
Employees	8.5%	4,700	5,100	5,500	6,200	6,600	7,200	7,900	8,900	10,500	9,800

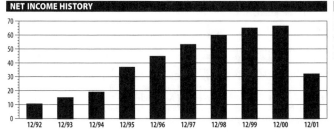

NET INCOME HISTORY

2001 FISCAL YEAR-END
Debt ratio: 43.6%
Return on equity: 7.8%
Cash ($ mil.): 10
Current ratio: 1.72
Long-term debt ($ mil.): 316

THE GREEN BAY PACKERS, INC.

On the frozen tundra of Lambeau Field, the legendary Green Bay Packers battle for pride in the National Football League. The team, founded in 1919 by Earl "Curly" Lambeau, has been home to such football icons as Bart Starr, Ray Nitschke, and legendary coach Vince Lombardi, and boasts a record 12 championship titles, including three Super Bowl victories. The team is also the NFL's only community-owned franchise, being a not-for-profit corporation with about 110,000 shareholders. The shares do not increase in value nor pay dividends, and can only be sold back to the team. No individual is allowed to own more than 200,000 shares.

After a couple of poor seasons, both athletically and financially, the Packers organization has high hopes for the future. Green Bay voters approved public financing for a $295 million renovation of historic Lambeau Field (which the city owns) in 2000. The project (scheduled to be completed by 2003) will add 10,000 seats to the stadium, which is one of the smallest in the NFL, as well as additional luxury seats. (The team's waiting list for season tickets boasts more than 56,000 names.) The team is also optimistic about its young head coach, Mike Sherman (who was named general manager in 2001), and a group of up-and-coming young players.

HISTORY

In 1919 Earl "Curly" Lambeau helped organize a professional football team in Green Bay, Wisconsin, with the help of George Calhoun, the sports editor of the *Green Bay Press-Gazette*. At 20 years old, Lambeau was elected team captain; he convinced the Indian Packing Company to back the team, giving the squad its original name, the Indians. The local paper, however, nicknamed the team the Packers and the name stuck. Playing on an open field at Hagemeister Park, the team collected fees by passing the hat among the fans. In 1921 the team was admitted into the American Professional Football Association (later called the National Football League), which had been organized the year before.

The Packers went bankrupt after a poor showing in the team's first season in the league, and Lambeau and Calhoun bought the team for $250. With debts continuing to mount, *Press-Gazette* general manager Andrew Turnbull helped reorganize the team as the not-for-profit Green Bay Football Corporation and sold stock at $5 a share. Despite winning three straight championships from 1929-31, the team again teetered on the brink of bankruptcy, forcing another stock sale in 1935. With fortunes on and off the field dwindling, Lambeau retired in 1950.

A third stock sale was called for that year, raising $118,000. City Stadium (renamed Lambeau Field in 1965) was opened in 1957. In 1959 the team hired New York Giants assistant Vince Lombardi as head coach.

Under Lombardi, the Packers dominated football in the 1960s, winning five NFL titles. With players such as Bart Starr and Ray Nitschke, the team defeated the Kansas City Chiefs in the first Super Bowl after the 1966 season. Lombardi resigned after winning Super Bowl II (he passed away in 1970), and the team again fell into mediocrity. Former MVP Starr was called upon to coach in 1974 but couldn't turn the tide before he was released in 1983.

Bob Harlan, who had joined the Packers as assistant general manager in 1971, became president and CEO in 1989. He hired Ron Wolf as general manager in 1991, who in turn hired Mike Holmgren as head coach early the next year. With a roster including Brett Favre, Reggie White, and Robert Brooks, the Packers posted six straight playoff appearances and won their third Super Bowl in 1997. A fourth stock sale (preceded by a 1,000:1 stock split) netted the team more than $24 million.

After Holmgren resigned in 1999 (he left to coach the Seattle Seahawks), former Philadelphia Eagles coach Ray Rhodes tried to lead the team but lasted only one dismal season. In 2000 former Holmgren assistant Mike Sherman was named the team's 13th head coach. Prompted by falling revenue, the team announced plans to renovate Lambeau Field, and voters in Brown County later approved a sales tax increase to help finance the $295 million project. The next year Wolf retired and coach Sherman was tapped as general manager. That year the team signed quarterback Favre to a 10-year, $100 million contract extension.

OFFICERS

President and CEO: Robert E. Harlan, age 65
EVP and COO: John M. Jones, age 50
EVP, General Manager, and Head Coach:
  Michael F. Sherman, age 47
VP: John J. Fabry
VP Football Operations: Mark Hatley, age 51
VP Player Finance and General Counsel:
  Andrew Brandt, age 41
Secretary: Peter M. Platten III
Treasurer: John R. Underwood
Executive Director of Public Relations: Lee Remmel,
  age 78
Corporate Counsel: Jason Wied
Director of Accounting: Duke Copp
Director of Administrative Affairs: Mark Schiefelbein
Director of College Scouting: John Dorsey
Director of Corporate Security: Jerry Parins

Director of Corporate Sponsorships: Craig Benzel
Director of Information Technology: Wayne Wichlacz
Director of Facility Operations: Ted Eisenreich
Director of Finance: Vicki Vannieuwenhoven
Director of Player Development: Edgar Bennett
Director of Premium Guest Services: Jennifer Ark
Director of Pro Personnel: Reggie McKenzie, age 39
Director of Public Relations: Jeff Blumb
Director of Research and Development: Mike Eayrs
Director of Special Events: Dee Geurts-Bengtson
Director of Ticket Operations: Mark Wagner
**Assistant to the General Manager and Director of
Football Administration:** Bruce Warwick
Manager of Community Relations: Cathy Dworak
Auditors: Wipfli Ullrich Bertelson LLP

LOCATIONS

HQ: 1265 Lombardi Ave., Green Bay, WI 54304
Phone: 920-496-5700   **Fax:** 920-496-5712
Web: www.packers.com

The Green Bay Packers play at Lambeau Field in Green
Bay, Wisconsin. The team holds its training camp at St.
Norbert College in De Pere, Wisconsin.

PRODUCTS/OPERATIONS

Championship Titles
Super Bowl I (1967)
Super Bowl II (1968)
Super Bowl XXXI (1997)
NFC Championships (1996-97)
NFC Central Division (1972, 1995-97)
NFC North Division (2002)
NFL Championships (1929-31, 1936, 1939, 1944, 1961-
62, 1965-67)
NFL Western Conference (1936, 1938-39, 1944, 1960-62,
1965-67)

COMPETITORS

Chicago Bears
Detroit Lions
Minnesota Vikings

HISTORICAL FINANCIALS & EMPLOYEES

Not-for-profit FYE: March 31	Annual Growth	3/93	3/94	3/95	3/96	3/97	3/98	3/99	3/00	3/01	3/02
Sales ($ mil.)	10.4%	54	66	62	70	75	82	103	109	118	132
Employees	8.7%	72	74	80	82	90	92	95	95	140	—

SALES HISTORY

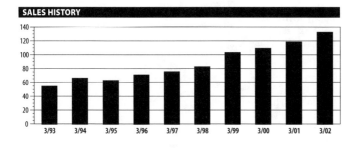

GUARDIAN INDUSTRIES CORP.

Giving its customers a break would never occur to Guardian Industries, one of the world's largest glassmakers. With facilities on five continents, Guardian primarily produces float glass and fabricated glass products for the automobile and construction markets. It also makes architectural glass, fiberglass, and automotive trim parts. Through its Guardian Building Products Group, the company operates Guardian Fiberglass, Builder Marts of America (which is 20% owned by Ace Hardware), and Cameron Ashley Building Products. President and CEO William Davidson took Guardian Industries public in 1968 and bought it back for himself in 1985. Davidson is also the managing partner of the Detroit Pistons NBA team.

Guardian has been expanding primarily through international acquisitions and by increasing its already significant position in the building materials business. In 2002 the company announced plans to build a second float glass plant in Brazil.

HISTORY

Guardian Glass began as a small maker of car windshields in Detroit in 1932 during the Great Depression. The company spent the 1930s and 1940s building its business to gain a foothold in glassmaking, historically one of the world's most monopolized industries. In 1949 PPG Industries and Libbey-Owens-Ford (now owned by the UK's Pilkington) agreed to stop their alleged monopolistic activity. William Davidson took over Guardian Glass from his uncle in 1957. As president, he tried to boost the enterprise's standing in the windshield niche, but PPG and Libbey-Owens-Ford refused to sell him raw glass. That year Guardian Glass filed for bankruptcy to reorganize.

The company emerged from bankruptcy in 1960 (the same year Pilkington developed the float process for glassmaking), and in 1965 it was hit with its first patent-infringement lawsuit. Three years later the company went public, changed its name to Guardian Industries, and was refused a license to use Pilkington's float technology. Guardian began an aggressive acquisition strategy in 1969, and in 1970 it hired Ford's top glass man (who knew the float process) and proceeded to build its first float-glass plant in Michigan. PPG sued Guardian in 1972. Davidson bought the Detroit Pistons in 1974. He applied a do-or-die style that might best be illustrated by the 1979 firing of Pistons' coach Dick Vitale, who claims Davidson axed him on his own front doorstep while a curbside limo waited with the motor running.

In 1980 Guardian started making fiberglass and began hiring former workers from insulation maker Manville to duplicate that company's patented technology for fiberglass insulation. Manville successfully sued Guardian in 1981. Guardian opened a Luxembourg plant that year. Pilkington sued Guardian in 1983, but the case was settled out of court three years later. Davidson took Guardian private in 1985, and in 1988 he bought an Indiana auto trim plant. He also built The Palace of Auburn Hills sports arena in 1988.

The 1990s brought more international expansion for Guardian, with plants added in India, Spain, and Venezuela. It also set up a distribution center in Japan, a country known for its tight control of the glass industry. In 1992 Guardian bought OIS Optical Imaging Systems, a maker of computer display screens. Guardian moved its headquarters to Auburn Hills, Michigan, in 1995. Its 1996 purchase of Automotive Moulding boosted its position in the auto plastics and trim market. In 1997 some 30 class-action lawsuits that alleged price-fixing were filed against the top five US glassmakers, including Guardian. The US Justice Department began investigating the matter.

Guardian booted its OIS Optical Imaging Systems unit in 1998, citing ongoing losses. That year the company's fiberglass subsidiary bought 50% of building materials buying group Builder Marts of America, giving Guardian a foothold in the markets for lumber and roofing products. Also in 1998 Davidson made a failed attempt to buy the Tampa Bay Lightning hockey team.

In 1999 Guardian bought Siam Guardian Glass Ltd. from Siam Cement Plc, the company's partner in Thailand. The next year Guardian acquired Cameron Ashley Building Products, a distributor with more than 160 branches in the US and Canada. Cameron Ashley distributes pool and patio enclosures, roofing, siding, insulation, industrial metals, and millwork materials to independent building materials dealers, builders, large contractors, and mass retailers.

OFFICERS

President and CEO: William M. Davidson
Group VP, Finance and CFO: Jeffrey A. Knight
VP, Human Resources: Bruce Cummings
Treasurer: Ann Waichunas
Director of Communications: Gayle Joseph
President and CEO, Automotive Products Group: D. James Davis

LOCATIONS

HQ: 2300 Harmon Rd., Auburn Hills, MI 48326
Phone: 248-340-1800   **Fax:** 248-340-9988
Web: www.guardian.com

Guardian Industries operates worldwide manufacturing and distribution facilities.

PRODUCTS/OPERATIONS

Selected Products and Services

Architectural Glass
Custom fabrication
Float glass
Insulating glass
Laminated glass
Mirrors
Patterned glass
Reflective coated glass
Tempered glass

Automotive Systems
Bodyside (mud flaps, wheel covers)
Front and rear end (grilles, rub strips)
Side window (door-frame moldings)
Windshield (window-surround moldings)

Cameron Ashley
Aluminum screen doors
Carports
Ceiling tile
Door frames
Doors
Fiberglass insulation
Formica
Metal roofing
Patio covers
Plywood
Rebar
Sheetrock
Storm doors
Windows

Guardian Fiberglass
Fiberglass insulation

Retail Auto Glass
Auto glass repair
Auto glass replacement
Insurance claim processing

COMPETITORS

Apogee Enterprises
Asahi Glass
Corning
CRH
Donnelly
Johns Manville
Nippon Sheet Glass
Owens Corning
Pilkington
PPG
Safelite Glass
Saint-Gobain
Vitro

HISTORICAL FINANCIALS & EMPLOYEES

Private FYE: December 31	Annual Growth	12/92	12/93	12/94	12/95	12/96	12/97	12/98	12/99	12/00	12/01
Estimated sales ($ mil.)	14.3%	1,200	1,200	1,500	1,700	1,900	2,000	2,200	3,650	4,000	4,000
Employees	7.4%	10,000	9,000	10,000	12,000	13,000	14,000	15,000	15,000	20,000	19,000

SALES HISTORY

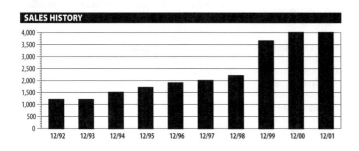

THE GUARDIAN LIFE INSURANCE

When your guardian angel fails you, there's Guardian Life Insurance Company of America. The mutual company, boasting nearly 3 million policy-holding owners, offers life insurance, disability income insurance, and — more recently — retirement programs. Guardian's employee health indemnity plans provide HMO, PPO, and dental and vision plans, as well as disability plans.

In the retirement area, Guardian has long offered the Park Avenue group of mutual funds and annuity products, managed by its Guardian Investor Services.

To meet competition in the quickly deregulating financial services area, the company is building its wealth management capabilities to target baby boomers getting ready for retirement. It created broker-dealer Park Avenue Securities and launched Guardian Trust Company to offer trust and investment management services.

As part of these initiatives, Guardian has been on the move to improve customer service and to raise its profile through national advertising. It has also continued acquiring complementary insurers including the acquisition of disability insurance (one of the company's designated growth areas) specialist Berkshire Life Insurance.

HISTORY

Hugo Wesendonck came to the US from Germany in 1850 to escape a death sentence for his part in an abortive 1848 revolution. After working in the silk business in Philadelphia, he moved to New York, which was home to more ethnic Germans than any city save Berlin and Vienna.

In 1860 Wesendonck and other expatriates formed an insurance company to serve the German-American community. Germania Life Insurance was chartered as a stock mutual, which paid dividends to shareholders and policy owners. Wesendonck was its first president.

The Civil War blocked the company's growth in the South, but it expanded in the rest of the US and by 1867 even operated in South America. After the Civil War, many insurers foundered from high costs. Wesendonck battled this by implementing strict cost controls and limiting commissions, allowing the company to continue issuing dividends and rebates on its policyholders' premiums.

In the 1870s Germania opened offices in Europe, and for the next few decades much of the company's growth was there. By 1910, 46% of sales originated in Europe. The company's target clientele in the US decreased between the 1890s and WWI as German immigration slowed, and its market share dropped from ninth in 1880 to 21st in 1910.

During WWI the company lost contact with its German business. Prodded by anti-German sentiment in the US, the company changed its name to The Guardian Life Insurance Company of America in 1917. After WWI the company began winding down its German business (a process that lasted until 1952).

In 1924 Guardian began mutualizing but could not complete the process until 1944 because of probate problems with a shareholder's estate. After WWII, Guardian offered noncancelable medical insurance (1955) and group insurance (1957). The company formed Guardian Investor Services in 1969 to offer mutual funds; two years later it established Guardian Insurance & Annuity to sell variable contracts. In 1989 it organized Guardian Asset Management to handle pension funds.

In 1993, as indemnity health costs rose, the company moved into managed care through its membership in Private Health Care Systems, a consortium of commercial insurance carriers offering managed health care products and services. This allowed Guardian to offer HMO and PPO products.

Guardian entered a joint marketing agreement in 1995 with HMO Physicians Health Services, which contracts with physicians and hospitals in the New York tri-state area. In 1996 the company acquired Managed Dental Care of California and an interest in Physicians Health Services. Facing deregulation and consolidation in the financial services area, as well as the demutualization of some of its largest competitors, Guardian in the late 1990s decided to add depth to its employee benefits lines and breadth to its wealth management lines.

In 1999 Guardian formed its broker-dealer subsidiary and received a thrift license to facilitate creation of a trust business. Acquisitions included Innovative Underwriters Services, Fiduciary Insurance Co. of America, and managed dental care companies First Commonwealth and First Choice Dental Network. In 2001 the company moved to boost its disability business with the purchase of Berkshire Life Insurance.

OFFICERS

Chairman and CEO: Joseph D. Sargent, age 72
President, COO, and Director: Dennis J. Manning, age 55
EVP and CFO: Robert E. Broatch, age 49
EVP and Chief Investment Officer: Frank J. Jones
EVP and Director: Edward K. Kane
EVP and Chief Actuary: Armand M. dePalo
SVP and CIO: Dennis S. Callahan
SVP and Corporate Secretary: Joseph A. Caruso

EVP, Equity Products: Bruce C. Long
EVP, Group Insurance, Group Pensions, and Corporate Administration: Gary B. Lenderink
SVP, Corporate Marketing: Nancy E. Rogers
SVP, Financial Management and Control: Stephen A. Scarpati
SVP, Group Insurance: Richard A. White
SVP, Human Resources and Administrative Support: Douglas C. Kramer
SVP, Individual Markets: Eileen C. McDonnell
Senior Managing Director, Fixed Income Securities: Thomas G. Sorell
Auditors: PricewaterhouseCoopers LLP

LOCATIONS

HQ: Guardian Life Insurance Company of America
7 Hanover Sq., New York, NY 10004
Phone: 212-598-8000   Fax: 212-919-2170
Web: www.glic.com

Guardian Life Insurance Company of America has operations in all 50 states, the District of Columbia, and Puerto Rico.

PRODUCTS/OPERATIONS

2001 Assets

	$ mil.	% of total
Cash & equivalents	1,274	3
Bonds	14,012	41
Stocks	2,358	7
Real estate	292	1
Mortgage loans	1,680	5
Policy loans	1,412	4
Assets in separate account	8,513	25
Other assets	4,792	14
Total	**34,333**	**100**

Selected Services
Employee benefits
Group pensions and 401(k) products
Individual life and disability income insurance
Investment products (stocks, bonds, mutual funds, and variable annuities & life insurance)

Selected Subsidiaries
Berkshire Life Insurance Company of America
First Commonwealth, Inc.
Guardian Baillie Gifford, Ltd. (Scotland)
The Guardian Insurance & Annuity Company, Inc.
Guardian Investor Services LLC
The Guardian Trust Company, FSB
Innovative Underwriters, Inc.
Managed Dental Care of California
Managed DentalGuard of Texas
Park Avenue Life Insurance Company
Park Avenue Securities LLC

COMPETITORS

Aetna
Allstate
American General
Anthem
AXA Financial
Charles Schwab
CIGNA
Citigroup
CNA Financial
FMR
GeneralCologne Re
The Hartford
John Hancock Financial Services
Liberty Mutual

MassMutual
Merrill Lynch
MetLife
New York Life
Northwestern Mutual
Oxford Health Plans
Pacific Mutual
Principal Financial
Prudential
UBS PaineWebber
UnitedHealth Group
USAA
WellPoint Health Networks

HISTORICAL FINANCIALS & EMPLOYEES

Mutual company FYE: December 31	Annual Growth	12/92	12/93	12/94	12/95	12/96	12/97	12/98	12/99	12/00	12/01
Assets ($ mil.)	14.3%	10,271	12,336	13,567	15,811	18,196	22,089	25,854	31,696	32,359	34,333
Net income ($ mil.)	2.8%	132	249	144	125	173	299	160	325	563	170
Income as % of assets	—	1.3%	2.0%	1.1%	0.8%	1.0%	1.4%	0.6%	1.0%	1.7%	0.5%
Employees	(2.5%)	7,502	7,126	7,602	5,322	5,155	4,800	—	5,465	6,000	6,000

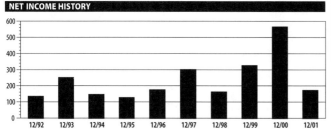

NET INCOME HISTORY

2001 FISCAL YEAR-END
Equity as % of assets: 16.0%
Return on assets: 0.5%
Return on equity: 3.2%
Long-term debt ($ mil.): —
Sales ($ mil.): 6,947

HALLMARK CARDS, INC.

As the #1 producer of warm fuzzies, Hallmark Cards is the Goliath of greeting cards. The company's cards are sold under brand names such as Hallmark, Shoebox, and Ambassador, and can be found in more than 47,000 US retail stores (about 7,500 of these stores bear the Hallmark name; the company owns less than 5% of these stores, and the rest are franchised). Hallmark also owns Binney & Smith (maker of Crayola brand crayons) and portrait studio chain The Picture People. The company offers electronic greeting cards and flowers through its Web site, Hallmark.com, and produces television movies through Hallmark Entertainment's majority-owned Crown Media unit. Members of the founding Hall family own two-thirds of Hallmark.

Not resting on well-engraved laurels, Hallmark has announced its intention to triple its revenue by 2010. While it plans to continue expanding its greeting card empire, the company is also intent on stretching its reach in markets such as personal development and family entertainment. Hallmark is bringing a literary slant to its products with a new line of cards and products developed by Pulitzer Prize nominee and poet Maya Angelou.

HISTORY

Eighteen-year-old Joyce Hall started selling picture postcards from two shoe boxes in his room at the Kansas City, Missouri, YMCA in 1910. His brother Rollie joined him the next year, and the two added greeting cards to their line in 1912. The brothers opened Hall Brothers, a store that sold postcards, gifts, books, and stationery, but it was destroyed in a 1915 fire. The Halls got a loan, bought an engraving company, and produced their first original cards in time for Christmas.

In 1921 a third brother, William, joined the firm, which started stamping the backs of its cards with the phrase "A Hallmark Card." By 1922 Hall Brothers had salespeople in all 48 states. The firm began selling internationally in 1931. Hall Brothers patented the "Eye-Vision" display case for greeting cards in 1936 and sold it to retailers across the country. The company aired its first radio ad in 1938. The next year it introduced a friendship card, displaying a cart filled with purple pansies. The card became the company's best-seller. During WWII Joyce Hall persuaded the government not to curtail paper supplies, arguing that his greeting cards were essential to the nation's morale.

The company opened its first retail store in 1950. The following year marked the first production of *Hallmark Hall of Fame*, TV's longest-running dramatic series and winner of more Emmy awards than any other program. Hall Brothers changed its name to Hallmark Cards in 1954 and introduced its Ambassador line of cards five years later.

Hallmark introduced paper party products and started putting *Peanuts* characters on cards in 1960. Donald Hall, Joyce Hall's son, was appointed CEO in 1966. Two years later Hallmark opened Crown Center, which surrounded company headquarters in Kansas City. Disaster struck in 1981 when two walkways collapsed at Crown Center's Hyatt Regency hotel, killing 114 and injuring 225.

Joyce Hall died in 1982, and Donald Hall became both chairman and CEO. Hallmark acquired Crayola Crayon maker Binney & Smith in 1984. It introduced Shoebox Greetings, a line of nontraditional cards, in 1986. Irvine Hockaday replaced Donald Hall as CEO the same year (Hall continued as chairman).

The company joined with Information Storage Devices in 1993 to market recordable greeting cards. It unveiled its Web site, Hallmark.com, in 1996 and began offering electronic greeting cards. Hallmark's 1998 acquisition of UK-based Creative Publications boosted the company into the top spot in the British greeting card market. The following year the company acquired portrait studio chain The Picture People and Christian greeting card maker DaySpring Cards. Hallmark also introduced Warm Wishes, a line of 99-cent cards. In addition, the company unveiled the Hallmark Home Collection, a line of home furnishings.

The company began testing overnight flower delivery in the US just in time for Valentine's Day 2000. Hallmark Entertainment subsidiary Crown Media went public in that same year. Hockaday retired as president and CEO at the end of 2001; vice chairman Donald Hall Jr. took the additional title of CEO in early 2002.

OFFICERS

Chairman: Donald J. Hall, age 46
Vice Chairman, President, and CEO: Donald J. Hall Jr., age 45
EVP and CFO: Robert J. Druten, age 55
SVP Corporate Strategy: Anil Jagtiani
SVP Human Resources and Director: David E. Hall
SVP Public Affairs and Communication: Steve Doyal
SVP Sales: Steve Paoletti
VP Marketing: Jan Murley
VP Operations: Wayne Herran
Director of Marketing: Jen Weiss
President and CEO, Hallmark Entertainment; Chairman, Crown Media: Robert Halmi Jr., age 44
President and CEO, Crown Media: David J. Evans Jr., age 61

HQ: 2501 McGee St., Kansas City, MO 64108
Phone: 816-274-5111   **Fax:** 816-274-5061
Web: www.hallmark.com

Hallmark Cards has operations in Australia, Belgium, Canada, China, Denmark, France, Japan, Mexico, the Netherlands, New Zealand, Puerto Rico, Spain, the UK, and the US. It markets its products in more than 100 countries.

COMPETITORS

1-800-FLOWERS.COM	Faber-Castell
American Greetings	Lifetouch
Amscan	Olan Mills
Andrews McMeel Universal	Party City
AOL Time Warner	PCA International
Blyth, Inc.	SPS Studios
CPI Corp.	Syratech
CSS Industries	Thomas Nelson
Dixon Ticonderoga	Viacom
Enesco Group	Walt Disney

PRODUCTS/OPERATIONS

Selected Product Lines
Ambassador (greeting cards)
Fresh Ink (greeting cards)
Life Mosaic (cards and gifts by poet Maya Angelou)
Hallmark.com (electronic greeting cards, gifts, flowers)
Hallmark en Español (products celebrating Latino heritage)
Hallmark Flowers (flower delivery)
Keepsake (holiday ornaments and other collectibles)
Mahogany (products celebrating African-American heritage)
Maxine (greeting cards)
Shoebox (greeting cards)
Tree of Life (products celebrating Jewish heritage)

Selected Subsidiaries
Binney & Smith (Crayola brand crayons and markers)
Crown Center Redevelopment (retail complex)
Crown Media Holdings (67%, pay television channels)
DaySpring (Christian greeting cards)
Hallmark Entertainment (television, movies, and home video production; majority stake in Crown Media)
Halls Merchandising (department store)
Image Arts (greeting card distributors)
InterArt (Mary Engelbriet and Boyds Bears products)
Irresistible Ink (handwriting service)
Litho-Krome (lithography)
The Picture People (portrait studio chain)
Tapper Candies (maker of candies, party favors)
William Arthur (invitations, stationery)

HISTORICAL FINANCIALS & EMPLOYEES

Private FYE: December 31	Annual Growth	12/92	12/93	12/94	12/95	12/96	12/97	12/98	12/99	12/00	12/01
Sales ($ mil.)	2.9%	3,100	3,400	3,800	3,400	3,600	3,700	3,900	4,200	4,200	4,000
Employees	5.4%	12,487	12,600	12,800	12,100	12,600	12,554	20,945	21,000	24,500	20,000

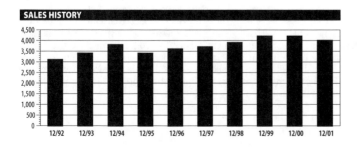

SALES HISTORY

HARPO, INC.

Everyone knows Oprah Winfrey is an exceptional businesswoman; there's no need to Harpo on it. Unrelated to the silent Marx brother, Harpo controls the entertainment interests of talk show host/actress/producer extraordinaire Oprah Winfrey. *The Oprah Winfrey Show* is the highest-rated TV talk show in history, seen in almost every US market and in 110 countries. Harpo also produces feature films (*Beloved*, which also starred Winfrey) and made-for-TV movies (*Oprah Winfrey Presents: Tuesdays with Morrie*) and launched *O, The Oprah Magazine* in 2000 with Hearst at a circulation of about 2.5 million.

Winfrey is worth about $800 million, according to *Forbes* magazine's Top 400 Richest Americans list. Her innovative ideas (such as Oprah's Book Club, which sent many previously little known titles to the top of bestseller lists) have earned her show more than 30 Emmys. Each week her show has some 22 million viewers, about three-fourths of which are women. The talk show icon has announced that her show will end in 2006, which will mark the 20th anniversary of the program. Winfrey founded Harpo (Oprah spelled backwards) in 1986.

Winfrey also owns about 8% of women's cable company Oxygen Media. Oxygen airs her *Oprah After the Show* program, where viewers can see the candid conversations Oprah has with her studio audience.

HISTORY

Oprah Winfrey began her broadcasting career in 1973 at age 19 as a news anchor at Nashville's WTVF-TV. She became an evening news co-anchor in Baltimore in 1976, where she was recruited to co-host WJZ-TV's local talk show *People Are Talking*. At first station management was apprehensive about Winfrey (a black woman in a field dominated by white men), but positive viewer response and healthy ratings put their fears to rest. She moved to Chicago in the early 1980s to host ABC affiliate WLS-TV's *AM Chicago*, which quickly became the city's top morning talk show. It was renamed *The Oprah Winfrey Show* in 1985.

That year Winfrey's performance in Steven Spielberg's *The Color Purple* (her first-ever acting role) won her an Oscar nomination. That recognition also boosted her ratings in 1986 when *The Oprah Winfrey Show* debuted nationally in 138 cities, thanks to a syndication deal with King World Productions secured by her agent (now Harpo president and COO) Jeffrey Jacobs. Harpo was founded that year.

Winfrey obtained full ownership of her program in 1988. Two years later Harpo Films was created, and Winfrey bought a Chicago studio to produce *Oprah*, becoming only the third woman to own her own production studio (Mary Pickford and Lucille Ball were the others). She introduced the popular Oprah's Book Club in 1996, a show segment in which she selects a book for viewers to read and then discusses it on a future show. In 1997 Winfrey launched her Web site, Oprah.com.

A lawsuit brought by Texas cattlemen as the result of a show that year on the UK outbreak of mad cow disease claimed that she had caused a drop in beef futures prices (Winfrey didn't emphasize that the disease had not appeared in the US). However, jurors ruled in Winfrey's favor in early 1998. Also that year Winfrey renewed her contract until the 2001-02 TV season.

After more than a dozen years at the top, Winfrey saw her program fall to second place in the ratings in 1998 behind Jerry Springer's trash TV talk show (which she called a "vulgarity circus"). Railing against the degeneration of the medium, Winfrey started a new show format called "Change Your Life TV," which aimed to improve viewers' lives by focusing on spirituality and personal empowerment (more poets and pop psychology, fewer prostitutes and porno queens).

In 1998 Winfrey agreed to produce original programming for Oxygen, a new cable network for women, in exchange for an equity stake. CBS bought King World in 1999, and the deal gave King World stockholder Winfrey a $100 million stake in CBS (which is now a stake in Viacom following its buy of CBS). The following year Winfrey launched her own magazine (*O, The Oprah Magazine*) with Hearst that focuses on relationships, health, and fashion.

As part of a strategy of media integration, the magazine, TV show, and Web site began to feature various parts of the same interview in all three formats. Also that year Winfrey renewed her contract with King World to host and produce the Oprah Winfrey Show through the 2003-04 television season.

The talk show diva announced in 2002 that her show would end after its 2005-06 season. In 2002, she also decided that Oprah's Book Club would be an occasional, instead of a regular, segment on her TV program (much to the dismay of many book publishers). In addition, a spin-off talk show hosted by Dr. Phil McGraw (a regular on the Oprah show) premiered that year.

Chairman: Oprah Winfrey, age 48
President and COO: Jeffrey Jacobs
CFO: Doug Pattison
President, Harpo Productions: Tim Bennett
President, Harpo Films: Kate Forte
Director of Media and Corporate Relations:
Lisa Halliday
Director of Human Resources: Bernice Smith

LOCATIONS

HQ: 110 N. Carpenter St., Chicago, IL 60607
Phone: 312-633-0808   **Fax:** 312-633-1976
Web: www.oprah.com

PRODUCTS/OPERATIONS

Selected Operations
Harpo Entertainment Group
  Harpo Films
    Beloved (1998)
    Oprah Winfrey Presents: Before Women Had Wings
      (1997)
    Oprah Winfrey Presents: The Wedding (1998)
    Overexposed (1992)
    There Are No Children Here (1993)
  Harpo Productions
    Oprah Winfrey Presents: Amy & Isabelle (2001)
    Oprah Winfrey Presents: David and Lisa (1998)
    Oprah Winfrey Presents: Tuesdays with Morrie
      (1999)
    The Oprah Winfrey Show
    The Women of Brewster Place (1989)
  Harpo Video

COMPETITORS

AOL Time Warner
Hallmark
Hearst
iVillage
Lifetime
MSO
News Corp.
Rainbow Media
Sony Pictures Entertainment
Universal Television
Viacom

HISTORICAL FINANCIALS & EMPLOYEES

Private FYE: December 31	Annual Growth	12/92	12/93	12/94	12/95	12/96	12/97	12/98	12/99	12/00	12/01
Sales ($ mil.)	7.4%	105	110	120	130	140	150	162	170	180	200
Employees	6.4%	—	135	141	166	176	175	190	200	200	221

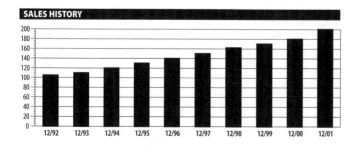

SALES HISTORY

HARVARD UNIVERSITY

Many parents dream of sending their children to Harvard; at more than $27,400 a year (undergrad), some even dream of being able to afford it. The oldest institution of higher learning in the US, Harvard is home to Harvard College (undergraduate studies) and 10 graduate schools (including John F. Kennedy School of Government, the Harvard Business School, Harvard Law School, and Harvard Medical School). The Radcliffe Institute for Advanced Study at Harvard was created when Radcliffe College and Harvard University merged in 1999. Harvard has more than 19,500 students, nearly two-thirds of whom are enrolled in graduate programs. At more than $18 billion, Harvard's endowment is the largest of any US university (Yale ranks #2).

It's usually a toss-up whether Harvard or one of its Ivy League rivals Princeton or Yale will rank at the top of the list of America's premiere schools or programs, but the university's reputation for academic excellence is well-founded. More than 30 Harvard faculty members have won Nobel Prizes over the years. Additionally, among Harvard's alumni are six US presidents — John Adams, John Quincy Adams, Rutherford B. Hayes, John F. Kennedy, Franklin Delano Roosevelt, and Theodore Roosevelt.

HISTORY

In 1636 the General Court of Massachusetts appropriated 400 pounds sterling for the establishment of a college. The first building was completed at Cambridge in 1639 and was named for John Harvard, who had willed his collection of about 400 books and half of his land to the school. The first freshman class consisted of four students.

During its first 150 years, Harvard adhered to the education standards of European schools, with emphasis on classical literature and languages, philosophy, and mathematics. It established its first professorship in 1721 (the Hollis Divinity Professorship) and soon after added professorships in mathematics and natural philosophy. In 1783 the school appointed its first professor of medicine.

Harvard updated its curriculum in the early 1800s, after professor Edward Everett returned from studying abroad with reports of the modern teaching methods in Germany. The university established the Divinity School in 1816, the Law School in 1817, and two schools of science in the 1840s.

In 1869 president Charles Eliot began engineering the development of graduate programs in arts and sciences, engineering, and architecture. He raised standards at the medical and law schools and laid the groundwork for the Graduate School of Business Administration and the School of Public Health. Radcliffe College was founded as "Harvard Annex" in 1879, 15 years after a group of women had begun studying privately with Harvard professors in rented rooms.

Harvard's enrollment, faculty, and endowment grew tremendously throughout the 20th century. The Graduate School of Education opened in 1920, and the first undergraduate residential house opened in 1930. In the 1930s and 1940s, the school established a scholarship program and a general education curriculum for undergraduates. During WWII Harvard and Radcliffe undergraduates began attending the same classes.

A quota limiting the number of female students was abolished in 1975, and in 1979 Harvard introduced a new core curriculum. Princeton-educated Neil Rudenstine became president in 1991 and vowed to cut costs and to seek additional funding so that no one should be denied a Harvard education for financial reasons.

Harvard made dubious headlines during its 1994-95 academic year, enduring a bank robbery in Harvard Square, three student suicides, and one murder-suicide. The following year Harvard paid a fine of $775,000 after the US Attorney's Office claimed the school's pharmacy had not properly controlled drugs, including antidepressants and codeine cough syrup. The fine was the largest ever paid in the US under the Controlled Substance Act.

In 1998 Harvard's endowment fund acquired insurance services firm White River in one of the largest direct investments ever made by a not-for-profit institution. Also that year the school altered some of its graduation processes and introduced stress-reducing programs in the wake of another student suicide.

In 1999 Radcliffe College merged with Harvard and the Radcliffe Institute for Advanced Study at Harvard was established. In 2000 president Neil Rudenstine announced he would step down in June 2001. Former US Treasury Secretary Lawrence Summers replaced him.

President: Lawrence H. Summers, age 47
Provost: Steven E. Hyman
VP Administration: Sally H. Zeckhauser
VP Alumni Affairs and Development:
  Thomas M. Reardon, age 54
VP Government, Community, and Public Affairs:
  Alan Stone
VP and General Counsel: Anne Taylor
Treasurer: D. Ronald Daniel
Auditors: PricewaterhouseCoopers LLP

LOCATIONS

HQ: Massachusetts Hall, Cambridge, MA 02138
Phone: 617-495-1000   **Fax:** 617-495-0754
Web: www.harvard.edu

PRODUCTS/OPERATIONS

Selected Programs and Schools
Undergraduate
  Harvard College
Graduate
  Graduate School of Arts and Sciences
  Graduate School of Design
  Graduate School of Education
  Harvard Business School
  Harvard Divinity School
  Harvard Law School
  Harvard Medical School
  Harvard School of Public Health
  John F. Kennedy School of Government
  School of Dental Medicine

HISTORICAL FINANCIALS & EMPLOYEES

School FYE: June 30	Annual Growth	6/92	6/93	6/94	6/95	6/96	6/97	6/98	6/99	6/00	6/01
Sales ($ mil.)	7.0%	1,210	1,306	1,377	1,467	1,519	1,565	1,679	1,788	2,023	2,228
Employees	3.5%	11,000	11,000	11,000	11,100	12,150	12,782	9,701	10,500	11,360	15,000

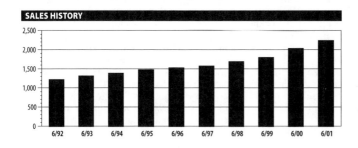

SALES HISTORY

HAWORTH INC.

Haworth isn't as square thinking as you might think it would be. The company is one of the top office furniture manufacturers in the US (behind #1 Steelcase and neck and neck with HON INDUSTRIES). Haworth offers a full range of furniture known for its innovative design, including partitions, desks, chairs, tables, and storage products. Nonetheless, Dilbert and other long-suffering office drones have Haworth to thank for inventing the pre-wired partitions that make today's cubicled workplace possible. Haworth is owned by the family of Gerrard Haworth, who founded the company in 1948.

The company sells its products in more than 120 countries worldwide through more than 800 dealers. Haworth, known as an aggressive competitor, has been expanding its presence in Europe, mostly through acquisitions. Operations include Germany's Nestler and Roder, Spain's Kemen, and Canada's SMED International and Groupe Lacasse.

Though the company has a reputation for being efficient, the soft market for furniture has hit Haworth as hard as its competitors and it has had to lay off some employees.

HISTORY

Gerrard Haworth, an industrial arts high school teacher in Holland, Michigan, started a woodworking business in his garage in 1938. Ten years later, he quit his teaching job, took out a mortgage on his house, borrowed $10,000 from his father, and started Modern Products. The fledgling company employed only six workers, but that changed two years later when Modern Products received a contract with the United Auto Workers in Detroit. The contract called for an innovative product: a "bank partition" — a partition constructed with wood below but with glass at the top. Believing other companies would want these partitions, Gerrard concentrated on their production. His hunch was correct, and Modern Products boomed throughout the 1950s, gaining a national presence by the decade's end.

Another Haworth, Gerrard's son Richard, went to work for the company in the 1960s, starting with sweeping floors but rising quickly to VP of research and development. When competitor Herman Miller introduced a set of movable panels, shelves, and desktops, it was Richard who developed the counterstroke for Modern Products, creating an insulated movable panel that also reduced noise. The insulated panels started shipping in 1971, helping fuel the company's continued growth.

Four years later, Richard — who would visit

competitors' showrooms and take apart their furniture surreptitiously — invented, developed, and patented an even more innovative panel, this one with electrical wiring inside. These panels, called Uni-Group, eliminated the need to call electricians in for rewiring, boosting sales by millions — and ushering in the age of cubicles for office workers everywhere. Also in 1975 Modern Products changed its name to Haworth; the next year Gerrard became chairman and made Richard president.

As president, Richard was at the helm for Haworth's most explosive period of growth; not only was the office furniture industry booming during the 1980s, but Haworth was growing at more than twice the industry's rate. The company expanded overseas as well, setting up a European division after buying German chair maker Comforto (1988). Seeking to emulate Haworth's success with the pre-wired electrical panel, competitor Steelcase introduced its own version. Haworth, claiming patent infringement, sued Steelcase in 1985, lost in 1988, but then successfully appealed in 1989. Haworth filed a similar patent claim against Herman Miller three years later.

With the office furniture industry tightening in the late 1980s (due in part to a glut of used office supplies), Haworth turned to its international markets. The company purchased two Portuguese furniture makers in 1991 and French and Italian companies, Ordo and Castelli, respectively, the next year. Haworth continued to expand its business line through domestic acquisitions as well, acquiring Globe Business Furniture in 1992 and United Chair and Anderson Hickey three years later.

Haworth's patents on pre-wired partitions entered public domain in 1994. In 1996 and 1997 it had a successful resolution of both its lawsuits against its top two competitors: Herman Miller settled out of court in 1996 for about $44 million, and the next year Steelcase was ordered to pay $211.5 million, one of the largest judgments in patent-litigation history.

In May 1999 Haworth expanded its international presence with its purchase of office furniture companies in Germany (dyes, Nestler, Roder, and Art Collection) and Spain (Kemen). The company paid about $290 million for Canada-based SMED International, a designer and manufacturer of office furniture and systems, in January 2000. The next month it bought a majority stake in Canadian office furniture maker Groupe Lacasse. For the first time ever, Haworth was forced in 2001 to cut jobs as a result of a slowdown throughout the industry. It also closed a wood-products plant that year.

Chairman: Richard G. Haworth
President and CEO: Gerald B. Johanneson, age 61
VP, Finance and CFO; President of SMED International: Calvin W. Kreuze
VP, Human Resources: Nancy Teutsch
CEO, SMED International: Mogens F. Smed
VP, Asia/Pacific: John Amell
VP, European Operations: Gerhard Rolf
VP, Global Manufacturing; President/General Manager, First Source: Craig Speck
VP, Global Marketing: Kristen Manos
VP, Global Order Fulfillment: Kathryn Farynowski
VP, Global Sales: Al Lanning
VP, Global Information Systems: Michael Moon

LOCATIONS

HQ: 1 Haworth Center, Holland, MI 49423
Phone: 616-393-3000   **Fax:** 616-393-1570
Web: www.haworth.com

Haworth operates in more than 120 countries throughout Asia, the Caribbean, Europe, the Middle East, and North, Central, and South America.

PRODUCTS/OPERATIONS

Products
Desks and casegoods
Files and storage
Seating
Systems
Tables
Work tools

Selected Brands

Castelli	PLACES
Causeway	PREMISE
Composites	RACE
Crossings	Scamps
DataThing	S-Con
Haworth Ten	System 58
if	System x-99
Improv	TAS
Jump Stuff	Tempo
MindSpace	Tripoli
Neon	UniGroup
Orlando	Varia
P.O.S.	

COMPETITORS

Boise Office Solutions	Neutral Posture
Bush Industries	Ergonomics
Facom	O'Sullivan Industries
Falcon Products	Sauder Woodworking
Herman Miller	Shelby Williams
HON INDUSTRIES	Steelcase
KI	Teknion
Kimball International	Vitra
Knoll	

HISTORICAL FINANCIALS & EMPLOYEES

Private FYE: December 31	Annual Growth	12/92	12/93	12/94	12/95	12/96	12/97	12/98	12/99	12/00	12/01
Sales ($ mil.)	11.3%	650	848	1,005	1,150	1,370	1,510	1,540	1,580	2,065	1,710
Employees	5.8%	6,000	7,000	7,400	8,900	9,000	10,000	10,000	10,000	14,500	10,000

SALES HISTORY

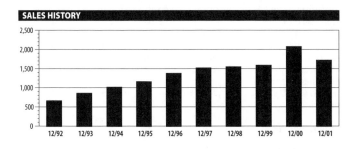

H. E. BUTT GROCERY COMPANY

The Muzak bounces between Tejano and country, and the tortillas and ribs are big sellers at H. E. Butt Grocery (H-E-B). Texas' largest private company and the #1 food retailer in South and Central Texas, H-E-B owns some 300 supermarkets, including a growing number of large (70,000 sq. ft.) gourmet Central Markets in major metropolitan areas and more than 80 smaller (24,000-30,000 sq. ft.) Pantry Foods stores, often in more rural areas. H-E-B also has one store in Louisiana and 17 upscale and discount stores in Mexico. H-E-B processes some of its own meat, dairy products, bread, and tortillas. The company is owned by the Butt family, which founded H-E-B in 1905.

The Texas grocery chain is familiar with the tastes of Latinos (about half of its market is Hispanic), and H-E-B has moved into Monterrey's more affluent neighborhoods, with stores operating under the H-E-B banner and the Economax name (a discount supermarket format). The company plans to have about 40 stores in Mexico by 2004.

To cement its #1 spot in Central Texas and fend off Wal-Mart, which is expanding in the region, H-E-B recently lowered prices on some 12,000 items in the Austin market. H-E-B is also acquiring nine stores in Texas from rival Albertson's. About 40% of the H-E-B stores have gasoline outlets, and most have pharmacies.

HISTORY

Charles C. Butt and his wife, Florence, moved to Kerrville, in the Texas Hill Country, in 1905, hoping the climate would help Charles' tuberculosis. Since Charles was unable to work, Florence began peddling groceries door-to-door for A&P. Later that year she opened a grocery store, C. C. Butt Grocery. However, Florence, a dyed-in-the-wool Baptist, refused to carry such articles of vice as tobacco. The family lived over the store, and all three of the Butt children worked there. The youngest son, Howard, began working in the business full-time in his teens and took over the business after WWI.

By adopting modern marketing methods such as price tagging (and deciding to sell tobacco), the Butts earned enough to begin expanding. In 1927 Howard opened a second store in Del Rio in West Texas, and over the next few years he opened other stores in the Rio Grande Valley. The company gained patron loyalty by making minimal markups on staples. It moved from Kerrville to Harlingen, Texas, in 1928 (it moved to Corpus Christi, Texas, in 1940 and to San Antonio in 1985).

The company began manufacturing foods in the 1930s, and it invested in farms and orchards. In 1935 Howard (who had adopted the middle name Edward) rechristened the chain the H. E. Butt Grocery Company (H-E-B). He put his three children to work for the company, grooming son Charles for the top spot after Howard Jr. took over the H. E. Butt Foundation from his mother.

While other chains updated their stores during the 1960s, H-E-B plodded. Howard Sr. resigned in 1971 and Charles took over, bringing in fresh management. But this was not enough. Studies showed that the reasons for its lagging market share were its refusal to stock alcohol and its policy of Sunday closing — policies abandoned in 1976. It also drastically undercut competitors, driving many independents out of business. Winning the price wars, H-E-B emerged the dominant player in its major markets.

H-E-B's first superstore, a 56,000-sq.-ft. facility offering general merchandise, photofinishing, and a pharmacy, opened in Austin, Texas, in 1979, and it concentrated on building more superstores over the next decade. It also installed in-store video rentals and added 35 freestanding Video Central locations (sold to Hollywood Entertainment in 1993).

In 1988 H-E-B launched its H-E-B Pantry division, which remodeled and built smaller supermarkets, mostly in rural Texas towns. Three years later it launched another format, the 93,000-sq.-ft. H-E-B Marketplace in San Antonio, which included restaurants. It also opened the upscale Central Market in Austin with extensive cheese, produce, and wine departments in 1994 (it later opened similar stores in San Antonio and Houston).

Chairman and CEO Charles retired as president in 1996, and James Clingman became the first non-family member to assume the office. That year H-E-B opened its first non-Texas store, in Lake Charles, Louisiana. In 1997 it opened its first Mexican store in an affluent area of Monterrey, followed the next year by a discount supermarket there under the Economax banner. In 1999 the company said it would expand further in Mexico with six to eight new stores per year (it opened seven in 2001). Also in 2001 H-E-B opened its first store — a Central Market — in the Dallas/Ft. Worth area.

In mid-2002 H-E-B opened a new Central Market in Dallas, its seventh Central Market in Texas and the company's 300th store.

Chairman and CEO: Charles C. Butt
President and COO: James F. Clingman Jr., age 64
SVP, Human Resources: Susan Allford
SVP, Information Solutions and Chief Information Officer: Don Beaver
VP Public Affairs and Communications, CFO, and Chief Administrative Officer: Jack C. Brouillard
Chief Merchandising Officer: Scott McClelland
Director, Foodservice Marketing: Ed Howie

LOCATIONS

HQ: 646 S. Main Ave., San Antonio, TX 78204
Phone: 210-938-8000   **Fax:** 210-938-8169
Web: www.heb.com

H. E. Butt Grocery Company operates grocery stores and gas stations in Central, East, and South Texas; Louisiana; and Mexico. The company also operates bakeries; a photo processing lab; and meat, milk, and ice cream plants.

2002 Stores

	No.
Central Texas	63
San Antonio and West Texas	58
Houston Metro	55
Border	42
Gulf Coast	29
Houston Rural East	24
Houston Rural West	23
Mexico	17
Total	**311**

PRODUCTS/OPERATIONS

Private Labels
H-E-B Own Brand
Hill Country Fare

Store Formats
Central Market (about 70,000 sq. ft., upscale supermarkets with expanded organic and gourmet foods; located in major metropolitan markets)
Economax (discount supermarkets, Mexico)
Gas 'N Go (gas stations)
H-E-B (large supermarkets)
H-E-B Marketplace (large supermarkets with specialty departments)
H-E-B Pantry (24,000-30,000 sq. ft., no-frills supermarkets with basic groceries; often located in rural or suburban areas)

COMPETITORS

7-Eleven
Albertson's
Brookshire Brothers
Chedraui
Comerci
Grupo Corvi
Costco Wholesale
Eckerd
Fiesta Mart
Fleming Companies
Gerland's Food Fair
Gigante
IGA
Kmart
Kroger
Randall's
Rice Food Markets
Soriana
Walgreen
Wal-Mart de México
Wal-Mart
Whole Foods
Winn-Dixie

HISTORICAL FINANCIALS & EMPLOYEES

Private FYE: October 31	Annual Growth	10/93	10/94	10/95	10/96	10/97	10/98	10/99	10/00	10/01	10/02
Sales ($ mil.)	9.2%	4,500	4,844	5,137	5,800	6,500	7,000	7,500	8,200	8,965	9,900
Employees	13.1%	19,772	25,000	25,000	42,000	45,000	45,000	45,000	50,000	60,000	60,000

SALES HISTORY

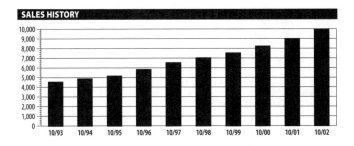

HEALTH CARE SERVICE

Health Care Service Corporation (HCSC) has the Blues. HCSC is made up of Blue Cross Blue Shield of Illinois (that state's oldest and largest health insurer), Blue Cross and Blue Shield of Texas, and Blue Cross and Blue Shield of New Mexico. A licensee of the Blue Cross and Blue Shield Association, the mutual company provides a range of group and individual insurance and medical plans to some eight million members, including indemnity insurance and managed care programs. HCSC also offers prescription drug plans, Medicare supplement insurance, dental and vision coverage, life and disability insurance, workers' compensation, retirement services, and medical financial services through subsidiaries.

HCSC also covers federal employees in its three states through the Federal Employee Program, a contract with the US government.

To better compete in the health care industry and to benefit from economies of scale, HCSC had planned an alliance with The Regence Group, which owns the Blues of Idaho, Utah, Oregon, and Washington, to serve some 10 million members and be the largest not-for-profit health insurance organization in the US. However, the two organizations changed their minds and instead teamed to cooperate on initiatives aimed at reducing administrative expenses.

HISTORY

The seeds of the Blue Cross organization were sown in 1929, when an official at Baylor University Hospital in Dallas began offering schoolteachers 21 days of hospital care for $6 a year. Fundamental to its coverage was a community rating system, which based premiums on the community's claims experience rather than subscribers' conditions.

In 1935 Elgin Watch Co. owner Taylor Strawn, Charles Schweppe, and other Chicago civic leaders pooled resources to form Hospital Services Corporation to provide the same type of coverage. (The firm adopted the Blue Cross symbol in 1939.) Employees of the Rand McNally cartography company were the first to be covered by the plan.

Soon, four similar plans were launched in other Illinois towns. Between 1947 and 1952, Hospital Services Corp. and these other four joined forces, offering coverage nearly statewide.

Meanwhile, Blue Shield physicians' fee plans in several cities were incorporated as Illinois Medical Service. Hospital Services Corp. and Illinois Medical Service operated independently but shared office space and personnel.

A 1975 change in state legislation let the entities merge to become Health Care Service

Corp. (HCSC), which offered both Blue Cross and Blue Shield coverage. Following the merger, the company's board of directors (which had been primarily composed of care providers) became dominated by consumers, which helped HCSC become more responsive to its members.

For the next six years, the state denied HCSC any rate increases, leaving it with a frighteningly low $12 million in reserves in 1982.

HCSC achieved statewide market presence in 1982 when it merged with Illinois' last independent Blue Cross plan, Rockford Blue Cross. In 1986, as managed care swept through the health care industry, only 14% of HCSC's members were enrolled in managed care plans. HCSC created its Managed Care Network Preferred point-of-service plan in 1991; the idea caught on with both employers and individuals and enrollment skyrocketed. By 1994 more than two-thirds of the firm's subscribers participated in some sort of managed care plan. That year it picked up Medicare payment processing for the state of Michigan.

In 1995 HCSC and Blue Cross and Blue Shield of Texas (BCBST) formed an affiliation they hoped would culminate in a merger giving the combined company $6 billion in sales and reserves of more than $1 billion. Texas consumer groups objected to the merger, claiming that Texas residents own BCBST and that Texans should be compensated for the transfer of ownership — especially since BCBST had received state tax breaks for decades in exchange for accepting all applicants. (A Texas judge ruled in favor of the merger in 1998.)

Citing high risks and low margins, HCSC in 1997 dropped its Medicare payment processing contract, which it had held for some 30 years. The next year HCSC agreed to pay $144 million after it pleaded guilty to covering up its poor performance in processing Medicare claims.

In 1999 HCSC agreed to buy Aetna's NylCare of Texas, giving it large, profitable HMOs in Houston and Dallas (completed in 2000). The next year it bested Anthem and Wellmark in wooing the troubled Blue Cross Blue Shield of New Mexico (completed in 2001).

President and CEO: Raymond F. McCaskey
SVP, Finance and CFO: Sherman M. Wolff
SVP, Information Technology and Subscriber Services: Joanne M. Rounds
VP, Health Care Division, Blue Cross and Blue Shield of New Mexico: Thomas A. MacLean
Corporate VP, Marketing and Commercial Accounts, Blue Cross Blue Shield of Illinois: Paula Steiner
President of Blue Cross and Blue Shield of Illinois: Gail Boudreaux, age 42
President, Blue Cross and Blue Shield of New Mexico: Norm Becker
President, Blue Cross and Blue Shield of Texas: Pat Hemingway Hall
Director, Human Resources: Robert Ernst

LOCATIONS

HQ: Health Care Service Corporation
300 E. Randolph, Chicago, IL 60601
Phone: 312-653-6000   **Fax:** 312-819-1220

PRODUCTS/OPERATIONS

2001 Sales

	$ mil.	% of total
Premium business	4,632	75
HMO business	1,498	24
Investment income & other	68	1
Total	**6,198**	**100**

Selected Products and Services
Dental insurance
Disability insurance
Indemnity insurance
Life insurance
Managed health care plans
Prescription drug coverage
Retirement plans
Supplemental Medicare coverage
Vision insurance
Workers' compensation

Selected Subsidiaries
Group Medical and Surgical Service
Preferred Financial Group
    Colorado Bankers Life Insurance Company
    Fort Dearborn Life Insurance Co.
    Medical Life Insurance Company
Rio Grande HMO, Inc.
Texas Gulf Coast HMO, Inc.
Texas Health Plan, Inc.
West Texas Health Plans, L.C.

COMPETITORS

Aetna
AFLAC
Anthem
CIGNA
Guardian Life
Humana
Kaiser Foundation
Mutual of Omaha
New York Life
Prudential
UnitedHealth Group

HISTORICAL FINANCIALS & EMPLOYEES

Mutual company FYE: December 31	Annual Growth	12/92	12/93	12/94	12/95	12/96	12/97	12/98	12/99	12/00	12/01
Assets ($ mil.)	13.9%	1,111	1,314	1,452	1,621	1,749	1,864	2,509	2,650	3,282	3,587
Net income ($ mil.)	21.1%	69	98	166	139	89	71	50	111	174	387
Income as % of assets	—	6.2%	7.5%	11.4%	8.6%	5.1%	3.8%	2.0%	4.2%	5.3%	10.8%
Employees	0.9%	—	—	—	5,600	5,650	5,700	—	—	—	—

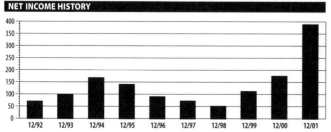

NET INCOME HISTORY

2001 FISCAL YEAR-END
Equity as % of assets: 32.9%
Return on assets: 11.3%
Return on equity: 31.1%
Long-term debt ($ mil.): —
Sales ($ mil.): 6,198

THE HEARST CORPORATION

Like legendary founder William Randolph Hearst's castle, The Hearst Corporation is sprawling. The company owns 12 daily newspapers (including the *San Francisco Chronicle* and the *Houston Chronicle*) and 18 weekly newspapers, 16 US consumer magazines (such as *Cosmopolitan* and *Esquire*), TV and radio stations (through 40%-owned Hearst Argyle Television), and a cartoon and features service (King Features). Hearst is also active in cable networks through stakes in A&E, Lifetime, and ESPN, and online services through its 30% stake in iVillage, the Web network aimed at women. The company is owned by the Hearst family, but managed by a board of trustees.

Hearst sold the *San Francisco Examiner* to the Fang family to satisfy antitrust regulators in conjunction with its 2000 purchase of the larger *San Francisco Chronicle*. Although it no longer owns Hearst Castle (deeded to the State of California in 1951), the company has extensive real estate holdings.

Using the selling power of its popular *Cosmopolitan* magazine, the company has capitalized with a TV channel in Spain and Portugal based on the magazine. The company is adding another one in Latin America and is considering a US launch.

Hearst also plans to turn a TV channel into a magazine; the company will launch *Lifetime* magazine in 2003 in a joint venture with women's cable channel Lifetime. The move will probably help take some of the sting out of its high profile failure of *Talk* magazine, a joint venture with movie studio Miramax. Led by Tina Brown, the famous former editor of *The New Yorker*, the magazine only lasted two years before the partners shut it down, citing the downturn in the economy and poor circulation.

Upon his death, William Randolph Hearst left 99% of the company's common stock to two charitable trusts controlled by a 13-member board that includes five family and eight non-family members. The will includes a clause that allows the trustees to disinherit any heir who contests the will.

HISTORY

William Randolph Hearst, son of a California mining magnate, started as a reporter — having been expelled from Harvard in 1884 for playing jokes on professors. In 1887 he became editor of the *San Francisco Examiner*, which his father had obtained as payment for a gambling debt. In 1895 he bought the *New York Morning Journal* and competed against Joseph Pulitzer's *New York World*. The "yellow journalism" resulting

from that rivalry characterized American-style reporting at the turn of the century.

Hearst branched into magazines (1903), film (1913), and radio (1928). Also during this time it created the Hearst International News Service (it was sold to E.W. Scripps' United Press in 1958 to form United Press International). By 1935 Hearst was at its peak, with newspapers in 19 cities, the largest syndicate (King Features), international news and photo services, 13 magazines, eight radio stations, and two motion picture companies. Two years later Hearst relinquished control of the company to avoid bankruptcy, selling movie companies, radio stations, magazines, and, later, most of his San Simeon estate. (Hearst's rise and fall inspired the 1941 film *Citizen Kane*.)

In 1948 Hearst became the owner of one of the US's first TV stations, WBAL-TV in Baltimore. When Hearst died in 1951, company veteran Richard Berlin became CEO. Berlin sold off failing newspapers, moved into television, and acquired more magazines.

Frank Bennack, CEO since 1979, expanded the company, acquiring newspapers, publishing firms (notably William Morrow, 1981), TV stations, magazines (*Redbook*, 1982; *Esquire*, 1986), and 20% of cable sports network ESPN (1991). Hearst branched into video via a joint venture with Capital Cities/ABC (1981) and helped launch the Lifetime and Arts & Entertainment cable channels (1984).

In 1991 Hearst launched a New England news network with Continental Cablevision. The following year it brought on board former Federal Communications Commission chairman Alfred Sikes, who quickly moved the company onto the Internet. In 1996 Randolph A. Hearst passed the title of chairman to nephew George Hearst (the last surviving son of the founder, Randolph died in 2000). Broadcaster Argyle Television merged with Hearst's TV holdings in 1997 to form publicly traded Hearst-Argyle Television.

In 1999 Hearst combined its HomeArts Web site with Women.com to create one of the largest online networks for women. It also joined with Oprah Winfrey's Harpo Entertainment to publish *O, The Oprah Magazine* (launched in 2000). In 1999 the company sold its book publishing operations to News Corp.'s HarperCollins unit. It also agreed to buy the *San Francisco Chronicle* from rival Chronicle Publishing. That deal was called into question over concerns that the *San Francisco Examiner* would not survive and the city would be left with one major paper. To resolve the issue, the next year Hearst sold the *Examiner* to ExIn (a group of investors affiliated with the Ted Fang family and other owners of the *San Francisco Independent*). Also in 2000 Hearst bought the UK magazines of Gruner + Jahr, the newspaper and magazine unit of German media juggernaut Bertelsmann.

The following year Hearst gained a 30% stake in iVillage following that company's purchase of rival Women.com Networks. In mid-2002 Victor Ganzi took over as CEO and president following Bennack's retirement.

OFFICERS

Chairman: George R. Hearst Jr., age 74
President and CEO: Victor F. Ganzi, age 55
EVP, Hearst Newspapers: Steven R. Swartz
SVP; President, Hearst Newspapers: George B. Irish
SVP and President, Hearst Entertainment:
Raymond E. Joslin
VP and CFO: Ronald J. Doerfler
VP and General Counsel: Eve Burton
President, Hearst Magazines: Cathleen P. Black
President, Hearst Business Media: Richard P. Malloch
President, Hearst Interactive Media:
Kenneth A. Bronfin, age 42
SVP, Human Resources, Hearst Magazines: Ruth Diem

LOCATIONS

HQ: 959 8th Ave., New York, NY 10019
Phone: 212-649-2000   **Fax:** 212-765-3528
Web: www.hearstcorp.com

Hearst newspapers are located throughout the US. Hearst Magazines are distributed in more than 110 countries.

PRODUCTS/OPERATIONS

Selected Operations

Broadcasting
Hearst-Argyle Television (40%)

Business Publications
Black Book
Diversion
Electronic Products
First DataBank
Motor Magazine

Entertainment and Syndication
A&E Television Networks (37.5%, with ABC & NBC)
  The History Channel
Cosmopolitan Television Iberia (Spain)
ESPN (20%)
King Features Syndicate
Lifetime Entertainment Services (50%, with ABC)
New England Cable News (with AT&T Broadband)

Interactive Media
drugstore.com (invested in online pharmacy site)
Hire.com (invested in career job site)
iVillage (30%, Internet site geared towards women)

Magazines
Company (UK magazine)
Cosmopolitan
Esquire
Good Housekeeping
Harper's Bazaar
House Beautiful
Marie Claire (with Marie Claire Album)
O, The Oprah Magazine (with Harpo)
Popular Mechanics
Redbook
SmartMoney (with Dow Jones)
Town & Country

Major Newspapers
Albany Times Union (New York)
Houston Chronicle
San Antonio Express-News
San Francisco Chronicle
Seattle Post-Intelligencer

COMPETITORS

Advance	E. W. Scripps	New York Times
Publications	Freedom Com-	News Corp.
Andrews McMeel	munications	PRIMEDIA
Universal	Gannett	Reader's Digest
AOL Time	Hachette	Reed Elsevier
Warner	Filipacchi	Group
Belo	Médias	Rodale
Bertelsmann	IPC Media	Seattle Times
Bloomberg	Knight Ridder	Tribune
Cox Enterprises	Liberty Media	Viacom
Dennis	McGraw-Hill	Walt Disney
Publishing	MediaNews	Washington Post
Emap	Meredith	

HISTORICAL FINANCIALS & EMPLOYEES

Private FYE: December 31	Annual Growth	12/92	12/93	12/94	12/95	12/96	12/97	12/98	12/99	12/00	12/01
Sales ($ mil.)	5.9%	1,973	2,174	2,299	2,513	2,568	2,833	2,200	2,740	3,400	3,300
Employees	3.1%	13,000	13,500	14,000	14,000	14,000	15,000	13,555	14,000	18,300	17,170

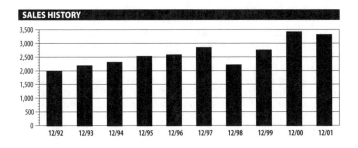

SALES HISTORY

HELMSLEY ENTERPRISES, INC.

What word rhyming with "itch" describes Leona Helmsley? Rich! Helmsley Enterprises is the repository of the real estate empire amassed by the late Harry Helmsley over a period of 50 years. Helmsley's widow and heir, Leona, has interests in such high-profile properties as Carlton House, the Helmsley Park Lane, and the Helmsley Windsor. Other holdings include apartment buildings and millions of square feet of primarily New York real estate, not to mention a lease held on the Empire State Building (which is owned by Donald Trump and others) until 2075.

The portfolio was valued at $5 billion before Leona Helmsley began to sell properties from it after her husband's death in 1997; the company still controls real estate valued at about half that amount.

Helmsley has ended a relatively quiet half-decade of staying out of the limelight. After quietly selling off a number of properties, many at a premium in New York's stratospheric real estate market, the "Queen of Mean" is grabbing headlines again: She appears to be winning a public fight with Donald Trump over the terms of the Empire State Building lease, and is being sued for millions for the alleged mistreatment of gay hotel employees.

At its apex, Helmsley's real estate empire included interests in more than 25 million sq. ft. of office space, more than 20,000 apartments, some 7,500 hotel rooms, 50 retail projects, warehouse space, land, garages, restaurants, and real estate companies. To keep the money in the family, the properties were managed by Helmsley-Spear (then 99%-owned by Helmsley, sold in 1997) and Helmsley-Noyes.

HISTORY

In 1925 Harry Helmsley began his career as a Manhattan rent collector; the work, then done in person, taught him to evaluate buildings and acquainted him with their owners. During the Depression, Helmsley obtained property at bargain prices. He paid $1,000 down for a building with a $100,000 mortgage and later quipped that he did so to provide a job for his father, whom he hired as superintendent. In 1946 he sold the building for $165,000.

In the late 1940s Helmsley teamed up with lawyer Lawrence Wien. Helmsley located properties; Wien financed them through a device of his own invention, the loan syndicate. Prominent properties Helmsley bought into in the 1950s included the Flatiron (1951), Berkeley (1953), and Equitable (1957) buildings. He moved into management in 1955 with the purchase of Leon Spear's property management

firm. In 1961 Helmsley bought the Empire State Building for $65 million and sold it to Prudential for $29 million with a 114-year leaseback (which expires in 2075); a public offering for the newly created Empire State Building Co. made up the balance.

In the mid-1960s Helmsley moved into property development, erecting office buildings and shopping centers. He bought the 30-building Furman and Wolfson trust, borrowing $78 million of the $165 million price on the strength of his reputation — the largest signature loan ever.

In 1969 Spear introduced Helmsley to Leona Roberts, a real estate broker who had sold Spear an apartment. Helmsley hired Leona and promoted her to SVP at his Brown, Harris, Stevens real estate brokerage. He divorced his wife and married Leona in 1971. In 1974 he leased an historic building and delegated the renovation to Leona (who built the company's hotel business). The Helmsley Palace opened in 1980 (now the New York Palace, sold 1993).

As Harry's health began to fail in the 1980s, Leona gained control of the empire. Maintenance deteriorated, bookkeeping went lax, and the couple's lavish spending became notorious. In 1988 they were charged with tax evasion. Harry was ruled incompetent to stand trial, but in 1989 Leona was convicted, fined $7.1 million, and sentenced to jail. She spent 21 months incarcerated, the last part of it in a halfway house.

After her 1994 release, Leona was banned from management of the hotels by laws forbidding felon involvement in businesses that serve liquor. She became more involved in the management of Harry's interests and began reshuffling assets, moving management contracts from Helmsley-Spear to Helmsley-Noyes, and selling buildings.

A 1995 suit brought by Harry's partners in Helmsley-Spear accused Leona of looting the company by depriving it of management contracts and loading it with debt to render worthless their right to buy the company under a 1970 option agreement.

In 1997 Harry died, and Leona announced she would sell the 125-property Helmsley portfolio. Wien's son-in-law Peter Malkin, partner in 13 top-notch Manhattan buildings, contested the control granted to her by Harry's will. They resolved their differences late that year. Leona also settled her differences with the Helmsley-Spear partners in 1997, agreeing to sell them the firm for less than $1 million.

Leona sold her favorite, the Helmsley Building on 230 Park Place, in 1998 to the Bass family on condition the building retain the name. That year, partly to avoid estate taxes, she formed the Harry and Leona Helmsley Foundation, a charity to which she contributed more than $30 million in 1999.

Leona moved closer to a deal in 2000 to buy back the Empire State Building from current owner Donald Trump and partners. The following year Malkin moved to challenge her, forming a plan to buy the skyscraper himself; Leona vowed to block his proposal.

OFFICERS

Owner and CEO: Leona Helmsley
CFO: Abe Wolf
VP Sales: Earle Altman
VP Finance: Robert Hecht
VP Data Processing: Frank Ambrosio
VP and General Counsel: Harold Meriam
Human Resources Director: Yogesh Mathur
Purchasing Agent: Senora Fraser
Auditors: Eisner & Lubin LLP

LOCATIONS

HQ: 230 Park Ave., Room 659, New York, NY 10169
Phone: 212-679-3600   **Fax:** 212-953-2810

Helmsley Enterprises operates primarily in New York City.

PRODUCTS/OPERATIONS

Selected Owned and/or Managed Properties
Empire State Building (office building, New York City)
Helmsley Carlton House (hotel, New York City)
Helmsley Middletowne (hotel, New York City)
Helmsley Park Lane (hotel, New York City)
Helmsley Sandcastle (hotel, Sarasota, Florida)
Helmsley Windsor (hotel, New York City)
Lincoln Building (office building, New York City)
New York Helmsley (hotel, New York City)

COMPETITORS

Alexander's
JMB Realty
Lefrak Organization
Lincoln Property
Port Authority of NY & NJ
Tishman Realty
Trammell Crow
Trizec Properties
Trump
Vornado

HISTORICAL FINANCIALS & EMPLOYEES

Private FYE: December 31	Annual Growth	12/92	12/93	12/94	12/95	12/96	12/97	12/98	12/99	12/00	12/01
Estimated sales ($ mil.)	(2.0%)	1,200	1,200	1,700	1,770	1,900	1,000	1,000	1,000	1,000	1,000
Employees	(15.0%)	13,000	13,000	13,000	13,000	13,000	7,800	7,800	3,000	3,000	3,000

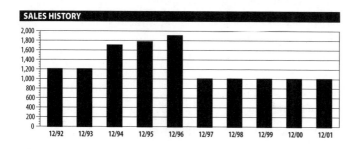

SALES HISTORY

HERBALIFE INTERNATIONAL, INC.

Rooted in the medicinal value provided by Mother Nature, Herbalife International sells more than 160 products containing herbs and other natural ingredients. Products include weight-control mixes and tablets, food and dietary supplements, shampoos, lotions, sunscreens, and body oils. The multilevel marketer sells its products through a network of independent distributors in more than 50 countries; salespeople earn money from their own efforts, as well as from the sales of those whom they have recruited into the organization. The estate of founder Mark Hughes owned about 40% of the company until its sale in 2002.

Distributors in emerging markets in Africa, Asia, and Eastern Europe have been attracted to Herbalife by the low startup costs. After buying promotional materials (at an average cost of $60), distributors buy products from Herbalife at a discount of up to 50% and resell them at retail prices. Nearly two-thirds of the company's gross sales are made outside the US.

The company's sales were hit hard by the economic crises in Asia and Russia, two key sales areas. Herbalife's continued struggle with slumping sales and industrywide questions of product efficacy were exacerbated by challenges brought on by the unexpected death of Hughes. The company, hoping to turn the tables on its troubles, was acquired by a group of venture capital firms including Whitney & Co. and Golden Gate Capital.

HISTORY

Mark Hughes' mother's death from an overdose of prescription diet pills was the catalyst for Herbalife. Hughes, a high-school dropout, founded the company with diet supplement maker Richard Marconi in 1980. Herbalife went public in 1986 after rapid growth, but it got into trouble for some of its product claims. Following federal and state investigations and US Senate hearings, Herbalife paid a hefty fine and removed some of its products from the market. Hughes was able to resurrect the firm by taking it overseas. Sales also got a boost from the success of the Thermojetics weight-control systems.

In 1995 Herbalife introduced a line of herbal and botanical skin care products (Dermajetics). In 1997 insider selling of stock prompted a major slide in the price of Herbalife shares. Earnings tanked in 1998 when economic crises hit such big revenue contributors as Russia and Asia.

In 1999 Hughes planned to buy the company's outstanding shares and take the company private; investors sued. In 2000 he dropped the attempt. That year 44-year-old Hughes died in what was ruled an accidental death caused by a combination of alcohol and antidepressant medication. Hughes' longtime associate (and former Herbalife COO) Christopher Pair moved into the positions of president and CEO. He stepped down a year later after the company's board criticized his management. Later in 2000, the Mark Hughes Family Trust turned down a $173 million bid for control of the company from Internet retailer Rbid.com. A group of investment firms bought the company in 2002 and Hughes' hopes to take the company private came to fruition without him.

OFFICERS

Chairman and EVP: John Reynolds, age 68
President, CEO, and Director: Francis X. Tirelli, age 48, $301,384 pay
EVP and COO: Brian L. Kane, age 56, $1,492,000 pay
EVP, Chief Administrative Officer, and CFO: Douglas G. Sages, age 51, $30,769 pay (partial-year salary)
EVP, Chief Business Affairs Officer, and Director: Conrad Lee Klein, age 73
EVP, Sales: Carol Hannah, age 53, $1,544,500 pay
VP, Human Resources: Jim Esterle
Auditors: Deloitte & Touche LLP

LOCATIONS

HQ: 1800 Century Park East, Los Angeles, CA 90067
Phone: 310-410-9600   **Fax:** 310-216-5169
Web: www.herbalife.com

Herbalife International sells its products in more than 50 countries worldwide.

2001 Sales

	% of total
Americas	37
Asia/Pacific Rim	35
Europe	28
Total	**100**

PRODUCTS/OPERATIONS

2001 Sales

	% of total
Nutritional supplements	45
Weight management	43
Personal care products	11
Literature, promotional & other	1
Total	**100**

Selected Products

Nutritional Supplements
A.M. Replenishing
Aminogen
Cell-U-Loss
Dinomins
DinoShakes
Echinacea Plus
Extreme C
Florafiber
Herbal Calmative
Herbal-Aloe
Herbalifeline
Kindermins
Male Factor 1000
Male Performance Complex
P.M. Cleansing
RoseOx
Schizandra Plus
Sleep Now
Tang Kuei Plus
Thermo-bond
Ultimate Prostate Formula
Woman's Choice
Women's Advantage
Xtra-Cal

Weight Management
Formula 1 Protein Mix
Thermojetics
Thermojetics Gold Herbal Supplement Tablets
Thermojetics Herbal Concentrate
Thermojetics High-Protein, Low-Carb Program

Personal Care
Colour cosmetics
Dermajetics
  AromaVie
  Good Hair Day
  Nature's Mirror
  Parfums Vitessences
  Skin Survival Kit

Subsidiaries
H & L (Suzhou) Health Products Ltd. (China)
HBL International Maroc, LLC (Morocco)
Herbalife Australasia Pty., Ltd. (Australia)
Herbalife Europe Limited (UK)
Herbalife Indonesia
Herbalife Internacional de Mexico, S.A. de C.V.
Herbalife International Argentina, S.A.
Herbalife International Belgium, S.A./N.V.
Herbalife International de Espana, S.A. (Spain)
Herbalife International Deutschland GmbH (Germany)
Herbalife International Do Brasil Ltda. (Brazil)
Herbalife International Finland OY
Herbalife International France, S.A.
Herbalife International Greece S.A.
Herbalife International Netherlands, B.V.
Herbalife International of America, Inc.
Herbalife International of Hong Kong Limited
Herbalife International of Israel (1990) Ltd.
Herbalife International of Japan, K.K.
Herbalife International Philippines, Inc.
Herbalife International Russia 1995 Ltd. (Israel)
Herbalife International, S.A. (Portugal)
Herbalife International Urunleri Tic. Ltd. Sti. (Turkey)
Herbalife Italia S.p.A. (Italy)
Herbalife Korea Co., Ltd. (South Korea)
Herbalife Norway Products A/S
Herbalife (N.Z.) Limited (New Zealand)
Herbalife of Canada, Ltd.
Herbalife Polska Sp.zo.o (Poland)
Herbalife Products de Mexico, S.A. de C.V.
Herbalife South Africa, Ltd.
Herbalife Sweden Aktiebolag
Herbalife (U.K.) Limited

COMPETITORS

Advanced	Mannatech	Shaklee
Nutraceuticals	Mary Kay	Slim-Fast
Alticor	Nature's	Sunrider
Avon	Sunshine	Vitamin Shoppe
BeautiControl	NBTY	Industries
Cosmetics	Nestlé	Weider Nutrition
GNC	Nu Skin	International
Heinz	Reliv	Whole Living
Jenny Craig	Rexall Sundown	Wyeth

HISTORICAL FINANCIALS & EMPLOYEES

Private FYE: December 31	Annual Growth	12/92	12/93	12/94	12/95	12/96	12/97	12/98	12/99	12/00	12/01
Sales ($ mil.)	18.9%	214	365	467	489	632	783	867	956	944	1,020
Net income ($ mil.)	8.7%	20	41	46	20	45	55	49	57	37	43
Income as % of sales	—	9.4%	11.3%	9.9%	4.0%	7.1%	7.0%	5.6%	6.0%	3.9%	4.2%
Employees	20.3%	464	638	862	1,060	1,180	1,459	1,742	2,170	2,391	2,445

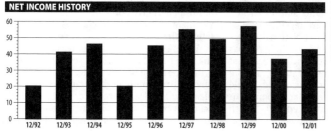

NET INCOME HISTORY

2001 FISCAL YEAR-END
Debt ratio: 0.5%
Return on equity: 17.6%
Cash ($ mil.): 179
Current ratio: 2.08
Long-term debt ($ mil.): 1

HICKS, MUSE, TATE & FURST

These Texas Hicks know an investment pool ain't no cement pond and like to buy, buy & buy. (They sell sometimes, too.) Hicks, Muse, Tate & Furst creates investment pools in the form of limited partnerships. Investors are mostly pension funds but also include financial institutions and wealthy private investors. The leveraged buyout firm assembles limited partnership investment pools, targets underperforming companies in specific niches, builds them up, and uses them to form a nucleus for other investments. Hicks, Muse also has holdings in manufacturing and real estate.

As its target industries consolidated — making US acquisitions scarce — Hicks, Muse had increasingly turned to foreign markets. The firm (which sold its AMFM to Clear Channel Communications to create the US's largest radio, television, and outdoor advertising group) exported its media mogul strategy through investments in Europe and Latin America. Hicks, Muse, along with US-based Liberty Media International, owns CableVision SA, Argentina's largest cable operator. Hicks, Muse's late 1990s hopes for a tidy profit on the more than $1 billion it invested in the South American nation have turned into a 2002 headache as that country wades through an economic depression.

At home, Hicks, Muse has suffered losses in telecommunications and has considered closing funds before they reach their original target amounts. It abandoned plans to buy out manufacturing firm Johns Manville with Bear Stearns when its stock took a dive. It also closed down offices in Argentina and New York.

Hicks, Muse owns the North American assets of bankrupt Vlasic Foods International Inc., including Vlasic pickles, Open Pit barbecue sauces, and Swanson frozen dinners. In addition, the company owns 54% of ConAgra's meat-packing operations (with Booth Creek Management and British Telecommunication's yellow pages firm Yell (with UK-based Apax Partners & Co.). Yell, in turn, is buying US directories publisher McLeod USA Publishing.

HISTORY

The son of a Texas radio station owner, Thomas Hicks became interested in leveraged buyouts as a member of First National Bank's venture capital group. Hicks and Robert Haas formed Hicks & Haas in 1984; the next year that firm bought Hicks Communications, a radio outfit run by Hicks' brother Steven. (This would be the first of many media companies bought or created by the buyout firm, often with Steven Hicks' involvement.)

Hicks & Haas' biggest coup was its mid-1980s buy of several soft drink makers, including Dr Pepper and Seven Up. The firm took Dr Pepper/Seven Up public just 18 months after merging the two companies. In all, Hicks & Haas turned $88 million of investor funding into $1.3 billion. The pair split up in 1989; Hicks wanted to raise a large pool to invest, but Haas preferred to work deal by deal.

Hicks raised $250 million in 1989 and teamed with former Prudential Securities banker John Muse. Early investments included Life Partners Group (life insurance, 1990; sold 1996). In 1991 Morgan Stanley's Charles Tate and First Boston's Jack Furst became partners.

As part of its buy-and-build strategy, Hicks, Muse bought DuPont's connector systems unit in 1993, renamed it Berg Electronics, added six more companies to it, and doubled its earnings before selling it in 1998. Not every move was a star in the Hicks, Muse crown. Less-than-successful purchases included bankrupt brewer G. Heileman, bought in 1994 and sold two years later for an almost $100 million loss.

The buyout firm's Chancellor Media radio company went public in 1996. That year Hicks, Muse gained entry into Latin America with its purchases of cash-starved Mexican companies, including Seguros Commercial America, one of the country's largest insurers. That year also brought International Home Foods (Jiffy Pop, Chef Boyardee) into the Hicks, Muse fold.

In 1997 Chancellor and Evergreen Media merged to form Chancellor Media (renamed AMFM in 1999). The next year Hicks, Muse continued buying US and Latin American media companies, as well as a few oddities (a UK software maker, a Danish seed company, and US direct-seller Home Interiors & Gifts). Hicks, Muse and Kohlberg Kravis Roberts merged their cinema operations to form the US's largest theater chain. The company that year also moved into the depressed energy field (Triton Energy) and formed a $1.5 billion European fund.

Buys in 1999 included UK food group Hillsdown Holdings, one-third of Mexican flour maker Grupo Minsa, and (just in time for millennial celebrations) popular champagne brands Mumm and Perrier-Jouët (it quadrupled its investment when it sold the champagne houses in late 2000).

Amid assorted media and other buys in 2000, the firm helped put together several joint deals. With investment bank Bear Stearns, it planned to buy construction-materials manufacturer Johns Manville; the deal soured later that year as the economy cooled. After vying with another buyout group for UK food concern United Biscuits,

Hicks, Muse teamed up with its rival to complete the deal.

Hicks, Muse sold International Home Foods to food giant ConAgra in 2000. The next year Hicks, Muse bought bankrupt Vlasic Foods International Inc.'s North American assets, including Vlasic pickles, Open Pit barbecue sauces, and Swanson frozen dinners. Along with UK-based Apax Partners & Co., the firm bought British Telecommunication's yellow pages firm Yell, which is buying US directories publisher McLeodUSA Publishing.

OFFICERS

Chairman and CEO: Thomas O. Hicks, age 56
COO: John R. Muse, age 51
CFO: Darron Ash
General Counsel: Marian Brancaccio
Partner: Lyndon Lea
Partner: Peter Brodsky
Human Resources Manager: Lynita Jessen
Senior Counselor: M. Brian Mulroney, age 63
Senior Counselor, Europe Strategy: Henry A. Kissinger, age 78
Latin America Strategy: Richard W. Fisher

LOCATIONS

HQ: Hicks, Muse, Tate & Furst Incorporated
200 Crescent Ct., Ste. 1600, Dallas, TX 75201
Phone: 214-740-7300   **Fax:** 214-720-7888

Hicks, Muse, Tate & Furst has offices in Dallas and London.

PRODUCTS/OPERATIONS

Selected Holdings
CCI/Triad Systems Corp. (computer systems)
CEI Citicorp Holding (40%, telecommunications and publishing)
Glass Group (automotive information services software)
Grupo Minsa, S.A. de C.V. (32%, corn flour producer, Mexico)
Grupo Vidrio Formas (69%, glass container supplier, Mexico)
Hillsdown Holdings PLC (food production, office furniture)
Home Interiors & Gifts, Inc. (80%, direct-selling of decorative accessories and gift items)
Ibero-American Media Partners (50%, Latin American media buyout fund)
International Outdoor Advertising (97%; billboards in Argentina, Chile, and Uruguay)
International Wire Holdings Corp. (60%; wire, wire harnesses, and cable)
LIN Holdings (69%, television stations)
Metrocall Inc. (paging systems)
OmniAmerica Wireless LP (45%, broadcast towers)
Pan-American Sports Network (80%, regional cable sports network)
RCN Corp. (fiber-optic telecommunications networks)
Rhythms NetConnections (8%, high-speed Internet access)
Sunrise Television Corp. (87%, small-market television stations)
Traffic (49%, broadcasting, Brazil)
United Biscuits (Holdings) plc (87%, with Finalrealm; food products; UK)
Viasystems Group (printed circuit boards)
Walden (REIT)

COMPETITORS

Bain Capital	Jordan Company
Berkshire Hathaway	KKR
Boston Ventures	Leonard Green
Clayton, Dubilier	Maseca
CVC Capital Partners	Texas Pacific Group
Equity Group Investments	Thomas Lee
Haas Wheat	Vestar Capital Partners
Heico	Vulcan Northwest
Investcorp	Wingate Partners

HIGHMARK INC.

Highmark is walking the tightrope between high-minded and high income. Highmark provides health-related coverage to nearly 25 million customers, primarily in Pennsylvania. The company offers medical, dental, vision, life, casualty, and other health insurance, as well as such community service programs as the Western Pennsylvania Caring Foundation, which offers free health care coverage to children whose parents earn too much to qualify for public aid but too little to afford private programs. Highmark also processes Medicare claims (Veritus Medicare and HGSAdministrators Medicare Services) and offers administrative and information services (Alliance Ventures).

Highmark continues to operate in western Pennsylvania under the Highmark Blue Cross Blue Shield name and as Pennsylvania Blue Shield statewide. National subsidiaries include United Concordia Companies (dental coverage) and Highmark Life and Casualty Group (disability and life insurance).

HISTORY

Highmark was created from the merger of Blue Cross of Western Pennsylvania (founded in 1937) and Pennsylvania Blue Shield, created in 1964 when the Medical Service Association of Pennsylvania (MSAP) adopted the Blue Shield name.

The Pennsylvania Medical Society, in conjunction with the state of Pennsylvania, had formed MSAP to provide medical insurance to the poor and indigent. MSAP borrowed $25,000 from the Pennsylvania Medical Society to help set up its operations, and Chauncey Palmer (who had originally proposed the organization) was named president. Individuals paid 35 cents per month, and families paid $1.75 each month to join MSAP, which initially covered mainly obstetrical and surgical procedures.

In 1945 Arthur Daugherty replaced Palmer as president (he served until his death in 1968) and helped MSAP recruit major new accounts, including the United Mine Workers and the Congress of Industrial Organizations. MSAP in 1946 became a chapter of the national Blue Shield association, which was started that year by the medical societies of several states to provide prepaid health insurance plans.

In 1951 MSAP signed up the 150,000 employees of United States Steel, bringing its total enrollment to more than 1.6 million. Growth did not lead to prosperity, though, as the organization had trouble keeping up with payments to its doctors. This shortfall in funds led MSAP to raise its premiums in 1961, at which point the state reminded the association of its social mission and

suggested it concentrate on controlling costs instead of raising rates.

MSAP changed its name to Pennsylvania Blue Shield in 1964. Two years later the association began managing the state's Medicare plan and started the 65-Special plan to supplement Medicare coverage. In the 1970s Pennsylvania Blue Shield again could not keep up with the cost of paying its doctors, which led to more rate increases and closer scrutiny of its expenses. Competition increased in the 1980s as HMOs cropped up around the state. Pennsylvania Blue Shield fought back by creating its own HMO plans — some of which it owned jointly with Blue Cross of Western Pennsylvania — in the 1980s.

After years of slowly collecting noninsurance businesses, Blue Cross of Western Pennsylvania changed its name to Veritus in 1991 to reflect the growing importance of its for-profit operations.

In 1996 Pennsylvania Blue Shield overcame physicians' protests and state regulators' concerns to merge with Veritus. The company adopted the name Highmark to represent its standards for high quality; it took a loss as it failed to meet cost-cutting goals and suffered early-retirement costs related to the merger consolidation. To gain support for the merger, Highmark sold for-profit subsidiary Keystone Health Plan East to Independence Blue Cross in 1997.

In 1999 Highmark teamed with Mountain State Blue Cross Blue Shield to become West Virginia's primary licensee. Rate hikes and investment returns helped propel the company into the black as the decade closed.

In 2001 Highmark announced that it had uncovered almost $5 million in health care insurance fraud over the course of the previous year.

OFFICERS

Chairman: John N. Shaffer
Vice Chairman: John A. Carpenter
President, CEO, and Director: John S. Brouse, age 62
Group EVP, Health Insurance Operations:
James Klingensmith
EVP, Government Business and Corporate Affairs:
George F. Grode
EVP, Strategic Business Development:
Kenneth R. Melani, age 48
SVP, CFO, and Treasurer: Robert C. Gray
SVP, Corporate Secretary, and General Counsel:
Gary R. Truitt
SVP and General Auditor: Elizabeth A. Farbacher
SVP, Human Resources and Administrative Services:
S. Tyrone Alexander
Assistant Secretary: Carrie J. Pecht
Assistant Treasurer: Joseph F. Reichard
Corporate Compliance Officer: George A. Welsh
Auditors: PricewaterhouseCoopers LLP

COMPETITORS

Aetna
CIGNA
Coventry Health Care
Guardian Life
Humana
New York Life
Prudential
UnitedHealth Group
U.S. Healthcare, Inc.

LOCATIONS

HQ: 5th Avenue Place, 120 5th Ave.,
Pittsburgh, PA 15222
Phone: 412-544-7000   **Fax:** 412-544-8368
Web: www.highmark.com

PRODUCTS/OPERATIONS

Selected Health Plans and Divisions
Alliance Ventures
Clarity Vision
Davis Vision
HealthGuard (managed care organization)
HGSAdministrators
Highmark Life & Casualty Group
Insurer Physician Services Organization
Keystone Health Plan Central (HMO; central
Pennsylvania)
Keystone Health Plan West (HMO; western
Pennsylvania)
United Concordia (dental)
Veritus Medicare Services

HISTORICAL FINANCIALS & EMPLOYEES

Not-for-profit FYE: December 31	Annual Growth	12/92	12/93	12/94	12/95	12/96	12/97	12/98	12/99	12/00	12/01
Sales ($ mil.)	9.2%	3,083	3,113	3,221	3,367	6,619	7,405	7,544	8,190	9,000	6,799
Net income ($ mil.)	(0.8%)	141	132	128	43	(50)	101	62	69	242	132
Income as % of sales	—	4.6%	4.2%	4.0%	1.3%	—	1.4%	0.8%	0.8%	2.7%	1.9%
Employees	6.2%	—	—	7,200	8,000	10,500	12,000	12,000	11,000	11,000	11,000

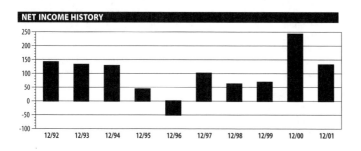

NET INCOME HISTORY

HUNTSMAN CORPORATION

Huntsman has managed to find some cover from its creditors. Having renegotiated some of its massive debt, the world's largest privately held chemical company can now focus more on the basics: basic chemicals and such. Huntsman is a major producer of basic chemicals and petrochemicals such as ethylene and propylene. The company also produces surfactants (used in cleaning and personal care products) and specialty chemicals such as polyurethanes, propylene oxides (used as a raw material for making polyurethanes), and propylene glycol. The company is the largest maker of titanium dioxide, the world's most commonly used white pigment.

Huntsman has been hamstrung by about $2 billion in debt, higher raw material costs, and a depressed chemicals market. As a result, the company stopped paying interest on debt and sought a financial restructuring. Credit Suisse First Boston's Global Opportunities Partners held much of Huntsman's debt but has swapped its bonds for a 49.9% equity in a holding company that owns Huntsman, Huntsman International (its joint venture with ICI), and Huntsman Polymers. The Huntsman family owns the rest and continues to run the company.

Founder and chairman Jon Huntsman, a cancer survivor, has directed hundreds of millions of dollars of company profits and his own money to educational and charitable causes and medical research. He donated $100 million to fund the Huntsman Cancer Institute at the University of Utah and has pledged an additional $125 million to fund research.

HISTORY

First exposed to the use of plastics in the manufacture of egg cartons, Jon Huntsman spent three frustrating years at Dow Chemical. Then he and his brother Blaine raised $300,000 and received a $1 million loan from Hambrecht & Quist to found Huntsman Container in 1970. When chemical supplies began to run short, Huntsman sold the company to Keyes Fiber in 1976.

After six years, half of which had been spent doing missionary work for the Mormon Church, Huntsman took over polystyrene operations and set his sights on an underused Shell plant in Ohio. With oil and gas titan Atlantic Richfield's backing, Huntsman convinced Shell and a bank to lend him the balance of the purchase price and formed Huntsman Chemical in 1982.

With the acquisition of Hoechst Celanese's polystyrene business in 1986, Huntsman became the #1 producer of styrene in the US. In 1987 Huntsman sold 40% of Huntsman Chemical for $52 million and then acquired a New Jersey

polypropylene plant from Shell. Huntsman reentered the packaging business in 1989 by acquiring Keyes, the European firm that had once been a part of Huntsman Container.

In 1991 hamburger dynasty McDonald's succumbed to environmentalist pressure and ceased to use the Huntsman-developed polystyrene clamshell containers; as a result, Huntsman lost about 10% of its business. The company acquired packaging assets from Goodyear Tire & Rubber in 1992 and named the new subsidiary Huntsman Packaging. The next year Huntsman bought 50% of Chemplex Australia Limited from Consolidated Press Holdings (controlled by Australian tycoon Kerry Packer).

Huntsman and Packer joined forces again in 1994 to buy most of Texaco's unprofitable petrochemical operations (renamed Huntsman Corporation) for $1 billion, doubling Huntsman's size and adding 24 plants in 12 countries. Also that year Huntsman bought Eastman Chemical's worldwide polypropylene business. The next year it formed a joint venture with Texaco to operate Texaco's worldwide lubricant-additives line, and Huntsman reacquired the 17% stake held by Great Lakes Chemical, which had been the only stock in the company held by outsiders at that time.

In 1996 Huntsman placed all of his businesses under a single entity, the Huntsman Corporation. The company bought the last of Texaco's chemicals operations in 1997, moving Huntsman into the propylene oxide market. Huntsman also bought packaging maker Rexene that year.

Huntsman sold its polystyrene and styrene monomer businesses in the US and Europe to NOVA Chemicals in 1998; it retained its expandable polystyrene unit when federal regulators objected to its sale. In 1999 the company doubled its size with the purchase of Imperial Chemical Industries' polyurethane, aromatics, titanium dioxide, petrochemical, and olefins businesses. (Huntsman established Huntsman International, a joint venture with ICI in which Huntsman owns a 70% stake, to manage these assets. Huntsman later agreed to buy ICI's 30% stake.)

In 2000 Huntsman sold Huntsman Packaging to J. P. Morgan Partners in a deal worth $1 billion. Also, Jon Huntsman stepped down as CEO (but remained as chairman). He was succeeded by his son, Peter Huntsman. Late in the year Huntsman acquired Rohm and Haas' thermoplastic polyurethane (TPU) business for about $120 million.

OFFICERS

Chairman: Jon M. Huntsman Sr., age 64
Vice Chairman: Jon M. Huntsman Jr.
President, CEO, and Director: Peter R. Huntsman, age 39
EVP and COO: Donald J. Stanutz, age 51
SVP and CFO: J. Kimo Esplin, age 39
SVP and General Counsel; SVP, Chief Legal Officer, and Secretary of Huntsman Polymers: Robert B. Lence, age 44
SVP, Environmental, Health, and Safety of Huntsman Corporation, Huntsman Polymers, and Huntsman Petrochemical: Michael J. Kern, age 52
SVP, North American Petrochemicals and Huntsman Polymers: Thomas J. Keenan, age 49
SVP, Public Affairs of Huntsman Corporation and Huntsman Polymers: Don H. Olsen, age 56
VP, Finance: L. Russell Healy, age 46
VP, Marketing/Commercial: Monte G. Edlund, age 46
VP and Treasurer: Samuel D. Scruggs
VP, Administration; VP, Huntsman Polymers: Sean Douglas, age 37

LOCATIONS

HQ: 500 Huntsman Way, Salt Lake City, UT 84108
Phone: 801-584-5700 **Fax:** 801-584-5781
Web: www.huntsman.com

Huntsman Corporation has operations worldwide.

PRODUCTS/OPERATIONS

Divisions
Gas Treating Products (such as gas-scrubbing agents)
Polymers (including resins)
Polyurethanes (used in products from adhesives to automotive parts)
Surfactants (including oxides and propylene)
Tioxides (titanium dioxides)

Selected Joint Ventures
CONDEA-Huntsman GmbH & Co. KG (automobile parts, boat hulls, and marble bath fixtures; Germany)
Huntsman Chemical Company Australia Limited (joint venture with Consolidated Press Holdings)
Huntsman International (joint venture with ICI)
Polystyrene Australia (joint venture with Dow Chemical (Australia) Ltd.)

COMPETITORS

Akzo Nobel	Imperial Chemical
BASF AG	Kerr-McGee
Bayer AG	Lyondell Chemical
BP Chemicals	Millennium Chemicals
BP	Novartis
ChevronTexaco	OxyChem
Degussa	Occidental Petroleum
Dow Chemical	Owens Corning
Eastman Chemical	PPG
DuPont	Rohm and Haas
Exxon Mobil	Sinopec Shanghai
Formosa Plastics	Petrochemical
Henkel	Teknor Apex
Hercules	Wyeth
Houghton Chemical	

HISTORICAL FINANCIALS & EMPLOYEES

Private FYE: December 31	Annual Growth	12/92	12/93	12/94	12/95	12/96	12/97	12/98	12/99	12/00	12/01
Sales ($ mil.)	21.0%	—	1,850	3,400	4,300	4,500	4,750	5,200	7,000	8,000	8,500
Employees	15.3%	3,900	5,000	8,100	8,000	8,000	9,550	10,000	14,000	16,000	14,000

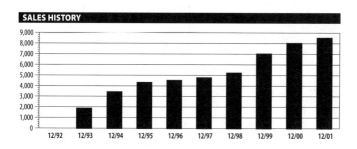

SALES HISTORY

HYATT CORPORATION

Hyatt is at your service. One of the nation's largest hotel operators, the company has more than 120 full-service luxury hotels and resorts in North America and the Caribbean (Hyatt International, its overseas branch, operates some 80 hotels and resorts in 37 countries). Many of Hyatt's hotels and resorts feature professionally designed golf courses and supervised activities for children (Camp Hyatt). The company also operates casinos and luxury retirement communities (Classic Residence by Hyatt). Led by chairman, president, and CEO Thomas Pritzker, the company is owned by the Pritzker family, one of the wealthiest in the US.

Hyatt caters to business travelers, convention-goers, and upscale vacationers. The company offers specially designed Business Plan rooms with fax machines and 24-hour access to copiers, printers, and other business necessities. Camp Hyatt targets family travelers with educational games, activities, and programs for children. The company, through Hyatt International, is doing much of its growing outside the US. It has some 17 hotels under construction in places such as China, India, Poland, Thailand, and the United Arab Emirates.

HISTORY

Nicholas Pritzker left Kiev, Russia, for Chicago in 1881, where his family's ascent to the ranks of America's wealthiest families began. His son A. N. left the family law practice in the 1930s and began investing in a variety of businesses. He turned a 1942 investment (Cory Corporation) worth $25,000 into $23 million by 1967. A. N.'s son Jay followed in his father's wheeling-and-dealing footsteps. In 1953, with the help of his father's banking connections, Jay purchased Colson Company and recruited his brother Bob, an industrial engineer, to restructure a company that made tricycles and US Navy rockets. By 1990 Jay and Bob had added 60 industrial companies, with annual sales exceeding $3 billion, to the entity they called the Marmon Group.

The family's connection to Hyatt hotels was established in 1957 when Jay bought a hotel called Hyatt House, located near the Los Angeles airport, from Hyatt von Dehn. Jay added five locations by 1961 and hired his gregarious youngest brother, Donald, to manage the hotel company. Hyatt went public in 1967, but the move that opened new vistas for the hotel chain was the purchase that year of an 800-room hotel in Atlanta that both Hilton and Marriott had turned down. John Portman's design, incorporating a 21-story atrium, a large fountain, and a revolving rooftop restaurant, became a Hyatt trademark.

The Pritzkers formed Hyatt International in 1969 to operate hotels overseas, and the company grew rapidly in the US and abroad during the 1970s. Donald Pritzker died in 1972, and Jay assumed control of Hyatt. The family decided to take the company private in 1979. Much of Hyatt's growth in the 1970s came from contracts to manage, under the Hyatt banner, hotels built by other investors. When Hyatt's cut on those contracts shrank in the 1980s, the company launched its own hotel and resort developments under Nick Pritzker, a cousin to Jay and Bob. In 1988, with US and Japanese partners, it built the Hyatt Regency Waikoloa on Hawaii's Big Island for $360 million — a record at the time for a hotel.

The Pritzkers took a side venture into air travel in 1983 when they bought bedraggled Braniff Airlines through Hyatt subsidiaries as it emerged from bankruptcy. After a failed 1987 attempt to merge the airline with PanAm, the Pritzkers sold Braniff in 1988.

Hyatt opened Classic Residence by Hyatt, a group of upscale retirement communities, in 1989. The company joined Circus Circus (now Mandalay Resort Group) in 1994 to launch the Grand Victoria, the nation's largest cruising gaming vessel, at Elgin, Illinois. The next year, as part of a new strategy to manage both freestanding golf courses and those near Hyatt hotels, the company opened its first freestanding course: an 18-hole par 71 championship course on Aruba.

President Thomas Pritzker, Jay's son, took over as chairman and CEO of Hyatt following his father's death in early 1999. In 2000 Hyatt announced plans to join rival Marriott International in launching an independent company to provide an online procurement network to serve the hospitality industry. The following year the company announced plans to begin building a new headquarters in 2002. The skyscraper, to be called the Hyatt Center, will be located in Chicago's West Loop.

OFFICERS

Chairman, President, and CEO; Chairman, Hyatt International Corporation: Thomas J. Pritzker, age 51
Vice Chairman; Chairman and President, Hyatt Development Corporation; President, Hyatt Equities: Nicholas J. Pritzker
Chairman, Classic Residence by Hyatt: Penny S. Pritzker
President, Classic Residence by Hyatt: Randal J. Richardson
President, Hyatt Hotels Corporation: Scott D. Miller
President, Hyatt International Corporation: Bernd Chorengel
EVP and COO, Hyatt Hotels Corporation: Edward W. Rabin

SVP Human Resources, Hyatt Hotels Corporation:
Linda Olson
SVP Marketing, Hyatt Hotels Corporation: Tom O'Toole
SVP Operations, Hyatt Hotels Corporation:
Chuck Floyd
VP Finance: Kirk A. Rose
Divisional VP (Southern), Hyatt Hotels Corporation:
Tim Lindgren
Divisional VP (Resorts), Hyatt Hotels Corporation:
Victor Lopez, age 51
Divisional VP (Western), Hyatt Hotels Corporation:
John Orr
Divisional VP (Central), Hyatt Hotels Corporation:
Steve Sokal

COMPETITORS

Accor
Cendant
Four Seasons Hotels
Helmsley
Hilton
Host Marriott
Marriott International
Ritz-Carlton
Sandals Resorts
Six Continents Hotels
Starwood Hotels & Resorts
Trump

LOCATIONS

HQ: 200 W. Madison St., Chicago, IL 60606
Phone: 312-750-1234   **Fax:** 312-750-8550
Web: www.hyatt.com

Hyatt Corporation and Hyatt International, a separate
entity also controlled by the Pritzker family, own and
operate hotels in Argentina, Australia, Azerbaijan,
Canada, Chile, China, Egypt, France, Germany, Greece,
Guatemala, Hungary, India, Indonesia, Israel, Japan,
Jordan, Kazakhstan, Kyrgyzstan, India, Indonesia, Japan,
Malaysia, Micronesia, Mexico, Morocco, Nepal, New
Zealand, Oman, the Philippines, Puerto Rico, Saudi
Arabia, Serbia and Montenegro, Singapore, South Africa,
South Korea, Spain, Taiwan, Thailand, Turkey, the UK,
the United Arab Emirates, the US, and the West Indies.

PRODUCTS/OPERATIONS

Selected Operations
Camp Hyatt (activities for children)
Classic Residence by Hyatt (upscale retirement
communities)
Hyatt Hotels and Resorts
Regency Casinos

HISTORICAL FINANCIALS & EMPLOYEES

Private FYE: January 31	Annual Growth	1/91	1/92	1/93	1/94	1/95	1/96	1/97	1/98	1/99	1/00
Estimated sales ($ mil.)	14.4%	—	1,350	1,460	950	1,240	2,500	2,900	3,000	3,400	3,950
Employees	5.7%	—	51,275	52,275	47,000	54,000	65,000	80,000	80,000	80,000	80,000

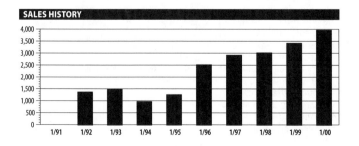

SALES HISTORY

IGA, INC.

IGA grocers are independent, but not that independent. The world's largest voluntary supermarket network, IGA has more than 4,400 stores, including members in nearly all 50 US states and in about 40 other countries. Collectively, its members are among North America's leaders in terms of supermarket sales. IGA (for either International or Independent Grocers Alliance, the company says) is owned by 37 worldwide distribution companies, including Fleming Companies and SUPERVALU. Members can sell IGA Brand private-label products and take advantage of joint operations and services such as advertising and volume buying. Some stores in the alliance, which primarily caters to smaller towns, also sell gas.

The first US grocer in China and Singapore, IGA has moved into Europe with its operations in Poland and Spain. Its international operations account for about 65% of its total sales. IGA realigned its corporate structure in 2001, setting up IGA North America, IGA Southern Hemisphere/Europe/Caribbean, and IGA Asia, each with its own president.

HISTORY

IGA was founded in Chicago in 1926 by a group led by Frank Grimes. During the 1920s chains began to dominate the grocery store industry. Grimes, an accountant for many grocery wholesalers, saw an opportunity to develop a network of independent grocers that could compete with the burgeoning chains. Grimes and five associates — Gene Flack, Louis Groebe, W. K. Hunter, H. V. Swenson, and William Thompson — created IGA.

Their idea was to "level the playing field" for independent grocers and chain stores by taking advantage of volume buying and mass marketing. IGA originally acted as a purchasing agent for its wholesalers but eventually passed that duty to the wholesalers. The group's first members were Poughkeepsie, New York-based grocery distributor W. T. Reynolds Company and the 69 grocery stores it serviced.

IGA focused on adding distributors and retailers, and soon added wholesaler Fleming-Wilson (now Fleming Companies) and Winston & Newell (currently SUPERVALU). In 1930 it hired Babe Ruth as a spokesman; other celebrity endorsers during the period included Jackie Cooper, Jack Dempsey, and Popeye. IGA also sponsored a radio program called the IGA Home Town Hour.

In 1945 the company introduced the Foodliner format, a design for stores larger than 4,000 sq. ft. The next year IGA introduced the 30-ft.-by-100-ft. Precision Store — designed so customers

had to pass all the other merchandise in the store to get to the dairy and bread sections.

Grimes retired as president in 1951. He was succeeded by his son, Don, who continued to expand the company. Don was succeeded in 1968 by Richard Jones, head of IGA member company J. M. Jones Co.

Thomas Haggai was named chairman of the company in 1976. A Baptist minister, radio commentator, and former CIA employee, Haggai had come to the attention of Grimes in 1960 when he praised Christian Scientists in one of his radio broadcasts. Grimes, a Christian Scientist, asked Haggai to speak at an IGA convention and eventually asked him to join the IGA board. Haggai, who became CEO in 1986, tightened the restrictions for IGA members, weeding out many of the smaller, low-volume mom-and-pop stores making up much of the group's network.

Haggai also began a push for international expansion. In 1988 the organization signed a deal with Japanese food company C. Itoh (now ITOCHU) to open a distribution outlet in Tokyo.

The 1990s saw expansion into Australia, Papua New Guinea, the Caribbean, China, Singapore, South Africa, and Brazil. IGA also expanded outside the continental US when it entered Hawaii. In 1993 IGA began an international television advertising campaign, a first for the supermarket industry. The next year the company launched its first line of private-label products for an ethnic food market, introducing several Mexican food products. In 1998 the group developed a new format for its stores that included on-site gas pumps.

SUPERVALU signed 54 independent grocery stores (primarily in Mississippi and Arkansas and Trinidad in the Caribbean) to the IGA banner in August 1999. With more than 60% of sales coming from international operations, IGA realigned its corporate structure in 2001, setting up IGA North America, IGA Southern Hemisphere/Europe/Caribbean, and IGA Asia, each with its own president.

OFFICERS

Chairman and CEO: Thomas S. Haggai
CFO: Robert Grottke
President, IGA Institute: Paulo Goelzer
VP, Events and Communications: Barbara G. Wiest
VP, Information Technology: Nick Liakopulos
VP, Retail Operations: William Benzing
Controller: John Collins
Director, Human Resources: Pat Smiftana
Director, Packaging: Tim Considine

LOCATIONS

HQ: 8725 W. Higgins Rd., Chicago, IL 60631
Phone: 773-693-4520   **Fax:** 773-693-4532
Web: www.igainc.com

IGA has operations in 48 states and about 40 other countries, commonwealths, and territories.

PRODUCTS/OPERATIONS

Distributors/Owners
Bozzuto's Inc.
C.I. Foods Systems Co., Ltd. (Japan)
The Copps Corporation
Davids Limited (Australia)
Fleming Companies, Inc.
Foodland Associated Limited (Australia)
Great North Foods
IGA Brasil (includes 16 individual companies)
Ira Higdon Grocery Company
Laurel Grocery Company
Martahari Putra Prima Tbk (Indonesia)
McLane Polska (Poland)
Merchants Distributors, Inc.
Metro Cash & Carry (Africa)
Nash Finch Company
NTUC Fairprice (Singapore)
Pearl River Distribution Ltd. (China)
SUPERVALU INC.
Tasmania Independent Wholesalers (Tasmania)
Tripifoods, Inc.
Villa Market JP Co., Ltd. (Thailand)
W. Lee Flowers & Co., Inc.
WALTERMART SUPERMARKETS (Philippines)

Affiliates
H.Y. Louie (fraternal relationship, Canada)
Sobey's (fraternal relationship, Canada)

Selected Joint Operations and Services
Advertising
Community service programs
Equipment purchase
IGA Brand (private-label products)
IGA Grocergram (in-house magazine)
Internet services
Marketing
Merchandising
Red Oval Family (manufacturer/IGA collaboration on sales, marketing, and other activities)
Volume buying

COMPETITORS

Albertson's
AWG
BJs Wholesale Club
C&S Wholesale
Carrefour
Casino Guichard
Coles Myer
Daiei
Dairy Farm International
Delhaize
George Weston
A&P
Hannaford Bros.
H-E-B
Ito-Yokado
Kroger
Meijer
Metro Cash and Carry
Penn Traffic
Publix
Roundy's
Royal Ahold
Safeway
Spartan Stores
Topco Associates
Wakefern Food
Wal-Mart
Winn-Dixie

HISTORICAL FINANCIALS & EMPLOYEES

Holding company FYE: December 31	Annual Growth	12/92	12/93	12/94	12/95	12/96	12/97	12/98	12/99	12/00	12/01
Estimated sales ($ mil.)	3.1%	15,900	16,500	17,000	17,100	16,800	18,000	18,000	19,000	21,000	21,000
Employees	(5.6%)	—	—	—	130,000	128,000	135,000	92,000	92,000	92,000	92,000

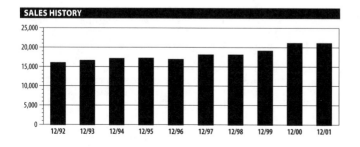

SALES HISTORY

INGRAM INDUSTRIES INC.

Ingram Industries is heavy into books, boats, and bad drivers. Ingram Book Group is one of the largest wholesale book distributors in the US; it ships more than 175 million books and audiotapes annually, serving some 32,000 retail outlets and 13,000 publishers. Ingram Marine Group operates Ingram Materials and ships grain, ore, and other products through about 1,800 barges. Ingram Insurance Group covers high-risk drivers in nine states through Permanent General Insurance. The Ingram family, led by chairman Martha Ingram (America's wealthiest active businesswoman), owns and runs Ingram Industries and controls about 75% of the voting shares of Ingram Micro (a top computer products wholesaler).

Ingram Book Group (operating out of eight fulfillment centers) is also a leading distributor to libraries, and the entire book division accounts for over half of Ingram Industries' total sales. Its Lightning Source subsidiary offers conversion and distribution services for print-on-demand and e-books.

Ingram Industries spun off its largest segment, Ingram Micro, in 1996. Ingram Entertainment (the US's top distributor of videotapes) was spun off the following year and is now owned by Martha's son, David.

HISTORY

Orrin Ingram and two partners founded the Dole, Ingram & Kennedy sawmill in 1857 in Eau Claire, Wisconsin, on the Chippewa River, about 50 miles upstream from the Mississippi River. By the 1870s the company, renamed Ingram & Kennedy, was selling lumber as far downstream as Hannibal, Missouri.

Ingram's success was noticed by Frederick Weyerhaeuser, a German immigrant in Rock Island, Illinois, who, like Ingram, had worked in a sawmill before buying one of his own. In 1881 Ingram and Weyerhaeuser negotiated the formation of Chippewa Logging (35%-owned by up-river partners, 65% by down-river interests), which controlled the white pine harvest of the Chippewa Valley. In 1900 Ingram paid $216,000 for 2,160 shares in the newly formed Weyerhaeuser Timber Company. Ingram let his sons and grandsons handle the investment and formed O.H. Ingram Co. to manage the family's interests. He died in 1918.

In 1946 Ingram's descendants founded Ingram Barge, which hauled crude oil to the company's refinery near St. Louis. After buying and then selling other holdings, in 1962 the family formed Ingram Corp., consisting solely of Ingram Barge. Brothers Bronson and Fritz Ingram

(the great-grandsons of Orrin) bought the company from their father, Hank, before he died in 1963, and in 1964 they bought half of Tennessee Book, a textbook distributing company founded in 1935. In 1970 they formed Ingram Book Group to sell trade books to bookstores and libraries.

Ingram Barge won a $48 million Chicago sludge-hauling contract in 1971, but later the company was accused of bribing city politicians with $1.2 million in order to land the contract. The brothers stood trial in 1977 for authorizing the bribes; Bronson was acquitted, but the court convicted Fritz on 29 counts. Before Fritz entered prison (he served 16 months of a four-year sentence), he and his brother split their company. Fritz took the energy operations and went bust in the 1980s. Bronson took the barge and book businesses and formed Ingram Industries.

The new company formed computer products distributor Ingram Computer in 1982 and between 1985 and 1989 bought all the stock of Micro D, a computer wholesaler. Ingram Computer and Micro D merged to form Ingram Micro. In 1992 it acquired Commtron, the world's #1 wholesaler of prerecorded videocassettes, and merged it into Ingram Entertainment.

When Bronson died in mid-1995, his wife Martha (the PR director) became chairman and began a restructuring. Ingram Industries closed its non-bookstore rack distributor (Ingram Merchandising) in 1995 and sold its oil-and-gas machinery subsidiary (Cactus Co.) in 1996. It spun off Ingram Micro in 1996, followed in 1997 by Ingram Entertainment. Ingram Industries purchased Christian books distributor Spring Arbor that year and also introduced an on-demand book publishing service (Lightning Print).

The company in late 1998 agreed to sell its book group to Barnes & Noble for $600 million, but FTC pressure killed the deal in mid-1999. With customers and competitors increasing distribution capacity in the western US, a resulting drop in business led Ingram Industries to cut more than 100 jobs at an Oregon warehouse in 1999.

In early 2000 Ingram renamed Lightning Print as Lightning Source. Also that year Ingram announced plans to distribute products other than books for e-tailers (starting with gifts). In March 2001 Ingram took over the specialty-book distribution for Borders.

In July 2002 Ingram completed its acquisition of Midland Enterprises LLC, a leading US inland marine transportation company that includes The Ohio River Company LLC and Orgulf Transport LLC.

OFFICERS

Chairman: Martha Ingram
Vice Chairman; Chairman, Ingram Book Group:
John R. Ingram, age 40
**President and CEO; Chairman, Ingram Barge
Company:** Orrin H. Ingram II
VP, Treasurer, and Controller: Mary K. Cavarra
VP, Human Resources: Dennis Delaney
President and CEO, Ingram Book Group:
Michael Lovett
**COO, Ingram Book Group and President, Ingram Book
Company:** Jim Chandler
President, Spring Arbor Distributors: Steve Arthur

LOCATIONS

HQ: 1 Belle Meade Place, 4400 Harding Rd.,
Nashville, TN 37205
Phone: 615-298-8200   **Fax:** 615-298-8242
Web: www.ingram.com

PRODUCTS/OPERATIONS

Selected Operations

Ingram Book Group
Ingram Book Company (wholesaler of trade books and
audiobooks)
Ingram Customer Systems (computerized systems and
services)
Ingram International (international distribution of
books and audiobooks)
Ingram Library Services (distributes books, audiobooks,
and videos to libraries)
Ingram Periodicals (direct distributor of specialty
magazines)
Ingram Publisher Relations (publishing services for
publishers)
Lightning Source (on-demand printing and electonic
publishing)
Specialty Retail (book distributor to nontraditional book
market)
Spring Arbor Distributors (product and services for
Christian retailers)

Ingram Insurance Group
Permanent General Insurance Co. (automobile
insurance in California, Florida, Georgia, Indiana,
Louisiana, Ohio, South Carolina, Tennessee, and
Wisconsin)

Ingram Marine Group
Ingram Barge (ships grain, ore, and other products)
Ingram Materials Co. (produces construction materials
such as sand and gravel)

COMPETITORS

Advanced Marketing
Allstate
American Commercial Lines
American Financial
Baker & Taylor
Chas. Levy
Follett
Hudson News
Kirby
Media Source
Progressive Corporation
SAFECO
State Farm
TECO Energy
Thomas Nelson
Times Publishing

HISTORICAL FINANCIALS & EMPLOYEES

Private FYE: December 31	Annual Growth	12/92	12/93	12/94	12/95	12/96	12/97	12/98	12/99	12/00	12/01
Sales ($ mil.)	(9.3%)	4,657	6,163	8,010	11,000	1,463	1,796	2,000	2,135	2,075	1,929
Employees	(3.4%)	8,407	9,658	10,000	13,000	5,300	6,362	6,500	6,080	6,494	6,148

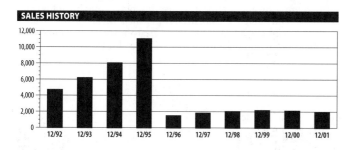

SALES HISTORY

TEAMSTERS

The International Brotherhood of Teamsters is the largest and arguably most (in)famous labor union in the US. With about 1.4 million members, the Teamsters represent 16 trade groups, including truckers, UPS workers, warehouse employees, cab drivers, airline workers, construction crews, and other workers. The union negotiates with employers for contracts that guarantee members fair wages and raises, health coverage, job security, paid time off, promotions, and other benefits. The Teamsters union has about 570 local chapters in the US and Canada.

Elected in 1998, Teamsters chief James P. Hoffa (son of assumed-dead union leader Jimmy Hoffa) is working to shed the union's notorious image and has proposed ethics policies aimed at rooting out internal corruption and ties to organized crime. Hoffa wants the Teamsters to police themselves and put an end to the close governmental supervision under which the union has operated since 1988. Working to re-establish the union as a power in national politics, he also lobbied against plans to allow trucks from Mexico to traverse US highways.

HISTORY

Two rival team-driver unions, the Drivers International Union and the Teamsters National Union, merged to form the International Brotherhood of Teamsters in 1903. Led by Cornelius Shea, the Teamsters established headquarters in Indianapolis. Daniel Tobin (president for 45 years, starting in 1907) demanded that union locals obtain executive approval before striking. Membership expanded from the team-driver base, prompting the union to add Chauffeurs, Stablemen, and Helpers to its name (1909).

Following the first transcontinental delivery by motor truck (1912), the Teamster deliverymen traded their horses for trucks. The union then recruited food processing, brewery, and farm workers, among others, to augment Teamster effectiveness during strikes. It joined the American Federation of Labor in 1920.

Until the Depression the Teamsters were still a small union of predominantly urban deliverymen. Then Farrell Dobbs, a Trotskyite Teamster from Minneapolis, organized the famous Minneapolis strikes in 1934 to protest local management's refusal to allow the workers to unionize. Workers clashed with police and National Guard units for 11 days before management acceded to the workers' demands. The strikes demonstrated the potential strength of unions, and Teamsters membership swelled. Although union power ebbed during WWII, the union continued to grow. The union moved its headquarters to Washington, DC, in 1953.

The AFL-CIO expelled the Teamsters in 1957 when Teamster ties to the mob became public during a US Senate investigation. New Teamsters boss Jimmy Hoffa eluded indictment and took advantage of America's growing dependence on trucking to negotiate the powerful National Master Freight Agreement (1964). Hoffa also organized industrial workers. He used a union pension fund to make mob-connected loans and was later convicted of jury tampering and sent to prison. In 1975, four years after his release, Hoffa vanished without a trace and is believed to have been the victim of a Mafia hit.

The Teamsters rejoined the AFL-CIO in 1987 and the following year settled a racketeering lawsuit filed by the US Justice Department by allowing government appointees to discipline corrupt union leaders, help run the union, and oversee its elections. The election of self-styled reformer Ronald Carey in 1991 (he received 49% of the vote) seemed to portend real changes for the union; each of his six predecessors had been accused of or imprisoned for criminal activities. However, membership dropped by 40,000 in both 1991 and 1992.

Carey won re-election as union president in 1996 over rival, and son of former boss Jimmy Hoffa, James P. Hoffa (whom Carey accused of having ties to organized crime). A 15-day strike by the Teamsters' UPS employees in 1997 led to the delivery company's agreement to combine part-time jobs into 10,000 new full-time positions. That year Carey's re-election was overturned amid a campaign finance investigation that netted guilty pleas from three Carey associates, and the Teamsters leader was disqualified from running for re-election in 1998. Carey was officially expelled from the Teamsters by the federal government, and Hoffa won the 1998 election over Tom Leedham (who was backed by the union's reform wing).

Promising to fight corruption, Hoffa hired former federal prosecutor Edwin Stier and several former FBI agents to help him operate Project RISE (respect, integrity, strength, and ethics), a new in-house anti-corruption program. In 2001 the union began lobbying against plans to allow Mexican trucking companies to transport goods across the US.

OFFICERS

General President: James P. Hoffa, age 61
General Secretary-Treasurer: Tom Keegel
VP At-Large: Randy Cammack
VP At-Large: Fred Gegare
VP At-Large: Carl E. Haynes
VP At-Large: Thomas R. O'Donnell
VP At-Large: Ralph J. Taurone
VP, Canada; President, Teamsters Canada:
Robert Bouvier
VP, Canada: Joseph McLean
VP, Canada: Garnet Zimmerman
VP, Central Region: Patrick Flynn
VP, Central Region: Walter Lytle
VP, Central Region: Dotty W. Malinsky
VP, Central Region: Lester A. Singer
VP, Central Region: Philip E. Young
VP, Eastern Region: Jack Cipriani
VP, Eastern Region: John Murphy
VP, Eastern Region: Dan De Santi
VP, Eastern Region: Richard Volpe
VP, Southern Region: Tyson Johnson
VP, Southern Region: Ken Wood
VP, Western Region: Al Hobart
VP, Western Region: Chuck Mack
VP, Western Region: Jim Santangelo
Director of Human Resources Department: Lynda Sist

LOCATIONS

HQ: International Brotherhood of Teamsters
25 Louisiana Ave. NW, Washington, DC 20001
Phone: 202-624-6800   **Fax:** 202-624-6918
Web: www.teamster.org

2001 Membership

	% of total
United States	
Central	32
East	28
West	26
South	7
Canada	7
Total	**100**

PRODUCTS/OPERATIONS

Trade Divisions
Airline
Bakery and Laundry
Brewery and Soft Drink
Building Material and Construction
Carhaul
Dairy
Freight
Industrial Trades
Motion Picture and Theatrical Trade
Newspaper, Magazine, and Electronic Media
Parcel and Small Package
Port
Public Services
Tankhaul
Trade Show and Convention Centers
Warehouse

INTERNATIONAL DATA GROUP

International Data Group (IDG) is a publishing giant with digital appeal. The world's top technology publisher, IDG produces some 300 magazines and newspapers in 85 countries, including *PC World* and *CIO*. In addition to publishing, IDG provides technology market research through its IDC unit and produces a number of industry events. In 2001 the firm sold its 75% stake in Hungry Minds (formerly IDG Books Worldwide), the oracle for the tech-unsavvy with its *For Dummies* series of books. Chairman Patrick McGovern, who founded IDG in 1964, holds a majority stake in the company; an employee stock plan owns the rest.

While a downturn in the economy hurt publishers in 2000 and 2001, IDG weathered the storm in part by concentrating on growing its market research and event marketing businesses. The company's IDC unit has hundreds of analysts in 43 countries, and its industry events include Macworld Expo and the Internet Commerce Expo. It also offers career services through JobUniverse.com and ITcareers.com and operates 330 Web sites featuring technology content. IDG has acquired some assets of *Industry Standard* publisher Standard Media (subscriber lists, trademarks, newsletters) following that company's bankruptcy liquidation.

HISTORY

Patrick McGovern began his career in publishing as a paperboy for the *Philadelphia Bulletin*. As a teenager in the 1950s, McGovern was inspired by Edmund Berkeley's book *Giant Brains; or Machines That Think*. He later built a computer and won a scholarship to MIT. There he edited the first computer magazine, *Computers and Automation*. McGovern started market research firm International Data Corporation in 1964 after interviewing the president of computer pioneer UNIVAC. Three years later he launched *Computerworld*, and within a few weeks the eight-page tabloid had 20,000 subscribers. Combined under the name International Data Group, McGovern's company reached $1 million in sales by 1968.

Taking the "International" in its name to heart, IDG began publishing in Japan in 1971 and expanded to Germany in 1975. Following the collapse of communism, the company had 10 publications in Russia and Eastern Europe by 1990. That year two teenage hackers broke into the company's voice mail system and erased orders from customers and messages from writers. The prank cost IDG about $2.4 million. Also in 1990, IDG launched IDG Books Worldwide (renamed Hungry Minds in 2000), which hit it big the next year with *DOS for Dummies*.

With the technology boom of the 1990s, competition in tech publishing heated up. By 1993 several of IDG's magazines, including *InfoWorld, Macworld,* and *PC World,* began losing ad pages to rivals Ziff Davis and CMP Media. To help stem advertiser attrition, IDG started an incentive program tied to its new online service. In 1995 IDG bought a stake in software companies Architect Software (now Excite@Home) and Netscape (now owned by AOL Time Warner) as part of its move toward Internet-based services.

In 1996 IDG launched *Netscape World: The Web,* a magazine covering the Internet, and introduced more than 30 industry newsletters delivered by e-mail. The company also bought *PC Advisor,* the UK's fastest-growing computer magazine. IDG kicked off its online ad placement service, Global Web Ad Network, in 1997. That year IDG merged *Macworld* with rival Ziff Davis' *MacUser* in a joint venture called Mac Publishing.

In 1998 IDG pledged $1 billion in venture capital for high-tech startups in China. It also introduced new publications in China, including a Chinese edition of *Cosmopolitan* (with Hearst Magazines) and *China Computer Reseller World.* Later that year the company launched *The Industry Standard* and spun off 25% of IDG Books to the public.

In 1999 it sold a 20% stake in Industry Standard Communications (renamed Standard Media International) to private investors and began laying plans for a possible spinoff in 2000. However, a weakening economy and slowing ad sales in 2000 quieted those plans.

The next year both Standard Media and Hungry Minds announced staff cuts and restructuring. IDG eventually sold its majority interest in Hungry Minds to John Wiley & Sons for about $90 million. Standard Media filed for bankruptcy and liquidated its assets, some of which were bought by IDG. The company also purchased Ziff Davis' 50% stake in their joint-venture Mac Publishing. In 2002 IDG CEO Kelly Conlin left the business and was replaced by company executive Pat Kenealy.

OFFICERS

Chairman: Patrick J. McGovern
CEO: Pat Kenealy
VP Finance: Jim Ghirardi
VP Human Resources: Karen Budreau
President and CEO, Bio-IT World Inc.: Morris R. Levitt
President, CXO Media: Walter Manninen
Auditors: Deloitte & Touche LLP

HQ: 1 Exeter Plaza, 15th Fl., Boston, MA 02116
Phone: 617-534-1200   **Fax:** 617-262-2300
Web: www.idg.com

International Data Group publishes more than 300 magazines and newspapers in 85 countries.

PRODUCTS/OPERATIONS

Selected Operations
IDC (market research)
IDG Events & Conferences
IDG Publications (periodical publishing)
IDG Recruitment Solutions (employment services)
IDG.net (online publications hub)

Selected Events
ComNet
Internet Commerce Expo
LinuxWorld Conference & Expo
Macworld Expo

Selected Periodicals
CIO
Computerworld
Darwin Magazine
GamePro
InfoWorld
Macworld
Network World
PC World
Publish

COMPETITORS

CNET Networks
Forrester Research
Freeman Companies
Future Network
Gartner
Jupitermedia
Key3Media
McGraw-Hill
Microsoft
Pearson
Penton Media
Reed Elsevier Group
SYS-CON Media
UMAC
United Business Media
Vivendi Universal Publishing
VNU
Ziff Davis Media

HISTORICAL FINANCIALS & EMPLOYEES

Private FYE: September 30	Annual Growth	9/93	9/94	9/95	9/96	9/97	9/98	9/99	9/00	9/01	9/02
Sales ($ mil.)	12.7%	880	1,100	1,400	1,700	1,876	2,050	2,560	3,100	3,010	2,580
Employees	11.2%	5,000	7,200	8,200	8,500	9,500	11,500	12,000	13,400	13,200	13,050

SALES HISTORY

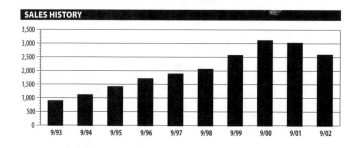

INTERNATIONAL MANAGEMENT

Show me the money! Led by founder and owner Mark McCormack, International Management Group (IMG) is the world's largest sports talent and marketing agency. The firm's list of clients includes the hippest athletes of the day, including Venus and Serena Williams, Tiger Woods, and Wayne Gretzky. In addition to representing sports idols, IMG also counts artists (Placido Domingo), models (Tyra Banks), and broadcasters (Bob Costas) among its clients. Its Trans World International division produces more than 5,000 hours of sports TV programming each year. In addition, IMG represents corporate clients (Cisco Systems), acts as a literary agent, and is active in real estate and golf course design among other things.

IMG is credited with having invented the field of sports management. While representing VIP clients may be how IMG gained its fame, the company is involved in several other aspects of sports promotion as well. It gives many of its clients venues in which to compete by promoting sporting events, and when athletes need training, they can take advantage of IMG's various sports academies.

The company is active in financial consulting through a joint venture with Merrill Lynch (McCormack Advisors International). IMG continues to expand internationally, organizing sporting events such as basketball, baseball, golf, and rugby across Asia, Australia, and Europe.

HISTORY

When former amateur golfer Mark McCormack went to Yale Law School in the 1950s, he didn't desert golf entirely. In his free time he set up paid exhibitions for pro golfers he knew from his days on the links, and in 1960 one of these players, Arnold Palmer, asked McCormack to manage his finances so he could concentrate on his game. McCormack went above and beyond the call of duty, signing Palmer to endorsement deals and licensing his name and image.

In two years Palmer's annual income skyrocketed from $60,000 to more than $500,000 — a fiscal triumph that would be the bedrock of IMG's business. Throughout the early and mid-1960s, IMG signed up more big-name golfers, as well as stars from other sports such as Jackie Stewart (car racing) and Jean-Claude Killy (skiing).

The addition of foreign stars such as Stewart (Scotland), Killy (France), and Gary Player (South Africa) allowed IMG access to global markets. In the late 1960s as television began to bring sports and its stars into living rooms around the world, IMG used its clients to promote products and services internationally. In

1967 McCormack created a new division of IMG — a TV production company that filmed and distributed sporting events called Trans World International (TWI). The next year IMG signed a contract with Wimbledon's organizers to coordinate video and television licensing.

IMG's entrepreneurial spirit came to the forefront with a vengeance in the 1980s. In addition to managing athletes, sporting events, and sponsors, the company began to skip the middleman and create the sports event itself. IMG debuted the Skins Game in 1983, a golf invitational featuring four of the sport's top athletes playing for high stakes. IMG also created Saturday afternoon sports staples such as *The Battle of the Network Stars*, shows that featured sports or TV stars competing in a series of events such as the tug-o-war and obstacle courses.

By the 1990s McCormack had situated IMG to take advantage of almost every aspect of televised sports events: Typically, an IMG event involved working with the athletes, the sponsor or sponsors, the event itself, and the television distribution rights. The company continued to expand its clientele beyond sports, adding names such as musician Placido Domingo. By 1997 IMG also counted the Rock and Roll Hall of Fame, the Americas Cup, and the Mayo Clinic as clients.

IMG teamed up with Chase Capital Partners (now J.P. Morgan Partners) in 1998 to form IMG/Chase Sports Capital, a private equity fund expected to raise some $200 million to invest in the sports industry. The next year IMG demonstrated a well-honed knack for capitalizing on its clients' appeal by staging a televised golf match between clients Tiger Woods and David Duval, and again in 2000 between Woods and Sergio Garcia. Also that year IMG tried to create a new cable network between TWI and the New York Yankees, but the New York Supreme Court blocked the deal, saying it violated the Yankees' current deal with MSG Network. In 2001 the Yankees broke ties with MSG, paying them $30 million, to do its own network.

OFFICERS

Chairman and CEO: Mark H. McCormack
CFO: Arthur J. LaFave
Senior Corporate VP: Peter Johnson
Senior Corporate VP: Stephanie Tolleson, age 45
President, IMG Football: Tom Condon
SVP Golf; President, Basketball: Mark Steinberg, age 35
VP Human Resources: Susie Austin
Director of Africa/Europe/Middle East Operations: Ian T. Todd, age 55
Director of Asia/Pacific Regions Operations: Alastair Johnston
Director of North/South American Operations: Robert D. Kain

HQ: International Management Group
    1360 E. 9th St., Ste. 100, Cleveland, OH 44114
Phone: 216-522-1200   **Fax:** 216-522-1145
Web: www.imgworld.com

IMG has 85 offices in 33 countries.

PRODUCTS/OPERATIONS

Selected Clients
All England Lawn Tennis & Croquet Club (Wimbledon)
Tyra Banks
Jose Carreras
Cisco Systems
Bob Costas
Placido Domingo
David Duval
Sergio Garcia
Wayne Gretzky
Stephen Hawking
International Olympic Committee
Heidi Klum
Nancy Lopez
John Madden
Joe Montana
Colin Montgomerie
Martina Navratilova
Greg Norman
Mark O'Meara
Arnold Palmer
Rugby World Cup
Serena Williams
Venus Williams
Tiger Woods
United States Golf Association

Selected Sports Academies
The David Leadbetter Golf Academy
IMG Hockey Academy
International Performance Institute
Nick Bollettieri Tennis Academy
The Soccer and Baseball Academies

Other Operations
IMG Golf Course Services (designs, manages, and
    markets golf courses worldwide)
Trans World International (sports television production)

COMPETITORS

Bull Run
Clear Channel Entertainment
CAA
Dentsu
the Firm
Golden Bear Golf
International Creative Management
Interpublic Group
Magnum Sports & Entertainment
TBA
United Talent
William Morris
WPP Group

HISTORICAL FINANCIALS & EMPLOYEES

Private FYE: December 31	Annual Growth	12/92	12/93	12/94	12/95	12/96	12/97	12/98	12/99	12/00	12/01
Estimated sales ($ mil.)	4.5%	—	—	—	1,000	1,000	1,100	1,100	1,100	1,260	1,300
Employees	7.7%	—	—	—	1,600	1,959	2,000	2,125	2,150	2,900	2,500

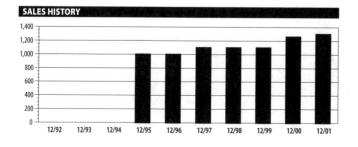

SALES HISTORY

THE IRVINE COMPANY INC.

At The Irvine Company, everything is going according to plan. Master plan, that is. The company creates master-planned communities in well-heeled Orange County, of which the company owns some 50,000 acres (making it California's largest landowner). The company's land is called Irvine Ranch and includes the US's largest planned community, Irvine, with more than 150,000 residents; some 30,000 acres have been set aside for wildlife habitat and open spaces. Its core holdings are derived from the 120,000-acre Irvine Ranch, formed in the mid-1800s when James Irvine bought out the debts of Mexican land-grant holders. Chairman Donald Bren, one of America's wealthiest men, owns the company.

The Irvine Company's portfolio includes the Irvine Spectrum development, one of the nation's largest high-tech research and business centers, as well as two hotels, five marinas, and three golf courses.

The University of California, Irvine, is built on company-donated land.

The Irvine Company also owns Irvine Apartment Communities, a real estate investment trust (REIT) that owns some 75 apartment complexes in the Irvine Ranch area, as well as in San Diego, San Jose, and Los Angeles.

Bren has continued the 35-year-old master plan created by the Irvine Foundation (the former parent of the Irvine Company), which calls for gradual development of rigorously planned communities. The plan — which has so far helped form the communities of Laguna Beach, Newport Beach, Orange, and Tustin, as well as centerpiece Irvine — has entered its final phase (set for completion around 2040), but the company faces increasing political opposition to its plans from area residents, who tend to become development-weary after they get their piece of the Irvine Ranch.

HISTORY

A wholesale merchant in San Francisco during the gold rush, James Irvine and two others assembled vast holdings in Southern California in the mid-1800s by buying out the debts of Mexican and Spanish land-grant holders. Irvine bought his partners' shares in 1876 and passed the ranch of 120,000 acres to his son, James II, upon his death in 1886. Eight years later James II incorporated the ranch as The Irvine Company and began turning it into an agribusiness empire, shifting from sheep ranching to cash crop farming.

James II owned the ranch and company until the 1930s, when the death of his son, James III,

prompted him to transfer a controlling interest in the company to the not-for-profit Irvine Foundation. James III's wife, Athalie, and daughter, Joan, inherited 22% of Irvine.

In 1959 company president Myford Irvine, a grandson of James I and uncle to Joan, was found dead from two shotgun wounds. Officials ruled it a suicide, but others weren't so sure.

With Athalie and Joan's encouragement, the company donated land in the early 1960s for the construction of the University of California, Irvine. The company would continue contributing to educational and philanthropic causes as well as donating property for green space to improve Orange County's suburban areas.

The 1960s also saw the Irvine Foundation forming its definitive master plan for prearranged communities and marked the company's entry into the real estate development sector. The plan was designed to anticipate and control growth, with provisions for green space and a mix of pricing levels.

Super-rich firebrand Joan, who had long accused Irvine Foundation officers of serving their own interests at the expense of other stockholders, lobbied Congress in the late 1960s to change tax laws pertaining to the foundation. Along with a group of investors led by Donald Bren, Alfred Taubman, and Herbert Allen, Joan trumped a bid by Mobil Oil and in 1977 gained control of the company from the foundation.

When California's real estate market went sour in 1983, Bren bought a majority interest of the firm. Joan returned to court to protest the price, gaining extra money when the court valued the land at $1.4 billion. In 1993 Bren sought cash from his holdings by offering apartment developments as a real estate investment trust, Irvine Apartment Communities.

Orange County's record-setting bankruptcy in 1994 (the county lost $1.7 billion in risky investments) threatened the value of The Irvine Company's property portfolio, most of which is located in Orange County. Thanks in part to a frothy economy and settlements from brokerage firms, Orange County and The Irvine Company were spared another 1983-esque bust.

In 1996 Bren bought the company's remaining stock. As part of its expansion into R&D, retail, and office properties in the Silicon Valley area, The Irvine Company opened an office in San Jose the next year, followed by its Eastgate Technology Park in San Diego in 1998. An industry-wide slide in REIT stock prices prompted Bren to take Irvine Apartment Communities private in 1999.

The company continued to expand its retail and office holdings into the aughts — including the purchase of Century City's Fox Plaza. In 2002, the Irvine City Council approved the Irvine Company's plans to develop the last phase of the company's master plan (to be completed in 2040) — bringing over 12,000 homes, 730,000 sq. ft. of retail space, and about 6.5 million sq. ft. of industrial space to the city's Northern Sphere area.

OFFICERS

Chairman: Donald L. Bren
Vice Chairman and COO: Michael D. McKee
Vice Chairman: Raymond L. Watson, age 75
Group SVP and CFO: Marc Ley
Group SVP and Chief Marketing Officer: W. E. Mitchell
Group SVP, Corporate Affairs: Monica Florian
Group SVP, Entitlement: Daniel Young
Group SVP, Public Affairs: Larry Thomas
Group SVP, Urban Planning and Design: Robert N. Elliott
SVP, Human Resources: Bruce Endsley
VP and Corporate Controller: Mary J. Vietze
President, Investment Properties Group: Clarence W. Barker
President, Irvine Community Development: Joseph D. Davis
President, Apartment Communities, Investment Properties Group: Max L. Gardner, age 50
President, Retail Properties, Investment Properties Group: Keith Eyrich
President, Office Properties, Investment Properties Group: William Halford
EVP, Resort Properties, Investment Properties Group: L. K. Eric Prevette
VP, Commercial Land Sales, Investment Properties Group: Larry Williams
Director, Compensation and Benefits: Pat Neher
Director, Purchasing: Heather Colbert
Director, Training: Gail Jenson

LOCATIONS

HQ: 550 Newport Center Dr., Newport Beach, CA 92658
Phone: 949-720-2000   **Fax:** 949-720-2218
Web: www.irvineco.com

The Irvine Company owns and develops 54,000 acres of land in Orange County, California, including the City of Irvine and parts of Anaheim, Laguna Beach, Newport Beach, Orange, and Tustin. It also owns properties in Los Angeles, San Diego, and San Jose.

PRODUCTS/OPERATIONS

Selected Divisions
Investment Properties Group
  Irvine Commercial Land Sales
  Irvine Resort Properties (hotels, marinas, and golf courses)
  Irvine Office Company (7 million sq. ft. of office space)
  Irvine Retail Properties Company (6.3 million sq. ft. of shopping and retail space)
Irvine Apartment Communities
Irvine Community Development

COMPETITORS

Arden Realty
California Coastal Communities
Center Trust
C.J. Segerstrom & Sons
Corky McMillin
Intergroup
KB Home
Kilroy Realty
Majestic Realty
MBK Real Estate
Mission West Properties
Newhall Land and Farming
Pan Pacific
Tejon Ranch

HISTORICAL FINANCIALS & EMPLOYEES

Private FYE: June 30	Annual Growth	6/92	6/93	6/94	6/95	6/96	6/97	6/98	6/99	6/00	6/01
Sales ($ mil.)	8.8%	700	800	800	700	710	816	1,000	1,100	1,305	1,500
Employees	5.1%	300	200	200	200	190	200	236	250	435	470

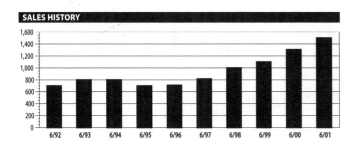

SALES HISTORY

JM FAMILY ENTERPRISES, INC.

Founder and honorory chairman Jim Moran and CEO Pat Moran (Jim's daughter) make JM Family Enterprises a family affair. JM, owned by the Moran family, is a holding company (Florida's second-largest private company, in fact, after Publix Super Markets) with about a dozen automotive-related businesses, including the nation's largest-volume Lexus retailer, JM Lexus, in Margate, Florida. JM's major subsidiary, Southeast Toyota Distributors, is the world's largest Toyota distribution franchise, delivering Toyota cars, trucks, and vans to more than 160 dealers in Alabama, Florida, Georgia, and North and South Carolina.

Among JM Family's other subsidiaries, JM&A Group provides insurance and warranty services to retailers nationwide. World Omni Financial handles leasing, dealer financing, and other financial services for US auto dealers.

Pat Moran is one of the top female business owners in the US.

HISTORY

Jim Moran first became visible as "Jim Moran, the Courtesy Man" in Chicago TV advertisements in the 1950s. At that time he ran Courtesy Motors, where he was so successful as the world's #1 Ford dealer that *Time* magazine put his picture on its cover in 1961.

Moran had entered the auto sales business after fixing up and selling a car for more than three times the price he had paid for it. That profit was much better than what he made at the Sinclair gas station he had bought, so he opened a used-car lot. Later, he moved to new-car sales when he bought a Hudson franchise (Ford had rejected him).

Seeing the promise of TV advertising, in 1948 Moran pioneered the forum for Chicago car dealers, not only as an advertiser and program sponsor but also as host of a variety show and a country/western music barn dance. The increased visibility positioned Moran as Hudson's #1 dealer, but the sales tactics at Courtesy Motors earned an antitrust suit that was settled out of court.

In 1955 Moran started with Ford and, with his TV influence as host of *The Jim Moran Courtesy Hour,* he became the world's #1 Ford dealer in his first month.

He moved to Florida in 1966 after being diagnosed with cancer and given one year to live. Successfully fighting the disease, he bought a Pontiac franchise and later started Southeast Toyota Distributors. In 1969 he formed JM Family Enterprises.

Legal problems cropped up in 1973 when the IRS investigated a Nassau bank serving as a tax haven for wealthy Americans. Moran and three Toyota executives were linked to the bank, and in 1978 Moran was indicted for tax fraud. When an immunity deal fell through, Moran pleaded guilty to seven tax fraud charges in 1984 and was sentenced to two years (suspended), fined more than $12 million, and ordered to perform community service. Moran's legal problems threatened his association with Toyota and were blamed for causing his stroke in 1983.

JM's legal problems continued in the 1980s, partly because of the imposition of auto import restrictions. To get more cars to sell, some Southeast Toyota managers encouraged auto dealers to file false sales reports. Some North Carolina dealers resisted and one sued, settling out of court for $22 million. Other dealers alleged racketeering and fraud on the part of Southeast Toyota, and by the beginning of 1994, JM had paid more than $100 million in fines and settlements for cases stretching back to 1988. In spite of that, Toyota renewed its contract with the company in 1993, a year ahead of schedule.

Pat Moran succeeded her father as JM president in 1992. Between 1991 and 1994 three suits were filed against Jim and Southeast Toyota alleging racism against blacks in establishing Toyota dealerships. All three suits were settled.

Jim teamed with Wayne Huizenga in 1996 to launch a national chain of used-car megastores under the name AutoNation USA, which Jim expected would draw buyers to his own auto dealerships. (AutoNation USA's first store was built just two blocks from JM's Coconut Creek Lexus Dealership.) Jim's interest in AutoNation USA was converted into a small percentage (less than 5%) of Republic Industries stock after Huizenga merged AutoNation into waste hauler Republic Industries (now called AutoNation) in 1997.

In late 1998 JM embarked on a national strategy to expand its presence outside the Southeast, establishing an office in St. Louis that handles indirect consumer leasing.

In 2000 Jim became honorary chairman while Pat was given the chairman position. Also that year the company was named the 51st Best Company to Work For in the United States by *Fortune* magazine. The company's rank in the the Best Company to Work For list rose to 20th place in 2001.

OFFICERS

Honorary Chairman: James M. Moran
Chairman and CEO: Patricia Moran, age 56
President: Colin Brown
EVP and CFO: James R. Foster
EVP and CIO: Scott Barrett
EVP: Louis Feagles
EVP, Human Resources: Gary L. Thomas

LOCATIONS

HQ: 100 NW 12th Ave., Deerfield Beach, FL 33442
Phone: 954-429-2000   Fax: 954-429-2244
Web: www.jmfamily.com

JM Family Enterprises operates auto retail, distribution, leasing, and financing businesses across the US, mainly in Alabama, Florida, Georgia, and North and South Carolina.

PRODUCTS/OPERATIONS

Selected Subsidiaries

Finance and Leasing
World Omni Financial Corp.

Insurance, Marketing, Consulting, and Related Companies
Fidelity Insurance Agency
JM&A Group (auto service contracts, insurance)
   Courtesy Insurance Co.
   Fidelity Insurance Agency, Inc.
   Fidelity Warranty Services, Inc.
   Jim Moran & Associates
   J.M.I.C. Life Insurance Co.

Retail Car Sales
JM Lexus

Vehicle Processing and Distribution
Parts Distribution Center
SET Inland Processing
SET Port Processing
Southeast Toyota Distributors, LLC

Selected Affiliates

Executive Incentives & Travel, Inc.

COMPETITORS

CarMax
Gulf States Toyota
Hendrick Automotive
Holman Enterprises
Island Lincoln-Mercury
Morse Operations
United Auto Group

HISTORICAL FINANCIALS & EMPLOYEES

Private FYE: December 31	Annual Growth	12/92	12/93	12/94	12/95	12/96	12/97	12/98	12/99	12/00	12/01
Sales ($ mil.)	13.0%	2,600	3,500	4,200	4,500	5,100	5,400	6,200	6,600	7,100	7,800
Employees	3.8%	2,300	2,300	2,000	2,000	3,000	2,900	3,000	3,304	3,400	3,227

SALES HISTORY

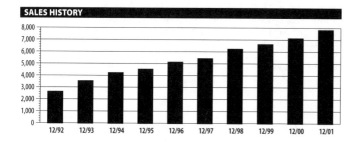

JOHNSON PUBLISHING COMPANY

Snubbed by advertisers when he founded his company 60 years ago, John Johnson has pushed his magazine company to the front of the pack. Led by its flagship publication, *Ebony*, Johnson Publishing Company stands as the largest black-owned publishing firm in the country. It also publishes *Jet* and operates a book division. In addition, Johnson Publishing produces a line of hair care products (Supreme Beauty) and cosmetics (Fashion Fair) marketed for African-American women, and each year it hosts the Ebony Fashion Fair, a traveling fashion show that raises money for scholarships and charities in cities across the US and Canada.

The company's book division features titles such as *The New Ebony Cookbook* and the more controversial *Forced Into Glory: Abraham Lincoln's White Dream*.

Johnson Publishing is owned and controlled by founder and chairman Johnson and his family. Johnson's daughter, Linda Johnson Rice, handles the day-to-day operations as president and CEO. His wife, Eunice, produces the Ebony Fashion Fair.

HISTORY

John H. Johnson launched his publishing business in 1942 while he was still in college in Chicago. The idea for a black-oriented magazine came to him while he was working part-time for Supreme Life Insurance Co. of America, where one of his jobs was to clip magazine and newspaper articles about the black community. Johnson used his mother's furniture as collateral to secure a $500 loan and then mailed $2 charter subscription offers to potential subscribers. He received 3,000 replies and used the $6,000 to print the first issue of *Negro Digest*, patterned after *Reader's Digest*. Circulation was 50,000 within a year.

Johnson started *Ebony* magazine in 1945 (which gained immediate popularity and is still the company's premier publication) and in 1951 launched *Jet*, a pocket-sized publication containing news items and features. In the early days Johnson was unable to obtain advertising, so he formed his own Beauty Star mail-order business and advertised its products (dresses, wigs, hair care products, and vitamins) in his magazines. He won his first major account, Zenith Radio, in 1947; Johnson landed Chrysler in 1954, only after sending a salesman to Detroit every week for 10 years. For 20 years, *Ebony* and *Jet* were the only national publications targeting blacks in the US.

By the 1960s Johnson had become one of the most prominent black men in the US. He posed with John F. Kennedy in 1963 to publicize a special issue of *Ebony* celebrating the Emancipation Proclamation. US magazine publishers named him Publisher of the Year in 1972. In 1973, Johnson launched *Ebony Jr!* (since discontinued), a magazine designed to provide "positive black images" for black preteens. His first magazine, *Negro Digest* (renamed *Black World*), became known for its provocative articles, but its circulation dwindled from 100,000 to 15,000. Johnson retired the magazine in 1975.

Unable to find the proper makeup for his *Ebony* models, Johnson founded his own cosmetics business, Fashion Fair Cosmetics, that year, which carved a niche beside Revlon (which introduced cosmetic lines for blacks) and another black cosmetics company, Johnson Products (unrelated) of Chicago. By 1982 Fashion Fair sales were more than $30 million.

The company got into broadcasting in 1972 when it bought Chicago radio station WGRT (renamed WJPC; that city's first black-owned station). It added WLOU (Louisville, Kentucky) in 1982 and WLNR (Lansing, Illinois; re-launched in 1991 as WJPC-FM) in 1985. By 1995, however, it had sold all of its stations.

Johnson and the company sold their controlling interest in the last minority-owned insurance company in Illinois (and Johnson's first employer), Supreme Life Insurance, to Unitrin (a Chicago-based life, health, and property insurer) in 1991. That year the company and catalog retailer Spiegel announced a joint venture to develop fashions for black women. The two companies launched a mail-order catalog called *E Style* in 1993 and an accompanying credit card the next year.

Johnson Publishing launched a South African edition of *Ebony* in 1995. Johnson was awarded the Presidential Medal of Freedom in 1996. The next year, however, circulation of *Ebony* fell 7% as mainstream magazines began covering black issues more thoroughly and a host of new titles appeared. In response, the company restructured its ventures and closed its *E Style* catalog. Johnson Publishing retired *Ebony Man* (launched in 1985) in 1998 and *Ebony South Africa* in 2000.

In 2002 John Johnson named his daughter Linda Johnson Rice as CEO of the company; Johnson will remain as chairman and publisher.

Chairman and Publisher: John H. Johnson, age 84
President and CEO: Linda Johnson Rice, age 44
Secretary and Treasurer; Producer and Director,
   EBONY Fashion Fair: Eunice W. Johnson
Executive Editor, EBONY Magazine: Lerone Bennett Jr.
VP, Fashion Fair Cosmetics: J. Lance Clark
Controller: Treak Owens
Director Personnel: LaDoris Foster

LOCATIONS

HQ: Johnson Publishing Company, Inc.
   820 S. Michigan Ave., Chicago, IL 60605
Phone: 312-322-9200   **Fax:** 312-322-0918
Web: www.ebony.com

PRODUCTS/OPERATIONS

Selected Operations

Fashion and Beauty Aids
Ebony Fashion Fair (traveling fashion show)
Fashion Fair Cosmetics (color cosmetics, fragrances,
   skincare)
Supreme Beauty Products (hair care)

Publishing
Books
   Forced Into Glory: Abraham Lincoln's White Dream
      by Lerone Bennett Jr.
   The New Ebony Cookbook by Charlotte Lyons
Magazines
   Ebony
   Jet

COMPETITORS

Advance Publications
Avon
Earl G. Graves
Essence Communications
Estée Lauder
Forbes
Hearst Magazines
LFP
L'Oréal
Mary Kay
Revlon
Time
Vanguarde Media

HISTORICAL FINANCIALS & EMPLOYEES

Private FYE: December 31	Annual Growth	12/92	12/93	12/94	12/95	12/96	12/97	12/98	12/99	12/00	12/01
Sales ($ mil.)	4.6%	274	294	307	316	326	361	372	387	400	412
Employees	(0.8%)	2,785	2,600	2,662	2,680	2,702	2,677	2,647	2,657	2,614	2,594

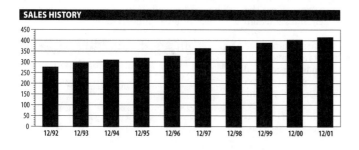

SALES HISTORY

THE JONES FINANCIAL COMPANIES

This is not your father's broker. Well, maybe it is. The Jones Financial Companies is the parent of Edward Jones (formerly called Edward D. Jones & Co.), an investment brokerage network catering to individual investors. Most of its clients are retired people and small-business owners in rural communities and suburbs. The "Wal-Mart of Wall Street" has thousands of satellite-linked offices in the US, Canada, and the UK. Brokers preach a conservative buy-and-hold approach, offering relatively low-risk investment vehicles such as government bonds, blue-chip stocks, and high-quality mutual funds.

The Jones Financial Companies' network of 7,500 offices make it one of the largest brokerage networks in the world. The company also sells insurance and engages in investment banking for such clients as Wal-Mart and public agencies. The firm embraces technology, maintaining one of the industry's largest satellite networks (including a dish for each office).

Preferring to groom brokers internally, the firm accepts applicants with no previous experience, trains them extensively, and monitors investment patterns to prevent account churning and trading in risky low-cap stocks. Before they are given such luxuries as office space, assistants — or even a computer — new brokers must make 1,000 cold calls in their chosen community. John Bachmann, managing partner of Edward Jones, has said the company has no plans to go public.

HISTORY

Jones Financial got its start in 1871 as bond house Whitaker & Co. In 1922 Edward D. Jones (no relation to the Edward D. Jones of Dow Jones fame) opened a brokerage in St. Louis. In 1943 the two firms merged.

Jones' son Edward "Ted" Jones Jr. joined the firm in 1948. Under Ted's leadership (and against his father's wishes), the company focused on rural customers, opening its first branch in the Missouri town of Mexico in 1955 and beginning its march across small-town America. Ted took over as managing partner in 1968, masterminding the company's small-town expansion. (The Wal-Mart comparison is apt; Ted Jones and Sam Walton were good friends.)

Almost from the start, the firm hammered home a conservative investment message focusing on blue-chip stocks and bonds. It expanded steadily throughout the years, adding offices with such addresses as Cedarburg, Wisconsin, and Paris, Illinois.

In the 1970s Edward D. Jones moved into underwriting with clients including Southern Co., Citicorp, and Humana. (It got burned in the mid-1980s on one such deal, when the SEC accused the company of fraud in a bond offering for life insurer D.H. Baldwin Co., which later filed for bankruptcy.)

The company's technological bent was spurred in 1978 after its Teletype network couldn't handle the demand generated by the firm's 220 offices. As a stopgap, the company nixed use of the Teletype for stock quotes, telling its brokers to call Merrill Lynch's toll-free number instead.

Managing partner John Bachmann took over from Ted Jones in 1980. (Bachmann started at the company as a janitor.) A follower of management guru Peter Drucker, Bachmann inculcated the company's brokers with Drucker's customer- and value-oriented principles.

Edward D. Jones began moving into the suburbs and into less-than-posh sections of big cities in the mid-1980s. In 1986 the company started a mortgage program, but the plan was never successful and was ended in 1988. The company weathered the 1987 stock market crash (many brokerages did not), albeit with thinner profit margins.

In 1990 Ted Jones died. The first half of the decade was a time of great expansion for the company as it doubled its number of offices. In 1993 the company opened an office in Canada.

In 1994 Jones Financial's acquisition of Columbia, Missouri-based thrift Boone National gave it the ability to offer trust and mortgage services to its clients, which helped sales as Jones started facing competition from Merrill Lynch in its small-town niche. The company's rapid expansion and relatively expensive infrastructure (all those one-person offices add up) began to eat at the bottom line, and in 1995 Bachmann stopped expansion so the firm could catch its breath.

In 1997 Edward Jones (which had unofficially dropped its middle "D" to boost name recognition) moved overseas, opening its first offices in the UK, a prime expansion target for the company. The next year the firm teamed up with Mercantile Bank to offer small-business loans. Jones resumed its expansionist push in 1999 and 2000, adding offices in all its markets, but continued to resist online trading.

OFFICERS

Managing Partner: John W. Bachmann, age 63, $205,202 pay
General Partner, Finance and Accounting: Steven Novik, age 52
General Partner, Product and Sales Division: Douglas E. Hill, age 57, $180,202 pay

General Partner, Human Resources: Michael R. Holmes, age 43
General Partner, Information Systems:
 Richie L. Malone, age 53, $160,000 pay
General Partner, Service Division: Darryl L. Pope, age 62
Limited Partner, Headquarters Administration:
 Robert Virgil Jr., age 67
Auditors: PricewaterhouseCoopers LLP

LOCATIONS

HQ: The Jones Financial Companies, L.L.L.P.
 12555 Manchester Rd., Des Peres, MO 63131
Phone: 314-515-2000   Fax: 314-515-2622
Web: www.edwardjones.com

The Jones Financial Companies operates more than 7,500 offices in the US, Canada, and the UK.

PRODUCTS/OPERATIONS

2001 Sales

	$ mil.	% of total
Commissions		
Mutual funds	740	35
Listed	219	10
Insurance	216	10
OTC	78	4
Principal transactions	370	17
Interest & dividends	176	8
Sub-transfer agent revenue	95	5
Mutual fund & insurance revenue	79	4
Money market fees	74	3
IRA custodial services fees	39	2
Investment banking	25	1
Other	31	1
Total	**2,142**	**100**

Selected Subsidiaries
EDJ Holding Co., Inc.
EDJ Leasing Co., LP
Edward D. Jones & Co. Canada Holding Co., Inc.
Edward D. Jones & Co., LP (broker-dealer)
Edward D. Jones Ltd. (UK)
EJ Insurance Agency Holding LLC
EJ Mortgage LLC
 Edward Jones Mortgage (50%)
LHC, Inc.
 Unison Capital Corp., Inc.
Passport Research Ltd. (50%, money market mutual fund adviser)
Unison Investment Trust

COMPETITORS

A.G. Edwards
Charles Schwab
Citigroup
FleetBoston
Merrill Lynch
Morgan Stanley
Raymond James Financial
TD Waterhouse
UBS PaineWebber
U. S. Bancorp Piper Jaffray
Wells Fargo

HISTORICAL FINANCIALS & EMPLOYEES

Private FYE: December 31	Annual Growth	12/92	12/93	12/94	12/95	12/96	12/97	12/98	12/99	12/00	12/01
Sales ($ mil.)	16.1%	557	642	661	722	952	1,135	1,450	1,787	2,212	2,142
Net income ($ mil.)	10.2%	62	66	54	58	93	114	199	187	230	149
Income as % of sales	—	11.2%	10.3%	8.2%	8.1%	9.8%	10.1%	13.7%	10.5%	10.4%	7.0%
Employees	15.5%	—	8,330	7,418	11,717	12,148	13,691	15,795	20,541	23,432	26,460

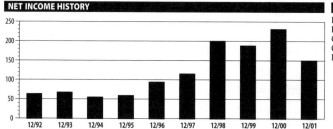

NET INCOME HISTORY

2001 FISCAL YEAR-END
Debt ratio: 6.4%
Return on equity: 22.4%
Cash ($ mil.): 197
Current ratio: —
Long-term debt ($ mil.): 46

J.R. SIMPLOT COMPANY

J.R. Simplot hopes you'll have fries with that. Potato potentate J.R. "Jack" Simplot simply shook hands with McDonald's pioneer Ray Kroc in the mid-1960s, and his company's french fry sales have sizzled ever since. The company still remains the major french fry supplier for McDonald's. J.R. Simplot produces more than 2 billion pounds of french fries, hash browns, and nuggets annually, making it one of the world's largest processors of frozen potatoes. It offers its potato products mainly to retail and food service customers under its Simplot brand and private labels.

The company's spuds sprouted other businesses, including cattle ranches and feedlots (which use feed made from potato peels). Its AgriBusiness Group mines phosphates (for fertilizer and feed) and silica. The company's Turf and Horticulture Group produces grass and turf seed and fertilizer.

Officially retired since 1994, J.R. Simplot remains one of the wealthiest Americans. After amassing a mountain of potato money, the spudillionaire moved on to semiconductors and invested heavily in Boise-based Micron Technology.

HISTORY

J.R. Simplot was born in Dubuque, Iowa, in 1909. His family moved to the frontier town of Declo, Idaho, about a year later. Frustrated with school and an overbearing father, Simplot dropped out at age 14 and moved to a local hotel, where he made money by paying cash for teachers' wage scrip, at 50 cents on the dollar. Simplot then got a bank loan using the scrip as collateral and moved into farming, first by raising hogs and then by growing potatoes. He met Lindsay Maggart, a leading farmer in the area, who taught him the value of planting certified potato seed, rather than potatoes.

Simplot purchased an electric potato sorter in 1928 and eventually dominated the local market by sorting for neighboring farms. By 1940 his company, J.R. Simplot, operated 33 potato warehouses in Oregon and Idaho. The company moved into food processing in the 1940s, first by producing dried onions and other vegetables for Chicago-based Sokol & Co. and later by producing dehydrated potatoes. Between 1942 and 1945 J.R. Simplot produced more than 50 million pounds of dehydrated potatoes for the US military. During the war the company also expanded into fertilizer production, cattle feeding, and lumber. It moved to Boise, Idaho, in 1947.

In the 1950s J.R. Simplot researchers developed a method to freeze french fries. In the mid-1960s Simplot persuaded McDonald's founder Ray Kroc to go with his frozen fries, a handshake deal that practically guaranteed Simplot's success in the potato processing industry. By the end of the 1960s, Simplot was the largest landowner, cattleman, potato grower, and employer in the state of Idaho. He also had established fertilizer plants, mining operations, and other businesses in 36 states, as well as in Canada and a handful of other countries.

During the oil crisis of the 1970s, J.R. Simplot began producing ethanol from potatoes. However, Simplot's empire-building was not without its rough edges. In 1977 he pleaded no contest to federal charges that he failed to report his income, and the next year he was forced to settle charges that he manipulated Maine potato futures.

The company entered the frozen fruit and vegetable business in 1983. Other ventures included using wastewater from potato processing for irrigation and using cattle manure to fuel methane gas plants. Simplot set up a Chinese joint venture in the 1990s to provide processed potatoes to McDonald's and other customers in East Asia.

The company bought the giant ZX cattle ranch near Paisley, Oregon, in 1994. Simplot retired from the board of directors that year to become chairman emeritus; Stephen Beebe was named president and CEO. The 1995 acquisition of the food operations of Pacific Dunlop (now Ansell) led to the creation of Simplot Australia, one of the largest food processors in Australia. Its 1997 stock swap with I. & J. Foods Australia enlarged the subsidiary's frozen food menu.

In 1999 the company sold its Simplot Dairy Products cheese business to France's Besnier Group, and it teamed with Dutch potato processor Farm Frites to enter new markets. In 2000 it launched agricultural Web site planetAg, bought the turf grass seed assets of AgriBioTech, and added the US potato operations of food giant Nestlé to its pantry.

In 2001 the firm said it would build an $80 million potato-processing plant in Manitoba. Also that year the company said it would not increase the value of its contracts with growers struggling amid low prices in a glutted market.

In 2002 Simplot sold its Australian pudding maker Big Sister to the Fowlers Vacola Group.

That same year Beebe retired and Lawrence Hlobik, president of the company's agribusiness unit, was named CEO.

Chairman Emeritus: J. R. Simplot
Chairman: Scott Simplot
CEO: Lawrence S. Hlobik
President and COO: Leigh Brinkerhoff
SVP Finance and CFO: Dennis Mogensen
SVP Sales and Marketing: Greg Ibsen
VP Human Resources: Ted Roper
VP Public Relations: Fred Zerza
VP Special Projects: Rick Fisch

LOCATIONS

HQ: 1 Capital Center, 999 Main St., Ste. 1300,
  Boise, ID 83702
Phone: 208-336-2110   **Fax:** 208-389-7515
Web: www.simplot.com

J.R. Simplot has operations in Australia, Canada, Mexico,
and the US.

PRODUCTS/OPERATIONS

Major Operating Groups
AgriBusiness Group
  Nitrogen and phosphate fertilizers
  Phosphate and silica ore mining
Corporate Group
  Corporate Development Department
  Corporate Information Systems
  Simplot Aviation (in-company flight services)
  SSI Food Services, Inc. (meat processing and
    packaging)
Food Group (Simplot Foods)
  Avocado products
  Fresh potatoes (Blue Ribbon, Golden Classic)
Frozen fruits and vegetables
  Frozen potato products (fries, nuggets, patties, sticks)
Land and Livestock Group
  Beef production
  Cattle feeding
  Hay, corn, grain production for feedlots

COMPETITORS

Cargill
ConAgra
ContiGroup
Del Monte Foods
Golden State Foods
Heinz
IBP
IMC Global
McCain Foods
Michael Foods
Potash Corporation
Pro-Fac
Seneca Foods

HISTORICAL FINANCIALS & EMPLOYEES

Private FYE: August 31	Annual Growth	8/93	8/94	8/95	8/96	8/97	8/98	8/99	8/00	8/01	8/02
Sales ($ mil.)	6.5%	1,700	2,100	2,200	2,700	2,800	2,800	2,730	2,700	3,000	3,000
Employees	4.2%	9,000	10,000	10,000	13,000	12,000	12,000	12,000	12,000	13,000	13,000

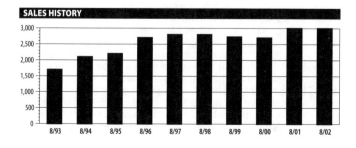

SALES HISTORY

KAISER FOUNDATION HEALTH

Kaiser Foundation Health Plan aims to be the emperor of the HMO universe. With more than 8 million members in nine states and the District of Columbia, it is one of the largest not-for-profit managed health care companies in the US. Kaiser has an integrated care model, offering both hospital and physician care through a network of hospitals and physician practices operating under the Kaiser Permanente name. Kaiser also sponsors the Permanente Medical Groups, associations consisting of more than 11,000 doctors that provide medical care to Kaiser health plan subscribers. The company also runs a network of Kaiser Foundation hospitals. California is the company's largest market with about 75% of its members.

A string of losses due to skyrocketing costs and stiff competition from commercial providers of managed care have prompted Kaiser to raise rates and divest underperforming units. Kaiser sold its unprofitable operations in North Carolina and plans to do the same in Kansas.

Like many competitors, Kaiser also faces the ever-rising costs of health care that threaten gains it has made to get back in the black.

HISTORY

Henry Kaiser — shipbuilder, war profiteer, builder of the Hoover and Grand Coulee dams, and founder of Kaiser Aluminum — was a bootstrap capitalist who did well by doing good. A high school dropout from upstate New York, Kaiser moved to Spokane, Washington, in 1906 and went into road construction. During the Depression, he headed the consortium that built the great WPA dams.

It was in building the Grand Coulee Dam that, in 1938, Kaiser teamed with Dr. Sidney Garfield, who earlier had devised a prepayment health plan for workers on California public works projects. As Kaiser moved into steelmaking and shipbuilding during WWII (turning out some 1,400 bare-bones Liberty ships — one per day at peak production), Kaiser decided healthy workers produce more than sick ones, and he called on Garfield to set up on-site clinics funded by the US government as part of operating expenses. Garfield was released from military service by President Roosevelt for the purpose.

After the war, the clinics became war surplus. Kaiser and his wife bought them — at a 99% discount — through the new Kaiser Hospital Foundation. His vision was to provide the public with low-cost, prepaid medical care. He created the health plan — the self-supporting entity that would administer the system — and the group medical organization, Permanente (named after

Kaiser's first cement plant site). He then endowed the health plan with $200,000. This health plan, the classic HMO model, was criticized by the medical establishment as socialized medicine performed by "employee" doctors.

But the plan flourished, becoming California's #1 medical system. In 1958 Kaiser retired to Hawaii and started his health plan there. But physician resistance limited national growth; HMOs were illegal in some states well into the 1970s. As health care costs rose, Congress legalized HMOs in all states. Kaiser expanded in the 1980s; as it moved outside its traditional geographic areas, the company contracted for space in hospitals rather than building them. Growth slowed as competition increased.

Some health care costs in California fell in the early 1990s as more medical procedures were performed on an outpatient basis. Specialists flooded the state, and as price competition among doctors and hospitals heated up, many HMOs landed advantageous contracts. Kaiser, with its own highly paid doctors, was unable to realize the same savings and was no longer the best deal in town. Its membership stalled.

To boost membership and control expenses, Kaiser instituted a controversial program in 1996 in which nurses earned bonuses for cost-cutting. Critics said the program could lead to a decrease in care quality; Kaiser later became the focus of investigations into wrongful death suits linked to cost-cutting in California (where it has since beefed up staffing and programs) and Texas (where it has agreed to pay $1 million in fines).

In 1997 Kaiser and Washington-based Group Health Cooperative of Puget Sound formed Kaiser/Group Health to handle administrative services in the Northwest. Kaiser also tried to boost membership by lowering premiums, but the strategy proved *too* effective: Costs linked to an unwieldy 20% enrollment surge brought a loss in 1997 — Kaiser's first annual loss ever.

A second year in the red in 1998 prompted Kaiser to sell its Texas operations to Sierra Health Services. It also entered the Florida market via an alliance with Miami-based AvMed Health Plan. In 1999 Kaiser announced plans to sell its unprofitable North Carolina operations (it closed the deal the following year).

In 2000 Kaiser announced plans to charge premiums for its Medicare HMO, Medicare+Choice, to offset the shortfall in federal reimbursements. In 2001 the company's hospital division bought the technology and assets of defunct Internet grocer Webvan, in an effort to increase its distribution activity. Also that year, the son of a deceased anthrax victim sued a Kaiser facility for failing to recognize and treat his father's symptoms.

Chairman Emeritus: David M. Lawrence, age 61
Chairman, President, and CEO: George C. Halvorson
EVP, Health Plan Operations: Arthur M. Southam
SVP and Chief Administration Officer: Robert M. Crane
SVP and CFO: Robert E. Briggs, age 54
SVP, National Contracting Purchasing and Distribution: Joseph W. Hummel
SVP, Workforce Development: Leslie A. Margolin
SVP, General Counsel, and Secretary: Kirk E. Miller
SVP and Director for Care and Services Quality: Patricia B. Siegel
SVP and CIO: Clifford Dodd
SVP and Chief Compliance Officer: Dan Garcia
VP, National HIPAA Compliance and Kaiser Permanente Information Technology (KP-IT) Compliance: Mary Henderson
VP, Human Resources, Regions Outside of California: Dresdene Flynn-White
President, Kaiser Permanente Northern California Region: Mary Ann Thode
President, Kaiser Permanente Southern California Region: Richard Cordova
Head of Annapolis Medical Center, Kaiser Permanente of the Mid-Atlantic States: Ruth A. Robinson
President, Mid-Atlantic Permanente Medical Group: Adrian E. Long
VP, Clinical Information System (CIS) Project: Bruce Turkstra

LOCATIONS

HQ: Kaiser Foundation Health Plan, Inc.
  1 Kaiser Plaza, Oakland, CA 94612
Phone: 510-271-5800   **Fax:** 510-271-6493
Web: www.kaiserpermanente.org

Kaiser Foundation Health Plan operates in California, Colorado, Georgia, Hawaii, Maryland, Ohio, Oregon, Virginia, Washington, and the District of Columbia.

PRODUCTS/OPERATIONS

Selected Operations
Kaiser Foundation Health Plans (health coverage)
Kaiser Foundation Hospitals (community hospitals and outpatient facilities)
Permanente Medical Groups (physician organizations)

COMPETITORS

Aetna
Blue Cross
Catholic Health East
Catholic Health Initiatives
Catholic Healthcare Network
Catholic Healthcare Partners
Catholic Healthcare West
CIGNA
HCA
Health Net
Humana
Oxford Health Plans
PacifiCare
Sierra Health
UnitedHealth Group
WellPoint Health Networks

HISTORICAL FINANCIALS & EMPLOYEES

Not-for-profit FYE: December 31	Annual Growth	12/92	12/93	12/94	12/95	12/96	12/97	12/98	12/99	12/00	12/01
Sales ($ mil.)	6.7%	11,032	11,930	12,268	12,290	13,241	14,500	15,500	16,841	17,700	19,700
Employees	3.3%	82,858	84,885	84,845	85,000	90,000	100,000	100,000	90,000	90,000	111,000

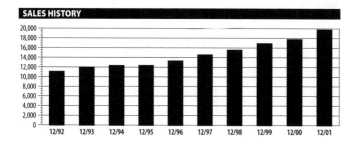

SALES HISTORY

KEMPER INSURANCE COMPANIES

Customers of all types keep company with Kemper Insurance Companies. Kemper offers an array of personal, risk management, and commercial property and casualty products. Its Lumbermens Life Agency offers personal term life and disability income insurance, wealth accumulation programs, and other services. Kemper's Business Customer Group provides workers' compensation and property coverage lines, and the Individual and Family Group offers auto, homeowners, and general liability insurance. The Kemper Casualty Company offers casualty and risk management services to large businesses.

Over the past few years, Kemper has completed a realignment of its operations — selling its reinsurance operations and building its specialty casualty business. The company is also selling its personal lines business to property and casualty insurer Unitrin.

Kemper has entered into a relationship with investment giant Berkshire Hathaway, including an equity investment by Berkshire Hathaway in Kemper's casualty operations (through a newly formed subsidiary).

HISTORY

James Kemper started Lumbermens Mutual in 1912 to provide workers' compensation coverage to Illinois lumberyard owners. The 26-year-old insurance agent perceived a niche when yard owners complained that insurers were overcharging by lumping lumberyards in with the more dangerous logging business. The next year Kemper expanded into fire insurance for lumberyards by founding National Underwriters. Lumbermens began growing, adding offices in Philadelphia, Boston, and Syracuse, New York. By 1921 the company was based in Chicago.

Lumbermens was one of the first auto insurers in the US, and in 1926 it formed American Motorists Insurance Co. specifically for personal and commercial auto insurance. In the early 1930s the firm added boiler and machinery, surety bond, and inland marine coverage. After a receptionist began greeting callers with "Kemper Insurance," Lumbermens subsidiaries all began to be known as the "Kemper companies."

The Kemper family was active in philanthropy, founding a traffic safety institute at Northwestern University in the 1930s and endowing a scholarship fund.

In 1957 Lumbermens began offering marine coverage. The Kemper companies grew to include Federal Kemper Life Assurance in 1961 and American Protection Insurance the next year.

In 1967 Lumbermens, responding to concerns about how a mutual company could own

so many subsidiaries, formed public holding company Kemperco (later Kemper Corp.), in which Lumbermens owned controlling interest. In 1981, at age 94, James Kemper died.

Like many other companies, Kemper Corp. set its sights in the 1980s on becoming a financial services powerhouse, buying three brokerages. As cyclic losses inherent in property/casualty insurance dragged down earnings growth, the company in 1989 began selling those operations back to Lumbermens for stock, decreasing Lumbermens' interest in Kemper Corp. (Property/casualty premiums had dropped from 60% of operating income in 1980 to 49% in 1981 and continued to fall until 1985.)

Additionally, reorganization gave separate management and boards of directors to Kemper Corp. and Kemper National Insurance Cos. (formed by Lumbermens Mutual Casualty Company, American Motorists Insurance Company, and American Manufacturers Mutual Insurance Company). In 1992 the companies' chairmanships were separated as well. Kemper Insurance (originally Kemper National) was formed just in time to be pummeled by the longest and costliest string of natural disasters in the 20th century.

Kemper Corp., meanwhile, became a financial services company with mutual fund offerings. In 1995 it sold its brokerage unit, and in 1996 it was bought by Insurance Partners and Zurich Insurance Group (now Zurich Financial).

Kemper Insurance, meanwhile, was devastated by the 1994 bond crash; earnings sank again in 1996 when the company bolstered environmental and asbestos reserves. Toward the end of the decade, the firm began realigning its insurance offerings, acquiring specialty coverage players (including Integrated DisAbility Management in 1997, Eagle Insurance in 1998, and Universal Bonding in 1999) and selling Kemper Reinsurance to GE Capital (1998). In 1999 Kemper took advantage of continuing deregulation when it announced plans to open LMC, a thrift serving Illinois. Kemper joined forces with Sumitomo Marine & Fire to sell discounted insurance products to Japanese corporations.

In 2000 Kemper bolstered its presence in the workers' compensation market when it acquired the policy renewal rights from the Superior National Insurance companies, which were under supervision by the California Insurance Department. The next year Kemper sold its Canadian subsidiary to UK-based Royal & Sun Alliance Insurance.

OFFICERS

Chairman and CEO: David B. Mathis, age 64
President, COO, and Director: William D. Smith, age 58
EVP, Capital Development: William A. Hickey
EVP, Client Services Group: Patricia A. Drago
SVP and CFO: Art Chandler
SVP and Chief Actuary: Frederick O. Kist
SVP and General Counsel: Mark Ohringer
SVP, Corporate Planning and Administration:
Mary Ann Eddy
SVP, Human Resources: Sue A. Coughlin
SVP and CFO, Lumbermens Mutual Casualty:
Mural R. Josephson
VP, Marketing: Joel Borgardt
VP, Sales: Robert Gwinn
Treasurer: Michael A. Finelli Jr.
General Auditor: Kent L. Suarez
President and CEO, GreatLand Insurance Co.:
W. Taylor
President and CEO, Kemper Casualty Company; EVP,
Lumbermens Mutual Casualty: Dennis P. Kane
President, Kemper Technology Services; SVP,
Lumbermens Mutual Casualty Company:
Jack E. Scott
Auditors: KPMG LLP

PRODUCTS/OPERATIONS

2001 Assets

	$ mil.	% of total
Cash	348	4
Bonds	5,067	57
Stocks	250	3
Mortgage loans	344	4
Real estate	114	1
Receivables	1,842	21
Other	916	10
Total	**8,881**	**100**

Subsidiaries and Affiliates
American Manufacturers Mutual Insurance Company
Eagle Insurance
Financial Insurance Solutions
GreatLand
Juris Prudent, Inc.
Kemper Alternative Risks
Kemper National Services, Inc.
Kemper Risk Management
Kemper Surety
KEMPES
Lumbermens Life Agency
NATLSCO

LOCATIONS

HQ: 1 Kemper Dr., Long Grove, IL 60049
Phone: 847-320-2000   **Fax:** 847-320-7992
Web: www.kemperinsurance.com

Kemper Insurance Companies has operations in
Australia, Belgium, Canada, Germany, Japan, Singapore,
and the US.

COMPETITORS

Acordia	CNA Financial
Allstate	Liberty Mutual
American Family	Mutual of Omaha
Insurance	New York Life
American Financial	Prudential
AIG	Reliance Group Holdings
American Safety Insurance	St. Paul Companies
Chubb	Travelers
CIGNA	

HISTORICAL FINANCIALS & EMPLOYEES

Mutual company FYE: December 31	Annual Growth	12/92	12/93	12/94	12/95	12/96	12/97	12/98	12/99	12/00	12/01
Assets ($ mil.)	1.3%	8,460	9,137	8,956	9,023	8,962	9,834	9,810	9,738	9,409	8,881
Net income ($ mil.)	3.9%	86	119	25	169	19	222	227	167	115	121
Income as % of assets	—	1.0%	1.3%	0.3%	1.9%	0.2%	2.3%	2.3%	1.7%	1.2%	1.4%
Employees	0.0%	—	9,000	8,295	8,837	10,068	9,500	9,000	—	8,500	9,000

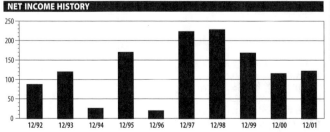

NET INCOME HISTORY

2001 FISCAL YEAR-END
Equity as % of assets: 16.9%
Return on assets: —
Return on equity: —
Long-term debt ($ mil.): —
Sales ($ mil.): —

KING RANCH, INC.

Meanwhile, back at the ranch ... the sprawling King Ranch, that is. King Ranch, founded in 1853, extends way beyond the original 825,000 acres that are still home to about 60,000 cattle and a wide variety of animal species. King Ranch oversees ranching and farming interests in Texas and Florida, but these days it also benefits from oil and gas royalties, farming (cotton, citrus, and sugar), and retail operations (designer saddles, leather goods). In addition, King Ranch also beefs up revenues with tourist dollars from bird-watchers, hunters, and sightseers who visit the Texas ranch. The descendants of founder Richard King own King Ranch.

Considered the birthplace of the American ranching industry, King Ranch has introduced the new highly fertile breed of beef cattle: the King Ranch Santa Cruz, which is one-fourth Gelbvieh, one-fourth Red Angus, and one-half Santa Gertrudis. Raising animals isn't the only thing King Ranch cottons to — this sprawl of four noncontiguous ranches is also one of the US's largest cotton producers.

Like a good western movie, some things ride into the sunset at King Ranch. The company sold its 670-acre Kentucky Thoroughbred breeding and racing farm, as well as most of its foreign ranches, and its primary oil and gas subsidiary. The company's operations are managed from its Houston corporate headquarters.

HISTORY

King Ranch was founded in 1853 by former steamboat captain Richard King and his wife Henrietta, the daughter of a Brownsville, Texas, missionary. On the advice of his friend Robert E. Lee, King used his steamboating profits and occasional strong-arm tactics to buy land — miles of flat, brush-filled, coastal plain and desert south of Corpus Christi, Texas, valued at pennies an acre. The next year King relocated the residents of an entire drought-ravaged village to the ranch and employed them as ranch hands, known ever after as *kineños* ("King's men"). The Kings built their homestead in 1858 at a site recommended by Lee.

King Ranch endured attacks from Union guerrillas during the Civil War and Mexican bandits after the war. Times were tough, but King was up to the challenge, always traveling armed and with outriders.

In 1867 the ranch used its famed Running W brand for the first time. After King's death in 1885, Robert Kleberg, who married King's daughter Alice, managed the 1.2 million-acre ranch for his mother-in-law. Henrietta died in 1925 and left three-fourths of the ranch to Alice.

Before Robert's death in 1932, control of the ranch passed to sons Richard and Bob. In 1933 Bob negotiated an exclusive oil and gas lease with Houston-based Humble Oil, which later became part of Exxon.

While Richard served in Congress, Bob ran the ranch. He developed the Santa Gertrudis, the first breed of cattle ever created in the US, by crossing British shorthorn cattle with Indian Brahmas. The new breed was better suited to the hot, dry South Texas climate.

Bob made King Ranch a leading breeder of quarter horses, which worked cattle, and Thoroughbreds, which he raced. He bought Kentucky Derby winner Bold Venture in 1936 and a Kentucky breeding farm in 1946; that year a King Ranch horse, Assault, won racing's Triple Crown.

When Bob died in 1974, the family asked James Clement, husband of one of the founders' great-granddaughters, to become CEO and bypassed Robert Shelton, a King relative and orphan whom Bob had raised as his own son. Shelton severed ties with the ranch in 1977 over a lawsuit he filed against Exxon, and partially won, alleging underpayment of royalties.

Under Clement, King Ranch became a multinational corporation. In 1980 it formed King Ranch Oil and Gas (also called King Ranch Energy) to explore for and produce oil and gas in five states and the Gulf of Mexico. In 1988 Clement retired, and Kimberly-Clark executive Darwin Smith became the first CEO not related to the founders. Smith left after one year, and the reins passed to petroleum geologist Roger Jarvis and then to Jack Hunt in 1995.

With the help of scientists, in the early 1990s the company developed a leaner, more fertile breed of the Santa Gertrudis called the Santa Cruz. In 1998 Stephen "Tio" Kleberg, the only King descendant still actively working the ranch, was pushed from the saddle of daily operations to a seat on the board. King Ranch sold its Kentucky horse farm in 1998 and teamed up with Collier Enterprises that year to purchase citrus grower Turner Foods from utility holding company FPL Group. In 2000 King Ranch sold King Ranch Energy to St. Mary Land and Exploration Co. for $60 million.

OFFICERS

Chairman: James H. Clement
President and CEO: Jack Hunt
CFO: Bill Gardiner
VP Livestock: Paul Genho
VP Audit: Richard Nilles
Secretary and General Counsel: Frank Perrone
Director of Human Resources: Martha Breit

LOCATIONS

HQ: 3 River Way, Ste. 1600, Houston, TX 77056
Phone: 832-681-5700   **Fax:** 832-681-5759
Web: www.king-ranch.com

King Ranch operates ranching and farming interests in
South Texas as well as in Florida.

Selected Agricultural Operations
Florida
    3,100 acres (St. Augustine sod)
    12,000 acres (sugar cane)
    40,000 acres (orange and grapefruit groves)
Texas
    60,000 acres (cotton and grain)

PRODUCTS/OPERATIONS

Selected Operations
King Ranch Museum
King Ranch Nature Tour Program
King Ranch Saddle Shop (leather products)
Consolidated Citrus Limited
    Partnership (southern Florida citrus groves)

COMPETITORS

Alico
AzTx Cattle
Bartlett and Company
Cactus Feeders
Calcot
ContiGroup
Devon Energy
Friona Industries
Koch
Lykes Bros.
Southern States

HISTORICAL FINANCIALS & EMPLOYEES

Private FYE: December 31	Annual Growth	12/91	12/92	12/93	12/94	12/95	12/96	12/97	12/98	12/99	12/00
Estimated sales ($ mil.)	(1.2%)	—	330	250	250	250	250	300	300	300	300
Employees	0.0%	—	700	700	700	700	700	700	700	700	700

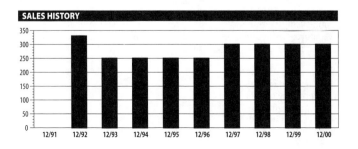

SALES HISTORY

KINKO'S, INC.

Kinko's has come a long way since its founding as a college town copy shop. It operates more than 1,100 business service centers (open 24 hours a day) in Asia, Australia, Europe, and North America. Originally providing self-service copying, Kinko's now offers a full range of services, including binding and finishing services, color printing, document management, and Internet access. The company primarily serves small office/home office customers, but also provides digital document services to large companies. Kinko's allows customers to design products and place orders through its Kinkos.com Web site. Buyout firm Clayton, Dubilier & Rice owns 42% of Kinko's.

Kinko's has continued to add services to its branch stores. The company plans to add more than 200 sign and banner centers to its stores by the end of 2002. Kinko's also has formed strategic alliances with FedEx Corporation (in-store shipping for customers) and America Online (marketing and co-branding).

New CEO Gary Kusin, a longtime Dallas businessman, relocated the company's headquarters to Dallas in early 2002. He cited the area's central location and low tax rate as reasons for uprooting the company. About 350 staffers lost jobs as a result of a restructuring of field support positions.

HISTORY

Kinko's is the creation of Paul Orfalea, who suffers from dyslexia and was inappropriately placed for six weeks in a school for the mentally retarded. The red-haired, Afro-sporting Orfalea (nicknamed Kinko) started selling pencils and spiral notebooks on the campus of UC Santa Barbara in 1970. When he saw a 10-cents-a-page photocopy machine in the library, he decided selling copies would be even better. The self-described hippie borrowed $5,000 that year and opened his first Kinko's shop in a former taco stand near the university. He sold school supplies and made copies on a wheeled copy machine that had to be moved outside because the shop was so small.

Orfalea opened a second California store in San Luis Obispo in 1972, and in the mid-1970s he started providing custom publishing materials for colleges. His innovative approach caught on, and by 1980 he had 80 stores in operation, mostly located near colleges.

In 1983 Kinko's opened its first store outside the US, in Canada, and in 1985 it opened its first 24-hour store, in Chicago. The company moved to Ventura, California, in 1988 and shifted its focus to the growing home office market in 1989 following the loss of a $1.9 million copyright infringement suit for photocopying texts for professors. By 1990 Kinko's had 420 stores.

Kinko's began positioning itself as "Your Branch Office" in 1992. The next year it teamed up with telecommunications company Sprint and introduced videoconferencing services in 100 stores.

Kinko's opened an office in South Korea in 1995 and launched Kinkonet, its electronic communications network. The company teamed up with UUNET in 1996 to make Internet access available at its stores.

Until that year Orfalea was the sole owner of 110 stores and had partnership arrangements with more than 120 other entrepreneurs, a relationship that allowed Orfalea to control the company's rapidly growing network, while giving plenty of incentive for local expansion. This relaxed style of management also led to some unprofitable operations.

To remedy this, Kinko's went corporate in 1996, selling about 30% of the company to buyout firm Clayton, Dubilier & Rice for $219 million; the funds have been used for expansion and new technology. (The buyout firm later increased its stake to 42 percent.) As part of the deal, Kinko's established a single, unified corporation, rolling into it all of the decentralized joint venture, corporate, and partnership companies operating under the Kinko's name.

In 1997 the company opened its first branch in China and made its first acquisition, document management company Electronic Demand Publishing, which became the core of Kinko's corporate document unit. In 1998 Kinko's opened its first stores in the UK (through a joint venture with the Virgin Group) and in the Middle East. The next year it began offering Internet-based custom printing services through an alliance with online print services firm iPrint.com.

In 2000 the company launched a new majority-owned Web firm, Kinkos.com, to offer Internet-based printing services. Orfalea resigned as chairman in 2000. In early 2001 Kinko's bought the rest of Kinkos.com (from Liveprint.com) and absorbed it into the company. Also that year Joseph Hardin Jr. (who had been CEO for more than three years) resigned from the company; Gary Kusin replaced him. The company relocated its headquarters to Dallas in 2002, a move that Orfalea criticized as unnecessary.

OFFICERS

Chairman Emeritus: Paul Orfalea
Chairman: George Tamke Jr.
President, CEO, and Director: Gary M. Kusin, age 51
CFO: William P. Benac
EVP Operations: Sue Parks
SVP and CTO: Allen Dickason
SVP, General Counsel, and Secretary: Leslie Klaassen
SVP and General Manager: Diana Ingram
SVP Human Resources and Administration:
Paul Rostron
SVP International: Mark Seals
SVP Operations and Sales: Scott Seay
VP Global Sourcing: Steve Grupe
VP Leasing and Site Selection: Paul Myrick
VP Marketing: Laura Kurzu
VP Sales: Jennifer Goodwyn
VP Treasury and Tax: Mark A. Blinn
Controller: Gary Golden
Marketing Director: Heather Clark
Manager of Environmental Affairs: Larry Rogero
Director of Public Relations: Maggie Thill
Corporate Communications: Chris Barnes

LOCATIONS

HQ: 13155 Noel Road, Ste. 1600, Dallas, TX 75240
Phone: 214-550-7000   **Fax:** 214-550-7001
Web: www.kinkos.com

Kinko's operates more than 1,100 stores in Australia,
Canada, China, Japan, the Netherlands, South Korea, the
UK, the United Arab Emirates, and the US.

PRODUCTS/OPERATIONS

Selected Products and Services
Binding and finishing services
Business and specialty papers
Computer rentals
Custom printing
Digital printing
E-mail
Fax services
FedEx services
Folding
Instant posters and banners
Internet access
Laminating
Laser printing
Office supplies
Overhead transparencies
Photocopying (black-and-white, color, full-service,
    self-service, oversize)
Pick up and delivery
Presentation materials
Scanning

COMPETITORS

Allegra
Black Dot Graphics
Champion Industries
EagleDirect.com
Franchise Services
General Binding
IKON
iPrint
Mail Boxes Etc.
Merrill
Office Depot
OfficeMax
PIP
Pitney Bowes
Staples
TRM
Xerox

HISTORICAL FINANCIALS & EMPLOYEES

Private FYE: June 30	Annual Growth	6/93	6/94	6/95	6/96	6/97	6/98	6/99	6/00	6/01	6/02
Estimated sales ($ mil.)	9.7%	—	—	1,100	1,350	1,500	1,600	1,800	2,000	2,200	2,100
Employees	0.7%	—	—	19,000	23,000	24,000	24,000	25,000	26,000	25,000	20,000

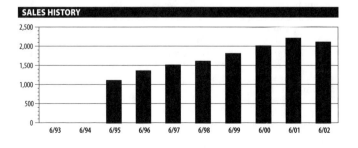

SALES HISTORY

KNOWLEDGE UNIVERSE, INC.

Is knowledge power? Knowledge Universe (KU) thinks so. The company invests in Internet-oriented companies, day care and childhood learning companies, and B2B companies, principally in business and human resources consulting and online training. The company's investments include firms such as Hoover's, Inc. (the publisher of this profile); Knowledge Learning Corp., operator of more than 300 day-care centers; private school operator Nobel Learning Communities; LeapFrog, maker of educational toys and books; and Productivity Point International, which provides comprehensive learning services to business. KU also owns a controlling stake in technology consulting business Nextera Enterprises.

KU's portfolio is divided into Knowledge Universe Business Group and Knowledge Universe Learning Group. The business group focuses on companies whose products and services aim to improve the productivity of client businesses. The learning group invests in companies that provide education venues such as interactive learning Web sites for children.

Founded in 1996, KU is an investment vehicle for Drexel Burnham Lambert vet Michael Milken; his brother Lowell, who oversees the Milken family philanthropies; and Oracle CEO Larry Ellison. Michael Milken is known for his innovative use of high-yield bonds and cancer-research philanthropy, or his term in jail for securities violations, depending on your perspective.

The Milken and Ellison names have attracted a lineup of business luminaries to KU's board: Directors include Rupert Murdoch, former Warner Brothers chairman Terry Semel, and former baseball commissioner Peter Ueberroth.

HISTORY

After returning from his sojourn "Up North" (as insiders delicately refer to a stretch in prison for SEC rules infractions relating to 1980s-era corporate finance innovations), and after vanquishing cancer, Michael Milken found a new crusade. In 1996 he and his brother Lowell, along with Larry Ellison, founded Knowledge Universe to invest a seed fund of $500 million in human capital. Cadence Design Systems vet Joe Costello was tapped to lead KU, but he left a few months later, citing strategic differences, and was replaced as president by former Mattel CEO Thomas Kalinske.

With an aim of providing crib-to-cane educational resources, Knowledge Universe began making acquisitions in 1997 with the purchase of Symmetrix. The management and information technology consulting company, renamed Nextera (from NextERA), then acquired other IT and human resources consultancies (including SiGMA Consulting, Planning Technologies and Sibson & Company) and went public in 1999. When the Milken name failed to wow investors into a meaningful IPO pop, Nextera began repositioning itself as an e-commerce specialist.

KU also bought into Nobel Educational Dynamics (now Nobel Learning Communities, which operates private and specialty schools) and bought up Children's Discovery Centers (now Knowledge Learning Corp., which runs about 300 preschools and day care centers). Also in the educational field, KU announced the formation of Knowledge University, an online university that was designed to offer access to top-notch scholars. But the project languished and eventually morphed into UNext, an online business training venture.

Additional investments reflected Milken's personal interests, including Oncology.com and Tasteforliving.com, a Web site named for a cookbook co-written by Milken, who became a vegetarian during his battle with cancer.

Although KU's aggregate sales exceeded $1 billion by 1999, the company began soft-pedaling its lifetime learning activities in favor of focusing on its incubator and venture capital activities in the area of B2B Internet informational services. In 2000 KU continued to emphasize B2B services with an investment in interactive Webcaster MShow.com.

Knowledge Universe companies made a push into China in 2000. KU's Community of Science, which produces a Web site for university researchers and R&D professionals, launched an Internet portal for Chinese researchers, COS China. Also that year KU's Nobel Learning Communities and South Ocean Development, the largest private school operator in China, signed a deal that includes student and teacher interchange programs, linking of the companies' schools via Web, and the development of preschools in China.

In 2001 KU invested $10 million to launch K12, an Web-based school providing tutoring through complete home school curricula, led by former US Secretary of Education and *Book of Virtues* author William Bennett. Also in 2001 KU's Nibblebox animation company merged with Vivendi Universal's Hypnotic. The following year educational toy maker subsidiary LeapFrog began trading on the NYSE.

Chairman: Michael Milken
Vice Chairman: Steven B. Fink, age 51
Vice Chairman: Lowell Milken
Vice Chairman: Gregory J. Clark, age 59
President and Director: Thomas Kalinske, age 57
**President, Knowledge Universe Business Group and
Knowledge Universe Capital; CFO and Director:**
Randolph C. Read, age 49
SVP, Corporate Communications: Geoffrey E. Moore
Human Resources: Gerry Wentworth

LOCATIONS

HQ: 3551 El Camino Real, Ste. 200,
Menlo Park, CA 94027
Phone: 650-549-3200   **Fax:** 650-549-3222
Web: www.knowledgeu.com

Knowledge Universe has offices in Menlo Park and Los
Angeles, California.

PRODUCTS/OPERATIONS

Selected Investments

Business Group
AdvanceOnline
eMind.com
EMVentures
Hoover's
KnowledgePlanet.com
MeansBusiness
Nextera Enterprises
Productivity Point International
Spring Group
TEC Worldwide
TeckChek
UNext

Learning Group
Charter School USA
Community of Science
K12
Knowledge Learning Corp.
LeapFrog Enterprises, Inc.
Nobel Learning Communities

COMPETITORS

Bain Capital
BancBoston Capital, Inc.
Fenway Partners
Gores Technology
Internet Capital
Madison Dearborn
Onex
Redbus Group
Veronis Suhler Stevenson
Vulcan Northwest
Warburg Pincus
Welsh Carson

HISTORICAL FINANCIALS & EMPLOYEES

Private FYE: December 31	Annual Growth	12/91	12/92	12/93	12/94	12/95	12/96	12/97	12/98	12/99	12/00
Estimated sales ($ mil.)	25.7%	—	—	—	—	—	600	1,200	1,200	1,500	1,500
Employees	11.2%	—	—	—	—	—	—	8,000	8,000	11,000	11,000

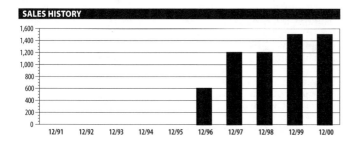

SALES HISTORY

KOCH INDUSTRIES, INC.

Koch Industries is the real thing when there's money to be made. Koch (pronounced "coke") is the second-largest private US company, after Cargill; it has extensive holdings in petroleum, agriculture, and chemicals. Its two refineries process about 600,000 barrels of crude oil a day. Koch also processes natural gas liquids and operates gas gathering systems and a 35,000-mile pipeline system between Texas and Canada. Its KoSa unit is a leading polyester producer. Other operations include minerals trading and transport, asphalt marketing, manufacturing equipment for processing industries, and ranching. Brothers Charles and David Koch control the company.

Ever alert for strategic acquisitions, Koch has named several top officers to a business development board to help identify growth opportunities.

HISTORY

Fred Koch grew up poor in Texas and worked his way through MIT. In 1928 Koch developed a process to refine more gasoline from crude oil, but when he tried to market his invention, the major oil companies sued him for patent infringement. Koch eventually won the lawsuits (after 15 years in court), but the controversy made it tough to attract many US customers. In 1929 Koch took his process to the Soviet Union, but he grew disenchanted with Stalinism and returned home to become a founding member of the anticommunist John Birch Society.

Koch launched Wood River Oil & Refining in Illinois (1940) and bought the Rock Island refinery in Oklahoma (1947). He folded the remaining purchasing and gathering network into Rock Island Oil & Refining (though later sold the refineries).

After Koch's death in 1967, his 32-year-old son Charles took the helm and renamed the company Koch Industries. He began a series of acquisitions, adding petrochemical and oil trading service operations.

During the 1980s Koch was thrust into various arenas, legal and political. Charles' brother David, also a Koch Industries executive, ran for US vice president on the Libertarian ticket in 1980. That year the other two Koch brothers, Frederick and William (David's fraternal twin), launched a takeover attempt, but Charles retained control, and William was fired from his job as VP.

The brothers traded lawsuits, and in a 1983 settlement Charles and David bought out the dissident family members for just over $1 billion. William and Frederick continued to challenge their brothers in court, claiming they had been shortchanged in the deal (the two estranged brothers eventually lost their case in 1998, and their appeals were rejected in 2000). In 1987 they even sued their mother over her distribution of trust fund money.

Despite this legal wrangling, Koch Industries continued to expand, purchasing a Corpus Christi, Texas, refinery in 1981. It expanded its pipeline system, buying Bigheart Pipe Line in Oklahoma (1986) and two systems from Santa Fe Southern Pacific (1988).

In 1991 Koch purchased the Corpus Christi marine terminal, pipelines, and gathering systems of Scurlock Permian (a unit of Ashland Oil). In 1992 the company bought United Gas Pipe Line (renamed Koch Gateway Pipeline) and its pipeline system extending from Texas to Florida.

To strengthen its engineering services presence worldwide, Koch acquired Glitsch International (a maker of separation equipment) from engineering giant Foster Wheeler in 1997. It also acquired USX-Delhi Group, a natural gas processor and transporter.

In 1998 Koch bought Purina Mills, the largest US producer of animal feed, and formed the KoSa joint venture with Mexico's Saba family to buy Hoechst's Trevira polyester unit. (Koch acquired the Saba family's stake in KoSa in 2001.) Lethargic energy and livestock prices in 1998 and 1999, however, led Koch to lay off several hundred employees, sell its feedlots, and divest portions of its natural gas gathering and pipeline systems. Purina Mills filed for bankruptcy protection in 1999 (later, it emerged from bankruptcy and held an IPO in 2000, and was acquired by #2 US dairy co-op Land O'Lakes in 2001).

William Koch sued Koch Industries in 1999, claiming the company had defrauded the US government and Native Americans in oil payments on Indian lands. A jury found for William, but he, Charles, and David agreed to settle the case in 2001 — and sat down to dinner together for the first time in 20 years.

In other legal matters, in 2000 Koch agreed to pay a $30 million civil fine and contribute $5 million toward environmental projects to settle complaints over oil spills from its pipelines in the 1990s. The company agreed to pay $20 million in 2001 to settle a separate environmental case concerning a Texas refinery.

Koch combined its pipeline system and trading units with the power marketing businesses of electric utility Entergy in 2001 to form Entergy-Koch, a joint venture that ranks among the biggest energy commodity traders in the US.

In 2002 Koch acquired Valero Energy's 40% stake in a Mont Belvieu, Texas, natural gas liquids fractionator, boosting its ownership to 80%.

Chairman and CEO: Charles G. Koch, age 66
President, COO, and Director: Joseph W. Moeller
EVP and Director: David H. Koch, age 62
EVP and Director: Richard H. Fink
EVP Operations; Chairman, KoSa: William R. Caffey
SVP and CFO: Steve Feilmeier
SVP Chemicals: Cy S. Nobles
SVP Human Resources: Paul Wheeler
SVP Corporate Strategy: John C. Pittenger
SVP: John M. Van Gelder
SVP; President, Koch Capital Markets: Sam Soliman
VP Business Development: Ron Vaupel
VP, General Counsel, and Secretary: Paul Kaleta
President, Flint Hills Resources: David L. Robertson
President, Koch Hydrocarbon: Steve Tatum
President, Koch Mineral Services: Jeff Gentry
President, Koch Ventures: Ray Gary
President and CEO, Entergy-Koch: Kyle D. Vann
President and CEO, Koch Financial:
  Randall A. Bushman
President and CEO, TrueNorth Energy: David G. Park
Managing Director, Environmental and Regulatory
  Affairs: Don Clay
Managing Director, Koch Metal Trading: Frans Pettinga
Compliance Director: Chris Wilkins
Director, Audit and Assurance: Tim Durkin
Assistant General Counsel: William Frerking
Auditors: KPMG LLP

Selected Operations
Flint Hills Resources (formerly Koch Petroleum, crude
  oil and refined products)
Koch Agriculture Group
  Koch Matador Cattle Company
Koch Chemicals Group
  Koch Chemicals (paraxylene)
    KoSa (polyester)
  Koch Microelectronic Service Co. (semiconductor
    chemicals)
  Koch Specialty Chemicals (high-octane missile fuel)
Koch Chemical/Environ Technology Group (specialty
  equipment & services for refining and chemical industry)
  Brown Fintube Company
  Iris Power Engineering, Inc.
  Koch-Glitsch, Inc.
  Koch Membrane Systems Inc.
  Koch Modular Process Systems, LLC
Koch Energy Group
  Entergy-Koch L.P. (50%)
  Koch Exploration
Koch Financial Services, Inc.
  Koch Financial Corp.
Koch Gas Liquids Group
Koch Materials Co. (asphalt)
Koch Mineral Services (bulk ocean transportation and
  fuel supply)
Koch Supply & Trading, LLC

HQ: 4111 E. 37th St. N, Wichita, KS 67220
Phone: 316-828-5500   Fax: 316-828-5739
Web: www.kochind.com

Koch Industries has operations in Argentina, Australia,
Brazil, Belgium, Canada, China, the Czech Republic,
France, Germany, India, Italy, Japan, Luxembourg, the
Netherlands, Poland, Spain, South Africa, Switzerland,
the US, the UK, and Venezuela.

ADM	Enron	Peabody Energy
AEP	Entergy	PEMEX
Aquila	EOTT	PG&E
Ashland	Exxon Mobil	Royal
Avista	Imperial Oil	Dutch/Shell
BP	Kerr-McGee	Group
Cargill	King Ranch	Shell Oil
CenterPoint	Lyondell	Products
Energy	Chemical	Southern
ChevronTexaco	Marathon Oil	Company
ConocoPhillips	Motiva	Sunoco
ContiGroup	Enterprises	Tractebel
Duke Energy	Occidental	Williams
Dynegy	Petroleum	Companies

Private FYE: December 31	Annual Growth	12/92	12/93	12/94	12/95	12/96	12/97	12/98	12/99	12/00	12/01
Sales ($ mil.)	8.1%	19,914	20,000	23,725	25,200	30,000	36,200	35,000	33,050	40,000	40,000
Employees	(1.0%)	12,000	12,000	12,000	12,500	13,000	15,600	16,000	12,500	11,500	11,000

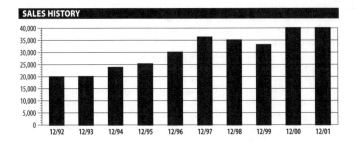

SALES HISTORY

KOHLBERG KRAVIS ROBERTS & CO.

The barbarians at the gate are now knocking more politely. The master of the 1980s buyout universe, Kohlberg Kravis Roberts (popularly known as KKR) has shed its hostile takeover image for a kinder, gentler, buy-and-build strategy. KKR assembles funds to buy low and sell high. An active investor, the firm supervises or installs new management and revamps strategy and corporate structure, selling underperforming units or adding new ones. KKR profits not only from its direct interest in these companies but also from fund and company management fees.

KKR's investments include stakes in publishing company PRIMEDIA (*Seventeen*, Channel One), diversified manufacturer Borden, and online mortgage lender Nexstar Financial. Kohlberg Kravis Roberts also has a joint venture with venture capital firm Accel to provide support for companies integrating online and brick-and-mortar businesses. Cousins Henry Kravis and George Roberts are the senior partners in KKR.

KKR is shopping in Europe, where bloated corporations are shedding noncore operations to streamline. Along with Wendel Investissement, KKR is slated to pick up French electrical product maker Legrand from Schneider Electric SA. Other European acquisitions in the works include seven businesses being spun off by German conglomerate Siemens. The businesses are noncore operations such as Mannesmann Plastics Machinery and Demag Cranes & Components. KKR will roll up its acquisitions into a new company called Demag Holding upon completion of the transactions. The firm has also announced plans to buy a 60% stake in the telephone directory subsidiaries of BCE in Cananda.

Since 1976 KKR has invested $100 billion in more than 90 companies, with investors receiving returns of around 23%. As the economy cools, though, the firm is weathering its fair share of tumult. KKR is no longer the top fund raiser in the investment industry and has written off investments in such firms as Birch Telecom, which have subsequently slid into bankruptcy.

HISTORY

In 1976 Jerome Kohlberg left investment bank Bear Stearns to form his own leveraged buyout firm; with him he brought protégé Henry Kravis and Kravis' cousin George Roberts. They formed Kohlberg Kravis Roberts & Co. (KKR).

Kohlberg believed LBOs, by giving management ownership stakes in their companies, would yield better results. KKR orchestrated friendly buyouts funded by investor groups and debt. The firm's first buyout was machine-toolmaker Houdaille Industries in 1979.

KKR lost money on its 1981 investment in the American Forest Products division of Bendix. But by 1984 the firm had raised its fourth fund and made its first $1 billion buyout: Wometco Enterprises. The next year KKR turned mean with a hostile takeover of Beatrice. The deal depended on junk bond financing devised by Drexel Burnham Lambert's Michael Milken and on the sale of pieces of the company. KKR funded the buyouts of Safeway Stores and Owens-Illinois (1986), Jim Walter Homes (1987), and Stop & Shop (1988, sold in 1996).

Unhappy with the firm's hostile image, Kohlberg left in 1987 to form Kohlberg & Co. His suit against KKR over the alleged undervaluing of companies in relation to his departure settlement was resolved for an undisclosed amount.

The Beatrice LBO triggered a rash of similar transactions as the financial industry sought fat fees. The frenzy culminated in 1988 with the $31 billion RJR Nabisco buyout, which brought KKR $75 million in fees. As the US slid into recession in 1989, LBOs dwindled and KKR turned to managing its acquisitions.

In 1991 KKR joined with what is now Fleet-Boston to buy Bank of New England. The next year it picked up 47% of what was then Advantica Restaurant Group (now just plain Denny's). It sold that holding in 1997. KKR made its first international foray in 1993 with Russian truck maker Kamaz; it later stalled when Kamaz refused to pay management fees. The next year it freed itself from the RJR morass by swapping its investment in RJR for troubled food company Borden.

In the latter half of the decade, KKR reaped mixed results on its investments, including what is now Spalding Holdings (sporting goods and Evenflo baby products), supermarket chain Bruno's, and KinderCare Learning Centers. The $600 million KKR had sunk into magazine group K-III (now PRIMEDIA) between 1990 and 1994 didn't revive interest in the stock, and it sent Bruno's into bankruptcy in 1998. Disgruntled investors complained about low returns, and in 1996 KKR booted activist megafund CalPERS from its investor ranks.

In 1998 KKR's niche buying continued when it joined with Hicks, Muse, Tate & Furst to buy Regal Cinemas, which it combined with Act III to form the biggest theater chain in the US. The chain's expansion left it on the brink of bankruptcy, and investor Philip Anschutz bought a chunk of its debt and possible control of the company in 2001.

The next year KKR departed from course and unveiled online mortgage lender Nexstar Financial, its first company built from the ground up.

Still focused on Europe, in 2000 the firm

claimed the telecommunications business of Robert Bosch (now Tenovis), UK private equity fund Wassall PLC, and Siemens' banking systems unit. The next year it bought the speciality chemicals and pigments operations of Laporte plc to create Rockwood Specialities.

Also in 2000, KKR joined with Internet VC firm Accel Partners to form Accel-KKR, Inc. to invest in companies that combine traditional business and Internet assets. It lost its place as the top fund-raiser to Thomas H. Lee, which closed a record-setting $6.1 billion fund in early 2001.

OFFICERS

Founding Partner: Henry R. Kravis, age 58
Founding Partner, California: George R. Roberts, age 58
General Partner, London: Edward A. Gilhuly, age 42
General Partner: Perry Golkin, age 48
General Partner, California: James H. Greene Jr., age 51
General Partner, California: Robert I. MacDonnell
General Partner: Michael W. Michelson
General Partner: Paul E. Raether
General Partner: Scott M. Stuart, age 42
Managing Director, London: Johannes Huth
Chairman, Accel-KKR, Inc.: Paul M. Hazen, age 60
Office Manager: Sandy Cisneros
Auditors: Deloitte & Touche LLP

LOCATIONS

HQ: 9 W. 57th St., Ste. 4200, New York, NY 10019
Phone: 212-750-8300   **Fax:** 212-750-0003
Web: www.kkr.com

Kohlberg Kravis Roberts & Co. has offices in London; Menlo Park, California; and New York City.

PRODUCTS/OPERATIONS

Selected Investments
Accuride Corporation
Alea Group Holdings AG
Amphenol Corporation
Birch Telecom, Inc.
Borden, Inc.
The Boyds Collection, Ltd.
Bristol West Insurance Group
DPL Inc.
Evenflo Company, Inc.
FirstMark Communications Europe SA
IDEX Corporation
Intermedia Communications Inc.
KinderCare Learning Centers, Inc.
KSL Recreation Corporation
MedCath Incorporated
NewSouth Communications
Nexstar Financial Corporation
Owens-Illinois, Inc.
PRIMEDIA Inc.
Shoppers Drug Mart Inc.
Spalding Holdings Corporation
Walter Industries, Inc.
Willis Group Limited
Wincor Nixdorf Holding GmbH & Co.
Zhone Technologies, Inc.
Zumtobel AG

COMPETITORS

AEA Investors	Hicks, Muse
American Financial	Interlaken Investment
Apollo Advisors	Investcorp
Bear Stearns	Jordan Company
Berkshire Hathaway	Lehman Brothers
Blackstone Group	Leonard Green
Carlyle Group	MacAndrews & Forbes
Clayton, Dubilier	Merrill Lynch
CVC Capital Partners	Salomon Smith Barney
Dresdner Kleinwort	Holdings
Wasserstein	Texas Pacific Group
Equity Group Investments	Thomas Lee
Forstmann Little	Veronis Suhler Stevenson
Goldman Sachs	Vestar Capital Partners
Haas Wheat	Wingate Partners
Heico	

KOHLER CO.

When plumbing powerhouse Kohler says profits are in the toilet, it's not complaining. Kohler makes bathroom products under the names Ann Sacks (ceramic tile, marble, stone products); Kallista (bathroom fixtures and accessories); and Hytec, Kohler, and Sterling (plumbing products). European brands include Jacob Delafon and Neomediam plumbing products and Sanijura bath cabinetry and related products. Kohler also makes small engines, generators, electrical switchgear, and high-end furniture. In addition, Kohler owns The American Club resort, golf courses, and other real estate.

Herbert Kohler Jr., the founder's grandson, has reorganized the company. Herbert, who now controls most of the company along with his sister Ruth, has vowed the company would never go public. The company is building a new manufacturing facility in Mexico and is expanding some of its US factories.

In 1873 29-year-old Austrian immigrant John Kohler and partner Charles Silberzahn founded Kohler & Silberzahn in Sheboygan, Wisconsin. That year they purchased a small iron foundry that made agricultural products for $5,000 from Kohler's father-in-law. In 1880, two years after Silberzahn left the firm, its machine shop was destroyed by fire.

The company introduced enameled plumbing fixtures in the rebuilt factory in 1883. The design caught on, and the business sold thousands of sinks, kettles, pans, and bathtubs. By 1887, when Kohler was incorporated, enameled items accounted for 70% of sales. By 1900 the 250-person company received 98% of its sales from enameled iron products. That year, shortly after John Kohler began building new facilities near Sheboygan (which later became the company village of Kohler), he died at age 56. More trouble followed: Kohler's new plant burned down in 1901, and two of the founder's sons died — Carl at age 24 in 1904 and Robert at age 35 in 1905.

Eldest surviving son Walter built a boarding hotel to house workers and introduced other employee-benefit programs. He also set up company-paid workmen's compensation before the state made it law in 1917.

By the mid-1920s, when Kohler premiered colors in porcelain fixtures and added brass fittings and vitreous china toilets and washbasins to its line, it was the #3 plumbing-product company in the US. As a testament to the design quality of its products, Kohler items were displayed at the New York Museum of Modern Art in 1929. The company also began developing products that would grow in importance in later decades: electric generators and small gasoline engines. During the 1950s Kohler's engines virtually conquered Southeast Asia, where they were used to power boats, drive air compressors, and pump water for rice paddies in Vietnam and Thailand. While strikes against Kohler in 1897 and 1934 had been resolved quickly, a 1954 strike against the firm lasted six years. The strike gave Kohler the dubious honor of enduring the longest strike in US history.

Small-engine use grew in the US in the 1960s, and Kohler's motors were used in lawn mowers, construction equipment, and garden tractors. The founder's last surviving son, Herbert (a child from John Kohler's second marriage), died in 1968. Under the leadership of Herbert's son, Herbert Jr. (appointed chairman 1972), Kohler expanded its operations, buying Sterling Faucet (1984); Baker, Knapp & Tubbs (1986); and Jacob Delafon (1986). More recent acquisitions include Sanijura (bathroom furniture, France) in 1993; Osio (enamel baths, Italy) in 1994; Robern (mirrored cabinets) in 1995; Holdiam (baths, whirlpools, and sinks, France) in 1995; and Canac (cabinets, Canada) in 1996.

The company entered a growing plumbing market in China through four joint ventures formed in that country in 1996 and 1997. In 1998 several family and non-family shareholders claimed a reorganization plan unfairly forced them out and undervalued their stock. Legal battles over the stock's fair price continued in 1999, and a settlement was reached in 2000 that granted shareholders a fair price and Herbert and his sister Ruth gained firm control of the company. More legal battles continued in 2001 when the company sued Kohler International Ltd., a Canada-based company, for trademark infringement.

Chairman and President: Herbert V. Kohler Jr.
SVP, Finance: Jeffery P. Cheney
VP, Human Resources: Laura Kohler

HQ: 444 Highland Dr., Kohler, WI 53044
Phone: 920-457-4441   **Fax:** 920-457-1271
Web: kohlerco.com

Kohler Co. operates 44 manufacturing plants, 26 subsidiaries and affiliates, and sales offices worldwide.

PRODUCTS/OPERATIONS

Selected Operations

Engines
Commercial turf equipment engines
Consumer lawn and garden equipment engines
Industrial, construction, and commercial equipment engines
Recreational equipment engines

Furniture
Baker Furniture
McGuire Furniture Company
Milling Road Furniture

Generators
Kohler rental power
Marine generators
Mobile generators
On-site power systems
Residential generators
Small business generators

Kitchen and Bath Products
Cabinets and vanities
  Canac (bathroom cabinetry)
  Robern (lighting and mirrored bath cabinetry)
  Sanijura (vanities and other bath furniture)
Plumbing products
  Jacob Delafon (bathtubs, faucets, lavatories, and toilets)
  Kallista (bathroom and kitchen sinks and faucets)
  Kohler (bath and shower faucets, baths, bidet faucets, bidets, body spa systems, glass showers and shower doors, kitchen and bathroom sinks and faucets, masterbaths, toilets, toilet seats, vanities, whirlpool baths)
  Sterling (bathing fixtures, faucets, sinks, tub/shower enclosures, vitreous china bath fixtures)
Tile and stone products
  Ann Sacks (art tile, glazed tile, knobs and pulls, mosaics, terra cotta)

Real Estate
The American Club (resort hotel)
Blackwolf Run golf course
Inn on Woodlake
Kohler Stables
Whistling Straits golf course

COMPETITORS

American Standard
Armstrong Floor
Armstrong Holdings
Bassett Furniture
Black & Decker
Briggs & Stratton
Carlson
Chicago Faucet
Cooper Industries
Crane
Dal-Tile
Dyson-Kissner-Moran
Elkay Manufacturing
Geberit
Geberit Manufacturing
Gerber Plumbing Fixtures
Grohe
Honda
Klaussner Furniture
Leggett & Platt
Masco
Moen
Mueller Industries
Newell Rubbermaid
NIBCO
Samuel Heath
Starwood Hotels & Resorts
Tecumseh Products
TOTO
U.S. Industries
Villeroy & Boch
Waxman
Yamaha

HISTORICAL FINANCIALS & EMPLOYEES

Private FYE: December 31	Annual Growth	12/92	12/93	12/94	12/95	12/96	12/97	12/98	12/99	12/00	12/01
Estimated sales ($ mil.)	8.4%	1,350	1,450	1,600	1,850	2,020	2,210	2,400	2,500	2,700	2,800
Employees	4.2%	13,778	14,257	14,500	15,000	18,000	18,000	18,000	20,000	20,000	20,000

SALES HISTORY

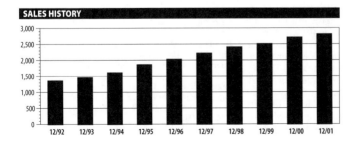

KPMG INTERNATIONAL

Businesses all over the world count on KPMG for accounting. The firm is the most geographically dispersed of accounting's Big Four, which also includes Deloitte Touche Tohmatsu, Ernst & Young, and PricewaterhouseCoopers. KPMG has reorganized its operations from a confederation of accounting firms into three more closely linked regional units: the Americas, Europe/Middle East/Africa, and Asia/Pacific. The firm also offers assurance, tax, and financial advisory services; its KLegal International network includes some 1,600 lawyers around the world.

After much regulatory pressure, KPMG separated its accounting and consulting operations; it sold a chunk of the consulting business to networking equipment maker Cisco Systems, then took it public and sold off its shares in 2002. The consulting unit, formerly known as KPMG Consulting, in 2002 changed its name to BearingPoint, to which KPMG is selling its Austrian, German, and Swiss consulting businesses.

HISTORY

Peat Marwick was founded in 1911, when William Peat, a London accountant, met James Marwick during an Atlantic crossing. University of Glasgow alumni Marwick and Roger Mitchell had formed Marwick, Mitchell & Company in New York in 1897. Peat and Marwick agreed to ally their firms temporarily, and in 1925 they merged as Peat, Marwick, Mitchell, & Copartners.

In 1947 William Black became senior partner, a position he held until 1965. He guided the firm's 1950 merger with Barrow, Wade, Guthrie, one of the US's oldest firms, and built its consulting practice. Peat Marwick restructured its international practice as PMM&Co. (International) in 1972 (renamed Peat Marwick International in 1978).

The next year several European accounting firms led by Klynveld Kraayenhoff (the Netherlands) and Deutsche Treuhand (Germany) began forming an international accounting federation. Needing an American member, the European firms encouraged the merger of Main Lafrentz and Hurdman Cranstoun, two American firms founded around the turn of the century. Main Hurdman & Cranstoun joined the Europeans to form Klynveld Main Goerdeler (KMG), named after two of the member firms and the chairman of Deutsche Treuhand, Reinhard Goerdeler. Other members were C. Jespersen (Denmark), Thorne Riddel (Canada), Thomson McLintok (UK), and Fides Revision (Switzerland).

Peat Marwick merged with KMG in 1987 to form Klynveld Peat Marwick Goerdeler (KPMG). KPMG lost 10% of its business as competing client companies departed. Professional staff departures followed in 1990 when, as part of a consolidation, the firm trimmed its partnership rolls.

In the 1990s the then-Big Six accounting firms all faced lawsuits arising from an evolving standard holding auditors responsible for the substance, rather than merely the form, of clients' accounts. KPMG was hit by suits stemming from its audits of defunct S&Ls and litigation relating to the bankruptcy of Orange County, California (settled for $75 million in 1998). Nevertheless KPMG kept growing; expanding its consulting division with the acquisition of banking consultancy Barefoot, Marrinan & Associates in 1996.

In 1997, after Price Waterhouse and Coopers & Lybrand announced their merger, KPMG and Ernst & Young announced one of their own. But they called it quits the next year, fearing that regulatory approval of the deal would be too onerous.

The creation of PricewaterhouseCoopers (PwC) and increasing competition in the consulting sides of all of the Big Five brought a realignment of loyalties in their national practices. KPMG Consulting's Belgian group moved to PwC and its French group to Computer Sciences Corporation. Andersen nearly wooed away KPMG's Canadian consulting group, but the plan was foiled by the ever-sullen Andersen Consulting group (now Accenture) and by KPMG's promises of more money. Against this background, KPMG sold 20% of its consulting operations to Cisco Systems for $1 billion. In addition to the cash infusion, the deal allowed KPMG to provide installation and system management to Cisco's customers.

In 2000 KPMG announced its IPO plans for the consulting group but continued to rail against the calls by the SEC for the severing of relationships between consulting and auditing organizations. That IPO took place in 2001. The next year the company sold its British and Dutch consultancy units to France's Atos Origin.

OFFICERS

Chairman, KPMG International and KPMG UK:
Mike Rake
CEO: Robert W. Alspaugh
COO: Colin Holland
CFO: Joseph E. Heintz
Chairman and CEO, KPMG LLP: Eugene D. O'Kelly, age 50
Deputy Chairman, KPMG LLP: Jeffrey M. Stein, age 48
CEO, KLegal International: Robert Glennie
International Chairman of Corporate Finance:
Stephen Barrett
Regional Executive Partner, Americas: Lou Miramontes
Regional Executive Partner, Asia-Pacific: John Sim
International Managing Partner, Assurance:
Hans de Munnik

International Managing Partner, Consulting:
Jim McGuire
International Managing Partner, Financial Advisory
Services: Gary Colter
International Managing Partner, Markets:
Alistair Johnston
International Managing Partner, Tax and Legal:
Hartwich Lübmann
Chief Marketing Officer, KPMG LLP:
Timothy R. Pearson
General Counsel, KPMG LLP: Claudia L. Taft
National Industry Director, Banking Practice, KPMG
LLP: Robert F. Arning
Partner, Human Resources, KPMG LLP:
Timothy P. Flynn

LOCATIONS

HQ: Burgemeester Rijnderslaan 20,
1185 MC Amstelveen, The Netherlands
Phone: +31-20-656-7890   Fax: +31-20-656-77-00
US HQ: 345 Park Ave., New York, NY 10154
US Phone: 212-758-9700   US Fax: 212-758-9819
Web: www.kpmg.com

KPMG International has offices in more than 150
countries.

2001 Sales

	$ mil.	% of total
Europe/Middle East/Africa	6,300	54
Americas	4,300	37
Asia/Pacific	1,100	9
Total	**11,700**	**100**

PRODUCTS/OPERATIONS

2001 Sales

	$ mil.	% of total
Assurance	5,800	50
Tax & legal	3,100	26
Consulting	1,500	13
Financial advisory	1,200	10
Other	100	1
Total	**11,700**	**100**

Selected Services

Assurance
Advisory services
Financial statement audits
Information Risk Management
Management Assurance Services

Financial Advisory
Corporate recovery
Corporate finance
Forensic & litigation services
Transaction services

Tax and Legal
Business tax services
Global tax services
Indirect tax/customs services
Legal services pertaining to corporate and commercial,
banking and financial services, competition,
employment/labor, intellectual property, e-commerce,
and estates and trusts law
State, local, and property tax services

COMPETITORS

Aon	Hewitt Associates
Bain & Company	Marsh & McLennan
BDO International	McKinsey & Company
Booz Allen	PricewaterhouseCoopers
Deloitte Touche Tohmatsu	Towers Perrin
Ernst & Young	Watson Wyatt
H&R Block	

HISTORICAL FINANCIALS & EMPLOYEES

Partnership FYE: September 30	Annual Growth	9/92	9/93	9/94	9/95	9/96	9/97	9/98	9/99	9/00	9/01
Sales ($ mil.)	7.4%	6,150	6,000	6,600	7,500	8,100	9,200	10,600	12,200	10,700	11,700
Employees	3.8%	73,488	76,200	76,200	72,000	77,000	83,500	85,300	102,000	108,000	103,000

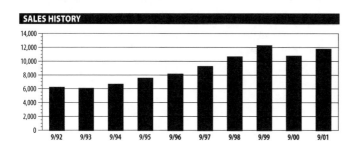

SALES HISTORY

LAND O'LAKES, INC.

Land O'Lakes butters up its customers. Its network of more than 1,100 community cooperatives serves 300,000 farmers and ranchers. The dairy co-op (#3 in the US, behind Dariy Farmers of America and California Dairies) provides its members with wholesale fertilizer and crop protection products, seed, and animal feed. Its oldest product, LAND O' LAKES butter, is the #1 butter brand in the US. Land O'Lakes also produces packaged milk, margarine, sour cream, and cheese. The co-op's animal feed division is a leading animal and pet food maker. The dairy industry and its markets have been consolidating, and the co-op has responded with acquisitions and joint ventures.

In addition to its Land O'Lakes Farmland Feeds and Agriliance agronomy divisions, its Land O'Lakes swine division raises feeder pigs for members, and sees the pigs to market. The co-op's subsidiary Land O'Lakes Finance provides financing services for beef, dairy, pork, and poultry producers.

In response to changes in the agriculture business and the rapidly consolidating dairy market, Land O'Lakes has positioned itself as a national player, and formed an alliance with Dean Foods to market value-added dairy products under the Land O'Lakes brand.

HISTORY

In the old days, grocers sold butter from communal tubs and it often went bad. Widespread distribution of dairy products had to await the invention of fast, reliable transportation. By 1921 the necessary transportation was available. That year about 320 dairy farmers in Minnesota formed the Minnesota Cooperative Creameries Association and launched a membership drive with $1,375, mostly borrowed from the US Farm Bureau.

The co-op arranged joint shipments for members; imposed strict hygiene and quality standards; and aggressively marketed its sweet cream butter nationwide, packaged for the first time in the familiar box of four quarter-pound sticks. A month after the co-op's New York sales office opened, it was ordering 80 shipments a week.

Minnesota Cooperative Creameries, as part of its promotional campaigns, ran a contest in 1924 to name that butter. Two contestants offered the winning name — Land O'Lakes. The distinctive Indian Maiden logo first appeared about the same time, and in 1926 the co-op changed its name to Land O'Lakes Creameries. By 1929, when it began supplying feed, its market share approached 50%.

During WWII civilian consumption dropped, but the co-op increased production of dried milk to provide food for soldiers and newly liberated concentration camp victims.

In the 1950s and 1960s, Land O'Lakes added ice cream and yogurt producers to its membership and fought margarine makers, yet butter's market share continued to melt. The co-op diversified in 1970 through acquisitions, adding feeds and agricultural chemicals. Two years later Land O'Lakes threw in the towel and came out with its own margarine. Despite the decreasing use of butter nationally, the co-op's market share grew.

Land O'Lakes formed a marketing joint venture, Cenex/Land O'Lakes Agronomy, with fellow co-op Cenex in 1987. As health consciousness bloomed in the 1980s, Land O'Lakes launched reduced-fat dairy products. It also purchased a California cheese plant, doubling its capacity. Land O'Lakes began ramping up its international projects at the same time: it built a feed mill in Taiwan, introduced feed products in Mexico, and established feed and cheese operations in Poland.

In 1997 the co-op bought low-fat cheese maker Alpine Lace Brands. Land O'Lakes took on the eastern US when it merged with the 3,600-member Atlantic Dairy Cooperative (1997), and it bulked up on the West Coast when California-based Dairyman's Cooperative Creamery Association joined its fold (1998).

During 2000 the co-op sold five plants to Dean Foods with an agreement to continue supplying the plants with raw milk. Also in 2000 Land O'Lakes combined its feed business with those of Farmland Industries to create Land O'Lakes Farmland Feed, LLC, with 69% ownership. That same year Cenex/Land O'Lakes Agronomy and Farmland Industries joined together their agronomy operations to create Agriliance LLC (now 50% owned).

In late 2001 the company spent $359 million to acquire Purina Mills (pet and livestock feeds). Purina Mills was folded into Land O'Lakes Farmland Feed, and as part of the purchase, Land O'Lakes increased its ownership of the feed business to 92%.

To take advantage of its nationally recognized brand, in 2002 Dean Foods formed an alliance with Land O'Lakes to develop and market value-added dairy products.

OFFICERS

Chairman: James D. Fife, age 52
President and CEO: John E. Gherty
EVP and COO, Agricultural Services: Duane Halverson
EVP; COO Dairy Foods: Chris Policinski
SVP and CFO: Daniel E. Knutson
SVP Western Region, Dairy Foods Group: Jack Prince
VP and General Counsel: John Rebane
VP, Human Resources: Karen Grabow
VP, Planning and Business Development:
Jim Wahrenbrock
VP, Public Affairs: Don Berg
VP, Research, Technology, and Engineering:
David Hettinga
President, Land O'Lakes Farmland Feed:
Bob DeGregorio
Auditors: KPMG LLP

LOCATIONS

HQ: 4001 Lexington Ave. North, Arden Hills, MN 55126
Phone: 651-481-2222   **Fax:** 651-481-2000
Web: www.landolakesinc.com

Land O'Lakes operates processing, manufacturing, warehousing, and distribution facilities across the US and internationally.

PRODUCTS/OPERATIONS

2001 Sales

	% of total
Dairy foods	60
Feeds	31
Seeds	7
Swine	2
Total	**100**

Selected Brands
Alpine Lace (low-fat cheese)
CROPLAN GENETICS (crop seed)
Land O'Lakes (animal feed)
LAND O' LAKES (consumer dairy products)
PMI Nutrition (animal feeds and pet foods)

Dairy Products
Butter
Cheese
Flavored butter
Light butter
Margarine
Milk
Sour cream

COMPETITORS

ADM
AMPI
California Dairies Inc.
Cargill
Dairy Farmers of America
Dean Foods
Foremost Farms
Kraft Foods
Northwest Dairy
Parmalat Finanziaria
Pioneer Hi-Bred
Prairie Farms Dairy
Saputo
Schreiber Foods
Unilever
WestFarm Foods

HISTORICAL FINANCIALS & EMPLOYEES

Cooperative FYE: December 31	Annual Growth	12/92	12/93	12/94	12/95	12/96	12/97	12/98	12/99	12/00	12/01
Sales ($ mil.)	9.9%	2,562	2,733	2,859	3,014	3,486	4,195	5,174	5,613	5,756	5,973
Net income ($ mil.)	2.5%	57	47	75	121	119	95	69	21	103	71
Income as % of sales	—	2.2%	1.7%	2.6%	4.0%	3.4%	2.3%	1.3%	0.4%	1.8%	1.2%
Employees	6.2%	5,000	5,700	5,500	5,500	5,500	5,500	6,500	6,500	6,500	8,600

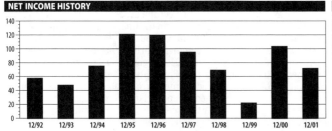

NET INCOME HISTORY

2001 FISCAL YEAR-END
Debt ratio: 57.8%
Return on equity: 8.7%
Cash ($ mil.): 130
Current ratio: 1.48
Long-term debt ($ mil.): 1,147

THE LEFRAK ORGANIZATION

Horace Greeley said "Go west, young man!" and The Lefrak Organization listened — if you take the famous New Yorker comic strip's view that you're in the Midwest once you cross the Hudson. The Lefrak Organization is one of the US's largest private landlords, with more than 60,000 apartments in New York City and New Jersey, another 30,000 units under management, and millions of square feet of commercial space. Owned by the LeFrak family, the company also owns and manages a variety of commercial and retail properties throughout New York City area.

Lefrak's flagship development, the 5,000-unit Lefrak City in Queens, has been home to successive waves of ethnic groups seeking a better life. The company is concentrating on its Newport City development, a 400-acre community of apartments, office towers, and stores on the waterfront in Jersey City across the Hudson River from Manhattan.

Lefrak has built half a dozen office towers on the site (occupied by CIGNA, UBS PaineWebber, and U.S. Trust, among others), and plans for further apartment developments and more office buildings are underway.

The company also has holdings in oil exploration (Lefrak Oil & Gas Organization) and entertainment (Lefrak Entertainment operates LMR, the record label that launched Barbra Streisand). It also owns stage and movie theaters and produces television programs, movies, and Broadway shows.

Chairman Samuel LeFrak, famed for his interpretation of the Golden Rule ("he who has the gold makes the rules"), is an active philanthropist, supporting the Guggenheim Museum. He has also contributed to the oceanographic studies of the late sea explorer Jacques Cousteau.

HISTORY

Harry Lefrak and his father came to the US from Palestine around 1900. They began building tenements to house the flood of immigrants then pouring into New York City. In 1901 they started what is now known as The Lefrak Organization. It diversified into glass and for some time provided raw material for the workshops of Louis Comfort Tiffany. After WWI the glass factory was sold, and the company expanded into Brooklyn, where it developed housing and commercial space in Bedford-Stuyvesant, among other areas.

Samuel, Harry's son, began working in the business early, assisting tradesmen at building sites. He then attended the University of Maryland and returned to the business.

After WWII business took off, as the company began building low-cost housing. Samuel took over the company in 1948. To keep costs down, Samuel bought clay and gypsum quarries, forests, and lumber mills and cement plants, eventually achieving 70% vertical integration of his operations.

The 1950s building boom was in part spurred by new laws in New York authorizing the issue of state bonds for financing low-interest construction loans, which Lefrak used to build more than 2,000 apartments in previously undeveloped coastal sections of Brooklyn. At its peak, Lefrak turned out an apartment every 16 minutes for rents as low as $21 per room.

In 1960 Lefrak broke ground for Lefrak City, a 5,000-apartment development built on 40 acres in Queens, which featured air-conditioned units and rented for $40 per room.

The next decade brought a real estate slump that endangered the organization's next project, Battery Park. Lefrak issued public bonds to save it. Samuel also picked up a few more properties during this period, and he capitalized the "F" in his family name but not the company name. (He later said that he did this to distinguish himself from other Lefraks at his club who had been posted for nonpayment of dues.)

Samuel's son Richard became increasingly involved in the business in the 1980s as the organization began an even bigger project: the 600-acre Newport City development, begun in 1989 with plans for almost 10,000 apartments and retail and commercial space.

The company bought 200 oil fields in 1994 to build up its reserves of gas and home-heating oil.

Meanwhile, Lefrak City had "turned," as its original Jewish occupants sought greener fields. As occupancy dropped, the company relaxed its tenant screening, and the development deteriorated (it was subsequently tagged "Crack City"). In the 1990s, however, it began attracting a mix of African, Jewish, and Central Asian immigrants, whose tightly knit communities improved the development's safety and equilibrium.

Construction of the company's Newport project continued throughout the 1990s with construction of office buildings, apartments, and a hotel (completed in 2000) on the site. As a tight Manhattan office market drove up lease prices, Lefrak's new offices across the Hudson attracted companies in the finance and insurance sectors. Lefrak filled about 3 million sq. ft. in its Newport development during 1999 and 2000.

In 2001 the company's Gateway complex in Battery Park City was damaged in the World Trade Center terrorist attack. The tenants threatened a rent strike, prompting Lefrak to lower rents to compensate for the difficulties attributed to living near the site.

OFFICERS

Chairman: Samuel J. LeFrak
President: Richard S. LeFrak, age 56
SVP Marketing: Edward Cortese
EVP and CFO: Richard N. Papert
VP Commercial: Marsilia Boyle
VP Commercial: Irwin Granville
VP Construction-Engineering: Anthony Scavo
VP Finance and Administration and Treasurer:
  Mitchell Ingerman
VP Management: Charles Mehlman
VP: Harrison LeFrak
General Counsel: Arnold S. Lehman
Director of Human Resources: John Farrelly
Auditors: Lewis Goldberg

LOCATIONS

HQ: 9777 Queens Blvd., Rego Park, NY 11374
Phone: 718-459-9021 **Fax:** 718-897-0688
Web: www.lefrak.com

The Lefrak Organization operates primarily in the New York metropolitan area.

Selected Properties

Commercial Space
Manhattan
  40 W. 57th St.
Gateway Plaza at Battery Park City
James Tower
Jersey City, New Jersey
  Newport development

Residential Apartments
Jersey City, New Jersey
  Atlantic
  East Hampton
  James Monroe
  Presidential Plaza
  Riverside
  Southampton
  Towers of America
Manhattan
  Gateway Plaza at Battery Park City
Queens
  Lefrak City

Residential Co-op Properties
Brooklyn
  Bay Ridge
  Bensonhurst
  Flatbush
  Park Slope
  Sheepshead Bay
Queens
  Elmhurst
  Flushing
  Forest Hills
  Key Gardens
  Rego Park
  Woodside

Retail
Jersey City, New Jersey
  Newport Centre Mall

PRODUCTS/OPERATIONS

Selected Operations

Energy
Lefrak Oil & Gas Organization

Entertainment
Lefrak Entertainment Co.

Real Estate
Commercial properties
Residential apartments
Residential co-op properties
Retail properties

COMPETITORS

Alexander's
Boston Properties
Equity Office Properties
  Trust
Hartz Mountain
Helmsley
Mack-Cali Realty

Port Authority of NY & NJ
Reckson Associates Realty
Starrett Corporation
Tishman Realty
Trizec Properties
Trump
Vornado

HISTORICAL FINANCIALS & EMPLOYEES

Private FYE: November 30	Annual Growth	11/91	11/92	11/93	11/94	11/95	11/96	11/97	11/98	11/99	11/00
Sales ($ mil.)	2.2%	—	3,200	3,200	3,100	3,300	3,500	3,400	2,750	3,200	3,800
Employees	(1.3%)	—	18,000	18,000	17,500	17,400	17,500	18,000	16,000	16,110	16,200

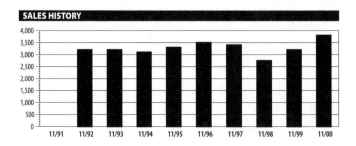

SALES HISTORY

LEVI STRAUSS & CO.

Levi Strauss & Co. (LS&CO.) has been caught with its pants down in the minds of America's tastemakers: teenagers. LS&CO., the world's #1 maker of brand-name clothing, sells jeans and sportswear under the Levi's, Dockers, and Slates names in more than 100 countries. Levi's jeans — department store staples — were once the uniform of American youth, but LS&CO. lost touch with the trends in recent years. To re-tap the youth market, LS&CO. is adding hip styles such as its unusually cut Engineered Jeans and the Superlow for women. The Haas family (relatives of founder Levi Strauss) owns LS&CO.

Sales and profits have fallen over the last decade, and the company's US market share, which topped 30% when the 1990s began, has slipped drastically thanks to competition from discount jeans makers such as VF Corporation (Lee and Wrangler).

LS&CO. has spent the past few years closing factories and cutting jobs in North America and Europe to pare costs. Almost all of its manufacturing is now done overseas.

HISTORY

Levi Strauss arrived in New York City from Bavaria in 1847. In 1853 he moved to San Francisco to sell dry goods to the gold rushers. Shortly after, a prospector told Strauss of miners' problems in finding sturdy pants. Strauss made a pair out of canvas for the prospector; word of the rugged pants spread quickly.

Strauss continued his dry-goods business in the 1860s. During this time he switched the pants' fabric to a durable French cloth called serge de Nimes, soon known as denim. He colored the fabric with indigo dye and adopted the idea from Nevada tailor Jacob Davis of reinforcing the pants with copper rivets. In 1873 Strauss and Davis produced their first pair of waist-high overalls (later known as jeans). The pants soon became de rigueur for lumberjacks, cowboys, railroad workers, oil drillers, and farmers.

Strauss continued to build his pants and wholesaling business until he died in 1902. Levi Strauss & Co. (LS&CO.) passed to four nephews who carried on their uncle's jeans business while maintaining the company's philanthropic reputation. After WWII Walter Haas and Peter Haas (a fourth-generation Strauss family member) assumed leadership of LS&CO. In 1948 they ended the company's wholesaling business to concentrate on Levi's clothing. In the 1950s Levi's jeans ceased to be merely functional garments for workers: They became the uniform of American youth. In the 1960s LS&CO. added women's attire and expanded overseas.

The company went public in 1971. That year it added a women's career line and bought Koret sportswear (sold in 1984). By the mid-1980s profits declined. Peace Corps veteran-turned-McKinsey consultant Robert Haas (Walter's son) grabbed the reins at LS&CO. in 1984 and took the company private the next year. He also instilled a touchy-feely corporate culture often at odds with the bottom line.

In 1986 LS&CO. introduced Dockers casual pants. The company's sales began rising in 1991 as consumers forsook designer duds of the 1980s for more practical clothes. LS&CO. says seven out of every ten American men own a pair of Dockers. However, LS&CO. missed out on the birth of another trend: the split between the fashion sense of US adolescents and their Levi's-loving, baby boomer parents.

In 1996 the company introduced Slates dress slacks. That year LS&CO. bought back nearly one-third of its stock from family and employees for $4.3 billion. Grappling with slipping sales and debt from the buyout, in 1997 LS&CO. closed 11 of its 37 North American plants, laying off 6,400 workers and 1,000 salaried employees; it granted generous severance packages even to those earning minimum wage.

In 1998, citing improved labor conditions in China, LS&CO. announced it would step up its use of Chinese subcontractors. Further restructuring added a third of its European plants to the closures list that year. LS&CO.'s sales fell 13% in fiscal 1998. The next year LS&CO. closed 11 of 22 remaining North American plants. It also unleashed several new jeans brands that eschewed the company's one-style-fits-all approach of old.

In 1999 Haas handed his CEO title to Pepsi executive Philip Marineau. The company continued to record losses from 1999 to 2001, but fought back with innovations such as the ICD+ line that features techno jackets wired with a mobile phone, MP3 player, headset, and remote control, introduced in Europe in 2000, and the hip-revealing Superlow for women that debuted in 2001. LS&CO. introduced a cotton-polyester blend with a Teflon coating, the Go Khaki, in 2002.

In April 2002 LS&CO. announced it would close six of its last eight US plants and cut 20% of its worldwide staff (3,300 workers).

OFFICERS

Chairman: Robert D. Haas, age 59, $1,148,077 pay
President, CEO, and Director: Philip A. Marineau, age 55, $1,450,000 pay
SVP and CFO: William B. Chiasson, age 49, $675,539 pay
SVP and CIO: David G. Bergen, age 46
SVP, General Counsel, and Assistant Secretary: Albert F. Moreno, age 58
SVP; President, Levi Strauss Asia Pacific: R. John Anderson, age 50, $546,413 pay
SVP; President, Levi Strauss Europe, Middle East, and Africa: Joseph Middleton, age 46, $628,185 pay
SVP, Worldwide Human Resources: Fred Paulenich, age 37
Auditors: KPMG LLP

LOCATIONS

HQ: 1155 Battery St., San Francisco, CA 94111
Phone: 415-501-6000   **Fax:** 415-501-7112
Web: www.levistrauss.com

Levi Strauss & Co. manufactures and sells its branded jeans, sportswear, and dress pants through retail locations and company-owned outlets in more than 100 countries.

2001 Sales

	% of total
Americas	67
Europe	25
Asia/Pacific	8
Total	**100**

PRODUCTS/OPERATIONS

2001 Sales

	% of total
Levi's	75
Dockers	25
Total	**100**

Selected Brand Names
501
Dockers
Dockers K-1
Dockers Recode
Red Tab Classics
Silvertab
Slates
Superlow

Operating Divisions
Asia/Pacific Division
Levi Strauss Europe, Middle East, Africa
Levi Strauss, the Americas
  Levi Strauss & Co. (Canada) Inc.
  Levi Strauss Argentina
  Levi Strauss do Brasil
  Levi Strauss Mexico
  Levi Strauss U.S.

COMPETITORS

Abercrombie & Fitch	J. Crew
American Eagle Outfitters	Limited Brands
Benetton	NIKE
Calvin Klein	OshKosh B'Gosh
Fruit of the Loom	Oxford Industries
The Gap	Polo
Guess?	Tommy Hilfiger
Haggar	VF
J. C. Penney	Warnaco Group

HISTORICAL FINANCIALS & EMPLOYEES

Private FYE: November 30	Annual Growth	11/92	11/93	11/94	11/95	11/96	11/97	11/98	11/99	11/00	11/01
Sales ($ mil.)	(2.9%)	5,570	5,892	6,074	6,707	7,136	6,861	5,959	5,139	4,645	4,259
Net income ($ mil.)	(9.3%)	362	492	558	735	465	138	103	5	223	151
Income as % of sales	—	6.5%	8.4%	9.2%	11.0%	6.5%	2.0%	1.7%	0.1%	4.8%	3.5%
Employees	(7.7%)	34,200	36,400	36,500	37,700	37,000	37,000	30,000	30,000	17,300	16,700

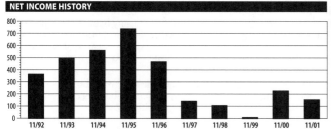

NET INCOME HISTORY

2001 FISCAL YEAR-END
Debt ratio: 100.0%
Return on equity: —
Cash ($ mil.): 103
Current ratio: 1.66
Long-term debt ($ mil.): 1,795

LIBERTY MUTUAL INSURANCE

Liberty Mutual wants more liberty. One of the largest workers' compensation insurers in the US, the company gained more flexibility in dealing with rapidly changing markets by reorganizing as a mutual holding company. Liberty Mutual Insurance has alliances with health care providers to manage disability care and also offers homeowners and auto insurance, retirement products, and group and individual life insurance. Other services include risk-prevention services (analyzing work sites and practices for safety), consulting, rehabilitation case management, and physical rehabilitation centers.

After failing to find a buyer, asset manager Liberty Financial is selling itself off little by little. Canadian insurer Sun Life has acquired Keyport Life Insurance and mutual fund distributor Independent Financial Marketing Group. Liberty Financial's investment management segment (including subsidiaries Crabbe Huston, Stein Roe & Farnham, and Liberty Wanger Asset Management) was snapped up by FleetBoston. The company plans to spend the money it receives from the sale of Liberty Financial on new acquisitions. Liberty Mutual has taken what is left of Liberty Financial private and merged it into one of its subsidiaries.

The company's diversification efforts include Liberty International, which provides insurance and occupational health and safety services in such countries as Canada, Japan, Mexico, Singapore, and the UK.

HISTORY

The need for financial aid to workers injured on the job was recognized in Europe in the late 19th century but did not make its way to the US until a workers' compensation law for federal employees was passed in 1908. Massachusetts was one of the first states to enact similar legislation. Liberty Mutual was founded in Boston in 1912 to fill this newly recognized niche.

Liberty Mutual followed the fire insurance practice of taking an active part in loss prevention. It evaluated clients' premises and procedures and recommended ways to prevent accidents. The company rejected the budding industry practice of limiting medical fees, instead studying the most effective ways to reduce the long-term cost of a claim by getting the injured party back to work.

In 1942 the company acquired the United Mutual Fire Insurance Company (founded 1908, renamed Liberty Mutual Fire Insurance Company in 1949). The next year it founded a rehabilitation center in Boston to treat injured workers and to test treatments.

In the 1960s and 1970s Liberty Mutual expanded its line to include life insurance (1963), group pensions (1970), and IRAs (1975).

Seeking to increase its national presence, the company formed Liberty Northwest Insurance Corporation in 1983. It continued expanding its offerings, with new subsidiaries in commercial, personal, and excess lines and, in 1986, by moving into financial services by buying Stein Roe & Farnham (founded 1958).

The expansion/diversification strategy seemed to work. Earnings between 1984 and 1986 more than tripled. Then came the downturn: Recession was followed by a string of natural disasters, and Liberty Mutual's income fell sharply between 1986 and 1988. In 1992 and 1993 the company lost suits to Coors and Outboard Marine for failing to back the companies in environmental litigation cases.

Liberty Mutual restructured in 1994, withdrawing from the group health business and reorganizing claims operations into two units: Personal Markets and Business Markets. The next year it gained a foothold in the UK when it received permission to invest in a Lloyd's of London syndicate management company.

The company expanded its financial services operations in 1995 and 1996, merging its Liberty Financial subsidiary with the already-public Colonial Group; it also acquired American Asset Management and Newport Pacific Management.

In a soft workers' compensation market, the company tried to build its position through key market acquisitions. In 1997 Liberty Mutual acquired bankrupt workers' comp provider Golden Eagle Insurance of California; the next year the firm bought Florida's Summit Holding Southeast. Mutual funds were also on the shopping list: Purchases included Société Générale's US mutual funds unit, led by international money dean Jean-Marie Eveillard. The firm also played suitor to high-performance trust fund SIFE; the $450 million proposal was rebuffed as ungenerous. In 1998 the company was slammed by increased claims — many related to a Condé Nast Building construction accident that shut down New York City's Times Square that summer. Liberty Mutual acquired erstwhile competitor Employers Insurance of Wausau that year.

In 1999 the company bought Guardian Royal Exchange's US operations. In a new international initiative that year, Liberty Mutual bought 70% of Singapore-based insurer Citystate Holdings (to be renamed Liberty Citystate) as its foothold in Asia. The following year the company made plans to form a mutual holding company to raise funds for acquisitions.

OFFICERS

Chairman Emeritus: Gary L. Countryman, age 63
Chairman, President, and CEO: Edmund F. Kelly, age 57
EVP, Auto & Home Markets: John B. Conners
EVP, Commercial Markets: Gary R. Gregg
EVP, Life Markets: John Tymochko
EVP, Regional Area Markets: Roger L. Jean
EVP; President, Liberty International:
  Thomas C. Ramey, age 57
SVP and CFO: J. Paul Condrin III
SVP and CIO: Terry L. Conner
SVP and Chief Investment Officer: A. Alexander Fontanes
SVP and General Counsel: Christopher C. Mansfield
**SVP and Manager of Human Resources and
  Administration:** Helen E.R. Sayles
SVP: Stephen G. Sullivan
VP and Corporate Actuary: Douglas M. Hodes
VP and Secretary: Dexter R. Legg
VP and Comptroller: Dennis J. Langwell
Auditors: Ernst & Young LLP

LOCATIONS

HQ: Liberty Mutual Insurance Companies
  175 Berkeley St., Boston, MA 02116
Phone: 617-357-9500   **Fax:** 617-350-7648
Web: www.libertymutual.com

Liberty Mutual Insurance has about 900 offices in the
US, as well as in Argentina, Australia, Bermuda, Brazil,
Canada, Colombia, Hong Kong, Ireland, Japan, Malaysia,
Mexico, Singapore, Spain, Thailand, the UK, and
Venezuela.

PRODUCTS/OPERATIONS

2001 Sales

	% of total
Commercial marketplace	32
Personal marketplace	28
Regional agency markets	16
International	15
Other	9
Total	**100**

Selected Product Lines
Annuities
Disability insurance
General liability
Individual and group auto and property insurance
Individual and group life
Investment advice and management
Mutual funds
Workers' compensation

Selected Operating Units
Liberty International
  Liberty ART SA (Argentina)
  Liberty Citystate (Singapore)
  Liberty International Canada
  Liberty International Underwriters
  Liberty Japan
  Liberty Mexico Seguros
  Liberty Mutual Insurance Company (Japan)
  Liberty Mutual Insurance Company (UK) Ltd.
  Liberty Paulista de Seguros (Brazil)
  Liberty Seguros SA (Colombia)
  Liberty Venezuela (merger between Seguros
    Panamerican and Seguros Caracas)
Liberty Mutual Group
  Colorado Casualty
  Golden Eagle Insurance Co.
  Indiana Insurance Company
  Liberty Northwest Insurance Corporation
  Merchants and Businessmen's Insurance Company
  Montgomery Mutual Insurance Company
  Peerless Insurance
  Summit Holding Southeast
  Wausau

COMPETITORS

21st Century	The Hartford	Prudential
AIG	Lincoln National	SAFECO
Allstate	MassMutual	St. Paul
Charles Schwab	MetLife	Companies
CIGNA	New York Life	State Farm
Citigroup	Northwestern	T. Rowe Price
CNA Financial	Mutual	Washington
Fremont General	Progressive	National
GenAmerica	Corporation	Corporation

HISTORICAL FINANCIALS & EMPLOYEES

Mutual company FYE: December 31	Annual Growth	12/92	12/93	12/94	12/95	12/96	12/97	12/98	12/99	12/00	12/01
Assets ($ mil.)	4.2%	20,216	20,544	20,644	21,791	22,690	25,230	26,254	55,259	30,264	29,375
Net income ($ mil.)	—	217	321	451	457	474	412	245	501	403	(289)
Income as % of assets	—	1.1%	1.6%	2.2%	2.1%	2.1%	1.6%	0.9%	0.9%	1.3%	—
Employees	7.0%	19,000	22,000	22,000	23,000	23,000	23,000	24,000	37,440	37,000	35,000

NET INCOME HISTORY

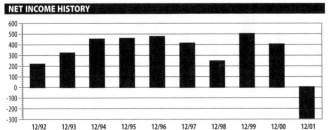

2001 FISCAL YEAR-END
Equity as % of assets: 19.7%
Return on assets: —
Return on equity: —
Long-term debt ($ mil.): —
Sales ($ mil.): 11,037

L.L. BEAN, INC.

With L.L. Bean, you can tame the great outdoors — or just look like you could. The outdoor apparel and gear maker mails more than 200 million catalogs per year. Products include outerwear, sportswear, housewares, footwear, camping and hiking gear, fishing gear, and the Maine hunting shoe upon which the company was built. L.L. Bean also operates four retail and 14 factory outlets in the US with nine additional stores in Japan. It also sells online through English- and Japanese-language Web sites. L.L. Bean was founded in 1912 by Leon Leonwood Bean and is controlled by his descendants.

From a pair of waterproof hunting boots in 1911, L.L. Bean's empire is based on catalogs mailed out under 95 different titles and advertising 16,000 products. Catalog sales account for 80% of L.L. Bean's revenue. L.L. Bean's flagship store in Freeport, Maine (known by locals as "the Bean") attracts 3 million visitors annually and is open 24 hours a day, 365 days a year. The company plans to open more retail outlets in hope that retail sales will one day equal catalog sales. Retail sales currently account for 20% of L.L. Bean's revenue; the company would like to see that number eventually rise to 50%. L.L. Bean also plans to scale back the number of catalog titles it offers.

L.L. Bean's famous customer service is exemplified by its liberal return policies and perpetual replacement of the rubber soles of its Maine Hunting Shoe. The company also offers seminars and events on such topics as fly fishing, sea kayaking, and outdoor photography.

HISTORY

Leon Leonwood Bean started out as a storekeeper in Freeport, Maine. Tired of wet, leaky boots, he experimented with various remedies and in 1911 came up with the Maine Hunting Shoe, a boot with rubber soles and feet and leather uppers. It became his most famous product.

From its outset in 1912, Bean's company was a mail-order house. The first batch of boots was a disaster: Almost all of them leaked. But Bean's willingness to correct his product's defects quickly, at his own expense, saved the company.

Maine's hunting licensing system, implemented in 1917, provided the company with a mailing list of affluent recreational hunters in the Northeast, and that year Bean opened a showroom to accommodate the customers stopping by his Freeport workshop.

Bean cultivated the image of the folksy Maine guide, offering durable, comfortable, weather-resistant clothes and reliable camping supplies. In 1920 Bean built a store on Main Street in Freeport. L.L. Bean continued to grow and add products, even during the Depression, and sales reached $1 million in 1937.

During WWII Bean helped design the boots used by the US military, and his company manufactured them, thus remaining afloat as the war years and rationing brought cutbacks in materials and outdoor activities. He began keeping the retail store open 24 hours a day in 1951, noting that he had "thrown away the keys." Bean added a women's department three years later.

Sales rose to $2 million in the early 1960s and were at $4.8 million when Bean died in 1967 at age 94. (He had resisted growing the business bigger, saying, "I'm eating three meals a day; I can't eat four.") The new president was Bean's grandson Leon Gorman, who had started with L.L. Bean in 1960. His early attempts at updating the mailing operations (mailing labels typed by hand and correspondence kept in cardboard boxes) had been vetoed by his grandfather. Gorman brought in new people and made improvements, including automating the mailing systems, improving the manufacturing systems, and targeting new, nonsporting markets (like women's casual clothes).

L.L. Bean continued its transition by targeting more of its classic customer profile — upper-middle-class college graduates — and sales grew about 20% annually for most of the 1980s. By 1989, however, sales had slowed and growth flattened as the national economy slumped and imitators carried away market share.

Unsolicited catalog orders had been coming in from Japan since the late 1980s, so in 1992 L.L. Bean began a joint venture with Seiyu and Matsushita Electric Industrial. Their first store opened that year (the company opened a catalog and service center in Japan in 1995). L.L. Kids began in 1993.

In 1996 the company began an online shopping service. Sparked by the success of its L.L. Kids division, which grew 300% in four years, the company opened a separate children's store in Freeport the next year. The company opened its second full-line store in 2000 near Washington, DC. L.L. Bean plans to continue opening retail stores in the eastern US.

L.L. Bean veteran Chris McCormick was named president and CEO in May 2001; Gorman remained chairman. McCormick is the first person outside of the Bean family to head the company.

In early 2002 L.L. Bean laid off 175 employees (about 4% of its workforce).

Chairman: Leon A. Gorman, age 67
President and CEO: Chris McCormick, age 46
SVP and CFO: Mark Fasold
SVP and COO: Bob Peixotto
Director of Human Resources: Anne Sowles
Director of IT Operations: Stafford Soule

LOCATIONS

HQ: Casco St., Freeport, ME 04033
Phone: 207-865-4761   **Fax:** 207-552-6821
Web: www.llbean.com

L.L. Bean sells through direct-mail catalogs and has retail stores and outlet stores in the US and Japan. It manufactures some of its merchandise in Maine.

PRODUCTS/OPERATIONS

Selected Catalogs
Corporate Sales (custom embroidered clothing and
   luggage)
Fly Fishing (equipment, outer wear, and accessories)
Home (linens, pillows, and decorating)
L.L. Bean
L.L. Bean Hunting
Outdoors (seasonal outdoor wear and accessories)
Outdoor Discovery Schools (classes and symposiums)
Traveler (clothing, luggage, and accessories)

Selected Products
Home and garden accessories
Men's, women's, and children's casual apparel
Outdoor classes
Outer wear
Shoes and boots
Sports gear and apparel
Travel apparel and luggage

COMPETITORS

Abercrombie & Fitch	Lands' End
American Eagle Outfitters	Levi Strauss
American Retail	Limited Brands
Bass Pro Shops	Lost Arrow
Brylane	May
Cabela's	Nautica Enterprises
Coldwater Creek	Norm Thompson
Coleman	North Face
Columbia Sportswear	Orvis Company
Dillard's	OshKosh B'Gosh
Eddie Bauer	Polo
Fast Retailing	REI
Federated	Sears
Foot Locker	Spiegel
The Gap	Sports Authority
Gart Sports	Sportsman's Guide
J. C. Penney	Talbots
J. Crew	Target
J. Jill Group	Timberland
Johnson Outdoors	Tommy Hilfiger

HISTORICAL FINANCIALS & EMPLOYEES

Private FYE: February 28	Annual Growth	2/93	2/94	2/95	2/96	2/97	2/98	2/99	2/00	2/01	2/02
Sales ($ mil.)	5.5%	743	867	976	1,078	1,040	1,068	1,070	1,100	1,100	1,200
Employees	2.8%	3,500	3,500	3,800	3,800	3,500	3,600	4,000	4,000	4,700	4,500

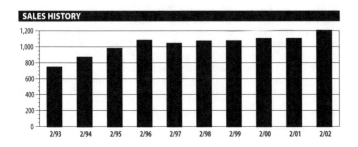

SALES HISTORY

LUCASFILM, LTD.

The Force is definitely with Emperor George Lucas. With five of the 20 highest grossing films of all time, Lucasfilm is one of the most successful independent production companies in the history of cinema. One of five companies owned by filmmaker George Lucas (the brains behind the *Star Wars* and *Indiana Jones* films), Lucasfilm's productions have garnered 17 Academy Awards. The company's most recent production is 2002's *Star Wars: Episode II — Attack of the Clones*; Lucasfilm's previous release, 1999's *Episode I — The Phantom Menace*, has grossed about $920 million worldwide and claims the #3 spot on the all-time list. Created in 1971, the company handles the business affairs of each firm in the Lucas empire.

These companies include LucasArts (video games), Lucas Digital (special effects house Industrial Light + Magic and Skywalker Sound), Lucas Learning (educational software), and Lucas Licensing (consumer products).

In 2002 Lucas spun off digital sound systems firm THX as an independent company. Lucasfilm is building a new headquarters and production center at the Presidio, a former Army base in San Francisco. A final sequel to the *Star Wars* series is slated for release in 2005.

HISTORY

After attending film school at the University of Southern California, George Lucas started his career as a documentary filmmaker, chronicling the production of Francis Ford Coppola's *Finian's Rainbow* in 1968. The two men became fast friends and founded American Zoetrope in 1969, which two years later released Lucas' feature film debut, the science-fiction film *THX 1138* (a full-length version of a student film he made at USC). The film flopped, and Coppola went into production on *The Godfather*. Lucas left American Zoetrope and created his own company, Lucasfilm, in 1971.

Two years later Lucas released *American Graffiti* through Universal Pictures (with some financial help from Coppola). The film was a smash hit; it raked in $115 million in the US and made him a millionaire before the age of 30. It also gave him the clout to try and get his most ambitious project off the ground, a space opera called *Star Wars*. Universal, frustrated with cost overruns on *Graffiti*, wanted no part of Lucas' seemingly ridiculous idea, so he went to 20th Century Fox, which agreed to finance the $10 million film. Lucas gave up his directing fee for a percentage of the box-office take and all merchandising rights. He created Industrial Light + Magic (ILM) and Sprocket Systems (later Skywalker Sound) in

1975 to produce the visual and sound effects needed for the film.

Star Wars cost about $12 million, and almost everyone involved was sure it would bomb. Released in 1977, the movie shattered every box-office record, and the merchandising rights Lucas obtained made him a multimillionaire. With his take from *Star Wars,* Lucas was able to finance the film's sequel, *The Empire Strikes Back* (1980), out of his own pocket, meaning he would receive most of the profits (it grossed more than $220 million domestically). Lucasfilm's next production was *Raiders of the Lost Ark* (1981), directed by Lucas' friend Steven Spielberg. It went on to gross more than $380 million worldwide.

The next year Lucas began developing the THX sound system in preparation for the 1983 release of the third *Star Wars* film, *Return of the Jedi* (which hauled in more than $260 million domestically). He also founded LucasArts in 1982 to develop video games. Lucasfilm completed Skywalker Ranch (a facility housing many of its various companies in Marin County, California) in the mid-1980s and filled out the decade with two *Raiders* sequels — *Indiana Jones and the Temple of Doom* (1984, $333 million worldwide) and *Indiana Jones and the Last Crusade* (1989, $495 million worldwide).

Lucasfilm reorganized in 1993 by spinning off LucasArts into a separate company and regrouping ILM and Skywalker Sound into a new company called Lucas Digital. Lucasfilm won local government approval to build an $87 million film studio near Skywalker Ranch in 1996, and the following year it re-released the *Star Wars Trilogy* to theaters with new special effects in celebration of the 20th anniversary, adding another $250 million to its take. Anticipating the release of the first of three prequels to the *Star Wars Trilogy*, Lucasfilm started signing marketing agreements in 1998 (including deals with Hasbro and Pepsi) that resulted in advance licensing of nearly $3 billion.

Star Wars: Episode I — The Phantom Menace opened in May 1999 and has grossed about $920 million worldwide (it finished its initial run second only to *Titanic*). Later in 1999 Lucas announced plans to develop a $250 million digital arts center at the old Presidio army base in San Francisco to house ILM, LucasArts, Lucas Learning, Lucas Online, THX, and the George Lucas Educational Foundation.

The next film in the *Star Wars* series, *Episode II — Attack of the Clones*, opened in May 2002.

Chairman: George W. Lucas Jr., age 58
President: Gordon Radley
VP Marketing: Jim Ward
Director Content Management Marketing:
Steve Sansweet
Director Corporate Real Estate: Chris Glennon
Acting General Manager, THX Ltd.: Mike Hewitt

LOCATIONS

HQ: PO Box 2009, San Rafael, CA 94912
Phone: 415-662-1800   **Fax:** 415-662-2437
Web: www.lucasfilm.com

COMPETITORS

Alliance Atlantis Communications
Artisan Entertainment
Dolby
DreamWorks SKG
Fox Entertainment
Lions Gate Entertainment
MGM
Pixar
Sony Pictures Entertainment
Time Warner Entertainment
Universal Studios
Viacom
Walt Disney

PRODUCTS/OPERATIONS

Selected Productions
American Graffiti (1973)
Howard the Duck (1986)
Indiana Jones and the Last Crusade (1989)
Indiana Jones and the Temple of Doom (1984)
Labyrinth (1986)
More American Graffiti (1979)
Radioland Murders (1994)
Raiders of the Lost Ark (1981)
Star Wars: Episode I — The Phantom Menace (1999)
Star Wars: Episode II — Attack of the Clones (2002)
Star Wars: Episode III (slated for 2005)
Star Wars: Episode IV — A New Hope (1977)
Star Wars: Episode V — The Empire Strikes Back
(1980)
Star Wars: Episode VI — Return of the Jedi (1983)
Tucker: The Man and His Dream (1988)
Willow (1988)
The Young Indiana Jones Chronicles (1992-96, TV
movies)

HISTORICAL FINANCIALS & EMPLOYEES

Private FYE: March 31	Annual Growth	3/92	3/93	3/94	3/95	3/96	3/97	3/98	3/99	3/00	3/01
Estimated sales ($ mil.)	37.7%	—	—	160	160	200	250	400	600	1,100	1,500
Employees	95.3%	—	—	—	36	100	200	500	1,300	1,800	2,000

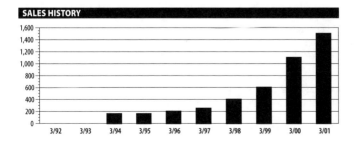

SALES HISTORY

MACANDREWS & FORBES

Through MacAndrews & Forbes Holdings, financier Ron Perelman is focused on makeup and money. The holding company has investments in an array of public and private companies, most notably Revlon (the #3 cosmetics company in the US), M&F Worldwide (licorice flavors), and WeddingChannel.com. Perelman is intent on reversing the fortunes of Revlon, which has been hobbled by debt and dwindling market share; his stake in Sunbeam (small appliances and Coleman camping equipment) became worthless when that company declared bankruptcy in 2001. He did make a hefty profit when Consolidated Cigar Holdings (the #1 US cigar maker) was sold to French tobacco maker Seita in 1999.

MacAndrews & Forbes Holdings owns 83% of Revlon. Most of Perelman's business strategy involves improving his cash position and paying down debt — hence his IPO of Revlon (1996), the sale of The Coleman Company to Sunbeam (1998), and the sale of two of Revlon's noncore units.

Perelman's holdings have dwindled in value since 1999. Revlon is struggling with debt and dwindling market share and Marvel Entertainment went bankrupt under his control.

Perelman is still a media curiosity, largely because of his very public courtship and wedding to wife #4, actress Ellen Barkin.

HISTORY

Ron Perelman grew up working in his father's Philadelphia-based conglomerate, Belmont Industries, but he left at the age of 35 to seek his fortune in New York. In 1978 he bought 40% of jewelry store operator Cohen-Hatfield Industries. The next year Cohen-Hatfield bought a minority stake in MacAndrews & Forbes (licorice flavoring). Cohen-Hatfield acquired MacAndrews & Forbes in 1980.

In 1984 Perelman reshuffled his assets to create MacAndrews & Forbes Holdings, which acquired control of Pantry Pride, a Florida-based supermarket chain, in 1985. Pantry Pride then bought Revlon for $1.8 billion with the help of convicted felon Michael Milken. After Perelman acquired Revlon, he added several other cosmetics vendors, including Max Factor and Yves Saint Laurent's fragrance and cosmetic lines.

In 1988 MacAndrews & Forbes agreed to invest $315 million in five failing Texas savings and loans (S&Ls), which Perelman combined and named First Gibraltar (sold to BankAmerica, now Bank of America, in 1993). The next year MacAndrews & Forbes bought The Coleman Company, a maker of outdoor equipment.

With a growing reputation for purchasing struggling companies, revamping them, and then selling them at a higher price, Perelman bought Marvel Entertainment Group (Marvel Comics) in 1989 and took it public in 1991. That year he sold Revlon's Max Factor and Betrix units to Procter & Gamble for over $1 billion.

MacAndrews & Forbes acquired 37.5% of TV infomercial producer Guthy-Renker and SCI Television's seven stations and merged them to create New World Television. That company was combined with TV syndicator Genesis Entertainment and TV production house New World Entertainment to create New World Communications Group, which Perelman took public in 1994. That year MacAndrews & Forbes and partner Gerald J. Ford bought Ford Motor's First Nationwide, the US's fifth-largest S&L at that time.

Subsidiaries Mafco Worldwide and Consolidated Cigar Holdings merged with Abex (aircraft parts) to create Mafco Consolidated Group in 1995. Following diminishing comic sales, Perelman placed Marvel in bankruptcy in 1996 and subsequently lost control of the company.

In 1997 First Nationwide bought California thrift Cal Fed Bancorp for $1.2 billion. In addition, Perelman sold New World to Rupert Murdoch's News Corp.

In 1998 Perelman orchestrated a $1.8 billion deal in which First Nationwide merged with Golden State Bancorp to form the US's third-largest thrift. Sunbeam bought Perelman's stake in Coleman that year, making Perelman a major Sunbeam shareholder. Also in 1998 MacAndrews & Forbes bought a 72% stake in Panavision (movie camera maker, later increased to 91%), invested in WeddingChannel.com, and sold its 64% stake in Consolidated Cigar to French tobacco giant Seita (netting Perelman a smoking $350 million profit).

Still burdened by debt, Revlon sold its professional products business in 2000.

Perelman's stock in Sunbeam was rendered worthless when the company initiated bankruptcy proceedings in February 2001. He was also sued by angry shareholders after the board of M&F Worldwide, the licorice company he controls, bought Perelman's stock in Panavision at more than five times its market value. In order to settle the litigation surrounding the purchase, in 2002 M&F agreed to return Pereleman's 83% stake in Panavision to Mafco. Golden State Bancorp also left the MacAndrews fold in 2002 when it was acquired by Citigroup.

Chairman, CEO, and CFO: Ronald O. Perelman, age 59
Co-Vice Chairman: Donald G. Drapkin, age 54
Co-Vice Chairman: Howard Gittis
Director of Human Resources: Herb Vallier

LOCATIONS

HQ: MacAndrews & Forbes Holdings Inc.
35 E. 62nd St., New York, NY 10021
Phone: 212-688-9000   **Fax:** 212-572-8400

MacAndrews & Forbes Holdings' consumer products
operations are principally in the US.

PRODUCTS/OPERATIONS

Selected Holdings
M&F Worldwide Corp. (32%, licorice extract)
Revlon Inc. (83%, cosmetics and personal care products)
Sunbeam Corporation (about 37%, small appliances and
  Coleman camping gear)
WeddingChannel.com

COMPETITORS

Alberto-Culver
Alticor
Avon
Bank of America
Body Shop
Brunswick
Chattem
Colgate-Palmolive
Dial
Estée Lauder
Golden West Financial
Johnson & Johnson
Kellwood
L'Oréal USA
LVMH
Mary Kay
Procter & Gamble
Ulta
Unilever
Washington Mutual
Wells Fargo

HISTORICAL FINANCIALS & EMPLOYEES

Private FYE: December 31	Annual Growth	12/92	12/93	12/94	12/95	12/96	12/97	12/98	12/99	12/00	12/01
Sales ($ mil.)	5.6%	3,496	2,748	3,030	4,413	6,196	6,071	4,900	5,400	5,500	5,700
Employees	(2.9%)	25,700	23,500	22,328	22,800	30,000	29,854	19,500	19,500	19,500	19,800

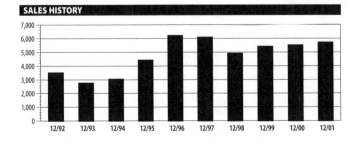

SALES HISTORY

MAJOR LEAGUE BASEBALL

It may be the national pastime, but Major League Baseball (MLB) is a big business whose troubled finances and disconnect with fans almost led it to yet another strike(out). MLB runs the game of professional baseball and oversees 30 franchises in 28 cities. Each team operates as a separate business but is regulated and governed by MLB. It sets official rules, regulates team ownership, and collects licensing fees for merchandise. It also sells national broadcasting rights and distributes fees to the teams. (Regional broadcast rights are held by each franchise.) The MLB was formed when the rival National and American Leagues joined together in 1903.

MLB has enjoyed a resurgence in popularity, thanks in large part to Mark McGwire and Sammy Sosa's race to set a new home run record in 1998. But the league and commissioner Bud Selig have made some tough decisions as financial disparity grows between small- and big-market teams.

The team owners and the league struggled throughout the 2002 season to negotiate a new labor agreement with players after the last contract, forged after a disastrous strike in 1994, expired at the end of the 2001 season. The cloud of the MLB's ninth work stoppage since 1972 hovered over the entire 2002 season, but another strike was narrowly avoided in late August at the 11th hour. The agreement forces the MLB to delay its plans to eliminate two teams until 2006 (the league had planned on contraction as early as 2003) and also places a luxury tax on teams with high payrolls. The money acquired from the tax will be distributed to smaller-market teams in an effort to allow those poorer clubs to compete with the high-priced talent of such teams as the New York Yankees.

Baseball fans became increasingly disgusted with both players and team owners as the threat of a strike loomed. But, now that a new labor agreement is in place, the MLB still has image problems that have to be addressed. Allegations that large amounts of players habitually abuse steroids are particularly troublesome.

HISTORY

The first baseball team to field professional players was the Cincinnati Red Stockings in 1869. Teams in Boston, New York City, and Philadelphia followed suit. In 1876 eight professional teams formed the National League. Competing leagues sprang up and folded, but Ban Johnson's Western League (formed in 1892) seized on territory abandoned by the National league in 1900 and began luring National League players with higher salaries. Renamed the American League, it also

began drawing away fans. The two leagues agreed to join forces in 1903 by having their champions meet in the World Series.

The sport flourished until the "black sox" scandal of 1919, in which eight Chicago White Sox players were accused of taking bribes to throw the World Series. The owners hired Judge Kenesaw Mountain Landis as baseball's first commissioner in 1921 to clean up the game's image. He served until his death in 1944. A joint committee of owners and players introduced more reforms in 1947, including a player pension fund.

The players formed the Major League Baseball Players' Association (MLBPA) in 1954 and signed the first collective-bargaining agreement with the owners in 1968. The players called their first strike in 1972, a 13-day walkout that won an improved pension plan. They won the right to free agency in 1976; another seven-week strike interrupted the 1981 season.

Salary increases slowed, and the free agent market dried up in the mid-1980s, prompting the MLBPA to sue the owners for collusion. The owners agreed to a settlement of $280 million in 1990. Baseball's eighth commissioner, Fay Vincent, resigned in 1992 after the owners effectively removed all power from the commissioner's office. An executive council of owners led by Milwaukee Brewers owner Bud Selig took control.

Prompted by the owners' decision to unilaterally restrict free agency and withdraw salary arbitration, the players started a 232-day strike in August 1994 that forced the cancellation of the World Series and stretched into the 1995 season. Revenue and income plummeted. Play resumed in 1995 when the owners and the MLBPA approved a new collective-bargaining agreement. Selig stepped down from the Brewers in 1998 to become the game's ninth commissioner.

Having alienated countless fans, baseball was resuscitated in 1998 by Mark McGwire and Sammy Sosa as they pursued Roger Maris' 37-year-old single-season home run record of 61. (McGwire's record of 70 only lasted until the 2001 season when the San Francisco Giants' outfielder Barry Bonds hit 72 homers.) The next year MLB umpires walked out for higher salaries, but the strategy backfired and 22 umpires lost their jobs. Later that year MLB signed a new six-year, $800 million TV contract with ESPN.

Sweeping changes took place in 2000 when owners, who had voted the previous year to eliminate the American and National league offices (centralizing power with the commissioner's office), also voted to restore the "best interests of baseball" powers to the commissioner, giving Selig full authority to redistribute wealth, block trades, and fine teams and players. The MLB also scored a financial home run when Fox Entertainment agreed to pay $2.5 billion for exclusive rights to televise all postseason contests through the 2006 season.

Due to the consistent financial disparity between large- and small-market teams, the league in 2001 voted to eliminate two teams before the start of the 2003 season. The next year Bob DuPuy was named president and COO of the league. (Former president Paul Beeston resigned after talks over a new collective bargaining agreement stalled.) The following year another strike was avoided late in the season. The new labor agreement pushes back the league's contraction plans until 2006 and also places a luxury tax on teams with high payrolls, which is then distributed to small-market franchises.

OFFICERS

Commissioner: Allan H. "Bud" Selig
President and COO: Robert A. DuPuy, age 55
EVP Administration: John McHale Jr.
EVP Baseball Operations: Sandy Alderson
EVP Business: Timothy J. Brosnan
EVP Labor and Human Resources: Rob Manfred
SVP and CFO: Jonathan D. Mariner, age 46
SVP Baseball Operations: Jimmie Lee Solomon
SVP International Business: Paul Archey
SVP Media Relations: Richard Levin
SVP Security and Facilities Management:
Kevin M. Hallinan
VP International Baseball Operations: Lou Melendez
VP Advertising: Jaqueline Parkes
VP Broadcasting: Bernadette McDonald
VP Community Affairs: Tom Brasuell
VP Corporate Sales and Marketing: Justin Johnson
Executive Director of Human Resources: Wendy Lewis
Auditors: Deloitte & Touche LLP

LOCATIONS

HQ: 245 Park Ave., New York, NY 10167
Phone: 212-931-7800   **Fax:** 212-949-8636
Web: www.mlb.com

PRODUCTS/OPERATIONS

Major League Franchises

American League
Anaheim Angels (California)
Baltimore Orioles
Boston Red Sox
Chicago White Sox
Cleveland Indians
Detroit Tigers
Kansas City Royals (Missouri)
Minnesota Twins (Minneapolis)
New York Yankees (New York City)
Oakland Athletics (California)
Seattle Mariners
Tampa Bay Devil Rays
Texas Rangers (Arlington)
Toronto Blue Jays

National League
Arizona Diamondbacks (Phoenix)
Atlanta Braves
Chicago Cubs
Cincinnati Reds
Colorado Rockies (Denver)
Florida Marlins (Miami)
Houston Astros
Los Angeles Dodgers
Milwaukee Brewers (switched from American League, 1998)
Montreal Expos
New York Mets (New York City)
Philadelphia Phillies
Pittsburgh Pirates
St. Louis Cardinals
San Diego Padres
San Francisco Giants

COMPETITORS

FIFA
NASCAR
NBA
NFL
NHL
PGA
World Wrestling Entertainment

HISTORICAL FINANCIALS & EMPLOYEES

Association FYE: October 31	Annual Growth	10/92	10/93	10/94	10/95	10/96	10/97	10/98	10/99	10/00	10/01
Sales ($ mil.)	8.6%	1,663	1,775	1,134	1,411	1,847	2,216	3,174	2,838	3,178	3,500
Employees	7.5%	—	150	150	170	200	200	—	—	—	—

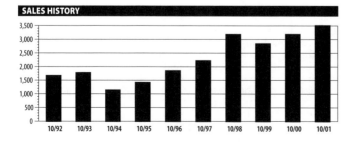

SALES HISTORY

THE MARMON GROUP, INC.

With more monikers than most, The Marmon Group monitors a melange of more than 100 autonomous manufacturing and service companies. Marmon's manufacturing units make medical products, mining equipment, industrial materials and components, consumer products (including Wells Lamont gloves), transportation equipment, building products, and water-treatment products. Services include marketing and distribution and consumer credit information (Trans Union). Overall, Marmon companies operate about 500 facilities in more than 40 countries. Chicago's Pritzker family (owners of the Hyatt hotel chain) owns The Marmon Group.

Each Marmon company operates under its own management, and a small corporate office (fewer than 100 employees) oversees and pulls together the conglomerate, acting as combination CFO, tax lawyer, accountant, and broker to member companies.

Marmon continues to grow through acquisitions, largely to complement its existing businesses, which include retail display equipment, fasteners and metal products, and consumer credit information.

HISTORY

Although the history of The Marmon Group officially begins in 1953, the company's roots are in the Chicago law firm Pritzker and Pritzker, started by Nicholas Pritzker in 1902. Through the firm the family made connections with First National Bank of Chicago, which A. N. Pritzker, Nicholas' son, used to get a line of credit to buy real estate. By 1940 the firm had stopped accepting outside clients to concentrate on the family's growing investment portfolio.

In 1953 A. N.'s son Jay used his father's connections to get a loan to buy Colson Company, a small, money-losing manufacturer of bicycles, hospital equipment, and other products. Jay's brother, Robert, a graduate of the Illinois Institute of Technology, took charge of Colson and turned it around. Soon Jay began acquiring more companies for his brother to manage.

In 1963 the brothers paid $2.7 million for about 45% of the Marmon-Herrington Company (whose predecessor, Marmon Motor Car, built the car that in 1911 won the first Indianapolis 500). The family now had a name for its industrial holdings — The Marmon Group.

It became a public company in 1966 when it merged with door- and spring-maker Fenestra. However, Jay began to take greater control of the group through a series of stock purchases, and by 1971 The Marmon Group was private once again.

A year earlier, in 1970, the group acquired a promising industrial pipe supplier, Keystone Tubular Service (which later became Marmon/Keystone). In 1973 Marmon began to acquire stock in Cerro Corp., which had operations in mining, manufacturing, trucking, and real estate; by 1976 the group had bought all of Cerro, thereby tripling its revenues. The brothers sold Cerro's trucking subsidiary, ICX, in 1977 and bought organ maker Hammond Corp., along with Wells Lamont, Hammond's glove-making subsidiary.

Marmon acquired conglomerate Trans Union in 1981. Trans Union brought many operations, including railcar and equipment leasing, credit information services, international trading, and water- and wastewater-treatment systems. Jay acquired Ticketmaster in 1982.

The Pritzkers made a foray into the airline business in 1984 by buying Braniff Airlines. After unsuccessfully bidding for Pan Am in 1987, they sold Braniff in 1988. Disappointments in other Pritzker businesses didn't slow Marmon, which added to its transportation equipment business in 1984 with Altamil, a maker of products for the trucking and aerospace industries.

To mark its 40th anniversary, the company sponsored a car, the Marmon Wasp II, at the 1993 Indianapolis 500. That year the Pritzkers sold 80% of Ticketmaster to Microsoft co-founder Paul Allen but retained a minority interest. Marmon sold Arzco Medical Systems in 1995 and Marmon/Keystone acquired Anbuma Group, a Belgian steel tubing distributor.

The Anbuma purchase and Marmon/Keystone's 1997 acquisition of UK tube distributor Wheeler Group exemplify Marmon's practice of building strength through acquisitions in its established markets. In 1998 Marmon purchased more than 30 companies, and opened a business development office in Beijing.

Marmon splashed out more than $500 million in 1999 to make 35 acquisitions, including Kerite (power cables), OsteoMed (specialty medical devices), and Bridport (medical and aviation products). Jay Pritzker died that year, and the company announced that his title of chairman will not be filled.

In 2000 Marmon spent another $500 million on more than 20 acquisitions, buying operations engaged in the production of retail display equipment, tank containers, and metal products, among others.

Former Illinois Tool Works chief John Nichols took over the Marmon CEO responsibilities from Robert Pritzker in 2001.

President and CEO: John D. Nichols
EVP: Robert C. Gluth
SVP and CFO: Robert K. Lorch
SVP, Secretary, and General Counsel: Robert W. Webb
SVP: Henry J. West
VP Human Resources: Larry Rist
VP: Mike Hartley
President, Comtran: John DeMarco
Auditors: Ernst & Young LLP

LOCATIONS

HQ: 225 W. Washington St., Chicago, IL 60606
Phone: 312-372-9500   **Fax:** 312-845-5305
Web: www.marmon.com

PRODUCTS/OPERATIONS

Selected Member Companies

Automotive Equipment
Fontaine Modification Co.
Fontaine Trailer Co.
Marmon-Herrington Co.
Perfection HY-Test Co.

Building Products and Fasteners
Anderson Copper and Brass Co.
Atlas Bolt & Screw Company
Shepherd Caster Corporation

Casters
Albion Industries, Inc.
Colson Caster Corporation

Consumer Products, Marketing, and Financial Services
Beijing Huilian Food Co., Ltd.
Getz Bros. & Co., Inc.
MarCap Corp.
Wells Lamont Corporation

Credit Data and Information Management
Trans Union LLC

Industrial Products
Amarillo Gear Co.
Enersul Inc.
Koehler-Bright Star, Inc.
Solidstate Controls, Inc.

Medical Products
American Medical Instruments, Inc.
B.G. Sulzle, Inc.
MicroAire Surgical Instruments, Inc.
OsteoMed Corporation

Metal Products and Materials
Cerro Copper Products Co.
Cerro Metal Products Co.
Penn Aluminum International, Inc.

Pipe and Tube Distribution
Marmon/Keystone Corporation
Future Metals, Inc.
M/K Huron Steel

Railway and Transportation Services
Penn Machine Co.
Railserve, Inc.
Trackmobile, Inc.
Union Tank Car Co.

Retail and Food-service Equipment
L.A. Darling Co.
Store Opening Solutions, Inc.
Thorco Industries, Inc.

Seat Belts and Cargo Restraints
Am-Safe Inc.
Bridport Aviation

Water Treatment Systems
Ecodyne Limited
EcoWater Systems, Inc.
Spectrum Labs, Inc.

Wire and Cable Products
Cable USA, Inc.
Hendrix Wire & Cable, Inc.
The Kerite Co.
Owl Wire and Cable, Inc.
Rockbestos-Surprenant Cable Corp.

COMPETITORS

Alcatel	Illinois Tool	Superior
Balfour Beatty	Works	TeleCom
Cable Design	Ingersoll-Rand	Terex
Technologies	ITT Industries	TRW
Eaton	LEONI	USG
Equifax	Masco	Wolverine Tube
GE	Pirelli S.p.A.	

HISTORICAL FINANCIALS & EMPLOYEES

Private FYE: December 31	Annual Growth	12/92	12/93	12/94	12/95	12/96	12/97	12/98	12/99	12/00	12/01
Sales ($ mil.)	5.4%	4,008	4,319	5,302	6,083	5,776	6,003	6,032	6,530	6,786	6,414
Employees	2.9%	27,000	27,700	28,000	30,000	35,000	33,000	35,000	40,000	40,000	35,000

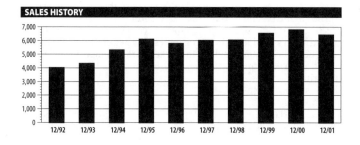

SALES HISTORY

7,000
6,000
5,000
4,000
3,000
2,000
1,000
0

12/92 12/93 12/94 12/95 12/96 12/97 12/98 12/99 12/00 12/01

MARS, INCORPORATED

Mars knows chocolate sales are nothing to snicker at. The #2 US candy maker (behind Hershey) makes such worldwide favorites as M&M's, Snickers, and the Mars bar. Its other products include 3 Musketeers, Dove, Milky Way, Skittles, Twix, and Starburst sweets; Combos and Kudos snacks; Uncle Ben's rice; and pet food under the names Pedigree, Sheba, and Whiskas. Mars also makes drink vending equipment and electronic automated payment systems. The Mars family (including siblings Forrest Mars Jr., president and CEO John Mars, and VP Jacqueline Badger Mars) owns the highly secretive firm — making the Mars family one of the richest in the country. Mars also offers ice-cream versions of several of its candy bars. Its automated payment systems include electronic coin changers and bill acceptors. The company, surpassed in candymaking in the US by Hershey, is ahead of its rival internationally. Mars stays virtually debt free and uses its profits for international expansion. It now sells its products in more than 100 countries on five continents.

Mars agreed to buy French pet food company Royal Canin in July 2001. In summer 2002 the two companies agreed to sell five pet food brands in order to gain regulatory approval. Upon the EU's approval of the sale, Mars will acquire a 10% stake in Royal Canin; it hopes to acquire full control of the company by 2003.

HISTORY

Frank Mars invented the Milky Way candy bar in 1923 after his previous three efforts at the candy business left him bankrupt. After his estranged son Forrest graduated from Yale, Mars hired him to work at his candy operation. When Forrest demanded one-third control of the company and Frank refused, Forrest moved to England with the foreign rights to Milky Way and started his own company (Food Manufacturers) in the 1930s. He made a sweeter version of Milky Way for the UK, calling it a Mars bar. Forrest also ventured into pet food with the 1934 purchase of Chappel Brothers (renamed Pedigree). At one point he controlled 55% of the British pet food market.

During WWII Forrest returned to the US and introduced Uncle Ben's rice (the world's first brand-name raw commodity) and M&M's (a joint venture between Forrest and Bruce Murrie, son of the then-Hershey president). The idea for M&M's was borrowed from British Smarties, for which Forrest obtained rights (from Rowntree Mackintosh) by relinquishing similar rights to the Snickers bar in some foreign markets. The ad slogan "Melts in your mouth, not in your hand" (and the candy's success in non-air-conditioned stores and war zones) made the company an industry leader. Mars introduced M&M's Peanut in 1954. It was one of the first candy companies to sponsor a television show — *Howdy Doody* in the 1950s.

Forrest merged his firm with his deceased father's company in 1964, after buying his dying half sister's controlling interest. (He renamed the business Mars at her request.) The merger was the end of an alliance with Hershey, who had supplied Frank with chocolate since his Milky Way inception.

In 1968 Mars bought Kal Kan. (The division now oversees all pet food operations.) In 1973 Forrest, then 69 years old, delegated his company responsibility to sons Forrest Jr. and John. Five years later the brothers, looking for snacks to offset dwindling candy sales from a more diet-conscious America, bought the Twix chocolate-covered cookie brand. During the late 1980s they bought ice-cream bar maker Dove Bar International and Ethel M Chocolates, producer of liqueur-flavored chocolates, a business their father had begun in his retirement.

Hershey passed Mars as the US's largest candy maker in 1988 when it acquired Cadbury Schweppes' US division (Mounds and Almond Joy). In response to the success of Hershey's Symphony Bar, Mars introduced its dark-chocolate Dove bar in 1991.

While Hershey chose to stick close to home, Mars ventured abroad. The company entered the huge confectionery market of India in 1989 by building a $10 million factory there. In 1996 the company opened a confectionery processing plant in Brazil. Back home, the company expanded its Starburst candy line in 1996 and in 1997 launched new ad campaigns, including M&M's spots featuring a trio of animated M&M candies. Mars introduced Uncle Ben's Rice Bowl frozen meals in the late 1990s.

Forrest Sr. died in 1999, spurring rumors that Mars would go public or be sold. Instead, the company dismantled most of its sales force, opting to use less costly food brokers. Also in 1999 Forrest Jr. retired, leaving brother John as president and CEO. Still far behind its rival, Mars received a modest boost in US market share when Hershey experienced computer troubles. In 2000 the company established its Effem India subsidiary to market Mars' products in India.

Chairman, President, and CEO: John Franklyn Mars, age 66
VP: Jacqueline Badger Mars, age 63
VP and Secretary: D. M. Newby
VP and Treasurer: R. E. Barnes
VP, Licensing Masterfoods USA: Michele Brown

LOCATIONS

HQ: 6885 Elm St., McLean, VA 22101
Phone: 703-821-4900 **Fax:** 703-448-9678
Web: www.mars.com

PRODUCTS/OPERATIONS

Selected Products

Candy	Brekkies
3 Musketeers	Cesar
Bounty	Chappie
Dove	Dine
Ethel M Chocolates	Frolic
Maltesers	KiteKat
M&M's	Loyal
Mars	My Dog
Milky Way	Pedigree
Opal Fruit	Sheba
Revels	Trill
Skittles	Waltham
Snickers	Whiskas
Starburst	
Twix	**Snacks**
	Combos
Ice Cream Bars	Kudos
3 Musketeers	
DoveBars	**Rice and Other Food and**
M&M Cookie Ice Cream	**Drinks**
Sandwiches	Dolmio sauces
Milky Way	Flavia drinks
Snickers	Masterfoods condiments
Starburst Ice Bars	and sauces
	Suzi Wan Chinese food
Pet Food	Uncle Ben's Rice
Bounce	

Other Products

Coin changers
Flavia office beverage systems
Klix beverage vending equipment
Lockets medicated lozenges
Smart card payment systems
Tunes medicated lozenges

Selected Divisions

Information Services International (information and systems technology for Mars units)
Masterfoods USA (US business units of M&M/Mars, Kal Kan, and Uncle Ben's)
MEI (electronic bill acceptors, coin changers, and card-based cashless payment systems)

COMPETITORS

Archibald Candy	Heinz
Brach's	Kraft Foods
Cadbury Schweppes	Lindt & Sprüngli
Campbell Soup	Meiji Seika
Colgate-Palmolive	Nestlé
ConAgra	Riviana Foods
CSM	Rocky Mountain Chocolate
Doane Pet Care Company	Russell Stover
Ezaki Glico	See's Candies
Ferrara Pan Candy	Thorntons
Ferrero	Tootsie Roll
General Mills	Unilever
Grupo Corvi	World's Finest Chocolate
Guittard	Wrigley
Hershey	

HISTORICAL FINANCIALS & EMPLOYEES

Private FYE: December 31	Annual Growth	12/92	12/93	12/94	12/95	12/96	12/97	12/98	12/99	12/00	12/01
Estimated sales ($ mil.)	3.5%	12,500	13,000	12,500	13,000	14,000	14,400	15,500	15,200	15,400	17,000
Employees	0.8%	28,000	27,000	28,000	28,000	28,000	28,500	30,000	28,500	30,000	30,000

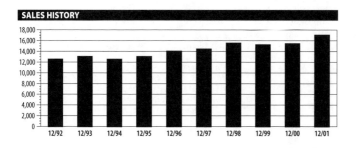

SALES HISTORY

MARY KAY INC.

Mary Kay is in the pink (and in Avon's shadow) as the US's #2 direct seller of beauty products. It sells more than 200 products in eight product categories: facial skin care, cosmetics, fragrances, nutritional supplements, sun protection, nail care, body care, and men's skin care. Some 850,000 direct-sales consultants demonstrate Mary Kay products in the US and about 35 other countries. Consultants vie for prizes such as the use of cars (including pink Cadillacs, first awarded in 1969). The family of late founder Mary Kay Ash owns most of the company.

Founded by a woman for women, Mary Kay has an overwhelmingly female workforce. Although the company stands by Mary Kay's original goal of providing financial and career opportunities for women, men exert quite a bit of power at the company: Mary Kay's chairman/CEO (Ash's son Richard Rogers) and CFO are both men.

The company gives bonuses each year, ranging from jewelry to the company's trademark pink Cadillacs. During her lifetime Ash was known for her religious nature as well as her generosity. However, she suffered a debilitating stroke in 1996 and she died on Thanksgiving Day 2001.

HISTORY

Before founding her own company in 1963, Mary Kay Ash worked as a Stanley Home Products sales representative. Impressed with the alligator handbag awarded to the top saleswoman at a Stanley convention, Ash was determined to win the next year's prize — and she did. Despite that accomplishment and having worked at Stanley for 11 years, a male assistant she had trained was made her boss after less than a year on the job. Tired of not receiving recognition, Ash and her second husband used their life savings ($5,000) to go into business for themselves. Although her husband died of a heart attack shortly before the business opened, Ash forged ahead with the help of her two grown sons.

She bought a cosmetics formula invented years earlier by a hide tanner. (The mixture was originally used to soften leather, but the tanner noticed how the formula made his hands look younger, and he began applying the mixture to his face, with great results.) Ash kept her first line simple — 10 products — and packaged her wares in pink to contrast with the typical black and red toiletry cases of the day. Ash also enlisted consultants, who held "beauty shows" with five or six women in attendance. Mary Kay grossed $198,000 in its first year.

The company introduced men's skin care products in 1965. Ash bought a pink Cadillac the following year and began awarding the cars as prizes three years later. (By 1981 orders were so large — almost 500 — that GM dubbed the color "Mary Kay Pink.")

Ash became a millionaire when her firm went public in 1968. Mary Kay grew steadily through the 1970s. Foreign operations began in 1971 in Australia, and over the next 25 years the company entered 24 more countries, including nations in Asia, Europe, Central and South America, and the Pacific Rim.

Sales plunged in the early 1980s, along with the company's stock prices (from $40 to $9 between 1983 and 1985). Ash and her family reacquired Mary Kay in 1985 through a $375 million LBO. Burdened with debt, the firm lost money in the late 1980s. Mary Kay took a number of steps to boost sales and income, doing a makeover on the cosmetics line and advertising in women's magazines again (after a five-year hiatus) to counter its old-fashioned image. The company also introduced recyclable packaging. In 1989 Avon rebuffed a buyout offer by Mary Kay, and both companies halted animal testing.

Mary Kay introduced a bath and body product line in 1991, and its Skin Revival System, launched in 1993, raked in $80 million in its first six months. It began operations in Russia that year; sales there reached $25 million by 1995. Ash suffered a debilitating stroke in 1996.

In 1998 the company began selling through retail outlets in China because of a government ban on direct selling. Changing with the times, Mary Kay added a white sport utility vehicle and new shades of pink to its fleet of 10,000 GM cars that year. Chairman John Rochon was named CEO in 1999. Also in 1999 Mary Kay launched *Women & Success* (a magazine for consultants) and Atlas (its electronic ordering system).

In June 2001 Richard Rogers, company chairman and son of Ash, replaced Rochon as CEO.

OFFICERS

Chairman and CEO: Richard Rogers, age 59
President and COO: David Holl
EVP, Global Manufacturing: Dennis Greaney
EVP, Global Marketing, and Chief Scientific Officer: Myra O. Barker
EVP and CIO: Kregg Jodie
SVP, Global Human Resources and Operations: Darrell Overcash
SVP, Finance: Terry Smith
President, Global Sales and Marketing: Tom Whatley
VP, Global Corporate Communications: Randall Oxford
General Counsel: Brad Glendening
e-Business Project Manager: Lou Silvey

LOCATIONS

HQ: 16251 Dallas Pkwy., Addison, TX 75001
Phone: 972-687-6300   **Fax:** 972-687-1609
Web: www.marykay.com

Mary Kay employs about 850,000 direct-sales consultants who sell the company's merchandise in 35 countries in Asia, Australia, Europe, North America, and South America.

PRODUCTS/OPERATIONS

Selected Product Lines
Body care
Cosmetics
Facial skin care
Fragrances
Men's skin care
Nail care
Nutritional supplements for men
Nutritional supplements for women
Sun protection

COMPETITORS

Alberto-Culver	Johnson & Johnson
Allou	L'Oréal
Alticor	L'Oréal USA
Avon	Merle Norman
Bath & Body Works	New Dana Perfumes
BeautiControl Cosmetics	Nu Skin
Body Shop	Perrigo
Clarins	Procter & Gamble
Colgate-Palmolive	Reliv
Coty	Revlon
Del Labs	Schwarzkopf & DEP
Dial	Scott's Liquid Gold
Estée Lauder	Shaklee
Helen of Troy	Shiseido
Herbalife	Sunrider
Intimate Brands	Unilever
John Paul Mitchell	Wella

HISTORICAL FINANCIALS & EMPLOYEES

Private FYE: December 31	Annual Growth	12/92	12/93	12/94	12/95	12/96	12/97	12/98	12/99	12/00	12/01
Sales ($ mil.)	8.7%	613	737	850	950	1,000	1,050	1,000	1,000	1,200	1,300
Employees	6.2%	2,100	2,400	2,400	2,800	3,000	3,500	3,500	3,250	3,600	3,600

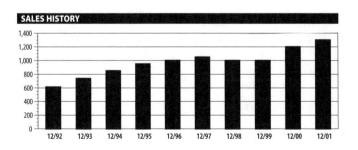

SALES HISTORY

MASHANTUCKET PEQUOT GAMING

Mashantucket Pequot Gaming Enterprise has propelled the Mashantucket Pequot Tribal Nation (with roughly 600 members) from the depths of intense poverty to its lofty position as the wealthiest Native American tribe in the US. It owns and operates Foxwoods Resort Casino, one of the largest casinos in the world and, many believe, the most profitable. The complex offers more than 6,400 slot machines and 350 gaming tables in five casinos, three hotels (Grand Pequot Tower, Great Cedar Hotel, Two Trees Inn), 21 restaurants, live entertainment, and a string of retail shops.

The Mashantucket Pequot reservation is a sovereign nation, and the Pequot tribe is not obligated to pay local property or business taxes, or reveal all of its finances. However, estimates of Foxwoods' annual revenues exceed $1 billion. The state of Connecticut receives 25% of the casino's slot machine revenues.

In addition to its gaming operations, the Mashantucket Pequot Tribal Nation owns Fox Navigation (high-speed ferry service) and the Pequot Pharmaceutical Network (mail-order and discount pharmaceuticals). It also owns three Connecticut hotels (Hilton Mystic, Norwich Inn & Spa, Randall's Ordinary Inn) and two golf courses (Foxwoods Golf & Country Club at Boulder Hills and Pequot Golf Club). The Mashantucket Pequot Tribal Nation has even established the Mashantucket Pequot Museum and Research Center dedicated to the tribe's life and history.

Two books released in 2000 and 2001, which questioned the authenticity of the Mashantucket Pequot tribe and claimed that the government was duped into giving them more land for their reservation than they were entitled to, sparked a series of lawsuits from neighboring communities. In early 2002 the Mashantucket Pequot tribe announced it had withdrawn its application to annex 165 acres of land close to its Foxwood Resort Casino, ending nearly 10 years of legal battles.

HISTORY

Once a powerful tribe, the Pequots were virtually wiped out in the 17th century by disease and attacks from colonists. More than 350 years later, Richard "Skip" Hayward, a pipefitter making $15,000 a year, led the fight for federal recognition of his nearly extinct Mashantucket Pequot tribe. He was elected tribal chairman in 1975, and the US government officially recognized the tribe in 1983.

The Indian Gaming Regulatory Act of 1988 opened the door for legal gambling on reservations, but tribes still had to negotiate with state governments for authorization. Hayward hired G. Michael "Mickey" Brown as a consultant and lawyer. Brown took the tribe's legal battle to the US Supreme Court, which eventually ruled that the Pequots could build a casino. When some 30 banks turned down the Pequots for a construction loan, Brown introduced Hayward and his tribe to Lim Goh Tong, billionaire developer of the successful Gentings Highlands Casino resort in Malaysia. Tong invested approximately $60 million, and the Foxwoods casino opened in 1992.

Brown brought in Alfred J. Luciani to serve as president and CEO of Foxwoods. Luciani stayed less than a year, however, resigning because of what he called philosophical differences with tribe leadership. Brown took over as CEO in 1993. Although Foxwoods grew rapidly, Brown often wrestled with members of the tribal council over how the business should be run. The next year Brown rehired Luciani to oversee the development of the Grand Pequot Tower hotel.

Brown resigned and Luciani was fired in 1997 after it was revealed that Brown had not fully disclosed his ties with Lim Goh Tong and that, in 1992, Luciani had accepted a $377,000 loan from Gamma International, a vendor that provided keno services to Foxwoods. The Pequots considered these actions to be conflicts of interest. A new management team was brought in, and Floyd "Bud" Celey, a veteran of Hilton Hotels, was appointed CEO.

The Pequots opened the Mashantucket Pequot Museum and Research Center in 1998. When tribal elections were held later that year, Kenneth Reels was elected chairman of the Pequot's tribal governing body, ousting Hayward from the position he had held for more than 20 years. Hayward was elected vice chairman. Mashantucket Pequot Gaming Enterprise concentrated on improving financial accountability in 1999, and the tribe began cutting costs by shuttering unprofitable holdings including Pequot River Shipworks, its shipbuilding business.

Former COO William Sherlock replaced Celey as CEO in 2000. That year the first of two books (the second was published in 2001), which questioned the tribe's legitimacy, created some controversy for the group. A federal audit in 2000 revealed that the tribe's pharmaceutical firm was giving discount drugs intended for Native Americans to its non-Native American employees.

Chairman, Tribal Council: Kenneth Reels
Vice Chairman, Tribal Council: Richard A. Hayward
CEO: William Sherlock
SVP Finance: John O'Brien
SVP Human Resources: Joanne Franks
Director, Casino Public Relations: Michael Dutton
Director, Public Relations: Arthur Henick
Director, Public Relations: Toni Parker-Johnson

COMPETITORS

Aztar
Connecticut Lottery
Harrah's Entertainment
Kerzner International
Mohegan Tribal Gaming
New York State Lottery
Park Place Entertainment
Trump Hotels & Casinos

LOCATIONS

HQ: Mashantucket Pequot Gaming Enterprise Inc.
  Rte. 2, Mashantucket, CT 06339
Phone: 860-312-3000   **Fax:** 860-312-1599
Web: www.foxwoods.com

The Mashantucket Pequot Gaming Enterprise has
holdings in Connecticut and Rhode Island.

PRODUCTS/OPERATIONS

Selected Operations
Foxwoods Resort Casino
  Foxwoods Golf & Country Club at Boulder Hills
    (Richmond, RI)
  Grand Pequot Tower
  Great Cedar Hotel
  Two Trees Inn

Selected Mashantucket Pequot Tribal Nation Holdings
Fox Navigation (ferry service)
Hilton Mystic (Mystic, CT)
Mashantucket Pequot Gaming Enterprise (Foxwoods
  Resort Casino; Ledyard, CT)
Mashantucket Pequot Museum and Research Center
  (Mashantucket, CT)
Norwich Inn & Spa (Norwich, CT)
Pequot Golf Club (Stonington, CT)
Pequot Pharmaceutical Network (mail-order and
  discount pharmaceuticals)
Randall's Ordinary Inn (North Stonington, CT)

HISTORICAL FINANCIALS & EMPLOYEES

Private FYE: September 30	Annual Growth	9/92	9/93	9/94	9/95	9/96	9/97	9/98	9/99	9/00	9/01
Estimated sales ($ mil.)	5.2%	—	1,000	1,000	1,030	1,100	1,000	1,000	1,200	1,300	1,500
Employees	4.8%	—	9,100	10,000	11,000	12,000	11,180	11,500	—	—	—

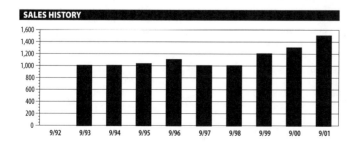

SALES HISTORY

HOOVER'S HANDBOOK OF PRIVATE COMPANIES 2003

MASSACHUSETTS MUTUAL LIFE

After flirting with the possibility of demutualizing, Massachusetts Mutual Life Insurance (MassMutual) has decided to stay the course. Founded in 1851, MassMutual sells small businesses and individuals a variety of life insurance and pension products through more than 1,300 offices in the US. Its Financial Services Group offers retirement plans for individuals and businesses, annuities, and trust services (through The MassMutual Trust Company). Other subsidiaries include OppenheimerFunds (mutual funds), David L. Babson & Co. (investor services), and Cornerstone Real Estate (real estate equities).

Like so many other insurance firms, MassMutual is determined to transform into a financial services firm. However, you won't catch the firm issuing stock to get the job done; the management of MassMutual has decided to keep things collective despite pressure from some policyholders (although the company has not ruled out going public in the future).

MassMutual International is exporting the company's operations worldwide, having established subsidiaries in Argentina, Bermuda, Chile, Hong Kong, Japan, Luxembourg, and Taiwan. It focuses on new product development (some 70% of sales come from products or channels developed within the last two years) and broadened distribution.

HISTORY

Insurance agent George Rice formed Massachusetts Mutual in 1851 as a stock company based in Springfield. The firm converted to a mutual in 1867. For its first 50 years MassMutual sold only individual life insurance, but after 1900 it branched out, offering first annuities (1917) and then disability coverage (1918).

The early 20th century was rough on MassMutual, which was forced to raise premiums on new policies during WWI, then faced the high costs of the 1918 flu epidemic. The firm endured the Great Depression despite policy terminations, expanding its product line to include income insurance. In 1946 MassMutual wrote its first group policy, for Jack Daniel's maker Brown-Forman Distillers. By 1950 the company had diversified into medical insurance.

MassMutual began investing in stocks in the 1950s, switching from fixed-return bonds and mortgages for higher returns. It also decentralized and in 1961 began automating operations. By 1970 the firm had installed a computer network linking it to its independent agents. During this period, whole life insurance remained the core product.

With interest rates increasing during the late 1970s, many insurers diversified by offering high-yield products like guaranteed investment contracts funded by high-risk investments. MassMutual resisted as long as it could, but as interest rates soared to 20%, the company experienced a rash of policy loans, which led to a cash crunch. In 1981, with its policy growth rate trailing the industry norm, MassMutual developed new products, including UPDATE, which offered higher dividends in return for adjustable interest on policy loans.

In the 1980s MassMutual reduced its stock investment (to about 5% of total investments by 1987), allowing it to emerge virtually unscathed from the 1987 stock market crash.

The firm changed course in 1990 and entered financial services. It bought a controlling interest in mutual fund manager Oppenheimer Management. MassMutual announced in 1993 that, with legislation limiting rates, it would stop writing new individual and small-group policies in New York.

The next year the company targeted the neglected family-owned business niche; in 1995 it sponsored the American Alliance of Family-Owned Businesses and rolled out new whole life products aimed at this segment. That year it bought David L. Babson & Company, a Massachusetts-based investment management firm, and opened life insurance companies in Chile and Argentina.

In 1996 MassMutual merged with Connecticut Mutual. It also acquired Antares Leveraged Capital Corp. (commercial finance) and Charter Oak Capital Management (investment advisory services). The next year MassMutual sold its Life & Health Benefits Management subsidiary.

Still in the mood to merge, the company entered discussions with Northwestern Mutual in 1998, but culture clashes terminated the talks. Also that year the company helped push through legislation that would allow insurers to issue stock through mutual holding companies, a move which MassMutual itself contemplated in 1999.

MassMutual expanded outside the US at the turn of the century. In 1999 it issued securities in Europe; opened offices in such locales as Bermuda and Luxembourg; and bought the Argentina operations of Jefferson-Pilot. A year later it expanded into Asia when it bought Hong Kong-based CRC Protective Life Insurance (now MassMutual Asia). In 2001 the company entered the Taiwanese market, buying a stake in Mercuries Life Insurance (now MassMutual Mercuries Life Insurance) and acquired Japanese insurer Aetna Heiwa Life (a subsidiary of US health insurer Aetna).

Chairman, President, and CEO: Robert J. O'Connell
EVP and CFO: Howard E. Gunton
EVP and CIO: Christine M. Modie
EVP and Chief Investment Officer: Stuart H. Reese
EVP and General Counsel: Lawrence V. Burkett Jr.
EVP, Disability Income Insurance and Long-Term Care Insurance; President, Financial Products Division: Toby J. Slodden
EVP, Human Resources and Communications: Susan A. Alfano
EVP, Individual Life Business: Matthew E. Winter
EVP, Life Services and Large Corporate Markets: James E. Miller
EVP, Retirement Services: Frederick C. Castellani
EVP; Chairman and CEO, OppenheimerFunds: John V. Murphy
SVP, Secretary, and Deputy General Counsel: Ann F. Lomeli
SVP, MassMutual Asia: Elroy Chan
SVP, Corporate Communications: Frances B. Emerson
SVP, Corporate Services: Colin C. Collins
SVP, Information Systems: Jonathan Picoult
SVP, Investments: Michael D. Hays
SVP, International: Andrew Oleksiw
SVP, Large Corporate Markets: Anne Melissa Dowling
SVP, Life Strategic Business and Annuities: Theresa H. Forde
SVP, Mergers and Acquisitions: Paul T. Pasteris
SVP and Actuary, Corporate Actuarial and Life Product Development: Isadore Jermyn
SVP and Chief Actuary: John R. Skar
SVP and Chief Compliance Officer: Margaret Sperry
SVP and General Auditor: Douglas J. Janik
Auditors: PricewaterhouseCoopers LLP

LOCATIONS

HQ: Massachusetts Mutual Life Insurance Company
1295 State St., Springfield, MA 01111
Phone: 413-788-8411   **Fax:** 413-744-6005
Web: www.massmutual.com

Massachusetts Mutual Life Insurance operates in Argentina, Bermuda, Chile, Hong Kong, Japan, Luxembourg, Taiwan, and the US.

PRODUCTS/OPERATIONS

2001 Assets

	$ mil.	% of total
Cash & equivalents	4,936	6
Bonds	27,804	35
Stocks	450	1
Mortgage loans	7,259	9
Real estate	1,924	3
Policy loans	6,262	8
Other investments	3,054	4
Assets in separate account	24,932	31
Other assets	2,313	3
Total	**78,934**	**100**

Selected Subsidiaries
Antares Capital Corporation (commercial finance)
C.M. Life Insurance Company
Cornerstone Real Estate Advisers, Inc. (real estate equities)
David L. Babson and Company, Inc. (institutional investment services)
MassMutual International, Inc.
Compañía de Seguros Vida Corp. S.A. (Chile)
MassLife Seguros de Vida S.A. (Argentina)
MassMutual Asia Ltd. (Hong Kong)
MassMutual Life Insurance Co. K.K. (Japan)
MassMutual Trust Company, F.S.B.
MML Bay State Life Insurance Company
OppenheimerFunds, Inc. (mutual funds)

COMPETITORS

AIG	FMR	Northwestern
Allianz	Guardian Life	Mutual
Allstate	The Hartford	Principal
American	Jefferson-Pilot	Financial
Financial	John Hancock	Prudential
American	Financial	St. Paul
General	Services	Companies
AXA Financial	Liberty Mutual	State Farm
Charles Schwab	Mellon Financial	TIAA-CREF
CIGNA	Merrill Lynch	Torchmark
Citigroup	MetLife	UBS
CNA Financial	Nationwide	PaineWebber
Conseco	New York Life	

HISTORICAL FINANCIALS & EMPLOYEES

Mutual company FYE: December 31	Annual Growth	12/92	12/93	12/94	12/95	12/96	12/97	12/98	12/99	12/00	12/01
Assets ($ mil.)	10.7%	31,495	34,699	35,720	38,632	55,752	61,069	66,979	70,586	73,739	78,934
Net income ($ mil.)	23.8%	116	139	93	159	239	262	359	441	740	791
Income as % of assets	—	0.4%	0.4%	0.3%	0.4%	0.4%	0.4%	0.5%	0.6%	1.0%	1.0%
Employees	4.5%	—	—	—	—	—	—	7,885	7,900	8,000	9,000

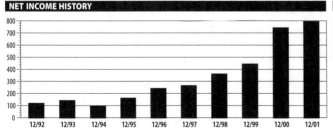

NET INCOME HISTORY

2001 FISCAL YEAR-END
Equity as % of assets: 6.5%
Return on assets: 1.0%
Return on equity: 17.6%
Long-term debt ($ mil.): —
Sales ($ mil.): 15,980

MASTERCARD INCORPORATED

Surpassing Visa in market share —*that* would be priceless. MasterCard is the US's #2 payment system. The company is owned by its more than 15,000 financial institution members worldwide. It markets the MasterCard (credit and debit cards) and Maestro (debit cards) brands; provides the transaction authorization network; and collects fees from members. Its cards are accepted at some 24 million global locations. MasterCard also operates the Cirrus ATM network and promotes Mondex chip-based smart cards; the organization owns 51% of Mondex International.

Citigroup, J.P. Morgan Chase, and BANK ONE each own about 7% of MasterCard.

Long considered more downmarket than Visa, MasterCard is working to add affluent users (the World MasterCard offers 24-hour concierge services). The company is working amid growing competition to make its electronic smart card (single-use or refillable chip-based cards used as cash) the industry standard through Mondex. Smart cards are common in Europe but have met consumer resistance in the US. MasterCard is launching smart card initiatives in Asia and moving into wireless e-commerce; it is teaming up with Oberthur Card Systems to develop secure methods to make purchases over mobile telephones.

MasterCard's quest for market share led to its merger with Europay, the firm's European counterpart, in mid-2002. European members now own about a third of the newly created holding company, MasterCard Inc. While the consolidation of Maestro's ownership (Europay and MasterCard had owned it 50-50) has given MasterCard control of the world's largest debit card network, it still trails Visa in credit cards.

HISTORY

A group of bankers formed The Interbank Card Association (ICA) in 1966 to establish authorization, clearing, and settlement procedures for bank credit card transactions. This was particularly important to banks left out of the rapidly growing BankAmericard (later Visa) network sponsored by Bank of America.

By 1969, ICA was issuing the Master Charge card throughout the US and had formed alliances in Europe and Japan. In the mid-1970s ICA modernized its system, replacing telephone transaction authorization with a computerized magnetic strip system. ICA had members in Africa, Australia, and Europe by 1979. That year the organization changed its name (and the card's) to MasterCard.

In 1980 Russell Hogg became president when John Reynolds resigned after disagreeing with the board over company performance and direction. Hogg made major organizational changes and consolidated data processing in St. Louis. MasterCard began offering debit cards in 1980 and traveler's checks in 1981.

MasterCard issued the first credit cards in China in 1987. The next year it bought Cirrus, then the world's largest ATM network. It also secured Eurocard (now Europay) to supervise MasterCard's European operations and help build the brand.

Hogg resigned in 1988 after disagreements with the board and was succeeded by Alex Hart. In 1991 the Maestro debit card was unveiled.

The 1990s were marked by trouble in Europe: The Europay pact hadn't resulted in the boom MasterCard had hoped for, customer service was below par, and competition was keen. Alex Hart retired in 1994 and was succeeded by Eugene Lockhart, who tackled the European woes. Lockhart considered ending the relationship but eventually worked things out with Europay. By the end of the decade, Europay was locked in a vicious battle to undercut Visa's market share through lower fees.

MasterCard in 1995 invested in UK-based Mondex International (now 51% owned by MasterCard International), maker of electronic, set-value, refillable smart cards. But US consumer resistance to cash cards and competition in the more advanced European market delayed growth in this area.

Lockhart resigned in 1997 and was succeeded by former head of overseas operations Robert Selander. The next year the Justice Department sued MasterCard and Visa for prohibiting member banks from issuing competing credit cards, such as American Express' Optima. That year MasterCard and Visa came under scrutiny for attempting to create a debit card industry monopoly. Yet another management upheaval began in 1999 as the company moved to streamline its organizational structure and shift away from geographical divisions.

In 2000 the Justice Department charged MasterCard and Visa with antitrust practices stemming from the companies' cross-ownership structure and an alleged noncompetitive alliance between them. The next year a federal judge ordered the two companies to allow their member banks to issue rival credit cards, but the order has been stayed pending appeal.

In 2002 it merged with Europay International, the Belgium-based card company with which it already had close ties. As part of the transaction, holding company MasterCard Inc. was formed; MasterCard International become its main subsidiary, and Europay became its Europe Region.

Chairman Emeritus: Donald L. Boudreau
Chairman: Lance L. Weaver, age 47
President and CEO: Robert W. Selander, age 51,
$3,283,000 pay
President, Asia/Pacific Region: André Sekulic
President, Europe Region: Peter Hoch
President, Latin America/Caribbean Region:
Jean F. Rozwadowski
President, North American Region: Ruth Ann Marshall
SEVP, Customer Group: Alan J. Heuer, $1,475,000 pay
SEVP, Global Development: Christopher D. Thom,
$1,200,000 pay
SEVP, Global Technology and Operations:
Jerry McElhatton, $1,400,000 pay
EVP and CFO: Denise K. Fletcher, age 53, $825,000 pay
EVP and Chief Marketing Officer: Larry Flanagan
EVP, Central Resources: Michael W. Michl
EVP, Global Account Management: Gary Flood
Chief e-Business Officer, Global Development:
Arthur D. Kranzley
SVP and Controller: Spencer Schwarz
General Counsel and Secretary: Noah J. Hanft
President, MasterCard Canada: Walter M. Macnee
Regional President, South Asia/Middle East/Africa:
Sonny Sannon
Auditors: PricewaterhouseCoopers LLP

HQ: 2000 Purchase St., Purchase, NY 10577
Phone: 914-249-2000   **Fax:** 914-249-4206
Web: www.mastercard.com

MasterCard International has US offices in California, Delaware, Florida, Georgia, Illinois, Missouri, New York, and Washington, DC. It has international offices in Argentina, Australia, Belgium, Brazil, Canada, Chile, China, Colombia, Hong Kong, India, Indonesia, Japan, Malaysia, Mexico, the Philippines, Singapore, South Africa, South Korea, Taiwan, Thailand, the United Arab Emirates, the UK, and Venezuela. It provides services in more than 210 countries.

Products
Maestro (debit card)
MasterCard (credit card including standard, Gold, Platinum, and World cards, as well as business, business debit, corporate, corporate fleet, corporate purchasing, and executive cards)
MasterCard Global Service (telephone services)
MasterCard Online Exclusives (online promotions for cardholders)
MasterCard/Cirrus ATM network
Member Protection Program
Mondex (chip-based electronic cash card)

American Express
Morgan Stanley
Visa

Holding company FYE: December 31	Annual Growth	12/92	12/93	12/94	12/95	12/96	12/97	12/98	12/99	12/00	12/01
Sales ($ mil.)	16.5%	451	540	665	816	946	1,090	1,257	1,389	1,571	1,774
Net income ($ mil.)	42.7%	—	—	12	21	71	40	57	86	118	142
Income as % of sales	—	—	—	1.8%	2.6%	7.6%	3.6%	4.6%	6.2%	7.5%	8.0%
Employees	12.3%	—	1,300	1,975	2,000	2,025	2,357	2,400	2,700	3,100	3,300

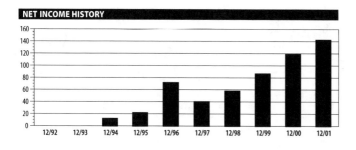

NET INCOME HISTORY

MAYO FOUNDATION

Mayo can whip up a medical miracle. The not-for-profit Mayo Foundation provides health care, most notably for difficult medical conditions, through its renowned Mayo Clinic in Rochester, Minnesota. Its multidisciplinary approach to care attracts some 500,000 patients a year, including such notables as Ronald and Nancy Reagan and the late King Hussein of Jordan. The Mayo Foundation also operates two major medical facilities, as well as a network of 13 affiliated community hospitals and clinics in several select states. The Mayo Foundation also conducts research and trains physicians, nurses, and other health professionals. The Mayo Foundation dates back to a frontier practice launched by William Mayo in 1863.

In addition to the Mayo Clinic, the foundation operates two other Rochester hospitals — Saint Mary's and Rochester Methodist. It has clinics in Arizona and Florida, and operates 13 hospitals in Iowa, Minnesota, and Wisconsin. At the University of Minnesota, the foundation's education programs include the Mayo Graduate School of Medicine and the Mayo School of Health-Related Sciences.

With managed care limiting patients' ability to use its facilities, Mayo forms referral alliances with hospital groups, HMOs, and other groups. Its charter prevents it from raising prices to compensate for rising health care costs, so the foundation commercializes medical technology, publishes medical literature, and invests in other medical startups to increase income. Also, affluent patients who can pay — well — for treatment (and who may contribute to the endowment) help subsidize care for those who can't pay.

HISTORY

In 1845 William Mayo came to the US from England. He was a doctor, veterinarian, river boatman, surveyor, and newspaper editor before settling in Rochester, Minnesota, in 1863.

When a tornado struck Rochester in 1883, Mayo took charge of a makeshift hospital. The Sisters of St. Francis offered to replace the hospital that was lost in the disaster if Mayo would head the staff. He agreed reluctantly. Not only were hospitals then associated with the poor and insane, but his affiliation with the sisters raised eyebrows among Protestants and Catholics.

Saint Marys Hospital opened in 1889. Mayo's sons William and Charles, who were starting their medical careers, helped him. After the elder Mayo retired, the sons ran the hospital. Although the brothers accepted all medical cases, they made the hospital self-sufficient, attracting paying patients by pioneering in specialization

at a time when physicians were jacks-of-all-medical-trades.

This specialization attracted other physicians, and by 1907 the practice was known as "the Mayo's clinic." The brothers, in association with the University of Minnesota, established the Mayo Foundation for Medical Research (now the Mayo Graduate School of Medicine), the world's first program to train medical specialists, in 1915.

In 1919 the brothers transferred the clinic properties and miscellaneous financial assets, primarily from patient care profits, into the Mayo Properties Association (renamed the Mayo Foundation in 1964). Under the terms of the endowment, all Mayo Clinic medical staff members became salaried employees. In 1933 the clinic established one of the first blood banks in the US. Both brothers died in 1939.

Part of the association's mission was to fund research. In 1950 two Mayo researchers won a Nobel Prize for developing cortisone to treat rheumatoid arthritis. The foundation opened its second medical school, the Mayo Medical School, in 1972.

As insurers in the 1980s pressured to cut hospital admissions and stays, the foundation diversified with for-profit ventures. In 1983 Mayo began publishing the *Mayo Clinic Health Letter*, its first subscription publication for a general audience, and the *Mayo Clinic Family Health Book*. It also began providing specialized lab services to other doctors and hospitals. The addition of Rochester Methodist Hospital (creating the largest not-for-profit medical group in the country) was also a response to financial pressures. Following the money south as affluent folks retired, the foundation opened clinics in Jacksonville (1986); Scottsdale, Arizona (1987); and in nearby Phoenix (1998).

Seeking to expand in its home market, Mayo in 1992 formed the Mayo Health System, a regional network of health care facilities and medical practices. In 1996 former patient Barbara Woodward Lips left $127.9 million to the foundation, the largest bequest in its history.

In the late 1990s the foundation increasingly looked to corporate partnerships to help defray costs and to expand research activities. In 1998 and 1999 Mayo boosted its presence overseas with nonmedical regional offices. Mayo scientists in 2000 announced they had regrown or repaired nerve coverings in mice; this type of damage in humans (caused by such conditions as multiple sclerosis) had been considered irreparable. The Mayo Foundation continues to push for breakthroughs in medical science.

Chairman, Mayo Foundation: Francis D. Fergusson, age 57
President and CEO, Mayo Foundation: Michael B. Wood
CFO and Treasurer, Mayo Foundation: David R. Ebel
VP and Director for Education:
Richard M. Weinshilboum
VP and Chief Administrative Officer: John H. Herrell, age 61
Chief Development Officer: David W. Lawrence
Secretary: Robert K. Smoldt
General Counsel: Jill A. Beed
Chair, Board of Governors, Mayo Clinic Jacksonville:
Leo F. Black
Chair, Board of Governors, Mayo Clinic Rochester:
Robert R. Hattery
Chair, Board of Governors, Mayo Clinic Scottsdale:
Michael B. O'Sullivan
Chair, Human Resources: Marita Heller

LOCATIONS

HQ: 200 1st St. SW, Rochester, MN 55905
Phone: 507-284-2511   **Fax:** 507-284-0161
Web: www.mayo.edu

The Mayo Foundation operates facilities in Rochester, Minnesota; Jacksonville, Florida; and Phoenix and Scottsdale, Arizona, it also has a network of community health care providers in Iowa, Minnesota, and Wisconsin.

PRODUCTS/OPERATIONS

Principal Divisions

Charter House, Rochester (retirement community)
Mayo Clinic Hospital, Phoenix
Mayo Clinic Jacksonville
Mayo Clinic Rochester
Mayo Clinic Scottsdale
Mayo Health System (network of clinics and hospitals in Iowa, Minnesota, and Wisconsin)
Rochester Methodist Hospital
St. Luke's Hospital, Jacksonville
Saint Marys Hospital, Rochester

Selected Mayo Publications

Publications for Patients
Inside Mayo Clinic (Rochester)
The Mayo Checkup (Jacksonville)
Mayo Clinic Complete Book of Pregnancy & Baby's First Year
Mayo Clinic Family Health Book
Mayo Clinic Guide to Self-Care
Mayo Clinic Health Letter
Mayo Clinic Heart Book
Mayo Clinic on Arthritis
Mayo Clinic on High Blood Pressure
The Mayo Clinic Williams-Sonoma Cookbook
Mayo Clinic Women's HealthSource
Perspectives on Mayo
Update (Scottsdale)

Publications for Physicians
Clinical Update
Dialogue
Mayo Clinic Cardiology Review
Mayo Clinic Proceedings
Mayo Medical Laboratories Communique
Mayo Medical Laboratories Interpretive Handbook
Medical Update (Jacksonville)

COMPETITORS

Allina Health
Ascension
Catholic Health Initiatives
Catholic Healthcare Partners
Detroit Medical Center
HCA
HEALTHSOUTH
Henry Ford Health System
HMA
Johns Hopkins Medicine
Memorial Sloan-Kettering
Methodist Health Care
New York City Health and Hospitals
Rush System for Health
Scripps
SSM Health Care
Tenet Healthcare
Trinity Health
Universal Health Services

HISTORICAL FINANCIALS & EMPLOYEES

Not-for-profit FYE: December 31	Annual Growth	12/92	12/93	12/94	12/95	12/96	12/97	12/98	12/99	12/00	12/01
Sales ($ mil.)	12.0%	1,490	1,579	1,873	2,189	2,348	2,566	2,370	2,750	3,710	4,135
Employees	9.2%	20,615	21,770	21,856	25,433	28,671	30,497	32,531	41,265	44,000	45,536

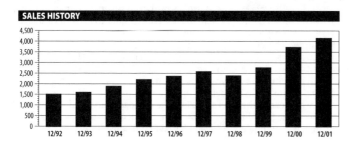

SALES HISTORY

MCKINSEY & COMPANY

Focusing on the big picture has made McKinsey & Company a big success. It is one of the world's top management consulting firms, with some 84 offices in 44 countries. The company provides a full spectrum of consulting services (finance, technology management, strategy) primarily to private companies. Recruiting the top graduates from business schools, it uses Darwinian "move up or get out" policies to weed out all but the best. McKinsey's reputation comes from a few basic ideals: The client's interests come first; be discreet; be honest; don't overextend yourself. Alumni include former American Express chairman Harvey Golub and former CBS chief Michael Jordan.

The Firm (as it is known to insiders) provides services in strategy, organization, corporate finance, and marketing, and is beefing up its capabilities in information technology, an area on which the consulting industry is increasingly focused. Its customers are mostly private companies, but McKinsey also serves government organizations, foundations, and associations. Additionally, the company runs the McKinsey Global Institute, an independent group that generates original research on economic, social, and geopolitical issues.

McKinsey's cachet comes from its devotion to the bottom line, meticulous data-gathering, discretion, and a carefully cultivated mystique. Its partners must survive a rigorous up-or-out weeding process in which failure to advance to higher levels means dismissal. The economic downturn has taken its toll on the consulting industry, and McKinsey has found itself competing fiercely with other firms for fewer clients and having more consultants on its hands. (Employees are staying put instead of leaving for Internet startups and venture capital firms.)

The company has also faced increasing scrutiny for its ties to and consulting done for such troubled companies as Enron, Global Crossing, and Kmart.

McKinsey is owned by its partners and led by a managing director.

HISTORY

McKinsey & Company was founded in Chicago in 1926 by University of Chicago accounting professor James McKinsey. The company evolved from an auditing practice of McKinsey and his partners, Marvin Bower and A. T. Kearney, who began analyzing business and industry and offering advice. McKinsey died in 1937; two years later, Bower, who headed the New York office, and Kearney, in Chicago, split the firm. Kearney renamed the Chicago office A. T. Kearney & Co., and Bower kept the McKinsey name and built up a practice structured like a law firm.

Bower focused on the big picture instead of on specific operating problems, helping boost billings to $2 million by 1950. He hired staff straight out of prestigious business schools, reinforcing the firm's theoretical bent. Bower implemented a competitive up-or-out policy requiring employees who are not regularly promoted to leave the firm. Only 20% of associates become partners.

Before becoming president in 1953, Dwight Eisenhower asked McKinsey to find out exactly what the government did.

By 1959 Bower had opened an office in London, followed by others in Amsterdam; Dusseldorf, Germany; Melbourne; Paris; and Zurich. In 1964 the company founded management journal *The McKinsey Quarterly*. When Bower retired in 1967, sales were $20 million and McKinsey was the #1 management consulting firm. During the 1970s, facing competition from firms with newer approaches, it lost market share. In response, then-managing director Ronald Daniel started specialty practices and expanded foreign operations.

The consulting boom of the 1980s was spurred by mergers and buyouts. By 1988 the firm had 1,800 consultants, sales were $620 million, and 50% of billings came from overseas.

The recession of the early 1990s hit white-collar workers, including consultants. McKinsey, scrambling to upgrade its technical side, bought Information Consulting Group (ICG), its first acquisition. But the corporate cultures did not meld, and most ICG people left by 1993.

In 1994 the company elected its first managing director of non-European descent, Indian-born Rajat Gupta. Two years later the traditionally hush-hush firm found itself at the center of that most-public 1990s arena, the sexual discrimination lawsuit. A female ex-consultant in Texas sued, claiming McKinsey had sabotaged her career. (The case was dismissed.)

In 1998 McKinsey joined with Northwestern University and the University of Pennsylvania to establish a world-class business school in India. The following year, graduating seniors surveyed in Europe, the UK, and the US named the company as their ideal employer.

Also in 1999 the company created @McKinsey to help "accelerate" Internet startups. The next year it increased salaries and offered incentives to better compete with Internet firms for employees. In 2001 the company expanded its branding business with the acquisition of Envision, a Chicago-based brand consultant.

OFFICERS

Managing Director: Rajat Gupta
CFO: Donna Rosenwasser
Director of Personnel: Jerome Vascellaro
Director of Communications: Javier Perez

LOCATIONS

HQ: 55 E. 52nd St., New York, NY 10022
Phone: 212-446-7000   **Fax:** 212-446-8575
Web: www.mckinsey.com

McKinsey & Company has 84 offices in 44 countries.

Selected Office Locations
Amsterdam
Atlanta
Bangkok
Beijing
Boston
Buenos Aires
Dublin
Geneva
Helsinki, Finland
Hong Kong
Kuala Lumpur, Malaysia
London
Los Angeles
Milan
Montreal
Moscow
Paris
Santiago, Chile
Singapore
Sydney
Tokyo
Toronto
Washington, DC
Zurich

PRODUCTS/OPERATIONS

Selected Areas of Practice
Automotive
Banking and securities
Chemicals
Consumer industries and packaged goods
Corporate finance
Corporate strategy
High tech
Insurance
Marketing
Operational effectiveness
Payors and providers
Pharmaceuticals and medical products
Pulp and paper
Retail
Telecommunications
Travel and logistics

COMPETITORS

Accenture
A.T. Kearney
Bain & Company
BearingPoint
Booz Allen
Boston Consulting
Cap Gemini
Computer Sciences
Deloitte Consulting
Grant Thornton International
IBM
Mercer Consulting
Perot Systems

HISTORICAL FINANCIALS & EMPLOYEES

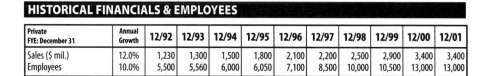

Private FYE: December 31	Annual Growth	12/92	12/93	12/94	12/95	12/96	12/97	12/98	12/99	12/00	12/01
Sales ($ mil.)	12.0%	1,230	1,300	1,500	1,800	2,100	2,200	2,500	2,900	3,400	3,400
Employees	10.0%	5,500	5,560	6,000	6,050	7,100	8,500	10,000	10,500	13,000	13,000

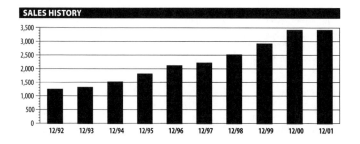

SALES HISTORY

MEIJER, INC.

Meijer (pronounced "Meyer") is the green giant of retailing in the Midwest. The company operates nearly 160 combination grocery and general merchandise stores; more than half are in Michigan, while the rest are in Illinois, Indiana, Kentucky, and Ohio. Its huge stores (which average 200,000 to 250,000 sq. ft. each, or about the size of four regular grocery stores) stock about 120,000 items, including Meijer private-label products. Customers can choose from about 40 departments, including hardware, apparel, toys, and electronics. Most stores also sell gasoline, offer banking services, and have multiple in-store restaurants. Founder Hendrik Meijer opened his first store in 1934; the company is still family-owned.

Although the discount superstore format is most often referred to in conjunction with rival Wal-Mart, Meijer is its pioneer. But that hasn't stopped the world's #1 retailer from muscling in on Meijer's markets. Wal-Mart has 14 supercenters in Michigan; eight in communities that also have a Meijer store. Meijer is responding by cutting prices, putting some expansion plans on hold, and renovating some older stores.

The retailer launched a "reinvented superstore format" at six Dayton, Ohio-area stores in late 2002. The makeover emphasizes discount fashion (featuring brands such as Levi's, Dockers, and Gotcha) in a department store atmosphere.

HISTORY

Dutch immigrant and barber Hendrik Meijer owned a vacant space next to his barbershop in Greenville, Michigan. Because of the Depression, he couldn't rent it out. So in 1934 he bought $338.76 in merchandise on credit and started his own grocery store, Thrift Market, with the help of his wife, Gezina; son, Fred; and daughter, Johanna. He made $7 the first day. Meijer had 22 competitors in Greenville alone, but his dedication to low prices attracted customers (he and Fred often traveled long distances to find bargains). In 1935, to encourage self-service, Meijer placed 12 wicker baskets at the front of the store and posted signs that read, "Take a basket. Help yourself."

A second store was opened in 1942. The company added four more in the 1950s. In 1962 Meijer — then with 14 stores — opened the first one-stop shopping Meijer Thrifty Acres store, similar to a hypermarket another operator had opened in Belgium a year earlier. By 1964, the year that Hendrik died and Fred took over, three of these general merchandise stores were operating. The company entered Ohio in the late 1960s.

In the early 1980s Meijer bought 14 Twin Fair stores in Ohio, 10 of them in Cincinnati. But it sold the stores by 1987 after disappointing results. Meijer had greater success in Columbus, Ohio, where it opened one store that year and immediately captured 20% of the market. In 1988 the company began keeping most stores open 24 hours a day.

In 1991 Meijer annihilated competitors in Dayton, Ohio, when it opened four stores. The company entered the Toledo market in 1993 with four stores; after one year it had taken 11.5% of the market. A foray into the membership warehouse market was abandoned in 1993. Meijer closed all seven SourceClubs in Michigan and Ohio just a few months after they had opened.

The company entered Indiana in 1994, opening 16 stores in less than two years; it also reached an agreement with McDonald's to open restaurants in several stores. The first labor strike in Meijer's history hit four stores in Toledo that year, leading to pickets at 14 others. Union officials accused the company of using intimidation tactics by its hiring of large, uniformed men in flak jackets and combat boots as security guards. After nine weeks Meijer agreed to recognize the workers' newly attained union affiliation.

In 1995 the company opened 13 stores, including its first in Illinois. It reentered the Cincinnati market in 1996, announcing the opening of two new stores there by mailing 80,000 videos to residents. By the end of the year, Meijer had a total of five stores in Cincinnati and had entered Kentucky.

In 1997 Meijer opened a central kitchen in Indiana to prepare deli salads and vegetables and to process orange juice for its stores. It opened its first two stores in Louisville, Kentucky, the following year. Meijer broke into the tough Chicago-area market with its first store in 1999.

The next year Meijer opened several "village-style" stores — scaled-down versions of its larger stores (about 155,000 sq. ft.). Later in 2000 Meijer unveiled what it claimed to be the largest superstore in North America. The 255,000-sq.-ft. behemoth (compared to a Wal-Mart Supercenter, which averages about 183,106 sq. ft.) features a gourmet coffee shop, a card shop, a bank open seven days a week, and restaurants serving pizza and sushi.

In February 2002 co-chairman Hank Meijer was named CEO, succeeding Jim McClean, who had run the company since 1999.

OFFICERS

Chairman Emeritus: Fred Meijer, age 82
Co-Chairman and CEO: Hendrik G. "Hank" Meijer, age 49
Co-Chairman: Doug Meijer, age 48
President and COO: Paul Boyer, age 56
SVP, Finance and Administration; CFO: Jim Walsh
SVP, Human Resources: Wendell Ray
SVP, Merchandising: Dave Perron
SVP, Public and Consumer Affairs: Brian Breslin
VP, Fashion Merchandising: Jo Ann Ogee
Director, Corporate Relations: John Zimmerman

LOCATIONS

HQ: 2929 Walker Ave. NW, Grand Rapids, MI 49544
Phone: 616-453-6711   **Fax:** 616-791-2572
Web: www.meijer.com

2002 Stores

	No.
Michigan	78
Ohio	36
Indiana	25
Kentucky	8
Illinois	7
Total	**154**

PRODUCTS/OPERATIONS

Selected Meijer Store Departments

Apparel	Jewelry
Auto supplies	Lawn and garden
Bakery	Music
Banking	Nutrition products
Books	Paint
Bulk foods	Pets and pet supplies
Coffee shop	Pharmacy
Computer software	Photo lab
Dairy	Portrait studio
Delicatessen	Produce
Electronics	Service meat and seafood
Floral	Small appliances
Food court	Soup and salad bar
Gas station	Sporting goods
Hardware	Tobacco
Health and beauty products	Toys
	Wall coverings
Home fashions	Wine

COMPETITORS

A&P	Kroger
Albertson's	Marsh Supermarkets
ALDI	Penn Traffic
CVS	Roundy's
D&W Food Centers	Schnuck Markets
Dollar General	Schottenstein Stores
Dominick's	Spartan Stores
Eagle Food	SUPERVALU
Family Dollar Stores	Target
Fleming Companies	Value City
Home Depot	Walgreen
IGA	Wal-Mart
Kmart	Winn-Dixie

HISTORICAL FINANCIALS & EMPLOYEES

Private FYE: January 31	Annual Growth	1/93	1/94	1/95	1/96	1/97	1/98	1/99	1/00	1/01	1/02
Estimated sales ($ mil.)	7.8%	5,390	4,250	5,160	5,640	6,000	6,900	8,300	9,500	10,000	10,600
Employees	3.7%	60,000	65,000	70,000	65,000	73,000	77,000	80,000	80,000	80,000	83,402

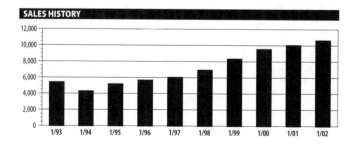

SALES HISTORY

MENARD, INC.

If sticks and stones break bones, what can two-by-fours and 2-inch nails do? That is what Menard is wondering now that its biggest rivals (#1 home-improvement giant The Home Depot and #2 Lowe's) are hammering away at its home turf. The third-largest home-improvement chain in the US, Menard has about 160 stores in Illinois, Indiana, Iowa, Michigan, Minnesota, Nebraska, North and South Dakota, and Wisconsin. The stores sell home-improvement products, such as floor coverings, hardware, millwork, paint, and tools; unlike its competitors, all the company's stores have full-service lumberyards. Menard is owned by president and CEO John Menard, who founded the company in 1972.

Although Menard outlets are typically smaller than those of Home Depot, they offer a similar selection of products by building large warehouses adjacent to stores, and then quickly restocking merchandise it's sold. The company has announced, however, that its average store size will be increased to 225,000 sq. ft., with plans to soon add 15 to 20 of these larger stores through new construction or renovation.

The company's products are laid out on easy-to-reach, supermarket-styled shelves. To help keep expenses low and prices cheap, Menard makes some of its merchandise, including picnic tables and doors.

Billionaire Menard runs the chain; other family members are engaged in its everyday operations. Menard also owns Team Menard, an Indy car-racing team.

HISTORY

John Menard was the oldest of eight children on a Wisconsin dairy farm. To pay for attending the University of Wisconsin at Eau Claire, he and some fellow college students built pole barns in the late 1950s. After learning that other builders had trouble finding lumber outlets open on the weekends, Menard began buying wood in bulk and selling it to them. He added other supplies in 1960, then sold his construction business in 1970 as building supply revenues became his chief source of income.

He founded Menard in 1972 as the do-it-yourself craze was beginning, but he wanted an operation run more like mass merchandiser Target, with easy-to-reach shelves, wide aisles, and tile floors rather than the cold, cumbersome layout used by lumberyards. To realize that concept, Menard built stockrooms and warehouses behind the stores so he could restock merchandise quickly.

Menard's vision worked, and he began building his midwestern empire, often acquiring abandoned retail sites that were inexpensive and in good locations. By 1986 Menard was in Iowa, Minnesota, North and South Dakota, and Wisconsin, and by 1990 it had 46 stores. In the early 1990s Menard began enlarging its operations to serve the ever-growing number of stores, opening a huge warehouse and distribution center and a manufacturing facility that made doors, Formica countertops, and other products. It entered Nebraska in 1990 and opened its first store in Chicago the next year. By 1992 there were more than 60 stores.

That year Menard made the *National Enquirer* with a story about the firing of a store manager who had built a wheelchair-accessible home for his 11-year-old daughter with spina bifida, violating a company theft-prevention policy forbidding store managers to build their own homes. The company insisted that the man was fired in part because of poor work performance.

Menard continued to expand to new areas, operating stores in Indiana and Michigan by 1992. As it continued expanding in the Chicago area, it offered varying store formats, ranging from a full line of building materials to smaller Menards Hardware Plus stores. By 1994 Menard had 85 stores, many larger than 100,000 sq. ft.

In 1995 and 1996 the company was plagued with lawsuits filed by customers charging false arrest and imprisonment for shoplifting. An on-duty police officer apprehending a shoplifting suspect at a store was even stopped and searched.

Competition also heated up during that time. The Home Depot's push into the Midwest — including opening several stores directly across the street from Menard — spurred Menard to fight back by lowering prices and opening nearly 40 stores. The fight forced smaller chains like Handy Andy out of business.

In 1997 Menard and his company were fined $1.7 million after dumping bags of toxic ash from the company's manufacturing facility at residential trash pick-up sites rather than at properly regulated outlets. (It had been fined for similar violations in 1989 and 1994.) In response to a price war initiated by Home Depot, in 1998 Menard dropped sales prices by 10%.

In 1999 competitor Lowe's began moving into Menard's biggest market, Chicago. Menard started opening larger stores in 2000 (about 162,000 sq. ft., some 74,000 sq. ft. bigger than the older stores). In 2001 it began beefing up its lines of home appliances, adding more washers, dryers, dishwashers, refrigerators, and ranges.

President and CEO: John R. Menard Jr., age 62
CFO and Treasurer: Earl R. Rasmussen
Operations Manager: Larry Menard
Director of Human Resources: Terri Jain
Senior Merchandiser: Ed Archibald
General Counsel: Dawn M. Sands

LOCATIONS

HQ: 4777 Menard Dr., Eau Claire, WI 54703
Phone: 715-876-5911   **Fax:** 715-876-2868
Web: www.menards.com/nindex.html

Menard owns home improvement stores in Illinois, Indiana, Iowa, Michigan, Minnesota, Nebraska, North Dakota, South Dakota, and Wisconsin.

PRODUCTS/OPERATIONS

Selected Departments
Appliances
Building materials
Electrical (wiring, lighting)
Floor coverings
Hardware
Lumberyard
Millwork (doors, cabinetry, molding)
Plumbing
Seasonal (Christmas, lawn and garden)
Tools
Wall coverings (wallpaper, paint)

COMPETITORS

84 Lumber
Ace Hardware
Carolina Holdings
Carter Lumber
Do it Best
Fastenal
Home Depot
Lanoga
Lowe's
Primus
Sears
Seigle's Home and Building Centers
Sherwin-Williams
Sutherland Lumber
TruServ
Wal-Mart
Wickes
Wolohan Lumber

HISTORICAL FINANCIALS & EMPLOYEES

Private FYE: January 31	Annual Growth	1/93	1/94	1/95	1/96	1/97	1/98	1/99	1/00	1/01	1/02
Estimated sales ($ mil.)	15.9%	1,400	1,750	2,300	2,700	3,200	3,700	4,000	4,500	5,000	5,300
Employees	7.9%	—	5,000	5,800	6,534	7,000	7,000	7,000	7,000	7,600	9,200

SALES HISTORY

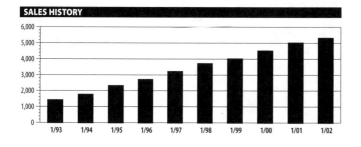

METROMEDIA COMPANY

Do you want a side of fiber optics with your steak? One of the US's largest private companies, Metromedia owns or franchises some 1,000 Ponderosa, Bennigan's, Bonanza, and Steak and Ale restaurants worldwide. Through Metromedia International Group, it has interests in telecommunications ventures in Eastern Europe and the former Soviet Union. These include cable TV, wireless and land-based phone systems, radio stations, and toll-calling services. Metromedia also controls Metromedia Fiber Network, which operates fiber-optic networks in urban areas. Its Metromedia Energy is an energy broker and provider of long-distance telephone services.

In 2002 Metromedia Fiber Network filed for Chapter 11 bankruptcy, citing a lower-than-expected demand for broadband connections in large cities. Billionaire investors John Kluge (chairman) and Stuart Subotnick (EVP) run the company through a partnership.

HISTORY

German immigrant John Kluge, born in 1914, came to Detroit at age eight with his mother and stepfather. He later worked at the Ford assembly line. At Columbia University he studied economics and (to the chagrin of college administrators) poker, building a tidy sum with his winnings by graduation. Kluge worked in Army intelligence during WWII. After the war he bought WGAY radio in Silver Spring, Maryland, and went on to buy and sell other small radio stations.

Kluge began to diversify, entering the wholesale food business in the mid-1950s. In 1959 he purchased control of Metropolitan Broadcasting, including TV stations in New York and Washington, DC, and took it public. He renamed the company Metromedia in 1960.

Metromedia added independent stations — to the then-legal limit of seven — in other major markets, paying relatively little compared to network affiliate prices. The stations struggled through years of infomercials but thrived in the late 1970s and early 1980s. Metromedia's stock price rose from $4.50 in 1974 to more than $500 in 1983. The company also acquired radio stations, the Harlem Globetrotters, and the Ice Capades.

In 1983 Kluge bought paging and cellular telephone licenses across the US. He later acquired long-distance carriers in Texas and Florida. In 1984 Metromedia went private in a $1.6 billion buyout and began to sell off its assets in 1985. It sold its Boston TV station to Hearst and its six other TV stations to Rupert Murdoch for a total of $2 billion. In 1986 it sold its outdoor advertising firm, nine of its 11 radio stations, and the

Globetrotters and Ice Capades. Kluge then sold most of the company's cellular properties to SBC Communications. In 1990 it sold its New York cellular operations to LIN Broadcasting and its Philadelphia cellular operations to Comcast.

Building what Kluge envisioned as his steakhouse empire, the firm bought the Ponderosa steak-house chain (founded in the late 1960s) in 1988 from Asher Edelman and later added Dallas-based USA Cafes (Bonanza steak houses, founded 1964) and S&A Restaurant Corp. (Steak and Ale, founded 1966; Bennigan's, founded 1976). Also in 1988 Kluge rescued friend Arthur Krim, whose Orion Pictures was threatened by Viacom, by buying control of the filmmaker.

Kluge's grand steak-house vision did not come to fruition. Increased competition squeezed profits at Ponderosa and Bonanza. The restaurant group also was plagued by management shake-ups, aging facilities, food-quality issues, and even bad press. (Bennigan's was ranked the worst casual dining chain in the US in a 1992 Consumer Reports poll.)

In 1989 Kluge merged Metromedia Long Distance with the long-distance operations of ITT. Renamed Metromedia Communications in 1991, the company merged with other long-distance providers to become MCI WorldCom. (Kluge sold his 16% of MCI WorldCom to the public in 1995.)

In 1995 Kluge created Metromedia International Group by merging Orion Pictures, Metromedia International Telecommunications, MCEG Sterling (film and television production), and Actava Group (maker of Snapper lawn mowers and sporting goods, sold 2002). Metromedia Restaurant Group announced a $190 million refinancing agreement for S&A Restaurant Corp. in 1998 to expand and refurbish its restaurants; it closed 28 unprofitable restaurants that year and launched a franchise program to grow its Bennigan's and Steak and Ale chains.

Metromedia expanded its Bennigan's units in South Korea in 1999, and the next year announced it would build 65 new restaurants in the US and expand to more than 200 units internationally. In 2001 Verizon Communications invested nearly $2 billion in Metromedia Fiber Network, but the latter company was forced to declare Chapter 11 bankruptcy the following year. It claimed that lower-than-expected demand for its metropolitan Internet services was due to stiff competition, which had driven down prices.

OFFICERS

Chairman and President: John W. Kluge, age 87
EVP; President and CEO, Metromedia International Group: Stuart Subotnick, age 60
SVP Finance; Treasurer: Robert A. Maresca
SVP, Secretary, and General Counsel: David A. Persing, age 44
SVP: Silvia Kessel, age 51
VP and Controller: David Gassler
President, Metromedia Restaurant Group: Michael Kaufman
President, Steak and Ale, Metromedia Restaurant Group: Bob Mandes
President, Ponderosa Steakhouse and Bonanza Steakhouse, Metromedia Restaurant Group: Doug Barber
International President and EVP Worldwide Franchising, Metromedia Restaurant Group: John Wright
EVP, Metromedia Restaurant Group: Bob Meyers
SVP Operations, Ponderosa Steakhouse and Bonanza Steakhouse, Metromedia Restaurant Group: Bill Spae
SVP Franchising, Ponderosa Steakhouse and Bonanza Steakhouse, Metromedia Restaurant Group: Gary Schneider
SVP Marketing, Ponderosa Steakhouse and Bonanza Steakhouse, Metromedia Restaurant Group: Craig Held
SVP Human Resources, Ponderosa Steakhouse and Bonanza Steakhouse, Metromedia Restaurant Group: Dave Evans
VP Corporate and Brand Relationships, Metromedia Restaurant Group: Peggy Marshall-Mims
VP Culinary Services, Metromedia Restaurant Group: Paul Freeman
VP Research and Analysis, Metromedia Restaurant Group: Sonja Partin
VP Business Process and Education, Bennigan's, Metromedia Restaurant Group: Gilbert Melott
VP Finance, Bennigan's, Metromedia Restaurant Group: Ted Beaman
VP Franchise Operations, Bennigan's, Metromedia Restaurant Group: Hank Simpson
VP Human Resources, Bennigan's, Metromedia Restaurant Group: Maureen Underwood
VP Marketing, Bennigan's, Metromedia Restaurant Group: John Beck

LOCATIONS

HQ: 1 Meadowlands Plaza, East Rutherford, NJ 07073
Phone: 201-531-8000   **Fax:** 201-531-2804
Web: www.metromediarestaurants.com

PRODUCTS/OPERATIONS

Selected Subsidiaries and Affiliates
Metromedia Energy (energy and long-distance telephone service)
Metromedia Fiber Network, Inc. (competitive local-exchange carrier)
AboveNet Communications, Inc. (data center operations)
SiteSmith, Inc. (Internet infrastructure management services)
Metromedia International Group, Inc. (telecommunications)
Metromedia Restaurant Group (Bennigan's, Bonanza, Ponderosa, Steak and Ale)

COMPETITORS

AT&T
Applebee's
Brinker
BT
Buffets
Carlson Restaurants Worldwide
Darden Restaurants
Deutsche Telekom
Hellenic Telecommunications
Level 3 Communications
Lone Star Steakhouse
O'Charley's
Outback Steakhouse
The Restaurant Company
Rostelecom
Ryan's Family Steak Houses
Sprint FON
Verizon
WorldCom
Worldwide Restaurant Concepts

HISTORICAL FINANCIALS & EMPLOYEES

Private FYE: December 31	Annual Growth	12/92	12/93	12/94	12/95	12/96	12/97	12/98	12/99	12/00	12/01
Estimated sales ($ mil.)	(2.8%)	1,804	1,900	2,000	1,900	1,900	1,950	1,500	1,610	1,500	1,400
Employees	(18.0%)	—	—	—	—	—	63,000	62,700	32,000	29,500	28,500

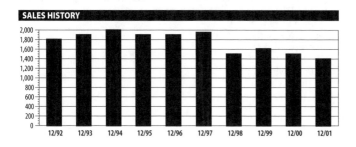

SALES HISTORY

MTA

No Sigma Chi or Delta Delta Delta chapter has anything on New York City's Metropolitan Transportation Authority (MTA) — it rushes almost 8 million people on an average day. The largest public transportation system in the US, the government-owned MTA moves more than 2.3 billion passengers a year. The MTA runs a fleet of about 5,000 buses in New York City's five boroughs, provides subway service to all but Staten Island, and operates the Staten Island Railway. It also offers bus and rail service to Connecticut and Long Island and maintains toll bridges and tunnels.

The MTA, a public-benefit corporation chartered by the New York Legislature, is working to become more self-sufficient. It has cut expenses through more efficient administration and maintenance. The agency also has introduced electronic fare collection (MetroCard) and toll collection (E-Z Pass).

Facing a $663 million budget gap for the 2003 fiscal year, the MTA has authorized the sale of nearly $2.9 billion worth of transportation bonds, the largest bond issue in the agency's history. The MTA hopes the proceeds from the bonds will help stave off a fare increase.

HISTORY

Mass transit began in New York City in the 1820s with the introduction of horse-drawn stagecoaches run by small private firms. By 1832 a horse-drawn railcar operating on Fourth Avenue offered a smoother and faster ride than its street-bound rivals.

By 1864 New York residents were complaining that horsecars and buses were overcrowded and that drivers were rude. (Horsecars were transporting 45 million passengers annually.) In 1870 a short subway under Broadway was opened, but it remained a mere amusement. Elevated steam railways were built, but people avoided them because of the smoke, noise, and danger from explosions. Cable cars arrived in the 1880s, and by the 1890s electric streetcars became important.

Construction of the first commercial subway line was completed in 1904. The line was operated by Interborough Rapid Transit (IRT), which leased the primary elevated rail line in 1903 and had effective control of rail transit in Manhattan and the Bronx. In 1905 IRT merged with the Metropolitan Street Railway, which ran most of the surface railways in Manhattan, giving the firm almost complete control of the city's rapid transit. Public protests led the city to grant licenses to Brooklyn Rapid Transit (later BMT), creating the Dual System. The two rail firms covered most of the city.

By the 1920s the transit system was again in crisis, largely because the two lines were not allowed to raise their five-cent fares. With the IRT and BMT in receivership in 1932, the city decided to own and operate part of the rail system and organized the Independent (IND) rail line. Pressure for public ownership and operation of the transit system resulted in the city's purchase of all of IRT's and BMT's assets in 1940 for $326 million.

In 1953 the legislature created the New York City Transit Authority, the first unified system. In 1968, two years after striking transit workers left the city in a virtual gridlock, the Metropolitan Transit Authority began to coordinate the city's transit activities with other commuter services.

The 1970s and 1980s saw the city's transit infrastructure and service deteriorate as crime, accidents, and fares rose. But by the early 1990s a modernization program had begun to make improvements: Subway stations were repaired, graffiti was removed from trains, and service was extended. By 1994 the agency said subway crime was down 50% from 1990, and ridership had increased.

The MTA set up a five-year plan in 1995 to cut expenses by $3 billion. Only 18 months later and already two-thirds of the way to reaching the goal, the authority said it would cut another $230 million and return the savings to customers as fare discounts. The agency agreed in 1996 to sell Long Island Rail Road's freight operations. The next year it began selling its one-fare/free-transfer MetroCard Gold.

In 1998 the MTA capital program completed the $200 million restoration of the Grand Central Terminal. The next year the MTA ordered 500 new clean-fuel buses. But the agency suffered a setback in 2000 when New York State's $3.8 billion Transportation Infrastructure Bond Act, which included $1.6 billion for MTA improvements, was rejected by voters.

MTA subway lines in lower Manhattan suffered extensive damage from the September 11, 2001, terrorist attacks that destroyed the World Trade Center's twin towers. The attacks left the MTA (which was already seeking billions of dollars for improvements) facing $530 million worth of damage.

OFFICERS

Chairman and CEO: Peter S. Kalikow
Vice Chairman: David S. Mack
Executive Director and COO: Katherine N. Lapp
Deputy Executive Director Corporate Affairs and Communications: Christopher P. Boylan
Deputy Executive Director and Director of Security: Louis R. Anemone
Deputy Executive Director, General Counsel, and Secretary: Mary J. Mahon
President, MTA Bridges and Tunnels: Michael C. Ascher
President, MTA Long Island Bus: Neil S. Yellin
President, MTA Long Island Rail Road: Kenneth J. Bauer
President, MTA Metro-North Railroad: Peter A. Cannito
President, MTA New York City Transit: Lawrence G. Reuter
Director Budgets and Financial Management: Gary G. Caplan
Director Human Resources: Margaret Connor
Auditor General: Paul Spinelli
Chief of Staff: Maureen E. Boll
Auditors: PricewaterhouseCoopers LLP

LOCATIONS

HQ: Metropolitan Transportation Authority
347 Madison Ave., New York, NY 10017
Phone: 212-878-7000   **Fax:** 212-878-0186
Web: www.mta.nyc.ny.us

MTA New York City Transit operates buses in all five New York City boroughs and provides subway service to all but Staten Island. It also maintains seven bridges and two tunnels in New York City. The MTA Staten Island Railway extends from the Staten Island Ferry landing 14 miles south to Tottenville. MTA Metro-North Railroad has rail lines to outlying counties in New York and Connecticut. MTA Long Island Bus operates buses in Nassau, Queens, and Suffolk counties. MTA Long Island Rail Road has rail lines to Nassau and Suffolk counties.

PRODUCTS/OPERATIONS

Selected Operating Units
The Long Island Rail Road Company (MTA Long Island Rail Road)
Metro-North Commuter Railroad Company (MTA Metro-North Railroad)
Metropolitan Suburban Bus Authority (MTA Long Island Bus)
New York City Transit Authority (MTA New York City Transit)
Staten Island Rapid Transit Operating Authority (MTA Staten Island Railway)
Triborough Bridge and Tunnel Authority (MTA Bridges and Tunnels)

COMPETITORS

Amtrak
BostonCoach
Coach USA
Laidlaw
Port Authority of NY & NJ
SuperShuttle International

HISTORICAL FINANCIALS & EMPLOYEES

Government-owned FYE: December 31	Annual Growth	12/92	12/93	12/94	12/95	12/96	12/97	12/98	12/99	12/00	12/01
Sales ($ mil.)	(2.0%)	4,845	5,036	5,189	5,005	5,381	5,511	5,707	5,590	4,033	4,052
Net income ($ mil.)	—	(173)	(136)	(156)	(154)	440	(93)	(7)	(489)	(386)	(1,170)
Income as % of sales	—	—	—	—	—	8.2%	—	—	—	—	—
Employees	0.1%	63,868	64,838	65,465	58,201	56,551	57,563	57,551	58,000	62,800	64,169

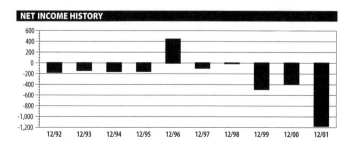

NET INCOME HISTORY

MIDAMERICAN ENERGY HOLDINGS

There's a new kind of twister tearin' up Tornado Alley. MidAmerican Energy Holdings generates, transmits, and distributes electricity to more than 670,000 customers and distributes natural gas to 650,000 customers in four Midwest states through subsidiary MidAmerican Energy Company. Its UK regional distribution subsidiary, Northern Electric, serves about 3.6 million electricity customers. MidAmerican Energy Holdings also has independent power production; real estate; and gas exploration, production, and pipeline operations. Warren Buffett's Berkshire Hathaway and other investors own the company.

MidAmerican Energy Company distributes electricity in Iowa, South Dakota, and Illinois; it distributes natural gas in those three states plus Nebraska. It also generates 4,500 MW of electricity (primarily from coal-fired plants) and sells wholesale energy to other utilities and marketers. MidAmerican Energy Holdings' residential real estate brokerage, HomeServices.Com, operates in 14 states in the US. Subsidiary CalEnergy has nearly 1,600 MW of capacity from independent power projects in the US and the Philippines.

MidAmerican Energy Holdings, which once focused on building and operating geothermal, hydroelectric, and natural gas power plants worldwide, now gets most of its revenues from its energy distribution operations. While deregulation led many utilities into the independent power production business, MidAmerican Energy Holdings diversified by purchasing regulated utilities in the US and abroad.

MidAmerican Energy Holdings was purchased by Berkshire Hathaway and other investors in 2000. Because of regulatory restrictions on utility ownership, Berkshire owns the majority of MidAmerican Energy Holdings' stock but has less than 10% of its voting control. Buffett business partner and Berkshire director Walter Scott controls a majority of MidAmerican Energy Holdings' voting rights.

HISTORY

Amid oil shortages, polluted air, and concerns about the safety of nuclear power plants, Charles Condy formed California Energy in 1971 to sell oil and gas partnerships and to consult on the development of geothermal power plants.

In 1978 Congress passed the Public Utility Regulatory Policies Act (PURPA) to wean the US from foreign oil by encouraging efficient use of fossil fuels and development of renewable and alternative energy sources. Grasping the potential of the changing energy environment, CalEnergy signed a 30-year deal with the US government in 1979 to develop the geothermal Coso Project

northeast of Los Angeles. In the 1980s CalEnergy focused entirely on geothermal development. It started producing power at the Coso Project in 1987, the year the company went public.

Omaha, Nebraska-based construction firm Peter Kiewit Sons' injected some much-needed capital by buying a stake in the company in 1990. CalEnergy restructured in 1991, moving its headquarters from San Francisco to Omaha. It also acquired Desert Peak and Roosevelt Hot Springs geothermal areas in the US and made plans to enter markets in Asia. In 1993 the Philippine government contracted CalEnergy to develop geothermal projects. CalEnergy also obtained the rights to exploit geothermal fields in Indonesia. In 1994 the company opened a geothermal plant in Yuma, Arizona.

In 1996 CalEnergy doubled its size by acquiring rival Magma Power, and it began geothermal projects in the Salton Sea and the Imperial Valley in California. It also took advantage of the growing deregulation trend in the UK by acquiring a controlling stake in Northern Electric, a major British regional electricity company with about 1.5 million customers in northeast England and Wales.

Completing its transformation into a global power player, CalEnergy acquired gas plants in Poland and Australia in 1997. It also attracted 300,000 new gas customers in the UK. The company bought back Kiewit's stake that year. In 1998 CalEnergy subsidiary CalEnergy International Ltd. was part of a consortium (the PowerBridge Group) that won a contract to develop, synchronize, and transmit up to 1,000 MW of electricity from Lithuania to Poland at an estimated cost of $400 million.

The next year CalEnergy bought MidAmerican Energy Holdings, an electric utility, for about $2.4 billion. CalEnergy took the MidAmerican name and moved its headquarters to Des Moines, Iowa. Subsidiary MidAmerican Realty Services went public as HomeServices.Com; MidAmerican Energy Holdings retained a majority stake. In 2000 Warren Buffett's Berkshire Hathaway led an investor group, which included MidAmerican Energy Holdings CEO David Sokol, in purchasing MidAmerican Energy Holdings for about $2 billion and $7 billion in assumed debt.

In 2001 MidAmerican Energy Holdings bought out minority shareholders in HomeServices.Com, making it a wholly owned subsidiary. It also traded Northern Electric's electricity and gas retail supply operations for Innogy's Yorkshire Electricity distribution business.

The following year the company purchased The Williams Companies' Kern River Gas Transmission subsidiary, which operates a 926-mile interstate pipeline in the western US, in a $960 million deal. Also in 2002 MidAmerican Energy Holdings purchased the Northern Natural Gas pipeline from Dynegy for $928 million plus $950 million in assumed debt.

OFFICERS

Chairman and CEO: David L. Sokol
President: Gregory E. Abel, age 38
SVP and CFO: Patrick J. Goodman
SVP and Chief Administrative Officer: Keith D. Hartje
SVP and General Counsel: Douglas Anderson
VP Human Resources: Maureen Sammon
President and COO, Northern Electric: P. Eric Connor, age 52
Managing Director, CalEnergy Gas: Peter Youngs
Auditors: Deloitte & Touche LLP

LOCATIONS

HQ: MidAmerican Energy Holdings Company
666 Grand Ave., Des Moines, IA 50303
Phone: 515-242-4300   **Fax:** 515-281-2389
Web: www.midamerican.com

MidAmerican Energy Holdings has energy operations in Illinois, Iowa, Nebraska, and South Dakota, and in Australia, the Philippines, Poland, and the UK.

PRODUCTS/OPERATIONS

2001 Sales

	$ mil.	% of total
MidAmerican Energy Co.	2,796	53
CE Electric UK	1,459	27
HomeServices.Com	645	12
CalEnergy	283	5
Other	154	3
Total	**5,337**	**100**

Selected Subsidiaries
CalEnergy Company (develops power production facilities)
CE Electric UK Funding
CalEnergy Gas (Holdings) Limited (exploration and production: Australia, Poland, and the UK)
Northern Electric plc
Northern Electric Distribution Ltd (electricity distribution, UK)
Yorkshire Electricity Distribution plc (95%, electricity distribution, UK)
HomeServices.Com Inc. (real estate brokerage)
Kern River Gas Transmission Company (natural gas pipeline)
MidAmerican Energy Company (electricity and natural gas distribution)
Northern Natural Gas Company (natural gas pipeline)

COMPETITORS

AES	Mirant
Alliant Energy	National Power
Ameren	Nebraska Public Power
Aquila	Nicor
Calpine	Peoples Energy
Dynegy	Scottish and Southern
Edison International	Energy
El Paso	Scottish Power
Entergy	Trigen Energy
International Power	TXU Europe

HISTORICAL FINANCIALS & EMPLOYEES

Private FYE: December 31	Annual Growth	12/92	12/93	12/94	12/95	12/96	12/97	12/98	12/99	12/00	12/01
Sales ($ mil.)	52.8%	117	132	155	355	519	2,166	2,555	4,399	5,103	5,337
Net income ($ mil.)	17.4%	34	47	37	63	93	(84)	127	167	133	143
Income as % of sales	—	28.8%	35.7%	23.8%	17.9%	17.8%	—	5.0%	3.8%	2.6%	2.7%
Employees	52.1%	225	249	278	593	4,400	4,300	3,703	9,700	9,550	9,780

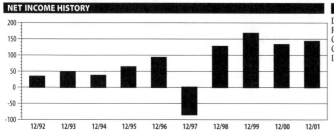

NET INCOME HISTORY

2001 FISCAL YEAR-END
Debt ratio: 70.8%
Return on equity: 5.4%
Cash ($ mil.): 417
Current ratio: 0.72
Long-term debt ($ mil.): 6,589

MILLIKEN & COMPANY INC.

Milliken & Company makes fabrics and chemicals used in products ranging from crayons to space suits. One of the world's largest textile companies, Milliken produces finished fabrics for uniforms, space suits, rugs, and carpets, as well as textiles used in automobiles, sails, tennis balls, and printer ribbons. It also makes chemicals (used in plastics) and petroleum products. Milliken's dyes infuse products such as Crayola crayons with color, its clarifying agents make plastics clear, and its chemicals are used in such things as the production of car dashboards. Milliken holds more than 1,300 patents and operates about 65 plants worldwide. The company has about 200 shareholders (most from the Milliken family).

Although the company has 200 shareholders, brothers Roger and Gerrish Milliken control the company. Roger, a billionaire who supports conservative causes, has led Milliken since 1947.

HISTORY

Seth Milliken and William Deering formed a company in 1865 to become selling agents for textile mills in New England and the southern US. Deering left the partnership, and in 1869 he founded Deering Harvester (now Navistar).

Milliken set up operations in New York before the turn of the century. He began buying the accounts receivable of cash-short textile mill operators and invested in some of the companies.

In his position as agent and financier, Milliken was able to spot failing mills. He bought out the distressed owners at a discount and soon became a major mill owner himself. In 1905 Milliken and his allies waged a bitter proxy fight and court case to win control of two mills, earning Milliken a fearsome reputation.

H. B. Claflin, a New York dry-goods wholesaler that also operated department stores, owed money to Milliken. When Claflin went bankrupt in 1914, Milliken got some of the stores, which became Mercantile Stores. The Milliken family retained about 40% of the chain (sold to Dillard's in 1998).

Roger Milliken, grandson of the founder, became the president of the company in 1947 and has ruled with a firm hand. He fired brother-in-law W. B. Dixon Stroud in 1955, and none of Roger's children, nephews, or nieces has ever been allowed to work for the company. The workers at Milliken's Darlington, South Carolina, mill voted to unionize in 1956. The next day Milliken closed the plant, beginning 24 years of litigation that ended at the US Supreme Court. Milliken settled with its workers for $5 million.

In the 1960s the company introduced Visa, a finish for easy-care fabrics. Milliken launched its Pursuit of Excellence program in 1981; the program stressed self-managed teams of employees and eliminated 700 management positions. Tom Peters dedicated his 1987 bestseller, *Thriving on Chaos*, to Roger.

Away from that limelight, Milliken is (and has always been) a secretive, closely held business. In 1989 that secrecy and family control were threatened when members of the Stroud branch of the family sued the company in the Delaware courts and then sold a small number of shares to Erwin Maddrey and Bettis Rainsford, executives of Milliken competitor Delta Woodside. The courts ruled in favor of Milliken in 1992; Maddrey and Rainsford were required to sign confidentiality agreements before receiving Milliken information.

In 1991 the company introduced Fashion Effects, a process that allowed it to customize drapery designs. Roger financially backed opponents of NAFTA in 1993.

Milliken is known by competitors for its unofficial motto: "Steal ideas shamelessly." Woven-filament maker NRB sued Milliken in 1997 for corporate spying, and the following year industrial textile maker Johnston Industries filed a similar lawsuit. Milliken settled both cases out of court.

In 1999 Milliken began using its Millitron dye technology to produce residential carpets and rugs. The company also introduced new brands of patterned rugs (including Royal Dynasty, Prestige, and American Heritage). In 2000 Milliken built a manufacturing facility in South Carolina to expand its production of Millard-brand clarifying agents.

OFFICERS

Chairman and CEO: Roger Milliken, age 87
Vice Chairman: Thomas J. Malone
President and COO: Ashley Allen
CFO: Jerry Pribanic
VP, Human Resources: Curtis Pressley
President, Milliken Chemical: John Rekers
Director, Public Affairs: Richard Dillard

LOCATIONS

HQ: 920 Milliken Rd., Spartanburg, SC 29304
Phone: 864-503-2020   **Fax:** 864-503-2100
Web: www.milliken.com

Milliken & Company has about 65 manufacturing facilities worldwide, including operations in Australia, Brazil, China, Hong Kong, Israel, Japan, Singapore, South Africa, the UK, and the US.

PRODUCTS/OPERATIONS

Selected Products

Chemicals
Carpet cleaner (Capture)
Clarifying agents for plastics (Millard)
Colorants and tints (ClearTint, Liquitint, Palmer, Reactint)
Electroconductive powders (Zelec)
Resin intermediates
Specialty chemicals
Textile chemicals
Turf maintenance chemicals

Fabrics, Carpet, and Rugs
Area rugs
Carpet and carpet tiles
Commercial table linen fabrics (Ambassador, Embassy, and Visa)
Entrance and logo mats (KEX)
Knit and woven apparel fabrics
Lining fabrics (Bemburg)
Mops (KEX)
Pool table cloth
Tennis ball felt
Towels

COMPETITORS

Asahi Kasei
Avondale Incorporated
Beaulieu of America
Burlington Industries
Collins & Aikman
Crompton
Dixie Group
Dow Chemical
DuPont
Galey & Lord
Interface
Johnston Industries
Mohawk Industries
Reliance Industries
Shaw Industries
Springs Industries
WestPoint Stevens

HISTORICAL FINANCIALS & EMPLOYEES

Private FYE: November 30	Annual Growth	11/93	11/94	11/95	11/96	11/97	11/98	11/99	11/00	11/01	11/02
Estimated sales ($ mil.)	3.2%	2,707	2,706	2,800	3,000	3,200	3,100	3,500	4,000	3,900	3,600
Employees	0.0%	14,000	13,500	13,500	15,000	16,000	16,000	18,000	21,000	20,000	14,000

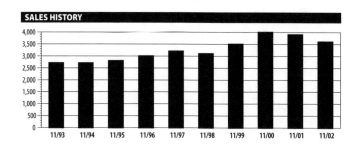

SALES HISTORY

MOTIVA ENTERPRISES LLC

Making money is a major motive behind Motiva Enterprises, which operates the eastern and southeastern US refining and marketing businesses of Royal Dutch/Shell's Shell Oil unit and Saudi Aramco. The company operates four refineries with a total capacity of 860,000 barrels a day, and it sells fuel at 13,000 Shell and Texaco branded gas stations. Motiva and sister company Shell Oil Products US (formerly Equilon; it operates in the West and Midwest) together make up the #1 US gasoline retailer. Motiva is a 50-50 joint venture of Shell and Saudi Aramco.

Motiva, with a long-term agreement with Saudi Aramco for crude oil supply, has holdings in almost 50 product terminals and operates three refineries on the Gulf Coast and one in Delaware.

Motiva was formed in 1998 to combine the eastern and southeastern US refining and marketing businesses of Texaco, Shell Oil, and Saudi Aramco. Texaco and Saudi Aramco each owned 35% of Motiva, and Shell owned 30%. In 2001 Texaco agreed to sell its stakes in Motiva (to Shell and Saudi Aramco) and Equilon (to Shell) to gain regulatory clearance to be acquired by Chevron. The deals were completed in 2002. Shell took full ownership of Equilon, which was renamed Shell Oil Products US.

HISTORY

Although Motiva was not created until 1998, two of its key players, Texaco and Saudi Aramco, had been doing business together in various ventures since 1936. But they had never tried anything on the scale of the Star Enterprise joint venture approved by Texaco CEO James Kinnear and Saudi Oil Minister Hisham Nazer in late 1988. The deal, valued at nearly $2 billion, was the largest joint venture of its kind in the US.

The agreement to create Star Enterprise sprang, in part, from Texaco's tumultuous ride following its purchase of Getty Oil in 1983. Texaco was sued by Pennzoil for pre-empting Pennzoil's bid for Getty; Pennzoil won a $10.5 billion judgment in 1985. Texaco filed for bankruptcy in 1987 and eventually settled with Pennzoil for $3 billion.

In 1988 Texaco emerged from bankruptcy after announcing a deal with Saudi Aramco at a stockholder meeting. Texaco got a much-needed injection of cash, and Saudi Aramco gained a steady US outlet for its supply of crude. The Saudis had been at odds with their OPEC partners for several years, and in late 1985 then-Saudi Oil Minister Sheikh Yamani and Saudi Aramco began increasing production, leading to an oil price crash in 1986. Nazer replaced Yamani and changed Saudi Aramco's strategy. To

secure market share, the Saudis started signing long-term supply contracts.

The deal with Texaco gave Saudi Aramco a 50% interest in Texaco's refining and marketing operations in the East and on the Gulf Coast — about two-thirds of Texaco's US downstream operations — including three refineries and its Texaco-brand stations. In return, the Saudis paid $812 million cash and provided three-fourths of Star's initial inventory, about 30 million barrels of oil. They also agreed to a 20-year, 600,000-barrel-a-day commitment of crude. Each company named three representatives to Star's management.

The new company soon initiated a modernization and expansion program: It acquired 65 stations, built 30 new outlets, and remodeled another 172 during 1989. In 1994 the company began franchising its Texaco-brand Star Mart convenience stores. By mid-1995 it had sold 30 franchises. Facing a more competitive oil marketing environment in the US, Shell Oil approached Texaco in 1996 with the possibility of merging some of their operations. In 1998 Shell and Texaco formed Equilon Enterprises, a joint venture that combined their western and midwestern refining and marketing activities.

Later that year Shell and Texaco/Saudi Aramco (Star Enterprises) formed Motiva to merge the companies' refining and marketing businesses on the East Coast and Gulf Coast. Shell and Texaco also formed two more Houston companies as satellite firms for Motiva and Equilon: Equiva Trading Company, a general partnership that provides supplies and trading services, and Equiva Services, which provides support services. L. Wilson Berry, the former president of Texaco Refining and Marketing, took over as CEO of Motiva.

In 1999 Motiva and Equilon together bought 15 product terminals from Premcor. To boost profits, in 2000 the Motiva board appointed Texaco downstream veteran Roger Ebert as its new CEO, replacing Berry, who announced his resignation after a Motiva board meeting.

In 2001 US government regulators required that Texaco sell its Motiva and Equilon stakes in order to be acquired by Chevron. That year Texaco veteran John Boles replaced Ebert (who retired) as CEO. Shell agreed to buy Texaco's stake in Equilon, and Shell and Saudi Aramco agreed to buy Texaco's stake in Motiva. The deals were completed in 2002.

President and CEO: John Boles
CFO: William M. Kaparich
VP Commercial Marketing and Distribution:
Ralph Grimmer
VP Human Resources and Corporate Services, Motiva Enterprises and Equilon Enterprises:
Bruce Culpepper
VP Refining, Motiva Enterprises and Equilon Enterprises: Carmine Falcone
VP Sales and Marketing: Larry Burch
VP Sales and Marketing: Hugh Cooley
Chief Diversity Officer, Motiva Enterprises and Equilon Enterprises: John Jefferson
General Counsel: Rick Frazier

COMPETITORS

7-Eleven
BP
CITGO
Cumberland Farms
Dairy Mart
Exxon Mobil
Gulf Oil
Marathon Ashland Petroleum
Racetrac Petroleum
Sunoco
Valero Energy
Wawa

LOCATIONS

HQ: 1100 Louisiana St., Houston, TX 77002
Phone: 713-277-8000   **Fax:** 713-277-9099
Web: www.motivaenterprises.com

Motiva Enterprises operates gas stations in the northeastern and southeastern US. It has refineries in Convent and Norco, Louisiana; Delaware City, Delaware; and Port Arthur, Texas.

Major Operations

Alabama	New Hampshire
Arkansas	New Jersey
Connecticut	New York
Delaware	North Carolina
Florida	Pennsylvania
Georgia	Rhode Island
Louisiana	Tennessee
Maryland	Texas
Massachusetts	Vermont
Mississippi	Virginia

HISTORICAL FINANCIALS & EMPLOYEES

Joint venture FYE: December 31	Annual Growth	12/91	12/92	12/93	12/94	12/95	12/96	12/97	12/98	12/99	12/00
Sales ($ mil.)	90.3%	—	—	—	—	—	—	—	5,371	12,196	19,446
Net income ($ mil.)	143.1%	—	—	—	—	—	—	—	78	(69)	461
Income as % of sales	—	—	—	—	—	—	—	—	1.5%	—	2.4%
Employees	46.1%	—	—	—	—	—	—	—	3,750	—	8,000

NET INCOME HISTORY

2000 FISCAL YEAR-END

Debt ratio: 30.1%
Return on equity: 14.1%
Cash ($ mil.): 9
Current ratio: 1.20
Long-term debt ($ mil.): 1,429

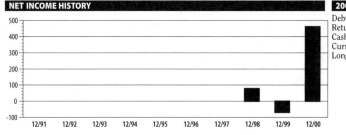

MTS, INCORPORATED

Whether pop music rocks your world or Broadway tunes set your feet a-tappin', MTS offers a tower of choices. MTS — owner of Tower Records — is one of the largest specialty retailers of music in the US, with nearly 120 company-owned music, book, and video stores in five countries; its franchise agreements encompass 9 additional countries. MTS also runs WOW! stores (a joint venture with electronics retailer The Good Guys) and publishes several free music magazines. International operations account for more than 40% of sales (expected to drop dramatically following the 2002 sale of its Japanese operations). Founder and chairman Russell Solomon, a high-school dropout, and his son and CEO Michael own 99% of MTS.

Though it helped pioneer specialty retailing's superstore concept, MTS has fewer stores than other major music chains; it is known for broad selection and high volume. Unlike other specialty retailers, managers at each store are granted discretion in maintaining the level and mix of their inventories.

The chain has faced increasing competition from discounters such as Wal-Mart, from industry consolidation, and from online retailers. Big losses prompted the company to adopt a restructuring plan, and it has indefinitely postponed the idea of going public.

Russell Solomon has described himself as an "aging hippie" who scorns corporate stuffiness and is known for confiscating neckties from visiting executives and displaying them outside his office. MTS was named for his son, Michael T. Solomon.

HISTORY

Russell Solomon began selling used jukebox records in 1941 in his father's Tower Cut Rate Drug Store at age 16. He joined the Army after dropping out of high school and went back to work in his father's store after his 1946 discharge. In 1952 he took over the record inventory from his father's store and began wholesaling, setting up record departments in drugstores and department stores.

Solomon's record wholesaling business went broke and creditors forced him to liquidate in 1960. Days later, with $5,000 from his father, Solomon incorporated MTS (named after his son Michael T.) and soon opened the first Tower Records in Sacramento, California. A month later a second Sacramento store was born. The first Tower Books opened in 1963, adjacent to one of the record stores.

By the 1967 "Summer of Love," Solomon was noticing the diverse musical tastes of the flower children who hung out in his stores. With the music business exploding, he figured serving the market would require stocking stores with a huge selection. In 1968 the first store outside Sacramento was opened, Tower Records' landmark Columbus Street store in San Francisco. At the time it was the largest record store in the US.

In 1970 Tower Records opened in Los Angeles on the Sunset Strip. The company started expanding outside California in 1976 (mainly in the West) and overseas in 1979 (Japan). The first Tower Video opened in Sacramento in 1981; three more opened the next year. The East Coast got its first Tower Records in 1983 (New York City); at the time the 35,000-sq.-ft. store was the world's largest. That year the company debuted *Pulse!* magazine, an in-store freebie with record reviews and artist interviews. The company's real expansion began in 1989; by 1994 Tower Records, with 127 outlets, had more than doubled its stores. That year it opened its first multimedia store, offering books, videos, records, and CD-ROMs under one roof.

MTS opened the largest record shop in the world (an eight-floor megastore in Tokyo) and the first WOW! store (a joint venture with electronics retailer The Good Guys) in Las Vegas in 1995. That year the company started selling CDs on the Internet via America Online; it added its own online store in 1996. In 1998 MTS sold $110 million in bonds to raise money for expansion. Also in 1998 president and CEO Russell Solomon passed his Tower-guarding duties and his titles to son Michael.

To counteract growing losses, the company began several experiments in 2000, including digital-downloading kiosks that allow customers to download songs and burn their own CDs. A similar project allows customers to pay for music from Tower's Web site and then immediately download it.

In 2001 MTS adopted a restructuring plan that included closing and liquidating most stand-alone and combination bookstores and selling the company's operations in Argentina, Hong Kong, Taiwan, and Singapore and converting them to franchises. It also decided to shut down its operations in Canada. The company's large losses in fiscal 2001 were attributed mostly to the restructuring and the closure of some of its international operations. As part of the September 2002 settlement of a CD price-fixing case, MTS is one of three music retailers and five recording companies that agreed to pay more than $67 million to compensate consumers. The companies will also distribute more than $75 million worth of CDs to US public entities and nonprofits. In October 2002 MTS sold off Japanese operations.

OFFICERS

Chairman: Russell M. Solomon, age 77, $932,780 pay
President, CEO, and Director: Michael T. Solomon, age 54, $460,400 pay
EVP, CFO, Secretary, Treasurer, and Director: DeVaughn D. Searson, age 58, $328,106 pay
SVP, European Operations: Andy D. Lown, age 37
SVP, Far East Operations: Keith Cahoon, age 46, $199,917 pay
SVP, Technology and Supply Chain and CIO: William Baumann, age 40
Director of Human Resources: Shauna Pompei
Auditors: KPMG LLP

LOCATIONS

HQ: 2500 Del Monte St., West Sacramento, CA 95691
Phone: 916-373-2500   **Fax:** 916-373-2535
Web: www.towerrecords.com

2002 Sales

	% of total
US	56
Japan	38
UK & Ireland	5
Other countries	1
Total	**100**

US Locations

Arizona	Massachusetts
California	Nevada
Colorado	New Jersey
Connecticut	New York
District of Columbia	Oregon
Georgia	Pennsylvania
Hawaii	Tennessee
Illinois	Texas
Louisiana	Virginia
Maryland	Washington

PRODUCTS/OPERATIONS

2002 Sales

	% of total
Recorded music	84
Video products	11
Complementary products	5
Total	**100**

Selected Operations
Internet
  TowerRecords.com
Music magazines
  Bounce (Japan)
  Pass (Taiwan)
  Pulse! (US)
  Pulse Latino (Latin America)
  Top (UK)
Stores
  Tower
  WOW! (jointly operated with The Good Guys)

COMPETITORS

Amazon.com	HMV
Barnes & Noble	Hollywood Entertainment
Bertelsmann	Kmart
Best Buy	Movie Gallery
Blockbuster	MP3.com
BMG Entertainment	Musicland
Books-A-Million	Target
Borders	Trans World
CDnow	Entertainment
Circuit City	Virgin Group
Columbia House	Wal-Mart
Costco Wholesale	Wherehouse
EMI Group	Entertainment
Hastings Entertainment	WHSmith

HISTORICAL FINANCIALS & EMPLOYEES

Private FYE: July 31	Annual Growth	7/93	7/94	7/95	7/96	7/97	7/98	7/99	7/00	7/01	7/02
Sales ($ mil.)	3.9%	699	809	951	1,001	992	1,008	1,026	1,100	1,080	983
Net income ($ mil.)	—	15	17	15	10	4	10	(8)	(10)	(90)	(57)
Income as % of sales	—	2.1%	2.1%	1.6%	1.0%	0.4%	1.0%	—	—	—	—
Employees	(6.6%)	—	—	—	—	6,800	7,200	7,500	7,158	6,795	4,828

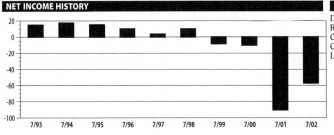

NET INCOME HISTORY

2002 FISCAL YEAR-END
Debt ratio: 100.0%
Return on equity: —
Cash ($ mil.): 37
Current ratio: 0.77
Long-term debt ($ mil.): 116

MUTUAL OF OMAHA

In the wild kingdom that is today's insurance industry, The Mutual of Omaha Companies wants to distinguish itself from the pack. The company provides individual health and accident coverage (through subsidiary Mutual of Omaha Insurance); its United of Omaha unit offers life insurance and annuities. The firm also offers personal property/casualty lines (homeowners, boat, auto, and flood coverage), disability coverage, brokerage services, pension plans, and mutual funds. Mutual of Omaha, which is owned by its policyholders, offers its products mainly through agent networks.

Clout-wielding managed care organizations, increasingly cost conscious, have put traditional indemnity insurers — which have less power to bargain for lower-cost services — at a disadvantage, as have state laws mandating coverage for persons regardless of underwriting policy. Mutual of Omaha is exiting the health business in some areas and is adding managed care services. It is focused on growing its health care networks internally, rather than by acquisition, to ensure its standards are met. These networks are largely in underserved rural areas, where the firm has kept a strong presence. The insurer is also working to increase sales of its life insurance and annuities products.

Mutual of Omaha is involved in wildlife conservation and protection. Starting with sponsorship of the long-running *Mutual of Omaha's Wild Kingdom,* this interest has evolved into a grant and scholarship program run by the company's Wildlife Heritage Center.

HISTORY

Charter Mutual Benefit Health & Accident Association got its start in Omaha, Nebraska, in 1909. A year later, half of its founders quit, leaving a group headed by pharmaceuticals businessman H. S. Weller in charge. He tapped C. C. Criss as principal operating officer, general manager, and treasurer. Criss brought in his wife Mabel and brother Neil to help run the business.

Formed to offer accident and disability protection at a time when there were many fraudulent benefit societies, Charter Mutual Benefit Health faced consumer resistance that slowed growth in its first 10 years. By 1920 it was licensed in only nine states. Experience helped it refine its products and improve its policies' comprehensibility. By 1924 the firm had more than doubled its penetration, gaining licensing in 24 states.

The US was nearing the depths of the Depression when Weller died in 1932. Criss succeeded him as president. The stock crash had brought a steep decline in the value of the firm's asset base, and premium income dropped (accompanied by an increase in claims). Even so, Mutual Benefit Health expanded its agency force, the scope of its benefits, and its operations. It went into Canada in 1935 and began a campaign to obtain licensing throughout the US.

By 1939 the company was licensed in all 48 states. During WWII it wrote coverage for civilians killed or injured in acts of war in the US (including Hawaii) and Canada. With paranoia running high and consumer goods in short supply, the insurance industry boomed during the war (and payouts on stateside act-of-war claims were low to nonexistent). Criss retired in 1949.

Gearing up its postwar sales efforts, in 1950 the company changed its name to Mutual of Omaha and adopted its distinctive chieftain logo. During the 1950s it added specialty accident and group medical coverage.

In 1963 it made an advertising coup when it launched *Mutual of Omaha's Wild Kingdom.* Hosted by zoo director Marlin Perkins and, later, naturalist sidekick Jim Fowler, the show was one of the most popular nature programs of all time. Later that decade the company added investment management to its services.

Changes in the health care industry during the 1990s led Mutual of Omaha to de-emphasize its traditional indemnity products in favor of building managed care alternatives. In 1993 it joined with Alegent Health System to form managed care company Preferred HealthAlliance. Mutual of Omaha also stopped writing new major medical coverage in such states as California, Florida, New Jersey, and New York, where state laws made providing health care onerous. This led the company to cut its workforce by about 10% in 1996.

In 1999 it bought out Alegent's interest in their joint venture and entered the credit card business (offering First USA Visa cards). The firm also lifted its $25,000 limit for coverage of AIDS-related illnesses (its standard limit is $1 million); the company had been sued over the policy.

OFFICERS

Chairman and CEO: John W. Weekly, age 70
President and COO; President, United World Life Insurance: John A. Sturgeon
EVP and Chief Investment Officer; President, Mutual of Omaha Investor Services: Richard A. Witt
EVP, Treasurer, and Comptroller: Tommie D. Thompson
EVP and Chief Actuary: Cecil D. Bykerk
EVP and Executive Counsel: Lawrence F. Harr
EVP and General Counsel: Thomas J. McCusker
EVP, Corporate Services and Corporate Secretary: M. Jane Huerter
EVP, Government Affairs: William C. Mattox

EVP, Individual Financial Services; President, Companion Life Insurance: Randall C. Horn
EVP, Group Benefit Services: Daniel P. Neary
EVP, Health Care Management: Stephen R. Booma
EVP, Information Services: James L. Hanson
SVP, Human Resources: John Brown
Public Relations Officer: Joe Clauson
President and CEO, innowave: Thomas P. Weekly
President and CEO, Kirkpatrick, Pettis, Smith, Polian: L.C. Petersen
President and CEO, Omaha Property and Casualty Insurance: Martin W. Dourney
Auditors: Deloitte & Touche LLP

LOCATIONS

HQ: The Mutual of Omaha Companies
Mutual of Omaha Plaza, Omaha, NE 68175
Phone: 402-342-7600   Fax: 402-351-2775
Web: www.mutualofomaha.com

The Mutual of Omaha Companies operate throughout the US.

PRODUCTS/OPERATIONS

Selected Services and Products
Annuities
Dental insurance
Disability insurance
Individual life and health insurance
Long-term-care insurance
Major medical
Mutual funds
Property/casualty coverage

Selected Subsidiaries and Affiliates
Companion Life Insurance Company
innowave Incorporated (water purification products)
Kirkpatrick, Pettis, Smith, Polian Inc. (brokerage)
Mutual of Omaha Insurance Company
Mutual of Omaha Investor Services (mutual funds)
Omaha Property and Casualty Insurance Company
United of Omaha Life Insurance Company
United World Life Insurance Company

COMPETITORS

Aetna	Liberty Mutual
Allstate	MassMutual
American National	MetLife
Insurance	MONY
Assurant Group	Morgan Stanley
AXA Financial	New York Life
Blue Cross	Northwestern Mutual
CIGNA	Prudential
CNA Financial	State Farm
Guardian Life	USAA
John Hancock Financial	
Services	

HISTORICAL FINANCIALS & EMPLOYEES

Mutual company FYE: December 31	Annual Growth	12/92	12/93	12/94	12/95	12/96	12/97	12/98	12/99	12/00	12/01
Assets ($ mil.)	(8.1%)	7,714	8,600	9,551	10,659	11,726	12,639	13,231	13,959	14,465	3,590
Net income ($ mil.)	(8.1%)	65	94	82	122	105	181	117	90	156	31
Income as % of assets	—	0.8%	1.1%	0.9%	1.1%	0.9%	1.4%	0.9%	0.6%	1.1%	0.8%
Employees	(1.5%)	—	7,665	8,330	8,163	7,047	7,309	7,111	—	—	—

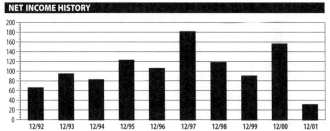

NET INCOME HISTORY

2001 FISCAL YEAR-END
Equity as % of assets: 47.2%
Return on assets: 0.3%
Return on equity: 1.5%
Long-term debt ($ mil.): —
Sales ($ mil.): 2,053

MUZAK LLC

The hills are alive with the sound of Muzak. The king of canned music, Muzak offers 60 music channels delivered via satellite, local broadcast transmission, tapes, and CDs.

The company counts retailers, grocery stores, hotels, office buildings, and factories among its 335,000 customers, and an estimated 80 million people hear Muzak tunes each day. In addition to providing music from genres such as classical, country, Latin, oldies, and contemporary, the company also sells, installs, and maintains such equipment as sound systems and intercoms. Investment firm ABRY Partners owns about 64% of the company.

Music delivered via satellite accounts for 74% of Muzak's business. The company made numerous acquisitions in the late 1990s and hopes to restore profitability by renewing its focus on its core services. Radio station giant Clear Channel owns about 21% of Muzak.

HISTORY

George Squier patented a system for transmitting phonograph music over electrical lines in 1922. He sold the rights to utility North American Company, and together they formed a subsidiary to begin testing the system in Cleveland. In 1934 Squier coined the term Muzak ("muz" from music and "ak" from Kodak, his favorite company); he died later that year. The company moved to New York in 1936.

In the 1930s Muzak was used in the then-newfangled elevators to calm riders (hence the term "elevator music"). In 1938 Warner Bros. bought the company but sold it the next year to US Senator William Benton (who was also the publisher of *Encyclopaedia Britannica*). Experiments showed that music could increase productivity, and during WWII Muzak systems were installed in factories.

After the war the company continued to work on Stimulus Progression — the idea of regulating worker productivity through music. During the 1950s the company began using audio tapes to deliver its music to customers. The company was sold to Wrather Corp. in 1957.

In 1972 Teleprompter bought the company and began distributing its music via satellite. Westinghouse bought Teleprompter in 1981 and sold it to Marshall Field V in 1986. Field bought Seattle-based Yesco, a producer of "foreground" music for retailers, and merged the two the next year. Muzak moved its headquarters from New York to Seattle.

Led by Yesco's management, Muzak greatly expanded the number of channels it offered, from one to 12, and it began updating its sound

to appeal to baby boomers. The new channels did not offer the traditional symphonic re-recordings of soft favorites; instead they featured original recordings, including jazz, contemporary pop, and country music. The company also introduced music video feeds for retailers, nightclubs, restaurants, and bars. Field sold Muzak to its management and New York investment firm Centre Capital in 1992.

In 1996 the company called off plans to go public. Saddled with debt from the buyout and mounting losses, it ousted CEO John Jester in 1997 and replaced him with William Boyd, who refocused the company on its core music business. In 1998 the company began buying competitors and its own independent affiliates.

In 1999 Muzak merged with Audio Communications Network, a Muzak franchiser owned by media investment firm ABRY Partners, and the Muzak affiliates owned by Capstar (Capstar later became part of AMFM, which was subsequently acquired by radio station owner Clear Channel). Later that year Muzak made a string of acquisitions, including Data Broadcasting's InStore Satellite Network, a music and ad business.

In 2000 Muzak moved its headquarters to Fort Mill, South Carolina. Extending its acquisitive streak, the company acquired Telephone Audio Productions (audio marketing and messaging) and Muzak franchisee Vortex Sound Communications. To pay for all those acquisitions, Muzak sold $85 million worth of preferred stock to Bank of America, New York Life, L.P., and Northwestern Investment in late 2000.

OFFICERS

CEO: William A. Boyd, age 60, $300,023 pay
COO, CFO, and Treasurer: Stephen P. Villa, age 38, $174,995 pay
SVP Owned Operations: Steven M. Tracy, age 51, $164,995 pay
SVP Technical Operations: David M. Moore, age 38, $119,995 pay
VP: Royce G. Yudkoff, age 45
VP and General Manager, Audio Marketing: Robert Boyd
VP and Secretary: Peni Garber, age 38
VP, General Counsel, and Assistant Secretary: Michael F. Zendan II, age 38, $117,304 pay
VP Marketing: Kenny Kahn
VP Team Member Services (HR): Frank Messana
Auditors: PricewaterhouseCoopers LLP

LOCATIONS

HQ: 3318 Lakemont Blvd., Fort Mill, SC 29708
Phone: 803-396-3000   **Fax:** 803-396-3136
Web: www.muzak.com

Muzak offers its services in 15 countries.

PRODUCTS/OPERATIONS

2001 Sales

	$ mil.	% of total
Music & related services	150	74
Equipment & related services	53	26
Total	**203**	**100**

Selected Music Genres
Classical
Country
Jazz
Latin
Mature adult
Oldies
Popular contemporary
Popular contemporary instrumentals
Specialty
Urban

Selected Products
Audio Architecture (music programming)
Voice (music and messages for phone systems)

COMPETITORS

DMX MUSIC
MP3.com
PlayNetwork
TM Century

HISTORICAL FINANCIALS & EMPLOYEES

Private FYE: December 31	Annual Growth	12/92	12/93	12/94	12/95	12/96	12/97	12/98	12/99	12/00	12/01
Sales ($ mil.)	15.8%	55	59	83	87	87	91	100	130	192	203
Net income ($ mil.)	—	(6)	(4)	(7)	(6)	(11)	(13)	(12)	(22)	(44)	(44)
Income as % of sales	—	—	—	—	—	—	—	—	—	—	—
Employees	11.1%	—	—	—	715	751	667	1,041	1,324	1,395	1,347

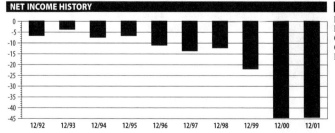

NET INCOME HISTORY

2001 FISCAL YEAR-END
Debt ratio: 67.1%
Return on equity: —
Cash ($ mil.): 3
Current ratio: 0.99
Long-term debt ($ mil.): 298

NASD

Bull market or bear, NASD will be there. NASD (formerly known as The National Association of Securities Dealers) is parent of the #2 and #3 US stock markets: The NASDAQ Stock Market and the American Stock Exchange (AMEX). Listed companies and investors can choose between auction (AMEX) or electronic trading (NASDAQ). The exchanges may lack the clout and market capitalization of the New York Stock Exchange, but — with some 4,100 and 600 listed companies, respectively — they surpass the NYSE's count. Per SEC orders, NASD Regulation oversees over-the-counter securities trading and disciplines traders; virtually all US securities dealers are members.

Despite the tech bust and economic slowdown, 55%-owned NASDAQ has proceeded with foreign expansion plans, some of which have been less than successful. It launched NASDAQ Canada and acquired a controlling interest in NASDAQ Europe (formerly Easdaq), but pulled the plug on an economically unviable NASDAQ Japan in 2002. To stay competitive with electronic communications networks (ECNs), NASDAQ in 2002 launched its own, SuperMontage. NASD plans to spin off NASDAQ, making it a publicly traded exchange.

HISTORY

NASD was founded in 1939 as a self-regulating entity for over-the-counter (OTC) securities traders who traded directly with companies or with market makers authorized to trade their stock. Traders shopped by phone to get the best price from the market makers, and up-to-date OTC quotes were unobtainable. NASD set trading qualifications, administered licensing tests, set standards for underwriting compensation, and disciplined wayward traders.

In 1963 the SEC asked the NASD to develop an automated OTC quotations system. Work began in 1968 on facilities in Trumbull, Connecticut, and Rockville, Maryland. The system went online in 1971 and soon turned into an electronic trading medium because it made dealer quotes more competitive and instantly visible. By 1972 volume exceeded 2 billion shares, and two years later the NASDAQ claimed a share volume nearly one-third of NYSE's. By 1980 it reported having almost 60% of the NYSE's volume, although NASDAQ counted both sides of many trades.

In 1975 Congress gave NASD responsibility for regulating the municipal securities market and asked the SEC to develop a national market system for share trading. The SEC handed the task to NASD. The market started trading in 1982 with 40 stocks, establishing a two-tier system: one for the crème de la crème, such as MCI (now WorldCom) and Microsoft, and one for smaller or newer issues. The system is continually updated; new technology has made it a model for other exchanges.

To improve responsiveness to small investors, NASD instituted the SOES (small order entry system) after the 1987 stock crash, when many traders bailed themselves out before executing customer sell orders. So-called SOES bandits (dealers who used the system to make frequent small trades) increased the market's volatility and made NASDAQ vulnerable to NYSE's contention that auction exchanges were fairer to investors. An SEC investigation resulted in a requirement that dealers execute small customer orders along with their own and at the best prices. In 1997 the new rules were phased in and spreads dropped by an average of 35% without affecting volume.

But NASD teetered between appeasing the public and looking out for its own. A 1997 proposal to cap investor arbitration awards at $750,000, regardless of actual damages, met with criticism, since arbitration had been instituted in 1987 because the parties could receive remedies comparable to those available in court.

Reform-minded Wall Streeter Frank Zarb took over in 1997. NASDAQ and the American Stock Exchange (AMEX) merged the next year. NASD reluctantly complied when the SEC asked it to join the NYSE in real-time trade price reporting.

With for-profit, around-the-clock competitors like The Island ECN and Archipelago in mind, NASD prepared in 1999 to spin off NASDAQ as a for-profit exchange (overwhelmingly approved in 2000). NASDAQ also extended official pricing to 6:30 p.m. (Eastern time) and agreed to share listings with the Hong Kong Stock Exchange.

In 2000 NASDAQ converted stock prices from fractions to decimals, mandated by regulators. That year it joined with SOFTBANK to build NASDAQ Japan, an Internet-based market of primarily Japanese tech companies. In 2001 the flaccid economy led NASDAQ to trim about 10% of its staff — its first job cuts since just after the 1987 crash. Zarb also retired that year.

In the wake of the terrorism attacks that shook Wall Street and the nation in 2001, NASDAQ and the NYSE began discussing a disaster plan under which the two would cooperate should a future incident cripple either market. NASDAQ continued to refine its focus toward regulation, with plans to spin off NASDAQ and to dispose of AMEX. In 2002 NASD wrote off its investment in NASDAQ Japan and decided to shutter the market.

OFFICERS

Chairman, President, and CEO: Robert R. Glauber,
age 63
**Vice Chairman; Chairman and CEO,The American
Stock Exchange:** Salvatore F. Sodano
Vice Chairman and President, NASD Regulation:
Mary L. Schapiro, age 46
EVP and CFO: Todd T. DiGanci
EVP and Chief Administrative Officer: Michael D. Jones
EVP, Corporate Development, Strategy & Technology:
Douglas H. Shulman
**SVP and Corporate Secretary, NASD, NASD
Regulation, and NASD Dispute Resolution:**
Barbara Z. Sweeney
SVP and General Counsel: T. Grant Callery
SVP and CTO: Martin P. Colburn
SVP, Market Operations: Steven A. Joachim
SVP and Investment Officer: James R. Allen
SVP, Affinity Marketing: Richard A. Bachman
SVP and Corporate Controller: Eileen M. Famiglietti
SVP, Human Resources: Andrew C. Goresh
**SVP, Corporate Communications and Government
Relations:** Howard M. Schloss
SVP and Corporate Secretary: Daniel S. Shook
SVP, Corporate Real Estate: Catherine C. Tighe
VP, Technology Administration: Lawrence E. Fitzpatrick
VP and Associate General Counsel: John J. Flood
VP, Internal Audit: Michael P. Hourigan
VP, Technology Administration: Stephen A. Machlis
VP, Finance: Gregory B. Raymond
VP, Market Operations: Karen J. Sancilio
VP, Financial Systems: Nanci L. Schimizzi
VP, Office of the Ombudsman: William B. Thompson
VP, Fixed Income: Justin Tubiolo
VP, Internal Audit: John P. Withington
VP, Finance: Robert L. Wood
**Director; Chairman and CEO, The NASDAQ Stock
Market:** Hardwick Simmons, age 61
CEO, NASDAQ Europe: Michael O. Sanderson, age 58
**President, NASD Dispute Resolution; EVP and Chief
Hearing Officer, NASD Regulation:** Linda D. Fienberg
**EVP and Director of Arbitration, NASD Dispute
Resolution:** George H. Friedman
EVP and COO, NASD Regulation: Elisse Barbara Walter
Auditors: Ernst & Young LLP

LOCATIONS

HQ: 1735 K St. NW, Washington, DC 20006
Phone: 202-728-8000   **Fax:** 202-293-6260
Web: www.nasd.com

NASD has regulation and dispute resolution offices
throughout the US. The company's stock exchange
operations have US offices in Chicago; Menlo Park,
California; New York; Rockville, Maryland; Trumbull,
Connecticut; and Washington, DC, and other offices in
Brussels, London, Montreal, Paris, Sao Paulo, Shanghai,
and Tokyo.

PRODUCTS/OPERATIONS

2001 Sales

	$ mil.	% of total
NASDAQ Stock Market	860	56
NASD	409	26
American Stock Exchange	281	18
Adjustments	(11)	—
Total	**1,539**	**100**

Selected Subsidiaries & Affiliates
The American Stock Exchange, LLC
NASD Dispute Resolution, Inc.
NASD Regulation, Inc.
NASDAQ Europe S.A./N.V. (60%)
NASDAQ LIFFE Markets, LLC
The NASDAQ Stock Market, Inc. (55%)
Securities Industry Automation Corporation

COMPETITORS

Archipelago
Bloomberg
E*TRADE
Goldman Sachs
Instinet
Island ECN
MarketXT
NYSE

HISTORICAL FINANCIALS & EMPLOYEES

Not-for-profit FYE: December 31	Annual Growth	12/92	12/93	12/94	12/95	12/96	12/97	12/98	12/99	12/00	12/01
Sales ($ mil.)	21.6%	264	332	372	438	556	634	740	1,177	1,555	1,539
Net income ($ mil.)	13.8%	35	39	21	17	55	36	47	154	114	112
Income as % of sales	—	13.2%	11.7%	5.6%	3.9%	9.9%	5.7%	6.4%	13.1%	7.3%	7.3%
Employees	5.4%	1,991	2,145	2,328	2,000	2,218	2,200	2,900	3,000	3,200	3,200

NET INCOME HISTORY

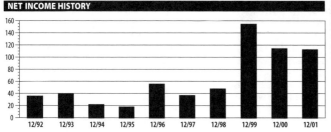

2001 FISCAL YEAR-END

Debt ratio: 19.3%
Return on equity: 10.8%
Cash ($ mil.): 562
Current ratio: 2.45
Long-term debt ($ mil.): 289

NBA

The National Basketball Association has shot a lot fewer airballs lately. The NBA is shaking off its fiscal and image problems with a little magic from the Washington Wizards, which added superstar Michael Jordan to its roster after he came out of retirement for the second time in 2001. The prospect of seeing Jordan play again boosted fan interest as well as attendance throughout the league. The 29-team NBA is divided into Eastern and Western Conferences and includes one Canadian team. The league also operates the WNBA (women's basketball), which features sister teams in 15 NBA cities.

After a less than stellar 1998-99 season that saw a contentious lockout and the second retirement of Jordan, the NBA saw its attendance figures and TV ratings decline dramatically. Add to that a host of on-and-off court image problems (such as boring play and a laundry list of player scandals), and 18-year commissioner David Stern has his work cut out for him to return the league to its glory days of the 1980s.

Despite the attendance and ratings declines, the league still manages to bring in the dough through lucrative merchandising deals and TV contracts. In 2002 the NBA cut a new six-year TV contract with Walt Disney's ABC and ESPN, and it secured a contract with AOL Time Warner's Turner Sports worth a reported $4.6 billion.

Expansion is also still very much alive for the NBA. After the Charlotte Hornets moved to New Orleans for the 2002-03 season, the league voted to give the city another franchise that will begin play in 2004-05. Robert Johnson, founder of BET, has been chosen as the majority owner of the new club. He is the first black owner of a major league sports team.

The NBA has also decided to rethink its strategy regarding the WNBA. The league has restructured the previous ownership rules for a WNBA franchise that dictated that only the current owners of NBA clubs could own a sister team. The move allows the league to expand into cities where there isn't already an NBA franchise. But the new rules also force WNBA teams to find their own corporate sponsors and pay player salaries themselves.

HISTORY

Dr. James Naismith, a physical education teacher at the International YMCA Training School in Springfield, Massachusetts, invented Basketball in 1891. Naismith nailed peach baskets at both ends of the school's gym, gave his students a soccer ball, and one of the world's most popular sports was born.

In the beginning, many YMCAs deemed the game too rough and banned it, so basketball was limited to armories, gymnasiums, barns, and dance halls. To pay the rent for the use of the hall, teams began charging spectators fees for admission, and leftover cash was divided among the players. The first pro basketball game was played in 1896 in Trenton, New Jersey.

A group of arena owners looking to fill their halls when their hockey teams were on the road formed the Basketball Association of America in 1946. It merged with the midwestern National Basketball League in 1949 to form the 17-team National Basketball Association (NBA).

Six teams dropped out in 1950. The league got an unexpected boost the next year when a point-shaving scandal rocked college basketball. The bad publicity for the college game made the pros look relatively clean, and it helped attract more fans. Another boost came through innovation when the league introduced the 24-second shot clock in 1954, which sped up the game and increased scoring.

Basketball came into its own in the late 1950s and 1960s, thanks to the popularity of such stars as Wilt Chamberlain, Bill Russell, and Bob Cousy. A rival league, the American Basketball Association (ABA), appeared on the scene in 1967 with its red, white, and blue basketball. Salaries escalated as the two leagues competed for players. The leagues merged in 1976.

By the early 1980s the NBA was suffering major image problems (drugs, fighting, racial issues) and began to wane in popularity. The league was resuscitated by exciting new players such as Magic Johnson, Larry Bird, and Michael Jordan and, in 1984, a new commissioner, David Stern. Although increased commercialism drove some purists crazy, big-name players and big-time rivalries helped sell the NBA's most important commodity — sport as entertainment.

Stern went to work cleaning up the league's image and financial problems, pushing through a strict anti-drug policy and a salary cap (the first such cap in major US sports). He also signed big marketing deals with such sponsors as Coca-Cola and McDonald's. The NBA added its first two non-US teams in 1995, the Toronto Raptors and the Vancouver Grizzlies. (The Grizzlies moved to Memphis, Tennessee, in 2001.) The league also created the Women's NBA (WNBA) in 1996.

On July 1, 1998, the NBA owners voted to lock out players, leading to the first work stoppage in the NBA's 52-year history. The dispute lasted six months, and the NBA's 1998-99 season was pared down to 50 games from the standard 82.

Concerned with the rash of players either leaving college early or skipping it entirely for the NBA, the league announced the formation of a developmental league (akin to baseball's minor leagues) in 2000, which started play in 2001. Also in 2001 the NBA got a much-needed shot in the arm when Michael Jordan came out of retirement for a second time to play for the Washington Wizards.

The following year the league signed a new TV contract. Former owner NBC decided not to pursue the league after its $1.3 billion bid failed to measure up to a six-year, $4.6 billion deal offered by Walt Disney's ABC and ESPN and AOL Time Warner's Turner Sports.

OFFICERS

Commissioner: David J. Stern, age 58
Deputy Commissioner and COO: Russell T. Granik
SVP Basketball Operations: Stu Jackson
SVP Business Affairs: Harvey E. Benjamin
SVP Communications: Timothy P. Andree
SVP Consumer Products: Christopher Heyn
SVP Finance: Robert Criqui
SVP International: Andrew Messick, age 36
SVP Marketing and Team Business Operations:
Bernie Mullin
SVP New League Development: Rob Levine
VP Internet Services: Brenda Spoonemore
VP Marketing Partnerships: Jonathan Press
VP Team Marketing Services: Bill Sutton
President and COO, NBA Entertainment: Adam Silver
President, NBA Television and New Media Ventures:
Ed Desser
President, Women's National Basketball Association:
Valerie B. Ackerman
**EVP Global Media Properties and Marketing
Partnerships:** Heidi Ueberroth
**EVP Programming and Executive Producer, NBA
Entertainment:** Gregg Winik
SVP and COO, WNBA: Paula Hanson
Human Resources: Patrica E. Swedin

LOCATIONS

HQ: National Basketball Association
Olympic Tower, 645 5th Ave., New York, NY 10022
Phone: 212-407-8000   **Fax:** 212-754-6414
Web: www.nba.com

PRODUCTS/OPERATIONS

NBA Teams

Eastern Conference:	Western Conference:
Atlantic Division	**Midwest Division**
Boston Celtics	Dallas Mavericks
Miami Heat	Denver Nuggets
New Jersey Nets	Houston Rockets
New York Knicks	Memphis Grizzlies
Orlando Magic	Minnesota
Philadelphia 76ers	Timberwolves
Washington Wizards	San Antonio Spurs
Central Division	Utah Jazz
Atlanta Hawks	**Pacific Division**
Chicago Bulls	Golden State Warriors
Cleveland Cavaliers	Los Angeles Clippers
Detroit Pistons	Los Angeles Lakers
Indiana Pacers	Phoenix Suns
Milwaukee Bucks	Portland Trail Blazers
New Orleans Hornets	Sacramento Kings
Toronto Raptors	Seattle SuperSonics

WNBA Teams

Eastern Conference	Western Conference
Charlotte Sting	Houston Comets
Cleveland Rockers	Los Angeles Sparks
Detroit Shock	Minnesota Lynx
Indiana Fever	Phoenix Mercury
New York Liberty	Portland Fire
Orlando Miracle	Sacramento Monarchs
Washington Mystics	Seattle Storm
	Utah Starzz

COMPETITORS

AFL
CART
Major League Baseball
NASCAR
NFL
NHL
PGA
World Wrestling Entertainment

HISTORICAL FINANCIALS & EMPLOYEES

Association FYE: August 31	Annual Growth	8/91	8/92	8/93	8/94	8/95	8/96	8/97	8/98	8/99	8/00
Sales ($ mil.)	12.5%	—	843	999	1,030	1,259	1,403	1,664	1,874	956	2,164
Employees	12.2%	—	—	—	450	550	650	850	1,000	800	—

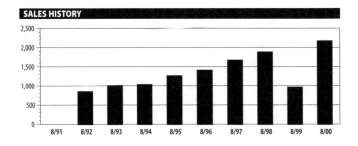

SALES HISTORY

2,500
2,000
1,500
1,000
500
0
8/91 8/92 8/93 8/94 8/95 8/96 8/97 8/98 8/99 8/00

NATIONAL FOOTBALL LEAGUE

In the world of professional sports, the National Football League (NFL) is blitzing the competition. The organization oversees America's most popular spectator sport, acting as a trade association for 32 franchise owners. The teams operate as separate businesses but share much of the revenue generated through broadcasting and merchandising. The NFL was founded as the American Professional Football Association in 1920. The league reorganized its two conferences, the AFC and NFC, for the 2002-03 season when the Houston Texans joined the league as the latest, and probably last, expansion team. Fans initially protested the move but quieted down once it was clear the reorganization made more geographic sense.

The NFL's primary operations consist of subsidiaries NFL Properties, which generates billions through merchandising and licensing, and NFL Enterprises, the entity that negotiates national broadcasting rights for the teams. The league's current eight-year, $17.6 billion TV contract was struck in 1998. Other subsidiaries include NFL Charities and NFL Films. The league is also capitalizing on the Internet as a revenue source, signing a four-year, $300 million deal with SportsLine.com, AOL, and CBS in 2001 to promote and maintain the league's NFL.com site.

HISTORY

Descended from the English game of rugby, American football was developed in the late 1800s by Walter Camp, a player from Yale University who is generally credited with introducing new rules for downs and scoring. Professional teams sprang up in the 1890s, but football remained relatively unorganized until 1920, when George Halas and college star Jim Thorpe helped organize the American Professional Football Association. The new league featured 14 teams from the Midwest and East, including Halas' Staleys (now the Chicago Bears) and the Racine Cardinals (now the Arizona Cardinals). In 1922 the association changed its name to the National Football League.

The new league suffered many growing pains over the next decade, but by the 1930s the NFL had settled on 10 teams including the Green Bay Packers (joined in 1921), the New York Giants (1925), and the Philadelphia Eagles (1933). Interest in the game remained somewhat regional, however, until the late 1940s and 1950s. In 1946 the Cleveland Rams moved to Los Angeles, and in 1950 the NFL expanded when three teams joined from the defunct All-American Football Conference. Television showed its potential in 1958 when that year's championship game, the first to be televised nationally, kept audiences riveted with an overtime victory by the Baltimore Colts over the Giants. In 1962 the NFL signed its first league-wide television contract with CBS, for $4.65 million.

The 1960s brought a new challenge in the form of the upstart American Football League (AFL). Concerned that the AFL would steal players with higher salaries and draw away fans, NFL commissioner Pete Rozelle negotiated a deal in 1966 to combine the leagues. That season concluded with the first AFL-NFL World Championship Game, which was renamed the Super Bowl in 1969. When the merger was completed in 1970, the new NFL sported 26 teams.

During the 1970s, football's popularity exploded, helped by the rise of franchise dynasties such as the Pittsburgh Steelers (four Super Bowl wins) and the Dallas Cowboys (five NFC titles). In 1982 the Oakland Raiders moved to Los Angeles after a jury ruled against the NFL's attempts to keep the team in Oakland. The decision prompted other teams to relocate in search of better facilities and more revenue. (The Raiders returned to Oakland in 1995.) Rozelle stepped down in 1989 and was replaced by Paul Tagliabue.

During the 1990s the league expanded to 30 teams, adding the Carolina Panthers and Jacksonville Jaguars in 1995. The next year Art Modell moved his Cleveland Browns franchise to Baltimore to become the Ravens. (The city of Cleveland held onto the rights to the Browns name and history and the franchise was revived in 1999.) In 1997 the Houston Oilers defected to Tennessee and were renamed the Titans. The next year brought new television deals worth $17.6 billion over eight years.

The NFL made plans for new expansion in 1999, awarding a franchise to Robert McNair of Houston, who paid a record $700 million franchise fee and $310 million for a new stadium. Named the Houston Texans, the team began play in 2002. (Also in 2002 the NFL realigned the NFC and AFC, shifting to eight divisions with four teams each.)

OFFICERS

Commissioner: Paul J. Tagliabue, age 61
CFO: Barbara A. Kaczynski
COO: Roger Goodell
EVP Communications and Government Affairs: Joe Browne
EVP Labor Relations; Chairman, NFLMC: Harold R. Henderson
EVP and League Counsel: Jeff Pash
EVP New Media and Enterprises: Thomas E. Spock
SVP Broadcast Planning: Dennis Lewin
SVP Corporate Sponsorships: Jim Schwebel
SVP Events: Jim Steeg

SVP New Media: Christopher J. Russo
VP Football Development and Operations: John Beake
VP Human Resources and Administration: Nancy Gill
VP NFL International: Gordon Smeaton
VP Player and Employee Development: Mike Haynes
VP Security: Milt Ahlerich
Senior Director of Brand and Consumer Marketing:
  Marjorie Rodgers, age 33
Director of Community Affairs: Beth Colleton
Executive Director, NFLPA: Gene Upshaw
Managing Director, NFL Europe: Jim Connelly
SVP and Managing Director, NFL International:
  Douglas Quinn
Auditors: Deloitte & Touche

LOCATIONS

HQ: 280 Park Ave., New York, NY 10017
Phone: 212-450-2000   **Fax:** 212-681-7573
Web: www.nfl.com

The National Football League oversees 32 franchises in
31 cities. It also has six franchises in Europe.

PRODUCTS/OPERATIONS

National Football League Franchises

American Football Conference
Baltimore Ravens
Buffalo Bills (New York)
Cincinnati Bengals
Cleveland Browns
Denver Broncos
Houston Texans
Indianapolis Colts
Jacksonville Jaguars (Florida)
Kansas City Chiefs (Missouri)
Miami Dolphins
New England Patriots (Foxboro, MA)
New York Jets (New York City)
Oakland Raiders (California)
Pittsburgh Steelers
San Diego Chargers
Tennessee Titans (Nashville)

National Football Conference
Arizona Cardinals (Phoenix)
Atlanta Falcons
Carolina Panthers (Charlotte, NC)
Chicago Bears
Dallas Cowboys
Detroit Lions
Green Bay Packers (Wisconsin)
Minnesota Vikings (Minneapolis)
New Orleans Saints
New York Giants (New York City)
Philadelphia Eagles
St. Louis Rams
San Francisco 49ers
Seattle Seahawks
Tampa Bay Buccaneers
Washington Redskins (Washington, DC)

Selected Business Units

NFL Charities
NFL Enterprises (media development)
NFL Films (highlight packages)
NFL Properties (licensing, marketing, promotions,
  and publishing)

COMPETITORS

CART
FIFA
Major League Baseball
NASCAR
NBA
NHL
PGA
World Wrestling Entertainment

HISTORICAL FINANCIALS & EMPLOYEES

Association FYE: March 31	Annual Growth	3/92	3/93	3/94	3/95	3/96	3/97	3/98	3/99	3/00	3/01
Sales ($ mil.)	13.3%	—	—	1,753	1,730	2,059	2,331	2,448	3,271	3,602	4,200
Employees	4.0%	—	—	—	—	—	—	400	400	450	450

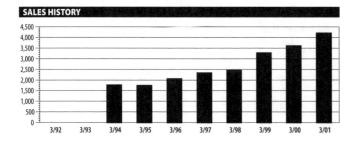

SALES HISTORY

NATIONAL GEOGRAPHIC SOCIETY

It's not your father's National Geographic Society anymore. Still publishing its flagship *National Geographic* magazine, the not-for-profit organization with some 10 million members has expanded into an array of venues to enhance our knowledge of the big blue marble. For-profit subsidiary National Geographic Ventures is fortifying the organization's presence on television and the Web and in map-making and retail. The organization owns part of the National Geographic Channel, a cable channel it operates jointly with NBC and FOX. The National Geographic Society also supports geographic expeditions (it has funded more than 7,000 scientific research projects) and sponsors exhibits, lectures, and education programs.

As competition from relative newcomers such as Discovery Communications intensifies, the commercialization of the National Geographic Society has been accelerating.

HISTORY

In 1888 a group of scientists and explorers gathered in Washington, DC, to form the National Geographic Society. Gardiner Hubbard was its first president. The organization mailed the first edition of its magazine, dated October 1888, to 165 members. The magazine had a brown cover and contained a few esoteric articles, such as "The Classification of Geographic Forms by Genesis." The organization's tradition of funding expeditions began in 1890 when it sent geologist Israel Russell to explore Alaska. It began issuing regular monthly editions of *National Geographic* in 1896.

Following Hubbard's death in 1897, his son-in-law, inventor Alexander Graham Bell, became president. Aiming to boost the magazine's popularity, he hired Gilbert Grosvenor (who later married Bell's daughter) as editor. Grosvenor turned the magazine from a dry, technical publication to one of more general interest.

Under Grosvenor the magazine pioneered the use of photography, including rare photographs of remote Tibet (1904), the first hand-tinted colored photos (1910), the first underwater color photos (1920s), and the first color aerial photographs (1930).

The organization sponsored Robert Peary's trek to the North Pole in 1909 and Hiram Bingham's 1912 exploration of Machu Picchu in Peru. National Geographic expanded into cartography with the creation of a maps division in 1915. Grosvenor became president in 1920. By 1930 circulation was 1.2 million (up from 2,200 in 1900). Grosvenor's policy of printing only "what is of a kindly nature ... about any

country or people" resulted in two articles that were criticized for their kindly portrayal of prewar Nazi Germany. (However, National Geographic maps and photographs were used by the US government for WWII intelligence.) That policy eased over the years, and in 1961 a *National Geographic* article described the growing US involvement in Vietnam.

Grosvenor retired in 1954. His son Melville Bell Grosvenor, who became president and editor in 1957, accelerated book publishing and created a film unit that aired its first TV documentary in 1965. Melville retired in 1967.

Melville's son Gilbert Melville Grosvenor took over as president in 1970. The organization debuted its *National Geographic Explorer* television series in 1985. National Geographic branched into commercial ventures in 1995 when it created for-profit subsidiary National Geographic Ventures to expand its presence on television, the Internet, maps, and retail.

Grosvenor became chairman in 1996, and Reg Murphy took over as president. Murphy shook up the organization by laying off nearly a quarter of its staff and stepping up its profit-making activities. National Geographic branched into cable television in 1996 when it partnered with NBC to launch a documentary channel. (FOX bought into the partnership three years later.)

John Fahey replaced Murphy as president in 1998. The following year National Geographic unveiled its *Adventure* magazine. To fight a circulation decline, the organization began offering *National Geographic* on newsstands for the first time in 1999. In 2000 National Geographic Ventures acquired recreational topographic map company Wildflower Productions. As part of an agreement to buy 30% of travel portal iExplore, National Geographic also agreed to license the use of its name for the first time in the organization's history.

OFFICERS

President and CEO, National Geographic Ventures:
C. Richard Allen
President, National Geographic Television:
Timothy T. Kelly
President, NationalGeographic.com: Mitch Praver
EVP and President, Books and School Publishing
Group: Nina D. Hoffman
EVP Mission Programs: Terry D. Garcia
SVP Human Resources: Thomas Sablo
SVP School Publishing: Ericka Markman
SVP International: Robert W. Hernandez
SVP Communications: Betty Hudson
Executive Director, Education Foundation:
Lanny M. Proffer
Editor in Chief, National Geographic Magazine:
William L. Allen
Managing Editor, National Geographic: Robert L. Booth
Associate Editor, National Geographic:
Bernard Ohanian

LOCATIONS

HQ: 1145 17th St. NW, Washington, DC 20036
Phone: 202-857-7000   Fax: 202-775-6141
Web: www.nationalgeographic.com

PRODUCTS/OPERATIONS

Selected Operations
Books
 Cuba
 Eyewitness to the 20th Century
 *Last Climb: The Legendary Everest Expeditions
  of George Mallory*
 Return to Midway
 The World of Islam
Education products
Magazines
 Adventure
 National Geographic
 Traveler
 World
Maps and atlases
Sponsorship of expeditions, lectures, and education
 programs
Television
 National Geographic Channel (25%, cable channel)
 National Geographic Explorer
 PBS specials
 Really Wild Animals
 Tales from the Wild

COMPETITORS

AOL Time Warner
DeLorme
Discovery Communications
Educational Insights
Encyclopaedia Britannica
ESRI
Lonely Planet
MapQuest.com
Rand McNally
Time

HISTORICAL FINANCIALS & EMPLOYEES

Not-for-profit FYE: December 31	Annual Growth	12/92	12/93	12/94	12/95	12/96	12/97	12/98	12/99	12/00	12/01
Sales ($ mil.)	0.6%	453	423	419	423	401	489	537	600	500	476
Employees	(3.2%)	2,005	1,700	1,493	1,551	1,300	1,214	1,410	—	1,500	1,500

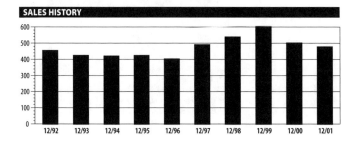

SALES HISTORY

NATIONAL HOCKEY LEAGUE

Contrary to popular humor, you don't have to go to a fight to see a hockey match break out in the National Hockey League. Nevertheless, for the NHL's 30 US and Canadian teams, there's plenty of opportunity for fisticuffs in each game. The clubs are organized into two conferences with three divisions each. Seven minor and semi-pro hockey leagues also fly under the NHL banner. Two expansion teams started play in the 2000-01 season (Columbus Blue Jackets, Minnesota Wild), which also began a new $600 million five-year TV deal with ABC and ESPN secured by commissioner Gary Bettman.

Despite the increase in league revenue over the past few seasons, the NHL still has a long way to go to catch up to the other professional sports leagues in popularity. Bettman's top priorities include changing the slow, low-scoring image of the game. (Rule changes have helped improve the pace.) The league has also been marred by violence, including a near epidemic of concussions. It is investigating the type of equipment used by players, such as the size and construction of elbow and shoulder pads, which increasingly have become weapons. In addition, the league lacks marquee players of Wayne Gretsky-esque stature.

HISTORY

The National Hockey League traces its roots to 1893, when the Stanley Cup (donated by Lord Stanley, Governor General of Canada) was first awarded to the Montreal Amateur Athletic Association hockey club of the Amateur Hockey Association of Canada. The National Hockey Association (NHA) was the first professional league to award the Cup (a large silver chalice with a new layer added each year, passed to the winning team and engraved with the names of that team's players) in 1910. The NHA folded in 1917 when feuding brought the need for a new image. That year Frank Calder, a British scholar and former sports journalist who came to Canada to be a soccer player, decided to keep the NHA's teams intact, rename the organization the National Hockey League (NHL), and appoint himself president. The league consisted of four teams that played a 22-game schedule.

The original Ottawa Senators (the team went under in 1934 and reemerged as an expansion team in 1992) were the league's first dynasty, winning four Cups from 1920-27. The NHL added its first US team in 1925 when the Boston Bruins joined the league. The 1920s saw continued expansion, but the NHL remained amorphous as many teams joined up and dropped out during the decade. Hordes of players went to WWII, forcing the NHL to field teams whose players were too young, too old, or barely able to skate. The league almost shut down, but the Canadian government encouraged play to continue, claiming it boosted national morale.

The Montreal Canadiens (winners of 24 Stanley Cups, more than any other franchise by far) dominated the NHL for most of the next three decades. The NHL, after representing a small number of teams for many years, launched its largest expansion in league history in 1967 when six US-based franchises joined up. The league expanded to 21 teams in 1979 by absorbing its rival professional league, the World Hockey Association. US interest in the sport stagnated for many years, however, as it was largely considered a Canadian sport, and its reputation for brutal violence turned off many fans. The NHL tried to put an end to its slugfest image by implementing new rules in 1992, reducing violent play and emphasizing a quicker game based on skill and style.

Several expansion teams (Anaheim, Florida, Tampa Bay, Ottawa, San Jose) were added to the NHL throughout the 1990s, a decade marred by the only major labor dispute in the league's history. Team owners instituted a player lockout in 1994 and delayed the season but ultimately failed in their goal of implementing a salary cap. (The current contract between the players' union and owners runs through 2004.) In 1997 the NHL added four new expansion teams (Atlanta; Columbus, Ohio; Minnesota; and Nashville), introducing them over a four-year period.

The league's plan to boost popularity by using pro players in the 1998 Winter Olympics games in Nagano, Japan, was thwarted by limited, late-night coverage. Later that year NHL team owners agreed to a $600 million, five-year television contract with Walt Disney's ABC and ESPN starting with the 2000-01 season. That season also marked further expansion as the Minnesota Wild and the Columbus Blue Jackets took to the ice. The league got a shot in the arm from the 2002 Winter Olympics in Salt Lake City, which featured many NHL players in a hotly contested US vs. Canada final. The Canadians took the gold medal with a 5-2 victory.

OFFICERS

Commissioner: Gary B. Bettman, age 50
EVP and COO: Jon Litner
EVP and CFO: Craig Harnett
EVP and Chief Legal Officer: William Daly
SVP New Business Development and President, NHL ICE: Keith Ritter
SVP Television and Media Ventures: Doug Perlman
VP Broadcasting and Programming: Adam Acone
VP Club Marketing: Scott Carmichael

Group VP Consumer Products Marketing:
Brian Jennings
Group VP Corporate Marketing: Andrew Judelson
Group VP and Managing Director, NHL International:
Ken Yaffe
President, NHL Enterprises: Ed Horne
Director of Human Resources: Janet A. Meyers
Director of Officiating: Andy van Hellemond
Auditors: PricewaterhouseCoopers LLP

LOCATIONS

HQ: 1251 Avenue of the Americas, 47th Fl.,
New York, NY 10020
Phone: 212-789-2000   Fax: 212-789-2020
Web: www.nhl.com

The National Hockey League has 24 teams in the US and
six in Canada.

PRODUCTS/OPERATIONS

Eastern Conference

Atlantic Division
New Jersey Devils
New York Islanders
New York Rangers
Philadelphia Flyers
Pittsburgh Penguins

Northeast Division
Boston Bruins
Buffalo Sabres
Montreal Canadiens
Ottawa Senators
Toronto Maple Leafs

Southeast Division
Atlanta Thrashers
Carolina Hurricanes
Florida Panthers
Tampa Bay Lightning
Washington Capitals

Western Conference

Central Division
Chicago Blackhawks
Columbus Blue Jackets
Detroit Red Wings
Nashville Predators
St. Louis Blues

Northwest Division
Calgary Flames
Colorado Avalanche
Edmonton Oilers
Minnesota Wild
Vancouver Canucks

Pacific Division
Dallas Stars
Los Angeles Kings
Mighty Ducks of Anaheim
Phoenix Coyotes
San Jose Sharks

Minor and Semi-Pro Leagues
American Hockey League
Central Hockey League
East Coast Hockey League
International Hockey League
United Hockey League
West Coast Hockey League
Western Professional Hockey League

COMPETITORS

AFL
CART
Indy Racing League
Major League Baseball
NASCAR
NBA
NFL
PGA

HISTORICAL FINANCIALS & EMPLOYEES

Association FYE: June 30	Annual Growth	6/91	6/92	6/93	6/94	6/95	6/96	6/97	6/98	6/99	6/00
Sales ($ mil.)	18.8%	—	—	—	604	763	728	1,099	1,336	1,476	1,697
Employees	27.3%	—	—	—	110	150	200	257	289	—	—

SALES HISTORY

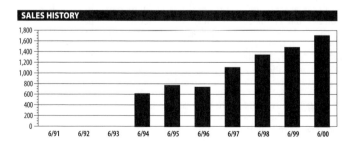

AMTRAK

Fueled by government dollars, Amtrak keeps on chugging, hoping to operate on its own steam. The National Railroad Passenger Corporation, better known as Amtrak, carries more than 23 million passengers a year in 46 states. A for-profit company that has never been profitable, Amtrak is almost wholly owned by the US Department of Transportation and receives large subsidies from the federal government, which wants Amtrak to be self-sufficient by the end of 2002. But Amtrak may not have the chance to do so — the Amtrak Reform Council (formed in 1997 to govern the rail operator) has proposed to Congress that Amtrak be split into three groups and that competition be allowed on some passenger routes.

Amtrak has announced plans to cut $285 million of its operations budget, including reducing its workforce of 24,600 by 1,000, deferring 23% of its planned capital investments, and reducing spending for marketing and advertising. Although it has asked the federal government for $1.2 billion in assistance for fiscal 2003, Amtrak has been promised only $521 million. If it doesn't receive the requested $1.2 billion, the rail company is threatening to shut down nearly half of its 41 long-distance routes.

But the Amtrak Reform Council, which sets a December 2002 deadline for the carrier to support itself, may soon derail Amtrak's plans. It has proposed to Congress that Amtrak be divided into three sections: a federal agency to oversee national rail programs, a company to manage tracks, and another company to manage rail service. It also calls for Amtrak's monopoly on rail passenger service to end, allowing competition within two to three years on certain routes. Congress, set to vote on the proposal in 2002, must now decide Amtrak's fate.

HISTORY

US passenger train travel peaked in 1929, with 20,000 trains in operation. But the spread of automobiles, bus service, and air travel cut into business, and by the late 1960s only about 500 passenger trains remained running in the US. In 1970 the combined losses of all private train operations exceeded $1.8 billion in today's dollars. That year Congress passed the Rail Passenger Service Act, which created Amtrak to preserve America's passenger rail system. Although railroads were offered stock in the corporation for their passenger equipment, most just wrote off the loss.

Amtrak began operating in 1971 with 1,200 cars, most built in the 1950s. Although the company lost money from the outset ($153 million in

1972), it continued to be bankrolled by Uncle Sam, despite much criticism. Amtrak ordered its first new equipment in 1973, the year it also began taking over stations, yards, and service staff. The company didn't own any track until 1976, when it purchased hundreds of miles of right-of-way track from Boston to Washington, DC.

After a 1979 study showed Amtrak passengers to be by far the most heavily subsidized travelers in the US, Congress ordered the company to better utilize its resources. The 1980s saw Amtrak leasing its rights-of-way along its tracks in the Northeast corridor to telecommunications companies (which installed fiber-optic cables) and beginning mail and freight services for extra revenue.

In the early 1990s Amtrak faced a number of challenges: Midwest flooding, falling airfares, and safety concerns over a number of rail accidents, particularly the 1993 wreck of the Sunset Limited near Mobile, Alabama, in which 47 people were killed. (It was the worst accident in Amtrak's history.) In 1994 Amtrak's board of directors (at Congress' behest) adopted a plan to be free of federal support by 2002. In 1995 the company began planning high-speed trains for its heavily traveled East Coast routes.

In 1997 Amtrak finalized agreements to buy the high-speed cars and locomotives central to its self-sufficiency plan. The company also began increasing its freight hauling and had its first profitable product line: the Metroliner route between New York and Washington, DC.

Amtrak's board of directors was replaced by Congress in 1997 with a seven-member Reform Board appointed by President Clinton. Chairman and president Thomas Downs resigned that year, and Tommy Thompson, then governor of Wisconsin, took over as chairman. Former Massachusetts governor Michael Dukakis was named vice chairman, and George Warrington stepped in as Amtrak's president and CEO.

Technical problems in 1999 delayed Amtrak's introduction of the Acela high-speed train in the Northeast until late 2000, when service began in the Boston-Washington, DC, corridor. In 2001 Amtrak pitched a 20-year plan, involving an annual outlay of $1.5 billion in federal funds, for expanding and modernizing its passenger service to help alleviate highway and airport congestion nationwide. Thompson left the Amtrak board in 2001 after he was named US secretary of health and human services.

Realizing Amtrak would not meet its December 2002 deadline to be self-sufficient, in 2002 the Amtrak Reform Council sent a proposal to Congress that Amtrak be divided into three groups: one to oversee operations and funding, a second to maintain certain Amtrak-owned tracks and properties, and a third to operate trains. It also called for competition to be allowed on some passenger routes within two to three years.

Also in 2002 Warrington resigned and was replaced by David Gunn, who formerly headed the metropolitan transit systems in New York and Toronto. Gunn began moving to cut costs, and he worked to secure new federal money to avert a threatened shutdown of rail service in July 2002.

OFFICERS

Chairman: John Robert Smith
Vice Chairman: Michael S. Dukakis
President and CEO: David L. Gunn
CFO: Arlene R. Friner
EVP Operations and COO: E. S. Bagley Jr.
EVP Marketing and Sales: Barbara J. Richardson
VP and Counsel, Business Diversity and Strategic Initiatives: Wanda Morris Hightower
VP Freight Railroad Affairs: Lee W. Bullock
VP Government Affairs: Sandy J. Brown
VP High-Speed Rail Development: David J. Carol
VP Human Resources: Lorraine A. Green
VP Labor Relations: Joseph M. Bress
VP Procurement: Michael Rienzi
VP Service Operations: Anne W. Hoey
President, Amtrak Intercity: Edward V. Walker
President, Amtrak Mail & Express: Lee H. Sargrad
General Manager, Eastern Operations: Bill Lerch
SVP, Amtrak West: Gilbert O. Mallery
Corporate Secretary: Stewart G. Simonson
Auditors: KPMG LLP

LOCATIONS

HQ: National Railroad Passenger Corporation
  60 Massachusetts Ave. NE, Washington, DC 20002
Phone: 202-906-3000   **Fax:** 202-906-3306
Web: www.amtrak.com

The National Railroad Passenger Corporation (or Amtrak) is the only intercity passenger rail service in the US with routes across the entire country. The company serves some 600 stations in 46 states.

COMPETITORS

America West
AMR
Burlington Northern Santa Fe
Coach USA
Continental Airlines
Delta
Greyhound
Metra
Northwest Airlines
Port Authority of NY & NJ
Roadway
Southwest Airlines
UAL
Union Pacific
UPS
US Airways
U.S. Postal Service
Yellow

HISTORICAL FINANCIALS & EMPLOYEES

Government-owned FYE: September 30	Annual Growth	9/92	9/93	9/94	9/95	9/96	9/97	9/98	9/99	9/00	9/01
Sales ($ mil.)	5.9%	1,325	1,403	1,413	1,497	1,555	1,674	2,285	2,042	2,111	2,100
Employees	0.3%	24,000	24,000	24,000	24,100	23,000	23,000	24,000	25,000	25,000	24,600

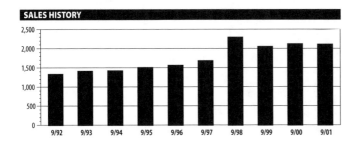

SALES HISTORY

NATIONWIDE

Call it truth in advertising — Nationwide has offices throughout the US. The company is a leading US property/casualty insurer that, though still a mutual firm, operates in part through publicly held insurance subsidiary Nationwide Financial. In addition to personal and commercial property/casualty coverage, life insurance, and financial services, the company offers surplus lines, professional liability, workers' compensation, managed health care, and other coverage. Nationwide sells its products through such affiliates as Farmland Insurance, Scottsdale Insurance, GatesMcDonald, and asset manager Gartmore.

Nationwide has sold German auto insurer Neckura, focusing on personal and small business lines in the US. The firm has also exited claims administration for Medicare. Nationwide Financial has bought Provident Mutual Life Insurance (now Nationwide Provident); the acquisition made the company the fourth-largest US provider of variable life insurance.

A decline in investment income set the company back in 2001, mainly due to the slump in equity-linked products.

HISTORY

In 1919 members of the Ohio Farm Bureau Federation, a farmers' consumer group, established their own automobile insurance company. (As rural drivers, they didn't want to pay city rates.) To get a license to operate from the state, the company, called Farm Bureau Mutual, needed 100 policyholders. It gathered more than 1,000. Founder Murray Lincoln headed the company until 1964.

The insurer expanded into Delaware, Maryland, North Carolina, and Vermont in 1928, and in 1931 it began selling auto insurance to city folks. It expanded into fire insurance in 1934 and life insurance the next year.

During WWII growth slowed, although the company had operations in 12 states and Washington, DC, by 1943. It diversified in 1946 when it bought a Columbus, Ohio, radio station. By 1952 the firm had resumed expansion and changed its name to Nationwide.

The company was one of the first auto insurance companies to use its agents to sell other financial products, adding life insurance and mutual funds in the mid-1950s. Nationwide General, the country's first merit-rated auto insurance firm, was formed in 1956.

Nationwide established Neckura in Germany in 1965 to sell auto and fire insurance. Four years later the company bought GatesMcDonald, a provider of risk, tax, benefit, and health care management services. In 1979 Nationwide reorganized and brought all of its property/casualty operations under the Nationwide Property & Casualty umbrella.

Throughout the 1980s the company experienced solid growth by establishing or purchasing insurance firms, among them Colonial Insurance of California (1980), Financial Horizons Life (1981), Scottsdale (1982), and the largest, Employers Insurance of Wausau (1985). Wausau wrote the country's first workers' compensation policy in 1911.

Earnings were up and down in the 1990s as the company invested in Wausau and in consolidating office operations. Nationwide set up an ethics office in 1995, a time of increased scrutiny of insurance industry sales practices, and made an effort to hire more women as agents. In 1996 the Florida Insurance Commission claimed the company discriminated against customers on the basis of age, gender, health, income, marital status, and location. Nationwide countered that the allegations originated from displeased agents.

In 1997 the firm settled a lawsuit by agreeing to stop its redlining practices. (It avoided selling homeowners' insurance to urban customers with homes valued at less than $50,000 or more than 30 years old, which allegedly discriminated against minorities.) It also dropped a year-old sales quota system that was under investigation.

As the century came to a close, Nationwide began to narrow its focus on its core businesses. It spun off Nationwide Financial Services so the unit could have better access to capital, and it expanded both at home and abroad through such purchases as ALLIED Group (multiline insurance), CalFarm (agricultural insurance in California), and AXA subsidiary PanEuroLife (asset management in Europe). It jettisoned such operations as West Coast Life Insurance, its Wausau subsidiary, and its ALLIED Life operations. The company's discrimination woes came back to haunt it in 1999, so it created a $750,000 fund to help residents of poor Cincinnati neighborhoods buy homes.

At the end of 2000 Nationwide Health Plans asked regulators for permission to exit the profit-poor HMO business. The division plans to maintain its more popular PPO operations. In 2001 Nationwide's expansion in Europe continued with the purchase of UK fund manager Gartmore Investment Management.

OFFICERS

Chairman and CEO: William G. Jurgensen, age 51
EVP and CFO: Robert A. Oakley, age 55
EVP and Chief Administrative Officer: Donna A. James, age 44
EVP and Chief Investment Officer: Robert J. Woodward Jr., age 60
EVP, Finance and Investments: Robert A. Rosholt
President, Strategic Investments and Chief Strategic Officer: Michael S. Helfer, age 56
SVP and Chief Communications Officer: John R. Cook Jr., age 58
SVP and Chief Investment Officer: Edwin P. McCausland Jr.
SVP, General Counsel, and Secretary: Patricia R. Hatler, age 47
SVP, Corporate Relations: Gregory Lashutka, age 57
SVP and Corporate Controller: David A. Diamond, age 46
VP and CIO: George McKinnon
President and CEO, Gartmore Group: Paul J. Hondros
President and Managing Director, Nationwide Global Holdings: Richard D. Headley, age 53
President and COO, Nationwide Financial, Nationwide Life Insurance, and Nationwide Life & Annuity Insurance: Joseph J. Gasper, age 58
President and COO, Nationwide Insurance: Galen R. Barnes, age 54
President and COO, Scottsdale Insurance Companies: R. Max Williamson
President and COO, Allied Insurance: Steve S. Rasmussen
Auditors: KPMG LLP

LOCATIONS

HQ: One Nationwide Plaza, Columbus, OH 43215
Phone: 614-249-7111   **Fax:** 614-249-7705
Web: www.nationwide.com

Nationwide operates in more than 35 countries around the world.

PRODUCTS/OPERATIONS

2001 Assets

	$ mil.	% of total
Cash & equivalents	1,062	1
Bonds	30,813	27
Stocks	3,781	3
Mortgage loans & real estate	8,591	8
Assets in separate account	61,222	54
Other assets	7,994	7
Total	**113,463**	**100**

Selected Subsidiaries and Affiliates

Gartmore Group (UK)
GatesMcDonald
Nationwide Agribusiness
Farmland Insurance
Nationwide Federal Credit Union
Nationwide Financial (81.5%)
401k Company
National Deferred Compensation
Nationwide Home Mortgage Company
Nationwide Retirement Plan Services, Inc.
Pension Associates, Inc.
Nationwide Global
PanEuroLife
Nationwide Insurance
Allied Insurance
CalFarm Insurance
Nationwide Health Plans
Nationwide Realty Investors
Scottsdale Insurance

COMPETITORS

Allstate	The Hartford	Pacific Mutual
American	John Hancock	Principal
Financial	Financial	Financial
AXA	Services	Prudential
AXA Financial	Liberty Mutual	St. Paul
Blue Cross	MassMutual	Companies
CIGNA	MetLife	State Farm
Citigroup	New York Life	UnitedHealth
CNA Financial	Northwestern	Group
Guardian Life	Mutual	USAA

HISTORICAL FINANCIALS & EMPLOYEES

Mutual company FYE: December 31	Annual Growth	12/92	12/93	12/94	12/95	12/96	12/97	12/98	12/99	12/00	12/01
Assets ($ mil.)	13.1%	37,582	42,213	47,696	57,420	67,624	83,214	98,280	115,760	117,039	113,463
Net income ($ mil.)	—	69	501	445	183	250	1,031	963	526	331	(295)
Income as % of assets	—	0.2%	1.2%	0.9%	0.3%	0.4%	1.2%	1.0%	0.5%	0.3%	—
Employees	0.8%	32,500	32,583	32,600	32,949	33,184	29,051	32,815	35,000	35,000	35,000

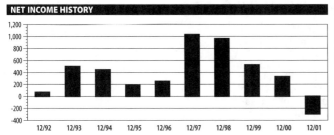

NET INCOME HISTORY

2001 FISCAL YEAR-END
Equity as % of assets: 7.1%
Return on assets: —
Return on equity: —
Long-term debt ($ mil.): —
Sales ($ mil.): 29,538

NUMMI

What do you get when a Japanese production process meets a California lifestyle? New United Motor Manufacturing, Inc. (NUMMI), a 50-50 joint venture between General Motors (GM) and Toyota. NUMMI makes Tacoma pickup trucks and Corolla sedans for Toyota. The Tacoma pickup is made only at the NUMMI plant in Fremont, California. The company also makes GM's Pontiac division's newest model — the Vibe sport wagon. NUMMI can produce 220,000 cars and 150,000 pickups a year. Together GM and Toyota are researching alternative-fuel vehicles to meet strict emissions requirements.

In addition to the Vibe, NUMMI has also debuted the Voltz — a right-hand-drive car that is exported to Japan for Toyota. NUMMI began as an experiment to see if Japanese management techniques emphasizing team decision-making would work in the US. The experiment has been a success story. Toyota's strategy to build more vehicles in the markets it serves (rather than transport them) helps the company reduce costs. NUMMI's production methods are considered to be among the world's most efficient.

HISTORY

Rivals General Motors (GM) and Toyota applied the old adage, "If you can't beat 'em, join 'em," in forming their 50-50 joint venture New United Motor Manufacturing, Inc. (NUMMI). During the early 1980s, GM was sagging in the small-car market, and Japan's Toyota wanted to build cars in the US to ease trade tension. GM head Roger Smith and Toyota chairman Eiji Toyoda met in 1982 to discuss ways to achieve their goals.

After a year of negotiations, the two companies announced their partnership at GM's plant (which GM had closed in 1982) in Fremont, California. Toyota put up $100 million, and GM provided the plant (valued at $89 million) and $11 million cash. The companies also raised $350 million to build a stamping plant.

To gain FTC approval, the companies agreed to limit the venture to 12 years (extended later), make no more than 250,000 cars a year for GM, and refrain from sharing strategic information. In 1984 the FTC approved the deal and NUMMI was born.

The Fremont plant had a reputation for poor labor relations, and Toyota originally refused to rehire any of the workers from the plant; after prolonged negotiations with the United Auto Workers (UAW), it agreed to hire 50% plus one of the former workers. From the outset NUMMI was different, with fewer management layers and a blurred distinction between blue- and white-collar workers.

NUMMI's first car, a Chevy Nova, rolled off the assembly line in late 1984. The company began producing the Corolla FX, a two-door version of the four-door Nova, in 1986. NUMMI earned kudos for high worker morale and productivity and was selected that year as a case study on positive labor-management relations for the International Labor Organization Conference.

Despite its success on some fronts, NUMMI's sales slid during the late 1980s. It had earned a reputation for high-quality cars, but it struggled with high overhead and weak Nova sales. In 1988 NUMMI halted Nova and Corolla FX production to build Geo Prizm and Corolla sedans.

By late 1989 NUMMI's production numbers had begun to rebound. In 1990 NUMMI began a major expansion as it geared up to build Toyota's half-ton pickup. Its first Toyota 4X2 pickup (the Toyota Hi-Lux) rolled off the assembly line in 1991, followed by the Toyota 4X4 pickup the next year.

In 1993 the FTC approved an indefinite extension of the original 12-year GM-Toyota agreement. Also that year NUMMI began building the Toyota Xtracab (an extended version of Toyota's pickup), and it began constructing a plastics plant to build bumper coverings for Prizms and Corollas. It also expanded the paint, body welding, and assembly plant facilities.

Although Toyota had produced half of its North America-bound pickups in Japan and half in the US for years, it shifted all compact truck production to the NUMMI plant with the 1995 launch of the Tacoma. NUMMI built its 3 millionth vehicle in 1997 and marked the event by donating three vehicles to charitable agencies in the Fremont area.

In 1998 Toyota introduced an updated Tacoma compact pickup, and GM changed the name of the Geo Prizm to the Chevrolet Prizm. The companies agreed in 1999 to a five-year partnership to develop and possibly produce alternative-fuel vehicles. GM alluded to the possible discontinued production of the Prizm in 2000; it could be replaced by a next-generation model.

OFFICERS

President and CEO: Kanji Ishii
SVP: Yuji Niimi
VP Finance and Purchasing; Treasurer: Toshiki Amano
VP Legal, Human Resources, Environmental and Government Affairs: Patricia Salas Pineda, age 50
VP: Ernesto Gonzalez-Beltram, age 40
General Manager Purchasing: Linda McClogan
Manager of Community Relations: Jean-Yves Jault
Sr. Specialist, Community Relations: Thom Faulkner

LOCATIONS

HQ: New United Motor Manufacturing, Inc.
45500 Fremont Blvd., Fremont, CA 94538
Phone: 510-498-5500   **Fax:** 510-770-4116
Web: www.nummi.com

PRODUCTS/OPERATIONS

Selected Models
Pontiac Vibe (sport wagon)
Toyota Corolla (sedan)
Toyota Tacoma (pickup)
Voltz (right-hand-drive sport wagon)

COMPETITORS

DaimlerChrysler
Fiat
Ford
Fuji Heavy Industries
Honda
Isuzu
Kia Motors
Mack Trucks
Mazda
Nissan
Peugeot Motors of America, Inc.
Saab Automobile
Suzuki Motor
Volkswagen

HISTORICAL FINANCIALS & EMPLOYEES

Joint venture FYE: December 31	Annual Growth	12/92	12/93	12/94	12/95	12/96	12/97	12/98	12/99	12/00	12/01
Estimated sales ($ mil.)	13.5%	2,200	2,700	3,700	4,500	4,700	4,600	4,699	—	—	—
Employees	2.9%	3,969	4,300	4,500	4,800	4,700	4,800	4,800	4,800	4,600	5,000

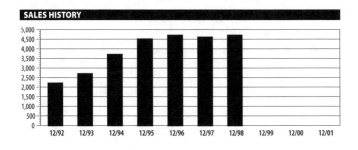

SALES HISTORY

NYC HEALTH AND HOSPITALS

New York City Health and Hospitals Corporation (HHC) takes care of the Big Apple. HHC has facilities in all five boroughs of New York City. As one of the largest municipal health service systems in the US, HHC operates a health care network consisting of 11 acute-care hospitals (including Bellevue, the nation's oldest public hospital), community clinics, diagnostic and treatment centers, long-term-care facilities, and a home health care agency. HHC also provides medical services to New York City's correctional facilities and operates MetroPlus, a health maintenance organization.

In recent years HHC has lost paying patients to newer, better-equipped facilities, and is left caring for a deluge of medically indigent and Medicaid patients, who tend to be sicker than the general population since they wait longer to seek care. To streamline, HHC has slashed jobs, worked to reduce the average length of stay of patients, and cut back on unnecessary facilities.

HISTORY

The City of New York in 1929 created a department to manage its hospitals for the poor. During the Depression, more than half of the city's residents were eligible for subsidized care, and its public hospitals operated at full capacity. Four new hospitals opened in the 1950s, but the city was already having trouble maintaining existing facilities and attracting staff. (Young doctors preferred private, insurance-supported hospitals catering to the middle class.) Meanwhile, technological advances and increased demand for skilled nurses made hospitals more expensive to operate. The advent of Medicaid in 1965 was a boon for the system because it brought in federal money.

In 1969 the city created the New York City Health and Hospitals Corporation (HHC) to manage its public health care system and, it was hoped, to distance it from the political arena. But HHC was still dependent on the city for funds, arousing criticism from those who had hoped for more autonomy. A 1973 state report claimed "the people of New York City are not materially better served by the Health and Hospitals Corporation than by its predecessor agencies."

City budget shortfalls in the mid-1970s led to cutbacks at HHC, including nearly 20% of staff. Later in the decade, several hospitals closed and some services were discontinued.

Ed Koch became mayor in 1978 and gained more control over HHC's operations. Struggles between his administration and the system led three HHC presidents to resign by 1981. That year Koch crony Stanley Brezenoff assumed the post and helped to transform HHC into a city pseudo-department.

The early 1980s brought greater prosperity to the system. Reimbursement rates and collections procedures improved, allowing HHC to upgrade its record-keeping and its ambulatory and psychiatric care programs. In the late 1980s, sharp increases in AIDS and crack addiction cases strained the system, and a sluggish economy decreased city funding. Criticism mounted in the early 1990s, with allegations of wrongful deaths, dangerous facilities, and lack of Medicaid payment controls. HHC lost patients to managed-care providers, and revenues plummeted. In 1995 a city panel recommended radically revamping the system.

Faced with declining revenues and criticism from Mayor Rudolph Giuliani that HHC was "a jobs program," the company began cutting jobs and consolidating facilities in 1996. Under Giuliani's direction, HHC made plans to sell its Coney Island, Elmhurst, and Queens hospital centers. In 1997 the New York State Supreme Court struck down Giuliani's privatization efforts, saying the city council had a right to review and approve each sale. In 1998 Giuliani continued to seek to restructure HHC, and the agency itself contended it was making progress toward its restructuring goals, which were aimed at giving HHC more autonomy as well as more fiscal responsibility. In anticipation of a budget shortfall that year, the system laid off some 900 support staff employees. In 1999 the state court of appeals ruled HHC could not legally lease or sell its hospitals.

In 2000 HHC launched its effort to improve its physical infrastructure by beginning the rebuilding and renovation of facilities in Brooklyn, Manhattan, and Queens. The organization also began converting to an electronic (and thus more efficient) clinical information system. In 2001 HHC forged ahead with further restructuring initiatives. It introduced the Open Access plan, a cost-cutting measure designed to expedite the processes involved in outpatient visits.

OFFICERS

Chairman: Richard T. Roberts
Vice Chairman: Edward J. Rappa
President, CEO, and Director: Benjamin K. Chu
SVP, Corporate Planning, Community Health, and Intergovernmental Relations: LaRay Brown
SVP, Operations: Frank J. Cirillo
SVP, North Brooklyn Health Network; Executive Director, Woodhull Medical and Mental Health Center: Lynda D. Curtis
SVP, Medical and Professional Affairs: Van Dunn
SVP, Finance and Capital; CFO: Rick Langfelder

SVP, Long Term Care Policy: Samuel Lehrfeld
SVP, Central Brooklyn Family Health Network;
Executive Director, Kings County Hospital Center:
Jean Leon
SVP, North Bronx HealthCare Network; Executive
Director, Jacobi Medical Center and North Central
Bronx Hospital: Joseph S. Orlando
SVP, South Manhattan Network; Executive Director,
Bellevue Hospital Center: Carlos Perez
SVP, Generations Plus Northern Manhattan Health
Network; Executive Director, Lincoln Medical and
Mental Health Center and Metropolitan Hospital
Center: Jose R. Sanchez
SVP, Queens Health Network; Executive Director,
Elmhurst Hospital Center: Pete Velez
SVP, South Brooklyn/Staten Island Health Network;
Executive Director, Coney Island Hospital:
William P. Walsh
General Counsel: Alan D. Aviles
Auditors: KPMG LLP

LOCATIONS

HQ: New York City Health and Hospitals Corporation
125 Worth St., Ste. 510, New York, NY 10013
Phone: 212-788-3321   Fax: 212-788-0040
Web: www.ci.nyc.ny.us/html/hhc

HHC Networks

Brooklyn Staten Island Family Health Network
Coney Island Hospital
Dr. Susan Smith McKinney Nursing and Rehabilitation
Center
East New York Diagnostic & Treatment Center
Kings County Hospital Center
Seaview Hospital Rehabilitation Center and Home

Generations Plus Northern Manhattan Health Network
Harlem Hospital Center
Lincoln Medical and Mental Health Center
Metropolitan Hospital Center
Morrisania Diagnostic & Treatment Center
Renaissance Diagnostic & Treatment Center
Segundo Ruiz Belvis Diagnostic & Treatment Center

North Bronx Network
Jacobi Medical Center
North Central Bronx Hospital

North Brooklyn Health Network
Cumberland Diagnostic & Treatment Center
Woodhull Medical and Mental Health Center

Queens Health Network
Elmhurst Hospital Center
Queens Hospital Center

South Manhattan Healthcare Network
Bellevue Hospital Center
Coler/Goldwater Memorial Hospital
Gouverneur Nursing Facility and Diagnostic &
Treatment Center

COMPETITORS

Carondelet Health
Catholic Healthcare Network
Columbia University
Cornell University
Memorial Sloan-Kettering
Montefiore Medical
Mount Sinai
NYU
North Shore-Long Island Jewish Health System
Saint Vincent Catholic Medical Centers

HISTORICAL FINANCIALS & EMPLOYEES

Government-owned FYE: June 30	Annual Growth	6/92	6/93	6/94	6/95	6/96	6/97	6/98	6/99	6/00	6/01
Sales ($ mil.)	2.7%	—	3,468	3,949	4,134	4,460	4,069	3,835	4,131	4,100	4,300
Employees	(4.1%)	—	—	45,000	41,711	35,000	33,000	31,600	33,403	33,500	33,600

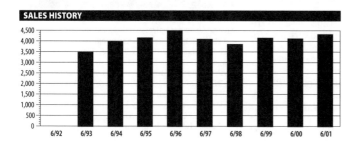

SALES HISTORY

NEW YORK LIFE INSURANCE

New York Life Insurance has been in the Big Apple since it was just a tiny seed. The company (the top mutual life insurer in the US) is adding products but retaining its core business: Life insurance and annuities. Its New York Life International is reaching out geographically, where the life insurance market is not yet mature. New York Life has added such products and services as mutual funds and securities brokerage for individuals. It also offers its asset management services to institutional investors. Other lines of business include special group policies sold through AARP and to federal government contractors.

After state legislators failed to approve a mutual holding company structure, New York Life announced it would not follow its rivals in demutualizing for fear of being gobbled up in a merger. The insurer will instead use its considerable war chest to further build international and asset management operations.

Streamlining operations, New York Life has put all of its asset management operations under one umbrella (New York Life Asset Management).

HISTORY

In 1841 actuary Pliny Freeman and 56 New York businessmen founded Nautilus Insurance Co., the third US policyholder-owned company. It began operating in 1845 and became New York Life in 1849.

By 1846 the company had the first life insurance agent west of the Mississippi River. Although the Civil War disrupted southern business, New York Life honored all its obligations and renewed lapsed policies when the war ended. By 1887 the company had developed its branch office system.

By the turn of the century, the company had established an agent compensation plan that featured a lifetime income after 20 years of service (discontinued in 1991). New York Life moved into Europe in the late 1800s but withdrew after WWI. In the early 1950s the company simplified insurance forms, slashed premiums, and updated mortality tables from the 1860s. In 1956 it became the first life insurer to use data-processing equipment on a large scale.

In the 1960s New York Life helped develop variable life insurance, which featured variable benefits and level premiums; it added variable annuities in 1968. Steady growth continued into the late 1970s, when high interest rates led to heavy policyholder borrowing. The outflow of money convinced New York Life to make its products more competitive as investments.

The company formed New York Life and Health Insurance Co. in 1982. It acquired MacKay-Shields Financial, which oversees its MainStay mutual funds, in 1984. The company's first pure investment product, a real estate limited partnership, debuted that year. When these limited partnerships proved riskier than most insurance customers bargained for, investors sued New York Life; in 1996 the company negotiated a plan to liquidate the partnerships and reimburse investors.

Expansion continued in 1987 when it bought a controlling interest in a third-party insurance plan administrator and group insurance programs. The company also acquired Sanus Corp. Health Systems.

New York Life formed an insurance joint venture in Indonesia in 1992 and entered South Korea and Taiwan. The next year it bought Aetna UK's life insurance operations.

In 1994 New York Life grew its health care holdings, adding utilization review and physician practice management units. Allegations of churning (agents inducing customers to buy more expensive policies), led New York Life to overhaul its sales practices in 1994; it settled the resulting lawsuit for $300 million in 1995. Soon came claims that agents hadn't properly informed customers that some policies were vulnerable to interest-rate changes and that customers might be entitled to share in the settlement. Some agents lashed out, saying New York Life fired them so it wouldn't have to pay them retirement benefits.

As health care margins decreased and the insurance industry consolidated, New York Life sold its health insurance operations in 1998 and said it would demutualize — a plan ultimately foiled by the state legislature.

In 2000 the company bought two Mexican insurance firms, including the nation's #2 life insurer, Seguros Monterrey. It received Office of Thrift Supervision permission to open a bank, New York Life Trust Company. Also that year, the company created a subsidiary to house its asset management businesses and entered the Indian market through its joint venture with Max India.

OFFICERS

Chairman and CEO: Seymour Sternberg, age 58
Vice Chairman; Chairman and CEO, New York Life International: Gary G. Benanav, age 56
Vice Chairman and President: Frederick J. Sievert, age 54
EVP: Phillip J. Hildebrand
EVP; Chairman and CEO, New York Life Investment Management LLC: Gary E. Wendlandt
EVP and Secretary: George J. Trapp
SVP and CFO: Michael E. Sproule
SVP and CIO: Judith E. Campbell

SVP and Chief Actuary: Joel M. Steinberg
SVP and Chief Investment Officer: Anne F. Pollack
SVP, General Auditor, and Chief Privacy Officer:
Thomas J. Warga
SVP and General Counsel: Shelia K. Davidson
SVP and Treasurer: Jay S. Calhoun
SVP, Human Resources: Leonard J. Elmer
SVP, Agency Department; President and CEO, NYLEX
Benefits: Albert J. Schiff
VP and Chief Marketing Officer, Life & Annuity:
Patricia Spencer Favreau
Chairman and CEO, MacKay Shields; Vice Chairman,
New York Life Investment Management: Ravi Akhoury
President and CEO, McMorgan & Company:
Terry O'Toole
Auditors: PricewaterhouseCoopers LLP

LOCATIONS

HQ: New York Life Insurance Company
51 Madison Ave., New York, NY 10010
Phone: 212-576-7000   Fax: 212-576-8145
Web: www.newyorklife.com

New York Life Insurance Company operates in
Argentina, China, Hong Kong, India, Indonesia, Mexico,
the Philippines, South Korea, Taiwan, Thailand, the US,
and Vietnam.

PRODUCTS/OPERATIONS

2001 Assets

	$ mil.	% of total
Cash	763	—
Bonds	64,214	58
Stocks	3,898	4
Mortgage loans	9,630	9
Real estate	513	—
Policy loans	6,153	6
Assets in separate account	14,039	13
Other assets	10,751	10
Total	**109,961**	**100**

Selected Operations

Asset Management
New York Life Asset Management LLC
MacKay Shields LLC
Madison Square Advisors LLC
MainStay Management LLC,
Monitor Capital Advisors LLC
New York Life Benefit Services LLC

Individual Operations
New York Life Insurance and Annuity Corporation
(individual life insurance and annuities)

International Operations
New York Life International, Inc.

Special Markets
NYLIFE Administration Corp. (long-term care and other
specialty programs)
New York Life Benefit Services, Inc. (retirement benefits
administration)

COMPETITORS

AEGON	John Hancock Financial
AIG	Services
Allianz	Kemper Insurance
Allstate	MassMutual
American General	Merrill Lynch
American National	MetLife
Insurance	MONY
AXA	Morgan Stanley
AXA Financial	Mutual of Omaha
Charles Schwab	Northwestern Mutual
CIGNA	Principal Financial
Citigroup	Prudential
CNA Financial	State Farm
Fortis	T. Rowe Price
Guardian Life	TIAA-CREF
The Hartford	UBS PaineWebber
Jefferson-Pilot	

HISTORICAL FINANCIALS & EMPLOYEES

Mutual company FYE: December 31	Annual Growth	12/92	12/93	12/94	12/95	12/96	12/97	12/98	12/99	12/00	12/01
Assets ($ mil.)	7.1%	59,169	66,791	68,926	74,281	78,809	84,067	90,367	94,979	97,101	109,961
Net income ($ mil.)	16.7%	271	368	404	625	579	650	753	555	1,205	1,086
Income as % of assets	—	0.5%	0.6%	0.6%	0.8%	0.7%	0.8%	0.8%	0.6%	1.2%	1.0%
Employees	5.5%	—	—	8,130	8,442	12,190	12,570	13,000	7,349	11,800	11,800

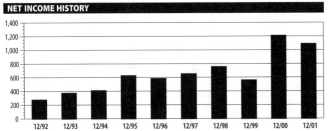

NET INCOME HISTORY

2001 FISCAL YEAR-END
Equity as % of assets: 7.9%
Return on assets: 1.0%
Return on equity: 12.4%
Long-term debt ($ mil.): —
Sales ($ mil.): 22,514

NEW YORK STATE LOTTERY

Winning the New York State Lottery could make you king of the hill, top of the heap. The New York State Lottery is one of the largest and oldest state lotteries in the US (only New Hampshire's lottery is older). It offers players both instant-win games, as well as the multimillion-dollar jackpots of its lotto games. In addition, the New York lottery operates Quick Draw, a Keno-style game in which numbers are picked every five minutes. The lottery sells tickets through more than 17,000 retailers and some 14,000 on-line terminals (maintained by GTECH Holdings).

The New York State Lottery has raised some $20 billion for state educational programs (which get 33% of sales) since its inception. In addition to education, proceeds from the lottery have helped pay for the construction of New York City Hall, as well as bridges and roads for the state. The lottery returns more than half the money it takes in as prizes; 2% of sales are used to cover administrative costs, while retailers get 6%.

The New York State lottery is facing competition from the multistate Powerball and The Big Game lotteries available in neighboring states. New York's legislature resisted approving a multistate game, but finally caved late in 2001 and authorized a bill allowing New Yorkers to buy Powerball tickets.

HISTORY

In the mid-1960s the New York state legislature succeeded in sending a lottery amendment to voters, and 60% of New Yorkers voted in favor of the amendment in 1966. Lottery sales began in 1967 with a raffle-style drawing game. In its first year of operation, the lottery contributed more than $26 million to the state's education fund.

New York introduced its first instant game in 1976, with sales topping $18 million the first week. The state debuted its six-of-six lotto game two years later. Sales were slow until 1981, when Louie "the Light Bulb" Eisenberg — the state's first lottery celebrity — won $5 million, the largest single-winner prize at that time.

GTECH Holdings won the contract to operate New York's lottery terminal sales in 1987. The Quick Pick option — through which a terminal chooses a player's numbers — was introduced in 1989, as was a new lotto game and the state's first online computer terminal game. Autoworker Antonio Bueti set a record for the largest individual prize, winning $35 million in 1990. A jackpot of $90 million was split among nine players in 1991.

Through the mid-1990s, however, lackluster lottery sales were blamed on the Persian Gulf War, the recession, and poor publicity. During 1993 and 1994, lottery management revamped the state's lottery infrastructure and redesigned some games. The investment paid off in October 1994 when lotto fever pushed a jackpot to $72.5 million. During the height of the frenzy, sales reached $46,000 a minute.

Quick Draw, which lets players choose numbers every five minutes, was added in 1995. Sales of the game topped $1 million on the second day and soon it was grossing nearly $12 million a week. Real estate mogul Donald Trump unsuccessfully sued to stop Quick Draw, claiming that it was more addictive than (his) casinos and would encourage organized crime. That year the New York State Lottery became the first to reach $3 billion in sales in a single year.

In 1996 the state pulled its Quick Draw advertising after critics complained it encouraged compulsive gambling. Lottery officials replaced enticing ads with advertising stressing the lottery's benefits to state education. The lottery was the subject of a sting operation that year led by Governor George Pataki to crack down on lottery vendors selling tickets to minors. In 1997 the lottery spawned its own game show with the debut of *NY Wired*, a half-hour weekly program pitting vendor representatives against each other for cash prizes given to audience members and schools.

With sales slipping, the state left longtime ad partner DDB Needham Worldwide (now DDB Worldwide) in 1998 and signed a $28 million contract with Grey Advertising. Lottery director Jeff Perlee resigned the next year. He was replaced by Margaret DeFrancisco, who helped drum up sales with Millennium Millions, which paid out a record $100 million prize to Johnnie Ely, a cook from the South Bronx, on the eve of 2000. Two players shared a record $130 million jackpot later in the year.

After holding out for years, the New York legislature in late 2001 authorized a bill that would allow state residents to participate in the multistate Powerball lottery.

OFFICERS

Director: Margaret R. DeFrancisco
Director of Financial Administration: Gerald Woitkoski
Director of Marketing and Sales: Connie H. Laverty
Director of Operations: Daniel J. Codden
Director of Human Resources: Charles Titus
Auditors: KPMG LLP

LOCATIONS

HQ: 1 Broadway Center, Schenectady, NY 12301
Phone: 518-388-3300   **Fax:** 518-388-3368
Web: www.nylottery.org

PRODUCTS/OPERATIONS

Selected Games
Numbers games
 New York Lotto
 Numbers
 Pick 10
 Quick Draw
 Take Five
 Win 4
Instant-win games
 Blackjack
 Cash Flurries
 Fortune Cookie
 Go for the Green
 Ho Ho Doubler
 Hot Shots
 Loose Change
 Lucky 7s
 Pot o' Gold
 Red Hot Hearts
 Take 5
 Top 10
 Win 4

COMPETITORS

Connecticut Lottery
Massachusetts State Lottery
Multi-State Lottery
New Hampshire Lottery
New Jersey Lottery
Pennsylvania Lottery
Vermont Lottery

HISTORICAL FINANCIALS & EMPLOYEES

Government-owned FYE: March 31	Annual Growth	3/92	3/93	3/94	3/95	3/96	3/97	3/98	3/99	3/00	3/01
Sales ($ mil.)	8.2%	2,063	2,360	2,369	3,028	3,752	4,136	4,185	3,831	3,674	4,185
Net income ($ mil.)	5.9%	867	1,001	1,011	1,244	1,400	1,543	1,529	1,413	1,365	1,447
Income as % of sales	—	42.0%	42.4%	42.7%	41.1%	37.3%	37.3%	36.5%	36.9%	37.2%	34.6%
Employees	4.7%	231	233	241	239	310	340	350	345	350	350

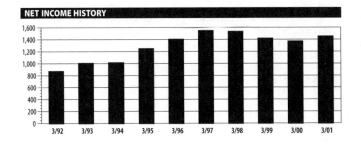

NET INCOME HISTORY

NEW YORK STOCK EXCHANGE, INC.

It's not called the Big Board for nothing: The New York Stock Exchange (NYSE) is the US's oldest and the world's largest stock market. The member-owned, not-for-profit group lists nearly 2,800 companies, including most of the largest US corporations, and is actively recruiting foreign companies seeking the liquidity available only in US markets. The NYSE is an auction exchange, meaning that stock prices are set largely by a throng of traders in an area the size of a football field, where the opening and closing of the day's action is punctuated by the NYSE's famous bell.

The NYSE touts its people-driven exchange against the electronic exchange run by archrival NASDAQ. The Big Board also faces competition from foreign exchanges and such electronic communications networks (ECNs) as The Island (now owned by its former rival Instinet). Even though the NYSE argues that such trades hamper investors' ability to see the big picture, the exchange accommodates brokers making large-block trades off the floor.

To better compete, the NYSE has boosted technology spending to improve execution times and has begun offering more and more new products, including ETFs (exchange-traded funds), such as the Qs. It also launched Open Book, a product that offers traders real-time access to specialist firms' buy and sell order information.

The exchange had also bandied about plans to go public as a for-profit company, but has shelved the idea.

HISTORY

To prevent a monopoly on stock sales by securities auctioneers, 24 New York stockbrokers and businessmen agreed in 1792 to avoid "public auctions," to charge a commission on sales of stock, and to "give preference to each other" in their transactions. The Buttonwood Agreement, named after a tree on Wall Street under which they met, established the first organized stock market in New York. The Bank of New York was the first corporate stock traded under the Buttonwood tree. Excluded traders continued dealing on the streets of New York until 1921 and later formed the American Stock Exchange.

In 1817 the brokers created the New York Stock & Exchange Board, a stock market with set meeting times. The NYS&EB began to require companies to qualify for trading (listing) by furnishing financial statements in 1853. Ten years later the board became the New York Stock Exchange.

Stock tickers began recording trades in 1867, and two years later the NYSE consolidated with competitors the Open Board of Brokers and the Government Bond Department. Despite repeated panics and recessions in the late 1800s, the stock market remained unregulated until well into the 20th century.

In the 1920s the NYSE installed a centralized stock quote service. Post-war euphoria brought a stock mania that fizzled in the crash of October 1929. The subsequent Depression brought investigation and federal regulation to the securities industry.

The NYSE registered as an exchange in 1934. In 1938 it reorganized, with a board of directors representing member firms, nonmember brokers, and the public; it also hired its first full-time president, member William McChesney Martin. As a self-regulating body, the NYSE policed the activities of its members.

The NYSE began electronic trading in the 1960s; in 1968 it broke 1929's one-day record for trading volume (16 million shares). It became a not-for-profit corporation in 1971.

Despite upgrades, technology was at least partly to blame for the 1987 crash: A cascade of large sales triggered by computer programs fueled the market's fall. NYSE's income suffered, leading to a $3 million loss in 1990.

In 1995 Richard Grasso became the first NYSE staff employee named chairman. The NYSE followed the other US stock markets in 1997 by switching trade increments from one-eighth point to one-sixteenth point (known as a "teenie" by arbitrageurs). New circuit-breaker rules halted trading on October 27 when the Dow Jones Industrial Average dropped 550 points in a day (the NYSE increased the trigger to 1,050 points in 1999).

The NYSE used a veiled threat to move to New Jersey to win itself the promise of some growing space. In 1999 the exchange named Karen Nelson Hackett as its first woman governor.

The Big Board in 2000 announced plans to go public, but the move frequently stalled, then died altogether. It also extended its official pricing until 6:30 p.m. (Eastern). In the wake of the terrorism attacks that shook Wall Street and the nation, the NYSE and NASDAQ in 2001 began discussing a disaster plan that would see the two cooperating should a future incident cripple either market. Also that year, the NYSE moved entirely to decimal pricing, in accordance with SEC mandates.

OFFICERS

Chairman and CEO: Richard A. Grasso, age 55
Vice Chairman: David H. Komansky, age 62
Executive Vice Chairman, President and Co-COO: Robert G. Britz, age 51
Executive Vice Chairman, President and Co-COO: Catherine R. Kinney, age 50
Group EVP, Regulation: Edward A. Kwalwasser, age 61
Group EVP, International: Georges Ugeux, age 56
EVP, Corporate Services: Frank Z. Ashen, age 57
EVP and General Counsel: Richard P. Bernard, age 51
EVP, Enforcement: David P. Doherty, age 61
EVP, Market Operations: Richard A. Edgar, age 56
EVP, Communications: Robert T. Zito, age 48
SVP, Floor Operations: Anne E. Allen
SVP and Chief Economist: Paul B. Bennett, age 51
SVP, International: Dorothy A. Carey
SVP, Strategic Planning and Chief Economist: James L. Cochrane, age 59
SVP, New Listings and Client Services: Noreen M. Culhane, age 51
SVP and Associate General Counsel: James F. Duffy, age 53
SVP and CFO: Keith R. Helsby, age 57
SVP, Competitive Position: Robert J. McSweeney, age 49
SVP, International Relations: Alain Y. Morvan, age 63
SVP, Market Surveillance: Regina C. Mysliwiec
SVP, Member Firm Regulation: Salvatore Pallante, age 55
SVP, Government Relations: Richard L. Ribbentrop, age 55
VP, Corporate Communications: Richard C. Adamonis, age 46
VP, Compensation: Dale B. Bernstein, age 43
VP, Corporate Audit/Regulatory Quality Review: Daniel Beyda, age 48
VP, Marketing Communications: Michael H. Cohen, age 39
VP, Security: James C. Esposito, age 58
VP, Market Data: Thomas E. Haley, age 63
VP, Government Relations: Douglas R. Nappi, age 39
VP, Corporate Compliance: Janice O'Neill, age 44
CTO: Roger Burkhardt, age 41
Corporate Secretary: Darla C. Stuckey, age 42
Controller: Alan Holzer, age 51
Auditors: PricewaterhouseCoopers LLP

LOCATIONS

HQ: 11 Wall St., New York, NY 10005
Phone: 212-656-3000   **Fax:** 212-656-2126
Web: www.nyse.com

PRODUCTS/OPERATIONS

2001 Sales

	$ mil.	% of total
Listing fees	295	34
Market data fees	160	18
Regulatory fees	152	17
Trading fees	145	16
Facility & equipment fees	48	6
Membership fees	12	1
Other	72	8
Total	**884**	**100**

Services
Market regulation
Member regulation
Securities clearing
Securities depository
Securities information

COMPETITORS

Archipelago
Bloomberg TRADEBOOK
CBOE
Chicago Mercantile Exchange
E*TRADE
Instinet
Investment Technology
Island ECN
Knight Trading
London Stock Exchange
NASD
NYFIX

HISTORICAL FINANCIALS & EMPLOYEES

Not-for-profit FYE: December 31	Annual Growth	12/92	12/93	12/94	12/95	12/96	12/97	12/98	12/99	12/00	12/01
Sales ($ mil.)	8.7%	418	445	452	501	562	639	729	735	815	884
Net income ($ mil.)	(2.8%)	41	54	44	57	74	86	101	75	73	32
Income as % of sales	—	9.8%	12.1%	9.7%	11.3%	13.3%	13.5%	13.9%	10.2%	8.9%	3.6%
Employees	0.0%	—	1,500	1,450	1,450	1,475	1,475	1,500	—	—	—

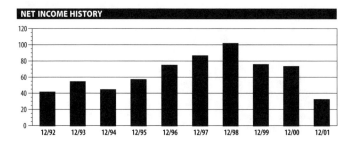

NET INCOME HISTORY

NORTHWESTERN MUTUAL

Making sure it's not all quiet on the Northwestern front, Northwestern Mutual's 7,500 agents (meticulously recruited and trained) sell a lineup of life and health insurance and retirement products, including fixed and variable annuities and mutual funds to a clientele of small businesses and prosperous individuals. Other lines of business include Midwestern investment bank Robert W. Baird & Co. and pension manager Frank Russell Company (known for the Russell 2000 stock index). Targeting wealthy individuals over 55, the company also operates its own trust services subsidiary, Northwestern Mutual Trust.

Northwestern Mutual would "enter the 21st Century as we left the 19th," according to its former chairman and CEO, John Ericson (who retired in mid-2001).

Well not exactly. Although the company has resisted the industry trend of demutualizing and remains committed to ownership by its about 3 million policyholders, The Quiet Company has begun blowing its own horn — in a diffident upper Midwest way. Reorganized to highlight its wealth management products, life insurance still accounts for the majority of the company's revenue.

HISTORY

In 1854, at age 72, John Johnston, a successful New York insurance agent, moved to Wisconsin to become a farmer. Three years later Johnston returned to the insurance business when he and 36 others formed Mutual Life Insurance (changed to Northwestern Mutual Life Insurance in 1865). From the beginning the company's goal was to become better, not just bigger.

The company continued to offer level-premium life insurance in the 1920s, while competitors offered new types of products. This failure to rise to new demands brought a decline in market share that lasted into the 1940s.

Northwestern automated in the late 1950s. In 1962 it introduced the Insurance Service Account, whereby all policies owned by a family or business could be consolidated into one monthly premium and paid with pre-authorized checks. In 1968 Northwestern inaugurated Extra Ordinary Life, which combined whole and term life insurance, using dividends to convert term to paid-up whole life each year. EOL soon became the company's most popular product.

Suffering from a low profile, in 1972 the insurer kicked off its "The Quiet Company" ad campaign during the summer Olympics. Public awareness of Northwestern jumped. But even in advertising, the company was staid; a revamped Quiet Company campaign made a return Olympic

appearance 24 years later in another effort to raise the public's consciousness.

In the 1980s Northwestern began financing leveraged buyouts, thus gaining direct ownership of companies. Investments included two-thirds of flooring maker Congoleum (with other investors); it also bought majority interests in Milwaukee securities firm Robert W. Baird (1982; now 64%) and mortgage guarantee insurer MGIC Investment (1985; now 11%).

The firm stayed out of the 1980s mania for fast money and high-risk diversification. Instead, it devoted itself almost religiously to its core business, despite indications that it was a shrinking market.

In the early 1990s new life policy purchases slowed and the agency force declined — ominous signs, since insurers make their premium income on retained policies, and continued sales are crucial to growth. Northwestern reversed the trend, adding administrative support for its agents, using database marketing to target new customers, and increasing the cross-selling of products among existing customers. The result was a record-setting 1996.

With the financial services industry consolidating, in 1997 Northwestern moved into the mutual fund business by setting up its nine Mason Street Funds.

In the 1990s many large mutuals sought to demutualize, and in 1998 Northwestern, politically influential in Wisconsin, successfully lobbied for legislation to permit demutualization, citing the need to be able to move quickly in shifting markets.

The next year the company acquired Frank Russell Co., a pension management firm. The acquisition gave Northwestern a foothold in global investment management and analytical services (the Russell 2000 index).

The company followed up with an all-out reorganization, separating the office of president from the duties of chairman and CEO, and naming, for the first time, an EVP of marketing. In 2001 the firm opened Northwestern Mutual Trust, a wholly owned personal trust services subsidiary.

OFFICERS

CEO and President: Edward J. Zore, age 56
SEVP, COO, and Chief Compliance Officer:
John M. Bremer
SEVP, Insurance: Peter W. Bruce
EVP, Agencies: William H. Beckley
EVP, Planning and Technology: Deborah A. Beck
EVP, Marketing: Bruce L. Miller
SVP and CFO: Gary A. Poliner
SVP and Chief Investment Officer: Mason G. Ross
SVP and Chief Actuary: William C. Koenig

SVP, Annuity and Accumulation Products:
Leonard F. Stecklein
SVP, Corporate and Government Relations:
Frederic H. Sweet
SVP, Information Systems: Walt J. Wojcik
SVP, Investment Products and Services:
Charles D. Robinson
SVP, Life Insurance: Richard L. Hall
SVP, Public Markets: Mark G. Doll
SVP, Securities and Real Estate: John E. Schlifske,
age 43
VP, Secretary, and General Counsel: Robert J. Berden
VP and Controller: Steven T. Catlett
VP, Disability Income: Meridee J. Maynard
VP, Communications: W. Ward White
VP, Information Systems: Martha M. Valerio
VP, Human Resources: Susan A. Lueger
VP, Information Systems: Barbara F. Piehler
VP, Tax and Financial Planning: James F. Reiskytl
VP, Marketing: J. Edward Tippetts
VP, Policyowner Services: Marcia Rimai
VP, Government Relations: Michael L. Youngman
Auditors: PricewaterhouseCoopers LLP

LOCATIONS

HQ: 720 E. Wisconsin Ave., Milwaukee, WI 53202
Phone: 414-271-1444   Fax: 414-299-7022
Web: www.northwesternmutual.com

Northwestern Mutual Life Insurance has agents and
offices throughout the US.

PRODUCTS/OPERATIONS

2001 Assets

	$ mil.	% of total
Bonds & cash	46,324	47
Stocks	5,369	6
Mortgage loans	15,164	15
Real estate	1,671	2
Policy loans	9,028	9
Other investments	4,817	5
Assets in separate account	11,786	12
Other assets	4,233	4
Total	**98,392**	**100**

Selected Subsidiaries
Frank Russell Company (investment management and
securities brokerage)
Mason Street Funds (mutual funds)
Robert W. Baird & Co. Incorporated (asset management)

COMPETITORS

Alliance Capital
American General
AXA Financial
CIGNA
Citigroup
CNA Financial
Conseco
FMR
Fortis
GenAmerica
Guardian Life
The Hartford
John Hancock Financial Services
Liberty Mutual
MassMutual
Merrill Lynch
MetLife
MONY
Morgan Stanley
Mutual of Omaha
Nationwide
New York Life
Pacific Mutual
Principal Financial
Prudential
T. Rowe Price
TIAA-CREF

HISTORICAL FINANCIALS & EMPLOYEES

Mutual company FYE: December 31	Annual Growth	12/92	12/93	12/94	12/95	12/96	12/97	12/98	12/99	12/00	12/01
Assets ($ mil.)	10.6%	39,679	44,061	48,112	54,876	62,680	71,081	77,995	85,985	92,125	98,392
Net income ($ mil.)	11.5%	244	330	279	459	620	689	809	1,337	1,829	650
Income as % of assets	—	0.6%	0.7%	0.6%	0.8%	1.0%	1.0%	1.0%	1.6%	2.0%	0.7%
Employees	2.4%	3,298	3,500	3,300	3,344	3,513	3,818	4,117	3,700	3,900	4,100

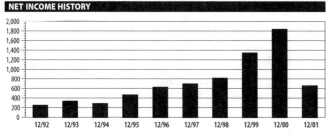

NET INCOME HISTORY

2001 FISCAL YEAR-END
Equity as % of assets: 7.0%
Return on assets: 0.7%
Return on equity: 10.2%
Long-term debt ($ mil.): —
Sales ($ mil.): 15,345

NORTHWESTERN UNIVERSITY

Near the city of big shoulders is a place that shapes broad minds. With its main campus in the Chicago suburb of Evanston, Northwestern University serves its 17,500 students through 12 schools and colleges such as the McCormick School of Engineering and Applied Sciences and the Medill School of Journalism. Its Chicago campus houses the schools of law and medicine, as well as several hospitals of the McGaw Medical Center. Northwestern is home to several research centers, continuing education services, and community outreach programs. The university also supports 19 intercollegiate athletic programs. Founded in 1851, Northwestern is the only private institution in the Big 10 conference.

With tuition and expenses running more than $30,000 a year, about 60% of undergraduates receive some form of financial aid from the school.

Among Northwestern's top-ranked programs are its law school, medical school, and its engineering program. Its J. L. Kellogg Graduate School of Management is ranked second in the nation by *Business Week*. Its journalism and drama programs produced such alumni as Charlton Heston, Gary Marshall, and Julia Louis-Dreyfus. Current US Supreme Court Justice John Paul Stevens is also a former Wildcat.

The school's endowment has also swelled to more than $2.8 billion, and it has exceeded its goal to raise $1 billion, Campaign Northwestern, by more than $15 million. The money will be used to increase endowment for student scholarships and fellowships, to help repair and build facilities, and to fund more faculty positions.

HISTORY

Northwestern University's Methodist founders met in 1850 to create an institution of higher learning serving the original Northwest Territory. The university was chartered in 1851, and two years later it acquired 379 acres of property north of Chicago on Lake Michigan. The town of Evanston was later named after John Evans, one of the school's founders.

Classes began in the fall of 1855 with two professors and 10 students. By 1869 Northwestern had more than 100 students and began to admit women. In 1870 Northwestern signed an affiliation agreement with the Chicago Medical College (founded 1859), and three years later it joined with the original University of Chicago (no relation to the current institution) to create the Union College of Law. When the University of Chicago closed in 1886 due to financial difficulties, Northwestern took control of the law school. The university reorganized in 1891, consolidating its

affiliated professional schools (dentistry, law, medicine, and pharmacy) into the university.

By 1900 Northwestern had become the third-largest university in the US (after Harvard and Michigan), with an enrollment of 2,700. During the 1920s the university created the Medill School of Journalism, named for the founder of the *Chicago Tribune*, Joseph Medill. In 1924 the school's athletic teams adopted the nickname Wildcats, and two years later the university completed the primary buildings that form its Chicago campus. Northwestern suffered a drop in enrollment during the Depression, but after WWII it saw student numbers swell as veterans took advantage of the GI Bill. Expansion continued throughout the 1960s and 1970s.

In 1985 the school and the City of Evanston began developing a research center to attract more high-tech industries to the area. The university's graduate school of business achieved national prominence in 1988 after it was ranked #1 in the US by *Business Week*. In 1995 Henry Bienen, a dean at Princeton, became the school's 15th president. That year Northwestern's football team, forever the doormat of the Big 10, achieved national fame when it won the conference championship.

In 1998 faculty member Professor John Pople won the Nobel Prize in Chemistry, the first Nobel Prize awarded to a faculty member while teaching at the university. To help pay for needed expansion, Bienen launched Campaign Northwestern that year with the goal of raising $1 billion. Northwestern won a significant legal battle in 1998 when a judge ruled that the university was not obligated to pay a faculty member simply because he had been granted tenure. Encouraged by their successful efforts, in 2000 the college raised its fund-raising goal to $1.4 billion from $1 billion.

The university's dental school closed its doors in 2001, citing the difficulties posed for private schools to afford to provide a competitive dental education.

OFFICERS

Chairman, Board of Trustees: Patrick G. Ryan, age 64
President: Henry S. Bienen
President Emeritus: Arnold R. Weber, age 71
Provost: Lawrence B. Dumas
SVP Business and Finance: Eugene S. Sunshine
VP and General Counsel: Thomas G. Cline
VP and Chief Investment Officer: David L. Wagner
VP Administration and Planning: Marilyn McCoy
VP Information Technology: Morteza A. Rahimi
VP Research and Graduate Studies: Lydia Villa-Komaroff

VP Student Affairs: William J. Banis
VP University Development and Alumni Relations:
Ronald D. Vanden Dorpel
VP University Relations: Alan K. Cubbage
Associate VP Human Resources: Guy E. Miller
Director Media Relations: Charles R. Loebbaka
Auditors: PricewaterhouseCoopers LLP

LOCATIONS

HQ: 633 Clark St., Evanston, IL 60208
Phone: 847-491-3741   Fax: 847-491-8406
Web: www.nwu.edu

Northwestern University has one campus in Chicago and
one in Evanston, Illinois.

PRODUCTS/OPERATIONS

Selected Undergraduate Colleges and Schools
Medill School of Journalism
Robert McCormick School of Engineering and Applied
Sciences
School of Education and Social Policy
School of Music
School of Speech
Weinberg College of Arts and Sciences

Selected Graduate Schools
The Graduate School
J. L. Kellogg Graduate School of Management
Medill School of Journalism
Medical School
Robert McCormick School of Engineering and Applied
Sciences
School of Education and Social Policy
School of Law
School of Music
School of Speech

Selected Research Centers and Institutes
Banking Research Center
Center for Biotechnology
Center for Catalysis and Surface Science
Center for Sleep and Circadian Biology
Center for Mathematical Studies in Economics and
Management Science
Center for Reproductive Science
Center for the Study of Ethical Issues in Business
Center for Quantum Devices
Center for Quality Engineering and Failure Prevention
Heizer Center for Entrepreneurial Studies
Institute for Environmental Catalysis
Institute for Health Services Research and Policy
Studies
Institute for Neuroscience
Institute for Policy Research
Kellogg Environmental Research Center
Materials Research Center
Program of African Studies
Traffic Institute
Transportation Center

HISTORICAL FINANCIALS & EMPLOYEES

School FYE: August 31	Annual Growth	8/92	8/93	8/94	8/95	8/96	8/97	8/98	8/99	8/00	8/01
Sales ($ mil.)	5.6%	587	628	676	708	779	721	816	782	875	959
Employees	0.1%	—	5,650	5,650	5,800	5,800	5,978	5,985	—	5,700	5,700

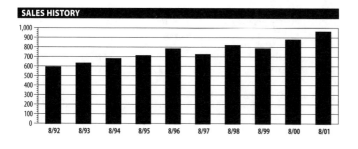

SALES HISTORY

OCEAN SPRAY CRANBERRIES, INC.

Ocean Spray Cranberries has transformed cranberries from turkey sidekick to the stuff of everyday beverages, cereal, and mixed drinks. Known for its blue-and-white wave logo, the company controls about 50% of the US cranberry drinks market. A marketing cooperative owned by more than 900 cranberry and citrus growers in the US and Canada, Ocean Spray has blended the cranberry with fruits ranging from apples to tangerines to produce its line of juices. It also makes other cranberry products (sauce, snacks), grapefruit juice, and Ocean Spray Premium 100% juice drinks.

Ocean Spray was started in 1912 as a cranberry sauce marketer and became a co-op in 1930. Surplus harvests of cranberries and competition from store brands have cut into its market share and forced layoffs. Competition from industry giants such as Coca-Cola and Pepsi, both of which are trying to increase market share in the non-carbonated drinks sector, also have hurt the company. Ocean Spray's chief competitor, Northland Cranberries, filed suit against the company in 2002, alleging it engaged in illegal, anticompetitive behavior.

To expand beyond the berry's traditional role, Ocean Spray has turned the fruit into a chewy snack (Craisins), and cranberries now show up in co-branded cookies and cereal. It has also introduced a "white juice" made from pre-ripened cranberries that are less tart. Promotion efforts have been aided by research showing that cranberry juice can reduce urinary tract infections.

Ocean Spray's Washington State-based subsidiary, Milne Fruit Products, processes fruit into juice ingredients.

HISTORY

Ocean Spray Cranberries traces its roots to Marcus Urann, president of the Cape Cod Cranberry Company. In 1912 Urann, who became known as the "Cranberry King," began marketing a cranberry sauce that was packaged in tins and could be served year-round. Inspired by the sea spray that drifted off the Atlantic and over his cranberry bogs, Urann dubbed his concoction Ocean Spray Cape Cod Cranberry Sauce.

It didn't take long for other cranberry growers to make their own sauces, and rather than compete, the Cranberry King consolidated. In 1930 Urann merged his company with A.D. Makepeace Company and with Cranberry Products, forming a national cooperative called Cranberry Canners. During the 1940s it added growers in Wisconsin, Oregon, and Washington and, to reflect its new scope, changed its name to National Cranberry Association.

Canadian growers were added to the fold in 1950. Urann retired in 1955, and two years later the co-op introduced its first frozen products. To take advantage of the popular Ocean Spray brand name, in 1959 the company changed its name to Ocean Spray Cranberries.

Two weeks before Thanksgiving that year, the US Department of Health mistakenly announced that aminotriazole, a herbicide used by some cranberry growers, was linked to cancer in laboratory rats. Sales of what consumers called "cancer berries" plummeted, and Ocean Spray nearly folded. However, the US government came to the rescue with subsidies in 1960, and the company stayed afloat.

The scare convinced Ocean Spray it needed to cut its dependence on seasonal demand, and it began to diversify more aggressively into the juice business, introducing a heavily promoted new line of juices blending cranberries with apples, grapes, and other fruits.

Ocean Spray allowed Florida's Indian River Ruby Red grapefruit growers to join the co-op in 1976. The company acquired Milne Food Products, a manufacturer of fruit concentrates and purees, in 1985, and three years later it signed a Japanese distribution deal.

To maintain its edge in a growing but increasingly competitive market, Ocean Spray automated plants and allied with food giants to create cranberry-flavored treats such as cookies (Nabisco, 1993) and cereal (Kraft Foods, 1996). In 1998 it unsuccessfully sued to block PepsiCo's purchase of juice maker Tropicana on grounds that it would interfere with PepsiCo's distribution of Ocean Spray's drinks. Ocean Spray also introduced a line of 100% juice blends to compete with rivals such as former co-op member Northland Cranberries.

Bumper harvests from 1997 through 1999 led to lower cranberry prices. As a result, in 1999 the company announced its third round of layoffs since 1997 (bringing the total to 500, or nearly one-fifth of its workforce). It also suspended its practice of buying back the stock of its growers, who must buy shares to join the co-op.

Amid criticism that it has been unable to compete effectively with for-profit rivals, Ocean Spray hired former Pillsbury executive Robert Hawthorne as CEO in 2000. Grower-owners voted not to explore a sale of the company at its 2001 annual meeting, a vote of confidence for the new management. The company supported a 32% crop reduction to help eliminate the crop surpluses that cause depressed prices. Ocean Spray also sold its interest in Nantucket Allserve (Nantucket Nectars) to Cadbury Schweppes.

CEO: Barbara S. Thomas
President and COO: Randy Papadellis
CFO & SVP: Tim C. Chan
VP, Cranberry Marketing: Stewart Gallagher
VP, Human Resources: John Soi
Manager, Corporate Communications and Public Affairs: Chris Phillips

LOCATIONS

HQ: 1 Ocean Spray Dr., Lakeville-Middleboro, MA 02349
Phone: 508-946-1000   **Fax:** 508-946-7704
Web: www.oceanspray.com

Ocean Spray Cranberries has seven receiving stations and eight processing and bottling plants in Florida, Massachusetts, Nevada, New Jersey, Oregon, Texas, Washington, Wisconsin, and British Columbia, Canada.

PRODUCTS/OPERATIONS

Selected Juice Products and Labels

Apple Juice
Black Cherry Blast
Cranapple
Cranberry Juice Cocktail
Cran*Blueberry
Cran*Cherry
Cran*Currant
Cran*Grape
Cranicot
Cran*Mango
Cran*Raspberry
Cran*Strawberry
Cran*Tangerine
Fruit Punch
Grapefruit Juice
Kiwi Strawberry
Lightstyle (Cranberry,
  Cran*Grape,
  Cran*Mango,
  Cran*Raspberry)
Mandarin Magic
¡Mango Mango!

Mauna La'i (Island Guava,
  ParadisePassion)
Orange Juice
Pink Grapefruit
Premium 100% Juice
  (Cranberry, Cranberry &
  Concord Grape,
  Cranberry & Georgia
  Peach, Cranberry &
  Granny Smith Apple,
  Cranberry & Key Lime,
  Cranberry & Pacific
  Raspberry)
Reduced (Cranapple,
  Cranberry Juice
  Cocktail, Cran-
  Raspberry)
Ruby Red Grapefruit
Ruby Red & Mango
Ruby Red & Tangerine
  Grapefruit

Other Products

Craisins (sweetened dried cranberries)
Cran Raspberry sauce
Cranberry sauce (jellied, whole)
Fresh cranberries

COMPETITORS

Cadbury Schweppes
Campbell Soup
Chiquita Brands
Clement Pappas
Cliffstar
Coca-Cola
Dole
Florida's Natural
Hansen Natural
J. M. Smucker
National Grape Cooperative
Northland Cranberries
Odwalla
Pepsi-Cola
Philip Morris
Sunkist
Triarc
Tropicana Products

HISTORICAL FINANCIALS & EMPLOYEES

Cooperative FYE: August 31	Annual Growth	8/93	8/94	8/95	8/96	8/97	8/98	8/99	8/00	8/01	8/02
Sales ($ mil.)	(0.7%)	1,168	1,221	1,361	1,433	1,438	1,480	1,360	1,400	1,104	1,100
Employees	(0.6%)	2,300	2,300	2,300	2,300	2,300	2,350	2,000	2,000	2,200	—

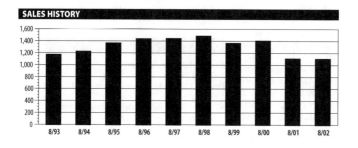

SALES HISTORY

THE OHIO STATE UNIVERSITY

The first class at Ohio State University (OSU) comprised 24 students. Today the university is Ohio's largest institution of higher learning and has the nation's second-largest single-campus enrollment (about 48,000 students at its Columbus campus), behind The University of Texas at Austin. OSU also boasts four regional campuses and two agricultural institutes. OSU's more than 4,500 faculty members offer instruction in more than 175 undergraduate programs, 120 master's degree programs, and nearly 100 doctoral programs. Its colleges and schools range from the Austin E. Knowlton School of Architecture to the College of Medicine and Public Health to the Fisher College of Business.

Noteworthy university alumni include astronaut Nancy Sherlock Currie, golfer Jack Nicklaus, author John Jakes, and Olympian Jesse Owens.

Near the close of 2000, OSU unveiled a five-year academic plan under which the university will spend $750 million to advance its national academic standing.

HISTORY

In 1870 the Ohio legislature, prompted by Governor Rutherford B. Hayes, agreed to establish the Ohio Agricultural and Mechanical College in Columbus on property provided by the Morrill Act of 1862 (the land-grant institution act, which gave land to states and territories for the establishment of colleges).

After a heated battle over whether the college should teach only agricultural and mechanical arts or foster a broad-based liberal arts curriculum, the college opened in 1873 offering agriculture, ancient languages, chemistry, geology, mathematics, modern languages, and physics courses. Two years later the school appointed its first female faculty member. The Ohio State University became the school's name in 1878; that year it graduated its first class. OSU graduated its first female student the next year.

OSU grew dramatically, adding schools of veterinary medicine (1885), pharmacy (1885), law (1891), and dairy sciences (1895). It awarded its first Masters of Arts degree in 1886.

The university continued to expand in the early 20th century, with enrollment surpassing 3,000 in 1908; by 1923 it had reached 10,000. New schools were added in education (1907), medicine and dentistry (1913), and commerce and journalism (1923). During WWI Ohio State designated part of its campus as training grounds and established the only college schools in the nation for airplane and balloon squadrons. Ohio Stadium was dedicated in 1922.

During the Great Depression Ohio State cut back salaries and course offerings. In the 1940s the school geared for war once again by establishing radiation and war research labs, as well as programs and services for students who were drafted. OSU captured its first national football championship in 1942.

The 1950s ushered in the era of legendary OSU football coach Woody Hayes. Hayes led his beloved Buckeyes to three national championships and nine Rose Bowl appearances before he was discharged for striking a Clemson player in 1978. The 1950s also saw the addition of four regional campuses at Lima, Mansfield, Marion, and Newark.

In the early 1960s the university was engaged in internal free-speech battles. By the end of that decade, enrollment had surpassed 50,000. OSU opened its School of Social Work in 1976.

In 1986 OSU and rival Michigan shared the Big 10 football conference title. Enrollment at OSU topped 54,000 in 1990 but then began declining. In response, the university tried to cut costs and beef up revenues. One way was through alliances: In 1992 it teamed with research group Battelle to develop a testing system for new drugs for the Food and Drug Administration. But when more savings were needed in 1995 and 1996, the university began streamlining operations, merging journalism and communications, and consolidating several veterinary departments. However, it also approved the creation of a new school of public health to provide education in environmental health, epidemiology, and health care management and financing.

But sports were not forgotten, and in 1996 OSU broke ground on the $84 million Schottenstein Center, a multipurpose facility for the university's basketball and ice hockey teams. In 1997 president Gordon Gee announced that he was leaving OSU for Brown University. The next year William Kirwan from the University of Maryland came on board as president.

In 2000 the university's "Affirm Thy Friendship" contribution campaign came to a close. The campaign increased OSU's endowment from $493 million in 1993 to $1.3 billion in 2000.

Ohio State won the national football championship in early 2003.

OFFICERS

President: Karen A. Holbrook
EVP and Provost: Edward J. Ray
Dean of the Graduate School: Susan L. Huntington
SVP Business & Finance and CFO: William Shkurti
VP Agricultural Administration and University Outreach: Bobby D. Moser
VP Research: C. Bradley Moore

VP Student Affairs: William H. Hall
VP University Development: Jerry A. May
VP University Relations: Lee Tashjian
Assistant VP Human Resources: Nancy K. Campbell
CIO: Ilee Rhimes
Executive Assistant to the President and General Counsel: Virginia M. Trethewey
Secretary of the Board of Trustees, Special Assistant to the President for Government Relations: William Napier
Controller: Greta J. Russell
Auditors: Deloitte & Touche LLP

LOCATIONS

HQ: 1800 Cannon Dr., Columbus, OH 43210
Phone: 614-292-3980   **Fax:** 614-292-4818
Web: www.osu.edu

The Ohio State University has campuses in Columbus, Lima, Mansfield, Marion, and Newark. It has two agricultural centers in Wooster, Ohio.

PRODUCTS/OPERATIONS

Selected Colleges and Schools
Austin E. Knowlton School of Architecture
College of Biological Sciences
College of Dentistry
College of Education
College of Engineering
College of Food, Agricultural, and Environmental Sciences
College of Human Ecology
College of Humanities
College of Law
College of Mathematical and Physical Sciences
College of Medicine and Public Health
College of Nursing
College of Optometry
College of Social and Behavioral Sciences
College of Social Work
College of the Arts
College of Veterinary Medicine
Graduate School
Max M. Fisher College of Business
School of Natural Resources
University College

HISTORICAL FINANCIALS & EMPLOYEES

School FYE: June 30	Annual Growth	6/92	6/93	6/94	6/95	6/96	6/97	6/98	6/99	6/00	6/01
Sales ($ mil.)	0.0%	1,656	1,409	1,506	1,575	1,531	1,630	1,749	1,923	1,554	1,661
Employees	0.9%	29,565	29,576	29,658	29,500	29,266	29,000	31,268	29,502	31,302	32,000

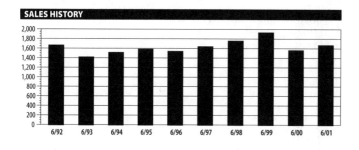

SALES HISTORY

PACIFIC MUTUAL

Life insurance is Pacific Mutual Holding's stock-in-trade. Pacific Mutual owns stock company Pacific LifeCorp, which, through its primary subsidiary Pacific Life Insurance, is the largest California-based life insurance outfit. Pacific Life offers fixed and variable life insurance policies, annuities, and pension plans; other subsidiaries manage health plans and provide real estate advice. Through Pacific Select Distributors, the company markets such investment products as annuities, mutual funds, and index funds. Pacific Mutual also owns almost a third of Allianz Dresdner Asset Management of America (formerly PIMCO Advisors), a major investment management firm majority-owned by insurer Allianz.

Pacific Mutual's conversion from a pure mutual to a mutual holding company gives it more flexibility and the option of an IPO; meanwhile, policyholders retain ownership of the company, but hold no stock.

Targeting individuals and small businesses, the company has opted out of the reinsurance business. It sold UK-based World-Wide Reassurance to Scottish Annuity & Life in exchange for a nearly 25% stake in the annuity reinsurer.

HISTORY

Pacific Mutual began business in 1868 in Sacramento, California, as a stock company. Its board was dominated by California business and political leaders, including three of the "Big Four" who created the Central Pacific Railroad (Charles Crocker, Mark Hopkins, and Leland Stanford) and three former governors (Stanford, Newton Booth, and Henry Huntley Haight). Stanford (founder of Stanford University) was the company's first president and policyholder.

By 1870 Pacific Mutual was selling life insurance throughout most of the western US. Expansion continued in the early 1870s into Colorado, Kentucky, Nebraska, New York, Ohio, and Texas. The company ventured into Mexico in 1873 but sold few policies. It had more luck in China, accepting its first risk there in 1875, and in Hawaii, where it started business in 1877. In 1881 Pacific Mutual moved to San Francisco.

Leland Stanford died in 1893. His widow and eponymous university, though rich in assets, found themselves struggling through a US economic depression. The benefit from Stanford's policy kept the university open until the estate was settled.

In 1905 Conservative Life bought the firm. The Pacific Mutual name survived the acquisition just as its records survived the fire that ravaged San Francisco after the 1906 earthquake. Pacific Mutual then relocated to Los Angeles.

The company squeaked through the Depression after a flood of claims on its noncancellable disability income policies forced Pacific Mutual into a reorganization plan initiated by the California insurance commissioner (1936). After WWII, Pacific Mutual entered the group insurance and pension markets.

After 83 years as a stock company and an eight-year stock purchasing program, Pacific Mutual became a true mutual in 1959.

Pacific Mutual relocated to Newport Beach in 1972. During the 1980s it built up its financial services operations, including its Pacific Investment Management Co. (PIMCO, founded 1971). The company was in trouble even before the stock crash of 1987 because of health care costs and over-investment in real estate. That year it brought in CEO Thomas Sutton, who sold off real estate and emphasized HMOs and fee-based financial services.

In the 1990s the firm cut costs and increased its fee income. PIMCO Advisors, L.P. was formed in 1994 when PIMCO merged with Thomson Advisory Group. The merger gave Pacific Mutual a retail market for its fixed-income products, a stake in the resulting public company, and sales that offset interest rate variations and changes in the health care system.

The company assumed failed Confederation Life Insurance Co.'s corporate-owned life insurance business and merged insolvent First Capital Life into Pacific Life as Pacific Corinthian Life in 1997. That year Pacific Mutual became the first top-10 US mutual to convert to a mutual holding company, thus allowing it the option of issuing stock to fund acquisitions. Because the firm remained partially mutual, however, policyholders retained ownership but got no shares of Pacific LifeCorp, its new stock company.

To compete with one-stop financial service behemoths such as Citigroup, Pacific Mutual began selling annuities through a Compass Bank subsidiary in 1998. The next year it bought controlling interests in broker-dealer M.L. Stern and investment adviser Tower Asset Management. In 2000 the world's #2 insurer, Allianz, bought all of PIMCO Advisors other than the interest retained by Pacific Mutual when it spun off the investment manager.

Chairman and CEO, Pacific Mutual Holding, Pacific
LifeCorp, and Pacific Life: Thomas C. Sutton, age 60
President, Pacific Life: Glenn S. Schafer, age 52
EVP and CFO, Pacific Life: Khanh T. Tran, age 46
EVP, Pacific Life, Annuities and Mutual Funds
Division; Chairman and CEO, Pacific Select
Distributors: Gerald W. Robinson
EVP, Pacific Life, Group Insurance Division:
David W. Gartley
EVP, Pacific Life, Institutional Products Division; EVP
and Chief Credit Officer, Pacific Financial Products:
Mark W. Holmlund
EVP, Pacific Life, Real Estate Division: Michael S. Robb
EVP, Pacific Life, Securities Division; EVP and Chief
Credit Officer, Pacific Financial Products:
Larry J. Card
SVP and General Counsel, Pacific Life:
David R. Carmichael
SVP, Administration, Pacific Life, Annuities and
Mutual Funds Division: Robert C. Hsu
SVP, Finance and Administration, Pacific Life, Life
Insurance Division: S. Gene Schofield
SVP, Guaranteed Products, Pacific Life, Institutional
Products Division: John E. Milberg
SVP, Human Resources, Pacific Life: Anthony J. Bonno
SVP, Public Affairs, Pacific Life: Robert G. Haskell
SVP, Risk and Financial Management, Pacific Life,
Institutional Products Division: Henry M. McMillan
SVP, Marketing Operations, Pacific Life, Life Insurance
Division: Michael A. Bell
SVP, Sales, Pacific Life, Annuities and Mutual Funds
Division: Dewey P. Bushaw
SVP, Strategic Planning and Development, Pacific Life:
Marc S. Franklin
Auditors: Deloitte & Touche LLP

HQ: Pacific Mutual Holding Company
700 Newport Center Dr., Newport Beach, CA 92660
Phone: 949-219-3011   Fax: 949-219-7614
Web: www.pacificlife.com

Pacific Mutual Holding has insurance operations
throughout the US (except in New York).

2001 Assets

	$ mil.	% of total
Cash & equivalents	510	1
Bonds	17,047	31
Stocks	266	—
Mortgage loans	2,933	5
Policy loans	4,899	9
Other investments	3,437	6
Assets in separate account	23,458	42
Other assets	3,132	6
Total	**55,682**	**100**

Selected Subsidiaries and Affiliates
Allianz Dresdner Asset Management of America L.P.
(31%)
Associated Securities Corp.
Aviation Capital Group
M.L. Stern & Co., LLC
Mutual Service Corporation
Pacific Financial Products, Inc.
Pacific Life & Annuity Company
Pacific LifeCorp.
Pacific Life Insurance Company
Pacific Select Distributors, Inc.
PMRealty Advisors, Inc.

Acordia	MetLife
Aetna	MONY
AXA Financial	Nationwide
Blue Cross	New York Life
Charles Schwab	Northwestern Mutual
CIGNA	PacifiCare
Citigroup	Principal Financial
GenAmerica	Provident Mutual
Guardian Life	Prudential
Hartford	St. Paul Companies
Health Net	StanCorp Financial Group
John Hancock Financial	State Farm
Services	USAA
Liberty Mutual	WellPoint Health
Lincoln National	Networks
MassMutual	

Mutual company FYE: December 31	Annual Growth	12/92	12/93	12/94	12/95	12/96	12/97	12/98	12/99	12/00	12/01
Assets ($ mil.)	19.1%	11,547	13,346	14,728	17,589	27,065	34,009	39,884	50,123	54,773	55,682
Net income ($ mil.)	13.2%	79	119	81	85	167	176	242	371	995	241
Income as % of assets	—	0.7%	0.9%	0.5%	0.5%	0.6%	0.5%	0.6%	0.7%	1.8%	0.4%
Employees	5.3%	2,265	2,400	2,400	2,700	2,750	3,422	2,700	3,799	3,600	3,600

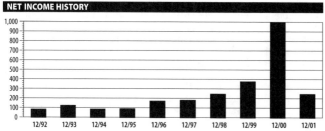

NET INCOME HISTORY

2001 FISCAL YEAR-END
Equity as % of assets: 6.7%
Return on assets: 0.4%
Return on equity: 6.9%
Long-term debt ($ mil.): —
Sales ($ mil.): 3,653

PARSONS CORPORATION

Almost evangelically, Parsons carries its message — and its engineering, procurement, and construction management services — worldwide. The company provides design, planning, and construction management through five operating groups: advanced technologies, communications, energy and chemicals, infrastructure and technology, and transportation. Among its many projects, Parsons has designed power plants; built dams, resorts, and shopping centers; and provided environmental services such as the cleanup of hazardous nuclear wastes. Parsons has also added improvements to airports and rail systems, bridges, and highways. Customers of the employee-owned company include government agencies and private industries.

The company has diversified in order to compete in every major region of the world. It has even provided vehicle emissions and inspections as part of its advanced technologies offerings. Through its communications group it provides such services as wireline and wireless network deployment and maintenance and data center and Web hosting deployment.

Among Parsons' projects has been its participation since 1998 in the US Army's programs for alternative technologies for chemical weapons disposal. The company established the Parsons Fabrication Facility in Pasco, Washington, to test process systems for chemical weapon and bulk agent disposal. The events of September 11, 2001, prompted the US Army to accelerate the destruction of its chemical weapons, and Parsons' Newport, Indiana, chemical agent disposal facility has been developing a plan for speedy neutralization of the weapons. Parsons has also provided engineering management support for the construction of the Russian Chemical Weapons Destruction Complex.

HISTORY

Ralph Parsons, the son of a Long Island fisherman, was born in 1896. At age 13 he started his first business venture, a garage and machine shop, which he operated with his brother. After a stint in the US Navy, Parsons joined Bechtel as an aeronautical engineer. The company changed its name to Bechtel-McCone-Parsons Corporation in 1938. However, Parsons later sold his shares in that company and left in 1944 to start his own design and engineering firm, the Ralph M. Parsons Co., after splitting with partner John McCone (who later headed the CIA).

Parsons Co. expanded into the chemical and petroleum industries in the early 1950s. During that decade it oversaw the building of several

natural gas and petroleum refineries overseas, including the world's largest, in Lacq, France.

In the early 1960s the company began working in Kuwait, which later proved to be one of its biggest markets. By 1969 Parsons had built oil refineries for all of the major oil companies, designed launch sites for US missiles, and constructed some of the largest mines in the world. In 1969 the company went public. With annual sales of about $300 million, it ranked second only to Bechtel in the design and engineering field. Ralph Parsons died in 1974.

The company built oil and gas treatment and production plants in Alaska in the 1970s and reorganized itself into The Parsons Corporation and RMP International in 1978. It went private in 1984 as The Parsons Corporation, taking advantage of a new tax law that favored corporations with employee stock ownership plans (ESOPs). Not all employees were happy, though. Several groups sued, maintaining that the plan disproportionately benefited executives, and that the buyout left the ESOP with all of the debt but no decision-making power. A Labor Department investigation later exonerated Parsons executives.

Parsons had just finished work on a power plant in Kuwait when Iraq invaded in 1990. Several employees were detained by the Iraqis but were released shortly before the Persian Gulf War. Two years later the company returned to Kuwait to rebuild some of the country's demolished infrastructure.

James McNulty, who had led the company's infrastructure and technology group, replaced Leonard Pieroni as CEO in 1996 after Pieroni died in the Bosnia plane crash that also claimed the life of US Secretary of Commerce Ronald Brown. Later that year a Parsons-led consortium won a $164.5 million contract for infrastructure projects in Bosnia.

In 1998 a Parsons/Inelectra joint venture won a construction contract to develop Cerro Negro's heavy oil production facilities in Venezuela; the next year Parsons was chosen to manage construction of a $5 billion refinery in Bahrain, a $1.4 billion gas plant in Saudi Arabia, and a $1 billion polyethylene project in Abu Dhabi.

Parsons partnered with TRW in 2000 to create TRW Parsons Management & Operations to bid on the DOE's Yucca Mountain site in Nevada, a potential repository for the US's high-level radioactive waste and spent nuclear fuel. It also was awarded a three-year contract to help rebuild the war-torn Serbian province of Kosovo and the next year was awarded a similar contract for Bosnia-Herzegovina.

In 2001 the firm won a US Federal Aviation

Administration contract to upgrade air traffic control towers and other equipment and systems, a contract that had been held by rival Raytheon since 1988. Parsons also strengthened its 80-year-old bridge division by acquiring bridge engineering firm Finley McNary. That year the company's joint venture with construction giant Fluor was awarded a contract for design and engineering work for the first offshore oil field in Kazakhstan.

The next year Parsons won a contract from Dallas Area Rapid Transit (DART) to provide systems engineering and construction management services for the second phase of the buildout for the light-rail system, the largest expansion of its kind in North America.

OFFICERS

Chairman and CEO: James F. McNulty
President and COO: Frank A. DeMartino
EVP and CFO: Curtis A. Bower
SVP and General Counsel: Gary L. Stone
SVP, Government Relations: James E. Thrash
VP, Human Resources: David R. Goodrich
VP and General Manager, Asset Management: Ronald L. Freeland
President, Parsons Advanced Technologies: Clifford E. Eby
President, Parsons Energy and Chemicals Group: William E. Hall
President, Parsons Infrastructure and Technology Group: John A. Scott
President, Parsons Transportation: James R. Shappell
President, Parsons Communications: Charles Harrington

LOCATIONS

HQ: 100 W. Walnut St., Pasadena, CA 91124
Phone: 626-440-2000 **Fax:** 626-440-2630
Web: www.parsons.com

Parsons Corporation provides heavy construction services in all states in the US and 80 other countries in Africa, Europe, Latin America, the Middle East, and Southeast Asia.

PRODUCTS/OPERATIONS

Selected Markets and Services

Parsons Advanced Technologies Group
Call centers
Criminal justice
Energy market data
Environmental data management
Revenue collection and management systems
Transportation data management
Vehicle inspection and compliance

Parsons Communications Group
Cable and component assembly
Equipment testing and system commissioning
Network planning and installation
Physical plants
Procurement, planning, and logistics
Project management
Wireless and wireline network management systems

Parsons Energy and Chemicals Group
Gas processing   Power
Oil and gas production   Refining
  and gas treatment   Sulfur management
Petrochemical and
  chemical plants

Parsons Infrastructure and Technology Group
Commercial and   Infrastructure
  institutional facilities   Mobile source air quality
Entertainment   Water resources

Parsons Transportation Group
Aviation   Railroads   Tunneling
Bridges   Systems   Urban transport
Highways   Engineering

COMPETITORS

ABB	Foster Wheeler	Michael Baker
AECOM	Gilbane	Peter Kiewit
BE&K	Granite	Turner
Bechtel	Halliburton	Tutor-Saliba
Black & Veatch	Hyundai	URS
Bouygues	Jacobs	Washington
Day &	Lend Lease	Group
Zimmermann	Louis Berger	
Fluor	M. A. Mortenson	

HISTORICAL FINANCIALS & EMPLOYEES

Private FYE: December 31	Annual Growth	12/92	12/93	12/94	12/95	12/96	12/97	12/98	12/99	12/00	12/01
Sales ($ mil.)	(0.4%)	1,556	1,547	1,597	1,467	1,600	1,263	1,600	1,800	2,400	1,500
Employees	(0.6%)	10,000	10,000	9,500	10,600	10,000	10,400	11,000	11,000	13,500	9,500

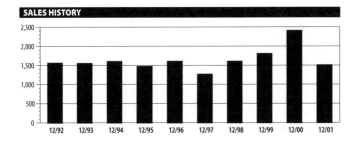

SALES HISTORY

PENSION BENEFIT GUARANTY

Underfunded pension plans give the heebie-jeebies to PBGC, or Pension Benefit Guaranty Corporation. The government corporation was established to promote the growth of defined-benefit pension plans, provide payment of retirement benefits, and keep pension premiums as low as possible. It protects the pensions of more than 40 million workers and monitors employers to ensure that plans are adequately funded. The agency receives no tax funds; its income is generated by insurance premiums paid by employers (about $19 per employee), investments, and assets recovered from terminated plans.

PBGC terminates pension plans when it determines that a company can no longer pay benefits; it can take a portion of a company's assets to ensure that pension obligations are met. When PBGC takes over a failed plan, it pays each individual pensioner covered by the plan up to $40,000 annually.

Many companies are moving from traditional defined benefit pension plans to so-called defined contribution plans, usually reducing the benefits of long-time workers in the process. Workers and their advocates criticize the switched plans, but they don't come under PBGC's jurisdiction unless they fail.

HISTORY

The Employment Retirement Income Security Act (ERISA) of 1974 established the Pension Benefit Guaranty Corporation (PBGC) to protect workers' pension benefits. The poor economy of the day guaranteed PBGC plenty of business. By 1975 more than 1,000 companies were unable to meet pension obligations. Other companies tried to avoid entering the system by terminating their plans before a 1996 deadline; the Supreme Court in 1980 upheld PBGC's contention that these companies were obligated to pay benefits to vested workers.

ERISA's provisions initially let companies voluntarily terminate their plans by paying PBGC a portion of their assets; many companies took this route until Congress limited the provision. Pensions faced a new threat in the late 1980s, as many buyout deals were structured to use company pension plans as part of their funding; Congress put a stop to that practice in 1990.

Companies found themselves caught between conflicting requirements of the PBGC (ever watchful for underfunded pension plans) and the IRS (which penalized overfunded plans). PBGC's deficit grew as it took on more and more pension payment liabilities; companies continued to jeopardize plans by using funds for other purposes. On behalf of 40,000 workers, PBGC in 1988 sued companies that allegedly terminated their plans illegally between 1976 and 1981 (the suit was settled in 1995 for $100 million.)

In 1989 new director James Lockhart began airing PBGC's plight, claiming that the pension system would follow the savings and loan industry into collapse. In the early 1990s his predictions seemed reasonable; PBGC's deficit was driven sky-high by such bankruptcies as Pan Am (1991), TWA, and Munsingwear (1992). Under Lockhart's guidance, the PBGC began publishing the "iffy fifty" — the 50 most underfunded pensions in the country.

Martin Slate succeeded Lockhart in 1993 and toned down the Chicken Little rhetoric, although that year PBGC announced that underfunding had nearly doubled between 1987 and 1992. Help arrived in the form of 1994's Retirement Protection Act, which put some teeth into pension laws. Under the reforms, PBGC required some employers to notify workers and retirees about the funding of their plans; it also changed the rules for annual reporting to the PBGC. The next year President Clinton vetoed the budget bill, which would have allowed companies to take money from their pension plans.

Slate died in 1997 and David Strauss took over. After two decades in the red, PBGC in 1998 marked its third consecutive year in the black. The organization was sued by several former Pan Am workers who claimed PBGC had shorted their benefits. That year PBGC announced that LTV, the giant steel company that went bankrupt in 1993, could resume monthly pension payments to retired workers.

In 1999 PBGC defended itself against critics who claimed it took too long to determine benefits from bankrupt companies, and often required pensioners to repay thousands of dollars that had been paid in estimated benefits.

In 2000 with a $10 billion surplus under PBGC's belt, Strauss said that Congress should permit well-funded pensions a holiday from paying premiums.

Chairman: Elaine L. Chao
Executive Director: Steve A. Kandarian
Deputy Executive Director and COO: Joseph Grant
Deputy Executive Director and CFO: Hazel Broadnax
Chief Management Officer: John Seal
Chief Negotiator: Andrea E. Schneider
Director, Communications and Public Affairs:
E. William Fitzgerald
Director, Human Resources: Sharon Barbee-Fletcher
Auditors: PricewaterhouseCoopers LLP

COMPETITORS

CIGNA
Putnam Investments
Vanguard Group

LOCATIONS

HQ: Pension Benefit Guaranty Corporation
1200 K St. NW, Washington, DC 20005
Phone: 202-326-4000   **Fax:** 202-326-4042
Web: www.pbgc.gov

PRODUCTS/OPERATIONS

2000 Assets

	$ mil.	% of total
Cash	349	2
Fixed maturity securities	12,390	58
Equities	8,189	38
Other investments	48	—
Recievables	431	2
Other	2	—
Total	**21,409**	**100**

HISTORICAL FINANCIALS & EMPLOYEES

Government agency FYE: September 30	Annual Growth	9/91	9/92	9/93	9/94	9/95	9/96	9/97	9/98	9/99	9/00
Assets ($ mil.)	16.3%	—	—	—	8,659	10,848	12,548	15,910	18,376	19,123	21,409
Net income ($ mil.)	9.6%	—	—	—	1,578	920	1,116	2,707	1,653	1,884	2,734
Income as % of assets	—	—	—	—	18.2%	8.5%	8.9%	17.0%	9.0%	9.9%	12.8%
Employees	2.2%	—	—	—	687	660	764	750	750	—	—

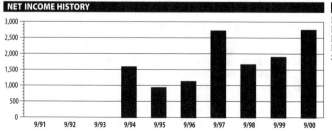

NET INCOME HISTORY

2000 FISCAL YEAR-END

Equity as % of assets: 46.6%
Return on assets: 13.5%
Return on equity: 31.8%
Long-term debt ($ mil.): —
Sales ($ mil.): 3,298

PENSKE CORPORATION

Penske, headed by race-car legend Roger Penske, seems to be on the right track as a diversified transportation company. Closely held Penske has stakes in Penske Truck Leasing Company (79%-owned by GE Capital), the US's #2 truck-rental operation, after Ryder. Penske Automotive operates five car dealerships in California and owns nearly 60% of publicly traded UnitedAuto Group, which runs about 120 franchise dealerships. Penske owns 15% of electronic fuel-injection system maker Diesel Technology (Robert Bosch owns the rest). Roger Penske owns 59% of the company.

The company's relationship with Kmart has become strained since the retailer filed Chapter 11 early in 2002. Penske eventually responded by closing 500 of its Penske Auto Centers at Kmart locations nationwide.

Penske just can't seem to resist that new car smell. The company has sold its racetrack interests and upped its stake in the struggling UAG. Roger Penske personally visited most of UAG's dealerships to help return the chain to profitablity. He now heads UAG and holds a 57% stake in Penske Corporation. Mr. Penske has said he would like to increase his stake in UAG to as much as 80%, and maybe even take the company private. Penske has sold its 49% stake in heavy-duty truck engine maker Detroit Diesel to DaimlerChrysler. The company has souped-up its Penske Truck Leasing unit with the purchase of Rollins Truck Leasing, the US's third-largest truck rental and leasing player.

HISTORY

As a teen Roger Penske earned money by repairing and reselling cars. At the age of 21 he entered his first auto race; he was running second when his car overheated. His winning ways, however, were soon apparent, and in 1961 *Sports Illustrated* named him race car driver of the year.

Nonetheless, in 1965 Penske went looking for a day job. With a $150,000 loan from his father, he bought a Chevrolet dealership in Philadelphia and retired from racing to avoid loading his balance sheet with steep life-insurance premiums for the CEO. Penske teamed with driver Mark Donohue in 1966 to form the Penske Racing Team. Donohue died in a crash in 1975, but team Penske continued.

In 1969 Penske started a regional truck-leasing business, incorporated under the name Penske. The company established auto dealerships in Pennsylvania and Ohio in the early 1970s. In 1975 the company bought the Michigan International Speedway. Penske and fellow racing team owner Pat Patrick started the race-sponsoring organization Championship Auto Racing Teams (CART) in 1978.

In 1982 Penske's truck-leasing business and rental company Hertz formed Hertz Penske Truck Leasing, a joint venture. Penske expanded its auto dealerships in the 1980s by acquiring dealerships in California, including Longo Toyota in 1985.

Racing legend Al Unser Sr. surprised Indy 500 watchers in 1987 by driving a car borrowed from an exhibition in a hotel lobby to a first place finish for the Penske Racing Team.

In 1988 Penske bought 80% of GM's Detroit Diesel engine-making unit, which had a market share of only 3% and had lost some $600 million over the previous five years. Penske trimmed $70 million from the unit's budget by firing 440 salaried employees, streamlining manufacturing processes, and cutting administration expenses. Detroit Diesel's market share doubled in its first two years as a Penske unit. Also in 1988 Penske purchased Hertz's stake in Hertz Penske Truck Leasing, which it later combined with the truck-rental division of appliance maker General Electric to create Penske Truck Leasing.

By 1993 Detroit Diesel's market share had grown to more than 25%. That year the engine maker went public. Penske bought 860 Kmart auto centers for $112 million in 1995. The company's racing business, Penske Motorsports, went public in 1996, but Penske retained a 55% stake in the company. Also that year Penske bought Truck-Lite, Quaker State's automotive lighting unit.

Penske Truck Leasing formed Penske Logistics Europe in 1997 to offer information systems and other integrated logistics services on that continent. The next year it formed a logistics joint venture with Brazil-based Cotia Trading to serve US-based clients in the South American market, and Penske Logistics Europe opened a pan-European transport routing center in the Netherlands.

Penske sold its Penske Motorsports operations, which included racetracks in California, Michigan, North Carolina, and Pennsylvania, to International Speedway in 1999. The same year Penske invested about $83 million for a 38% stake in car retailer UnitedAuto Group (UAG) and Roger Penske became CEO of Penske. In 2000 the company sold its 48.6% stake in Detroit Diesel to DaimlerChrysler.

The following year Penske Corp. increased its stake in UAG to 57%, and added three additional dealerships. Later in 2001 Penske Truck Leasing acquired Rollins Truck Leasing (the US's third-largest player behind Ryder and Penske). After Kmart filed Chapter 11 early in 2002, Penske expressed a "wait and see" strategy about the fate of its Penske Auto Centers business. Later that year Penske's Truck-Lite Industries bought Federal-Mogul's lighting business for $23 million.

Early in April 2002 Penske had waited long enough, and didn't like what it saw. It closed 500 of its Penske Auto Centers at Kmart locations nationwide. The move sparked a legal battle with Kmart filing a restraining order to block the store closures, but the decision came too late. The matter was then remanded to federal bankruptcy court in Chicago.

OFFICERS

Chairman and CEO: Roger S. Penske, age 66
EVP, Administration: Paul F. Walters
SVP, Corporate Finance: J. Patrick Conroy
VP, Human Resources: Randall W. Johnson

LOCATIONS

HQ: 13400 Outer Dr. West, Detroit, MI 48239
Phone: 313-592-5000   **Fax:** 313-592-5256
Web: www.penske.com

Penske operations include Penske Automotive, with five dealerships in southern California; Penske Auto Centers, with about 630 repair shops located in Kmart stores; Penske Truck Leasing, with about 700 worldwide rental locations; and UnitedAuto Group, with more than 127 franchise dealerships in 19 states, Brazil, and Puerto Rico.

PRODUCTS/OPERATIONS

Selected Subsidiaries and Affiliates
Davco, Inc. (fuel filters and engine accessories)
Diesel Technology (15%, fuel-injection system manufacturing)
Penske Auto Centers, Inc. (retail auto-service outlets)
Penske Automotive (retail auto sales)
Penske Truck Leasing Co. LP (21%, truck rental and leasing)
Truck-Lite (automotive lighting)
UnitedAuto Group (57%, retail auto sales)

COMPETITORS

AMERCO
AutoNation
DaimlerChrysler
Discount Tire
Fiat
General Motors
Goodrich
Isuzu
Mack Trucks
Navistar
PACCAR
Prospect Motors
Ryder
Tasha Inc.
Volvo

HISTORICAL FINANCIALS & EMPLOYEES

Private FYE: December 31	Annual Growth	12/92	12/93	12/94	12/95	12/96	12/97	12/98	12/99	12/00	12/01
Sales ($ mil.)	16.4%	2,800	3,250	3,287	3,900	5,200	5,800	6,000	6,400	10,000	11,000
Employees	14.2%	10,906	11,500	16,000	16,700	25,000	28,000	28,000	34,000	34,000	36,000

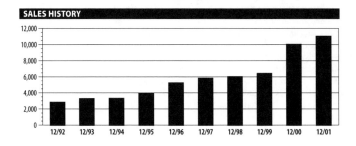

SALES HISTORY

PERDUE FARMS INCORPORATED

James Perdue makes Big Bird nervous. His family's company is one of the largest in the US poultry market, selling 48 million pounds of distinctly yellow chicken products and nearly 4 million pounds of turkey products each week. Vertically integrated, Perdue Farms sees its birds from the egg to the supermarket meat case. Perdue is expanding its value-added chicken parts and food service products and has established a plant in China through a joint venture. It also processes grain and makes vegetable oils and pet food ingredients. Founded by Arthur Perdue (James' grandfather) in 1920, the company sells its products in the East, Midwest, and South, and it exports to more than 50 countries.

While the company breeds and hatches the eggs, it ships the chicks off to supervised contract growers, who then send back fully grown birds. The company processes grain to make its own feeds and vegetable oils, and turns poultry by-products into pet food ingredients. And in a joint venture with AgriRecycle it makes fertilizer from used chicken litter.

James Perdue — like his famous father, Frank, had before him — appears in the company's advertisements. Perdue produces its own breed of chicken, the skin of which is a distinct yellow color, resulting from a diet that includes marigold petals.

HISTORY

If asked which came first, the chickens or the eggs, the Perdue family will tell you the eggs did. Arthur Perdue, a railroad express worker, bought 23 layer hens in 1920 and started supplying the New York City market with eggs from a henhouse in his family's backyard in Salisbury, Maryland. His son Frank joined the business in 1939.

The Perdues sold broiling chickens to major processors, such as Swift and Armour, in the 1940s and pioneered chicken crossbreeding to develop new breeds. The family started contracting with farmers in the Salisbury area in 1950 to grow broilers for them. Frank became president of the company in 1952. The next year the company began mixing its own feed.

Frank persuaded his father to borrow money to build a soybean mill in 1961. (Arthur had not willingly gone into debt in his previous 40-plus years in the poultry industry.) The soybean mill was part of Frank's plan to vertically integrate the company — with grain storage facilities, feed milling operations, soybean processing plants, mulch plants, hatcheries, and 600 contract chicken farmers — to counter the threat of processors buying chickens directly from farmers rather than through middlemen like the Perdues.

To differentiate their products, the Perdue name was applied to packages on retail meat counters in 1968.

Two years later the company began a breeding and genetic research program. During the following years Frank transformed himself from country chicken salesman to media poultry pitchman when the company decided to use him as spokesperson in its print, radio, and TV ads. Catchy slogans ("It takes a tough man to make a tender chicken") combined with Frank's whiny voice and sincere face helped sales. As Perdue Farms expanded geographically into new eastern markets such as Philadelphia, Boston, and Baltimore, it acquired the broiler facilities of other processors.

In 1983 James Perdue, Frank's only son, joined the company as a management trainee. In 1984 Perdue added processors in Virginia and Indiana and introduced turkey products. Two years later it acquired Intertrade, a feed broker, and FoodCraft, a food equipment maker. However, after enjoying a rising demand for poultry by a health-conscious society in the 1970s and early 1980s, the company found its sales leveling off in the late 1980s. When North Carolina fined Perdue for unsafe working conditions in 1989, the company increased its emphasis on safety.

James, who had become chairman of the board in 1991, replaced his folksy father in 1994 as the company's spokesman in TV ads. In the early 1990s Perdue's management determined future sales growth lay in food service and international sales; therefore, the poultry company quietly began laying the groundwork to support these new markets.

Perdue launched its Cafe Perdue entrée meal kits in 1997. The following year it purchased food service poultry processor Gol-Pak and, through a joint venture, opened a poultry processing plant in Shanghai, China.

Settlements to chicken catchers and line workers in 2001 and 2002 cost the company over $12 million in back wages. Also in 2002 Perdue announced it would be shuttering a deboning plant purchased only three years earlier, and put its money-losing Italian entrée De Luca business (purchased in 1998) up for sale.

Chairman and CEO: James A. Perdue
President and COO: Robert Turley
SVP of Retail, Sales, and Marketing: Steve Evans
SVP of Supply Chain Management: Larry Winslow
VP of Human Resources: Rob Heflin
President and General Manager, Specialty Foods: Randy Day
President and General Manager, Grain and Oilseed Division: Dick Willey
Director of Public Relations: Tita Cherrier
Director of Environmental Service: John Chlada

LOCATIONS

HQ: 31149 Old Ocean City Rd., Salisbury, MD 21804
Phone: 410-543-3000   **Fax:** 410-543-3292
Web: www.perdue.com

Perdue Farms has operations in Alabama, Connecticut, Delaware, Florida, Indiana, Kentucky, Maryland, New Jersey, North Carolina, Pennsylvania, South Carolina, Tennessee, Virginia, and West Virginia.

PRODUCTS/OPERATIONS

Selected Poultry Products and Brands

Fresh Poultry
Chicken parts (Prime Parts)
Cornish hens
Ground chicken
Roasters and turkeys (Oven Stuffer)
Seasoned chicken
Skinless, boneless poultry cuts (Fit 'N Easy)
Turkey burgers
Turkey sausage

Fully Cooked Poultry
Cutlets
Nuggets (Fun Shapes)
Rotisserie-style chicken (Tender Ready, food service)
Tenders

Other Brands
Chef's Choice
Cookin' Good
Gol-pak
Shenandoah
Short Cuts

Other Products
Pet food ingredients
Vegetable oils

COMPETITORS

AJC International
Cagle's
Cargill
ConAgra
Foster Farms
Gold Kist
Hormel
Keystone Foods
Murphy-Brown
Pilgrim's Pride
Sanderson Farms
Townsends
Tyson Foods

HISTORICAL FINANCIALS & EMPLOYEES

Private FYE: March 31	Annual Growth	3/93	3/94	3/95	3/96	3/97	3/98	3/99	3/00	3/01	3/02
Sales ($ mil.)	8.5%	1,300	1,600	1,700	2,100	2,200	2,200	2,515	2,501	2,700	2,700
Employees	4.6%	13,300	18,600	18,600	19,000	18,000	18,000	20,500	19,500	19,500	20,000

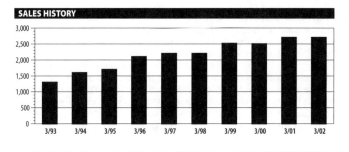

SALES HISTORY

PETER KIEWIT SONS', INC.

By building everything from tunnels to high-rises, Peter Kiewit Sons' has become a heavy-weight in the heavy construction industry. The employee-owned firm is one of the largest general contractors in the US, having projects in 46 states and the District of Columbia, as well as in Canada and Puerto Rico. Kiewit specializes in projects such as highways, commercial buildings, mining infrastructure, and waste-disposal systems. One of the leading transportation contractors, Kiewit builds bridges, highways, railroads, airports, and mass transit systems. Transportation contracts account for nearly 75% of Kiewit's jobs. The company is owned by current and former employees and Kiewit family members.

With most of its contracts dedicated to large-scale transportation projects, the company leads the US in highway construction projects, which include work for the Winter Olympics in Salt Lake City and for Denver's interstate highway system.

Water supply facilities and dams make up another 13% of the company's total contracts, and the balance comes from mining, power, heat and cooling, and other markets.

The company specializes in design/build projects and often works through joint ventures. Nearly 90% of its contract business is from government entities.

The construction business has the undivided attention of Kiewit these days. It has spun off its asphalt and ready-mix concrete business as Kiewit Materials and has created a unit to focus on construction for the offshore drilling industry. The company also continues to provides construction for telephone and data network operator Level 3 Communications, although it divested the telecom business in 1998.

HISTORY

Born to Dutch immigrants, Peter Kiewit and brother Andrew founded Kiewit Brothers, a brickyard, in 1884 in Omaha, Nebraska. By 1912 two of his sons worked at the yard, which was named Peter Kiewit & Sons. When Peter Kiewit died in 1914, his son Ralph took over, and the firm took the name Peter Kiewit Sons'. Another son, Peter, joined Ralph at the helm in 1924 after dropping out of Dartmouth and later took over.

During the Depression, Kiewit managed huge federal public works projects, and in the 1940s it focused on war-related emergency construction projects.

One of the firm's most difficult projects was top-secret Thule Air Force Base in Greenland, above the Arctic Circle. For more than two years 5,000 men worked around the clock, beginning in 1951; the site was in development for 15 years.

In 1952 the company won a contract to build a $1.2 billion gas diffusion plant in Portsmouth, Ohio. It also became a contractor for the US interstate highway system (begun in 1956).

Peter Kiewit died in 1979, after stipulating that the largely employee-owned company should remain under employee control and that no one employee could own more than 10%. His 40% stake, when returned to the company, transformed many employees into millionaires. Walter Scott Jr., whose father had been the first graduate engineer to work for Kiewit, took charge. Scott made his mark by parlaying money from construction into successful investments.

When the construction industry slumped, Kiewit began looking for other investment opportunities, and in 1984 it acquired packaging company Continental Can Co. (selling off non-core insurance, energy, and timber assets). Continental was saddled with a 1983 class action lawsuit alleging that it had plotted to close plants and lay off workers before they were qualified for pensions. In 1991 Kiewit agreed to pay $415 million to settle the lawsuit. In the face of a consolidating packaging industry, the company sold Continental in the early 1990s.

In 1986 Kiewit loaned money to a business group to build a fiber-optic loop in Chicago; by 1987 it had launched MFS Communications to build local fiber loops in downtown districts. In 1992 Kiewit split its business into two pieces: the construction group, which was strictly employee-owned; and a diversified group, to which it added a controlling stake in phone and cable TV company C-TEC in 1993. That year Kiewit took MFS public; by 1995 it had sold all its shares, and the next year MFS was bought by telecom giant WorldCom.

In 1996 Kiewit assisted CalEnergy (now MidAmerican Energy) in a hostile $1.3 billion takeover of the UK's Northern Electric. Kiewit got stock in CalEnergy and a 30% stake in the UK electric company, all of which it sold to CalEnergy in 1998.

That year Kiewit spun off its telecom and computer services holdings into Level 3 Communications. Scott, who had been hospitalized the year before for a blood clot in his lung, stepped down as CEO, and Ken Stinson, CEO of Kiewit Construction Group, took over Peter Kiewit Sons'.

In 1999 Kiewit acquired a majority interest in Pacific Rock Products, a construction materials firm in Canada. Kiewit spun off its asphalt, concrete, and aggregates operations in 2000 as Kiewit Materials. Also that year the company created Kiewit Offshore Services to focus on construction for the offshore drilling industry. In 2001 the company acquired marine construction firm General Construction Company (GCC). The next year it expanded its offshore business further by buying a Canadian subsidiary from oil and gas equipment services company Friede Goldman Halter, which was trying to emerge from bankruptcy.

OFFICERS

Chairman Emeritus: Walter Scott Jr., age 70
Chairman and CEO, Peter Kiewit Sons' and Kiewit Construction: Kenneth E. Stinson, age 59, $4,236,542 pay
President, COO, and Director: Bruce E. Grewcock, age 48, $913,000 pay
EVP and Director; EVP, Kiewit Pacific: Richard W. Colf, age 58, $1,045,900 pay
EVP and Director; EVP, Kiewit Pacific: Allan K. Kirkwood, age 58, $945,900 pay
EVP and Director: Roy L. Cline, age 64, $520,212 pay
EVP and Director: Douglas E. Patterson, age 50
VP and Treasurer: Michael J. Piechoski, age 48
VP, General Counsel, and Secretary: Tobin A. Schropp, age 39
VP, Human Resources and Administration: John B. Chapman, age 56
VP: Ben E. Muraskin, age 38
VP: Gerald S. Pfeffer, age 56
VP: Jerry Porter, age 58
VP: James Rowings, age 49
VP: Stephen A. Sharpe, age 50
Controller: Gregory D. Brokke, age 39
Auditors: KPMG LLP

LOCATIONS

HQ: Kiewit Plaza, Omaha, NE 68131
Phone: 402-342-2052   **Fax:** 402-271-2939
Web: www.kiewit.com

Peter Kiewit Sons' has 22 principal operating offices in North America.

Office Locations

US	New Jersey
Alaska	New Mexico
Arizona	New York
California	Pennsylvania
Colorado	Rhode Island
Florida	Texas
Georgia	Utah
Hawaii	Washington
Kansas	
Illinois	**Canada**
Maryland	Alberta
Massachusetts	British Columbia
Nebraska	Ontario
Nevada	Quebec

PRODUCTS/OPERATIONS

2001 New Contracts

	% of total
Transportation (highways, bridges, airports, railroads & mass transit)	74
Water supply/dams	13
Mining	5
Power, heat & cooling	4
Other	4
Total	**100**

COMPETITORS

ABB	Parsons
Bechtel	Perini
Black & Veatch	Raytheon
Bovis Lend Lease	Skanska USA Civil
Fluor	Turner Corporation
Foster Wheeler	Tutor-Saliba
Granite Construction	Washington Group
Halliburton	Whiting-Turner
ITOCHU	Williams Companies
Jacobs Engineering	

HISTORICAL FINANCIALS & EMPLOYEES

Private FYE: December 31	Annual Growth	12/92	12/93	12/94	12/95	12/96	12/97	12/98	12/99	12/00	12/01
Sales ($ mil.)	7.5%	2,020	2,179	2,991	2,902	2,904	2,764	3,403	4,013	4,463	3,871
Net income ($ mil.)	(0.4%)	181	261	110	244	221	155	288	165	179	175
Income as % of sales	—	9.0%	12.0%	3.7%	8.4%	7.6%	5.6%	8.5%	4.1%	4.0%	4.5%
Employees	8.6%	7,600	10,620	14,000	14,300	14,000	16,200	16,200	20,300	11,146	16,000

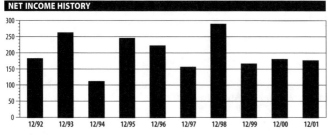

NET INCOME HISTORY

2001 FISCAL YEAR-END
Debt ratio: 2.9%
Return on equity: 22.9%
Cash ($ mil.): 216
Current ratio: 1.78
Long-term debt ($ mil.): 25

PORT AUTHORITY OF NY AND NJ

The Port Authority of New York and New Jersey bridges the often-troubled waters between the two states — and helps with other transportation needs of more than 400 million customers who rely on the Port Authority's services. The bi-state agency operates and maintains tunnels, bridges, airports, a commuter rail system, shipping terminals, and other facilities within the Port District, an area surrounding the Statue of Liberty. A self-supporting public agency, the Port Authority receives no state or local tax money but relies on tolls, fees, and rents. The governors of the two states each appoint six of the 12 members of the agency's board and review the board's decisions.

The Port Authority's facilities include such international symbols of transportation and commerce as the George Washington Bridge, the Holland and Lincoln tunnels, LaGuardia and John F. Kennedy airports, and the New York-New Jersey Port. The Port Authority Trans-Hudson (PATH) rapid-transit system carries nearly 75 million passengers per year.

The World Trade Center was counted among the agency's assets before its twin towers and much of the rest of the complex were destroyed in terrorist attacks on September 11, 2001. The Port Authority is working with other agencies, government officials, and real estate interests on the rebuilding of the World Trade Center site.

HISTORY

New York and New Jersey spent much of their early history fighting over their common waterways. In 1921 a treaty creating a single, bi-state agency, the Port of New York Authority, was ratified by the New York and New Jersey state legislatures.

The agency struggled at first, although its early projects, such as the Goethals Bridge (1928, linking Staten Island to New Jersey), far from timid. It merged with the Holland Tunnel Commission in 1930, which brought a steady source of revenue. In 1931 the George Washington Bridge (spanning the Hudson River from Manhattan to New Jersey) was completed. The Lincoln Tunnel (also linking Manhattan to New Jersey) opened in 1937.

After WWII the Port Authority broadened its focus to include commercial aviation. In 1947 the agency took over LaGuardia Airport, and the following year it dedicated the New York International Airport (renamed John F. Kennedy International Airport in 1963).

As trucking supplanted railroads in the late 1950s, The Port Authority experimented with more efficient ways of transferring cargo. In 1962 it built the first containerport in the world. That year the agency acquired a commuter rail line connecting Newark to Manhattan, which became the Port Authority Trans-Hudson (PATH).

In the early 1970s the Port Authority completed the World Trade Center. The agency changed its name to the Port Authority of New York and New Jersey in 1972 to reflect its role in mass transit between the two states. Critics, however, frequently assailed the agency for inefficiency and pork-barrel politics. In 1993 terrorists detonated a truck bomb in one of the World Trade Center towers, but within a year the building had largely recovered.

George Marlin became executive director in 1995. He cut operating expenses for the first time since 1943 and through budget cuts and layoffs, saved $100 million in 1996 and avoided hikes in tolls and fares. A privatization proponent, Marlin sold the World Trade Center's Vista Hotel to Host Marriott and arranged for the sale of other nontransportation businesses. He stepped down in 1997, and Robert Boyle took the post. That year the agency broke ground on the $1.2 billion Terminal 4 at JFK International Airport.

In 1998 the Port Authority authorized a $930 million design and construction contract for a light-rail line to JFK International Airport. New York City mayor Rudolph Giuliani proposed legislation in 1999 to place the Port Authority's LaGuardia and JFK airports under City Hall jurisdiction.

An 18-month standoff between the governors of New York and New Jersey regarding disputes over leases and agency spending was settled in 2000, which allowed the Port Authority to move forward with projects that had been blocked. Also in 2000 Boyle announced plans to resign. Neil Levin, New York's state insurance superintendent and a former Goldman Sachs vice president, replaced him the next year.

After the Port Authority and Vornado Realty Trust in 2001 failed to finalize an agreement for Vornado to lease the World Trade Center, the Port Authority that year signed a 99-year, $3.2 billion deal to lease portions of the World Trade Center's office space to a group led by Silverstein Properties while leasing the retail space to Westfield America.

Less than two months later, the World Trade Center's twin towers were destroyed when terrorists hijacked passenger jets and flew them into the buildings. Levin was killed, and 83 other Port Authority employees were listed as dead or missing.

The cleanup of the World Trade Center site, known as "Ground Zero," was completed in 2002, eight months after the attacks.

OFFICERS

Chairman, Port Authority of New York and New Jersey, Port Authority Trans-Hudson, Newark Legal and Communications Center, and New York & New Jersey Railroad: Jack G. Sinagra
Vice Chairman, Port Authority of New York and New Jersey, Port Authority Trans-Hudson, Newark Legal and Communications Center, and New York & New Jersey Railroad: Charles A. Gargano
Executive Director, Port Authority of New York and New Jersey, Port Authority Trans-Hudson, Newark Legal and Communications Center, and New York & New Jersey Railroad: Joseph J. Seymour
Deputy Executive Director: Michael R. DeCotiis
COO; VP and General Manager, Port Authority Trans-Hudson: Ernesto L. Butcher
CFO: Charles F. McClafferty
Director Human Resources: Paul Segalini
General Counsel; VP and Secretary, New York & New Jersey Railroad: Jeffrey S. Green
Auditors: Deloitte & Touche LLP

LOCATIONS

HQ: The Port Authority of New York and New Jersey
225 Park Ave. S., 18th Fl., New York, NY 10003
Phone: 212-435-7000   **Fax:** 212-436-7390
Web: www.panynj.gov

The Port Authority of New York and New Jersey has operations in the five boroughs of New York City and in 12 counties in New Jersey and New York. The agency has overseas offices in Belgium, China, Hong Kong, Japan, Singapore, South Korea, and the UK.

PRODUCTS/OPERATIONS

2001 Sales

	$ mil.	% of total
Air terminals	1,427	53
Interstate transportation	788	29
World Trade Center	291	11
Port commerce	118	4
Economic development	91	3
Total	**2,715**	**100**

Selected Locations

Aviation
Downtown Manhattan Heliport (New York)
John F. Kennedy International Airport (New York)
LaGuardia Airport (New York)
Newark Liberty International Airport (New Jersey)
Teterboro Airport (New Jersey)

Commercial Real Estate
Bathgate Industrial Park (Bronx, New York)
Essex County Resource Recovery Center (waste-to-energy electric generation plant; Newark, New Jersey)
Industrial Park at Elizabeth (New Jersey)
Queens West (mixed-use waterfront development; Queens, New York)
South Waterfront (mixed-use waterfront development; Hoboken, New Jersey)

Port Commerce
Auto Marine Terminal (Bayonne, New Jersey)
Brooklyn-Port Authority Marine Terminal (New York)
Howland Hook Marine Terminal (New York)
Port Newark/Elizabeth Marine Terminal (New Jersey)

Tunnels, Bridges, and Terminals
Bayonne Bridge (Staten Island to Bayonne, New Jersey)
George Washington Bridge (Manhattan to Ft. Lee, New Jersey)
George Washington Bridge Bus Terminal
Goethals Bridge (Staten Island to Elizabeth, New Jersey)
Holland Tunnel (Manhattan to Jersey City, New Jersey)
Lincoln Tunnel (Manhattan to Union City, New Jersey)
Port Authority Bus Terminal (Manhattan)

Other
The Port Authority Trans-Hudson System (PATH, rail transportation between New York and New Jersey)
World Trade Center (office complex, Manhattan, prior to its destruction by terrorists in 2001)

COMPETITORS

Coach USA	Amtrak
Covanta	Reckson Associates Realty
Helmsley	Tishman Realty
Lefrak Organization	Trump
MTA	

HISTORICAL FINANCIALS & EMPLOYEES

Government-owned FYE: December 31	Annual Growth	12/92	12/93	12/94	12/95	12/96	12/97	12/98	12/99	12/00	12/01
Sales ($ mil.)	3.8%	1,934	1,921	1,980	2,083	2,154	2,206	2,361	2,548	2,648	2,715
Net income ($ mil.)	4.6%	144	108	153	177	199	282	299	314	372	216
Income as % of sales	—	7.4%	5.6%	7.7%	8.5%	9.2%	12.8%	12.7%	12.3%	14.1%	7.9%
Employees	(3.7%)	9,500	9,350	9,200	9,250	8,100	7,500	7,200	7,200	7,000	—

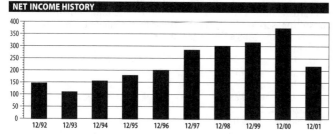

NET INCOME HISTORY

2001 FISCAL YEAR-END
Debt ratio: 56.8%
Return on equity: 4.3%
Cash ($ mil.): 47
Current ratio: 1.48
Long-term debt ($ mil.): 6,821

PRICEWATERHOUSECOOPERS

Not merely the firm with the longest one-word name, PricewaterhouseCoopers (PwC) is also the world's largest accountancy, formed when Price Waterhouse merged with Coopers & Lybrand in 1998, passing then-leader Andersen. The firm has offices around the world, providing clients with services in three lines of business: Assurance and Business Advisory Services (including financial and regulatory reporting); Tax and Legal Services; and Corporate Finance and Recovery. The company serves some of the world's largest businesses, as well as smaller firms.

PwC puts its heft to good use: Global clients make up about 40% of the firm's sales. Its bottom line, though, changed significantly in 2002, when PwC sold its consulting arm to IBM. A separation had been under consideration for years in light of SEC concerns about conflicts of interest when firms perform auditing and consulting for the same clients. The collapse of Enron and concomitant downfall of Enron's auditor and PwC's erstwhile peer Andersen undoubtedly hastened plans to spin off PwC's consultancy via an IPO, which was then scrapped in favor of the IBM deal.

Like the other members of the (now) Big Four, PwC picked up business and talent as scandal-felled Andersen was winding down its operations in 2002. The former Andersen organization in China and Hong Kong joined PwC, accounting for about 70% of the approximately 3,500 Andersen alumni that came aboard.

HISTORY

In 1850 Samuel Price founded an accounting firm in London and in 1865 took on partner Edwin Waterhouse. The firm and the industry grew rapidly, thanks to the growth of stock exchanges that required uniform financial statements from listees. By the late 1800s Price Waterhouse (PW) had become the world's best-known accounting firm.

US offices were opened in the 1890s, and in 1902 United States Steel chose the firm as its auditor. PW benefited from tough audit requirements instituted after the 1929 stock market crash. In 1935 the firm was given the prestigious job of handling Academy Awards balloting. It started a management consulting service in 1946. But PW's dominance slipped in the 1960s, as it gained a reputation as the most traditional and formal of the major firms.

Coopers & Lybrand, the product of a 1957 transatlantic merger, wrote the book on auditing. Lybrand, Ross Bros. & Montgomery was formed in 1898 by William Lybrand, Edward Ross, Adam Ross, and Robert Montgomery. In

1912 Montgomery wrote *Montgomery's Auditing*, which became the bible of accounting.

Cooper Brothers was founded in 1854 in London by William Cooper, eldest son of a Quaker banker. In 1957 Lybrand joined up to form Coopers & Lybrand. During the 1960s the firm expanded into employee benefits and internal control consulting, building its technology capabilities in the 1970s as it studied ways to automate the audit process.

Coopers & Lybrand lost market share as mergers reduced the Big Eight accounting firms to the Big Six. After the savings and loan debacle of the 1980s, investors and the government wanted accounting firms held liable not only for the form of audited financial statements but also for their veracity. In 1992 the firm paid $95 million to settle claims of defrauded investors in MiniScribe, a failed disk-drive maker. Other hefty payments followed, including a $108 million settlement relating to the late Robert Maxwell's defunct media empire.

In 1998 Price Waterhouse and Coopers & Lybrand combined PW's strength in the media, entertainment, and utility industries, and Coopers & Lybrand's focus on telecommunications and mining. But the merger brought some expensive legal baggage involving Coopers & Lybrand's performance of audits related to a bid-rigging scheme involving former Arizona governor Fife Symington.

Further growth plans fell through in 1999 when merger talks between PwC and Grant Thornton International failed. The year 2000 began on a sour note: An SEC conflict-of-interest probe turned up more than 8,000 alleged violations, most involving PwC partners owning stock in their firm's audit clients.

As the SEC grew ever more shrill in its denunciation of the potential conflicts of interest arising from auditing companies that the firm hoped to recruit or retain as consulting clients, PwC saw the writing on the wall and in 2000 began making plans to split the two operations. As part of this move, the company downsized and reorganized many of its operations.

The following year PwC paid $55 million to shareholders of MicroStrategy Inc., who charged that the audit firm defrauded them by approving the client firm's inflated earnings and revenues figures.

OFFICERS

Global Chairman: Andrew Ratcliffe
Global CEO and Global Board Member:
Samuel A. DiPiazza
Global CFO: Geoffrey E. Johnson
Global Board Member, France: Pierre B. Anglade
Global Board Member, Netherlands: Paul R. Baart
Global Board Member, South Africa: Colin Beggs
Global Board Member, Australia: Paul V. Brasher
Global Board Member, US: Jay D. Brodish
Global Board Member, Brazil:
Raimundo L.M. Christians
Global Board Member, Switzerland: Edgar Fluri
Global Board Member, UK: Alec N. Jones
Global Board Member, Germany: Jan Konerding
Global Board Member, US: Keith D. Levingston
Global Board Member, US: Dennis J. Lubozynski
Global Board Member, US: Donald A. McGovern
Global Board Member, Canada: Israel H. Mida
Global Board Member, Japan: Dean A. Yoost
Managing Partner, Global Markets: Willem L.J. Bröcker
Managing Partner, Global Operations:
Amyas C.E. Morse, age 52
Global General Counsel; Acting US General Counsel:
Lawrence Keeshan
Vice Chairman, Services (US): John O'Connor
Vice Chairman, Operations (US): Eugene Donnelly
**Human Resources, Learning, and Education Leader
(US):** Bob Daugherty
Marketing Leader (US): Dean Kern

LOCATIONS

HQ: 1301 Avenue of the Americas, New York, NY 10019
Phone: 646-471-4000   **Fax:** 646-394-1301
Web: www.pwcglobal.com

PricewaterhouseCoopers has offices in about 150
countries.

2002 Sales

	% of total
Europe, Middle East & Africa	45
North America	38
Asia/Pacific	13
South & Central America	4
Total	**100**

PRODUCTS/OPERATIONS

2002 Sales

	$ mil.	% of total
Assurance & business advisory services	7,990	57
Tax & legal services	4,180	29
Corporate finance & recovery	1,200	7
Other	430	7
Total	**13,800**	**100**

Selected Services

Audit, Assurance and Business Advisory Services
Accounting and regulatory advice
Audit
Corporate training
Public services audit and advisory

Global Risk Management Solutions
Audit and compliance services
Operational advisory
Risk and value management
Security and technology services
Sustainability services

**Financial Advisory (called Corporate Finance &
Recovery outside the US)**
Business recovery services
Corporate finance
Dispute analysis and investigations (forensics)
Valuation and strategy

Global Tax Services
Customs and duties
E-business services
Finance and treasure
Global visa solutions
International assignment solutions
Mergers and acquisitions
Tax compliance and outsourcing

COMPETITORS

Bain & Company	Hewitt Associates
BDO International	KPMG
Booz Allen	Marsh & McLennan
Boston Consulting	McKinsey & Company
Deloitte Touche Tohmatsu	Towers Perrin
Ernst & Young	Watson Wyatt
H&R Block	

HISTORICAL FINANCIALS & EMPLOYEES

Partnership FYE: June 30	Annual Growth	6/93	6/94	6/95	6/96	6/97	6/98	6/99	6/00	6/01	6/02
Sales ($ mil.)	15.1%	3,890	3,980	4,460	5,020	5,630	15,000	15,300	21,500	24,000	13,800
Employees	11.0%	48,781	50,122	53,000	56,000	60,000	140,000	155,000	150,000	160,000	124,563

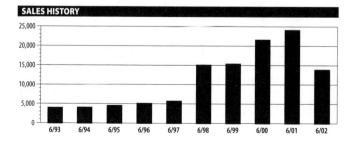

SALES HISTORY

PUBLIX SUPER MARKETS, INC.

Shoppers at Publix shouldn't have to worry about being checked out — although with its share of gender and race discrimination lawsuits, they might wonder. Publix Super Markets is one of the largest and most profitable US grocery chains. Most of its nearly 700 stores are in Florida, but it also operates in Alabama, Georgia, and South Carolina. Publix makes some of its own deli, bakery, and dairy goods, and many stores offer flowers, housewares, and pharmacies. Its online store, PublixDirect, offers delivery service in parts of Florida. Founder George Jenkins began offering stock to Publix employees in 1930. Employees own about 27% of Publix, which is still run by the Jenkins family.

By emphasizing service and a family-friendly image rather than price, Publix has grown faster and been more profitable than Winn-Dixie Stores and other rivals. While winning Florida's shoppers, Publix has lost a few legal battles brought by its employees. It has settled three suits (over gender and race discrimination) but currently is embroiled in another suit alleging it discriminated against Hispanics. Despite the lawsuits, Publix was named to *FORTUNE* magazine's "Most Admired Companies" list.

PublixDirect offers delivery in Broward County, Florida, with plans to expand to Orlando and Atlanta. Publix is also moving into the convenience store/gas station business with its "Pix" convenience stores. It has two stores in Polk County, Florida, and is opening two more in Deltona and Kissimmee. Publix opens about 30 new supermarkets each year. About 80% of the company's stores are in Florida. The grocery chain is entering the Nashville, Tennessee, market with the purchase of seven Albertson's supermarkets, a convenience store, and a fuel center.

HISTORY

George Jenkins, age 22, resigned as manager of the Piggly Wiggly grocery in Winter Haven, Florida, in 1930. With money he had saved to buy a car, he opened his own grocery store, Publix, next door to his old employer. The small store (named after a chain of movie theaters) prospered despite the Depression, and in 1935 Jenkins opened another Publix in the same town. Five years later, after the supermarket format had become popular, Jenkins closed his two smaller locations and opened a new, more modern Publix Market. With pastel colors and electric-eye doors, it was also the first US store to feature air conditioning.

In 1944 Publix Super Markets bought the All-American chain of Lakeland, Florida (19 stores), and moved its corporate headquarters to that city. The company began offering S&H Green Stamps in 1953, and in 1956 it replaced its original supermarket with a mall featuring an enlarged Publix and a Green Stamp redemption center. Publix expanded into South Florida in the late 1950s and began selling stock to employees.

As Florida's population grew, Publix continued to expand, opening its 100th store in 1964. Publix was the first grocery chain in the state to use bar-code scanners — all its stores had the technology by 1981. The company beat Florida banks in providing ATMs and during the 1980s opened debit card stations.

Publix continued to grow in the 1980s, safe from takeover attempts because of its employee ownership. In 1988 it installed the first automated checkout systems in South Florida, giving patrons an always-open checkout lane.

The chain quit offering Green Stamps in 1989, and most of the $19 million decrease in Publix advertising expenditures was attributed to the end of the 36-year promotion. That year, after almost six decades, "Mr. George" — as founder Jenkins was known — stepped down as chairman in favor of his son Howard. (George died in 1996.)

In 1991 Publix opened its first store outside Florida, in Georgia, as part of its plan to become a major player in the Southeast. Publix entered South Carolina in 1993 with one supermarket.

The United Food and Commercial Workers Union began a campaign in 1994 against alleged gender and racial discrimination in Publix's hiring, promotion, and compensation policies.

Publix opened its first store in Alabama in 1996. That year a federal judge allowed about 150,000 women to join a class-action suit filed in 1995 by 12 women who had sued Publix charging that the company consistently channeled female employees into low-paying jobs with little chance for good promotions. The case, said to be the biggest sex discrimination lawsuit ever, was set to go to trial, but in 1997 the company paid $82.5 million to settle and another $3.5 million to settle a complaint of discrimination against black applicants and employees.

Publix promised to change its promotion policies, but two more lawsuits alleging discrimination against women and blacks were filed in 1997 and 1998. The suit filed on behalf of the women was denied class-action status in 2000. Later that year the company settled the racial discrimination lawsuit for $10.5 million. Howard Jenkins stepped down as CEO in mid-2001; his cousin Charlie Jenkins took the helm.

In mid-2002 Publix invested in Florida-based Crispers, a chain of 13 quick-serve restaurants targeting health-conscious diners.

Chairman: Howard M. Jenkins, age 50
Vice Chairman: Hoyt R. Barnett, age 58, $324,600 pay
CEO and COO, Director: Charles H. Jenkins Jr., age 58, $466,093 pay
President: W. Edwin Crenshaw, age 51, $401,088 pay
CFO and Treasurer: David P. Phillips, age 42, $263,743 pay
SVP and CIO: Daniel M. Risener, age 61, $269,160 pay
SVP: Tina P. Johnson, age 42
SVP: James J. Lobinsky, age 62
SVP: Thomas M. O'Connor, age 54
VP, Assistant Secretary: Linda Kane
VP, Controller: Gino DiGrazia
VP, Controller: Sandy Woods
VP, Human Resources: James H. Rhodes II, age 57
Secretary: John A. Attaway Jr., age 43
Auditors: KPMG LLP

LOCATIONS

HQ: 1936 George Jenkins Blvd., Lakeland, FL 33815
Phone: 863-688-1188   **Fax:** 863-284-5532
Web: www.publix.com

Publix Super Markets operates nearly 700 grocery stores in Alabama, Florida, Georgia, and South Carolina. The company also has three dairy processing plants (Deerfield Beach and Lakeland, Florida, and Lawrenceville, Georgia) and a deli plant and a bakery in Lakeland. Publix operates eight distribution centers in Florida (Boynton Beach, Deerfield Beach, Jacksonville, Lakeland, Miami, Orlando, and Sarasota) and Georgia (Lawrenceville).

2001 Stores

	No.
Florida	534
Georgia	127
South Carolina	23
Alabama	4
Total	**688**

PRODUCTS/OPERATIONS

Selected Supermarket Departments

Bakery	Health and beauty care
Banking	Housewares
Dairy	Meat
Deli	Pharmacy
Ethnic foods	Photo processing
Floral	Produce
Groceries	Seafood

Foods Processed
Baked goods
Dairy products
Deli items

COMPETITORS

Albertson's
ALDI
BI-LO
Bruno's Supermarkets
Costco Wholesale
CVS
Delhaize America
Fleming Companies
IGA
Ingles Markets
Kerr Drug
Kmart
Kroger
Nash Finch
The Pantry
Rite Aid
Royal Ahold
Ruddick
Sedano's Management
Smart & Final
Walgreens
Wal-Mart
Whole Foods
Winn-Dixie

HISTORICAL FINANCIALS & EMPLOYEES

| Private
FYE: December 31 | Annual
Growth | 12/92 | 12/93 | 12/94 | 12/95 | 12/96 | 12/97 | 12/98 | 12/99 | 12/00 | 12/01 |
|---|---|---|---|---|---|---|---|---|---|---|---|
| Sales ($ mil.) | 9.7% | 6,664 | 7,473 | 8,665 | 9,393 | 10,431 | 11,224 | 12,067 | 13,069 | 14,724 | 15,370 |
| Net income ($ mil.) | 13.7% | 166 | 184 | 239 | 242 | 265 | 355 | 378 | 462 | 530 | 530 |
| Income as % of sales | — | 2.5% | 2.5% | 2.8% | 2.6% | 2.5% | 3.2% | 3.1% | 3.5% | 3.6% | 3.5% |
| Employees | 6.3% | 73,000 | 82,000 | 90,000 | 95,000 | 103,000 | 111,000 | 117,000 | 120,000 | 126,000 | 126,000 |

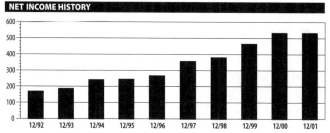

NET INCOME HISTORY

2001 FISCAL YEAR-END
Debt ratio: 0.0%
Return on equity: 19.6%
Cash ($ mil.): 251
Current ratio: 1.03
Long-term debt ($ mil.): 0

RAND MCNALLY & COMPANY

Rand McNally lets you know where you stand. The largest commercial mapmaker in the world, the company is famous for its flagship Rand McNally Road Atlas —the best-selling product in the history of mapmaking. In addition, the company produces travel-related software (TripMaker, StreetFinder) and educational products for classrooms (globes, atlases). Rand McNally also operates a Web site and makes mileage and routing software for the transportation industry. Founded in 1856, Rand McNally was owned by the McNally family until AEA Investors bought a controlling interest in 1997.

The company makes maps for the Canadian market through its Rand McNally Canada unit. It sells its products online and through some 50,000 retail outlets across the US, including 25 Rand McNally stores.

Although it created a Web site in 1996, the company didn't really begin focusing on the Internet until 1999, years later than online rivals such as MapQuest.com. In 2000 Rand McNally relaunched its Web site in hopes of catching up with its online competitors. Industry analysts have speculated that AEA Investors has been frustrated with Rand McNally's slow growth and may sell the company.

Rand McNally was founded by William Rand and Andrew McNally in 1856. In 1864 the pair bought the job-printing department of the *Chicago Tribune,* and expanded into the printing of railroad tickets and schedules. They published their first book, a Chicago business directory, in 1870.

In 1872 the company printed its first map for the *Railway Guide.* Rand McNally later expanded into publishing paperback novels (popular among train travelers), and by 1891 annual sales topped $1 million.

During the 1890s McNally bought Rand's share of the business, and the company branched into printing school textbooks. Rand McNally's first photo auto guide was issued in 1907, and the company introduced its first complete US road atlas in 1924. When Hitler invaded Poland in 1939, Rand McNally's New York stock of European maps sold out in one day. WWII necessitated the revision of a number of maps — a challenge that the company continued to face throughout the 20th century.

Although the company had abandoned adult fiction and nonfiction in 1914, it reentered the field in 1948 when a company official persuaded explorer Thor Heyerdahl to write a book for the company about his adventures. First published

in 1950, Heyerdahl's *Kon-Tiki* sold more than a million copies in its first six years.

Rand McNally produced its first four-color road atlas in 1960, and during the 1970s it began publishing travel guides for Mobil Oil. The next decade the company published several new road atlases to fill the void created when gas stations discontinued their practice of giving away free road maps. Rand McNally sold its textbook publishing business to Houghton Mifflin in 1980, and five years later it began computerizing its cartography operations.

In 1993 the company acquired Allmaps Canada Limited (now Rand McNally Canada). It introduced *TripMaker,* a CD-ROM vacation-planning program, the next year. Also in 1994 Rand McNally won a contract to create maps for a *Reader's Digest* atlas. The company debuted its StreetFinder street-level software in 1995 and created its Cartographic and Information Services division in 1996. It also established a Web site that year.

The next year, as part of a plan to focus on mapmaking and providing geographic information, Rand McNally sold a number of its subsidiaries (Book Services Group, DocuSystems Group). AEA Investors bought a controlling interest in the company later in 1997, bringing an end to more than 140 years of McNally family control (though it did retain a minority stake). While Rand McNally was still profitable, the sale to AEA underscored the challenges facing the company: Growth in earnings had slowed, and technological changes (Internet maps and software) had altered the mapmaking industry.

Rand McNally expanded in 1999 with acquisitions of mapmakers Thomas Bros. Maps and King of the Road Map Service. Later that year Henry Feinberg resigned as chairman and CEO. Richard Davis was appointed CEO, and John Macomber became chairman.

In 2000 the company relaunched its Web site with additional trip planning capabilities. Also that year it became the primary North American distributor of *National Geographic* maps and COO Norman Wells replaced Davis as CEO.

In 2001 Michael Hehir was named CEO, Wells replaced Macomber as chairman, and Macomber remained as a director on the board.

Chairman: Norman E. Wells Jr., age 52
President, CEO, and Director: Michael Hehir
SVP Consumer Travel: Victoria Donnowitz
SVP Business-to-Business Division: Robert P. Denaro
SVP Geographic Information Services: Joel Minster
Chief Administrative Officer: Dean Haskell
VP, Information Services: Ken Levin
General Manager, Transportation Data Management: Shel Greenberg
Group Controller: David Jones
Media Relations: Ditas Mauricio
Editorial Director: Laurie Borman

LOCATIONS

HQ: 8255 N. Central Park Ave., Skokie, IL 60076
Phone: 847-329-8100   **Fax:** 847-329-6361
Web: www.randmcnally.com

Rand McNally operates in the US and Canada. It has retail stores in California, Florida, Illinois, Massachusetts, Michigan, Minnesota, Missouri, New Jersey, New York, Pennsylvania, Texas, Virginia, and Washington, DC.

PRODUCTS/OPERATIONS

Selected Print Products
Business Travelers' Briefcase Atlas
Motor Carriers' Road Atlas
Rand McNally Pocket City Atlas
Rand McNally Road Atlas
The Thomas Guides

Selected Sales Channels
Rand McNally (retail stores)
randmcnally.com (e-commerce)

Selected Software
New Millennium World Atlas Deluxe Edition
Rand McNally StreetFinder Deluxe
Rand McNally TripMaker Deluxe

COMPETITORS

AAA
Analytical Surveys
DeLorme
ESRI
Expedia
Globe Pequot
Lonely Planet
MapInfo
MapQuest.com
Michelin
National Geographic
Piersen Graphics
R. L. Polk
TravRoute
Vicinity

HISTORICAL FINANCIALS & EMPLOYEES

Private FYE: December 31	Annual Growth	12/92	12/93	12/94	12/95	12/96	12/97	12/98	12/99	12/00	12/01
Sales ($ mil.)	(5.8%)	342	395	438	469	163	175	175	179	200	200
Employees	(14.3%)	4,000	4,000	4,200	4,650	1,000	1,000	1,000	920	1,000	1,000

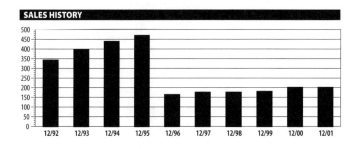

SALES HISTORY

THE ROCKEFELLER FOUNDATION

The Rockefeller Foundation is one of the nation's oldest private charitable organizations. It supports grants, fellowships, and conferences for programs that try to identify and alleviate need and suffering around the world. These programs (or themes) include initiatives to foster fair implementation of health care, job opportunities for America's urban poor, creative expression through the humanities and arts, and agricultural policies that ensure food distribution to people in developing countries. The foundation's cross theme of global inclusion binds its programs to a global focus, ensuring that globalization gets doled out democratically and helps populations typically alienated from the global economy.

President Gordon Conway has introduced the reorganization focusing on the role of globalization in aiding the poor. The foundation's former divisions — such as Agricultural Sciences, Equal Opportunity, and Health Sciences — now come under the themes of Food Security, Working Communities, and Health Equity. Its non-New York City offices (Bangkok; Mexico City; Nairobi, Kenya; Harare, Zimbabwe; and San Francisco) are taking on increasing responsibility in carrying out the group's global mission. The foundation maintains no ties to the Rockefeller family or its other philanthropies. An independent board of trustees sets program guidelines and approves all expenditures.

HISTORY

Oil baron John D. Rockefeller, one of America's most criticized capitalists, was also one of its pioneer philanthropists. Before founding The Rockefeller Foundation in 1913, he funded the creation of The University of Chicago (with $36 million over a 25-year period) and formed organizations for medical research (1901), the education of southern African-Americans (1903), and hookworm eradication in the southern US.

Rockefeller turned the control of the foundation over to his son John D. Rockefeller Jr. in 1916. The younger Rockefeller separated the foundation from the family's interests and established an independent board. (The board later rejected a proposal from John Sr. to replace school textbooks that he claimed promoted Bolshevism.)

In the mid-1920s the foundation started conducting basic medical research. In 1928 it absorbed several other Rockefeller philanthropies, adding programs in the natural and social sciences and the arts and humanities. During the 1930s the foundation developed the first effective yellow fever vaccine (1935), continued its worldwide battles against disease, and supported pioneering research in the field of biology. Other grants supported the performing arts in the US and social science research. During WWII it supplied major funding for nuclear science research tools (spectroscopy, X-ray diffraction).

After the war, with an increasing number of large public ventures modeled after the foundation (e.g., the UN's World Health Organization) taking over its traditional physical and natural sciences territory, the organization dissolved its famed biology division in 1951. The following year emphasis swung to agricultural studies under chairman John D. Rockefeller III. The organization took wheat seeds developed at its Mexican food project to Colombia (1950), Chile (1955), and India (1956); a rice institute in the Philippines followed (1960). The Green Revolution sprouted 12 more developing-world institutes.

In the 1960s the foundation began dispatching experts to African and Latin American universities in an effort to raise the level of training at those institutions. The long bear market of the 1970s caused the foundation's assets to drop to a low of $732 million (1977).

In 1990 the organization set up the Energy Foundation, a joint effort with the Pew Charitable Trusts and the MacArthur Foundation, to explore alternate energy sources.

In the mid-1990s the Republican-led Congress launched three probes into the foundation and several other not-for-profits over allegations of political activities that could jeopardize their tax status.

In 1998 Gordon Conway, a British agricultural ecologist, became the foundation's 12th (and first foreign) president. He implemented a retooling of the organization's programs in 1999. He also led an effective campaign against bioengineering giant Monsanto's (now part of Pharmacia Corp.) plan to market "sterile seeds" that do not regenerate. In 2000 James Orr III, a Rockefeller board member and CEO of Boston's United Asset Management Corporation, succeeded Alice Ilchman as chairman of the board of trustees.

OFFICERS

Chairman: James F. Orr III
President: Gordon R. Conway
EVP for Strategy: Lincoln C. Chen
VP, Administration and Communication:
  Denise Gray-Felder
VP: Robert W. Herdt
VP and Acting Director, Working Communities:
  Julia I. Lopez
Associate VP: Joyce L. Moock
Corporate Secretary: Lynda Mullen
Treasurer and Chief Investment Officer: Donna J. Dean
CTO: Fernando Mola-Davis

LOCATIONS

HQ: 420 Fifth Ave., New York, NY 10018
Phone: 212-869-8500   Fax: 212-764-3468
Web: www.rockfound.org

The Rockefeller Foundation has field offices in Kenya, Mexico, Thailand, Zimbabwe, and the US, and maintains the Bellagio Study and Conference Center in northern Italy.

PRODUCTS/OPERATIONS

2001 Grants

	$ mil.	% of total
Working communities	33	21
Health equities	26	17
Global inclusion	23	15
Food security	21	13
Creativity & culture	17	11
Regional activities	14	9
Special programs	14	9
Program venture investment	7	5
Total	**155**	**100**

Themes

Creativity & Culture (Renews and preserves the cultural heritage of people excluded from the globalizing economy; promotes public exchanges of ideas; supports diversity and creativity in humanities and arts)

Food Security (Generates agricultural institutions, policies, and innovations to help rural poor in developing countries)

Global Inclusion (Seeks to ensure that globalization processes are carried out fairly and democratically, benefiting those most in need)

Health Equity (Seeks to improve the implementation of health care in developing countries)

Working Communities (Seeks to increase employment, improve schools, and encourage democratic participation in poor urban neighborhoods in the US)

HISTORICAL FINANCIALS & EMPLOYEES

| Foundation
FYE: December 31 | Annual
Growth | 12/92 | 12/93 | 12/94 | 12/95 | 12/96 | 12/97 | 12/98 | 12/99 | 12/00 | 12/01 |
|---|---|---|---|---|---|---|---|---|---|---|---|
| Sales ($ mil.) | (6.9%) | 198 | 208 | 21 | 319 | 413 | 510 | 388 | 680 | 127 | 104 |
| Employees | 6.5% | 142 | 147 | 137 | 130 | 152 | 149 | 150 | 220 | 230 | 250 |

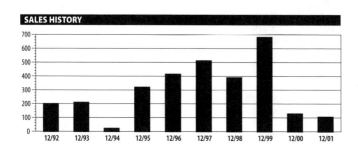

SALES HISTORY

ROSENBLUTH INTERNATIONAL

In the mood for a trip? Rosenbluth International will help you unravel the travel scene. A leading travel management company, Rosenbluth emphasizes services for corporate clients (ChevronTexaco, J.P. Morgan Chase, NIKE).

With 1,300 locations worldwide, the company is known for staying abreast of evolving travel technology and offers its services with the aid of travel systems such as its Discount Analysis Containing Optimal Decision Algorithms (DACODA), which maximizes savings on airline tickets. Founded in 1892 by Marcus Rosenbluth, the company still is owned and operated by his family, including his great-grandson, chairman and CEO Hal Rosenbluth.

Rosenbluth International makes billions by keeping its customers second. The company, whose corporate philosophy was revealed in chairman and CEO Hal Rosenbluth's 1992 book *The Customer Comes Second* (after employees), is a leader in travel management services. The company's mascot is a salmon, because of its ability to successfully swim upstream against the tide. In addition to providing traditional travel services (airline, hotel, and car rental reservations), Rosebluth has branched into virtual travel management, offering its clients services such as Web conferencing.

HISTORY

In 1892 Marcus Rosenbluth began selling immigration packages from his storefront shop to neighbors in Philadelphia's Brewerytown. After collecting $50 in various currencies, he would arrange passage for an immigrant family's European relative to Ellis Island, often greeting the American-to-be personally and helping complete forms in the new language.

Rosenbluth's travel company rode out the ups and downs of two world wars and the emerging commercial airline industry. By the time Rosenbluth's great-grandson Hal Rosenbluth came aboard in 1974, the mostly consumer leisure travel agency had sales of more than $20 million a year. In the year of airline deregulation (1978), a lightbulb went on as Hal Rosenbluth observed reservation agents working on corporate accounts. He soon demoted himself from vice president to reservations agent and began steering the company toward corporate accounts.

Before deregulation, airlines focused on service; fares were regulated by law and rarely changed. Businesses were interested mostly in who could deliver their tickets the fastest. With deregulation, fares changed with dizzying frequency. Yield management replaced service. Travelers needed help sorting through the confusion,

and Rosenbluth saw the opportunity to meet their needs.

In the early 1980s accounts with Bethlehem Steel and DuPont helped Rosenbluth gain a national presence. A less than ecstatic reception in Atlanta in 1985 motivated the company to upgrade its high-tech pricing and reservations system and lure corporate accounts with promises of savings and good service. Hal Rosenbluth became CEO in 1987, and the next year Rosenbluth sought to grow overseas by forming Rosenbluth International Alliance (RIA), a network of independent business travel agencies.

Hal Rosenbluth's book, *The Customer Comes Second*, was published in 1992. Rosenbluth abandoned RIA in 1993 (buying some of the businesses and setting up new ones) when it found it could not control the quality of service it offered to multinationals. Crunched by low air fares, the company began reorganizing operations in 1994 by breaking up the company into 100-plus branches serving specific clients and regions. It also laid off about 10% of its workforce.

In 1997 the company geared itself for global growth by forming a strategic alliance with The SABRE Group to integrate SABRE's technology into its travel reservations systems. One year later Rosenbluth bought Swedish travel firm Business Express.

In 1999 Rosenbluth acquired travel services firm Aquarius Travel. Later that year the company expanded into Web-based travel services when it bought a majority of Internet travel services company biztravel.com. In 2000 Rosenbluth unveiled Rosenbluth Everywhere, a custom online and wireless travel service. The firm also expanded into non-travel call center services and made headlines when biztravel.com offered travelers refunds for flights that arrived late (biztravel.com folded the next year in the wake of the September 11th terrorist attacks).

The company continued to seek out partnerships in 2001, adding large Chinese travel agency China Comfort to its list of business affiliates. In 2002 Rosenbluth landed another major corporate client, US publisher McGraw-Hill.

Chairman and CEO: Hal F. Rosenbluth, age 50
President and COO: Alex Wasilov
CFO: Thomas Sukay
SVP Marketing: Michael Boult
SVP North America: Ron DiLeo
SVP Upstream: Jerry Johnson
VP and Corporate Controller: Jeff Petrick
VP and General Counsel: Thomas Knoblauch
VP Business Development, Upstream: Joe Terrion
VP Marketing and Business Development North America: Gordon Locke
VP Human Resources Development: Cecily Carel
VP Central US: Yma Sherry
VP Western US: R. Timothy Small
CIO: John Dabek
Chief Marketing Officer: Kimberly Harrington-Martinez
Director Corporate Development: Mara Pagotto

HQ: 2401 Walnut St., Philadelphia, PA 19103
Phone: 215-977-4000   **Fax:** 215-977-4028
Web: www.rosenbluth.com

Rosenbluth International has operations in 24 countries worldwide.

Selected Products and Services
@Rosenbluth (business travel management system)
Custom-Res (global reservation system)
Discount Analysis Containing Optimal Decision Algorithms (DACODA, system for maximizing savings on airline tickets)
E-Ticket Tracking Solution (electronic ticket tracking System)
Global Distribution Network (electronic reservation system)
Res-Monitor (low-fare search system)
Rosenbluth's Electronic Messaging Services (e-mail based travel management system)
Travelution (discount airline tickets Web site)

American Express	MyTravel
Carlson Wagonlit	Pleasant Holidays
Expedia	priceline.com
JTB	Travelocity
Kuoni Travel	TUI
Maritz	WorldTravel

Private FYE: December 31	Annual Growth	12/92	12/93	12/94	12/95	12/96	12/97	12/98	12/99	12/00	12/01
Sales ($ mil.)	11.0%	—	—	—	3,200	3,500	4,000	3,500	4,500	5,500	6,000
Employees	2.9%	—	—	—	—	4,500	4,500	4,500	4,500	5,500	5,200

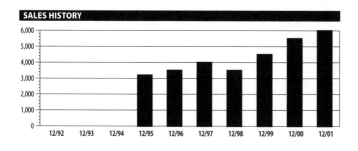

SALES HISTORY

ROTARY INTERNATIONAL

The rotary phone may be gone, but Rotary International is still going strong. The organization addresses issues such as AIDS, hunger, and illiteracy, and includes about 30,100 clubs across some 160 countries with nearly 1.2 million members (predominantly men, although women are its fastest-growing segment). Its not-for-profit Rotary Foundation invests in international education and humanitarian programs (funds are raised through voluntary contributions). Rotary International also sponsors Interact clubs for secondary school students and a network of more than 6,400 Rotaract clubs for members ages 18-30. It is governed by a 19-member board and maintains offices globally.

Membership in Rotary clubs is by invitation only. Each club strives to include representatives from major businesses, professions, and institutions in its community. Along with other service organizations, Rotary International has been confronted with a new issue — social and attitudinal trends that have made it more difficult to attract new members. While Rotary International has fared better than some of its counterparts, a decline in civic-mindedness and the fact that corporations no longer stress membership in service organizations present new challenges for the organization.

HISTORY

On February 23, 1905, lawyer Paul Harris met with three friends in an office in Chicago's Unity Building. Inspired by the fellowship and tolerance of his boyhood home in Wallingford, Vermont, Harris proposed organizing a men's club to meet periodically for the purpose of camaraderie and making business contacts. The new endeavor was organized as the Rotary Club of Chicago (the name arose from the club's custom of rotating its meeting place) and had 30 members by the end of the year.

As additional clubs followed, the organization assumed its role as a civic and service organization (the installation of public comfort stations in Chicago's City Hall was one of its first projects). At the first convention of the National Association of Rotary Clubs in 1910, Harris was elected president. International clubs soon followed, and by 1921 there were Rotary clubs on each continent.

In 1932, while struggling to revive a company with financial difficulties, Rotarian Herbert Taylor devised a statement of business ethics that later became the Rotarian mantra. Taylor's "4-Way Test" consisted of the following questions: "Is it the truth? Is it fair to all concerned? Will it

build goodwill and better friendships? Will it be beneficial to all concerned?"

During WWI Rotary clubs promoted war relief and peace fund efforts. Following WWII the clubs assisted in efforts to aid refugees and prisoners of war. The extent of Rotarian involvement in international issues became clear when 49 members assisted in drafting the United Nations Charter in 1945.

The first significant contributions to The Rotary Foundation followed Harris' death in 1947. These funds formed the bedrock for the foundation's programs, and in 1965 the foundation created its Matching Grants and Group Study Exchange programs. Rotary International also welcomed younger members in the 1960s by creating its Interact and Rotaract clubs in 1962 and 1968, respectively.

The largest meeting of Rotarians occurred in 1978 when almost 40,000 members attended the organization's Tokyo convention. But controversy was fast approaching the male-only organization. In 1978 a California Rotary club defied the male-only requirement and admitted two women. Claiming that the club had violated the organization's constitution, Rotary International revoked the club's charter. A lengthy court battle ensued, and a series of appeals landed the issue on the docket of the US Supreme Court. In 1987 the court ruled that the all-male requirement was discriminatory. Two years later Rotary International officially did away with its all-male status.

In the 1990s membership in Rotary clubs grew, but at a slower pace than in the organization's past. Mary Wolfenberger was appointed the organization's first female CFO in 1993 (she resigned in 1997). In 1998 Rotary International joined with the United Nations to launch a series of humanitarian service projects in developing areas. In 1999 the organization spearheaded events to help flood victims in North Carolina and refugees in the Balkans. In 2000 the group created a program specializing in peace and conflict resolution. Rotary International established its first Internet-based Rotary club in early 2002.

Chairman of the Rotary Foundation: Gen W. Kinross
President: Bhichai Rattakul
President-Elect: Jonathon Majiyagbe
VP: James R. Shamblin
General Secretary: Edwin H. Futa
Treasurer: Dong-Kurn Lee
Director Human Resources: Carolyn Engblom
Executive Committee Chairman and CFO:
  Gerald A. Meigs
Controller: Mark A. Vieth
Communications Services General Manager:
  Kathy Kessenich
Membership Services General Manager: Theresa Nissen
Rotary Foundation General Manager: Duane Sterling
Corporate Services Manager: Andrew McDonald
Public Relations Manager: Susan Ross

HQ: 1 Rotary Center, 1560 Sherman Ave.,
  Evanston, IL 60201
Phone: 847-866-3000   **Fax:** 847-328-8281
Web: www.rotary.org

Rotary International has clubs in some 160 countries.

Selected Issues Addressed
AIDS
Concern for the aging
Drug-abuse prevention
Environment
Hunger
Literacy
Polio
Service to women
Urban violence prevention
Youth

Selected Programs
Educational programs
  Ambassadorial Scholarships
  Grants for University Teachers
  Group Study Exchange (GSE)
  Rotary World Peace Scholarships
Humanitarian grants
  Discovery Grants
  Grants for Rotary Volunteers
  Matching Grants
  New Opportunities Grants
  Peace Program Grants
PolioPlus Program
  Polio Eradication Advocacy
  Polio Eradication Private Sector Campaign
  PolioPlus Partners

Not-for-profit FYE: June 30	Annual Growth	6/93	6/94	6/95	6/96	6/97	6/98	6/99	6/00	6/01	6/02
Sales ($ mil.)	0.8%	52	59	60	62	72	73	61	61	62	56
Employees	(2.3%)	617	450	350	400	400	400	450	450	500	500

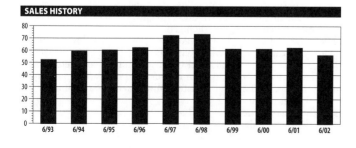

ROUNDY'S, INC.

Roundy's rounds up name-brand and private-label goods and distributes them to about 800 warehouse and grocery stores in 12 states, mostly in the Midwest and South. Founded in 1872, the company is a wholesale cooperative with 55 members that operate about 100 stores in Wisconsin and Illinois. Roundy's also services nearly 700 independent stores. Roundy's offers its members and customer stores support services, including accounting and inventory control, advertising, and store financing.

The supermarket operations of Roundy's 55 member companies in Wisconsin and Illinois account for about 20% of the cooperative's sales. Nearly 40% of its sales come from its distribution business to some 700 independent grocery stores across 14 states.

To boost its sales and profits, Roundy's has been acquiring independent stores, most recently four Pick 'n Save supermarkets in Milwaukee. With the addition of the four Milwaukee stores, Roundy's owns 44 Pick 'n Save stores and 21 Copps Food Centers, making it Wisconsin's leading supermarket chain.

The company has given up on its online shopping service at 10 Pick 'n Save stores. The service, which allowed customers to order groceries online and pick them up at the stores, was launched in 2001.

Private investment firm Willis Stein & Partners bought Roundy's in June 2002.

HISTORY

Migration from the eastern US and overseas was boosting Milwaukee's ranks when William Smith, Judson Roundy, and Sidney Hauxhurst formed grocery wholesaler Smith, Roundy & Co. in 1872. Smith left the firm in 1878 for his first of two terms as Wisconsin's governor, and William Peckham joined the company, which was then renamed Roundy, Peckham & Co. Two years later Charles Dexter joined the company, by then operating in five midwestern states and running a manufacturing business.

The wholesaler became Roundy, Peckham & Dexter Co. in 1902, following the death of Hauxhurst (Roundy died in 1907). The company introduced its first private-label product — salt — in 1922. In 1929 Dexter (then 84) came up with a plan to publicize the Roundy's name by handing out cookbooks that called for the company's goods.

Roy Johnson, who joined the company in 1912, was named president near the end of the Depression. In the 1940s the wholesaler acquired smaller companies in the region. The firm became Roundy's in 1952 when Roundy,

Peckham & Dexter was bought by a group comprising hundreds of Wisconsin grocery retailers. Johnson remained head of the new company until his death in 1962. James Aldrich led the company for the next 11 years.

In 1970 Roundy's started Insurance Planners, which offered insurance to retailers. Vincent Little became president of the company in 1973. Two years later Roundy's began a real estate subsidiary (Ronco Realty) and opened its first Pick 'n Save Warehouse Foods store.

The company expanded in the mid-1980s through the purchase of distributors. But expansion hurt profits, and dividends were suspended in 1984 and 1985. In the late 1980s several Pick 'n Save stores opened throughout Wisconsin and other midwestern states. Owners grew suspicious of Little's accounting practices and the special treatment given a Roundy's-owned store run by his son, and in 1986 they forced him out of his president and CEO positions. John Dickson replaced him.

By 1994 Pick 'n Save had vastly upgraded its image — one store sold $1,000 cognac and featured an $18,000 cappuccino machine. However, sales dropped off for the third straight year. COO Gerald Lestina was named CEO in 1995, replacing Dickson, who continued as chairman. Dickson died later that year.

Roundy's did not pay its members a dividend in 1995 as it made an effort to offset losses in Michigan and Ohio. To ease those losses, in 1997 the company closed 12 poorly performing stores in those states. A year later a fire destroyed its Evansville, Indiana, warehouse; the company rebuilt the facility in 1999. Also in 1999 Roundy's purchased three supermarkets in Indiana from Kroger and The John C. Groub Company.

The Mega Marts and Ultra Mart chains, which together operate 24 Pick 'n Save stores, primarily in Wisconsin, were acquired by Roundy's in 2000. In 2001 Roundy's launched an online grocery shopping service, called Pick 'n Save Online Shopping, in two test stores in Wisconsin (with plans for more locations). Also in 2001 the company purchased its competitor, The Copps Corporation, acquiring 21 stores in north and central Wisconsin and a wholesale business that distributes to retailers in Wisconsin and northern Michigan.

Chicago-based private equity investment firm Willis Stein & Partners bought Roundy's in June 2002. In October Roundy's completed the acquisition of four Gold's Pick 'n Save stores in northeastern Milwaukee for $26 million.

OFFICERS

President and CEO: Robert Mariano
CFO: Darren Karst
VP of Management Information Systems:
Larry C. Goddard, age 47
VP of Sales and Development: Michael J. Schmitt,
age 53, $275,250 pay
VP of Administration: David C. Busch, age 53
VP of Advertising: Londell J. Behm, age 51
VP of Corporate Retail: Gary L. Fryda, age 49,
$332,500 pay
VP of Distribution: John E. Paterson, age 54
VP of Human Resources: Debra A. Lawson, age 45
VP of Planning and Information Services:
Charles H. Kosmaler Jr., age 59
VP, Secretary, and Treasurer: Edward G. Kitz, age 48
VP of Wholesale: Ralph D. Beketic, age 55, $309,656 pay
Director of Natural and Organic Foods:
Robert E. Carlson
Auditors: Deloitte & Touche LLP

LOCATIONS

HQ: 23000 Roundy Dr., Pewaukee, WI 53072
Phone: 262-953-7999   **Fax:** 262-953-6580
Web: www.roundys.com

Roundy's distributes products to nearly 800 stores (including about 60 company-owned stores) in Arkansas, Illinois, Indiana, Kentucky, Michigan, Missouri, New Jersey, New York, Ohio, Oklahoma, Pennsylvania, Tennessee, West Virginia, and Wisconsin.

PRODUCTS/OPERATIONS

2001 Sales

	% of total
Independent retailers	38
Company-owned stores	40
Co-op members	22
Total	**100**

Product Lines
Bakery goods
Dairy products
Dry groceries
Fresh produce
Frozen foods
General merchandise
Meats

Selected Private and Controlled Labels
Buyers' Choice
Old Time
Roundy's
Shurfine

Selected Services
Centralized bakery purchasing
Financing
Group advertising
Insurance
Inventory control
Merchandising
Ordering assistance
Point-of-sale support
Pricing services
Purchasing reports
Real estate services
Retail accounting
Retail training
Store development
Store engineering

COMPETITORS

A&P
Albertson's
ALDI
AWG
Central Grocers
 Cooperative
Certified Grocers Midwest
Costco Wholesale
Dominick's
Eagle Food
Fleming Companies
GSC Enterprises
Hy-Vee
IGA
Kmart
Kroger
Meijer
Nash Finch
S. Abraham & Sons
Spartan Stores
SUPERVALU
Topco Associates
Wal-Mart

HISTORICAL FINANCIALS & EMPLOYEES

Private FYE: December 31	Annual Growth	12/92	12/93	12/94	12/95	12/96	12/97	12/98	12/99	12/00	12/01
Sales ($ mil.)	3.7%	2,491	2,480	2,462	2,488	2,579	2,611	2,579	2,717	2,984	3,449
Net income ($ mil.)	15.0%	7	8	7	9	10	11	12	18	21	26
Income as % of sales	—	0.3%	0.3%	0.3%	0.4%	0.4%	0.4%	0.5%	0.6%	0.7%	0.7%
Employees	11.4%	5,088	4,884	4,775	4,839	5,481	5,071	5,193	5,617	9,071	13,451

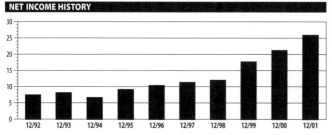

NET INCOME HISTORY

2001 FISCAL YEAR-END
Debt ratio: 54.1%
Return on equity: 16.1%
Cash ($ mil.): 46
Current ratio: 1.07
Long-term debt ($ mil.): 201

SALVATION ARMY USA

The largest civil army in the land, the Salvation Army is more than 3 million strong. Its programs assist alcoholics, drug addicts, the homeless, the handicapped, the elderly, prison inmates, people in crisis, and the unemployed through a range of services. These include day-care centers, programs for people with disabilities, substance abuse programs, and educational facilities for at-risk students. It also provides disaster relief in the US and abroad. The Salvation Army USA is a national unit of the Salvation Army, an international body based in London, which oversees Army activities in more than 100 countries.

Active as a church and a charity, the organization serves nearly 37 million people a year. The Salvation Army usually tops the list of US not-for-profits in terms of donations received: In 2000 contributions reached about $523 million.

Along with promoting charity, the Salvation Army seeks to save souls. As an evangelical church, it preaches the message of salvation through Jesus Christ. Before joining the organization and becoming a soldier (a lay member), one must sign an agreement known as the "Articles of War," a commitment to the avoidance of gambling, debt, and profanity and to abstention from alcohol, tobacco, and other recreational drugs. The US organization includes some 125,000 soldiers, more than 3 million volunteers, and nearly 5,400 officers, who are also ordained ministers.

Officers are expected to wear their uniforms at all times and to work full-time for the Salvation Army. They receive no salary; instead, they are provided with room and board and given a limited stipend.

The Salvation Army USA is only one of scores of national Salvation Army organizations around the world, which report to the group's global leader, General John Gowans, at its international headquarters in the UK.

HISTORY

William Booth (1829-1912) started preaching the gospel as a Wesleyan Methodist in the UK, but the church expelled him because he insisted on preaching outside and to everyone, including the poor. In 1865 he moved to the slums of London's East End and attracted large crowds with his volatile sermons. Opposition to his message of universal salvation for drunks, thieves, prostitutes, and gamblers often caused riots. In fact, the first women in the organization wore bonnets designed with a dual purpose in mind — warmth and protection from flying objects.

At a meeting in 1878, a sign was used referring to the "Salvation Army." Booth adopted the reference as both the name and the style of his organization. Members became soldiers, evangelists were officers, and Booth was referred to as "General." Prayers became knee drills, and contributions were called cartridges.

The Salvation Army marched across the Atlantic to the US in 1880, led by seven women and one man. Women have always played an active role in the Salvation Army, both as officers and soldiers. Booth's wife, Catherine Mumford, was a leading suffragette, and Booth advocated equal rights for women. In 1891 a crab pot was placed on a San Francisco street to collect donations, with a sign reading "Keep the Pot Boiling." The idea led to the Salvation Army's annual Christmas kettle program.

During WWI the organization became famous for the doughnuts that it served the doughboys fighting on the front lines. After some internal dissension, the Salvation Army took its only public political stance in 1928 with the endorsement of Herbert Hoover for his support of Prohibition during his presidential campaign. The charity opened its first home for alcoholics in 1939, in Detroit.

After WWII the Salvation Army began using such radio and TV programs as *Heartbeat Theater* and *Army of Stars* to spread its message.

Over the years the Salvation Army has provided assistance to victims of hurricanes, floods, and earthquakes. Volunteers rendered almost 70,000 service hours in the aftermath of the Oklahoma City bombing in 1995, counseling more than 1,600 victims and family members, helping with funeral arrangements, and providing food, clothing, and travel assistance. Indicative of the organization's readiness and extensive reach, its volunteers were helping victims in Guam within minutes of the 1997 Korean Air plane crash. The Salvation Army was quickly on the scene after a Jonesboro, Arkansas, shooting incident in 1998 when four students and one teacher were killed by fellow students. Late that year the organization received the largest donation in its history — $80 million from Joan Kroc, wife of McDonald's co-founder Ray Kroc.

In 2000 General Paul Rader retired, and with incoming General John Gowans the organization initiated its first reform in more than 100 years by allowing officers to marry outside the ranks. Following the September 11 attacks in 2001, the Salvation Army provided assistance to rescue workers and families affected by the tragedy through its Disaster Relief Fund.

General (International Director): John Gowans
Chairman National Advisory Board: Donald V. Fites
Commissioner (National Commander): John Busby
Colonel (National Chief Secretary): Thomas C. Lewis
Colonel (National Secretary for Personnel):
Myrtle V. Ryder
**Lieutenant Colonel (National Treasurer and Secretary
Business Administration):** Don McDougald
Commissioner (Southern Territorial Commander):
Raymond S. Cooper
Commissioner (Western Territorial Commander):
David Edwards
Commissioner (Central Territorial Commander):
Lawrence Moretz
Commissioner (Eastern Territorial Commander):
Joseph J. Noland
**Commissioner (National President Women's
Organizations):** Elsie Busby
Auditors: PricewaterhouseCoopers LLP

LOCATIONS

HQ: 615 Slaters Ln., Alexandria, VA 22313
Phone: 703-684-5500 **Fax:** 703-684-3478
Web: www.salvationarmyusa.org

Salvation Army USA operates service centers, local
churches, and social service programs and facilities
throughout the US and provides disaster relief
worldwide.

PRODUCTS/OPERATIONS

Selected Services
Alcohol and drug treatment centers
Clinics and hospitals
Convalescent homes
Counseling
Crisis counseling
Food distribution centers
Handicapped housing
Homeless shelters
Institutes for the blind
Leprosy clinics
Military canteens and hostels
Nurseries and day care centers
Occupational centers
Prison ministry
Probation housing
Refugee centers
Science and trade schools
Student housing
Welfare aid

HISTORICAL FINANCIALS & EMPLOYEES

Not-for-profit FYE: September 30	Annual Growth	9/92	9/93	9/94	9/95	9/96	9/97	9/98	9/99	9/00	9/01
Sales ($ mil.)	6.7%	1,287	1,398	1,355	1,421	2,070	2,525	2,078	1,707	1,803	2,313
Employees	1.8%	—	—	39,591	38,999	44,626	40,770	39,883	43,318	45,096	45,000

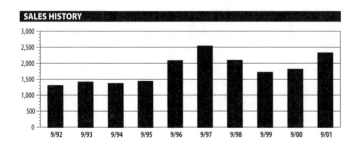

SALES HISTORY

S.C. JOHNSON & SON, INC.

S.C. Johnson & Son helped consumers move from the flyswatter to the spray can. The company is one of the world's largest makers of consumer chemical products. These include Drano-brand drain cleaner, Glade air freshener, Johnson floor wax, OFF! insect repellent, Pledge furniture polish, Raid insecticide, Shout stain remover, Windex window cleaner, and Ziploc plastic bags. The founder's great-grandson and one of the richest men in the US, chairman emeritus Samuel Johnson, and his immediate family own about 60% of S.C. Johnson; descendants of the founder's daughter own about 40%.

Many of S.C. Johnson's products have been and remain top sellers in their market categories. The company has operations in nearly 70 countries and its products are available in more than 100.

The company's commercial products division (Johnson Wax Professional and Johnson Polymer) has been spun off as a private company owned by the Johnson family. The company has also sold most of its personal care line. In 2002 the company agreed to buy the household insecticides unit of German drug giant Bayer AG for $734 million.

HISTORY

Samuel C. Johnson, a carpenter whose customers were as interested in his floor wax as in his parquet floors, founded S.C. Johnson in Racine, Wisconsin, in 1886. Forsaking carpentry, Johnson began to manufacture floor care products. The company, named S.C. Johnson & Son in 1906, began establishing subsidiaries worldwide in 1914. By the time Johnson's son and successor, Herbert Johnson, died in 1928, annual sales were $5 million. Herbert Jr. and his sister, Henrietta Lewis, received 60% and 40% of the firm, respectively. The original section of S.C. Johnson's headquarters, designed by Frank Lloyd Wright and called "the greatest piece of 20th-century architecture" in the US, was finished in 1939.

In 1954, with $45 million in annual sales, Herbert Jr.'s son Samuel Curtis Johnson joined the company as new products director. Two years later it introduced Raid, the first water-based insecticide, and soon thereafter, OFF! insect repellent. Each became a market leader. The company unsuccessfully attempted to diversify into paint, chemicals, and lawn care during the 1950s and 1960s. The home care products segment prospered, however, with the introduction of Pledge aerosol furniture polish and Glade aerosol air freshener.

After Herbert Jr. suffered a stroke in 1965, Samuel became president. In 1975 the firm banned the use of the chlorofluorocarbons (CFCs) in its products, three years before the US government banned CFCs. Samuel started a recreational products division that was bought by the Johnson family in 1986. That company went public in 1987 as Johnson Worldwide Associates, with the family retaining control.

The company launched Edge shaving gel and Agree hair products in the 1970s but had few products as successful in the 1980s. It moved into real estate with Johnson Wax Development (JWD) in the 1970s, but sold JWD's assets in the late 1980s.

S. Curtis Johnson, Samuel's son, joined the company in 1983. In 1986 S.C. Johnson bought Bugs Burger Bug Killers, moving into commercial pest control; in 1990 it entered into an agreement with Mycogen to develop biological pesticides for household use.

In 1993 it bought Drackett, bringing Drano and Windex to its product roster along with increased competition from heavyweights such as Procter & Gamble and Clorox. That year S.C. Johnson sold the Agree and Halsa lines to DEP. In 1996 it launched a line of water-soluble pouches for cleaning products that allow work to be done without touching hazardous chemicals. President William Perez became CEO the next year.

S.C. Johnson bought Dow Chemical's DowBrands unit, maker of bathroom cleaner (Dow), plastic bags (Ziploc), and plastic wrap (Saran Wrap), for $1.2 billion in 1998. It then sold off other Dow brands (cleaners Spray 'N Wash, Glass Plus, Yes, and Vivid) to the UK's Reckitt & Colman to settle antitrust issues.

A year later S.C. Johnson sold its skin care line, including Aveeno, to health care products maker Johnson & Johnson, and spun off its commercial products unit as a private firm owned by the Johnson family. Boosting its home cleaning line, in 1999 it introduced two new products: AllerCare (for dust mite control) and Pledge Grab-It (electrostatically charged cleaning sheets).

In 2000 S.C. Johnson pulled its AllerCare carpet powder and allergen spray from store shelves after some consumers had negative reactions to the fragrance additive in the products. That year H. Fisk Johnson succeeded his father (who became chairman emeritus) as chairman.

In 2001 the company was fined $950,000 for selling banned Raid Max Roach Bait traps in New York after agreeing to pull them from store shelves. Also that year S.C. Johnson's Japanese subsidiary agreed to buy that country's leading drain cleaner brand, Pipe Unish, from Unicharm.

OFFICERS

Chairman Emeritus: Samuel C. Johnson, age 75
Chairman: H. Fisk Johnson, age 44
President, CEO, and Director: William D. Perez, age 54
President, Asia/Pacific: Joseph T. Mallof, age 51
President, North America: David L. May
President, Europe, Africa, and Near East:
Steven P. Stanbrook
EVP, Americas: Pedro Cieza
SVP, General Counsel, and Secretary: David Hecker
SVP, Worldwide Corporate Affairs: Jane M. Hutterly
SVP, Worldwide Human Resources: Gayle P. Kosterman
SVP, Worldwide Manufacturing and Procurement:
Nico J. Meiland
SVP, Worldwide Research, Development & Engineering:
Darcy D. Massey
SVP and CFO: W. Lee McCollum, age 53
VP, Air Care Business and Canadian Operations:
Gregory J. Barron
VP, Corporate Tax Counsel: Robert S. Randleman
VP, Enterprise Resource Planning: David C. Henry
VP, Finance - North America: Mark H. Eckhardt
VP, Finance and Information Systems - EurAFNE:
Francis Foin
VP, Home Cleaning Business: John Rote
VP, Human Resources, Asia/Pacific: Wesley A. Coleman
VP, Insect Control and Shave Business:
William C. Thompson
VP, Marketing Services - Worldwide: Ralph D. Perry
VP, North American Sales: Darwin Lewis
**VP, Research, Development and Engineering - Global Air
Care:** Richard S. Hutchings
VP and Area Director - Asia: Frank F. Guerra
VP, Human Resources Asia/Pacific: Jeffrey M. Waller
VP and CIO: Daniel E. Horton
VP and Corporate Treasurer: William H. Van Lopik
Director, Corporate Public Affairs: Cynthia Georgeson
Director of Diversity: Maria Campbell

LOCATIONS

HQ: 1525 Howe St., Racine, WI 53403
Phone: 262-260-2000   **Fax:** 262-260-6004
Web: www.scjohnson.com

S.C. Johnson & Son has operations in nearly 70
countries worldwide.

Selected Countries with Manufacturing Facilities

Argentina	India	South Africa
Brazil	Indonesia	South Korea
Canada	Japan	Spain
Chile	Kenya	Taiwan
China	Mexico	UK
Egypt	The Netherlands	Ukraine
France	Nigeria	US
Germany	The Philippines	Venezuela
Ghana	Russia	Vietnam
Greece	Saudi Arabia	

PRODUCTS/OPERATIONS

Selected Products and Brands

Air Care
Air freshener (Glade, Glade Duet)
Pillow and mattress covers (AllerCare)

Home Cleaning
Bathroom/drain (Drano, Scrubbing Bubbles, Vanish,
Dow)
Cleaners (Fantastik, Windex, Windex Multi-Surface
Cleaner with Vinegar)
Floor care (Pledge, Pledge Grab-It, Johnson)
Furniture care (Pledge, Pledge Wipes, Pledge Grab-it
Dry Dusting Mitts)
Laundry/carpet care (Shout)

Home Storage
Plastic bags (Ziploc)
Plastic wrap (Handi-Wrap, Saran Wrap)

Insect Control
Insecticides (Raid, Raid Max)
Repellents (Deep Woods OFF!, OFF!, OFF! Mosquito
Lamp, OFF! Skintastic)

COMPETITORS

3M	Gillette
Alticor	IWP International
Blyth, Inc.	Procter & Gamble
Church & Dwight	Reckitt Benckiser
Clorox	Shaklee
Colgate-Palmolive	Unilever
Dial	United Industries
DuPont	Yankee Candle

HISTORICAL FINANCIALS & EMPLOYEES

Private FYE: June 30	Annual Growth	6/93	6/94	6/95	6/96	6/97	6/98	6/99	6/00	6/01	6/02
Estimated sales ($ mil.)	3.9%	3,550	3,800	4,000	4,000	4,300	5,000	4,200	4,200	4,500	5,000
Employees	(3.5%)	13,100	13,100	13,400	12,100	12,500	13,200	9,500	9,500	9,500	9,500

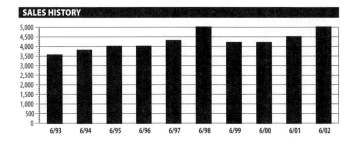

SALES HISTORY

SCHNEIDER NATIONAL, INC.

If you think that's the Great Pumpkin behind you, look again. With its signature bright-orange fleet of 14,000 trucks and more than 40,000 trailers, Schneider National is one of the top truckload carriers in the US. The company's Schneider National Carriers unit provides truckload service throughout North America, including one-way van, expedited, dedicated, and intermodal offerings, as well as truck brokerage.

The Schneider Dedicated Operations unit supplies customers with their own personal Schneider fleets, including trucks, trailers, and drivers. Other divisions include Schneider Bulk (liquid chemical transport), Schneider Specialized (trailers and hauling services for unique shipments), and Schneider TruckRail (containers and trailers designed for use on rail or over the road). The company also acts as a middleman through Schneider Brokerage, which finds carriers for shippers, and Schneider Finance, which sells and leases truck equipment.

Schneider National also rides the information superhighway. Its Logistics subsidiary cuts shipping costs of large US and European customers by finding efficient ways to use their supply chains, shipping routes, and carriers. The unit, which works with carriers in all modes of transportation, offers a real-time cargo tracking system with customer access over the Internet.

Known for being an early adopter of new transportation technology, Schneider National was one of the first carriers to link all its trucks by two-way satellite. More recently, the company has invested in an in-cab e-mail system to help drivers stay in touch with their families.

HISTORY

A. J. "Al" Schneider bought a truck in 1935 with money earned from selling the family car. He drove the truck for three years, got another, and then leased them both to another firm. Becoming general manager of Bins Transfer & Storage in 1938, Schneider bought the company that year and changed the name to Schneider Transport & Storage. In 1944 Schneider stopped storing household goods and continued as an intrastate carrier in Wisconsin through the 1950s, transporting food and household goods. The Interstate Commerce Commission granted its first interstate license to Schneider in 1958. Al's son Donald joined the company as general manager in 1961, and in 1962 the company dropped "Storage" from its name to become Schneider Transport. The 1960s also saw the first of many acquisitions. Donald became CEO in 1973, overseeing more acquisitions and the creation of Schneider National as a holding company

for the organization. Donald also saw to the installation of computerized control systems, the first of many technical innovations Schneider would use in its trucks.

With the Motor Carrier Act's passage in 1980, restrictions eased and interstate shipping opened up. Schneider (and its competitors) saw the sky as the limit and founded Schneider Communications, a long-distance provider, in 1982. Eager to escape the Teamsters' thrall but choosing not to go head-to-head with the powerful union, Schneider formed Schneider National Carriers as a nonunion company out of three 1985 acquisitions, which signed on new recruits, while Schneider Transport remained unionized. The company focused on guaranteeing on-time delivery in the deregulated market: In 1988 Schneider became the first trucking company to install a satellite-tracking system in its trucks, setting the industry standard.

Schneider further expanded its services in the 1990s, starting with Schneider Specialized Services for carrying difficult items. It moved into Canada and Mexico in 1991. In 1993 the company formed Schneider Logistics to help companies streamline their shipping operations. It sold Schneider Communications to Frontier Communications in 1995. The company moved into Europe in 1997.

It continued buying other US trucking firms, including Landstar Poole and Builder's Transport (both in 1998), mainly to acquire their drivers for its expanding fleet. In 1999 Schneider acquired the glass-transportation business of A. J. Metler & Rigging.

In 2000 Schneider acquired the freight payment services of Tranzact Systems and further boosted its e-commerce offerings through alliances with ContractorHub.com and Paperloop.com. The company also made plans to spin off Schneider Logistics and sell part of it to the public, but unfavorable market conditions put the IPO on hold. Schneider added expedited services to its portfolio in 2001 to provide time-definite delivery in Canada, Mexico, and the US.

OFFICERS

Chairman: Donald J. Schneider, age 66
President and CEO: Christopher B. Lofgren, age 43
CFO: Tom Gannon
CIO: Steve Matheys
VP Human Resources: Tim Fliss

LOCATIONS

HQ: 3101 S. Packerland Dr., Green Bay, WI 54306
Phone: 920-592-2000   **Fax:** 920-592-3063
Web: www.schneider.com

Schneider National has operations throughout Canada, parts of Mexico, and the US. Its Schneider Logistics subsidiary has operations throughout North America and Europe. The company's major operating centers in North America are located in Akron, Ohio; Charlotte, North Carolina; Chicago; Dallas; Des Moines, Iowa; Detroit; Evergreen, Alabama; Green Bay, Wisconsin; Harrisburg, Pennsylvania; Indianapolis; Los Angeles; Memphis; and Portland, Oregon.

PRODUCTS/OPERATIONS

Selected Operating Units
Schneider Finance (commercial financing and leasing services)
Schneider Logistics, Inc. (supply chain management services)
Schneider National Bulk Carriers (liquid chemical transport services)
Schneider National Carriers (full-truckload service, including intermodal, brokerage, expedited services, dedicated transport, and one-way van transport)
Schneider Specialized Carriers (open equipment transportation, specializing in industrial glass transport)

COMPETITORS

Burlington Northern Santa Fe
Cannon Express
Celadon
CHR
CSX
J. B. Hunt
Landstar System
Norfolk Southern
Roadway
Ryder
Swift Transportation
Union Pacific
Werner

HISTORICAL FINANCIALS & EMPLOYEES

Private FYE: December 31	Annual Growth	12/92	12/93	12/94	12/95	12/96	12/97	12/98	12/99	12/00	12/01
Sales ($ mil.)	9.4%	1,066	1,175	1,325	1,700	2,156	2,510	2,711	3,000	3,089	2,388
Employees	5.5%	12,000	13,950	15,300	15,500	17,550	16,500	17,000	19,000	18,775	19,349

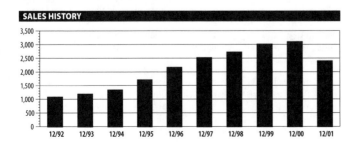

SALES HISTORY

THE SCHWAN FOOD COMPANY

Frozen pizza is the flashy part of The Schwan Food Company (formerly Schwan's Sales Enterprises). With pizza brands such as Tony's, Red Baron, and Freschetta, the company is the #2 frozen pizza maker in the US, behind Kraft Foods. Schwan is also a top supplier to the institutional frozen pizza market and has operations in Europe. But pizza isn't the only slice in the company's revenue — its core business is a fleet of home-delivery trucks. Schwan delivers casseroles, ice cream, and frozen foods to homes in the continental US. The family of late founder Marvin Schwan owns the company.

With a fleet of unintentionally retro-hip freezer trucks, Schwan is definitely cool. The Marshall, Minnesota-based company maintains a home delivery system that brings more than 300 frozen food products directly to customers in 48 mainland states. Orders can include bagels, casseroles, or pancakes, but it's Schwan's ice cream that has a devoted following.

In addition to its US pizza market, Schwan sells Freschetta and Chicago Town pizzas in Western Europe, and supplies schools and other institutional cafeterias with frozen pizza and sandwiches. Another Schwan unit produces food manufacturing equipment, and systems to convert vehicles to using liquid propane.

The family of late founder Marvin Schwan (who himself gave no interviews after 1982) is notoriously secretive.

HISTORY

Paul Schwan bought out his partner in their dairy in 1948 and began manufacturing ice cream using his own recipes. His son, Marvin Schwan, made deliveries for the dairy for a few years. After attending a two-year college, Marvin came back in 1950 to work at the dairy full-time. Two years later he began using his delivery experience to take advantage of the increase in homes with freezers. He bought an old truck for $100 and began a rural route selling ice cream to farmers. He quickly developed a loyal customer base and expanded to two routes the following year.

In the 1960s the company diversified with two acquisitions: a prepared sandwich company and a condensed fruit juice company. A new holding company, Schwan's Sales Enterprises, was established in 1964. Schwan's began delivering pizza the next year. Paul died in 1969.

Deciding that frozen pizza was not a fad, Marvin bought Kansas-based Tony's Pizza in 1970 and quickly rose to the top of the new industry. In the late 1970s Schwan's entered the commercial leasing business, and it later added more

leasing companies under the Lyon Financial Services umbrella (later sold in 2000).

The company entered the institutional pizza market in the mid-1980s and bought out competitors Sabatasso Foods and Better Baked Pizza. Schools liked Schwan's use of their government surplus cheese to make pizzas, which the company then sold to the schools at a discount.

In 1992 the company bought two Minnesota-based food companies: Panzerotti, a stuffed pastry business, and Monthly Market, a specialty retailer that sells groceries to fund-raising groups. It also began selling its pizzas in the UK. The next year Schwan's bought Chicago Brothers Frozen Pizza, a San Diego-based company specializing in deep-dish pizza.

Marvin died of a heart attack in 1993 at age 64, with his worth estimated at more than $1 billion. The previous year he had willed two-thirds of the company's stock to a charitable Lutheran trust, which was to be bought out by Schwan's after his death. In 1994 his brother, Alfred, and Marvin's friend Lawrence Burgdorf made arrangements to have the company repurchase the foundation's shares for a total of $1.8 billion. But Marvin's four children filed a lawsuit in 1995 against their uncle and Burgdorf over the action. They claimed the men did not have the financial health of the company at heart and were divided in their loyalty. The children, on the other hand, were called money-hungry and callous to their father's last wishes. (The case was settled in 1997 but no information was released.)

In 1994 more than 200,000 people in 28 states contracted salmonella food poisoning after eating E. coli-tainted Schwan's ice cream. The company's insurance company eventually paid out nearly $1 million to about 6,000 affected customers in exchange for their signed releases promising they would not sue Schwan's.

Lenny Pippin became the company's fourth CEO in 1999, replacing Alfred, who remained on as chairman. Schwan's exited the Canadian market at the end of 1999 due to perennial losses. In 2000 Schwan's introduced irradiated frozen ground beef patties and struck an agreement with another company to electronically pasteurize some of its products, and sold the assets and trademarks of its Chicago Brothers food operations.

In mid-2001 Schwan's expanded its offerings by acquiring frozen dessert maker Edwards Fine Foods from private equity firm Ripplewood Holdings. In early 2002 the company sold off its Orion Food Systems subsidiary to Kohlberg Investors. The company began a reorganization of its business units and changed its name from Schwan's Sales Enterprises to The Schwan Food Company at the beginning of 2003.

OFFICERS

Chairman: Alfred Schwan
President and CEO: M. Lenny Pippin
CFO, VP Finance: Tracy Burr
VP Administration, General Counsel: Dave Paskach
VP; General Manager, Schwan's Food Service:
John Drown
VP; General Manager, Schwan's Home Service:
Michael Ziebell
VP, Human Resources: Sue Beary
VP, Public Relations: Howard Miller
President and COO, Global Consumer Brands:
John Beadle
Director, Customer Relations: Jerry Matzner

LOCATIONS

HQ: 115 W. College Dr., Marshall, MN 56258
Phone: 507-532-3274   **Fax:** 507-537-8226
Web: www.schwansinc.com

The Schwan Food Company has manufacturing facilities
in the US and in Europe; its products are sold in the 48
contiguous states and Western Europe.

PRODUCTS/OPERATIONS

Selected Consumer Brands
Chicago Town (frozen pizza, UK)
Freschetta
Larry's (frozen potato side dishes)
Pagoda Café (frozen Oriental foods)
Red Baron
Tony's
Edwards Fine Foods (desserts)

COMPETITORS

Aurora Foods
Ben & Jerry's
Blue Bell
Celentano Brothers
Colorado Prime
ConAgra
Domino's Pizza
Dreyer's
Kraft Foods North America
Little Caesar
Luigino's
Nation Pizza Products
Nestlé
Omaha Steaks
Papa John's
SYSCO
Yum!

HISTORICAL FINANCIALS & EMPLOYEES

Private FYE: December 31	Annual Growth	12/92	12/93	12/94	12/95	12/96	12/97	12/98	12/99	12/00	12/01
Estimated sales ($ mil.)	6.0%	1,780	2,100	2,200	2,350	2,500	2,900	2,875	3,350	3,100	3,000
Employees	17.6%	—	6,000	6,000	6,000	6,000	6,000	6,000	6,000	—	22,000

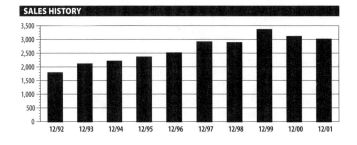

SALES HISTORY

SCIENCE APPLICATIONS

It definitely pays to have a rich Big Brother, or an Uncle Sam with deep pockets. Science Applications International Corporation (SAIC) is a leading provider of systems integration, engineering, and R&D services to the US government (which accounts for about 60% of sales). SAIC also provides professional services to the commercial sector, including consulting, software implementation, and network engineering. The company's Telcordia Technologies subsidiary (formerly the research arm of the Baby Bells) supplies a variety of software and services to the telecommunications sector. SAIC is the nation's largest employee-owned research and engineering company.

Following the terrorist attacks of September 11, 2001, the company has seen increased demand for homeland security-related projects, prompting it to install an emergency telecommunications system in New York, develop a training program for US sky marshals, and build a communications network for the US Central Command. SAIC also has its hands in undersea data collection and space systems engineering.

Founder, chairman, and CEO Robert Beyster — who has guided the company to record revenues for each of the last 32 years — asserts that employee ownership has been key to the company's success, and has shown little interest (or need) in pursuing an IPO; the company last received outside funding in 1970, when it received $200,000 from private investors.

HISTORY

Physicist Robert Beyster, who worked at Los Alamos National Laboratory in the 1950s, was hired by General Atomic in 1957 to establish and manage its traveling wave linear accelerator. When the company was sold to Gulf Oil in 1968, research priorities changed and Beyster left. He founded Science Applications Inc. (SAI) the following year and built his business from consulting contracts with Los Alamos and Brookhaven National Laboratories.

During the first year Beyster instituted an employee ownership plan that rewarded workers that brought onboard new business with stock in SAI. Beyster's idea was to share the success of SAI and to raise capital.

In 1970 the company established an office in Washington, DC, to court government contracts. Despite a recession, SAI continued to grow during the 1970s, and by 1979 sales topped $100 million. The following year SAI restructured, becoming a subsidiary of Science Applications International Corporation (SAIC), a new holding company.

During the 1980s defense buildup, an emphasis on high-tech weaponry and SAIC's high-level Pentagon connections (directors have included former defense secretaries William Perry and Melvin Laird and former CIA director John Deutch) brought in contracts for submarine warfare systems and technical development for the Strategic Defense Initiative ("Star Wars").

As defense spending slowed with the end of the Cold War, SAIC began casting a wider net. By 1991 computer systems integration and consulting accounted for 25% of sales, which surpassed the $1 billion mark.

SAIC made several purchases during the mid-1990s, including transportation communications firm Syntonic, Internet domain name registrar Network Solutions, Inc. (NSI), and government think tank Aerospace Corp. In 1997 SAIC acquired Bellcore (the research lab of the regional Bells, now Telcordia Technologies), and reduced its stake in NSI through a public offering. SAIC formed several alliances in 1998, including a joint venture with Rolls-Royce to service the aerospace, energy, and defense industries.

The next year SAIC expanded its information technology (IT) expertise with the acquisition of Boeing's Information Services unit. It also acquired the call center software operations of Elite Information Group. SAIC in 2000 realized a significant gain on its $5 million purchase of NSI when e-commerce software maker VeriSign bought the minority-owned (23%) subsidiary for $17 billion.

In 2001 SAIC signed a variety of large contracts, including an outsourcing agreement with BP to manage that company's North American application and hosting services, as well as a $3 billion deal to provide support (in conjunction with Bechtel Group) for the US Department of Energy's civilian radioactive waste management program.

OFFICERS

Chairman, President, and CEO: J. Robert Beyster, age 77
EVP and CFO: Thomas E. Darcy, age 51
EVP and Secretary: J. Dennis Heipt, age 59
EVP Commercial and International Business: Randy Walker
EVP Federal Business: Duane P. Andrews, age 57
EVP Strategic Initiatives: J. P. Walkush, age 49
EVP Systems Integration: John H. Warner Jr., age 61
EVP: N. E. Cox, age 52
EVP: D. H. Foley, age 57
EVP: John E. Glancy, age 55
EVP: S. D. Rockwood, age 58
EVP: William A. Roper Jr., age 56
EVP: R. A. Rosenberg, age 67
EVP: A. L. Slotkin, age 55

SVP: Bryan Bebb
SVP and Controller: P. N. Pavlics, age 41
SVP and General Counsel: D. E. Scott, age 45
SVP and Treasurer: Steven P. Fisher, age 41
SVP and Manager, Global Telecommunications Group:
Robert K. Young
SVP and Analyst: Lewis A. Dunn
SVP Business Development: Jim Russell
SVP Health Solutions Group: Michael A. Mark
SVP Human Resources: Bernard Theull
President and CEO, ANXeBusiness Corp.:
Alexander J. Preston
President and Managing Director, SAIC Venture
Capital: Kevin Werner
Director of Asia Technology Program: Wendy Frieman
Director of Business Development: Christopher A. Boyd
Director of Community Relations: Gerald E. Connolly
Auditors: Deloitte & Touche LLP

LOCATIONS

HQ: Science Applications International Corporation
10260 Campus Point Dr., San Diego, CA 92121
Phone: 858-826-6000 **Fax:** 858-826-6800
Web: www.saic.com

Science Applications International has offices in more
than 150 cities worldwide.

2002 Sales

	$ mil.	% of total
US	5,595	92
Venezuela	336	6
UK	155	2
Other countries	9	—
Total	**6,095**	**100**

PRODUCTS/OPERATIONS

2002 Sales by Customer

	% of total
Government	64
Commercial, telecom	23
Commercial, other	13
Total	**100**

Selected Services

Energy
Information systems
Plant monitoring systems
Project management
Quality assurance
Safety evaluations

Environmental
Monitoring
Regulatory compliance support and training
Remedial actions and investigations
Sampling
Site assessments

Health
Medical information systems
Research support
Technology development

Information Technology
Information protection and e-business security
Intranet consulting and network design
Outsourcing

National Security
Advanced research
Management support
Systems engineering and integration
Technical support
Technology development

Telecommunications
Consulting and engineering
Network design and implementation
Software development and enhancements

COMPETITORS

Accenture	Computer	SRA
American	Sciences	International
Management	DynCorp	SRI
Anteon	EDS	International
Battelle	GRCI	Titan
Memorial	IBM	TRW
CACI	Keane	Unisys
International	MITRE	Veridian
Cap Gemini		

HISTORICAL FINANCIALS & EMPLOYEES

Private FYE: January 31	Annual Growth	1/93	1/94	1/95	1/96	1/97	1/98	1/99	1/00	1/01	1/02
Sales ($ mil.)	16.8%	1,504	1,671	1,922	2,156	2,402	3,089	4,740	5,530	5,896	6,095
Net income ($ mil.)	(7.5%)	38	42	49	57	64	85	151	620	2,059	19
Income as % of sales	—	2.5%	2.5%	2.6%	2.7%	2.7%	2.7%	3.2%	11.2%	34.9%	0.3%
Employees	11.0%	15,839	17,800	20,500	21,100	22,600	30,300	35,200	39,078	41,500	40,400

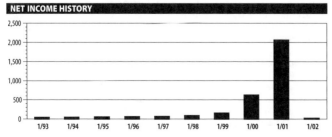

NET INCOME HISTORY

2002 FISCAL YEAR-END
Debt ratio: 4.7%
Return on equity: 0.6%
Cash ($ mil.): 480
Current ratio: 1.51
Long-term debt ($ mil.): 123

SEAGATE TECHNOLOGY HOLDINGS

Seagate Technology Holdings knows that if you want to survive in the storage market, you'd better have drive. The company is a leading independent maker of rigid disk drives (or hard drives) used to store data in computers. Its drives are used in systems ranging from personal computers and workstations to high-end servers and mainframes. The company, which is now registered in the Cayman Islands, was taken private in a deal led by Silver Lake Partners and Texas Pacific Group in 2000. Seagate, which is owned by a holding company called New SAC, filed to go public again in 2002.

In an industry hurt by falling PC prices, Seagate has managed to stay at the front of the disk drive provider line by significantly undercutting competitors' prices, instituting global layoffs, and consolidating facilities. About two-thirds of Seagate's sales are to computer hardware manufacturers, which include Hewlett-Packard (20% of sales) Dell, EMC, IBM, and Sun Microsystems. The company also sells through distributors.

Prior to being taken private — a transaction that allowed Seagate to realize the value of its large holding in VERITAS Software while avoiding certain tax liabilities — the company had operations that included a business intelligence software developer (Crystal Decisions) and a unit devoted to tape storage products. The new Seagate is composed of its core hard drive business (99% of sales) and a subsidiary called XIOtech that develops storage networking products. Seagate owner New SAC is made up of affiliates of investment firms Silver Lake Partners, Texas Pacific Group, August Capital, and J.P. Morgan Partners; investment funds affiliated with Goldman Sachs & Company; and Seagate management.

HISTORY

Seagate Technology was founded in 1979 by Alan Shugart, an 18-year veteran of IBM who had made floppy disks standard on microcomputers; manufacturing expert and longtime technology industry veteran Tom Mitchell; design engineer Douglas Mahon; and Finis Conner. Seagate pioneered the miniaturizing of larger mainframe hard disk drives for PCs. Seagate's first product, a 5.25-in. hard disk, sold briskly. With IBM as a customer, the company had grabbed half of the market for small disk drives by 1982; sales reached $344 million by 1984. But Seagate's heavy dependence on IBM showed its double edge as dwindling PC demand prompted IBM to cut orders. Sales in 1985 dropped to $215 million and profits to $1 million (from $42 million). Seagate transferred its manufacturing to Singapore and cut its California

workforce in half. That year Conner, after a quarrel with Shugart, left Seagate to start his own disk drive company, Conner Peripherals. (Mitchell later joined him.)

Using acquisitions to grow, the company purchased Grenex (thin-film magnetic media, 1984), Aeon (aluminum substrates, 1987), and Integrated Power Systems (custom semiconductors, 1987). Seagate also lured back IBM, which had turned to an alternate supplier in the interim.

With sales more than doubling in 1986 and again in 1987, Seagate continued to invest in 5.25-in. production, ignoring signs of a coming 3.5-in. drive standard. The strong market in 1988 for the smaller drives prompted Seagate's quick shift to 3.5-in. production. Seagate's purchase of Imprimis in 1989 made it the world's premier independent drive maker and a leader in high-capacity drives.

In 1993 the company acquired a stake in flash memory storage specialist Sundisk. That year, when Sun Microsystems accounted for 11% of sales, Seagate was the only profitable independent disk drive company. In 1994 Seagate began pursuing its software initiative, acquiring companies including Palindrome and Crystal Computer Services.

Shugart, an iconoclast who once ran his dog for Congress, had a small comeuppance in 1996 when Seagate paid just over $1 billion for Conner Peripherals, which had banked on 3.5-in. disk drives from the start and had gone public in 1988. By the time of the acquisition, Conner was a leading maker of disk and tape drives, storage systems, and software. Seagate merged Conner's software subsidiary with its own holdings to form Seagate Storage Management Group, and continued to expand by buying management software companies. In 1997 the company bought disk drive developer Quinta. Seagate took a charge that year following a ruling that it had sold faulty drives to Amstrad PLC.

An industry slump, production problems, and lowered PC demand prompted Seagate to cut 20% of its workforce, streamline development, fire Shugart, and replace him with president and COO — and former investment banker — Stephen Luczo. The downturn took its toll when the company suffered a $530 million loss for fiscal 1998. The next year Seagate gained a stake of about 33% in VERITAS Software when it sold its network and storage management software operations to that company for $3.1 billion. Seagate also announced that it would lay off another 10% of its workforce of nearly 80,000.

In early 2000 the company acquired XIOtech, a maker of virtual storage and storage area network systems, for about $360 million. Later that year Seagate entered into a deal with VERITAS whereby the software maker bought back the stake owned by Seagate. As part of the deal, Seagate was taken private in a buyout led by Silver Lake Partners and Texas Pacific Group.

Also in 2000, COO William Watkins, who joined Seagate when it bought Conner Peripherals, replaced Luczo as president; Luczo remained CEO. The company filed to go public again in 2002, completing its IPO in December.

OFFICERS

Chairman and CEO: Stephen J. Luczo, age 45
President, COO, and Director: William D. Watkins, age 49
EVP and Chief Administrative Officer: Donald L. Waite, age 69
EVP and CTO: Townsend H. Porter Jr., age 57
EVP, Business Development and Strategic Planning: Jeremy Tennenbaum, age 48
EVP, Finance and CFO: Charles C. Pope, age 47
EVP, Global Disc Storage Operations: David Wickersham, age 46
EVP, Worldwide Sales, Marketing, and Customer Service: Brian S. Dexheimer, age 39
SVP; General Manager, Asia Operations: James M. Chirico Jr., age 44
SVP, General Counsel, and Secretary: William L. Hudson, age 50
SVP, Heads and Media: Jaroslaw S. Glembocki, age 46
SVP, Research: Mark Kryder
President and CEO, XIOtech: Kathy Snouffer
Executive Director, IT Applications: Pranab Sinha
Director, E-Business Development: Jay Remley
Auditors: Ernst & Young LLP

LOCATIONS

HQ: 920 Disc Dr., Scotts Valley, CA 95066
Phone: 405-936-1234   **Fax:** 405-936-1220
Web: www.seagate.com

Seagate Technology has sales offices in Australia, China, France, Germany, India, Ireland, Japan, the Netherlands, Singapore, Sweden, Switzerland, Taiwan, the UK, and the US.

2002 Sales

	$ mil.	% of total
US	2,398	39
Singapore	1,627	27
The Netherlands	1,438	24
Other countries	624	10
Total	**6,087**	**100**

PRODUCTS/OPERATIONS

2002 Sales

	$ mil.	% of total
Disc drives	6,023	99
Other	64	1
Total	**6,087**	**100**

Selected Products
Disk drives
    Desktop (Barracuda)
    Server/multiuser and workstation systems (Barracuda, Cheetah)
Network storage systems

COMPETITORS

Fujitsu
Hitachi
IBM
Maxtor
Samsung Electronics
Toshiba
Western Digital

HISTORICAL FINANCIALS & EMPLOYEES

Private* FYE: June 30	Annual Growth	6/93	6/94	6/95	6/96	6/97	6/98	6/99	6/00	6/01	6/02
Sales ($ mil.)	0.1%	—	—	—	—	—	—	—	6,073	5,966	6,087
Net income ($ mil.)	(35.3%)	—	—	—	—	—	—	—	366	(522)	153
Income as % of sales	—	—	—	—	—	—	—	—	6.0%	—	2.5%
Employees	—	—	—	—	—	—	—	—	—	—	46,000

*IPO completed in December 2002

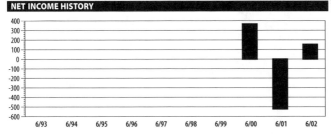

NET INCOME HISTORY

2002 FISCAL YEAR-END
Debt ratio: 53.9%
Return on equity: 23.6%
Cash ($ mil.): 612
Current ratio: 1.22
Long-term debt ($ mil.): 749

SEMATECH, INC.

SEMATECH (from "semiconductor manufacturing technology") is hardly semi-technical. The not-for-profit research consortium, which does business as International SEMATECH, pursues advances in design, lithography, and other facets of chip manufacturing. It also provides custom wafer processing and publishes technical reports for its members. The group is funded by member dues; employees from its members' companies — Agere, Advanced Micro Devices, Hewlett-Packard, Hynix, IBM, Infineon, Intel, Motorola, Philips, STMicroelectronics, Taiwan Semiconductor, and Texas Instruments — carry out research at its Texas site.

International SEMATECH is credited with updating the equipment used in American factories and helping US chip makers recover their global dominance.

The consortium has lost some of its original US members in recent years — in part because of the US chip industry's return to dominance, in part because of its inclusion of non-US firms — but continues to tackle difficult technological issues related to the shrinking size of chips and use of new materials. International SEMATECH is also teaming up with other international research organizations, including Selete, its Japanese counterpart.

HISTORY

In 1986 Japan surpassed the US to become the leading maker of semiconductors. The Semiconductor Industry Association (SIA), a US chip industry trade group, formed SEMATECH in 1987 with funding for five years from the US Defense Department's Defense Advanced Research Projects Agency, and another $100 million per year from 14 member companies.

Former Xerox research executive Bill Spencer became CEO of SEMATECH in 1990. Despite its technological advances, critics complained that the organization benefited its largest members. In the early 1990s Micron Technology and LSI Logic (its smallest members) and Harris Corp. dropped out.

SEMATECH's government funding was extended (although lowered) in 1992. When the US regained its world manufacturing chip title that year, many credited SEMATECH for the turnaround. In 1994 SEMATECH began phasing out federal backing. Citing the main challenge to US chip makers as technology limits, not foreign competition, the organization in 1996 invited European and Asian manufacturers to join an initiative to make larger semiconductor wafers. When government funding came to an end in 1996, SEMATECH formed an international branch and increased its dues (from $10 million to $15 million) to cover lost funding.

In 1997 Mark Melliar-Smith was named CEO; Spencer remains chairman. In 1998 five companies from Asia and Europe formed the new International SEMATECH. That year National Semiconductor left SEMATECH, citing financial difficulties.

In 1999 Motorola, concerned about the organization's international push, gave the required two years notice that it would withdraw. Compaq — which became a member when it acquired Digital Equipment (but not that company's chip operations) in 1997 — also made plans to leave. SEMATECH was instrumental in two major chip industry developments implemented in 1999: migration to 300 millimeter (12-in.) silicon wafers and adoption of copper interconnect technology.

By 2000 SEMATECH and International SEMATECH became a single entity. Also that year the research organization accelerated its international involvement through pacts with Selete, the organization's Japanese counterpart, and Belgian research agency IMEC.

Also in 2000 International SEMATECH began licensing its TP2 tool performance tracking software, which automatically collects performance data on operations and equipment in semiconductor manufacturing facilities.

The following year Bob Helms, a Texas Instruments engineer and Stanford University emeritus professor, succeeded Melliar-Smith as president and CEO. Early in 2002 the consortium announced plans to lay off about 60 employees — a tenth of its workforce — in response to smaller budgets and in the face of a sharp downturn across the semiconductor industry.

OFFICERS

Chairman: O. B. Bilous
President and CEO: Bob Helms
VP and COO, Advanced Technology: Betsy Weitzman
VP and COO, Manufacturing Operations and Technology: John Schmitz
Chief Administrative Officer: David Saathoff
General Counsel: Robert Falstad
Financial Planner: Stuart Clark
Director, Advanced Technology Development Facility: Juergen Woehl
Director, Environment, Safety, and Health: Coleen Miller
Director, Front End Processes: Mike Jackson
Director, Manufacturing Methods and Productivity: Scott Kramer
Director, Supplier Relations: David Anderson
Associate Director, Advanced Technology Development Facility: Dan Holladay
Associate Director, Interconnect: Ken Monnig

Associate Director, Manufacturing Methods and
  Productivity: Randy Goodall
Technical Manager, Metrology/Yield Management Tools:
  Alain Diebold
Program Manager, Copper Metallization: Klaus Pfeifer
Program Manager, e-Diagnostics: Harvey Wohlwend
Program Manager, Environmental Protection:
  Walter Worth
Program Manager, External Research and International
  SEMATECH/SRC Front End Processes Research
  Center: Ed Strickland
Program Manager, Guidelines and Standards:
  Jackie Ferrell
Program Manager, Low-k Dielectric: Jeff Wetzel
Program Manager, Mask Strategy: Wally Carpenter
Program Manager, Metrology/Yield Management Tools:
  Ron Remke
Program Manager, Next Generation Lithography:
  John Canning
Program Manager, Patterning: Gilden Shelden
Program Manager, Supplier Relations: Neil Gayle
Project Manager, Water Optimization: Jerry Chen
Program Manager, Worker Protection: Peter Dahlgren
Manager, Doping Program: Larry Larson
Manager, Manufacturing Operations: Bob Swartwout
Manager, Resist Development: Gene Feit
Manager, Strategic Development: Robert Noland
Manager, Supplier Relations: Chris Daverse
Contract Manager: Carri Crowe
Information Manager, International Technology
  Roadmap of Semiconductors: Linda Wilson
Webmaster, International Roadmap of Semiconductors:
  Sarah Mangum
Human Resources: Linda Cline
Equipment Engineering Maintenance Supervisor:
  Gerry Moore
Auditors: PricewaterhouseCoopers LLP

LOCATIONS

HQ: 2706 Montopolis Dr., Austin, TX 78741
Phone: 512-356-3500   Fax: 512-356-3086
Web: www.sematech.org

SEMATECH includes members from France, Germany,
the Netherlands, South Korea, Taiwan, and the US.

PRODUCTS/OPERATIONS

Research and Development Programs
Advanced technical development facilities and facilities
  design
Environment, safety, and health
Front-end processes
Interconnect
Lithography
Manufacturing methods and productivity

SEMATECH Members
Advanced Micro Devices
Agere
Hewlett-Packard
Hynix
IBM
Infineon
Intel
Motorola
Philips
STMicroelectronics
Taiwan Semiconductor Manufacturing Corp.
Texas Instruments

COMPETITORS

IBM
Intel
MCC
MIT
Research Triangle Institute
SAIC
Southwest Research Institute
SRI International
University of California

SKADDEN, ARPS

Have you heard about the law firm that sued the business information publisher for a profile that opened with a wickedly clever lawyer joke? Neither have we, and we would like to keep it that way. Skadden, Arps, Slate, Meagher & Flom, the largest US law firm and one of the largest in the world, employs about 1,700 attorneys in 22 offices around the world. Founded in 1948, the firm offers counsel for corporate dealings, litigation, and international concerns. Skadden, Arps, Slate, Meagher & Flom has first-rate bankruptcy, litigation, and securities practices.

Widely known for its mergers and acquisitions (M&A) practice, Skadden, Arps is a giant in the field; during the course of 1990 to 1999, the firm handled more than 1,000 deals. For example, the firm represented Germany's Mannesmann in the largest merger in history when it was acquired by Vodafone Group for about $180 billion.

HISTORY

Marshall Skadden, Leslie Arps, and John Slate hung out their shingle in New York City on April Fool's Day, 1948. Skadden and Arps came from a Wall Street law firm, and Slate had been counsel to Pan American World Airways. Without the reputation and connections of the established New York law firms, the firm found work one case at a time from referrals, handling mainly commercial, corporate, and litigations work. Marshall Skadden died in 1958.

Denied the luxury of steady clients, the firm was forced to be innovative and, at times, unorthodox. Joe Flom, who had joined as the firm's first associate, specialized in corporate law and proxy fights. During the 1960s, when tender offers and hostile takeovers increased, many of the more venerable firms referred clients engaged in the undignified corporate raids to Flom to preserve their gentlemanly reputations. With "white shoe" lawyers on Wall Street hesitant to tread into the uncivilized region of corporate takeovers, Skadden, Arps went for it, and the firm virtually pioneered the business of mergers and acquisitions (M&A) under Flom.

When Congress passed the Williams Act in 1968, which "legitimized" tender offers by providing regulation, other law firms started to get in on the act. Skadden, Arps was way ahead of the game, however, and as corporations and lawyers realized that aggressive legal tactics helped win corporate takeover battles, it also became apparent that Joe Flom was the expert. As takeover fights became more frequent in the early 1970s, the firm earned more than just respect. Earnings came not just from some of the highest hourly rates in the industry, but from hefty retainers (now a common practice at many firms) on the theory that association with Flom would scare raiders off. The only other name that could strike such fear in people's hearts was Marty Lipton of rival takeover specialists Wachtell, Lipton, Rosen & Katz. From the late 1970s through the 1980s, Skadden, Arps was involved in almost every important M&A case in the US.

The firm used its success in mergers and acquisitions to build its practice in other areas. In the early 1980s it branched into bankruptcy, product liability, and real estate law. By then it had opened offices in Boston; Chicago; Los Angeles; Washington, DC; and Wilmington, Delaware. Les Arps died in 1987.

With the boom in mergers and acquisitions activity and bankruptcies in the late 1980s, the firm grew to almost 2,000 lawyers by 1989. Then came the recession, and M&A work virtually dried up. Skadden, Arps responded by shedding more than 500 lawyers between 1989 and 1990. It also scrambled to diversify and expand internationally. As takeover activity rebounded in the mid-1990s, the diversification strategy actually began to work against Skadden, Arps because profits didn't skyrocket like those of M&A specialist firms.

The firm opened an office in Singapore in 1995 to coordinate its Asian business, signaling that city's growing importance as a financial center. Two years later two-thirds of the firm's Beijing team defected to a rival firm. Headquarters shrugged it off and flew in replacements. Skadden, Arps won one of its highest profile cases in 1998 when the sexual harassment suit brought against President Clinton by Paula Jones was thrown out.

With its M&A practice in full swing again, Skadden, Arps was involved in 70 announced M&A deals in 1999, including the $75 billion merger of oil companies Exxon and Mobil. It also became the first US law firm to reach $1 billion in revenue in 2000. (It passed the $1 billion mark again in 2001.) The company announced an alliance with Italian law firm Studio Chiomenti in mid-2001.

OFFICERS

Executive Partner: Robert C. Sheehan
Finance Director: Carol Sawdye
Director, Associate Development: Jodie R. Garfinkel
Director, Human Resources: Laurel Henschel
Director, Legal Hiring: Carol Lee H. Sprague
Director, Marketing & Communications: Sally Feldman
Director, Technology: Harris Z. Tilevitz
Senior Partner: Joseph H. Flom
Senior Partner, Corporate Practice: Roger S. Aaron

Senior Partner Litigation: William P. Frank
Managing Partner, Boston: Louis A. Goodman
Managing Partner, Chicago: Wayne W. Whalen
Managing Partner, Houston: Lyndon C. Taylor
Managing Partner, Los Angeles: Rand S. April
Managing Partner, New York: Irene A. Sullivan
Managing Partner, Palo Alto: Kenton J. King
Managing Partner, Reston: Ronald Barusch
Managing Partner, Washington: Michael P. Rogan
Managing Partner, Wilmington: Steven J. Rothschild
Managing Partner, Asian Practice: Phyllis G. Korff
Managing Partner, European Practice: Bruce M. Buck

LOCATIONS

HQ: Skadden, Arps, Slate, Meagher & Flom LLP
Four Times Square, New York, NY 10036
Phone: 212-735-3000   Fax: 212-735-2000
Web: www.skadden.com

US Offices
Boston
Chicago
Houston
Los Angeles
New York City
Newark, NJ
Palo Alto, CA
San Francisco
Washington, DC
Wilmington, DE

International Offices
Beijing
Brussels
Frankfurt
Hong Kong
London
Moscow
Paris
Singapore
Sydney
Tokyo
Toronto

PRODUCTS/OPERATIONS

Selected Practice Areas
Antitrust
Banking and institutional investing
Corporate finance
Government affairs
Health care
Insurance
Intellectual property
International trade
Internet and e-commerce
Labor and employment law
Litigation
Mass torts and insurance litigation
Mergers and acquisitions
Real estate
Tax
Trusts and estates
White-collar crime

COMPETITORS

Baker & McKenzie
Cleary, Gottlieb
Clifford Chance
Cravath, Swaine
Davis Polk
Debevoise & Plimpton
Jones, Day
Latham & Watkins
Mayer, Brown, Rowe & Maw
Paul, Weiss, Rifkind
Shearman & Sterling
Sidley Austin Brown & Wood
Simpson Thacher
Sullivan & Cromwell
Wachtell, Lipton
Weil, Gotshal
White & Case

HISTORICAL FINANCIALS & EMPLOYEES

Partnership FYE: December 31	Annual Growth	12/92	12/93	12/94	12/95	12/96	12/97	12/98	12/99	12/00	12/01
Sales ($ mil.)	12.0%	440	478	582	635	710	826	890	1,025	1,154	1,225
Employees	4.2%	3,000	3,200	3,100	3,000	3,150	3,000	3,200	3,600	4,235	4,350

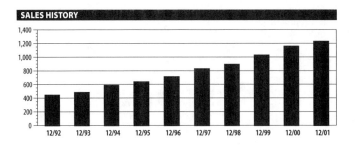

SALES HISTORY

SMITHSONIAN INSTITUTION

The Smithsonian Institution wears many hats, from the one worn by Harrison Ford in the Indiana Jones Trilogy to the one worn by Abraham Lincoln the night he was assassinated. The world's largest museum, the Smithsonian houses more than 140 million pieces in 16 museums and galleries. More than 40 million people every year come view its exhibits on art, music, TV and film, science, history, and other subjects. Admission to its museums, most of which are located on the National Mall in Washington, DC (two are in New York City), is usually free. The Smithsonian also operates the National Zoo and a handful of research facilities. The Smithsonian receives 57% of its operating revenue from the federal government.

The Smithsonian's exhibits display items such as the Declaration of Independence, the ruby slippers worn by Judy Garland in *The Wizard of Oz,* and the Wright Brothers' first airplane. A board of regents that includes Vice President Richard Cheney, Chief Justice William Rehnquist, six members of Congress, and nine private citizens leads the institution.

HISTORY

English chemist James Smithson wrote a proviso to his will in 1826 that would lead to the creation of the Smithsonian Institution. When he died in 1829, he left his estate to his nephew, Henry James Hungerford, with the stipulation that if Hungerford died without heirs, the estate would go to the US to create "an Establishment for the increase and diffusion of knowledge among men." Hungerford died in 1835 without any heirs, and the US government inherited more than $500,000 in gold.

Congress squandered the money after it was received in 1838, but perhaps feeling pangs of guilt, covered the loss. The Smithsonian was finally created in 1846, and Princeton physicist Joseph Henry was named as its first secretary. That year it established the Museum of Natural History, the Museum of History and Technology, and the National Gallery of Art. The Smithsonian's National Museum was developed around the collection of the US Patent Office in 1858. The Smithsonian continued to expand, adding the National Zoological Park in 1889 and the Smithsonian Astrophysical Observatory in 1890.

The Freer Gallery, a gift of industrialist Charles Freer, opened in 1923. The National Gallery was renamed the National Collection of Fine Arts in 1937, and a new National Gallery, created with Andrew Mellon's gift of his art collection and a building, opened in 1941. The Air and Space Museum was established in 1946.

More museums were added in the 1960s, including the National Portrait Gallery in 1962 and the Anacostia Museum (exhibits and materials on African-American history) in 1967. The Kennedy Center for the Performing Arts was opened in 1971. The Collection of Fine Arts was renamed the National Museum of American Art and the Museum of History and Technology was renamed the National Museum of American History in 1980.

The Smithsonian placed its first-ever contribution boxes in four of its museums in 1993. A planned exhibit featuring the Enola Gay — the plane that dropped the atomic bomb on Hiroshima — created a firestorm in 1994 with critics charging that the exhibit downplayed Japanese aggression and US casualties in WWII. The original exhibit was canceled in 1995, the director of the Air and Space Museum resigned, and a scaled-down version of the exhibit premiered.

Large contributions from private donors continued in the 1990s; the Mashantucket Pequot tribe gave $10 million from its casino operations in 1994 for a planned American Indian museum and prolific electronics inventor Jerome Lemelson donated $10.4 million in 1995. The museum celebrated its sesquicentennial in 1996 amid news that $500 million in repairs were needed over the next 10 years.

California real estate developer Kenneth Behring gave the largest cash donation ever to the museum in 1997 — $20 million for the National Museum of Natural History. Short of funds, the Smithsonian had to cut back on its 150th anniversary traveling exhibit that year. The Smithsonian announced a $26 million renovation for the National Museum of Natural History in 1998. Two years later Kenneth Behring quadrupled his record breaking 1997 donation of $20 million by giving $80 million to the National Museum of American History in 2000. Catherine Reynolds withdrew most of her $38 million gift in 2002 after the Smithsonian Institution refused to implement her ideas for an exhibit at the National Museum of American History.

OFFICERS

Director, Policy and Analysis: Carole Neeves
Director, National Museum of Art: Elizabeth Broun
Director, National Air and Space Museum: John Dailey
Director, National Portrait Gallery; Director, National
  Museum of American History: Marc Pachter
Director, National Zoological Park: Lucy H. Spelman,
  age 37
Director, Hirshhorn Museum: Ned Rifkin
Director, Planning, Management, and Budget:
  Bruce Dauer
General Counsel: John E. Huerta, age 57

LOCATIONS

HQ: 1000 Jefferson Dr. SW, Washington, DC 20560
Phone: 202-357-2700   Fax: 202-786-2377
Web: www.smithsonian.org

The Smithsonian Institution has museums and galleries
located in New York City and Washington, DC; its
research centers are located in the US and Panama.

PRODUCTS/OPERATIONS

Museums and Research Centers
Anacostia Museum and Center for African American
  History & Culture
Archives of American Art
Arthur M. Sackler Gallery
Arts and Industries Building
Center for Folklife Programs and Cultural Heritage
Conservation and Research Center
Cooper-Hewitt, National Design Museum (New York
  City)
Freer Gallery of Art
Hirshhorn Museum and Sculpture Garden
National Air and Space Museum
National Museum of African Art
National Museum of American History
National Museum of Natural History
National Museum of the American Indian (New York
  City)
National Portrait Gallery
National Postal Museum
National Zoological Park
Smithsonian American Art Museum
  Renwick Gallery
Smithsonian Astrophysical Observatory
Smithsonian Center for Latino Initiatives
Smithsonian Center for Materials Research and
  Education
Smithsonian Environmental Research Center
Smithsonian Institution Building (The Castle)
Smithsonian Marine Station at Fort Pierce
Smithsonian Tropical Research Institute

HISTORICAL FINANCIALS & EMPLOYEES

Not-for-profit FYE: September 30	Annual Growth	9/92	9/93	9/94	9/95	9/96	9/97	9/98	9/99	9/00	9/01
Sales ($ mil.)	(0.7%)	706	730	605	750	703	729	774	563	604	665
Employees	(0.6%)	6,800	6,800	6,671	6,600	6,487	6,469	—	6,400	6,500	—

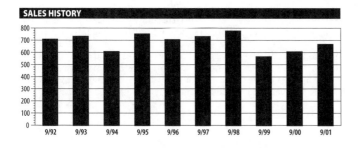

SALES HISTORY

SPRINGS INDUSTRIES, INC.

Watch out — Springs Industries wants to cozy up in your bedroom. The company makes sheets, pillows, shower curtains, bedspreads, towels, and bath rugs under the Springmaid and Wamsutta brands. Springs also makes infant apparel, baby bedding, fabrics, window blinds, and hardware (Bali, Graber brands). The firm makes private-label items for Wal-Mart and Target, and licensed brands such as Harry Potter and John Deere. Springs sells through department stores, mass retailers, and catalogs. The Close family, descendants of co-founder Leroy Springs (whose great-great-granddaughter Crandall Close Bowles is CEO), owns about 55% of Springs and has joined with Heartland Industrial Partners and taken the firm private.

Wal-Mart represents more than 30% of Springs' sales. The company also sells through about 60 of its own outlet stores. Historically an apparel textile maker, Springs has spent the past decade refocusing on home fashions through sales and acquisitions.

Heartland Industrial owns the remaining 45% of Springs.

HISTORY

Springs Industries began in 1887 as Fort Mill Manufacturing Co., a cotton miller organized by Samuel Elliott White and a group of investors, including Leroy Springs, White's future son-in-law. Springs later founded his own cotton mill, Lancaster Cotton Mills, in 1895 and gained control of Fort Mill Manufacturing in 1914, three years after White died.

Leroy's only son, Elliott Springs, became president in 1931 when his father died. Left with massive debt and six aging cotton mills, Elliott rejuvenated the company by modernizing mill equipment and consolidating the plants into the Springs Cotton Mills (1933). During WWII the company's seven mills made fabric for military use.

In 1945 Springs started the Springmaid line of bedding and fabrics. Elliott's satiric, risque, but effective ads (beginning in 1948) helped the company become a leading producer of sheets.

Elliott died in 1959 and his son-in-law, William Close, became president. With profits sharply declining, the company went public as Springs Mills in 1966.

The first non-family member to be president, Peter Scotese from Federated Department Stores, was hired in 1969. The next year Springs began working with designer Bill Blass. It diversified into synthetic fabrics in 1971 by buying a minority interest in a Japanese textile plant producing Ultrasuede for apparel and cars.

Springs acquired Graber Industries (window-decorating products) in 1979 and three years later changed its name to Springs Industries. In 1985 it acquired M. Lowenstein, which made Wamsutta home furnishings; the deal also gave it Clark-Schwebel Fiber Glass (industrial fabrics). Springs added Carey-McFall (Bali blinds) in 1989.

Declining economic conditions throughout the textile industry in the late 1980s and early 1990s forced Springs to close plants and trim its weakened finished-fabrics segment (the downsizing continued into 1993). A $70 million charge in 1990 led to a $7 million loss, its first in 25 years as a public company.

Historically a maker of apparel fabrics, Springs had grown vulnerable to imports and launched a long-term plan to focus on home furnishings through sales and acquisitions. In 1991 the company set up a bath group with the purchase of C. S. Brooks. Springs became a leading seller of home textiles in Canada the next year by buying the marketing and sales units of C. S. Brooks Canada and Springmaid distributor Griffiths-Kerr. A hostile takeover bid for rival Fieldcrest Cannon was rebuffed in 1993.

Expanding in 1995, Springs acquired Dundee Mills (baby and health care products, towels), Dawson Home Fashions (bath accessories, shower curtains), and Nanik Window Coverings (blinds, shutters). In 1996 the company sold its Clark-Schwebel subsidiary and the following year purchased half of American Fiber Industries (pillows, mattress pads, comforters).

Crandall Close Bowles became the eighth president of Springs in 1997. The next year she took over the chairman and CEO posts from Walter Elisha.

To further focus on its home furnishings business, in 1998 the company sold its UltraSuede business (but kept its UltraLeather business) and its industrial products division. In 1999 Springs finally exited the apparel fabrics business when it sold its Springfield division to a management group, then it purchased Regal Rugs (bath and accent rugs) and the remaining 50% of American Fiber Industries.

In April 2001 the Close family agreed to partner with private equity firm Heartland Industrial Partners to take Springs private. In September the deal was completed, increasing the family's stake to 55%, with Heartland owning the remaining 45%. In June 2002 Springs acquired Burlington Industries' window treatments and bedding consumer products businesses.

Chairman and CEO: Crandall Close Bowles, age 53,
$637,504 pay
EVP and CFO: Kenneth E. Kutcher
EVP and CIO: Ray E. Greer
EVP; President, Home Furnishings Operating Group:
Dean Riggs
EVP; President, Sales and Marketing Group:
Thomas P. O'Connor, age 54, $396,672 pay
SVP and Chief Purchasing Officer: John R. Cowart
SVP, General Counsel, and Secretary: C. Powers Dorsett
SVP, Global Sourcing and International Marketing:
Dale Williams
SVP, Human Resources: Gracie P. Coleman
VP and Treasurer: Samuel J. Ilardo
VP and Controller: Charles M. Metzler
VP, Corporate Communications and Public Affairs:
Ted Matthews
VP, Creative Development: Nancy W. Webster
Auditors: Deloitte & Touche LLP

LOCATIONS

HQ: 205 N. White St., Fort Mill, SC 29715
Phone: 803-547-1500   **Fax:** 803-547-1636
Web: www.springs.com

Springs Industries operates 40 manufacturing plants in
13 states.

PRODUCTS/OPERATIONS

Selected Products and Brand Names

Home Furnishings (sheets, comforters, infant bedding,
towels, shower curtains, bath rugs, ceramic bath
accessories, fabric)
Daisy Kingdom
Dundee
Performance
Regal
Springmaid
Texmade (in Canada)
Wabasso (in Canada)
Wamsutta

Window Furnishings and Related Hardware
Bali
CrystalPleat
FashionPleat
Graber
Maestro
Nanik

COMPETITORS

Avondale Incorporated
Burlington Industries
Carter's
Coats
Croscill
Crown Crafts
Dan River
Galey & Lord
Gerber Childrenswear
Guilford Mills
Hunter Douglas
Milliken
Mohawk Industries
National Textiles
Newell Rubbermaid
Pillowtex
R. B. Pamplin
WestPoint Stevens

HISTORICAL FINANCIALS & EMPLOYEES

Private FYE: December 31	Annual Growth	12/92	12/93	12/94	12/95	12/96	12/97	12/98	12/99	12/00	12/01
Sales ($ mil.)	2.2%	1,976	2,023	2,069	2,233	2,243	2,226	2,181	2,220	2,275	2,400
Employees	(2.3%)	20,900	20,300	20,500	23,700	20,700	19,500	17,500	18,500	18,200	17,000

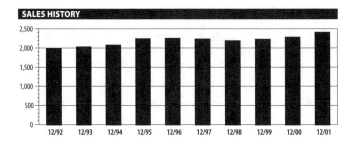

SALES HISTORY

SRI INTERNATIONAL

Business Week magazine has called SRI International "Silicon Valley's soul." The not-for-profit think tank ponders advances in biotechnology, chemicals and energy, computer science, electronics, and public policy — and ways to commercialize those advances.

SRI focuses on technology research and development, business strategies, and issues analysis. It has more than 800 patents and patent applications in such areas as information sciences, software development, communications, robotics, and pharmaceuticals. Among SRI's clients are Visa, Samsung, NASA, and the US Department of Defense. Originally founded in 1946 as Stanford Research Institute, SRI became fully independent of Stanford University in 1970.

The organization has conceived such innovations as the computer mouse, magnetic encoding for checks, the videodisc, and high-definition television, not to mention some of the foundations of personal computing, the Internet, and stealth technology. Its 1,400 scientists, researchers, policy experts, and support staff work at research centers worldwide.

SRI has two for-profit subsidiaries: Sarnoff (formerly a unit of General Electric) specializes in creating and commercializing electronic, biomedical, and information technologies, and SRI Consulting focuses on such issues as organizational management, marketing technologies, and the commercialization of processes. SRI and Sarnoff have together spun off more than 20 companies (*Business Week* has also called SRI "Spin-Off City").

HISTORY

In the 1920s Stanford University professor Robert Swain envisioned a research center devoted to chemistry, physics, and biology. Swain received support from university president Ray Lyman and alumnus Herbert Hoover, but the Great Depression and WWII postponed the venture.

Finally, in 1946, the Stanford Research Institute was formed in conjunction with the university. That year the David Sarnoff Research Center invented the color TV tube under the wing of RCA Laboratories.

During Stanford Research's early years, it worked on such projects as logistics for Disneyland, magnetic ink for character recognition, and strategies for combating air pollution. The think tank was the focus of student protests in the 1960s because of its defense work. In 1969 Stanford Research Institute was one of four nodes on the first computer network, the ARPANET. It became fully independent in 1970 as SRI International.

In the 1960s and 1970s, SRI won large contracts from the US Department of Defense for research in such areas as radar, speech recognition, and noise cancellation technologies. It got a tremendous boost in 1987 when longtime client General Electric gave SRI the Sarnoff Research Center (as a tax write-off) plus $250 million in business, along with $65.2 million in cash.

In 1993 SRI founded Pangene to commercialize gene cloning and analysis technology. The next year it founded GeneTrace to develop genetics-related products for biomedical research and Nuance Communications to commercialize speech recognition products. In 1995 it created Intuitive Surgical, which develops minimally invasive surgical technologies.

SRI developed two key components for use in an improved mail sorting program, which the US Postal Service announced in 1997 it would use to save millions in processing costs. The David Sarnoff Research Center changed its name to Sarnoff Corporation that year. SRI joined Motorola in 1997 to make semiconductors for digital TVs.

In 1998 SRI and the National Science Foundation teamed to develop innovative science and math teaching programs. The following year SRI began working with network equipment leader Cisco Systems and the US Army to develop a voice and multimedia communications system for the military.

In 2000 SRI spun off AtomicTangerine, an e-business venture consulting firm. That same year SRI and Palm, Inc. teamed together to launch the Palm Education Pioneers Program. The program will give Palm handheld computers to about 100 K-12 teachers. SRI will develop and conduct a research program to evaluate effectiveness of Palm technology in the classroom. The research group also announced in 2000 that it would team with Mattel to develop toys using the institute's research in robotics, embedded systems, speech recognition, and wireless systems.

In 2001 SRI partnered with SPEEDCOM Wireless to codevelop wireless technology.

OFFICERS

Chairman: Samuel H. Armacost, age 64
President and CEO: Curtis R. Carlson
SVP and CFO: Thomas J. Furst
VP, Engineering and Systems: John W. Prausa
VP, Information and Computing Sciences: William Mark
VP, Information, Telecommunications, and Automation: Michael S. Frankel

VP, Intellectual Property: Steven Weiner
VP, International Business Development:
Leonard Polizzotto
VP, Legal and Business Affairs and General Counsel:
Richard Abramson
VP, Corporate Business Development, Biotechnology:
Michael Tracy
VP, Physical Sciences: Lawrence H. Dubois
VP, Policy Division: Dennis Beatrice
VP, Ventures and Strategic Business Development:
Norman Winarsky
President and CEO, Sarnoff Corporation:
James E. Carnes, age 63
Senior Director, Corporate and Marketing
Communications: Alice R. Resnick
Senior Director, Human Resources: Jean E. Tooker
Director, Pharmaceutical Formulations Design:
Manoj Maniar
Program Director, Instrumentation and Simulation
Systems: Chris Terndrup

LOCATIONS

HQ: 333 Ravenswood Ave., Menlo Park, CA 94025
Phone: 650-859-2000   Fax: 650-326-5512
Web: www.sri.com

SRI International has offices in Greenland, Japan, South
Korea, and the UK, and throughout the US.

PRODUCTS/OPERATIONS

Business Areas
Automation and Robotics
Automotive and Commercial Equipment Technologies
Biopharmaceutical Development
Chemistry, Materials, and Applied Physics
Communications Technologies
Defense and Intelligence
Information Science and Software Development
   (human-computer interaction)
Medical Devices
Pharmaceutical Discovery
Policy (analysis of social, technological, and economic
   changes)
Product Engineering
Sensors and Measurement Systems
Systems and Services

Subsidiaries
Sarnoff Corporation (commercialization of innovative
   electronics, biomedical, and information technologies)
SRI Consulting (management consulting)

Selected SRI Spinoffs
AlterEgo Networks (wireless networking device services)
AtomicTangerine (information security consulting)
Intuitive Surgical, Inc. (technologies and techniques for
   minimally invasive surgery)
Nuance Communications, Inc. (speech recognition
   technology)
Pangene Corp. (genetic engineering technology)

Selected Sarnoff Spinoffs
Delsys Pharmaceutical Corp. (drug manufacturing and
   delivery technologies)
DIVA Systems Corporation (interactive video-on-demand
   services)
Orchid BioSciences, Inc. (gene analysis products and
   services)
Pyramid Vision Technologies (real-time video image
   systems)
Sarcon Microsystems, Inc. (infrared and chemical
   sensing technologies used in laboratory analysis,
   industrial monitoring, and commercial security
   applications)
Sarif (polysilicon active-matrix liquid crystal light valves
   for projection displays and head-mounted systems)
Secure Products (anticounterfeiting and anti-diversion
   systems)
Songbird Hearing, Inc. (development of a disposable
   hearing aid)

COMPETITORS

Aerospace	Educational	Research
Corporation	Testing Service	Triangle
Andersen	Kendle	Institute
Battelle	LECG	SAIC
Memorial	McKinsey &	Southwest
Bayer	Company	Research
Booz Allen	Mission Research	Institute
CACI	MIT	Teknowledge
International	MITRE	University of
The Charles	PAREXEL	California
Stark Draper	Quintiles	Wellcome Trust
Laboratory	Transnational	Westat
DuPont	Rand	

HISTORICAL FINANCIALS & EMPLOYEES

Not-for-profit FYE: December 31	Annual Growth	12/92	12/93	12/94	12/95	12/96	12/97	12/98	12/99	12/00	12/01
Sales ($ mil.)	(5.7%)	305	312	312	320	326	363	174	160	164	180
Employees	(5.5%)	2,321	2,170	1,973	1,900	2,700	2,783	1,500	1,400	1,400	1,400

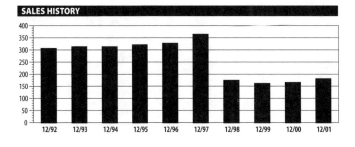

SALES HISTORY

STANFORD UNIVERSITY

Prospectors panning for gold in higher education can strike it rich at Stanford University. The school is one of the premier educational institutions in the US, boasting respected programs in business, engineering, law, and medicine, among others. Its campus is home to more than 14,000 students as well as 1,700 faculty members. A private institution, Stanford supports its activities through an $8 billion endowment, one of the largest in the US. The university was founded in 1885 by Leland Stanford Sr. and his wife, Jane, in memory of their son, Leland Jr.

Stanford is also widely recognized as one of the top US research universities and sports a host of laboratories and research centers, including the Stanford Institute for Economic Policy Research and the Stanford Linear Accelerator Center. Its faculty members include 17 Nobel Prize winners and 21 National Medal of Science winners.

In 2000 the school welcomed its 10th president, former provost John Hennessy, who then launched a campaign to raise $1 billion, the largest drive ever undertaken by a university. It quickly reached half that goal thanks to donations from such alumni as Jerry Yang (co-founder of Yahoo!), Charles Schwab, and Texas billionaire Robert Bass. However, its alumni ranks lost a prominent member in 2001 when William Hewlett (of Hewlett-Packard) died.

HISTORY

In 1885 Leland Stanford Sr. and his wife, Jane, established Leland Stanford Junior University in memory of their son Leland Jr., who had died of typhoid at age 15. Stanford made his fortune selling provisions to California gold miners and as a railroad magnate whose Central Pacific Railroad built tracks eastward and eventually completed the transcontinental railway. Stanford also served as California's governor and as a US senator.

The Stanfords donated more than 8,000 acres of land from their own estate to establish an unconventional university, one that was both co-educational and nondenominational. Stanford opened its doors in 1891 to a freshman class of 559 students. It awarded its first degrees four years later, and among the graduates was future US president Herbert Hoover. Leland Stanford Sr. died in 1893, and in 1903 Jane Stanford turned the university over to the board of trustees. After weathering significant damage in 1906 from the Great San Francisco Earthquake, the university established a law school in 1908 and its medical school five years later.

During WWI the university mobilized half of its students into the Students' Army Training Corps. The School of Education was established in 1917, followed by the School of Engineering and Graduate School of Business eight years later. In 1933 a rule limiting the number of women admitted to Stanford was abolished.

Wallace Sterling, who became president of the university after WWII, initiated the transformation of Stanford into a world-class institution with a reputation for teaching and research. Under Sterling the university initiated development on the Stanford Research Park.

In 1958 Stanford opened its first overseas campus (near Stuttgart, Germany), and the Stanford Medical Center was completed the following year. The university created a computer science department in 1965 and two years later opened the Stanford Linear Accelerator Center dedicated to physics research.

Donald Kennedy became president in 1980. During his tenure, it was revealed that Stanford had overcharged the Office of Naval Research for indirect costs associated with research. The scandal led to Kennedy's resignation in 1992, and in 1994 the Office of Naval Research and the university settled a related lawsuit for $1.2 million and a stipulation that Stanford had not committed any wrongdoing. Gerhard Casper succeeded Kennedy as president.

In 1997 Stanford and the University of California at San Francisco combined their teaching hospitals in a public/private merger. Two years later after the controversial experiment had harmed both hospitals' financial picture, the merger was terminated, and the two hospitals agreed to go their separate ways.

In 1999 Casper announced his intention to resign as president. The school tapped provost John Hennessy as his replacement. Soon after his appointment in 2000, Hennessey launched a campaign to raise $1 billion. Former Stanford professor and Netscape co-founder Jim Clark donated $150 million later that year to support Stanford's biomedical engineering and sciences program. (The donation was the university's largest since its founding grant.) The school also launched a new company, SKOLAR, which has developed an online search engine for the medical industry.

OFFICERS

President: John L. Hennessy, age 50
Provost: John W. Etchemendy
VP Business Affairs and CFO: Randall S. Livingston
VP Development: John B. Ford
VP Public Affairs: Gordon Earle
Vice Provost Campus Relations: LaDoris Cordell
Vice Provost Faculty Development: Patricia Jones
Vice Provost Student Affairs: Gene Awakuni
Vice Provost Undergraduate Education: John Bravman

CEO, Stanford Management Co.: Mike McCaffery
President, Alumni Association: Howard Wolf
Executive Director Human Resources: John Cammidge
Executive Director Information Technology Systems
  and Services: Christopher Handley
Director University Communications: Alan Acosta
General Counsel: Deborah Zumwalt

LOCATIONS

HQ: 857 Serra St., Stanford, CA 94305
Phone: 650-723-2300   Fax: 650-725-0247
Web: www.stanford.edu

Stanford University's campus is located in Stanford,
California. The university also offers study programs in
Argentina, Chile, France, Germany, Italy, Japan, Mexico,
Russia, and the UK.

PRODUCTS/OPERATIONS

Selected Schools
Undergraduate
  School of Earth Sciences
  School of Engineering
  School of Humanities and Sciences
Graduate
  School of Business
  School of Earth Sciences
  School of Education
  School of Engineering
  School of Humanities and Sciences
  School of Law
  School of Medicine

Selected Interdisciplinary Research Centers
Center for Computer Research in Music and Acoustics
Center for Integrated Facility Engineering
Center for Integrated Systems
Stanford Integrated Manufacturing Association

Selected Laboratories, Centers, and Institutes
Center for Research on Information Storage Materials
Center for the Study of Language and Information
Edward L. Ginzton Laboratory
Institute for International Studies
Institute for Research on Women and Gender
Stanford Center for Buddhist Studies
Stanford Humanities Center
Stanford Institute for Economic Policy Research
W.W. Hansen Experimental Physics Laboratory

Selected Medical Research Facilities
Center for Biomedical Ethics
Center for Research in Disease Prevention
Human Genome Center
Richard M. Lucas Center for Magnetic Resonance
  Spectroscopy & Imaging
Sleep Disorders Center

Other Selected Research Facilities
Hoover Institution on War, Revolution and Peace
Hopkins Marine Station
Martin Luther King, Jr. Papers Project
Stanford Linear Accelerator Center

HISTORICAL FINANCIALS & EMPLOYEES

School FYE: August 31	Annual Growth	8/92	8/93	8/94	8/95	8/96	8/97	8/98	8/99	8/00	8/01
Sales ($ mil.)	15.7%	—	—	—	—	1,416	1,474	1,558	1,749	1,957	2,940
Employees	4.7%	—	—	—	—	8,702	8,677	9,535	—	—	—

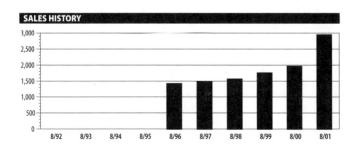

SALES HISTORY

STATE FARM INSURANCE

Like an enormous corporation, State Farm is everywhere. One of the US's largest personal lines property & casualty companies, State Farm Insurance Companies provide auto insurance, as well as homeowners, nonmedical health, and life insurance through some 16,000 agents. Competition has increased with the fall of barriers between the banking, securities, and insurance industries. State Farm's not-so-secret weapon is a federal savings bank charter that offers deposit accounts, CDs, mortgages, and auto and home equity loans online, on the phone, and face-to-face in Illinois and Missouri.

Expanding its financial services (the company has started offering mutual funds), insurance is still the company's main source of income. State Farm insures about 20% of the automobiles on US roads.

Taking advantage of the currently lucrative insurance climate, State Farm has formed Bermuda-based reinsurer Da Vinci Re together with RenaissanceRe. The company has stopped writing new homeowners policies in some 15 states in an effort to improve profitability.

Since its founding, the group's companies have been run by only two families, the Mecherles (1922-54) and the Rusts (1954-present).

HISTORY

Retired farmer George Mecherle formed State Farm Mutual Automobile Insurance in Bloomington, Illinois, in 1922. State Farm served only members of farm bureaus and farm mutual insurance companies, charging a one-time membership fee and a premium to protect an automobile against loss or damage.

Unlike most competitors, State Farm offered six-month premium payments. The insurer billed and collected renewal premiums from its home office, relieving the agent of the task. In addition, State Farm determined auto rates by a simple seven-class system, while competitors varied rates for each model.

State Farm in 1926 started City and Village Mutual Automobile Insurance to insure non-farmers' autos; it became part of the company in 1927. Between 1927 and 1931 it introduced borrowed-car protection, wind coverage, and insurance for vehicles used to transport schoolchildren. State Farm expanded to California in 1928 and formed State Farm Life Insurance the next year. In 1935 it established State Farm Fire Insurance. George Mecherle became chairman in 1937, and his son Ramond became president. In 1939 George challenged agents to write "A Million or More (auto policies) by '44." State Farm saw a 110% increase in policies.

During the 1940s State Farm focused on urban areas after most of the farm bureaus formed their own insurance companies. In the late 1940s and 1950s, it moved to a full-time agency force.

Homeowners coverage was added to the insurer's offerings under the leadership of Adlai Rust, who led State Farm from 1954 until 1958, when Edward Rust took over. He died in 1985 and his son, Edward Jr., currently holds the top spot.

Between 1974 and 1987 the insurer was hit by several gender-discrimination suits (a 1992 settlement awarded $157 million to 814 women). State Farm has since tried to hire more women and minorities.

In the early 1990s serial disasters, including Hurricane Andrew and the Los Angeles riots, proved costly. The 1994 Northridge earthquake alone generated more than $2.5 billion in claims and contributed to a 72% decline in earnings.

State Farm — the top US home insurer since the mid-1960s — canceled 62,500 residential policies in South Florida in 1996 to cut potential hurricane loss an estimated 11%. In response, Florida's insurance regulators rescinded a previously approved rate hike. That year the company agreed to open more urban neighborhood offices to settle a discrimination suit brought by the Department of Housing and Urban Development, which accused State Farm of discriminating against potential customers in minority-populated areas.

Legal trouble continued. In 1997 State Farm settled with a California couple who alleged the company forged policyholders' signatures on forms declining coverage and concealed evidence to avoid paying earthquake damage claims. That year a policyholder sued to keep State Farm from "wasting company assets" on President Clinton's legal defense against Paula Jones' sexual harassment charges (Clinton held a State Farm personal liability policy).

Relations with its sales force already rocky, State Farm in 1998 proposed to reduce up-front commissions and cut base pay in favor of incentives for customer retention and cross-selling. Reduced auto premiums and increased catastrophe claims from across the US eroded State Farm's bottom line that year. A federal thrift charter obtained in 1998 let the company launch banking operations the next year.

State Farm is appealing a 1999 Illinois state court judgment that it pay $1.2 billion to policyholders for using aftermarket parts in auto repairs. In 2000 the firm was hit with a class-action lawsuit about its denial of personal-injury claims; previous suits had been individual cases.

OFFICERS

Chairman and CEO: Edward B. Rust Jr., age 51
EVP and General Counsel: Kim M. Brunner
EVP, Financial Services: Jack W. North
EVP: Brian V. Boyden
EVP: John P. Coffey
EVP: Barbara Cowden
EVP: William K. King
SVP, Investments: Paul N. Eckley
SVP, Investments: Kurt G. Moser
VP, Corporate Secretary, and Counsel: Laura P. Sullivan
VP and Treasurer: Michael L. Tipsord
VP, Human Resources: Arlene Hogan
Vice Chairman, State Farm Mutual and Director:
Roger S. Joslin, age 66
**Vice Chairman, President, and COO, State Farm
Mutual:** Vincent J. Trosino
President and CEO, State Farm Federal Savings Bank:
Stanley R. Ommen
**SEVP, Chief Agency and Marketing Officer, and
Director, State Farm Mutual:** Charles R. Wright
**SEVP and Chief Administrative Officer, State Farm
Mutual Automobile Insurance:** James E. Rutrough
**SVP and Chief Administrative Officer, Life Company
Affiliates:** Susan D. Waring
Systems VP: Richard Shellito
Auditors: PricewaterhouseCoopers LLP

LOCATIONS

HQ: State Farm Insurance Companies
1 State Farm Plaza, Bloomington, IL 61710
Phone: 309-766-2311   **Fax:** 309-766-3621
Web: www.statefarm.com

State Farm Insurance Companies has operations in
Canada and throughout the US.

PRODUCTS/OPERATIONS

Group Companies
State Farm County Mutual Insurance Company of Texas
(high-risk auto insurance)
State Farm Federal Savings Bank
State Farm Fire and Casualty Company (homeowners,
boat owners, and commercial insurance)
State Farm Florida Insurance Company (homeowners
and renters insurance)
State Farm General Insurance Company (property
insurance)
State Farm Indemnity Company (auto insurance in New
Jersey)
State Farm Life Insurance Company
State Farm Mutual Automobile Insurance Company
(auto and health insurance)

COMPETITORS

AIG
Allstate
American Family Insurance
Berkshire Hathaway
GEICO
The Hartford
Liberty Mutual
MetLife
Nationwide
Progressive Corporation
Prudential
SAFECO
Travelers
USAA
Zurich Financial Services

HISTORICAL FINANCIALS & EMPLOYEES

Mutual company FYE: December 31	Annual Growth	12/92	12/93	12/94	12/95	12/96	12/97	12/98	12/99	12/00	12/01
Assets ($ mil.)	9.2%	—	—	—	—	—	82,296	88,366	80,114	119,602	117,162
Net income ($ mil.)	—	—	—	—	—	—	3,581	996	1,033	408	(5,000)
Income as % of assets	—	—	—	—	—	—	4.4%	1.1%	1.3%	0.3%	—
Employees	1.4%	—	—	—	—	—	—	76,257	79,300	79,300	79,400

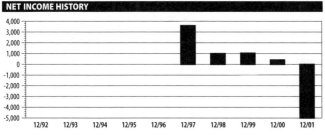

NET INCOME HISTORY

2001 FISCAL YEAR-END
Equity as % of assets: 38.9%
Return on assets: —
Return on equity: —
Long-term debt ($ mil.): —
Sales ($ mil.): 47,900

STATE UNIVERSITY OF NEW YORK

SUNY days are ahead for many New Yorkers seeking higher education. With nearly 390,000 students, the State University of New York (SUNY) is running neck-and-neck with California State University for the title of largest university system in the US. The school maintains 64 campuses around New York State, including 13 university colleges and four university centers, 30 community colleges, five technical colleges, and three health centers. Its institutions offer some 5,100 programs of study, including accounting, journalism, bioengineering, and computer science. The university system hands out some 70,000 diplomas each year, including nearly 9,000 post-graduate degrees.

Most students are residents of New York State (about a third of all New York State high school graduates enroll at SUNY institutions) and pay about $3,400 a year in tuition. SUNY is also top-notch in research, boasting more than $700 million in federal, state, and local grants and contracts. Its laboratories have helped pioneer magnetic resonance imaging, implantable heart pacemakers, and supermarket bar code scanners.

Chancellor Robert King is challenging SUNY administrators and the state to increase levels of funding to help keep the university competitive against other top-flight institutions. New York Governor George Pataki has pledged a $2 billion multi-year construction program for SUNY's facilities.

HISTORY

The State University of New York was organized in 1948, but it traces its roots back to several institutions founded in the 19th century. In 1844 the New York state legislature authorized the creation of the Albany Normal School, which was charged with educating the state's secondary school teachers. Two years later, the University of Buffalo was chartered to provide academic, theological, legal, and medical studies. More normal schools later were founded between 1861 and 1889 in Brockport, Buffalo, Cortland, Fredonia, Geneseo, New Paltz, Oneonta, Oswego, Plattsburgh, and Potsdam.

In the early 1900s the state established several agricultural colleges, including schools in Canton (1907), Alfred (1908), Morrisville (1910), Farmingdale (1912), and Cobleskill (1916). New York also set up several schools as units of Cornell University, including colleges of veterinary medicine (1894), agriculture (1909), home economics (1925), and industrial and labor relations (1945).

After WWII, veterans began to fill US colleges and universities, taking advantage of the GI Bill

to secure a college education. The legislature set up SUNY in 1948 to consolidate 29 institutions under a single board of trustees charged with meeting the growing demand. The board coordinated the state colleges into a single body and established four-year liberal arts colleges, professional and graduate schools, and research centers. During the 1950s and 1960s, new campuses were created at Binghamton, Stony Brook, Old Westbury, Purchase, and Utica/Rome, and enrollment began to take off, jumping from 30,000 in 1955 to 63,000 in 1959.

By the early 1970s SUNY had more than 320,000 students at 72 institutions. But budget constraints later that decade led to higher tuition, reduced enrollment goals, and employment cutbacks. In 1975 eight New York City community colleges were transferred to City University. SUNY's enrollment began growing again during the 1980s, reaching more than 400,000 by 1990. Early in the decade, the institution began implementing SUNY 2000, a plan that called for increasing access to education and diversifying undergraduate studies. Following his election in 1994, Governor George Pataki proposed more than $550 million in cuts to the SUNY system.

In 1997 John Ryan replaced Thomas Bartlett as chancellor. The following year SUNY became the exclusive sponsor of The College Channel, a guide to colleges and college life aimed at high school juniors and seniors and broadcast by PRIMEDIA's Channel One. In 1999 the governor's budget director, Robert King, was named chancellor to replace the retiring Bartlett. In 2000 SUNY faced rising budget shortfalls at its teaching hospitals, in part because money was being siphoned off to other areas. That year King announced a set of initiatives to raise an additional $1.5 billion in federal research grants and $1 billion in private donations over five years.

In 2001 the university announced its intention to keep tuition at $3,400 a year for the seventh year in a row.

OFFICERS

Chancellor: Robert L. King
Provost and Vice Chancellor Academic Affairs: Peter D. Salins
Vice Chancellor and COO: Richard P. Miller Jr.
Vice Chancellor and CFO: David Richter
Vice Chancellor Community Colleges: Robert T. Brown
Vice Chancellor Business and Industry Relations: R. Wayne Diesel
Vice Chancellor Legal Affairs and University Counsel: D. Andrew Edwards Jr.
Vice Chancellor and Secretary; President, Research Foundation of the State University of New York: John J. O'Connor

University Controller: Patrick J. Wiater
University Auditor: C. Kevin O'Donoghue
Assistant Vice Chancellor for Employee Relations:
  Joyce Villa
Director of Employee Relations: Raymond Haines
Associate Director of Employee Relations:
  Pam Williams
Assistant Director of Employee Relations:
  Liesl Zwicklbauer
Auditors: KPMG LLP

LOCATIONS

HQ: State University Plaza, Albany, NY 12246
Phone: 518-443-5500   Fax: 518-443-5387
Web: www.suny.edu

PRODUCTS/OPERATIONS

Selected Institutions
Colleges of Technology
  Alfred
  Canton
  Cobleskill
  Delhi
  Morrisville
  University Colleges of Technology
Health Science Centers
  Brooklyn
  Syracuse
Statutory Colleges
  College of Agriculture and Life Sciences at Cornell
    University
  College of Ceramics at Alfred University
  College of Human Ecology at Cornell University
  College of Veterinary Medicine at Cornell University
  School of Industrial and Labor Relations at Cornell
    University
University Centers
  Albany
  Binghamton
  Buffalo
  Stony Brook
University Colleges
  Brockport
  Buffalo State
  Cortland
  Empire State
  Fredonia
  Geneseo
  New Paltz
  Old Westbury
  Oneonta
  Oswego
  Plattsburgh
  Potsdam
  Purchase

HISTORICAL FINANCIALS & EMPLOYEES

School FYE: June 30	Annual Growth	6/92	6/93	6/94	6/95	6/96	6/97	6/98	6/99	6/00	6/01
Sales ($ mil.)	4.8%	3,407	3,692	4,018	4,167	4,136	4,244	4,564	4,628	5,076	5,211
Employees	4.6%	47,514	47,574	48,194	52,000	55,000	56,135	65,000	65,000	—	—

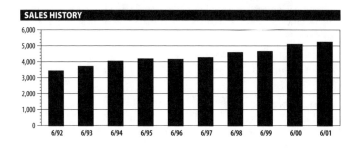

SALES HISTORY

STATER BROS. HOLDINGS INC.

Stater Bros. Markets has no shortage of major league rivals, operating in the same Southern California markets as Ralphs, Albertson's, and Safeway. Stater Bros. Holdings has about 155 Stater Bros. Markets, mostly in Riverside and San Bernardino counties. It also has stores in Kern, Los Angeles, Orange, and San Diego counties. In 1999 the company converted about 45 outlets it bought from Albertson's to the Stater Bros. Market name. It also has a 50% stake in milk and juice processor Santee Dairies. Stater Bros. is owned by La Cadena Investments, a general partnership consisting of Stater Bros. CEO Jack Brown and other company executives.

Competition from the grocery giants, and the purchase of the stores from Albertson's in 1999, has put a strain on the company's profits. To distinguish itself from rivals, the chain refuses to offer promotional games and frequent shopper cards, boasting everyday low prices instead. Kroger owns the other 50% of Santee Dairies; Santee serves Stater Bros. Markets and Ralph's, as well as independent grocers.

Stater Bros. Holdings is the largest privately held supermarket chain in Southern California.

HISTORY

In 1936, at age 23, Cleo Stater and his twin brother, Leo, mortgaged a Chevrolet to make a down payment on a modest grocery store where Cleo had been working for five years in their hometown of Yucaipa, California. Later that year the brothers bought their second grocery in the nearby community of Redlands. Their younger brother, Lavoy, soon joined them to help build the company. In 1938 the brothers opened the first Stater Bros. market in Colton; by 1939 they had a chain of four stores.

The small, family-owned grocery chain continued to grow. In 1948 Stater Bros. opened its first supermarket (which was several times larger than its other stores and had its own parking lot) in Riverside. By 1950 the company had 12 stores.

Stater Bros. consolidated its offices and warehouse in Colton in the early 1960s and continued its expansion into nearby communities. By 1964 it operated 27 supermarkets in 18 cities in Los Angeles, Orange, Riverside, and San Bernardino counties. In 1968 the brothers sold the company's 35 stores to Long Beach, California-based petroleum services provider Petrolane for $33 million. Lavoy succeeded Cleo as president.

As a division of Petrolane, Stater Bros. kept growing. In the 1970s the company introduced a new store design that expanded sales area but required less land and a smaller building. The

number of stores more than doubled (to over 80) between 1968 and 1979, when Lavoy retired.

Ron Burkle, VP of Administration for Petrolane, and his father, Joe, president of Stater Bros., attempted to buy the chain for $100 million in 1981. Infuriated by the low bid, Petrolane fired Ron and demoted his father, who left that year. Jack Brown was named president in his place. Petrolane sold the chain in 1983 to La Cadena Investments, a private company that included Brown and other top Stater Bros. executives.

Leo died in 1985. That year the company went public to reduce debt from the 1983 LBO and to provide funds for an extensive expansion plan. It also incorporated as Stater Bros. Inc. In 1986 a proxy fight for control of the company erupted between Brown's La Cadena group and chairman Bernard Garrett, who owned about 41% of Stater Bros. Brown had been suspended as president and CEO (Joe Burkle returned in his place), but Los Angeles-based investment firm Craig Corp. bought Garrett's stake and Brown returned; he was later elected chairman. That year Stater Bros. also became a co-owner in Santee Dairies with Hughes Markets.

The next year Craig and Stater Bros. executives took the grocery chain private again. Burkle bought a 9% stake in Craig in 1989 through Yucaipa Capital Partners. Also in 1987 Craig reduced its stake in Stater Bros., transferring some stock to La Cadena. Stater Bros. Holdings was created as a parent company for the grocery chain.

Stater Bros. expressed an interest in buying rival Alpha Beta stores when they were put up for sale, but Yucaipa Companies bought them in 1991. Craig considered selling its stake in Stater Bros. in 1992; it finally sold its half of the company to La Cadena in 1996.

In 1999 Stater Bros. acquired 33 Albertson's and 10 Lucky stores, as well as one store site. (The FTC required Albertson's to sell the stores in order to acquire American Stores, Lucky's parent.) The acquisition and the early retirement of debt resulted in its 1999 losses. In September 2001 company co-founder Cleo Stater died.

In early 2002 the company announced a partnership with Krispy Kreme Doughnuts to offer the treats at selected Stater Bros. supermarkets.

OFFICERS

Chairman, President, and CEO: Jack H. Brown, age 62, $1,178,500 pay
Vice Chairman: Thomas W. Field Jr., age 68
EVP and COO: Donald I. Baker, age 60, $412,000 pay
SVP and CFO: Phillip J. Smith, age 54, $187,000 pay
Group SVP Administration: A. Gayle Paden, age 65, $338,000 pay
Group SVP Development: H. Harrison Lightfoot, age 63, $334,000 pay
Group SVP Marketing: Dennis McIntyre
Group SVP Retail: Jim Lee
VP Construction and Maintenance: Scott Limbacher
VP Human Resources: Kathy Finazzo
Secretary: Bruce D. Varner, age 65
Property Development Manager: Mike McCasland
Auditors: Ernst & Young LLP

LOCATIONS

HQ: 21700 Barton Rd., Colton, CA 92324
Phone: 909-783-5000   **Fax:** 909-783-3930
Web: www.staterbrosmarkets.org

Stater Bros. Holdings operates one distribution center and about 155 supermarkets in Southern California.

2001 Stores

	No.
San Bernardino County	46
Riverside County	40
Orange County	30
Los Angeles County	27
San Diego County	10
Kern County	2
Total	**155**

PRODUCTS/OPERATIONS

Selected Departments and Products
Bakery
Dairy products
Delicatessen
Fresh produce
Frozen foods
General merchandise
Health & beauty aids
Liquor
Meats
Seafood

COMPETITORS

Albertson's
Arden Group
Costco Wholesale
Longs
Ralphs
Safeway
Smart & Final
Trader Joe's Co
Walgreen
Wal-Mart
Whole Foods

HISTORICAL FINANCIALS & EMPLOYEES

Private FYE: September 30	Annual Growth	9/92	9/93	9/94	9/95	9/96	9/97	9/98	9/99	9/00	9/01
Sales ($ mil.)	5.9%	1,538	1,526	1,540	1,580	1,705	1,718	1,726	1,830	2,418	2,574
Net income ($ mil.)	0.1%	8	6	9	7	16	13	3	(9)	(6)	8
Income as % of sales	—	0.5%	0.4%	0.6%	0.4%	0.9%	0.8%	0.1%	—	—	0.3%
Employees	4.5%	8,500	9,800	10,000	9,800	8,900	8,900	8,700	12,700	12,100	12,600

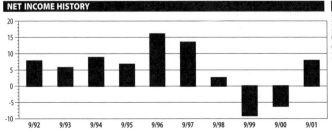

NET INCOME HISTORY

2001 FISCAL YEAR-END
Debt ratio: 100.0%
Return on equity: —
Cash ($ mil.): 102
Current ratio: 1.64
Long-term debt ($ mil.): 467

SUNKIST GROWERS, INC.

Perhaps the US enterprise least susceptible to an outbreak of scurvy, Sunkist Growers is a cooperative owned by 6,500 citrus farmers in California and Arizona. Sunkist markets fresh oranges, lemons, grapefruit, and tangerines in the US and overseas. Fruit that doesn't meet fresh market standards is turned into juices, oils, and peels for use in food products. The Sunkist brand is one of the most recognized names in the US; through licensing agreements the name also appears worldwide on dozens of beverages and other products, from vitamins to fruit rolls.

Sunkist is one of the 10 largest marketing cooperatives in America and the largest cooperative in the world's fruit and vegetable industry. Most of its sales come from US customers; Sunkist's biggest export customers are Hong Kong, Japan, and South Korea. Sunkist has licensing agreements with companies in more than 55 countries.

HISTORY

Sunkist Growers was founded in the early 1890s as the Pachappa Orange Growers, a group of California citrus farmers determined to control the sale of their fruit. Success attracted new members, and in 1893 the Southern California Fruit Exchange was born. The name "Sunkissed" was coined by an ad copywriter in 1908, and it was soon reworked into "Sunkist" and registered as a trademark, becoming the first brand name for a fresh produce item. Eventually the co-op renamed itself after its popular brand: It became Sunkist Growers in 1952. Sunkist began licensing its trademark to other companies in the early 1950s.

As early as 1916, efforts to increase citrus consumption included designing and marketing glass citrus juicers and encouraging homemakers to "Drink an Orange." The co-op also promoted the practice of putting lemon slices in tea or water and funded early research on the health benefits of vitamins (vitamin C in particular). In 1925 tissue wrappers gave way to stamping the Sunkist name directly on each piece of fruit.

Although Sunkist pioneered bottled orange juice in 1933, its juice marketing efforts were never as successful as those of its Florida competitors. Florida oranges are drippy and dowdy and thus better suited for juicing. Capitalizing on this aspect, Florida growers dominated the market for fresh and frozen juice.

In 1937 Congress created a system of citrus shipment quotas and limits (known as "marketing orders") that ultimately proved most beneficial to large citrus cooperatives. By the early 1990s the marketing order system was under political attack, and in 1992 the Justice Department filed civil prosecution against Sunkist, alleging that the co-op had reaped unfair extra profits by surpassing its lemon shipment limits. In 1994, after much legal wrangling, the quotas were abolished and the Justice Department dropped its case against Sunkist.

Inconveniently warm weather and increasing competition from imported citrus marked the harvests of 1996. That year the co-op had trouble maintaining discipline among its members; some undercut Sunkist price levels, while others flooded the market to sell their fruit at the higher early market prices, creating a supply surplus. Also that year the co-op relinquished the marketing of all Sunkist juices in North America to Florida-based Lykes Bros. in a licensing agreement.

The co-op agreed in 1998 to distribute grapefruit from Florida's Tuxedo Fruit, providing Sunkist with winter grapefruit supply and increasing its year-round consumer a-peel. Also in 1998 Russell Hanlin, Sunkist president and CEO since 1978, was succeeded by Vince Lupinacci. Lupinacci, who had held positions with Pepsi and Six Flags, became the first person from outside the citrus business to hold Sunkist's top post.

In 1998 the company sold 90 million cartons of fresh citrus — the greatest volume in its history — despite increased competition from imported Latin American, South African, and Spanish crops, a damaging California freeze, and the ill effects of El Nino. In 1999 production was almost halved due to adverse weather.

Lupinacci resigned in 2000, citing personal and family reasons. Chairman Emeritus James Mast then took the helm as acting president. Although the company grew its market through exports to China in 2000, its profits were squeezed that year by increasing foreign competition, a citrus glut, and lessened demand. In mid-2001 Jeff Gargiulo replaced Mast as Sunkist's president and CEO.

Chairman: Al Williams
President and CEO: Jeffrey D. Gargiulo
VP and COO: Jim Padden
VP of Corporate Relations: Michael Wooton
Corporate Secretary: Linda D. Shepler
Treasurer and Acting CFO: Richard French
Director of Human Resources: John R. McGovern

LOCATIONS

HQ: 14130 Riverside Dr., Sherman Oaks, CA 91423
Phone: 818-986-4800   **Fax:** 818-379-7405
Web: www.sunkist.com

2001 Sales

	$ mil.	% of total
Fresh fruit		
Domestic	574	58
Export	247	25
Fruit products	83	8
Other	89	9
Total	**993**	**100**

COMPETITORS

Alico
Chiquita Brands
Dole
Florida's Natural
Fresh Del Monte Produce
Louis Dreyfus Citrus
Minute Maid
Tropicana Products
UniMark Group
Vitality Beverages

HISTORICAL FINANCIALS & EMPLOYEES

Cooperative FYE: October 31	Annual Growth	10/92	10/93	10/94	10/95	10/96	10/97	10/98	10/99	10/00	10/01
Sales ($ mil.)	(0.4%)	1,029	1,093	1,005	1,096	1,025	1,075	1,069	862	847	993
Net income ($ mil.)	(9.8%)	—	—	—	—	—	—	6	6	(4)	4
Income as % of sales	—	—	—	—	—	—	—	0.5%	0.7%	—	0.4%
Employees	(0.5%)	900	1,200	1,138	1,150	878	813	875	—	—	—

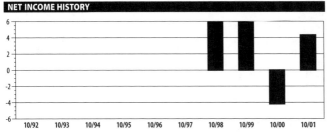

NET INCOME HISTORY

2001 FISCAL YEAR-END

Debt ratio: 35.0%
Return on equity: 7.9%
Cash ($ mil.): 3
Current ratio: 1.37
Long-term debt ($ mil.): 31

TIAA-CREF

It's punishment enough to write the name *once* on a blackboard. Teachers Insurance and Annuity Association - College Retirement Equities Fund (TIAA-CREF) is one of the US's largest, if not longest-named, private pension systems, providing for more than 2 million members of the academic community and for investors outside academia's ivied confines. It also serves some 12,000 institutional investors. TIAA-CREF's core offerings include financial advice, investment information, retirement accounts, pensions, annuities, individual life and disability insurance, tuition financing, and trust services (through savings bank TIAA-CREF Trust). The system also manages its own line of mutual funds.

TIAA-CREF — one of the nation's heftiest institutional investors — has not been afraid to throw its weight around corporate boardrooms. The organization is known for active and choosy investing, and is a vocal critic of extravagant executive compensation packages. With an increasing share of its investment assets overseas, TIAA-CREF is also leading the crusade for global corporate governance standards.

TIAA-CREF exited the group life and disability business, selling its operations to StanCorp Financial Group.

HISTORY

With $15 million, the Carnegie Foundation for the Advancement of Teaching in 1905 founded the Teachers Insurance and Annuity Association (TIAA) in New York City to provide retirement benefits and other forms of financial security to educators. When Carnegie's original endowment was found to be insufficient, another $1 million reorganized the fund into a defined-contribution plan in 1918. TIAA was the first portable pension plan, letting participants change employers without losing benefits and offering a fixed annuity. The fund required infusions of Carnegie cash until 1947.

In 1952 TIAA CEO William Greenough pioneered the variable annuity, based on common stock investments, and created the College Retirement Equities Fund (CREF) to offer it. Designed to supplement TIAA's fixed annuity product, CREF invested participants' premiums in stocks. CREF and TIAA were subject to New York insurance (but not SEC) regulation.

During the 1950s, TIAA led the fight for Social Security benefits for university employees and began offering group total disability coverage (1957) and group life insurance (1958).

In 1971 TIAA-CREF began helping colleges boost investment returns from endowments, then moved into endowment management. It helped found a research center to provide objective investment information in 1972.

For 70 years retirement was the only way members could exit TIAA-CREF. Their only investment choices were stocks through CREF or a one-way transfer into TIAA's annuity accounts based on long-term bond, real estate, and mortgage investments. In the 1980s CREF indexed its funds to the S&P average.

By 1987's stock crash, TIAA-CREF had a million members, many of whom wanted more protection from stock market fluctuations. After the crash, Clifton Wharton (the first African-American to head a major US financial organization) became CEO; the next year CREF added a money market fund, for which the SEC required complete transferability, even outside TIAA-CREF. Now open to competition, TIAA-CREF became more flexible, adding investment options and long-term-care plans.

John Biggs became CEO in 1993. After the 1994 bond crash, TIAA-CREF began educating members on the ABCs of retirement investing, hoping to persuade them not to switch to flashy short-term investments and not to panic during such cyclical events as the crash.

In 1996 it went international, buying interests in UK commercial and mixed-use property. TIAA-CREF filed for SEC approval of more mutual funds in 1997. Although Federal tax legislation took away TIAA-CREF's tax-exempt status in 1997, the change was made without decreasing annuity incomes for the year.

The status change let TIAA-CREF offer no-load mutual funds to the public in 1998. A trust company and financial planning services were added; all new products were sold at cost, with TIAA-CREF waiving fees. TIAA-CREF in 1998 became the first pension fund to force out an entire board of directors (that of sputtering cafeteria firm Furr's/Bishop's). Also that year TIAA-CREF's crusade to curb "dead hand" poison pills (an antitakeover defense measure) found favor with the shareholders of Bergen Brunswig (now AmerisourceBergen), Lubrizol, and Mylan Laboratories. Late in 1999, the organization sold half of its stake in the Mall of America to Simon Property Group, keeping 27%. The next year it made a grab for more market share when it launched five new mutual funds.

Biggs, who spearheaded TIAA-CREF's efforts to fight corporate malfeasance, retired at the end of his term in 2003; Herbert Allison took over.

Chairman, President, and CEO: Herbert M. Allison, age 59
Vice Chairman and Chief Investment Officer:
Martin L. Leibowitz
EVP and General Counsel: Charles H. Stamm
EVP and Chief Actuary: Harry I. Klaristenfeld
EVP, Finance and Planning: Richard L. Gibbs
EVP, Human Resources: Matina S. Horner, age 63
EVP, Consulting Services: David A. Shunk
EVP and President, Retirement Services: James A. Wolf
EVP, External Affairs: Don Harrell
EVP and President, Shared Services: Mary Ann Werner
EVP, CREF Investments: Scott C. Evans
EVP, TIAA Investments: John A. Somers
EVP, Information Technology: C. Victoria Apter
EVP, Financial Operations and Facilities: Ira J. Hoch
EVP, Retirement Services Administration: Frances Nolan
EVP, Marketing: Deanne J. Shallcross
Auditors: Deloitte & Touche LLP

LOCATIONS

HQ: Teachers Insurance and Annuity Association -
College Retirement Equities Fund
730 3rd Ave., New York, NY 10017
Phone: 212-490-9000   **Fax:** 212-916-4840
Web: www.tiaa-cref.com

Offices
Atlanta
Bloomington, MN (Minneapolis-St. Paul)
Boston
Chicago
Denver
Dublin, OH (Columbus)
Indianapolis
Kirkland, WA (Seattle)
Las Colinas, TX (Dallas)
Morrisville, NC (Raleigh-Durham)
New York
Newport Beach, CA (Los Angeles)
Philadelphia
Pittsburgh
Rochester, NY
San Francisco
Southfield, MI (Detroit)
Tampa
Washington, DC

PRODUCTS/OPERATIONS

2001 Sales

	$ mil.	% of total
Premiums & other considerations	11,422	49
Net investment income	11,140	47
Other	849	4
Total	**23,411**	**100**

Selected Subsidiaries and Units
Teachers Personal Investors Services, Inc. (mutual fund
management)
TIAA-CREF Individual & Institutional Services, Inc.
(broker-dealer)
TIAA-CREF Institute (think tank)
TIAA-CREF Life Insurance Company (insurance and
annuities)
TIAA-CREF Trust Company, FSB (trust services)
TIAA-CREF Tuition Financing, Inc. (state tuition savings
program management)

Selected Mutual Funds
Bond *Plus* Fund
Equity Index Fund
Growth & Income Fund
Growth Equity Fund
High-Yield Bond Fund
International Equity Fund
Managed Allocation Fund
Money Market Fund
Short-Term Bond Fund
Social Choice Equity Fund

COMPETITORS

Aetna	CIGNA	New York Life
AIG	Citigroup	Northwestern
American	FMR	Mutual
General	John Hancock	Principal
AXA Financial	Financial	Financial
Bank of New	Services	Prudential
York	J.P. Morgan	T. Rowe Price
Berkshire	Chase	U.S. Global
Hathaway	MassMutual	Investors
CalPERS	Merrill Lynch	USAA
Charles Schwab	MetLife	Vanguard Group

HISTORICAL FINANCIALS & EMPLOYEES

Not-for-profit FYE: December 31	Annual Growth	12/92	12/93	12/94	12/95	12/96	12/97	12/98	12/99	12/00	12/01
Sales ($ mil.)	(5.5%)	—	—	—	—	31,024	41,437	35,054	38,665	37,273	23,411
Employees	8.3%	—	—	—	—	4,490	4,920	5,000	5,000	5,000	6,700

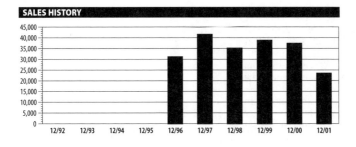

SALES HISTORY

TENNESSEE VALLEY AUTHORITY

Although the Tennessee Valley Authority (TVA) may not be an expert on Tennessee attractions like Dollywood and the Grand Ole Opry, it is an authority on power generation. TVA is the largest government-owned power producer in the US, with nearly 30,400 MW of generating capacity. The federal corporation transmits electricity to 158 local distribution utilities, which in turn serve 8.3 million consumers. It also provides power for industrial facilities and government agencies, and it manages the Tennessee River system for power production and flood control.

TVA is the sole power wholesaler, by law, in an 80,000-sq.-mi. territory that includes most of Tennessee and portions of six neighboring states (Alabama, Georgia, Kentucky, Mississippi, North Carolina, and Virginia). Generating and transmitting power to local distribution utilities accounts for about 84% of TVA's sales. Established by Congress during the Depression as part of the New Deal, TVA began as an effort to spur economic development in its area.

TVA's rates are among the nation's lowest, which would-be competitors attribute to its exemption from federal and state income and property taxes. To prepare for deregulation, the authority is trying to reduce its $25 billion debt.

HISTORY

In 1924 the Army Corps of Engineers finished building the Wilson Dam on the Tennessee River in Alabama to provide power for two WWI-era nitrate plants. With the war over, the question of what to do with the plants became a political football.

An act of Congress created the Tennessee Valley Authority (TVA) in 1933 to manage the plants and Tennessee Valley waterways. New Dealers saw TVA as a way to revitalize the local economy through improved navigation and power generation. Power companies claimed the agency was unconstitutional, but by 1939, when a federal court ruled against them, TVA had five operating hydroelectric plants and five under construction.

During the 1940s TVA supplied power for the war effort, including the Manhattan Project in Tennessee. During the postwar boom between 1945 and 1950, power usage in the Tennessee Valley nearly doubled. Despite adding dams, TVA couldn't keep up with demand, so in 1949 it began building a coal-fired unit. Because coal-fired plants weren't part of TVA's original mission, in 1955 a Congressional panel recommended the authority be dissolved.

Though TVA survived, its funding was cut. In 1959 it was allowed to sell bonds, but it no longer received direct government appropriations for power operations. In addition, it had to pay back the government for past appropriations.

TVA began to build the first unit of an ambitious 17-plant nuclear power program in Alabama in 1967. However, skyrocketing costs forced it to raise rates and cut maintenance on its coal-fired plants, which led to breakdowns. In 1985 five reactors had to be shut down because of safety concerns.

In 1988 former auto industry executive Marvin Runyon was appointed chairman of the agency. "Carvin' Marvin" cut management, sold three airplanes, and got rid of peripheral businesses, saving $400 million a year. In 1992 Runyon left to go to the postal service and was replaced by Craven Crowell, who began preparing TVA for competition in the retail power market.

TVA ended its nuclear construction program in 1996 after bringing two nuclear units on line within three months, a first for a US utility. The next year it raised rates for the first time in 10 years, planning to reduce its debt. In response to a lawsuit filed by neighboring utilities, it agreed to stop "laundering" power by using third parties to sell outside the agency's legally authorized area.

In 1999 the authority finished installing almost $2 billion in scrubbers and other equipment at its coal-fired plants so that it could buy Kentucky coal along with cleaner Wyoming coal. That year, however, the EPA charged TVA with violating the Clean Air Act by making major overhauls on some of its older coal-fired plants without getting permits or installing updated pollution-control equipment. It ordered TVA to bring most of its coal-fired plants into compliance with more current pollution standards. The next year TVA contested the order in court, stating compliance would jack up electricity rates.

Also in 2000 TVA agreed to produce tritium, a radioactive gas that boosts the power of nuclear weapons, for the US Department of Energy (a first for a civilian nuclear power generator). TVA was also fined by the US Nuclear Regulatory Commission for laying off a nuclear plant whistleblower. Crowell resigned in 2001, and Glenn McCullough Jr. was named chairman.

OFFICERS

Chairman: Glenn L. McCullough Jr.
President and COO: Oswald Zeringue
EVP and General Counsel: Maureen Dunn
EVP Administration: D. LaAnne Stribley
EVP Communications and Government Relations:
Ellen Robinson
EVP Customer Service and Marketing: Mark O. Medford
EVP Financial Services and CFO: David N. Smith
EVP Fossil Power Group: Joseph R. Bynum
EVP Human Resources: John E. Long Jr.
EVP River System Operations and Environment:
Kathryn J. Jackson
EVP Transmission and Power Supply: Terry Boston
EVP TVA Nuclear and Chief Nuclear Officer:
John A. Scalice
SVP Information Services: Diane Bunch
SVP Performance Initiatives: Ron Loving
SVP Power Resources and Operations Planning:
Gregory M. Vincent
VP Bulk Power Trading: Amy T. Bums
VP Economic Development: Katie Rawls
VP Investor Relations: Sylvia H. Caldwell
Auditors: PricewaterhouseCoopers LLP

LOCATIONS

HQ: 400 W. Summit Hill Dr., Knoxville, TN 37902
Phone: 865-632-2101   **Fax:** 865-632-2270
Web: www.tva.gov

The Tennessee Valley Authority's service area covers
most of Tennessee and parts of Alabama, Georgia,
Kentucky, Mississippi, North Carolina, and Virginia.

PRODUCTS/OPERATIONS

2001 Sales

	$ mil.	% of total
Electricity		
Municipalities & cooperatives	5,908	84
Industries	659	9
Federal agencies & other	330	5
Other	102	2
Total	**6,999**	**100**

HISTORICAL FINANCIALS & EMPLOYEES

Government-owned FYE: September 30	Annual Growth	9/92	9/93	9/94	9/95	9/96	9/97	9/98	9/99	9/00	9/01
Sales ($ mil.)	3.7%	5,065	5,276	5,401	5,375	5,693	5,552	6,729	6,595	6,762	6,999
Net income ($ mil.)	—	120	311	151	10	61	8	233	119	24	(3,311)
Income as % of sales	—	2.4%	5.9%	2.8%	0.2%	1.1%	0.1%	3.5%	1.8%	0.4%	—
Employees	(4.4%)	19,493	18,974	19,027	16,559	16,021	14,500	13,818	13,322	13,400	13,000

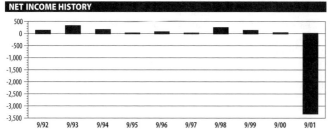

NET INCOME HISTORY

2001 FISCAL YEAR-END

Debt ratio: 93.2%
Return on equity: —
Cash ($ mil.): 343
Current ratio: 0.24
Long-term debt ($ mil.): 19,851

TEXAS A&M UNIVERSITY

Everything is bigger in Texas, even its universities. With more than 90,000 students at nine institutions, The Texas A&M University System ranks among the largest in the US. Its flagship school at College Station is well-known not only for its programs in engineering and agriculture, but also for its long-held traditions and school spirit. Other system institutions include Tarleton State University and Prairie View A&M. The system also runs eight state extension agencies and a health sciences center. Texas A&M was founded in 1876 as the Agricultural and Mechanical College of Texas. The A&M system was formed in 1948. It is funded in part by a $7.7 billion state endowment (shared with the University of Texas).

Texas A&M in College Station is the largest campus in the system, with an enrollment exceeding 44,000. A&M's schools are well regarded for business administration and veterinary medicine as well. The system also operates eight state agricultural and engineering extension agencies and a health sciences center (including Baylor College of Dentistry in Dallas).

In the wake of a bonfire collapse that took the lives of 12 students in 1999, A&M has been charged by outsiders with trying to conceal the university's involvement in the accident. Still others have called on A&M to loosen some of its traditions. However, the school, students, and alumni have all stood fast against the tide. A&M has also embarked on a mission to renovate its facilities, announcing a $2 billion capital spending campaign in 2000.

HISTORY

The Texas Constitution of 1876 created an agricultural and mechanical college and stated that "separate schools shall be provided for the white and colored children, and impartial provisions shall be made for both." The white school, the Agricultural and Mechanical College of Texas (later Texas A&M), began instruction that year. Texas A&M was a men's school at first, and membership in its Corps of Cadets was mandatory. The Agricultural and Mechanical College of Texas for Colored Youth (later Prairie View A&M) opened in 1878.

To help fund the agricultural colleges and The University of Texas, the Legislature established the Permanent University Fund in 1876 to hold more than 1 million acres of land in West Texas as an endowment. An additional 1 million acres was added in 1883. The Santa Rita well on the university land struck oil in 1923 and money flowed into the Permanent University Fund's coffers. Under the provisions of the constitution, The University of Texas got two-thirds of the income, and A&M got the rest.

In 1948 The Texas A&M College System was established to oversee Texas A&M, Prairie View A&M, Tarleton State, and Arlington State (which left the system in 1965 and is now The University of Texas at Arlington). By 1963 enrollment system-wide had reached 8,000. That year the system changed its name to The Texas A&M University System, the same year that Texas A&M went coed.

By the mid-1980s enrollment had surpassed 35,000 students. The system grew quickly in 1989 when it added Texas A&I University (now Texas A&M University-Kingsville), Corpus Christi State (now Texas A&M University-Corpus Christi), and Laredo State University (now Texas A&M International). West Texas State College in Canyon joined the system in 1990 and became West Texas A&M University in 1993.

The 91-year-old Baylor College of Dentistry (in Dallas) and East Texas State University, well-known for training future teachers, joined the A&M system in 1996 (East Texas State was divided into Texas A&M University-Commerce and Texas A&M-Texarkana). In 1997 the system opened the first portion of the $82 million George Bush Presidential Library and Museum. In early 1998 the system signed an alliance with the private South Texas College of Law in Houston, which was opposed by the Texas Higher Education Coordinating Board. (In 1999 a judge ruled that the two schools had to discontinue their affiliation.) That year Texas Instruments donated $5.1 million to the system (one of the largest donations in the institution's history) for the creation of an analog technology program. Chancellor Barry Thompson announced he would retire in 1999. The system appointed former Army general Howard Graves as the new chancellor.

Tragedy struck the College Station campus later that year when logs being stacked for the annual bonfire celebrating The University of Texas/Texas A&M football game collapsed and killed 12 people. Clinging to the 90-year tradition, many Aggies past and present insisted the bonfire go on in future years. In 2000 Graves announced a $2 billion, five-year capital improvement plan.

In 2002 Robert Gates, former interim dean of A&M's George Bush School of Government and Public Service, was named president of the university system.

Chairman, Board of Regents: Erle Nye, age 65
Vice Chairman: Dionel E. Avilés
President: Robert M. Gates, age 58
Chancellor: Howard D. Graves
Vice Chancellor of Academic and Student Affairs:
Leo Sayavedra
Vice Chancellor of Agriculture and Life Sciences:
Edward A. Hiler
Vice Chancellor of Business Services (CFO):
Tom D. Kale
Vice Chancellor of Governmental Affairs:
Stanton C. Calvert
Vice Chancellor of Health Affairs; President, The Texas A&M University System Health Science Center:
Nancy W. Dickey
Deputy Chancellor: Jerry Gatson
Associate Vice Chancelllor of Human Resources:
Patti Couger
Associate Vice Chancellor of Budgets and Accounting:
B. J. Crain
Associate Vice Chancellor and Treasurer:
Greg Anderson
Associate Vice Chancellor of Planning and Institutional Research: Glenn Dowling
Associate Vice Chancellor of Distance Learning and Information Technology: LeAnn McKinzie
President, Prairie View A&M University:
Charles A. Hines
President, Tarleton State University: Dennis P. McCabe
President, Texas A&M International University:
Ray Keck III
President, Texas A&M University-Commerce:
Keith McFarland
President, Texas A&M University-Corpus Christi:
Robert R. Furgason, age 66
President, Texas A&M University-Kingsville:
Rumaldo Juarez
President, Texas A&M University-Texarkana:
Stephen R. Hensley
President, West Texas A&M University: Russell Long
Chief of Staff: Tami Davis Sayko
Director of Communications: Brenda Sims
Auditors: Texas State Auditor

HQ: The Texas A&M University System
John B. Connally Bldg., 301 Tarrow, 3rd Fl.
College Station, TX 77840
Phone: 979-458-6000   **Fax:** 979-845-2490
Web: tamusystem.tamu.edu

Selected Texas A&M University System Components
Health Science Center
  Baylor College of Dentistry
  College of Medicine
  Graduate School of Biomedical Sciences
  Institute of Biosciences and Technology
  School of Rural Public Health
Universities
  Prairie View A&M University
  Tarleton State University
  Texas A&M International University
  Texas A&M University
  Texas A&M University-Commerce
  Texas A&M University-Corpus Christi
  Texas A&M University-Kingsville
  Texas A&M University-Texarkana
  West Texas A&M University
State agencies
  Texas Agricultural Experiment Station
  Texas Agricultural Extension Service
  Texas Engineering Experiment Station
  Texas Engineering Extension Service
  Texas Forest Service
  Texas Transportation Institute
  Texas Veterinary Medical Diagnostic Laboratory
  Texas Wildlife Damage Management Service

School FYE: August 31	Annual Growth	8/92	8/93	8/94	8/95	8/96	8/97	8/98	8/99	8/00	8/01
Sales ($ mil.)	5.7%	1,172	1,212	1,287	1,299	1,425	1,550	1,695	1,792	2,620	1,928
Employees	4.9%	15,670	15,966	16,367	20,000	22,600	22,800	23,300	23,000	23,000	24,000

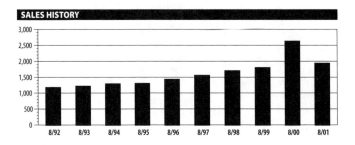

SALES HISTORY

TEXAS LOTTERY COMMISSION

The eyes of Texas are watching the lotto jackpot. The Texas Lottery Commission oversees one of the country's largest state lotteries, which has pumped more than $7 billion into state coffers since it was created in 1991. About 55% of lottery sales are paid out in prize money, while more than 30% goes to the state's Foundation School Fund; the remainder covers administration costs and commissions to retailers. The lottery offers four numbers games (Lotto Texas, Pick 3, Cash 5, and Texas Two Step) and several instant-win games sold through retailers around the state. Retailers such as grocery stores, gas stations, and liquor and convenience stores make a small commission on tickets they sell.

The Lone Star lottery seems to be rebounding, with rising sales after two years of losses. The company is discontinuing its slumping Texas Million lottery game. It also changed its Texas Lotto game so that customers must match six numbers out of 54 numbers instead of 50. The extra four numbers changed the odds of winning from about one in 16 million to one in 26 million.

HISTORY

A state lottery had been an issue in Texas for years before it was discussed in earnest in the mid-1980s. Falling oil and gas revenue had plunged the state into a recession, raising the specter of tax increases. In 1985 the state budget had a shortfall of $1 billion; that figure tripled by 1987. Adding fuel to the fire, the Texas Supreme Court ruled in 1989 that Texas had to change the way it funded public schools to avoid penalizing poor school districts. The ruling forced the state to seek new sources of revenue. In 1991 Governor Ann Richards called a special session of the legislature to deal with the fiscal crisis, and House Bill 54 was passed, creating the state lottery. The measure was approved by 64% of voters.

In May 1992 Richards bought the symbolic first ticket at an Austin feed store. (It was not a winner.) Fourteen hours later Texans had spent nearly $23 million on tickets — breaking the California Lottery's first-day sales record — and had won $10 million in prizes. More than 102 million tickets were sold the first week. GTECH Holdings was awarded a five-year contract that year for lotto operations. Lotto Texas started in November with a winner taking nearly $22 million. By the end of the year, lotto sales in Texas had topped $1 billion. In its first 15 months, it contributed $812 million to the state's coffers.

In March 1994 five winners split a record $77 million jackpot. By that autumn sales from the lottery's beginning had surpassed $5 billion.

In November, a Mansfield, Texas, gas station owner picked up the largest single-winner jackpot, $54 million. By the end of 1994, Texas had the largest state lottery in the US. Cumulative sales topped $8 billion in mid-1995. In its first 37 months of operation, the Texas Lottery contributed $2.5 billion to the state's general fund. Cash 5 debuted that year, and instant ticket vending machines were installed at some sites.

In 1996 lottery director Nora Linares was dismissed following allegations that one of her friends received $30,000 from GTECH as a "hunting consultant." When a GTECH official was convicted in New Jersey of taking kickbacks from a lobbyist, questions were raised concerning payments to GTECH's Texas lobbyist, former Texas Lieutenant Governor Ben Barnes. In 1997 the state canceled its contract with GTECH to operate the lottery through 2002 and reopened bidding; GTECH filed suit to enforce the contract. Executive director Lawrence Littwin later was dismissed by the commission. Littwin sued GTECH, claiming the company had gotten him fired. (The case was settled in 1999.) Linda Cloud, his replacement, reinstated GTECH's contract. That year the Texas legislature voted to increase the amount going to the state and to reduce prize payouts.

Lottery sales fell sharply in 1998, due in part to the reduced prize money. To combat suffering sales, the legislature reversed itself the next year and restored the level of prize payouts. The commission proposed lengthening the odds of winning to create larger jackpots, but public outcry scuttled the plan. In 2000 the commission agreed to change the wording on its scratch tickets after a San Antonio College professor and his students argued that breaking even is not winning. The following year it introduced its first new lottery game in about three years, Texas Two Step, and discontinued Texas Million following slumping sales.

OFFICERS

Chairman: C. Thomas Clowe
Executive Director: Linda Cloud
Deputy Executive Director: Patsy Henry
Director Communications: Keith Elkins
Director Financial Administration: Bart Sanchez
Director Human Resources: Jim Richardson
Director Lottery Operations: Gary Grief
Director Marketing: Toni Smith
Director Security: Mike Pitcock
General Counsel: Kimberly Kiplin

LOCATIONS

HQ: 611 E. Sixth St., Austin, TX 78701
Phone: 512-344-5000   **Fax:** 512-344-5080
Web: www.txlottery.org

PRODUCTS/OPERATIONS

2001 Allocation of Sales

	% of total
Prize money	57
Schools	31
Administrative costs	7
Retailers	5
Total	**100**

Selected Games

Lottery Games
Cash 5
Lotto Texas
Pick 3
Texas Two Step

Scratch-off Games
$25,000 Hearts
$50,000 Fortune
Big Bonus Bucks
Cattle Drive Cash Round Up
Cold Hard Cash
Deal Me In
Deluxe 7-11-21
Double Lucky Number
Prairie Dog Dollars
Ride to Riches
Star of Texas
Texas Trails
Treasure Hunt
Wild Cash
Wizard of Odds

COMPETITORS

Georgia Lottery
Multi-State Lottery
New Mexico Lottery Authority

HISTORICAL FINANCIALS & EMPLOYEES

Government-owned FYE: August 31	Annual Growth	8/92	8/93	8/94	8/95	8/96	8/97	8/98	8/99	8/00	8/01
Sales ($ mil.)	18.9%	594	1,863	2,772	3,052	3,449	3,761	3,106	3,156	2,658	2,826
Net income ($ mil.)	(11.1%)	250	660	932	1,014	1,101	1,421	1,213	(118)	(116)	87
Income as % of sales	—	42.1%	35.4%	33.6%	33.2%	31.9%	37.8%	39.0%	—	—	3.1%
Employees	0.4%	325	325	325	325	325	304	335	300	335	—

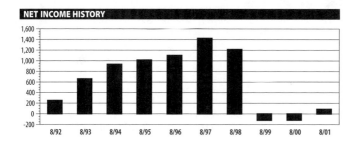

NET INCOME HISTORY

TEXAS PACIFIC GROUP

Yee-hah! Let's round us up some LBOs. Investment firm Texas Pacific Group (TPG) has staked its claim on the buyout frontier with a reputation for roping in companies other firms wouldn't touch with a ten-foot pole. TPG is an active investor, often taking control of the firms in which it invests. It profits not only from the rise in value of its holdings, but also from fund management. Like investor Warren Buffett, Texas Pacific Group invests in brands, buying and resuscitating consumer and *luxe* labels, as well as less-recognizable technology and telecommunication companies.

TPG goes where other firms fear to tread, targeting perennial losers that offer the potential for big payoffs such as US Airways, of which it planned to buy almost 40% as a part of that airline's Chapter 11 reorganization. TPG was upstaged, however, when The Retirement Systems of Alabama stepped in and offered the airline a better deal. With buying opportunities drying up in the US, the firm is looking for bargain prices on European firms. In the volatile Latin American market, however, TPG is curbing the size and pace of its investments.

TPG holdings include Oxford Health Plans, Magellan Health Services, Ducati Motor, J. Crew, Del Monte, Motorola, and ON Semiconductor. Its venture capital affiliate TPG Ventures invests in telecommunications and technology companies. TPG is leading a group of investors, including Bain Capital, in buying US-based Burger King from British firm Diageo. Co-founder and partner David "Bondo" Bonderman is known for turning around Continental Airlines. TPG usually holds onto a company for at least five years, although consistent moneymakers are likely to be kept indefinitely.

Affiliated funds include the Newbridge partnerships (overseas investments) and Colony Capital (real estate). Newbridge, which is also owned by Blum Capital Partners, is poised to take a share of China-based Shenzhen Development Bank in a landmark foreign investment in Mainland China.

HISTORY

The story of Texas Pacific Group is largely the story of David "Bondo" Bonderman. The magna cum laude Harvard law grad — an ardent Democrat and former law professor — built a reputation as an adviser who helped Texas billionaire Robert Bass rack up triple-digit returns.

After a decade with Bass, Bonderman struck out on his own in 1992. James Coulter, recruited to the Bass organization out of Stanford University's business school, went with him. William

Price, a former Bain & Company consultant who advised Bonderman on some of his Bass deals, joined them, as did Richard Schifter (airlines background) and David Stanton (technology expertise).

Bonderman raised eyebrows in 1993 when TPG affiliate Air Partners recapitalized Continental Airlines, then in its second bankruptcy. At the time the airline industry was losing billions, and Bonderman was a little-known quantity. After an extensive restructuring and management shakeup, Bonderman turned Continental into the US's #5 airline, logging record profits for four consecutive quarters.

This type of deal would become Bonderman's modus operandi: Jumping into troubled waters shunned by others, turning the company around, then (often) selling his interest for a profit. Of the head-rolling that frequently occurs after buyouts, Bonderman once said, "Generally speaking, you like to dance with the girl that brung you, and if you can't, sometimes you have to shoot her." In 1994 Bonderman worked his magic with America West Airlines. As with Continental, TPG sold shares in a second offering that made millions.

While the health care industry was debating reform in 1994, Bonderman seized the opportunity to buy a majority share in managed care company PPOM (sold in 1997). In 1995 affiliated fund Colony Capital teamed up with Virgin Group to buy 116 MGM Cinemas and bring the multiplex boom to the UK.

Taking a cue from Robert Mondavi, in 1996 TPG bought Nestlé's debt-ridden Wine World Estates (with help from investment group Silverado Partners), renamed it Beringer Wine Estates Holdings, and took it public in 1997 in an IPO twice as big as Mondavi's.

In 1997 TPG bought clothier J. Crew Group. In an era of falling petroleum prices, the firm gambled on Appalachian energy company Belden & Blake and teamed with Genesis Health Ventures and Cypress Group to buy a stake in ailing elder care operator Multicare. It also bought Del Monte Foods, the world's #1 maker of canned fruits and vegetables (taking it public in 1999).

In 1998 Bonderman and Air Partners sold their interest in Continental to Northwest Airlines. Following its strategy of buying turnarounds, TPG threw lifelines to HMO Oxford Health Plans (1998) and Magellan Health Services (1999). It also built its technology holdings, investing in integrated circuits maker ZiLOG (1998) and leading a management buyout of a Motorola unit that is now ON Semiconductor.

The group jumped into a European investment hotbed, taking a majority stake in Punch Taverns Group, which bought 3,600 pubs from

Allied Domecq. In 1999 TPG bought the Bally fashion house and a stake in Italian scooter maker Piaggio. It failed, however, to turn around Favorite Brands, selling the marshmallow and candy maker to Nabisco. In 2000 TPG said it would buy a stake in French "smart card" maker Gemplus and would sell more than 4 million of its 23 million shares of GlobeSpan Virata at about $100 per share. (TPG's original investment was about $850,000.) In 2002 TPG picked up Gate Gourmet, an airline catering company, from the bankrupt Switzerland-based Swissair Group. It also exited its participation in ZiLOG upon completion of that company's reorganization.

OFFICERS

Managing Partner: David Bonderman, age 59
CFO: Jim O'Brien
Vice President: John Viola
Treasurer: Michelle Reese
General Partner, TPG Ventures for European Investment: Badri Nathan
Human Resources Manager: Jennifer Dixon

LOCATIONS

HQ: 301 Commerce St., Ste. 3300,
   Fort Worth, TX 76102
Phone: 817-871-4000   **Fax:** 817-871-4001

Texas Pacific Group has offices in Fort Worth, Texas; San Francisco; Washington, DC; and London.

PRODUCTS/OPERATIONS

Selected Holdings
America West Airlines
Bally Management (shoes and accessories)
Belden & Blake Corp. (oil and gas)
Del Monte Foods Company
Denbury Resources Inc. (oil and gas)
Ducati Motor SpA
Gate Gourmet (airline catering)
Genesis Health Ventures Inc.
GlobeSpan (semiconductors)
J. Crew Group Inc.
Magellan Health Services Inc.
MEMC Electronic Materials (silicon wafers for
   semiconductors)
Motorola, Inc.
ON Semiconductor
Oxford Health Plans, Inc.
Paradyne Networks, Inc. (broadband accessory devices)
Piaggio
Punch Taverns Ltd.
Ryanair Holdings (airlines)
Zhone Technologies (data networking equipment)

COMPETITORS

AEA Investors
Apollo Advisors
Berkshire Hathaway
Blackstone Group
Carlyle Group
Clayton, Dubilier
Goldman Sachs
Haas Wheat
Heico
Hicks, Muse
Jordan Company
Keystone
KKR
Oaktree Capital
Sevin Rosen Funds
Thomas Lee
Wingate Partners

TOPCO ASSOCIATES LLC

Topco Associates is principally into private-label procurement. Topco uses the combined purchasing clout of more than 50 member companies (mostly supermarket operators) to wring discounts from suppliers. Serving grocery wholesalers, retailers, and food service firms, Topco markets more than 5,000 private-label items, including fresh meat, dairy and bakery goods, and health and beauty aids. Its brands include Food Club, Shurfine, and a line of "Top" labels such as Top Crest. In 2001 Topco Associates, Inc. merged operations with Shurfine International to form Topco Associates LLC. The new entity is 86%-owned by Topco Associates, Inc.

Holding company Shurfine International owns 14% of the merged entity, which also has members in Israel and Japan. But most of Topco's 54 member companies are in the consolidating US market, where many stores have been bought by giant chains.

Topco's cost-saving scheme goes beyond product offerings; its buying power cuts costs for its members' stores. Its warehouse equipment purchase and a financial services program also create savings for members.

In addition to the Shurfine, Food Club, and Top Crest brands, Topco distributes Ultimate Choice and Shurfresh products. Topco also helps members market their own brands.

HISTORY

Food Cooperatives was founded in Wisconsin in 1944 to procure dairy bags and paper products during wartime shortages. A few years later it merged with Top Frost Foods, with which it had some common members. In 1948 the name Topco Associates was adopted (created by combining the word "Top" from Top Frost with the "Co" in Cooperatives). The member companies involved in the merger included Alpha Beta, Big Bear Stores, Brockton Public Market, Fred Meyer, Furr's, Hinky Dinky, Penn Fruit Company, and Star Markets.

Topco initially sold basic commodities to private-label retailers. It added fresh produce in 1958 and expanded its product line further in 1960, moving into general merchandise, health and beauty care items, and store equipment. In 1961, when the company moved its headquarters to Skokie, Illinois, revenues topped the $100 million mark. In the 1960s other leading supermarkets, including Giant Eagle, King Soopers, McCarty-Holman, and Tom Thumb, joined Topco.

Also that decade it came under attack from the Justice Department when it was accused of antitrust activity in granting its members exclusive distribution rights for Topco-branded products.

In 1972 the Supreme Court ruled against Topco. Topco then agreed to sell products under the private labels of its members.

In the late 1970s the company introduced Valu Time, the first nationally marketed line of branded generic products. This concept was then adopted by many US supermarkets. By 1979 Topco surpassed $1 billion in annual revenues.

By the end of the 1980s, Topco's membership had expanded to include Randall's, Riser Foods, Pueblo International, Schnuck Markets, and Smith's Food & Drug Centers. In 1988 it introduced World Classics, a premium line of high-volume, high-margin products promoted as national brands.

During the early 1990s Topco ran through a number of CEOs. In 1990 Robert Seelert replaced 10-year CEO Marcel Lussier. In 1992 John Beggs took over, and the next year Steven Rubow was handed the reins.

The early 1990s also saw rapid growth, with 20 new members bringing the company's total to 46 by 1995. (Its membership later declined in number through acquisition and consolidation.) Topco also expanded internationally, with the membership of Oshawa Group in Canada and the associate membership of SEIYU in Japan in 1995. Also that year the company lured upscale Kings Super Markets away from distributor White Rose.

Topco began offering members utility accounting and natural gas services through Illinova Energy Partners in 1998. In 1999 the company expanded its Top Care line of personal care products, using a variety of packaging designed to resemble several name brands within a single category. CEO Rubow retired in late 1999 and was replaced by Steve Lauer. Topco took aim at consumers who prefer natural foods in 2000, launching the Full Circle line of organically grown items.

In November 2001 Topco combined operations with co-op operator Shurfine International and re-formed as a limited liability company. Topco Associates, Inc. and Shurfine International became holding companies with stakes in Topco Associates LLC. Lauer, CEO of Topco Associates, Inc., was named president and CEO of the new company.

OFFICERS

Chairman: Joseph V. Fisher
Vice Chairman: Steven C. Smith
President, CEO, and Director: Steven K. Lauer
SVP and Chief Procurement Officer: Jeffrey Posner
SVP and President, Wholesale Channel: John Stanhaus
SVP Center Store: Daniel F. Mazur

SVP Cost Containment Programs/Support Services:
Ian Grossman
SVP Member Development: Kenneth H. Guy
SVP Perishables: Russel Wolfe
SVP World Brands: Michael Ricciardi
VP Best Practices and Cost Containment:
David McMurray
VP Dairy: Laird Snelgrove
VP Finance: Deborah Byers
VP Grocery: Dennis Dangerfield
VP Non-Foods: Curt Maki
VP Produce and Floral Operations: Bert Boyd
VP Sales and Marketing, Wholesale Channel:
Mike Nugent
Manager Corporate Communications: Melissa Hilston
Manager Human Resources: Dennis Pieper
Auditors: KPMG LLP

LOCATIONS

HQ: 7711 Gross Point Rd., Skokie, IL 60077
Phone: 847-676-3030   **Fax:** 847-676-4949
Web: www.topco.com

Topco Associates purchases products on behalf of its
members in the US, Israel, Japan, and Puerto Rico.

PRODUCTS/OPERATIONS

Selected Private-Label Brands
Food Club
Full Circle
Pet Club
Price Saver
Savers Choice
Shurfine
Shurfresh
Shurtech
Top Care
Top Crest
Ultimate Choice

Selected Member Companies
Ace Hardware
Acme
Ahold USA
Alex Lee
Associated Grocers, Inc.
Big Y Foods
Blue Square-Israel
Eagle Food Centers
F.A.B.
Fred W. Albrecht Grocery Co.
Fresh Brands (Piggly Wiggly)
Furr's Supermarkets
Giant Eagle
Haggen
Hy-Vee
Kings Super Markets
K-VA-T Food Stores
Meijer
Penn Traffic
Piggly Wiggly Carolina
Pueblo International
Raley's Supermarkets
Schnuck Markets
THE SEIVU
Ukrop's Super Markets
Weis Markets

COMPETITORS

Ahold USA
C&S Wholesale
Kroger
SUPERVALU
SYSCO
Wakefern Food
Wal-Mart

HISTORICAL FINANCIALS & EMPLOYEES

Cooperative FYE: December 31	Annual Growth	3/92	3/93	3/94	3/95	3/96	3/97	3/98	3/99	3/00	*12/01
Sales ($ mil.)	2.1%	2,900	3,000	3,500	3,700	3,900	3,700	3,900	4,000	3,400	3,500
Employees	(3.1%)	400	375	400	375	390	400	365	359	275	284

* Fiscal year change

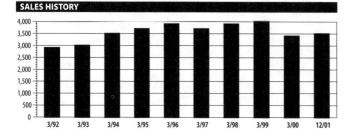

SALES HISTORY

THE TRUMP ORGANIZATION

When it comes to betting on big business, The Donald always pulls out a Trump card. Through the Trump Organization, The Donald can claim several pieces of prime real estate in the Big Apple, including Trump International Hotel and Tower, Trump Tower (26 floors of it, anyway), 40 Wall Street, and the General Motors Building (50%, with Conseco). Trump also owns 42% of publicly traded Trump Hotels & Casino Resorts, and is operator of three Atlantic City casinos (Trump Taj Mahal, Trump Plaza, and Trump Marina); a tribal casino in California (Trump 29); and a riverboat casino in Indiana. Other holdings include a Florida resort and 50% of the Miss USA, Miss Teen USA, and Miss Universe beauty pageants. (CBS owns the rest.)

The Donald continues to excel on the strength of his deal-making prowess; the flamboyant tycoon is renowned for setting up real estate partnerships in which other firms put up most of the cash while he retains most of the control. In the Trump World Tower, for example, he invested $6.5 million, while Korean firm Daewoo pumped in more than $58 million.

Trump also has profited from his famous moniker — which he has trademarked — and his public image: Developers now can pay to co-brand their properties using the Trump name, as long as they meet Trump's super-luxury standard.

Trump dumped his stake in the now-tallest building in New York City. His interest in the Empire State Building leasehold brought in only a paltry $2 million per year.

HISTORY

The third of four children, Donald Trump was the son of a successful builder in Queens and Brooklyn. After graduating from the Wharton School of Finance in 1968, his first job was to turn around a 1,200-unit foreclosed apartment complex in Cincinnati that his father had bought for $6 million with no money down. Managing the Cincinnati job gave Trump a distaste for the nonaffluent; he wanted to get to Manhattan to meet all the right people.

Operating as the Trump Organization, he took options on two Hudson River sites in 1975 for no money down and began lobbying the city to finance his construction of a convention center. The center was built, but not by Trump, who nevertheless got about $800,000 and priceless publicity. He and hotelier Jay Pritzker turned the Commodore Hotel near Grand Central Station into the Grand Hyatt Hotel in 1975. Trump married fashion model Ivana Zelnicek two years later.

In 1981 he built the posh Trump Tower on Fifth Avenue and proceeded to wheel and deal himself into 1980s folklore. In 1983 he joined with Holiday Inn to build the Trump Casino Hotel (now Trump Plaza) in Atlantic City using public-issue bonds (he bought out Holiday Inn's interest in 1986), and he bought the Trump Castle from Hilton in 1985. In 1987 he ended up with the unfinished Taj Mahal in Atlantic City, then the world's largest casino, after a battle with Merv Griffin for Resorts International (which Griffin won). He bought the Plaza Hotel in Manhattan in 1988, and the Eastern air shuttle (renamed the Trump Shuttle) the next year.

As the 1990s dawned, though, Trump's balance sheet was loaded with about $3 billion in debt. At the same time, his marriage to Ivana broke up in a splash of publicity. Trump's 70 creditor banks consolidated and restructured his debt in 1990. He married Marla Maples in 1993. (They divorced in 1998.)

In 1995 Trump formed Trump Hotels & Casino Resorts and took it public. He also paid a token $10 for 40 Wall St. (now home to American Express). The next year he sold his half-interest in the Grand Hyatt Hotel to the Pritzker family and unloaded more than $1.1 billion in debt by selling the Taj Mahal and Trump's Castle to Trump Hotels. That year Trump bought the Miss Universe, Miss USA, and Miss Teen USA beauty pageants.

In 1997 he published *The Art of the Comeback,* a follow-up to *The Art of the Deal* (1987), and started work on Trump Place, a residential development on New York's Upper West Side. He teamed with Conseco in 1998 to buy the famed General Motors Building for $800 million. In 1999 he began building the Trump World Tower — a 90-story residential building near the United Nations complex. Residents of nearby high-rises brought lawsuits in 2000, claiming that the new building would block their view and lower their property value. The court sided with Trump.

The following year Trump and publisher Hollinger International announced plans to transform the former riverfront headquarters of the *Chicago Sun-Times* into a residential and commercial development. Originally planned to be the world's tallest skyscraper, the development would have returned to Chicago the lofty title it lost to the Petronas Towers (Kuala Lumpur, Malaysia). Trump decided to scale back the project in the wake of terrorist attacks on the World Trade Center.

Chairman, President, and CEO: Donald J. Trump, age 55
CFO: Allen Weisselberg
EVP Acquisitions and Finance: Abraham Wallach
VP Finance: John P. Burke, age 53
VP: Norma Foerderer
Corporate Secretary: Rhona Graff-Riccio
General Counsel: Bernard Diamond

LOCATIONS

HQ: 725 Fifth Ave., New York, NY 10022
Phone: 212-832-2000   **Fax:** 212-935-0141
Web: www.trumponline.com

PRODUCTS/OPERATIONS

Trump Hotels & Casino Resorts, Inc.
Trump 29 Casino (tribal casino; Twentynine Palms Reservation, CA)
Trump Indiana (mooring for a 37,000-sq.-ft. yacht casino; Buffington Harbor, IN)
Trump Marina (casino resort; Atlantic City, NJ)
Trump Plaza (hotel/casino; Atlantic City, NJ)
Trump Taj Mahal (hotel/casino; Atlantic City, NJ)

Other Holdings
40 Wall Street
Briar Hall Country Club (Westchester County, NY)
General Motors Building at Trump International Plaza
Mar-A-Lago (private club; Palm Beach, FL)
Miss Teen USA pageant
Miss Universe pageant
Miss USA pageant
Ocean Trails Golf Course (private club; Ranchos Palos Verdes, CA)
Trump International Golf Club (West Palm Beach, FL)
Trump International Hotel and Tower
Trump Palace
Trump Parc
Trump Place
Trump Tower
Trump World Tower

COMPETITORS

Alexander's
Aztar
Harrah's Entertainment
Helmsley
Hyatt
Lefrak Organization
Marriott International
Mashantucket Pequot Gaming
MGM Mirage
Park Place Entertainment
Port Authority of NY & NJ
Ritz-Carlton
Rouse
Tishman Realty
Vornado

HISTORICAL FINANCIALS & EMPLOYEES

Private FYE: December 31	Annual Growth	12/92	12/93	12/94	12/95	12/96	12/97	12/98	12/99	12/00	12/01
Estimated sales ($ mil.)	22.2%	1,400	2,000	2,750	4,000	6,000	6,500	6,800	7,000	8,000	8,500
Employees	2.9%	17,000	15,000	15,000	19,000	19,000	22,000	22,000	—	22,000	22,000

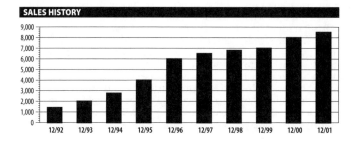

SALES HISTORY

TRUSERV CORPORATION

To survive against home improvement giants such as The Home Depot and Lowe's, TruServ is relying on pure service. Formed by the merger of Cotter & Company (which was the supplier to the True Value chain) and ServiStar Coast to Coast, the troubled cooperative serves some 7,000 retail outlets, including its flagship True Value hardware stores. The company sells building, home improvement, and garden supplies, as well as appliances, housewares, sporting goods, and toys. TruServ also manufactures its own brand of paints and the necessary applicators.

Additionally, the firm operates the Taylor Rental and Grand Rental Station chains and serves the Home & Garden Showplace chain.

The merger of Cotter & Company and Servi-Star Coast to Coast (operator of Coast to Coast and ServiStar hardware stores, most of which converted to the True Value banner) gave members — many of them mom-and-pop outlets — more buying clout to compete against the do-it-yourself mega-retailers, plus retail advice and advertising support.

Amid financial difficulties that include a $50.7 million loss in 2001, TruServ is selling its paint-manufacturing operations and plans to grow its business in the rental and maintenance, repair, and operation (MRO) arenas.

HISTORY

Noting that hardware retailers had begun to form wholesale cooperatives to lower costs, John Cotter, a traveling hardware salesman, and associate Ed Lanctot started pitching the wholesale co-op idea in 1947 to small-town and suburban hardware retailers; by early 1948 they had enrolled 25 merchants for $1,500 each. Cotter became chairman of the new firm, Cotter & Company.

The co-op created the Value & Service (V&S) store trademark in 1951 to emphasize the advantages of an independent hardware store. Acquisitions included the 1963 purchase of Chicago-based wholesaler Hibbard, Spencer, Bartlett, giving Cotter 400 new members and the well-known True Value trademark, which soon replaced V&S signs. Four years later Cotter broadened its focus by buying the General Paint & Chemical Company (Tru-Test paint). The V&S name was revived in 1972 for a five-and-dime store co-op, V&S Variety Stores.

Cotter died in 1989. By that time there were almost 7,000 True Value Stores. Cotter moved into Canada in 1992 by acquiring hardware distributor and store operator Macleod-Stedman (275 outlets).

Juggling merchandise for variety and hardware stores and delivering very small amounts of merchandise to a lukewarm co-op membership did not allow for economies of scale, so in 1995 the company quit its manufacturing operations and its US variety stores (though it still serves variety stores in Canada, operating as C&S Choices), tightened membership requirements, and introduced new services.

Two years later Cotter formed TruServ by merging with hardware wholesaler Servistar Coast to Coast. ServiStar had its origins in the nation's first hardware co-op, American Hardware Supply, which was founded in Pittsburgh in 1910 by M. R. Porter, John Howe, and E. S. Corlett. By 1988, the year it changed its name to Servistar, the co-op topped $1 billion in sales.

Servistar expanded in the upper Midwest and on the West Coast in 1990 when it acquired the assets of the Coast to Coast chain (founded in 1928 as a franchise hardware store in Minneapolis); Servistar brought Coast to Coast out of bankruptcy two years later, making it a co-op. Merging its 1992 acquisition of Taylor Rental Center with its Grand Rental Station stores in 1993 made Servistar the #1 general rental chain. In 1996 it consolidated Coast to Coast's operations into its own and changed its name to Servistar Coast to Coast.

President Don Hoye became CEO of the company in 1999. That year TruServ slashed 1,000 jobs and declared it would convert all its hardware store chains to the True Value banner. But TruServ lost $131 million in 1999 over bookkeeping gaffs, and co-op members received no dividends. Of 2,800 ServiStar dealers, only 1,900 raised the True Value flag. Others either declined to switch or were never offered the change because other True Value stores already shared their market area. In addition, stores began deserting the co-op because of inventory and other problems. In late 2000 the company sold its lumber and building materials business.

As competition continued to increase in 2001, the company was facing falling sales, lawsuits from shareholders, and accusations by retailers of unfair practices intended to pressure them into adopting the cooperative's flagship True Value banner. The company also faced a $200 million loan default. It made cuts in its corporate staff and divested its Canadian interests. In July 2001 Hoye resigned. The company's CFO and COO, Pamela Forbes Lieberman, was named the new CEO in November of that year.

In April 2002 the company reported a net loss of $50.7 million during 2001, which it attributed to restructuring charges, inventory write downs, and finance fees. Also that month the company announced that it had received $200 million in long-term financing. TruServ, under SEC investigation for alleged inventory, accounting, and other internal-control problems, was one of several companies that failed in August 2002 to meet a government requirement to swear by their past financial results.

Chairman: J.W. Blagg
Vice Chairman: James D. Howenstine, age 58
President, CEO, and Director:
  Pamela Forbes Lieberman, age 48, $530,525 pay
SVP and CFO: David A. Shadduck, age 41
SVP and CIO: Neil A. Hastie, age 53, $399,763 pay
SVP, Logistics: Michael D. Rosen, age 49
SVP, Merchandise Supply Chain: William F. Godwin, age 47, $426,057 pay
VP, Human Resources: Amy Mysel
VP, Marketing and Advertising: Carol Cruikshank-Wentworth
VP, MRO: Fred Kirst
VP, Retail Development: Brian Kiernan
General Counsel and Secretary: Robert Ostrov, age 52, $488,535 pay (prior to title change)
Auditors: PricewaterhouseCoopers LLP

LOCATIONS

HQ: 8600 W. Bryn Mawr Ave., Chicago, IL 60631
Phone: 773-695-5000   **Fax:** 773-695-6516
Web: www.truserv.com

TruServ is a hardware store cooperative serving some 7,000 stores in the US.

PRODUCTS/OPERATIONS

2001 Sales

	$ mil.	% of total
Hardware goods	551	21
Farm & garden	514	20
Electrical & plumbing	441	17
Painting & cleaning	379	14
Appliances & housewares	286	11
Sporting goods & toys	149	6
Lumber & building materials	79	3
Other	220	8
Total	**2,619**	**100**

Selected Operations
Grand Rental Station
Home & Garden Showplace
Induserve Supply
Party Central
Taylor Rental
True Value

COMPETITORS

84 Lumber	McCoy
Ace Hardware	Menard
Akzo Nobel	Northern Tool
Benjamin Moore	Réno-Dépôt
Carolina Holdings	Sears
Do it Best	Sherwin-Williams
Fastenal	Sutherland Lumber
Hertz	United Rentals
Home Depot	Valspar
Kmart	Wal-Mart
Lanoga	Wickes
Lowe's	Wolohan Lumber

HISTORICAL FINANCIALS & EMPLOYEES

Cooperative FYE: December 31	Annual Growth	12/92	12/93	12/94	12/95	12/96	12/97	12/98	12/99	12/00	12/01
Sales ($ mil.)	1.2%	2,356	2,421	2,574	2,437	2,442	3,332	4,328	4,502	3,994	2,619
Net income ($ mil.)	—	61	57	60	59	52	43	20	(131)	34	(51)
Income as % of sales	—	2.6%	2.4%	2.3%	2.4%	2.1%	1.3%	0.5%	—	0.9%	—
Employees	(1.1%)	4,400	4,400	4,200	4,186	3,825	5,800	6,500	5,500	4,300	4,000

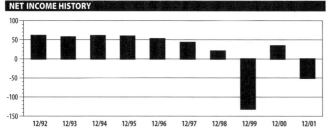

NET INCOME HISTORY

2001 FISCAL YEAR-END
Debt ratio: 74.2%
Return on equity: —
Cash ($ mil.): 89
Current ratio: 1.03
Long-term debt ($ mil.): 236

TY INC.

Take some fabric, shape it like an animal, fill it with plastic pellets, and you too could own luxury hotels. That's the lesson taught by Ty Warner, sole owner of Ty Inc., the firm behind Beanie Babies and their worldwide cult following — popular with kids and adults alike. Since 1993 Ty has produced more than 365 different Beanie Babies with colorful names such as Sequoia the bear (current) and Cheezer the mouse (retired). Other products include Beanie Buddies (bigger versions of traditional Beanies), Ty Classics (stuffed animals), Beanie Boppers (pre-teen dolls), and Punkies (squeezable beanbag pals). Beanie bucks enabled Warner to buy three luxury hotels (in New York and California) in recent years.

Ty's marketing smarts have kept Beanies popular for years rather than for a single holiday season, a la Furby or Tickle Me Elmo. The company limits production so that supply never outstrips demand, keeping only 40 or 50 Beanie Babies in circulation at any one time. Ty's "retirement" of a Beanie can cause its price among collectors to skyrocket from its $5-$7 retail debut to hundreds or even thousands of dollars.

Rather than flood the market with Beanies through the likes of Toys "R" Us and Wal-Mart, Ty sells them only through specialty toy and gift retailers. In addition, the firm doesn't advertise, relying instead on the word of mouth that is rampant in Beanie culture. Books, magazines, newsletters, and Web sites stoke collectors' enthusiasm. This collectors' market — which Ty frowns upon (officially, anyway) — shows signs of fading, however.

HISTORY

Ty Warner, the son of a plush-toy salesman, started his toy career selling stuffed animals to specialty shops for stuffed-bear manufacturer Dakin. Warner left Dakin in 1980, moved to Europe for a few years, and in the mid-1980s returned to the US and founded Ty Inc. The company first designed a line of $20, understuffed Himalayan cats.

Beanie Babies first debuted at a 1993 trade show. In January 1994 the first nine Beanies went on sale — at prices low enough for kids to afford — in Chicago specialty stores. As Warner had learned at Dakin, selling stuffed animals through specialty retailers rather than through mass merchandisers meant bigger profits for suppliers and longer-term popularity. By 1995 there were about 30 different Beanies, and Ty's estimated sales were $25 million.

The popularity of Beanies exploded in 1996, first in the Midwest, then along the East Coast, and then across the US. By midyear, Beanies —

and the public's mania for getting them before they sold out — were receiving widespread media coverage. Ty heightened the frenzy among collectors when it started announcing Beanie retirements on its Web site in 1997.

McDonald's got on the bandwagon in 1997: The fast-food giant issued some 100 million "teenie" Beanie Babies in a Happy Meal promotion. McDonald's ran out of the toys and had to end the promotion early, causing a public relations mess. McDonald's doubled its toy order in 1998 and teamed up with Ty again in 1999 and 2000.

In 1998 Warner paid $10 million for a 7% stake in marketing company Cyrk. In return, Cyrk developed the Beanie Babies Official Club, which turned stores that sell Beanies into "official headquarters" offering club membership kits. Ty introduced its Attic Treasures and Beanie Buddies lines that year.

By spring 1998 Beanies had become a customs issue at the Canadian border, where Ty's limit of one imported Beanie per person into the US resulted in tears and fisticuffs. (Ty later raised the personal limit to 30.) That summer the crowds at Major League Baseball games featuring Beanie giveaways were 26% bigger than average.

Warner bought the Four Seasons hotel in New York City in 1999. He also provided auditing documents and correspondence to *The New York Post* indicating that Ty had 1998 profits of more than $700 million — more than Hasbro and Mattel combined.

After an August 1999 announcement that it would retire the Beanies at the end of the year, the company held a New Year's vote to determine their fate. In the most shocking outcome since *Rocky IV*, the public voted overwhelmingly in favor of continuing the Beanies. Ty introduced its humanoid Beanie Kids line in early 2000. Later that year Warner bought the Four Seasons Biltmore Hotel and the San Ysidro Ranch — the hostelry where JFK and Jackie honeymooned; both are near Santa Barbara, California. In 2001 Ty debuted its pre-teen Beanie Boppers (boy and girl dolls designed for kids from 8 to 12 years of age).

President and CEO: H. Ty Warner
CFO: Michael W. Kanzler
Director of Human Resources: Susan McCrickard

LOCATIONS

HQ: 280 Chestnut Ave., Westmont, IL 60559
Phone: 630-920-1515   **Fax:** 630-920-1980
Web: www.ty.com

PRODUCTS/OPERATIONS

Selected Products
Attic Treasures
Baby Ty
Beanie Babies
Beanie Boppers
Beanie Buddies
Beanie Kids
Pluffies
Punkies
Teenie Beanie Boppers
Ty Classics

COMPETITORS

Applause
Boyds Collection
Enesco Group
Hasbro
Imperial Toy Corp.
Mattel
North American Bear
Pleasant
Russ Berrie
Vermont Teddy Bear

HISTORICAL FINANCIALS & EMPLOYEES

Private FYE: December 31	Annual Growth	12/92	12/93	12/94	12/95	12/96	12/97	12/98	12/99	12/00	12/01
Estimated sales ($ mil.)	76.3%	—	—	—	25	250	400	1,000	1,250	850	750
Employees	53.3%	—	—	—	50	200	500	1,000	1,000	1,000	650

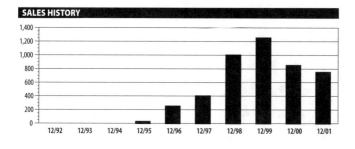

SALES HISTORY

UNIFIED WESTERN GROCERS, INC.

Unified Western Grocers guarantees that food and general merchandise reach about 3,700 mostly independent grocery stores in Arizona, California, Colorado, Hawaii, Nevada, Oregon, Utah, and Washington. The food wholesaler and cooperative supplies a full line of groceries, as well as its own bakery and dairy goods. In addition to name-brand items, its offerings include private labels Gingham, Springfield, and Western Family. The co-op also provides member support services such as store remodeling, financing, and insurance. Unified serves about 670 patrons, many of whom own shares in the company. It was formed in 1999 when Certified Grocers of California merged with United Grocers of Oregon.

Consolidation and the trend toward self-distribution among food retailers has hurt wholesale grocery distributors. The two co-ops merged to match the buying power afforded to large supermarket chains and wholesalers.

Unified is helping independent grocers capture an increasing share of the Hispanic market in places like Los Angeles by supplying ethnic foods and targeted marketing campaigns to its member stores.

Unified has begun its own store format, Apple Markets, to replace older stores. Unified also owns nine SavMax, three Apple Markets, and two Thriftway stores on the West Coast.

HISTORY

Certified Grocers of California evolved from a group of 15 independent Southern California grocers that formed a purchasing cooperative in 1922 to compete against large grocery chains. Certified Grocers of California incorporated in 1925 and issued stock to 50 members.

The co-op merged with a small retailer-owned wholesale company called Co-operative Grocers in 1928. It acquired Walker Brothers Grocery in 1929 and nearly tripled the previous year's sales. By 1938 the co-op had grown to 310 members and 380 stores, and sales passed $10 million.

Certified launched a line of private-label products under the Springfield name in 1947. In the early 1950s it added nonfood items and began processing its own private-label coffee and meat products. The co-op added delicatessen items in 1956. During the 1960s and 1970s, Certified added a meat center, a frozen food and deli warehouse, a produce distribution center, a creamery, a central bakery, and a specialty foods warehouse.

In 1989 the co-op opened several membership warehouse stores called Convenience Clubs. The Save Mart and Boys Markets chains left the fold in 1991. The co-op lost about 30% of its business during the next two years, including the Bel Air and Williams Bros. chains. After disappointing returns, in 1992 Certified sold its warehouse stores, cut staff, and consolidated warehouses.

CFO (and former Atlantic Richfield executive) Al Plamann was appointed CEO in 1994, succeeding Everett Dingwell. In 1996 the co-op began to convert its customers' older retail stores to Apple Markets in Southern California. Revenues began to dip in 1997 as the result of reduced purchases from some supermarkets and the sale in 1996 of one of its subsidiaries, Hawaiian Grocery Stores.

Member chain Stumps converted to the Apple Markets banner in 1998. Faced with a declining customer base, in 1999 Certified merged with United Grocers of Oregon to form Unified Western Grocers.

Dr. R. Norton, F. L. Freeburg, and A. C. Brinckerhoff founded United Grocers of Oregon in 1915 as a way for grocers in Portland to cooperate in purchasing merchandise. By the next year the co-op had 35 members. In the 1950s United formed a trucking department and established a general merchandise division. It also grew rapidly in the 1950s through acquisitions, buying Northwest Grocery Company and the Fridegar Grocery Company. In 1963 United formed its frozen food department when it purchased Raven Creamery.

By 1975 the company's Northwest Grocery Company subsidiary had 14 Cash and Carry warehouses that sold goods to small grocers and restaurants. In 1995 the company bought California food distributor Market Wholesale. Three years later United sold its Cash and Carry warehouse-style stores to Smart & Final.

Upon completion of the merger in 1999, Certified's president and CEO, Plamann, was named to head the new organization. Soon after, Unified consolidated warehouse operations, eliminated duplicate personnel, and combined its private labels. Also in 1999 the company acquired California-based Gourmet Specialties.

The next year it bought the specialty foods business of J. Sosnick and Son, another California company, and Central Sales of Washington state. The company attributed net losses during 2001 to delays in moving the source for northern California specialty merchandise from southern California to northern California, and to the costs of entering the Washington marketplace, among other factors.

President and CEO: Alfred A. Plamann, age 59,
$500,000 pay
EVP Finance and Administration; CFO:
Richard J. Martin, $270,000 pay
EVP, General Counsel, and Secretary:
Robert M. Ling Jr., $245,000 pay
VP and CIO: Gary S. Herman
SVP Procurement: Philip S. Smith, age 51
SVP Distribution: Rodney L. VanBebber, age 46
SVP Retail Support Services: Daniel J. Murphy, age 54,
$184,615 pay
VP and Controller: William O. Cote, age 44
VP and Treasurer: David A. Woodward, age 59
VP Insurance: Joseph A. Ney, age 53
VP Human Resources: Don Giltin
Auditors: Deloitte & Touche LLP

LOCATIONS

HQ: 5200 Sheila St., Commerce, CA 90040
Phone: 323-264-5200   **Fax:** 323-265-4006
Web: www.uwgrocers.com

Unified Western Grocers distributes to about 3,700
member stores in Arizona, California, Colorado, Hawaii,
Nevada, Oregon, Utah, and Washington.

PRODUCTS/OPERATIONS

Selected Co-op Members
Alamo Market
Andronico's Markets
Bales For Food
Berberian Enterprises, Inc.
Bristol Farms Markets, Inc.
Estacada Foods, Inc.
Evergreen Markets, Inc.
Gelson's Markets
Goodwin & Sons, Inc.
Howard's On Scholls
Joe Notrica, Inc.
K. V. Mart Co.
Mar-Val Food Stores, Inc.
Mollie Stone's Markets
Pioneer Super Save, Inc.
Pokerville Select Market
Pro & Son's, Inc.
Sentry Market
Stump's Market, Inc.
Super A Foods, Inc.
Super Center Concepts, Inc.
Sweet Home Thriftway
Tresierras Bros. Corp.
Wright's Foodliner

Selected Support Services
Financing
Information technology
Insurance
Private labels
Real estate development
Security
Store design

COMPETITORS

Albertson's	Safeway
Associated Food	Shurfine International
Associated Grocers	SUPERVALU
Fleming Companies	Topco Associates
Kroger	Wal-Mart
Nash Finch	WinCo Foods

HISTORICAL FINANCIALS & EMPLOYEES

Cooperative FYE: September 30	Annual Growth	9/92	9/93	9/94	9/95	9/96	9/97	9/98	9/99	9/00	9/01
Sales ($ mil.)	2.3%	2,378	2,007	1,874	1,823	1,949	1,927	1,832	1,894	3,067	2,929
Net income ($ mil.)	—	(4)	0	(2)	1	2	2	3	3	(11)	(13)
Income as % of sales	—	—	—	—	0.0%	0.1%	0.1%	0.2%	0.1%	—	—
Employees	3.8%	3,000	2,500	2,600	2,470	2,400	2,400	2,200	3,945	4,000	4,200

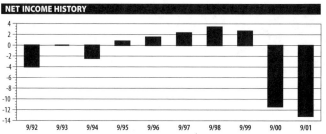

NET INCOME HISTORY

2001 FISCAL YEAR-END
Debt ratio: 76.5%
Return on equity: —
Cash ($ mil.): 15
Current ratio: 0.15
Long-term debt ($ mil.): 288

UNITED STATES POSTAL SERVICE

Through snow, rain, heat, and gloom of night, the United States Postal Service (USPS) delivers more than 45% of the world's mail, more than 200 billion pieces a year. The independent government agency relies on postage and fees to fund operations. Though it has a monopoly on delivering nonurgent letters, the USPS faces competition for services such as package delivery. The US president appoints nine of the 11 members of the board that oversees the USPS. The presidential appointees select the postmaster general, who, along with the deputy postmaster general, is a board member.

A challenge for the agency is the growing use of the Internet, which the USPS expects will cause the volume of "snail mail" to decline. To keep pace, the USPS is launching e-commerce initiatives such as computerized postage. The agency has also tapped into online shopping with its priority mail, merchandise return, and delivery confirmation services. It has formed limited alliances with express delivery companies, including a deal in which FedEx provides air transportation for express mail, priority, and first-class mail shipments (but doesn't deliver the mail).

At the same time, the agency has been hit hard by rising fuel costs. With an eye on its bottom line, the USPS has scaled down its construction program and accelerated the pace of its rate increases. Often-rocky employee relations haven't helped matters.

HISTORY

The second-oldest agency of the US government (after Indian Affairs), the Post Office was created by the Continental Congress in 1775 with Benjamin Franklin as postmaster general. The postal system came to play a vital role in the development of transportation in the US.

At that time, postal workers were riders on muddy paths delivering letters without stamps or envelopes. Letters were delivered only between post offices. Congress approved the first official postal policy in 1792: Rates ranged from six cents for less than 30 miles to 25 cents for more than 450. Letter carriers began delivering mail in cities in 1794.

First based in Philadelphia, in 1800 the Post Office moved to Washington, DC. In 1829 Andrew Jackson elevated the position of postmaster general to cabinet rank — it became a means of rewarding political cronies. Mail contracts subsidized the early development of US railroads. The first adhesive postage stamp appeared in the US in 1847.

Uniform postal rates (not varying with distance) were instituted in 1863, the year free city

delivery began. The start of free rural delivery in 1896 spurred road construction in isolated US areas. Parcel post was launched in 1913, and new mail-order houses such as Montgomery Ward and Sears, Roebuck flourished.

The famous pledge beginning "Neither snow nor rain ..." — not an official motto — was first inscribed at the main New York City post office in 1914. Scheduled airmail service between Washington, DC, and New York City began in 1918, stimulating the development of commercial air service. The ZIP code was introduced in 1963.

As mail volume grew, postal workers became increasingly militant under work stress. (Franklin's pigeonhole sorting method had barely changed.) A work stoppage in the New York City post office in 1970 spread within nine days to 670 post offices, and the US Army was deployed to handle the mail. Later that year the Postal Reorganization Act was passed. The new law established a board of governors to handle postal affairs and choose the postmaster general, who became CEO of an independent agency, the United States Postal Service (USPS). The next year USPS negotiated the first US government collective bargaining labor contract. Express mail service began in 1977; at this time the service stepped up automation efforts.

In 1995 USPS launched Global Package Link, a program to expedite major customers' shipments to Canada, Japan, and the UK. The next year it overhauled rates, cutting prices for larger mailers who prepared their mail for automation and raising prices for small mailers who didn't.

Postmaster General Marvin Runyon — whose six-year tenure took the agency from the red into the black — retired in 1998 and was succeeded by USPS veteran William Henderson. The next year a one-cent hike in the price of first-class postage took effect. (Another one-cent increase took effect in 2001, and the rate rose once again the following year.) In a nod to the Internet, USPS in 1999 contracted with outside vendors to enable customers to buy and print stamps online.

In 2001 USPS formed a strategic alliance with rival FedEx through which FedEx agreed to provide air transportation for USPS mail, in return for the placement of FedEx drop boxes in post offices. Henderson stepped down at the end of May 2001, and EVP Jack Potter was named to replace him. That year several postal workers in a Washington, DC, branch office were exposed to anthrax-tainted letters.

Chairman: Robert F. Rider, age 73
Vice Chairman: S. David Fineman
Postmaster General and CEO: John E. Potter
Deputy Postmaster General: John Nolan
EVP and COO: Patrick R. Donahoe
EVP and CFO: Richard J. Strasser Jr.
SVP and Chief Marketing Officer: Anita J. Bizzotto
SVP and CTO: Charles E. Bravo
SVP Government Relations and Public Policy:
Debrorah K. Willhite
SVP Human Resources: Suzanne Medvidovich
SVP Operations: John A. Rapp
VP and Consumer Advocate: Francia G. Smith
VP and Treasurer: Michele C. Purton
VP and General Counsel: Mary Gibbons
VP Area Operations, Eastern Area: Gary McCurdy
VP Area Operations, Great Lakes Area: Danny Jackson
VP Area Operations, New York Metro Area:
David Solomon
VP Area Operations, Northeast Area: Jon M. Steele
VP Area Operations, Pacific Area: Al Iniguez
VP Area Operations, Southeast Area: William J. Brown
VP Area Operations, Southwest Area: George Lopez
VP Area Operations, Western Area: Craig G. Wade
VP Delivery and Retail: Henry A. Pankey
VP Diversity Development: Benjamin Ocasio
VP Employee Resource Management: Dewitt Harris
VP Engineering: Thomas G. Day
VP Facilities: Rudolph K. Umscheid
VP Finance and Controller: Donna M. Peak
VP Information Technology: Robert L. Otto
VP International Business: James P. Wade
VP Labor Relations: Anthony Vegliante
VP Pricing and Classification: Stephen M. Kearney
VP Product Development: Nicholas F. Barranca
VP Public Affairs and Communications:
Azeezaly S. Jaffer
VP Retail Consumers and Small Business:
Patricia M. Gibert
VP Service and Market Development: John R. Wargo
Secretary: William T. Johnstone
Inspector General: Karla W. Corcoran
Judicial Officer: James A. Cohen
Auditors: Ernst & Young LLP

LOCATIONS

HQ: 475 L'Enfant Plaza SW, Washington, DC 20260
Phone: 202-268-2500   **Fax:** 202-268-4860
Web: www.usps.gov

PRODUCTS/OPERATIONS

2001 Sales

	$ mil.	% of total
First-class mail	35,876	54
Standard mail	15,705	24
Priority mail	4,916	7
Periodicals	2,205	3
Packages	1,994	3
International	1,732	3
Express mail	996	2
Other services	2,495	4
Adjustments	(85)	—
Total	**65,834**	**100**

Selected Services

Certified mail	Merchandise return
Collection-on-delivery	(downloadable return-
(COD)	mail labels)
Delivery confirmation (via	Money orders
Web)	Passport applications
Digital Certificate (proof of	PC Postage
identification for	Periodicals
electronic transactions)	Post office boxes
Express mail	Postage meters
First-class mail	Priority mail
Free mail for the blind and	Registered mail
handicapped	Return receipt
International mail	Special delivery
Mail forwarding	Standard mail

COMPETITORS

Airborne	FedEx
BAX Global	Mail Boxes Etc.
CNF	Roadway
DHL Worldwide Express	UPS

HISTORICAL FINANCIALS & EMPLOYEES

Government-owned FYE: September 30	Annual Growth	9/92	9/93	9/94	9/95	9/96	9/97	9/98	9/99	9/00	9/01
Sales ($ mil.)	4.0%	46,151	47,418	49,252	54,294	56,402	58,216	60,072	62,726	64,540	65,834
Net income ($ mil.)	—	(536)	(1,765)	(914)	1,770	1,567	1,264	550	363	(199)	(1,680)
Income as % of sales	—	—	—	—	3.3%	2.8%	2.2%	0.9%	0.6%	—	—
Employees	1.1%	725,290	691,723	728,944	753,384	760,966	765,174	792,041	800,000	787,538	797,795

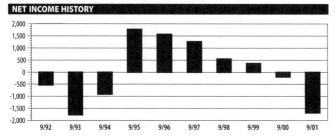

NET INCOME HISTORY

2001 FISCAL YEAR-END

Debt ratio: 100.0%
Return on equity: —
Cash ($ mil.): 1,005
Current ratio: 0.11
Long-term debt ($ mil.): 5,751

UNITED WAY OF AMERICA

United Way of America (UWA) has been described as a mutual fund for charitable causes, and with about 43,000 agencies receiving financial support from UWA's 1,400 local organizations, the epithet seems fitting. The not-for-profit organization focuses on health and human services causes. Its local organizations help to fund a multitude of endeavors, including the American Cancer Society, Big Brothers/Big Sisters, Catholic Charities, Girl Scouts and Boy Scouts, and the Salvation Army. During a fund-raising campaign that began in 2000, UWA raised about $3.9 billion (some 50% from employee contributions and about 23% from corporations). Its administrative expenses average 13% of funds raised.

Each of the local organizations is an independent entity governed by local volunteers, and UWA acts as a national services and training center, supporting the local organizations with services such as national advertising and research. To advance the understanding of its role, UWA has launched an initiative to raise awareness of how it serves local communities.

HISTORY

The first modern Community Chest was created in 1913, laying the foundation for the practice of allocating funds among multiple causes. Five years later, representatives from 12 fundraising organizations met in Chicago and established the American Association for Community Organizations, the predecessor of the present-day United Way. By 1929 more than 350 Community Chests had been established.

Payroll deductions for charitable contributions debuted in 1943. In 1946 the United Way's predecessor organization initiated a cooperative relationship with the American Federation of Labor and the Congress of Industrial Organizations (which merged to become the AFL-CIO in 1955); the two groups agreed to provide services to members of organized labor. (The relationship continues today, with the organizations collaborating on projects such as recruiting members of organized labor to lead health and human services organizations.)

The Uniform Federal Fund-Raising Program was created by order of President Dwight Eisenhower in 1957, enabling federal employees to contribute to charities of their choice. (The program later evolved into the Combined Federal Campaign.) Six years later, Los Angeles became the first city to adopt the United Way name when more than 30 local United Fund organizations and Community Chests merged.

The national organization, which had been operating under the United Community Funds and

Councils (UCFCA) name, adopted the United Way of America (UWA) name in 1970. It established its headquarters in Alexandria, Virginia, in 1971.

Congress made its first grant for emergency food and shelter to the private sector in 1983, and UWA was selected as its fiscal agent. UWA created its Emergency Food and Shelter National Board Program the same year. In 1984 UWA created the Alexis de Tocqueville Society to solicit larger donations from individuals. (It attracted such members as Bill Gates and Walter Annenberg.)

In 1992 William Aramony, UWA's president for more than two decades, resigned after coming under fire for his lavish expenditures. Former Peace Corps head Elaine Chao was tapped to replace him, and in 1995 Aramony was sentenced to seven years in prison for defrauding the organization of about $600,000. Former UWA CFO Thomas Merlo and Stephen Paulachak (former president of a UWA spinoff) were convicted on related charges. After four years spent burnishing UWA's tarnished image, Chao resigned in 1996, and was succeeded in 1997 by Betty Beene, who had headed UWA operations in Houston and New York's tri-state area.

In an effort to stress the manner in which its local organizations benefit their communities, UWA launched a brand-initiative campaign in 1998. The following year UWA's local organization in Santa Clara, California, found itself in serious financial straits when donations began slipping despite its location in the wealthy Silicon Valley. Infoseek (now Walt Disney Internet Group's GO.com) founder Steve Kirsch and Microsoft founder Gates chipped in $1 million and $5 million, respectively, to help keep the organization afloat.

Beene, who drew the ire of some chapters for suggesting a national pledge-processing center and national standards, stepped down in January 2001. Later that year the United Way named Brian Gallagher as its new president and CEO. Also in 2001 UWA began funneling more funds into smaller community projects instead of national charities.

OFFICERS

Chairman: Len Roberts
President and CEO: Brian A. Gallagher
CFO: Vernon McHargue
VP External Communications: Ann Andrews
Director Public Relations: Philip Jones
Legal Counsel: Patti Turner
Human Resources: Evelyn Amador

HQ: 701 N. Fairfax St., Alexandria, VA 22314
Phone: 703-836-7112   **Fax:** 703-683-7840
Web: national.unitedway.org

United Way of America has 1,400 local organizations
across the US.

PRODUCTS/OPERATIONS

Selected Recipients of United Way Funds
American Cancer Society
American Red Cross
Big Brothers/Big Sisters of America
Boy Scouts of America
Catholic Charities USA
Girl Scouts of the United States of America
The Salvation Army
The Urban League

HISTORICAL FINANCIALS

Not-for-profit FYE: December 31	Annual Growth	12/92	12/93	12/94	12/95	12/96	12/97	12/98	12/99	12/00	12/01
Sales ($ mil.)	3.1%	3,040	3,050	3,078	3,148	3,250	3,400	3,580	3,770	3,910	4,000

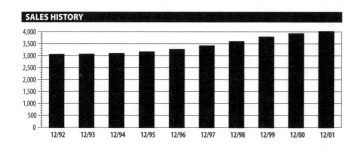

SALES HISTORY

UNIVERSITY OF CALIFORNIA

Along with celebrities and smog, California boasts one of the nation's leading systems of higher education. The University of California (UC) offers areas of study in more than 150 disciplines. It has more than 187,000 students at its nine undergraduate and graduate campuses (which include three law schools and five medical schools): Berkeley, Davis, Irvine, Los Angeles, Riverside, San Diego, San Francisco, Santa Barbara, and Santa Cruz. The university's 10th campus, UC Merced, is scheduled to open in 2004. UC also operates three US Department of Energy research labs in California and New Mexico. While no longer using affirmative action admissions, UC is making efforts to boost minority enrollment.

In the wake of California's Proposition 209, which eliminated state affirmative action programs, enrollment of minorities dropped, as well as the hiring of female faculty. To help raise minority admissions, UC guarantees admission to the top 4% of students at each California high school or the top 12.5% statewide. A proposal by former president Richard Atkinson would accept the top 12.5% of students at each school who first complete a transfer program at a California community college.

HISTORY

The founders of California's government provided for a state university via a clause written into the state's constitution in 1849. The origins of the College of California, opened in Oakland in 1869, date back to the Contra Costa Academy, a small school established by Yale alumnus Henry Durant in 1853. Durant ran Contra Costa, and then the college, until 1872. Women were allowed to enter the school in 1870. The college moved to Berkeley and graduated its first class (12 men) in 1873.

As California's economy and population grew, so did its university system. Renamed University of California (UC) in 1879, it had 1,000 students by 1895. Agriculture, mining, geology, and engineering were among its first fields. A second campus was established at Davis in 1905, followed by campuses in San Diego (1912) and Los Angeles (1919).

The Depression brought cutbacks in funding for UC, but the system rebounded in the 1940s. It opened its fifth campus (Santa Barbara) in 1944, and during WWII it also began gaining recognition for research. Between 1945 and 1965 enrollment quadrupled, spurred by GI Bill-sponsored veterans and a population shift to the West. The state legislature formulated the Master Plan for Higher Education in 1960, which reorganized university administration and established admission requirements. Campuses were established at Irvine and Santa Cruz in 1965.

The first of several important demonstrations in the 1960s at UC Berkeley came in 1964 over the university's attempts to ban political activity on a strip of UC-owned land. The People's Park riot of 1969, which touched off when UC tried to close a parcel of land in Berkeley that students had turned into a kind of playground for the counterculture, left one dead and more than 50 wounded.

Aware of the changing demographics of its student body, especially its growing Asian enrollment (28% in 1990), UC Berkeley gave the chancellor's job to Chang-Lin Tien in 1990 — the first person of Asian descent to hold that position at a major US university. (Tien served as chancellor until 1997.) A California recession in the early 1990s resulted in budget cuts for UC. Strapped for cash, the university launched a for-profit entity in 1992 to tap its extensive library of patents.

UC San Diego chancellor Richard Atkinson succeeded Jack Peltason as UC president in 1995, the same year the UC Board of Regents approved a new campus — the university's 10th — in the San Joaquin Valley. That year the board also voted to phase out race- and sex-based affirmative action. In 1997, in an effort to be competitive with other top universities in recruiting faculty, the board voted to offer health benefits to the partners of gay employees. Also that year UC created the California Digital Library and began putting its library collection online.

Entrepreneur Alfred Mann donated $100 million to UCLA in 1998 for biomedical research. Admissions of non-Asian-American minorities to the fall freshman classes of UCLA and UC Berkeley fell sharply that year. The following year the UC system began guaranteeing admission to the top 4% of students in each of the state's high schools. UC took some heat in 1999 and 2000 for two separate instances of security breaches at the Los Alamos National Laboratory. In late 2002 Atkinson retired.

Chairman: John J. Moores, age 58
SVP Academic Affairs and Provost: C. Judson King, age 67
SVP Business and Finance: Joseph P. Mullinix
SVP University Affairs: Bruce B. Darling
VP Agriculture and Natural Resources: W. R. Gomes
VP Budget: Lawrence C. Hershman
VP Clinical Services: William H. Gurtner
VP Educational Outreach: Winston C. Doby
VP Financial Management: Anne C. Broome
VP Health Affairs: Michael V. Drake
VP Investments and Treasurer: David H. Russ
VP Laboratory Management: John P. McTague
VP Legal Affairs and General Counsel: James E. Holst
Assistant VP Policy, Planning, and Research: Lubbe Levin
Secretary: Leigh Trivette
Auditors: PricewaterhouseCoopers LLP

LOCATIONS

HQ: 1111 Franklin St., Oakland, CA 94607
Phone: 510-987-9173   **Fax:** 510-987-0894
Web: www.ucop.edu

Campuses
UC Berkeley (32,128 students)
UC Davis (27,292)
UC Irvine (21,491)
UC Los Angeles (37,494)
UC Merced (to open in 2004)
UC Riverside (14,429)
UC San Diego (19,484)
UC San Francisco (2,578)
UC Santa Barbara (18,822)
UC Santa Cruz (13,147)

PRODUCTS/OPERATIONS

2001 Sales

	$ mil.	% of total
Sales & services	4,313	27
State appropriations	3,368	21
Department of Energy Laboratories	3,101	20
Federal appropriations	1,851	12
Tuition & fees	1,190	7
Private gifts	1,034	6
Investment income	628	4
Local government grants & contracts	121	1
Other	281	2
Total	**15,887**	**100**

Department of Energy Laboratories
Ernest Orlando Lawrence Berkeley National Laboratory (Berkeley, CA)
Lawrence Livermore National Laboratory (Livermore, CA)
Los Alamos National Laboratory (New Mexico)

HISTORICAL FINANCIALS & EMPLOYEES

School FYE: June 30	Annual Growth	6/92	6/93	6/94	6/95	6/96	6/97	6/98	6/99	6/00	6/01
Sales ($ mil.)	8.9%	7,394	7,548	7,895	7,958	8,363	9,022	9,375	13,074	14,048	15,887
Employees	(2.1%)	132,279	131,661	132,964	131,660	137,874	130,000	130,000	99,890	103,767	108,827

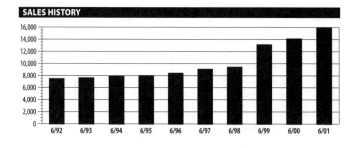

SALES HISTORY

THE UNIVERSITY OF CHICAGO

The University of Chicago ranks as one of the world's youngest and most esteemed universities. Home to more than 70 Nobel Prize recipients (Enrico Fermi, Milton Friedman, Saul Bellow), the College of the university offers a common core curriculum based on the "Great Books." Undergraduates can major in more than 40 areas, not including business and engineering. Among the U of C's graduate divisions and professional schools are the University of Chicago Law School and Graduate School of Business, both of which are ranked in the top 10 by *U.S. News & World Report*. Founded in 1890 by John D. Rockefeller, the university has an endowment exceeding $3.8 billion. Nearly 12,800 students attend the U of C.

The University of Chicago has steadfastly stood its ground against trendiness in education curricula. All students take courses that expose them to the social, biological, and physical sciences, as well as humanities, mathematics, and language. Rare is the student who is not versed in Thucydides. While the University's list of those who graduated is impressive, the list of those who did not is equally prominent, including Oracle's Larry Ellison and author Kurt Vonnegut.

Students attending the U of C study primarily at its 200-acre main campus on the South Side of Chicago, but the university's Graduate School of Business also maintains campuses in downtown Chicago; Barcelona, Spain; and Singapore. Among the many institutions affiliated with the U of C are the University of Chicago Medical Center, the Enrico Fermi Institute, the Argonne National Laboratory, and the Yerkes Observatory. The University of Chicago Press publishes 250 to 300 new titles each year, as well as more than 50 journals, and is the largest university press in the US.

HISTORY

The University of Chicago took its name from the first U of C, a small Baptist school that operated from 1858-1886. In 1891, William Rainey Harper, the man who was to become the University's first president, convinced Standard Oil's John D. Rockefeller to provide a founding gift of $600,000. Members of the American Baptist Education Society chipped in another $400,000, and department store owner Marshall Field donated the land for the campus.

The university opened in 1892 with a faculty of 103 and 594 students. As it grew, the university took over property that had been used in the Columbian Exposition of 1892-93, eventually surrounding the fair's former midway. (The school's football team later earned the nickname "Monsters of the Midway" while being coached

by the legendary Amos Alonzo Stagg; this was before withdrawing from intercollegiate play in 1939.) Legend has it that the University retains the right to rejoin the Big Ten.

Only four years after its founding, the university's enrollment of 1,815 exceeded Harvard's. By 1907, 43% of its 5,000 students were women. Robert Maynard Hutchins, president from 1929-1951, revolutionized the university and American higher education by insisting on the study of original sources (the Great Books) and competency testing through comprehensive exams. He organized the college and graduate divisions into their present structure, reaffirming the role of the university as a place for intellectual exploration rather than vocational training. In 1942 the U of C ushered in the nuclear age when Enrico Fermi created the first controlled nuclear chain reaction in the school's abandoned football stadium.

From the 1950s through the 1970s, the university purchased and restored Frank Lloyd Wright's famed Robie House and built the Joseph Regenstein Library (1970). In 1978 Hanna Holborn Gray became the first woman to be named president of a major university. Gray abolished the decade old Lascivious Costume Ball, a major social event (some would say the only social event) at the university. Hugo Sonnenschein succeeded Gray in 1993. The beginning of his tenure coincided with a period of financial difficulty for the school, as increases in costs outpaced revenue growth. In 1996 Sonnenschein announced plans to boost enrollment by as much as 30% in order to invigorate the school's finances.

U of C graduate and former professor Myron Scholes shared the Nobel Prize in economics in 1997. The next year the school announced plans for a $35 million athletics center to be named after Gerald Ratner, a former student who donated $15 million toward construction of the facility. The university later signed an agreement to supply content to Internet distance-learning startup UNext.com, founded by trustee Andrew Rosenfield. (This agreement was controversial within the university community.) Cardean University, UNext.com's online university, began operating in 2000.

Sonnenschein resigned in 2000 and was replaced by Don Randel, former provost of Cornell University. The same year the University of Chicago Graduate School of Business opened a campus in Singapore, and U of C economist James Heckman was awarded the Nobel Prize for his work in microeconomics.

OFFICERS

Chairman, Board of Trustees: Edgar D. Jannotta
President: Don M. Randel, age 61
Provost: Richard P. Saller
VP Administration and CFO: Donald J. Reaves, age 54
VP Community and Government Affairs: Henry Webber
VP Development and Alumni Relations:
Randy L. Holgate
VP and CIO: Gregory A. Jackson
VP and Chief Investment Officer: Philip Halpern
VP and Dean, College of Enrollment:
Michael C. Behnke
VP and Dean of Students: Margo P. Marshak
VP and General Counsel: Beth A. Harris
VP for Medical Affairs: James L. Madara
Associate VP Human Resources Management:
G. Chris Keeley
Secretary, Board of Trustees: Kineret S. Jaffe
Comptroller: William J. Hogan Jr.
Auditors: KPMG LLP

LOCATIONS

HQ: 5801 S. Ellis Ave., Chicago, IL 60637
Phone: 773-702-1234   **Fax:** 773-702-4155
Web: www.uchicago.edu

The University of Chicago has campuses in the Hyde
Park area of Chicago; downtown Chicago; Barcelona,
Spain; and Singapore.

PRODUCTS/OPERATIONS

Selected Affiliated Institutions
Argonne National Laboratory
Center for Gender Studies
Center for Middle Eastern Studies
Chapin Hall Center for Children and the Laboratory
Schools
Enrico Fermi Institute
James Franck Institute
The MacLean Center for Clinical Medical Ethics
Oriental Institute

Selected Graduate Schools and Programs
Divinity School
Graduate School of Business
Graham School of General Studies
Harris Graduate School of Public Policy Studies
Law School
Pritzker School of Medicine
School of Social Service Administration

Selected Libraries
D'Angelo Law Library
Eckhart Library (mathematics, mathematical statistics,
and computer science)
Harper Memorial Library for the College
John Crerar Library (natural sciences, medicine, and
technology)
Joseph Regenstein Library (humanities and social
sciences)
School of Social Service Administration Library
Yerkes Observatory Library (astronomy and
astrophysics)

HISTORICAL FINANCIALS & EMPLOYEES

School FYE: June 30	Annual Growth	6/92	6/93	6/94	6/95	6/96	6/97	6/98	6/99	6/00	6/01
Sales ($ mil.)	4.2%	1,113	1,150	1,217	1,313	1,395	1,377	892	848	1,639	1,617
Employees	0.2%	—	11,800	11,400	10,954	12,000	12,000	12,869	11,900	11,900	12,000

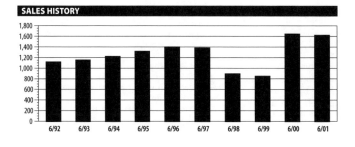

SALES HISTORY

THE UNIVERSITY OF TEXAS SYSTEM

These students are hooked on higher education. The University of Texas System runs nine universities throughout the Lone Star State with a total enrollment of nearly 170,000 students, making it one of the largest university systems in the US. (Its flagship school in Austin, with some 50,000 students, ranks as the largest campus population in the nation.) UT also runs six health centers and four medical schools and receives more than $1 billion a year for research. Its $10-billion endowment fund (managed by the University of Texas Investment Management Co.) is the third largest in the country (after Harvard and Yale). Established in 1876, UT Austin opened in 1883. The UT System was formally organized in 1950.

With the bulging ranks of Generation Y looming on the horizon, the UT System expects its enrollment to swell to 250,000 by the end of the decade. To accommodate the increase, the system has laid out plans for nearly $3 billion in capital spending for new and improved facilities. It also hopes the improvements will put it on par with research institutions such as California State.

HISTORY

The Texas Declaration of Independence (1836) admonished Mexico for having failed to establish a public education system in the territory, but attempts to start a state-sponsored university were stymied until after Texas achieved US statehood and fought in the Civil War. A new constitution in 1876 provided for the establishment of "a university of the first class," and in 1883 The University of Texas (UT) opened in Austin. Eight professors taught 218 students in two curricula: academics and law.

The school's first building opened in 1884, and in 1891 the university's medical school opened in Galveston. By 1894 UT Austin had 534 students and a football team. UT opened a Graduate School in 1910 and various other colleges over the years. The university added its first academic branch campus when the Texas State School of Mines and Metallurgy (opened in 1914 in El Paso) became part of the system in 1919.

UT's financial future was secured in 1923 when oil was found on West Texas land that had been set aside by the legislature as an education endowment. The income from oil production, as well as the proceeds of surface-use leases, became the Permanent University Fund (PUF), from which only interest and earnings on the revenues can be used: two-thirds by UT and one-third by Texas A&M University. UT continued to grow, thanks to the PUF, which topped $100 million by 1940.

UT sported the black eye of racial prejudice (as did many other institutions at the time) when it refused to admit Heman Sweatt, a black student, to its law school in 1946. The Supreme Court ordered UT to admit him in 1950, the same year the UT System was officially organized. Sixteen years later, in one of the nation's most highly publicized crimes, Charles Whitman killed 14 people and wounded 31 others with a high-powered rifle fired from atop the UT Austin administration tower. The observation deck wasn't closed until 1975, however, after a series of suicides. (It was later reopened in 1999.)

In the meantime, UT added a medical center in Dallas and several graduate schools in Austin. The 1960s through the 1980s were a time of geographic expansion for the system as it absorbed other institutions, started several new campuses, and expanded its network of medical centers. In 1996 the UT System became the first public university to establish a private investment management company (University of Texas Investment Management Co.) to invest PUF money (by that time over $9 billion) and other funds.

The race issue reared its head again in 1996 when a federal court ruled in the Hopwood decision (named for the plaintiff) that the UT System could no longer use race to determine scholarships and admissions. Minority enrollments declined the following year, prompting the Texas Legislature to enact a law granting admission to the top 10% of graduates from any Texas high school to the state university of their choice. Chancellor William Cunningham announced plans in 2000 to expand the UT System by 100,000 students over the decade. After he resigned that year, R. D. Burck took over as his successor. In 2001 UT received a $50 million donation, the largest gift in its history, from Texas businessman and Minnesota Vikings owner Red McCombs. The following year Burck stepped down and was replaced by Mark Yudof, former president of the University of Minnesota.

OFFICERS

Chairman, Board of Regents: Charles Miller
Vice Chairman, Board of Regents: Rita C. Clements
Vice Chairman, Board of Regents: Woody L. Hunt
Vice Chairman, Board of Regents: A. W. Riter Jr.
Counsel and Executive Secretary, Board of Regents:
Francie A. Frederick
Chancellor: Mark G. Yudof
Executive Vice Chancellor Academic Affairs:
Teresa Sullivan
Executive Vice Chancellor Business Affairs:
Kerry L. Kennedy
Acting Executive Vice Chancellor Health Affairs:
James C. Guckian

Vice Chancellor and General Counsel:
Cullen M. Godfrey
Vice Chancellor Administration: Tonya Brown
Vice Chancellor Development and External Relations:
Shirley B. Perry
Vice Chancellor Educational System Alignment:
Edwin R. Sharpe Jr.
Vice Chancellor Federal Relations: William H. Shute
Vice Chancellor Governmental Relations: Tom A. Scott
Vice Chancellor Special Engineering Programs:
Charles Sorber
President, University of Texas at Arlington:
Robert E. Witt
President, University of Texas at Austin:
Larry R. Faulkner
President, University of Texas at Brownsville:
Juliet V. García
President, University of Texas at Dallas:
Franklyn G. Jenifer, age 63
President, University of Texas at El Paso:
Diana S. Natalicio, age 61
President, University of Texas Pan American:
Miguel A. Nevárez
President, University of Texas of the Permian Basin:
W. David Watts
President, University of Texas at San Antonio:
Ricardo Romo
President, University of Texas at Tyler:
Rodney H. Mabry
Executive Director Public Affairs: Michael L. Warden
Director Human Resources: John Poole
Director Information Resources: Lewis Watkins
Auditors: Texas State Auditor

LOCATIONS

HQ: 601 Colorado St., Austin, TX 78701
Phone: 512-499-4200   **Fax:** 512-499-4218
Web: www.utsystem.edu

PRODUCTS/OPERATIONS

University of Texas System Component Institutions

Academic Institutions
The University of Texas at Arlington (est. 1895; 19,148 students)
The University of Texas at Austin (est. 1883; 50,010 students)
The University of Texas at Brownsville (est. 1991; 9,094 students)
The University of Texas at Dallas (est. 1961; 10,137 students)
The University of Texas at El Paso (est. 1914; 14,695 students)
The University of Texas-Pan American (Edinburg; est. 1927; 12,520 students)
The University of Texas of the Permian Basin (Odessa; est. 1969; 2,222 students)
The University of Texas at San Antonio (est. 1969; 18,607 students)
The University of Texas at Tyler (est. 1971; 3,392 students)

Health Institutions
The University of Texas Health Science Center at Houston (est. 1972; 3,170 students)
The University of Texas Health Science Center at San Antonio (est. 1959; 2,557 students)
The University of Texas Health Center at Tyler (est. 1947)
The University of Texas M.D. Anderson Cancer Center (Houston; est. 1941)
The University of Texas Medical Branch at Galveston (est. 1891; 1,952 students)
The University of Texas Southwestern Medical Center at Dallas (est. 1943; 1,554 students)

HISTORICAL FINANCIALS & EMPLOYEES

School FYE: August 31	Annual Growth	8/92	8/93	8/94	8/95	8/96	8/97	8/98	8/99	8/00	8/01
Sales ($ mil.)	7.3%	3,433	3,744	4,030	4,300	4,624	4,803	5,244	4,131	5,943	6,461
Employees	2.0%	67,210	67,985	70,000	72,395	74,364	75,517	77,112	—	79,430	80,000

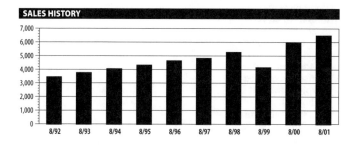

SALES HISTORY

UNIVERSITY OF WISCONSIN

There is no School of Cheese in the University of Wisconsin System, but there are 13 four-year universities, 13 two-year campuses, and a statewide extension program. The University of Wisconsin System is one of the largest public university systems in the US, with some 157,000 students. Its top school is the University of Wisconsin at Madison, which offers undergraduate, graduate, and doctoral degrees and regularly ranks as one of the top public schools in the US. It has some 40,900 students and a nationally recognized graduate program in sociology. The system's other major campus is the University of Wisconsin at Milwaukee, with more than 23,800 students.

The University of Wisconsin System is ranked in the top 10 of US public schools by *U.S. News & World Report*. One-third of the UW System's annual budget comes from state funds. Student fees, federal grants, fund raising, and other sources account for the remainder.

HISTORY

When Wisconsin became a state in 1848, its constitution called for the establishment of a state university. A board of regents was named, and it first established a preparatory school because regents felt Wisconsin's secondary schools were not advanced enough to prepare students for university studies. The school began classes in 1849 with 20 students in the Madison Female Academy Building. The University of Wisconsin's first official freshman class began studies in the fall of 1850. A campus was established a mile west of the state capitol in Madison. By 1854, when it held its first commencement (with two graduates), the school had 41 students.

Enrollment dipped during the Civil War (all but one of the school's senior class joined the army) but soon rebounded, and by 1870 the university had almost 500 students. Meanwhile, it established a school of agriculture (in 1866) and a school of law (1868). The state established normal schools (teachers colleges) in Platteville (1866), Whitewater (1868), Oshkosh (1871), and River Falls (1874).

There was also a teachers' course for women at the university in Madison. However, when John Bascom became president in 1874, he transformed the university into a truly coeducational institution, putting women "in all respects on precisely the same footing" with the men.

While the university at Madison remained Wisconsin's central seat of learning, the state continued to establish normal schools. It opened institutions in Milwaukee (1885), Superior (1893), Stevens Point (1894), La Crosse (1909),

and Eau Claire (1916). The nine normal schools eventually became a system of state colleges called Wisconsin State Universities.

The university at Madison also continued to grow, and by the late 1920s it had almost 9,000 students. WWII brought a drop in enrollment, but afterward it took off, jumping from about 7,000 in 1945 to over 22,000 by the late 1950s. The University of Wisconsin-Milwaukee branch was founded in 1956. Other branch campuses were established in Green Bay (1965) and Kenosha (1968).

The Madison campus became a focal point for student protests during the Vietnam War. Events came to a head in 1970 when President Fred Harrington resigned during a four-day standoff between students and the National Guard. War protesters also placed a bomb outside Sterling Hall, which housed the Army Math Research Center; the explosion killed one student and injured three others.

The state legislature merged the University of Wisconsin and the Wisconsin State Universities in 1971 to create The University of Wisconsin System. By the early 1980s it had an enrollment of nearly 160,000. Later that decade, however, it tightened admission standards, and enrollment began to fall.

A property-tax reform bill passed by the legislature in 1994 cut into The University of Wisconsin System's funding the next year. The system announced it would cut 500 jobs in 1997, use more part-time instructors, and increase class sizes to deal with the $43 million it lost in the budget cuts.

UW-Madison broke ground on the $22 million Fluno Center for Executive Education in 1998, a 100-room dorm, classroom building, and dining hall rolled into one. The next year enrollment at The University of Wisconsin System's two-year colleges broke 10,000 for the first time in five years. The licensing of technologies invented at the UW-Madison campus was expanded to include all four-year universities in the UW System in 2000. The System's mandatory student-fee policy was ruled unconstitutional later that year.

OFFICERS

President: Katharine C. Lyall, age 60
SVP Academic Affairs: Cora B. Marrett
SVP Administration: David W. Olien
VP Finance: Deborah A. Durcan
VP University Relations: Linda Weimer
Assistant VP Academic Affairs; Senior Advisor of President, Multicultural Affairs: Andrea-Teresa Arenas
Assistant VP Administrative Services: Ellen James
Assistant VP Capital Planning and Budget: Nancy J. Ives
Associate VP Academic Affairs: Ron Singer
Associate VP Budget and Planning: Freda Harris
Associate VP Human Resources: George H. Brooks
Associate VP Learning and Information Technology: Edward Meachen
Associate VP Policy Analysis and Research: Frank Goldberg
Director Budget Planning: Melissa Kepner
Director Information Services: Nancy Crabb
Director Internal Audit: Ronald L. Yates
General Counsel: Patricia Brady
Auditors: State of Wisconsin Legislative Audit Bureau

LOCATIONS

HQ: The University of Wisconsin System
Van Hise Hall, 1220 Linden Dr., Madison, WI 53706
Phone: 608-262-2321   **Fax:** 608-262-3985
Web: www.uwsa.edu

University Campuses
UW-Baraboo/Sauk County (two-year college; 653 students)
UW-Barron County (two-year college; 570)
UW-Eau Claire (four-year university; 10,643)
UW-Fond Du Lac (two-year college; 684)
UW-Fox Valley (two-year college; 1,776)
UW-Green Bay (four-year university; 5,558)
UW-La Crosse (four-year university; 9,092)
UW-Madison (four-year university; 40,877)
UW-Manitowoc (two-year college; 647)
UW-Marathon County (two-year college; 1,292)
UW-Marinette (two-year college; 535)
UW-Marshfield/Wood County (two-year college; 643)
UW-Milwaukee (four-year university; 23,835)
UW-Oshkosh (four-year university; 10,929)
UW-Parkside (four-year university; 5,016)
UW-Platteville (four-year university; 5,511)
UW-Richland (two-year college; 496)
UW-River Falls (four-year university; 5,822)
UW-Rock County (two-year college; 981)
UW-Sheboygan (two-year college; 768)
UW-Stevens Point (four-year university; 8,735)
UW-Stout (four-year university; 7,780)
UW-Superior (four-year university; 2,787)
UW-Washington County (two-year college; 939)
UW-Waukesha (two-year college; 2,245)
UW-Whitewater (four-year university; 10,471)

PRODUCTS/OPERATIONS

2001 Sales

	$ mil.	% of total
State appropriations	1,047	34
Tuition & fees	712	23
Federal grants & contracts	429	14
Private gifts, grants & contracts	273	9
Auxiliary enterprises	235	7
Educational activities	189	6
State grants & contracts	39	1
UW Hospital Authority	31	1
Endowment income	19	—
Federal appropriations	19	—
Local grants & contracts	12	—
Other	155	5
Total	**3,160**	**100**

HISTORICAL FINANCIALS & EMPLOYEES

School FYE: June 30	Annual Growth	6/92	6/93	6/94	6/95	6/96	6/97	6/98	6/99	6/00	6/01
Sales ($ mil.)	4.0%	2,226	2,309	2,442	2,556	2,612	2,399	2,543	2,558	2,922	3,160
Employees	(2.5%)	30,090	30,269	30,341	30,410	28,626	25,399	25,500	25,889	23,981	24,000

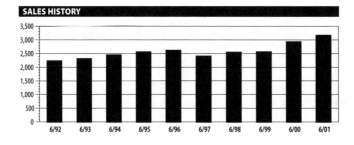

SALES HISTORY

USAA

USAA has a decidedly military bearing. The mutual insurance company serves more than 4 million customers, primarily military personnel and their families. Its products and services include property & casualty (sold only to military personnel) and life insurance, banking, discount brokerage, and investment management. USAA relies largely on technology and direct marketing to sell its products, reaching clients via the telephone and Internet. The company also has a large mail-order catalog business (computers, furniture, giftware, jewelry, and home and auto safety items), and it offers long-distance telephone services.

The company is expecting its membership to continue growing, projecting it to nearly double by 2010. In an attempt to increase revenue, the company has entered new markets by making efforts to target people less affluent than military officers.

Facing rising claims and a decline in value of its investments, USAA has streamlined operations by reducing staff and closing down divisions (including mailing, printing, and information technology offices).

HISTORY

In 1922 a group of 26 US Army officers gathered in a San Antonio hotel and formed their own automobile insurance association. The reason? As military officers who often moved, they had a hard time getting insurance because they were considered transient. So the officers decided to insure each other. Led by Major William Garrison, who became the company's first president, they formed the United States Army Automobile Insurance Association.

In 1924, when US Navy and Marine Corps officers were allowed to join, the company changed its name to United Services Automobile Association. By the mid-1950s the company had some 200,000 members. During the 1960s the company formed USAA Life Insurance Company (1963) and USAA Casualty Insurance Company (1968).

In 1969 Robert McDermott, a retired US Air Force brigadier general, became president. He cut employment through attrition, established education and training seminars for employees, and invested in computers and telecommunications (drastically cutting claims-processing time). McDermott added new products and services, such as mutual funds, real estate investments, and banking. Under McDermott, USAA's membership grew from 653,000 in 1969 to more than 3 million in 1993.

During the 1970s, in an effort to go paperless,

USAA became one of the insurance industry's first companies to switch from mail to toll-free (800) numbers. In the early 1980s the company introduced its discount purchasing program, USAA Buying Services. In 1985 it opened the USAA Federal Savings Bank. In the late 1980s USAA began installing an optical storage system to automate some customer service operations.

McDermott retired in 1993 and was succeeded by Robert Herres. The following year USAA Federal Savings Bank began developing a home banking system, offering members information and services over advanced screen telephones provided by IBM.

In the early 1990s USAA's real estate activities increased dramatically. In 1995 USAA restructured its interest in the Fiesta Texas theme park in San Antonio in order to focus on previously developed properties in geographically diverse areas. That year Six Flags Theme Parks (now Six Flags, Inc.) assumed operation and management of Fiesta Texas (which it purchased from USAA in 1998).

In 1997 USAA began including enlisted military personnel as members. It also started to experiment with a "plain English" mutual fund prospectus. In 1998 USAA also began offering Choice Ride in Orlando, Florida. For about $1,100 per quarter and a promise not to drive except in emergencies, the pilot program provided 36 round trips and a 90% discount on car insurance, in hopes of keeping older drivers from unnecessarily getting behind the wheel.

Also in 1998, as part of its new Financial Planning Network, USAA began offering retirement and estate planning assistance aimed at 25- to 55-year-olds for a yearly $250 fee. In 1999 claims doubled largely due to the impact of Hurricane Floyd and spring hail storms hitting military communities in North Carolina and Virginia.

In 1998 USAA also moved to consolidate its customers' separate accounts (such as mutual fund holdings, stocks and bonds, and life insurance products) into one main account to strengthen customer relationships and reduce operational costs. The next year, after completing a number of technology projects, it laid off workers for the first time in its history.

OFFICERS

Chairman, President, and CEO: Robert G. Davis
SVP, CFO, and Corporate Treasurer: Josue Robles Jr.
SVP, Secretary, and General Counsel: Bradford W. Rich
SVP, Corporate Communications: Wendi E. Strong
SVP, Corporate Services: David H. Garrison
SVP, Enterprise Business Operations:
  Robert T. Handren
SVP, Human Resources: Elizabeth D. Conklyn

SVP, Marketing: Karen B. Presley
President and CEO, USAA Alliance Services:
Donna M. Bhatia
President and CEO, USAA Federal Savings Bank:
Mark H. Wright
President and CEO, USAA Investment Management:
Christopher W. Claus
President and CEO, USAA Life Insurance:
James M. Middleton
President and CEO, USAA Real Estate and La Cantera
Development: Edward B. Kelley
President, USAA Information Technology:
Stephen E. Yates, age 54
President, USAA Property and Casualty Insurance:
Henry Viccellio Jr.
Auditors: KPMG LLP

LOCATIONS

HQ: 9800 Fredericksburg Rd., San Antonio, TX 78288
Phone: 210-498-2211   **Fax:** 210-498-9940
Web: www.usaa.com

USAA has major regional offices in California, Colorado,
Florida, Virginia, and Washington. It maintains
international offices in London and Frankfurt.

PRODUCTS/OPERATIONS

Selected Operations
USAA Alliance Services Company (merchandising &
member services)
USAA Federal Savings Bank
USAA Investment Management Company (mutual funds,
investment & brokerage services)
USAA Property & Casualty (including automobile, home,
boat, and flood insurance)
USAA Real Estate Company

COMPETITORS

21st Century
Allstate
American Express
American Financial
American General
AXA Financial
Berkshire Hathaway
Charles Schwab
Chubb
CIGNA
Citigroup
CNA Financial
FMR
Guardian Life
The Hartford
John Hancock Financial Services
Kemper Insurance
Liberty Mutual
MassMutual
MetLife
Morgan Stanley
Mutual of Omaha
Nationwide
New York Life
Northwestern Mutual
Pacific Mutual
Prudential
St. Paul Companies
State Farm
T. Rowe Price
UBS PaineWebber

HISTORICAL FINANCIALS & EMPLOYEES

Mutual company FYE: December 31	Annual Growth	12/92	12/93	12/94	12/95	12/96	12/97	12/98	12/99	12/00	12/01
Assets ($ mil.)	8.5%	16,235	18,494	19,548	22,244	23,622	25,007	28,831	30,323	32,794	33,829
Net income ($ mil.)	17.6%	140	676	564	730	855	1,189	980	765	669	604
Income as % of assets	—	0.9%	3.7%	2.9%	3.3%	3.6%	4.8%	3.4%	2.5%	2.0%	1.8%
Employees	4.6%	14,667	15,905	15,233	15,677	16,571	17,967	20,120	21,795	22,000	22,000

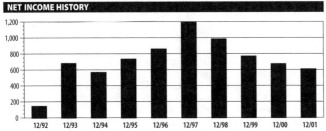

NET INCOME HISTORY

2001 FISCAL YEAR-END
Equity as % of assets: 21.9%
Return on assets: 1.8%
Return on equity: 8.3%
Long-term debt ($ mil.): —
Sales ($ mil.): 8,970

VISA INTERNATIONAL

Paper or plastic? Visa International hopes you'll choose the latter. Visa operates the world's largest consumer payment system (ahead of MasterCard and American Express), with more than 1 billion credit and other payment cards in circulation. The company is owned by 21,000 banks, each of which issues and markets its own Visa products in competition with the others. They all participate in the VisaNet payment system, which provides authorization, transaction processing, and settlement services for purchases from 24 million merchants worldwide. In addition to credit cards, Visa also provides its customers with debit cards, Internet payment systems, value-storing smart cards, and traveler's checks.

Visa International operates through six autonomous regional organizations.

Visa is accelerating its push to introduce chip cards over magnetic-strip technology, and it is maneuvering its Open Platform technology into position against the MasterCard-supported Mondex platform and Microsoft's Smart Card for Windows. Winner takes all in this contest, with losers having to adapt to new systems or face a shrinking market share.

Both Visa's US unit and MasterCard are in some four million retailers' sights. Led by Wal-Mart, the merchants seek up to $200 billion in damages in their class-action suit over fees the card issuers charge for certain debit-card transactions. The two defendants are still appealing antitrust litigation brought against them by the US Department of Justice.

HISTORY

Although the first charge card was issued by Western Union in 1914, it wasn't until 1958 that Bank of America (BofA) issued its BankAmericard, which combined the convenience of a charge account with credit privileges. When BofA extended its customer base outside California, the interchange system controlling payments began to falter because of design problems and fraud.

In 1968 Dee Hock, manager of the BankAmericard operations of the National Bank of Commerce in Seattle, convinced member banks that a more reliable system was needed. Two years later National BankAmericard Inc. (NBI) was created as an independent corporation (owned by 243 banks) to buy the BankAmericard system from BofA.

With its first ad slogan, "Think of it as Money," the Hock-led NBI developed BankAmericard into a widely used form of payment in the US. Multinational corporation IBANCO was formed in 1974 to carry the operations to other countries.

People outside the US resisted BankAmericard's nominal association with BofA, so in 1977 Hock changed the card's name to Visa. NBI became Visa USA, and IBANCO became Visa International.

By 1980 Visa had debuted debit cards, begun issuing traveler's checks, and created an electromagnetic point-of-sale authorization system. Visa developed a global network of ATMs in 1983; it was expanded in 1987 by the purchase of a 33% stake in the Plus System of ATMs, then the US's second-largest system. Hock retired in 1984 with the company well on its way to realizing his vision of a universal payment system.

The company built the Visa brand with aggressive advertising, such as sponsorship of the 1988 and 1992 Olympics, and by co-branding (issuing cards through other organizations with strong brands, such as Blockbuster and Ford).

In 1994 Visa teamed up with Microsoft and others to develop home-banking services and software. Visa Cash was introduced during the 1996 Olympics. Visa pushed its debit cards in 1996 and 1997 with humorous ads featuring presidential nominee Bob Dole and showbiz success story Daffy Duck.

Visa expanded its smart card infrastructure in 1997. Along with MasterCard, it published encryption and security software for online transactions. The gloves came off the next year as the companies vied to convince the world to rally around their respective e-purse technology standards.

During the 1990s, Visa fought American Express' attempts to introduce a bank credit card of its own by forbidding Visa members in the US from issuing the product; the Justice Department responded with an antitrust suit against Visa and MasterCard. The case went to trial in 2000 with the government claiming that Visa and MasterCard stifle competition and enjoy an exclusive cross-ownership structure.

Also in 2000 the company made a deal with Gemplus, the French smart-card company, to enable payments over wireless networks; Visa also inked a billing deal with wireless technology company Aether Systems, as well as e-commerce agreements with telecommunications companies Nokia and LM Ericsson.

Visa continued its technology push in 2000 through a deal with Financial Services Technology Consortium to test biometrics — the use of fingerprints, irises, and voice recognition to identify cardholders. The company also launched a prepaid card, Visa Buxx, targeted at teenagers.

In 2000 the European Union launched an investigation into the firm's transaction fees, alleging that the fees could restrict competition. The following year Visa International agreed to drop its fee to 0.7% of the transaction value over five years. In 2001 a federal judge ordered Visa and MasterCard to allow their member banks to issue rival credit cards; the card firms are appealing the case.

OFFICERS

President and CEO: Malcolm Williamson, age 63
CFO: Ken Sommer
EVP and General Counsel: Guy Rounsaville
EVP, Global Marketing Partnerships and Sponsorships: Tom Shepard
EVP, Human Resources: Elizabeth Rounds
SVP, Public Policy: Mark MacCarthy
President, Inovant: John Partridge
President, Visa Canada: Derek A. Fry
President, Visa Central and Eastern Europe, Middle East, and Africa Region: Anne L. Cobb
President, Visa European Union (EU): Johannes I. van der Velde
President, Visa Latin America and Caribbean: Eduardo Eraña
President and CEO, Visa Asia Pacific: Rupert G. Keeley
President and CEO, Visa USA: Carl F. Pascarella, age 58
EVP and COO, Visa USA: Paul Vessey
EVP, General Counsel, and Secretary, Visa USA: Paul A. Allen
EVP and CFO, Visa USA: Victor W. Dahir
EVP, Sales and Integrated Solutions, Visa USA: John T. Gardner Jr.
EVP, Product Management, Visa USA: Anthony N. McEwen
EVP, Operations and Risk Management, Visa USA: Steve Ruwe
EVP, Brand Management, Visa USA: Rebecca Saeger, age 47
EVP, Systems Group and CTO, Visa USA: Scott Thompson
EVP, Human Resources, Visa USA: Jan van der Voort
VP, Public Affairs, Visa USA: Kelly Presta
EVP and Chief Administrative Officer, Visa Asia Pacific: David Lee
EVP and General Manager, Operations, Visa Asia Pacific: Dennis Wlasichuk
EVP and Regional Legal Counsel, Visa Asia Pacific: Lyn Boxall

LOCATIONS

HQ: 900 Metro Center Blvd., Foster City, CA 94404
Phone: 650-432-3200   **Fax:** 650-432-3087
Web: www.visa.com

Visa International provides consumer payment services at more than 21 million locations worldwide.

PRODUCTS/OPERATIONS

Products and Services
ATMs (almost 650,000 locations)
Electron (debit card outside of US)
Interlink (debit card)
smartVisa card (computer-chip-embedded card accepted worldwide)
Visa Business card (for small businesses and professionals)
Visa Cash (smart cards)
Visa Classic card (credit/debit card issued by Visa's 21,000 member banks)
Visa Corporate card (for travel and entertainment expenses)
Visa Debit card (accesses bank account for immediate settlement of payments)
Visa Gold card (higher spending limits)
VisaNet (electronic-transaction processing network)
Visa Purchasing card (for corporate purchases)
Visa Travelers Cheques
Visa TravelMoney (prepaid card in any currency)

COMPETITORS

American Express
Citigroup
MasterCard
Morgan Stanley

HISTORICAL FINANCIALS & EMPLOYEES

Private FYE: September 30	Annual Growth	9/92	9/93	9/94	9/95	9/96	9/97	9/98	9/99	9/00	9/01
Estimated sales ($ mil.)	16.4%	920	1,040	1,260	1,330	1,650	2,050	2,550	2,800	3,000	3,600
Employees	10.2%	2,500	3,000	3,500	4,000	4,800	5,000	5,000	5,000	5,000	6,000

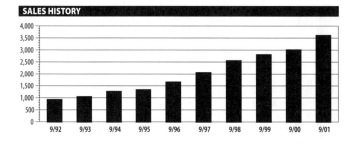

SALES HISTORY

VULCAN NORTHWEST INC.

Even with all his Vulcan logic, could Spock invest like *this?* Brainy billionaire Paul Allen organizes his business and charitable ventures under Vulcan Northwest. Vulcan Northwest includes Allen's slim stake in the industry-defining juggernaut Microsoft, as well as holdings in dozens of companies providing computer, technology, multimedia, and communications products and services. Vulcan Northwest holds stakes in some six charitable organizations. Allen also owns professional sports teams like the NBA's Portland Trail Blazers and the NFL's Seattle Seahawks.

Vulcan Northwest's charities support the arts, medical research, land conservation, and other causes. Allen, who co-founded Microsoft with Bill Gates, promotes a "wired world" vision, in which everyone is united through interconnecting communications, entertainment, and information systems. His Vulcan Ventures finds investment opportunities. CEO Jody Patton, Allen's sister, oversees both his business and charitable ventures. He has also paid for a sponsorship of the OneWorld Challenge yachting team that will compete in the famous America's Cup race in 2003.

Many of Allen's investments in the "wired world" took a beating with the stock market downturn. He even saw his own personal wealth take a dip, but that hasn't stopped him from looking for ways to wring goodness out of technological advances. Among his latest projects is the Final Encyclopedia. Straight out of a sci-fi novel, the project is looking to put together the ultimate reference source in a form accessible to everyone.

HISTORY

Paul Allen and Bill Gates first worked together on computer projects as schoolmates in Seattle. They developed a program to determine traffic patterns and launched Traf-O-Data, an operation that failed because the state provided the information for free. When Allen saw an article on the MITS Altair 8800 minicomputer in 1975, the two realized it needed a simplified programming language to make it useful. They offered MITS a modified version of BASIC they had written for Traf-O-Data. The company set them up in an office in Albuquerque, New Mexico. They then began their biggest collaboration of all: Microsoft. While Gates concentrated on business, Allen focused on technical issues.

They moved to Bellevue, a Seattle suburb, in 1979. The next year IBM asked them to create a programming language for a PC project. Allen bought Q-DOS (quick and dirty operating system) from Seattle Computer; the pair tweaked it and renamed it MS-DOS. Allen and Gates made a key decision to structure their contract with

IBM to allow clones. They also helped design many aspects of the original IBM PC.

Allen developed Hodgkin's disease in 1982. Facing his own mortality, he ended his daily involvement in Microsoft (keeping a chunk of the company and a board seat) and began to play more (traveling and playing the electric guitar). With his cancer in remission in 1985, Allen founded multimedia software company Asymetrix. The next year he set up Vulcan Northwest to hold his diversified interests and Vulcan Ventures. He also began helping startups, indulging his interests (buying the NBA's Portland Trail Blazers in 1988 and donating some $60 million to build a museum honoring his musical idol, Jimi Hendrix, and other Pacific Northwest artists). He also funded Seattle-area civic improvements.

In 1990 Allen hired William Savoy to help organize his finances; Savoy later became president of Vulcan Ventures. Seeing a need for more R&D in the US, Allen in 1992 started Interval Research. He also invested in America Online (sold 1994). In 1993 Allen bought 80% of Ticketmaster (sold 1997), and in 1995 he invested in DreamWorks SKG, the multimedia company of Steven Spielberg, Jeffrey Katzenberg, and David Geffen.

Allen made a rare buy outside the entertainment and high-tech worlds through a 1996 investment in power turbine maker Capstone Turbine. To prevent the Seattle Seahawks from moving to California, Allen bought the team in 1997 and made plans for a new stadium. He consolidated his management operations under Vulcan Northwest and dissolved Paul Allen Group (founded 1994), keeping Vulcan Ventures.

Allen moved into cable in 1998 and 1999; his Charter Communications eventually became the #4 US cable firm. In 1999 several Allen investments (Charter Communications, Vulcan Ventures, RCN, High Speed Access, and Go2Net) joined to form wired-world venture Broadband Partners.

In 2000 it was nearly impossible to ignore Allen's influence on Seattle as several major projects took shape or were completed, including the new Seahawks' arena, the rock 'n' roll museum, and the renovation of a 90-year-old train station as part of a complex that will include Vulcan's new headquarters. Also in 2000 Allen provided a $100 million infusion to struggling Oxygen Media. The next year Vulcan Ventures bought sports games Web site operator Small World Media to boost its sports holdings.

Chairman: Paul G. Allen
CEO: Jody Patton
CFO: Joseph Franzi
Senior Executive; President, Vulcan Ventures:
William D. Savoy, age 37
VP Real Estate: Ada M. Healey
VP Art, Design, and Construction: John H. Thomas
VP Finance: Buster Brown
VP Corporate Communications: Steven C. Crosby
VP Operations: Pamela Faber
VP Media Development: Richard E. Hutton
VP and General Counsel: Richard Leigh
VP Technology: Dave Leinweber
VP Information Management Services: Chris Purcell
VP Investment Management: Nathan Troutman
VP Corporate Leadership: Denise Wolf
VP Public Relations: Michael Nank

LOCATIONS

HQ: 505 5th Ave. South, Ste. 900, Seattle, WA 98104
Phone: 206-342-2000   **Fax:** 206-342-3000
Web: www.vulcan.com

PRODUCTS/OPERATIONS

Selected Holdings
800.com (online consumer electronics retailer)
Charter Communications (cable TV system)
Click2learn, Inc. (multimedia development software)
Digeo Broadband Inc. (broadband services)
DreamWorks SKG (entertainment company)
Drugstore.com (online retailer)
HealthAnswers, Inc. (healthcare communications)
High Speed Access Corp. (digital subscriber line
provider)
IFILM (film industry online-content provider)
iVAST (broadband content provider)
Kestrel Solutions (optical fiber networking)
Metricom, Inc. (wireless data-transmission products)
myplay, inc. (digital music services)
NETSchools Corp. (educational technology equipment
and services)
Oxygen Media (Internet and television-content provider)
Portland Trail Blazers (professional basketball team)
RCN Corporation (broadband fiber-optic networks)
Replay TV, Inc. (television-programming technology
provider)
Seattle Seahawks (professional football team)
Sharewave Inc. (digital wireless technology)
Small World (online fantasy sports)
The Sporting News (print and online sports magazine)
Stamps.com (online postage retailer)
Telescan, Inc. (online investor information)
TiVo (television-programming technology provider)
USA Networks (broadcasting and other media, retail, and
Internet services)
Vulcan Ventures, Inc. (investments)
Wavtrace (wireless technology)

COMPETITORS

Accel Partners	Institutional	SOFTBANK
Austin Ventures	Venture	Sutter Hill
Benchmark	Partners	Trinity Ventures
Capital	Kleiner Perkins	US Venture
Boston Ventures	Matrix Partners	Partners
Draper Fisher	Mayfield Fund	Venrock
Jurvetson	Menlo Ventures	Associates
Flatiron Partners	Microsoft	Veronis Suhler
Hummer	Small-	Stevenson
Winblad	Technology	

WAKEFERN FOOD CORPORATION

Started by seven men who invested $1,000 each, Wakefern Food has grown into the largest supermarket cooperative in the US. The co-op is owned by 40 independent grocers who operate about 180 ShopRite supermarkets in Connecticut, Delaware, New Jersey (where it is a dominant chain), New York, and Pennsylvania. More than half of ShopRite stores offer pharmacies. In addition to name-brand and private-label products (ShopRite, Chef's Express, Reddington Farms), Wakefern supports its members with advertising, merchandising, insurance, and other services. Wakefern's ShopRite Supermarkets subsidiary acquired the assets of Florida-based Big V Supermarkets, which filed for bankruptcy in 2000.

Wakefern Food is remodeling, upgrading technology, and expanding product selection at the newly acquired Big V stores.

The company provides members and other customers with more than 20,000 name-brand items, including groceries, dairy and meat products, produce, frozen foods, and general merchandise. It also sells more than 3,000 items under the ShopRite label.

All members are given one vote in the co-op, regardless of size.

HISTORY

Wakefern Food was founded in 1946 by seven New York- and New Jersey-based grocers: Louis Weiss, Sam and Al Aidekman, Abe Kesselman, Dave Fern, Sam Garb, and Albert Goldberg (the company's name is made up of the letters of the first five of those founders). Like many cooperatives, the association sought to lower costs by increasing its buying power as a group.

They each put in $1,000 and began operating a 5,000-sq.-ft. warehouse, often putting in double time to keep both their stores and the warehouse running. The shopkeepers' collective buying power proved valuable, enabling the grocers to stock many items at the same prices as their larger competitors.

In 1951 Wakefern members began pooling their resources to buy advertising space. A common store name — ShopRite — was chosen, and each week co-op members met to decide which items would be sale priced. Within a year, membership had grown to over 50. Expansion became a priority, and in the mid-1950s co-op members united in small groups to take over failed supermarkets. One such group, called the Supermarkets Operating Co. (SOC), was formed in 1956. Within 10 years it had acquired a number of failed stores, remodeled them, and given them the ShopRite name.

During the late 1950s sales at ShopRite stores slumped after Wakefern decided to buck the supermarket trend of offering trading stamps (which could then be exchanged for gifts), figuring that offering the stamps would ultimately lead to higher food prices. The move initially drove away customers, but Wakefern cut grocery prices across the board and sales returned. The company also embraced another supermarket trend: stocking stores with nonfood items.

The co-op was severely shaken in 1966 when SOC merged with General Supermarkets, a similar small group within Wakefern, becoming Supermarkets General Corp. (SGC). SGC was a powerful entity, with 71 supermarkets, 10 drugstores, six gas stations, a wholesale bakery, and a discount department store. Many Wakefern members opposed the merger and attempted to block the action with a court order. By 1968 SGC had beefed up its operations to include department store chains as well as its grocery stores. In a move that threatened to break Wakefern, SGC broke away from the co-op, and its stores were renamed Pathmark.

Wakefern not only weathered the storm, it grew under the direction of chairman and CEO Thomas Infusino, elected shortly after the split. The co-op focused on asserting its position as a seller of low-priced products. Wakefern developed private-label brands, including the ShopRite brand. In the 1980s members began operating larger stores and adding more nonfood items to the ShopRite product mix. With its number of superstores on the rise, and facing increased competition from club stores in 1992, Wakefern opened a centralized, nonfood distribution center in New Jersey.

In 1995, 30-year Wakefern veteran Dean Janeway was elected president of the co-op. In 1996 the company debuted its ShopRite MasterCard, co-branded with New Jersey's Valley National Bank. The following year the co-op purchased two of its customers' stores in Pennsylvania, then threatened to close them when contract talks with the local union deteriorated. In 1998 Wakefern settled the dispute, then sold the stores.

The company partnered with Internet bidding site priceline.com in 1999, offering customers an opportunity to bid on groceries and then pick them up at ShopRite stores. Big V, Wakefern's biggest customer, filed for Chapter 11 bankruptcy protection in 2000 and said it was ending its distribution agreement with the co-op. In July 2002, however, Wakefern's ShopRite Supermarkets subsidiary acquired all of Big V's assets for approximately $185 million in cash and assumed liabilities.

Chairman and CEO: Thomas Infusino
President: Dean Janeway
CFO: Ken Jasinkiewicz
EVP: Joseph Sheridan
VP Corporate and Consumer Affairs: Mary Ellen Gowin
VP Human Resources: Ernie Bell
CIO: Natan Tabak

LOCATIONS

HQ: 600 York St., Elizabeth, NJ 07207
Phone: 908-527-3300   **Fax:** 908-527-3397
Web: www.shoprite.com

Wakefern Food's 40-plus members operate about 200 ShopRite supermarkets in Connecticut, Delaware, New Jersey, New York, and Pennsylvania.

PRODUCTS/OPERATIONS

Major Members
Foodarama Supermarkets
Inserra Supermarkets
Village Super Market

Selected Private Labels
Black Bear (deli items)
Chef's Express
Reddington Farms (poultry)
ShopRite

COMPETITORS

A&P
C&S Wholesale
Di Giorgio
Fleming Companies
IGA
King Kullen Grocery
Krasdale Foods
Pathmark
Royal Ahold
Shurfine International
Stop & Shop
SUPERVALU
Wal-Mart

HISTORICAL FINANCIALS & EMPLOYEES

Cooperative FYE: September 30	Annual Growth	9/92	9/93	9/94	9/95	9/96	9/97	9/98	9/99	9/00	9/01
Sales ($ mil.)	6.7%	—	—	3,740	3,700	4,304	4,613	5,000	5,500	5,800	5,900
Employees	7.6%	—	—	3,000	3,700	3,000	3,200	3,000	4,000	5,000	5,000

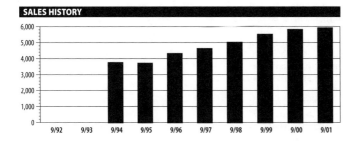

SALES HISTORY

WINGATE PARTNERS

Wingate Partners gets by on more than a wing and a prayer, rescuing lackluster manufacturing, distribution, and service businesses. With three funds worth some $290 billion, the investment firm avoids banking, media, high-tech, real estate, and certain other companies, investing instead in companies that are underperforming or that are in transitional industries. Targets often have revenues between $100 million and $500 million, and may or may not be profitable at the time of purchase. Wingate will invest between $10 million and $20 million in a holding. Its portfolio includes holdings in Kevco (manufactured-housing building products distributor) and auto parts distributor Pro Parts Xpress.

Wingate often makes more expensive purchases in conjunction with other investors. An active investor, Wingate usually takes seats on the boards of companies it holds, and sometimes manages them. Wingate has launched three investment funds with a combined capitalization of $290 million. Investors include Yale University, The Ford Foundation, BankAmerica Capital, and the Hall family (of Hallmark cards fame).

HISTORY

In 1987 experienced investors Frederick Hegi and James Callier teamed up with Tom Sturgess, a former senior executive with the distribution arm of meatpacker Swift Independent, to form Wingate. Hegi, who began his career as an investment manager at First National Bank of Chicago, was part of an investment group that had acquired Swift. Callier had been a McKinsey & Company management consultant and an investor in his own right.

The trio found 11 prominent individual and institutional investors — including Carl Lindner, Henry Hillman, Hughes Aircraft Pension Fund, the University of Texas endowment fund, and several insurance companies — to establish the $67 million Wingate Partners L.P. fund to support Wingate's acquisition strategy.

The investment fund's initial purchase was manufactured-home builder Redman Industries and its aluminum window manufacturing unit, Redman Building Products, in 1988. To bring the underperforming Redman operations into profitability, Wingate began cutting costs and paring noncore businesses. Wingate also bought children's car seat and crib maker Century Products (an unprofitable subsidiary of Gerber Products) that year.

In 1991 the company bought Loomis Armored; it took three years for Wingate to return the armored-car company to profitability. (Loomis

Armored had recorded three years of losses prior to its purchase by Wingate.) In 1992 Wingate bought Associated Stationers, a network of stationery distribution centers.

By the time Wingate took Redman Industries public in 1993 (earning about $69 million), it had turned the company around. Wingate held on to Redman Building Products (the window unit) until 1997, when it was sold to Robert Bass' Keystone Inc.

When Wingate launched its second investment fund in 1994, it raised $130 million. Investors included BankAmerica Capital Corp., Common Fund, Duke University, The Ford Foundation, the Hall family, the Hughes Aircraft Pension Fund, the Kauffman Foundation, The University of Texas, Yale University, and several wealthy families in Dallas, Denver, and Kansas City.

With Wingate Partners II, the firm jumped on the health care bandwagon. Teaming with the former CEO of a hospital chain, Wingate formed rollup company AmeriStat Mobile Medical Services in 1994 to acquire ambulance companies. After making 10 such buys, Wingate sold the business to ambulance operator Laidlaw in 1995.

Wingate bought Associated Stationers' rival United Stationers in 1995 and merged the former competitors under the United name. Wingate co-founder Sturgess served as United Stationers' chairman, CEO, and president until his resignation in 1996. (He still serves on Wingate's advisory board.) Wingate acquired independent tire distributor ITCO Tire that year. In 1997 Wingate merged its Loomis Armored unit with Borg-Warner Security's Wells Fargo Armored Service subsidiary to form Loomis, Fargo & Co.

In 1998 the firm separately sold Century Products' stroller and car seat operations and its crib-making division, Okla Homer Smith. Also that year Wingate sold ITCO to Heafner Tire Group, a nationwide tire distributor and retailer. In 1999 the company bought 46% of manufactured-housing building products distributor Kevco and acquired three automotive parts distributors to form Pro Parts Xpress.

In 2000 Wingate launched its third fund and sold its stake in United Stationers. The next year it sold its half of Loomis.

OFFICERS

Founding Partner and Principal: Frederick B. Hegi Jr.,
  age 58
Senior Associate: Bradley F. Brenneman, age 31
Principal: Jay I. Applebaum, age 40
Principal: Michael B. Decker
Principal: V. Edward Easterling Jr., age 42
Principal: James A. Johnson, age 47
VP: Jason H. Reed, age 34
Controller: Alma Evans

LOCATIONS

HQ: 750 N. St. Paul St., Ste. 1200, Dallas, TX 75201
Phone: 214-720-1313   **Fax:** 214-871-8799
Web: www.wingatepartners.com

PRODUCTS/OPERATIONS

Selected Holdings
ENSR International (environmental consulting)
Kevco, Inc. (building products)
National Spirit Group (student sports and spirit
  products and services)
Pro Parts Xpress (auto parts distributor)

COMPETITORS

AEA Investors
Apollo Advisors
Berkshire Hathaway
Blackstone Group
Clayton, Dubilier
Forstmann Little
Haas Wheat
Heico
Hicks, Muse
Interlaken Investment
KKR
Texas Pacific Group
Thomas Lee

W.K. KELLOGG FOUNDATION

Charitable grants from W.K. Kellogg Foundation are gr-r-reat! Founded in 1930 by cereal industry pioneer Will Keith Kellogg, the foundation provides about $200 million in grants each year to programs focused on youth and education, as well as health issues. It also funds many rural development and agricultural projects and works to foster greater volunteerism. Most of its grants go to initiatives in the US, though it also makes grants throughout Latin America and Africa. The foundation's work is funded primarily from its nearly $6 billion trust.

W.K. Kellogg Foundation is guided by its founder's desire "to help people help themselves" and prefers funding programs that offer long-term solutions rather than quick handouts. In 1934 Kellogg donated $66 million in stock to the foundation, which now ranks as one of the largest charitable organizations in the world.

W.K. Kellogg Foundation, which owns nearly a third of the Kellogg Company, is governed by an independent board of trustees.

Born in 1860, Will Keith Kellogg's early jobs included those of stock boy and traveling broom salesman. He also went to work as a clerk (and later, bookkeeper and manager) at the Battle Creek Sanitarium, a renowned homeopathic hospital where his older brother, John Harvey Kellogg, was physician-in-chief. In 1894 the brothers' experiments to improve vegetarian diets led to a happy accident that resulted in the first wheat flakes. In 1906 W.K. Kellogg started the Battle Creek Toasted Corn Flake Company. Through marketing genius and innovative products, Kellogg's company became a leader in the industry.

A philanthropist by inclination, Kellogg established the Fellowship Corporation in 1925 to build an agricultural school and a bird sanctuary, as well as to set up an experimental farm and a reforestation project. He also gave $3 million to hometown causes such as the Ann J. Kellogg School for disabled children, and for the construction of an auditorium, a junior high school, and a youth recreation center.

After attending a White House Conference on Child Health and Protection, Kellogg established the W.K. Kellogg Child Welfare Foundation in 1930. A few months later he broadened the focus of the charter and renamed the institution the W.K. Kellogg Foundation. That year the foundation began its landmark Michigan Community Health Project (MCHP), which opened public health departments in counties once thought too small and poor to sustain them. In 1934 Kellogg placed more than $66 million in Kellogg

Company stock and other investments in a trust to fund his foundation.

During WWII the foundation expanded its programming to Latin America, funding advanced schooling for dentists, physicians, and other health professionals. After the war, it broadened its programming to include agriculture to help war-torn Europe. It funded projects in Germany, Iceland, Ireland, Norway, and the UK. Following Kellogg's death in 1951, the organization began providing support for graduate programs in health and hospital administration, as well as for rural leadership and community colleges.

During the 1970s the foundation lent its support to the growing volunteerism movement and to aiding the disadvantaged, with a special emphasis on programs for minorities. A review of operations in the late 1970s led the Kellogg Foundation to reassert its emphasis on health, education, agriculture, and leadership. The foundation also expanded its programs to southern Africa.

In 1986 The Kellogg Foundation began funding the Rural America Initiative — a series of 28 projects meant to develop leadership, train local government officials, and revitalize rural areas. William Richardson became president and CEO of the foundation in 1995, leaving his post as president of The Johns Hopkins University. Also during the 1990s, the foundation supported the Community-Based Public Health Initiative, which assisted universities in educating public health professionals by presenting community-based approaches to students and faculty.

In 1998 the organization announced a five-year, $55 million plan to bring health care to the nation's poor and homeless. Also that year it gave Portland State University a $600,000 grant to develop its Institute for Nonprofit Management. In 1999 the Kellogg Foundation started its first geographically based program, pledging $15 million in grants for development of Mississippi River Delta communities in Arkansas, Louisiana, and Mississippi. In 2001 the foundation pledged an additional $20 million to support economic growth in the region through the Emerging Markets Partnership.

President and CEO: William C. Richardson, age 61
SVP and Corporate Secretary: Gregory A. Lyman
SVP Programs: Anne C. Petersen
VP and Chief Investment Officer: Paul J. Lawler
VP Finance and Treasurer: La June Montgomery-Tally
VP Programs: Richard M. Foster
VP Programs: Marguerite M. Johnson
VP Programs: Robert F. Long
VP Programs: Gail D. McClure
Director Human Resources: Norm Howard
Director Marketing and Communications:
 Karen E. Lake
Director Technology: Tim Dechant
Controller: Gloria Dickerson
Senior Counsel and Assistant Corporate Secretary:
 Mary C. Cotter
Auditors: PricewaterhouseCoopers LLP

HQ: 1 Michigan Ave. East, Battle Creek, MI 49017
Phone: 269-968-1611   **Fax:** 269-968-0413
Web: www.wkkf.org

2001 Grants

	$ mil.	% of total
US	156.1	79
Latin America & the Caribbean	23.3	12
Africa	17.2	9
Total	**196.6**	**100**

2001 Grants

	$ mil.	% of total
Youth & education	40.2	20
Health	28.6	15
Latin America & the Caribbean	23.3	12
Program activities	17.9	9
Africa	17.2	9
Food systems & rural development	16.4	8
Philanthropy & volunteerism	13.9	7
Special opportunities	10.7	5
Cross program initiative	7.9	4
Greater Battle Creek	7.0	4
Recurring grants	6.9	4
Cross-cutting themes	6.6	3
Total	**196.6**	**100**

Foundation FYE: August 31	Annual Growth	8/92	8/93	8/94	8/95	8/96	8/97	8/98	8/99	8/00	8/01
Sales ($ mil.)	(0.2%)	226	256	235	271	298	374	330	327	277	223
Employees	(3.8%)	—	—	—	264	276	280	286	290	250	209

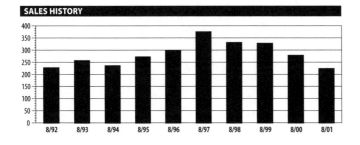

THE YUCAIPA COMPANIES LLC

Yucaipa has a hungry eye for picking out ripe bargains in different industries, but made its name with grocery stores. The investment company forged its reputation as the ultimate grocery shopper, executing a series of grocery chain mergers and acquisitions that put the company on the supermarket map. The Yucaipa Companies owns Jurgensen's, Falley's, and Alpha Beta, among other chains. The company's chairman, billionaire Ron Burkle, is a prominent Democratic activist and fundraiser; former president Bill Clinton and the Rev. Jesse Jackson serve on the company's board.

Yucaipa maintains a 70% stake in Golden State Foods, one of McDonald's largest suppliers; 9% of Fleming, a major food distributor; and 2% of Kroger. In addition, it has a minority stake in Simon Worldwide (formerly Cyrk), a promotional marketing company whose largest customer is McDonald's. Yucaipa's portfolio also includes Alliance Entertainment (a distributor of music, videos and games) and a 6% interest in Kmart Corporation.

Some of its investments have run into bumps in the road: Kmart filed for bankruptcy in 2002, and Simon faces numerous lawsuits stemming from a scandal after an employee allegedly rigged its client McDonald's Monopoly games and stole the cash.

Yucaipa is teaming up with California Public Employees' Retirement System (CalPERS) to form Yucaipa American Funds, which will seek to raise funds from union pensions and invest in labor-friendly businesses.

HISTORY

Ronald Burkle launched his career in the grocery industry as a box boy at his dad's Stater Bros. grocery store. By age 28 Burkle had moved up to SVP of administration, but he was fired after botching a buyout of the company in 1981.

Burkle and former Stater Bros. colleagues Mark Resnik and Douglas McKenzie founded Yucaipa (named after Burkle's hometown of Yucaipa, California) in 1986 when they bought Los Angeles gourmet grocery chain Jurgensen's. The next year Yucaipa bought Kansas-based Falley's, which had 20 Food 4 Less stores in California.

In 1989 Yucaipa merged with Breco Holding, operator of 70 grocery stores, and bought Northern California's Bell Markets. It acquired ABC Markets in Southern California in 1990. The next year the company bought the 142-store chain Alpha Beta. Thirty-six Yucaipa stores were damaged in the 1992 Los Angeles riots, but Yucaipa rebuilt, working with unions to keep workers employed until the stores were operational.

The company acquired the 28-store Smitty's Super Valu chain (now Fred Meyer Marketplace) in 1994. The following year Yucaipa bought the 70-year-old family-owned chain Dominick's Finer Foods. Later in 1995 Yucaipa's Food 4 Less chain merged with Los Angeles competitor Ralphs Grocery (founded in 1873 by George Ralphs), making Yucaipa #1 in Southern California.

Yucaipa sold Smitty's to Utah-based Smith's in 1996, acquiring a minority stake in Smith's. (Burkle became Smith's CEO). Dominick's went public in 1996, and Yucaipa retained a minority stake. The next year Fred Meyer bought Smith's for $1.9 billion. Burkle became the acquired company's chairman, and Yucaipa gained a 9% interest in Fred Meyer.

In 1998 Fred Meyer bought Ralphs and 155-store Quality Food Centers (QFC). Yucaipa and Wetterau Associates, a management firm, bought Golden State Foods, giving Yucaipa a 70% stake in the McDonald's food supplier. Also that year Yucaipa sold Dominick's to Safeway.

After Kroger bought Fred Meyer in 1999, Yucaipa turned away from the consolidating grocery industry and moved into cyberspace. That year Burkle and former Walt Disney president Michael Ovitz launched CheckOut Entertainment Network, which operated CheckOut.com, an entertainment Web site at which Web surfers could buy books, music, and videogames. Yucaipa hired Richard Wolpert, former president of Disney Online, to oversee its Internet and technology activities.

Yucaipa added to its portfolio in 1999 by taking stakes in GameSpy (online games), Talk City (later LiveWorld, online chat service), OneNetNow (online communities), ClubMom (Web site for mothers), and Cyrk (now Simon Worldwide, promotional marketing). Yucaipa also bought music, video, and games distributor Alliance Entertainment. The company also holds a minority stake in Simon Worldwide.

Music and video retailer Wherehouse Entertainment became a 50% owner of CheckOut.com after it merged its online retailing operations with CheckOut.com in 1999. (As the Internet economy faltered, Yucaipa sold CheckOut.com in 2001.)

In 2000 the company digressed from its focus on the Web to invest in Kole Imports, an importer of merchandise sold in discount stores.

Managing Partner: Ronald W. Burkle, age 49
CFO: Steve Mortensen
Senior Advisor: William J. "Bill" Clinton, age 56
Partner: Carlton J. Jenkins, age 45
Partner: Erika Paulson, age 27
Partner: Ed Renwick
Partner: Scott Stedman
Partner: Nick Tasooji
Partner: Ira Tochner
**Chief Adminstration Officer and Human Resources
  Director:** Bill Bailey
Legal: Robert P. Bermingham
Public Relations/Corporate Communications:
  Ari Swiller
Investor Relations and Business Development:
  Adrienne Gaines

Bain Capital
Berkshire Hathaway
Blackstone Group
Carlyle Group
Hicks, Muse
KKR
Leonard Green
Texas Pacific Group
Thomas Lee

HQ: 9130 W. Sunset Blvd., Los Angeles, CA 90069
Phone: 310-789-7200   **Fax:** 310-228-2873

Selected Investments
Alliance Entertainment (music, videos, and game
  distribution)
Fleming Companies (9%, wholesale food distributor)
Golden State Foods (70%, McDonald's supplier)
Kmart Corporation (6%, discount retailer)
Kole Imports (minority stake, discount-merchandise
  importer)
The Kroger Co. (2%, grocery stores)
Simon Worldwide (20%, promotional marketing)

Hoover's Handbook of Private Companies

OTHER MAJOR COMPANIES

24 HOUR FITNESS WORLDWIDE INC.

5020 Franklin Dr.	CEO: Mark S. Mastrov	2001 Sales: $1,029.0 million
Pleasanton, CA 94588	CFO: Colin Heggie	1-Yr. Sales Change: 13.0%
Phone: 925-416-3100	HR: John Putereaugh	Employees: 27,000
Fax: 925-416-3146	Type: Private	FYE: December 31
Web: www.24hourfitness.com		

If you're holding too much weight, 24 Hour Fitness Worldwide has the solution. It owns and operates some 437 fitness centers (under the 24 Hour Fitness, Q Clubs, and Hart's Athletic Clubs names) that offer aerobic, cardiovascular, and weight lifting activities. Some facilities also feature squash, racquetball, and basketball courts; swimming pools; steam and sauna rooms; tanning rooms; and whirlpools. The centers (the majority of which are open 24 hours a day) are located in 15 states in the US, as well as in Europe and Asia. Investment partnership McCown De Leeuw & Co. is the leading investor in the firm, which was founded in 1983 by Mark Mastrov.

KEY COMPETITORS
Bally Total Fitness
The Sports Club
World Gym

84 LUMBER COMPANY

1019 Route 519	CEO: Joseph A. Hardy Sr.	2001 Sales: $1,904.0 million
Eighty Four, PA 15330	CFO: Dan Wallach	1-Yr. Sales Change: 2.9%
Phone: 724-228-8820	HR: Steve Cherry	Employees: 5,400
Fax: 724-228-8058	Type: Private	FYE: December 31
Web: www.84lumber.com		

With its no-frills stores (most don't have air conditioning or heating), 84 Lumber has built itself to be a low-cost provider of lumber and building materials. Through more than 430 stores, the company sells lumber, siding, drywall, windows, and other supplies, as well as kits to make barns, playsets, decks, and even homes. Its stores are in about 35 states, mainly in the East, Southeast, and Midwest; 84 Lumber also sells products internationally. CEO Joseph Hardy Sr. founded 84 Lumber in 1956; his daughter, president Maggie Hardy Magerko, owns about 80% of the firm.

KEY COMPETITORS
Carolina Holdings
Home Depot
Lowe's

A&E TELEVISION NETWORKS

235 E. 45th St.	CEO: Nickolas Davatzes	2001 Sales: $804.0 million
New York, NY 10017	CFO: Gerard Gruosso	1-Yr. Sales Change: 4.4%
Phone: 212-210-1400	HR: Rosalind Clay Carter	Employees: —
Fax: 212-850-9304	Type: Joint venture	FYE: December 31
Web: www.aande.com		

A&E Television Networks is defying the notion that TV rots the brain. It offers a smorgasbord of programming in history, the arts, current events, and nature through its two main cable networks: A&E (more than 84 million subscribers) and The History Channel (more than 72 million subscribers). The company's flagship program is A&E's *Biography*. A&E Television also operates two digital cable channels (Biography Channel, History Channel International) and a handful of Web sites. A&E is a joint venture of media giants Hearst (37.5%), Walt Disney's ABC Cable (37.5%), and General Electric's NBC (25%).

KEY COMPETITORS
Discovery Communications
Turner Broadcasting
Viacom

📖 **In-depth profiles of an additional 200 key private companies are found on pages 36–435.**

ABBEY CARPET COMPANY, INC.

3471 Bonita Bay Blvd.
Bonita Springs, FL 34134
Phone: 941-948-0900
Fax: 941-948-0999
Web: www.abbeycarpet.com

CEO: Philip Gutierrez
CFO: Herb Gray
HR: —
Type: Private

2000 Sales: $1,280.0 million
1-Yr. Sales Change: 28.0%
Employees: —
FYE: December 31

Beating out even McDonald's as the first registered franchise in California, Abbey Carpet Company has become one of the nation's top franchise operations. The company runs a network of more than 750 independently owned and operated stores across the US, the Bahamas, and Puerto Rico. It sells brand-name carpet at mill-direct prices, as well as area rugs; hardwood, laminate, and vinyl floorings; ceramic tile; and window coverings. It also offers its own line of carpet and home fashion products. Founded in 1958 by Milton Levinson, Abbey Carpet began as a single floor-covering store in Sacramento, California. Chairman and CEO Phil Gutierrez has owned Abbey Carpet since 1983.

KEY COMPETITORS
Carpet One
Home Depot
Lowe's

ACADEMY SPORTS & OUTDOORS, LTD.

1800 N. Mason Rd.
Katy, TX 77449
Phone: 281-646-5200
Fax: 281-646-5204
Web: www.academy.com

CEO: David Gochman
CFO: Michael Ondruch
HR: Sylvia Barrera
Type: Private

2002 Sales: $775.0 million
1-Yr. Sales Change: 7.6%
Employees: 5,000
FYE: January 31

Academy Sports & Outdoors is near the head of the class among sporting goods retailers. The company is the third-largest full-line sporting goods chain in the US, behind The Sports Authority and Gart Sports. Academy's low-frills stores carry clothing, shoes, and equipment for almost any sport, including hunting, fishing, and boating. Academy has about 60 stores in Alabama, Florida, Louisiana, Mississippi, Oklahoma, Tennessee, and Texas. The company dates back to a San Antonio tire shop opened by Max Gochman in 1938. The business moved into military surplus items and during the 1980s began focusing on sports and outdoor merchandise. The Gochman family still owns Academy.

KEY COMPETITORS
Gart Sports
Sports Authority
Wal-Mart

ACF INDUSTRIES, INC.

620 N. 2nd St.
St. Charles, MO 63301
Phone: 636-940-5000
Fax: 636-940-5024
Web: www.acfindustries.com

CEO: Roger Wynkoop
CFO: Laura Parli
HR: Gary Rager
Type: Private

2001 Est. Sales: $620.0 mil.
1-Yr. Sales Change: (0.5%)
Employees: 3,000
FYE: December 31

ACF Industries (ACF) has been around for more than a century, but it is still on track. The company makes railroad tank and covered hopper cars (a category that it revolutionized with its Center Flow design). Through ACF Acceptance, the company also provides financing for its customers. ACF Industries has manufacturing operations in Pennsylvania and West Virginia. Formed in 1899 and originally known as American Car & Foundry, ACF is the oldest builder of railcars in the US and is owned by billionaire financier Carl Icahn, who also is ACF's chairman.

KEY COMPETITORS
GATX
Greenbrier
Trinity Industries

📖 **In-depth profiles of an additional 200 key private companies are found on pages 36–435.**

ACT MANUFACTURING, INC.

2 Cabot Rd.	CEO: John Young	2001 Sales: $1,536.0 million
Hudson, MA 01749	CFO: Pauline F. Taylor	1-Yr. Sales Change: 12.1%
Phone: 978-567-4000	HR: —	Employees: —
Fax: 978-562-8395	Type: Private	FYE: December 31
Web: www.actmfg.com		

ACT Manufacturing is trying to keep its PCB act together long enough to sell it. Most of ACT's business comes from printed circuit board, or PCB, assemblies, though it also makes cable and harness assemblies and electromechanical subassemblies. It also offers advanced manufacturing, product testing, and order fulfillment services. Top customers include Efficient Networks, EMC, and Nortel Networks. In the face of brutal market conditions and a steep decline in its business, ACT has filed for Chapter 11 bankruptcy protection and has announced plans to sell the company. Chairman John Pino and his family own 28% of ACT.

KEY COMPETITORS
Flextronics
Sanmina-SCI
Solectron

ADVANTAGE/ESM FEROLIE

2 Van Riper Rd.	CEO: Lawrence J. Ferolie	2001 Est. Sales: $1,200.0 mil.
Montvale, NJ 07645	CFO: Cathy Ross	1-Yr. Sales Change: 9.1%
Phone: 201-307-9100	HR: Julie Shasteen	Employees: 615
Fax: 201-782-0878	Type: Private	FYE: December 31
Web: www.feroliegroup.com		

A food broker serving the northeastern US, Advantage/ESM Ferolie broke into the business in 1948. The company provides sales and marketing services for packaged food and packaged goods companies. Through exclusive area and regional contracts, the group arranges distribution to warehouse stores, drugstores, supermarkets, and mass merchandisers. Some of Advantage/ESM Ferolie's biggest clients are Gillette's Duracell, Georgia-Pacific's Fort James, Kraft Foods, Unilever's Lipton, and McCormick & Company. The company is affiliated with Advantage Sales & Marketing, a partnership of food brokerages operating across the US. Founded by A. Joseph Ferolie, the company remains family-owned.

KEY COMPETITORS
Atlantic Mktg
Crossmark
Richfood

ADVENTIST HEALTH

2100 Douglas Blvd.	CEO: Donald R. Ammon	2001 Sales: $2,868.6 million
Roseville, CA 95661	CFO: Douglas E. Rebok	1-Yr. Sales Change: 14.3%
Phone: 916-781-2000	HR: Roger Ashley	Employees: 16,500
Fax: 916-783-9909	Type: Not-for-profit	FYE: December 31
Web: www.adventisthealth.org		

Adventist Health is a not-for-profit health care system with strong ties to the Seventh-Day Adventist Church. The West Coast wing of an international organization operating more than 160 Adventist health care operations, Adventist Health runs about 20 hospitals (with some 3,200 beds), almost 20 home health services agencies, and various other outpatient facilities and hospices in California, Hawaii, Oregon, and Washington. The organization also works with its own churches and those of other denominations to offer such preventative health services as medical screenings, immunizations, and health education.

KEY COMPETITORS
Catholic Healthcare West
Los Angeles County
  Department of Health
Tenet Healthcare

📖 **In-depth profiles of an additional 200 key private companies are found on pages 36–435.**

ADVOCATE HEALTH CARE

2025 Windsor Dr.
Oak Brook, IL 60523
Phone: 630-572-9393
Fax: 630-572-9139
Web: www.advocatehealth.com

CEO: James H. Skogsbergh
CFO: Lawrence J. Majka
HR: Ben Grigaliunas
Type: Not-for-profit

2000 Sales: $1,675.2 million
1-Yr. Sales Change: 4.7%
Employees: 24,500
FYE: December 31

Advocating wellness in Chicagoland from Palos Heights to Palatine, Advocate Health Care is an integrated health care network with more than 200 sites serving the Chicago area. Advocate's operations include eight acute-care hospitals (including Christ Medical Center and Lutheran General Hospital) with more than 3,000 beds, two children's hospitals, and home health care and ambulatory care services. Advocate also has teaching affiliations with area medical schools such as the University of Illinois at Chicago. In addition, Advocate manages a medical ethics center that helps its staff and clients address such issues as cloning and physician-assisted suicide.

KEY COMPETITORS
HCA
Provena Health
Rush System for Health

AECOM TECHNOLOGY CORPORATION

555 S. Flower St., Ste. 3700
Los Angeles, CA 90071
Phone: 213-593-8000
Fax: 213-593-8729
Web: www.aecom.com

CEO: Richard G. Newman
CFO: Glenn Robson
HR: —
Type: Private

2002 Est. Sales: $1,700.0 mil.
1-Yr. Sales Change: 88.2%
Employees: 15,500
FYE: September 30

AECOM Technology means never having to say Architecture, Engineering, Consulting, Operations, and Maintenance. One of the world's leading engineering and design groups, the company offers a range of professional technical services, mostly to government agencies and large corporations. AECOM is a top design firm in Asia and the Middle East and a global leader in the water, transportation, and wastewater sectors. It has expanded in Europe by acquiring UK-based companies such as transportation infrastructure groups Maunsell and Oscar Faber and water and wastewater construction group Metcalf & Eddy UK. AECOM employees control the company with a 44% stake.

KEY COMPETITORS
ABB
Bechtel
Louis Berger Group

AFFILIATED FOODS INCORPORATED

1401 Farmers Ave.
Amarillo, TX 79118
Phone: 806-372-3851
Fax: 806-372-3647
Web: www.afiama.com

CEO: George Lankford
CFO: Wayne Smith
HR: Gene Blackburn
Type: Cooperative

2002 Sales: $854.0 million
1-Yr. Sales Change: 22.0%
Employees: 1,000
FYE: September 30

Actually, it's the stores — 700 of them — that are affiliated with grocery distributor Affiliated Foods. The cooperative distributes food and nonfood items to its member-owners' stores in Arizona, Colorado, Kansas, New Mexico, Oklahoma, Texas, and Wyoming. Founded in 1946 as Panhandle Associated Grocers, Affiliated Foods helps retailers implement computer systems and software. In addition, the co-op operates Tri-State Baking (TenderCrust and Always Fresh brands) and owns the Plains Dairy, which processes 60,000 gallons of milk a day, and bottles water, juice, tea, and fruit drinks. It also owns a stake in private-label products supplier Western Family Foods (Western Family and Shurfine brands).

KEY COMPETITORS
AWG
Fleming Companies
SUPERVALU

📖 In-depth profiles of an additional 200 key private companies are found on pages 36–435.

A. G. SPANOS COMPANIES

1341 W. Robinhood Dr., Ste. A-1
Stockton, CA 95207
Phone: 209-478-7954
Fax: 209-473-3703
Web: www.agspanos.com

CEO: Dean A. Spanos
CFO: Jeremiah T. Murphy
HR: Charlene Flynn
Type: Private

2002 Est. Sales: $1,400.0 mil.
1-Yr. Sales Change: (10.3%)
Employees: 600
FYE: September 30

Spanning the land from California to Florida, A.G. Spanos Companies bridges many operations: building, managing, and selling multi-family housing units; constructing master-planned communities; and developing land. The firm has built more than 80,000 apartments in 18 states since its founding in 1960. Major projects include Spanos Park, a $1 billion master-planned community on 3,000 acres in founder and chairman Alex Spanos' hometown of Stockton, California, and the construction of luxury apartments across the nation. Alex Spanos, owner of the NFL's San Diego Chargers, stills owns the firm, which is operated by sons Dean (president and CEO) and Michael Spanos (EVP).

KEY COMPETITORS
Centex
Del Webb
Irvine Company

AGAMERICA, FCB

375 Jackson St.
St. Paul, MN 55101
Phone: 651-282-8800
Fax: 651-282-8666
Web: www.agamericafcb.com

CEO: William J. Collins
CFO: Diane M. Cole
HR: John E. Lovstad
Type: Cooperative

2001 Sales: $821.6 million
1-Yr. Sales Change: (1.5%)
Employees: —
FYE: December 31

AgAmerica aggrandizes farm credit in the western US. The cooperative is one of six regional banks in the federal Farm Credit System, providing loans and banking services to local Farm Credit offices. The bank ended its joint management agreement with sister Western Farm Credit Bank and is now co-managed with AgriBank, with which it plans to merge by 2003. AgAmerica offers operating and land loans, rural home mortgages, crop insurance, and financial services such as record-keeping and financial planning to aquatic producers, farmers, ranchers, rural homeowners, timber harvesters, and rural utility providers. The bank raises its funds through the sale of securities.

KEY COMPETITORS
Acceptance Insurance
AgFirst
National Rural Utilities
  Cooperative Finance

AGFIRST FARM CREDIT BANK

1401 Hampton St.
Columbia, SC 29202
Phone: 803-799-5000
Fax: 803-254-1776
Web: www.agfirst.com

CEO: F. A. Lowrey
CFO: Larry R. Doyle
HR: Pat N. Roche
Type: Cooperative

2001 Sales: $754.1 million
1-Yr. Sales Change: (32.0%)
Employees: —
FYE: December 31

AgFirst puts farms first. AgFirst Farm Credit Bank is a large agricultural lender for the southeastern US and Puerto Rico, offering more than $10 billion in loans to some 79,000 farmers, ranchers, and rural homeowners. It is one of six regional farm credit banks that make up the Farm Credit System (FCS) cooperative. AgFirst originates real estate, operating, and rural home mortgage loans. The company also offers crop, life, and other insurance; equipment leasing; and tax services. Clients include rural utility businesses, agricultural cooperatives, and agribusinesses. The bank does not accept deposits; it raises money by selling bonds and notes on the capital markets.

KEY COMPETITORS
AgAmerica
AgriBank
National Rural Utilities
  Cooperative Finance

📖 In-depth profiles of an additional 200
key private companies are found on pages 36–435.

AGRIBANK, FCB

375 Jackson
St. Paul, MN 55164
Phone: 651-282-8800
Fax: 651-282-8666
Web: www.agribank.com

CEO: William J. Collins
CFO: Diane M. Cole
HR: John E. Lovstad
Type: Cooperative

2001 Sales: $1,182.8 million
1-Yr. Sales Change: (33.3%)
Employees: —
FYE: December 31

AgriBank sees green in green acres. AgriBank is one of six intermediary banks in the Farm Credit System, a nationwide network of cooperatives that provide loans and financial services for farmers and rural homeowners. Farm Credit Services co-ops write loans for land, equipment, and other farm operating costs; they in turn own AgriBank, which provides loans and wholesale banking services to the co-ops. AgriBank also provides credit to rural electric, water, and telephone systems. The company has a co-management arrangement with AgAmerica; the two plan to merge in early 2003.

KEY COMPETITORS
Acceptance Insurance
Ag Services
AgFirst

AGRILINK FOODS, INC.

90 Linden Oaks
Rochester, NY 14602
Phone: 585-383-1850
Fax: 585-383-9153
Web: www.agrilinkfoods.com

CEO: Dennis M. Mullen
CFO: Earl L. Powers
HR: Lois Warlick-Jarvie
Type: Private

2002 Sales: $1,010.5 million
1-Yr. Sales Change: (22.5%)
Employees: 4,000
FYE: June 30

Agrilink is in the pink. As the #1 US maker of frozen vegetables, Agrilink Foods' veggie brands include Birds Eye, Birds Eye Voila!, Birds Eye Simply Grillin', Birds Eye Hearty Spoonfuls, Freshlike, and McKenzie's. The company also produces branded canned vegetables, pie fillings, chili and chili ingredients, salad dressings, and snacks. In addition, it makes private-label, food service, and industrial market foods, including canned and frozen vegetables, salad dressings, salsa, fruit fillings and toppings, and frozen vegetable specialty products. In 2002 Vestar Holdings acquired control of Agrilink from Pro-Fac Cooperative. Vestar and Pro-Fac now hold approximately 56% and 41% of Agrilink, respectively.

KEY COMPETITORS
ConAgra
Kraft Foods
Nestlé

AGWAY INC.

333 Butternut Dr.
DeWitt, NY 13214
Phone: 315-449-7061
Fax: 315-449-6008
Web: www.agway.com

CEO: Donald P. Cardarelli
CFO: Peter J. O'Neill
HR: Richard Opdyke
Type: Cooperative

2002 Sales: $899.9 million
1-Yr. Sales Change: (41.9%)
Employees: 4,200
FYE: June 30

It's either Agway or the highway for many farmers. The agricultural co-op has 69,000 members, primarily in the Northeast. The co-op's Agricultural Group sells feeds, seeds, fertilizers, and other farm supplies to members and other growers. Agway's Country Products Group processes and markets fresh produce (mostly under the Country Best label). It also invests in new agricultural technology. Agway Energy Products sells fuel and HVAC systems, and markets electricity and gas in deregulated states. The co-op also offers leasing services. In 2002 Agway filed for bankruptcy.

KEY COMPETITORS
ADM
Cenex Harvest States
Farmland Industries

In-depth profiles of an additional 200 key private companies are found on pages 36–435.

AID ASSOCIATION FOR LUTHERANS/LUTHERAN BROTHERHOOD

625 4th Ave. South	CEO: Bruce J. Nicholson	2001 Sales: $2,308.0 million
Minneapolis, MN 55415	CFO: Laurence W. Stranghoener	1-Yr. Sales Change: (0.6%)
Phone: 612-340-7000	HR: Jennifer H. Martin	Employees: 3,733
Fax: 612-340-4070	Type: Not-for-profit	FYE: December 31
Web: www.aal.org		

The Spirit has moved Aid Association for Lutherans (AAL) to merge with Lutheran Brotherhood. The resulting entity — a 3 million member-strong fraternal organization — has been christened Thrivent Financial for Lutherans. The merger brings under one steepled roof some $55 billion in assets under management in mutual funds, bank and trust services (AAL Bank and Trust and LB Community Bank & Trust are merging to become Thrivent Financial Bank), and other financial services. The combined organization also has about $145 billion in life insurance in force.

KEY COMPETITORS
Citigroup
FMR
State Farm

AIR WISCONSIN AIRLINES CORPORATION

W6390 Challenger Dr., Ste. 203	CEO: Geoffrey T. Crowley	2001 Sales: —
Appleton, WI 54914	CFO: James C. Clarke	1-Yr. Sales Change: —
Phone: 920-739-5123	HR: Lisa Conover	Employees: 2,600
Fax: 920-739-1325	Type: Private	FYE: December 31
Web: www.airwis.com		

Not limited to the state that shares its name, Air Wisconsin Airlines flies some 4 million passengers to about 45 cities in 21 states in the US. The regional carrier operates as United Express, providing connecting service to and from United Airlines' hubs in Denver and Chicago. Air Wisconsin's fleet consists mostly of regional jets. The smaller, more fuel-efficient aircraft make flying to less populated destinations more cost effective than using larger jets. The airline plans to expand its regional jet fleet and has firm orders to acquire 51 Canadair jets. Like many airlines in the wake of the September 11 US terrorist attacks, Air Wisconsin cut its flight schedule and trimmed its staff.

KEY COMPETITORS
Frontier Airlines
Mesa Air
Midwest Express

ALBERICI CONSTRUCTORS, INC.

2150 Kienlen Ave.	CEO: Robert F. McCoole	2001 Sales: $837.0 million
St. Louis, MO 63121	CFO: Gregory T. Hesser	1-Yr. Sales Change: 0.0%
Phone: 314-261-2611	HR: Carolyn Eskew	Employees: 480
Fax: 314-261-4225	Type: Private	FYE: December 31
Web: www.alberici.com		

When it comes to heavy construction, Alberici Constructors may not have written the book, but it has earned a footnote or two. Founded in 1918, Alberici Constructors (which changed its name in 2002 from J.S. Alberici Construction Co.) has worked on heavy construction projects ranging from a DaimlerChrysler plant to a Boeing rocket factory. It offers general contracting, construction management, design/build services, and specialty contracting such as heavy demolition and steel fabrication and erection. Markets served include aerospace, automotive, energy, health care, industrial process, and manufacturing. The Alberici family still has the largest share of the employee-owned firm, now part of Alberici Group.

KEY COMPETITORS
Fluor
Raytheon
Washington Group

📖 **In-depth profiles of an additional 200 key private companies are found on pages 36–435.**

ALCOA FUJIKURA LTD.

830 Crescent Centre Dr., Ste. 600	CEO: Robert S. Hughes II	2001 Sales: —
Franklin, TN 37067	CFO: Barbara Smith	1-Yr. Sales Change: —
Phone: 615-778-6000	HR: Brett Blair	Employees: 40,000
Fax: 615-778-5927	Type: Joint venture	FYE: December 31
Web: www.alcoa-fujikura.com		

Alcoa Fujikura offers the goods for driving and dialing. A joint venture between US-based aluminum producer Alcoa and Japanese wire and cable maker Fujikura, Alcoa Fujikura makes fiber-optic products for electric utilities and telecommunications networks, as well as electrical distribution systems used in automobiles. Its fiber-optic products range from cable and connectors to couplers and fusion-splicing systems. The automotive division makes electronic controllers, plastic components, printed circuit boards, and wiring. Alcoa Fujikura also offers engineering, installation, and testing services. The company's clients include BellSouth, Ford, Harley-Davidson, and Verizon.

KEY COMPETITORS
Corning
Furukawa Electric
Stoneridge

ALEX LEE, INC.

120 4th St. SW	CEO: Boyd L. George	2002 Est. Sales: $1,980.0 mil.
Hickory, NC 28602	CFO: Ronald W. Knedlik	1-Yr. Sales Change: 4.8%
Phone: 828-323-4424	HR: Glenn DeBiasi	Employees: 9,000
Fax: 828-323-4435	Type: Private	FYE: September 30
Web: www.alexlee.com		

The George family mixed food wholesaling and retail well before it became a trend among consolidators. Founded by Alex and Lee George, Alex Lee has been distributing food to retailers through Merchants Distributors, Inc. (MDI) since 1931. MDI serves more than 600 retailers in the Mid-Atlantic and Southeast, including IGA stores and Galaxy Food Centers. The company became a food service supplier in the 1960s through Institution Food House, and in 1984 it bought the Lowes Foods chain, which has more than 100 stores in North Carolina and Virginia. In 1998 Alex Lee started Consolidation Services to provide logistic services to vendors, distributors, and manufacturers. The George family controls Alex Lee.

KEY COMPETITORS
Fleming Companies
Kroger
SUPERVALU

ALLEGIS GROUP, INC.

6992 Columbia Gateway Dr.	CEO: John Carey	2001 Est. Sales: $2,700.0 mil.
Columbia, MD 21046	CFO: Dave Seandeven	1-Yr. Sales Change: (27.0%)
Phone: 410-579-4800	HR: Neil Mann	Employees: 8,000
Fax: —	Type: Private	FYE: December 31
Web: www.allegisgroup.com		

Clients in need of highly skilled technical and other personnel might want to take the pledge of Allegis. Allegis Group is one of the world's largest staffing and recruitment firms with more than 300 offices in North America and Europe. Its operating companies include Aerotek (engineering, automotive, and scientific professionals for short- and long-term assignments); Mentor 4 (recruitment for accounting, human resources, and customer support positions); and TEKsystems (IT staffing and consulting). In 1983 Steve Bisciotti and Jim Davis established Aerotek to provide contract engineering personnel to two clients in the aerospace industry; Bisciotti and Davis still control Allegis.

KEY COMPETITORS
Adecco
CDI
MPS

📖 **In-depth profiles of an additional 200 key private companies are found on pages 36–435.**

ALLIANCE CAPITAL MANAGEMENT L.P.

1345 Avenue of the Americas	CEO: Bruce W. Calvert	2001 Sales: $2,992.9 million
New York, NY 10105	CFO: Robert H. Joseph Jr.	1-Yr. Sales Change: 18.7%
Phone: 212-969-1000	HR: —	Employees: 4,542
Fax: 212-969-2229	Type: Private	FYE: December 31
Web: www.alliancecapital.com		

Alliance Capital Management has tons of funds. As one of the world's largest investment managers, Alliance Capital Management primarily serves such institutional investors as pension funds, foundations, endowments, government entities, and insurance companies. Alliance manages more than 80 mutual funds (with most of them invested in large-cap firms) and offers more than 100 additional funds from other managers. It also offers individuals managed accounts, retirement plans, and college savings plans. Alliance owns money manager and research firm Sanford C. Bernstein. French insurer AXA holds approximately 52% of Alliance Capital Management; publicly traded Alliance Capital Management Holding owns about 30%.

KEY COMPETITORS
FMR
ING
Merrill Lynch

ALLINA HEALTH SYSTEM

710 East 24th St.	CEO: John M. Morrison	2001 Sales: $1,700.0 million
Minneapolis, MN 55404	CFO: David Jones	1-Yr. Sales Change: (34.6%)
Phone: 612-775-5000	HR: Michael W. Howe	Employees: 22,102
Fax: —	Type: Not-for-profit	FYE: December 31
Web: www.allina.com		

Allina Health System is a not-for-profit health care system that focuses on prevention and community programs as an alternative means of keeping its members healthy. Allina Health System's health plans, doctors, and hospitals cover Minnesota and Wisconsin. The system's Medica Health Plans offers a variety of plans and serves more than 1 million members. The Allina Medical Group operates about 15 hospitals and nearly 50 clinics offering in-patient and ambulatory care. Allina Health System also operates nursing homes and provides home health care.

KEY COMPETITORS
HCA
Mayo Foundation
SSM Health Care

ALTICOR INC.

7575 Fulton St. East	CEO: Doug DeVos	2002 Sales: $4,500.0 million
Ada, MI 49355	CFO: Lynn Lyall	1-Yr. Sales Change: 28.6%
Phone: 616-787-1000	HR: Robin Horder-Koop	Employees: 10,500
Fax: 616-682-4000	Type: Private	FYE: August 31
Web: www.alticor.com		

At the core of Alticor, there is Amway. Alticor was formed in 2000 as a holding company for four businesses: direct-selling giant Amway, Web-based sales firm Quixtar, Pyxis Innovations (corporate development for Alticor and affiliates), and Access Business Network (manufacturing, logistics services). Access Business' biggest customers are Amway and Quixtar, but Access also serves outsiders. Amway, which accounts for the bulk of Alticor's revenues, sells more than 450 different products through 3 million independent distributors. Quixtar sells Amway and other products online. Alticor is owned by Amway founders, the DeVos and Van Andel families.

KEY COMPETITORS
Avon
CCL Industries
PFSweb

📖 **In-depth profiles of an additional 200 key private companies are found on pages 36–435.**

A-MARK FINANCIAL CORPORATION

100 Wilshire Blvd., 3rd Fl.	CEO: Steven C. Markoff	2002 Sales: $2,300.0 million
Santa Monica, CA 90401	CFO: Joseph Ozaki	1-Yr. Sales Change: (11.5%)
Phone: 310-319-0200	HR: —	Employees: 104
Fax: 310-319-0346	Type: Private	FYE: July 31
Web: www.amark.com		

Calling all gold bugs: A-Mark Financial trades, markets, and finances rare coins, precious metals, and collectibles. A-Mark Precious Metals trades in gold, silver, platinum, and palladium coins, bars, ingots, and medallions for central banks, corporations, and individuals around the world. A-Mark Financial distributes coins for government mints, including those of Australia, Canada, South Africa, and the US. Subsidiary A-M Handling provides melting and assay services. Chairman, president, and owner Steven Markoff founded A-Mark Financial in 1965.

KEY COMPETITORS
Anglo American
DGSE Companies
Degussa

AMERICAN BUILDERS & CONTRACTORS SUPPLY CO., INC.

1 ABC Pkwy.	CEO: Kenneth A. Hendricks	2001 Sales: $1,381.5 million
Beloit, WI 53511	CFO: Kendra Story	1-Yr. Sales Change: 11.5%
Phone: 608-362-7777	HR: Lisa Indgjer	Employees: 3,188
Fax: 608-362-2717	Type: Private	FYE: December 31
Web: www.abc-supply.com		

American Builders & Contractors Supply Co. (which operates as ABC Supply) has put roofs over millions of heads. A leading supplier of roofing, siding, windows, and related builder's supplies, ABC Supply has about 215 outlets in more than 40 states. It carries its own brand of products (Amcraft, Mule-Hide), and it offers doors, windows, tools and such from about 500 vendors. ABC Supply distributes its products via a fleet of some 2,900 vehicles. It also operates a building supply catalog. ABC Supply, which markets its products mostly to small and medium-sized professional contractors, was founded in 1982 by CEO Kenneth Hendricks. Hendricks and his wife, EVP Diane, own the company.

KEY COMPETITORS
Cameron Ashley
Georgia-Pacific Corporation
North Pacific Group

AMERICAN CAST IRON PIPE CO.

1501 N. 31st Ave. North	CEO: Van L. Richey	2001 Sales: $600.0 million
Birmingham, AL 35202	CFO: J. M. Cook	1-Yr. Sales Change: 0.0%
Phone: 205-325-7701	HR: Leann Barr	Employees: 2,313
Fax: 205-325-1942	Type: Private	FYE: December 31
Web: www.acipco.com		

American Cast Iron Pipe Co. (ACIPCO) has one of the largest individual ductile iron pipe casting plants in the world. Its divisions — American Centrifugal, American Ductile Iron Pipe, American Flow Control, and American Steel Pipe — make ductile iron pipe and fittings, cast steel tubes, electric resistance welded steel pipes, fire hydrants and fire truck pumps, and valves for water treatment and energy production. ACIPCO's newest subsidiary, American SpiralWeld Pipe, produces spiral-welded steel pipe. John Joseph Eagan founded ACIPCO in 1905, and in 1922 placed all of the company's stock into a beneficial trust for ACIPCO employees. Employees also receive generous quarterly bonuses.

KEY COMPETITORS
AK Steel Holding Corporation
McWane
Oregon Steel Mills

📖 In-depth profiles of an additional 200 key private companies are found on pages 36–435.

AMERICAN CENTURY COMPANIES, INC.

4500 Main St., Ste. 1500	CEO: William M. Lyons	2001 Sales: —
Kansas City, MO 64111	CFO: Robert T. Jackson	1-Yr. Sales Change: —
Phone: 816-531-5575	HR: Jerry Bartlett	Employees: 3,000
Fax: 816-340-7962	Type: Private	FYE: December 31
Web: www.americancentury.com		

American Century Companies, through subsidiary American Century Investment Management, oversees a family of more than 60 mutual funds. The firm administers four distinct groups of funds: capital preservation, income, growth and income, and growth. The company's brokerage services afford investors access to more than 9,000 additional mutual funds from approximately 250 other firms. American Century manages accounts for individuals, corporations, charitable organizations, and retirement plans. The company manages some $85 billion of client assets. J.P. Morgan Chase owns a 45% stake in American Century, which is controlled by founder James Stowers Jr. and his family.

KEY COMPETITORS
FMR
T. Rowe Price
Vanguard Group

AMERICAN CRYSTAL SUGAR COMPANY

101 N. Third St.	CEO: James J. Horvath	2002 Sales: $775.3 million
Moorhead, MN 56560	CFO: Joseph J. Talley	1-Yr. Sales Change: (10.5%)
Phone: 218-236-4400	HR: Randy Johnson	Employees: 1,243
Fax: 218-236-4422	Type: Cooperative	FYE: August 31
Web: www.crystalsugar.com		

Call it saccharine, but for American Crystal Sugar, business is all about sharing. The sugar beet cooperative is owned by more than 3,000 growers in the Red River Valley of North Dakota and Minnesota. American Crystal, formed in 1899 and converted into a co-op in 1973, divides the 35-mile-wide valley into five districts, each served by a processing plant. During an annual eight-month "campaign," the plants operate continuously, producing sugar, molasses, and beet pulp. Its products (under the Crystal name, the licensed Pillsbury brand, and private labels) are sold through marketing co-ops United Sugars and Midwest Agri-Commodities. American Crystal also owns 46% of corn-sweeteners joint venture ProGold.

KEY COMPETITORS
Florida Crystals
Imperial Sugar
U.S. Sugar

AMERICAN FOODS GROUP, INC.

544 Acme St.	CEO: Carl W. Kuehne	2001 Est. Sales: $650.0 mil.
Green Bay, WI 54308	CFO: Doug Hagen	1-Yr. Sales Change: 12.1%
Phone: 920-437-6330	HR: Marc Houston	Employees: 1,500
Fax: 920-436-6510	Type: Private	FYE: June 30
Web: www.american-foods.com		

American Foods Group is a bona fide Green Bay packer. It slaughters cattle and produces branded and private label bacon, beef cuts, deli meats, ham, and sausage for sale to the grocery and food service industries. Its beef plant cranks out 4 million pounds of ground beef each week. The company operates refrigerated trucking unit Americas Service Lines and offers meats and other gift foods direct to consumers through its Ackerman & Cooke catalogs and Web site. CEO and owner Carl Kuehne purchased American Foods in 1985 and expanded it through acquisitions and product development. After nixing plans to be acquired by Smithfield Foods, American Foods set up a joint venture with Iowa beef producers.

KEY COMPETITORS
Farmland Industries
IBP
Smithfield Foods

📖 In-depth profiles of an additional 200
key private companies are found on pages 36–435.

AMERICAN GOLF CORPORATION

2951 28th St.	CEO: Edward R. Sause	2001 Sales: $730.8 million
Santa Monica, CA 90405	CFO: —	1-Yr. Sales Change: (2.1%)
Phone: 310-664-4000	HR: Tom Norton	Employees: 20,000
Fax: 310-664-6160	Type: Private	FYE: December 31
Web: www.americangolf.com		

American Golf Corporation (AGC) is in the rough. The company — one of the largest golf-course management firms in the world with more than 300 public, private, and resort courses in the US, Australia, Japan, and the UK — is struggling with the weak US economy and increased competition. The firm has fallen behind in rental payments to sister firm National Golf Properties, from which it leases half its properties. National Golf had agreed to acquire AGC, although some National Golf shareholders challenged the deal on claims that the primary beneficiary would be David Price (chairman of both AGC and National Golf). In 2002 an investor group led by Goldman Sachs agreed to purchase both National Golf and ACG.

KEY COMPETITORS
ClubCorp
Golf Trust of America

AMERICAN PLUMBING AND MECHANICAL, INC.

1950 Louis Henna Blvd.	CEO: Robert A. Christianson	2001 Sales: $606.2 million
Round Rock, TX 78664	CFO: David C. Baggett	1-Yr. Sales Change: 8.7%
Phone: 512-246-5260	HR: Phil Thompson	Employees: 5,600
Fax: 512-246-5290	Type: Private	FYE: December 31
Web: www.ampam.com		

It would take a lot of Teflon tape to connect the far-flung companies of American Plumbing and Mechanical (AMPAM). AMPAM provides contract plumbing services, as well as HVAC and mechanical services, in more than a dozen states in the US. The company provides its services for single-family and multifamily residential structures, as well as for commercial and institutional projects. Founded in 1998 to acquire 10 regional contracting companies, AMPAM began operations in 1999 and has continued to acquire or create similar companies in new service areas. The firm's subsidiaries operate as separate entities, with AMPAM providing financial and accounting support. Management members own more than 80% of the company.

KEY COMPETITORS
American Residential Services
Chemed
Scott Co.

AMERICAN RETAIL GROUP INC.

6251 Crooked Creek Rd.	CEO: Hans Brenninkmeyer	2001 Est. Sales: $900.0 mil.
Norcross, GA 30092	CFO: Michele Toth	1-Yr. Sales Change: (28.0%)
Phone: 770-662-2500	HR: Elaine Gregg	Employees: 11,000
Fax: 770-448-1853	Type: Private	FYE: January 31

It's all in the family with retail clothing giant American Retail Group (ARG). ARG is the US piece of the Brenninkmeyer family's $7-billion global retail puzzle. The company sells mid-priced apparel and outdoor clothing through nearly 1,000 stores in the US. Its chains include Eastern Mountain Sports, Maurice's, Anchor Blue Clothing, Levi's Outlet by M.O.S.T., Dockers Outlet by M.O.S.T., and Juxtapose. The Brenninkmeyers, who entered US retailing in 1948, are a secretive bunch, sometimes sending their children to college under assumed names. The brood runs its empire from a secluded compound in the Netherlands and employs more than 200 family members.

KEY COMPETITORS
J. C. Penney
Kmart
Sears

📖 **In-depth profiles of an additional 200 key private companies are found on pages 36–435.**

AMERICAN SOCIETY OF COMPOSERS, AUTHORS AND PUBLISHERS

1 Lincoln Plaza	CEO: John LoFrumento	2001 Sales: $600.0 million
New York, NY 10023	CFO: Bob Candela	1-Yr. Sales Change: 20.0%
Phone: 212-621-6000	HR: Diane Pfadenhauer	Employees: 600
Fax: 212-874-8480	Type: Not-for-profit	FYE: December 31
Web: www.ascap.com		

While Frank Sinatra got the glory, Johnny Mercer got some of the money, and his estate still does, thanks to the American Society of Composers, Authors and Publishers (ASCAP). ASCAP is the #1 performance-rights organization in the world. The group protects the rights of composers, songwriters, lyricists, and music publishers by licensing and distributing royalties for the public performances of their copyrighted works. Whether they're played in a stadium, on the radio or Internet, on an airplane, or in a bar, songs of more than 135,000 members are covered.

KEY COMPETITORS
BMI
SESAC

AMERICAN UNITED LIFE INSURANCE COMPANY

1 American Sq.	CEO: Jerry D. Semler	2001 Sales: $1,317.8 million
Indianapolis, IN 46206	CFO: Constance E. Lund	1-Yr. Sales Change: 3.3%
Phone: 317-285-1877	HR: Mark Roller	Employees: —
Fax: —	Type: Mutual company	FYE: December 31
Web: www.aul.com		

American United Life Insurance Company specializes in pensions and annuities and also offers individual and group life insurance and disability coverage. The company touts its reinsurance unit (which dates from 1904) as the oldest in the US. American United Life Insurance was formed from the 1936 merger of United Mutual Life Insurance and American Central Life Insurance. Licensed in 49 states and the District of Columbia, it also does business in Latin America. The company has restructured into a mutual holding company, which gives it a more favorable tax status as well as allowing it to form publicly traded subsidiaries.

KEY COMPETITORS
CNA Financial
Lincoln National
Principal Financial

AMICA MUTUAL INSURANCE COMPANY

100 Amica Way	CEO: Thomas A. Taylor	2001 Sales: $954.0 million
Lincoln, RI 02865	CFO: Robert A. DiMuccio	1-Yr. Sales Change: (11.3%)
Phone: 800-242-6422	HR: Richard S. Glover	Employees: 3,600
Fax: 401-333-4610	Type: Mutual company	FYE: December 31
Web: www.amica.com		

Amica is an amicable source for your insurance needs. Amica Mutual Insurance Company provides a variety of personal insurance products, including auto, home, marine, personal liability, and life policies. The company is a mutual insurance company, which means it is owned by its policyholders. With about 60 offices in the US, Amica sells its policies directly to customers in all states except Hawaii. Its roots as an auto insurer go back to 1907, when fire coverage was a car owner's most important need, due to exploding gas tanks. Amica was formed in 1973 through the consolidation of Automobile Mutual Insurance Company of America and Factory Mutual Liability Insurance Company of America.

KEY COMPETITORS
Allstate
CNA Financial
State Farm

In-depth profiles of an additional 200 key private companies are found on pages 36–435.

AMSTED INDUSTRIES INCORPORATED

205 N. Michigan Ave., 44th Fl.	CEO: W. Robert Reum	2002 Est. Sales: $1,360.0 mil.
Chicago, IL 60601	CFO: Stephen Gregory	1-Yr. Sales Change: (17.6%)
Phone: 312-645-1700	HR: Thomas G. Berg	Employees: 9,000
Fax: 312-819-8494	Type: Private	FYE: September 30
Web: www.amsted.com		

Wilbur and Orville Wright's first flight might never have succeeded without an assist from Amsted's Diamond Chain subsidiary. A maker of roller chains for a variety of equipment and machinery, Diamond Chain also produced the propeller chain for the Wright brothers' aircraft. AMSTED's other subsidiaries include ASF-Keystone (side frames, bolsters, and cast-steel freight car components); Griffin Pipe Products (ductile iron pressure and sewer pipe); and Means Industries (automotive steering and transmission components). Customers include industrial distributors, locomotive and railcar manufacturers, and automotive OEMs. Employee-owned AMSTED has roughly 50 plants worldwide.

KEY COMPETITORS
ALSTOM
Bethlehem Steel
Meridian Rail

ANCIRA ENTERPRISES

6111 Bandera Rd.	CEO: Ernesto Ancira Jr.	2001 Sales: $648.0 million
San Antonio, TX 78238	CFO: Betty Ferguson	1-Yr. Sales Change: 10.0%
Phone: 210-681-4900	HR: Valerie Tackett	Employees: 675
Fax: 210-681-9413	Type: Private	FYE: December 31
Web: www.ancira.com		

Ancira Enterprises wants to help Texans hit the road: It sells cars, trucks, and recreational vehicles exclusively in the Lone Star State. The company's dealerships feature new vehicles under the Buick, Chevrolet, Chrysler, Ford, GMC, Jeep, Kia, Nissan, Pontiac, and Volkswagen brands, as well as used cars and trucks. Ancira Enterprises also sells new and used campers, motor homes, and recreational vehicles under the American Dream, Fleetwood, and Winnebago names, among others. The company is one of the nation's top fleet dealers and operates on-site parts and service departments. Ancira Enterprises, which was founded in 1984, is owned by president Ernesto Ancira Jr.

KEY COMPETITORS
AutoNation
David McDavid
Group 1 Automotive

ANDERSON NEWS COMPANY

6016 Brookvale Ln., Ste. 151	CEO: Charles Anderson	2001 Est. Sales: $1,100.0 mil.
Knoxville, TN 37919	CFO: John Campbell	1-Yr. Sales Change: 0.0%
Phone: 865-584-9765	HR: Donna Norris	Employees: 7,000
Fax: 865-584-3498	Type: Private	FYE: December 31
Web: www.andersonnews.com		

Anderson News is the covergirl of the magazine wholesale industry. The company (which bought ARAMARK's magazine distribution operations in 1998) leads the merger-happy industry with about a 40% US market share. Anderson News distributes thousands of magazine titles to about 40,000 outlets, including bookstores, mass merchants, grocery and convenience stores, discount retailers, and just about any other place that sells something to read. The company also distributes newspapers, books, videos, and music. Anderson News was founded in 1917 by CEO Charles Anderson's grandfather; it is still family-owned. The founding Anderson family also runs the #3 US bookstore chain, Books-A-Million.

KEY COMPETITORS
Chas. Levy
Hudson News
Jim Pattison Group

📖 **In-depth profiles of an additional 200 key private companies are found on pages 36–435.**

THE ANGELO IAFRATE COMPANIES

26400 Sherwood	CEO: Angelo E. Iafrate Sr.	2000 Sales: $675.0 million
Warren, MI 48091	CFO: George Ihm	1-Yr. Sales Change: —
Phone: 586-756-1070	HR: Eugene Polk	Employees: 2,000
Fax: 586-756-0467	Type: Private	FYE: December 31
Web: www.iafrate.com		

Included among the US's largest private firms, The Angelo Iafrate Companies also ranks among the nation's top environmental construction firms. The group's subsidiaries are engaged in surface paving and heavy civil and highway construction projects, turnkey industrial contracting, underground utility infrastructure installation, site preparation and excavation, and environmental construction and remediation. The company also has a materials division that processes and sells crushed concrete, sand and gravel, limestone, and asphalt. Founded in 1960, the company is owned by the Iafrate family, who developed a state-of-the-art process to crush and recycle concrete.

KEY COMPETITORS
Bechtel
Jacobs Engineering
Washington Group

APEX OIL COMPANY, INC.

8235 Forsyth Blvd., Ste. 400	CEO: P. Anthony Novelly	2002 Est. Sales: $1,400.0 mil.
Clayton, MO 63105	CFO: John L. Hank Jr.	1-Yr. Sales Change: (30.0%)
Phone: 314-889-9600	HR: Julie Cook	Employees: 175
Fax: 314-854-8539	Type: Private	FYE: September 30
Web: www.apexoil.com		

At the top of its game, Apex Oil is engaged in the wholesale sales, storage, and distribution of petroleum products. Its range of refined products includes asphalt, kerosene, fuel oil, diesel fuel, heavy oil, gasoline, and bunker fuels. The company's terminals are located on the East Coast, Gulf Coast, in California, and in the Midwest. Internationally, Apex Oil has a terminal in Caracas, Venezuela, and has additional activities in Bermuda, Monaco, and the Netherlands. The company is also engaged in a tug boats and barge business and has a storage and truck rack operation. Founded in 1932 by Samuel Goldstein, Apex Oil is controlled by CEO Tony Novelly.

KEY COMPETITORS
Chemoil
Crown Central Petroleum
Getty Petroleum Marketing

API GROUP, INC.

2366 Rose Place	CEO: Lee R. Anderson Sr.	2001 Sales: $750.0 million
St. Paul, MN 55113	CFO: Loren Rachey	1-Yr. Sales Change: 3.3%
Phone: 651-636-4320	HR: —	Employees: 5,000
Fax: 651-636-0312	Type: Private	FYE: December 31
Web: www.apigroupinc.com		

Holding company APi Group has a piece of the action in four business sectors: construction services, fire protection, manufacturing, and materials distribution. APi has more than 20 subsidiaries, which operate as independent companies. Services provided by the company's construction subsidiaries include energy conservation; electrical, industrial, and mechanical contracting; industrial insulation; and overhead door installation. Other units install fire protection systems, fabricate structural steel, and distribute building materials. The family-owned company was founded in 1926 by Reuben Anderson, father of CEO Lee Anderson.

KEY COMPETITORS
EMCOR
Scott Co.
Tyco Fire and Security Services

📖 **In-depth profiles of an additional 200 key private companies are found on pages 36–435.**

APPLEONE, INC.

327 W. Broadway	CEO: Bernard Howroyd	2000 Sales: $648.0 million
Glendale, CA 91209	CFO: Mike Hoyle	1-Yr. Sales Change: —
Phone: 818-240-8688	HR: Deborah Guzman	Employees: 1,922
Fax: 818-240-9958	Type: Private	FYE: December 31
Web: www.appleone.com		

An apple a day keeps the unemployment lines away. AppleOne is one of the nation's largest privately held employment agencies, with some 400 offices across the US and Canada. It places job seekers in a variety of temporary, temporary-to-permanent, and full-time positions in accounting, customer service, law, and information technology, among other fields. The company also offers its corporate clients human resources services, such as payroll and tax filing, continuing education, and outplacement. CEO Bernard Howroyd, who founded the company in 1964 after a conversation with an unhappy temp worker in a bar, controls AppleOne.

KEY COMPETITORS
Adecco
Kelly Services
Manpower

APPLETON PAPERS, INC.

825 E. Wisconsin Ave.	CEO: Doug Buth	2001 Sales: $1,000.0 million
Appleton, WI 54912	CFO: Dale Parker	1-Yr. Sales Change: (9.1%)
Phone: 920-734-9841	HR: Paul Karch	Employees: 2,500
Fax: 920-991-8080	Type: Private	FYE: December 31
Web: www.appletonpapers.com		

Appleton Papers shows that some things don't fall far from the tree. The company — formerly the US branch of Arjo Wiggins Appleton — manufactures and distributes paper and paperboard products. Its core business is carbonless paper (NCR Paper), a profitable but waning market. Appleton also produces thermal paper (Optima) for use with print technology and computer products, uncoated security paper (Docucheck) that protects documents against forgery, and coated paper (Avario) for design and communication printing. Appleton is truly owned by its employees; more than 90% of its employees bought the company from Arjo Wiggins by investing roughly 75% of their 401k plans (about $40,000 each).

KEY COMPETITORS
Boise Cascade
International Paper
Weyerhaeuser

ARBOR COMMERCIAL MORTGAGE, LLC

333 Earle Ovington Blvd., 9th Fl.	CEO: Ivan Kaufman	2001 Sales: $600.0 million
Uniondale, NY 11553	CFO: Rick Herbst	1-Yr. Sales Change: 20.0%
Phone: 516-832-8002	HR: Kevin McNulty	Employees: 125
Fax: 516-832-8045	Type: Private	FYE: December 31
Web: www.thearbornet.com		

Shake this tree and you might just end up with some money. Arbor Commercial Mortgage originates and services commercial real-estate loans with an emphasis on multifamily and assisted-living properties. Arbor is a Fannie Mae Delegated Underwriting and Servicing (DUS) lender for individual multifamily loans. DUS lenders can make loans for eventual sale to Fannie Mae without prior approval. Arbor also offers the Fannie Mae DUS Targeted Affordable Housing Product for the development and financing of low-income housing and the Fannie Mae DUS Small Loan Product for multifamily loans up to $3 million. Arbor was founded in 1983 by CEO Ivan Kaufman and operates nationwide.

KEY COMPETITORS
Citigroup
Ocwen Financial
Washington Mutual

📖 **In-depth profiles of an additional 200 key private companies are found on pages 36–435.**

ARCTIC SLOPE REGIONAL CORPORATION

301 Arctic Slope Ave., Ste. 300
Anchorage, AK 99518
Phone: 907-852-8633
Fax: 907-852-5733
Web: www.asrc.com

CEO: Jacob Adams
CFO: Frank Zirnkilton
HR: Karen Burnell
Type: Private

2001 Sales: $1,062.0 million
1-Yr. Sales Change: 2.3%
Employees: 6,413
FYE: December 31

The Inupiat people have survived the Arctic for centuries, and now they're surviving in the business world. The Inupiat-owned Arctic Slope Regional Corporation (ASRC) was set up to manage 5 million acres on Alaska's North Slope after the Alaska Native Claims Settlement Act in 1971 cleared the way for oil development in the area. ASRC gets about two-thirds of sales from its energy services subsidiaries (Natchiq) and its petroleum refining and marketing units (Petro Star). Other operations include construction, engineering, and manufacturing. Along with other native corporations, ASRC has formed Alaska Native Wireless which, in partnership with AT&T Wireless, has won more than 40 mobile licenses in the US.

KEY COMPETITORS
Alaska Communications
 Systems
Baker Hughes
Tesoro Petroleum

ASHLEY FURNITURE INDUSTRIES, INC.

1 Ashley Way
Arcadia, WI 54612
Phone: 608-323-3377
Fax: 608-323-6008
Web: www.ashleyfurniture.com

CEO: Todd Wanek
CFO: Richard Barclay
HR: Jim Dotta
Type: Private

2001 Est. Sales: $1,090.0 mil.
1-Yr. Sales Change: 14.5%
Employees: 6,000
FYE: December 31

Furniture buyers took a shine to Ashley Furniture Industries when it added a tough, high-gloss polyester finish to its furniture in 1986. The company is the nation's largest privately held furniture manufacturer. Ashley Furniture makes and imports upholstered, leather, and hardwood furniture, as well as bedding. It has manufacturing plants and distribution centers spread throughout the country and overseas. It runs more than 100 Ashley Furniture HomeStores — independently owned shops that sell only Ashley Furniture products. The firm was founded by Carlyle Weinberger in 1945. Father-and-son duos Ron and Todd Wanek and Chuck and Ben Vogel own Ashley Furniture.

KEY COMPETITORS
Furniture Brands International
Klaussner Furniture
La-Z-Boy

ASI CORP.

48289 Fremont Blvd.
Fremont, CA 94538
Phone: 510-226-8000
Fax: 510-226-8858
Web: www.asipartner.com

CEO: Marcel Liang
CFO: —
HR: Crystal Yuan
Type: Private

2001 Est. Sales: $1,000.0 mil.
1-Yr. Sales Change: 22.2%
Employees: 500
FYE: December 31

ASI has a whole lotta sales going on. The company, a wholesale distributor of computer software, hardware, and accessories, sells more than 3,000 products, including CD-ROM drives, modems, monitors, PCs, networking equipment, and storage devices. ASI also boasts a dedicated motherboard catalog site, motherboardmaster.com, and offers standard and custom configurations. The company sells to systems integrators and resellers throughout North America. Vendor partners include 3Com, Microsoft, Samsung, and Toshiba. President Christine Liang, who founded ASI in 1987, owns 51% of the company.

KEY COMPETITORS
Arrow Electronics
Ingram Micro
Tech Data

In-depth profiles of an additional 200 key private companies are found on pages 36–435.

ASPLUNDH TREE EXPERT CO.

708 Blair Mill Rd.
Willow Grove, PA 19090
Phone: 215-784-4200
Fax: 215-784-4493
Web: www.asplundh.com

CEO: Christopher B. Asplundh
CFO: Joseph P. Dwyer
HR: Jean Nichols
Type: Private

2001 Est. Sales: $1,400.0 mil.
1-Yr. Sales Change: (5.0%)
Employees: 24,000
FYE: December 31

How much wood would a woodchuck chuck, if a woodchuck could chuck wood? A lot, if the woodchuck were named Asplundh. The company is the world's largest tree-trimming business, clearing tree limbs from power lines for utilities and municipalities in Australia, Canada, New Zealand, and the US. The company also offers utility-related services such as meter reading, pipeline maintenance, storm emergency services, street light maintenance and construction, underground pipeline location, and utility pole maintenance. The Asplundh family owns and manages the company, which was founded in 1928.

KEY COMPETITORS
Davey Tree
Monroe and Lewis Tree Service
Wright Tree Service

ASSOCIATED FOOD STORES, INC.

1850 W. 2100 South
Salt Lake City, UT 84119
Phone: 801-973-4400
Fax: 801-978-8551
Web: www.afstores.com

CEO: Richard A. Parkinson
CFO: S. Neal Berube
HR: Fred Ferguson
Type: Cooperative

2002 Sales: $1,189.5 million
1-Yr. Sales Change: 9.6%
Employees: 1,400
FYE: March 31

Associated Food Stores, a regional cooperative wholesale distributor, goes to extremes — mountain cold and desert heat — in supplying nearly 600 independent supermarkets. Member stores (who own the cooperative) are spread throughout eight western states. The co-op owns about 25% of Western Family Foods, a grocery wholesalers' partnership that produces private-label merchandise under the Western Family brand. AFS acquired three of its four largest customers (Macey's, Dan's, and Lin) in 1999 to avoid losing them to acquisition-hungry supermarket chains. It currently owns and operates about 22 retail stores. The co-op was formed in 1940 by Donald Lloyd, president of the Utah Retail Grocers Association, and 34 other retailers.

KEY COMPETITORS
Fleming Companies
SUPERVALU
Unified Western Grocers

ASSOCIATED GROCERS, INC.

3301 S. Norfolk
Seattle, WA 98118
Phone: 206-762-2100
Fax: 206-764-7731
Web: agsea.com

CEO: Robert P. Hermanns
CFO: John L. Carrosino
HR: Dick Harding
Type: Private

2001 Est. Sales: $1,000.0 mil.
1-Yr. Sales Change: (9.1%)
Employees: 1,100
FYE: September 30

Associated Grocers (AG) feeds the ability of its member/owners to remain competitive. The cooperative distributes food and nonfood goods and provides support services to more than 300 independent grocery retailers in the Northwest, Hawaii, Alaska, Guam, and the Pacific Rim. It distributes more than 12,000 items, including products under the Western Family, Ovenworks, and Javaworks names. AG (not to be confused with Associated Grocers in other regions) was formed in 1934 to support 11 Seattle-based neighborhood grocers. Financial trouble led to a 15-month-long restructuring effort that resulted in asset sales and a new management team led by CEO Robert Hermanns, formerly the COO of Weis Markets.

KEY COMPETITORS
Kroger
Safeway
Unified Western Grocers

In-depth profiles of an additional 200 key private companies are found on pages 36–435.

ASSOCIATED MATERIALS INCORPORATED

2200 Ross Ave., Ste. 4100 E.	CEO: Michael Caporale	2001 Sales: $595.8 million
Dallas, TX 75201	CFO: D. Keith LaVanway	1-Yr. Sales Change: 19.3%
Phone: 214-220-4600	HR: Stephanie Johnson	Employees: 2,140
Fax: 214-220-4607	Type: Private	FYE: December 31
Web: www.associatedmaterials.com		

Associated Materials Incorporated (AMI) is quick to side with its customers. Through its Alside division (almost 90% of sales), the company makes vinyl siding and vinyl windows for the new construction and home remodeling markets. Other Alside products include vinyl fencing, decking, railing, and garage doors. Alside operates 89 company-owned supply centers and distributes metal siding and other building products made by other OEMs. AMI's AmerCable unit makes jacketed electrical cable for industrial, mining, marine, and telecommunications industries. Investment firm Harvest Partners acquired AMI in 2002.

KEY COMPETITORS
Nortek
Owens Corning
Royal Group Technologies

ASSOCIATED MILK PRODUCERS INCORPORATED

315 N. Broadway	CEO: Mark Furth	2001 Sales: $1,200.0 million
New Ulm, MN 56073	CFO: Steve Sorenson	1-Yr. Sales Change: 20.0%
Phone: 507-354-8295	HR: Leigh Heilman	Employees: 1,600
Fax: 507-359-8651	Type: Cooperative	FYE: December 31
Web: www.ampi.com		

Associated Milk Producers Incorporated might wear a cheesy grin, but it churns up solid sales. Shying away from the liquid stuff, it transforms more than 5 billion pounds of milk into butter, cheese, and other solid milk products each year. A regional cooperative of 4,600 dairy farms from Iowa, Minnesota, Missouri, Nebraska, North and South Dakota, and Wisconsin, AMPI operates 14 manufacturing plants. The co-op produces 60% of all the instant milk sold in the US and is a major cheddar producer. Aside from its own State brand of cheese and butter, AMPI primarily makes private-label products for retailers and food service customers.

KEY COMPETITORS
Dairy Farmers of America
Foremost Farms
Land O'Lakes

ASSOCIATED WHOLESALERS, INC.

Route 422, P.O. Box 67	CEO: J. Christopher Michael	2001 Sales: $923.0 million
Robesonia, PA 19551	CFO: Thomas C. Teeter	1-Yr. Sales Change: 5.0%
Phone: 610-693-3161	HR: Audrey Hausmann	Employees: 1,500
Fax: 610-693-3171	Type: Cooperative	FYE: July 31
Web: www.awiweb.com		

Being associated with Associated Wholesalers, Inc. (AWI) means having a supplier of food and nonfood items. The retailer-owned cooperative supplies health and beauty care items, meat, dairy products, produce, bakery products, and canned goods to independent grocers in Delaware, Maryland, New Jersey, New York, Pennsylvania, Virginia, and West Virginia. In addition to merchandise, the co-op also provides training and technical services to members, and it operates nine of its own Shurfine Markets in four Pennsylvania counties. AWI operates two distribution centers in Pennsylvania — one in Robesonia that supplies food, and one in York that handles general merchandise.

KEY COMPETITORS
Di Giorgio
Fleming Companies
SUPERVALU

📖 **In-depth profiles of an additional 200 key private companies are found on pages 36–435.**

ATLANTIC MUTUAL COMPANIES

140 Broadway	CEO: Klaus G. Dorfi	2001 Sales: $837.7 million
New York, NY 10005	CFO: Cornelius E. Golding	1-Yr. Sales Change: 1.1%
Phone: 212-943-1800	HR: Lisa Reciniti	Employees: 1,800
Fax: 212-428-6566	Type: Mutual company	FYE: December 31
Web: www.atlanticmutual.com		

Having set sail as a marine insurer more than 150 years ago, Atlantic Mutual Companies today provides commercial, personal, and marine property/casualty insurance to individuals and businesses. Through its subsidiaries (including Atlantic Mutual Insurance, Centennial Insurance, and Atlantic Specialty Insurance), the company offers insurance programs and loss control for large firms, and specialty coverage for small to midsized companies such as financial institutions, retailers, and wholesalers. Atlantic Mutual also provides auto and homeowners coverage for individuals. Independent agents and brokers sell the company's products throughout the US.

KEY COMPETITORS
ACE Limited
AIG
St. Paul Companies

AUSTIN ENERGY

721 Barton Springs Rd.	CEO: Juan Garza	2001 Sales: $811.0 million
Austin, TX 78704	CFO: Elaine Kuhlman	1-Yr. Sales Change: 3.6%
Phone: 512-322-9100	HR: Ken Andriessen	Employees: 1,362
Fax: 512-322-6005	Type: Government-owned	FYE: September 30
Web: www.austinenergy.com		

The capital city of Texas may have a laid-back reputation, but it uses plenty of energy. Austin Energy is a municipally owned electric utility that serves 360,000 residential and commercial customers. Its 2,600 MW of generation capacity comes primarily from its two gas-fired plants, part-ownership of a coal-fueled facility, and a 16% stake in a nuclear-powered plant in Bay City, Texas. The utility buys 100 MW of alternative energy from wind power and landfill methane sources. Austin Energy has been producing electricity since 1895, when a hydroelectric plant opened on the Colorado River. Power deregulation took effect in Texas in 2002, but as a city-owned utility, Austin Energy is not required to participate.

AUSTIN INDUSTRIES INC.

3535 Travis St., Ste. 300	CEO: Ronald J. Gafford	2001 Sales: $1,257.0 million
Dallas, TX 75229	CFO: Paul W. Hill	1-Yr. Sales Change: 3.3%
Phone: 214-443-5500	HR: Enrique Estrada	Employees: 6,000
Fax: 214-443-5581	Type: Private	FYE: December 31
Web: www.austin-ind.com		

Paving the way for progress, Austin Industries provides civil, commercial, and industrial construction services. Its oldest subsidiary, Austin Bridge & Road, provides road, bridge, and parking lot construction across Texas. Subsidiary Austin Commercial, known for its high-rises, builds corporate headquarters, technology sites, and hospitals in the central and southwestern US. Austin Commercial tackled its first major sports-arena project with American Airlines Center in Dallas. The group's Austin Industrial provides construction, maintenance, and electrical services for the chemical, refining, power, and manufacturing industries, mostly in the US South and Southeast. The employee-owned firm was founded in 1918.

KEY COMPETITORS
Beck Group
Granite Construction
Turner Industries

📖 **In-depth profiles of an additional 200 key private companies are found on pages 36–435.**

AVONDALE INCORPORATED

506 S. Broad St.	CEO: G. Stephen Felker	2002 Sales: $659.7 million
Monroe, GA 30655	CFO: Jack R. Altherr Jr.	1-Yr. Sales Change: (14.6%)
Phone: 770-267-2226	HR: Sharon L. Rodgers	Employees: 5,700
Fax: 770-267-5196	Type: Private	FYE: August 31

Family-owned Avondale has fabric in its genes — er, jeans. The vertically integrated company makes apparel fabrics (cotton and cotton-blend piece-dyed fabrics, indigo-dyed denim); greige fabrics (undyed, unfinished cotton and cotton blends); specialty fabrics (such as coated materials for awnings, boat covers, and tents); and yarns. Leading apparel makers such as VF Corporation (maker of Lee and Wrangler jeans, among others) buy from Avondale. The company operates about 20 manufacturing facilities in Alabama, Georgia, and North and South Carolina. Avondale was founded in Georgia in 1895 and is headed by G. Stephen Felker, great-grandson of the founder.

KEY COMPETITORS
Cone Mills
Galey & Lord
R. B. Pamplin

BAIN & COMPANY

2 Copley Place	CEO: Orit Gadiesh	2001 Sales: —
Boston, MA 02116	CFO: Len Banos	1-Yr. Sales Change: —
Phone: 617-572-2000	HR: Elizabeth Corcoran	Employees: 2,800
Fax: 617-572-2427	Type: Partnership	FYE: December 31
Web: www.bain.com		

"Bainies" are always ready when corporate titans need a little direction. One of the world leaders in strategic consulting, Bain & Company (whose consultants are called Bainies) offers services such as business unit, organizational, and corporate strategy; distribution and logistics advice; mergers, acquisitions, and divestiture consulting; and sales and marketing strategy. It works for clients in a variety of industries, including consumer products, financial services, technology, media and communications, and telecommunications. The firm also offers services for startups through its bainlab unit.

KEY COMPETITORS
Booz Allen
Boston Consulting
McKinsey & Company

BAKER & TAYLOR CORPORATION

2709 Water Ridge Pkwy.	CEO: Gary M. Rautenstrauch	2002 Sales: $1,122.0 million
Charlotte, NC 28217	CFO: David Finlon	1-Yr. Sales Change: 12.2%
Phone: 704-357-3500	HR: Claudette Hampton	Employees: 2,750
Fax: 704-329-8989	Type: Private	FYE: June 30
Web: www.btol.com		

If you've strolled through a library recently, you likely saw a lot of Baker & Taylor (B&T) without knowing it. The #1 book supplier to libraries, B&T maintains three operating units. Its institutional segment distributes books, calendars, music, and DVDs to about 8,000 school, public, and specialty libraries around the world. Its retail unit supplies storefront and Internet retailers, as well as independent booksellers, with nearly 4 million book titles and more than 135,000 video, DVD, and CD titles. Its Informata.com unit is B&T's business-to-business e-commerce arm. Investment firm The Carlyle Group and its affiliates own nearly 85% of B&T. Management, employees, and other private investors own the rest.

KEY COMPETITORS
Alliance Entertainment
Ingram Entertainment
Ingram Industries

In-depth profiles of an additional 200 key private companies are found on pages 36–435.

BANNER HEALTH SYSTEM

1441 N. 12th St.	CEO: Peter S. Fine	2002 Sales: —
Phoenix, AZ 85006	CFO: Ron Bunnell	1-Yr. Sales Change: —
Phone: 602-495-4000	HR: Gerri Toomey	Employees: 21,500
Fax: —	Type: Not-for-profit	FYE: December 31
Web: www.bannerhealth.com		

Formed from the merger of Lutheran Health Systems and Samaritan Health System, Banner Health System is one of the largest non-church affiliated, not-for-profit health systems in the country. The organization operates about 20 hospitals, long-term care centers, and family clinics in seven states, specializing in hospitals serving non-urban communities. Its Banner Health Arizona division provides home care, heart care, cancer care, women's health, and out-patient services, along with behavioral health and rehabilitation. The Banner Health Colorado division consists of a network of community hospitals; it also supplies home medical equipment in Colorado.

KEY COMPETITORS
Catholic Healthcare West
HCA
Triad Hospitals

BARNES & NOBLE COLLEGE BOOKSTORES, INC.

33 E. 17th St.	CEO: Max J. Roberts	2002 Est. Sales: $1,250.0 mil.
New York, NY 10003	CFO: Barry Brover	1-Yr. Sales Change: 4.2%
Phone: 212-539-2000	HR: Gail Gittleson	Employees: 9,500
Fax: 212-780-1866	Type: Private	FYE: April 30
Web: www.bkstore.com		

Barnes & Noble College Bookstores is the scholastic sister company of Barnes & Noble (B&N), the US's largest bookseller. Started in 1873, the company operates more than 450 campus bookstores nationwide, selling textbooks, trade books, school supplies, collegiate clothing, and emblematic merchandise. Universities, medical and law schools, and community colleges hire Barnes & Noble College Bookstores to replace traditional campus cooperatives. (The schools get a cut of the sales.) The company also runs online retailer textbooks.com. B&N's Chairman Leonard Riggio owns a controlling interest in Barnes & Noble College Bookstores.

KEY COMPETITORS
Follett
Nebraska Book
Wallace's Bookstores

BARTLETT AND COMPANY

4800 Main St., Ste. 600	CEO: James B. Heberstreit	2001 Est. Sales: $800.0 mil.
Kansas City, MO 64112	CFO: Arnie Wheeler	1-Yr. Sales Change: (1.2%)
Phone: 816-753-6300	HR: Bill Webster	Employees: 600
Fax: 816-753-0062	Type: Private	FYE: December 31

When the cows come home, Bartlett and Company will be ready. The company's primary business is grain merchandising, but it also runs cattle feedlots and mills flour. Bartlett operates grain storage facilities in Kansas City, Kansas; St. Joseph and Waverly, Missouri; and Nebraska City, Nebraska. It has terminal elevators in Iowa, Kansas, and Missouri, as well as more than 10 country elevators. Bartlett's cattle operations are based in Texas; its flour mills are in Kansas, North Carolina, and South Carolina. The Bartlett and Company Grain Charitable Foundation makes financial gifts to local causes. Founded in 1907 as Bartlett Agri Enterprises, the company is still owned by the founding Bartlett family.

KEY COMPETITORS
ADM
Cargill
DeBruce Grain

In-depth profiles of an additional 200 key private companies are found on pages 36–435.

BARTON MALOW COMPANY

226500 American Dr.
Southfield, MI 48034
Phone: 248-436-4500
Fax: 248-436-5001
Web: www.bmco.com

CEO: Ben C. Maibach III
CFO: Mark A. Bahr
HR: Judith Willard
Type: Private

2002 Sales: $1,251.0 million
1-Yr. Sales Change: 7.8%
Employees: 1,264
FYE: March 31

Barton Malow scores by building end zones and home plates. The construction management and general contracting firm also makes points for its schools, hospitals, offices, and plants. Barton Malow's services range from planning to completion of projects; it has experience in 37 US states and the District of Columbia, including Atlanta's Phillips Arena, Boston's Shriners Hospital, and General Motors' Truck Product Center. Barton Malow Design provides architecture and engineering services, and the company's Barton Malow Rigging unit installs process equipment and machinery. Chairman Ben Maibach Jr. and his family own a majority stake in the firm, which was founded in 1924 by C. O. Barton.

KEY COMPETITORS
Gilbane
Hunt Construction
Walbridge Aldinger

BASHAS' INC.

22402 S. Basha Rd.
Chandler, AZ 85248
Phone: 480-895-9350
Fax: 480-895-5394
Web: www.bashas.com

CEO: Edward N. Basha Jr.
CFO: Darl J. Andersen
HR: Michael Gantt
Type: Private

2001 Est. Sales: $1,359.0 mil.
1-Yr. Sales Change: 13.3%
Employees: 10,800
FYE: December 31

Bashas' has blossomed in the Arizona desert. Founded in 1932 and owned by the Basha family, the food retailer has grown to about 125 stores. These are located primarily throughout Arizona, but with one store each in California and New Mexico. Its holdings include Bashas' traditional supermarkets, AJ's Fine Foods (gourmet-style supermarkets), and Bashas' Mercado and Food City supermarkets, which cater to Hispanics in southern Arizona. Bashas' acquired 22 Southwest Supermarkets stores and is converting them to Food City supermarkets. It also operates a handful of supermarkets (including its New Mexico store) in the Navajo Nation. The company offers online grocery shopping through its Groceries On The Go service.

KEY COMPETITORS
Albertson's
Kroger
Safeway

BASS PRO SHOPS, INC.

2500 E. Kearney
Springfield, MO 65898
Phone: 417-873-5000
Fax: 417-873-4672
Web: www.basspro.com

CEO: John L. Morris
CFO: Toni Miller
HR: Mike Roland
Type: Private

2001 Est. Sales: $1,100.0 mil.
1-Yr. Sales Change: 11.1%
Employees: 8,800
FYE: December 31

Bass Pro Shops (BPS) knows how to reel in the shoppers. Each of its 15 Outdoor World stores (in 10 states) covers about 280,000 sq. ft. The cavernous outlets sell boats, campers, equipment, and apparel for most outdoor activities and offer features such as archery ranges, giant fish tanks, snack bars, and video arcades. The first Outdoor World store, in Missouri, has been that state's #1 tourist attraction since it opened in 1981. BPS catches shoppers at home with its seasonal and specialty catalogs and through its TV and radio programs. It owns Tracker Marine (boat manufacturing), American Rod & Gun (sporting goods wholesale), and runs a resort in the Ozark Mountains. Founder and CEO John Morris owns BPS.

KEY COMPETITORS
Academy
MarineMax
Wal-Mart

In-depth profiles of an additional 200
key private companies are found on pages 36–435.

BE&K INC.

2000 International Park Dr.	CEO: T. Michael Goodrich	2002 Sales: $1,478.0 million
Birmingham, AL 35243	CFO: Clyde M. Smith	1-Yr. Sales Change: (16.8%)
Phone: 205-972-6000	HR: Kimberly S. Patterson	Employees: 8,822
Fax: 205-972-6651	Type: Private	FYE: March 31
Web: www.bek.com		

Like a busy bee building hives for the queen, BE&K keeps up its reputation as a top US engineering and construction contractor. BE&K provides engineering, procurement, and construction and maintenance services worldwide for industrial process facilities, including the cement, chemical, petrochemical, pharmaceutical, and pulp and paper industries. It also serves the telecommunications, manufacturing, environmental, energy, and commercial sectors. The company was founded in 1972 by partners Peter Bolvig, William Edmonds, and chairman Ted Kennedy (who retain ownership). Overseas operations began in Poland in 1984 through a strategic relationship with International Paper; BE&K now operates on five continents.

KEY COMPETITORS
CH2M HILL
Parsons
URS

BEAULIEU OF AMERICA, LLC

1502 Coronet Dr.	CEO: Carl M. Bouckaert	2001 Est. Sales: $1,400.0 mil.
Dalton, GA 30720	CFO: Bayard Hollingsworth	1-Yr. Sales Change: (22.2%)
Phone: 706-695-4624	HR: Clint Hubbard	Employees: 10,000
Fax: 706-695-6237	Type: Private	FYE: December 31
Web: www.beaulieu-usa.com		

Products from Beaulieu of America (BOA) have floored a lot of customers. A vertically integrated manufacturer, BOA produces fibers and fabrics for its own carpets as well as for other carpet companies. Through its Coronet division, the company produces berber, commercial, indoor/outdoor, and needlepunched carpet. Its products also include artificial grass, mats, and wall coverings. BOA has sold its area rug division to Springs Industries and is currently closing and consolidating other operations in order to pay down debt. Chairman and CEO Carl Bouckaert and his wife, Mieke, whose family made carpets in Europe, founded Beaulieu in 1978; the Bouckaerts control BOA.

KEY COMPETITORS
Interface
Mohawk Industries
Shaw Industries

THE BECK GROUP

1700 Pacific Ave., Ste. 3800	CEO: Lawrence A. Wilson	2000 Sales: $990.0 million
Dallas, TX 75201	CFO: Patricia Priest	1-Yr. Sales Change: 69.5%
Phone: 214-965-1100	HR: Jerry Cooper	Employees: 710
Fax: 214-965-1300	Type: Private	FYE: December 31
Web: www.beckgroup.com		

At the beck and call of commercial developers, The Beck Group has built everything from racetracks to runways, retail centers, hotels, and hospitals. The firm provides design/build, general contracting, and construction management services in the US and Mexico. Focusing on commercial and institutional building, Beck offers services such as scheduling, contract administration, and procurement support. The company also provides real estate development services. Its projects include Dallas' Cotton Bowl, the Texas Motor Speedway outside Fort Worth, the Museum of Contemporary Art in Los Angeles, and California's Beverly Hills Hotel. Members of the Beck family own the company, which was founded in 1912 by Henry Beck.

KEY COMPETITORS
Austin Industries
Centex
Turner Corporation

📖 **In-depth profiles of an additional 200 key private companies are found on pages 36–435.**

BELLCO HEALTH CORP.

5500 New Horizons Blvd.
N. Amityville, NY 11701
Phone: 631-789-6300
Fax: 631-841-6185
Web: www.bellcohealth.com

CEO: Neil Goldstein
CFO: Vincent Russo
HR: —
Type: Private

2002 Sales: $877.0 million
1-Yr. Sales Change: 13.2%
Employees: 165
FYE: June 30

This Bellco is no baby. Bellco Health Corp. operates through three divisions. Its Bellco Drug division is an independent drug distributor selling primarily to pharmacies and retailers on Long Island and in New York City. The company distributes various name-brand and generic pharmaceutical products, as well as over-the-counter drugs and sundries. Its American Medical Distributors division sells professional products to specialty clinics and physicians. The company's third division, Dialysis Purchasing Alliance, is a group-purchasing organization focusing on dialysis equipment and supplies. The Schuss family, who founded Bellco in 1955, owns the company.

KEY COMPETITORS
AmerisourceBergen
Cardinal Health
McKesson

BEN E. KEITH COMPANY

601 E. 7th St.
Fort Worth, TX 76102
Phone: 817-877-5700
Fax: 817-338-1701
Web: www.benekeith.com/main.html

CEO: Robert Hallam
CFO: Mel Cockrell
HR: Sam Reeves
Type: Private

2002 Sales: $1,185.0 million
1-Yr. Sales Change: 11.0%
Employees: 2,526
FYE: June 30

Ben E. Keith is your bud if you like eating out and drinking Bud. The company delivers a full line of foods (produce, dry groceries, frozen food, meat), paper goods, equipment, and supplies to more than 12,000 customers in Arkansas, Kansas, Louisiana, New Mexico, Oklahoma, and Texas. It is one of the world's largest Anheuser-Busch distributors, delivering beer in 54 Texas counties. Ben E. Keith's customers include restaurants, hospitals, schools, and other institutional businesses. Founded in 1906 as Harkrider-Morrison, the company assumed its current name in 1931 in honor of Ben E. Keith, who served as the company's president until 1959. Its owners include Robert and Howard Hallam.

KEY COMPETITORS
McLane Foodservice
SYSCO
U.S. Foodservice

BERWIND GROUP

3000 Centre Square West, 1500 Market St.
Philadelphia, PA 19102
Phone: 215-563-2800
Fax: 215-563-8347
Web: www.berwind.com

CEO: Hellene Runtagh
CFO: James Cook
HR: Catherine Warrin
Type: Private

2001 Sales: —
1-Yr. Sales Change: —
Employees: 7,500
FYE: December 31

Berwind Group isn't workin' in a coal mine anymore. Founded in 1874 to mine Appalachian coal, the firm began leasing its mining operations in 1962 to fund investments in new ventures. Berwind's Interlogix subsidiary makes items such as intrusion and fire detection sensors, facility integration control systems, and surveillance equipment. Berwind Property Group owns commercial, retail, and residential real estate nationwide, and Berwind Financial Group provides investment banking services. Berwind Natural Resources and Berwind Pharmaceutical Services round out the group's operations. The Berwind family owns the company. A subsidiary of the company has agreed to acquire office supply firm Hunt Corporation.

KEY COMPETITORS
DuPont
FMC
W.W. Grainger

📖 **In-depth profiles of an additional 200 key private companies are found on pages 36–435.**

BIG Y FOODS, INC.

2145 Roosevelt Ave.
Springfield, MA 01102
Phone: 413-784-0600
Fax: 413-732-7350
Web: www.bigy.com

CEO: Donald H. D'Amour
CFO: Herb Dotterer
HR: Jack Henry
Type: Private

2002 Est. Sales: $1,200.0 mil.
1-Yr. Sales Change: 0.0%
Employees: 7,850
FYE: June 30

Why call it Big Y? Big Y Foods began as a 900-sq.-ft. grocery at a Y intersection in Chicopee, Massachusetts. It now operates about 45 supermarkets in Massachusetts and Connecticut. More than half of its stores are Big Y World Class Markets, offering specialty departments such as bakeries, floral shops, and in-store banking. The remaining stores consist of Big Y Supermarkets and one Table & Wine store, which sells gourmet food, wine, and liquor. Some Big Y stores provide child care, dry cleaning, photo processing, and even propane sales, and their delis and Food Courts offer to-go foods. Big Y is owned and run by the D'Amour family; Paul D'Amour bought the original store in 1936 and was quickly joined by teenage brother Gerald.

KEY COMPETITORS
SUPERVALU
Shaw's
Stop & Shop

BILL BLASS LTD.

550 7th Ave., 12th Fl.
New York, NY 10018
Phone: 212-221-6660
Fax: 212-302-5166

CEO: Michael Groveman
CFO: Ronald Fetzer
HR: Ronald Fetzer
Type: Private

2000 Est. Sales: $775.0 mil.
1-Yr. Sales Change: 2.0%
Employees: 45
FYE: December 31

Bill Blass' signature has marked sophisticated styles for over three decades. His namesake company makes tailored men's and women's clothing known to adorn the upper crust from Barbara Bush to Barbra Streisand. Blass started the company in 1970 and made a name for himself to create timeless, tailored designs using fine fabrics. Never yielding to trendy looks such as disco or grunge, the Bill Blass name has acquired a loyal fashion following. Most sales come from more than 40 licenses for items such as furniture, eyewear, and accessories. Blass, who retired in 2000 and passed away in 2002, sold the firm in 1999 to its jeanswear licensee, Resource Club, and Michael Groveman (CEO). Lars Nilsson is the head designer.

KEY COMPETITORS
Chanel
Christian Dior
St. John Knits

BILL HEARD ENTERPRISES

200 Brookstone Center Pkwy., Ste. 205
Columbus, GA 31904
Phone: 706-323-1111
Fax: 706-321-9488
Web: www.billheard.com

CEO: William T. Heard
CFO: Ronald A. Feldner
HR: Jim Matthews
Type: Private

2001 Sales: $2,600.0 million
1-Yr. Sales Change: 44.8%
Employees: 4,000
FYE: December 31

The Southern hills (and Western deserts) are alive with the sound of Chevys — music to the ears of Bill Heard Enterprises. The largest Chevrolet dealer in the world (according to Chevrolet Motor Division), Bill Heard has more than 15 dealerships in Alabama, Arizona, Florida, Georgia, Nevada, Tennessee, and Texas. The dealer sells new and used vehicles and auto supplies and offers repair services; it also owns Oldsmobile and Cadillac franchises in Georgia and sells Hyundais at its Memphis location. William Heard Sr. opened his first dealership in 1919. He switched to selling Chevrolets exclusively in 1932, and his son and grandsons, who now run the family-owned business, continue to focus on Chevy sales.

KEY COMPETITORS
AutoNation
CarMax
United Auto Group

In-depth profiles of an additional 200 key private companies are found on pages 36–435.

BJC HEALTH SYSTEM

4444 Forest Park Ave.	CEO: Steven H. Lipstein	2001 Sales: $2,200.0 million
St. Louis, MO 63108	CFO: Edward Stiften	1-Yr. Sales Change: 4.8%
Phone: 314-286-2000	HR: Robert Cannon	Employees: 25,801
Fax: 314-286-2060	Type: Not-for-profit	FYE: December 31
Web: www.bjc.org		

BJC brings Jews and Christians together for the good of its patients. BJC Health System is the product of the 1993 merger of Barnes-Jewish, Inc., and Christian Health System. The system operates 12 hospitals and about 100 primary care and home health facilities in and around St. Louis — both in Missouri and Illinois. Specialized services include hospice care, rehabilitation services, and occupational health and workers' compensation. BJC also offers a dental plan with HMO, PPO, and fee-for-service options. BJC Health System is affiliated with Washington University Medical Center.

KEY COMPETITORS
Ascension
SSM Health Care
Sisters of Mercy

BLACK & VEATCH

8400 Ward Pkwy.	CEO: Leonard C. Rodman	2001 Sales: $2,224.0 million
Kansas City, MO 64114	CFO: Karen L. Daniel	1-Yr. Sales Change: (5.7%)
Phone: 913-458-2000	HR: Shirley Gaufin	Employees: 8,500
Fax: 913-458-2934	Type: Private	FYE: December 31
Web: www.bv.com		

From Argentina to Zimbabwe, Black & Veatch provides the ABCs of construction and engineering. It engages in all phases of building projects, including design and engineering, financing and procurement, and construction. Since 1915 Black & Veatch has handled jobs ranging from the elegant (reconstructing a Renaissance building in the Czech Republic) to the industrial (building a coal-fired power plant in Guatemala). With more than 90 offices worldwide, Black & Veatch targets the infrastructure, process, and power markets. Other markets include high-tech, information technology, management consulting, telecommunications, and water/wastewater. The employee-owned firm is one of the US's largest private companies.

KEY COMPETITORS
Bechtel
Fluor
Shaw Group

BOB ROHRMAN AUTO GROUP

701 Sagamore Pkwy. South	CEO: Bob Rohrman	2001 Sales: $694.4 million
Lafayette, IN 47905	CFO: Tom Hanlan	1-Yr. Sales Change: 7.1%
Phone: 765-448-1000	HR: Kim Sharp	Employees: 1,200
Fax: 765-449-2266	Type: Private	FYE: December 31
Web: www.rohrman.com		

With about 35 dealerships in Indiana and around Chicago, Bob Rohrman Auto Group is after the lion's share of area car sales. The company sells more than 36,000 new and used vehicles annually from its dealerships in Chicago, and in Indianapolis, Fort Wayne, and Lafayette, Indiana. Bob Rohrman offers new vehicles from most major auto manufacturers, including DaimlerChrysler, General Motors, Honda, Hyundai, Isuzu, Kia, Mitsubishi, Nissan, and Toyota. It also sells auto parts and offers leasing and financing services. Its Web site features an inventory search for new and used cars, and offers auto repair coupons. President and namesake Bob Rohrman owns the company, which he founded in 1963.

KEY COMPETITORS
AutoNation
Jordan Automotive
Kelley Automotive

In-depth profiles of an additional 200 key private companies are found on pages 36–435.

BOLER CO.

500 Park Blvd., Ste.1010	CEO: John M. Boler	2001 Est. Sales: $600.0 mil.
Itasca, IL 60143	CFO: John Gaynor	1-Yr. Sales Change: (11.1%)
Phone: 630-773-9111	HR: Peter Quagliana	Employees: 500
Fax: 630-773-9121	Type: Private	FYE: December 31

Smooth — that's how Boler wants truck drivers to describe their ride. The holding company, which operates as Hendrickson International, makes truck and trailer suspension systems and auxiliary axle systems for the commercial heavy-duty vehicle market. The Hendrickson stamping division makes truck bumpers and stamped components. Hendrickson's spring division manufactures steel flat-leaf and parabolic taper-leaf springs. The company sells to OEMs in Europe and Latin America, as well as Australia, Japan, and the US. Chairman, president, and founder John Boler bought Hendrickson International in 1977 and remains the company's owner.

KEY COMPETITORS
ArvinMeritor, Inc.
Tower Automotive
Transportation Components

BON SECOURS HEALTH SYSTEM, INC.

1505 Marriottsville Rd.	CEO: Christopher M. Carney	2002 Sales: $2,300.0 million
Marriottsville, MD 21104	CFO: Michael W. Cottrell	1-Yr. Sales Change: —
Phone: 410-442-5511	HR: David D. Jones	Employees: 27,000
Fax: 410-442-1082	Type: Not-for-profit	FYE: August 31
Web: www.bshsi.com		

Bon Secours Health System succors the poor and sick. A not-for-profit organization dedicated to providing health care services to all, Bon Secours Health System was created in 1983 by the Sisters of Bon Secours, an international Roman Catholic order established in 1824 in Paris. Bon Secours Health System is composed of 24 acute-care hospitals, nine long-term-care facilities, and a psychiatric hospital. Bon Secours Health System also operates ambulatory sites, nursing care centers, assisted-living facilities, hospices, and home health care services.

KEY COMPETITORS
Catholic Health East
Johns Hopkins Medicine
MedStar

BONNEVILLE POWER ADMINISTRATION

905 NE 11th Ave.	CEO: Stephen J. Wright	2001 Sales: $4,278.7 million
Portland, OR 97232	CFO: James H. Curtis	1-Yr. Sales Change: 40.7%
Phone: 503-230-3000	HR: Roy P. Smithey	Employees: 2,878
Fax: 503-230-3816	Type: Government-owned	FYE: September 30
Web: www.bpa.gov		

Bonneville Power Administration (BPA) keeps the lights on in the Pacific Northwest. The US Department of Energy power-marketing agency operates a 15,000-mile high-voltage transmission grid that delivers 46% of the electrical power consumed in eight states. The electricity that BPA wholesales is generated primarily by 29 federal hydroelectric plants and one private nuclear facility. BPA has added hydroelectric power from British Columbia, gas-fired peak generators, and wind energy to its power mix. Founded in 1937, the utility sells primarily to public utilities; most of its big industrial customers, aluminum smelters, have shut down.

KEY COMPETITORS
AES
CenterPoint Energy
Dynegy

In-depth profiles of an additional 200 key private companies are found on pages 36–435.

BORDEN CHEMICAL, INC.

180 E. Broad St.	CEO: Craig O. Morrison	2001 Sales: $1,372.1 million
Columbus, OH 43215	CFO: William H. Carter	1-Yr. Sales Change: (10.0%)
Phone: 614-225-4000	HR: Nancy A. Reardon	Employees: 2,800
Fax: —	Type: Private	FYE: December 31
Web: www.bordenchem.com		

After giving Elsie the cow, the Cracker Jack boy, and Elmer's their pink slips, Borden Chemical (formerly Borden) is focused on industrial chemicals. The company — controlled by Kohlberg Kravis Roberts & Co. (KKR) — has sold its dairy division and its decorative products unit, as well as its Cracker Jack snack food, Eagle Brand foods, and Elmer's Products divisions. Borden Chemical's operations now include the production of formaldehyde, forest product resins, industrial resins, UV coatings, melamine, and oilfield products (proppants). Customers include businesses in the forest-products, foundry, automotive, construction, composites, electronics, and oilfield industries.

KEY COMPETITORS
Ashland
DuPont

BOSCOV'S DEPARTMENT STORES

4500 Perkiomen Ave.	CEO: Edwin A. Lakin	2002 Sales: $1,000.0 million
Reading, PA 19606	CFO: Russell C. Diehm	1-Yr. Sales Change: 0.0%
Phone: 610-779-2000	HR: Ed Elko	Employees: 12,000
Fax: 610-370-3495	Type: Private	FYE: January 31
Web: www.boscovs.com		

Outlet-mall capital Reading, Pennsylvania, has conceived more than bargain shopping. It's given us Boscov's Department Stores, which operates more than 35 department stores that anchor malls mainly in Pennsylvania, but also in Delaware, Maryland, New Jersey, and New York. The stores sell men's, women's, and children's apparel, shoes, and accessories; it also sells jewelry, cosmetics, housewares, appliances, toys, and sporting goods. Some stores also feature travel agencies, vision centers, hair salons, and restaurants. The firm's charge-card services are handled by its Boscov's Receivable Finance subsidiary. Boscov's was founded by Solomon Boscov in 1911 and is owned by the families of Albert Boscov and Edwin Lakin.

KEY COMPETITORS
Federated
J. C. Penney
Sears

BOSTON CAPITAL CORPORATION

1 Boston Place	CEO: John P. Manning	2001 Est. Sales: $700.0 mil.
Boston, MA 02108	CFO: —	1-Yr. Sales Change: —
Phone: 617-624-8900	HR: Ann Bowdoin	Employees: 120
Fax: 617-624-8999	Type: Private	FYE: December 31
Web: www.bostoncapital.com		

Boston Capital became one of the largest apartment owners in the US with a little help from Uncle Sam. Boston Capital takes advantage of federal tax credits, which it packages into public investment funds in exchange for developing apartment complexes targeted to low-income tenants. The firm also offers mezzanine, bridge, mortgage, and other kinds of financing for commercial and multifamily real estate. Subsidiary Boston Capital Housing purchases and refurbishes apartment properties; Boston Capital Partners provides equity financing for the construction of new properties and the renovation of older holdings. The company owns more than 2,200 properties (including more than 110,000 apartment units) in 48 states.

KEY COMPETITORS
AIMCO
American Community
  Properties Trust
Intergroup

📖 In-depth profiles of an additional 200
key private companies are found on pages 36–435.

THE BOSTON CONSULTING GROUP

Exchange Place, 31st Fl.
Boston, MA 02109
Phone: 617-973-1200
Fax: 617-973-1399
Web: www.bcg.com

CEO: Carl Stern
CFO: Hugh Simons
HR: —
Type: Private

2001 Sales: $1,050.0 million
1-Yr. Sales Change: (4.5%)
Employees: 4,450
FYE: December 31

Global corporations are willing to give much more than a penny for the thoughts of management consulting firm Boston Consulting Group (BCG). Founded in 1963 by consulting pioneer Bruce Henderson, BCG is one of the top-ranked consulting practices in the world, serving leading firms in such industries as consumer goods, financial services, and telecommunications. Its nearly 3,000 consultants assist clients in developing and implementing corporate strategies, improving efficiencies, and integrating new technologies. The firm is noted for developing and applying its own original consulting concepts, such as "time-based competition" (rapid response to change) and "deconstruction" (an end to vertical integration).

KEY COMPETITORS
Bain & Company
Booz Allen
McKinsey & Company

BOSTON UNIVERSITY

121 Bay State Rd.
Boston, MA 02215
Phone: 617-353-2000
Fax: 617-353-4048
Web: web.bu.edu

CEO: John Silber
CFO: Kenneth G. Condon
HR: Manuel Monteiro
Type: School

2001 Sales: $971.5 million
1-Yr. Sales Change: 2.2%
Employees: 8,900
FYE: June 30

You'll probably amount to a lot more than a hill of beans after graduating from Boston University. Founded as a Methodist seminary in 1839, BU has some 29,000 students at its campus on the banks of the Charles River. The private university has 21 graduate and undergraduate schools and colleges, including schools of education, law, management, medicine, social work, and theology. It also supports a number of research programs, such as the Center for Space Physics and the Center for Human Genetics. Four Nobel laureates — Elie Wiesel, Derek Walcott, Saul Bellow, and Sheldon Glashow — are among more than 3,000 faculty members.

BOZZUTO'S INC.

275 School House Rd.
Cheshire, CT 06410
Phone: 203-272-3511
Fax: 203-250-2953
Web: www.bozzutos.com

CEO: Michael A. Bozzuto
CFO: Mark G. Kindig
HR: Doug Vaughn
Type: Private

2001 Est. Sales: $850.0 mil.
1-Yr. Sales Change: 9.4%
Employees: 1,025
FYE: September 30

If you shop at an IGA supermarket within 250 miles of Cheshire, Connecticut, then Bozzuto's will keep you grinning. The company distributes food and other items to independent supermarkets belonging to the IGA network. The wholesaler supplies more than 100 stores with food, tobacco products, and household items under national brands as well as the IGA and Bestway labels. It also provides store design, administrative, marketing, and inventory management services. Bozzuto's owns Adams Super Food Stores, a Cheshire-based supermarket chain. Founded in 1945 as John Bozzuto & Sons, Bozzuto's serves stores in New England, New York, New Jersey, and Pennsylvania. Founder Adam Bozzuto passed away in mid-2002.

KEY COMPETITORS
C&S Wholesale
Di Giorgio
SUPERVALU

In-depth profiles of an additional 200 key private companies are found on pages 36–435.

BRADCO SUPPLY CORP.

13 Production Way	CEO: Barry Segal	2001 Sales: $800.0 million
Avenel, NJ 07001	CFO: Steven Feinberg	1-Yr. Sales Change: 14.3%
Phone: 732-382-3400	HR: Ginny DeLuca	Employees: 1,450
Fax: 732-382-6577	Type: Private	FYE: December 31
Web: www.bradcosupply.com		

Bradco Supply offers construction contractors everything they need to put a roof over their clients' heads. The company distributes roofing, siding, windows, and other building materials through about 90 locations in 25 states. Founded in 1966, Bradco Supply is one of the nation's largest distributors of roofing materials for commercial use. It also exports its construction materials to Africa, the Caribbean, the Far East, Latin America, the Middle East, and Russia. The company has been acquiring smaller roofing material businesses. CEO Barry Segal owns Bradco Supply.

KEY COMPETITORS
ABC Supply
Cameron Ashley
North Pacific Group

BRASFIELD & GORRIE, LLC

729 S. 30th St.	CEO: M. Miller Gorrie	2001 Sales: $943.0 million
Birmingham, AL 35233	CFO: Randall J. Freeman	1-Yr. Sales Change: 11.1%
Phone: 205-328-4000	HR: Kelly Crane	Employees: 2,000
Fax: 205-251-1304	Type: Private	FYE: December 31
Web: www.brasfieldgorrie.com		

Brasfield & Gorrie makes a big splash in the southeastern US. Among its construction projects are the VisionLand amusement and water park in Alabama and hotels, health care facilities, industrial plants, retail complexes, and water-treatment plants. Commercial and industrial construction together account for two-thirds of its revenues. It provides general contracting, design/build, and construction management services through offices in Alabama, Florida, Georgia, North Carolina, and Tennessee, and has completed projects in 16 states. Founded in 1922 by Thomas C. Brasfield, the company was sold to owner and CEO Miller Gorrie in 1964.

KEY COMPETITORS
H.J. Russell
Skanska USA Building
Turner Corporation

BREED TECHNOLOGIES, INC.

5300 Allen K. Breed Hwy.	CEO: John Riess	2002 Est. Sales: $1,100.0 mil.
Lakeland, FL 33811	CFO: Douglas D. Watts	1-Yr. Sales Change: (22.6%)
Phone: 863-668-6000	HR: Brenda Stanley	Employees: 16,000
Fax: 863-668-6007	Type: Private	FYE: June 30
Web: www.breedtech.com		

BREED Technologies is a leading manufacturer of air bags and air bag components. The company also makes steering wheels and seat belts. BREED's line of air bag products includes sensors, inflators, driver-side and steering-wheel air bag combinations, and side-impact air bag systems. BREED supplies air bag systems to most of the world's carmakers. The company also makes a line of interior trim products including automatic and manual shift knobs, park brake handles, shift and brake boots, armrest covers, pull handles, and other assorted trim components. BREED's bank lenders control the company.

KEY COMPETITORS
Autoliv
Robert Bosch

📖 **In-depth profiles of an additional 200 key private companies are found on pages 36–435.**

BROOKSHIRE BROTHERS, LTD.

1201 Ellen Trout Dr.	CEO: Tim Hale	2001 Est. Sales: $750.0 mil.
Lufkin, TX 75902	CFO: Donny Johnson	1-Yr. Sales Change: 7.1%
Phone: 936-634-8155	HR: Robert Gilmer	Employees: 6,000
Fax: 936-633-4611	Type: Private	FYE: April 30
Web: www.brookshirebrothers.com		

From its roots in East Texas, the Brookshire Brothers supermarket chain now has about 70 locations stretching from Louisiana to Central Texas. The company primarily operates under the Brookshire Brothers banner, although a few fly the B&B, Budget Chopper, and Celebration Foods flags. Nearly all of the stores feature outlets selling Conoco gasoline. (The company is one of Conoco's largest distributors.) Brookshire Brothers is not affiliated with Brookshire Grocery of Tyler, Texas. The companies share a common ancestry dating back to 1921, but a split between the founding brothers in the late 1930s resulted in separate grocery chains. Formerly family-owned, Brookshire Brothers is now 67%-owned by employees.

KEY COMPETITORS
H-E-B
Randall's
Wal-Mart

BROOKSHIRE GROCERY COMPANY

1600 W. South West Loop 323	CEO: Bruce G. Brookshire	2002 Est. Sales: $1,700.0 mil.
Tyler, TX 75701	CFO: Marvin Massey	1-Yr. Sales Change: 0.0%
Phone: 903-534-3000	HR: Tim Brookshire	Employees: 11,500
Fax: 903-534-2206	Type: Private	FYE: September 30
Web: www.brookshires.com		

By selling staples, specialties, and Southern hospitality, Brookshire Grocery Company has grown into a chain of about 135 Brookshire's and Super 1 Food supermarkets in Texas, Arkansas, Louisiana, and Mississippi. Brookshire also owns two distribution centers, a dairy, a fleet of nearly 350 trucks, and bakery, ice cream, drink, and ice manufacturing facilities. The company's stores average about 40,000 sq. ft., while its warehouse-style Super 1 Foods stores average 80,000 sq. ft. More than 40 of Brookshire Grocery's stores sell gasoline. Originally part of the Brookshire Brothers grocery chain (dating back to 1921), the company split from it in 1939. The Brookshire family is still among the company's owners.

KEY COMPETITORS
Albertson's
Kroger
Wal-Mart

BROWN AUTOMOTIVE GROUP LTD.

10287 Lee Hwy.	CEO: Charles S. Stringfellow Jr.	2001 Sales: $2,750.0 million
Fairfax, VA 22030	CFO: Charles S. Stringfellow Jr.	1-Yr. Sales Change: 10.0%
Phone: 703-352-5555	HR: —	Employees: 3,100
Fax: 703-352-5591	Type: Private	FYE: December 31
Web: www.brownscar.com		

Color them diverse: Brown Automotive Group, a leading auto dealer in the mid-Atlantic region, sells about 15 makes of automobiles from more than 20 dealerships in the Washington, DC, and Baltimore areas, as well as in Charlottesville and Richmond, Virginia. The company's new-car makes include DaimlerChrysler, General Motors, Honda, Jaguar, Mazda, Mercedes, Nissan, Saab, Subaru, Toyota, and Volkswagen. It also sells used cars and provides collision-repair services. Although the company was formed by William Schuiling in 1983, it traces its origins to Schuiling's purchase of one of Brown Automotive's Pontiac dealerships in Arlington, Virginia, in the early 1970s.

KEY COMPETITORS
Jim Koons Automotive
Ourisman Automotive
Rosenthal Automotive

In-depth profiles of an additional 200 key private companies are found on pages 36–435.

BUFFETS, INC.

1460 Buffet Way
Eagan, MN 55121
Phone: 651-994-8608
Fax: 651-365-2356
Web: www.buffet.com

CEO: Kerry A. Kramp
CFO: R. Michael Andrews
HR: K. Michael Shrader
Type: Private

2001 Sales: $1,045.0 million
1-Yr. Sales Change: 2.4%
Employees: 25,000
FYE: June 30

You don't have to worry about getting seconds at Buffets. The company operates one of the country's largest chains of buffet restaurants, with more than 400 locations in 36 states. Operating mostly under the Old Country Buffet and HomeTown Buffet brands, the company's locations are self-service buffets featuring entrees, sides, and desserts for an all-inclusive price. Buffets' other brands include Original Roadhouse Grill, Granny's Buffet, Country Roadhouse Buffet & Grill, and Tahoe Joe's Famous Steakhouse. Private equity firm Caxton-Iseman Capital owns Buffets.

KEY COMPETITORS
Investor's Management
Ryan's Family Steak Houses
Shoney's

BUILDER MARTS OF AMERICA, INC.

1 Independence Pointe
Greenville, SC 29615
Phone: 864-297-6101
Fax: 864-281-3201
Web: www.buildermarts.com

CEO: Duane Faulkner
CFO: R. Steven Robins
HR: Kay Gould
Type: Private

2000 Est. Sales: $1,000.0 mil.
1-Yr. Sales Change: 19.4%
Employees: 200
FYE: December 31

Business is building at Builder Marts of America (BMA). BMA supplies products and services to more than 5,000 building-supply retailers nationwide. Its offerings include lumber and other forest products; building materials; hardlines, including paint, power tools, and plumbing; and millwork such as steel doors and wood windows. In 2000 glassmaker Guardian Industries' Building Products Group bought the lumber and building materials division of TruServ and folded it into BMA, making it the US's largest buying group for such products. The same year BMA purchased Cameron Ashley Building Products. Guardian Industries owns a controlling share of BMA.

KEY COMPETITORS
Home Depot
Lowe's
Lumbermens Merchandising

BUILDERS FIRSTSOURCE

2001 Bryan St., Ste. 1600
Dallas, TX 75201
Phone: 214-880-3500
Fax: 214-880-3599
Web: www.buildersfirstsource.com

CEO: Floyd F. Sherman
CFO: Charles L. Horn
HR: —
Type: Private

2001 Sales: $1,561.0 million
1-Yr. Sales Change: (8.7%)
Employees: 6,800
FYE: December 31

Builders FirstSource, like an ambitious weight lifter, is bulking up an already well-built form. It aims to be a leading supplier to professional builders — it sells doors, hardware, windows, lumber, and other building products. It also provides engineering services. Since its founding in 1997 as Stonegate Resources, the company has grown, primarily through acquisitions, to include more than 70 distribution centers and about 60 manufacturing plants in 12 states. The company is focusing more on value-added products, such as wall panels, trusses, and specialty millwork. Builders FirstSource was founded by a management team headed by former CEO John Roach and private investment firm Littlejohn & Levy.

KEY COMPETITORS
84 Lumber
CertainTeed
U.S. Industries

📖 **In-depth profiles of an additional 200 key private companies are found on pages 36–435.**

BURT AUTOMOTIVE NETWORK

5200 S. Broadway	CEO: Lloyd G. Chavez	2001 Sales: $1,317.1 million
Englewood, CO 80110	CFO: John Held	1-Yr. Sales Change: 16.6%
Phone: 303-789-6700	HR: Todd van Maldeghem	Employees: 1,350
Fax: 303-789-6706	Type: Private	FYE: December 31
Web: www.burt.com		

John Elway may have retired, but Burt Automotive Network is still trying to sack him. In Denver, Burt goes head-to-head with the John Elway AutoNation USA dealerships, once owned by (and still named for) the former Broncos star. Burt operates seven dealerships in Colorado that sell new cars from DaimlerChrysler, Ford, GM, Honda, Mazda, and Toyota. It also sells commercial trucks and used cars, offers parts and repair services, and has partnered with another Denver auto dealer, Kuni, to acquire dealerships. Burt, owned by CEO Lloyd G. Chavez, is one of the largest Hispanic-owned businesses in the US. A salesman with Burt since 1950, Chavez became the majority owner in 1982 and bought the rest of the company in 1987.

KEY COMPETITORS
Autonation
MNL, Inc.
Phil Long Dealerships

CABELA'S INC.

1 Cabela Dr.	CEO: James Cabela	2001 Sales: —
Sidney, NE 69160	CFO: Dave Roehr	1-Yr. Sales Change: —
Phone: 308-254-5505	HR: Larry Hiers	Employees: 7,041
Fax: 308-254-4800	Type: Private	FYE: December 31
Web: www.cabelas.com		

Cabela's is a hunter's and fisherman's Disneyland. The seller of outdoor sporting goods operates mainly through the 70 million-plus catalogs it mails each year, but its eight stores are big attractions, too. Located in Kansas, Nebraska, Michigan, Minnesota, South Dakota, and Wisconsin, the stores are as big as 150,000 sq. ft. and include such features as waterfalls, mountain replicas, and exotic game trophies. Founded in 1961 by Dick Cabela and still owned by his family, the company sells footwear, clothing, and gear for fishing, hunting, camping, and other outdoor activities. Cabela's also sells merchandise online and has an outdoors show on ESPN2.

KEY COMPETITORS
Orvis Company
REI
Sportsman's Guide

CACTUS FEEDERS, INC.

2209 W. 7th St.	CEO: Paul F. Engler	2001 Est. Sales: $625.0 mil.
Amarillo, TX 79106	CFO: Matt Forrester	1-Yr. Sales Change: (3.8%)
Phone: 806-373-2333	HR: Kevin Hazelwood	Employees: 500
Fax: 806-371-4767	Type: Private	FYE: October 31
Web: www.cactusfeeders.com		

Cactus Feeders owner Paul Engler may operate the world's largest cattle feedlot business, but he is no match for Oprah Winfrey. Cactus Feeders has a capacity for about 480,000 head of cattle, which it beefs up and sells to beef packers. The company operates nine feedyards in Texas and Kansas, as well as three cattle ranches under the Spike Box brand in Texas and New Mexico. It also provides market analysis, marketing services, and financing for its rancher/suppliers. Engler and other cattle ranchers unsuccessfully sued Winfrey and a guest after a 1996 show disparaged the beef industry. Employees own 32% of Cactus Feeders, which Engler founded in 1975.

KEY COMPETITORS
AzTx Cattle
ContiGroup
King Ranch

In-depth profiles of an additional 200 key private companies are found on pages 36–435.

CALIFORNIA DAIRIES INC.

11709 E. Artesia Blvd.	CEO: Gary Korsmeier	2001 Est. Sales: $2,000.0 mil.
Artesia, CA 90701	CFO: Joe Heffington	1-Yr. Sales Change: 9.2%
Phone: 562-865-1291	HR: Holly Misenhimer	Employees: 530
Fax: 562-860-8633	Type: Cooperative	FYE: April 30

Herding dairies to give them greater "ag"-gregate strength has made California Dairies one of the largest dairy cooperatives in the US. Formed from the 1999 merger of three California dairy cooperatives (California Milk Producers, Danish Creamery Association, and San Joaquin Valley Dairymen), California Dairies' 700 members account for more than 40% of its home state's milk production. The co-op's five plants process milk, cheese, butter, and powdered milk. California Dairies, the nation's second-largest agricultural cooperative after Farmland Industries, also markets the milk its members produce.

KEY COMPETITORS
Dairy Farmers of America
Dean Foods
Land O'Lakes

CALIFORNIA STATE LOTTERY COMMISSION

600 N. 10th St.	CEO: Joan Wilson	2001 Sales: $2,894.8 million
Sacramento, CA 95814	CFO: Pat Eberhart	1-Yr. Sales Change: 11.4%
Phone: 916-323-7095	HR: —	Employees: 685
Fax: 916-327-0489	Type: Government-owned	FYE: June 30
Web: www.calottery.com		

There's still a gold rush going on in the Golden State, but you won't need a pick or a shovel to get in on the action. The California State Lottery Commission offers a string of scratch-off games (Ancient Riches, Double Doubler) and numbers games (Fantasy 5, SuperLotto Plus) for Californians' wagering pleasure. Scratch-off and Fantasy 5 players also can win chances to spin a wheel for prizes on the *Big Spin* TV show. State law requires that at least 34% of lottery proceeds go to public education in California; since its 1985 inception, the lottery has provided more than $13 billion to that cause. Most of those funds are used to attract and retain teachers.

KEY COMPETITORS
Multi-State Lottery
Oregon State Lottery
Washington State Lottery

CALIFORNIA STEEL INDUSTRIES, INC.

14000 San Bernardino Ave.	CEO: C. Lourenco Gonçalves	2001 Sales: $640.4 million
Fontana, CA 92335	CFO: Vicente Wright	1-Yr. Sales Change: (11.2%)
Phone: 909-350-6300	HR: Brett Guge	Employees: 952
Fax: 909-350-6223	Type: Joint venture	FYE: December 31
Web: www.californiasteel.com		

California Steel Industries (CSI) is into slab, steel slab. The company uses steel slab produced by third parties to manufacture steel products such as hot-rolled and cold-rolled steel, galvanized coils and sheets, and electric resistance weld (ERW) pipe. Its customers include construction and building suppliers, oil and gas producers, wheel and rim manufacturers, and packaging and container companies. CSI serves the western region of the US; about half of its flat-rolled steel is consumed by customers in Las Vegas, Phoenix, and Southern California. Japan's Kawasaki Steel and Brazilian iron-ore miner Companhia Vale do Rio Doce (CVRD) each own 50% of CSI.

KEY COMPETITORS
AK Steel Holding Corporation
Nucor
Steel Dynamics

In-depth profiles of an additional 200
key private companies are found on pages 36–435.

CANTOR FITZGERALD, L.P.

299 Park Ave.	CEO: Howard W. Lutnick	2001 Est. Sales: $900.0 mil.
New York, NY 10171	CFO: —	1-Yr. Sales Change: (9.1%)
Phone: 212-821-6710	HR: —	Employees: 450
Fax: —	Type: Private	FYE: —
Web: www.cantor.com		

Cantor Fitzgerald entered the spotlight tragically as one of the companies hit hardest by the September 11, 2001, attack on New York's World Trade Center. Although the firm lost 659 employees — two thirds of its workforce — it was back in operation just two days later. Cantor Fitzgerald is the largest trader of US Treasuries, and accounts for half of all government bond trading. The company trades securities, equities, derivatives, and foreign stocks. It operates the Cantor Exchange, an electronic US Treasury futures exchange, and offers electronic trading of sovereign debt. Its electronic trading platform eSpeed was spun off in 1999.

KEY COMPETITORS
BrokerTec Global
ICAP
Traditional Financial

CARILION HEALTH SYSTEM

1212 3rd St.	CEO: Edward Murphy	2001 Sales: $1,177.4 million
Roanoke, VA 24016	CFO: Donald E. Lorton	1-Yr. Sales Change: 9.1%
Phone: 540-981-8080	HR: Brucie Boggs	Employees: 10,200
Fax: 540-344-5716	Type: Not-for-profit	FYE: September 30
Web: www.carilion.com		

Carilion Health System rings true for residents of western Virginia. Founded in 1899 as the Roanoke Hospital Association, the system today includes about 10 hospitals, a nursing home, and a cancer center, with a total of about 1,300 beds. Its Medical Center for Children in Roanoke serves as a regional pediatric referral site, and its Carilion Behavioral Health has become one of the most comprehensive psychiatric-service networks in its area. Through its 60%-owned, for-profit Carilion Health Plans subsidiary, the system markets its own HMO and point-of-service health care plans.

KEY COMPETITORS
HCA
Mid Atlantic Medical
Sentara Healthcare

CARONDELET HEALTH SYSTEM

13801 Riverport Dr., Ste. 300	CEO: Andrew W. Allen	2001 Sales: $938.3 million
St. Louis, MO 63043	CFO: Paul Briggs	1-Yr. Sales Change: (5.7%)
Phone: 314-770-0333	HR: Nancy Heet	Employees: 16,000
Fax: 314-770-0444	Type: Not-for-profit	FYE: June 30
Web: www.chs-stl.com		

Through a network of some 16 facilities, Carondelet Health System carries on its healing mission in seven widely scattered states from New York to Washington. Besides hospitals, Carondelet Health System operates behavioral treatment centers, hospice centers, and rehabilitation facilities. The not-for-profit is sponsored by the Sisters of St. Joseph Carondelet, a Roman Catholic order founded in 17th century France. Some members of the order emigrated to the US in 1836; they founded a school for the deaf in St. Louis, and their mission spread across the country.

KEY COMPETITORS
Ascension
Catholic Health Initiatives
Tenet Healthcare

In-depth profiles of an additional 200 key private companies are found on pages 36–435.

CARPENTER CO.

5016 Monument Ave.
Richmond, VA 23220
Phone: 804-359-0800
Fax: 804-353-0694
Web: www.carpenter.com

CEO: Stanley F. Pauley
CFO: Dave Morman
HR: Tom Newport
Type: Private

2001 Est. Sales: $1,000.0 mil.
1-Yr. Sales Change: (7.0%)
Employees: 6,200
FYE: December 31

It's a cushy job for Carpenter Co., making polyurethane foam and chemicals and polyester fiber used as cushioning by the automotive, bedding, floor covering, and furniture industries, among others. The company started out making foam rubber; it now manufactures air-filter media, expanded polystyrene building materials, and a tire-fill product as a replacement for air in off-road construction vehicles. Carpenter has facilities throughout the US, as well as in Canada, Denmark, France, Germany, Spain, Sweden, and the UK. The company also sells consumer products — which include craft fiber products, mattress pads, and pillows — through retailers.

KEY COMPETITORS
Acordis
Foamex
Owens Corning

CARQUEST CORPORATION

2635 Millbrook Road
Raleigh, NC 27604
Phone: 919-573-2500
Fax: 919-573-2501
Web: www.carquest.com

CEO: A.E. Lottes III
CFO: John Gardner
HR: Ted Pattison
Type: Private

2000 Est. Sales: $2,000.0 mil.
1-Yr. Sales Change: 0.0%
Employees: 36,000
FYE: December 31

Searching for a sensor, solenoid, or switches? CARQUEST can steer you in the right direction. The replacement-auto-parts distribution group is owned by its seven member warehouse distributors. (The largest is North Carolina-based General Parts.) The CARQUEST group includes a network of about 60 distribution centers serving about 4,000 distributor-owned and independent jobbers in the US and Canada. The company sells its own line of auto parts (made by Moog Automotive, Dana, Gabriel, and others) to the jobbers, as well as wholesalers, for eventual resale to professional repair centers, service stations, dealerships, and, to a lesser degree, do-it-yourself (DIY) customers.

KEY COMPETITORS
AutoZone
Genuine Parts
Pep Boys

CARROLS CORPORATION

968 James St.
Syracuse, NY 13203
Phone: 315-424-0513
Fax: 315-475-9616
Web: www.carrols.com

CEO: Alan Vituli
CFO: Paul R. Flanders
HR: Jerry Digenova
Type: Private

2001 Sales: $656.3 million
1-Yr. Sales Change: 40.6%
Employees: 16,100
FYE: December 31

Carrols knows about royalty. The restaurant management company is the #1 Burger King franchisee in the US, with about 360 restaurants in 13 southeastern, midwestern, and northeastern states. The company has expanded beyond Whoppers, buying the Pollo Tropical grilled chicken chain, which includes about 60 company-owned restaurants in Florida and 26 franchised locations (primarily in Puerto Rico). It has also purchased the 125-unit Taco Cabana Mexican food chain. Carrols, which jettisoned its own brand-name restaurants and began franchising Burger Kings in 1976, is owned by investment firms BIB Holdings (44%) and Madison Dearborn Capital Partners (22%).

KEY COMPETITORS
McDonald's
Taco Bell
Wendy's

In-depth profiles of an additional 200 key private companies are found on pages 36–435.

CARTER LUMBER COMPANY

601 Tallmadge Rd.	CEO: Bryan Carter	2001 Est. Sales: $590.0 mil.
Kent, OH 44240	CFO: Jeff Donley	1-Yr. Sales Change: 3.5%
Phone: 330-673-6100	HR: David McCafferty	Employees: 4,400
Fax: 330-678-6134	Type: Private	FYE: December 31
Web: www.carterlumber.com		

Who says you can't teach an old log new tricks? Founded in 1932 by Warren Carter, Carter Lumber owns about 250 lumber and home-improvement stores in Ohio and eight other states from Michigan to South Carolina. The company caters to both contractors and do-it-yourselfers, supplying them with lumber, plywood, roofing, kitchen and bath products, windows, doors, plumbing and electrical products, heating equipment, tools, siding, and other products. The home-improvement retailer also operates two building supply centers and 72,000 acres of timberland in Arkansas. Warren Carter died in 2000, at the age of 101, but Carter Lumber continues to be a family-owned business.

KEY COMPETITORS
84 Lumber
Home Depot
Lowe's

CATHOLIC HEALTHCARE PARTNERS

615 Elsinore Place	CEO: Michael D. Connelly	2001 Sales: $2,601.8 million
Cincinnati, OH 45202	CFO: Rick Annis	1-Yr. Sales Change: 9.7%
Phone: 513-639-2800	HR: Rick Frederick	Employees: 30,000
Fax: 513-639-2700	Type: Not-for-profit	FYE: December 31
Web: www.health-partners.org		

Catholic Healthcare Partners offers health care services, primarily in Ohio but also in Indiana, Kentucky, Pennsylvania, and Tennessee through the more than 100 corporations that make up its system. Facilities include about 30 hospitals, some 30 long-term-care facilities, housing sites for the elderly, and wellness centers. The system also offers physician practices, hospice and home health care, and outreach services. Catholic Healthcare Partners is co-sponsored by the Sisters of Mercy in Cincinnati and in Dallas, Pennsylvania; The Sisters of the Humility of Mary in Villa Maria, Pennsylvania; The Franciscan Sisters of the Poor; and Covenant Health Systems.

KEY COMPETITORS
Catholic Health Initiatives
HCA
OhioHealth

CBRE HOLDING, INC.

355 S. Grand Ave.	CEO: Raymond E. Wirta	2001 Sales: $1,170.8 million
Los Angeles, CA 90071	CFO: Kenneth J. Kay	1-Yr. Sales Change: (11.5%)
Phone: 213-613-3333	HR: Pam Perry	Employees: 9,700
Fax: 213-613-3005	Type: Private	FYE: December 31
Web: www.cbre.com		

CBRE Holding believes that the most important things in real estate are location, location, location, but also *ubicacion* and *l'emplacement* — not to mention *posizione* and *Standort*. The company, better known by the name of its primary operating subsidiary CB Richard Ellis, is the largest commercial real estate services company in the US and a powerhouse throughout the world. Offerings range from real estate brokerage to property management to asset services. It manages hundreds of millions of square feet of commercial space. The company also offers mortgage banking (L.J. Melody) and advisory and management services for private pension funds and large investors (CB Richard Ellis Investors L.L.C.).

KEY COMPETITORS
Cushman & Wakefield
Jones Lang LaSalle
Trammell Crow

📖 In-depth profiles of an additional 200
key private companies are found on pages 36–435.

CCA GLOBAL PARTNERS

4301 Earth City Expwy.	CEO: Alan Greenberg	2001 Est. Sales: $4,000.0 mil.
Earth City, MO 63045	CFO: Ed Muchnick	1-Yr. Sales Change: 27.4%
Phone: 314-506-0000	HR: Lisa Miles	Employees: —
Fax: 314-291-6674	Type: Cooperative	FYE: September 30
Web: www.carpetone.com		

Business is "floor"ishing at CCA Global Partners. Formerly Carpet Co-op, the firm has about 2,400 locations selling name-brand carpets and floor coverings such as ceramic tile, laminates, and hardwoods. Although most stores operate under the Carpet One name, other names include Stone Mountain Carpet Mill Outlets, ProSource, and International Design Guild (high-end showrooms). Carpet One is the world's largest floor covering retailer, with stores in the US, Canada, Australia, and New Zealand. It's the exclusive US marketer of Bigelow and Lees carpet brands. Executives Howard Brodsky and Alan Greenberg founded the co-op in 1984.

KEY COMPETITORS
Abbey Carpet
Home Depot
Lowe's

CENTRA, INC.

12225 Stephen Rd.	CEO: Manuel Moroun	2000 Est. Sales: $800.0 mil.
Warren, MI 48089	CFO: Norman E. Harned	1-Yr. Sales Change: 6.7%
Phone: 586-939-7000	HR: Lisa Putty	Employees: 5,100
Fax: 586-755-5607	Type: Private	FYE: December 31
Web: www.centraltransportint.com		

At the center of CenTra is Manuel Moroun, who controls the holding company founded by his father, Tufick, in the 1940s. CenTra's holdings include Central Transport International, a privately held less-than-truckload carrier with 150 terminals, and Central Global Express, an air freight forwarder. Along with Canadian affiliate Central-McKinlay International, the trucking firm serves major markets in Canada, Mexico, and the US. The company's CTX subsidiary provides time-sensitive and door-to-door freight transport in North America. CenTra also owns the Ambassador Bridge, a private toll bridge that connects Detroit with Windsor, Ontario.

KEY COMPETITORS
Roadway
USFreightways
Yellow

CENTRAL GROCERS COOPERATIVE, INC.

11100 Belmont Ave.	CEO: Joe Caccamo	2001 Sales: $918.8 million
Franklin Park, IL 60131	CFO: Robert J. Wagner	1-Yr. Sales Change: 24.4%
Phone: 847-451-0660	HR: Annalee Robish	Employees: —
Fax: 847-288-8710	Type: Cooperative	FYE: July 31

In a city of big stores, Central Grocers Cooperative helps neighborhood markets stay afloat. The co-op distributes name-brand and private-label (Centrella and Silver Cup) food and nonfood merchandise to about 240 member-owner stores in the Chicago area and also in Indiana and Wisconsin. Founded in 1918, Central Grocers has clung to independence as national giants have bought up local chains. The cooperative bought stores itself in 1998 rather than lose them as customers; it now owns 10 in Indiana and two in Illinois. The cooperative-owned stores operate under the banners Centrella, Strack and Van Til, Town & Country, and Ultra Foods. It also owns 48% of the eight-store Sterk's chain in Indiana.

KEY COMPETITORS
Albertson's
Certified Grocers Midwest
Safeway

📖 **In-depth profiles of an additional 200
key private companies are found on pages 36–435.**

CENTRAL NATIONAL-GOTTESMAN INC.

3 Manhattanville Rd.	CEO: Kenneth L. Wallach	2001 Sales: $1,700.0 million
Purchase, NY 10577	CFO: Joshua J. Eisenstein	1-Yr. Sales Change: (6.8%)
Phone: 914-696-9000	HR: Louise Caputo	Employees: 900
Fax: 914-696-1066	Type: Private	FYE: December 31

Got pulp? Central National-Gottesman does. Founded in 1886, the family-owned company distributes pulp, paper, paperboard, and newsprint in about 75 countries worldwide. In addition to its North American operations, the company operates about 25 overseas offices in 22 countries located in Asia, Europe, and Latin America. The Central National-Gottesman network includes the Lindenmeyr family of companies, which specializes in the distribution of fine paper as well as papers for books and magazines. The company's extensive list of suppliers includes paper-industry leaders International Paper (#1) and Weyerhaeuser.

KEY COMPETITORS
Unisource

CERTIFIED GROCERS MIDWEST, INC.

1 Certified Dr.	CEO: Ken R. Koester	2001 Sales: $631.8 million
Hodgkins, IL 60525	CFO: Dan Caithamer	1-Yr. Sales Change: (7.0%)
Phone: 708-579-2100	HR: Marcy Meister	Employees: 540
Fax: 708-354-7502	Type: Cooperative	FYE: August 31
Web: www.certisaver.com		

If you shop at a Certi-Saver, you can be certain your groceries came from Certified Grocers Midwest (CGM). CGM is a cooperative wholesaler of baked goods, fresh produce, meat products, and health and beauty aids; it distributes brand-name and private-label goods to member and non-member stores. CGM provides support services such as advertising, market research, site analysis, and financial help to nearly 200 member stores, some of which operate under the Certi-Saver banner. The cooperative, established in 1940, covers Illinois, Indiana, Iowa, Michigan, and Wisconsin. To attract more Hispanic customers, CGM has expanded its selection of Hispanic items, which include the Gamesa and Los Pericos brands of foods.

KEY COMPETITORS
Central Grocers Cooperative
Nash Finch
Roundy's

CF INDUSTRIES, INC.

1 Salem Lake Dr.	CEO: R. C. Liuzzi	2001 Sales: $1,087.4 million
Long Grove, IL 60047	CFO: Stephen R. Wilson	1-Yr. Sales Change: (1.2%)
Phone: 847-438-9500	HR: Francie Lucente	Employees: 1,700
Fax: 847-438-0211	Type: Cooperative	FYE: December 31
Web: www.cfindustries.com		

The grass is always greener at CF Industries. Organized in 1946 as Central Farmers Fertilizer Company, CF Industries is an interregional agricultural cooperative that manufactures and markets fertilizers, including nitrogen products (ammonia, granular urea, and UAN solutions), phosphates, and potash (potassium) products to its members in 48 states and two Canadian provinces. The co-op is owned by nine regional agricultural co-ops, including GROWMARK, Land O'Lakes, and Cenex Harvest States Cooperatives. CF Industries operates nitrogen and phosphate plants, a phosphate mine, and a network of distribution terminals and storage facilities through which it offers products worldwide.

KEY COMPETITORS
IMC Global
Potash Corporation
Terra Industries

In-depth profiles of an additional 200 key private companies are found on pages 36–435.

CFM INTERNATIONAL, INC.

1 Neumann Way
Cincinnati, OH 45215
Phone: 513-563-4180
Fax: 513-552-3306
Web: www.cfm56.com

CEO: Pierre Fabre
CFO: —
HR: —
Type: Joint venture

2001 Est. Sales: $6,700.0 mil.
1-Yr. Sales Change: 0.0%
Employees: —
FYE: December 31

CFM International makes sure that hundreds of aircraft don't have to just wing it. The company, a joint venture of US-based General Electric (GE) and France's Snecma, manufactures aircraft engines for more than 300 commercial and military customers worldwide. The company's name stems from a combination of CF6 and M56, designations for commercial aircraft engines made, respectively, by GE and Snecma. GE manufactures CFM's engine cores and assembles roughly half of its engines; Snecma makes the fans and rotors and assembles the rest of the engines. CFM's engines can be found in Boeing 737s, the DC8, Airbus A320s, and the AWACS.

KEY COMPETITORS
Honeywell International
Pratt & Whitney
Rolls-Royce

CH2M HILL COMPANIES, LTD.

6060 S. Willow Dr.
Greenwood Village, CO 80111
Phone: 303-771-0900
Fax: 303-846-2231
Web: www.ch2m.com

CEO: Ralph R. Peterson
CFO: Samuel H. Iapalucci
HR: Robert C. Allen
Type: Private

2001 Sales: $1,940.5 million
1-Yr. Sales Change: 13.7%
Employees: 10,500
FYE: December 31

CH2M's name is a company (not a chemical) compound derived from the initials of its founders — Cornell, Howland and Hayes (2 H's) and Merryfield — plus HILL, from its first merger. CH2M HILL offers engineering consulting services related to industrial facility design, transportation, water treatment, and environmental remediation. Specialties include sewer and waste-treatment design, hazardous-waste cleanup, and transportation projects such as highways and bridges. CH2M HILL is also involved in US Department of Energy nuclear-waste cleanup projects. Founded in 1946 in Corvallis, Oregon, CH2M HILL is employee-owned and operates from about 150 offices worldwide.

KEY COMPETITORS
MWH Global
Tetra Tech
URS

CHAPMAN AUTOMOTIVE GROUP, LLC

PO Box 11550
Scottsdale, AZ 85271
Phone: 480-970-0740
Fax: 480-994-4096
Web: www.chapmanchoice.com

CEO: Jerry B. Chapman
CFO: —
HR: —
Type: Private

2001 Sales: $612.3 million
1-Yr. Sales Change: 17.4%
Employees: —
FYE: December 31

Spend a few hours with a dealer in Vegas and you might lose your shirt — or end up with a new car. Chapman Automotive Group annually sells about 20,000 new and used automobiles from about 10 dealerships in Nevada and Arizona. The group sells General Motors, DaimlerChrysler, BMW, Isuzu, Lincoln, and Volkswagen automobiles. The company's dealerships also offer parts and service departments. In addition to selling to individual consumers, Chapman Automotive supplies cars, trucks, and parts to government and corporate fleet buyers. CEO Jerry Chapman, who founded the group in 1978, owns and runs the company with his three sons.

KEY COMPETITORS
AutoNation
Tuttle-Click
VT

> In-depth profiles of an additional 200
> key private companies are found on pages 36–435.

CHAS. LEVY COMPANY LLC

1200 N. North Branch St.	CEO: Carol G. Kloster	2001 Sales: $715.0 million
Chicago, IL 60622	CFO: William Nelson	1-Yr. Sales Change: 16.3%
Phone: 312-440-4400	HR: Robert Blyth	Employees: 6,000
Fax: 312-440-7414	Type: Private	FYE: September 30
Web: www.chaslevy.com		

Chas. Levy keeps racking up sales. The wholesaler distributes magazines and books throughout the US, primarily in several midwestern states. It's one of four companies that control nearly 90% of single-copy sales at US magazine racks. The company has grown through acquisitions of other distributors. Chas. Levy distributes books through its Levy Home Entertainment subsidiary to retail chains including Best Buy, Kmart, Meijer, ShopKo, Stop & Shop, Target, and Wal-Mart. The company has shut down its newspaper distribution operation. Chair Barbara Levy Kipper owns the company her grandfather founded in 1893.

KEY COMPETITORS
Anderson News
Hudson News
Jim Pattison Group

CHARLES PANKOW BUILDERS, LTD.

2476 N. Lake Ave.	CEO: Rik Kunnath	2001 Sales: $600.0 million
Altadena, CA 91001	CFO: Tim Murphy	1-Yr. Sales Change: (40.0%)
Phone: 626-791-1125	HR: Patty Bevans	Employees: 220
Fax: 626-794-1539	Type: Private	FYE: December 31
Web: www.pankow.com		

Charles Pankow Builders has some concrete ideas on how to construct high-rises. The design/build general contractor specializes in quake-resistant concrete frames, putting up department stores, hotels, condominiums, medical facilities, and office buildings, primarily in California and Hawaii. The company also has operations in other US states. Affiliate Pankow Special Projects focuses on small-scale projects such as renovations and seismic upgrades. Pankow's new framing system, developed with researchers at the University of Washington and the National Institute of Standards and Technology, has been used for San Francisco's tallest precast concrete building. Chairman Charles Pankow founded the company in 1963.

KEY COMPETITORS
Hathaway Dinwiddie
 Construction
Swinerton
Webcor Builders

CHARMER INDUSTRIES, INC.

1950 48th St.	CEO: Steven Drucker	2001 Est. Sales: $790.0 mil.
Astoria, NY 11105	CFO: Steve Meresmen	1-Yr. Sales Change: 0.0%
Phone: 718-726-2500	HR: Annette Perry	Employees: 1,500
Fax: 718-726-3101	Type: Private	FYE: December 31
Web: charmer.com		

Not easily shaken by competition, Charmer Industries has not stirred from its top spot as New York State's #1 wine and liquor wholesaler. It is the state's exclusive distributor for Schieffelin & Sommerset (a joint venture between Diageo's United Distillers & Vintners and Moët-Hennessy), and Brown-Forman (maker of Jack Daniels and Southern Comfort). Charmer Industries also owns Connecticut Distributors and Washington (DC) Wholesale Liquor. Herman Merinoff owns the company and also holds a majority interest in Maryland-based Sunbelt Beverage. (The two companies are not consolidated for revenue purposes.)

KEY COMPETITORS
National Distributing
Peerless Importers
Southern Wine & Spirits

📖 **In-depth profiles of an additional 200
key private companies are found on pages 36–435.**

CHEMCENTRAL CORPORATION

7050 W. 71st St.	CEO: John R. Yanney	2001 Sales: $860.0 million
Bedford Park, IL 60499	CFO: John G. LaBahn	1-Yr. Sales Change: (6.2%)
Phone: 708-594-7000	HR: Ken Krausz	Employees: 982
Fax: 708-594-6382	Type: Private	FYE: December 31
Web: www.chemcentral.com		

CHEMCENTRAL is in the center of a chemically dependent world. The company is one of the top chemical distributors in North America. It carries products made by BASF, Dow Chemical, DuPont, and others. Key customers for CHEMCENTRAL's more than 8,000 chemical products include companies that manufacture adhesives, caulks, and sealants; cleaning agents; cosmetics and personal care products; inks and paint coatings; and plastic and rubber compounds. Established in 1926 as the William J Hough Company of Chicago, CHEMCENTRAL now has more than 100 warehouse, distribution, and sales units worldwide.

KEY COMPETITORS
Aceto
Ashland
Stinnes

CHEMOIL CORPORATION

4 Embarcadero Center, Ste. 1100	CEO: Robert V. Chandran	2001 Sales: $3,000.0 million
San Francisco, CA 94111	CFO: Manolete Gonzalez	1-Yr. Sales Change: 172.7%
Phone: 415-268-2700	HR: Lucius C. Conrad	Employees: —
Fax: 415-268-2701	Type: Private	FYE: December 31
Web: www.chemoil.com		

Chemoil is hunkered down in the bunker fuel distribution business. Founded in 1981, the company supplies marine bunker fuels to about 330 shipping companies worldwide. Chemoil operates refineries and terminals and distributes fuel from five US ports (including New York and Los Angeles), the Netherlands, Singapore, and Turkey. The company supplies more than 4,000 vessels a year. Fuel is delivered mostly by tankers, barges, and tugboats owned and operated by Chemoil or its affiliates, which include KC Marine (New York), King Shipping (Houston), Unilloyd (Rotterdam), and Westoil Marine (Los Angeles). Chemoil is 50%-owned by Japanese trading company ITOCHU, which is helping to fund its expansion to new ports.

KEY COMPETITORS
Apex Oil
BP
Tesoro Petroleum

CHEVRON PHILLIPS CHEMICAL COMPANY LP

10001 Six Pines Dr.	CEO: Jim Gallogly	2001 Sales: $6,010.0 million
The Woodlands, TX 77380	CFO: Kent Potter	1-Yr. Sales Change: (19.5%)
Phone: 832-813-4100	HR: Sherry Richard	Employees: 6,056
Fax: 800-231-3890	Type: Joint venture	FYE: December 31
Web: www.cpchem.com		

A coin toss determined which company's name would go first when Chevron (now ChevronTexaco) and Phillips Petroleum formed a new joint venture, Chevron Phillips Chemical Company (CPChem). CPChem derives plastics, resins, additives, specialty chemicals, and lubricants from petroleum and natural gas. A leading maker of olefins and polyolefins (synthetic fibers), CPChem also produces aromatics, olefins, and styrenics. North America's largest producer of high-density polyethylene (HDPE) — used in blow/injection molding, plastic bags and pipes, and films — CPChem is also near the top in ethylene and aromatics production. Most of CPChem's operations are located in the US.

KEY COMPETITORS
BP
Equistar Chemicals
Shell

📖 **In-depth profiles of an additional 200 key private companies are found on pages 36–435.**

CHICK-FIL-A INC.

5200 Buffington Rd.	CEO: S. Truett Cathy	2001 Sales: $1,242.0 million
Atlanta, GA 30349	CFO: James B. McCabe	1-Yr. Sales Change: 14.4%
Phone: 404-765-8000	HR: Renea Boozer	Employees: 40,000
Fax: 404-765-8971	Type: Private	FYE: December 31
Web: www.chick-fil-a.com		

Beloved by bovines, Chick-fil-A is the nation's #3 fast-food chicken restaurant chain (behind Yum! Brands' KFC and AFC's Popeye's). Chick-fil-A serves chicken entrees, sandwiches, and salads (as well as its famous waffle fries and fresh-squeezed lemonade) at more than 1,000 stores in 35 US states and in South Africa. Although about 40% of its restaurants are located in shopping malls, the company is focusing most of its expansion efforts on freestanding outlets. Chick-fil-A also licenses units inside hospitals, schools, airports, and other nontraditional locations.

KEY COMPETITORS
AFC Enterprises
KFC
McDonald's

CHRISTUS HEALTH

6363 N. Hwy. 161, Ste. 450	CEO: Thomas C. Royer	2001 Sales: $2,200.0 million
Irving, TX 75038	CFO: Jay Herron	1-Yr. Sales Change: 5.8%
Phone: 214-492-8500	HR: Mary Lynch	Employees: 8,000
Fax: 214-492-8540	Type: Not-for-profit	FYE: June 30
Web: www.christushealth.org		

CHRISTUS has plenty to be merry about. The not-for-profit system was formed in 1999 by a merger of Incarnate Word Health System and Sisters of Charity Health System. CHRISTUS Health operates more than 40 hospitals and other health care facilities in four states, as well as in Mexico. Facilities range from acute-care hospitals to outpatient centers and also include hospice centers, medical education centers, and long-term acute-care facilities. CHRISTUS' predecessor organizations have their roots in the religious order Sisters of Charity of the Incarnate Word, founded when three French nuns arrived in Texas in 1866 to care for the poor and sick.

KEY COMPETITORS
Memorial Hermann Healthcare
Sisters of Mercy
Triad Hospitals

CIC INTERNATIONAL LTD.

5 Marine View Plaza	CEO: Satiris G. Fassoulis	2002 Sales: $773.0 million
Hoboken, NJ 07030	CFO: Robert C. Perry	1-Yr. Sales Change: 9.0%
Phone: 201-792-1800	HR: Robert Volvo	Employees: 735
Fax: 201-792-5755	Type: Private	FYE: August 31
Web: www.cic-international.com		

Like a veteran goalie, CIC International holds its own on defense. The company makes military equipment and systems for governments and defense industries worldwide. It makes military products for land, sea, and air. The company's main products include night vision and optical devices, munitions, helicopters, and avionics components (jet engines, fuel systems, headup displays). CIC also upgrades tanks and armored personnel carriers. Its naval services include upgrading weapon systems and providing engineering for surface warfare problems. The defense contractor began in 1930 as a silk and fur trader. Company executives and employees control CIC.

KEY COMPETITORS
General Dynamics
Lockheed Martin
Northrop Grumman

In-depth profiles of an additional 200 key private companies are found on pages 36–435.

CIGARETTES CHEAPER

4457 Park Rd.	CEO: John Roscoe	2001 Est. Sales: $750.0 mil.
Benicia, CA 94510	CFO: Bob Mazur	1-Yr. Sales Change: 15.4%
Phone: 707-745-8146	HR: Jay Chapman	Employees: 2,350
Fax: 707-748-0855	Type: Private	FYE: March 31

Cigarettes Cheaper keeps packing them in. The #1 specialty retailer of cigarettes in the US operates nearly 600 Cigarettes Cheaper, Premium Tobacco Stores, and Customer Company outlets in 21 states; more than one-third of the stores are in California. In addition to the leading cigarette brands, Cigarettes Cheaper sells its own brands under names such as Geronimo and Noble. It also sells roll-your-own supplies. Because of its large sales volume, the company is able to negotiate with tobacco manufacturers and pass the savings along to its customers. The first Cigarettes Cheaper store opened in 1994 as an extension to a chain of grocery stores (now mostly defunct) owned by the family of CEO John Roscoe.

KEY COMPETITORS
7-Eleven
Houchens
Kroger

CINEMARK, INC.

3900 Dallas Pkwy., Ste. 500	CEO: Lee Roy Mitchell	2001 Sales: $853.7 million
Plano, TX 75093	CFO: Robert D. Copple	1-Yr. Sales Change: 8.6%
Phone: 972-665-1000	HR: Brad Smith	Employees: 8,000
Fax: 972-665-1004	Type: Private	FYE: December 31
Web: www.cinemark.com		

Cinemark has left its mark on the cinema landscape. The third-largest movie exhibitor in the US (following Regal Entertainment and AMC) has more than 3,000 screens in nearly 280 theaters in the US and several other countries (most are in Latin America). Cinemark operates multiplex theaters (the ratio of screens to theaters is about 11 to 1) in smaller cities and in suburban areas of major metropolitan markets. Some larger theaters operate under the Tinseltown name; other Cinemark theaters are "discount" theaters, as opposed to the houses which exhibit first-run movies. Chairman and CEO Lee Roy Mitchell owns about 91% of the company's voting stock.

KEY COMPETITORS
AMC Entertainment
Carmike Cinemas
Regal Entertainment

CINGULAR WIRELESS

5565 Glenridge Connector, Ste. 1401	CEO: Stanley T. Sigman	2001 Sales: $14,300.0 million
Atlanta, GA 30342	CFO: Richard G. Lindner	1-Yr. Sales Change: 13.1%
Phone: 404-236-6000	HR: Rickford D. Bradley	Employees: —
Fax: 404-236-6005	Type: Joint venture	FYE: December 31
Web: www.cingular.com		

BellSouth *plus* SBC *times* wireless assets *equals* Cingular Wireless. With a name chosen to emphasize unity and the individual customer, the two regional Bell companies have combined assets to create the #2 wireless carrier in the US, behind Verizon Wireless. With 22.1 million customers, the joint venture is 60%-owned by SBC and 40% by BellSouth, according to the contributions made by the two companies, which share control of Cingular Wireless. Eleven brand names used by the SBC and BellSouth wireless units have been replaced by the Cingular Wireless brand. The company, which has held talks to merge with VoiceStream Wireless (now T-Mobile USA), has announced cuts in 7% of its workforce, amounting to more than 2,500 jobs.

KEY COMPETITORS
AT&T Wireless
Sprint PCS
Verizon Wireless

In-depth profiles of an additional 200 key private companies are found on pages 36–435.

CLARK ENTERPRISES, INC.

7500 Old Georgetown Rd.	CEO: A. James Clark	2001 Est. Sales: $2,500.0 mil.
Bethesda, MD 20814	CFO: Lawrence C. Nussdorf	1-Yr. Sales Change: 4.2%
Phone: 301-272-8100	HR: Ann Timmons	Employees: 4,000
Fax: 301-272-1928	Type: Private	FYE: December 31
Web: www.clarkus.com		

Convention does not bind Clark Enterprises. Besides constructing convention centers, Clark Enterprises' Clark Construction unit builds hotels, office buildings, prisons, stadiums, and transportation facilities. The general builder has worked on several Maryland projects, including Oriole Park at Camden Yards (home to baseball's Baltimore Orioles), and many other recognizable structures around the country, such as the Los Angeles Convention Center, the US Federal Courthouse in Boston, and the 30th Street Station in Philadelphia. Services include general contracting, construction management, materials procurement, and project development. CEO James Clark owns Clark Enterprises.

KEY COMPETITORS
Hensel Phelps Construction
Skanska
Turner Corporation

CLARK RETAIL GROUP, INC.

3003 Butterfield Rd., Ste. 300	CEO: Brandon K. Barnholt	2001 Sales: $2,600.0 million
Oak Brook, IL 60523	CFO: Jeffrey W. Jones	1-Yr. Sales Change: 0.0%
Phone: 630-366-3000	HR: Deborah C. Paskin	Employees: 7,400
Fax: 630-366-3440	Type: Private	FYE: December 31
Web: www.clarkretail.com		

Clark Retail Group hopes to reach out to those on the go. It operates or franchises about 1,300 gas stations and convenience stores, many operated by subsidiary Clark Retail Enterprises. Store names include Clark, Lighthouse Smoke Shop, Minit Mart, Oh! Zone, On The Go, and White Hen Pantry. Clark Retail Enterprises was formed when an affiliate of investment firm Apollo Management bought the retail assets of oil refiner Clark USA in 1999. Clark Retail Group's holdings span much of the central US and Massachusetts, with more than 400 locations in the Chicago area. Struggling with weak gasoline margins and slow consumer spending, Clark Retail Enterprises filed for reorganization under Chapter 11 in October 2002.

KEY COMPETITORS
BP
CITGO
Exxon Mobil

COLLIERS INTERNATIONAL PROPERTY CONSULTANTS INC.

84 State St., 3rd Fl.	CEO: Margaret Wigglesworth	2001 Sales: $800.0 million
Boston, MA 02019	CFO: Margaret Carlson	1-Yr. Sales Change: (20.0%)
Phone: 617-722-0221	HR: Margaret Carlson	Employees: 6,600
Fax: 617-722-0224	Type: Private	FYE: December 31
Web: www.colliers.com		

Colliers International Property Consultants is one of the largest commercial real estate dealers in the world. With more than 250 offices in about 50 countries, the company is a partnership of more than 40 independently owned firms. Colliers International agencies provide brokerage, corporate, construction consulting, investment sales, and property development and management services to tenants, owners, and investors. Colliers Macauley Nicolls (dba Colliers International) is the group's largest member, with offices in nearly 90 cities worldwide. Originally founded in 1832, Colliers Jardine represents the Asia/Pacific region. All told, Colliers International firms manage about 400 million sq. ft. of property on six continents.

KEY COMPETITORS
CB Richard Ellis
Grubb & Ellis
Jones Lang LaSalle

In-depth profiles of an additional 200 key private companies are found on pages 36–435.

COLORADO BOXED BEEF COMPANY

302 Progress Rd.	CEO: Bryan Saterbo	2001 Sales: $740.0 million
Auburndale, FL 33823	CFO: Nathan Benn	1-Yr. Sales Change: 13.1%
Phone: 863-967-0636	HR: Jerry Heyman	Employees: 425
Fax: 863-965-2222	Type: Private	FYE: March 31
Web: www.coloradoboxedbeef.com		

Whether it runs, swims, or flies (or tries to), Colorado Boxed Beef will zap it and serve it up. Under brand names such as Bridgewater Farms and Colorado Gold, the company wholesales fresh and frozen beef, pork, lamb, poultry, fish, and some dairy products to grocery chains, cruise lines, food service distributors, and exporters throughout the US. It also manufactures quality portion-controlled food-service products. Colorado Boxed Beef was one of the first meat companies to provide ground beef that has been irradiated to reduce the danger of salmonella, E. coli, and other bacteria. The company is owned and operated by the family of the late Richard Saterbo, who founded it with his wife, Edith, in 1975.

KEY COMPETITORS
Cargill
ConAgra
IBP

COLSON & COLSON CONSTRUCTION COMPANY

2250 McGilchrist S.E., Ste. 200	CEO: William Colson	2001 Sales: $887.7 million
Salem, OR 97302	CFO: Gregory Tibbot	1-Yr. Sales Change: 28.7%
Phone: 503-370-7070	HR: Linda Livermore	Employees: 7,000
Fax: 503-364-5716	Type: Private	FYE: December 31

Colson & Colson Construction builds retirement communities for senior citizens worldwide. The company primarily develops affordable retirement properties nationwide for Holiday Retirement Corp. (HRC), the #1 owner and manager of retirement homes in the US and Europe. Colson & Colson has interests in some 20,000 HRC units. Generally located in a midsized town, the typical property is a traditional retirement facility of about 115 units. The company uses a prefabrication process to speed construction and keep costs down. William Colson is CEO of both Colson & Colson and HRC. The Colson family owns the majority of Colson & Colson and also holds a significant stake in HRC.

KEY COMPETITORS
Centex
Del Webb
Lennar

COLUMBIA FOREST PRODUCTS INC.

222 SW Columbia, Ste. 1575	CEO: Harry L. Demorest	2001 Est. Sales: $750.0 mil.
Portland, OR 97201	CFO: Cliff Barry	1-Yr. Sales Change: (6.3%)
Phone: 503-224-5300	HR: —	Employees: 3,300
Fax: 503-224-5294	Type: Private	FYE: December 31
Web: www.columbiaforestproducts.com		

Columbia Forest Products is a clear-cut leader as North America's largest manufacturer of hardwood plywood, veneer, and laminated products. The employee-owned company makes products used in flooring, cabinets, architectural millwork, and commercial fixtures. Specializing in Northern Appalachian hardwoods, Columbia Forest Products' rotary veneer is used by the cabinetry, door, furniture, and decorative plywood industries. The company sells its products to OEMs, wholesale distributors, and mass merchandisers. Columbia Forest Products operates 20 plants in the US and Canada.

KEY COMPETITORS
Armstrong Holdings
Roseburg Forest Products
Weyerhaeuser

In-depth profiles of an additional 200
key private companies are found on pages 36–435.

COLUMBIA HOUSE COMPANY

1221 Avenue of the Americas
New York, NY 10020
Phone: 212-596-2000
Fax: 212-596-2213
Web: www.columbiahouse.com

CEO: Scott Flanders
CFO: Neil Pennington
HR: Michael E. Pilnick
Type: Private

2001 Sales: $1,100.0 million
1-Yr. Sales Change: (8.3%)
Employees: 4,000
FYE: December 31

If the house is a-rockin', it's probably Columbia House. Initially a 50-50 joint venture between entertainment giants Sony and AOL Time Warner, Columbia House is the top club-based direct marketer of music, videos, and DVDs in North America. The company sells more than 16,000 music selections and 7,000 video titles via mail-order and its namesake Web site. Started in 1955, Columbia House boasts some 16 million members in the US, Canada, and Mexico. The company agreed to merge with online music retailer CDnow in 1999, but the deal was called off in early 2000. Investment firm Blackstone Group bought 85% of Columbia House in June 2002 (Sony and AOL Time Warner retain a 15% stake).

KEY COMPETITORS
Amazon.com
Bertelsmann
Musicland

CONAIR CORPORATION

1 Cummings Point Rd.
Stamford, CT 06904
Phone: 203-351-9000
Fax: 203-351-9180
Web: www.conair.com

CEO: Barry Haber
CFO: Pat Yannotta
HR: John Mayorek
Type: Private

2001 Sales: $1,151.0 million
1-Yr. Sales Change: 6.4%
Employees: 4,592
FYE: December 31

Counterintelligence has shown that Conair has a place in many bathrooms and kitchens. Personal products by Conair include curling irons, hair dryers, shavers, mirrors, and salon products (Jheri Redding, Rusk) designed for both home and professional salon use. Its small appliances include food blenders, food processors, and other kitchen appliances produced by its Cuisinart unit. Conair also sells electric toothbrushes (Interplak), telephones, answering machines, and private-label appliances and personal products for retailers. Lee Rizzuto, who founded Conair in 1959 with his parents, owns the company.

KEY COMPETITORS
Applica
Helen of Troy
SEB

CONCENTRA INC.

5080 Spectrum Dr., Ste. 400W
Addison, TX 75001
Phone: 972-364-8000
Fax: 972-387-1938
Web: www.concentra.com

CEO: Daniel J. Thomas
CFO: Thomas E. Kiraly
HR: Tammy Jackson
Type: Private

2001 Sales: $842.9 million
1-Yr. Sales Change: 12.1%
Employees: 10,276
FYE: December 31

Concentra (formerly CONCENTRA Managed Care) concentrates on getting people back to work cheaper. It is the holding company for Concentra Operating Corporation, which provides cost containment and case management services to employers and to occupational, auto, and group health payors throughout the US. Concentra offers specialized cost-containment services for occupational and auto injury cases, preferred-provider network management, telephone case management, and medical bill review. The company also operates more than 200 medical centers in about 30 states, providing occupational health care including pre-employment screening, injury care, and loss prevention.

KEY COMPETITORS
CORE
CorVel
NDCHealth

📖 **In-depth profiles of an additional 200
key private companies are found on pages 36–435.**

CONNECTICARE INC.

30 Batterson Park Rd.	CEO: Marcel L. Gamache	2001 Sales: $654.0 million
Farmington, CT 06032	CFO: Thomas L. Tran	1-Yr. Sales Change: 20.9%
Phone: 860-674-5700	HR: Dick Rogers	Employees: 540
Fax: 860-674-2030	Type: Private	FYE: December 31
Web: www.connecticare.com		

To profit or not to profit? That is no longer a question for ConnectiCare. The company, one of the largest HMOs in Connecticut, has converted to for-profit status in order to raise capital. In 1979 a group of doctors at Hartford Hospital planted the seeds for what would become ConnectiCare; today, the company's nearly 250,000 members in Connecticut and western Massachusetts choose from HMO or point-of-service options. The company has a network of more than 30 hospitals and about 8,000 care providers. ConnectiCare has established a charitable foundation as part of its reorganization to for-profit status.

KEY COMPETITORS
Aetna
Anthem
Health Net

THE CONNELL COMPANY

1 Connell Dr.	CEO: Grover Connell	2001 Sales: $2,525.0 million
Berkeley Heights, NJ 07922	CFO: Terry Connell	1-Yr. Sales Change: 4.1%
Phone: 908-673-3700	HR: Maureen Waldron	Employees: 245
Fax: 908-673-3800	Type: Private	FYE: December 31
Web: www.connellco.com		

The Connell Company can sell you a boatload of rice or lend you money for that power plant you've been meaning to install. Connell's core business is rice distribution, conducted through subsidiary Connell Rice & Sugar. The company's support operations have grown into full subsidiaries, including brokerage of flour and sweeteners, export sales of food manufacturing equipment, commercial real estate development, heavy equipment leasing, exporting, and financial services (such as underwriting airlines' purchases of aircraft). The company has offices in Taiwan, Thailand, and the US. Connell has remained a family-owned business since it was founded in 1926.

KEY COMPETITORS
Cargill
Riceland Foods
Riviana Foods

CONNELL LIMITED PARTNERSHIP

1 International Place	CEO: Francis A. Doyle	2001 Est. Sales: $1,200.0 mil.
Boston, MA 02110	CFO: Kurt Keady	1-Yr. Sales Change: 1.3%
Phone: 617-737-2700	HR: Kathy Gallager	Employees: 2,000
Fax: 617-737-1617	Type: Private	FYE: December 31

The die was cast in 1987 when several subsidiaries organized to create Connell Limited Partnership, a maker of aluminum and industrial equipment. The company's Danly Die Set makes die sets and supplies for die makers. Its Wabash Alloys unit recycles scrap aluminum for steelmakers and the die- and sand-casting industries. Its IEM unit offers bushings and wear plate products. Yuba Heat Transfer provides heat-transfer equipment and feedwater heaters to the petroleum, chemical, and pulp and paper industries. Connell sold its Mayville Metal products to APW Limited.

KEY COMPETITORS
Actuant
IMCO Recycling
TAT Technologies

📖 In-depth profiles of an additional 200 key private companies are found on pages 36–435.

CONRAIL INC.

2001 Market St., 16th Fl.
Philadelphia, PA 19103
Phone: 215-209-2000
Fax: 215-209-4068
Web: www.conrail.com

CEO: Gregory R. Weber
CFO: Joseph Rogers
HR: Anthony Carlini
Type: Private

2000 Sales: $985.0 million
1-Yr. Sales Change: (55.2%)
Employees: —
FYE: December 31

Conrail is the holding company for Consolidated Rail, a freight railroad in the heavily industrialized Northeast. Most of its former lines and facilities have been divided between its joint owners, rail operators CSX (42%) and Norfolk Southern (58%), following an agreement that took effect in 1999. Conrail, however, continues to manage and operate some lines and facilities in the Philadelphia and Detroit metropolitan areas and in much of New Jersey. To serve customers along those lines, both CSX and Norfolk Southern pay a fee to Conrail for line access; Conrail acts as the local switching and terminal management agent.

KEY COMPETITORS
Guilford Transportation
USFreightways

CONSOLIDATED ELECTRICAL DISTRIBUTORS INC.

31356 Via Colinas, Ste. 107
Westlake Village, CA 91362
Phone: 818-991-9000
Fax: 818-991-6842
Web: www.cedcareers.com

CEO: H. Dean Bursch
CFO: Thomas A. Lullo
HR: Marie Lipp
Type: Private

2001 Est. Sales: $2,600.0 mil.
1-Yr. Sales Change: 4.0%
Employees: 5,500
FYE: December 31

Electrical equipment wholesaler Consolidated Electrical Distributors (CED) has US distribution wired. With more than 500 locations nationwide, the family-owned business is one of the largest distributors of electrical products in the country. CED supplies load centers, panelboards, transformers, switches, motor controls, drives, and similar products to residential and commercial contractors and industrial customers. Founded in 1957 as The Electric Corporation of San Francisco, the company has grown by acquiring electrical distributors; since it usually keeps the acquired firm's name and management team, CED now does business under about 80 names. The Colburn family owns CED.

KEY COMPETITORS
Anixter International
Graybar Electric
WESCO International

CONTRAN CORPORATION

5430 LBJ Fwy., Ste. 1700
Dallas, TX 75240
Phone: 972-233-1700
Fax: 972-448-1444

CEO: Harold C. Simmons
CFO: Bob D. O'Brien
HR: Keith A. Johnson
Type: Private

2001 Sales: $1,100.0 million
1-Yr. Sales Change: (8.3%)
Employees: 7,300
FYE: December 31

Founded by Texas billionaire Harold Simmons, Contran is a holding company that controls around 94% of Valhi, Inc., a publicly traded company. Through subsidiaries and affiliations, Valhi conducts diversified operations involved in chemicals (NL Industries), titanium metals (Titanium Metals Corporation), waste management services (Waste Control Specialties), computer support systems, and precision ball-bearing slides and locking systems (CompX International). Contran also has a controlling interest in Keystone Consolidated Industries, a maker of fencing and wire products. Trusts benefiting Simmons' daughters and his grandchildren own almost all of Contran (Simmons is the sole trustee).

KEY COMPETITORS
Millennium Chemicals
RTI International Metals
Waste Management

In-depth profiles of an additional 200 key private companies are found on pages 36–435.

CORNELL UNIVERSITY

Cornell University Campus, 305 Day Hall	CEO: Hunter R. Rawlings III	2002 Sales: $1,666.1 million
Ithaca, NY 14853	CFO: Harold D. Craft Jr.	1-Yr. Sales Change: 14.2%
Phone: 607-255-2000	HR: Mary G. Opperman	Employees: 13,319
Fax: 607-255-5396	Type: School	FYE: June 30
Web: www.cornell.edu		

To excel at Cornell you'll need every one of your brain cells. The Ivy League university has been educating young minds since its founding in 1865. Its more than 20,000 students can select from seven undergraduate and four graduate and professional colleges and schools. In addition to its Ithaca, New York, campus, the university also offers two medical graduate and professional colleges and schools in New York City, and has set up education-outreach centers in every county and borough of New York. Cornell's faculty includes a handful of Nobel laureates, and the university has a robust research component studying everything from animal health to space to waste management.

CRESCENT ELECTRIC SUPPLY COMPANY

7750 Dunleith Dr.	CEO: James R. Etheredge	2001 Sales: $609.0 million
East Dubuque, IL 61025	CFO: Alice R. Vontalge	1-Yr. Sales Change: (3.6%)
Phone: 815-747-3145	HR: Dan Philippi	Employees: —
Fax: 815-747-7720	Type: Private	FYE: December 31
Web: www.cesco.com		

Crescent Electric Supply always plays it straight with its customers. The company was founded in 1919 by Titus Schmid as a lamp agent for General Electric. Today Crescent Electric distributes electrical supplies from leading manufacturers such as GE Lighting, Hubbell, Siemens, and Thomas & Betts. The company also offers bin management and other inventory services. Orders can be placed through Crescent Electric's online order system at any hour of the day. Customers include John Deere, Caterpillar, Mitsubishi, and various government agencies. Members of the Schmid family continue to own Crescent Electric.

KEY COMPETITORS
Graybar Electric
Kirby Risk
Mayer Electric

CROWLEY MARITIME CORPORATION

155 Grand Ave.	CEO: Thomas B. Crowley Jr.	2001 Sales: $1,001.0 million
Oakland, CA 94612	CFO: John Calvin	1-Yr. Sales Change: 25.1%
Phone: 510-251-7500	HR: Susan Rogers	Employees: 3,800
Fax: 510-251-7788	Type: Private	FYE: December 31
Web: www.crowley.com		

Crowley Maritime has pushed and pulled its way into prominence as one of the largest tug and barge operators in the world. The company transports freight, petroleum products, and breakbulk (structures that cannot be broken down) by ship. It provides ship assists, towing, logistics, and marine salvage. The company has some 60,000 containers and trailers and a 300-vessel fleet including tugboats, tankers, barges, and specialized cargo vessels. Crowley Maritime has more than 100 offices worldwide and has expanded with the acquisition of Marine Transport. CEO Thomas Crowley (grandson of the founder), his family, and employees own about 85% of the company, which was founded in 1892.

KEY COMPETITORS
APL
Alexander & Baldwin
CSX

📖 **In-depth profiles of an additional 200 key private companies are found on pages 36–435.**

CROWN CENTRAL PETROLEUM CORPORATION

1 North Charles St.	CEO: Frank B. Rosenberg	2001 Est. Sales: $1,700.0 mil.
Baltimore, MD 21201	CFO: John E. Wheeler Jr.	1-Yr. Sales Change: (13.3%)
Phone: 410-539-7400	HR: J. Michael Mims	Employees: 2,600
Fax: 410-659-4747	Type: Private	FYE: December 31
Web: www.crowncentral.com		

Independent oil refiner and marketer Crown Central Petroleum's family jewels include two refineries in Texas with a total capacity of 152,000 barrels per day, 346 retail service stations in the mid-Atlantic and southeastern US, and 13 product terminals. Crown Central also offers fleet fueling services. The company has come under attack for a four-year labor lockout at its Houston-area refinery, civil rights violations, and excessive toxic releases. It is considering selling its refineries and its terminals. Rosemore, Inc., the holding company of Crown Central chairman Henry Rosenberg and his family, took full ownership of Crown Central in 2001 after beating out a competing bid from rival Apex Oil.

KEY COMPETITORS
ConocoPhillips
Motiva Enterprises
Valero Energy

CROWN EQUIPMENT CORPORATION

40 S. Washington St.	CEO: James F. Dicke II	2002 Sales: $966.0 million
New Bremen, OH 45869	CFO: Kent Spille	1-Yr. Sales Change: (14.3%)
Phone: 419-629-2311	HR: Randy Niekamp	Employees: 7,000
Fax: 419-629-9241	Type: Private	FYE: March 31
Web: www.crownlift.com		

Crown Equipment is a leading maker of electric heavy-duty lift trucks for maneuvering goods in warehouses and distribution centers. The company's products include narrow-aisle stacking equipment, powered pallet trucks, order-picking equipment, and forklift trucks. Its equipment can move four-ton loads and stack pallets nearly 45 feet high. Crown Equipment sells its products globally through retailers. The company, founded in 1945 by brothers Carl and Allen Dicke, originally made temperature controls for coal furnaces. It began making material-handling equipment in the 1950s. The Dicke family still controls Crown Equipment.

KEY COMPETITORS
Caterpillar
Ingersoll-Rand Infrastructure
Komatsu

CUMBERLAND FARMS, INC.

777 Dedham St.	CEO: Lily Haseotes Bentas	2002 Sales: $1,700.0 million
Canton, MA 02021	CFO: Kevin Johnson	1-Yr. Sales Change: 13.3%
Phone: 781-828-4900	HR: Foster G. Macrides	Employees: 6,976
Fax: 781-828-9624	Type: Private	FYE: September 30
Web: www.cumberlandfarms.com		

Beginning as a one-cow dairy, Cumberland Farms now owns and operates more than 1,000 convenience stores (three-fourths of which sell gasoline) in 11 eastern seaboard states from Maine to Florida. The company has its own grocery distribution and bakery operations to supply its stores. Cumberland Farms owns a two-thirds limited partnership in petroleum wholesaler Gulf Oil, giving it the right to use and license Gulf trademarks in Delaware, New Jersey, New York, most of Ohio, Pennsylvania, and the New England states. The company, the first convenience-store operator in New England, was founded in 1938 by Vasilios and Aphrodite Haseotes. The Haseotes' children, including CEO Lily Haseotes Bentas, own the company.

KEY COMPETITORS
7-Eleven
BP
Exxon Mobil

📖 **In-depth profiles of an additional 200 key private companies are found on pages 36–435.**

CUNA MUTUAL GROUP

5910 Mineral Point Rd.	CEO: Michael B. Kitchen	2001 Sales: $2,030.0 million
Madison, WI 53701	CFO: —	1-Yr. Sales Change: —
Phone: 608-238-5851	HR: —	Employees: 5,000
Fax: —	Type: Mutual company	FYE: December 31
Web: www.cunamutual.com		

CUNA would soonah eat tuna than make its products available to banks. CUNA Mutual Group offers the more than 10,000 credit unions in the US (as well as those in 30 other countries) a range of products and services, including life insurance, investment advisory, and information technology. Entities that make up the group include CUNA Mutual Insurance Society (accident, health, and life insurance) and CUNA Mutual Mortgage Corporation (mortgage loan origination, purchasing, and servicing). The group also offers customers such technology services as Web site enhancement and automated lending software. CUNA was founded in 1935 by pioneers of the credit union movement and is owned by its credit union policyholders.

KEY COMPETITORS
BISYS
PrimeVest
U.S. Central Credit Union

CUSHMAN & WAKEFIELD INC.

51 W. 52nd St.	CEO: Arthur J. Mirante II	2001 Sales: $870.0 million
New York, NY 10019	CFO: Thomas P. Dowd	1-Yr. Sales Change: 6.1%
Phone: 212-841-7500	HR: Carolyn F. Sessa	Employees: 11,000
Fax: 212-841-7767	Type: Private	FYE: December 31
Web: www.cushwake.com		

Cushman & Wakefield serves the real estate needs of corporations and financial institutions around the globe. The commercial real estate brokerage and services company, founded in 1917 by J. Clydesdale Cushman and Bernard Wakefield, has more than 170 offices in about 50 countries. Cushman & Wakefield operates in Africa, Asia, Europe, the Middle East, and North and South America. Landmark projects include the American Express Tower in Manhattan and the Sears Tower in Chicago. The company has begun an Internet venture with Business Integration Group to offer online real estate management services. The Rockefeller Group, a Mitsubishi Estate subsidiary, owns about 80% of Cushman & Wakefield.

KEY COMPETITORS
CB Richard Ellis
Grubb & Ellis
Trammell Crow

DADE BEHRING INC.

1717 Deerfield Rd.	CEO: James Reid-Anderson	2001 Sales: $1,235.0 million
Deerfield, IL 60015	CFO: John Duffey	1-Yr. Sales Change: 4.3%
Phone: 847-267-5300	HR: Kathy Kennedy	Employees: 6,500
Fax: 847-267-5408	Type: Private	FYE: December 31
Web: www.dadebehring.com		

Dade Behring just wants to make *sure* that blood is thicker than water. Among the company's products are diagnostic instruments that test how well blood coagulates. Other products test for infectious diseases; measure levels of cholesterol, glucose, iron, or sodium in the body; diagnose cardiac disease; monitor therapeutic drugs; and test for illicit drug use. With sales offices worldwide, the company has almost 25,000 customers, mainly clinical laboratories and hospitals. Dade Behring's staff of more than 1,000 provides support services to its product's users. In order to battle its debt, the company is reorganizing under Chapter 11 bankruptcy protection.

KEY COMPETITORS
Beckman Coulter
Johnson & Johnson
Roche

📖 **In-depth profiles of an additional 200 key private companies are found on pages 36–435.**

DAIRYLEA COOPERATIVE INC.

5001 Brittonfield Pkwy.	CEO: Richard P. Smith	2002 Sales: $941.0 million
East Syracuse, NY 13057	CFO: Edward Bangel	1-Yr. Sales Change: 17.2%
Phone: 315-433-0100	HR: Edward Bangel	Employees: 115
Fax: 315-433-2345	Type: Cooperative	FYE: March 31
Web: www.dairylea.com		

Yes, the farmer takes a wife, then hi-ho, the derry-o, the farmer takes membership in milk-marketing organizations such as Dairylea Cooperative. Owned by more than 2,800 dairy farmers in the northeastern US, Dairylea markets 5 billion pounds of milk for its farmers annually to customers such as Kraft Foods and Great Lakes Cheese Company. The cooperative invests in dairy companies and provides members with financial and farm-management services, as well as insurance. Dairylea, the largest milk marketer in the Northeast, has a joint marketing venture with Dairy Farmers of America and other cooperatives. Dairylea's Empire Livestock subsidiary markets livestock.

KEY COMPETITORS
AMPI
Agri-Mark
Foremost Farms

D&H DISTRIBUTING CO., INC.

2525 N. 7th St.	CEO: Israel Schwab	2001 Sales: $875.0 million
Harrisburg, PA 17110	CFO: Robert Miller	1-Yr. Sales Change: 36.1%
Phone: 717-236-8001	HR: Jen Lieberman	Employees: —
Fax: 717-255-7838	Type: Private	FYE: April 30
Web: www.dandh.com		

D&H could stand for Distributing and How! D&H Distributing sells more than 6,000 computer and electronics products to resellers nationwide. Clients include large resellers and small retailers such as college bookstores. D&H also targets local, state, and federal government agencies. It operates five divisions: computer products, home entertainment, security, educational resources, and government services. Suppliers include Hewlett-Packard, Texas Instruments, and Microsoft. Founded in 1918 as a tire retreader, the company entered the electronics business in 1926. D&H has been employee-owned since 1999.

KEY COMPETITORS
Arrow Electronics
Ingram Micro
Tech Data

DARBY GROUP COMPANIES, INC.

865 Merrick Ave.	CEO: Carl Ashkin	2001 Est. Sales: $625.0 mil.
Westbury, NY 11590	CFO: Justina Sorraci	1-Yr. Sales Change: (7.4%)
Phone: 516-683-1800	HR: Susan Scanlon	Employees: 1,500
Fax: 516-832-7101	Type: Private	FYE: December 31
Web: www.darbygroup.com		

Dog-owning pill poppers with bad teeth drive the sales of the Darby Group. The group's Darby-Spencer-Mead Dental Supply uses more than 200 phone operators to take orders and distribute some 40,000 products in stock for dentists. Its Burns Veterinary Supply unit provides veterinary supplies and services through about 150 field and phone sales representatives. Darby Drug provides health care professionals with pharmaceuticals and disposable supplies. Other companies within the Darby Group include Bedford Chiropractic Supply, which distributes chiropractic equipment, nutritional supplements, and other items.

KEY COMPETITORS
Henry Schein
McKesson
Patterson Dental

📖 **In-depth profiles of an additional 200 key private companies are found on pages 36–435.**

DARCARS

9020 Lanham-Severn	CEO: John R. Darvish	2001 Sales: $845.4 million
Lanham, MD 20706	CFO: Michael Hancheruk	1-Yr. Sales Change: 8.0%
Phone: 301-459-1100	HR: Sam Bruner	Employees: 1,800
Fax: 301-459-5125	Type: Private	FYE: December 31
Web: www.darcars.com		

Buying a new vehicle in the Washington, DC, area can expose you to the Darcars side of human nature. Darcars, an automobile dealership holding company, has more than 20 automobile dealerships in Maryland and Virginia. Its dealerships sell a variety of new and used automobiles, including cars made by General Motors, DaimlerChrysler, Ford, Kia, Mitsubishi, Toyota, Volkswagen, and Volvo. Darcars offers a full range of automotive services, including parts and service departments and car body repair. Darcars was founded in 1977 by John Darvish, whose family still owns and runs the company.

KEY COMPETITORS
Brown Automotive
Jim Koons Automotive
Rosenthal Automotive

DAVID MCDAVID AUTO GROUP

3700 W. Airport Fwy.	CEO: David McDavid Sr.	2001 Est. Sales: $700.0 mil.
Irving, TX 75062	CFO: Jay Torda	1-Yr. Sales Change: 17.4%
Phone: 972-790-6100	HR: Kristy Pyatt	Employees: 1,200
Fax: 972-986-5689	Type: Private	FYE: December 31
Web: www.mcdavid.com		

David McDavid Auto Group is one of the largest vehicle vendors in Texas, with about a dozen dealerships in Austin, Houston, and Dallas. The company sells new cars made by Acura, Ford, General Motors, Honda, Kia, Nissan, and Suzuki, and it also sells used cars. David McDavid Auto Group is named for its founder and CEO, who started his first car dealership in 1962 at age 19; he is a former minority owner of the Dallas Mavericks basketball team. McDavid sold 70% of David McDavid Auto Group to automotive consolidator Asbury Automotive Group in 1997. Asbury Automotive is a joint venture of Ripplewood Holdings and LBO firm Freeman, Spogli & Co.

KEY COMPETITORS
Gulf States Toyota
Sonic Automotive
VT

DAVID WEEKLEY HOMES

1111 N. Post Oak Rd.	CEO: David M. Weekley	2001 Sales: $827.0 million
Houston, TX 77055	CFO: Jim Alexander	1-Yr. Sales Change: (0.1%)
Phone: 713-963-0500	HR: Mike Gentry	Employees: 1,037
Fax: 713-963-0322	Type: Private	FYE: December 31
Web: www.davidweekleyhomes.com		

A development home developed to *your* taste? David Weekley Homes will do it. Founded in 1976, it is the second-largest privately owned homebuilder in the US, annually building more than 3,400 single-family detached homes that range in size from about 1,500 sq. ft. to more than 4,000 sq. ft. Weekley builds homes from hundreds of floor plans and offers custom upgrades. Prices range from $120,000 to about $650,000. The company builds in its own planned communities in Texas, Oklahoma, Colorado, and in the Southeast, as well as on buyers' lots. For the past three years, it has been listed among the "Top 100 Companies to Work for in America" in *Fortune* magazine. Founder and chairman David Weekley owns the firm.

KEY COMPETITORS
D.R. Horton
Engle Homes
Town and Country Homes

📖 In-depth profiles of an additional 200 key private companies are found on pages 36–435.

DAVID WILSON'S AUTOMOTIVE GROUP

1400 N. Tustin	CEO: David Wilson	2001 Sales: $1,073.3 million
Orange, CA 92867	CFO: Ted Tomasek	1-Yr. Sales Change: 3.9%
Phone: 714-639-6750	HR: Vicki Murphy	Employees: 450
Fax: 714-771-0363	Type: Private	FYE: December 31

First Orange County, then the world — or at least Arizona. David Wilson's Automotive Group has its roots in Orange County, California. In 1985 owner David Wilson bought Toyota of Orange, the first of his 12 dealerships, which are all located in California and Arizona and sell Acura, Ford, Honda, and Lexus cars, as well as Toyotas. The company didn't expand east until 1998, when it opened a Honda dealership in Scottsdale, Arizona. The company then added a Toyota location in Arizona in 1999. The company's dealerships now sell more than 42,000 new and used cars annually. The dealerships run by David Wilson's Automotive Group also offer parts and service departments; some offer fleet services.

KEY COMPETITORS
Autonation
Marty Franich
Tuttle-Click

DAWN FOOD PRODUCTS, INC.

2021 Micor Dr.	CEO: Ronald L. Jones	2001 Est. Sales: $655.0 mil.
Jackson, MI 49203	CFO: Peter J. Staelens	1-Yr. Sales Change: 0.8%
Phone: 517-789-4400	HR: Bill Lambkin	Employees: 2,100
Fax: 517-789-4465	Type: Private	FYE: December 31
Web: www.dawnfoods.com		

A muffin at Starbucks, a cookie from Mrs. Fields, or a doughnut from Krispy Kreme — all just another day in the kitchen for Dawn Food Products. The company provides pre-baked and fully baked products — as well as bases, equipment, fillings, frozen dough, icings, ingredients, and mixes — to the food industry. Its customers include food service companies, institutional bakeries, restaurants, retail outlets, and supermarkets. Dawn Food Products also offers support services such as merchandising and marketing. Owned by the Jones family, Dawn Food Products was founded in 1920 in Jackson, Michigan, and now operates throughout the US and in 13 other countries.

KEY COMPETITORS
General Mills
International Multifoods
Interstate Bakeries

THE DAY & ZIMMERMANN GROUP, INC.

1818 Market St.	CEO: Harold L. Yoh III	2001 Sales: $1,300.0 million
Philadelphia, PA 19103	CFO: Joe Ritzel	1-Yr. Sales Change: (16.3%)
Phone: 215-299-8000	HR: Judith Jones Blanks	Employees: 20,000
Fax: 215-299-8355	Type: Private	FYE: December 31
Web: www.dayzim.com		

Day & Zimmermann offers services as distinct as day and night. The company provides engineering and construction management, security, munitions assembly and disposal, and technical- and administrative-staffing services worldwide. Its clients are US and foreign defense and energy agencies; utilities; and educational, financial, and health organizations. It also operates dedicated offices for individual clients, such as DuPont and Lucent. The company boosted its munitions business in 1999 by buying Mason & Hanger Engineering, which subsequently lost a contract at the Pantex nuclear bomb plant in Texas that it had held since 1956. Founded in 1901, Day & Zimmermann is owned by CEO Harold Yoh and his family.

KEY COMPETITORS
Bechtel
CDI
McDermott

📖 In-depth profiles of an additional 200
key private companies are found on pages 36–435.

DEBRUCE GRAIN, INC.

4100 N. Mulberry Dr.	CEO: Paul DeBruce	2002 Sales: $1,378.0 million
Kansas City, MO 64116	CFO: Curt Heinz	1-Yr. Sales Change: 14.7%
Phone: 816-421-8182	HR: Joni Hawn	Employees: 400
Fax: 816-584-2350	Type: Private	FYE: March 31
Web: www.debruce.com		

Got a few tons of wheat and no place to keep it? DeBruce Grain stores, handles, and sells grain and fertilizer for the agribusiness industry. The company runs 13 grain elevators in Iowa, Kansas, Nebraska, and Texas with a combined capacity of 60 million bushels of grain. DeBruce Grain's office in Mexico merchandises grain grown in both countries. The company also markets fertilizer (by the bag, truck, or barge-load), and it brokers truck freight through subsidiary DeBruce Transportation. DeBruce paid a $685,000 fine in relation to the 1998 explosion, which killed seven workers, of its Haysville, Kansas, facility — the largest grain elevator in the world. Owner and CEO Paul DeBruce founded the company in 1978.

KEY COMPETITORS
Ag Processing
Cargill
Scoular

DELAWARE NORTH COMPANIES INC.

40 Fountain Plaza	CEO: Jeremy M. Jacobs	2001 Sales: $1,600.0 million
Buffalo, NY 14202	CFO: —	1-Yr. Sales Change: 6.7%
Phone: 716-858-5000	HR: Karen Kemp	Employees: 25,000
Fax: 716-858-5479	Type: Private	FYE: December 31
Web: www.delawarenorth.com		

When it comes to corn dogs and nachos, Delaware North makes a lot of concessions. A giant in the food concession industry, the company has a string of subsidiaries ready to make hungry folks happy. Among the company's holdings are Sportservice (food service at sports stadiums), CA One Services (airport food service), and Delaware North Parks Services (visitor services for national parks and tourist attractions). The company also operates Boston's FleetCenter and owns a handful of pari-mutuel facilities across the US. Delaware North was founded in 1915 by brothers Charles, Louis, and Marvin Jacobs. The Jacobs family (including CEO Jeremy Jacobs, owner of the NHL's Boston Bruins) still controls the company.

KEY COMPETITORS
ARAMARK
HMSHost
Sodexho Alliance

DELCO REMY INTERNATIONAL, INC.

2902 Enterprise Dr.	CEO: Thomas J. Snyder	2001 Sales: $1,053.5 million
Anderson, IN 46013	CFO: Raj Shah	1-Yr. Sales Change: (3.4%)
Phone: 765-778-6499	HR: Roderick English	Employees: 7,422
Fax: 765-778-6404	Type: Private	FYE: December 31
Web: www.delcoremy.com		

Carmakers get cranked up with the help of Delco Remy International, which manufactures and distributes starters and alternators for carmakers and light- and heavy-duty truck makers. The company, which is owned by Citicorp Venture Capital, also remanufactures engines, fuel systems, starters, transmissions, alternators, and torque converters for the automotive aftermarket. Delco's OEM customers include companies such as General Motors, Delphi, Navistar, and Caterpillar; retail customers include Pep Boys, AutoZone, and other automotive parts chains.

KEY COMPETITORS
Genuine Parts
Motorcar Parts
Robert Bosch

In-depth profiles of an additional 200 key private companies are found on pages 36–435.

DELTA DENTAL PLAN OF CALIFORNIA

100 1st St.	CEO: Gary D. Radine	2001 Sales: $3,300.0 million
San Francisco, CA 94105	CFO: Elizabeth Russell	1-Yr. Sales Change: 17.9%
Phone: 415-972-8300	HR: Teri Forestieri	Employees: 2,400
Fax: 415-972-8366	Type: Not-for-profit	FYE: December 31
Web: www.deltadentalca.org		

Delta Dental Plan of California doesn't just help keep the mouths of movie stars clean. A not-for-profit organization, the company is a member of the Delta Dental Plans Association and has affiliates nationwide. Delta Dental provides dental coverage through HMOs, preferred provider plans (PPOs), and such government programs as California's Denti-Cal. The company serves more than 15 million enrollees; its programs cover more than one-third of California residents. Together with Delta Dental of Pennsylvania, in 2000 Delta Dental of California formed Dentegra Group, a holding company that serves some 17 million members throughout the US.

KEY COMPETITORS
Health Net
MetLife
WellPoint Health Networks

DEMOULAS SUPER MARKETS INC.

875 East St.	CEO: Julien Lacourse	2001 Est. Sales: $2,000.0 mil.
Tewksbury, MA 01876	CFO: Donald Mulligan	1-Yr. Sales Change: 11.1%
Phone: 978-851-8000	HR: Lucille Lopez	Employees: 12,700
Fax: 978-640-8390	Type: Private	FYE: December 31

Supermarket or soap opera? Demoulas Super Markets runs almost 60 grocery stores under the Market Basket and Demoulas Super Market names in Massachusetts and New Hampshire. The firm also has real estate interests. The company was founded in 1954 when brothers George and Mike Demoulas bought their parents' mom-and-pop grocery. The men agreed that, upon one brother's death, the other would care for the deceased's family and maintain the firm's 50-50 ownership. In 1990 George's family alleged that Mike had defrauded them of all but 8% of the company's stock; the 10-year court battle was decided in favor of George's family, giving it 51% of the company. By then Mike had resigned as CEO.

KEY COMPETITORS
Hannaford Bros.
Shaw's
Stop & Shop

THE DEPOSITORY TRUST & CLEARING CORPORATION

55 Water St., 49th Fl.	CEO: Jill M. Considine	2001 Sales: —
New York, NY 10041	CFO: Richard R. Macek	1-Yr. Sales Change: —
Phone: 212-855-1000	HR: Kevin P. Carey	Employees: 3,250
Fax: 212-855-8440	Type: Private	FYE: December 31
Web: www.dtcc.com		

It's clear that securities trading just wouldn't be the same without The Depository Trust & Clearing Corporation (DTCC), parent to The Depository Trust Company (DTC) and the National Securities Clearing Company (NSCC). The companies provide the infrastructure for clearing, settlement, and custody of most US securities transactions. DTCC was founded in 1999 when the operating companies (both founded in the 1970s) were combined under a single holding structure. DTC is the world's largest securities depository and a clearinghouse for trading settlement; NSCC processes most broker-to-broker equity, corporate, and municipal-bond trades in the US.

📖 In-depth profiles of an additional 200
key private companies are found on pages 36–435.

DESERET MANAGEMENT CORPORATION

60 E. South Temple, Ste. 575
Salt Lake City, UT 84111
Phone: 801-323-4216
Fax: 801-323-4236
Web: www.deseretmanagement.com

CEO: Rodney H. Brady
CFO: —
HR: Roland A. Radack
Type: Private

2000 Est. Sales: $780.0 mil.
1-Yr. Sales Change: 17.3%
Employees: 3,100
FYE: December 31

While the Church of Jesus Christ of Latter-Day Saints handles the spiritual, Deseret Management takes care of the worldly. The holding company oversees a portfolio of for-profit ventures for the Mormon Church, including about 20 radio stations, several TV stations, and Salt Lake City's *Deseret News* newspaper. Its Deseret Book Company publishes primarily inspirational books under four imprints, and operates a chain of more than 30 book stores in about a dozen states. Deseret also houses life insurance, hotel and restaurant management, and property management services. Founded in 1932, Deseret Management does not accept advertising for alcohol or other goods objectionable to the church.

KEY COMPETITORS
Christian Science Publishing
Reader's Digest
Thomas Nelson

DETROIT MEDICAL CENTER

3663 Woodward Ave., Ste. 200
Detroit, MI 48201
Phone: 313-578-2000
Fax: 313-578-3225
Web: www.dmc.org

CEO: Arthur T. Porter
CFO: Nickolas Vitale
HR: Ruthann Voelker
Type: Not-for-profit

2000 Sales: $1,600.0 million
1-Yr. Sales Change: 10.2%
Employees: 16,500
FYE: December 31

The seeds for the Detroit Medical Center were planted in 1955, when four Detroit hospitals joined efforts to provide coordination between the hospitals and Wayne State University's medical school. Today the medical center (which became a not-for-profit corporation in 1985) serves patients in southeastern Michigan with more than 2,000 beds and some 3,000 physicians. The center is made up of seven hospitals, more than 100 outpatient facilities, and two nursing centers. The Detroit Medical Center is the teaching and clinical research site for Wayne State, now one of the US's largest medical schools; the medical center is also allied with the Barbara Ann Karmanos Cancer Institute and the Kresge Eye Institute.

KEY COMPETITORS
Henry Ford Health System
Trinity Health
William Beaumont Hospital

DEVCON CONSTRUCTION INCORPORATED

690 Gibraltar Dr.
Milpitas, CA 95035
Phone: 408-942-8200
Fax: 408-262-2342
Web: www.devcon-const.com

CEO: Gary Filizetti
CFO: Bret Sisney
HR: Jennifer Cooke
Type: Private

2001 Sales: $1,351.0 million
1-Yr. Sales Change: 3.9%
Employees: 550
FYE: March 31

The dot-com deathwatch hasn't stopped Devcon Construction — it's still riding the coattails of Silicon Valley's business boom. One of the area's top general-building contractors, Devcon has constructed more than 35 million sq. ft. of office, industrial, and commercial space in Northern California. Founded in 1976, Devcon specializes in high-tech projects, including industrial research-and-development facilities for clients such as Cisco Systems and Silicon Graphics. Devcon also provides engineering, design/build, and interior design services. In addition to building company facilities and offices, Devon works on projects such as hotels, restaurants, retail stores, and schools.

KEY COMPETITORS
DPR Construction
Rudolph & Sletten
Webcor Builders

In-depth profiles of an additional 200 key private companies are found on pages 36–435.

DFS GROUP LIMITED

First Market Tower, 525 Market St., 33rd Fl.
San Francisco, CA 94105
Phone: 415-977-2700
Fax: 415-977-4289
Web: www.dfsgroup.com

CEO: Edward J. Brennan
CFO: Steve Mangnum
HR: Peggy Tate
Type: Private

2001 Sales: $1,000.0 million
1-Yr. Sales Change: (33.3%)
Employees: 8,600
FYE: December 31

Some world travelers prefer seeing the sights, but as DFS Group knows, some prefer checking out a good sale. The world's largest travel retailer, DFS (Duty Free Shoppers) runs some 150 stores, located primarily in the Asia/Pacific region and on the US West Coast. The stores offer upscale brands of perfume, jewelry, liquor, tobacco, clothing, and other high-end goods. DFS is famous for its airport stores, but it also runs about 15 Galleria centers in resorts and downtown areas. French conglomerate LVMH owns 61% of the company. Co-founder Robert Miller owns 38%.

KEY COMPETITORS
BAA
King Power
Richemont

DHL AIRWAYS, INC.

50 California St., 5th Fl.
San Francisco, CA 94111
Phone: 415-677-6100
Fax: 415-677-7268

CEO: Vicki Bretthauer
CFO: Jeffrey J. Simmons
HR: Chuck Thomson
Type: Private

2001 Sales: $1,462.0 million
1-Yr. Sales Change: (2.3%)
Employees: 10,087
FYE: December 31

A US arm of DHL International, cargo carrier DHL Airways helps its parent company take on delivery giants FedEx and UPS on their own turf. DHL Airways operates about 35 aircraft and enables its parent and other customers to offer same-day and overnight delivery of virtually any kind of cargo, including temperature-sensitive materials. Investor William A. Robinson owns 75% of the company's voting shares. Brussels-based DHL International, which operates through DHL Worldwide Express, owns 52% of DHL Airways, but because of limits on foreign ownership of US-based airlines, it controls only 23% of the voting shares. German postal service Deutsche Post controls about 75% of DHL International.

KEY COMPETITORS
Airborne
FedEx
UPS

DHL WORLDWIDE EXPRESS, INC.

50 California St.
San Francisco, CA 94111
Phone: 415-677-6100
Fax: 415-677-7268
Web: www.dhl-usa.com

CEO: Uwe R. Dörken
CFO: —
HR: Gary Sellers
Type: Private

2001 Sales: $6,000.0 million
1-Yr. Sales Change: 9.1%
Employees: 71,480
FYE: December 31

By bus, boat, or bicycle, from Albania to Kyrgyzstan, Qatar to Zimbabwe, DHL Worldwide Express delivers. The company is the world leader in cross-border express deliveries, ahead of FedEx and UPS. Overall, DHL links 120,000 destinations in about 230 countries and territories. The company has about 4,000 offices worldwide, and it operates a fleet of more than 250 aircraft. Affiliate DHL Airways provides air cargo services in the US. Brussels-based DHL International, which is 75%-owned by Deutsche Post, owns 100% of DHL Worldwide Express and 52% of DHL Airways. Deutsche Post has agreed to take full ownership of DHL International.

KEY COMPETITORS
CNF
FedEx
UPS

📖 **In-depth profiles of an additional 200 key private companies are found on pages 36–435.**

DI GIORGIO CORPORATION

380 Middlesex Ave.	CEO: Richard B. Neff	2001 Sales: $1,538.8 million
Carteret, NJ 07008	CFO: Lawrence S. Grossman	1-Yr. Sales Change: 3.4%
Phone: 732-541-5555	HR: Jackie Simmons	Employees: 1,353
Fax: 732-541-3590	Type: Private	FYE: December 31
Web: www.whiterose.com		

Di Giorgio delivers little apples (and other foods) to the Big Apple. Founded in 1920, the firm is a food wholesaler and distributor primarily in New York City, Long Island, and New Jersey. It offers more than 17,000 products to more than 1,800 stores ranging from independents and members of co-ops to regional chains. (A&P accounts for about 25% of sales.) Although Di Giorgio distributes national brands, it also supplies frozen and refrigerated products under its White Rose brand, a name known in New York for well over a century. Di Giorgio co-chairman and CEO Richard Neff owns more than 99% of the company, primarily through his sole general partnership in Rose Partners; co-chairman and president Stephen Bokser owns about 1%.

KEY COMPETITORS
C&S Wholesale
Krasdale Foods
Wakefern Food

DICK CORPORATION

300 Stadium Circle	CEO: David E. Dick	2001 Sales: $1,100.0 million
Pittsburgh, PA 15212	CFO: Jeffrey L. Konn	1-Yr. Sales Change: 4.8%
Phone: 412-384-1000	HR: Janet Love	Employees: 3,500
Fax: 412-384-1150	Type: Private	FYE: December 31
Web: www.dickcorp.com		

Without any help from Tom or Harry, Dick Corporation, a general contracting, construction, and construction management firm, builds commercial, institutional, power, industrial, bridge, and highway projects. Subsidiary Dick International is expanding the company's overseas operations beyond the Caribbean into Europe, Latin America, and the Middle East. Major projects include construction of PNC Park, the new home of the Pittsburgh Pirates, and the preservation of Fallingwater, a home designed by Frank Lloyd Wright. CEO David Dick and president Douglas Dick, part owners of the Pittsburgh Pirates, run the family-owned firm, founded by their grandfather, Noble Dick, in 1922.

KEY COMPETITORS
Jacobs Engineering
Peter Kiewit Sons'
Turner Corporation

DILLINGHAM CONSTRUCTION CORPORATION

5960 Inglewood Dr.	CEO: D. E. Sundgren	2001 Est. Sales: $1,258.0 mil.
Pleasanton, CA 94588	CFO: Larry L. Magelitz	1-Yr. Sales Change: 1.5%
Phone: 925-463-3300	HR: Bob Schwab	Employees: 6,500
Fax: 925-847-7029	Type: Private	FYE: October 31
Web: www.dillinghamconstruction.com		

Dillingham Construction doesn't dillydally around when it comes to civil, commercial, industrial, and marine construction. Founded in the 1880s by Benjamin Dillingham to build a railroad through the swamps of Hawaii, the firm now completes projects internationally. It offers design/build, construction management, maintenance, and emergency response services for such projects as dams, highways, industrial plants, offices, housing, and rapid transit systems. It also makes hot-mix asphalt, recycles pavement, and performs seismic retrofits. Subsidiaries include Nielsen Dillingham Builders and Dillingham Dredging. The group has agreed to sell subsidiary Hawaiian Dredging to Kajima Engineering and Construction.

KEY COMPETITORS
Bechtel
DPR Construction
Peter Kiewit Sons'

📖 In-depth profiles of an additional 200
key private companies are found on pages 36–435.

DISCOUNT TIRE CO.

14631 N. Scottsdale Rd.	CEO: Gary T. Van Brunt	2001 Sales: $1,320.0 million
Scottsdale, AZ 85254	CFO: Christian Roe	1-Yr. Sales Change: 10.7%
Phone: 480-951-1938	HR: Staci Adams	Employees: 8,415
Fax: 480-483-4431	Type: Private	FYE: December 31
Web: www.discounttire.com		

Concerned about that upcoming "re-tire-ment"? Discount Tire, one of the largest independent tire dealers in the US, can provide several options. With about 500 stores in some 20 states, the company sells leading brands (Michelin, Goodyear, Uniroyal) and private-label tires, as well as wheels and suspension products. Discount Tire operates mostly in the Midwest and Southwest. It fixes flat tires for free, regardless of where they were bought. Some of the company's West Coast stores operate as America's Tire Co. because of a name conflict. Discount Tire also sells tires online through Discount Tire Direct. Owner Bruce Halle founded the company in 1960 with six tires — four of them recaps.

KEY COMPETITORS
Sears
TBC
Wal-Mart

DO IT BEST CORP.

6502 Nelson Rd.	CEO: Bob Taylor	2002 Sales: $2,390.0 million
Fort Wayne, IN 46801	CFO: Dave Dietz	1-Yr. Sales Change: 8.6%
Phone: 260-748-5300	HR: Nancy Harris	Employees: —
Fax: 260-748-5620	Type: Cooperative	FYE: June 30
Web: www.doitbest.com		

If you're building a house or fixing one up, you might as well Do it Best — at least, that's the hope of the hardware industry's third-largest cooperative. Trailing TruServ and Ace Hardware, Do it Best has about 4,300 member-owned stores in the US and more than 40 other countries. The stores stock some 70,000 hardware and building products, which are also sold online. (Its Web site offers advice for do-it-yourselfers.) The co-op, whose buying power enables members to get retail products at competitive prices, also offers unifying branding programs using the Do it Best and Do it center names. Do it Best (formerly Hardware Wholesalers) began in 1945; it bought the Our Own Hardware co-op in 1998.

KEY COMPETITORS
Ace Hardware
Home Depot
TruServ

DOANE PET CARE COMPANY

210 Westwood Place South, Ste. 400	CEO: Douglas J. Cahill	2001 Sales: $895.8 million
Brentwood, TN 37027	CFO: Philip K. Woodlief	1-Yr. Sales Change: 0.4%
Phone: 615-373-7774	HR: Debra J. Shecterle	Employees: 2,730
Fax: 615-309-1187	Type: Private	FYE: December 31

Doane Pet Care has no quibble with kibble. A leading maker of private-label dog and cat food both in North America and in Europe, the company makes dry and semi-moist foods, as well as soft treats and dog biscuits. Wal-Mart accounts for more than 40% of its sales; other customers include about 600 mass merchandisers, grocery and pet store chains, and farm and feed stores. Doane also makes products for other pet food companies. The highly lever-aged company has expanded into Asia, Europe, and Latin America through several domestic and overseas acquisitions. Doane is owned by investors and investment firms, including an affiliate of J.P. Morgan Chase & Co. and New York buyout firm Bruckmann, Rosser, Sherrill & Co.

KEY COMPETITORS
Heinz
Mars
Nestlé Purina PetCare

In-depth profiles of an additional 200 key private companies are found on pages 36–435.

DOT FOODS, INC.

Route 99 South
Mount Sterling, IL 62353
Phone: 217-773-4411
Fax: 217-773-3321
Web: www.dotfoods.com

CEO: Patrick F. Tracy
CFO: William Metzinger
HR: Mike Hulsen
Type: Private

2001 Sales: $1,500.0 million
1-Yr. Sales Change: 35.5%
Employees: 1,750
FYE: December 31

Dot Foods, the largest food-service redistributor in the US, began as a station wagon that hauled dairy goods around as Associated Dairy Products. The company now runs over 400 trucks (under the name Dot Transportation) that receive groceries, flatware, serving ware, and janitorial supplies from food and equipment makers and redistribute them to food processors and food-service distributors. Dot owns facilities in California, Georgia, Illinois, Maryland, and Missouri, and has customers in 49 states. Its edotfoods subsidiary handles Dot's e-commerce. Dot also owns Principle Resource, a provider of marketing services to food manufacturers. Robert and Dorothy Tracy founded the family-owned company in 1960.

KEY COMPETITORS
Purity Wholesale Grocers
SYSCO
U.S. Foodservice

DPR CONSTRUCTION, INC.

1450 Veterans Blvd.
Redwood City, CA 94063
Phone: 650-474-1450
Fax: 650-474-1451
Web: www.dprinc.com

CEO: Peter Nosler
CFO: Ron Davidowski
HR: Brian Longway
Type: Private

2001 Sales: $1,800.0 million
1-Yr. Sales Change: (8.1%)
Employees: 3,100
FYE: December 31

Building on its success, DPR Construction caters to microelectronics, biotechnology, pharmaceuticals, and health care companies. It operates primarily in the western US, and is one of Silicon Valley's biggest contractors. DPR also specializes in corporate office construction and entertainment projects (such as theme parks and studios); clients include Apple Computer, Disney, Kaiser Permanente, Pixar Animation, and WorldCom. The company has expanded in the southeastern US by opening an office in Atlanta in 2002. DPR is owned by President Doug Woods, CEO Peter Nosler, and CFO Ron Davidowski (the D, P, and R), who founded the company in 1990 after leaving rival Rudolph & Sletten.

KEY COMPETITORS
Devcon Construction
Turner Corporation
Webcor Builders

DR PEPPER/SEVEN UP BOTTLING GROUP, INC.

Sherry Ln., Ste. 500
Dallas, TX 75225
Phone: 214-530-5000
Fax: 214-530-5036

CEO: Jim L. Turner
CFO: Holly Lovvorn
HR: Kellie Defratus
Type: Private

2001 Sales: $1,820.0 million
1-Yr. Sales Change: (4.2%)
Employees: 8,800
FYE: December 31

Dr Pepper/Seven Up Bottling Group (DPSUBG) rings up sweet results for Cadbury Schweppes, the world's #3 soft-drink firm. The group is a leading bottler of soft drinks in the US, distributing in much of California, Texas, and a number of western states from 14 distribution centers. Besides the Dr Pepper and 7 UP brands (owned by Cadbury Schweppes), it also bottles A&W Root Beer, Canada Dry, Hawaiian Punch, and RC Cola. DPSUBG was formed in 1999 when Dr Pepper Bottling Company of Texas and American Bottling merged. Cadbury Schweppes and The Carlyle Group own 40% and 53% of the company, respectively. CEO Jim Turner joined Dr Pepper Bottling Company of Texas in 1982 and built it by acquiring franchises.

KEY COMPETITORS
Coca-Cola Enterprises
Cott
Pepsi Bottling

📖 In-depth profiles of an additional 200
key private companies are found on pages 36–435.

THE DREES CO.

211 Grandview Dr., Ste. 300	CEO: David Drees	2002 Sales: $848.4 million
Fort Mitchell, KY 41017	CFO: Mark Williams	1-Yr. Sales Change: 61.1%
Phone: 859-578-4200	HR: Effie McKeehan	Employees: 1,100
Fax: 859-341-5854	Type: Private	FYE: March 31
Web: www.dreeshomes.com		

A family-operated tradition since 1928, The Drees Co. helps other families start their own traditions by building homes for them. The company, which is one of the leading home builders in Cincinnati, offers almost 100 floor plans ranging from about $90,000 to $500,000. Besides Cincinnati, the builder operates in seven other cities. It is expanding to high-growth areas yet to be built-out, such as Austin, Texas. Drees added Zaring National's homebuilding assets in Cincinnati, Indianapolis, and Nashville, Tennessee with its acquisition (2000), and created the Zaring Premier Homes brand. Drees also owns apartment complexes, and its First Equity Mortgage subsidiary helps buyers finance their homes.

KEY COMPETITORS
Crossmann Communities
Fischer Homes
M/I Schottenstein Homes

DRESSER, INC.

15455 Dallas Pkwy., Ste. 1100	CEO: Patrick M. Murray	2001 Sales: $1,545.8 million
Addison, TX 75001	CFO: James A. Nattier	1-Yr. Sales Change: —
Phone: 972-361-9800	HR: James F. Riegler	Employees: 8,500
Fax: 972-361-9929	Type: Private	FYE: December 31
Web: www.dresser.com		

All dressed up and no place to flow? Not Dresser. The company, formerly Dresser Industries (and formerly a part of Halliburton), makes flow control products, measurement systems, and power systems. Dresser's flow control segment makes injection pumps, diagnostic equipment, and valves. Its measurement systems division consists of Dresser Wayne (gas pumps and outdoor payment systems used by gas stations) and Dresser Measurement (pressure and temperature gauges, natural gas meters, and regulators). Dresser's power systems include natural-gas-powered engines, rotary blowers, and vacuum pumps bearing the Waukesha and ROOTS brands. DEG Acquisitions, a US-based investment firm, owns more than 90% of Dresser.

KEY COMPETITORS
Flowserve
IDEX
Tokheim

DRUMMOND COMPANY, INC.

530 Beacon Pkwy. W., Ste. 900	CEO: Garry N. Drummond	2001 Est. Sales: $600.0 mil.
Birmingham, AL 35209	CFO: Walter F. Johnsey	1-Yr. Sales Change: (2.4%)
Phone: 205-945-6500	HR: Andy Slentz	Employees: 2,500
Fax: 205-945-4254	Type: Private	FYE: December 31
Web: www.drummondco.com		

Drummond Company is building its business from the ground down. The company operates a surface coal mine and an underground coal mine, both located in Alabama. These mining operations extract about 6.4 million tons of coal annually. Through an affiliate, Drummond also mines in Colombia (producing some 6.8 million tons annually) and operates a port facility there. In addition, the company operates a coke plant in Alabama. It is involved in real-estate businesses that build housing communities and office parks in California and Florida. Heman Drummond began the company in 1935 on land homesteaded by his mother; eventually his five sons entered the business. The Drummond family still owns and manages the company.

KEY COMPETITORS
Arch Coal
Horizon Natural Resources
Peabody Energy

In-depth profiles of an additional 200 key private companies are found on pages 36–435.

DUCHOSSOIS INDUSTRIES, INC.

845 N. Larch Ave.
Elmhurst, IL 60126
Phone: 630-279-3600
Fax: 630-530-6091

CEO: Craig J. Duchossois
CFO: Robert L. Fealy
HR: Melody Ditori
Type: Private

2001 Est. Sales: $1,105.0 mil.
1-Yr. Sales Change: (7.9%)
Employees: 6,500
FYE: December 31

Business is no longer a horse race for holding company Duchossois Industries. The former owner of Chicago's Arlington International Racecourse, Duchossois Industries (pronounced Deshy-swa) sold its interests in the track to Churchill Downs. The Chamberlain Group, a Duchossois subsidiary, is the world's largest maker of residential and commercial door openers, and it is a leading maker of access control products. Duchossois also has interests in the consumer products, transportation, defense, and entertainment industries. The company sold its railroad car unit (Thrall) to Trinity Industries in 2001. Duchossois Industries is owned by the family of Richard Duchossois; he also holds a 24% stake in Churchill Downs.

KEY COMPETITORS
GATX
Johnstown America
Stanley Works

DUKE ENERGY FIELD SERVICES CORPORATION

370 17th St., Ste. 900
Denver, CO 80202
Phone: 303-595-3331
Fax: 303-595-0480
Web: www.defieldservices.com

CEO: Jim W. Mogg
CFO: Rose M. Robeson
HR: David Goode
Type: Joint venture

2001 Sales: $9,597.7 million
1-Yr. Sales Change: 5.5%
Employees: 3,600
FYE: December 31

Duke Energy Field Services (DEFS) is a midstream maven. Formed when Duke Energy and Phillips Petroleum (later ConocoPhillips) combined their gas-gathering, processing, and marketing operations, the company is one of the largest midstream natural-gas operators in the US, with 57,000 miles of gathering pipeline and 71 processing plants. DEFS also owns several NGL processing facilities and is the US's #1 NGL producer, at 400,000 barrels per day. The firm sells about 40% of its NGL production to ConocoPhillips under a long-term contract. Duke Energy owns about 70% of DEFS; ConocoPhillips owns 30%. DEFS is the general partner of TEPPCO Partners, L.P., which owns a network of refined products and crude oil pipelines.

KEY COMPETITORS
Dynegy
Enterprise
Koch

DUNAVANT ENTERPRISES, INC.

3797 New Getwell Rd.
Memphis, TN 38118
Phone: 901-369-1500
Fax: 901-369-1608
Web: www.dunavant.com

CEO: William B. Dunavant Jr.
CFO: —
HR: Mike Andereck
Type: Private

2001 Sales: $1,030.0 million
1-Yr. Sales Change: 0.8%
Employees: 2,400
FYE: June 30

King Cotton is alive and well in Memphis. Homegrown Dunavant Enterprises is one of the largest cotton traders in the world. The company was founded in 1960 by William Dunavant, his son Billy (who is allergic to cotton), and Samuel T. Reeves. (The elder Dunavant died shortly after the founding, and Reeves left in 1995 to form Pinnacle Trading.) The company, which grew by selling aggressively to China and the Soviet Union, maintains offices in Asia, Australia, Europe, Mexico, South America, the former Soviet Union, and the southern US. The company's other business interests include cotton ginning, trucking, and warehousing. Dunavant Enterprises is owned by the Dunavant family and company employees.

KEY COMPETITORS
Calcot
Cargill
Plains Cotton

In-depth profiles of an additional 200
key private companies are found on pages 36–435.

DUNN INDUSTRIES, INC.

929 Holmes	CEO: Terrence P. Dunn	2001 Sales: $1,533.0 million
Kansas City, MO 64106	CFO: Gordon Lansford	1-Yr. Sales Change: 16.9%
Phone: 816-474-8600	HR: —	Employees: 3,000
Fax: 816-391-2510	Type: Private	FYE: December 31

Although its beginnings date back to 1924, this company is far from done. Family-owned Dunn Industries, representing five generations of builders, owns construction companies, including flagship J. E. Dunn Construction, Witcher Construction, and Dunn Industrial Group. Dunn designs and builds institutional, commercial, and industrial projects; it also provides construction and program management. Long focusing on projects in western and midwestern states, the company has expanded into the Southeast with its acquisition of Atlanta-based general contractor R.J. Griffin. J.E. Dunn was construction manager for Sprint's world headquarters near Kansas City, one of the Midwest's largest construction projects.

KEY COMPETITORS
Alberici
Skanska USA Building
Turner Corporation

DYNCORP

11710 Plaza America Dr.	CEO: Paul V. Lombardi	2001 Sales: $1,960.4 million
Reston, VA 20190	CFO: Patrick C. FitzPatrick	1-Yr. Sales Change: 8.4%
Phone: 703-261-5000	HR: James A. Campbell	Employees: 23,300
Fax: 703-261-4800	Type: Private	FYE: December 31
Web: www.dyncorp.com		

Government work is more than good enough for DynCorp. One of the largest employee-owned professional services firms in the US, DynCorp offers a wide range of technical and outsourced services, primarily to agencies of the US government. Its practice areas include consulting, information systems integration, operations outsourcing, logistics, training, and engineering services. In addition, DynCorp owns a 40% stake in information services provider DynTek. Founded in 1946, DynCorp was taken private in a 1987 buyout led by management. Employee retirement plans control nearly 85% of the company.

KEY COMPETITORS
CACI International
Northrop Grumman
SAIC

THE DYSON-KISSNER-MORAN CORPORATION

565 5th Ave., 4th Fl.	CEO: Robert R. Dyson	2001 Est. Sales: $850.0 mil.
New York, NY 10017	CFO: Douglas I. Schwartz	1-Yr. Sales Change: 6.3%
Phone: 212-661-4600	HR: —	Employees: 4,600
Fax: 212-986-7169	Type: Private	FYE: January 31
Web: www.dkmcorp.com		

Privately held investment firm Dyson-Kissner-Moran, through takeovers and strategic acquisitions, has diversified its holdings to include businesses from manufacturing to arts and crafts. The firm typically uses its own capital to fund acquisitions and usually leaves them intact after the purchase. Founded in the mid-1950s, its purchases have included Household Finance and electronic-parts maker Kearney-National. Dyson-Kissner-Moran is controlled by the family of co-founder Charles Dyson (prominent philanthropist, LBO pioneer, and #5 on Richard Nixon's political enemies list), who died in 1997. His son Robert is the firm's chairman and CEO.

KEY COMPETITORS
Haas Wheat
Hicks, Muse
KKR

📖 In-depth profiles of an additional 200 key private companies are found on pages 36–435.

EAGLE-PICHER INDUSTRIES, INC.

250 E. 5th St., Ste. 500
Cincinnati, OH 45201
Phone: 513-721-7010
Fax: 513-721-2341
Web: www.epcorp.com

CEO: John H. Weber
CFO: Thomas R. Pilholski
HR: Jeffrey D. Sisson
Type: Private

2001 Sales: $692.5 million
1-Yr. Sales Change: (17.3%)
Employees: 4,100
FYE: November 30

From batteries to boron, Eagle-Picher Industries (EPI) provides products for the automotive, aerospace, telecommunications, pharmaceutical, and food and beverage industries. EPI's automotive group leads in sales (58%) with products that include precision-machined components, rubber-coated parts, and fluid systems. The company's Technologies Segment makes batteries for satellites, launch vehicles, and missiles, as well as boron for nuclear applications. Its Materials Segment produces diatomaceous earth and perlite filter aids. EPI has sold its Machinery Segment, which made elevating-wheel tractor scrapers (exclusively for Caterpillar). Dutch investment firm Granaria Holdings owns EPI.

KEY COMPETITORS
Federal-Mogul
Linamar
Newcor

EARLE M. JORGENSEN COMPANY

3050 E. Birch St.
Brea, CA 92821
Phone: 714-579-8823
Fax: 714-577-3784
Web: www.emjmetals.com

CEO: Maurice S. Nelson Jr.
CFO: William Johnson
HR: Inger Dickinson
Type: Private

2002 Sales: $895.1 million
1-Yr. Sales Change: (15.5%)
Employees: 1,725
FYE: March 31

Earle M. Jorgensen (EMJ) is one of the US's largest independent steel distributors. The company sells tubing, pipes, and bar, as well as structural, plate, and sheet metal products. EMJ makes its products from carbon steel, alloy steel, stainless steel, and aluminum. It markets to the automotive, agriculture, chemical, medical, oil, defense, food, petrochemical, and machinery-manufacturing industries. The company operates more than 35 service centers, a cutting center, and a tube-honing facility. Employees own about 27% of EMJ; investment firm Kelso & Company owns most of the rest.

KEY COMPETITORS
Gerdau AmeriSteel
Rouge Industries
United States Steel

EARNHARDT'S AUTO CENTERS

1301 N. Arizona Ave.
Gilbert, AZ 85233
Phone: 480-926-4000
Fax: 480-497-7238
Web: www.earnhardt.com

CEO: Hal J. Earnhardt III
CFO: Robbyn McDowell
HR: Sue Camrud
Type: Private

2001 Sales: $685.3 million
1-Yr. Sales Change: 0.8%
Employees: 2,000
FYE: December 31

Milking the Southwest for all it's worth, Earnhardt's Auto Centers (and its bull-riding founder) sell more than 32,000 new and used vehicles, including RVs, each year. The company's seven auto dealerships in Arizona feature Chrysler, Dodge, Ford, Honda, Hyundai, Jeep, Kia, Mazda, Plymouth, Suzuki, Th!nk (electric vehicles), and Volkswagen autos. The outlets also operate parts and service departments and offer financing. Earnhardt's Web site allows customers to "build" their next car online: Shoppers can select from a complete list of options before submitting their order electronically. Established in 1951 by Tex Earnhardt, the company is family-owned and -operated.

KEY COMPETITORS
AutoNation
Larry H. Miller Group
United Auto Group

In-depth profiles of an additional 200 key private companies are found on pages 36–435.

EBSCO INDUSTRIES INC.

5724 Hwy. 280 East
Birmingham, AL 35242
Phone: 205-991-6600
Fax: 205-995-1636
Web: www.ebscoind.com

CEO: James T. Stephens
CFO: Richard L. Bozzelli
HR: John Thompson
Type: Private

2002 Sales: $1,400.0 million
1-Yr. Sales Change: 1.8%
Employees: 5,000
FYE: June 30

Few portfolios are more diverse than that of EBSCO Industries (short for Elton B. Stephens Company). Among the conglomerate's information services, manufacturing, and sales subsidiaries are magazine subscription and fulfillment firms, a fishing lure manufacturer, a rifle manufacturer, a specialty office and computer furniture retailer, and a real estate company. EBSCO's main businesses revolve around the publishing industry: EBSCO operates a subscription management agency and is one of the largest publishers of information online and on CD-ROM. The family of founder Elton B. Stephens Sr. owns the company.

KEY COMPETITORS
Quebecor
Reed Elsevier Group
Thomson Corporation

EBY-BROWN COMPANY

280 W. Shuman Blvd., Ste. 280
Naperville, IL 60566
Phone: 630-778-2800
Fax: 630-778-2830
Web: www.eby-brown.com

CEO: Richard "Dick" Wake
CFO: Mark Smetana
HR: Rick Thorgesen
Type: Private

2001 Sales: $3,670.0 million
1-Yr. Sales Change: 7.9%
Employees: 2,100
FYE: December 31

Eby-Brown makes its money on vices such as munchies and nicotine. A leading supplier to convenience stores, the company offers more than 11,000 name-brand products, including tobacco, candy, snacks, health and beauty aids, and general merchandise. The company's eight distribution centers serve 28 midwestern and southeastern states and more than 25,000 stores, including the Speedway and SuperAmerica chains owned by Marathon Ashland Petroleum. Eby-Brown also has a marketing division that offers its customers advertising and promotion services. The century-old company is family-owned and run. Co-CEOs Tom and Dick Wake succeeded their father, Chairman William Wake Jr., in 1983.

KEY COMPETITORS
GSC Enterprises
McLane
Spartan Stores

EDUCATIONAL TESTING SERVICE

Rosedale Rd.
Princeton, NJ 08541
Phone: 609-921-9000
Fax: 609-734-5410
Web: www.ets.org

CEO: Kurt M. Landgraf
CFO: Frank R. Gatti
HR: Yvette Donado
Type: Not-for-profit

2002 Sales: $700.0 million
1-Yr. Sales Change: 41.8%
Employees: 2,500
FYE: June 30

Educational Testing Service (ETS) produces as many sweaty palms as the words, "We're from the IRS." The creator of the Scholastic Assessment Test (SAT) administers more than 12 million achievement, occupational, and admissions tests a year (including nearly 3.2 million SATs in 2000-01). Founded in 1947, the not-for-profit group is one of the nation's largest testing organizations. The ETS Research division conducts research projects focusing on education. For-profit subsidiary The Chauncey Group International designs, develops, and administers occupational certification and professional assessment tests. ETS is closing nearly 84 of its testing centers outside of the US.

KEY COMPETITORS
ACT
McGraw-Hill
NCS Pearson

> 📖 In-depth profiles of an additional 200
> key private companies are found on pages 36–435.

EMACHINES, INC.

14350 Myford Rd., Bldg. 100	CEO: Wayne R. Inouye	2000 Sales: $684.1 million
Irvine, CA 92606	CFO: —	1-Yr. Sales Change: (16.0%)
Phone: 714-481-2828	HR: —	Employees: 134
Fax: 714-505-5049	Type: Private	FYE: December 31
Web: www.emachines.com		

They're not cheap — they're *inexpensive*. eMachines' bargain PCs are designed for word processing, e-mail, and Web surfing. It sells its products through distributors and retailers such as Best Buy, Circuit City, and Office Depot. The company also sells products directly. eMachines saw early success as a pioneer seller of cut-rate PCs bundled with Internet service contracts, but it has struggled against larger PC makers with competitively priced products. Founded in 1998 by former CEO Steven Dukker, eMachines was acquired by director Lap Shun (John) Hui through a holding company and taken private in 2001.

KEY COMPETITORS
Dell Computer
Gateway
Hewlett-Packard

EMORY UNIVERSITY

1380 S. Oxford Rd. SE	CEO: William M. Chace	2002 Sales: $1,860.0 million
Atlanta, GA 30322	CFO: John L. Temple	1-Yr. Sales Change: 3.3%
Phone: 404-727-6123	HR: Alice R. Miller	Employees: 19,288
Fax: 404-727-0646	Type: School	FYE: August 31
Web: www.emory.edu		

"Have a Coke and a smile" means a little more to Emory University than it does to the rest of the world. The school, which boasts more than 11,400 students and 2,500 faculty members, was transformed from Emory College to Emory University in 1915 by a $1 million donation from Coca-Cola Company owner Asa Candler. Today, about 40% of Emory's endowment consists of Coca-Cola stock. The university offers undergraduate, graduate, and professional degrees in a wide range of fields, including medicine, theology, law, nursing, and business. Founded in 1836, the private university also maintains several research centers and operates a joint venture with HCA to offer managed health care.

EMPIRE BEEF COMPANY, INC.

171 Weidner Rd.	CEO: Steve H. Levine	2001 Sales: $703.0 million
Rochester, NY 14624	CFO: Michael Quinn	1-Yr. Sales Change: 3.1%
Phone: 585-235-7350	HR: Christopher Carretta	Employees: 200
Fax: 585-235-1776	Type: Private	FYE: December 31
Web: www.empirebeef.com/whower.html		

Protein has given Empire Beef its bulk. The wholesale meat distributor ships more than six million pounds of meat each week. Purchased from major packers such as IBP and Perdue Farms, Empire Beef distributes beef, lamb, pork, poultry, seafood, and veal. The firm also makes portion-controlled marinated and flavor-enhanced fresh and frozen meat products for food service and retail sale. Empire Beef serves customers east of the Mississippi, primarily in the Northeast, with its fleet of multi-temperature trucks. Harry Levine started the firm as a small slaughtering plant in 1937; slaughter operations later stopped. The Levine family owns Empire Beef (Harry's grandson Steve is CEO).

KEY COMPETITORS
Colorado Boxed Beef
SYSCO
Stock Yards Packing

In-depth profiles of an additional 200 key private companies are found on pages 36–435.

ENERSYS INC.

2366 Bernville Rd., PO Box 14145	CEO: John D. Craig	2002 Est. Sales: $900.0 mil.
Reading, PA 19612	CFO: Michael T. Philion	1-Yr. Sales Change: 125.0%
Phone: 610-208-1991	HR: Ted Fries	Employees: 7,000
Fax: 610-208-1671	Type: Private	FYE: March 31
Web: www.enersysinc.com		

EnerSys' battery operations are charging off in different directions. The company, formerly Yuasa Inc., makes stationary industrial batteries that provide uninterruptible power and backup power for electronic systems and motive-power batteries for big equipment such as forklifts. Other products include battery chargers and accessories. Company management and Morgan Stanley acquired Yuasa's Motive Power and Stationary Power operations in 2000 and renamed the company EnerSys. The remaining small vehicle battery operation, renamed Yuasa Battery, is wholly owned by Japan-based Yuasa Corporation. EnerSys has also acquired Invensys' Energy Storage products group.

KEY COMPETITORS
C&D Technologies
Exide
Rayovac

EPIX HOLDINGS CORPORATION

3710 Corporex Park Dr.	CEO: Thomas S. Taylor	2001 Sales: $1,842.0 million
Tampa, FL 33619	CFO: Thomas S. Taylor	1-Yr. Sales Change: 41.7%
Phone: 813-664-0404	HR: —	Employees: 400
Fax: 813-621-6816	Type: Private	FYE: December 31
Web: www.epixweb.com		

When it comes to epic human resources concerns, more and more employers are using EPIX solutions. EPIX Holdings (formerly Payroll Transfers) is one of the nation's leading professional employer organizations, providing human resources management for its clients' permanent full-time workers. The company's services include insurance, tax administration, employee benefits programs, regulatory compliance, and payroll processing. The company provides administrative services for more than 50,000 employees from some 3,500 small and midsized businesses throughout the US. EPIX, which was founded in 1989, is backed by Texas financier Robert Bass' Keystone group, among other investment firms.

KEY COMPETITORS
Administaff
Gevity HR
TeamStaff

EQUISTAR CHEMICALS, LP

1221 McKinney St., Ste. 700	CEO: Dan F. Smith	2001 Sales: $5,909.0 million
Houston, TX 77010	CFO: Charles L. Hall	1-Yr. Sales Change: (21.2%)
Phone: 713-652-7200	HR: John A. Hollinshead	Employees: 3,400
Fax: 713-652-4151	Type: Partnership	FYE: December 31
Web: www.equistarchem.com		

Petrochemicals are used to make polymers, and Equistar Chemical — a partnership of Lyondell Chemical (about 70%) and Millennium Chemicals (about 30%) — makes a lot of both. Equistar's largest business segment, petrochemicals (66% of sales) makes olefins (ethylene, propylene and butadiene); oxygenated products (ethylene oxide, ethylene glycol); and aromatics (benzene and toluene). Equistar's polymers segment makes polyolefins (polyethylenes, polypropylene) and performance polymers. Polyethylene is used in plastic bags and bottles; polypropylene is used in plastic caps, rigid packaging, automotive components, and carpet. Lyondell recently acquired Occidental's 30% stake in the company.

KEY COMPETITORS
Dow Chemical
ExxonMobil Chemical
Huntsman

📖 **In-depth profiles of an additional 200 key private companies are found on pages 36–435.**

ERGON, INC.

2829 Lakeland Dr.	CEO: Leslie Lampton Sr.	2001 Est. Sales: $1,460.0 mil.
Jackson, MS 39208	CFO: Kathy Stone	1-Yr. Sales Change: (23.2%)
Phone: 601-933-3000	HR: Lance Maserov	Employees: 2,000
Fax: 601-933-3350	Type: Private	FYE: December 31
Web: www.ergon.com		

That'll work! Ergon (named after the Greek word for work) operates in six major business segments: asphalt and emulsions; information technology; oil and gas; real estate; refining and marketing; and transportation and terminaling. In addition to providing a range of petroleum products and services, the company manufactures and markets computer-technology services and sells road maintenance systems, including emulsions and special coatings. Ergon also provides truck, rail, and marine transport services and sells residential and commercial real estate properties.

KEY COMPETITORS
Ferrellgas Partners
Koch
Marathon Oil

ESTES EXPRESS LINES

3901 W. Broad St.	CEO: Robey W. Estes Jr.	2001 Sales: $694.5 million
Richmond, VA 23230	CFO: Gary D. Okes	1-Yr. Sales Change: 0.5%
Phone: 804-353-1900	HR: Thomas Donahue	Employees: 8,531
Fax: 804-353-8001	Type: Private	FYE: December 31
Web: www.estes-express.com		

With customer satisfaction as its express purpose, Estes Express Lines is a multiregional less-than-truckload (LTL) transportation firm. The company operates a fleet of about 4,000 tractors and 11,500 trailers and has a network of more than 100 terminals in 33 US states. Estes Express also offers truck and trailer leasing. The carrier provides services to the rest of the US and Canada through its partners in the ExpressLINK regional LTL alliance: G.I. Trucking, Lakeville Motor Express, and TST Overland Express. Founded by W. W. Estes in 1931, the company is still owned and operated by the Estes family.

KEY COMPETITORS
Arkansas Best
Overnite Transportation
Yellow

EVERETT SMITH GROUP

800 N. Marshall St.	CEO: Anders Segerdahl	2001 Est. Sales: $700.0 mil.
Milwaukee, WI 53202	CFO: John Steelman	1-Yr. Sales Change: 5.3%
Phone: 414-273-3421	HR: —	Employees: 6,000
Fax: —	Type: Private	FYE: December 31

From skins to steel, Everett Smith Group has you covered. Through subsidiary Albert Trostel & Sons, the holding company owns Eagle Ottawa Leather, which makes upholstery leather for major carmakers including Ford and Toyota. Everett Smith Group also owns W.B. Place, a maker and retailer of custom leather garments that also provides deerskin tanning and taxidermy services. Everett Smith's Sivyer Steel makes steel castings for construction, mining, and railroads. The company's Maysteel subsidiary makes power distribution equipment and enclosures for the utility industry. Descendants of Everett G. Smith control the company.

KEY COMPETITORS
Kawasho
ROHN Industries
Tandy Brands

📖 In-depth profiles of an additional 200 key private companies are found on pages 36–435.

EXPRESS PERSONNEL SERVICES

8516 NW Expwy.	CEO: Robert A. Funk	2001 Sales: $781.0 million
Oklahoma City, OK 73162	CFO: Thomas Richards	1-Yr. Sales Change: (14.7%)
Phone: 405-840-5000	HR: Larry Ferree	Employees: 224,000
Fax: 405-720-9390	Type: Private	FYE: December 31
Web: www.expresspersonnel.com		

When you need a worker fast, Express Personnel Services delivers. The professional staffing company provides work for some 225,000 employees from more than 400 offices in the US, Canada, and South Africa. In addition to temporary staffing, the company provides professional placement and contract staffing through Express Professional Staffing and offers workplace services (consulting, training, development) through Express Business Solutions. The company is owned by founder and CEO Robert Funk, who also owns the Oklahoma City Blazers hockey team and Express Ranches, one of the nation's largest cattle breeders.

KEY COMPETITORS
Adecco
Kelly Services
Manpower

E-Z MART STORES, INC.

602 W. Falvey Ave.	CEO: Sonja Y. Hubbard	2001 Est. Sales: $655.0 mil.
Texarkana, TX 75501	CFO: Stacy Y. Floyd	1-Yr. Sales Change: 2.2%
Phone: 903-832-6502	HR: Kim Fowler	Employees: 3,200
Fax: 903-832-3731	Type: Private	FYE: September 30
Web: www.e-zmart.com		

In 1970, when small-town America closed at 6 p.m., E-Z Mart Stores founder Jim Yates kept his first convenience store in Ashdown, Arkansas, open until 11. The company rode the wave of convenience-store growth, adding more than 85 locations in Arkansas and Oklahoma in 1999 alone. It now boasts 400 outlets across five southern states (Arkansas, Louisiana, Missouri, Oklahoma, and Texas). E-Z Mart prefers to expand through acquisitions. The company is remodeling many of its stores, adding features such as canopies for gas-pump islands and enhanced lighting. Yates died in late 1998 when the plane he was piloting crashed, leaving his daughter Sonja Hubbard at the company's helm as CEO.

KEY COMPETITORS
7-Eleven
Exxon Mobil
Valero Energy

THE F. DOHMEN CO.

W194 N11381 McCormick Dr.	CEO: John Dohmen	2002 Sales: $838.0 million
Germantown, WI 53022	CFO: Tracy Pearson	1-Yr. Sales Change: 12.0%
Phone: 262-255-0022	HR: Robert Dohmen	Employees: 450
Fax: 262-255-0041	Type: Private	FYE: April 30
Web: www.dohmen.com		

The F. Dohmen Co. helps pharmacists with just about everything except interpreting handwriting. The company is one of the largest private pharmaceutical wholesalers in the US. Its Dohmen Medical division distributes brand-name and generic products, including medical and surgical supplies. F. Dohmen also makes pharmaceutical management systems that perform an array of services, including prescription processing, physician and insurer information management, and chronic disease management. The company's additional services include advertising assistance; it sells National Brand Equivalent products that permit pharmacies to use their own store labels. German immigrant Frederick Dohmen founded the firm in 1858.

KEY COMPETITORS
AmerisourceBergen
Cardinal Health
McKesson

📖 In-depth profiles of an additional 200 key private companies are found on pages 36–435.

FAREWAY STORES, INC.

2300 E. 8th St.	CEO: F. William Beckwith	2001 Est. Sales: $635.0 mil.
Boone, IA 50036	CFO: Craig Shepley	1-Yr. Sales Change: 5.8%
Phone: 515-432-2623	HR: Mike Mazour	Employees: 4,900
Fax: 515-433-4416	Type: Private	FYE: March 31

Fareway Stores makes the green through groceries. The supermarket chain operates Fareway stores primarily throughout Iowa, but it has also expanded into Illinois. Its more than 70 stores average about 23,500 sq. ft. Eschewing such amenities as video rentals and dry-cleaning services, Fareway Stores stick to the basics — meat (all cut to order) and groceries only. Former Safeway workers Paul Beckwith and Fred Vitt founded Fareway Stores in 1938; the Beckwith family still controls the company. Because of the founders' biblical beliefs, the stores are closed on Sundays, and if you've got a 2 a.m. brisket craving, you're out of luck: Not even shelf-stocking night crews can be found at the stores after hours.

KEY COMPETITORS
Hy-Vee
IGA
Wal-Mart

THE FAULKNER ORGANIZATION

4437 Street Rd.	CEO: Hank Faulkner	2001 Sales: $818.0 million
Trevose, PA 19053	CFO: Bill Febold	1-Yr. Sales Change: (0.4%)
Phone: 215-364-3980	HR: Walt Huber	Employees: 1,100
Fax: 215-364-0706	Type: Private	FYE: December 31
Web: www.faulknerfamily.com		

The sound and the fury of Buicks moving off the lot is coming from The Faulkner Organization, one of the Delaware Valley's largest-volume automotive dealers. The company operates about 20 automobile dealerships in Pennsylvania and Delaware. Its domestic car franchises include Buick, Cadillac, Chevrolet, Ford, GMC, Mercury, Oldsmobile, Pontiac, and Saturn; its import franchises sell Hondas, Mazdas, Mitsubishis, and Toyotas. In addition to new and used cars, the company sells auto parts and offers automotive repairs, car financing, fleet services, and credit life insurance. Founded in 1932 by Henry Faulkner, the company is still owned and operated by the Faulkner family.

KEY COMPETITORS
Brown Automotive
Pacifico
Planet Automotive Group

FEDERATED INSURANCE COMPANIES

121 E. Park Sq.	CEO: Al Annexstad	2000 Sales: $1,153.2 million
Owatonna, MN 55060	CFO: Raymond R. Stawarz	1-Yr. Sales Change: 8.6%
Phone: 507-455-5200	HR: Bryan Brose	Employees: 3,100
Fax: 507-455-5452	Type: Mutual company	FYE: December 31
Web: www.federatedinsurance.com		

Federated Insurance is a mutual company with a specific focus. Consistent with its century-old roots as an insurer for Minnesota farm implement dealers, Federated offers group life and health coverage; it also provides workers' compensation, automobile, property/casualty, retirement planning, and individual life insurance to a narrow niche of businesses — auto and tire dealers, service stations, building contractors, equipment dealers, machine shops, and printers. Operating nationwide, Federated Insurance markets its policies directly and through an independent sales force.

KEY COMPETITORS
Blue Cross
CNA Financial
State Farm

In-depth profiles of an additional 200 key private companies are found on pages 36–435.

FELLOWES, INC.

1789 Norwood Ave.	CEO: James Fellowes	2002 Sales: $700.0 million
Itasca, IL 60143	CFO: Joseph T. Koch	1-Yr. Sales Change: 7.7%
Phone: 630-893-1600	HR: —	Employees: 1,750
Fax: 630-893-1648	Type: Private	FYE: March 31
Web: www.fellowes.com		

Fellowes, Inc. (formerly Fellowes Manufacturing Company) produces office products that can organize or obliterate. A leading maker of paper shredders (Powershred, Shredmate), it also makes office storage boxes, computer accessories (such as ergonomic wrist rests and glare filters), and office desk accessories. The company has moved further into the digital age with new offerings such as notebook security locks and PDA accessories. Fellowes' products are sold through office-products stores and mass merchandisers in more than 100 countries. Still owned and run by the Fellowes family, the company was started in 1917 when Harry Fellowes paid $50 for Bankers Box, a maker of storage boxes for bank records.

KEY COMPETITORS
Avery Dennison
General Binding
TAB Products

FIESTA MART, INC.

5235 Katy Fwy.	CEO: Louis Katopodis	2001 Sales: $770.0 million
Houston, TX 77007	CFO: Vicki Baum	1-Yr. Sales Change: 5.5%
Phone: 713-869-5060	HR: Wanda Parish	Employees: 7,600
Fax: 713-865-5514	Type: Private	FYE: May 31
Web: www.fiestamart.com		

Fiesta Mart celebrates food every day of the year. The company runs about 50 stores in Texas that sell ethnic and conventional groceries, including items popular with its target customers: Mexican- and Asian-Americans. Its stores are located mainly in the Houston area, but Fiesta also owns stores in Austin and the Dallas/Ft. Worth metroplex. Fiesta purchased three supermarkets from Winn-Dixie Stores when the grocer left the Texas market. At its supermarkets, Fiesta leases kiosks to vendors who offer such items as jewelry and cellular phones. The company also runs 16 Beverage Mart liquor stores. Donald Bonham and O. C. Mendenhall founded Fiesta Mart in 1972. Their families, along with employees, own the company.

KEY COMPETITORS
H-E-B
Kroger
Randall's

FINDLAY INDUSTRIES, INC.

4000 Fostoria Rd.	CEO: Thomas Zigler	2002 Est. Sales: $800.0 mil.
Findlay, OH 45840	CFO: Raymond Lowry	1-Yr. Sales Change: 3.1%
Phone: 419-422-1302	HR: Geneva Frennell	Employees: 3,500
Fax: 419-427-3390	Type: Private	FYE: April 30
Web: www.findlayindustries.com		

Findlay Industries doesn't need a room to show off its interior designs. The automotive interiors supplier makes door and sidewall trim panels (quarter-trim panels), seat back and trunk covers, headliners, and sleeper cabs. It makes these components for customers including BMW, Ford, General Motors, Toyota, and other car and heavy truck makers around the world. Findlay Industries' brands include the ProBond family of molded headliner material. The company has 24 manufacturing facilities in Europe and North America. The company, founded by Philip D. Gardner in 1959, is controlled by Gardner and former president Philip J. Gardner.

KEY COMPETITORS
Delphi
Johnson Controls
Lear

> 📖 **In-depth profiles of an additional 200 key private companies are found on pages 36–435.**

FISHER DEVELOPMENT, INC.

1485 Bayshore Blvd., Ste. 152	CEO: Ken Pickart	2000 Sales: $1,229.0 million
San Francisco, CA 94124	CFO: Dennis Kreuser	1-Yr. Sales Change: 113.0%
Phone: 415-468-1717	HR: Barry Langford	Employees: 1,229
Fax: 415-468-6241	Type: Private	FYE: December 31
Web: www.fisherinc.com		

Retail contractor Fisher Development leaves Gaps wherever it goes. Founded in 1971, the company serves as general contractor for The Gap clothing chain on as many as 500 jobs a year. Keeping it all in the family, Fisher Development founder and owner Bob Fisher is the brother of Gap retail stores founder Donald Fisher; an audit committee at The Gap reviews the deals annually. The company also builds and renovates for Gap-owned Banana Republic and Old Navy, as well as Harry and David, Pottery Barn, Williams-Sonoma, and others. The #1 retail interior contractor in the US, Fisher Development has expanded its work into Europe.

KEY COMPETITORS
PCL Construction
Skanska USA Building
Whiting-Turner

FLINT INK CORPORATION

4600 Arrowhead Dr.	CEO: H. Howard Flint II	2001 Sales: $1,400.0 million
Ann Arbor, MI 48105	CFO: Michael J. Gannon	1-Yr. Sales Change: 29.6%
Phone: 734-622-6000	HR: Glenn T. Autry	Employees: 4,000
Fax: 734-622-6060	Type: Private	FYE: December 31
Web: www.flintink.com		

The world's #2 ink maker (behind Sun Chemical), Flint Ink sells its products across several continents and has drawn a bull's-eye on becoming #1. The company hopes to accomplish this goal through its acquisition strategy. Flint Ink has plants throughout the Americas, Australasia, and Europe. The company's customers include printing facilities that produce magazines, newspapers, catalogs, and packaging materials. Flint Ink also makes specialty inks (for example, for printing lottery tickets) and environment-friendly vegetable-oil-based inks. The Flint family owns the company; Howard Flint II represents the third generation of the family to head the firm, which was founded in 1920.

KEY COMPETITORS
Akzo Nobel
Borden Chemical
Dainippon Ink and Chemicals

FLORIDA'S NATURAL GROWERS

650 Hwy. 27	CEO: Stephen Caruso	2001 Sales: $620.0 million
Lake Wales, FL 33853	CFO: W.J. Hendry	1-Yr. Sales Change: 2.5%
Phone: 863-676-1411	HR: Susan Langley	Employees: —
Fax: 863-676-0114	Type: Cooperative	FYE: August 31
Web: floridanatural.com		

Florida's Natural Growers (formerly Citrus World) is known for squeezing out profits. It is the third largest citrus juice seller (behind Tropicana and Minute Maid), producing more than 20 million boxes of oranges from 60,000 acres of citrus groves. The cooperative produces frozen concentrated and not-from-concentrate juices (orange, apple, grapefruit, lemonade, and fruit blends) under the Florida's Natural, Grower's Pride, Donald Duck, Bluebird, Adams, and Texsun brand names. The company was founded in 1933 by a group of citrus growers who wanted to process grapefruit.

KEY COMPETITORS
Coca-Cola
Louis Dreyfus Citrus
Tropicana Products

In-depth profiles of an additional 200 key private companies are found on pages 36–435.

FLYING J INC.

1104 Country Hills Dr.	CEO: J. Phillip Adams	2002 Sales: $3,150.0 million
Ogden, UT 84403	CFO: Paul F. Brown	1-Yr. Sales Change: (27.6%)
Phone: 801-624-1000	HR: Jerry Beckman	Employees: 11,500
Fax: 801-624-1587	Type: Private	FYE: January 31
Web: www.flyingj.com		

Flying J puts out a welcome mat for truck drivers in North America. From its humble beginnings in 1968 with four locations, the company is now one of the largest US truck-stop operators — running more than 150 amenity-loaded Flying J Travel Plazas in more than 40 states and Canada. Flying J and its subsidiaries go beyond the usual truck-stop fare (food, fuel, showers) by offering truckers extra services, including advertising, banking, bulk-fuel programs, fuel cost analysis, insurance, and truck fleet sales. The company also owns oil and gas reserves, as well as a 25,000-barrel-a-day oil refinery. Founder and chairman Jay Call owns a majority stake in Flying J. The company plans to add more than 30 plazas by 2003.

KEY COMPETITORS
Petro Stopping Centers
Pilot
TravelCenters of America

FM GLOBAL

1301 Atwood Ave.	CEO: Shivan S. Subramaniam	2001 Sales: $1,052.2 million
Johnston, RI 02919	CFO: Jeffrey A. Burchill	1-Yr. Sales Change: 1.1%
Phone: 401-275-3000	HR: Enzo Rebula	Employees: 4,000
Fax: 401-275-3029	Type: Mutual company	FYE: December 31
Web: www.fmglobal.com		

If you're looking to protect your corporation, turn your insurance dial to FM Global. The insurer provides commercial and industrial property insurance and a variety of risk management services, ranging from all-risk programs to specialized products for ocean cargo and machinery equipment. FM Global operates through such subsidiaries as Factory Mutual Insurance, Mutual Boiler Re, Affiliated FM Insurance, and Bermuda-based New Providence Mutual (which offers alternative risk financing for hard-to-find coverage). In addition to the US, the company has offices in Asia, Australia, Canada, Europe, and South America.

KEY COMPETITORS
GE Global Insurance Holding
Gerling
Travelers

FOLLETT CORPORATION

2233 West St.	CEO: Christopher Traut	2002 Sales: $1,733.0 million
River Grove, IL 60171	CFO: Kathryn A. Stanton	1-Yr. Sales Change: 11.5%
Phone: 708-583-2000	HR: Richard Ellspermann	Employees: 10,000
Fax: 708-452-9347	Type: Private	FYE: March 31
Web: www.follett.com		

Not all kids like to read, but (fortunately for Follett) by the time they reach college, they don't have a choice. Follett is the #1 operator of US college bookstores and has about 600 campus bookstores throughout the US and Canada. The company's business groups operate in about 60 countries, and provide books and audiovisual materials to grade school and public libraries. The groups also provide library automation and management software, textbook reconditioning, and other services. The efollett.com Web site sells new and used college textbooks (its database has about 16 million titles). The Follett family has owned and managed the company for four generations.

KEY COMPETITORS
Baker & Taylor
Barnes & Noble College
 Bookstores
Ingram Industries

In-depth profiles of an additional 200
key private companies are found on pages 36–435.

FOREMOST FARMS USA, COOPERATIVE

E10889A Penny Lane	CEO: Dave Fuhrmann	2001 Sales: $1,332.1 million
Baraboo, WI 53913	CFO: Duaine Kamenick	1-Yr. Sales Change: 21.9%
Phone: 608-355-8700	HR: Joan Behr	Employees: 1,705
Fax: 608-355-8699	Type: Cooperative	FYE: December 31
Web: www.foremostfarms.com		

No jokes about "herd mentality," please. Foremost Farms USA — owned by about 4,700 dairy farmers in seven midwestern states, mainly Wisconsin — is one of the largest dairy cooperatives in the US. Operating 24 plants, the cooperative churns out solid and fluid dairy products for retail and food-service customers under the Golden Guernsey Dairy and Morning Glory Dairy brands, as well as private labels. To reduce dependence on commodity products, the co-op is developing new products (flavored milks, natural fruit juices), and has expanded its mozzarella capacity to meet consumer demand. Cheese makes up 50% of its sales.

KEY COMPETITORS
AMPI
Dairy Farmers of America
Land O'Lakes

FOREVER LIVING PRODUCTS INTERNATIONAL, INC.

7501 E. McCormick Pkwy.	CEO: Rex Maughan	2001 Sales: $1,300.0 million
Scottsdale, AZ 85258	CFO: David Hall	1-Yr. Sales Change: 8.3%
Phone: 480-998-8888	HR: Glen B. Banks	Employees: 2,000
Fax: 480-998-8887	Type: Private	FYE: December 31
Web: www.foreverliving.com		

Forever Living Products International might not lead you to immortality, but its aloe vera-based health-care products are intended to improve your well-being. The firm sells an aloe vera juice drink, as well as aloe vera-based aromatherapy products, cosmetics, dietary and nutritional supplements, lotion, soap, and tooth gel products. Owner Rex Maughan also owns aloe vera plantations in the Dominican Republic, Mexico, and Texas; Aloe Vera of America, a processing plant; and Forever Resorts' US resorts/marinas, including Dallas-area South Fork Ranch (of *Dallas* TV show fame). Forever Living Products sells its goods through a global network of independent distributors.

KEY COMPETITORS
Herbalife
Nature's Sunshine
Sunrider

FORMICA CORPORATION

10155 Reading Rd.	CEO: Frank A. Riddick III	2000 Sales: $773.7 million
Cincinnati, OH 45241	CFO: Edward Case	1-Yr. Sales Change: 32.2%
Phone: 513-786-3400	HR: Linda Farfing	Employees: 5,400
Fax: 513-786-3024	Type: Private	FYE: December 31
Web: www.formica.com		

Formica — an adjective *and* a laminate. Formica Corporation points out that Formica is a product brand of adhesives and surfacing materials, as well as the material itself that is used in countertops and cabinets. Its brand names include Formica, Formica DecoMetal, ColorCore, Fountainhead, and Surell. Formica has subsidiaries in Asia, Europe, and the Americas. A top laminate supplier, Formica offers its products worldwide; the Americas account for more than half of its sales. Formica has filed for Chapter 11 bankruptcy protection in order to restructure — Credit Suisse First Boston Private Equity is its majority shareholder. Other owners include Citicorp Venture Capital, Ltd., and CVC Capital Partners Limited.

KEY COMPETITORS
Dal-Tile
DuPont
Perstorp

In-depth profiles of an additional 200 key private companies are found on pages 36–435.

FORSYTHE TECHNOLOGY, INC.

7500 Frontage Rd.	CEO: Richard A. Forsythe	2001 Sales: $691.0 million
Skokie, IL 60077	CFO: Albert Weiss	1-Yr. Sales Change: 9.5%
Phone: 847-675-8000	HR: Julie A. Fusco	Employees: 521
Fax: 847-763-7557	Type: Private	FYE: December 31
Web: www.forsythetech.com		

Forsythe Technology believes it has the foresight to provide businesses with the right computer equipment and network technology. Its Forsythe Solutions Group helps companies select, install, and manage computer systems and software, and its Forsythe McArthur subsidiary leases computer equipment. Forsythe Technology also owns a stake in management-service provider SevenSpace. The company works with vendors such as Cisco, Hewlett-Packard, and Sun Microsystems, and it serves more than 3,000 clients from offices throughout the US. CEO Richard Forsythe holds a majority interest in the employee-owned company, which he founded in 1971.

KEY COMPETITORS
Comdisco
EDS
IBM Global Services

FOSTER POULTRY FARMS

1000 Davis St.	CEO: Paul Carter	2001 Sales: $1,269.0 million
Livingston, CA 95334	CFO: Larry Keillor	1-Yr. Sales Change: 12.6%
Phone: 209-394-7901	HR: Tim Walsh	Employees: 11,000
Fax: 209-394-6342	Type: Private	FYE: December 31
Web: www.fosterfarms.com		

As the West Coast's top poultry company, Foster Poultry Farms has a secure place in the pecking order. The company's vertically integrated operations see chickens and turkeys from the incubator to grocers' meat cases (under the Foster Farms brand). In addition to hatching, raising, slaughtering, and processing chickens and turkeys for the grocery and food-service industries, the company grinds its own feed. Already #1 in its home state, Foster Poultry Farms bought the chicken operations of local rival Zacky Farms, making it even larger. Max and Verda Foster founded the company in 1939; it is still owned by the Foster family, who also operate a separate dairy company under the Foster Farms name.

KEY COMPETITORS
Gold Kist
Hormel
Tyson Foods

FRANK CONSOLIDATED ENTERPRISES

666 Garland Place	CEO: James S. "Jim" Frank	2002 Sales: $1,575.0 million
Des Plaines, IL 60016	CFO: Mary Ann O'Dwyer	1-Yr. Sales Change: 5.0%
Phone: 847-699-7000	HR: Joan Richards	Employees: 550
Fax: 847-699-4047	Type: Private	FYE: August 31
Web: www.wheels.com		

Frank Consolidated Enterprises has an old lease on life. Its Wheels subsidiary, which claims to have pioneered the auto leasing concept, provides administrative, management, and financing services to help corporations manage their vehicle fleets. The company manages more than 240,000 vehicles. It operates in the US as Wheels and in other countries through Interleasing, an alliance of international fleet management and leasing companies. Wheels was founded in 1939 by Zollie Frank. Frank's family still owns the parent company; his widow serves as its chair, and son Jim is its president and CEO. Frank Consolidated Enterprises also owns Z Frank Chevrolet, a Chicago-based auto dealership, which another son runs.

KEY COMPETITORS
Donlen
Enterprise Rent-A-Car
PHH Arval

In-depth profiles of an additional 200 key private companies are found on pages 36–435.

FREEDOM COMMUNICATIONS, INC.

17666 Fitch Ave.	CEO: Alan J. Bell	2001 Est. Sales: $760.0 mil.
Irvine, CA 92614	CFO: David Kuykendall	1-Yr. Sales Change: (10.6%)
Phone: 949-253-2300	HR: Marcy Bruskin	Employees: —
Fax: 949-474-7675	Type: Private	FYE: December 31
Web: www.freedom.com		

Southern California is the real cradle of Freedom. Media conglomerate Freedom Communications owns more than two dozen daily newspapers, including its flagship, California's *Orange County Register,* with a circulation of about 360,000. In addition, the company owns 37 weekly papers, eight television stations, and a handful of niche magazines (primarily health-care titles such as *Clinical Geriatrics* and *Home HealthCare Consultant*). Freedom Communications also operates more than 50 Web sites, which range from online versions of its printed properties to regional information guides. The company is owned by the family of founder R. C. Hoiles.

KEY COMPETITORS
Advance Publications
E. W. Scripps
Gannett

THE FREEMAN COMPANIES

1421 W. Mockingbird Ln.	CEO: Donald S. Freeman Jr.	2001 Sales: $878.0 million
Dallas, TX 75247	CFO: Ellis Moseley	1-Yr. Sales Change: 17.1%
Phone: 214-670-9000	HR: Suzanne Bragg	Employees: 34,000
Fax: 214-670-9100	Type: Private	FYE: June 30
Web: www.freemanco.com		

The Freeman Companies knows there's no business like the trade show business. The firm stages thousands of conventions, corporate meetings, expositions, and trade shows every year for which it also prepares exhibits for its clients. Freeman's operations include Freeman Decorating (event design and production), Freeman Exhibit (exhibit rental and production), Sullivan Transfer (heavy hauling), and Stage Rigging (theatrical rigging). The company's AVW Audio Visual (presentation technologies) unit has merged with Berkshire Partners' TELAV to form AVW/TELAV. Freeman Companies was founded by D.S. "Buck" Freeman in 1927; the company is owned by the Freeman family (including chairman and CEO Donald Freeman) and company employees.

KEY COMPETITORS
Key3Media
VNU
Viad

THE GALE COMPANY

200 Campus Dr., Ste. 200	CEO: Stanley C. Gale	2001 Sales: —
Florham Park, NJ	CFO: Kathleen Wielkopolski	1-Yr. Sales Change: —
Phone: 973-301-9500	HR: —	Employees: 500
Fax: 973-301-9501	Type: Private	FYE: December 31
Web: www.thegalecompany.com		

Real estate is a breeze for The Gale Company. The firm offers real estate services in the US and UK, including consulting, property management, and construction. Formerly known as Gale & Wentworth, the company manages maintenance, security, and other concerns for property owners; represents businesses in sales and leasing; provides outsourcing services; and oversees construction projects. The Gale Company, which manages some 50 million sq. ft., also invests in property through joint ventures with such financiers as Morgan Stanley and J.P. Morgan. Workstage, the firm's joint venture with office-furniture maker Steelcase, develops customized office buildings. CEO Stanley Gale controls the firm.

KEY COMPETITORS
CB Richard Ellis
Colliers International
Shorenstein

In-depth profiles of an additional 200 key private companies are found on pages 36–435.

GALPIN MOTORS, INC.

15505 Roscoe Blvd.	CEO: Herbert F. Boeckmann II	2001 Sales: $665.9 million
North Hills, CA 91343	CFO: Phil Marshall	1-Yr. Sales Change: 1.7%
Phone: 818-787-3800	HR: Joyce McNeely	Employees: 750
Fax: 818-778-2019	Type: Private	FYE: December 31
Web: www.gogalpin.com		

Galpin Motors will do just about anything to get you to buy a car, even feed you in its Horseless Carriage restaurant. Claiming to have sold the first Saturn, it also sells Jaguar, Lincoln, Mazda, and Mercury models, as well as used cars, from four dealerships and a Web site. It also rents and customizes — or "Galpinizes" — cars, such as its 1978 "Gucci Thunderbird," sold with matching handbag, wallet, and scarf. Galpin Motors' dealerships have featured a King Tut exhibit, a miniature circus, and a $1 million presentation to Mother Teresa. Founded in 1946, Galpin Motors is owned and run by the Boeckmann family.

KEY COMPETITORS
Autonation
David Wilson's
Penske Automotive

GATE PETROLEUM COMPANY

9540 San Jose Blvd.	CEO: Herbert H. Peyton	2001 Sales: $615.0 million
Jacksonville, FL 32257	CFO: P. Jeremy Smith	1-Yr. Sales Change: 11.8%
Phone: 904-737-7220	HR: Marlene Giese	Employees: 4,000
Fax: 904-732-7660	Type: Private	FYE: June 30
Web: www.gatepetro.com		

Gate Petroleum swings three ways. The company runs a chain of more than 150 gas stations in seven southeastern states, selling gas and groceries and offering fleet management services. The company is also in the real estate and construction materials businesses. In Florida the company owns three private clubs (the Epping Forest Yacht Club, the Ponte Vedra Inn & Club, and the Ponte Vedra Lodge & Club), as well as office buildings and business parks. It is also developing a huge residential and commercial complex in Jacksonville. Subsidiary Gate Concrete has plants in seven states, making and selling concrete and building materials. CEO Herbert Peyton, who founded the company in 1960, owns the majority of Gate Petroleum.

KEY COMPETITORS
7-Eleven
Exxon Mobil
The Pantry

GEISINGER HEALTH SYSTEM

100 N. Academy Ave.	CEO: Glenn Steele Jr.	2002 Est. Sales: $1,200.0 mil.
Danville, PA 17822	CFO: Kevin Brennan	1-Yr. Sales Change: 9.1%
Phone: 570-271-6211	HR: Russell Showers	Employees: 7,817
Fax: 570-271-7498	Type: Not-for-profit	FYE: June 30
Web: www.geisinger.org		

Geisinger Health System is one of Pennsylvania's largest health care providers, serving the central and northeastern portions of the state. Founded in 1915, the system operates Geisinger Medical Center, Geisinger Wyoming Valley Medical Center, The Janet Weis Children's and Women's Hospital, and an alcohol and chemical dependency treatment facility. The system's HMO, Geisinger Health Plan, boasts some 300,000 members and a network of about 40 hospitals and more than 3,100 physicians. For-profit Geisinger Medical Management offers pharmacy-contract-management services to health care providers.

KEY COMPETITORS
Catholic Health East
Highmark
Universal Health Services

📖 In-depth profiles of an additional 200
key private companies are found on pages 36–435.

GENERAL PARTS, INC.

2635 Millbrook Rd.	CEO: O. Temple Sloan Jr.	2001 Sales: $1,562.0 million
Raleigh, NC 27604	CFO: John Gardner	1-Yr. Sales Change: 7.1%
Phone: 919-573-3000	HR: Ed Wharty	Employees: 13,000
Fax: 919-573-3553	Type: Private	FYE: December 31

Feel free to salute General Parts, distributor of replacement automotive parts, supplies, and tools for every make and model of foreign and domestic car, truck, bus, and farm or industrial vehicle. The largest member of the CARQUEST network, employee-owned General Parts, with more than 1,200 company-owned stores, distributes its products to about 4,000 CARQUEST and other auto parts stores across North America through 35 distribution centers. The company, which has been growing through acquisitions, sells its parts to do-it-yourself mechanics, professional installers, body shops, farmers, and fleet owners (commercial customers account for about 85% of sales). The company owns CARQUEST Canada.

KEY COMPETITORS
Advance Auto Parts
AutoZone
Genuine Parts

GENLYTE THOMAS GROUP LLC

10350 Ormsby Park Place, Ste. 601	CEO: Larry K. Powers	2001 Sales: $985.2 million
Louisville, KY 40223	CFO: William G. Ferko	1-Yr. Sales Change: (2.2%)
Phone: 502-420-9500	HR: Manny Cadima	Employees: 5,314
Fax: 502-420-9540	Type: Joint venture	FYE: December 31
Web: www.genlytethomas.com		

At the marriage of The Genlyte Group and Thomas Industries, which formed Genlyte Thomas Group, they must have played "You Light Up My Life." The joint venture — of which Genlyte owns 68%, Thomas 32% — plays a leading role in the North American lighting market. Genlyte Thomas' lighting fixtures and controls are used both indoors and outdoors, for decoration, landscaping, and tracking. Brand names include Bronzelite, Capri, Lightolier, and ZED. The company markets to distributors, who resell the products for use in the construction and remodeling of residential, commercial, and industrial facilities. Genlyte Thomas' flagship Lightolier division is teaming up with Steelcase to develop workplace lighting.

KEY COMPETITORS
Catalina Lighting
Cooper Industries
GE

GENMAR HOLDINGS, INC.

80 S. 8th St.	CEO: Grant E. Oppegaard	2002 Est. Sales: $1,200.0 mil.
Minneapolis, MN 55402	CFO: Roger R. Cloutier II	1-Yr. Sales Change: 21.2%
Phone: 612-339-7600	HR: David Vigdal	Employees: 6,500
Fax: 612-337-1930	Type: Private	FYE: June 30
Web: www.genmar.com		

Genmar Holdings trolls for sales by cruising the pleasure boat market with a line of luxury yachts, recreational powerboats, and fishing boats. The company builds more than 400 different boat models ranging in size from 60-foot yachts (servants not included) to fishing skiffs. Its brands include Glastron, Ranger, and Wellcraft. Genmar markets its boats through about 1,800 independent dealers in the US and 30 other countries. The company — which is a combination of 16 different boat manufacturers acquired over 24 years — is controlled by chairman Irwin Jacobs (investor and former corporate raider). In 2001, through JTC Acquisitions, Genmar acquired bankrupt Outboard Marine's US boating and trailer assets.

KEY COMPETITORS
Brunswick
Fountain Powerboat
Yamaha Motor

📖 In-depth profiles of an additional 200 key private companies are found on pages 36–435.

GEOLOGISTICS CORPORATION

1251 E. Dyer Rd.
Santa Ana, CA 92705
Phone: 714-513-3000
Fax: 714-513-3120
Web: www.geo-logistics.com

CEO: William J. Flynn
CFO: Michael Bible
HR: Bob Westman
Type: Private

2001 Sales: $1,000.0 million
1-Yr. Sales Change: (33.3%)
Employees: 6,000
FYE: December 31

GeoLogistics gets goods going, globally. The company's integrated logistics offerings include multimodal freight-forwarding, customs brokerage, warehousing and distribution, supply chain management, and trade-show logistics. GeoLogistics provides real-time shipment tracking through its Internet-based GeoVista logistics software system. The company has operations in 140 countries. To focus on core logistics operations, GeoLogistics has sold its moving van unit, The Bekins Company. Investment firms Questor Management, William E. Simon & Sons, and Oaktree Capital Management control GeoLogistics, which was founded in 1996.

KEY COMPETITORS
EGL
Exel
Panalpina

GEORGE E. WARREN CORPORATION

605 17th St.
Vero Beach, FL 32960
Phone: 772-778-7100
Fax: 772-778-7171
Web: www.gewarren.com

CEO: Thomas L. Corr
CFO: Michael E. George
HR: Martin Paris
Type: Private

2001 Est. Sales: $1,400.0 mil.
1-Yr. Sales Change: 7.7%
Employees: 25
FYE: December 31

By barge, by pipeline, by tank truck by George, George E. Warren is a major private wholesale distributor of petroleum in the eastern US. Founded in Boston by George E. Warren in 1907 as a coal and oil distributor, it moved to Florida in the early 1990s. The company distributes product mostly by barge and pipeline, though it uses some tank trucks as well. Warren has distribution facilities in the southeastern and southwestern US. It distributes products including propane, propylene, ethylene, gasoline, and heating oil to various industries. President Thomas Corr owns the company.

KEY COMPETITORS
Martin Resource Management
Penn Octane
Sun Coast Resources

GEORGIA CROWN DISTRIBUTING COMPANY

7 Crown Circle
Columbus, GA 31908
Phone: 706-568-4580
Fax: 706-561-1647
Web: www.georgiacrown.com

CEO: Donald M. Leebern Jr.
CFO: Orlene Bovaird
HR: Mary Beth Gibbon
Type: Private

2001 Sales: $730.0 million
1-Yr. Sales Change: 2.8%
Employees: 1,665
FYE: July 31

Aptly named Fate D. Leebern may have died for Georgia Crown Distributing, a beverage bottler and distributor. He founded Georgia Crown as Columbus Wine Company Distributor in 1938, the same year Georgia prohibition was repealed. After the first rail shipment of legal liquor was received, someone — reportedly the Dixie Mafia — murdered Leebern. Today the family-owned company distributes beer, wine, liquor, bottled water, juices, and soft drinks to Georgia, Alabama, and Tennessee. The bottler also distributes its own brand of bottled water, Melwood Springs. CEO Donald Leebern Jr. is the grandson of the company's founder. The Leebern family owns the business.

KEY COMPETITORS
Coca-Cola Enterprises
National Distributing
Southern Wine & Spirits

In-depth profiles of an additional 200 key private companies are found on pages 36–435.

G-I HOLDINGS INC.

1361 Alps Rd.	CEO: Susan B. Yoss	2000 Est. Sales: $1,200.0 mil.
Wayne, NJ 07470	CFO: —	1-Yr. Sales Change: 5.3%
Phone: 973-628-3000	HR: Gary Schneid	Employees: 5,500
Fax: 973-628-3326	Type: Private	FYE: December 31

G-I Holdings (formerly GAF Corporation) works to keep a roof over your head. It is one of the US's oldest sources for commercial and residential roofing materials, with more than 25 plants in the US. Subsidiary Building Materials Corporation of America makes flashing, vents, and complete roofing systems. Other products include residential shingles (Timberline and Sovereign brands) and GAF CompositeRoof for commercial asphalt roofing. Customers include contractors, distributors, and retail outlets such as The Home Depot. G-I Holdings has filed for bankruptcy protection due to asbestos liability claims. Chairman Samuel Heyman owns 99% of the company and 81% of affiliate International Specialty Products Inc.

KEY COMPETITORS
Bridgestone/Firestone
ElkCorp
Owens Corning

GILBANE, INC.

7 Jackson Walkway	CEO: Paul J. Choquette Jr.	2001 Sales: $2,658.0 million
Providence, RI 02903	CFO: Ken Alderman	1-Yr. Sales Change: 11.3%
Phone: 401-456-5800	HR: Dan M. Kelly	Employees: 1,700
Fax: 401-456-5936	Type: Private	FYE: December 31
Web: www.gilbaneco.com		

Family-owned Gilbane has been the bane of its rivals for four generations. Subsidiary Gilbane Building provides construction management, contracting, and design and build services to construct office buildings, manufacturing plants, schools, prisons, and more for the firm's governmental, commercial, and industrial clients. Projects include the National Air and Space Museum, Lake Placid's 1980 Winter Olympics facilities, and the new WWII memorial in Washington, DC. The other subsidiary, Gilbane Properties, develops and finances public and private projects and acts as a property manager. Chairman and CEO Paul Choquette is a descendant of William and Thomas Gilbane, who founded the firm in 1873.

KEY COMPETITORS
Bechtel
Bovis Lend Lease
Parsons

GILSTER-MARY LEE CORPORATION

1037 State St.	CEO: Donald Welge	2001 Sales: $615.0 million
Chester, IL 62233	CFO: Michael Welge	1-Yr. Sales Change: 5.1%
Phone: 618-826-2361	HR: Robert Welge	Employees: 4,000
Fax: 618-826-2973	Type: Private	FYE: December 31
Web: www.gilstermarylee.com		

Breakfast is the most important meal of the day, especially at Gilster-Mary Lee. One of the largest private-label cereal manufacturers in the US (along with Ralcorp Holdings), Gilster-Mary Lee makes nearly 500 private-label products including cereal, cake, cocoa, dinner, and drink mixes; pasta; and popcorn. The company's customers include major US grocery chains and food wholesalers. The firm also offers products under its own Hospitality brand. The Gilster family founded the company as a flour mill in 1895 and began making cake mixes in the 1950s. Gilster-Mary Lee's 90 or so shareholders are led by president and CEO Donald Welge and his brother, CFO Michael Welge; the two are great-nephews of the company's founders.

KEY COMPETITORS
General Mills
Kraft Foods
Ralcorp

In-depth profiles of an additional 200 key private companies are found on pages 36–435.

GLAZER'S WHOLESALE DRUG COMPANY INC.

14860 Landmark Blvd.	CEO: Bennett Glazer	2001 Sales: $1,600.0 million
Dallas, TX 75240	CFO: Cary Rossel	1-Yr. Sales Change: 8.1%
Phone: 972-702-0900	HR: Rusty Harmount	Employees: 3,600
Fax: 972-702-8508	Type: Private	FYE: December 31
Web: www.glazers.com		

Glazer's Wholesale Drug, named during Prohibition when only drugstores and drug wholesalers could deal in liquor, is a wholesale distributor of alcoholic beverages. It is the largest distributor of malts, spirits, and wines in Texas and one of the largest US wine and spirits distributors. It also operates in Arizona (Alliance Beverage), Arkansas, Indiana (Olinger Distributing), Iowa, Kansas, Louisiana, Missouri, and Ohio. The company distributes Robert Mondavi wines and Brown-Forman and Bacardi spirits, among others. Glazer's has been acquiring wholesalers and distributors in the Midwest, including Mid-Continent Distributor (Missouri). CEO Bennett Glazer and family own Glazer's.

KEY COMPETITORS
Gallo
National Wine & Spirits
Southern Wine & Spirits

GLOBAL EXCHANGE SERVICES, INC.

100 Edison Park Dr.	CEO: Harvey F. Seegers	2001 Sales: $602.0 million
Gaithersburg, MD 20878	CFO: Jean-Jacques Charhon	1-Yr. Sales Change: (5.9%)
Phone: 301-340-4000	HR: —	Employees: 2,100
Fax: 301-340-5840	Type: Private	FYE: December 31
Web: www.gxs.com		

Global eXchange Services (GXS) wants to bring good IT to life. Founded in the early 1960s as the information technology division of General Electric (GE), GXS offers e-commerce supply chain automation services and software for companies in the retail, manufacturing, energy, and transportation industries. The company uses Web-based electronic data interchange and XML technology to automate the exchange of data, build and manage online trading communities, facilitate data and document sharing, and automate procurement and supply chain functions. Technology buyout firm Francisco Partners owns 90% of GXS.

KEY COMPETITORS
EDS
IBM
SAP

GOLD KIST INC.

244 Perimeter Center Pkwy. NE	CEO: John Bekkers	2002 Sales: $1,863.8 million
Atlanta, GA 30346	CFO: Stephen O. West	1-Yr. Sales Change: 2.9%
Phone: 770-393-5000	HR: Harry T. McDonald	Employees: 18,000
Fax: 770-393-5262	Type: Cooperative	FYE: June 30
Web: www.goldkist.com		

At Gold Kist, the chickens don't even get to see the road, much less cross it. An agricultural cooperative of 2,500 farmers (mainly in the South), Gold Kist is the #3 US chicken producer (behind Tyson Foods and Pilgrim's Pride). It markets whole and cut-up chickens, chicken parts, and other processed products under brands such as Gold Kist Farms and Young 'n Tender to grocery chains, the food service industry, and school and military systems. It also markets hogs, conducts peanut research, and builds and installs industrial wastewater treatment systems. The co-op provides financing for farmers and produces nuts through its 25% stake in US pecan processor Young Pecan Company.

KEY COMPETITORS
Perdue
Pilgrim's Pride
Tyson Foods

In-depth profiles of an additional 200 key private companies are found on pages 36–435.

GOLDEN RULE INSURANCE COMPANY

712 11th St.	CEO: John Whelan	2001 Sales: $829.0 million
Lawrenceville, IL 62439	CFO: Patrick F. Carr	1-Yr. Sales Change: 0.0%
Phone: 618-943-8000	HR: Rick Lane	Employees: 1,084
Fax: 618-943-8031	Type: Private	FYE: December 31
Web: www.goldenrule.com		

Follow the golden rule and you will find insurance. Golden Rule Insurance provides health insurance, life insurance, and annuities. Other products include Asset-Care (a long-term care insurance policy that combines life insurance and asset management), ValuTerm (term life insurance), and WealthBuilder (fixed-rate annuities). Golden Rule operates in all states except New York. Throughout the 1980s and 1990s the company was accused of hardball tactics aimed at denying policyholder claims and "cherry picking" (denying sick and therefore high-risk) customers.

KEY COMPETITORS
Aetna
UnitedHealth Group
WellPoint Health Networks

THE GOLUB CORPORATION

501 Duanesburg Rd.	CEO: Neil M. Golub	2002 Est. Sales: $2,100.0 mil.
Schenectady, NY 12306	CFO: John Endres	1-Yr. Sales Change: 5.0%
Phone: 518-355-5000	HR: Margaret Davenport	Employees: 19,700
Fax: 518-379-3597	Type: Private	FYE: April 30
Web: www.pricechopper.com		

Supermarket operator The Golub Corporation offers tasty come-ons such as table-ready meals, gift certificates, automatic discount cards, and a hotline where cooks answer food-related queries. Golub operates 100-plus Price Chopper supermarkets in Connecticut, Massachusetts, New Hampshire, upstate New York, northeastern Pennsylvania, and Vermont. It also runs Mini Chopper service stations and convenience stores. Golub has discontinued its HouseCalls home delivery service. Brothers Bill and Ben Golub founded the company in 1932. The Golub family owns 56% of Golub and has turned down offers to sell the company. Employees own the other 44% of Golub.

KEY COMPETITORS
Ahold USA
Big Y Foods
Hannaford Bros.

GOODMAN MANUFACTURING COMPANY, L.P.

2550 N. Loop West, Ste. 400	CEO: Charles A. Carroll	2001 Est. Sales: $1,150.0 mil.
Houston, TX 77092	CFO: Larry Blackburn	1-Yr. Sales Change: 4.5%
Phone: 713-861-2500	HR: Donald R. King	Employees: 3,750
Fax: 713-861-2176	Type: Private	FYE: December 31
Web: www.goodmanmfg.com		

Goodman knows how to cool off a hot situation. Goodman Manufacturing Company, through its Amana Heating and Air Conditioning, Goodman Manufacturing, and Quietflex divisions, makes air-conditioning, ventilation, and heating equipment for residential and commercial use. Goodman, which sells its products through independent installers and distributors worldwide, is among the top US makers of air conditioners. Its brands include Amana, Caloric, Goodman, GmC, Modern Maid, and Janitrol. The company sold its Amana Appliance division (washers, dryers, microwaves, and refrigerators) to Maytag. Goodman is owned by the family of Harold Goodman, who founded the company in 1977.

KEY COMPETITORS
Carrier
Fedders
GE Consumer Products

In-depth profiles of an additional 200 key private companies are found on pages 36–435.

GOODTIMES ENTERTAINMENT LIMITED

16 E. 40th St.	CEO: Andrew Greenberg	2001 Est. Sales: $760.0 mil.
New York, NY 10016	CFO: Jonathan Boon	1-Yr. Sales Change: 60.0%
Phone: 212-951-3000	HR: —	Employees: 800
Fax: 212-951-9319	Type: Private	FYE: December 31
Web: www.goodtimes.com		

GoodTimes Entertainment hopes you find its celebrity-endorsed products Dy-No-Mite! The company distributes videos and DVDs through direct marketing and retail outlets in niches such as animated features (*Rudolph the Red-Nosed Reindeer and the Island of Misfit Toys*), Christian entertainment (*Charlton Heston Presents The Bible*), and fitness instruction (Richard Simmons). It also distributes videos and DVDs of Broadway shows through an agreement with the Broadway Television Network. The company also offers products such as fitness devices (Cableflex, endorsed by Jackie Chan) and cosmetics (*Results* Skin Care, endorsed by Joan Rivers). The family of chairman Joseph Cayre owns GoodTimes Entertainment.

KEY COMPETITORS
AOL Time Warner
Viacom
Walt Disney

GOODWILL INDUSTRIES INTERNATIONAL, INC.

9200 Rockville Pike	CEO: George W. Kessinger	2001 Sales: $1,940.0 million
Bethesda, MD 20814	CFO: —	1-Yr. Sales Change: 4.9%
Phone: 301-530-6500	HR: Alison Jenkens	Employees: 61,766
Fax: 301-530-1516	Type: Not-for-profit	FYE: December 31
Web: www.goodwill.org		

Founded to give those in need "a hand up, not a handout," Goodwill Industries International supports the operations of about 210 independent Goodwill chapters worldwide. Though known mainly for its some 1,900 thrift stores, Goodwill focuses on providing rehabilitation, training, placement, and employment services for those with disabilities and other barriers to employment. Goodwill is one of the world's largest providers of such services, as well as one of the world's largest employers of the disabled. Funding comes primarily from the retail stores, contract services provided to local employers, and grants. Nearly 86% of revenues go to job training and rehabilitation programs.

GORDON FOOD SERVICE

333 50th St. SW	CEO: Dan Gordon	2002 Est. Sales: $2,750.0 mil.
Grand Rapids, MI 49501	CFO: Steve Whitteberry	1-Yr. Sales Change: 5.8%
Phone: 616-530-7000	HR: David Vickery	Employees: 5,000
Fax: 616-261-7600	Type: Private	FYE: October 31
Web: www.gfs.com		

Gordon Food Service (GFS) caters to the tastes of Midwesterners and Canadians. A food distributor serving schools, restaurants, and other institutions, GFS boasts more than 12,000 products ranging from fresh produce to sanitation systems. The company also makes its own foods under names such as Triumph Packaging and Ready, Set, Serve. GFS also sells food in bulk through some 85 GFS Marketplace stores in four states. GFS acquired in 2002 the Pacific Division of SERCA Foodservice from Sobeys and renamed it Neptune Food Service. The late Isaac VanWestenbrugge (great-grandfather of CEO Dan Gordon) founded the company as a butter and egg distributor in 1897. GFS is still owned and run by the Gordon family.

KEY COMPETITORS
McLane Foodservice
SYSCO
U.S. Foodservice

In-depth profiles of an additional 200 key private companies are found on pages 36–435.

GORES TECHNOLOGY GROUP

10877 Wilshire Blvd., Ste. 1805	CEO: Alec Gores	2001 Sales: $2,000.0 million
Los Angeles, CA 90024	CFO: Cathy Scanlon	1-Yr. Sales Change: 66.7%
Phone: 310-209-3010	HR: David Strain	Employees: 10,000
Fax: 310-209-3310	Type: Private	FYE: December 31
Web: www.gores.com		

In the gory aftermath of the Tech Wreck, Gores Technology Group can probably find a bargain. The company buys and manages software, hardware, technology services, and telecommunications concerns. Targets typically have revenues between $10 million and $1 billion and are often spinoffs of noncore operations from Global 2000 companies. Gores Technology usually takes full ownership. Since its founding by chairman Alec Gores in 1992, it has bought some 35 companies around the world worth about $2 billion. These include the personal computer operations of Micron Electronics (now Interland) and software maker The Learning Company, which subsequently sold its education business to Ireland's Riverdeep software firm.

KEY COMPETITORS
Carlyle Group
KKR
Platinum Equity

GOSS HOLDINGS, INC.

700 Oakmont Ln.	CEO: Thomas R. Cochill	2001 Est. Sales: $650.0 mil.
Westmont, IL 60559	CFO: Joseph P. Gaynor III	1-Yr. Sales Change: 4.3%
Phone: 630-850-5600	HR: Angela Lewis	Employees: 2,700
Fax: 630-850-6310	Type: Private	FYE: December 31
Web: www.gossgraphic.com		

Goss Holdings always has some pressing news. The company operates through its Goss Graphic Systems subsidiary, making web-offset printing presses for newspapers and commercial printers, as well as advertising insert presses. Goss offers its presses, related parts, and services (sensitive to publishing schedules) through sales offices and plants in North America, Europe, and Asia. The company serves newspaper publishers in more than 120 countries. Customers have included *The Asahi Shimbun* (Japan), *The People's Daily* (China), and *The Financial Times* (UK). Goss has emerged from Chapter 11 bankruptcy, and investment firm Stonington Partners controls 91% of the company.

KEY COMPETITORS
Baldwin Technology
MAN
Pamarco Technologies

GOULD PAPER CORPORATION

11 Madison Ave.	CEO: Harry E. Gould Jr.	2001 Est. Sales: $820.0 mil.
New York, NY 10010	CFO: Carl Matthews	1-Yr. Sales Change: 1.2%
Phone: 212-301-0000	HR: Barbara O'Grady	Employees: 455
Fax: 212-481-0067	Type: Private	FYE: December 31
Web: www.gouldpaper.com		

Paper is as good as gold for Gould Paper, one of the largest privately owned distributors of printing and fine papers in the US. The company distributes and sells paper for multiple markets including fine papers, commercial printing, lithography, newsprint, direct mail, catalogs, envelopes, and specialty papers. The Gould North America division oversees business within the US and Canada, while Gould National produces paper rolls (wholesale). Its International Packaging Group makes specialty packaging (paperboard, plastics). Harry Gould Sr. (father of chairman, president, CEO, and company owner Harry Gould Jr.) formed the company in 1924. Gould Paper has expanded over the years by acquiring other paper companies.

KEY COMPETITORS
Clifford Paper
International Paper
Midland Paper

In-depth profiles of an additional 200
key private companies are found on pages 36–435.

GRAHAM PACKAGING HOLDINGS COMPANY

2401 Pleasant Valley Rd.	CEO: Philip R. Yates	2001 Sales: $923.1 million
York, PA 17402	CFO: John E. Hamilton	1-Yr. Sales Change: 11.9%
Phone: 717-849-8500	HR: George Lane	Employees: 4,100
Fax: 717-848-4836	Type: Private	FYE: December 31
Web: www.grahampackaging.com		

Grocery stockers and mechanics handle Graham Packaging's products every day. The company makes blow-molded plastic containers for food and beverages (55% of sales), household and personal care products, and automotive lubricants. Customers such as Minute Maid, Hershey Foods, Procter & Gamble, and Pennzoil-Quaker State use the containers for juices, sauces, teas, fabric and dish detergents, and motor oil. One-third of Graham Packaging's manufacturing plants are located on the grounds of its customers' production facilities. The company, which is controlled by Blackstone Group, has postponed its IPO until market conditions improve. North America accounts for 80% of sales.

KEY COMPETITORS
Amcor
Consolidated Container
Constar International

GREAT DANE LIMITED PARTNERSHIP

602 E. Lathrop Ave.	CEO: C. F. Hammond III	2001 Est. Sales: $1,100.0 mil.
Savannah, GA 31402	CFO: Tom Horan	1-Yr. Sales Change: (16.0%)
Phone: 912-644-2100	HR: Thor Egede-Nissen	Employees: 3,400
Fax: 912-644-2166	Type: Private	FYE: December 31
Web: www.greatdanetrailers.com		

Great Dane is really going places — the company is one of the largest manufacturers of truck trailers in North America. Great Dane makes refrigerated (reefer) and freight vans and platform trailers. The company has nine manufacturing plants in the US and sales, parts, and service centers across the US, Canada, Mexico, and South America. It also sells used trailers. Great Dane is a unit of Chicago-based investment group CC Industries, which is controlled by the Henry Crown family. The company started in 1900 as a maker of steel products and switched to trailer making in 1931.

KEY COMPETITORS
Lufkin Industries
Utility Trailer
Wabash National

GREAT LAKES CHEESE COMPANY, INC.

17825 Great Lakes Pkwy.	CEO: Gary Vanich	2001 Sales: $800.0 million
Hiram, OH 44234	CFO: Russ Mullins	1-Yr. Sales Change: 11.6%
Phone: 440-834-2500	HR: Beth Wendell	Employees: 1,200
Fax: 440-834-1002	Type: Private	FYE: December 31
Web: www.greatlakescheese.com		

Great Lakes Cheese Company understands the power of provolone and the charm of cheddar. The firm manufactures and distributes natural and processed cheeses, including cheddar, Swiss, mozzarella, and provolone. The company packages shredded, chunk, and sliced cheese under retailers' private labels. Additionally it imports cheeses, and produces cheese for deli, bulk, and food service sale. The firm has five plants in New York, Ohio, and Wisconsin and is expanding into Utah. Hans Epprecht, a Swiss immigrant, founded the company in 1958 as a bulk-cheese distributor in Cleveland. Chairman Epprecht and Great Lakes Cheese employees own the company.

KEY COMPETITORS
Kraft Foods
Land O'Lakes
Saputo

In-depth profiles of an additional 200 key private companies are found on pages 36–435.

GREDE FOUNDRIES, INC.

9898 W. Bluemound Rd.	CEO: Bruce E. Jacobs	2001 Sales: $591.0 million
Milwaukee, WI 53226	CFO: Kristen Z. Reilly	1-Yr. Sales Change: (6.6%)
Phone: 414-257-3600	HR: W. Stewart Davis	Employees: 4,500
Fax: 414-256-9399	Type: Private	FYE: December 31
Web: www.grede.com		

Many industries would be lost without Grede Foundries. The company produces gray iron, ductile iron, and steel castings for use in farm and construction equipment, motor vehicles, and a host of other products. Grede's cast products include axles, brackets, crankshafts, hydraulic end caps, and sprockets. The company also offers services such as design assistance, painting, machining, and subassembly. Grede operates 11 foundries in the US and one in the UK. In a partnership with Grupo Proeza, the company is constructing a ductile iron foundry near Monterrey, Mexico. William Grede founded the company as Liberty Foundry in 1920. The business is still owned by Grede's descendants, including chairman Burleigh Jacobs.

KEY COMPETITORS
Atchison Casting
Citation
INTERMET

GREEN BAY PACKAGING INC.

1700 N. Webster Ct.	CEO: William F. Kress	2001 Sales: $800.0 million
Green Bay, WI 54307	CFO: Joseph Baemmert	1-Yr. Sales Change: (3.1%)
Phone: 920-433-5111	HR: —	Employees: 2,800
Fax: 920-433-5337	Type: Private	FYE: December 31
Web: www.gbp.com		

Green Bay Packaging is always packed and ready to go. The company is an integrated and diversified paperboard packaging manufacturer. In addition to corrugated containers, the company makes pressure-sensitive label stock, folding cartons, linerboard, and lumber products. Its Fiber Resources division in Arkansas manages 195,000 acres of company-owned forests and, through contractors, produces lumber, woodchips, recycled paper, and wood fuel. Green Bay Packaging also offers fiber procurement, wastepaper brokerage, and paper-slitting services. Founded by corrugated paper pioneer George Kress in 1933, the company operates 29 divisions in 14 states. The Kress family controls Green Bay Packaging.

KEY COMPETITORS
Chesapeake Corporation
Smurfit-Stone Container
Temple-Inland

GREENVILLE HOSPITAL SYSTEM

701 Grove Rd.	CEO: Frank D. Pinckney	2001 Sales: $691.1 million
Greenville, SC 29605	CFO: Susan Bichel	1-Yr. Sales Change: 16.8%
Phone: 864-455-7000	HR: Douglas Dorman	Employees: 6,500
Fax: 864-455-6218	Type: Not-for-profit	FYE: September 30
Web: www.ghs.org		

Greenville Hospital System is a not-for-profit community hospital system serving South Carolina's "Golden Strip" (the I-85 corridor connecting Charlotte, North Carolina, with Atlanta). Founded in 1912 as a community hospital, the system today includes four acute-care hospitals (about 900 beds), as well as a children's hospital, a cancer center, and a nursing home. Greenville Hospital System offers a full range of services, including a primary-care physician network, a health plan, and outpatient care. The company, which also operates a charitable foundation, has teaching affiliations with two medical schools and a research affiliation with Clemson University.

KEY COMPETITORS
Bon Secours Health
HMA
Novant Health

In-depth profiles of an additional 200
key private companies are found on pages 36–435.

THE GROCERS SUPPLY CO., INC.

3131 E. Holcombe Blvd.	CEO: Milton Levit	2001 Sales: $1,500.0 million
Houston, TX 77021	CFO: Michael Castleberry	1-Yr. Sales Change: 7.1%
Phone: 713-747-5000	HR: Terry Collins	Employees: 2,400
Fax: 713-746-5611	Type: Private	FYE: December 31
Web: www.grocerssupply.com		

Need crackers in Caracas or vanilla in Manila? Grocers Supply Co. distributes groceries near and far. The company (not to be confused with fellow Texas distributor GSC Enterprises) distributes food, health and beauty items, household products, and school and office supplies to more than 1,200 convenience stores, 650 supermarkets, and 200 schools within a 350-mile radius of Houston. Its Grocers Supply International (GSI) division ships supplies to oil company operations, other commercial customers, and US embassies around the world. GSI boasts that it will buy anything to ship anywhere for anyone, including macaroons in Rangoon, or even oleo in Tokyo. Grocers Supply is owned by the Levit family.

KEY COMPETITORS
C.D. Hartnett
GSC Enterprises
McLane

GROUP HEALTH COOPERATIVE OF PUGET SOUND

521 Wall St.	CEO: Cheryl M. Scott	2001 Sales: $1,436.0 million
Seattle, WA 98121	CFO: Jim Truess	1-Yr. Sales Change: 2.6%
Phone: 206-326-3000	HR: Brenda Tolbert	Employees: 10,500
Fax: 206-448-4010	Type: Not-for-profit	FYE: December 31
Web: www.ghc.org		

Group Health Cooperative of Puget Sound is a not-for-profit managed health care group serving counties in Washington and northern Idaho. Members may participate in HMO, PPO, or point-of-service health plans. The co-op is governed by an 11-person board elected by the organization's members. Specialized services include mental health and substance abuse treatment, hospice services, and HIV/AIDS case management. Group Health Cooperative of Puget Sound has an alliance with Virginia Mason Medical Center (to share medical centers and hospitals), as well as with Kaiser Permanente, one of the nation's largest nonprofit health care systems. The organization is owned by its nearly 600,000 members.

KEY COMPETITORS
Aetna
CIGNA
PacifiCare

GROWMARK, INC.

1701 Towanda Ave.	CEO: Bill Davisson	2002 Sales: $1,242.4 million
Bloomington, IL 61701	CFO: Jeff Solberg	1-Yr. Sales Change: (14.9%)
Phone: 309-557-6000	HR: Wes Ehler	Employees: 697
Fax: 309-829-8532	Type: Cooperative	FYE: August 31
Web: www.growmark.com		

Retail farm-supply and grain-marketing cooperative GROWMARK can mark its growth by the grain. Through its member-owner co-ops — about 100 in retail and 250-plus in grain marketing — GROWMARK serves farmers in the midwestern US and Ontario, Canada. Under the Fast Stop name, the co-op runs fuel stations and convenience stores. Its FS- and NK-brand grains include alfalfa, corn, wheat, and soybeans. GROWMARK also offers fertilizer, seeds, and buildings such as grain bins. GROWMARK partners with Archer Daniels Midland, fertilizer maker and distributor CF Industries, and pet food producer PRO-PET, and has an energy alliance with Countrymark Cooperative and Land O'Lakes.

KEY COMPETITORS
Agway
Cenex Harvest States
Farmland Industries

📖 In-depth profiles of an additional 200 key private companies are found on pages 36–435.

GS INDUSTRIES, INC.

1901 Roxborough Rd., Ste. 200
Charlotte, NC 28211
Phone: 704-366-6901
Fax: 704-365-4340
Web: www.gsind.com

CEO: Mark Essig
CFO: —
HR: Richard Luzzi
Type: Private

2000 Sales: $700.0 million
1-Yr. Sales Change: 3.5%
Employees: 2,000
FYE: December 31

GS Industries (GSI) is a leading maker of cast wear parts and grinding media for the mining industry, as well as North America's top maker of steel wire rod. Wire rod is used by automakers in the production of tire cord, shocks, and brake pads. GSI's mining products include steel grinding balls and rods and mill liners. The company has operations in Asia, Australia, Europe, and the Americas. It is part owner of Siderperu, a Peruvian maker of steel products. GSI was established by the 1995 merger of Georgetown Steel and GS Technologies, two steel minimills. Investment firm Bain Capital controls the company, which is restructuring under bankruptcy protection.

KEY COMPETITORS
Insteel
Keystone Consolidated
Nucor

GSC ENTERPRISES, INC.

130 Hillcrest Dr.
Sulphur Springs, TX 75482
Phone: 903-885-0829
Fax: 903-885-6928
Web: www.grocerysupply.com

CEO: Michael K. McKenzie
CFO: Kerry Law
HR: Theresa Patterson
Type: Private

2001 Est. Sales: $1,100.0 mil.
1-Yr. Sales Change: 1.7%
Employees: 1,100
FYE: December 31

GSC Enterprises brings the groceries to the grocery store. The wholesale distributor (whose name stands for "Grocery Supply Company," not to be confused with Grocers Supply Co.) supplies independently owned convenience stores, grocers, discounters, and other retailers and wholesalers. It serves some 15,000 stores in about 15 states in the Southwest, Southeast, and Midwest. GSC stocks and distributes tobacco, candy, grocery items, prepared foods (Chicago Style Pizza, Chester Fried Chicken, Deli-Fast Foods), and other items. The firm also owns Fidelity Express, which sells money orders in stores. GSC is owned by the McKenzie family, descendants of two of the men who founded it in 1947.

KEY COMPETITORS
Eby-Brown
Fleming Companies
SUPERVALU

GULF OIL LIMITED PARTNERSHIP

90 Everett Ave.
Chelsea, MA 02150
Phone: 617-889-9000
Fax: 617-884-0637
Web: www.gulfoil.com

CEO: John Kaneb
CFO: Alice Kuhne
HR: Karen Channel
Type: Partnership

2002 Est. Sales: $1,680.0 mil.
1-Yr. Sales Change: (14.7%)
Employees: 150
FYE: September 30

Gulf Oil bridges the gap between petroleum producers and retail sales outlets. The petroleum wholesaler distributes gasoline and diesel fuel to 1,800 Gulf-branded stations in 11 northeastern states. Gulf Oil, which owns and operates 12 storage terminals, also distributes motor oils, lubricants, and heating oil to commercial, industrial, and utility customers. The company has alliances with terminal operators in areas in the Northeast where it does not have a proprietary terminal. Noteworthy for providing the world's first drive-in service station, Gulf Oil was established in 1901 with an oil strike in Spindletop, Texas. The oil company restructured into seven operating companies in the 1970s.

KEY COMPETITORS
Amerada Hess
Getty Petroleum Marketing
Motiva Enterprises

In-depth profiles of an additional 200 key private companies are found on pages 36–435.

GULF STATES TOYOTA, INC.

7701 Wilshire Place Dr.	CEO: Toby Hynes	2001 Est. Sales: $3,800.0 mil.
Houston, TX 77040	CFO: Frank Gruen	1-Yr. Sales Change: 16.9%
Phone: 713-580-3300	HR: Dominic Gallo	Employees: 3,000
Fax: 713-580-3332	Type: Private	FYE: December 31

Even good ol' boys buy foreign cars from Gulf States Toyota. One of only two US Toyota distributors not owned by Toyota Motor Sales (the other is JM Family Enterprises' Southeast Toyota Distributors), the company distributes Toyota and Lexus cars, trucks, and sport utility vehicles in Arkansas, Louisiana, Mississippi, Oklahoma, and Texas. Founded in 1969 by Thomas Friedkin and still owned by The Friedkin Companies, Gulf States distributes new Toyotas, parts, and accessories to around 140 dealers in its region. Because Toyota has had success converting Internet leads into actual sales, Gulf States offers customizable Web site packages to its entire dealership network.

KEY COMPETITORS
Ford
General Motors
Nissan North America

GUTHY-RENKER CORP.

41-550 Eclectic St., Ste. 200	CEO: Greg Renker	2001 Sales: $700.0 million
Palm Desert, CA 92260	CFO: Kevin Knee	1-Yr. Sales Change: 40.0%
Phone: 760-773-9022	HR: Aleida Hernadez	Employees: —
Fax: 310-581-3232	Type: Private	FYE: December 31
Web: www.guthy-renker.com		

What do Kathie Lee Gifford, Victoria Principal, and Tony Robbins have in common? Each has starred in an infomercial produced by Guthy-Renker, one of the largest infomercial producers in the US. The company's pitchpeople hawk products, including fitness equipment, cosmetics, and motivational tapes. Guthy-Renker has expanded into other areas of electronic retailing such as its Choice Mall Internet shopping mall. The company also pursues marketing opportunities through direct mail, retail, and telemarketing. The company was founded in 1988 by Bill Guthy and Greg Renker, after being spun off from Guthy's Cassette Productions Unlimited (CPU).

KEY COMPETITORS
Access Television Network
Summit America Television
ValueVision Media

HAGGEN, INC.

2211 Rimland Dr.	CEO: Dale Henley	2001 Est. Sales: $700.0 mil.
Bellingham, WA 98226	CFO: Tom Kenney	1-Yr. Sales Change: 5.1%
Phone: 360-733-8720	HR: Janel Ernster	Employees: 4,000
Fax: 360-650-8235	Type: Private	FYE: December 31
Web: www.haggen.com		

Haggen showers shoppers in the Pacific Northwest with salmon, coffee, and other essentials. The area's largest independent grocer, Haggen operates 28 combination supermarket/drugstores in Washington and Oregon. Most upscale Haggen Food and Pharmacy stores feature specialty departments, while the TOP Food & Drug outlets are generally discount outfits; however, both may offer such amenities as Starbucks Coffee shops, Blockbuster Video outlets, or child-care centers. To keep up with the Joneses of supermarket fame and fortune, Haggen partnered with ShopEaze.com (an e-commerce service provider), which failed, leaving Haggen without an online store. Brothers and co-chairmen Don and Rick Haggen own the chain.

KEY COMPETITORS
Albertson's
Brown & Cole Stores
Fred Meyer Stores

In-depth profiles of an additional 200 key private companies are found on pages 36–435.

HALE-HALSELL CO.

9111 E. Pine St.	CEO: Robert D. Hawk	2001 Est. Sales: $950.0 mil.
Tulsa, OK 74115	CFO: Michael Owens	1-Yr. Sales Change: 10.6%
Phone: 918-835-4484	HR: Ron Stacey	Employees: 4,500
Fax: 918-641-5471	Type: Private	FYE: December 31
Web: www.hale-halsell.com		

Hale-Halsell Co. doesn't make cattle drives, but the food retailer and wholesaler does round up and move out grocery goods throughout Arkansas, Kansas, Missouri, Oklahoma, and Texas. On the retail side, the company operates some 120 Git-N-Go convenience stores and about 10 Super H Foods supermarkets, primarily in small Oklahoma towns. Hale-Halsell also runs a restaurant supply business. Tom Hale and Hugh Halsell started the company in 1901 to supply settlers in the newly opened Native American lands in Oklahoma. Hale-Halsell is majority-owned by Hale's descendant, Elmer Hale Jr.

KEY COMPETITORS
Fleming Companies
Kroger
Wal-Mart

HAMPTON AFFILIATES

9600 SW Barnes Rd., Ste. 200	CEO: Ronald C. Parker	2002 Sales: $700.0 million
Portland, OR 97225	CFO: Steven J. Zika	1-Yr. Sales Change: (2.9%)
Phone: 503-297-7691	HR: Darrell Eng	Employees: 1,300
Fax: 503-203-6607	Type: Private	FYE: January 31
Web: www.hamptonlumber.com		

As a vertically integrated lumber company, Hampton Affiliates knows trees from seedling to stud. One of Oregon's top timber firms, Hampton churns out about 900 million board feet of lumber annually. The company has more than 180,000 acres of timberland and owns mills in Oregon and Washington. It owns California Builders' Supply, a distributor of doors, windows, and other building materials, and Lane Stanton Vance, a maker of imported and domestic hardwood lumber. Hampton has added stud lumber and distribution operations to supply home-building centers and is exploring import/export opportunities in the Pacific Rim region. L. M. "Bud" Hampton founded the company in 1942, and the Hampton family still owns it.

KEY COMPETITORS
Georgia-Pacific Corporation
Sierra Pacific Industries
Simpson Investment

HARBOUR GROUP INDUSTRIES, INC.

7701 Forsyth Blvd., Ste. 600	CEO: Sam Fox	2001 Est. Sales: $2,800.0 mil.
St. Louis, MO 63105	CFO: Mike Santoni	1-Yr. Sales Change: —
Phone: 314-727-5550	HR: Harriet Lovins	Employees: —
Fax: 314-727-9912	Type: Private	FYE: December 31
Web: www.harbourgroup.com		

Troubled manufacturers can seek refuge with Harbour Group Industries, a conglomerate that acquires and consolidates manufacturing companies in fragmented industries. Harbour's current portfolio includes companies in 24 different industries, including auto accessories, chimney and fireplace products, fluid handling equipment, industrial cleaning, paint sundries, plastics-processing equipment, heat exchangers, and textile machinery. Since its founding in 1976, Harbour Group has acquired about 125 companies; most have been combined with similar acquisitions.

KEY COMPETITORS
Albert Trostel & Sons
AptarGroup
Swagelok

In-depth profiles of an additional 200 key private companies are found on pages 36–435.

HAROLD LEVINSON ASSOCIATES

1 Enterprise Place	CEO: Edward Berro	2001 Est. Sales: $1,000.0 mil.
Hicksville, NY 11801	CFO: Andrew P. DeFrancesco	1-Yr. Sales Change: 37.0%
Phone: 516-822-0068	HR: Mirabella Barrasso	Employees: 350
Fax: 516-822-2182	Type: Private	FYE: December 31
Web: www.hladistributors.com		

Harold Levinson Associates (HLA) can soothe your nicotine fit with a fat cigar, light it, satisfy your sweet tooth, and even help you make a long-distance phone call. From its warehouse and distribution facility in Hicksville, New York, HLA ships out cigars imported from around the world, tobaccos, and smoking accessories such as lighters. Besides tobacco products (85% of sales), HLA distributes groceries and candy to 16,000 delis, gas stations, and convenience stores in the New York area. Following price hikes by cigarette manufacturers, HLA launched its cigars and other smokes into cyberspace with an e-commerce Web site. The company also distributes prepaid, long-distance phone cards. HLA was founded in 1975.

KEY COMPETITORS
800-JR Cigar
Holt's Cigar
Synergy Brands

THE HARTZ MOUNTAIN CORPORATION

400 Plaza Dr.	CEO: Robert Devine	2001 Est. Sales: $1,100.0 mil.
Secaucus, NJ 07094	CFO: Chris Bridgnell	1-Yr. Sales Change: 12.8%
Phone: 201-271-4800	HR: Kelly Shevlin	Employees: 2,200
Fax: 201-271-0164	Type: Private	FYE: December 31
Web: www.hartz.com		

Hartz Mountain has something for pets of all sizes. The company markets about 1,500 pet care products including nutritional products for small pets, birds, and aquariums; over-the-counter animal health products (including flea and tick treatments); and toys and accessories for dogs, cats, and birds. Hartz Mountain is buying the Alley Cat and Meow Mix brands from Nestlé Purina PetCare. Max Stern founded the company in 1926 after emigrating from Germany. The Stern family operated the company for more than 75 years under the Hartz Group umbrella along with the family's real estate operations. An investment group, including members of Hartz management, bought the Hartz Mountain pet products business in 2000.

KEY COMPETITORS
Iams
Mars
Nestlé Purina PetCare

HARVARD PILGRIM HEALTH CARE, INC.

93 Worcester St.	CEO: Charles D. Baker Jr.	2001 Sales: $1,700.0 million
Wellesley, MA 02481	CFO: Joseph C. Capezza	1-Yr. Sales Change: (19.0%)
Phone: 617-745-1000	HR: Deborah Hicks	Employees: 1,800
Fax: 617-509-7590	Type: Not-for-profit	FYE: December 31
Web: www.harvardpilgrim.org		

This Harvard once bled green rather than crimson. Harvard Pilgrim Health Care provides managed health care for Massachusetts and New England. The company offers its 730,000 members HMO, preferred provider organization (PPO), point-of-service, and Medicaid/Medicare plans through more than 120 affiliated hospitals in New England. Harvard Pilgrim Health Care also offers HPHConnect, for online benefits administration. Harvard Pilgrim has recovered after being placed into receivership by the state of Massachusetts in 1999. Restructuring and raising premiums brought a healthier bottom line but also a significant reduction in membership.

KEY COMPETITORS
Aetna
Blue Cross (MA)
Tufts Health Plan

In-depth profiles of an additional 200 key private companies are found on pages 36–435.

THE HASKELL COMPANY

111 Riverside Ave.	CEO: Steven T. Halverson	2001 Sales: $700.0 million
Jacksonville, FL 32202	CFO: Edward W. Mullinix	1-Yr. Sales Change: —
Phone: 904-791-4500	HR: John B. Morgan	Employees: 1,300
Fax: 904-791-4699	Type: Private	FYE: December 31
Web: www.thehaskellco.com		

Design-build services lie at the heart of Haskell. The company ranks among the US's top design-build firms, which oversee not only the architectural and engineering design but also the construction of a project. Haskell offers a full portfolio of architectural, engineering, construction, facility management, and real estate services. Projects include industrial, commercial, and institutional facilities. Chairman Preston Haskell founded the employee-owned firm in 1965 and also led the establishment of the Design-Build Institute of America in 1993.

KEY COMPETITORS
BE&K
Hensel Phelps Construction
Turner Corporation

HBE CORPORATION

11330 Olive Street Rd.	CEO: Fred S. Kummer	2001 Sales: $614.0 million
St. Louis, MO 63141	CFO: Gene Kemp	1-Yr. Sales Change: (6.7%)
Phone: 314-567-9000	HR: Kevin Farrell	Employees: 9,100
Fax: 314-567-0602	Type: Private	FYE: December 31
Web: www.hbecorp.com		

HBE derives a healthy business out of designing and building health care facilities. The firm provides planning, architectural, engineering, management, interior design, and construction services throughout the US. Hospital Building & Equipment is the group's chief operating division. HBE also designs and builds financial institutions and hotels and is engaged in the hospitality industry through its ownership of 24 Adam's Mark Hotels & Resorts properties. HBE is owned by chairman, president, and CEO Fred Kummer, who founded the firm as a small construction company in 1960.

KEY COMPETITORS
Marriott International
Pepper Construction
Turner Corporation

HEAFNER TIRE GROUP, INC.

12200 Herbert Wayne Ct., Ste. 150	CEO: Richard P. Johnson	2001 Sales: $1,107.9 million
Huntersville, NC 28078	CFO: William E. Berry	1-Yr. Sales Change: 1.9%
Phone: 704-992-2000	HR: J. David Phillips	Employees: 2,025
Fax: 704-992-1384	Type: Private	FYE: December 31
Web: www.heafnertiregroup.com		

Heafner Tire Group's business starts where the rubber meets the road. The company is the largest independent distributor of tires and related products in the US. Tire brands include industry leaders Michelin and Bridgestone/Firestone as well as Goodyear, which also makes Heafner's Monarch house brand through its Kelly-Springfield subsidiary. Heafner Tire's distribution business is split into four divisions, which operate 65 distribution centers that serve 35 states. To focus on national distribution, Heafner Tire has sold 130 Winston Tire Centers on the West Coast and about 30 T.O. Haas Tire outlets. Charlesbank Equity Fund IV owns more than 96% of the company.

KEY COMPETITORS
Discount Tire
Goodyear
TBC

In-depth profiles of an additional 200
key private companies are found on pages 36–435.

HEALTH INSURANCE PLAN OF GREATER NEW YORK

7 W. 34th St.	CEO: Anthony L. Watson	2000 Sales: $2,409.7 million
New York, NY 10001	CFO: Michael Fullwood	1-Yr. Sales Change: 8.4%
Phone: 212-630-5000	HR: Fred Blickman	Employees: —
Fax: 212-630-8747	Type: Not-for-profit	FYE: December 31
Web: www.hipusa.com		

This firm says it's HIP to be healthy. Health Insurance Plan of Greater New York (HIP) is a not-for-profit HMO founded in the 1940s to provide low-cost health care to New York City employees; HIP now boasts nearly 800,000 members. The organization provides medical, lab, and pharmacy services through some 16,000 physicians and about 100 facilities around New York City. Efforts in the 1990s to expand out-of-state proved disastrous; its New Jersey effort was closed by regulators, and HIP sold its Florida affiliate after accumulating huge losses. Back home, HIP has faced allegations from regulators of lavish executive lifestyles and too-cozy relationships with contractors.

KEY COMPETITORS
Aetna
Oxford Health Plans
WellChoice

HEALTH MIDWEST

2304 E. Meyer Blvd.	CEO: Richard Brown	2000 Sales: $863.8 million
Kansas City, MO 64132	CFO: Thomas Langenberg	1-Yr. Sales Change: (2.3%)
Phone: 816-751-3751	HR: Dennis Johnson	Employees: 12,000
Fax: 816-276-9250	Type: Subsidiary	FYE: December 31
Web: www.healthmidwest.org		

Health Midwest operates about 15 hospitals in the metropolitan Kansas City area. With 2,500 physicians, Health Midwest is not only a huge health care provider, but also a major employer. Services include primary care, rehabilitation, and home health care. Specialized programs include childbirth classes, health screenings, hospice services, and behavioral health services. Health care giant HCA-The Healthcare Company exited the Kansas City area after confronting intense competition from Health Midwest, but HCA recently bought up Health Midwest's hospitals and other assets.

KEY COMPETITORS
Catholic Health Initiatives
Sisters of Charity of
Leavenworth
Triad Hospitals

HENDRICK AUTOMOTIVE GROUP

6000 Monroe Rd.	CEO: Jim C. Perkins	2001 Sales: $2,638.7 million
Charlotte, NC 28212	CFO: James F. Huzl	1-Yr. Sales Change: 6.3%
Phone: 704-568-5550	HR: Tim Taylor	Employees: 4,700
Fax: 704-566-3295	Type: Private	FYE: December 31
Web: www.hendrickauto.com		

For megadealer Hendrick Automotive Group, variety is the spice of life. The company sells new and used cars and light trucks from more than 20 automakers, including General Motors, Honda, and Porsche. Hendrick has a network of more than 50 dealerships in nine states ranging from the Carolinas to California. The company also offers financing, as well as automobile parts, accessories, service, and body repair. Founder Rick Hendrick pleaded guilty in 1997 to mail fraud relating to alleged bribes of American Honda executives; he was later pardoned by President Bill Clinton. Hendrick owns the company, which began in 1976 as a single dealership in Bennettsville, South Carolina.

KEY COMPETITORS
AutoNation
Sonic Automotive
United Auto Group

In-depth profiles of an additional 200 key private companies are found on pages 36–435.

HENKELS & MCCOY, INC.

985 Jolly Rd.
Blue Bell, PA 19422
Phone: 215-283-7600
Fax: 215-283-7659
Web: www.henkelsandmccoy.com

CEO: Kenneth L. Rose
CFO: Robert Delark
HR: Vincent Benedict
Type: Private

2001 Sales: $675.0 million
1-Yr. Sales Change: (9.8%)
Employees: 5,000
FYE: September 30

When utilities and telecommunications companies need the real McCoy to install or repair their transmission networks, they can call on Henkels & McCoy. The specialty contractor provides engineering, construction, and maintenance for electric and gas transmission and distribution firms and communications companies. It installs aerial and underground electrical distribution systems, fiber-optic networks on electric transmission towers or along railroad rights-of-way, and gas transmission lines at sites around the world. It also offers training and storm restoration services. John Henkels Jr. founded the company in 1923 as a tree-trimming and landscaping firm. Employees and the Henkels family own the company.

KEY COMPETITORS
Dycom
MasTec
Quanta Services

HENRY FORD HEALTH SYSTEM

1 Ford Place
Detroit, MI 48202
Phone: 313-876-8700
Fax: 313-876-9243
Web: www.henryfordhealth.org

CEO: Gail L. Warden
CFO: David Mazurkiewicz
HR: Robert Rieny
Type: Not-for-profit

2001 Sales: $2,000.0 million
1-Yr. Sales Change: 5.3%
Employees: 15,000
FYE: December 31

In 1915 automaker Henry Ford founded the hospital that would be the starting point for southeastern Michigan's not-for-profit Henry Ford Health System, a hospital network that is also involved in medical research and education. The system includes six hospitals with about 2,000 beds, more than 30 other health care facilities, and over 2,000 physicians representing a wide range of specialties. The system's Health Alliance Plan provides managed care and health insurance to more than 500,000 members. The Henry Ford Health Sciences Center Research Institute, the Josephine Ford Cancer Center, and other research centers and affiliated hospitals are also part of the health care system.

KEY COMPETITORS
Detroit Medical Center
Trinity Health
William Beaumont Hospital

HENSEL PHELPS CONSTRUCTION CO.

420 6th Ave.
Greeley, CO 80632
Phone: 970-352-6565
Fax: 970-352-9311
Web: www.henselphelps.com

CEO: Jerry L. Morgensen
CFO: Stephen J. Carrico
HR: —
Type: Private

2002 Sales: $1,771.0 million
1-Yr. Sales Change: 29.5%
Employees: 2,200
FYE: May 31

Hensel Phelps Construction builds it all, from the courthouse to the Big House. Launched as a home building firm by Hensel Phelps in 1937, the employee-owned company now focuses on such nonresidential projects as prisons, airport facilities, hotels, government and corporate complexes, convention centers, sport arenas, and department stores. Hensel Phelps offers design/build, construction management, and turnkey services to clients, as well as financing and cost estimates. Through offices in six states, Hensel Phelps operates nationwide. Major clients include ChevronTexaco, IBM, the Pentagon, United Airlines, and Neiman Marcus.

KEY COMPETITORS
Clark Enterprises
PCL Construction
Turner Corporation

In-depth profiles of an additional 200 key private companies are found on pages 36–435.

HERB CHAMBERS COMPANIES

259 McGrath Hwy.
Somerville, MA 02145
Phone: 617-666-8333
Fax: 617-666-8448
Web: www.chamberscars.com

CEO: Herbert G. Chambers
CFO: Bruce Spatz
HR: —
Type: Private

2001 Sales: $987.1 million
1-Yr. Sales Change: 1.3%
Employees: 1,000
FYE: December 31

Step into the chambers of Herb Chambers Companies and you'll find a wide range of cars. The company runs about 20 dealerships in New England that sell just about everthing from pricey new cars from BMW, Cadillac, Lexus, Mercedes-Benz, and Porsche to more affordable offerings from Honda, Hyundai, Kia, Mazda, Saturn, and Toyota; dealerships also offer used cars. All of its cars are available online, and customers can buy a car, sight unseen, via fax, phone, or e-mail, and have the dealer deliver it. Herb Chambers also offers parts and service and online credit applications. Owner and CEO Herb Chambers started his automotive empire with a Cadillac/Oldsmobile dealership in New London, Connecticut, in 1985.

KEY COMPETITORS
AutoNation
Group 1 Automotive
United Auto Group

HINES INTERESTS L.P.

2800 Post Oak Blvd.
Houston, TX 77056
Phone: 713-621-8000
Fax: 713-966-2053
Web: www.hines.com

CEO: Gerald D. Hines
CFO: C. Hastings Johnson
HR: David LeVrier
Type: Private

2001 Est. Sales: $750.0 mil.
1-Yr. Sales Change: 0.0%
Employees: 2,800
FYE: December 31

Hines Interests has been involved in many developments, but none of them include ketchup. Founded by Gerald Hines in 1957, the company is a private commercial real estate development company. Hines handles most aspects of real estate development, including site selection, rezoning, design, construction management, and financing. Its portfolio includes corporate headquarters, industrial facilities, and master-planned resorts and residential communities. Hines also manages almost 80 million sq. ft. of real estate in the US and 11 other countries. Management services include public relations, security, tenant relations, and vendor contract-negotiation services. Hines Interests is controlled by the Hines family.

KEY COMPETITORS
CB Richard Ellis
Jones Lang LaSalle
Trammell Crow

HOBBY LOBBY STORES, INC.

7707 SW 44th St.
Oklahoma City, OK 73179
Phone: 405-745-1100
Fax: 405-745-1636
Web: www.hobbylobby.com

CEO: David Green
CFO: Patrick Jones
HR: Bill Owens
Type: Private

2001 Sales: $1,015.0 million
1-Yr. Sales Change: 12.2%
Employees: 15,000
FYE: December 31

If something wicker this way comes, Hobby Lobby Stores may be the source. The company runs about 280 stores in 24 mostly midwestern states, selling arts and craft supplies, baskets, candles, frames, home decorating accessories, and silk flowers. The #3 craft retailer (after Michaels Stores and Jo-Ann Stores), Hobby Lobby prefers to set up shop in second-generation retail sites (such as vacated supermarkets and Wal-Marts). Sister companies supply Hobby Lobby with merchandise, and products are distributed through a center in Oklahoma City. CEO David Green, who owns the company with his wife, Barbara, founded the company in 1972 and operates it according to biblical principles, including closing stores on Sunday.

KEY COMPETITORS
Garden Ridge
Jo-Ann Stores
Michaels Stores

In-depth profiles of an additional 200 key private companies are found on pages 36–435.

HOFFMAN CORPORATION

805 SW Broadway, Ste. 2100
Portland, OR 97205
Phone: 503-221-8811
Fax: 503-221-8934
Web: www.hoffmancorp.com

CEO: Cecil W. Drinkward
CFO: Scott Fredricks
HR: Sheri Sundstrom
Type: Private

2001 Sales: $1,165.0 million
1-Yr. Sales Change: 22.1%
Employees: 1,200
FYE: December 31

Hoffman cherishes a challenge — such as building the nation's deepest subway station in Portland, Oregon, or the snakelike, metal-clad Experience Music Project in Seattle. The company's main subsidiary, Hoffman Construction, builds civic, commercial, and industrial facilities, primarily in the western and midwestern US. One of the top builders of manufacturing facilities, Hoffman also serves such sectors as education, health care, and power generation. Its in-house abilities include plumbing and high-tech cleanroom process systems (Hoffman Mechanical), substructures and superstructures (Hoffman Structures), and specialty electrical wiring (HT Electric). Employees own the company, which was founded in 1922.

KEY COMPETITORS
Bovis Lend Lease
Skanska
Turner Corporation

HOLIDAY COMPANIES

4567 W. 80th St.
Bloomington, MN 55437
Phone: 952-830-8700
Fax: 952-830-8864
Web: holidaystationstores.com

CEO: Ronald A. Erickson
CFO: Dennis Lindahl
HR: Bob Nye
Type: Private

2001 Est. Sales: $1,300.0 mil.
1-Yr. Sales Change: 8.3%
Employees: 5,500
FYE: December 31

Wholesaling has taken a vacation at Holiday Companies. It sold its Fairway Foods distributions buiness to Fleming Companies in 2000 and now owns convenience stores and sporting good stores in the upper Midwest and Northwest. Holiday Companies owns more than 250 Holiday Stationstores in 11 states and also has 37 franchised stores. These sell gas supplied by the company's Erickson Petroleum subsidiary. It also owns about 55 Gander Mountain sporting goods stores. The company was founded in 1928 as a general store in a small Wisconsin town by two Erickson brothers, whose descendants own and operate the company.

KEY COMPETITORS
7-Eleven
Casey's General Stores
Exxon Mobil

HOLIDAY RETIREMENT CORP.

2250 McGilchrist St. SE, Ste. 200
Salem, OR 97302
Phone: 503-370-7070
Fax: 503-364-5716
Web: www.holidayretirementcorp.com

CEO: William Colson
CFO: Donald Harris
HR: Linda Livermore
Type: Private

2001 Sales: —
1-Yr. Sales Change: —
Employees: 7,500
FYE: December 31

With meal and maid services and organized social activities for their enjoyment, residents of Holiday Retirement communities probably feel like they're on a permanent vacation. The company — with more than 260 facilities in 39 states, Canada, the UK, and France — is a leading retirement community operator in Europe and the US. It has its own property developer (Colson & Colson Construction), architects (Curry-Brandaw), and builders (Colson & Colson General Contractors). Colson & Colson owns the properties, and Holiday Retirement manages them, hiring a few couples to live on-site. The Peverel Group, a wholly owned subsidiary, is a top operator of retirement homes in the UK.

KEY COMPETITORS
Emeritus
Life Care Centers
Nationwide Health Properties

In-depth profiles of an additional 200 key private companies are found on pages 36–435.

HOLMAN ENTERPRISES

7411 Maple Ave.	CEO: Joseph S. Holman	2001 Sales: $2,105.1 million
Pennsauken, NJ 08109	CFO: Robert Campbell	1-Yr. Sales Change: (4.3%)
Phone: 856-663-5200	HR: Paul Toepel	Employees: 2,600
Fax: 856-665-3444	Type: Private	FYE: December 31
Web: www.holmanauto.com		

Holman sells a whole lot of cars. Family-owned Holman Enterprises owns about 20 car and truck dealerships in southern New Jersey and southern Florida. Founded in 1924, Holman sells BMW, Ford, Infiniti, Jaguar, Lincoln, Mercury, Rolls-Royce, and Saturn cars, as well as Ford, Kenworth, and Sterling trucks. The company also offers collision repair services. Holman's RMP engine and parts distributor sells small parts and powertrains authorized by Ford. Its Automotive Resources International unit, one of the largest independently owned vehicle fleet leasing management groups in the world, also operates a truck parts and accessories company.

KEY COMPETITORS
Autonation
Penske
United Auto Group

THE HOLMES GROUP, INC.

One Holmes Way	CEO: Peter J. Martin	2001 Sales: $628.0 million
Milford, MA 01757	CFO: John M. Kelliher	1-Yr. Sales Change: 22.4%
Phone: 508-634-8050	HR: Louis F. Cimini	Employees: 7,500
Fax: 508-634-1211	Type: Private	FYE: December 31
Web: www.holmesproducts.com		

The Holmes Group makes what it takes to condition the air, open canned goods, and slow-cook meals. The company (formerly Holmes Products) makes Bionaire, Holmes, Family Care, Pollenex, and other brands of air purifiers, fans, filters, heaters, and humidifiers. It also offers Rival kitchen appliances, including can openers and Crock-Pots. Holmes' other products include shower heads and massagers, and it distributes decorative lighting products. It has plants in the US and China and sells its goods in Asia, Europe, North America, and South America. Wal-Mart, Kmart, and Target ring up nearly half of Holmes' sales. Investment firm Berkshire Partners owns 74% of Holmes, and founder and chairman Jordan Kahn owns 12%.

KEY COMPETITORS
Honeywell International
NACCO Industries
Sunbeam

HONICKMAN AFFILIATES

8275 Rte. 130	CEO: Jeffrey Honickman	2001 Est. Sales: $1,100.0 mil.
Pennsauken, NJ 08110	CFO: Walt Wilkinson	1-Yr. Sales Change: 12.2%
Phone: 856-665-6200	HR: June Raufer	Employees: 5,000
Fax: 856-661-4684	Type: Private	FYE: December 31

Honickman Affiliates doesn't mind bottling its creative juices. The firm is one of the nation's largest private bottlers — bottling and distributing soft drinks primarily in Maryland, New Jersey, New York, Ohio, and Virginia through more than 10 plants. A major bottler of Pepsi-Cola brands and Cadbury Schweppes brands including 7 UP, it also sells Canada Dry, Mott's, Snapple, and South Beach Beverage Company's SoBe beverages. It distributes Coors beers in New York and brews up private-label soft drinks. Honickman is buying smaller bottlers and is a PepsiCo anchor bottler candidate. Chairman and owner Harold Honickman started the company in 1957 when his father-in-law built a bottling plant for him.

KEY COMPETITORS
Coca-Cola Enterprises
Cott
Philadelphia Coca-Cola

📖 **In-depth profiles of an additional 200 key private companies are found on pages 36–435.**

HORIZON NATURAL RESOURCES COMPANY

2000 Ashland Dr.	CEO: Robert C. Scharp	2001 Sales: $1,413.0 million
Ashland, KY 41101	CFO: Michael Nemser	1-Yr. Sales Change: (5.8%)
Phone: 606-920-7400	HR: Lance G. Sogen	Employees: 4,000
Fax: 606-920-7720	Type: Private	FYE: December 31
Web: www.horizonnr.com		

Horizon Natural Resources (formerly AEI Resources) is one of the US's largest producers of steam (bituminous) coal. The company operates mines in six states. It sells mainly to electric utilities in the eastern US. Horizon's Mining Technologies subsidiary makes Addcar-brand highwall mining equipment, while its Mining Machinery subsidiary provides trucking services, major equipment rebuilds, and mining equipment. Horizon's ties to the founding Addington family were severed as part of a reorganization that bought the company out of bankruptcy in 2002; however, later that year it again filed to reorganize under Chapter 11. Horizon's heavy debt was caused in part by numerous acquisitions during the late 1990s.

KEY COMPETITORS
CONSOL Energy
Massey Energy
Peabody Energy

HORSEHEAD INDUSTRIES INC.

110 E. 59th St.	CEO: William E. Flaherty	2001 Sales: $765.0 million
New York, NY 10022	CFO: Peter W. Nelson	1-Yr. Sales Change: (0.6%)
Phone: 212-527-3000	HR: —	Employees: 2,925
Fax: 212-527-3008	Type: Private	FYE: December 31
Web: www.horseheadinc.com		

Formed by a management-led buyout of Gulf+Western Industries' New Jersey Zinc Company in 1981, Horsehead Industries operates mainly through four subsidiaries. Its Horsehead Resources Development company recovers and recycles leftover zinc from steelmaking operations. Horsehead sells its zinc products through Zinc Corporation of America. Horsehead's Sterling Resources offers environmental consulting services such as remediation design, engineering and production management, and regulatory compliance consulting. Through ZCA Mines, Horsehead is selling its zinc mine in Balmat, New York for $20 million. CEO William Flaherty and other former Gulf+Western executives, along with private investors, control the company.

KEY COMPETITORS
Mitsui Mining & Smelting
Noranda
Teck Cominco

HORSESHOE GAMING HOLDING CORP.

18454 S. West Creek Dr.	CEO: Jack B. Binion	2001 Sales: $933.3 million
Tinley Park, IL 60477	CFO: Kirk C. Saylor	1-Yr. Sales Change: (7.9%)
Phone: 708-429-8300	HR: David S. Carroll	Employees: 7,843
Fax: 708-429-8315	Type: Private	FYE: December 31
Web: www.horseshoegaming.com		

Bring your lucky charms to casinos owned by Horseshoe Gaming Holding Corp. The company owns a Horseshoe Casino and Hotel in Bossier City, Louisiana, as well as one in Tunica, Mississippi. In 2001 Horseshoe Gaming sold its Empress Casino riverboat and hotel in Joliet, Illinois, but it retains an Empress location in Hammond, Indiana. Illinois officials denied the company a license to operate the Empress riverboat in Joliet, alleging that owner and CEO Jack Binion failed to comply with state regulations after buying the casino. The company appealed the decision, but later struck a deal that forced it to sell the location to Argosy Gaming.

KEY COMPETITORS
Casino Magic
Park Place Entertainment
Pinnacle Entertainment

In-depth profiles of an additional 200 key private companies are found on pages 36–435.

HOUCHENS INDUSTRIES INC.

900 Church St.
Bowling Green, KY 42101
Phone: 270-843-3252
Fax: 270-781-6377

CEO: Jim Gipson
CFO: Mark Iverson
HR: Sharon Grooms
Type: Private

2002 Est. Sales: $1,727.0 mil.
1-Yr. Sales Change: 110.6%
Employees: 5,850
FYE: September 30

Houchens Industries operates stores for shoppers more interested in supper than super. Eschewing the industry trend toward massive superstores, the company's 31 Houchens Markets in Kentucky average less than 20,000 sq. ft. Its nearly 200 Save-A-Lot stores (licensed from SUPERVALU) offer limited selections and cover 15,000 sq. ft. or less. Houchens has stores in 13 states from eastern Texas to New York. The company also owns more than 40 Jr. Foods convenience stores and 23 Tobacco Shoppe discount cigarette outlets, mostly in Kentucky and Tennessee. It bought cigarette maker Commonwealth Brands in 2001. Founded as BG Wholesale in 1918 by Ervin Houchens, the company is entirely owned by its employees.

KEY COMPETITORS
K-VA-T Food Stores
Kroger
Winn-Dixie

H.P. HOOD INC.

90 Everett Ave.
Chelsea, MA 02150
Phone: 617-887-3000
Fax: 617-887-8484
Web: www.hphood.com

CEO: John A. Kaneb
CFO: Gary R. Kaneb
HR: Bruce W. Bacon
Type: Private

2001 Sales: $800.0 million
1-Yr. Sales Change: 14.3%
Employees: 1,600
FYE: December 31

H.P. Hood is busily trying to cream its competition — with ice cream, sour cream, and whipping cream. The company, one of New England's leading dairies, also produces milk, cottage cheese, and juices. Besides its own brands, H.P. Hood makes private-label, licensed, and franchise products. It specializes in extended shelf-life products which are distributed nationally under licensing agreements. The company has plants in Connecticut, Maine, Massachusetts, New York, Vermont, and Virginia. Founded in 1846 by Harvey P. Hood as a one-man milk-delivery service, H.P. Hood still offers home delivery. The family of CEO John Kaneb owns the company.

KEY COMPETITORS
Dean Foods
Parmalat North America
Unilever

H.T. HACKNEY CO.

502 S. Gay St.
Knoxville, TN 37902
Phone: 865-546-1291
Fax: 865-546-1501
Web: www.hthackney.com

CEO: William B. Sansom
CFO: Mike Morton
HR: —
Type: Private

2001 Sales: $2,500.0 million
1-Yr. Sales Change: 8.7%
Employees: 3,100
FYE: December 31

The H.T. Hackney Company began delivering goods to small grocers by horse and buggy in 1891; it now supplies more than 30,000 independent grocers and convenience stores in about 20 states east of the Mississippi. H.T. Hackney distributes more than 25,000 items, including frozen food, tobacco products, health and beauty items, and deli products. In addition, it owns Tennessee-based Natural Springs Water Group, has furniture-making operations (Volunteer Fabricators), and distributes petroleum through its Hackney Petroleum division. Looking to expand its convenience store business, in September 2000 the company acquired six gas stations from Aztex Enterprises. Chairman and CEO Bill Sansom owns H.T. Hackney.

KEY COMPETITORS
Eby-Brown
GSC Enterprises
McLane

📖 In-depth profiles of an additional 200 key private companies are found on pages 36–435.

HUBBARD BROADCASTING INC.

3415 University Ave.	CEO: Stanley S. Hubbard	2001 Est. Sales: $600.0 mil.
St. Paul, MN 55114	CFO: Ronald Lindwall	1-Yr. Sales Change: 0.0%
Phone: 651-646-5555	HR: Suzanne Cook	Employees: 1,344
Fax: 651-642-4172	Type: Private	FYE: December 31

This Hubbard's cupboard is stuffed with broadcasting treats. Hubbard Broadcasting owns eight TV stations and three radio stations, mainly in Minnesota and New York. Hubbard Broadcasting also owns Conus Communications (satellite news gathering) and TV production companies such as Diamond P. Sports. Since selling its 51% stake in United States Satellite Broadcasting (USSB) to Hughes Electronics (DIRECTV) in 1999 for $1.25 billion, Hubbard has launched several satellite and cable channels of its own, like the All News Channel and Moviewatch. Late founder Stanley E. Hubbard started his broadcasting empire when he launched Minneapolis radio station WAMD in 1923. Hubbard's family still owns the company.

KEY COMPETITORS
Clear Channel
Granite Broadcasting
Sinclair Broadcast Group

HUDSON NEWS COMPANY

1305 Paterson Plank Rd.	CEO: James Cohen	2001 Est. Sales: $600.0 mil.
North Bergen, NJ 07047	CFO: Catherine Oberg	1-Yr. Sales Change: 0.4%
Phone: 201-867-3600	HR: Cynthia Simmons	Employees: 2,225
Fax: 201-867-0067	Type: Private	FYE: December 31
Web: www.hudsongroupusa.com		

As a large wholesale distributor and retailer of magazines and books in the New York area, Hudson News Company has been keeping people up-to-date on current events for years. The company distributes *Talk*, *Business Week*, and other publications. The company's retail business, Hudson Group, operates more than 200 newsstands, cafes, and specialty shops, mainly in East Coast airports and train stations. Hudson News sold its Metropolitan News Company and its holdings in the Newark Newsdealer Supply Company (which handled about half of the circulation of *The New York Times*) to The New York Times Company in 1992. Formerly Hudson County News, the firm was renamed in 1997. Hudson News is owned by chairman Robert Cohen.

KEY COMPETITORS
Chas. Levy
Ingram Industries
WH Smith USA Travel Retail

HUNT CONSOLIDATED INC.

Fountain Place 1445 Ross at Field, Ste. 1400	CEO: Ray L. Hunt	2001 Sales: $1,500.0 million
Dallas, TX 75202	CFO: Donald Robillard	1-Yr. Sales Change: (25.0%)
Phone: 214-978-8000	HR: Jim Clark	Employees: 2,600
Fax: 214-978-8888	Type: Private	FYE: December 31

Hunt Consolidated is a holding company for the oil and real estate businesses of Ray Hunt, son of legendary Texas wildcatter and company founder H.L. Hunt. Founded in 1934 (reportedly with H.L.'s poker winnings), Hunt Oil is an oil and gas production and exploration company with primary interests in North and South America. Hoping to repeat huge discoveries in Yemen, Hunt is exploring in Canada, Ghana, Madagascar, and Oman. It has also teamed up with Repsol YPF and S.K. Corp. on an exploration project in Peru, and has expanded its Canadian operations through the acquisition of Chieftain International. Hunt Realty handles commercial and residential real estate development and investment management activities.

KEY COMPETITORS
BP
Exxon Mobil
Lincoln Property

📖 In-depth profiles of an additional 200
key private companies are found on pages 36–435.

HUNT CONSTRUCTION GROUP

2450 S. Tibbs Ave.	CEO: Robert G. Hunt	2001 Sales: $1,811.0 million
Indianapolis, IN 46241	CFO: Steve Atkins	1-Yr. Sales Change: 33.9%
Phone: 317-227-7800	HR: —	Employees: 850
Fax: 317-227-7810	Type: Private	FYE: December 31
Web: www.huntconstructiongroup.com		

Hunt Construction Group knows that if they build it, you will come. A private company held by Hunt Corporation of Scottsdale, Arizona, the construction firm is a leading builder of sports complexes, from the old Three Rivers Stadium to the new Pittsburgh Steelers Stadium complex. The company's portfolio also includes aviation facilities, convention centers, corporate office buildings, government buildings, hospitals, hotels, industrial operations, research development centers, and universities. Founded in 1944 as Huber, Hunt & Nichols, the group changed its name in 2000 to more accurately reflect the ownership of the corporation, which is now under its third generation of Hunt leadership.

KEY COMPETITORS
Barton Malow
Gilbane
Turner Corporation

HY-VEE, INC.

5820 Westown Pkwy.	CEO: Ronald D. Pearson	2002 Est. Sales: $4,100.0 mil.
West Des Moines, IA 50266	CFO: John Briggs	1-Yr. Sales Change: 5.1%
Phone: 515-267-2800	HR: Jane Knaack-Esbeck	Employees: 46,000
Fax: 515-267-2817	Type: Private	FYE: September 30
Web: www.hy-vee.com		

Give Hy-Vee a high five for being one of the largest privately owned US supermarket chains, despite serving some modestly sized midwestern towns. The company runs more than 200 Hy-Vee supermarkets in Illinois, Iowa, Kansas, Minnesota, Missouri, Nebraska, and South Dakota. About half of its supermarkets are in Iowa, as are most of its 25-plus Drug Town drugstores. It distributes products to its stores through several subsidiaries, including Lomar Distributing (specialty foods), Perishable Distributors of Iowa (fresh foods), and Florist Distributing (flowers). Charles Hyde and David Vredenburg founded the employee-owned firm in 1930. The company's moniker is a combination of the founders' names.

KEY COMPETITORS
Albertson's
Eagle Food
Fareway Stores

IASIS HEALTHCARE CORPORATION

113 Seaboard Ln., Ste. A200	CEO: David R. White	2002 Sales: $949.9 million
Franklin, TN 37067	CFO: W. Carl Whitmer	1-Yr. Sales Change: 6.8%
Phone: 615-844-2747	HR: Russ Follis	Employees: 8,000
Fax: 615-846-3006	Type: Private	FYE: September 30
Web: www.iasishealthcare.com		

If you're sick in the suburbs, IASIS Healthcare provides a medical oasis. Formed largely from castoffs of hospital operators Tenet Healthcare and Paracelsus Healthcare (now Clarent Hospital Corporation) and a series of management buyouts in 1999, the company owns and operates 14 hospitals in Arizona, Florida, Texas and Utah. IASIS also operates four outpatient surgical centers, and Health Choice, a Medicaid-managed health plan that serves nearly 60,000 individuals in Arizona. Private equity firm Joseph Littlejohn & Levy owns more than 85% of the company.

KEY COMPETITORS
HCA
Tenet Healthcare
Triad Hospitals

📖 In-depth profiles of an additional 200
key private companies are found on pages 36–435.

ICC INDUSTRIES INC.

460 Park Ave.	CEO: John Oram	2001 Sales: $1,600.0 million
New York, NY 10022	CFO: Susan Abinder	1-Yr. Sales Change: 23.1%
Phone: 212-521-1700	HR: Frances Foti	Employees: 3,200
Fax: 212-521-1970	Type: Private	FYE: December 31
Web: www.iccchem.com		

ICC Industries keeps pharmaceutical companies supplied with the raw materials used in manufacturing drugs. An international maker and marketer of chemicals, plastics, and pharmaceutical products, ICC also trades and distributes nutritional supplements and food ingredients. Its main subsidiary, ICC Chemical Corporation, maintains trading and marketing offices in Asia, Europe, South America, and the US. The company's Prior Energy Corporation has natural gas distribution interests in several southern states. ICC Industries also owns nearly 90% of Pharmaceutical Formulations, a manufacturer and distributor of generic over-the-counter drugs. The Farber family, including chairman John Farber, owns ICC.

KEY COMPETITORS
Formosa Plastics
IFF
IVAX

ICON HEALTH & FITNESS, INC.

1500 S. 1000 West	CEO: Scott R. Watterson	2002 Sales: $896.1 million
Logan, UT 84321	CFO: S. Fred Beck	1-Yr. Sales Change: 5.4%
Phone: 435-750-5000	HR: Doug Younker	Employees: 5,000
Fax: 435-750-3917	Type: Private	FYE: May 31
Web: www.iconfitness.com		

ICON Health & Fitness has brawn as the leading US maker of home fitness equipment. ICON's products include treadmills, elliptical trainers, and weight benches. Brands include Weider, HealthRider, IMAGE, NordicTrack, ProForm, JumpKing, Weslo, and the licensed Reebok name. ICON also offers fitness accessories, spas, and commercial fitness equipment. It makes most of its products in Utah and sells them through retailers, infomercials, the Web, and its catalog, Workout Warehouse. Sears has an exclusive license to sell NordicTrack-brand apparel. Bain Capital, Credit Suisse, and founders Scott Watterson and Gary Stevenson collectively own more than 90% of ICON. The company intends to license its brand names to other manufacturers.

KEY COMPETITORS
Brunswick
Cybex International
Guthy-Renker

INDIANA UNIVERSITY

107 S. Indiana Ave.	CEO: Myles Brand	2001 Sales: $1,782.5 million
Bloomington, IN 47405	CFO: Judith G. Palmer	1-Yr. Sales Change: 7.5%
Phone: 812-855-4848	HR: Daniel Rives	Employees: 16,070
Fax: 812-855-7002	Type: School	FYE: June 30
Web: www.indiana.edu		

Indiana University has been educating residents of the Hoosier state since being founded in 1820. With a total student population exceeding 96,200, the university has eight campuses including flagship institution IU-Bloomington and seven commuter campuses in Fort Wayne, Gary, Indianapolis, Kokomo, New Albany, Richmond, and South Bend. IU-Bloomington offers students more than 100 academic programs in more than a dozen schools. Its graduate schools offer advanced degrees in a variety of areas ranging from business to music to law. IU-Bloomington also is home to a string of centers and institutes including the Advanced Research & Technology Institute and the Center for International Business Education and Research.

📖 **In-depth profiles of an additional 200 key private companies are found on pages 36–435.**

INDUCTOTHERM INDUSTRIES, INC.

10 Indel Ave.	CEO: Henry M. Rowan	2002 Est. Sales: $700.0 mil.
Rancocas, NJ 08073	CFO: Frank D. Manley	1-Yr. Sales Change: (4.8%)
Phone: 609-267-9000	HR: David L. Braddock	Employees: 5,000
Fax: 609-267-5705	Type: Private	FYE: April 30
Web: www.inductothermindustries.com		

The heat is on at Inductotherm Industries, the parent of an international group of more than 50 engineering and technology companies that produce a variety of products, primarily for the metals industry. Inductotherm is a leading maker of induction-heating equipment, with more than 10,000 units installed worldwide. Group companies produce welding equipment, electrical components, electronics, engineered products, metal components, and plastic products. Services range from metals fabrication to silkscreen printing. Chairman and majority owner Hank Rowan (namesake of New Jersey's Rowan University) and his late wife Betty financed the company's startup in 1953 from the sale of their home.

KEY COMPETITORS
Astronics
Milacron
SPX

INGERSOLL INTERNATIONAL INC.

707 Fulton Ave.	CEO: Andries Ruijssenaars	2001 Est. Sales: $600.0 mil.
Rockford, IL 61103	CFO: William Shannon	1-Yr. Sales Change: 0.0%
Phone: 815-987-6000	HR: Patrick Winn	Employees: 3,500
Fax: 815-987-6725	Type: Private	FYE: November 30
Web: www.ingersoll.com		

Ingersoll International cuts to the chase — or at least through the metal. One of the US's top machine tool companies, Ingersoll supplies machine tools, manufacturing systems, and metal-cutting tools to the metalworking, transportation, construction, agriculture, and power-generation industries worldwide. Its products include drills, boring tools, crankshaft-broaching tools, saws, and automated transfer lines that produce engine parts. Ingersoll produces about 60% of its machines in the US and the rest in Germany. The company was founded in 1887 by Winthrop Ingersoll and is owned by his heirs. One grandson, Robert Gaylord Jr., is seeking to block the company's sale of two subsidiaries to Israeli firm Iscar.

KEY COMPETITORS
Giddings & Lewis
Greenfield Industries
Milacron

INGRAM ENTERTAINMENT HOLDINGS INC.

2 Ingram Blvd.	CEO: David B. Ingram	2001 Sales: $871.0 million
La Vergne, TN 37089	CFO: William D. Daniel	1-Yr. Sales Change: (17.6%)
Phone: 615-287-4000	HR: Andy Grossberg	Employees: 928
Fax: 615-287-4982	Type: Private	FYE: December 31
Web: www.ingramentertainment.com		

Companies selling books and CDs might get the star treatment, but Ingram Entertainment Holdings doesn't mind its supporting role. Ingram is the #1 independent video, DVD, and computer game distributor in the US. It also distributes software, audio books, electronics, and used videos and games. From 22 US locations, Ingram serves more than 10,000 video stores, mass retailers, e-tailers, drugstores, and supermarkets (including Blockbuster, Tower Records, and Walgreens). Ingram offers direct-to-consumer fulfillment services for e-commerce sites and has a majority stake in ad agency Frank, Best & Ingram. Chairman David Ingram owns 95% of Ingram Entertainment, which was spun off from family-owned Ingram Industries in 1997.

KEY COMPETITORS
Alliance Entertainment
Baker & Taylor
Handleman

📖 In-depth profiles of an additional 200
key private companies are found on pages 36–435.

THE INLAND GROUP, INC.

2901 Butterfield Rd.
Oak Brook, IL 60523
Phone: 630-218-8000
Fax: 630-218-4957
Web: www.inlandgroup.com

CEO: Daniel L. Goodwin
CFO: Alan Kremin
HR: Barbara White
Type: Private

2001 Sales: $685.0 million
1-Yr. Sales Change: 0.0%
Employees: —
FYE: June 30

This company's in land, and not just because it's in the Midwest. The Inland Group invests in apartments, land, and "big box" retail buildings. Other operations include brokerage, mortgage financing, property management, syndication, and development, as well as a venture capital lending program for commercial and multifamily properties. Inland is one of the largest landholders in the Chicago metropolitan area, selling and leasing primarily commercial and retail space. It also operates Inland Retail Real Estate Trust, a commercial REIT. In 1967 teacher Daniel Goodwin (CEO) teamed up with three friends (also teachers) and pooled $1,000 to start the group.

KEY COMPETITORS
Jones Lang LaSalle
Lincoln Property
Trammell Crow Residential

INOVA HEALTH SYSTEM

2990 Telestar Ct.
Falls Church, VA 22042
Phone: 703-289-2000
Fax: 703-205-2161
Web: www.inova.org

CEO: Knox Singleton
CFO: Richard Magenheimer
HR: Ellen Menard
Type: Not-for-profit

2000 Sales: $1,009.4 million
1-Yr. Sales Change: 4.8%
Employees: 13,000
FYE: December 31

Inova keeps NoVa healthy. Founded in 1956 as a country hospital in Fairfax, Virginia, Inova Health System is a not-for-profit health care provider, offering acute care, long-term care, home health care, mental health, and satellite emergency care services in the North Virginia suburbs of Washington, DC. Inova's network includes five hospitals (including a children's hospital) with about 1,400 beds, as well as assisted living centers for seniors and several family practice locations. Through the Inova Health System Foundation, the company coordinates philanthropy programs for the community.

KEY COMPETITORS
HCA
Johns Hopkins Medicine
MedStar

INSERRA SUPERMARKETS, INC.

20 Ridge Rd.
Mahwah, NJ 07430
Phone: 201-529-5900
Fax: 201-529-1189

CEO: Lawrence R. Inserra
CFO: Theresa Inserra
HR: Marie Larson
Type: Private

2001 Sales: $800.0 million
1-Yr. Sales Change: (4.1%)
Employees: 3,900
FYE: December 31

The Big Apple need never be short of apples (or oranges, for that matter) thanks to Inserra Supermarkets. Inserra owns and operates about 20 ShopRite supermarkets and superstores in northern New Jersey and southeastern New York State (most are in the Rockland county area). Inserra's superstores feature bagel bakeries, cafes, and pharmacies. The company also offers banking services in selected stores through agreements with Poughkeepsie Savings Bank, Statewide Savings Bank, and others. Owned by the Inserra family, the retailer is one of 40-plus members that make up cooperative Wakefern Food, the owner of the ShopRite name.

KEY COMPETITORS
A&P
Kings Super Markets
Royal Ahold

📖 In-depth profiles of an additional 200
key private companies are found on pages 36–435.

INTELSAT, LTD.

3400 International Dr. NW
Washington, DC 20008
Phone: 202-944-6800
Fax: 202-944-7890
Web: www.intelsat.com

CEO: Conny L. Kullman
CFO: Joseph Corbett
HR: Benjamin Katcoff
Type: Private

2001 Sales: $1,084.0 million
1-Yr. Sales Change: (1.2%)
Employees: 850
FYE: December 31

Intelsat's geostationary satellites enjoy a bird's-eye view of earth. The former International Telecommunications Satellite Organization, set up by governments around the world in 1964, reorganized in 2001 as a private company and by the end of 2003 plans to conduct a US public offering. Intelsat is owned by the telecom companies that are its major customers, accounting for more than 75% of sales. The Intelsat system provides Internet, broadcast, telephony, and corporate network services worldwide. Intelsat is upgrading its satellite fleet, which it plans to expand to 24 by 2003, and it is developing a terrestrial infrastructure to complement its "birds." Lockheed Martin owns a 24% stake in the company.

KEY COMPETITORS
Eutelsat
Hughes Electronics
SES GLOBAL

INTERACTIVE BROKERS GROUP LLC

1 Pickwick Plaza
Greenwich, CT 06830
Phone: 203-618-5700
Fax: 203-618-5770
Web: www.interactivebrokers.com

CEO: Thomas Peterffy
CFO: Paul Brody
HR: Tammy Silby
Type: Private

2001 Sales: $746.0 million
1-Yr. Sales Change: 5.5%
Employees: 479
FYE: December 31

Interactive Brokers Group provides brokerage services for investors interested in trading on world markets. The company daily executes more than 200,000 trades in stocks, options, futures, and foreign exchange. Customers may trade on 45 different markets located in 16 countries. The company caters to both individual and institutional investors, who execute their trades through the Internet or their home computer via the company's IB Trader Workstation software. The firm's affiliate, Timber Hill LLC, acts as a market maker. Interactive Brokers Group is owned by chairman Thomas Peterffy.

KEY COMPETITORS
ICAP
Jefferies Group
William Blair

INTERLINE BRANDS, INC.

303 Harper Dr.
Moorestown, NJ 08057
Phone: 856-439-1222
Fax: 856-439-1333
Web: www.wilmar.com

CEO: Michael J. Grebe
CFO: William E. Sanford
HR: Annette A. Ricciuti
Type: Private

2001 Sales: $609.0 million
1-Yr. Sales Change: 2.0%
Employees: 2,200
FYE: December 31

When something breaks, bursts, or drips, you can call Interline Brands (formerly Wilmar Industries), a national distributor of repair and maintenance products. The firm sells plumbing, hardware, electrical, janitorial, and related products under private labels (Wilmar and Wilflo) as well as brand names. It uses a direct salesforce, telephone sales, and direct mailings. The company more than doubled its size in October 2000 with its purchase of plumbing supplier Barnett (Premier, ProPlus, Barnett, Rx, U.S. Lock, and Legend brands). Interline Brands runs about 60 distribution centers in the US. Investment firm Parthenon Capital and an investor group including management bought the firm in May 2000.

KEY COMPETITORS
Hughes Supply
Noland
Wolseley

📖 **In-depth profiles of an additional 200 key private companies are found on pages 36–435.**

INTERMOUNTAIN HEALTH CARE, INC.

36 S. State St.
Salt Lake City, UT 84111
Phone: 801-442-2000
Fax: 801-442-3327
Web: www.ihc.com

CEO: William H. Nelson
CFO: Everett Goodwin
HR: Phyllis A. Domm
Type: Not-for-profit

2001 Sales: $2,652.3 million
1-Yr. Sales Change: 3.9%
Employees: 23,000
FYE: December 31

Intermountain Health Care (IHC) is a not-for-profit health care organization operating more than 20 hospitals, 16 home health care agencies, an air ambulance service, and some 75 physician and urgent care clinics in Utah and Idaho. IHC has affiliations with more than 2,000 physicians, including about 400 in its IHC Physician Group. IHC Health Plans offers health insurance programs to large and small employers. The company was formed in 1975 when the Church of Jesus Christ of Latter Day Saints (the Mormons) decided to donate 15 of its hospitals to the communities they served.

KEY COMPETITORS
HCA
IASIS Healthcare
Trinity Health

INVESTORS MANAGEMENT CORP.

5151 Glenwood Ave.
Raleigh, NC 27612
Phone: 919-781-9310
Fax: 919-881-4686
Web: www.goldencorral.net

CEO: Ted Fowler
CFO: Richard Urquhart
HR: Paul Weber
Type: Private

2001 Sales: $1,030.0 million
1-Yr. Sales Change: 6.4%
Employees: 16,500
FYE: December 31

Investors Management Corporation hopes you'll join them in an eat-out at the Golden Corral. The holding company has more than 470 Golden Corral family-style restaurants (about 75% are franchised, the rest company-owned) in some 40 states. The restaurants offer hot meats, pasta, pizza, and fresh vegetables on the trademark 140-item Golden Choice Buffet, which averages about $6 a plate. Golden Corral restaurants also feature a steak menu, as well as a Brass Bell Bakery, which serves fresh pastries and baked goods every fifteen minutes. Founded in 1973 by chairman James Maynard, Golden Corral is one of the nation's largest family-style restaurant chains.

KEY COMPETITORS
Buffets
Denny's
Ryan's Family Steak Houses

J. CREW GROUP, INC.

770 Broadway
New York, NY 10003
Phone: 212-209-2500
Fax: 212-209-2666
Web: www.jcrew.com

CEO: Kenneth S. Pilot
CFO: Scott M. Rosen
HR: David F. Kozel
Type: Private

2002 Sales: $777.9 million
1-Yr. Sales Change: (5.8%)
Employees: 7,800
FYE: January 31

The crews depicted in the flashy catalogs of the J. Crew Group are far from motley. 60% of J. Crew's sales come from classic-styled jeans, khakis, and other basic (but pricey) items sold to young professionals through its catalogs and Web site and in about 175 retail and factory outlets in the US. It also has about 60 outlets in Japan through a joint venture with Itochu. Asian contractors produce about 80% of the company's merchandise. Texas Pacific Group owns more than 60% of J. Crew; Emily Cinader Woods, daughter of founder Arthur Cinader, owns nearly 20%.

KEY COMPETITORS
The Gap
L.L. Bean
Lands' End

📖 In-depth profiles of an additional 200 key private companies are found on pages 36–435.

JEA

21 W. Church St.	CEO: Walter P. Bussells	2001 Sales: $983.2 million
Jacksonville, FL 32202	CFO: Ronald M. Baker	1-Yr. Sales Change: 5.3%
Phone: 904-665-6000	HR: Joan Clark	Employees: 2,318
Fax: 904-665-7008	Type: Government-owned	FYE: September 30
Web: www.jea.com		

As long as sparks are flying in Jacksonville, everything is A-OK with JEA. The municipal utility provides electricity to more than 360,000 customers in Jacksonville and parts of three adjacent counties in Florida. Established in 1895, JEA has a generating capacity of 2,825 MW (about 53% of its power is derived from coal-fired plants). The company also resells electricity to other utilities, including FPL, which accounts for 15% of electricity sales. JEA also provides water and wastewater services; it serves 198,000 water customers from 100 wells and 32 treatment plants and 147,000 wastewater customers with six regional treatment plants.

KEY COMPETITORS
FPL
Florida Public Utilities
United Water Resources

JELD-WEN, INC.

401 Harbor Isles Blvd.	CEO: Roderick C. Wendt	2001 Est. Sales: $2,000.0 mil.
Klamath Falls, OR 97601	CFO: Brent Cap	1-Yr. Sales Change: 0.0%
Phone: 541-882-3451	HR: Eileen Harris	Employees: 20,000
Fax: 541-885-7454	Type: Private	FYE: December 31
Web: www.jeld-wen.com		

JELD-WEN can improve your outlook — whether it's by providing new windows for your home, or by offering accommodations at a scenic resort. A leading maker of windows and doors, JELD-WEN owns more than 150 companies in the Americas, Asia, and Europe. These companies manufacture such products as interior and exterior doors, garage doors, door frames, moldings, windows, and patio doors. JELD-WEN also sells time-shares at resorts such as Oregon's Eagle Crest and Running Y Ranch. The company's other interests include specialty wood products (including wood pellets used in fireplaces), real estate, marketing communications, and education. Chairman Richard Wendt and his siblings founded JELD-WEN in 1960.

KEY COMPETITORS
Andersen Corporation
Nortek
Pella

J.F. SHEA CO., INC.

655 Brea Canyon Rd.	CEO: John F. Shea	2001 Sales: $1,968.0 million
Walnut, CA 91789	CFO: James G. Shontere	1-Yr. Sales Change: 5.6%
Phone: 909-594-9500	HR: Howard Hulme	Employees: 2,288
Fax: 909-594-0935	Type: Private	FYE: December 31
Web: www.jfshea.com		

J.F. Shea helped construct the Washington, DC, subway system, the Golden Gate Bridge, and the Hoover Dam, and now it wants to build your house. Its Shea Homes division builds single-family houses and planned communities, mainly for move-up buyers. J.F. Shea also manages apartments and commercial buildings. The company's Heavy Construction division specializes in underground projects, including dams, pipelines, and tunnels, and its Redding division produces gravel, asphalt, and concrete products. J.F. Shea's proposed buyout of Sun City developer Del Webb in 2000 was rebuffed (rival Pulte bought Del Webb the next year). Founded as a plumbing company in 1876, J.F. Shea is still owned by the Shea family.

KEY COMPETITORS
KB Home
Pulte Homes
Tutor-Saliba

📖 In-depth profiles of an additional 200
key private companies are found on pages 36–435.

JIM KOONS AUTOMOTIVE COS.

2000 Chain Bridge Rd.
Vienna, VA 22182
Phone: 703-356-0400
Fax: 703-442-5765
Web: www.koons.com

CEO: James E. Koons
CFO: Ed Waugh
HR: Ed Waugh
Type: Private

2001 Sales: $992.6 million
1-Yr. Sales Change: 5.5%
Employees: 1,400
FYE: December 31

Wheelin' and dealin' on the Web, Jim Koons Automotive sells new and used cars the old-fashioned way and through the Internet. Its 15 locations in the Washington, DC, area (Virginia and Maryland) offer cars made by Daimler-Chrysler, Ford, GM, Mazda, Toyota, and Volvo. Three locations specialize in used cars. Internet customers can select new car options, obtain quotes, make appointments for parts and service, and access online coupons for oil changes and other services. President Jim Koons' father, John Koons Sr., the first auto dealer to enter the Automotive Hall of Fame, founded the company in 1964. The Koons family owns the company.

KEY COMPETITORS
Brown Automotive
Ourisman Automotive
Rosenthal Automotive

J. M. HUBER CORPORATION

333 Thornall St.
Edison, NJ 08837
Phone: 732-549-8600
Fax: 732-549-2239
Web: www.huber.com

CEO: Peter T. Francis
CFO: Philip Betsch
HR: Gary Crowell
Type: Private

2001 Est. Sales: $1,700.0 mil.
1-Yr. Sales Change: 66.3%
Employees: 5,000
FYE: December 31

Toothpaste, paint, and tires — J. M. Huber claims to make them even better. Founded in 1883 by Joseph Maria Huber (and still owned by his heirs), the company makes specialty additives and minerals used to thicken and improve the cleaning properties of toothpaste, the brightness and gloss of paper, the strength and durability of rubber, and the flame retardant properties of wire and cable. The diverse company also makes oriented strand board (a plywood substitute). Huber manages a half-million acres of timberland in Maine and the southeastern US, and explores for and produces oil and gas in Texas, Colorado, Wyoming, and Utah.

KEY COMPETITORS
Baker Hughes
Georgia-Pacific Corporation
Minerals Technologies

JMB REALTY CORPORATION

900 N. Michigan Ave., Ste. 1100
Chicago, IL 60611
Phone: 312-440-4800
Fax: 312-915-2310

CEO: Rigel Barber
CFO: Steve Lovelett
HR: Gail Silver
Type: Private

2001 Est. Sales: $1,000.0 mil.
1-Yr. Sales Change: 0.0%
Employees: —
FYE: December 31

JMB wants to make State Street a great street again and bring glitter back to the Steel City's Golden Triangle. A major US commercial real estate investment firm, JMB Realty owns, develops, and manages real estate projects throughout North America, including regional malls, hotels, planned communities, and office complexes. JMB is heavily involved in ambitious retail developments in Chicago's Loop and downtown Pittsburgh. JMB was founded in 1968 by Robert Judelson, Judd Malkin, and Neil Bluhm; Judelson (the "J" of JMB) is no longer involved with JMB, but Malkin remains as chairman and Bluhm is president.

KEY COMPETITORS
DeBartolo
Lincoln Property
Trammell Crow

In-depth profiles of an additional 200
key private companies are found on pages 36–435.

JOHN PAUL MITCHELL SYSTEMS

9701 Wilshire Blvd., Ste. 1205	CEO: John Paul DeJoria	2001 Sales: $600.0 million
Beverly Hills, CA 90212	CFO: Rick Battaglini	1-Yr. Sales Change: 0.0%
Phone: 310-248-3888	HR: Luke Jacobellis	Employees: 100
Fax: 310-248-2780	Type: Private	FYE: December 31
Web: www.paulmitchell.com		

From pomades to pompadours, John Paul Mitchell Systems does 'dos. The #1 privately owned hair care firm in the US makes over 90 different hair care products that sell in more than 100,000 hair salons worldwide. John Paul Mitchell was founded in Hawaii in 1980 by John Paul "J. P." DeJoria and the late Paul Mitchell. The company's signature white bottles with distinctive black lettering have attracted the attention of counterfeiters on more than one occasion. Chairman and CEO DeJoria, a former gang member who sports a black ponytail and beard (and is seen in company TV commercials), is a vocal supporter for consumer product safety.

KEY COMPETITORS
L'Oréal
Revlon
Unilever

THE JOHNS HOPKINS UNIVERSITY

3400 N. Charles St.	CEO: William R. Brody	2001 Sales: $2,100.0 million
Baltimore, MD 21218	CFO: James T. McGill	1-Yr. Sales Change: 5.0%
Phone: 410-516-8000	HR: Audrey Smith	Employees: 28,000
Fax: —	Type: School	FYE: June 30
Web: www.jhu.edu		

Founded in 1876 with a $7 million bequest from its namesake, The Johns Hopkins University established its reputation from the beginning by molding itself in the image of a European research institution. While renowned for its School of Medicine, the private university offers eight academic divisions spanning fields of study including business, engineering, and music. Its some 18,000 students and 2,600 full-time faculty members are scattered across campuses in the Baltimore and Washington, DC, areas, as well as at international programs in Nanjing, China; Bologna, Italy; and Florence, Italy.

JONES, DAY, REAVIS & POGUE

Northpoint, 901 Lakeside Ave.	CEO: Patrick F. McCartan	2001 Sales: $790.0 million
Cleveland, OH 44114	CFO: Derald Hunt	1-Yr. Sales Change: 17.0%
Phone: 216-586-3939	HR: Julie Dressing	Employees: —
Fax: 216-579-0212	Type: Partnership	FYE: December 31
Web: www.jonesday.com		

Legal leviathan Jones, Day, Reavis & Pogue ranks as one of the world's largest law firms, providing counsel to about half of the *FORTUNE* 500 companies. It has more than 1,600 attorneys in some two dozen offices across the US, as well as in Asia and Europe. The firm's practice groups include litigation, tax, government regulation, and business. Jones, Day has counted Bridgestone/Firestone, General Motors, IBM, RJR Nabisco, and Texas Instruments among its top clients. Other notable clients include America Online, Aventis, and BP Amoco. The firm traces its roots to the Cleveland law partnership founded by Edwin Blandin and William Rice in 1893.

KEY COMPETITORS
Baker & McKenzie
Clifford Chance
Skadden, Arps

📖 **In-depth profiles of an additional 200 key private companies are found on pages 36–435.**

THE JORDAN AUTOMOTIVE GROUP

609 E. Jefferson Blvd.	CEO: Craig Kapson	2000 Est. Sales: $2,000.0 mil.
Mishawaka, IN 46545	CFO: George Merryman	1-Yr. Sales Change: 0.0%
Phone: 574-259-1981	HR: Cheryl Scialpi	Employees: 200
Fax: 574-254-7552	Type: Private	FYE: December 31
Web: www.jordanauto.com		

Jordan Automotive scores points for being one of the nation's largest Ford dealers and one of the largest fleet dealers. The family-owned company runs six franchises in Indiana that sell new and used vehicles, including Ford, Toyota, Volvo, Mitsubishi, Lincoln-Mercury, and Kia models. It also has parts and service departments. Jordan Automotive's fleet business, Jordan Fleet Sales, provides flatbeds, dump trucks, construction trucks, and other heavy-duty vehicles. Chairman Jordan Kapson founded the company as a single Dodge dealership in 1949 after working at his father-in-law's dealership; his son Craig is the company's president.

KEY COMPETITORS
Bob Rohrman Auto
Kelley Automotive
United Auto Group

JORDAN INDUSTRIES, INC.

Arborlake Center, Ste. 550, 1751 Lake Cook Rd.	CEO: John W. Jordan II	2001 Sales: $722.8 million
Deerfield, IL 60015	CFO: Thomas C. Spielburger	1-Yr. Sales Change: (10.4%)
Phone: 847-945-5591	HR: —	Employees: 6,500
Fax: 847-945-5698	Type: Private	FYE: December 31
Web: www.jordanindustries.com		

Although not related to Michael, with a name like Jordan Industries, it's no wonder this company does it all. The company is involved in markets as diverse as automotive products, bicycle reflector kits, software application development, electric motors, and specialty advertising products. It owns more than 20 companies, which are divided into five separate business units: Kinetek (electric motors and gears), Jordan Auto Aftermarket (torque converters), Consumer and Industrial Products (food flavorings, gift items), Specialty Printing and Labeling (promotional products), and Jordan Specialty Plastics (plastic products and parts). Chairman and CEO John W. Jordan II owns more than 40% of the company.

KEY COMPETITORS
Aftermarket Technology
Baldor Electric
BorgWarner

JOSTENS, INC.

5501 Norman Center Dr.	CEO: Robert C. Buhrmaster	2001 Sales: $736.6 million
Minneapolis, MN 55437	CFO: John A. Feenan	1-Yr. Sales Change: (8.5%)
Phone: 952-830-3300	HR: Steven A. Tighe	Employees: 6,100
Fax: 952-830-3293	Type: Private	FYE: December 31
Web: www.jostens.com		

Are you *sure* you want to remember high school? Well, if you do, look to Jostens, the leading US producer of yearbooks and class rings. Class rings are sold on school campuses and through bookstores, retail jewelers, and the Internet, while Jostens' sports rings commemorate professional sports champions (it has made 23 of 35 Super Bowl rings). Jostens sells other graduation products including diplomas, announcements, caps, and gowns, and it takes and sells class and individual pictures for schools in the US and Canada. A private investment group led by Investcorp took Jostens private in May 2000.

KEY COMPETITORS
American Achievement
Herff Jones
Walsworth

In-depth profiles of an additional 200 key private companies are found on pages 36–435.

JOURNAL COMMUNICATIONS INC.

333 W. State St.
Milwaukee, WI 53203
Phone: 414-224-2000
Fax: 414-224-2469
Web: www.jc.com

CEO: Steven J. Smith
CFO: Paul M. Bonaiuto
HR: Daniel L. Harmsen
Type: Private

2001 Sales: $824.8 million
1-Yr. Sales Change: (1.7%)
Employees: 6,600
FYE: December 31

Journal Communications can easily chronicle its operations. The diversified media company generates most of its sales from newspaper publishing, including its flagship *Milwaukee Journal Sentinel*, nearly 50 weekly newspapers and community shoppers, and about a dozen business and specialty publications. It also owns 36 radio stations and six TV stations. In addition, Journal Communications has commercial printing operations, offers direct marketing services, and owns Norlight Telecommunications. The *Journal Sentinel* resulted from a merger between *The Milwaukee Journal* (1882) and *The Milwaukee Sentinal* (1837) in 1995. An employee stock trust owns 90% of the company.

KEY COMPETITORS
Gannett
Lee Enterprises
Tribune

JPI

600 E. Las Colinas Blvd., Ste. 1800
Irving, TX 75039
Phone: 972-556-1700
Fax: 972-556-3784
Web: www.jpi.com

CEO: Frank Miller III
CFO: Frank B. Schubert
HR: —
Type: Private

2001 Sales: $1,135.0 million
1-Yr. Sales Change: 13.5%
Employees: 1,000
FYE: December 31

JPI can walk your dog or rent you a bike but what it does best is build and manage apartments. One of the largest luxury multifamily apartment developers in the US, JPI also manages more than 24,000 units in about a dozen states. The company typically buys underperforming properties in desirable areas and upgrades them with such features as parking garages, fitness centers, and 24-hour concierge services. JPI's student complexes include game rooms and fitness centers. Founded in 1976 as Jefferson Properties, Inc., JPI was a subsidiary of Southland Financial until the early 1990s when Hunt Realty invested in it.

KEY COMPETITORS
Castle & Cooke
Gables Residential Trust
Trammell Crow Residential

KB TOYS

100 West St.
Pittsfield, MA 01201
Phone: 413-496-3000
Fax: 413-496-3616
Web: www.kbtoys.com

CEO: Michael L. Glazer
CFO: Robert J. Feldman
HR: Gerry Murray
Type: Private

2002 Sales: $2,000.0 million
1-Yr. Sales Change: 0.0%
Employees: 25,000
FYE: January 31

KB Toys hopes toy buyers will take their haul from the mall. One of the largest toy retailers in the US, KB Toys operates more than 1,300 stores under four main formats: KB Toys stores in malls, KB Works neighborhood stores, KB Toy Outlets and KB Toy Liquidator in outlet malls, and KB Toy Express in malls selling closeout toys during the Christmas season. It has stores throughout the US and in Guam and Puerto Rico, and it sells toys online through Kbkids.com and eToys.com (KB Toys bought the inventory and rights to the defunct eToys business in 2001). It also offers a business-to-business gift program. The firm, founded as a wholesale candy company in 1922, is owned by private equity firm Bain Capital.

KEY COMPETITORS
Target
Toys "R" Us
Wal-Mart

📖 In-depth profiles of an additional 200
key private companies are found on pages 36–435.

KENTUCKY LOTTERY CORPORATION

1011 W. Main St.	CEO: Arthur L. Gleason Jr.	2001 Sales: $590.9 million
Louisville, KY 40202	CFO: Howard Kline	1-Yr. Sales Change: 1.2%
Phone: 502-560-1500	HR: Church Saufley	Employees: —
Fax: 502-560-1670	Type: Government-owned	FYE: June 30
Web: www.kylottery.com		

Kentucky's grass may be blue, but many Kentuckians prefer green — the kind they can stuff into their wallets. For optimists looking to bag some bucks, the Kentucky Lottery offers numbers games (Pick 3, Pick 4, Lotto South) and an array of scratch-off and pull-tab games (One-Eyed Jack, Pool Party, Speed Bingo). Kentucky also participates in the multistate Powerball game. The lottery's proceeds (some $1.6 billion) have gone to education, Vietnam veterans, affordable housing, college scholarships, literacy programs, and Kentucky's General Fund. Launched in 1989, the lottery has introduced new games as it struggles with intense competition from nearby casinos.

KEY COMPETITORS
Churchill Downs
Hoosier Lottery
Illinois Lottery

KERR DRUG, INC.

2522 S. Tri-Center Blvd.	CEO: Anthony N. Civello	2001 Est. Sales: $750.0 mil.
Durham, NC 27713	CFO: Richard D. Johnson	1-Yr. Sales Change: 15.4%
Phone: 919-544-3896	HR: Briony Voorhees	Employees: 3,500
Fax: 919-544-7138	Type: Private	FYE: December 31
Web: www.kerrdrug.com		

Oh, you can buy knick-knacks and doo-dads at a Kerr Drug store, but the company that bills itself as "Carolina's Drugstore" puts its primary focus on pharmacy operations, which account for the majority of sales. Kerr Drug operates more than 130 stores in the Carolinas in several formats, ranging from upscale stores featuring cosmetologists, expanded gift sections, and even Starbucks coffee to the Smart Dollar Stores format offering more cleaning supplies, health and beauty aids, and soft goods. Founded by Banks Kerr in 1951, the chain was sold in 1995 to retailer J. C. Penney. A management group led by Kerr CEO Anthony Civello and COO Richard Johnson took Kerr Drug private in 1996.

KEY COMPETITORS
CVS
Eckerd
Walgreen

KEYSTONE FOODS LLC

300 Barr Harbor Dr., Ste. 600	CEO: Herbert Lotman	2001 Est. Sales: $2,700.0 mil.
West Conshohocken, PA 19428	CFO: —	1-Yr. Sales Change: 1.9%
Phone: 610-667-6700	HR: Jerry Gotro	Employees: 6,700
Fax: 610-667-1460	Type: Private	FYE: December 31
Web: www.keystonefoods.com		

Keystone Foods hopes you won't just have the salad. The company is one of the largest makers of hamburger patties and processed poultry. It's a major supplier to McDonald's restaurants; in the 1970s Keystone persuaded the fast-food giant to switch to frozen beef to reduce the health risks associated with fresh beef. Overseas, operations include McKey Food Services and MacFood Services (some are joint ventures). In addition to its worldwide meat processing plants, which produce millions of burgers daily, Keystone also operates M&M Restaurant Supply, and has begun to supply fresh beef to a U.S. grocery retailer. Chairman and CEO Herbert Lotman owns the company, which began as a beef-boning business in the 1960s.

KEY COMPETITORS
Golden State Foods
IBP
Tyson Foods

In-depth profiles of an additional 200 key private companies are found on pages 36–435.

KI

1330 Bellevue St.	CEO: Richard J. Resch	2001 Est. Sales: $625.0 mil.
Green Bay, WI 54302	CFO: Mark Olsen	1-Yr. Sales Change: (1.0%)
Phone: 920-468-8100	HR: Kristine Hackbarth-Horn	Employees: 3,500
Fax: 920-468-0280	Type: Private	FYE: December 31
Web: www.ki.com		

KI can be found in cubicles, classrooms, cafeterias, and college dorms. Formerly known as Krueger International, KI makes ergonomic seating, cabinets, and other furniture used by businesses, health care organizations, schools, and government agencies. The company offers everything from desks to daybeds, not to mention tables, wall and storage systems, and even trash cans. KI operates manufacturing facilities in Canada, Italy, and the US, and it markets its products through sales representatives, furniture dealers, architects, and interior designers. Founded in 1941, KI was bought in the 1980s by its managers, who later allowed their employees to buy company stock. The company is now 100% owned by employees.

KEY COMPETITORS
Haworth
Herman Miller
Steelcase

KIMBALL HILL HOMES

5999 New Wilke Rd., Ste. 504	CEO: David K. Hill Jr.	2002 Sales: $700.0 million
Rolling Meadows, IL 60008	CFO: Gene Rowehl	1-Yr. Sales Change: 4.0%
Phone: 847-364-7300	HR: Jo Ann Peterson	Employees: 654
Fax: 847-439-0875	Type: Private	FYE: June 30
Web: www.kimballhill.com		

Chicagoland members of the GI generation and their offspring, who have long thrived in the 'burbs, can thank lawyer-turned-builder D. Kimball Hill, founder of Kimball Hill Homes as a pioneer of Chicago's suburbs. Today Kimball Hill Homes has expanded into California, Florida, Nevada, Ohio, Oregon, Texas, Washington, and Wisconsin. The company mainly targets first-time or move-up buyers, although it also builds 3,000 to 4,000 sq. ft. houses priced between $600,000 and $800,000. It offers mortgage financing and refinancing of investment properties in five states through its KH Financial subsidiary. Kimball Hill Homes is owned by the Hill family, including the founder's son, chairman and CEO David Hill Jr.

KEY COMPETITORS
David Weekley Homes
Pulte Homes
Ryland

KINDERCARE LEARNING CENTERS, INC.

650 NE Holladay, Ste. 1400	CEO: David J. Johnson	2002 Sales: $829.4 million
Portland, OR 97232	CFO: Robert Abeles	1-Yr. Sales Change: 11.6%
Phone: 503-872-1300	HR: Edward L. Brewington	Employees: 27,000
Fax: 503-872-1304	Type: Private	FYE: May 31
Web: www.kindercare.com		

KinderCare helps prepare the kids of today for the world of tomorrow. The #1 US for-profit operator of preschool and child care facilities, KinderCare Learning Centers provides child care and age-specific educational programs for kids from six weeks to 12 years old. Some 129,000 children are enrolled in more than 1,260 centers in 39 states and two centers in the UK; the average weekly full-time tuition is around $135. Operations include KinderCare Learning Centers, KinderCare At Work (at nearly 50 corporate sites), and Mulberry Child Care Centers. The company also runs several high school distance learning programs. Affiliates of Kohlberg Kravis Roberts own almost 80% of KinderCare.

KEY COMPETITORS
ARAMARK
Knowledge Learning
La Petite Academy

In-depth profiles of an additional 200 key private companies are found on pages 36–435.

KING KULLEN GROCERY COMPANY INC.

185 Central Ave.
Bethpage, NY 11714
Phone: 516-733-7100
Fax: 516-827-6325
Web: www.kingkullen.com

CEO: Bernard D. Kennedy
CFO: J. D. Kennedy
HR: Thomas Nagle
Type: Private

2002 Est. Sales: $790.0 mil.
1-Yr. Sales Change: 1.0%
Employees: —
FYE: September 30

How's this for a crowning achievement? King Kullen Grocery Company claims to have been the originator of the supermarket format. Heralding itself as "America's first supermarket," the firm operates nearly 50 supermarkets, mainly on Long Island, New York. King Kullen also owns an 18,000-sq.-ft. Wild By Nature natural foods store (and plans to open more), and it offers a line of vitamins and supplements under the same name in some regular stores. Most stores average about 35,000 sq. ft., but it has a 62,000-sq.-ft. upscale market with features such as ethnic fare, catering, and a Wild By Nature section. Started in a Queens warehouse in 1930 by Michael Cullen, the firm is owned and operated by Cullen's relatives.

KEY COMPETITORS
A&P
C&S Wholesale
Pathmark

KINGSTON TECHNOLOGY COMPANY, INC.

17600 Newhope St.
Fountain Valley, CA 92708
Phone: 714-435-2600
Fax: 714-435-2699
Web: www.kingston.com

CEO: John Tu
CFO: Koichi Hosokawa
HR: Daniel Hsu
Type: Private

2001 Sales: $900.0 million
1-Yr. Sales Change: (43.8%)
Employees: 1,900
FYE: December 31

Kingston Technology cuts a kingly figure in the realm of memory. The company is a top maker of memory modules — circuit boards loaded with memory chips that increase the capacity and speed of printers and computers. Kingston also makes flash memory cards used in portable electronic devices such as digital cameras, wireless phones, and personal digital assistants. Kingston has taken on some manufacturing chores for its customers through its Payton Technology Project, a specialized factory that tests and packages memory chips before assembling them into customized memory modules. Founders John Tu (president and CEO) and David Sun (COO) own the company.

KEY COMPETITORS
Micron Technology
SanDisk
Unigen

KINRAY INC.

152-35 10th Ave.
Whitestone, NY 11357
Phone: 718-767-1234
Fax: 718-767-4388
Web: www.kinray.com

CEO: Stewart Rahr
CFO: Bill Bodinger
HR: Howard Hershberg
Type: Private

2001 Sales: $2,000.0 million
1-Yr. Sales Change: 17.0%
Employees: 600
FYE: December 30

Kinray, the US's largest privately held wholesale drug distributor, is nothing if not independent. It provides generic, branded, and repackaged drugs, health and beauty products, medical equipment, vitamins and herbals, and diabetes-care products; it also has a 750-item private-label program. The company serves nearly 2,000 pharmacies in the northeastern US. Kinray spearheaded the creation of the Wholesale Alliance Cooperative, a group of independent regional drug distributors that aims to help preserve the viability of independent pharmacies (who are customers to the wholesalers). The company was founded in 1944 by Joseph Rahr. His son, CEO and president Stewart Rahr, has owned the company since 1975.

KEY COMPETITORS
Cardinal Distribution
McKesson
Quality King

In-depth profiles of an additional 200 key private companies are found on pages 36–435.

KLAUSSNER FURNITURE INDUSTRIES, INC.

405 Lewallen Rd.	CEO: J. B. Davis	2001 Sales: $955.0 million
Asheboro, NC 27205	CFO: Dave Bryant	1-Yr. Sales Change: (9.6%)
Phone: 336-625-6174	HR: Mark Walker	Employees: 6,900
Fax: 336-626-0905	Type: Private	FYE: December 31
Web: www.klaussner.com		

Klaussner Furniture Industries makes furniture for the couch potato in all of us. It is one of the US's largest makers of upholstered furniture. Klaussner sells fabric- and leather-upholstered sofas and recliners, dining furniture, and office furniture under the JDI, Realistic, Revolution Motion, Paoli, Tellus, and Klaussner brand names. It also offers sofas and chairs under the licensed Sealy name. Its 20 plants produce items exported to about 60 countries. Klaussner also owns about 20% of furniture retailer Jennifer Convertibles. Chairman Hans Klaussner has owned the company since 1979; it was founded in 1964 as Stuart Furniture Industries.

KEY COMPETITORS
Furniture Brands International
Steelcase

KNOLL, INC.

1235 Water St.	CEO: Andrew B. Cogan	2001 Sales: $985.4 million
East Greenville, PA 18041	CFO: Barry L. McCabe	1-Yr. Sales Change: (15.3%)
Phone: 215-679-7991	HR: S. David Wolfe	Employees: 3,863
Fax: 215-679-1755	Type: Private	FYE: December 31
Web: www.knoll.com		

Designer cubicles make for happier workers, or so goes the gospel at Knoll. The company makes a variety of distinctively designed, curvilinear office furniture and related accessories, including office systems (a.k.a. cubicles) sold under such names as Equity, Dividends, and Currents. Other products include rolling chairs and other seating, tables, metal and wood desks, file cabinets, computer and desk accessories, textiles, and leather upholstery. Knoll also sells textiles and leather upholstery. Knoll management and investment firm Warburg Pincus own the company.

KEY COMPETITORS
Haworth
Herman Miller
Steelcase

KOCH ENTERPRISES, INC.

10 S. 11th Ave.	CEO: Robert L. Koch II	2001 Est. Sales: $650.0 mil.
Evansville, IN 47744	CFO: Susan E. Parsons	1-Yr. Sales Change: 5.3%
Phone: 812-465-9800	HR: Debbie Alexander	Employees: 3,500
Fax: 812-465-9613	Type: Private	FYE: December 31
Web: www.kochenterprises.com		

Koch gets straight A's. Koch Enterprises is a diversified company with interests including aluminum, automotive finishing systems, air-conditioning equipment, and adhesives. Subsidiaries include George Koch Sons (engineers, installs, and services a range of finishing systems for the automotive industry), Koch Air (distributes heating and air-conditioning equipment), Gibbs Die Casting (supplies automotive aluminum die-castings products), Brake Supply Company (repairs and replaces brakes and hydraulic systems for the automotive and mining industries), and Uniseal (makes adhesives and sealants for automobile manufacturers, as well as connectors for drain and waste pipes). The Koch family owns the company.

KEY COMPETITORS
Dana
Illinois Tool Works
Kaiser Aluminum

In-depth profiles of an additional 200 key private companies are found on pages 36–435.

KOPPERS INDUSTRIES, INC.

436 7th Ave.
Pittsburgh, PA 15219
Phone: 412-227-2001
Fax: 412-227-2333
Web: www.koppers.com

CEO: Walter W. Turner
CFO: Donald E. Davis
HR: Joseph E. Boan
Type: Private

2001 Sales: $707.6 million
1-Yr. Sales Change: (2.2%)
Employees: 2,085
FYE: December 31

Koppers Industries treats wood right. The company makes carbon compounds and treated-wood products for the chemical, railroad, aluminum, utility, and steel markets. Its carbon materials and chemicals unit (nearly 60% of sales) makes materials for producing aluminum, polyester resins, plasticizers, and wood preservatives. The railroad and utility products segment supplies treated crossties and utility poles and treats wood for vineyard, construction, and other uses. Koppers owns 50% of KSA Limited Partnership, which produces about 150,000 concrete crossties annually. The company operates in the Australasia region, Europe, and the US. Private investment firm Saratoga Partners III, L.P., owns Koppers.

KEY COMPETITORS
Kerr-McGee
RailWorks
Stepan

KRAUS-ANDERSON, INCORPORATED

525 S. 8th St.
Minneapolis, MN 55404
Phone: 612-332-7281
Fax: 612-332-8739
Web: www.krausanderson.com

CEO: Bruce W. Engelsma
CFO: Thomas L. Dunleavy
HR: Jim Brenk
Type: Private

2000 Sales: $710.0 million
1-Yr. Sales Change: 16.4%
Employees: 1,000
FYE: December 31

Kraus-Anderson builds on experience. The group's Kraus-Anderson Construction firm, founded in 1897, is one of the top building contractors in the US. Serving as general contractor, construction manager, or designer, the firm completes about 400 projects a year, including hotels, conference centers, department stores, and sports facilities. Other companies under the Kraus-Anderson umbrella are Kraus-Anderson Realty (property management and leasing), Kraus-Anderson Insurance (personal and commercial insurance), Kraus-Anderson Capital (equipment financing), and Kraus-Anderson Communications (advertising). Chairman and CEO Bruce Engelsma and his family own the company, which was purchased from the founders in 1937.

KEY COMPETITORS
M. A. Mortenson
Turner Corporation
Walsh Group

K-VA-T FOOD STORES, INC.

201 Trigg St.
Abingdon, VA 24210
Phone: 276-628-5503
Fax: 276-628-1592
Web: www.foodcity.com

CEO: Steven C. Smith
CFO: Robert L. Neeley
HR: Donnie Meadows
Type: Private

2001 Est. Sales: $1,000.0 mil.
1-Yr. Sales Change: 3.8%
Employees: 8,700
FYE: December 31

What do you call a chain of supermarkets in Kentucky, Virginia, and Tennessee? How about K-VA-T Food Stores? K-VA-T is one of the largest grocery chains in the region, with about 85 supermarkets primarily under the Food City banner (and a handful of Super Dollar Supermarkets). Originally a Piggly Wiggly franchise with three stores, K-VA-T was founded in 1955. It has expanded by acquiring stores from other regional food retailers, opening new stores, and adding services such as more than 30 pharmacies, about 20 Gas'N Go gasoline outlets, and banking. Its Mid-Mountain Foods provides warehousing and distribution services. The founding Smith family owns a majority of K-VA-T; employees own the rest of the company.

KEY COMPETITORS
Delhaize America
Kroger
Wal-Mart

In-depth profiles of an additional 200 key private companies are found on pages 36–435.

LANDMARK COMMUNICATIONS, INC.

150 W. Brambleton Ave.	CEO: Decker Anstrom	2001 Sales: $732.0 million
Norfolk, VA 23510	CFO: Lemuel E. Lewis	1-Yr. Sales Change: (9.1%)
Phone: 757-446-2000	HR: Charlie W. Hill	Employees: —
Fax: 757-446-2983	Type: Private	FYE: December 31
Web: www.landmarkcom.com		

Landmark Communications' media properties are all over the map. Owner of cable station The Weather Channel, Landmark is also a leading community newspaper publisher. It publishes three metro newspapers (*The Virginian-Pilot, News & Record,* and *The Roanoke Times*) in North Carolina and Virginia and about 50 daily, semiweekly, and weekly community papers in the East and Midwest. The company also publishes 70 free newspapers and special-interest publications, including some focusing on college sports. Chairman Frank Batten Jr. and his family own the company.

KEY COMPETITORS
Community Newspaper Holdings
Knight Ridder
Media General

LANE INDUSTRIES, INC.

1 Lane Center, 1200 Shermer Rd.	CEO: Forrest M. Schneider	2001 Sales: $870.0 million
Northbrook, IL 60062	CFO: —	1-Yr. Sales Change: (13.0%)
Phone: 847-498-6789	HR: Linda Datz	Employees: 6,350
Fax: 847-498-2104	Type: Private	FYE: December 31

From the seeds of a humble office machine and supplies manufacturer grew the mighty oak of Lane Industries. The diversified holding company's oldest investment is its nearly two-thirds stake in General Binding, a maker of binding and laminating equipment, marker boards, and paper shredders, founded by William Lane II in 1947. Lane Industries is also active in the lodging industry through Lane Hospitality, which owns or operates about 30 hotels, resorts, and time-share properties. Through Lane Security, the company owns Protection Service Industries, a security alarm firm in California, Arizona, and New Mexico. Lane Industries also has farming and ranching interests. The Lane family owns the company.

KEY COMPETITORS
Fellowes
Starwood Hotels & Resorts
Tyco International

LANOGA CORPORATION

17946 NE 65th St.	CEO: Paul Hylbert	2001 Sales: $1,400.0 million
Redmond, WA 98052	CFO: William Brakken	1-Yr. Sales Change: 7.7%
Phone: 425-883-4125	HR: —	Employees: 5,500
Fax: 425-882-2959	Type: Private	FYE: December 31
Web: www.lanogacorp.com		

Lanoga is a lumbering giant. The company is one of the top US retailers of lumber and building materials, catering to professional contractors as well as consumers. Operating about 240 stores in 18 states, Lanoga has grown through dozens of small acquisitions. Its divisions include United Building Centers (Midwest and Rocky Mountain states), Lumbermen's Building Centers (Northwest and Arizona), Spenard Builders Supply (Alaska), and the Home Lumber Company (Colorado). The firm is buying 31 lumberyards and three manufacturing plants in Wisconsin and northern Michigan from Wickes. Lanoga was founded in 1855 by cousins William Laird and Matthew Norton. Descendants of the company's founders own Lanoga.

KEY COMPETITORS
84 Lumber
Home Depot
Lowe's

📖 In-depth profiles of an additional 200 key private companies are found on pages 36–435.

LARRY H. MILLER GROUP

9350 S. 150 E. Rte. 1000
Sandy, UT 84070
Phone: 801-563-4100
Fax: 801-563-4198
Web: www.lhm.com

CEO: Larry H. Miller
CFO: Clark Whitworth
HR: Linda Jeppesen
Type: Private

2001 Sales: $1,550.1 million
1-Yr. Sales Change: 13.4%
Employees: —
FYE: December 31

You wouldn't hire the Larry H. Miller Group for your late night bebop, but the firm does know a little something about all that jazz. Its interests include automobiles, television, and basketball. The company operates more than 35 auto dealerships in Arizona, Colorado, Idaho, New Mexico, Oregon, and Utah. Its dealerships sell Cadillac, Chevrolet, Honda, Lexus, Toyota, and other makes of cars. The company also owns the Utah Jazz professional basketball team, its home (the Delta Center arena), the WNBA's Utah Starzz, and Salt Lake City TV station KJZZ. In addition the group, owned by its CEO with the same name, operates two movie theaters with a total of about 30 screens in Salt Lake City and Sandy, Utah.

KEY COMPETITORS
AutoNation
Burt Automotive
Earnhardt's Auto Centers

LATHAM & WATKINS

633 W. 5th St., Ste. 4000
Los Angeles, CA 90071
Phone: 213-485-1234
Fax: 213-891-8763
Web: www.lw.com

CEO: Robert Dell
CFO: Michael Eichenseer
HR: Mimi Krumholz
Type: Partnership

2001 Sales: $769.5 million
1-Yr. Sales Change: 19.8%
Employees: —
FYE: December 31

Latham & Watkins' founders Dana Latham and Paul Watkins flipped a coin in 1934 to determine which of their names would go first on the company's shingle. From that coin toss, the law firm has grown into one of the largest in the US. With more than 1,400 lawyers, the firm ranks high in corporate finance, mergers and acquisitions, technology law, and litigation. Latham was a key player in the financing for the Venetian Resort Hotel and Casino in Las Vegas and Gemstar's acquisition of TV Guide. Headquartered in Los Angeles, the firm has 12 locations worldwide. Latham counts Amgen, AOL Time Warner, Lucent, and Morgan Stanley among its clients.

KEY COMPETITORS
Gibson, Dunn & Crutcher
O'Melveny & Myers
Skadden, Arps

LEINER HEALTH PRODUCTS LLC

901 E. 233rd St.
Carson, CA 90745
Phone: 310-835-8400
Fax: 310-952-7760
Web: www.leiner.com

CEO: Robert M. Kaminski
CFO: Robert Reynolds
HR: John L. Kelly
Type: Private

2001 Sales: $612.1 million
1-Yr. Sales Change: (7.6%)
Employees: 2,606
FYE: March 31

Whether you're looking for prevention or a cure, Leiner Health Products has a pill for you. The company is a top maker of vitamins, minerals, supplements, and OTC drugs sold primarily under private labels, but also under its own labels (such as YourLife, Nature's Origin, and Pharmacist Formula). It makes more than 400 vitamin and supplement products. Its OTC pharmaceuticals include cold medicines and analgesics; Leiner also makes bath, skin, and hair products. The company's products are sold at more than 50,000 US supermarkets, drugstores, and other outlets, including Wal-Mart and Costco. North Castle Partners, a private investment firm, controls the company.

KEY COMPETITORS
GNC
NBTY
Perrigo

In-depth profiles of an additional 200 key private companies are found on pages 36–435.

LEPRINO FOODS COMPANY

1830 W. 38th Ave.	CEO: Wes Allen	2002 Est. Sales: $1,750.0 mil.
Denver, CO 80211	CFO: Ron Klump	1-Yr. Sales Change: 2.9%
Phone: 303-480-2600	HR: Dave Swan	Employees: 3,000
Fax: 303-480-2605	Type: Private	FYE: October 31
Web: www.leprinofoods.com		

To pizza chains such as Domino's, Pizza Hut, and Little Caesar, Leprino Foods really is the big cheese. The company is the world's largest maker of mozzarella cheese, which it sells to pizza chains and food manufacturers. Leprino's other dairy products include premium block mozzarella and provolone, as well as whey protein concentrate, and lactose for use in animal feeds, baby formula, and baked goods. The firm gets its milk supply from the nation's large dairy co-ops. Subsidiary Leprino Transportation Company operates refrigerated tractor trailers that transport the company's products nationwide. Italian immigrant Michael Leprino Sr. founded the company in 1950. It is still owned by the Leprino family.

KEY COMPETITORS
Kraft Foods
Saputo
Schreiber Foods

LES SCHWAB TIRE CENTERS

646 NW Madras Hwy.	CEO: Philip Wick	2001 Sales: $1,000.0 million
Prineville, OR 97754	CFO: Tom Freedman	1-Yr. Sales Change: 25.0%
Phone: 541-447-4136	HR: Larry Smith	Employees: 6,000
Fax: 541-416-5208	Type: Private	FYE: December 31
Web: www.lesschwab.com		

If you're seeking tires, Les Schwab Tire Centers aims to help. Of course, it doesn't hurt that the owner wrote the bible of tire retailing: *Pride in Performance — Keep It Going*. Les Schwab Tire Centers prides itself on continued customer service; it sells tires and batteries and does alignment, brake, and shock work at about 350 stores in Alaska, California, Idaho, Montana, Nevada, Oregon, Utah, and Washington. With a story that rivals Moses', founder and chairman Les Schwab was reared in a logging camp and went to school in a converted boxcar. In 1952 he bought a tire shop that eventually became Les Schwab Tire Centers. The firm, owned by Schwab and his family, plans to open about 15 to 20 new stores a year.

KEY COMPETITORS
Discount Tire
Sears
Wal-Mart

LEVITZ HOME FURNISHINGS, INC.

300 Crossways Park Dr.	CEO: Alan Rosenberg	2002 Sales: $915.0 million
Woodbury, NY 11797	CFO: Carl Landeck	1-Yr. Sales Change: (0.5%)
Phone: 516-496-9560	HR: Maria Infante	Employees: 4,900
Fax: 631-927-1780	Type: Private	FYE: April 30

The lamps stay lit a lot at Levitz Home Furnishings, the holding company for Levitz Furniture and Seaman Furniture. Levitz Furniture has about 60 stores (half of them in California), while Seaman has more than 50 stores in the northeastern US. The creation of Levitz Home Furnishings in 2001 allowed Levitz Furniture to emerge from Chapter 11 bankruptcy (originally filed in 1997), in part by distributing management of its 15 East Coast stores to Seaman. The alliance also combines the two companies' administration, advertising, distribution, merchandising, and warehousing efforts. Chairman James Rubin, also co-chairman of M.D. Sass Associates, controls Levitz Home Furnishings.

KEY COMPETITORS
Ethan Allen
IKEA
La-Z-Boy

> **In-depth profiles of an additional 200 key private companies are found on pages 36–435.**

LIBERTY TRAVEL, INC.

69 Spring St.	CEO: Gilbert Haroche	2000 Sales: $1,400.0 million
Ramsey, NJ 07446	CFO: Richard Cowlan	1-Yr. Sales Change: 0.7%
Phone: 201-934-3500	HR: Susan Brennen	Employees: 2,500
Fax: 201-934-3651	Type: Private	FYE: December 31
Web: www.libertytravel.com		

Give me liberty, or give me travel? Liberty Travel gives you both. The company is one of the US leaders in leisure vacations and owns 200 offices in the Northeast and in Florida; it sells directly to the holiday traveler. Liberty's sister company GOGO Worldwide Vacations serves the travel agent community with customized land-only and air-inclusive travel packages from almost 90 offices in more than 30 states. It also operates Air France Holidays. CEO Gilbert Haroche and the late Fred Kassner founded the privately held Liberty Travel in 1951; Haroche still owns the company.

KEY COMPETITORS
American Express
Carlson Wagonlit
WorldTravel

LIFE CARE CENTERS OF AMERICA

3570 Keith St. NW	CEO: Forrest L. Preston	2000 Est. Sales: $1,265.0 mil.
Cleveland, TN 37312	CFO: Steve Ziegler	1-Yr. Sales Change: 4.5%
Phone: 423-472-9585	HR: Mark Gibson	Employees: 29,350
Fax: 423-339-8337	Type: Private	FYE: December 31
Web: www.lcca.com		

Life Care Centers of America is a privately owned operator of retirement and health care centers in the US. The company manages more than 240 facilities in 28 states — including retirement communities, assisted-living facilities, and nursing homes — and provides specialized services such as home health care. Founder Forrest Preston opened his first center in 1970, and the company continues to tout a "corporate culture grounded in the Judeo-Christian ethic." However Life Care has faced complaints of poor-quality care, part of a situation that plagues the industry overall.

KEY COMPETITORS
Beverly Enterprises
Mariner Health Care
Sun Healthcare

LIFETIME ENTERTAINMENT SERVICES

309 W. 49th St.	CEO: Carole Black	2001 Sales: $727.0 million
New York, NY 10019	CFO: James Wesley	1-Yr. Sales Change: 10.0%
Phone: 212-957-4610	HR: Patricia Langer	Employees: —
Fax: 212-957-4449	Type: Joint venture	FYE: December 31
Web: www.lifetimetv.com		

Lifetime Entertainment Services hopes viewers make a long-term commitment to its television programs. The company operates three women-oriented cable TV networks (Lifetime, Lifetime Movie Network, and Lifetime Real Women) offering original movies, talk shows, sports (including the Women's National Basketball Association), and syndicated shows. Its Lifetime channel reaches some 85 million US households and is the highest-rated cable network in prime time. Its Lifetime Online unit offers information and entertainment on the Web. Lifetime was formed through the merger of channels Daytime and Cable Health Network in 1984. It is jointly owned by Walt Disney (through ABC Cable) and Hearst.

KEY COMPETITORS
Harpo
Oxygen Media
Rainbow Media

In-depth profiles of an additional 200 key private companies are found on pages 36–435.

LIFETOUCH INC.

11000 Viking Dr., Ste. 400	CEO: Paul Harmel	2001 Sales: $750.0 million
Eden Prairie, MN 55344	CFO: Randy Pladson	1-Yr. Sales Change: 7.1%
Phone: 952-826-4000	HR: Ted Koenecke	Employees: 17,000
Fax: 952-826-4557	Type: Private	FYE: June 30
Web: www.lifetouch.com		

When it's picture day at school and the kids are all lined up with new haircuts and scrubbed faces, odds are good that their toothy grins are directed at someone from Lifetouch. One of the largest US portrait photographers, employee-owned Lifetouch also runs about 570 photography studios in J. C. Penney (420) and Target stores (150) across the nation. In addition, Lifetouch takes baby, family, business, and sports portraits; publishes church directories and year-books; and offers event digital imaging (which combines photography, graphics, and text), CD business imaging, and video production services. The company operates in the US and Canada. Lifetouch was founded in 1936 as National School Studios.

KEY COMPETITORS
CPI Corp.
Olan Mills
PCA International

LINCOLN PROPERTY COMPANY

3300 Lincoln Plaza, 500 N. Akard	CEO: A. Mack Pogue	2002 Sales: $1,766.0 million
Dallas, TX 75201	CFO: Nancy Davis	1-Yr. Sales Change: 30.6%
Phone: 214-740-3300	HR: Luanne Hudson	Employees: 5,000
Fax: 214-740-3441	Type: Private	FYE: June 30
Web: www.lincolnproperty.com		

Lincoln Property is one of the US's largest diversified real estate companies — honest! Lincoln began by building apartments in the Dallas area, then expanded into commercial and retail projects. It now has residential properties comprising more than 140,000 units, and has developed about 140 million sq. ft. of commercial properties nationwide (still managing 90 million). It has joint ventures with Lend Lease to develop commercial property and with Sam Zell's Equity Residential Properties to build apartments. Its joint venture with American International Group is active in Central Europe and Spain. CEO Mack Pogue cofounded Lincoln in 1965 with Trammell Crow, whose stake Pogue bought out in 1977.

KEY COMPETITORS
JMB Realty
Tishman Realty
Trammell Crow Residential

LINSCO/PRIVATE LEDGER CORP.

9785 Town Center Dr.	CEO: Todd A. Robinson	2001 Sales: —
San Diego, CA 92121	CFO: Scott Hansen	1-Yr. Sales Change: —
Phone: 858-450-9606	HR: Gina Cannella	Employees: 800
Fax: 858-546-8324	Type: Private	FYE: December 31
Web: www.lpl.com		

Linsco/Private Ledger (LPL), repeatedly ranked as the largest independent brokerage firm in the US, was created from the 1989 merger of brokerage firms Linsco and Private Ledger. The company advises clients on stocks and bonds, mutual funds, commodities, options, annuities, insurance, real estate investment trusts (REITs), and other investment vehicles. As an independent, LPL doesn't sell its own investment products, but provides access to others' across the nation. LPL executes nearly two million trades and invests approximately $40 billion annually.

KEY COMPETITORS
Charles Schwab
Merrill Lynch
Morgan Keegan

In-depth profiles of an additional 200 key private companies are found on pages 36–435.

LOEWS CINEPLEX ENTERTAINMENT CORPORATION

711 5th Ave., 11th Fl.	CEO: Travis Reid	2002 Sales: $856.2 million
New York, NY 10022	CFO: John J. Walker	1-Yr. Sales Change: (5.2%)
Phone: 212-833-6200	HR: Allan Fox	Employees: 16,500
Fax: 212-833-6277	Type: Private	FYE: February 28
Web: www.loewscineplex.com		

Running a theater chain has its highs and Loews. With more than 2,700 screens in some 280 theaters throughout the globe, Loews Cineplex Entertainment (the oldest theater circuit in North America) hopes to maintain the highs as one of the world's leading theater chains. The company operates under the Loews and Sony names in 19 US states, including major cities such as Boston, Chicago, New York, and San Francisco, as well as Washington, DC. In addition, the company owns and operates the Cineplex Odeon name in Canada. Loews Cineplex also owns 50% stakes in theaters in Spain (Yelmo Cineplex) and South Korea (Megabox Cineplex).

KEY COMPETITORS
AMC Entertainment
Cinemark
Regal Entertainment

THE LONGABERGER COMPANY

1500 E. Main St.	CEO: Tami Longaberger	2001 Sales: $970.0 million
Newark, OH 43055	CFO: Stephanie Imhoff	1-Yr. Sales Change: (3.0%)
Phone: 740-322-5000	HR: Anne Dunlap	Employees: 7,000
Fax: 740-322-5240	Type: Private	FYE: December 31
Web: www.longaberger.com		

A tisket, a tasket, a Longaberger basket. The Longaberger Company is the #1 maker of handmade baskets in the US, selling nearly 10 million a year. The baskets are sold in the US through in-home shows conducted by Longaberger's 70,000 independent sales associates. Baskets account for half of sales, but the company also sells pottery, fabrics, window treatments, and wrought-iron home accessories. Longaberger's home office is a seven-story rendition of a basket with two 75-ton handles on top. The company also owns a golf course, a hotel, and Longaberger Homestead (an events area with shops and restaurants). The family-owned firm is run by the daughters of the late Dave Longaberger, who founded the company in 1973.

KEY COMPETITORS
Euromarket Designs
Pier 1 Imports
Williams-Sonoma

LOS ANGELES DEPARTMENT OF WATER AND POWER

111 N. Hope St.	CEO: David H. Wiggs Jr.	2002 Sales: $2,784.2 million
Los Angeles, CA 90012	CFO: Ron Vazquez	1-Yr. Sales Change: (23.3%)
Phone: 213-367-1338	HR: —	Employees: —
Fax: 213-367-1455	Type: Government-owned	FYE: June 30
Web: www.ladwp.com		

The Los Angeles Department of Water and Power (LADWP) keeps the movie cameras running and the swimming pools full. The largest municipally owned utility in the US, LADWP provides electricity to 1.4 million residential and business customers and water to 650,000 customers (or 3.7 million people). The company has power plant interests that give it 2,000 MW of generating capacity; it also buys and sells wholesale power. Most of the city's water supply is transported through two aqueduct systems from the Sierra Nevada Mountains; other water sources include wells and local groundwater basins. Because LADWP is city-owned, its retail monopoly status was unaffected by utility deregulation in California.

KEY COMPETITORS
Avista
Sacramento Municipal
Sempra Energy

In-depth profiles of an additional 200 key private companies are found on pages 36–435.

LOWER COLORADO RIVER AUTHORITY

3700 Lake Austin Blvd.	CEO: Joseph J. Beal	2001 Sales: $689.4 million
Austin, TX 78703	CFO: John Meismer	1-Yr. Sales Change: 28.2%
Phone: 512-473-3200	HR: Karen Farabee	Employees: 1,910
Fax: 512-473-3298	Type: Government-owned	FYE: June 30
Web: www.lcra.org		

The stars at night are big and bright, but Texans in 58 counties still need electricity from the Lower Colorado River Authority (LCRA). The utility supplies wholesale electricity to 42 utility customers, comprising 9 electric cooperatives and 33 towns. The LCRA has interests in fossil-fueled, hydroelectric, and wind-powered generation facilities that give it a capacity of about 2,700 MW; it also has power transmission assets. The company's water unit operates 30 water and wastewater systems, three irrigation systems, and six dams in its service territory; it also monitors the water quality of the lakes formed by its dams. LCRA's revenues provide funding for its more than 40 recreation areas.

KEY COMPETITORS
Brazos Electric Power
TNP Enterprises

LUMBERMENS MERCHANDISING CORPORATION

137 W. Wayne Ave.	CEO: Anthony J. DeCarlo	2001 Est. Sales: $1,700.0 mil.
Wayne, PA 19087	CFO: David J. Gonze	1-Yr. Sales Change: (19.0%)
Phone: 610-293-7000	HR: John Broomell	Employees: 200
Fax: 610-293-7098	Type: Cooperative	FYE: September 30
Web: www.lmc.net		

Membership has its privileges. Through Lumbermens Merchandising Corporation (LMC), lumber retailers in the eastern half of the US pool their buying resources to leverage volume discounts from vendors and increase their own efficiency. LMC's network of members includes more than 1,000 building material locations. The cooperative is the largest dealer-owned lumber building materials buying group in the US. It holds members to strict confidentiality, in part to safeguard vendor contracts. In addition to lumber and panel products, LMC also supplies its members with non-wood products, millwork, and hardware. LMC is planning to expand into the western portion of the US.

KEY COMPETITORS
BMA
Cameron Ashley
Do it Best

M. FABRIKANT & SONS, INC.

1 Rockefeller Plaza, 28th Fl.	CEO: Matthew Fabrikant Fortgang	2002 Sales: $900.0 million
New York, NY 10020	CFO: Sheldon L. Ginsberg	1-Yr. Sales Change: (3.2%)
Phone: 212-757-0790	HR: Susan Fortgang	Employees: 800
Fax: 212-262-9757	Type: Private	FYE: July 31
Web: www.fabrikant.com		

Diamonds have been around practically forever, and so has M. Fabrikant & Sons, a major US diamond wholesaler. Four generations of the Fabrikant and Fortgang families run the family-owned firm, which claims to be one of the oldest diamond and jewelry companies in the world (it was founded as a loose diamond wholesaler in New York City in 1895). Fabrikant purchases and sells loose and polished diamonds and other precious and semi-precious stones, plus diamond, gold, and silver jewelry. Customers include retailers such as Wal-Mart and major jewelry chains. Affiliates include Susan Fortgang's Royal Asscher Cut branded-diamond company, Japanese joint venture Leer Tokyo Pearl, and about 20% of jeweler Lazare Kaplan.

KEY COMPETITORS
LJ International
Lazare Kaplan
Michael Anthony Jewelers

In-depth profiles of an additional 200 key private companies are found on pages 36–435.

MA LABORATORIES, INC.

2075 N. Capitol Ave.	CEO: Abraham Ma	2001 Sales: $805.0 million
San Jose, CA 95132	CFO: Ricky Chow	1-Yr. Sales Change: (5.8%)
Phone: 408-941-0808	HR: Shareen Wu	Employees: 300
Fax: 408-941-0909	Type: Private	FYE: December 31
Web: www.malabs.com		

If you need a computer part, just ask your MA. Distributor MA Laboratories, one of the largest privately held companies in the Silicon Valley, provides computer resellers and systems integrators with more than 3,000 high-tech gadgets and computer items. MA Labs specializes in memory modules but sells just about everything commonly found in or near a computer, including hard drives, motherboards, CD-ROMs, and video cards. Other products include monitors, software, fax modems, network cards, digital cameras, notebook computers, and accessories. Among MA's suppliers are 3Com, Advanced Micro Devices, Hewlett-Packard, IBM, Intel, Microsoft, Sony, and Toshiba. MA Labs was founded in 1983 by owner and CEO Abraham Ma.

KEY COMPETITORS
Bell Microproducts
Ingram Micro
Tech Data

M. A. MORTENSON COMPANY

700 Meadow Ln. North	CEO: M. A. Mortenson Jr.	2001 Sales: $1,127.5 million
Minneapolis, MN 55422	CFO: Peter A. Conzemius	1-Yr. Sales Change: 4.4%
Phone: 763-522-2100	HR: Daniel R. Haag	Employees: 1,800
Fax: 763-520-3430	Type: Private	FYE: December 31
Web: www.mortenson.com		

It's all bricks and mortar for M. A. Mortenson, one of the largest general contractors in the US. The company's services include site selection and design, financing, construction, and construction and facility management. M. A. Mortenson builds aviation, education, health care, and sports facilities, as well as power plants and dams. Mortenson works primarily in the US, where its latest projects include a new arena for the NBA's Memphis Grizzlies and the Walt Disney Concert Hall, the new home for the Los Angeles Philharmonic Orchestra. The family-owned company was founded in 1954 by M. A. Mortenson Sr., whose son M. A. Mortenson Jr. now serves as chairman and CEO.

KEY COMPETITORS
Hunt Construction
Turner Corporation
Walsh Group

MARATHON ASHLAND PETROLEUM LLC

539 S. Main St.	CEO: Gary R. Heminger	2001 Sales: $27,348.0 million
Findlay, OH 45840	CFO: Garry L. Peiffer	1-Yr. Sales Change: (5.3%)
Phone: 419-422-2121	HR: Rodney P. Nichols	Employees: 27,462
Fax: 419-425-7040	Type: Joint venture	FYE: December 31
Web: www.mapllc.com		

It's not hard to find Marathon Ashland Petroleum (MAP) on the map — the company has operations in 21 states in the US and is charting a course to sustain its position as one of the US's leading oil refiners. A joint venture between Marathon Oil (which owns 62%) and Ashland (38%), MAP operates seven refineries with the combined capacity to process 935,000 barrels of crude oil a day. MAP sells refined products at 3,755 Marathon- and 100 Ashland-branded gas stations, and through retail subsidiary Speedway SuperAmerica, which has more than 2,000 outlets. MAP also holds stakes in more than 6,000 miles of pipeline, and it is the largest US producer of asphalt (with a 100,000 barrels-per-day refining capacity).

KEY COMPETITORS
BP
ChevronTexaco
Exxon Mobil

In-depth profiles of an additional 200 key private companies are found on pages 36–435.

MARATHON CHEESE CORPORATION

304 East St.	CEO: John Skoug	2001 Est. Sales: $600.0 mil.
Marathon, WI 54448	CFO: Gary Peterson	1-Yr. Sales Change: 3.4%
Phone: 715-443-2211	HR: Ronald Leszczynski	Employees: 1,400
Fax: 715-443-2211	Type: Private	FYE: June 30

Which 50 year-old firm has a reason to say "cheese" and mean it? Marathon Cheese, one of the world's largest independent cheese packagers. The company packages cheese for such clients as Kraft Foods, Land O'Lakes, Sysco, Sargento, and Schreiber Foods. It offers sizes from shredded and cubed cheese for consumer convenience to 22-pound blocks. Marathon Cheese packages about five million pounds per week of cheddar, Swiss, and other varieties. Ray and Marie Goldbach started the company in their basement in 1952; the Goldbach family owns the majority of Marathon Cheese.

KEY COMPETITORS
Dairy Farmers of America
Great Lakes Cheese
Leprino Foods

MARC GLASSMAN INC.

5841 W. 130th St.	CEO: Kevin Yaugher	2001 Est. Sales: $750.0 mil.
Parma, OH 44130	CFO: Beth Weiner	1-Yr. Sales Change: 0.7%
Phone: 216-265-7700	HR: Beth Weiner	Employees: 6,100
Fax: 216-362-0041	Type: Private	FYE: December 31
Web: www.marcs.com		

Marc Glassman wants to prove that low prices can lead to big things. The retailer operates about 50 drugstores, most of which are Marc's Deep-Er Discount stores in northeast Ohio, but also a handful of Xpect Discount Drugs in Connecticut and Massachusetts. Marc Glassman's no-frills stores (sorry, credit cards not accepted) range in size from 18,000 sq. ft. to 48,000 sq. ft. Most have pharmacies and offer a constantly changing mix of closeout and excess merchandise, including clothing, cosmetics, housewares, toys, and tools. The company specializes in seasonal products (Christmas, Halloween, lawn and garden). Owner and chairman Marc Glassman founded the company in Middleburg Heights, Ohio, in 1979.

KEY COMPETITORS
CVS
Rite Aid
Walgreen

MARITZ INC.

1375 N. Highway Dr.	CEO: W. Stephen Maritz	2002 Sales: $1,500.0 million
Fenton, MO 63099	CFO: James W. Kienker	1-Yr. Sales Change: 13.8%
Phone: 636-827-4000	HR: Terry L. Goring	Employees: 6,000
Fax: 636-827-3312	Type: Private	FYE: March 31
Web: www.maritz.com		

Not only can Maritz send your employees on business trips, it can motivate them to go. With about 240 offices in more than 40 countries, Maritz offers travel, employee motivation, and marketing services. Its performance improvement and incentive programs help client companies improve workforce quality and customer satisfaction. The company is also one of the nation's largest custom market research companies. In addition, TQ3 Maritz Travel Solutions TUI AG co-own TQ3 Travel Solutions, Europe's top travel firm and a leading global agency with some 1,600 locations in more than 60 countries. The Maritz family owns the company.

KEY COMPETITORS
American Express
Carlson
J.D. Power

In-depth profiles of an additional 200 key private companies are found on pages 36–435.

MARK IV INDUSTRIES, INC.

501 John James Audubon Pkwy.	CEO: William P. Montague	2002 Sales: $1,200.0 million
Amherst, NY 14226	CFO: Mark G. Barberio	1-Yr. Sales Change: (40.0%)
Phone: 716-689-4972	HR: Michelle Acquilina	Employees: 8,000
Fax: 716-689-6098	Type: Private	FYE: February 28
Web: www.mark-iv.com		

Mark IV Industries' engineered components and systems are on the mark when it comes to fluid-handling and power-steering uses. The company's automotive division manufactures idlers, pulleys, belts, power-steering and air-conditioning hoses, manifolds, and water pumps. Mark IV's industrial unit manufactures circulating liquid temperature control systems used to regulate and monitor the temperature of injection molding machines. Mark IV primarily targets aftermarket and OEM customers. European private equity firm BC Partners controls the company.

KEY COMPETITORS
Dana
Dover
United Technologies

THE MARTIN-BROWER COMPANY, L.L.C.

9500 West Bryn Mawr Ave., Ste. 700	CEO: Richard DiStasio	2001 Est. Sales: $2,800.0 mil.
Rosemont, IL 60018	CFO: John Roussel	1-Yr. Sales Change: 12.0%
Phone: 847-227-6500	HR: Phil Menzel	Employees: 2,900
Fax: 847-227-6550	Type: Private	FYE: December 31

Ronald McDonald is worth his weight in gold(en arches) to Martin-Brower, the largest supplier of distribution services to the McDonald's restaurant chain. The company is the exclusive distributor to about half of the McDonald's restaurants in the US, and all of its outlets in Brazil, Canada, Central America, and Puerto Rico, supplying such items as crew hats, first-aid kits, lightbulbs, and trash bags. The company operates 31 distribution centers in seven countries. Martin-Brower changed hands in 1998 when privately owned food and beverage distributor Reyes Holdings purchased the company from UK-based Sygen International (previously PIC International).

KEY COMPETITORS
Anderson-DuBose
Golden State Foods
Keystone Foods

MARTY FRANICH AUTO CENTER

550 Auto Center Dr.	CEO: Steven Franich	2001 Sales: $815.3 million
Watsonville, CA 95076	CFO: Tim Liebel	1-Yr. Sales Change: (11.8%)
Phone: 831-722-4181	HR: —	Employees: —
Fax: 831-724-1853	Type: Private	FYE: December 31
Web: www.franichford.com		

Fleet customers can sail on into Marty Franich Auto Center dealerships. Founded in 1948, the company consists of two full-service dealerships in Watsonville, California, that sell Chrysler, Dodge, Eagle, Ford, Jeep, Lincoln, Mercury, and Plymouth vehicles. The dealer also sells used vehicles, and it operates parts and service departments. The company specializes in sales to fleet buyers and sells to rental outfits nationwide, including Hertz, Budget Rent-a-Car, and Avis Group. President and CEO Steven Franich is the son of founder Martin (Marty) Franich, whose family owns the company.

KEY COMPETITORS
AutoNation
Prospect Motors

📖 In-depth profiles of an additional 200 key private companies are found on pages 36–435.

MARYLAND STATE LOTTERY AGENCY

6776 Reisterstown Rd., Ste. 204
Baltimore, MD 21215
Phone: 410-318-6200
Fax: 410-764-4263
Web: www.msla.state.md.us

CEO: Buddy Roogow
CFO: Gina Smith
HR: Bobby Sinclair
Type: Government-owned

2002 Sales: $1,300.0 million
1-Yr. Sales Change: 7.4%
Employees: 150
FYE: June 30

The Maryland State Lottery Agency offers players a variety of ways to amass a fortune. Among its games of chance are scratch-offs bearing titles such as Betty Boop, High Stakes, Hot Cherries, and Slingo. The agency's numbers games include Lotto, Pick 3, and Pick 4. Maryland State Lottery also participates in the seven-state The Big Game lottery. The agency, which was created in 1973, distributes about 55% of its revenue as prizes; the rest goes to state-funded programs, retailers, and operational expenses. Proceeds from lottery sales helped build Camden Yards, home of Major League Baseball's Baltimore Orioles.

KEY COMPETITORS
Multi-State Lottery
New Jersey Lottery
Pennsylvania Lottery

MASSACHUSETTS INSTITUTE OF TECHNOLOGY

77 Massachusetts Ave.
Cambridge, MA 02139
Phone: 617-253-1000
Fax: 617-253-8000
Web: web.mit.edu

CEO: Charles M. Vest
CFO: Allan S. Bufferd
HR: Laura Avakian
Type: School

2001 Sales: $1,465.0 million
1-Yr. Sales Change: (33.1%)
Employees: 8,700
FYE: June 30

It's patently clear that the Massachusetts Institute of Technology (MIT) takes the prize. A leading research university, the school receives hundreds of patents a year and Nobel Prizes have been awarded to 56 people associated with MIT. Blending that science and engineering acumen with a top business program, MIT graduates have started more than 4,000 companies — Hewlett-Packard and Intel to name just two. Research, much of it federally sponsored, accounts for more than half of the school's revenue. Tuition for MIT's more than 10,200 students runs about $28,230 a year. The faculty of the 26 academic departments includes nearly 960 professors. Founded in 1865, MIT is privately endowed.

MASSACHUSETTS STATE LOTTERY COMMISSION

60 Columbian St.
Braintree, MA 02184
Phone: 781-849-5555
Fax: 781-849-5509
Web: www.masslottery.com

CEO: Jay Mitchell
CFO: Michael Sullivan
HR: Deborah Keyes
Type: Government-owned

2001 Sales: $3,935.9 million
1-Yr. Sales Change: 5.9%
Employees: 410
FYE: June 30

For a lucky few, the Commonwealth creates uncommon wealth. The Massachusetts State Lottery Commission offers several numbers games (Mass Cash, Mass Millions, Megabucks) and scratch-off games (Draw Poker, Lifetime Cash, High Roller). Massachusetts also participates in the seven-state The Big Game lottery. State law requires that at least 45% of lottery proceeds must go to pay prizes, a maximum of 15% can be used for operating expenses, and the remainder must be distributed to the state's 351 cities and towns. The Massachusetts State Lottery Commission was created in 1971.

KEY COMPETITORS
Multi-State Lottery
New Hampshire Lottery
Vermont Lottery

📖 **In-depth profiles of an additional 200 key private companies are found on pages 36–435.**

MBM CORPORATION

2641 Meadowbrook Rd.	CEO: Jerry L. Wordsworth	2001 Est. Sales: $4,236.0 mil.
Rocky Mount, NC 27802	CFO: Jeff Kowalk	1-Yr. Sales Change: 10.8%
Phone: 252-985-7200	HR: Tim Ozment	Employees: 3,500
Fax: 252-985-7241	Type: Private	FYE: December 31

What's on the menu at your favorite restaurant? Just ask MBM Corporation, one of the leading privately owned custom food service distributors in the US. The company specializes in providing food to national restaurant chains such as Arby's, Burger King, Chick-fil-A, and Darden Restaurants (Red Lobster, Olive Garden, Bahama Breeze). MBM fills its customers' orders through its network of about 30 distribution centers across the US. J. R. Wordsworth founded the company about 50 years ago as a retail food distributor. MBM made the transition to its present role in restaurant food distribution after Wordsworth's children bought the business in the 1970s.

KEY COMPETITORS
McLane Foodservice
SYSCO
U.S. Foodservice

MCCARTHY BUILDING COMPANIES, INC.

1341 N. Rock Hill Rd.	CEO: Michael D. Bolen	2002 Sales: $1,050.0 million
St. Louis, MO 63124	CFO: George F. Scherer	1-Yr. Sales Change: (12.9%)
Phone: 314-968-3300	HR: Jan Kraemer	Employees: 2,500
Fax: 314-968-3037	Type: Private	FYE: March 31
Web: www.mccarthy.com		

A company that was in construction before Reconstruction, McCarthy Building Companies is one of the oldest privately held builders in the US. The general contractor and construction manager has projects worldwide and ranks among the top builders of health care facilities in the US. Contracts include heavy construction projects (bridges and water and waste-treatment plants), industrial projects (biopharmaceutical, food processing, and micro-electronics facilities), commercial projects (retail and office buildings), and institutional projects (airports, schools, and prisons). Timothy McCarthy founded the firm in 1864. His great-grandson, chairman emeritus Michael McCarthy, sold the firm to its employees in 2002.

KEY COMPETITORS
Bovis Lend Lease
Skanska
Turner Corporation

MCJUNKIN CORPORATION

835 Hillcrest Dr.	CEO: H. Barnard Wehrle III	2001 Sales: $830.0 million
Charleston, WV 25311	CFO: Michael H. Wehrle	1-Yr. Sales Change: 12.0%
Phone: 304-348-5211	HR: Chilton Mueller	Employees: 1,600
Fax: 304-348-4922	Type: Private	FYE: December 31
Web: www.mcjunkin.com		

McJunkin is a nationwide distributor of steel, pipe, valves and fittings, oil-field tubular goods, and drilling, electrical, and mining supplies. It also provides services such as assembly, electropolishing, valve actuation and servicing, and project management. McJunkin's clients include companies from the power, pulp and paper, mining, and automotive industries. McJunkin's subsidiaries include Precision Clean Piping, McA Target Oil Tools, and McJunkin Controls. The company, which has more than 100 US locations, operates in Mexico through its Trottner-McJunkin joint venture. Founded in 1921, the firm is owned by descendants of the McJunkin family.

KEY COMPETITORS
American Cast Iron
Cooper Cameron
Tyco International

📖 In-depth profiles of an additional 200 key private companies are found on pages 36–435.

MCKEE FOODS CORPORATION

10260 McKee Rd.	CEO: Jack McKee	2002 Sales: $970.0 million
Collegedale, TN 37315	CFO: Barry Patterson	1-Yr. Sales Change: 7.8%
Phone: 423-238-7111	HR: Eva L. Disbro	Employees: 6,500
Fax: 423-238-7101	Type: Private	FYE: June 30
Web: www.mckeefoods.com		

When Little Debbie smiles up out of your lunch bag, you know you are loved. McKee Foods' Little Debbie is the US's leading brand of snack cake, named for and featuring the smiling face of the company's founders' granddaughter. The company makes snack cakes, creme-filled cookies, crackers, and candy. McKee Foods also sells granola bars, fruit snacks, and cereals under its Sunbelt brand. Low prices and family packs of individually wrapped treats have driven sales. McKee Foods is the largest independent bakery in the U.S. The company started in 1934 with founder O. D. McKee and his wife, Ruth, selling nickel cakes from the back seat of their car. The company is still owned and operated by the McKee family.

KEY COMPETITORS
Interstate Bakeries
Lance
Tasty Baking

MCWANE CORP.

2900 Hwy. 280, Ste. 300	CEO: John J. McMahon Jr.	2001 Est. Sales: $800.0 mil.
Birmingham, AL 35223	CFO: Charles Nowlin	1-Yr. Sales Change: 6.0%
Phone: 205-414-3100	HR: —	Employees: 5,200
Fax: 205-414-3180	Type: Private	FYE: December 31

As a leading manufacturer of fire hydrants, McWane may just be a dog's best friend. The privately held company is also a leading maker of ductile iron pipe and water valves. With the acquisition of Amerex in Trussville, Alabama, McWane has become one of the world's leading makers of fire extinguishers and fire suppression systems. Through its Manchester Tank division, the company also produces gas grills, as well as propane tanks for recreational vehicles. McWane was founded in 1921 and continues to be family-owned. Its Clow Water subsidiary has been making fire hydrants since 1890.

KEY COMPETITORS
American Cast Iron
INTERMET
McJunkin

MEDIANEWS GROUP, INC.

1560 Broadway, Ste. 2100	CEO: William Dean Singleton	2002 Sales: $711.7 million
Denver, CO 80202	CFO: Ronald A. Mayo	1-Yr. Sales Change: (16.6%)
Phone: 303-563-6360	HR: Charles M. Kamen	Employees: 11,200
Fax: 303-894-9327	Type: Private	FYE: June 30
Web: www.medianewsgroup.com		

Paper cuts can really hurt, especially when they're made by newspaper predator MediaNews Group. Known for ruthlessly cutting staff at unprofitable newspapers, the company publishes 50 dailies (including *The Denver Post* and *The Salt Lake Tribune*) and about 95 non-dailies in a dozen states. It also operates Web sites for most of its daily papers and operates a small number of radio and television stations. The company is a joint venture of vice chairman and CEO Dean Singleton and chairman Richard Scudder, who began buying newspapers together in 1983.

KEY COMPETITORS
E. W. Scripps
Gannett
Tribune

In-depth profiles of an additional 200 key private companies are found on pages 36–435.

MEDLINE INDUSTRIES, INC.

1 Medline Place	CEO: Charles S. Mills	2001 Sales: $1,231.0 million
Mundelein, IL 60060	CFO: Bill Abington	1-Yr. Sales Change: 21.2%
Phone: 847-949-5500	HR: Joseph Becker	Employees: 3,500
Fax: 800-351-1512	Type: Private	FYE: December 31
Web: www.medline.com		

Medline Industries, a private medical equipment distributor and manufacturer, goes toe-to-toe with the bigger guns, selling more than 100,000 products, such as furnishings for hospital rooms, exam equipment, housekeeping supplies, and surgical gloves and garments. The company manufactures about 70% of its products and then distributes them to such customers as hospitals, extended care facilities, and home health care providers. Marketing efforts are handled by Medline's some 600 sales representatives and roughly 20 distribution centers. The company is owned by the Mills family, which founded Medline in 1910 as a manufacturer of nurses' gowns.

KEY COMPETITORS
Allegiance
Owens & Minor
Tyco Healthcare

MEDSTAR HEALTH

5565 Sterrett Place, 5th Fl.	CEO: John P. McDaniel	2001 Sales: $1,990.0 million
Columbia, MD 21044	CFO: Michael A. Curran	1-Yr. Sales Change: 10.6%
Phone: 410-772-6500	HR: David Noe	Employees: 21,700
Fax: 410-715-3905	Type: Not-for-profit	FYE: June 30
Web: www.medstarhealth.org		

Whether you've been knocked out and are seeing stars or you're just plain sickly, MedStar Health can cater to you. The not-for-profit organization runs seven hospitals in Baltimore and Washington, DC. With more than 4,000 affiliated physicians, MedStar offers such services as acute care, rehabilitation, assisted living, hospice, long-term care, and emergency services. Its MedStar Physician Partners contracts with private physicians in the Baltimore/Washington, DC area. MedStar also manages an independent practice association, which includes both primary and specialty care physicians. After continued financial losses, Georgetown University sold a controlling interest in its hospital to MedStar.

KEY COMPETITORS
Ascension
Bon Secours Health
Johns Hopkins Medicine

MEMORIAL SLOAN-KETTERING CANCER CENTER

1275 York Ave.	CEO: Harold Varmus	2001 Sales: $959.4 million
New York, NY 10021	CFO: Michael P. Gutnick	1-Yr. Sales Change: 9.5%
Phone: 212-639-2000	HR: Michael Browne	Employees: 7,609
Fax: 212-639-3576	Type: Not-for-profit	FYE: December 31
Web: www.mskcc.org		

Ranked as one of the nation's top cancer centers, Memorial Sloan-Kettering Cancer Center includes Memorial Hospital for pediatric and adult cancer care and the Sloan-Kettering Institute for cancer research activities. The center specializes in bone-marrow transplants and chemotherapy and offers programs in cancer prevention, treatment, research, and education. Memorial Sloan-Kettering offers inpatient and outpatient services to more than 10,000 patients every year. Other services include pain management, rehabilitation, and psychological programs.

KEY COMPETITORS
Johns Hopkins Medicine
New York City Health and Hospitals
University of Texas

📖 **In-depth profiles of an additional 200 key private companies are found on pages 36–435.**

MEMPHIS LIGHT, GAS AND WATER DIVISION

220 S. Main St.	CEO: Herman Morris Jr.	2000 Sales: $1,160.0 million
Memphis, TN 38103	CFO: John McCullough	1-Yr. Sales Change: 8.0%
Phone: 901-528-4011	HR: Michael Magness	Employees: 2,600
Fax: 901-528-4758	Type: Government-owned	FYE: December 31
Web: www.mlgw.com		

Memphis Light, Gas and Water Division (MLGW) helps lighten up the Memphis blues. The municipally owned utility provides electricity, water, and natural gas services for all of Shelby County, Tennessee, including the city of Memphis. It serves primarily residential and commercial customers. MLGW buys electricity from the Tennessee Valley Authority and distributes it to more than 409,000 customers. The company purchases natural gas on the spot market, transmits it through open access pipelines, and delivers it to 308,000 customers. Through its artesian water system, the company supplies water to nearly 250,000 customers. MLGW is also building a fiber-optic network in Memphis.

KEY COMPETITORS
AGL Resources
American Water Works
Nashville Electric

MENASHA CORPORATION

1645 Bergstrom Rd.	CEO: Harold R. Smethills Jr.	2001 Sales: $1,000.0 million
Neenah, WI 54957	CFO: Arthur Huge	1-Yr. Sales Change: (10.8%)
Phone: 920-751-1000	HR: Linda Mingus	Employees: 5,500
Fax: 920-751-1236	Type: Private	FYE: December 31
Web: www.menasha.com		

Menasha has the whole package. Founded in 1849 as a woodenware business, the holding company now owns businesses that make packaging and paperboard, returnable material handling systems, product labels, and promotional materials. Each company is independently operated. The company's main subsidiaries are Menasha Packaging Company (corrugated packaging), ORBIS Corporation (returnable materials handling products), Poly Hi Solidur (polymers), and Promo Edge Company (printing). It also has investments in other manufacturing companies. Menasha operates nearly 70 facilities across the US and in seven other countries. Descendants of founder Elisha Smith own a majority of Menasha.

KEY COMPETITORS
Boise Cascade
Smurfit-Stone Container
Sonoco Products

MERIDIAN AUTOMOTIVE SYSTEMS, INC.

550 Town Center Dr., Ste. 475	CEO: H. H. Wacaser	2001 Sales: $976.8 million
Dearborn, MI 48126	CFO: Richard Newsted	1-Yr. Sales Change: 21.6%
Phone: 313-336-4182	HR: Thomas C. Eggebeen	Employees: 5,900
Fax: 313-253-4026	Type: Private	FYE: December 31
Web: www.meridianautosystems.com		

From bumper to bumper, Meridian Automotive Systems has the line on what it takes to keep a vehicle together. The auto parts company operates three business segments: Exterior Composites (body panels, fenders, tailgates); Interiors and Exterior Lighting (floor consoles, fog lamps, instrument panels, signal lamps); and Front and Rear End Modules (bumpers, energy-absorbing foam, plastic fascias). Meridian's major customers include Ford, General Motors, and DaimlerChysler. The company operates 20 primary manufacturing plants in North and South America. Meridian is owned by Windward Capital Partners, Capital d'Amerique CDPQ Inc., Credit Suisse First Boston, and Northwestern Mutual Life Insurance.

KEY COMPETITORS
A.G. Simpson
Faurecia
Tower Automotive

In-depth profiles of an additional 200 key private companies are found on pages 36–435.

MERRILL CORPORATION

1 Merrill Circle	CEO: John W. Castro	2000 Sales: $587.7 million
St. Paul, MN 55108	CFO: Robert H. Nazarian	1-Yr. Sales Change: 15.4%
Phone: 651-646-4501	HR: Kathleen A. Larkin	Employees: 4,157
Fax: 651-646-5332	Type: Private	FYE: January 31
Web: www.merrillcorp.com		

This company merrily manages documents and provides data and printing services. Merrill Corporation is among the largest document management firms in the US and a leading provider of financial document services, such as preparing and delivering electronic filings to the SEC, producing annual reports, and creating other time-sensitive documents. It also provides software and services to help its clients manage electronic documents and maintains data centers at a number of client sites. In addition, Merrill provides corporate communication materials and traditional printing services. The company, controlled by Credit Suisse First Boston, has nearly 50 offices worldwide.

KEY COMPETITORS
Bowne
Mail-Well
R. R. Donnelley

METALDYNE CORPORATION

47603 Halyard Dr.	CEO: Timothy D. Leuliette	2001 Sales: $2,127.8 million
Plymouth, MI 48170	CFO: William M. Lowe	1-Yr. Sales Change: 28.9%
Phone: 734-207-6200	HR: Jim Strahley	Employees: 12,500
Fax: 734-207-6500	Type: Private	FYE: December 31
Web: www.metaldyne.com		

Whether you're cruising down the highway or being towed, Metaldyne products may be involved. The metal-forming and -machining company's Chassis Group, Engine Group, and Transmission and Driveline Group make automotive components for passenger cars and commercial vehicles. Products include components and assemblies for engines, noise and vibration control, transmissions, wheels, suspensions, axles, and drivelines. Metaldyne's Diversified Industrial Group subsidiary makes packaging and sealing products, towing systems, insulation facing, and cutting tools. Metaldyne, now part of Heartland Industrial Partners, was formed through the consolidation of MascoTech, Simpson Industries, and Global Metal Technologies.

KEY COMPETITORS
Dana
Delphi
Visteon

METHODIST HEALTH CARE SYSTEM

6565 Fannin St.	CEO: Peter Butler	2000 Sales: $795.0 million
Houston, TX 77030	CFO: Albert Zimmerli	1-Yr. Sales Change: 31.3%
Phone: 713-790-3333	HR: Donald T. Benson	Employees: 8,100
Fax: 713-790-4885	Type: Not-for-profit	FYE: December 31
Web: www.methodisthealth.com		

The not-for-profit Methodist Health Care System owns and operates several Houston-area hospitals, including Methodist Hospital, San Jacinto Methodist Hospital, Methodist Diagnostic Hospital, and Methodist Health Center-Sugar Land. Flagship Methodist Hospital is the Baylor College of Medicine's teaching facility and is also known for innovations in urology and neurosurgery, among other specialties. Methodist Health Care's health care plan, MethodistCare, offers HMO, PPO, and point-of-service options; its Visiting Nurse Association provides home health services. The Methodist Health Care System was founded in 1919.

KEY COMPETITORS
HEALTHSOUTH
Memorial Hermann Healthcare
St. Luke's

In-depth profiles of an additional 200 key private companies are found on pages 36–435.

METHODIST HEALTHCARE

1211 Union Ave., Ste. 700
Memphis, TN 38104
Phone: 901-726-7000
Fax: 901-726-2300
Web: www.methodisthealth.org

CEO: Gary S. Shorb
CFO: Chris McLean
HR: Carol Ross-Spang
Type: Not-for-profit

2000 Sales: $771.7 million
1-Yr. Sales Change: (0.1%)
Employees: 13,000
FYE: December 31

Methodist Healthcare operates hospitals, home health agencies, and clinics in the Memphis area. Founded in 1918 by John Sherard, the not-for-profit health care system serves patients of all denominations and operates about a dozen hospitals, including the Le Bonheur Children's Medical Center. Methodist Healthcare's other offerings — some of which are operated through affiliations and joint ventures — include home health and extended care services, substance abuse recovery programs, sleep disorder centers, and physical therapy. Methodist Healthcare also operates physician practices and a physician referral service.

KEY COMPETITORS
Baptist Hospital
Catholic Healthcare Partners
HMA

MFA INCORPORATED

201 Ray Young Dr.
Columbia, MO 65201
Phone: 573-874-5111
Fax: 573-876-5430
Web: www.mfa-inc.com

CEO: Don Copenhaver
CFO: Allen Floyd
HR: Janice Schuerman
Type: Cooperative

2001 Sales: $620.8 million
1-Yr. Sales Change: 10.7%
Employees: —
FYE: June 30

Begun in 1914 when seven Missouri farmers got together to buy 1,150 pounds of binder twine, agricultural cooperative MFA today ties together 45,000 farmers in Missouri and adjacent states. MFA, the US's oldest regional co-op, supplies its member-owners with manufacturing, distribution, and purchasing services. It runs about 150 retail service centers and works with some 400 independent dealers. MFA produces and markets beef, dairy, horse, and swine feeds, as well as soybean, corn, wheat, grass, grain, and alfalfa seeds. The co-op also provides crop protection services, animal health products, and farm supplies.

KEY COMPETITORS
Ag Processing
Cenex Harvest States
Farmland Industries

MICHAEL FOODS, INC.

5353 Wayzata Blvd., Signal Bank Bldg., Ste. 324
Minneapolis, MN 55416
Phone: 952-546-1500
Fax: 952-546-3711
Web: www.michaelfoods.com

CEO: Gregg A. Ostrander
CFO: John D. Reedy
HR: —
Type: Private

2001 Sales: $1,161.3 million
1-Yr. Sales Change: 7.5%
Employees: 4,050
FYE: December 31

For Michael Foods, the egg comes first (to answer that age-old riddle). The diversified food processor and distributor has four divisions, but eggs account for about 55% of sales. With the help of 14 million hens, Michael Foods is a leading US producer of long-shelf-life liquid eggs to industry and consumers. Its other divisions produce Kohler dairy-mix products and Northern Star refrigerated potato products and distribute refrigerated foods such as cheese, eggs, and butter. Customers include food processors, food service companies, and grocery stores. A group led by management, the Michael family, and two investment firms took the company private in 2001.

KEY COMPETITORS
Cal-Maine Foods
Kraft Foods
Primera Foods

📖 In-depth profiles of an additional 200 key private companies are found on pages 36–435.

MICHIGAN LOTTERY

101 E. Hillsdale	CEO: James E. Kipp	2001 Sales: $1,614.7 million
Lansing, MI 48933	CFO: Scott Matteson	1-Yr. Sales Change: (4.7%)
Phone: 517-335-5756	HR: —	Employees: 200
Fax: 517-335-5644	Type: Government-owned	FYE: December 31
Web: www.michigan.gov/lottery		

Michigan's kids win in the Michigan Lottery, which has contributed some $9.8 billion to public education in the Great Lakes State since the lottery was started in 1972. The Michigan Lottery runs the Michigan Millions jackpot game, as well as daily numbers games and instant-win games such as 3 For The Money, Silver Dollars, and Cashword. About half of ticket sales are awarded in prizes, while more than 35% goes to the state's K-12 education fund. Retailers also get a small commission on ticket sales (about 7%). In addition, Michigan takes part in the multistate lottery, The Big Game, with Georgia, Illinois, Maryland, Massachusetts, New Jersey, and Virginia.

KEY COMPETITORS
Hoosier Lottery
Multi-State Lottery
Ohio Lottery

MICRO ELECTRONICS, INC.

4119 Leap Rd.	CEO: Dale Brown	2001 Est. Sales: $900.0 mil.
Hilliard, OH 43026	CFO: James Koehler	1-Yr. Sales Change: 20.0%
Phone: 614-850-3000	HR: Angie Miller	Employees: 2,300
Fax: 614-850-3001	Type: Private	FYE: September 30
Web: www.microelectronics.com		

Micro Electronics is the parent of several technologically gifted children: its divisions. The company's nearly 20 Micro Center computer retail stores which average 45,000 sq.ft. feature about 36,000 products organized in more than a dozen specialized departments. Micro Center is the largest of Micro Electronics' divisions and operates in 13 states. Micro Electronics sells its own brands of notebook and desktop computers under the WinBook and PowerSpec names. Micro Center Online is the company's online and phone order operation; training is provided through the Micro Center Computer Education unit. The company is owned by founder and president John Baker and other private investors.

KEY COMPETITORS
Best Buy
Circuit City
CompUSA

MICRO WAREHOUSE, INC.

535 Connecticut Ave.	CEO: Jerome B. York	2001 Est. Sales: $2,200.0 mil.
Norwalk, CT 06854	CFO: Laurie Schmalkuche	1-Yr. Sales Change: (15.4%)
Phone: 203-899-4000	HR: Larry Midler	Employees: 2,700
Fax: 203-899-4203	Type: Private	FYE: December 31
Web: www.warehouse.com		

Do you count disks instead of sheep? Micro Warehouse lets you shop in the middle of the night. The company sells computer products through catalogs, the Internet, and telemarketers. Serving individual, corporate, education, and government customers, the company distributes more than 120 million catalogs worldwide each year. Micro Warehouse offers more than 30,000 items, including computers, hardware, software, peripherals, and networking equipment. Most of the company's sales are in the US. An investor group including CEO Jerome York, Gary Wilson, and Freeman Spogli & Co. bought the company in early 2000.

KEY COMPETITORS
CDW Computer Centers
CompuCom
Insight Enterprises

In-depth profiles of an additional 200 key private companies are found on pages 36–435.

MICRONPC, LLC

906 E. Karcher Rd.
Nampa, ID 83687
Phone: 208-898-3434
Fax: 208-898-3424
Web: www.micronpc.com

CEO: Michael S. Adkins
CFO: —
HR: —
Type: Private

2002 Sales: —
1-Yr. Sales Change: —
Employees: 1,000
FYE: August 31

MicronPC is a chip off the old Micron block. Once the personal computer division of Micron Electronics (now Interland), MicronPC manufactures desktop and notebook computers, and servers. The company also resells accessories such as Lexmark printers and Intel wireless LAN equipment (access points, PC cards). MicronPC, which has found success primarily in government markets, is focusing on growth in small and medium-sized business, education, and consumer markets. Gores Technology Group, a specialist in the acquisition and management of technology companies, bought MicronPC in 2001.

KEY COMPETITORS
Dell Computer
Gateway
Hewlett-Packard

MINNESOTA MUTUAL COMPANIES, INC.

400 Robert St. North
St. Paul, MN 55101
Phone: 651-665-3500
Fax: 651-665-4488
Web: www.minnesotamutual.com

CEO: Robert L. Senkler
CFO: Gregory S. Strong
HR: Kathy L. Pinkett
Type: Private

2001 Sales: $1,801.4 million
1-Yr. Sales Change: (9.9%)
Employees: 4,400
FYE: December 31

With 10,000 lakes in their state, Minnesotans have learned to be careful. Minnesota Mutual's flagship Minnesota Life Insurance helps them take care, with individual and group life and disability insurance and annuities. Other business units include Advantus Capital Management, which provides asset management. Two other subsidiaries, Securian Holding and Securian Financial (offering advisory programs, mutual funds, and annuities), were created by the conversion of Minnesota Mutual Life into the mutual holding company Minnesota Mutual Companies.

KEY COMPETITORS
New York Life
Northwestern Mutual
Prudential

MINYARD FOOD STORES, INC.

777 Freeport Pkwy.
Coppell, TX 75019
Phone: 972-393-8700
Fax: 972-462-9407
Web: www.minyards.com

CEO: Gretchen Minyard Williams
CFO: Mario J. LaForte
HR: Alan Vaughan
Type: Private

2001 Est. Sales: $910.0 mil.
1-Yr. Sales Change: (9.0%)
Employees: 6,700
FYE: June 30

Everything's bigger in Texas, including regional grocery chains such as Minyard Food Stores. Its 70-plus supermarkets are located primarily in the competitive Dallas/Fort Worth market, where it has about a 10% share. Company banners include about 30 Minyard supermarkets, some 20 Sack 'n Save warehouse stores (low-cost shopping with customers bagging their own groceries), and more than 20 Carnival Food Stores, which offer more ethnic fare. Minyard also owns 14 On the Go gas stations. The Minyard family started the company in 1932 with a single store in east Dallas. Minyard Food Stores is among the largest US private companies owned and run by women: sisters Elizabeth Minyard and Gretchen Minyard Williams.

KEY COMPETITORS
Albertson's
Kroger
Randall's

📖 **In-depth profiles of an additional 200 key private companies are found on pages 36–435.**

MODERN CONTINENTAL COMPANIES, INC.

600 Memorial Dr.
Cambridge, MA 02139
Phone: 617-864-6300
Fax: 617-864-8766
Web: www.moderncontinental.com

CEO: Lelio Marino
CFO: Peter Grela
HR: Edward Burns
Type: Private

2002 Sales: $1,117.0 million
1-Yr. Sales Change: (0.1%)
Employees: 4,823
FYE: June 30

Modern Continental Companies is a modern concern with Old World values. Italian immigrant Lelio Marino founded the company in 1967 after he and co-worker Kenneth Anderson left a Boston construction firm. A heavy construction leader in New England, Modern Continental Companies focuses on highways, mass transit systems, and other infrastucture projects. Its most notable current job is on Boston's Central Artery Tunnel, "The Big Dig," due for completion in 2003. The company also develops residential, commercial, and marina projects; Marino's personal interests have led the company to dabble in health care, restaurant operation, organic farming, and tourism. CEO Marino owns 75% of the company; Anderson, 25%.

KEY COMPETITORS
Bechtel
Granite Construction
Peter Kiewit Sons'

MODUS MEDIA, INC.

690 Canton St.
Westwood, MA 02090
Phone: 781-407-2000
Fax: 781-407-3800
Web: www.modusmedia.com

CEO: Terence M. Leahy
CFO: Laki Nomicos
HR: Mike Quinn
Type: Private

2001 Sales: $606.0 million
1-Yr. Sales Change: (11.1%)
Employees: 3,860
FYE: December 31

The meaning of life is mysterious, so Modus Media keeps its customers fulfilled in another sense. Formerly Modus Media International, the company provides outsourced manufacturing, fulfillment, and distribution services for such hardware and software firms as Sun Microsystems, Dell, Sony, and Microsoft. The company has more than 20 globally linked supply centers in a dozen countries. In addition, it offers online transaction services such as e-commerce Web site design, payment processing, and fulfillment. Modus Media also provides customer relations services. The company was spun off from Stream International in 1998.

KEY COMPETITORS
Sykes Enterprises
West Corporation
Zomax

MOHEGAN TRIBAL GAMING AUTHORITY

1 Mohegan Sun Blvd.
Uncasville, CT 06382
Phone: 860-862-8000
Fax: 860-862-7167
Web: www.mohegansun.com

CEO: William J. Velardo
CFO: Jeffrey E. Hartmann
HR: Kevin Vogel
Type: Private

2001 Sales: $786.6 million
1-Yr. Sales Change: 6.3%
Employees: 7,583
FYE: September 30

The sun also rises at Mohegan Sun Casino, a complex run by the Mohegan Tribal Gaming Authority for the Mohegan Tribe of Indians of Connecticut. The Native American-themed facility's 315,000 sq. ft. of gaming space in the Casino of the Earth (opened in 1996) and Casino of the Sky (2001) includes more than 6,100 slot machines, 240 gaming and 42 poker tables, and simulcast horse race wagering. A $1 billion expansion has added a 10,000-seat arena, 300-seat cabaret, and dozens of stores and restaurants. Gambling revenues go to after-school and cultural programs for the tribe and financial assistance to other tribes, and to pay for college education for tribal members; a quarter of the slots revenue goes to the state.

KEY COMPETITORS
Harrah's Entertainment
Mashantucket Pequot Gaming
Trump Hotels & Casinos

📖 **In-depth profiles of an additional 200 key private companies are found on pages 36–435.**

MONTEFIORE MEDICAL CENTER

111 E. 210th St.	CEO: Spencer Foreman	2001 Sales: $1,379.3 million
Bronx, NY 10467	CFO: Joel A. Perlman	1-Yr. Sales Change: 5.6%
Phone: 718-920-4321	HR: Roberta Cash	Employees: 11,000
Fax: 718-920-6321	Type: Not-for-profit	FYE: December 31
Web: www.montefiore.com		

As the university hospital for the Albert Einstein College of Medicine, Montefiore Medical Center is a leading teaching and research center. More than a century old, the hospital serves residents of New York City (particularly the Bronx, where it is located) and southern Westchester County through more than 30 locations. It also offers skilled nursing care, home health care, psychiatric services, and a children's medical center. Specialties include cardiology, oncology, women's health, and AIDS research. The hospital has a partnership with Bentley Health Care, created by renowned oncologist Bernard Salick, to open cancer clinics in the Bronx, Manhattan, and Westchester County.

KEY COMPETITORS
Catholic Healthcare Network
New York City Health and Hospitals
Saint Vincent Catholic Medical Centers

MOTOR COACH INDUSTRIES INTERNATIONAL, INC.

1700 E. Golf Rd.	CEO: Stephen K. Clough	2001 Est. Sales: $700.0 mil.
Schaumburg, IL 60173	CFO: Horst Sieben	1-Yr. Sales Change: 1.1%
Phone: 847-285-2000	HR: Barry Melnkovic	Employees: 4,200
Fax: 847-285-2013	Type: Private	FYE: December 31
Web: www.ridemci.com		

Do you know what NFL analyst John Madden and inmates of the Los Angeles County jail have in common? Both of them take a bus — a bus made by Motor Coach Industries International (MCII). The company builds luxury buses under the MCII and Dina brands. MCII's buses are up to 45 feet long and, if you buy one like Madden's, offer such creature comforts as full kitchens and marble bathtubs (inmates enjoy fewer amenities). The company's commuter coaches feature vacuum flush toilets and six-monitor video systems. MCII also makes ISTV prison buses and offers motor coach service, financing, and refurbishing. Investment firm Joseph Littlejohn & Levy owns more than 60% of MCII; Mexico's Gómez-Flores family owns the rest.

KEY COMPETITORS
Fleetwood Enterprises
Monaco Coach
Thor Industries

MSX INTERNATIONAL, INC.

22355 W. Eleven Mile Rd.	CEO: Thomas T. Stallkamp	2001 Sales: $929.3 million
Southfield, MI 48034	CFO: Frederick K. Minturn	1-Yr. Sales Change: (10.2%)
Phone: 248-299-1000	HR: Paul Wagner	Employees: 10,142
Fax: 248-829-6250	Type: Private	FYE: December 31
Web: www.msxi.com		

MSX International (MSXI) never tires of steering its clients into the driver's seat. The company provides staffing, engineering, and other business services to clients primarily from the auto industry. MSXI generates about 75% of its sales by providing services to automotive companies, including DaimlerChrysler, Ford, and GM. Among its offerings are temporary and permanent staffing, executive search, training, product engineering, program management, supply chain management, and custom communications. Citigroup owns more than 75% of the company.

KEY COMPETITORS
ADP
Adecco
EDS

📖 **In-depth profiles of an additional 200 key private companies are found on pages 36–435.**

MTD PRODUCTS INC.

5965 Grafton Rd.	CEO: Curtis E. Moll	2001 Est. Sales: $800.0 mil.
Valley City, OH 44280	CFO: —	1-Yr. Sales Change: 6.7%
Phone: 330-225-2600	HR: Regis A. Dauk	Employees: 6,500
Fax: 330-273-4617	Type: Private	FYE: July 31
Web: www.mtdproducts.com		

MTD Products wants to mow down its foes. The outdoor power equipment manufacturer makes walk-behind and tractor mowers, snow throwers, edgers, and tillers under the Cub Cadet, White Outdoor, Yard-Man, and Yard Machines brands. Its Cub Cadet Commercial line is aimed at landscapers. MTD's Mechanical Systems also makes transmission systems for the appliance industry. The company owns 56% of Shiloh Industries, which bought MTD's auto parts division in 1999. Two years later MTD bought the Troy-Bilt tiller and mower business from Garden Way, which filed for bankruptcy. MTD was formed in 1932 by German immigrants Theo Moll, Emil Jochum, and Erwin Gerhard as the Modern Tool and Die Company. The Moll family owns MTD.

KEY COMPETITORS
Black & Decker
Deere
Toro

MULTI-STATE LOTTERY ASSOCIATION

1701 48th St., Ste. 210	CEO: Charles Strutt	2001 Sales: $1,130.3 million
West Des Moines, IA 50266	CFO: J. Bret Toyne	1-Yr. Sales Change: 5.2%
Phone: 515-453-1400	HR: —	Employees: —
Fax: 515-453-1420	Type: Association	FYE: June 30
Web: www.musl.com		

It takes a lot of MUSL to produce some of the largest jackpots in the world. Made up of 24 member lotteries, the Multi-State Lottery Association (MUSL) operates the Powerball drawing, which has produced one of the world's biggest jackpot prizes — $295 million in 1998. Through MUSL, states can combine their buying power to get large jackpots and drive lottery sales. The not-for-profit association, which pays out half of its ticket sales in prizes and uses the other half to help fund state legislature projects, allows the states to share the cost of lottery operation. MUSL was founded in 1988 by six state lotteries. Although Powerball is its most popular game, MUSL also offers 2by2 and Wild Card 2, among others.

KEY COMPETITORS
Massachusetts State Lottery
New York State Lottery
Texas Lottery

MWH GLOBAL, INC.

300 N. Lake Ave., Ste. 1200	CEO: Robert B. Uhler	2001 Sales: $722.0 million
Pasadena, CA 91101	CFO: David J. D. Harper	1-Yr. Sales Change: 31.3%
Phone: 626-796-9141	HR: Gary Melillo	Employees: 5,500
Fax: 626-568-6619	Type: Private	FYE: September 30
Web: www.mw.com		

MWH Global's initials tell the story of this energy and environmental engineering, construction, and water resource management firm formed by the 2001 merger of Montgomery Watson and HARZA Engineering. Montgomery Watson has brought water, wastewater, and environmental specialties to the table, while HARZA has added its expertise in power plant design to the mix. MWH Global offers design, construction, finance, operation, and maintenance services for projects in more than 30 countries in the Americas, the Asia/Pacific Rim region, Europe, and the Middle East. The new company has deep roots: Montgomery Watson was founded in 1945, and HARZA was founded in 1920. MWH Global employees own the company.

KEY COMPETITORS
Bechtel
Black & Veatch
Dick Corporation

In-depth profiles of an additional 200 key private companies are found on pages 36–435.

NASHVILLE ELECTRIC SERVICE

1214 Church St.	CEO: Donald Kohanski	2001 Sales: $716.2 million
Nashville, TN 37246	CFO: Decosta E. Jenkins	1-Yr. Sales Change: 2.3%
Phone: 615-747-3981	HR: Herb Deberry	Employees: 992
Fax: 615-747-3596	Type: Government-owned	FYE: June 30
Web: www.nespower.com		

The "Nashville Sound" would be hard to hear without Nashville Electric Service (NES), the power distributor to nearly 330,000 customers in central Tennessee. One of the largest government-owned utilities in the US, the company is required to purchase its power from another government-owned operator, the Tennessee Valley Authority (TVA). With state and national energy deregulation in the offing, both NES and TVA are expecting changes in their relationship. NES is ready to rock 'n' roll after the divorce. Anticipating deregulation, the company wants to cut its obligations to TVA and join the rush to pursue other power sources, including purchasing on the open market and self-generation.

KEY COMPETITORS
AEP
Duke Energy
Memphis Light

NATIONAL ASSOCIATION FOR STOCK CAR AUTO RACING

1801 W. International Speedway Blvd.	CEO: Mike Helton	2000 Est. Sales: $2,000.0 mil.
Daytona Beach, FL 32115	CFO: Doris Rumery	1-Yr. Sales Change: 33.3%
Phone: 386-253-0611	HR: Starr Gsell	Employees: —
Fax: 386-252-8804	Type: Private	FYE: December 31
Web: www.nascar.com		

NASCAR: It's not just for rednecks anymore. The National Association for Stock Car Auto Racing is one of the fastest-growing spectator sports in the US, appealing to all demographics, including women, who make up 40% of its audience. NASCAR runs more than 90 races each year in 25 states through three racing circuits: the Busch, Craftsman Truck, and its signature Winston Cup Series. The Winston Cup Series, featuring popular drivers like Jeff Gordon and Dale Jarrett, alone draws more than 6 million race fans each year. NBC, FOX, and Turner Broadcasting have taken note, paying $2.4 billion over six years for broadcast rights. NASCAR was founded in 1947 by Bill France and is still owned by the France family.

KEY COMPETITORS
CART
Indy Racing League
NFL

NATIONAL DISTRIBUTING COMPANY, INC.

1 National Dr. SW	CEO: Jay M. Davis	2001 Est. Sales: $1,700.0 mil.
Atlanta, GA 30336	CFO: John A. Carlos	1-Yr. Sales Change: 6.3%
Phone: 404-696-9440	HR: Bruce E. Carter	Employees: 2,500
Fax: 404-691-6238	Type: Private	FYE: December 31
Web: www.ndcweb.com		

Although National Distributing Company tries to be a wallflower, the beverages it sells often make it the life of the party. An intensely private company founded in the 1900s by Chris Carlos (joined by Alfred Davis in 1942), National Distributing is among the nation's top three wholesale wine, spirits, and beer vendors. The company distributes such brands as Jack Daniels whiskey, Jose Cuervo tequila, Korbel wine, and Smirnoff vodka. National Distributing operates in Colorado, Florida, Georgia, Maryland, New Mexico, Ohio, South Carolina, Virginia, and Washington, DC. The Carlos and Davis families own and operate National Distributing.

KEY COMPETITORS
Georgia Crown Distributing
Southern Wine & Spirits
Sunbelt Beverage

📖 **In-depth profiles of an additional 200 key private companies are found on pages 36–435.**

NATIONAL ENVELOPE CORPORATION

29-10 Hunters Point Ave.
Long Island City, NY 11101
Phone: 718-784-0505
Fax: 718-706-7663
Web: www.nationalenvelope.com

CEO: Leslie F. Stern
CFO: Nathan F. Moser
HR: Karen Schreck
Type: Private

2001 Est. Sales: $625.0 mil.
1-Yr. Sales Change: 38.9%
Employees: 5,000
FYE: December 31

Pushing the envelope is this company's business. National Envelope makes some 100 million envelopes each day, ranging from regular office envelopes to customized envelopes for direct-mail use. Products under its Printmaster brand include envelopes with windows, translucent envelopes, booklet-style envelopes, envelopes with clasps, and presentation portfolios. National Envelope serves paper distributors and wholesalers throughout Canada and the US. The company's 20 divisions include New York Envelope, Alcor, Williamhouse, and Old Colony Envelope, a supplier of fine paper products. William Ungar owns National Envelope, which he founded in 1952.

KEY COMPETITORS
Mail-Well
National Service Industries
Workflow Management

NATIONAL GRAPE COOPERATIVE ASSOCIATION, INC.

2 S. Portage St.
Westfield, NY 14787
Phone: 716-326-5200
Fax: 716-326-5494
Web: www.nationalgrape.com

CEO: Fredrick P. Kilian
CFO: Thomas E. Callahan
HR: Thomas E. Gettig
Type: Cooperative

2001 Sales: $649.6 million
1-Yr. Sales Change: (4.3%)
Employees: 1,333
FYE: August 31

Well, of course grape growers want to hang out in a bunch! The 1,400 or so grower-owners in the National Grape Cooperative Association grow and harvest purple, red, and white grapes from more than 49,000 acres of vineyards in order to supply its well-known, wholly owned subsidiary Welch Foods. Welch's sells juices, jams, and jellies under the Welch's and BAMA brands. Other products include co-branded candy (with Russell Stover) and fresh grapes (distributed by C.H. Robinson Worldwide). Welch's is the world's #1 marketer of Concord and Niagara grape products.

KEY COMPETITORS
Cadbury Schweppes
J. M. Smucker
Ralcorp

NATIONAL GYPSUM COMPANY

2001 Rexford Rd.
Charlotte, NC 28211
Phone: 704-365-7300
Fax: 800-392-6421
Web: www.national-gypsum.com

CEO: Thomas C. Nelson
CFO: Bill Parmelle
HR: Nick Rodono
Type: Private

2001 Est. Sales: $1,500.0 mil.
1-Yr. Sales Change: (0.7%)
Employees: 2,650
FYE: December 31

New NGC, Inc., doing business as National Gypsum Company, produces an array of wall supplies and is the second-largest gypsum wallboard manufacturer in the US. The company sells wallboard under the Gold Bond and Durabase brand names. It also produces joint treatment compounds (ProForm), cement board (PermaBase), plaster, and framing systems and tests acoustical, fire, and structural properties of building materials. National Gypsum sells its products worldwide to the construction industry. Delcor Inc., a subsidiary of Golden Eagle Industries, owns the company.

KEY COMPETITORS
Lafarge North America
Temple-Inland
USG

In-depth profiles of an additional 200 key private companies are found on pages 36–435.

NATIONAL LIFE INSURANCE CO.

1 National Life Dr.
Montpelier, VT 05604
Phone: 802-229-3333
Fax: 802-229-9281
Web: www.natlifeinsco.com

CEO: Thomas H. MacLeay
CFO: —
HR: —
Type: Mutual company

2001 Sales: $1,025.9 million
1-Yr. Sales Change: (2.9%)
Employees: 1,000
FYE: December 31

Founded in 1848, National Life Insurance is one of the oldest life insurance firms in the US. Through its subsidiaries, the company offers a full range of individual life insurance and annuity products and is shifting its status from that of an insurance outfit to that of a financial services company by increasing its investment services segment. Affiliates include Life Insurance Company of the Southwest (annuities) and the Sentinel Funds (investment products and services). National Life is a mutual company owned by its policyholders, but it is restructuring to become a public stock company.

KEY COMPETITORS
MetLife
New York Life
Prudential

NATIONAL RURAL UTILITIES COOPERATIVE FINANCE CORPORATION

2201 Cooperative Way
Herndon, VA 20171
Phone: 703-709-6700
Fax: 703-709-6778
Web: www.nrucfc.org

CEO: Sheldon C. Petersen
CFO: Steven L. Lilly
HR: Melanie Smith
Type: Cooperative

2001 Sales: $1,388.3 million
1-Yr. Sales Change: 36.0%
Employees: 200
FYE: May 31

Forget *Sesame Street* morals — try Wall Street money. Because cooperation alone only goes so far, the National Rural Utilities Cooperative Finance Corporation in 1969 set up the National Rural Electric Cooperative Association, a lobby representing more than 1,000 electric co-ops in 49 states. Owned by the electric and telecommunications cooperatives that make up its membership, the financial organization supplements government loans that traditionally fueled rural electric utilities. The organization sells commercial paper, medium-term notes, and collateral trust bonds to its members. The firm also offers short-term lines of credit and finances intermediate and long-term loans.

KEY COMPETITORS
AgFirst
FINOVA
GE

NATIONAL TEXTILES, L.L.C.

480 Hanes Mill Rd.
Winston-Salem, NC 27105
Phone: 336-714-8400
Fax: 336-714-8786
Web: www.nationaltextiles.com

CEO: Jerry D. Rowland
CFO: Keith G. Huskins
HR: David V. Shirlen
Type: Private

2002 Sales: $700.0 million
1-Yr. Sales Change: (12.5%)
Employees: 4,325
FYE: June 30

Have you heard the one about National Textiles? Boy, has this company got a yarn to spin. National Textiles makes open-end and ring-spun cotton, cotton-polyester blend yarns, knit fabrics, finished tubular fabrics, and cut parts. Sara Lee (maker of Hanes) is the company's primary customer, for use in brands such as Just My Size, Hanes Beefy-Ts, Hanes Her Way, and Champion. It has about 10 production facilities, acquired from Sara Lee, and a cotton distribution center in the southern US; its Georgia location is among the world's largest spinning plants and its Tennessee location is a leading US ring-spun facility. Chairman Marty Granoff and his son, Michael, own most of the company.

KEY COMPETITORS
Avondale Incorporated
Galey & Lord
Parkdale Mills

📖 **In-depth profiles of an additional 200 key private companies are found on pages 36–435.**

NATIONAL WINE & SPIRITS, INC

700 W. Morris St.
Indianapolis, IN 46206
Phone: 317-636-6092
Fax: 317-685-8810
Web: www.nwscorp.com

CEO: James E. LaCrosse
CFO: James E. LaCrosse
HR: Karin Lijana Matura
Type: Private

2002 Sales: $681.6 million
1-Yr. Sales Change: 3.1%
Employees: 1,618
FYE: March 31

Bartender to the nation's breadbasket, National Wine & Spirits is one of the largest wine and liquor distributors in the Midwest. Serving 36,000 locations, the company distributes to restaurants, liquor stores, and retailers in Illinois, Indiana, and Michigan and owns an interest in a Kentucky distributor. The company's suppliers include Fortune Brands (Jim Beam), Diageo (Bailey's), and Beringer Blass Wine Estates. The company sold its Cameron Springs bottled water operation to Perrier. The company owns 25% of Commonwealth Wine & Spirits. CEO James LaCrosse and director Norma Johnston own National Wine & Spirits, which was founded in 1935.

KEY COMPETITORS
Glazer's Wholesale Drug
Johnson Brothers
Southern Wine & Spirits

NAVY EXCHANGE SERVICE COMMAND

3280 Virginia Beach Blvd.
Virginia Beach, VA 23452
Phone: 757-463-6200
Fax: 757-631-3659
Web: www.navy-nex.com

CEO: William J. Maguire
CFO: Michael P. Good
HR: Craig Sinclair
Type: Government-owned

2002 Sales: $1,915.9 million
1-Yr. Sales Change: (3.0%)
Employees: 16,000
FYE: January 31

Before Old Navy, there was the Navy Exchange Service Command (NEXCOM). Active-duty military personnel, reservists, retirees, and their family members can shop at more than 100 NEXCOM retail stores (brand-name and private-label merchandise ranging from apparel to home electronics), about 190 NEXCOM Ships Stores (basic necessities), and its 100 Uniform Support Centers (the sole source of authorized uniforms). NEXCOM also runs about 40 Navy Lodges in the US and six foreign countries. NEXCOM receives tax dollars for its shipboard stores, but it is otherwise self-supporting. Most of the profits fund morale, welfare, and recreational programs for sailors.

KEY COMPETITORS
Kmart
Target
Wal-Mart

NAVY FEDERAL CREDIT UNION

820 Follin Ln.
Vienna, VA 22180
Phone: 703-255-8000
Fax: 703-255-8741
Web: www.navyfcu.org

CEO: Brian L. McDonnell
CFO: Brady Cole
HR: Louise Foreman
Type: Cooperative

2001 Sales: $1,138.6 million
1-Yr. Sales Change: 12.1%
Employees: —
FYE: December 31

"Once a member always a member" promises Navy Federal Credit Union (NFCU). This policy undoubtedly helped NFCU become one of the nation's largest credit unions, claiming more than 2 million members. Formed in 1933, Navy Federal Credit Union provides US Navy and Marine Corps personnel and their families with checking and savings accounts, mortgages, IRAs, and a variety of loans (including auto and student loans). Members (who can retain their credit union privileges even after discharge from the armed services) get access to approximately 620,000 ATMs in Visa's PLUS Network and the Armed Forces Financial Network. NFCU has some 90 locations in the US and about 25 overseas.

KEY COMPETITORS
Bank of America
U.S. Central Credit Union
USAA

In-depth profiles of an additional 200 key private companies are found on pages 36–435.

NCH CORPORATION

2727 Chemsearch Blvd.
Irving, TX 75062
Phone: 972-438-0211
Fax: 972-438-0186
Web: www.nch.com

CEO: Irvin L. Levy
CFO: Tom F. Hetzer
HR: Neil Thomas
Type: Private

2002 Est. Sales: $650.0 mil.
1-Yr. Sales Change: (4.4%)
Employees: 8,000
FYE: April 30

NCH Corporation has been cleaning up for years. The company makes and sells about 450 chemical, maintenance, repair, and supply products for customers in more than 60 countries. NCH markets its products — including many types of cleaners — through a direct sales force to the agricultural, home-improvement, industrial, recreational, and utility industries. Specialty chemical products, including cleaning and water treatment chemicals, deodorizers, lubricants, paints and paint strippers, patching compounds, and flooring and carpet treatments, account for the majority of sales. Other products include fasteners, welding supplies, and plumbing parts. Descendants of founder Milton Levy own the company.

KEY COMPETITORS
Cintas
Ecolab
Hughes Supply

NESCO, INC.

6140 Parkland Blvd.
Mayfield Heights, OH 44124
Phone: 440-461-6000
Fax: 440-449-3111
Web: www.nescoinc.com

CEO: Robert J. Tomsich
CFO: Frank Rzicznek
HR: —
Type: Private

2001 Est. Sales: $1,100.0 mil.
1-Yr. Sales Change: (8.3%)
Employees: 10,250
FYE: December 31

NESCO doesn't take diversification lightly. The holding company's operations include industrial equipment manufacturing, real estate investment, and staffing services. NESCO's industrial group includes material handlers Continental Conveyor (conveyor systems for the mining industry) and Goodman Conveyor (bulk conveyor equipment). Other industrial group companies include ACC Automation, which makes dip molding equipment for manufacturing everything from rubber gloves to condoms, Penn Union (copper and aluminum electrical connectors), NESCO Service Co. (staffing), and Rogers Company (trade show exhibits). Founder and CEO Robert Tomsich owns the company, which is not related to Oklahoma-based NESCO, a specialty contractor.

KEY COMPETITORS
FKI
Ingersoll-Rand
MAN

NEW AGE ELECTRONICS INC.

21950 Arnold Center Rd.
Carson, CA 90810
Phone: 310-549-0000
Fax: 310-835-7765
Web: www.newageinc.com

CEO: Lee Perlman
CFO: Mark Tipton
HR: Michelle Olsen
Type: Private

2000 Sales: $1,024.0 million
1-Yr. Sales Change: 37.1%
Employees: 124
FYE: December 31

New Age Electronics probably can't hook you up with an automatic patchouli oil dispenser, crystal polisher, or wicca spell encyclopedia software. No, this company distributes computers and electronic office products, manufactured largely in Asia, to resellers in the US including Costco and Sam's Club wholesale outlets. New Age deals in computers and peripherals, printers, copiers, fax machines, cash registers, and related supplies and accessories. It also sells such manufacturer-refurbished products as computers, printers, and fax machines. New Age was founded in 1988 by partners Lee Perlman (chairman and CEO) and Adam Carroll (president and COO).

KEY COMPETITORS
Arrow Electronics
Ingram Micro
Tech Data

In-depth profiles of an additional 200 key private companies are found on pages 36–435.

NEW BALANCE ATHLETIC SHOE, INC.

Brighton Landing, 20 Guest St.	CEO: James S. Davis	2001 Sales: $1,160.0 million
Boston, MA 02135	CFO: John Gardner	1-Yr. Sales Change: 5.5%
Phone: 617-783-4000	HR: Carol O'Donnell	Employees: 2,400
Fax: 617-787-9355	Type: Private	FYE: December 31
Web: www.newbalance.com		

New Balance Athletic Shoe's everyman appeal is what gives it a boost. Unlike rivals NIKE and adidas-Salomon, the company shuns celebrity endorsers; its lesser-known athletes show its emphasis on substance versus style. The approach attracts a clientele of aging boomer jocks who are less fickle than the teens chased by other shoe firms. New Balance is known for its wide selection of shoe widths. Besides men's and women's shoes for running, cross-training, basketball, tennis, hiking, and golf, the company offers fitness apparel and kids' shoes and owns leather boot maker Dunham. Founded in 1906 to make arch supports, owner, chairman, and CEO Jim Davis bought New Balance on the day of the 1972 Boston Marathon.

KEY COMPETITORS
adidas-Salomon
NIKE
Reebok

NEW YORK UNIVERSITY

70 Washington Sq. South	CEO: John E. Sexton	2002 Sales: —
New York, NY 10012	CFO: Harold T. Read	1-Yr. Sales Change: —
Phone: 212-998-1212	HR: Karen Bradley	Employees: 10,136
Fax: 212-995-4040	Type: School	FYE: August 31
Web: www.nyu.edu		

Higher education is at the core of this Big Apple institution. The setting and heritage of New York University (NYU) have helped make it one of the nation's most popular educational institutions. With nearly 50,000 students attending its 14 schools and colleges, NYU is among the largest private schools in the US. It is well regarded for its arts and humanities studies, and its law school and Leonard N. Stern School of Business are also considered among the best in the country. In addition to a Manhattan campus, NYU has branch campuses in Westchester and Rockland counties. The school was started in 1831. Its alumni include Federal Reserve Chairman Alan Greenspan and film producer Ismail Merchant (*The Remains of the Day*).

THE NEWARK GROUP, INC.

20 Jackson Dr.	CEO: Fred G. von Zuben	2002 Sales: $800.0 million
Cranford, NJ 07016	CFO: Joseph Byrne	1-Yr. Sales Change: (9.4%)
Phone: 908-276-4000	HR: Carl R. Crook	Employees: 4,200
Fax: 908-276-2888	Type: Private	FYE: April 30
Web: www.newarkgroup.com		

The Newark Group is proof that one man's trash is another man's treasure. The company, founded in 1912, is a major producer of paper products from recycled materials. Its recycled fibers division operates paper mills across the US and converts the 2.5 million tons of wastepaper it collects annually into several grades of paper and fiber products, including envelopes, corrugated cardboard, and newspaper. The paperboard division produces 1.3 million tons of paperboard per year from its 15 US mill sites. Recycled paperboard ends up in such products as books, puzzles, gameboards, and packaging.

KEY COMPETITORS
Oji Paper
Smurfit-Stone Container
Weyerhaeuser

In-depth profiles of an additional 200 key private companies are found on pages 36–435.

NIKKEN GLOBAL INC.

52 Discovery Rd.	CEO: Toshizo Watanabe	2001 Est. Sales: $1,500.0 mil.
Irvine, CA 92618	CFO: Alex Bond	1-Yr. Sales Change: 0.0%
Phone: 949-789-2000	HR: Rick Knudson	Employees: —
Fax: 800-669-8856	Type: Private	FYE: December 31
Web: www.nikken.com		

Nikken Global wants to attract you — and your friends and relatives — to buy and sell magnetic therapeutic devices through its global distribution network (think Amway). The company has pulled in independent distributors to sell its magnetic "wellness" products, such as pillows, sleep masks, support wraps, shoe inserts, jewelry, and blankets. Nikken tugs at Fido and Fluffy, too, offering pet products such as blankets and vitamins. The company also provides human nutritional supplements and skin care products. The company does business in more than 20 countries in the Asia/Pacific region, Europe, and North America. Nikken is owned by Isamu Masuda, who founded the company in Japan in 1975.

KEY COMPETITORS
Biomagnetics
Magnetherapy

NORTH BROWARD HOSPITAL DISTRICT

303 SE 17th St.	CEO: Wil Trower	2001 Sales: $670.2 million
Fort Lauderdale, FL 33316	CFO: Patricia Mahaney	1-Yr. Sales Change: 17.0%
Phone: 954-355-5100	HR: Wilhelmena Mack	Employees: —
Fax: 954-355-4966	Type: Government-owned	FYE: June 30
Web: www.nbhd.org		

North Broward Hospital District takes care of shark bites and more. The district serves Broward County (the Fort Lauderdale area) with four acute-care hospitals and a host of community-based centers. Flagship hospital Broward General features a sleep disorders lab and the Chris Evert Women and Children's Center. The system's more than 40 additional facilities include family health centers, hospice programs, and a diagnostic treatment center for children. North Broward Hospital District, founded in 1938, has suffered from reduced government reimbursements, high health care costs, and — most recently — budget cuts courtesy of the state legislature.

KEY COMPETITORS
Bon Secours Health
Catholic Health East
HCA

NORTH CAROLINA ELECTRIC MEMBERSHIP CORPORATION

3400 Sumner Blvd.	CEO: Charles W. Terrill	2001 Sales: $659.8 million
Raleigh, NC 27616	CFO: Lark S. James	1-Yr. Sales Change: (0.8%)
Phone: 919-872-0800	HR: Sally Stevens	Employees: 146
Fax: 919-878-3970	Type: Cooperative	FYE: December 31
Web: www.ncemcs.com		

It's a cooperative effort: North Carolina Electric Membership generates and transmits electricity to 26 of 27 of the state's electric cooperatives. The co-op owns two peaking generators (18 MW of power) and a 28% share (644 MW) in the Catawba Nuclear Station of York County, South Carolina. It also buys power from Progress Energy, American Electric Power, and other for-profit utilities. North Carolina Electric Membership's cooperatives serve more than 800,000 businesses and homes in North Carolina. The wholesale co-op also operates an energy operations center and offers training programs, engineering and construction management, and power supply planning to all 27 cooperatives.

KEY COMPETITORS
Dominion
SCANA
TVA

In-depth profiles of an additional 200 key private companies are found on pages 36–435.

NORTH PACIFIC GROUP, INC.

815 NE Davis St.	CEO: Thomas J. Tomjack	2001 Sales: $1,100.0 million
Portland, OR 97232	CFO: Christopher D. Cassard	1-Yr. Sales Change: (8.3%)
Phone: 503-231-1166	HR: Karen Austin	Employees: 850
Fax: 503-238-2641	Type: Private	FYE: December 31
Web: www.north-pacific.com		

Paneling, poles, pilings, or pipes, North Pacific Group (NOR PAC) is building on the construction industry. The company is one of North America's largest wholesale distributors of building materials. Employee-owned since the 1986 retirement of its founder, Doug David, NOR PAC distributes wood, steel, agricultural, and food products. Wood products, which make up the majority of its business, include lumber, millwork, poles, and logs. NOR PAC operates through 30 sales facilities and over 175 inventory locations, selling its products to furniture makers, retailers, and metal fabricators. Its more than 30 subsidiaries and divisions include Saxonville USA, Landmark Building Products, and Cascade Imperial Mills.

KEY COMPETITORS
Georgia-Pacific Corporation
Louisiana-Pacific
Weyerhaeuser

NORTH SHORE-LONG ISLAND JEWISH HEALTH SYSTEM

145 Community Dr.	CEO: Michael J. Dowling	2001 Sales: $3,200.0 million
Great Neck, NY 11021	CFO: Bob Shapiro	1-Yr. Sales Change: 38.5%
Phone: 516-465-8100	HR: Ronald Stone	Employees: 30,000
Fax: 516-465-8396	Type: Not-for-profit	FYE: December 31
Web: www.nslij.com		

This hospital system has a scope that stretches long beyond Long Island. The product of a merger between the North Shore Health System and Long Island Jewish Medical Center, North Shore-Long Island Jewish Health System runs 18 hospitals in Long Island and New York's outer boroughs; several of these are affiliated with regional medical schools (including New York University and the Albert Einstein College of Medicine). The system has a mental health facility, long-term care facilities, trauma centers, rehabilitation, outpatient surgery centers, and also offers home care and hospice services.

KEY COMPETITORS
Catholic Healthcare Network
New York City Health and Hospitals
Saint Vincent Catholic Medical Centers

NORTHERN TOOL & EQUIPMENT CO.

2800 Southcross Dr. West	CEO: Donald L. Kotula	2001 Est. Sales: $750.0 mil.
Burnsville, MN 55306	CFO: John Manning	1-Yr. Sales Change: 15.4%
Phone: 952-894-9510	HR: Jean Erath	Employees: 2,400
Fax: 952-882-6927	Type: Private	FYE: December 31
Web: www.northerntool.com		

Serious do-it-yourselfers put their kids to sleep with bedtime stories from the catalogs of Northern Tool & Equipment. The company sells snowblowers, log splitters, pressure washers, power generators, and other heavy-duty tools and equipment, primarily to construction contractors, landscape crews, auto shops, and the do-it-yourself crowd. About two-thirds of its sales are through its catalogs, but the company also sells through its Web site and in about 40 retail stores in 10 states. Northern Tool & Equipment makes about 10% of the products it sells. CEO Donald Kotula and his family own the company. Kotula started the business in 1981 as a mail-order shop out of his garage.

KEY COMPETITORS
Home Depot
Lowe's
Tractor Supply

In-depth profiles of an additional 200 key private companies are found on pages 36–435.

NOVANT HEALTH, INC.

2085 Frontis Plaza Blvd.
Winston-Salem, NC 27103
Phone: 336-718-7028
Fax: 336-718-9258
Web: www.novanthealth.org

CEO: Paul M. Wiles
CFO: Dean Swindle
HR: Mel Asbury
Type: Not-for-profit

2000 Sales: $801.9 million
1-Yr. Sales Change: 4.9%
Employees: 12,000
FYE: December 31

Novant Health is a not-for-profit health system in North Carolina. Formed in 1997 by a merger of Carolina Medicorp and Presbyterian Healthcare System, Novant serves nearly 4 million people in more than 30 counties across North and South Carolina and Virginia. The system includes eight inpatient hospitals with about 2,000 beds, in addition to a women's health and wellness center, long-term-care facilities, and numerous outpatient offices. Novant Health also includes the for-profit PARTNERS National Health Plans of North Carolina, an HMO covering more than 300,000 members.

KEY COMPETITORS
Greenville Hospital System
Sentara Healthcare
Wake Forest University Baptist Medical Center

NOVEON INTERNATIONAL, INC.

9911 Brecksville Rd.
Cleveland, OH 44141
Phone: 216-447-5000
Fax: 216-447-5669
Web: www.noveoninc.com

CEO: Steven J. Demetriou
CFO: Michael D. Friday
HR: Christopher R. Clegg
Type: Private

2001 Sales: $1,063.4 million
1-Yr. Sales Change: —
Employees: 2,790
FYE: December 31

Polymers and additives add up to big business for Noveon. The specialty chemical maker, formerly the Performance Materials segment of what is now Goodrich Corporation, was spun off as PMD Group in early 2001 and renamed Noveon that May. Its products include performance polymers and additives (colorants, fragrance enhancers) used in food and beverages, personal and home care products, and pharmaceuticals. Noveon's additives also are found in paints, coatings, water treatments, lubricants, and rubber. In addition, the company manufactures post-chlorinated polyvinyl chloride (CPVC) resins and compounds, and thermoplastic polyurethanes (TPUs). Noveon is owned by AEA Investors, DLJ Merchant Banking, and DB Capital Partners.

KEY COMPETITORS
BASF AG
Dow Chemical
DuPont

NRT INCORPORATED

339 Jefferson Rd.
Parsippany, NJ 07054
Phone: 973-240-5000
Fax: 973-240-5241
Web: www.nrtinc.com

CEO: Robert M. Becker
CFO: Daniel J. Happer
HR: Ross Anthony
Type: Private

2001 Est. Sales: $3,159.0 mil.
1-Yr. Sales Change: 12.8%
Employees: 51,000
FYE: December 31

NRT is Not a Realty Trust anymore. The #1 residential real estate company in the US began life in 1996 as National Realty Trust, established by real estate franchisor HFS (now Cendant) to own the nearly 400 real estate offices that came with the purchase of Coldwell Banker. Cendant and a subsidiary of Apollo Advisors restructured the trust into NRT to snap up successful independent realtors in hot metropolitan markets and rebrand them under Cendant's franchise names (Century 21, Coldwell Banker, and ERA). The realtor has more than 950 offices in about 26 markets. After a planned IPO was aborted due to a tumbling market, NRT remains controlled by Cendant. The company has purchased The DeWolfe Companies.

KEY COMPETITORS
Baird & Warner
Kennedy-Wilson
RE/MAX

In-depth profiles of an additional 200 key private companies are found on pages 36–435.

NYPRO INC.

101 Union St.
Clinton, MA 01510
Phone: 978-365-9721
Fax: 978-368-0236
Web: www.nypro.com

CEO: Brian S. Jones
CFO: Nicholas D. Aznoian
HR: —
Type: Private

2002 Sales: $589.6 million
1-Yr. Sales Change: 19.2%
Employees: 9,000
FYE: June 30

Nypro is a real pro when it comes to injection molding. The company makes plastic parts used in devices that range from cell phones, electric razors, and seat belts to inkjet printer cartridges and personal computers. Customers in the electronics and telecommunications industries together account for nearly half of sales. Although custom-precision plastic-injection molding is Nypro's core business, the company also offers assembly services to other manufacturers. Nypro's products can be found around the world, but North America accounts for most of its sales. The company has 27 molding plants in 14 countries. Chairman Gordon Lankton sold Nypro to employees in 1999 through an employee stock ownership plan.

KEY COMPETITORS
Atlantis Plastics
Berry Plastics
Hoffer Plastics

OGLETHORPE POWER CORPORATION

2100 E. Exchange Place
Tucker, GA 30085
Phone: 770-270-7600
Fax: 770-270-7325
Web: www.opc.com

CEO: Thomas A. Smith
CFO: Anne F. Appleby
HR: W. Clayton Robbins
Type: Cooperative

2001 Sales: $1,139.3 million
1-Yr. Sales Change: (5.0%)
Employees: 175
FYE: December 31

Not-for-profit Oglethorpe Power Corporation is one of the largest electricity cooperatives in the US, with contracts to supply wholesale power to 39 member/owners (making up most of Georgia's retail electric suppliers) until 2025. Oglethorpe's member/owners, which also operate as not-for-profits, serve about 1.5 million residential, commercial, and industrial customers. Oglethorpe, which was formed in 1974, has a generating capacity of nearly 3,700 MW (primarily from coal-fired and nuclear facilities). Along with the generating plants Oglethorpe owns or leases, it has power contracts with other suppliers, which account for nearly 20% of its energy supply.

KEY COMPETITORS
MEAG Power
Southern Company
TVA

OHIO FARMERS INSURANCE COMPANY

1 Park Circle
Westfield Center, OH 44251
Phone: 330-887-0101
Fax: 330-887-0840
Web: www.westfield-cos.com

CEO: Cary Blair
CFO: Robert Krisowaty
HR: Debra Cummings
Type: Private

2001 Est. Sales: $745.0 mil.
1-Yr. Sales Change: (6.9%)
Employees: —
FYE: December 31

Ohio Farmers Insurance has plowed beyond the crop and cattle biz. The 150-year-old company is chartered as a stock company without stockholders. Its affiliates — including Beacon Insurance, Old Guard Insurance, Westfield Insurance, and Westfield National — are known by the umbrella name Westfield Group. The company offers such standard personal lines as auto and homeowners insurance; its niche products include fidelity and surety bonds and specialty coverage for farmers, auto repair shops, and religious organizations. The company has opened Westfield Bank, offering personal and business banking services through a referral program involving independent insurance agents in northeastern Ohio.

KEY COMPETITORS
Allstate
Prudential
State Farm

In-depth profiles of an additional 200 key private companies are found on pages 36–435.

OHIO LOTTERY COMMISSION

615 W. Superior Ave.
Cleveland, OH 44113
Phone: 216-787-3200
Fax: 216-787-5215
Web: www.ohiolottery.com

CEO: Dennis G. Kennedy
CFO: Mark M. Polatajko
HR: Renee Bianchi
Type: Government-owned

2002 Sales: $1,983.1 million
1-Yr. Sales Change: (0.8%)
Employees: 350
FYE: June 30

The year was 1974 — Nixon resigned, an energy crisis gripped the nation, and Ray Stevens ignited a streaking sensation. But were residents of the Buckeye State paying attention? Maybe not — they had a brand new state lottery to play! Since selling its first lottery ticket that fateful year, the Ohio Lottery Commission has raised more than $9 billion for education in Ohio, the cause to which lottery proceeds are dedicated. The commission offers a variety of instant ticket games (Count Cashula, Fat Cat) and numbers games (Pick 3, Pick 4) for Ohioans' wagering pleasure. Facing slumping sales, in 2000 the Ohio Lottery Commission debuted numbers game Super Lotto Plus, which offered players better odds of winning.

KEY COMPETITORS
Michigan Lottery
Multi-State Lottery
Pennsylvania Lottery

OHIO NATIONAL FINANCIAL SERVICES

1 Financial Way
Cincinnati, OH 45242
Phone: 513-794-6100
Fax: 513-794-4504
Web: www.ohionatl.com

CEO: David B. O'Maley
CFO: Ronald J. Dolan
HR: Anthony G. Esposito
Type: Mutual company

2001 Sales: $2,000.0 million
1-Yr. Sales Change: 177.1%
Employees: 700
FYE: December 31

Ohio National Financial Services subsidiary Ohio National Life Insurance sells individual and group life insurance, disability insurance, pension plans, and annuities. Other company subsidiaries include Ohio National Equities and O.N. Equity Sales, which offer wholesale and retail brokerage services, and Ohio National Investments, an investment adviser to the ONE Fund series mutual fund. The firm's products are sold in 47 states, the District of Columbia, and Puerto Rico. The company has expanded into New York with the acquisitions of asset manager Suffolk Capital Management and First ING Life Insurance Company of New York (renamed National Security Life and Annuity).

KEY COMPETITORS
American United Life
Minnesota Mutual
StanCorp Financial Group

OHIOHEALTH

1087 Dennison Ave., 3rd Fl.
Columbus, OH 43201
Phone: 614-566-5424
Fax: 614-544-5244
Web: www.ohiohealth.com

CEO: David P. Blom
CFO: John Kowalski
HR: John Boswell
Type: Not-for-profit

2001 Est. Sales: $2,000.0 mil.
1-Yr. Sales Change: 66.7%
Employees: 15,340
FYE: June 30

With nearly 4,000 affiliated physicians in more than half of the state's 88 counties, not-for-profit OhioHealth aims to keep Buckeyes healthy. Established in 1984, the system operates eight acute-care hospitals and is affiliated with four more. Additional facilities include outpatient centers, long-term care facilities, rehabilitation centers, radiology and imaging centers, women's health centers, and sleep centers. Subsidiary HomeReach provides home health care and medical supply services. Its WorkHealth program offers workers' compensation care management and occupational rehabilitation services. OhioHealth's joint venture, OhioHealth Group, operates the HealthReach PPO.

KEY COMPETITORS
Catholic Health Initiatives
Catholic Healthcare Partners
Trinity Health

📖 **In-depth profiles of an additional 200 key private companies are found on pages 36–435.**

OMEGA WORLD TRAVEL

3102 Omega Office Park
Fairfax, VA 22301
Phone: 703-359-0200
Fax: 703-359-8880
Web: www.owt.net

CEO: Gloria Bohan
CFO: —
HR: Betsy Amos
Type: Private

2001 Est. Sales: $750.0 mil.
1-Yr. Sales Change: 5.6%
Employees: 1,000
FYE: December 31

Omega is the last word in travel. Omega World Travel is one of the largest travel agencies in the US, with 100 offices in more than 30 states, the District of Columbia, Japan, and the UK. The company specializes in corporate travel arrangements (60% of its business), but also handles government contracts, group travel, and plain old vacationers. The company also serves clients though 100 on-site locations and an online travel site. Most of Omega's sales come from airline reservations. In addition, the company offers discounts on all major cruise lines at its CRUISE.COM Web site and provides travel agent training through its Omega Travel School. President Gloria Bohan founded the company in 1972.

KEY COMPETITORS
American Express
Carlson Wagonlit
Navigant International

OMNISOURCE CORPORATION

1610 N. Calhoun St.
Fort Wayne, IN 46808
Phone: 260-422-5541
Fax: 260-424-0307
Web: www.omnisource.com

CEO: Leonard I. Rifkin
CFO: Gary Rohrs
HR: Ben Eisbart
Type: Private

2002 Sales: $840.0 million
1-Yr. Sales Change: 2.4%
Employees: 1,350
FYE: September 30

OmniSource lives on scraps. Irving Rifkin founded the private, family-owned scrap-metal processor and trader in 1943 to supply scrap for WWII. OmniSource was a pioneer in adopting formal quality-control programs and in turning scrap into briquettes for foundry and steel-mill furnace use. Today the company rates as one of the largest scrap recycling firms in North America. Through a network of six brokerage offices, it tracks national and international scrap prices and activities. OmniSource operates 26 processing facilities, a secondary aluminum smelting plant, and a heavy-media separation facility. The founder's son, Leonard Rifkin, is chairman and CEO.

KEY COMPETITORS
Commercial Metals
David J. Joseph
Metal Management

O'NEAL STEEL, INC.

744 41st St. North
Birmingham, AL 35222
Phone: 205-599-8000
Fax: 205-599-8037
Web: www.onealsteel.com

CEO: Bill Jones
CFO: Don Freriks
HR: Shawn Smith
Type: Private

2001 Est. Sales: $742.0 mil.
1-Yr. Sales Change: (21.1%)
Employees: 2,500
FYE: December 31

O'Neal Steel has an angle on the steel industry. One of the US's leading private metals service companies, O'Neal sells a full range of metal products — including angles, bars, beams, coil, pipe, plate, and sheet — made from steel, aluminum, brass, and bronze. The company operates around 40 plants in the US, from which it offers such metal-processing services as cutting, forming, bending, and machining. Its Weldment Fabrication Division makes subassemblies, bracket weldments, and precision parts for the mining and the mobile crane industries. Founded by Kirkman O'Neal in 1922 in Alabama, the company has expanded largely through mergers and acquisitions. It is still owned and run by the O'Neal family.

KEY COMPETITORS
Reliance Steel
Ryerson Tull
Worthington Industries

In-depth profiles of an additional 200 key private companies are found on pages 36–435.

OPUS CORPORATION

10350 Bren Rd. West	CEO: Mark H. Rauenhorst	2001 Sales: $1,200.0 million
Minnetonka, MN 55343	CFO: Ronald W. Schiferl	1-Yr. Sales Change: (14.3%)
Phone: 952-656-4444	HR: Janet A. Maistrovich	Employees: 1,400
Fax: 952-656-4529	Type: Private	FYE: December 31
Web: www.opuscorp.com		

This Opus can be heard from coast to coast. Founded in 1953 as Rauenhorst Construction Company, the commercial real estate development and management firm builds custom facilities (office buildings, warehouses, and malls) for purchase or lease and develops business parks. The company also offers architecture, engineering, construction, property management, and financing and leasing. Opus operates through five independent operating companies and has several subsidiaries that provide support functions. The company has nearly 30 offices across the US. The Gerald Rauenhorst family owns the company.

KEY COMPETITORS
Brookfield Properties
Lincoln Property
Structure Tone

ORIUS CORP.

1401 Forum Way, 4th Fl.	CEO: Ronald L. Blake	2001 Sales: —
West Palm Beach, FL 33401	CFO: Robert E. Agres	1-Yr. Sales Change: —
Phone: 561-687-8300	HR: Gregory W. Castle	Employees: 3,859
Fax: 561-687-8080	Type: Private	FYE: December 31
Web: www.oriuscorp.com		

Orius lies within the cosmos of telecommunications infrastructure. The company designs, engineers, installs, and maintains telecom and cable networks (fiber-optic, coaxial, and copper). Services include digging trenches, laying cable, and placing poles and manholes for new or expanding networks. Customers are primarily cable TV operators and telecom providers. Orius also provides on-premise communications wiring for businesses, government agencies, and utilities. Founded in 1997, Orius operates through subsidiaries in 48 states in the US. Chicago investment firm Willis Stein & Partners owns a majority stake in Orius, which has filed for Chapter 11 bankruptcy protection after a downturn in the telecom industry.

KEY COMPETITORS
Dycom
MasTec
Quanta Services

ORMET CORPORATION

1233 Main St., Ste. 4000	CEO: R. Emmett Boyle	2001 Sales: $700.0 million
Wheeling, WV 26003	CFO: Rich Caruso	1-Yr. Sales Change: 0.0%
Phone: 304-234-3900	HR: Lisa Riedle	Employees: 3,000
Fax: 304-234-3929	Type: Private	FYE: December 31
Web: www.ormet.com		

Ormet's canny business skills have made it one of the US's leading producers of aluminum. Through its Ormet Primary Aluminum subsidiary, the company smelts aluminum ore (bauxite) and manufactures aluminum ingot, billet (pressed bars), sheet, foil, and other products for the fabrication, extrusion, and conversion markets. The company's Ormet Aluminum Mill Products subsidiary further processes the aluminum into auto trim, cans, gift wrap, packaging, and other products. Ormet operates nine plants (including alumina plants, rolling mills, recycling facilities, and marine terminals), primarily in the midwestern US. CEO Emmett Boyle owns the company, which was founded in Hannibal, Ohio, in 1954.

KEY COMPETITORS
Alcan
Alcoa
Norsk Hydro

In-depth profiles of an additional 200
key private companies are found on pages 36–435.

OURISMAN AUTOMOTIVE ENTERPRISES

4400 Branch Ave.	CEO: Mandell J. Ourisman	2001 Sales: $655.6 million
Marlow Heights, MD 20748	CFO: Mohamed Reshed	1-Yr. Sales Change: 5.5%
Phone: 301-423-4028	HR: —	Employees: 1,000
Fax: 301-423-5725	Type: Private	FYE: December 31
Web: www.ourisman.com		

Whether you buy American or foreign, Ford or Chevy, Ourisman Automotive Enterprises can satisfy your vehicular proclivity. Serving the Washington, DC, area, Ourisman operates 12 dealerships throughout Maryland and Virginia. Its Chevrolet, DaimlerChrysler, Ford, Honda, Mitsubishi, Suzuki, and Toyota dealerships sell both new and used vehicles. Ourisman also operates a leasing office that offers free dealership-to-door delivery of newly leased vehicles. In addition, the company sells parts and offers service. The Ourisman family, which owns the company, founded Ourisman in 1921.

KEY COMPETITORS
Brown Automotive
Jim Koons Automotive
Rosenthal Automotive

OUTSOURCING SOLUTIONS INC.

390 S. Woods Mill Rd., Ste. 350	CEO: Timothy G. Beffa	2001 Sales: $612.3 million
Chesterfield, MO 63017	CFO: Gary L. Weller	1-Yr. Sales Change: 12.8%
Phone: 314-576-0022	HR: Brenda Hicks	Employees: 9,000
Fax: 314-576-1867	Type: Private	FYE: December 31
Web: www.osi.to		

Pay now or deal with Outsourcing Solutions (OSI) later. The accounts-receivable management firm provides a variety of collection, portfolio purchasing, and outsourcing services to its customers, which include credit card, financial, utility, and health care companies, as well as education, government, and retail clients. The acquisitive company operates some 70 offices in about 25 states; it also offers its services in Canada, Mexico, and Puerto Rico. Services include providing call centers for credit authorization and customer service. OSI also purchases new and delinquent accounts from creditors. OSI is majority owned by Madison Dearborn Partners.

KEY COMPETITORS
Asta Funding
IntelliRisk Management
NCO Group

OXFORD AUTOMOTIVE, INC.

1250 Stephenson Hwy.	CEO: John W. Potter	2002 Est. Sales: $800.0 mil.
Troy, MI 48083	CFO: Aurelian Bukatko	1-Yr. Sales Change: (2.9%)
Phone: 248-577-1400	HR: Dennis Bemis	Employees: 7,000
Fax: 248-577-3388	Type: Private	FYE: March 31
Web: www.oxauto.com		

Oxford Automotive, a supplier of metal car and truck components, is riding the sport utility vehicle (SUV) boom all the way to the bank. The company manufactures suspension and structural systems, leaf springs, and other components for the automotive manufacturing industry. A majority of those components roll out on SUVs, minivans, and light trucks made by such companies as GM, Ford, Renault, Peugeot, and DaimlerChrysler. The company's products can be found on Ford's F-Series pickups and on DaimlerChrysler's Ram pickups. Chairman Selwyn Isakow owns about 56% of the company.

KEY COMPETITORS
Magna International
Tower Automotive
thyssenkrupp budd

In-depth profiles of an additional 200 key private companies are found on pages 36–435.

PACIFIC COAST BUILDING PRODUCTS INCORPORATED

3001 I St.	CEO: David J. Lucchetti	2001 Sales: $725.0 million
Sacramento, CA 95816	CFO: Dave Pringle	1-Yr. Sales Change: 4.9%
Phone: 916-444-9304	HR: Mark Ingram	Employees: 3,200
Fax: 916-325-3630	Type: Private	FYE: March 31
Web: www.paccoast.com		

Protecting Ronald Reagan's papers and propping up the San Francisco art world seems like a tall order, but Pacific Coast Building Products does both. The building materials manufacturer and distributor provided roof tiles for Reagan's presidential library and concrete blocks for the San Francisco Museum of Modern Art. It makes and distributes building products for residential, commercial, and industrial construction, selling to builders and contractors at 30 locations in 10 western states. Pacific Coast Building Products also provides services such as roofing, waterproofing, and insulation. The late Fred Anderson (father-in-law of president and CEO David Lucchetti) founded the company in 1953; his family owns the firm.

KEY COMPETITORS
ABC Supply
Building Materials Holding
Home Depot

THE PAMPERED CHEF, LTD.

1 Pampered Chef Ln.	CEO: Doris K. Christopher	2001 Sales: $740.0 million
Addison, IL 60101	CFO: Rick Geu	1-Yr. Sales Change: 4.4%
Phone: 630-261-8900	HR: Catherine Landman	Employees: 1,110
Fax: 630-261-4049	Type: Private	FYE: December 31
Web: www.pamperedchef.com		

Got a hankerin' for crinkle-cut watermelons, perfectly wedged apples, or artfully zested lemons? Then call The Pampered Chef, a direct seller of about 150 gourmet kitchen gadgets, cookware, cookbooks, and foodstuffs. The company has about 66,000 independent sales reps who sell products at in-home kitchen parties (à la Tupperware) throughout Canada, Germany, the UK, and the US. The reps demonstrate product use and care and then share recipes. As incentive (à la Mary Kay), they can ultimately receive ruby and diamond rings, as well as trips. Founded in 1980 by home economist, educator, and CEO Doris Christopher, the firm is being bought by Berkshire Hathaway, the conglomerate controlled by billionaire Warren Buffett.

KEY COMPETITORS
Lifetime Hoan
Tupperware
WKI Holding

PARKDALE MILLS, INC.

P.O. Box 1787	CEO: Anderson D. Warlick	2002 Est. Sales: $900.0 mil.
Gastonia, NC 28053	CFO: Dan Wilson	1-Yr. Sales Change: (10.1%)
Phone: 704-874-5000	HR: Reid Baker	Employees: 3,500
Fax: 704-874-5176	Type: Private	FYE: September 30
Web: www.parkdalemills.com		

Like that nice, soft-spun cotton in your undies? Thank Parkdale Mills. Parkdale, founded in 1916, is the largest independent yarn spinner in the US. The company manufactures cotton and cotton-polyester blend yarns and specializes in spun yarn that winds up in consumer goods such as sheets, towels, underwear, and hosiery. Parkdale has customers worldwide, including Jockey International, Lands' End, Fieldcrest Cannon, L.L. Bean, and Springmaid. The company operates and owns 66% of Parkdale America, a joint venture with polyester and nylon yarn maker Unifi. It also operates mills in Mexico through a joint venture with Burlington Industries. Chairman Duke Kimbrell owns about half of Parkdale.

KEY COMPETITORS
Avondale Incorporated
Guilford Mills
National Textiles

In-depth profiles of an additional 200 key private companies are found on pages 36–435.

PARSONS & WHITTEMORE, INCORPORATED

4 International Dr.	CEO: George Landegger	2002 Est. Sales: $1,100.0 mil.
Rye Brook, NY 10573	CFO: Steven Sweeney	1-Yr. Sales Change: 0.0%
Phone: 914-937-9009	HR: Suzanne Henry	Employees: 2,500
Fax: 914-937-2259	Type: Private	FYE: March 31

Parsons & Whittemore is one of the world's largest producers of market pulp, the raw material used in papermaking. It is also a supplier of bleached kraft pulp, which is used to make paper bags, butcher wrap, newsprint, strong bond and ledger paper, and tissue. Parsons & Whittemore has pulp mills in Alabama and in Canada. It also produces newsprint through its Alabama River Newsprint joint venture with Canada's Abitibi-Consolidated, the world's largest newsprint maker. Chairman and CEO George Landegger and his family own the company. Landegger's father, Karl, came to the US from Austria in 1938 and bought Parsons & Whittemore, then a small pulp-trading firm founded in 1909.

KEY COMPETITORS
Pope & Talbot
Potlatch
Weyerhaeuser

PARSONS BRINCKERHOFF INC.

1 Penn Plaza	CEO: Thomas J. O'Neill	2002 Est. Sales: $1,350.0 mil.
New York, NY 10119	CFO: Richard A. Schrader	1-Yr. Sales Change: 13.2%
Phone: 212-465-5000	HR: John J. Ryan	Employees: 9,294
Fax: 212-465-5096	Type: Private	FYE: October 31
Web: www.pbworld.com		

After converting (and covering) the US, Parsons Brinckerhoff is spreading its word (and pavement) around the globe. As one of the top US transportation engineering firms, the company provides planning, design, management, and maintenance for construction projects. The company specializes in transit systems, tunnels, bridges, highways, and airports, as well as telecommunications, energy, and environmental projects. Founded in 1885 by William Barclay Parsons, the company designed New York City's first subway. Other projects include the Sabiya Power Station in Kuwait and the Austin-Bergstrom International Airport in Texas. Employee-owned Parsons Brinckerhoff operates more than 250 offices in nearly 80 countries.

KEY COMPETITORS
HNTB
Louis Berger Group
URS

P.C. RICHARD & SON

150 Price Pkwy.	CEO: Gary Richard	2002 Sales: $925.0 million
Farmingdale, NY 11735	CFO: Tom Pohmer	1-Yr. Sales Change: 5.1%
Phone: 631-843-4300	HR: Bonni Richard	Employees: 2,134
Fax: 631-843-4469	Type: Private	FYE: January 31
Web: www.pcrichard.com		

P.C. Richard & Son is out to beat The Wiz — and short out Circuit City, too. Founded in 1909 by Dutch immigrant milkman and jack-of-all-trades Peter Christiana Richard, the family-owned company has more than 40 stores in the New York City metropolitan area. Once a hardware store, P.C. Richard now gets about half of its sales from appliances (air conditioners, stoves, microwaves, vacuum cleaners), and it also sells home electronics (televisions, DVD players, VCRs, sound systems) and computers. The firm is operated by fourth-generation Richard family members. P.C. Richard attempted to go public in 1993 but withdrew its offering after a tepid response.

KEY COMPETITORS
Cablevision Electronics
 Investments
Circuit City
Sears

In-depth profiles of an additional 200 key private companies are found on pages 36–435.

PEERLESS IMPORTERS, INC.

16 Bridgewater St.
Brooklyn, NY 11222
Phone: 718-383-5500
Fax: 718-389-5708
Web: www.peerimp.com

CEO: Nino Magliocco
CFO: Mario Gottesmann
HR: Pat Prisinzano
Type: Private

2001 Est. Sales: $710.0 mil.
1-Yr. Sales Change: 2.9%
Employees: 1,200
FYE: December 31

Peerless Importers has some of the most beloved liquid assets around. The company, founded in 1943, distributes wine and spirits in New York and Connecticut. Its spirits catalog includes blends, brandy and cognac, cordials and liqueurs (including Baileys Irish Cream), gin, rum, scotch (including J&B), and vodka. Wines are imported from Australia, Chile, and Western Europe. Unfortunately, Peerless Importers does have peers and has, in the past, lost business from liquor giants Diageo and Bacardi Limited to New York rivals like Charmer Industries. The Magliocco family (through its Quaker Equities holding company) owns and operates Peerless Importers and its Johnny Barton subsidiary.

KEY COMPETITORS
Charmer Industries
Gallo
Johnson Brothers

PELLA CORPORATION

102 Main St.
Pella, IA 50219
Phone: 641-628-1000
Fax: 641-628-6070
Web: www.pella.com

CEO: Gary Christenson
CFO: Herbert Liennenbrugger
HR: Karin Peterson
Type: Private

2001 Est. Sales: $900.0 mil.
1-Yr. Sales Change: (1.1%)
Employees: 6,800
FYE: November 30

Window and door maker Pella got out of a jamb by offering its products through retailers. Originally Pella focused on upscale homeowners, builders, and designers, marketing its products through a network of distribution centers and upscale Pella Window Stores retail outlets. The company has expanded its market, allowing do-it-yourselfers to buy its ProLine windows and doors through building supply stores. Pella's products include sliding French and contemporary doors and awning, clad casement, and bay windows. Pella was founded in 1925 as Rolscreen Company (after its first product, a roll-up window screen). The descendants of founder Pete Kuyper own the company.

KEY COMPETITORS
Andersen Corporation
Atrium
JELD-WEN

PENN MUTUAL LIFE INSURANCE CO.

600 Dresher Rd.
Horsham, PA 19044
Phone: 215-956-8000
Fax: 215-956-8347
Web: www.pennmutual.com

CEO: Robert E. Chappell Jr.
CFO: Nancy S. Brodie
HR: Michael A. Biondolillo
Type: Mutual company

2001 Sales: $1,065.7 million
1-Yr. Sales Change: (12.7%)
Employees: —
FYE: December 31

Founded in 1847, Penn Mutual Life Insurance offers life insurance, annuities, and investment products. The company has five main subsidiaries, including Penn Insurance and Annuity and brokerages Janney Montgomery Scott and Hornor, Townsend & Kent. Penn sells its products to high-net-worth individuals, professionals, and small businesses. Products include term, whole life, universal life, variable universal life, and disability income insurance policies, as well as a full range of deferred and immediate annuity products. The company also provides trust services and asset management to individuals and institutions.

KEY COMPETITORS
MetLife
Pacific Mutual
Prudential

📖 In-depth profiles of an additional 200
key private companies are found on pages 36–435.

THE PENNSYLVANIA LOTTERY

2850 Turnpike Industrial Dr.
Middletown, PA 17057
Phone: 717-986-4699
Fax: 717-986-4767
Web: www.palottery.com

CEO: Robert F. Mars III
CFO: Larry P. Williams
HR: Sabrina Theiss
Type: Government-owned

2002 Sales: $1,947.0 million
1-Yr. Sales Change: 8.0%
Employees: —
FYE: June 30

Even if they don't become millionaires, senior citizens in Pennsylvania can still benefit from the state lottery. Established in 1971, Pennsylvania Lottery proceeds are dedicated to programs geared toward seniors (property-tax relief, rent rebates, reduced-cost transportation, co-pay prescriptions). Proceeds also fund more than 50 Area Agencies on Aging across Pennsylvania. State law mandates that at least 40% of lottery proceeds must be awarded in prizes, and at least 30% must be used for benefit programs. Games range from traditional lottery game Super 6 Lotto to daily wagering game Big 4. IGT Online Entertainment Systems (formerly Automated Wagering International) operates the lottery's computer systems.

KEY COMPETITORS
New Jersey Lottery
New York State Lottery
Ohio Lottery

THE PENNSYLVANIA STATE UNIVERSITY

408 Old Main
University Park, PA 16802
Phone: 814-865-4700
Fax: 814-863-0701
Web: www.psu.edu

CEO: Graham B. Spanier
CFO: Gary C. Schultz
HR: —
Type: School

2001 Sales: $2,150.4 million
1-Yr. Sales Change: 9.1%
Employees: 27,112
FYE: June 30

Chartered in 1855 to apply scientific principles to farming, The Pennsylvania State University system is one of the largest in the US. Penn State has an enrollment of more than 81,700 students (about 15% are graduate students) and more than 5,100 faculty members. It offers 160 undergraduate and 150 graduate programs at 24 campuses. The school's largest campus, with about half of the undergraduate students, and its oldest is at University Park in central Pennsylvania. Other sites include the College of Medicine in Hershey and the Dickinson School of Law in Carlisle. Fisher-Price cofounder Herman Fisher, football great Roosevelt Grier, and former US Secretary of Defense William Perry attended Penn State.

PENSKE TRUCK LEASING

Rte. 10 Green Hills
Reading, PA 19607
Phone: 610-775-6000
Fax: 610-775-6432
Web: www.pensketruckleasing.com

CEO: Brian Hard
CFO: Frank Cocuzza
HR: John W. Kaisoglus
Type: Joint venture

2001 Sales: $3,400.0 million
1-Yr. Sales Change: (2.2%)
Employees: 21,000
FYE: December 31

Penske Truck Leasing is positioning itself as a top player in commercial truck leasing. With its 2001 acquisition of Rollins Truck Leasing, the company ranks #2 in the industry behind rival Ryder. Penske Truck Leasing operates more than 145,000 vehicles from about 1,000 locations in the US, Canada, Europe, Mexico, and South America. The company offers full-service leasing, contract maintenance, and commercial and consumer truck rental. Through Penske Logistics, it provides global transportation management, distribution and warehouse management, and integrated logistics. Founded in 1988, Penske Truck Leasing is a joint venture of GE Equipment Management and race-car legend Roger Penske's Penske Corporation.

KEY COMPETITORS
AMERCO
Ryder
UniGroup

In-depth profiles of an additional 200 key private companies are found on pages 36–435.

PEPPER CONSTRUCTION GROUP, LLC

643 N. Orleans St.	CEO: J. Stanley Pepper	2001 Sales: $834.0 million
Chicago, IL 60610	CFO: Joel D. Thomason	1-Yr. Sales Change: 15.4%
Phone: 312-266-4700	HR: John Beasley	Employees: 1,250
Fax: 312-266-2792	Type: Private	FYE: September 30
Web: www.pepperconstruction.com		

Although Pepper Construction Group sprinkles buildings across the US, it mainly spices up the construction landscape in the US Midwest. A top general contractor and construction manager in the region, Pepper builds commercial buildings, hotels, malls, and schools. Commercial, health care, and retail markets account for two-thirds of sales. The firm, which outsources its design and engineering tasks, can perform concrete, drywall, masonry, and millwork jobs and offers hazardous waste services through Pepper Environmental Technologies. Regular clients include Marshall Field's and Northwestern University. Founded by Stanley Pepper in Chicago in 1927, the company is owned and run by his family.

KEY COMPETITORS
Bovis Lend Lease
Turner Corporation
Walsh Group

PETRO STOPPING CENTERS, L.P.

6080 Surety Dr.	CEO: James A. "Jack" Cardwell Sr.	2001 Sales: $684.3 million
El Paso, TX 79905	CFO: Edward Escudero	1-Yr. Sales Change: (30.2%)
Phone: 915-779-4711	HR: Walter Kalinowski	Employees: 4,108
Fax: 915-774-7382	Type: Private	FYE: December 31
Web: www.petrotruckstops.com		

Petro Stopping Centers is the center of attention for truckers who need a petro stop. The firm operates 55 truck stops (almost half of them franchised) in 30 states. Its truck stops sell Mobil-brand diesel fuel, gas, and travel merchandise such as food, toiletries, truck accessories, and electronics. (Fuel accounts for almost 75% of sales.) The centers also provide Petro:Lube facilities (preventive maintenance services), showers, laundry services, game rooms, and Iron Skillet restaurants (home-style cooking). Chairman and CEO Jack Cardwell, who founded the company in 1975, and his son, COO Jim, own more than 50% of the company. Volvo Petrol Holdings has a 29% stake.

KEY COMPETITORS
Flying J
Pilot
TravelCenters of America

PHIL LONG DEALERSHIPS, INC.

1212 Motor City Dr.	CEO: Jay Cimino	2001 Sales: $782.6 million
Colorado Springs, CO 80906	CFO: Duane Sessions	1-Yr. Sales Change: 11.8%
Phone: 719-575-7100	HR: Linda Bonewell	Employees: 1,800
Fax: 719-575-7837	Type: Private	FYE: November 30
Web: www.phillong.com		

The list of car models being sold by Phil Long Dealerships is getting longer. Founded in 1945 by a WWII US Navy pilot, the late Philip Long, the company sells new and used vehicles through more than a dozen dealerships in Colorado Springs and Denver, Colorado. The makes sold by the dealerships include Audi, Chrysler, Ford, Hyundai, Kia, Mercedes-Benz, Mitsubishi, Nissan, Saturn, and Suzuki. In addition, the company allows customers to search for a vehicle, apply for credit, and complete the purchase through its Web site. The dealerships also provide parts and service. The company is owned by a partnership that includes CEO Jay Cimino and other managers.

KEY COMPETITORS
AutoNation
Braman Management
Burt Automotive

📖 In-depth profiles of an additional 200 key private companies are found on pages 36–435.

PILOT CORPORATION

5508 Lonas Rd.
Knoxville, TN 37909
Phone: 865-588-7487
Fax: 865-450-2800
Web: www.pilotcorp.com

CEO: James A. Haslam III
CFO: Jeffrey L. Cornish
HR: Mark A. Rowan
Type: Private

2001 Est. Sales: $1,700.0 mil.
1-Yr. Sales Change: (3.8%)
Employees: 7,200
FYE: December 31

Pilot offers a salve to those suffering from white-line fever. Catering to truckers and travelers alike, Pilot operates more than 240 travel centers in 38 states (through a joint venture with Marathon Ashland Petroleum); each features one or more national food chains, such as Subway, Dairy Queen, Wendy's, and Taco Bell. Pilot features fuel islands large enough to service several 18-wheelers at a time and private showers for its customers. Pilot also operates more than 65 convenience stores in Tennessee and Virginia. James Haslam II got Pilot off the ground in 1958 as a gas station that sold cigarettes and soft drinks; now his son, CEO James Haslam III, pilots the firm. The Haslam family owns the company.

KEY COMPETITORS
Flying J
Petro Stopping Centers
TravelCenters of America

PINNACLE FOODS CORPORATION

6 Executive Campus
Cherry Hill, NJ 08002
Phone: 856-969-7100
Fax: 856-969-7311
Web: www.pinnaclefoodscorp.com

CEO: C. Dean Metropoulos
CFO: Mike Dion
HR: Joy Telenson
Type: Private

2001 Sales: $750.0 million
1-Yr. Sales Change: —
Employees: 2,600
FYE: July 31

Pinnacle Foods is in a pickle and in the pits, and that's right where it wants to be. Under the Vlasic brand, the company sells the #1 pickle in the US, as well as jalapeños and other peppers. Through its Swanson unit, Pinnacle sells frozen dinners, pot pies, and other heat-and-serve comestibles under the Hungry-Man and Great Starts labels, among others. It also owns Open Pit barbecue sauce. The company was formed in 2001 when buyout firm Hicks, Muse, Tate & Furst bought the Swanson, Vlasic, and Open Pit brands from Vlasic Foods International. Pinnacle Foods plans to continue acquiring national brands.

KEY COMPETITORS
Heinz
International Multifoods
Kraft Foods

PITMAN COMPANY

721 Union Blvd.
Totowa, NJ 07512
Phone: 973-812-0400
Fax: 973-812-1630
Web: www.pitman.com

CEO: Joseph A. Demharter
CFO: John A. Eichner
HR: Hal Snyder
Type: Private

2001 Sales: $600.0 million
1-Yr. Sales Change: (2.3%)
Employees: 517
FYE: March 31

Pitman's history illustrates how the graphic arts landscape has shifted. Founded by Harold Pitman in 1906 as a producer of copper plates and steel dies, the company is now one of North America's largest graphic arts suppliers. It distributes traditional prepress and pressroom products, digital imaging systems, and graphics software from such manufacturers as Agfa, Kodak, and Imation. It also offers support services such as financial consulting and technical workshops. Its 22 US branches serve commercial, corporate printing and packaging, and newspaper publishing customers, and it sells online through PrintNation, which it acquired in 2001. Employees and members of chairman Peter Schmidt Jr.'s family own Pitman.

KEY COMPETITORS
Buhrmann
Enovation Graphics Systems
Matthews International

📖 In-depth profiles of an additional 200 key private companies are found on pages 36–435.

PLANET AUTOMOTIVE GROUP, INC.

2333 Ponce De Leon Blvd., Ste. 600
Coral Gables, FL 33134
Phone: 305-774-7690
Fax: 305-774-7697
Web: www.planetautomotive.com

CEO: Alan Potamkin
CFO: David Yusko
HR: Andy Pfeifer
Type: Private

2001 Sales: $1,411.3 million
1-Yr. Sales Change: 4.5%
Employees: 1,600
FYE: December 31

Expect a lot of iron, glass, and rubber on the surface of Planet Automotive Group. Formerly Potamkin Manhattan, the company coalesced from a network of auto dealerships owned by the Potamkin family. The company's 40-plus dealerships operate primarily in Florida, but also in California, Illinois, Iowa, Massachusetts, New York, Pennsylvania, and Texas. It has grown through acquisitions of new- and used-car dealerships. The company's dealerships also offer parts and service departments. The late Victor Potamkin opened his first dealership in 1946, and his two sons, Robert and Alan, now run the company.

KEY COMPETITORS
AutoNation
Holman Enterprises
United Auto Group

PLASTIPAK PACKAGING, INC.

9135 General Court
Plymouth, MI 48170
Phone: 734-455-3600
Fax: 734-354-7391
Web: www.plastipak.com

CEO: William C. Young
CFO: Mary E. Young
HR: Matt Leslie
Type: Private

2001 Sales: $812.0 million
1-Yr. Sales Change: 43.5%
Employees: 3,300
FYE: October 31

Plastipak Packaging likes to keep things bottled up. The company supplies plastic containers for products such as carbonated and noncarbonated beverages, cleaning products, distilled spirits, and processed juices. It makes high-density polyethylene (HDPE) resins and polyethylene terephthalate (PET) at its plants in the US and South America. In conjunction with Canada-based Husky Injection Molding Systems, Plastipak has pioneered a molding process, EXI-PAK, that allows products that were once confined to glass or metal containers to be packaged in plastic. Plastipak also licenses its technologies to manufacturers, including customers in Brazil, Germany, and New Zealand. The Young family owns and runs Plastipak.

KEY COMPETITORS
PolyOne
PVC Container
Silgan

PLATINUM EQUITY HOLDINGS

2049 Century Park East, Ste. 2700
Los Angeles, CA 90067
Phone: 310-712-1850
Fax: 310-712-1848
Web: www.peh.com

CEO: Tom T. Gores
CFO: William Foltz
HR: Kathleen A. Wilkinson
Type: Private

2001 Sales: —
1-Yr. Sales Change: —
Employees: 15,000
FYE: December 31

Platinum Equity Holdings knows "an oldie but a goodie" when it sees one. The information technology investment firm buys underperforming businesses, including units of large corporations. These companies, many of them 20 years old, usually offer legacy products and services and have well-established customer bases and distribution operations. Platinum focuses on companies offering products and/or services in such sectors as call center and help desk operations, data communications and networking, information systems, and software. The firm has operations in the US, Europe, Asia, and South America. Platinum is owned by CEO Tom Gores, brother of Alec, who founded investment firm Gores Technology Group.

KEY COMPETITORS
Apollo Advisors
Clayton, Dubilier
KKR

📖 **In-depth profiles of an additional 200 key private companies are found on pages 36–435.**

PLIANT CORPORATION

1515 Woodfield Rd., Ste. 600
Schaumburg, IL 60173
Phone: 847-969-3300
Fax: 847-969-3338
Web: www.pliantcorp.com

CEO: Jack E. Knott II
CFO: Brian E. Johnson
HR: Larry Shepler
Type: Private

2001 Sales: $840.4 million
1-Yr. Sales Change: (0.4%)
Employees: 3,500
FYE: December 31

Pliant is flexible when it comes to packaging. The company makes flexible packaging products and value-added films for a variety of applications. Among Pliant's three product segments, its specialty films segment (45% of sales) includes diapers, adult incontinence and feminine care products, and sterile packaging. The industrial films division (some 30% of sales) makes stretch films (used to bundle palletized loads during shipping) and PVC films (used to wrap food products). Products such as printed rollstock, bags, and sheets make up Pliant's design segment. The US accounts for nearly 85% of sales. Former chairman and CEO Richard Durham and his family own almost 30% of the company; J.P. Morgan Partners owns about 53%.

KEY COMPETITORS
AEP Industries
Griffon
Polymer Group

PMC GLOBAL, INC.

12243 Branford St.
Sun Valley, CA 91352
Phone: 818-896-1101
Fax: 818-897-0180
Web: www.pmcglobalinc.com

CEO: Philip E. Kamins
CFO: Thian C. Cheong
HR: Karen Ferguson
Type: Private

2001 Sales: $800.0 million
1-Yr. Sales Change: 2.0%
Employees: 4,300
FYE: December 31

Multifaceted PMC Global can make Teletubbies brand kiddie soap *and* the pipe that drains the soap suds away. The diversified international company produces memory chips, connectors, film, packaging, plastics, plastic-molding equipment, and specialty chemicals, among other things. It operates through more than a dozen specialized divisions such as ASC Group (electronics), Cosrich (children's bath, cosmetics, and toiletry products, including Disney brands), PMC Specialties Group (specialty chemicals), and VCF Films (PVC and acrylic films). CEO Philip Kamins (who owns the company) founded PMC (an acronym for Plastic Management Corporation) in 1971 as an outgrowth of a small plastics scrap yard he founded in 1964.

KEY COMPETITORS
BASF AG
DuPont
Pactiv

POWER AUTHORITY OF THE STATE OF NEW YORK

123 Main St.
White Plains, NY 10601
Phone: 914-681-6200
Fax: 212-468-6360
Web: www.nypa.gov

CEO: Eugene W. Zeltmann
CFO: Michael H. Urbach
HR: Vincent C. Vesce
Type: Government-owned

2001 Sales: $2,016.0 million
1-Yr. Sales Change: (0.9%)
Employees: —
FYE: December 31

Question authority? Well, without question authority for power lies in the Power Authority of the State of New York (commonly referred to as the New York Power Authority, or NYPA). The company generates and transmits more than 20% of New York's electricity, making it the largest state-owned public power provider in the US. It is also New York's only statewide electricity supplier. NYPA owns 21 hydroelectric and fossil-fueled generating facilities that produce about 5,700 MW of electricity, and it operates more than 1,400 circuit-miles of transmission lines.

KEY COMPETITORS
Con Edison
Energy East
KeySpan Energy

In-depth profiles of an additional 200 key private companies are found on pages 36–435.

PRAIRIE FARMS DAIRY INC.

1100 N. Broadway St.	CEO: Roger Capps	2001 Sales: $1,104.7 million
Carlinville, IL 62626	CFO: Paul Benne	1-Yr. Sales Change: 0.2%
Phone: 217-854-2547	HR: Tom Weber	Employees: 2,300
Fax: 217-854-6426	Type: Cooperative	FYE: September 30
Web: www.prairiefarms.com		

The bittersweet torture Prairie Farms Dairy inflicts upon the lactose intolerant! With about 800 members, Prairie Farms is one of the largest dairy cooperatives in the Midwest. It produces milk, butter, cottage cheese, sour cream, and orange juices, primarily under the Prairie Farms label. It also makes goodies such as ice cream, yogurt, sherbet, and dips. The company's products are sold in stores, schools, and to institutional clients in the Midwest. Subsidiary PFD Supply distributes food and paper products to fast-food restaurants, including Burger King and McDonald's.

KEY COMPETITORS
AMPI
Dairy Farmers of America
Land O'Lakes

PSF GROUP HOLDINGS, INC.

423 W. 8th St., Ste. 200	CEO: John M. Meyer	2002 Sales: $674.9 million
Kansas City, MO 64105	CFO: Stephen A. Lightstone	1-Yr. Sales Change: 24.9%
Phone: 816-472-7675	HR: Jeffrey K. Gough	Employees: 4,200
Fax: 816-843-1450	Type: Holding company	FYE: March 31
Web: www.psfarms.com		

PSF Group Holdings doesn't actually hold the hogs — that's done by its wholly owned subsidiary Premium Standard Farms, the second-largest US hog producer after Smithfield Foods. Vertically integrated Premium Standard controls production from birth to slaughter, making feed and selling live hogs, fresh pork, and processed products. It distributes its fresh and frozen pork to retailers, food service customers, and food manufacturers through its facilities in northern Missouri, North Carolina, and Texas. Agribusiness giant ContiGroup Companies holds 53% of PSF Group Holdings.

KEY COMPETITORS
Farmland Industries
Seaboard
Smithfield Foods

PRESBYTERIAN HEALTHCARE SERVICES

2501 Buena Vista SE	CEO: James H. Hinton	2001 Sales: $1,007.0 million
Albuquerque, NM 87106	CFO: Dale Maxwell	1-Yr. Sales Change: 0.7%
Phone: 505-841-1234	HR: Renee Reimer	Employees: 7,253
Fax: 505-923-6141	Type: Not-for-profit	FYE: December 31
Web: www.phs.org		

Established in the early 1900s as a sanatorium for tuberculosis patients, not-for-profit Presbyterian Healthcare Services (PHS) now cares for more than 400,000 New Mexicans. PHS's Presbyterian Health Plan serves individuals, spouses, and dependents, covering everything from preventive to emergency care. PHS hospitals offer small group plans for companies with less than 50 employees and group health plans with HMO and point-of-service options. Enrollees include the State of New Mexico, University of New Mexico, and Intel. The PHS network of eight hospitals and about 15 community health centers and clinics stretches from Cimarron to Ruidoso.

KEY COMPETITORS
Banner Health System
CIGNA
Triad Hospitals

In-depth profiles of an additional 200 key private companies are found on pages 36–435.

PRIMUS, INC.

3110 Kettering Blvd.
Dayton, OH 45439
Phone: 937-294-6878
Fax: 937-293-9591
Web: www.winholesale.com

CEO: Richard W. Schwartz
CFO: Jack W. Johnston
HR: —
Type: Private

2002 Sales: $1,001.0 million
1-Yr. Sales Change: (3.7%)
Employees: 3,195
FYE: January 31

You Win some, you Win some more. So it goes for Primus, which invests in a collection of some 425 small wholesale distributors in about 40 states that sell plumbing, heating, air-conditioning, electrical, and other supplies to contractors and other customers. The companies are easily recognizable by their Win-prefixed names, such as Columbia Winnelson (plumbing products), Salt Lake Windustrial (pipes and valves), and Dayton Winfastener (specialty fasteners). Primus supports its companies, through units Dapsco and Distro, with bulk purchasing, warehousing, and data processing. Primus is owned mostly by heirs of the investors, including chairman Richard Schiewetz, who founded Primus in 1956.

KEY COMPETITORS
Ferguson Enterprises
Hughes Supply
W.W. Grainger

PRINCETON UNIVERSITY

1 Nassau Hall
Princeton, NJ 08544
Phone: 609-258-3000
Fax: 609-258-1294
Web: www.princeton.edu

CEO: Shirley M. Tilghman
CFO: Christopher McCrudden
HR: —
Type: School

2002 Sales: $767.0 million
1-Yr. Sales Change: 20.1%
Employees: 12,238
FYE: June 30

Princeton rules the Ivy League. The highly selective university accepts about 11% of those who apply. Founded in 1746, Princeton is one of the US's richest universities, with an endowment of more than $8 billion (behind Harvard, Yale, and Texas). It offers degrees in 35 departments. Princeton's more than 6,300 students pay a tuition of more than $27,000 a year; 50% receive some financial aid. Nobel prize winners associated with Princeton include Woodrow Wilson (who was Princeton's president before becoming US president), writer Toni Morrison, and physicist Richard Feynman. The university also is loosely affiliated with the Institute for Advanced Study where Albert Einstein once taught.

PRINTPACK, INC.

4335 Wendell Dr.
Atlanta, GA 30336
Phone: 404-691-5830
Fax: 404-699-7122
Web: www.printpack.com

CEO: Dennis M. Love
CFO: R. Michael Hembree
HR: Nicklas D. Stucky
Type: Private

2002 Est. Sales: $1,100.0 mil.
1-Yr. Sales Change: 7.2%
Employees: 4,300
FYE: June 30

Printpack wraps its flexible packaging around salty snacks, confections, baked goods, cookies, crackers, and cereal, as well as tissues and paper towels. The company's packaging includes plastic film, aluminum foil, metallized films and paper with specialized coatings, and cast and blown monolayer and co-extruded films. Customers include Frito-Lay, Georgia-Pacific, General Mills, and Quaker Oats. Printpack manufactures packaging materials at about 20 plants in the US, Mexico, and the UK. The founding Love family owns and manages the company, which was founded in 1956.

KEY COMPETITORS
Alcoa
Pechiney
Pliant

In-depth profiles of an additional 200
key private companies are found on pages 36–435.

PROVENA HEALTH

9223 W. St. Francis Rd.
Frankfort, IL 60423
Phone: 815-469-4888
Fax: 815-469-4864
Web: www.provena.org

CEO: William Foley
CFO: William M. Wheeler
HR: Terry S. Solem
Type: Not-for-profit

2000 Sales: $869.0 million
1-Yr. Sales Change: 20.8%
Employees: 11,400
FYE: December 31

The offspring of a very holy union, Provena Health was created from the merger of Illinois Roman Catholic hospital groups Franciscan Sisters Health Care (Frankfort), ServantCor (Kankakee), and Mercy Center for Health Care Services (Aurora), in an effort to stay competitive in an era of managed care. Provena has seven hospitals, 14 nursing homes, more than 40 clinics, six home health agencies, and its own PersonalCare HMO. It also has a hospice program, and its HealthCare Equipment unit sells a large selection of medical equipment. Provena is sponsored by Franciscan Sisters of the Sacred Heart, Servants of the Holy Heart of Mary, and Sisters of Mercy of the Americas.

KEY COMPETITORS
Advocate Health Care
BJC Health
Rush System for Health

PROVIDENCE HEALTH SYSTEM

506 2nd Ave., Ste. 1200
Seattle, WA 98104
Phone: 206-464-3355
Fax: 206-464-3038
Web: www.providence.org

CEO: Henry G. Walker
CFO: Michael Butler
HR: Sue Byington
Type: Not-for-profit

2001 Sales: $3,274.1 million
1-Yr. Sales Change: 1.4%
Employees: 32,929
FYE: December 31

Sisterhood is powerful in health care. The order of the Sisters of Providence runs not-for-profit Providence Health System in the Pacific Northwest (with outposts in Alaska and California). The system operates more than 20 acute care hospitals, as well as long-term care and assisted-living facilities and primary care centers. In addition the company offers health plans, low-income housing, and home health, hospice, and various community outreach services. The Sisters were founded in 1843 in Montreal; their work in the US began in 1856, when five members of the order established a mission in what was then Washington Territory.

KEY COMPETITORS
Adventist Health
Legacy Health System
Tenet Healthcare

PUERTO RICO ELECTRIC POWER AUTHORITY

Ave. Ponce De Leon 17 1/2
San Turce, PR 00909
Phone: 787-289-3434
Fax: 787-289-4665
Web: www.prepa.com

CEO: Hector Rosario
CFO: Luis Figueroa
HR: Ana Blanes
Type: Government-owned

2002 Sales: —
1-Yr. Sales Change: —
Employees: 9,550
FYE: June 30

No man is an island, but Puerto Rico Electric Power Authority (PREPA) stands alone on one. Founded in 1941, the government-owned utility is the sole electricity distributor for Puerto Rico, where it serves nearly 1.4 million residential and business customers. PREPA owns five primarily fossil-fueled power plants that give it nearly 4,400 MW of generating capacity, and it has more than 31,000 miles of transmission and distribution lines. In order to keep up with increasing demand, the Puerto Rican government has allowed independent power producers to build cogeneration plants on the island to sell power to PREPA.

In-depth profiles of an additional 200 key private companies are found on pages 36–435.

PURDUE PHARMA L.P.

1 Stamford Forum, 201 Tresser Blvd.	CEO: Raymond R. Sackler	2001 Sales: $1,500.0 million
Stamford, CT 06901	CFO: Edward B. Mahony	1-Yr. Sales Change: 25.0%
Phone: 203-588-8000	HR: David Long	Employees: 3,000
Fax: 203-588-8850	Type: Private	FYE: December 31
Web: www.purduepharma.com		

Purdue Pharma's mantra could be "no pain, no gain." The pharmaceutical firm (formerly Purdue Frederick), known for OTC medicines like Betadine (an antiseptic) and Senokot (a laxative), concentrates its research and development on pain management and cancer. Prescription drugs include pain relievers MS Contin and OxyContin. It is also developing cardiac and respiratory therapies, as well as inhaled drug delivery systems. The firm markets products from other manufacturers in addition to its own products. Purdue Pharma also sponsors the pain control organization Partners Against Pain. Founded in 1892, the firm is part of a network of affiliates with operations in Asia, North and South America, and Europe.

KEY COMPETITORS
Elan Corporation
Endo Pharmaceuticals
Johnson & Johnson

PURITY WHOLESALE GROCERS, INC.

5400 Broken Sound Blvd. NW, Ste. 100	CEO: Salvatore Ricciardi	2002 Sales: $1,600.0 million
Boca Raton, FL 33487	CFO: Alan Rutner	1-Yr. Sales Change: 10.3%
Phone: 561-994-9360	HR: Karen McGrath	Employees: 490
Fax: 561-241-4628	Type: Private	FYE: June 30
Web: www.pwg-inc.com		

Untainted by grocery retailing, Purity Wholesale Grocers (PWG) sticks to getting the goods to grocers. The company takes advantage of the discounts granted to large wholesalers and retailers (and of the promotional pricing offered in certain regions) by purchasing items and selling them to retailers not privy to those discounts. PWG moves groceries, health and beauty care items, pharmaceutical products, dairy foods, and dry goods to US grocery chains, drugstores, and convenience stores. PWG's marketing network is made up of 12 independently operated food distributors, marketers, and transportation firms in the US and Puerto Rico. The company is owned by Jeff Levitetz, who founded PWG in 1982.

KEY COMPETITORS
Dot Foods
Nash Finch
Spartan Stores

QUAD/GRAPHICS, INC.

W224 N3322 Duplainville Rd.	CEO: Thomas A. Quadracci	2001 Sales: $1,700.0 million
Pewaukee, WI 53072	CFO: John C. Fowler	1-Yr. Sales Change: (5.6%)
Phone: 414-566-6000	HR: Emmy M. LaBode	Employees: 10,500
Fax: 414-566-4668	Type: Private	FYE: December 31
Web: www.qg.com		

Your mailbox may be filled with Quad/Graphics' handiwork. One of the largest privately held printers in the US, the company prints catalogs, magazines, books, direct mail, and other items. It offers a full range of services, including design, photography, desktop production, printing, binding, wrapping, and (through subsidiary Parcel/Direct) distribution and transportation. At 15 printing facilities — five of which are in Wisconsin — the company prints catalogs for Bloomingdale's and Victoria's Secret, among others, as well as periodicals such as *People, Newsweek, National Geographic,* and *Sports Illustrated.* Company employees and relatives of the founding Quadracci family own Quad/Graphics.

KEY COMPETITORS
Dai Nippon Printing
Quebecor World
R. R. Donnelley

📖 In-depth profiles of an additional 200
key private companies are found on pages 36–435.

QUALITY CHEKD DAIRIES, INC.

1733 Park St.
Naperville, IL 60563
Phone: 630-717-1110
Fax: 630-717-1126
Web: www.qchekd.com

CEO: Peter Horvath
CFO: Tom Bruce
HR: —
Type: Cooperative

2001 Sales: $2,500.0 million
1-Yr. Sales Change: —
Employees: 14
FYE: September 30

The founders of Quality Chekd Dairies were better dairymen than proofreaders. The non-profit cooperative provides marketing, purchasing, and training services to its some 40 member dairies and dairy product processors in the US, Mexico, El Salvador, and Colombia. Along with access to the co-op's marketing, accounting, and purchasing services, members can attend its COW TECH training programs. Quality Chekd also offers food quality and safety testing services through an independent lab. Most of its members are smaller regional dairies and processors, but they all enjoy the use of the red check mark logo, familiar to grocery shoppers.

KEY COMPETITORS
Dairy Farmers of America
Foremost Farms
MMPA

QUALITY KING DISTRIBUTORS INC.

2060 9th Ave.
Ronkonkoma, NY 11779
Phone: 631-737-5555
Fax: 631-439-2388
Web: www.qkd.com

CEO: Glenn Nussdorf
CFO: Dennis Barkey
HR: Jane Midgal
Type: Private

2001 Sales: $2,400.0 million
1-Yr. Sales Change: 17.1%
Employees: 1,300
FYE: October 31

Quality King Distributors rules a gargantuan gray market empire. It buys US name-brand products that have been exported to overseas markets, re-imports them, then sells them below suggested retail prices. The practice is deeply disliked by US manufacturers, but has been ruled legal by the Supreme Court. Quality King distributes groceries and hair, health, and beauty care products to pharmacy and grocery chains, grocery distributors, and wholesale clubs throughout the US. Bernard Nussdorf and his wife Ruth founded Quality King in 1960 in Queens, New York. The Nussdorf family still owns the company, which has transferred its pharmaceutical distribution business to affiliate QK Healthcare prior to spinning it off.

KEY COMPETITORS
Cardinal Health
D & K Healthcare Resources
McKesson

QUARK, INC.

1800 Grant St.
Denver, CO 80203
Phone: 303-894-8888
Fax: 303-894-3398
Web: www.quark.com

CEO: Farhad F. Ebrahimi
CFO: Farhad F. Ebrahimi
HR: Marlene Gresh
Type: Private

2000 Est. Sales: $600.0 mil.
1-Yr. Sales Change: 0.0%
Employees: 1,000
FYE: December 31

Quark has all the quirks of desktop publishing down. Founded in 1981, the private company makes the leading desktop publishing software — QuarkXPress. Available for Macs and PCs, the page layout tool is used by graphics designers to arrange text and images for books, newspapers, magazines, and other publications. The company also offers digital asset management software (Quark Digital Media System) for managing text, images, and other files over networks and the Internet. Quark's customers represent the commercial publishing, graphic arts, and multimedia production markets. CEO Farhad Ebrahimi is the majority shareholder.

KEY COMPETITORS
Adobe
Corel
Microsoft

In-depth profiles of an additional 200 key private companies are found on pages 36–435.

QUEXCO INCORPORATED

2777 N. Stemmons Fwy.	CEO: Howard M. Meyers	2001 Est. Sales: $2,000.0 mil.
Dallas, TX 75207	CFO: —	1-Yr. Sales Change: —
Phone: 214-688-4000	HR: —	Employees: 7,000
Fax: 214-630-5864	Type: Private	FYE: December 31

Quexco gets the lead out and puts it back in. A leading secondary lead producer, this private holding company recycles scrapped lead acid batteries into refined lead and lead products. Quexco's RSR Corporation subsidiary is one of the largest lead smelters in the US, with operations in California, Indiana, New York, and Texas. Quexco also owns Eco-Bat Technologies plc, a UK-based battery recycler with operations in Europe and South Africa. The company's RSR Technologies subsidiary (formerly its R&D unit) offers technology and product development services to the metals industry. Chairman and CEO Howard Meyers, who also heads Bayou Steel Corporation, controls Quexco.

KEY COMPETITORS
Exide
Noranda
Renco

QUIKTRIP CORPORATION

4705 S. 129th East Ave.	CEO: Chester Cadieux	2002 Sales: $3,050.0 million
Tulsa, OK 74134	CFO: Terry Carter	1-Yr. Sales Change: 4.1%
Phone: 918-615-7700	HR: Kim Owen	Employees: 6,575
Fax: —	Type: Private	FYE: April 30
Web: www.quiktrip.com		

QuikTrip provides a quick fix for people on the go. QuikTrip (QT) owns and operates more than 400 gasoline and convenience stores primarily in the Midwest. QT stores, which average 4,500 to 5,000 sq. ft., feature the company's own brand of gas, as well as brand-name beverages, candy, and tobacco, and QT's own Quik 'n Tasty and HOTZI lines of sandwiches. QuikTrip travel centers offer CAT scales, food, fuel, showers, and other services for truckers. The company's FleetMaster program offers commercial trucking companies detailed reports showing drivers' product purchases, amounts spent, and odometer readings. QuikTrip was founded in 1958 by chairman, president, and CEO Chester Cadieux and partners.

KEY COMPETITORS
ChevronTexaco
Hale-Halsell

R.A.B. HOLDINGS, INC.

444 Madison Ave.	CEO: Richard A. Bernstein	2002 Sales: $596.3 million
New York, NY 10022	CFO: Steven M. Grossman	1-Yr. Sales Change: (8.6%)
Phone: 212-688-4500	HR: Hal B. Weiss	Employees: 1,770
Fax: 212-888-5025	Type: Private	FYE: March 31

R.A.B. Holdings holds the reins on two fast-growing grocery segments: kosher foods and health foods. It owns one of the top US kosher food makers, The B. Manischewitz Company, which makes matzos and other foods. It also operates Millbrook Distribution Services, which distributes specialty and natural foods, health and beauty care products, and general merchandise items to retailers in 42 states. R.A.B. has increased sales of its products by offering items such as rice pilafs and soup mixes to attract health-conscious non-Jewish consumers. The company also offers merchandising services to its retailers through Millbrook Retail Solutions. Founder, chairman, president, and CEO Richard Bernstein owns 40% of R.A.B.

KEY COMPETITORS
Fleming Companies
Hain Celestial
SUPERVALU

In-depth profiles of an additional 200 key private companies are found on pages 36–435.

RACETRAC PETROLEUM, INC.

300 Technology Ct.	CEO: Carl E. Bolch Jr.	2001 Sales: $2,942.0 million
Smyrna, GA 30082	CFO: Robert J. Dumbacher	1-Yr. Sales Change: 4.7%
Phone: 770-431-7600	HR: —	Employees: 3,850
Fax: 770-431-7612	Type: Private	FYE: December 31
Web: www.racetrac.com		

RaceTrac Petroleum hopes it is a popular pit stop for gasoline and snacks in the Southeast. The company operates about 500 company-owned and franchised gas stations and convenience stores in Alabama, Arkansas, Florida, Georgia, Kentucky, Louisiana, Mississippi, North Carolina, South Carolina, Tennessee, Texas, and Virginia under the RaceTrac and Raceway names. Carl Bolch founded RaceTrac in Missouri in 1934. His son, chairman and CEO Carl Bolch Jr., moved the company into high-volume gas stations with long, self-service islands that can serve many vehicles at once. RaceTrac's convenience stores also sell fresh deli food, rent videos, and offer some fast-food fare. The Bolch family owns the company.

KEY COMPETITORS
ChevronTexaco
Exxon Mobil
Motiva Enterprises

RALEY'S INC.

500 W. Capitol Ave.	CEO: William J. Coyne	2002 Sales: $3,200.0 million
West Sacramento, CA 95605	CFO: William Anderson	1-Yr. Sales Change: 6.7%
Phone: 916-373-3333	HR: Dan Abfalter	Employees: 17,000
Fax: 916-371-1323	Type: Private	FYE: June 30
Web: www.raleys.com		

Raley's has to stock plenty of fresh fruit and great wines — it sells to the people that produce them. The company operates about 150 supermarkets and larger-sized superstores, mostly in Northern California, but also in Nevada and New Mexico. In addition to its flagship Raley's Superstores, the company operates Bel Air Markets, Nob Hill Foods (an upscale Bay Area chain), and a discount warehouse chain, Food Source. Raley's stores typically offer groceries, natural foods, liquor, and pharmacies. Readers of *Consumer Reports* named Raley's the #1 supermarket chain in the US in 2000. Founded during the Depression by Tom Raley, the company is owned by Tom's daughter Joyce Raley Teel and is run by the family.

KEY COMPETITORS
Albertson's
Safeway
Save Mart Supermarkets

R. B. PAMPLIN CORP.

805 SW Broadway, Ste. 2400	CEO: Robert Boisseau Pamplin Jr.	2001 Est. Sales: $800.0 mil.
Portland, OR 97205	CFO: David Hastings	1-Yr. Sales Change: (10.1%)
Phone: 503-248-1133	HR: —	Employees: 8,500
Fax: 503-248-1175	Type: Private	FYE: December 31
Web: www.pamplin.org		

Founded by a man of the cloth, R. B. Pamplin casts a wide net. The family-owned conglomerate, started in 1957 by minister and company CEO Robert Pamplin Jr. (Robert Sr. is chairman), has operations ranging from entertainment to retail stores to manufacturing interests (asphalt, concrete, and textiles.) The company's Mount Vernon Mills is one of the largest denim producers in the US. Pamplin's entertainment concerns include radio broadcasting, newspapers, and record labels in the northwestern US. The company's other units are as diverse as retail stores offering Christian products to Columbia Empire Farms, which grows berries and grapes used in preserves and wine, then sold through its Your NorthWest stores.

KEY COMPETITORS
Avondale Incorporated
Cone Mills
U.S. Concrete

In-depth profiles of an additional 200
key private companies are found on pages 36–435.

RECREATIONAL EQUIPMENT, INC.

6750 S. 228th St.
Kent, WA 98032
Phone: 253-395-3780
Fax: 253-395-4352
Web: www.rei.com

CEO: Dennis Madsen
CFO: Brad Johnson
HR: Glen Simmons
Type: Cooperative

2001 Sales: $740.1 million
1-Yr. Sales Change: 6.0%
Employees: 6,000
FYE: December 31

Outdoor gear and clothing from Recreational Equipment, Inc. (REI) outfits everyone from mountain climbers to mall walkers. The company is one of the nation's largest consumer cooperatives, with about 2 million member-owners. Through about 60 outlets in 24 states, REI sells high-end gear, clothing, and footwear (including private-label goods) for adventurous outdoor activities such as climbing, kayaking, and skiing, as well as for hiking, bicycling, and camping. The company also repairs gear, and it sells merchandise online and through occasional catalogs.

KEY COMPETITORS
L.L. Bean
Lost Arrow
North Face

RED APPLE GROUP, INC.

823 11th Ave.
New York, NY 10019
Phone: 212-956-5803
Fax: 212-247-4509
Web: www.jacny.com

CEO: John A. Catsimatidis
CFO: Gary Pokrassa
HR: John Gedea
Type: Private

2001 Sales: $1,100.0 million
1-Yr. Sales Change: 10.0%
Employees: 3,117
FYE: February 28

Red Apple Group sells apples (and more) in the Big Apple. Subsidiary United Refining, which processes 72,000 barrels of oil a day, distributes fuel to its 400 KwikFill/Red Apple gas stations/convenience stores in New York, Pennsylvania, and Ohio. Red Apple controls Gristede's Foods, a leading New York City supermarket chain. It also has real estate, aircraft leasing, and newspaper operations. CEO John Catsimatidis owns the Red Apple Group, which lost out to Russian oil giant LUKOIL in a bid to acquire East Coast gasoline retailer Getty Petroleum Marketing. Red Apple owns and operates regional gas retailer Country Fair (68 gas stations).

KEY COMPETITORS
A&P
Getty Petroleum Marketing
Motiva Enterprises

RED CHAMBER GROUP

1912 E. Vernon Ave.
Vernon, CA 90058
Phone: 323-234-9000
Fax: 323-231-8888
Web: www.redchamber.com

CEO: Ming Bin Kou
CFO: Ming Shin Kou
HR: —
Type: Private

2001 Sales: $680.0 million
1-Yr. Sales Change: 2.3%
Employees: —
FYE: December 31

Ahoy, matey! If it's seafood you'd be awanting, the Red Chamber Group can accommodate. The third-largest seafood supplier in North America (after StarKist and ConAgra) and the largest importer of seafood from India, the Red Chamber Group imports and exports all manner of seafood — from shrimp to fish to lobster — around the world. It also operates aqua farms. Red Chamber Group serves as an umbrella for a number of companies, including Red Chamber Co. (which started as a small family-owned restaurant in Los Angeles), Aqua Star, Neptune Foods, Mid-Pacific Seafoods, OFI Markesa International, and Tampa Bay Fisheries. The Kou family owns and operates Red Chamber.

KEY COMPETITORS
Maruha
Pacific Seafood
Trident Seafoods

In-depth profiles of an additional 200 key private companies are found on pages 36–435.

RENCO GROUP INC.

30 Rockefeller Plaza	CEO: Ira L. Rennert	2002 Sales: $2,175.0 million
New York, NY 10112	CFO: Roger L. Fay	1-Yr. Sales Change: 1.2%
Phone: 212-541-6000	HR: Justin W. D'Atri	Employees: 13,500
Fax: 212-541-6197	Type: Private	FYE: October 31

Renco Group is a holding company for a diverse bunch of businesses. Its AM General subsidiary makes the HUMVEE, an extra-wide all-terrain vehicle used by the military, and the HUMMER, the HUMVEE's civilian counterpart. Renco Steel and WCI Steel manufacture, fabricate, and distribute steel. Other Renco Group companies include Doe Run, the world's #2 smelter; coal miner Rencoal; and Consolidated Sewing Machine, which makes industrial sewing machines. Renco was established in 1980 and is owned by industrialist Ira Rennert, a former business consultant whose Long Island, New York, home is double the size of the White House and is said to include 29 bedrooms, 42 bathrooms, a 100-car garage, and an English pub.

KEY COMPETITORS
Oshkosh Truck
Singer
United States Steel

REPUBLIC ENGINEERED PRODUCTS LLC

3770 Embassy Pkwy.	CEO: Joseph F. Lapinsky	2001 Sales: $993.7 million
Akron, OH 44333	CFO: John B. George	1-Yr. Sales Change: (21.5%)
Phone: 330-670-3000	HR: John Willoughby	Employees: 2,500
Fax: 330-670-7031	Type: Private	FYE: December 31
Web: www.republicengineered.com		

Republic Engineered Products (formerly Republic Technologies International) has set the bar higher after once being under Chapter 11 bankruptcy protection. The company is one of the largest producers of special bar quality (SBQ) used to make automobiles, heavy equipment, and similar products. Customers — including DaimlerChrysler, Ford, GM, and their suppliers — turn the company's steel into components such as bearings, crankshafts, and spark plug shells. The company's steelmaking facilities are located in Indiana, Ohio and New York. Private investment firms KPS Special Situations Fund L.P. (New York) and Hunt Investment Group L.P. (Dallas) acquired the company for approximately $463 million.

KEY COMPETITORS
AK Steel Holding Corporation
Nucor
United States Steel

RESOLUTION PERFORMANCE PRODUCTS LLC

1600 Smith Street, Ste. 2400	CEO: Marvin O. Schlanger	2001 Sales: $863.0 million
Houston, TX 77002	CFO: J. Travis Spoede	1-Yr. Sales Change: —
Phone: 832-366-2300	HR: Dennis F. White	Employees: 940
Fax: 832-366-2584	Type: Private	FYE: December 31
Web: www.resins.com		

The name Resolution Performance Products (RPP) is beginning to resin-ate throughout the chemical industry. Once the Resins and Versatics business of Shell Chemicals, the unit was sold to private investment firm Apollo Management in 2000 and thus renamed. The company is the world's leading maker of epoxy resins, which are used in coatings, adhesives, and printed circuit boards because of their insulating and adhesive properties. While RPP gets nearly two-thirds of its sales from epoxy resins, it also produces vesatic acids, which are used in pharmaceuticals, personal care products, and coatings. Bayer accounts for about 10% of sales. Apollo Management owns about 90% of the company; Shell Oil owns nearly 8%.

KEY COMPETITORS
Dow Chemical
ExxonMobil Chemical
Sunoco Chemicals

In-depth profiles of an additional 200 key private companies are found on pages 36–435.

RETAIL BRAND ALLIANCE, INC.

100 Phoenix Ave.	CEO: Claudio Del Vecchio	2002 Sales: —
Enfield, CT	CFO: Brian K. Baumann	1-Yr. Sales Change: —
Phone: 860-741-0771	HR: Susan Eyvazzadeh	Employees: 10,036
Fax: 860-745-9714	Type: Private	FYE: July 31

Given a food court and some seasonal kiosks, Retail Brand Alliance could open its own shopping mall. The holding company's portfolio includes over 1,000 mostly mall-based women's apparel shops in about 45 states under the Casual Corner, August Max, and Petite Sophisticate banners. Retail Brand Alliance also owns 160-store chain Brooks Brothers (men's suits and women's clothing); Carolee Designs (jewelry and accessories designer); and Adrienne Vittadini, a women's sportswear designer. President and CEO Claudio Del Vecchio owns Retail Brand Alliance, which he acquired as the Casual Corner Group in 1997 from his father's company, Luxottica Group (operator of LensCrafters and Sunglass Hut).

KEY COMPETITORS
AnnTaylor
Federated
Limited Brands

REYES HOLDINGS LLC

9500 West Bryn Mawr Ave., Suite 700	CEO: J. Christopher Reyes	2001 Sales: $3,900.0 million
Rosemont, IL 60018	CFO: Daniel P. Doheny	1-Yr. Sales Change: 11.4%
Phone: 847-227-6500	HR: —	Employees: 3,877
Fax: 847-227-6550	Type: Private	FYE: December 31

Closely held Reyes Holdings has a kingly grasp over two things that are often held closely together — food and beer. Through its subsidiary companies Reyes Holdings distributes products throughout North, Central, and South America. One of these, The Martin-Brower Company, supplies McDonald's restaurants in the US and Canada. Martin-Brower also serves McDonald's in Brazil, Central America, and Puerto Rico. Reyes Holdings also counts Premium Distributors of Virginia, Chicago Beverage Systems, and California's Harbor Distributing among the wholesalers it owns. The company operates more than 35 distribution centers in US and six other countries. Chairman Chris Reyes, Jude Reyes, and David Reyes own the company.

KEY COMPETITORS
McLane Foodservice
SYSCO
U.S. Foodservice

RGIS INVENTORY SPECIALISTS

2000 E. Taylor Rd.	CEO: Mike Nicholson	2001 Sales: —
Auburn Hills, MI 48326	CFO: Mark Papak	1-Yr. Sales Change: —
Phone: 248-651-2511	HR: Susan Kingman	Employees: 40,000
Fax: —	Type: Private	FYE: December 31
Web: www.rgisinv.com		

With RGIS Inventory Specialists, you can count on a lot of counting. The company is a leading third-party inventory taker in the US, with more than 400 offices worldwide. RGIS employees work during the day or at night to count inventory for their customers, primarily large retailers but also manufacturers and warehouses. Using scanners to send information to a sophisticated computer system at RGIS headquarters, the company performs more than 400,000 inventories per year. RGIS, which stands for "Retail Grocery Inventory Service," was founded in 1958 by Thomas Nicholson, whose descendants still own the company.

KEY COMPETITORS
Kelly Services

In-depth profiles of an additional 200 key private companies are found on pages 36–435.

RICH PRODUCTS CORPORATION

1150 Niagara St.	CEO: Robert E. Rich Jr.	2001 Sales: $1,702.0 million
Buffalo, NY 14213	CFO: Charles R. Trego	1-Yr. Sales Change: 5.1%
Phone: 716-878-8000	HR: Brian Townson	Employees: 6,500
Fax: 716-878-8765	Type: Private	FYE: December 31
Web: www.richs.com		

Starting in 1945 with "the miracle cream from the soya bean," Rich Products has grown from a niche maker of soy-based whipped toppings and frozen desserts to a major US frozen foods manufacturer. Since the 1960s the company has developed new products, such as Coffee Rich (nondairy coffee creamer), and expanded through acquisitions to include frozen bakery and pizza doughs and ingredients for the food service and in-store bakery markets, plus SeaPak (seafood) and Byron's (barbecue). Rich Products markets some 2,300 products in about 75 countries. The company, owned and operated by the founding Rich family, also owns the Wichita Wranglers and Buffalo Bisons minor league baseball teams.

KEY COMPETITORS
ConAgra
Kraft Foods
Nestlé

RITZ CAMERA CENTERS, INC.

6711 Ritz Way	CEO: David M. Ritz	2000 Est. Sales: $800.0 mil.
Beltsville, MD 20705	CFO: Jay Sloan	1-Yr. Sales Change: (40.7%)
Phone: 301-419-0000	HR: Alan MacDonald	Employees: 7,000
Fax: 301-419-2995	Type: Private	FYE: December 31
Web: www.ritzcamera.com		

Ritz Camera Centers began as a one-man portrait studio and developed into the largest photographic chain in the US. The company has more than 1,275 stores nationwide offering one-hour photofinishing, cameras, film, and related photographic and optical products and services. Other items include cellular phones. Stores operate under names such as Ritz and Wolf; the company also sells online. Subsidiary Boater's World Marine Centers has more than 100 stores nationwide that offer gear and clothing for fishing, boating, and watersports. CEO David Ritz owns Ritz Camera, which was founded in 1918. Ritz's cousin, Chuck Wolf, owned Wolf Camera, the #2 photo chain in the US, which Ritz Camera acquired in 2001.

KEY COMPETITORS
Wal-Mart
Walgreen
West Marine

RIVERWOOD HOLDING, INC.

3350 Riverwood Pkwy., Ste. 1400	CEO: Stephen M. Humphrey	2001 Sales: $1,249.9 million
Atlanta, GA 30339	CFO: Daniel J. Blount	1-Yr. Sales Change: 10.7%
Phone: 770-644-3000	HR: Wayne E. Juby	Employees: 4,100
Fax: 770-644-2962	Type: Private	FYE: December 31
Web: www.riverwood.com		

Riverwood International is a CUK above the rest. It's one of only two major producers of coated, unbleached kraft (CUK) paperboard for packaged goods (MeadWestvaco is the other). The company's CUK board is used primarily for packaging beverages (carrierboard) and consumer products (folding cartons). Beverage customers include Anheuser-Busch (almost 15% of sales), Miller Brewing (about 10%), Coke and Pepsi bottlers, and Asahi; consumer packaging clients include Kraft, Nestlé, Unilever, and Mattel. Riverwood also leases packaging machinery. The company was taken private in 1995 by a group of investment firms and filed to go public in 2002. Clayton, Dubilier, & Rice and EXOR Group each own about 30% of Riverwood.

KEY COMPETITORS
MeadWestvaco
Smurfit-Stone Container
Sonoco Products

📖 **In-depth profiles of an additional 200 key private companies are found on pages 36–435.**

ROLL INTERNATIONAL CORPORATION

11444 W. Olympic Blvd., 10th Fl.	CEO: Stewart A. Resnick	2001 Est. Sales: $800.0 mil.
Los Angeles, CA 90064	CFO: Robert A. Kors	1-Yr. Sales Change: (3.0%)
Phone: 310-966-5700	HR: —	Employees: 5,100
Fax: 310-914-4747	Type: Private	FYE: December 31

Churning out collectible family heirlooms (or flea market fodder) is the primary business of Stewart and Lynda Resnick's Roll International. The centerpiece of their empire is The Franklin Mint, the world's largest collectibles company, with operations in 15 countries. The Franklin Mint sells goods by mail order, through its Web site, and in 50 company-owned and independent retail stores. It also operates The Franklin Mint Museum, which has displayed such authentic items as a Jacqueline Kennedy Onassis necklace and a Princess Diana gown. Other Roll operations include Paramount Farms (pistachios and almonds), Paramount Citrus (citrus products), Teleflora (floral delivery service), and Suterra (pest control).

KEY COMPETITORS
Enesco Group
FTD
Sun Growers

ROOMS TO GO

11540 Hwy. 92 East	CEO: Jeffrey Seaman	2001 Sales: $1,260.0 million
Seffner, FL 33584	CFO: Lou Stein	1-Yr. Sales Change: 21.2%
Phone: 813-623-5400	HR: Linda Garcia	Employees: 5,500
Fax: 813-620-1717	Type: Private	FYE: December 31
Web: www.roomstogo.com		

Need that sofa, recliner, table, and lamp in a hurry? Rooms To Go — with over 80 stores in Florida, Georgia, North Carolina, South Carolina, Tennessee, and Texas — has transformed itself into the top-selling furniture retailer in the US. The company markets its limited selection of furniture to brand-conscious, time-pressed customers. It packages low- to moderately priced furniture and accessories and offers discounts for those willing to buy a roomful. Rooms To Go also operates a Rooms to Go Kids chain with about 20 stores in the Southeast, Texas, and Puerto Rico. President and owner Jeffrey Seaman and his father, Morty, founded the firm in 1990 after selling Seaman Furniture Company.

KEY COMPETITORS
Havertys
J. C. Penney
Sears

ROONEY BROTHERS COMPANY

5601 S. 122nd East Ave.	CEO: Timothy P. Rooney	2002 Sales: $1,201.0 million
Tulsa, OK 74146	CFO: Jim Lawson	1-Yr. Sales Change: 14.1%
Phone: 918-583-6900	HR: Jackie Proffitt	Employees: 2,500
Fax: 918-592-4334	Type: Private	FYE: September 30

Film star Mickey isn't the only Rooney to have landed big contracts. Rooney Brothers, through its Manhattan Construction unit, builds hospitals, government buildings (George Bush Presidential Library in Texas), offices, highways, and sports arenas (Reliant Stadium in Houston). It offers construction manager, general contractor, and design/build services to its clients, located mainly in the southwestern and mid-Atlantic states. Rooney Brothers also makes construction materials, operates building supply stores, and manufactures electronics. Family-owned Rooney Brothers was organized in 1984 to acquire Manhattan Construction, which was founded by patriarch L. H. Rooney in 1896.

KEY COMPETITORS
Austin Industries
Hensel Phelps Construction
M. A. Mortenson

In-depth profiles of an additional 200 key private companies are found on pages 36–435.

ROSEBURG FOREST PRODUCTS CO.

Old Hwy. 99 South
Dillard, OR 97432
Phone: 541-679-3311
Fax: 541-679-9683
Web: www.rfpco.com

CEO: Allyn Ford
CFO: Ron Burgess
HR: Hank Snow
Type: Private

2001 Est. Sales: $750.0 mil.
1-Yr. Sales Change: 2.7%
Employees: 3,600
FYE: December 31

With roots in a Depression-era sawmill, Roseburg Forest Products has branched out with a comprehensive line of wood products. The company produces specialty panels (melamine, particleboard, and vinyl laminates), and plywood products such as concrete forming panel and siding. Its standard lumber offerings include pine, Douglas fir, and Hemlock products. Roseburg manages nearly 800,000 acres of land in northern California and southern Oregon. The company is owned by the heirs of philanthropist Kenneth Ford, who established the Ford Family Foundation.

KEY COMPETITORS
Georgia-Pacific Corporation
Louisiana-Pacific
Weyerhaeuser

ROSEN'S DIVERSIFIED, INC.

1120 Lake Ave.
Fairmont, MN 56031
Phone: 507-238-4201
Fax: 507-238-9966

CEO: Thomas J. Rosen
CFO: Rob Hovde
HR: Dominick Driano
Type: Private

2001 Est. Sales: $800.0 mil.
1-Yr. Sales Change: 14.3%
Employees: 2,000
FYE: September 30

Rosen's Diversified has the goods to make the grass greener for the cows it slaughters. The agricultural holding company has interests in meatpacking, including Long Prairie Packing and Skylark Meats, and in companies that distribute chemical fertilizers for farms in nearly 15 states. Its beef-slaughtering operations consist of meatpacking plants in three states, with the capacity to slaughter about 3,500 head of cattle a day. Rosen's Diversified processes meat for restaurants, government customers, and food manufacturers in the US. The company was founded in 1946 by brothers Elmer and Ludwig Rosen. CEO Thomas Rosen (the son of Elmer) and other family members share ownership of Rosen's Diversified.

KEY COMPETITORS
Cargill
ConAgra
Farmland Industries

ROSENTHAL AUTOMOTIVE ORGANIZATION

1100 S. Glebe Rd.
Arlington, VA 22204
Phone: 703-553-4300
Fax: 703-553-8435

CEO: Robert M. Rosenthal
CFO: Michael Baron
HR: Jeraldine Mendez
Type: Private

2001 Sales: $861.7 million
1-Yr. Sales Change: 4.4%
Employees: 1,500
FYE: December 31

A dealer of wheels in a city of wheeler-dealers, Rosenthal Automotive operates about 15 auto dealerships in the Washington, DC, area. Rosenthal's dealerships sell more than 22,000 new cars a year, including Chevrolets, Hondas, Jaguars, Mazdas, Nissans, Toyotas, Volkswagens, and Volvos. The company also sells used cars and has wholesale and fleet operations. Chairman and owner Robert Rosenthal founded Rosenthal Automotive in 1954 when he opened his first Chevrolet dealership in Arlington, Virginia. In 1997 Rosenthal joined other dealers in the Washington, DC, area to form Capital Automotive REIT, the first automotive-only real estate investment trust in the US.

KEY COMPETITORS
Brown Automotive
Jim Koons Automotive
Ourisman Automotive

In-depth profiles of an additional 200 key private companies are found on pages 36–435.

ROYSTER-CLARK, INC.

600 Fifth Ave., 25th Fl.
New York, NY 10020
Phone: 212-332-2965
Fax: 212-332-2473
Web: www.roysterclark.com

CEO: Francis P. Jenkins Jr.
CFO: Walter R. Vance
HR: Kenneth W. Carter
Type: Private

2001 Sales: $953.8 million
1-Yr. Sales Change: 4.4%
Employees: 3,130
FYE: December 31

Royster-Clark has been spreading it on thick for more than 125 years. The company makes fertilizer and crop-protection products. It processes seed for leading seed companies and sells seed under its own label. Operations include granulation, blending, and seed-processing plants, 400 retail farm supply centers, and a network of distribution terminals and warehouses. The company offers such agronomic services as custom blending and spreading and soil sampling. Royster-Clark operates in the eastern, southern, and midwestern US. Chairman and CEO Francis Jenkins owns about 38% of the company. Investment firm 399 Venture Partners (a Citigroup affiliate) also owns about 38%.

KEY COMPETITORS
Agrium
Tractor Supply
Wilbur-Ellis

RTM RESTAURANT GROUP

5995 Barfield Rd.
Atlanta, GA 30328
Phone: 404-256-4900
Fax: 404-256-7277
Web: www.rtmrestaurantgroup.com

CEO: Russell V. Umphenour Jr.
CFO: Doug Benham
HR: Sharron Barton
Type: Private

2002 Sales: $800.0 million
1-Yr. Sales Change: 6.7%
Employees: 25,000
FYE: May 31

RTM is motivated by roast beef. RTM Restaurant Group is the largest franchise group in the US, operating more than 1,000 restaurants in 24 states. The company is the nation's largest franchiser of Arby's Roast Beef restaurants, with some 770 units. Through its 20% stake in Winners International, RTM franchises nearly 170 Mrs. Winner's Chicken & Biscuits and Lee's Famous Recipe Chicken units. RTM also operates Del Taco, T.J. Cinnamon's Classic Bakery, Sbarro, and Pasta Connection restaurants. The company was founded in 1973 by president Russ Umphenour. He retains majority ownership in the company.

KEY COMPETITORS
Hardee's
McDonald's
Subway

RUDOLPH AND SLETTEN, INC.

989 E. Hillsdale Blvd., Ste. 100
Foster City, CA 94404
Phone: 650-572-1919
Fax: 650-577-1558
Web: www.rsconstruction.com

CEO: Allen Rudolph
CFO: Jim Evans
HR: Norma Adjmi
Type: Private

2002 Est. Sales: $1,002.0 mil.
1-Yr. Sales Change: 17.6%
Employees: 800
FYE: June 30

Rudolph and Sletten builds on shaky ground in California, but the force is with it. The firm built Lucasfilm's Skywalker Ranch production facility and is a leading player in the Silicon Valley, where it raised corporate campuses for Apple Computer, Microsoft, and Sun Microsystems, among others. Acting as on-site general contractor or construction manager, the company specializes in projects for the health care, high-tech research and manufacturing, biotechnology, and entertainment industries; it also takes on such unique projects as the Monterey Bay Aquarium. Onslow "Rudy" Rudolph, father of president Allen Rudolph, founded the company in 1960 and was joined by Kenneth Sletten in 1962.

KEY COMPETITORS
Devcon Construction
DPR Construction
Webcor Builders

In-depth profiles of an additional 200 key private companies are found on pages 36–435.

S. ABRAHAM & SONS, INC.

4001 Three Mile Rd. NW
Grand Rapids, MI 49501
Phone: 616-453-6358
Fax: 616-453-9346
Web: www.sasinc.com

CEO: Alan Abraham
CFO: James Leonard
HR: Keith Anderson
Type: Private

2001 Est. Sales: $850.0 mil.
1-Yr. Sales Change: 9.5%
Employees: 1,000
FYE: December 31

Impudence won't get you anywhere in the grocery business, but SAS might. Regional wholesale food distributor S. Abraham & Sons (SAS) serves convenience stores and small grocers in seven midwestern states. The company distributes name-brand groceries, health and beauty aids, snacks, store supplies, and tobacco. SAS offers private-label products such as Smart Choice health and beauty aids and Red & White groceries; its fast-food programs include Beantown (coffee), Salubre (pizza), and Subsations (sandwiches). Founded in 1927 by Sleyman Abraham, SAS is family-owned and operated. SAS also provides services such as category management (shelf management).

KEY COMPETITORS
Fleming Companies
McLane
Spartan Stores

SACRAMENTO MUNICIPAL UTILITY DISTRICT

6201 S St.
Sacramento, CA 95817
Phone: 916-452-3211
Fax: 916-732-5835
Web: www.smud.org

CEO: Jan E. Schori
CFO: Gail R. Hullibarger
HR: Shirley Lewis
Type: Government-owned

2001 Sales: $1,524.4 million
1-Yr. Sales Change: 57.5%
Employees: 2,140
FYE: December 31

Because it doesn't want its name to be mud, the Sacramento Municipal Utility District (SMUD) is powering up for competition. One of the largest locally owned electric utilities in the US, SMUD serves nearly 530,000 customers in California's Sacramento and Placer counties. It generates half of its electricity (its 1,200-MW capacity is derived primarily from hydroelectric and cogeneration power plants) and buys the rest. Having one of the US's largest solar energy distribution systems, it is a leader in advanced and renewable generation technology. In response to deregulation, SMUD is increasing its generation capacity and selling wholesale power.

KEY COMPETITORS
Edison International
Los Angeles Water and Power
PG&E

SAFELITE GLASS CORP.

2400 Farmers Dr.
Columbus, OH 43216
Phone: 614-210-9000
Fax: 614-210-9451
Web: www.safelite.com

CEO: John F. Barlow
CFO: Douglas A. Herron
HR: Elizabeth A. Wolszon
Type: Private

2002 Sales: $634.2 million
1-Yr. Sales Change: (12.5%)
Employees: 6,000
FYE: March 31

Safelite Glass has the answer to what blew into your windshield. The company, the US's largest auto glass retailer, operates more than 700 Safelite AutoGlass service centers, more than 3,200 mobile vans, and about 80 auto glass warehouses in all 50 states. It makes its own windshields at two factories, one in Kansas and the other in North Carolina. Safelite also operates two national call centers for auto glass service scheduling and claims processing. Heavy debt led Safelite to file for Chapter 11 bankruptcy in 2000; later that year it emerged from bankruptcy and restructured. Founded in 1947, Safelite merged with rival Vistar in 1997. Safelite is 90%-owned by a 35-bank syndicate.

KEY COMPETITORS
Apogee Enterprises
Guardian Industries
PPG

In-depth profiles of an additional 200 key private companies are found on pages 36–435.

SAINT VINCENT CATHOLIC MEDICAL CENTERS OF NEW YORK

85-25 153rd St.	CEO: David J. Campbell	2000 Sales: $1,465.2 million
Jamaica, NY 11432	CFO: Gary Zuar	1-Yr. Sales Change: 2.8%
Phone: 718-558-6900	HR: Ira Warm	Employees: —
Fax: 718-558-7286	Type: Not-for-profit	FYE: December 31
Web: www.svcmc.org		

If you get bit by a snake at the Bronx Zoo, you'll have to leave the borough if you want to be treated at any of the facilities of Saint Vincent Catholic Medical Centers of New York. The not-for-profit system operates eight hospitals serving New York City (except the Bronx) and Westchester County. It also runs three home health care agencies, four skilled nursing facilities, a hospice center, and more than 60 clinics that provide a range of services. Catholic Medical Center of Brooklyn and Queens, Saint Vincents Hospital and Medical Center of Manhattan, and Sisters of Charity Healthcare of Staten Island merged under the Saint Vincent name in 2000.

KEY COMPETITORS
Catholic Healthcare Network
New York City Health and Hospitals
North Shore-Long Island Jewish Health System

SAMMONS ENTERPRISES, INC.

5949 Sherry Ln., Ste. 1900	CEO: Robert W. Korba	2001 Est. Sales: $3,085.0 mil.
Dallas, TX 75225	CFO: Joseph A. Ethridge	1-Yr. Sales Change: 59.5%
Phone: 214-210-5000	HR: Carol Cochran	Employees: 3,000
Fax: 214-210-5099	Type: Private	FYE: December 31

Sammons Enterprises summons its revenues from several sources. The diversified holding company's interests include insurance (Midland National Life Insurance and North American Company for Life and Health Insurance), and water bottling (Mountain Valley Spring). Sammons Enterprises also owns The Grove Park Inn Resort in Asheville, North Carolina. The company has sold industrial equipment distribution unit Briggs-Weaver in order to focus on its core niche businesses. The late Charles Sammons, an orphan who became a billionaire philanthropist, founded the company in 1962. His estate still owns the company, and his widow, Elaine Sammons, serves as chairman.

KEY COMPETITORS
MetLife
Nestlé
Prudential

S&P COMPANY

100 Shoreline Hwy., Bldg. B, Ste. 395	CEO: Bernard Orsi	2001 Est. Sales: $750.0 mil.
Mill Valley, CA 94941	CFO: Brian Bizer	1-Yr. Sales Change: (25.0%)
Phone: 415-332-0550	HR: —	Employees: 300
Fax: 415-332-0567	Type: Private	FYE: June 30

After years of chugging along, S&P's days of brewing the blue ribbon are over. S&P owns Pabst Brewing, which in 2001 shut down its 115-year old Texas brewery and its Pennsylvania plant. The company transferred production of its brands (Pabst Blue Ribbon, Pearl, Lone Star, Old Milwaukee, Schlitz, and Colt 45) to Miller Brewing. Pabst pays Miller to brew the beers, but retains ownership of the brands and markets the products. Once the #4 US brewer, Pabst has been unable to compete with the nation's top brewing giants. The Kalmanovitz Charitable Trust (established by the late founder Paul Kalmanovitz) was granted ownership of the company in 2000.

KEY COMPETITORS
Adolph Coors
Anheuser-Busch
Miller Brewing

📖 **In-depth profiles of an additional 200 key private companies are found on pages 36–435.**

SANTA MONICA FORD CORPORATION

1230 Santa Monica Blvd.	CEO: L. Wayne Harding	2001 Sales: $800.0 million
Santa Monica, CA 90404	CFO: Dean Chow	1-Yr. Sales Change: 0.0%
Phone: 310-451-1588	HR: Ricky Berardy	Employees: —
Fax: 310-394-8115	Type: Private	FYE: December 31

You can get a new car from Santa Monica Ford if the other Santa doesn't bring one. Santa Monica Ford is one of the top-selling Ford dealers in the US, selling about 24,000 vehicles a year. The dealership sells new Ford cars and trucks, with most of its business from fleet sales (mass quantities to corporate customers). Santa Monica Ford also operates a parts and service department and a body shop. Established in 1948, Santa Monica Ford offers a customer satisfaction program that includes surveys, follow-up phone calls, and keep-in-touch letters. Chairman and CEO L. Wayne Harding owns the company.

KEY COMPETITORS
AutoNation
Galpin Motors
Tuttle-Click

SAS INSTITUTE INC.

100 SAS Campus Dr.	CEO: James H. Goodnight	2001 Sales: $1,130.0 million
Cary, NC 27513	CFO: W. Greyson Quarles Jr.	1-Yr. Sales Change: 0.9%
Phone: 919-677-8000	HR: W. Greyson Quarles Jr.	Employees: 8,636
Fax: 919-677-4444	Type: Private	FYE: December 31
Web: www.sas.com		

SAS Institute answers SOS cries from companies drowning in data. The world's largest privately held software specialist leads the market in data warehousing and data mining software used to gather, manage, and analyze the enormous amounts of information stored on mainframes and databases. Clients such as GE, Nabisco, and Wells Fargo use its software to find patterns in customer purchases, create mailing lists for repeat buyers, and target new business. SAS also offers industry-specific integrated software and support packages. Chairman, president, and CEO James Goodnight owns about two-thirds of the company; co-founder and EVP John Sall owns the remainder.

KEY COMPETITORS
Cognos
Hyperion
Information Builders

SAUDER WOODWORKING CO.

502 Middle St.	CEO: Kevin Sauder	2001 Sales: $700.0 million
Archbold, OH 43502	CFO: Arnold Moshier	1-Yr. Sales Change: 0.0%
Phone: 419-446-2711	HR: Steve Webster	Employees: 3,500
Fax: 419-446-3692	Type: Private	FYE: December 31
Web: www.sauder.com		

Sauder Woodworking takes the fear out of furniture and makes furniture for the God-fearing. The firm is the #1 US maker of ready-to-assemble (RTA) furniture (ahead of Bush Industries and O'Sullivan Industries) and, through Sauder Manufacturing, is also a top maker of church furniture and institutional seating. RTA products include computer workstations, desks, entertainment centers, and wardrobes. Subsidiary Archbold Container makes corrugated packaging and displays. Sauder's products are sold through retailers in more than 70 countries. In April 2001 Sauder acquired Progressive Furniture, which makes fully assembled furniture. Sauder was founded in 1934 by Erie Sauder and is still family owned and operated.

KEY COMPETITORS
Bush Industries
IKEA
O'Sullivan Industries

In-depth profiles of an additional 200 key private companies are found on pages 36–435.

SAVE MART SUPERMARKETS

1800 Standiford Ave.	CEO: Robert M. Piccinini	2002 Sales: $1,600.0 million
Modesto, CA 95350	CFO: Ron Riesenbeck	1-Yr. Sales Change: 5.0%
Phone: 209-577-1600	HR: Mike Silveira	Employees: 7,300
Fax: 209-577-3857	Type: Private	FYE: March 31

Save Mart Supermarkets is one of the big wheels in the California grocery business. A sponsor of the NASCAR Dodge/Save Mart 350, the company has about 100 grocery stores in northern and central California. Its supermarkets and warehouse stores operate under the S-Mart, Save Mart Foods, and Food Maxx banners. The chain has been trying out different formats, including an upscale prototype with its own coffeehouse and expanded offerings of ethnic and organic foods and its popular private-label salad mix line, Fresh Favorites. Save Mart also owns distributor SMART Refrigerated Transport. CEO Robert Piccinini owns most of Save Mart, which was founded in 1952 by his father, Mike Piccinini, and uncle, Nick Tocco.

KEY COMPETITORS
Albertson's
Raley's
Safeway

JOHNSONDIVERSEY, INC.

8310 16th St.	CEO: Gregory E. Lawton	2001 Sales: $2,641.0 million
Sturtevant, WI 53177	CFO: Michael J. Bailey	1-Yr. Sales Change: 103.2%
Phone: 262-631-4001	HR: —	Employees: 14,500
Fax: 262-260-4282	Type: Private	FYE: December 31
Web: www.johnsondiversey.com		

JohnsonDiversey is the industrial-strength version of S.C. Johnson & Son. Split off from the well-known private company in 1999, JohnsonDiversey consists of two units: Professional and Polymer. Professional provides commercial cleaning, hygiene, pest control, and food sanitation products to retailers, building service contractors, hospitality firms, and food service operators. Polymer produces acrylic resins used in printing, packaging, coatings, and adhesives. The Johnson family controls two-thirds of the company; Unilever controls the rest. The firm changed its name from SC Johnson Commercial Markets, Inc. to JohnsonDiversey in 2002 after acquiring Unilever's industrial cleaning business (DiverseyLever).

KEY COMPETITORS
Colgate-Palmolive
Ecolab
Procter & Gamble

SCHENECTADY INTERNATIONAL, INC.

1302 Congress St.	CEO: Wallace A. Graham	2001 Est. Sales: $600.0 mil.
Schenectady, NY 12303	CFO: John C. Obst	1-Yr. Sales Change: (7.7%)
Phone: 518-370-4200	HR: J. Richard Wyles	Employees: 2,500
Fax: 518-346-3111	Type: Private	FYE: December 31
Web: www.siigroup.com		

Schenectady International came to life by bringing good varnishes to life for General Electric. Founded by Howard Wright in 1906, the company was established to develop insulating varnishes for GE's early electrical devices. Today Schenectady International still makes chemical coatings for insulating copper and aluminum magnet wire, as well as friction material resins for use in making brake linings and clutch facings. The company's other products include chemicals used in the production of semiconductors, imaging products, rubber compounds, agrochemicals, dyes, fuel additives, and flavoring agents. Descendants of Wright still own the company.

KEY COMPETITORS
Dow Chemical
DuPont

In-depth profiles of an additional 200 key private companies are found on pages 36–435.

SCHNUCK MARKETS, INC.

11420 Lackland Rd.	CEO: Craig D. Schnuck	2002 Est. Sales: $2,107.0 mil.
St. Louis, MO 63146	CFO: Todd R. Schnuck	1-Yr. Sales Change: 5.4%
Phone: 314-994-9900	HR: William Jones	Employees: 18,000
Fax: 314-994-4465	Type: Private	FYE: October 31
Web: www.schnucks.com		

If you'll meet me in St. Louis, then chances are there'll be a Schnuck Market in sight. The region's largest food chain, Schnuck Markets operates more than 100 stores, mostly in the St. Louis area, but also in other parts of Missouri and in Illinois, Indiana, Mississippi, Tennessee, and Wisconsin. All stores offer a full line of groceries, and most have pharmacies, video rental outlets, in-store banking, and florist shops. Although most stores operate under the Schnuck banner, the company also runs several Logli supermarkets and a Sentry Drug in Illinois. The company acquired 12 Seessel's stores in Memphis from Albertson's in 2002. Founded in 1939, the company is owned by the Schnuck family.

KEY COMPETITORS
Dierbergs Markets
Kroger
SUPERVALU

SCHONFELD SECURITIES, LLC

One Jericho Plaza	CEO: Steven Schonfeld	2001 Sales: $612.0 million
Jericho, NY 11753	CFO: Howie Brammen	1-Yr. Sales Change: —
Phone: 516-822-0202	HR: Rosalee Mandracchia	Employees: 1,158
Fax: 516-822-0590	Type: Private	FYE: December 31
Web: www.schonfeld.com		

Want to watch Schonfeld Securities in action? Don't blink or you might miss it. Founded in 1988 by Steven Schonfeld as part of the Schonfeld Group, the company's specialty is the fast-paced world of short-term trading. Schonfeld Securities is also among the rare breed of proprietary traders, meaning the firm seeks profit through direct gain on sales rather than a commission on each trade. Schonfeld is one of the largest of such firms in the US in both the number of traders and volume traded on the NYSE and NASDAQ. The company relies heavily on technology to analyze the market, and designs and implements its own complex quantitative software.

KEY COMPETITORS
Charles Schwab
Hold Brothers
UBS PaineWebber

SCHOTTENSTEIN STORES CORPORATION

1800 Moler Rd.	CEO: Jay L. Schottenstein	2001 Est. Sales: $650.0 mil.
Columbus, OH 43207	CFO: —	1-Yr. Sales Change: (56.7%)
Phone: 614-221-9200	HR: Susan Daugherty	Employees: 5,300
Fax: 614-449-0403	Type: Private	FYE: July 31

Schottenstein Stores is where the Schottenstein family keeps its retail holdings. The firm owns interests in a host of retail businesses, including nearly 68% of Value City Department Stores (about 115 Value City stores, 20 Filene's Basement stores, and some 125 DSW Shoe Warehouse stores). Schottenstein Stores also owns Value City Furniture (about 70 superstores in the Midwest and East Coast states), 26% of casual clothing chain American Eagle Outfitters (675 mall stores in the US and Canada), and retail liquidator Schottenstein Bernstein Capital Group, as well as 50 shopping centers. The company launched American Signature Home stores in 2002 with plans for 25 of the furniture outlets throughout the Southeast.

KEY COMPETITORS
The Gap
Sears
Wal-Mart

📖 **In-depth profiles of an additional 200**
key private companies are found on pages 36–435.

SCHREIBER FOODS, INC.

425 Pine St.	CEO: Larry Ferguson	2002 Est. Sales: $1,450.0 mil.
Green Bay, WI 54301	CFO: Brian Liddy	1-Yr. Sales Change: 7.4%
Phone: 920-437-7601	HR: Jeff Ottum	Employees: 4,400
Fax: 920-437-1617	Type: Private	FYE: September 30
Web: www.sficorp.com		

If you order cheese on that burger, you might well get a taste of Schreiber Foods. The cheese processor is a major supplier of the cheese used on hamburgers by US fast-food restaurants. Schreiber also supplies process, natural, and substitute cheese to grocery stores, delis, schools, distributors, and food manufacturers. Its brands include American Heritage, Cache Valley, Cooper, and Clearfield. Subsidiary Green Bay Machinery makes cheese-slicing and -wrapping equipment, and Schreiber's Arden International Kitchens unit makes frozen entrees. Schreiber International exports cheese worldwide. Founded in 1945, Schreiber opted in 1999 to transfer its ownership into an employee stock ownership plan.

KEY COMPETITORS
Dairy Farmers of America
Great Lakes Cheese
Kraft Foods

THE SCOULAR COMPANY

2027 Dodge St.	CEO: Randal L. Linville	2002 Sales: $2,100.0 million
Omaha, NE 68102	CFO: Timothy J. Regan	1-Yr. Sales Change: 0.1%
Phone: 402-342-3500	HR: Yvonne Lutz	Employees: 330
Fax: 402-342-5568	Type: Private	FYE: May 31
Web: www.scoular.com		

The people who grow the wheat aren't usually the ones who grind it. The Scoular Company handles the process that goes on between the two groups. The company is best known for grain marketing, trading more than 400 million bushels of grain and more than 1 million tons of grain byproducts (used for animal feed) annually throughout North America. Other divisions offer fishmeal products for animal and aquaculture feeds, ingredients for food manufacturing, truck freight brokering, and livestock marketing. Founded in 1892 to run grain elevators, employee-owned Scoular still operates 13 elevators in Nebraska.

KEY COMPETITORS
ADM
Cargill
Farmland Industries

SCRIPPS

4275 Campus Point Ct.	CEO: Stan Pappelbaum	2001 Est. Sales: $715.0 mil.
San Diego, CA 92121	CFO: —	1-Yr. Sales Change: 2.1%
Phone: 858-678-7000	HR: Claudia Mazanec	Employees: 10,000
Fax: 858-678-6558	Type: Not-for-profit	FYE: September 30
Web: www.scrippshealth.org		

Scripps has its lines down cold. Founded in 1924, the not-for-profit hospital group serves the San Diego area with five acute-care hospitals, two skilled nursing facilities, and several outpatient clinics. The system also offers home health care and operates community outreach programs. Scripps consists of two partners: Scripps Health (overseeing hospitals, clinics, and home health care) and Scripps Physicians (a managed care network of 2,000 affiliated physicians). Scripps is affiliated with The Scripps Research Institute, which performs biomedical research; Scripps Foundation for Medicine and Science serves as a fundraiser for both the hospital group and the research institute.

KEY COMPETITORS
Adventist Health
HCA
Tenet Healthcare

📖 **In-depth profiles of an additional 200 key private companies are found on pages 36–435.**

SEALY CORPORATION

Sealy Dr., One Office Pkwy.	CEO: David J. McIlquham	2001 Sales: $1,196.7 million
Trinity, NC 27370	CFO: Jim Hirshorn	1-Yr. Sales Change: 8.6%
Phone: 336-861-3500	HR: Jeffrey C. Claypool	Employees: 6,410
Fax: 336-861-3501	Type: Private	FYE: November 30
Web: www.sealy.com		

Sealy is a slumbering giant. The company, North America's #1 maker of bedding products, manufactures mattresses and box springs and sells them at more than 7,000 stores. Its brands include Sealy, Barrett, and Stearns & Foster. Sealy's customers include sleep shops, furniture and department stores, warehouse clubs, and mass merchandisers, as well as the hospitality industry. Sealy also licenses its name to makers of other bedding products (pads, pillows) and home furnishings (sofas, futons). The company runs more than 30 factories in Argentina, Brazil, Canada, Mexico, Puerto Rico, and the US. Boston-based investment firm Bain Capital, along with company management, owns Sealy.

KEY COMPETITORS
Serta
Simmons
Spring Air

SEATTLE CITY LIGHT

700 5th Ave., Ste. 3300	CEO: Gary Zarker	2001 Sales: $627.6 million
Seattle, WA 98104	CFO: Jim Ritch	1-Yr. Sales Change: 58.5%
Phone: 206-684-3000	HR: Bill Kolden	Employees: 1,628
Fax: 206-625-3709	Type: Government-owned	FYE: December 31
Web: www.cityofseattle.net/light		

Seattle City Light keeps guitars humming and coffee grinders running in the Seattle metropolitan area. One of the US's largest municipally owned power companies, Seattle City Light transmits and distributes electricity to more than 350,000 residential, commercial, industrial, and government customers and owns about 1,900 MW of mostly hydroelectric generation capacity. It also sells power to wholesale customers. Seattle City Light owns or contracts for about 80% of its power supply and obtains most of the rest from the Bonneville Power Administration. Evolving from several neighborhood electric companies that began powering Seattle in 1886, the company was created in 1910 to power the city's streetlights.

KEY COMPETITORS
Avista
PacifiCorp
Puget Energy

SECURITY BENEFIT GROUP OF COMPANIES

One Security Benefit Pl.	CEO: Kris Robbins	2001 Sales: $1,385.7 million
Topeka, KS 66636	CFO: Donald Schepker	1-Yr. Sales Change: (7.6%)
Phone: 785-438-3000	HR: Craig Anderson	Employees: 600
Fax: —	Type: Private	FYE: December 31
Web: www.securitybenefit.com		

Security Benefit Group of Companies is the largest life insurer in the Jayhawk State. The group operates through Security Benefit Life Insurance Company, which offers variable life insurance, annuities, mutual funds, and asset management services through about 16,500 sales representatives. Security Benefit is highlighting its asset management skills by opening several new funds. After more than 100 years as a mutual company, the company has made plans to convert to stock ownership but has not followed through on those plans. Security Benefit's roots go back to the Knights and Ladies of Security, a benefit society begun in 1892 in Topeka, Kansas.

KEY COMPETITORS
Aetna
American United Life
John Hancock Financial Services

📖 In-depth profiles of an additional 200
key private companies are found on pages 36–435.

SEMINOLE ELECTRIC COOPERATIVE, INC.

16313 N. Dale Mabry Hwy.
Tampa, FL 33618
Phone: 813-963-0994
Fax: 813-264-7906
Web: www.seminole-electric.com

CEO: Richard J. Midulla
CFO: John W. Geeraerts
HR: W. Tip English
Type: Cooperative

2001 Sales: $669.1 million
1-Yr. Sales Change: 14.8%
Employees: 455
FYE: December 31

This Seminole may not be a native Floridian, but it has provided electricity in the state since 1948. Seminole Electric Cooperative (SECI) generates and transmits electricity for 10 member distribution cooperatives that serve more than 720,000 residential and business customers in 45 Florida counties. SECI has 1,500 MW of primarily coal-fired generating capacity. The cooperative also buys electricity from other utilities and independent power producers, and it owns 350 miles of transmission lines. SECI was formed to aggregate the power demands of its members and is governed by a board of trustees representing the 10 member utilities.

KEY COMPETITORS
FPL
Progress Energy
TECO Energy

SENTRY INSURANCE, A MUTUAL COMPANY

1800 North Point Dr.
Stevens Point, WI 54481
Phone: 715-346-6000
Fax: 715-346-7516
Web: www.sentry.com

CEO: Dale R. Schuh
CFO: William J. Lohr
HR: Greg Mox
Type: Mutual company

2001 Sales: $1,880.0 million
1-Yr. Sales Change: 9.6%
Employees: 4,300
FYE: December 31

Vigilant for its policyholders, Sentry Insurance (of the famous Minuteman statue logo) offers a variety of insurance coverage, including life, group health, auto, and property/casualty insurance. The mutual company (owned by its policyholders) offers coverage through several subsidiaries. Sentry also provides specialized insurance to small and large businesses, including manufacturers and retailers. The company's Sentry Equity Services offers mutual fund services through its Sentry Fund. Sentry was founded in 1904 to provide insurance to members of the Wisconsin Retail Hardware Association.

KEY COMPETITORS
Allstate
Prudential
State Farm

SERTA, INC.

325 Spring Lake Dr.
Itasca, IL 60143
Phone: 630-285-9350
Fax: 630-285-9330
Web: www.serta.com

CEO: Edward F. Lilly
CFO: —
HR: —
Type: Private

2001 Sales: $870.0 million
1-Yr. Sales Change: 1.4%
Employees: 4,800
FYE: December 31

Serta, the #2 mattress manufacturer in the world (behind Sealy), hopes to keep the competition awake at night. It is the nation's #1 mattress supplier to hotels and motels; its Perfect Sleeper mattress line, which it has been selling since the 1930s, is the best-selling premium mattress in the US. Serta's top-of-the-line mattress collection is sold under the Perfect Night name. Founded in 1931 by 13 mattress makers who licensed the Serta name, the company is now owned by eight independent licensees; each licensee has separate marketing, manufacturing, and sales operations. The group has 27 factories in the US, four in Canada, and another 27 throughout Asia, Europe, and the Middle East, and South America.

KEY COMPETITORS
Sealy
Simmons
Spring Air

📖 **In-depth profiles of an additional 200 key private companies are found on pages 36–435.**

SERVICES GROUP OF AMERICA

4025 Delridge Way SW, Ste. 500
Seattle, WA 98106
Phone: 206-933-5225
Fax: 206-933-5247
Web: www.fsafood.com

CEO: Thomas J. Stewart
CFO: Peter Smith
HR: Lanett Draper
Type: Private

2002 Sales: $1,650.0 million
1-Yr. Sales Change: 11.5%
Employees: 3,300
FYE: January 31

Though it bears a rather vague company name, Services Group of America's operations are pretty specific. Its subsidiary, Food Services of America, is a food service distributor, supplying hospitals, schools, and restaurants in 15 western and midwestern states. Its DSA Meats subsidiary provides custom meat cutting services to retail and foodservice customers in Washington state. Service Group's other operations include fresh fruit and vegetable marketing, commercial real estate development and management, and natural Black Angus beef production and marketing. The company, formed in 1985, bought fast-food distributor McCabe's Quality Foods in January 2001 and meat producer S&P Foods in mid-2002.

KEY COMPETITORS
Gordon Food Service
SYSCO
U.S. Foodservice

THE SF HOLDINGS GROUP, INC.

373 Park Ave. S.
New York, NY 10016
Phone: 212-779-7448
Fax: 212-779-9562

CEO: Dennis Mehiel
CFO: Hans H. Heinsen
HR: Jeffery Seidman
Type: Private

2002 Est. Sales: $1,277.0 mil.
1-Yr. Sales Change: (3.0%)
Employees: 6,370
FYE: September 30

The words "Can I get that to go?" are like money in the bank for the SF Holdings Group. Through subsidiaries the company produces disposable paper and plastic cups, plates, cutlery, and food packaging sold under brand names such as Centerpiece, Hoffmaster, Lily, Preference, and Sweetheart. Its Sweetheart Cup subsidiary accounts for almost 75% of sales and primarily sells its wares to institutional food service customers such as restaurant chains, schools, theaters, and airlines. The Fonda Group, another subsidiary, also sells to institutional food service customers and to consumer markets, as well as through supermarkets and warehouse clubs. Chairman and CEO Dennis Mehiel owns about 72% of SF Holdings.

KEY COMPETITORS
Dart Container
Huhtamäki
Solo Cup

SHAMROCK FOODS COMPANY

2228 N. Black Canyon Hwy.
Phoenix, AZ 85009
Phone: 602-272-6721
Fax: 602-233-2791
Web: www.shamrockfoods.com

CEO: Norman McClelland
CFO: Philip Giltner
HR: Robert Beake
Type: Private

2002 Sales: $1,093.0 million
1-Yr. Sales Change: (0.6%)
Employees: 2,143
FYE: September 30

Milk does a business good, too. Thanks to that udder delight, Shamrock Foods has fortified itself from a tiny mom-and-pop dairy into a food processor and distributor serving supermarkets, convenience stores, restaurants, and institutional clients in 10 states in the West and Southwest, including California, Colorado, and Texas. Most of the company's business is dedicated to processing dairy products, including milk, cottage cheese, sour cream, and eggnog. Production of the company's ice cream is outsourced. Its products are sold under the Shamrock Farms and Sunland brands, as well as under private labels. Started in 1922, Shamrock Foods is owned and run by the founding McClelland family.

KEY COMPETITORS
Dairy Farmers of America
Dean Foods
Land O'Lakes

In-depth profiles of an additional 200 key private companies are found on pages 36–435.

SHEARMAN & STERLING

599 Lexington Ave.	CEO: Robert C. Treuhold	2001 Sales: $620.0 million
New York, NY 10022	CFO: Kenneth W. Johnson	1-Yr. Sales Change: 5.1%
Phone: 212-848-4000	HR: Barbara Gannet	Employees: 2,000
Fax: 212-848-7179	Type: Partnership	FYE: December 31
Web: www.shearman.com		

Law firm Shearman & Sterling has secured its place in history. Founded in 1873, the firm helped railroad baron Jay Gould fight for control of US railroads, aided in brokering a deal to free hostages in Iran, and represented women suing the Citadel military academy for admission. Today Shearman & Sterling has more than 1,000 lawyers in 18 domestic and international offices. Its practice areas include antitrust, bankruptcy, capital markets, intellectual property, litigation, mergers and acquisitions, project development and finance, and tax. Shearman & Sterling clients have included Viacom, Mpower Communications, and the Algerian oil and gas ministry.

KEY COMPETITORS
Cleary, Gottlieb
Davis Polk
Skadden, Arps

SHEEHY AUTO STORES

12450 Fair Lakes Circle, Ste. 380	CEO: Vincent A. Sheehy	2001 Sales: $599.5 million
Fairfax, VA 22033	CFO: Michael Larkin	1-Yr. Sales Change: 20.0%
Phone: 703-802-3480	HR: —	Employees: —
Fax: 703-802-3481	Type: Private	FYE: December 31
Web: www.sheehy.com		

Don't blame Sheehy Auto Stores (formerly VinCo Management) for heavy traffic on the beltway around the nation's capital. Sheehy just sells cars; *people* drive. Sheehy Auto Stores operates 16 Sheehy auto franchises in the Washington, DC, area: seven in Maryland and nine in Virginia. The company's dealerships sell new Dodge, Ford, Honda, Isuzu, Kia, Mitsubishi, and Nissan vehicles. All Sheehy dealerships sell used cars and offer financing, leasing, and service. Customers can order parts and make service appointments online through the company's Web site. CEO Vince Sheehy owns the company.

KEY COMPETITORS
Brown Automotive
Ourisman Automotive
Rosenthal Automotive

SHEETZ, INC.

5700 Sixth Ave.	CEO: Stanton R. Sheetz	2002 Est. Sales: $1,920.0 mil.
Altoona, PA 16602	CFO: Joseph S. Sheetz	1-Yr. Sales Change: 1.1%
Phone: 814-946-3611	HR: Phil Freeman	Employees: 8,500
Fax: 814-946-4375	Type: Private	FYE: September 30
Web: www.sheetz.com		

You might say Sheetz is to the convenience store business what Wal-Mart is to discount shopping. Noted for being exceptionally large (stores average 4,200 sq. ft., nearly twice the size of the average 7-Eleven, but new stores are planned to be 4,700 sq. ft.), Sheetz stores sell groceries, fountain drinks, baked goods, and made-to-order sandwiches and salads, as well as discount gas and cigarettes. The company operates more than 270 combination convenience stores and gas stations, mostly in small and midsized towns in Pennsylvania, but also in towns throughout Maryland, Ohio, Virginia, and West Virginia. Founded in 1952 by Bob Sheetz, the company is owned and run by the Sheetz family.

KEY COMPETITORS
7-Eleven
Uni-Marts
Wawa

In-depth profiles of an additional 200
key private companies are found on pages 36–435.

SHONEY'S, INC.

1727 Elm Hill Pike
Nashville, TN 37210
Phone: 615-391-5201
Fax: 615-231-2531
Web: www.shoneys.com

CEO: V. Michael Payne
CFO: —
HR: Sergio Garza-Caballero
Type: Private

2001 Sales: $665.5 million
1-Yr. Sales Change: (20.4%)
Employees: 15,000
FYE: October 31

Shoney's satisfies your craving for the hearty kind of food Grandma used to make. The company owns or franchises about 900 restaurants in 28 states, primarily in the southern US. Its flagship chain has about 350 Shoney's units in 24 states, and it offers full-service family dining and an all-you-can-eat buffet. Shoney's also operates or franchises some 560 Captain D's quick-service seafood restaurants. Shoney's has sold off noncore operations such as its Pargo's and Fifth Quarter chains and a distribution business. The company was taken private in 2002 by an investor group.

KEY COMPETITORS
CBRL Group
Denny's
Long John Silver's

SHORENSTEIN COMPANY, L.P.

Bank of America Ctr., 555 California St., 49th Fl.
San Francisco, CA 94104
Phone: 415-772-7000
Fax: 415-398-6682
Web: www.shorenstein.com

CEO: Douglas W. Shorenstein
CFO: Richard A. Chicotel
HR: —
Type: Private

2001 Est. Sales: $750.0 mil.
1-Yr. Sales Change: 0.0%
Employees: 550
FYE: December 31

Shorenstein helps businesses shore up in new places. The company is one of the US's largest and oldest privately owned real estate firms, owning interests in or managing some 20 million sq. ft. of office space. It is also one of the largest office landlords in San Francisco, where about 7 million sq. ft. of its properties are located. Shorenstein invests in large, high-quality office buildings which it operates and manages itself; a subsidiary manages office properties for institutional investors. The firm also offers a line of closed-end funds that invest in office properties. Founded by Walter Shorenstein after WWII, the company is now owned by his son, chairman and CEO Douglas Shorenstein.

KEY COMPETITORS
Boston Properties
Equity Office Properties Trust
Helmsley

SIDLEY AUSTIN BROWN & WOOD LLP

Bank One Plaza, 10 S. Dearborn
Chicago, IL 60603
Phone: 312-853-7000
Fax: 312-853-7036
Web: www.sidley.com

CEO: Thomas A. Cole
CFO: Christian Cooley
HR: Michael Prapuolenis
Type: Partnership

2001 Sales: $715.0 million
1-Yr. Sales Change: 6.7%
Employees: —
FYE: December 31

Sidley Austin Brown & Wood aims to be a one-stop shop for corporate clients needing legal help. The law firm was created in 2001 by the merger of Chicago-based Sidley & Austin (founded by Norman Williams and John Thompson in 1866) and Wall Street-based Brown & Wood (established in 1914 in New York City). The firm employs more than 1,400 attorneys around the world, including Chicago and six other US cities. International offices are located in Beijing, Hong Kong, London, Shanghai, Singapore, and Tokyo. The firm's practices include financial transactions, antitrust, bankruptcy, intellectual propety and taxes. Clients have included AT&T and Citigroup.

KEY COMPETITORS
Baker & McKenzie
Mayer, Brown, Rowe & Maw
Skadden, Arps

In-depth profiles of an additional 200
key private companies are found on pages 36–435.

SIERRA PACIFIC INDUSTRIES

19794 Riverside Ave.	CEO: A. A. "Red" Emmerson	2001 Est. Sales: $1,500.0 mil.
Anderson, CA 96007	CFO: Mark Emmerson	1-Yr. Sales Change: 0.0%
Phone: 530-378-8000	HR: Ed Bond	Employees: 3,600
Fax: 530-378-8109	Type: Private	FYE: December 31
Web: www.spi-ind.com		

Sierra Pacific Industries (SPI) isn't your run-of-the-mill company. One of the largest US landowners, it manufactures millwork products and lumber in Northern California. Subsidiary Sierra Pacific Windows makes aluminum clad and wood patio doors and specialty windows. It also owns 1.5 million acres of California timberlands. SPI's cogeneration plants recycle wood waste into electricity that is used to power its plants; excess electricity is sold to local utilities and energy service providers. SPI traces its roots to a company started in the late 1920s by R. H. "Curly" Emmerson, father of CEO Red Emmerson. The third generation of the Emmerson family owns and operates Sierra Pacific.

KEY COMPETITORS
Georgia-Pacific Corporation
Louisiana-Pacific
Weyerhaeuser

SIGMA PLASTICS GROUP

Page & Schuyler Ave., Bldg. #8	CEO: Alfred S. Teo	2001 Sales: $765.0 million
Lyndhurst, NJ 07071	CFO: John Reier	1-Yr. Sales Change: 6.3%
Phone: 201-933-6000	HR: Debra Barbour	Employees: 3,100
Fax: 201-933-6429	Type: Private	FYE: October 31

The plastic sheeting and film business is not Greek to Sigma Plastics. Having grown through acquisitions, the company (one of North America's largest) produces plastic film and sheet for industrial, institutional, and government markets. The company's Zeta Consumer Products subsidiary filed for bankruptcy and was then sold, marking the end of Sigma's foray into the housewares business. The company manufactures its diverse range of plastic products on 700 extrusion lines at its plants in 23 different North American locations. Chairman and CEO Alfred Teo owns Sigma Plastics.

KEY COMPETITORS
Bemis
DuPont
Sealed Air

SIMMONS COMPANY

One Concourse Pkwy., Ste. 800	CEO: Charles R. Eitel	2001 Sales: $679.5 million
Atlanta, GA 30328	CFO: William S. Creekmuir	1-Yr. Sales Change: (6.5%)
Phone: 770-512-7700	HR: Rhonda Rousch	Employees: 2,800
Fax: 770-392-2560	Type: Private	FYE: December 31
Web: www.simmonsco.com		

Simmons sleeps tight as the #3 US mattress maker, behind Sealy and Serta. The firm makes and distributes mattresses and accessories under the Simmons, Beautyrest, BackCare, DreamScapes, Deep Sleep, and Olympic Queen labels. It licenses its trademarks for retail stores and to makers of beds and sleeping aids. Simmons sells through nearly 8,000 furniture outlets, department stores, and specialty shops. Simmons also owns about 60 retail World of Sleep and Gallery mattress outlets in the US. Directors Peter Lamm, Richard Dresdale, and Mark Genender, through Investment firm Fenway Partners, own nearly 85% of Simmons; Simmons' employees and Investcorp own the rest. Zalmon Simmons founded the firm in 1871.

KEY COMPETITORS
Sealy
Serta
Spring Air

📖 **In-depth profiles of an additional 200 key private companies are found on pages 36–435.**

SIMPSON INVESTMENT COMPANY

1301 Fifth Ave., Ste. 2800	CEO: Colin Moseley	2001 Est. Sales: $800.0 mil.
Seattle, WA 98101	CFO: —	1-Yr. Sales Change: 1.9%
Phone: 206-224-5000	HR: Linda Cronin	Employees: 4,300
Fax: 206-224-5060	Type: Private	FYE: December 31
Web: www.simpson.com		

Simpson Investment Company is one of the oldest privately owned forest products companies in the northwestern US. The holding company makes paper and lumber products through its subsidiaries, Simpson Timber and Simpson Paper. Simpson Timber owns timberlands and operates converting facilities in California, Oregon, and Washington, where it produces dimension lumber and plywood; its Simpson Door Company makes stile and rail wood-panel doors. Simpson Paper, through subsidiary Simpson Tacoma Kraft, makes bleached and unbleached kraft pulp and linerboard used in packaging (boxes and grocery bags). Simpson Paper also recycles cardboard into paper. The Simpson family has controlled the firm since its founding in 1890.

KEY COMPETITORS
Georgia-Pacific Corporation
International Paper
Weyerhaeuser

SINCLAIR OIL CORPORATION

550 E. South Temple	CEO: Robert E. Holding	2001 Est. Sales: $2,300.0 mil.
Salt Lake City, UT 84102	CFO: Charles Barlow	1-Yr. Sales Change: 21.1%
Phone: 801-524-2700	HR: Lowell Hardy	Employees: 6,900
Fax: 801-526-3000	Type: Private	FYE: December 31
Web: www.sinclairoil.com		

Way out west, where fossils are found, brontosaur signs litter the ground. They belong to Sinclair Oil's more than 2,600 service stations and convenience stores in 22 western and midwestern US states. The company also operates three oil refineries, two pipelines (one jointly owned with ConocoPhillips), exploration operations, and a trucking fleet, all in the western US. It owns the Grand America Hotel, the Little America hotel chain, and two ski resorts (Sun Valley in Idaho and Snowbasin in Utah). Snowbasin was a venue of the 2002 Winter Olympics. The man behind all of this is Earl Holding, whose storied company, founded in 1916 by Harry Sinclair, was a central figure in the infamous Teapot Dome scandal.

KEY COMPETITORS
Exxon Mobil
Vail Resorts
Valero Energy

SIRVA

5001 US Hwy. 30 West	CEO: Ron Milewski	2001 Sales: $2,249.0 million
Fort Wayne, IN 46818	CFO: —	1-Yr. Sales Change: (5.2%)
Phone: 260-429-2511	HR: Todd Schorr	Employees: 6,800
Fax: 260-429-1853	Type: Private	FYE: December 31
Web: www.sirva.com		

Whether you're moving across the street, across town, or across the ocean, SIRVA (formerly Allied Worldwide) will get your belongings where they need to be. Formed in 1999 through a merger of North American Van Lines and Allied Van Lines, the group is one of the largest moving companies in the world. SIRVA operates in more than 30 countries in Asia, Australia, Europe, and North America. Besides North American and Allied, its brands include Pickfords. SIRVA plans to expand all aspects of its operations, which include logistics, household and business relocation, and insurance. The company is controlled by investment firm Clayton, Dubilier & Rice.

KEY COMPETITORS
AMERCO
Atlas World
UniGroup

In-depth profiles of an additional 200 key private companies are found on pages 36–435.

SITHE ENERGIES, INC.

335 Madison Ave., 28th Fl.
New York, NY 10017
Phone: 212-351-0000
Fax: 212-351-0005
Web: www.sithe.com

CEO: William Kriegel
CFO: Thomas Boehlert
HR: Steven Atamanchulo
Type: Joint venture

2001 Sales: $1,000.0 million
1-Yr. Sales Change: —
Employees: —
FYE: December 31

Sithe Energies wants to slice through the competition to become a leading independent power producer. Sithe owns stakes in more than 20 operational facilities in North America with a total generating capacity of about 2,200 MW. Sithe also owns power plants in Asia and Australia that generate 1,400 MW of capacity. The firm sells energy to utilities, industrial companies, governments, and other institutions. Sithe is selling some noncore domestic and overseas assets. Utility holding company Exelon owns 49.9% of Sithe and has an option to buy the rest. Other investors include French utility giant Vivendi Environnement (34%), Japanese trading firm Marubeni (15%), and Sithe managers (1%).

KEY COMPETITORS
AES
Calpine
NRG Energy

SOAVE ENTERPRISES L.L.C.

3400 E. Lafayette St.
Detroit, MI 48207
Phone: 313-567-7000
Fax: 313-567-0966
Web: www.soaveenterprises.com

CEO: Anthony L. Soave
CFO: Michael L. Piesko
HR: Marcia Moss
Type: Private

2001 Est. Sales: $900.0 mil.
1-Yr. Sales Change: 2.5%
Employees: 2,000
FYE: December 31

Soave Enterprises is suave enough to manage multiple lines of business. The company provides capital to small businesses. Its diverse interests are divided into four groups: Industrial (including demolition and waste collection services), Metals Recycling (metals shredding and recycling), Real Estate (including residential, industrial, and recreational projects in six states), and Diversified (ranging from auto dealerships to beer distribution, hydroponic tomato gardening, ground transportation around Detroit Metro Airport, and insurance sales). The bulk of Soave's operations are in Michigan. President and CEO Anthony Soave, who founded the company in 1961, owns Soave Enterprises.

KEY COMPETITORS
David J. Joseph
Nucor
Waste Management

SOFTWARE HOUSE INTERNATIONAL, INC.

2 Riverview Dr.
Somerset, NJ 08873
Phone: 732-764-8888
Fax: 732-764-8889
Web: www.shi.com

CEO: Thai Lee
CFO: Paul Ng
HR: Anthony Salina
Type: Private

2001 Sales: $1,800.0 million
1-Yr. Sales Change: 28.6%
Employees: —
FYE: December 31

Software House International (SHI) wants to put software in houses across the globe. The company distributes more than 100,000 hardware and software products from suppliers such as Adobe, Corel, Microsoft, and IBM. SHI also offers professional services such as systems integration and application development through its Software House Enterprise Solutions division. The company counts Agilent, AT&T, Boeing, and Hewlett-Packard among its clients. Founded in 1982, SHI has grown from a company with less than $1 million in annual revenue in 1989, when entrepreneur Thai Lee assumed ownership, to a company worth more than $1 billion.

KEY COMPETITORS
ASI Corp.
Ingram Micro
Tech Data

In-depth profiles of an additional 200 key private companies are found on pages 36–435.

SOLO CUP COMPANY

1700 Old Deerfield Rd.	CEO: Robert L. Hulseman	2001 Est. Sales: $900.0 mil.
Highland Park, IL 60035	CFO: Ronald L. Whaley	1-Yr. Sales Change: 8.0%
Phone: 847-831-4800	HR: Kathleen Wolf	Employees: 4,700
Fax: 847-831-5849	Type: Private	FYE: December 31
Web: www.solocup.com		

Solo Cup's goodies are best enjoyed in the company of others. A leader in the disposable product market, the company makes cups, plates, bowls, storage containers, cutlery, and drinking straws. In addition to mass-market retailers, Solo Cup's items are sold to end users, including restaurants, schools, hospitals, and coffee shops. The company has 14 manufacturing facilities and about a dozen warehouses. The firm's plastic, paper, and foam goods are sold, soiled, and thrown out around the world. Leo J. Hulseman founded the Paper Container Manufacturing Company in 1936; it became Solo Cup in 1946, named for the cone-shaped paper cup that made it famous. His descendants own and operate the company.

KEY COMPETITORS
CP&P
Dart Container
SF Holdings

SOUTH CAROLINA PUBLIC SERVICE AUTHORITY

1 Riverwood Dr.	CEO: John H. Tiencken Jr.	2001 Sales: $973.0 million
Moncks Corner, SC 29461	CFO: Elaine G. Peterson	1-Yr. Sales Change: 12.8%
Phone: 843-761-8000	HR: Ronald H. Holmes	Employees: 1,695
Fax: 843-761-7060	Type: Government-owned	FYE: December 31
Web: www.santeecooper.com		

Someone's got to turn on those bright lights in the big city — and in the small cities, too. South Carolina Public Service Authority, known as Santee Cooper, provides wholesale electricity to 20 cooperatives and two municipalities that serve about 600,000 customers in South Carolina. It directly retails electricity to more than 130,000 additional customers. One of the largest US state-owned utilities, Santee Cooper operates in all 46 counties in South Carolina and has interests in power plants (hydroelectric, coal-fired, nuclear, and combustion turbine) that give it 4,300 MW of generating capacity. The Santee Cooper Regional Water System treats and distributes water to nearly 95,000 consumers in the state.

KEY COMPETITORS
MEAG Power
North Carolina Electric Membership
SCANA

SOUTHERN STATES COOPERATIVE, INCORPORATED

6606 W. Broad St.	CEO: Thomas Scribner	2001 Sales: $1,739.0 million
Richmond, VA 23230	CFO: Bob West	1-Yr. Sales Change: 12.4%
Phone: 804-281-1000	HR: Richard G. Sherman	Employees: 5,700
Fax: 804-281-1413	Type: Cooperative	FYE: June 30
Web: www.southernstates-coop.com		

Founded in 1923 to provide affordable, high-quality seed to Virginia farmers, Southern States Cooperative serves about 321,000 members, mainly in midwestern and southern states. It offers its farmer-owners feed and fertilizer manufacturing, seed processing, grain marketing, and petroleum and propane services, as well as wholesale farm supplies. The co-op's GardenSouth and Southern States stores sell farm supplies, garden products, and fuel through about 740 outlets. Other services include GrowMaster Crop Services, sales financing, and an aquaculture program. Southern States Cooperative merged with Michigan Livestock Exchange in 1998 and purchased Agway Inc.'s consumer wholesale dealer business.

KEY COMPETITORS
Ag Processing
Cenex Harvest States
Farmland Industries

In-depth profiles of an additional 200 key private companies are found on pages 36–435.

SOUTHERN WINE & SPIRITS OF AMERICA, INC.

1600 NW 163rd St.	CEO: Harvey Chaplin	2001 Sales: $3,750.0 million
Miami, FL 33169	CFO: Steven Becker	1-Yr. Sales Change: 7.1%
Phone: 305-625-4171	HR: Mark Krauss	Employees: 5,680
Fax: 305-625-4720	Type: Private	FYE: December 31
Web: www.southernwineandspirits.com		

Fueled by alcohol and nicotine, Southern Wine & Spirits of America delivers market dominance. The firm is the #1 US distributor of wine and spirits, serving nine states. In addition to importing and distributing wine and spirits, it distributes imported brews, such as Grolsch and Steinlager; cigars, such as Don Diego and Montecristo; and nonalcoholic beverages, including Clamato and Rose's Lime Juice. The company also owns Pacific Wine & Spirits and Romano Bros. Beverage, the largest spirits wholesaler in Illinois; it is also entering new markets elsewhere. Chairman and CEO Harvey Chaplin and his secretive family own more than 50% of the company.

KEY COMPETITORS
National Distributing
Sunbelt Beverage
Young's Market

SOUTHWIRE COMPANY

One Southwire Dr.	CEO: Stuart Thorn	2001 Sales: $1,700.0 million
Carrollton, GA 30119	CFO: J. Guyton Cochran Jr.	1-Yr. Sales Change: 13.3%
Phone: 770-832-4242	HR: Mike Wiggins	Employees: 3,000
Fax: 770-832-4929	Type: Private	FYE: December 31
Web: www.southwire.com		

Southwire hopes everyone's cable-ready. One of the world's largest cable and wire manufacturers, Southwire makes building wire and cable, utility cable products, industrial power cable, telecommunications cable, copper and aluminum rods, and cord products. The company also provides engineering and machining and fabrication services. Its Forte Power Systems subsidiary provides turnkey services for high-voltage systems using extruded-dielectric cable. The purchase of General Cable Corporation's building wire assets made the company one of North America's largest producers of building wire. Founded in 1950 by Roy Richards Sr. (the chairman's father), Southwire is owned by the Richards family.

KEY COMPETITORS
AFC Cable
Phelps Dodge
Superior TeleCom

SPITZER MANAGEMENT, INC.

150 E. Bridge St.	CEO: Alan Spitzer	2000 Est. Sales: $850.0 mil.
Elyria, OH 44035	CFO: —	1-Yr. Sales Change: 0.0%
Phone: 440-323-4671	HR: —	Employees: 1,700
Fax: 440-323-3623	Type: Private	FYE: December 31
Web: www.spitzer.com		

Pick a car, any car. Spitzer Management, with more than 30 franchises in Ohio, Pennsylvania, and Florida, sells almost every kind of car from A to V (Acura, Buick, Chevy, Chrysler, Dodge, Ford, GMC, Jeep, Lincoln, Mazda, Mercury, Mitsubishi, Nissan, Oldsmobile, Plymouth, Pontiac, Toyota, and Volkswagen). Spitzer dealerships sell both new and used cars and offer parts, service, and collision-repair departments. The company, founded in 1904, also has interests in real estate, hotels, and marinas and manages a golf course. Owner and CEO Alan Spitzer's statewide (Ohio) campaign to legalize gambling failed, ruining plans to build a casino on company-owned land. He is now building homes and condos on the site.

KEY COMPETITORS
AutoNation
Ricart Automotive

In-depth profiles of an additional 200 key private companies are found on pages 36–435.

SRP

1521 N. Project Dr.	CEO: William P. Schrader	2002 Sales: $2,214.4 million
Tempe, AZ 85281	CFO: Mark B. Bonsall	1-Yr. Sales Change: (26.8%)
Phone: 602-236-5900	HR: L.J. U'Ren	Employees: 4,222
Fax: 602-236-2170	Type: Government-owned	FYE: April 30
Web: www.srpnet.com		

One of the US's largest publicly owned utilities, SRP (Salt River Project) provides Phoenix with two types of current: electric and water. Electricity comes from the Salt River Project Agricultural Improvement and Power District, which is a political subdivision of the State of Arizona. The District has a generating capacity of 6,600 MW and distributes power to more than 770,000 customers; its subsidiary New West Energy provides related services. Water comes from the Salt River Valley Water Users' Association, a private firm that delivers about 1 million acre-feet of water to residents and agricultural irrigators; it also operates canals, reservoirs, and wells in its service area.

KEY COMPETITORS
Pinnacle West
Southwest Gas
UniSource Energy

SSM HEALTH CARE SYSTEM INC.

477 N. Lindbergh Blvd.	CEO: Sister Mary J. Ryan	2001 Sales: —
St. Louis, MO 63141	CFO: Elizabeth A. Alhand	1-Yr. Sales Change: —
Phone: 314-994-7800	HR: Steven M. Barney	Employees: 22,000
Fax: 314-994-7900	Type: Not-for-profit	FYE: December 31
Web: www.ssmhc.com		

The health care mission of SSM Health Care System began with five nuns who fled religious persecution in Germany in 1872 only to arrive in St. Louis in the midst of a smallpox epidemic. They formed their first hospital there in 1877 and later became pioneers in bringing health care to the rural frontier, founding the Oklahoma Territory's first hospital in 1898. Today the not-for-profit, sponsored by the Franciscan Sisters of Mary, owns and operates some 20 acute care hospitals with more than 5,000 licensed beds. The company also operates nursing homes and rehabilitation clinics, and offers home health and hospice care. SSM's facilities are located in Illinois, Missouri, Oklahoma, and Wisconsin.

KEY COMPETITORS
BJC Health
HCA
Tenet Healthcare

STAPLE COTTON COOPERATIVE ASSOCIATION

214 W. Market St.	CEO: Woods E. Eastland	2001 Sales: $1,050.0 million
Greenwood, MS 38930	CFO: Mack L. Alford	1-Yr. Sales Change: 0.9%
Phone: 662-453-6231	HR: Eugene A. Stansel Jr.	Employees: 230
Fax: 662-453-6274	Type: Cooperative	FYE: August 31
Web: www.staplcotn.com		

Wear underwear? Chances are Staplcotn had a hand in it. Staple Cotton Cooperative Association, best known for its Staplcotn cotton marketing arm, serves more than 12,000 member-owners in 50 states. Founded in 1921 by Mississippi cotton producer Oscar Bledsoe and 10 Delta growers, it sells about 3 million bales of cotton annually. Most of the yield is sold to the US textile industry to make men's knit underwear, T-shirts, sheets, towels, and denim. Customers include Fruit of the Loom and Levi Strauss & Co. The co-op's Stapldiscount subsidiary offers low-interest loans for equipment, buildings, and land. Staplcotn is represented worldwide by Amcot, which also represents three other US cotton co-ops.

KEY COMPETITORS
Calcot
Dunavant Enterprises
Plains Cotton

📖 **In-depth profiles of an additional 200 key private companies are found on pages 36–435.**

STATE OF FLORIDA DEPARTMENT OF THE LOTTERY

250 Marriott Dr.	CEO: David Griffin	2002 Sales: $2,330.0 million
Tallahassee, FL 32301	CFO: David Faulkenberry	1-Yr. Sales Change: 2.4%
Phone: 850-487-7777	HR: Karen Boulding	Employees: 482
Fax: 850-487-4541	Type: Government-owned	FYE: June 30
Web: www.flalottery.com		

No dimpled chads here — unless it's a grinning guy named Chad holding a winning ticket. The State of Florida Department of the Lottery runs instant-play scratch tickets and lotto games, including Florida Lotto (the big jackpot), Fantasy 5, and Cash 3. Lotto tickets are sold at thousands of retail outlets statewide. The Florida Lottery gives 38 cents of every dollar generated to Florida's Educational Enhancement Trust Fund, which provides funding for programs from pre-kindergarten up to the state university. The Florida Lottery pays out half of sales in prize money. Lottery officials have stepped up marketing efforts in hopes of reviving lagging sales.

KEY COMPETITORS
Florida Gaming
Georgia Lottery
Multi-State Lottery

STEINER CORPORATION

505 E. South Temple	CEO: Kevin Steiner	2001 Sales: $712.0 million
Salt Lake City, UT 84102	CFO: Kevin Steiner	1-Yr. Sales Change: 6.3%
Phone: 801-328-8831	HR: Tim Weiler	Employees: 10,000
Fax: 801-363-5680	Type: Private	FYE: June 30
Web: www.amlinen.com		

Steiner tells its clients, "It pays to keep clean," and provides uniforms, linens, and other products and services worldwide to achieve that goal. Operating under the name Alsco (American linen supply company), the company supplies towels, linens, and uniforms to the medical and hospitality industries, among others. It also rents, sells, and manufactures uniforms, provides workplace restroom services, launders specialized garments, and manages gownrooms at high-tech sites. In addition, Steiner supplies air and liquid filtration products and manufactures uniform lockers. Founded in 1889 by George Steiner, the company is family owned.

KEY COMPETITORS
ARAMARK
Cintas
G&K Services

STEVEDORING SERVICES OF AMERICA INC.

1131 SW Klickitat Way	CEO: Jon Hemingway	2002 Est. Sales: $1,046.0 mil.
Seattle, WA 98134	CFO: Charles Sadowski	1-Yr. Sales Change: 4.6%
Phone: 206-623-0304	HR: —	Employees: 10,000
Fax: 206-623-0179	Type: Private	FYE: January 31
Web: www.ssofa.com		

"Stevedoring" is a romantic-sounding way to say heavy lifting, which Stevedoring Services of America (SSA) does a lot of. The largest marine terminal operator in the US, SSA loads and unloads ships at ports from Seattle to New Zealand. The company handles a variety of cargo, including steel, coal, and cars. It also provides rail terminal services, warehousing, and shipment tracking. SSA's Tideworks Technology division offers administrative and operational software and technology services for terminal operators. Founded in the 1880s, SSA has been owned by the Smith and Hemingway families since 1949; CEO Jon Hemingway is the third generation of his family to head the company.

KEY COMPETITORS
Evergreen Marine
Hutchison Whampoa
P&O

In-depth profiles of an additional 200 key private companies are found on pages 36–435.

STEWART'S SHOPS CORP.

2907 Route 9
Balston Spa, NY 12020
Phone: 518-581-1200
Fax: 518-581-1209
Web: www.stewartsicecream.com

CEO: William Dake
CFO: William Dake
HR: Jim Botch
Type: Private

2001 Sales: $700.0 million
1-Yr. Sales Change: 8.0%
Employees: 3,000
FYE: December 31

I scream, you scream, we all scream for Stewart's ice cream, especially if we live in upstate New York or Vermont, home to more than 300 Stewart's Shops. Stewart's Shops (formerly known as Stewart's Ice Cream Company) runs a chain of convenience stores selling some 3,000 different products, including dairy items, groceries, food to go, beer, gasoline, and, of course, ice cream. Stewart's makes its own ice cream — more than 50 flavors both hand-dipped and packaged — and dairy products, and it has several private-label products. It also sells national brands. The founding Dake family owns about two-thirds of the company; employee compensation plans own the rest of Stewart's Shops.

KEY COMPETITORS
7-Eleven
Ben & Jerry's
Cumberland Farms

STRATEGIC HOTEL CAPITAL LLC

77 W. Wacker Dr., Ste. 4600
Chicago, IL 60601
Phone: 312-658-5000
Fax: 312-658-5799
Web: www.shci.com

CEO: Laurence S. Geller
CFO: Chasen Syr
HR: —
Type: Private

2001 Est. Sales: $1,000.0 mil.
1-Yr. Sales Change: 0.0%
Employees: 50
FYE: December 31

Strategic Hotel Capital (SHC) strategically invests capital in hotels. The private investment group owns more than 30 hotel properties, which operate on a "fee for service" basis, in the US, Europe, and Mexico. Its affiliated brands include Four Seasons, Hilton, Marriott, and Ritz-Carlton, as well as trophy properties such as Manhattan's Marriott East Side and Essex House Westin and San Diego's Hyatt Regency. In early 2002 SHC began considering an IPO but plans seemed to fizzle as the economy headed south that summer. The company receives funding from Goldman Sachs and Prudential; CEO Laurence Geller also owns a stake in the company.

KEY COMPETITORS
Hilton
Marriott International
Starwood Hotels & Resorts

THE STRUCTURE TONE ORGANIZATION

15 East 26th St.
New York, NY 10010
Phone: 212-481-6100
Fax: 212-685-9267
Web: www.structuretone.com

CEO: Anthony Carvette
CFO: Ray Froimowitz
HR: Tony Tursy
Type: Private

2002 Est. Sales: $2,100.0 mil.
1-Yr. Sales Change: 0.0%
Employees: 1,600
FYE: October 31

Structured to set the right tone for its clients, The Structure Tone Organization develops corporate and commercial properties for major clients down the block and around the world. Through four main companies, the group provides general contracting, construction management, and project management services for building construction, interior fit-outs and renovations, and infrastructure upgrades. A top builder in the New York City area (it is a leader in telecommunications projects there as well), the company also works in Asia, Europe, and South America. Structure Tone was founded to focus on building interiors in 1971 by Lou Marino and Patrick Donaghy, whose family now owns the company.

KEY COMPETITORS
Bovis Lend Lease
Skanska USA Building
Turner Corporation

📖 **In-depth profiles of an additional 200 key private companies are found on pages 36–435.**

SUFFOLK CONSTRUCTION COMPANY, INC.

65 Allerton St.	CEO: John F. Fish	2002 Sales: $701.9 million
Boston, MA 02119	CFO: Mike Azarela	1-Yr. Sales Change: 5.9%
Phone: 617-445-3500	HR: Jodi Grant	Employees: 487
Fax: 617-445-2343	Type: Private	FYE: August 31
Web: www.suffolk-construction.com		

The bricks fly at Suffolk Construction. The company provides general contracting, construction management, preconstruction, and design/build services to clients in the public and private sectors across the US. Commercial and residential projects include university halls, senior housing, hotels (Marriott, Hilton), corporate offices, and retail facilities. A top Boston contractor, Suffolk Construction is owned by president John Fish and his father Edward, who created Suffolk Construction in 1982. It also operates in Florida and California. The Fish family has been in the construction business for four generations (since the 1890s). Another construction company is owned by John's brother Ted Fish.

KEY COMPETITORS
Kraus-Anderson
Modern Continental Companies
Perini

SUNBELT BEVERAGE CORPORATION

60 E. 42nd St.	CEO: Charles Merinoff	2001 Est. Sales: $910.0 mil.
New York, NY 10165	CFO: Gene Luciano	1-Yr. Sales Change: 7.1%
Phone: 212-699-7000	HR: Paul Puca	Employees: 1,700
Fax: 212-699-7099	Type: Private	FYE: March 31
Web: www.charmer-sunbelt.com		

Sunbelt Beverage has become one of the biggest swigs in its business. A leading wine and spirits wholesaler in a rapidly consolidating industry, the company operates through a number of joint ventures and subsidiaries including Premier Beverage (Florida), Reliable Churchill (Maryland), Ben Arnold-Sunbelt Beverage (South Carolina), and others in Alabama, Colorado, Connecticut, Mississippi, Pensylvania, and Washington, DC. Division management bought Sunbelt Beverage from McKesson (drugs and sundries wholesaler) and took it private in 1988 with the backing of investment firm Weiss, Peck & Greer. Herman Merinoff, owner of New York-based wholesaler Charmer Industries, has a majority stake in Sunbelt Beverage.

KEY COMPETITORS
Glazer's Wholesale Drug
National Distributing
Southern Wine & Spirits

SUPERIOR GROUP, INC.

3 Radnor Corporate Center, Ste. 400	CEO: William G. Warden IV	2001 Est. Sales: $800.0 mil.
Radnor, PA 19087	CFO: David Davies	1-Yr. Sales Change: 6.7%
Phone: 610-964-2000	HR: Patricia H. Wilson	Employees: 3,400
Fax: 610-964-2001	Type: Private	FYE: December 31
Web: www.superior-group.com		

Metal-centric holding company Superior Group makes and sells tubing through subsidiaries Fine Tubes (precision tubing), Superior Tube (small metal tubing), Swepco Tube (corrosion-resistant tubing and pipe), and Western Pneumatic Tube (thin-walled tubing). Its TW Metals subsidiary is a metals distributor and processor for such customers as Air France, FedEx, and United Airlines. Superior's Drever Group designs and sells industrial furnaces to steel mills and metal manufactures, while Sharp Corp. makes consumer-friendly packaging for pharmaceuticals such as carded blister packaging and child-resistant bottles. SGI Capital is Superior's investment arm. Superior is owned by the Warden family, heirs of its founder.

KEY COMPETITORS
Earle M. Jorgensen
Inductotherm
Lone Star Technologies

📖 In-depth profiles of an additional 200
key private companies are found on pages 36–435.

SUTHERLAND LUMBER COMPANY, L.P.

4000 Main St.	CEO: Steve Scott	2001 Est. Sales: $850.0 mil.
Kansas City, MO 64111	CFO: Steve Scott	1-Yr. Sales Change: 3.0%
Phone: 816-756-3000	HR: Shanna Wilson	Employees: 2,300
Fax: 816-756-3594	Type: Private	FYE: December 31
Web: www.sutherlands.com		

Who says lumber can't be high tech? Sutherland Lumber operates more than 60 lumber and home improvement stores in 15 states. Subsidiary Housemart.com offers more than 40,000 items online, fulfilling orders through four Oklahoma stores. Sutherland's stores range in size from 50,000 to 190,000 sq. ft. They sell lumber, paints, tools, and building packages for houses, sheds, garages, and farm buildings. In addition the stores sell lawn and garden equipment, plumbing supplies, and materials for hobbies and crafts. The company, which is owned and operated by the Sutherland family, was founded in 1917 as an oilfield supplier. The family also has holdings in ranching, farmland, timber, and manufacturing.

KEY COMPETITORS
Ace Hardware
Home Depot
Lowe's

SUTTER HEALTH

2200 River Plaza	CEO: Van R. Johnson	2000 Sales: $3,500.0 million
Sacramento, CA 95833	CFO: Robert D. Reed	1-Yr. Sales Change: 19.9%
Phone: 916-733-8800	HR: Ken Buback	Employees: 35,000
Fax: 916-286-6841	Type: Not-for-profit	FYE: December 31
Web: www.sutterhealth.org		

Sutter Health is one of the nation's largest not-for-profit health care systems. It was organized in 1996 through the merger of Sutter Health and California Healthcare System. Today the company caters to residents in more than 100 northern California communities. Its services are provided through the firm's approximately 5,000 affiliated doctors, from facilities of various types, including: acute care hospitals, home health/hospice networks, medical groups, occupational health services centers, and skilled nursing facilities. Sutter Health's network also boasts several research institutes.

KEY COMPETITORS
Adventist Health
Catholic Healthcare West
Tenet Healthcare

SWAGELOK COMPANY

29500 Solon Rd.	CEO: William R. Cosgrove	2001 Sales: $1,000.0 million
Solon, OH 44139	CFO: Frank J. Roddy	1-Yr. Sales Change: (16.7%)
Phone: 440-248-4600	HR: James L. Francis	Employees: 3,000
Fax: 440-349-5970	Type: Private	FYE: December 31
Web: www.swagelok.com		

With sales partners worldwide, Swagelok Company has to speak many languages, *fluidly*. The company makes fluid system components, which include plug, pinch, and radial diaphragm valves, sanitary fittings, welding systems, and 8,400 other products. Its products are used by bioprocessing and pharmaceuticals research companies and in the oil and gas, power, and semiconductor industries. Swagelok has more than 200 manufacturing, research, sales, and distribution facilities worldwide. Founded in 1947 by Fred Lennon in his kitchen, the company requires all prospective sales people and their families to tour company facilities for two months before coming on board. The Lennon family still controls the company.

KEY COMPETITORS
CIRCOR International
ITT Industries
Tyco International

📖 In-depth profiles of an additional 200 key private companies are found on pages 36–435.

SWIFT & COMPANY

1770 Promontory Circle	CEO: John S. Simons	2002 Sales: $7,733.0 million
Greeley, CO 80634	CFO: Danny Herron	1-Yr. Sales Change: —
Phone: 970-506-8000	HR: Jack Shandley	Employees: 21,400
Fax: 970-506-8307	Type: Private	FYE: May 30

Swift & Company has a hoof up on other newcomers to the meat industry. Once the meat processing business of ConAgra, the company was spun off and is now 54% owned by an investment group led by Hicks, Muse, Tate & Furst and Booth Creek Management. ConAgra has kept 46% of the company and will continue to obtain fresh beef, pork, and lamb from its former subsidiary. With operations in Australia as well as the US, the company is the #3 US beef processor — behind Tyson's IBP Fresh Meats and Cargill's Excel unit. Swift & Company intends to focus on fresh, branded, and value-added meats.

KEY COMPETITORS
Cargill
IBP
Smithfield Foods

SWINERTON INCORPORATED

580 California St., 11th Fl.	CEO: David H. Grubb Sr.	2001 Sales: $1,549.0 million
San Francisco, CA 94104	CFO: Michael Re	1-Yr. Sales Change: (0.1%)
Phone: 415-421-2980	HR: Paul Smolinski	Employees: 1,200
Fax: 415-984-1201	Type: Private	FYE: December 31
Web: www.swinerton.com		

Swinerton is building up the West just as it helped rebuild San Francisco after the 1906 earthquake. The construction group, formerly Swinerton & Walberg, builds commercial, industrial, and government facilities, including resorts, subsidized housing, public schools, Hollywood soundstages, hospitals, and airport terminals. Swinerton offers general contracting through Swinerton Builders, Westwood Swinerton, and Harbison-Mahony-Higgins; it also provides engineering construction, property management, and project management and property assessment. The employee-owned company, which has been acquiring other contractors in the past decade to expand in the Northwest and Southwest, traces its family tree to 1888.

KEY COMPETITORS
DPR Construction
Turner Corporation
Webcor Builders

SYNNEX INFORMATION TECHNOLOGIES, INC.

3797 Spinnaker Ct.	CEO: Robert Huang	2001 Sales: $3,340.0 million
Fremont, CA 94538	CFO: Lawrence S. Leong	1-Yr. Sales Change: (9.7%)
Phone: 510-656-3333	HR: Rebecca Chou	Employees: 1,600
Fax: 510-668-3777	Type: Private	FYE: November 30
Web: www.synnex.com		

SYNNEX's approach to contract manufacturing and distribution services is far from cynical. SYNNEX Information Technologies custom-builds electronics for manufacturers such as 3Com, Hewlett-Packard, and IBM, as well as for systems integrators and resellers. The company makes and configures PCs, printed circuit boards (PCBs), networking equipment, and other electronic gear. SYNNEX also provides design, distribution, and support services; its online services include parts catalogs, configuration, and ordering. The company works closely with majority shareholder MiTAC International, a Taiwan-based computer and PCB maker that owns 56% of SYNNEX. CEO Robert Huang founded SYNNEX (pronounced "Sin-nuks") in 1980.

KEY COMPETITORS
Avnet
Sanmina-SCI
Solectron

In-depth profiles of an additional 200 key private companies are found on pages 36–435.

TAC WORLDWIDE COMPANIES

850 Washington St.	CEO: Gary T. DiCamillo	2001 Sales: $850.0 million
Dedham, MA 02026	CFO: Paul Salvucci	1-Yr. Sales Change: (22.7%)
Phone: 781-251-8000	HR: Bob Moritz	Employees: 1,150
Fax: 781-251-8064	Type: Private	FYE: December 31
Web: www.1tac.com		

TAC Worldwide wants to be a permanent fixture in the temporary staffing business. The company offers contract and temporary staffing services through 150 offices in all 50 states and more than 20 countries in Europe, North America, and Southeast Asia. TAC offers staffing in fields such as information technology, engineering, office support, and entertainment. Each year it places 50,000 contract and temporary employees with more than 6,500 companies. Chairman Salvatore Balsamo, who controls TAC Worldwide, founded the company as Technical Aid Corporation in 1969.

KEY COMPETITORS
Adecco
Manpower
Randstad

TANG INDUSTRIES, INC.

3773 Howard Hughes Pkwy., Ste. 350N	CEO: Cyrus Tang	2001 Est. Sales: $1,300.0 mil.
Las Vegas, NV 89109	CFO: Kurt R. Swanson	1-Yr. Sales Change: 4.0%
Phone: 702-734-3700	HR: Vaughn Kuerschner	Employees: 3,800
Fax: 702-734-6766	Type: Private	FYE: December 31
Web: www.tangindustries.com		

Although it's not a good source of Vitamin C, Tang Industries *is* a diversified holding company; its largest holding is National Material, a metal-fabricating and -distributing company that engages in steel stamping and recycles and trades aluminum and scrap metal. SKD Tooling Company, a subsidiary out of China, supplies tooling operations aimed at the automobile industry. The company also has steel operations in China. Tang Industries' holdings include real estate, manufacturer GF Office Furniture, and Curatek Pharmaceuticals, which specializes in niche markets overlooked by large drugmakers. The company was founded in 1964 by Chinese immigrant Cyrus Tang after he bought a small metal-stamping shop in Illinois.

KEY COMPETITORS
Commercial Metals
Ryerson Tull
Steelcase

TAP PHARMACEUTICAL PRODUCTS INC.

675 North Field Dr.	CEO: H. Thomas Watkins	2001 Sales: $3,787.2 million
Lake Forest, IL 60045	CFO: Kevin Dolan	1-Yr. Sales Change: 7.0%
Phone: 847-582-2000	HR: Denise Kitchen	Employees: 3,000
Fax: 800-830-6936	Type: Joint venture	FYE: December 31
Web: www.tap.com		

TAP Pharmaceutical Products taps into hot drug industry trends. The joint venture between Abbott Laboratories and Takeda Chemical Industries develops and sells drugs in the US and Canada. Products target cancer, gastroenterology, gynecology, and urology. Its Lupron treats prostate cancer and endometriosis. It also markets gastric acid inhibitor Prevacid with Abbott and has gained FDA approval for antibiotic Spectracef. Although erectile dysfunction treatment Uprima won European approval, TAP withdrew it from FDA consideration after questions arose over its efficacy and safety.

KEY COMPETITORS
AstraZeneca
PRAECIS PHARMACEUTICALS
Pfizer

In-depth profiles of an additional 200 key private companies are found on pages 36–435.

TAUBER OIL COMPANY

55 Waugh Dr., Ste. 700	CEO: David W. Tauber	2001 Sales: $1,800.0 million
Houston, TX 77210	CFO: Stephen E. Hamlin	1-Yr. Sales Change: 80.0%
Phone: 713-869-8700	HR: Debbie Moseley	Employees: 60
Fax: 713-869-8069	Type: Private	FYE: September 30
Web: www.tauberoil.com		

No petrochemical product is taboo for oil refiner and marketer Tauber Oil. The company, which was founded by O. J. Tauber Sr. in 1953, markets refined petroleum products, natural gas, carbon black feedstocks, liquefied petroleum gases, chemicals, and petrochemicals (including benzene, styrene monomer, and methanol). The company is one of the US's leading suppliers of feedstocks for reforming and olefin cracking. Subsidiary Tauber Petrochemical was created in 1997 to beef up the company's international petrochemical business. Tauber maintains a fleet of more than 100 rail cars.

KEY COMPETITORS
Exxon Mobil
Lyondell Chemical
Valero Energy

TAYLOR CORPORATION

1725 Roe Crest Dr.	CEO: Bradley Schreier	2001 Est. Sales: $1,300.0 mil.
North Mankato, MN 56003	CFO: Bill Kozitza	1-Yr. Sales Change: (0.8%)
Phone: 507-625-2828	HR: Deb Newman	Employees: 14,000
Fax: 507-625-2988	Type: Private	FYE: December 31
Web: www.taylorcorp.com		

Taylor Corporation is wedded to invitations. One of the largest specialty printers in the US, Taylor was founded in 1951 as wedding invitation printer Carlson Craft. Taylor operates through some 90 firms in Australia, Europe, and North America. Its subsidiaries print wedding invitations, company stationery, Post-it Notes, and graduation announcements, among other items. The company also owns greeting card company Current and offers direct marketing, office supplies, and online sales of printed products. Chairman Glen Taylor — who bought the company in 1975 — has relinquished his CEO title to spend more time on philanthropy, agribusiness, and basketball (Taylor is majority owner of the Minnesota Timberwolves).

KEY COMPETITORS
Hallmark
Quebecor World
R. R. Donnelley

TEAM HEALTH, INC.

1900 Winston Rd.	CEO: Lynn Massingale	2001 Sales: $965.3 million
Knoxville, TN 37919	CFO: David Jones	1-Yr. Sales Change: 5.0%
Phone: 865-693-1000	HR: Lisa Courtney	Employees: 3,500
Fax: 865-539-8003	Type: Private	FYE: December 31
Web: www.teamhealth.com		

Team Health hopes to score some points with its outsourced physician services. It has contracts with more than 350 hospitals in about 30 states to provide medical staffing, management, administrative, and other support services. With some 2,000 physicians in its network, the firm specializes in emergency medicine, radiology, pediatrics, anesthesia, and hospitalists (hospital physicians who coordinate care during patients' stays with their primary physicians and other medical professionals). It operates through physician-managed regional affiliates. A group of emergency physicians founded Team Health in 1979. Team Health Holdings owns more than 90% of the company.

KEY COMPETITORS
EmCare
PhyAmerica
RehabCare

In-depth profiles of an additional 200 key private companies are found on pages 36–435.

TELCOBUY.COM LLC

60 Weldon Pkwy.	CEO: James P. Kavanaugh	2001 Sales: $604.0 million
St. Louis, MO 63043	CFO: Thomas W. Strunk	1-Yr. Sales Change: (1.0%)
Phone: 314-569-7000	HR: Ann W. Marr	Employees: 400
Fax: 314-569-8310	Type: Private	FYE: December 31
Web: www.telcobuy.com		

telcobuy.com helps the phone company make a connection. The company operates an online business-to-business marketplace for the telecommunications industry. Its site includes more than 500,000 telecommunications infrastructure products and services representing some 3,000 suppliers. telcobuy.com also provides electronic procurement, technical consulting, and contract manufacturing, among other services. Its major clients include SBC Communications and Verizon. Founders David Steward (chairman) and James Kavanaugh (CEO) control telcobuy.com through an entity called World Wide Technology.

KEY COMPETITORS
Anixter International
Graybar Electric
Verticalnet

TEXAS HEALTH RESOURCES INC.

611 Ryan Plaza Dr., Ste. 900	CEO: Douglas D. Hawthorne	2000 Sales: $1,340.1 million
Arlington, TX 76011	CFO: Ron Bourland	1-Yr. Sales Change: 3.8%
Phone: 817-462-7900	HR: Bonnie Bell	Employees: 16,000
Fax: —	Type: Not-for-profit	FYE: December 31
Web: www.texashealth.org		

This company is takin' care of Texas, with about 25 health care facilities in the Dallas/Fort Worth and North Texas region. Formed by the merger of Harris Methodist Health System, Presbyterian Healthcare System, and Arlington Memorial Hospital Foundation, the not-for-profit system includes acute-care hospitals, mental health centers, a retirement community, senior care centers, and home health services. Its network includes more than 4,000 physicians and more than 4,200 beds. Texas Health Resources sold its unprofitable St. Paul Medical Center to the University of Texas.

KEY COMPETITORS
Baylor Health
HCA
Triad Hospitals

TEXAS PETROCHEMICALS LP

3 Riverway, Ste. 1500	CEO: Bill W. Waycaster	2002 Sales: $599.6 million
Houston, TX 77056	CFO: Carl Stutts	1-Yr. Sales Change: (30.2%)
Phone: 713-627-7474	HR: Jimmy Rhodes	Employees: 323
Fax: 713-626-3650	Type: Private	FYE: June 30
Web: www.txpetrochem.com		

Texas Petrochemicals has kept motoring along thanks to the US Clean Air Act of 1990, which requires an oxygenate in gasoline in heavily populated areas. The company derives about 55% of its sales from the production of MTBE, the predominate oxygenate used in US gasoline; however, it has been reducing its dependence on MTBE after several contamination incidents. (MTBE also might be banned.) Other products include butadiene, butene-1, high-purity isobutylene, and diisobutylene, which are used in the manufacture of synthetic rubber, plastic resins, and lubricants. Texas Petrochemicals operates its own cogeneration power plant and sells the excess capacity. Several investment firms and officers own the company.

KEY COMPETITORS
Lyondell Chemical
Methanex
Millennium Chemicals

In-depth profiles of an additional 200
key private companies are found on pages 36–435.

TIC HOLDINGS INC.

2211 Elk River Rd.
Steamboat Springs, CO 80487
Phone: 970-879-2561
Fax: 970-879-6078
Web: www.tic-inc.com

CEO: Ron McKenzie
CFO: Jim Kissane
HR: Barbara Judd
Type: Private

2001 Sales: $1,123.0 million
1-Yr. Sales Change: 12.5%
Employees: 5,000
FYE: December 31

TIC Holdings doesn't flinch when it comes to constructing heavy industrial projects. Founded in 1974, the holding company offers services including civil engineering, heavy equipment erection, pipeline construction, and electrical installation. Main subsidiary TIC - The Industrial Company provides industrial construction services in the US through seven regional units. Subsidiary Western Summit Constructors focuses on water and wastewater projects. TIC also has an international unit. The management-owned firm ranks among leading contractors in the wastewater, petrochemical, power, refining, mining, and industrial process markets, as well as in the electrical and instrumentation and pulp and paper industries.

KEY COMPETITORS
Black & Veatch
Foster Wheeler
Zachry

TIME WARNER ENTERTAINMENT COMPANY, L.P.

75 Rockefeller Plaza
New York, NY 10019
Phone: 212-484-8000
Fax: 212-333-3987

CEO: Richard D. Parsons
CFO: Wayne H. Pace
HR: —
Type: Partnership

2001 Sales: $15,302.0 million
1-Yr. Sales Change: 9.4%
Employees: 35,300
FYE: December 31

Time Warner Entertainment (TWE) will show you a good time. The company's Warner Bros. subsidiary oversees film and TV productions and home video and DVD operations. TWE also owns HBO (which, in turn, owns 50% of Comedy Central) and 50% of Court TV. Its cable systems (Time Warner Cable and the 65%-owned TWE-Advance/Newhouse partnership) serve nearly 13 million subscribers. Comcast owns 27% of TWE, but 73%-owner AOL Time Warner (AOLTW) controls the management of TWE. Comcast gained its stake in the firm by buying its previous owner AT&T Broadband. Comcast has agreed to sell the stake back to AOLTW. Once completed, AOLTW plans to take Time Warner Cable public.

KEY COMPETITORS
Comcast
Viacom
Walt Disney

TIMEX CORPORATION

555 Christian Rd.
Middlebury, CT 06762
Phone: 203-346-5000
Fax: 203-346-7019
Web: www.timex.com

CEO: Jose Santana
CFO: Edward F. Pytka
HR: M. A. Saleh
Type: Private

2000 Est. Sales: $600.0 mil.
1-Yr. Sales Change: 0.0%
Employees: 7,500
FYE: December 31

Branching out from its original "Takes a licking" designs, Timex is strapping on new faces in order to tap new markets worldwide. The US's largest watch producer has expanded its lines from simple, low-cost watches to include high-tech tickers capable of paging or downloading computer data. Its sports watches have gone upscale and gadgety with lines such as Reef Gear and Ironman. (The brightness of its Indiglo watch helped a man lead a group of people down 34 flights of dark stairs after the first World Trade Center bombing in 1993.) Timex also makes watches for Nautica and Guess? under license. Founded in 1854 as Waterbury Clock, Timex is owned by Fred Olsen, whose father bought the company in 1942.

KEY COMPETITORS
Casio Computer
Seiko
Swatch

In-depth profiles of an additional 200 key private companies are found on pages 36–435.

TISHMAN REALTY & CONSTRUCTION CO. INC.

666 Fifth Ave.
New York, NY 10103
Phone: 212-399-3600
Fax: 212-397-1316
Web: www.tishman.com

CEO: John L. Tishman
CFO: Larry Schwarzwalder
HR: Gina Perrone
Type: Private

2001 Sales: $1,640.0 million
1-Yr. Sales Change: 47.9%
Employees: 920
FYE: June 30

Tishman Realty & Construction is an immigrant success story writ large. The company builds office, hospitality, recreational, industrial, and other kinds of property for its own account and for other owners. The firm offers third-party developers a full menu of real estate design, construction, management, and financing services. High-profile projects handled by the company (or its publicly owned predecessor) include Disney World's EPCOT Center, Madison Square Garden, the ill-fated World Trade Center, and Chicago's John Hancock Center. Chairman and CEO John Tishman and his family — scions of immigrant founder Julius Tishman, who began building tenements in 1898 — own the company.

KEY COMPETITORS
CB Richard Ellis
Gilbane
Trammell Crow

TNP ENTERPRISES, INC.

4100 International Plaza Tower II
Fort Worth, TX 76109
Phone: 817-731-0099
Fax: 817-737-1343
Web: www.tnpe.com

CEO: William J. Catacosinos
CFO: Theodore A. Babcock
HR: Melissa D. Davis
Type: Private

2001 Sales: $658.9 million
1-Yr. Sales Change: 2.3%
Employees: 786
FYE: December 31

The sleepy little utility from the Southwest has made a big splash in its industry. The company's main subsidiary, Texas-New Mexico Power (TNMP), transmits and distributes electricity to more than 240,000 customers in Texas and New Mexico. TNP has formed First Choice Power to compete in Texas' retail electric supply market, which has been deregulated. It has also sold its 300-MW power plant. TNP was acquired in 2000 by a private investor group in the first LBO of a US electric utility. Industry veteran William Catacosinos of Laurel Hill Capital Partners led the buyout and became TNP's CEO. Other investors include CIBC World Markets.

KEY COMPETITORS
El Paso Electric
PNM Resources
TXU

TOPA EQUITIES, LTD.

1800 Avenue of the Stars, Ste. 1400
Los Angeles, CA 90067
Phone: 310-203-9199
Fax: 310-557-1837

CEO: John E. Anderson
CFO: Brenda Seuthe
HR: Virginia Flores
Type: Private

2001 Est. Sales: $875.0 mil.
1-Yr. Sales Change: 1.2%
Employees: 1,600
FYE: December 31

Holding company Topa Equities casts a wide net. Owned by John Anderson, Topa has about 30 businesses involved in automobile dealerships (Silver Star Automotive), beer distribution, insurance, real estate, and more. Topa's beverage operations include Ace Beverage, Mission Beverages, and Paradise Beverages; the firm dominates the Hawaiian and Caribbean beer markets and serves California. Brands sold include all major US brews and leading US imports Corona, Guinness, Heineken, and Labatt, among others. Anderson started in 1956 as a distributor of Hamm's beer. UCLA's Anderson School of Business, to which Anderson donated $15 million, is named for him.

KEY COMPETITORS
Citigroup
Prospect Motors
Young's Market

📖 In-depth profiles of an additional 200 key private companies are found on pages 36–435.

TOWERS PERRIN

One Stamford Plaza, 263 Tresser Boulevard
Stamford, CT 06901
Phone: 203-326-5400
Fax: 203-326-5499
Web: www.towers.com

CEO: Mark Mactas
CFO: Mark L. Wilson
HR: Anne Donovan Bodnar
Type: Private

2001 Sales: $1,469.0 million
1-Yr. Sales Change: 1.5%
Employees: 9,009
FYE: December 31

Refusing to live in an ivory tower, this company aims to offer practical advice. One of the leading management consulting firms in the world, Towers Perrin serves an extensive list of corporate clients, including more than 700 of the *FORTUNE* 1000 companies. The firm's core focus is on human resources consulting. Its Tillinghast-Towers Perrin unit focuses on risk management and actuarial services to financial companies, and its Towers Perrin Reinsurance serves clients primarily as a reinsurance intermediary. In addition to consulting, the company produces several publications and surveys investigating business trends and challenges.

KEY COMPETITORS
Hewitt Associates
PricewaterhouseCoopers
Watson Wyatt

TRADER JOE'S COMPANY

800 S. Shamrock Ave.
Monrovia, CA 91016
Phone: 626-599-3700
Fax: 626-301-4431
Web: www.traderjoes.com

CEO: Dan Bane
CFO: Randy Scoville
HR: Carol Impara
Type: Private

2001 Est. Sales: $1,900.0 mil.
1-Yr. Sales Change: 13.8%
Employees: 7,488
FYE: June 30

When it comes to grocery chains, Trader Joe's isn't your average Joe. With more than 175 stores in 15 mostly West and East Coast states, the company offers upscale grocery fare such as health foods, organic produce, and nutritional supplements. To keep costs down, its stores have no service departments and average about 9,000 sq. ft. (and thus have a more limited selection than typical supermarkets). The company's specialty is its line of more than 2,000 private-label products, including beverages, soup, snacks, and frozen items. Started by Joe Coulombe as a Los Angeles convenience store chain in 1958, the company was bought in 1979 by German billionaires Karl and Theo Albrecht, who also own the ALDI food chain.

KEY COMPETITORS
Safeway
Whole Foods
Wild Oats Markets

TRAMMELL CROW RESIDENTIAL

2859 Paces Ferry Rd. #1100
Atlanta, GA 30339
Phone: 770-801-1600
Fax: 770-801-5395
Web: www.tcresidential.com

CEO: J. Ronald Terwilliger
CFO: Thomas J. Patterson
HR: Tim Swango
Type: Private

2001 Sales: —
1-Yr. Sales Change: —
Employees: 2,000
FYE: December 31

Trammell Crow Residential (TCR) builds quite a nest. A builder and manager of upscale apartment complexes, the company operates regionally through some 30 national and divisional partners. These partners work with the company to handle the purchase, development, and building of multi-family projects. TCR has more than 60,000 units; heaviest concentrations of properties are in the Southeast, the West Coast, and Texas. Trammell Crow Residential Services manages the complexes. The company split off from mammoth Trammell Crow in 1977 but is still associated with the Crow family empire of real estate development firms.

KEY COMPETITORS
Gables Residential Trust
JPI
Lincoln Property

 In-depth profiles of an additional 200 key private companies are found on pages 36–435.

TRANSAMMONIA, INC.

350 Park Ave.	CEO: Ronald P. Stanton	2001 Sales: $2,434.0 million
New York, NY 10022	CFO: Edward G. Weiner	1-Yr. Sales Change: (0.5%)
Phone: 212-223-3200	HR: Marguerite Harrington	Employees: 237
Fax: 212-759-1410	Type: Private	FYE: December 31
Web: www.transammonia.com		

Fertilizer, liquefied petroleum gas (LPG), and petrochemicals form the lifeblood of international trader Transammonia. The company trades, distributes, and transports these commodities around the world. Transammonia's fertilizer business includes ammonia, phosphates, and urea. Transammonia's Sea-3 subsidiary imports propane from Algeria, the North Sea region, and Venezuela to its terminals in Newington, New Hampshire, and Tampa, Florida. The company's Trammochem unit trades in petrochemicals, specializing in aromatics, methanol, methyltertiary butyl ether (MTBE), and olefins. Trammo Gas trades in LPG.

KEY COMPETITORS
Cargill
ConAgra
Norsk Hydro

TRAVELCENTERS OF AMERICA, INC.

24601 Center Ridge Rd., Ste. 200	CEO: Edwin P. Kuhn	2001 Sales: $1,935.0 million
Westlake, OH 44145	CFO: James W. George	1-Yr. Sales Change: (6.1%)
Phone: 440-808-9100	HR: Bruce Sebera	Employees: 10,255
Fax: 440-808-3306	Type: Private	FYE: December 31
Web: www.tatravelcenters.com		

TravelCenters of America is in the food, fuel, and relaxation business for the long haul. The company's network of about 160 interstate highway travel centers in 40 states is the nation's largest. Company-owned and franchised truck stops provide gas, fast-food and sit-down restaurants (Country Pride, Buckhorn Family), convenience stores, and lodging. With professional truck drivers accounting for most of the customers, some outlets also offer "truckeronly" services such as laundry and shower facilities, telephone and TV rooms, and truck repair services. The company is owned by a group of investors led by Oak Hill Capital Partners, Freightliner, and company officers.

KEY COMPETITORS
Flying J
Petro Stopping Centers
Pilot

TRIDENT SEAFOODS CORPORATION

5303 Shilshole Ave. NW	CEO: Charles "Chuck" Bundrant	2002 Sales: $650.0 million
Seattle, WA 98107	CFO: Philip Bishop	1-Yr. Sales Change: 8.3%
Phone: 206-783-3818	HR: Mike Ryan	Employees: 4,000
Fax: 206-782-7195	Type: Private	FYE: August 31
Web: www.tridentseafoods.com		

Something's *supposed* to be fishy at Trident Seafoods. The vertically integrated seafood business hauls in salmon, crab, and assorted finfish from the chilly waters of Alaska and the Pacific Northwest and cans or freezes the catch for retail and food service customers around the world. Trident Seafoods operates a fleet of processing boats and trawlers and more than 10 processing plants ashore. The company's brands include Arctic Ice, PubHouse, and the Sea Legs brand of surimi (crab-flavored processed fish). Founder and president Chuck Bundrant is a majority owner of Trident Seafoods; ConAgra holds a minority stake.

KEY COMPETITORS
ConAgra
Maruha
Red Chamber Group

In-depth profiles of an additional 200 key private companies are found on pages 36–435.

TRINITY HEALTH

27870 Cabot Dr.	CEO: Judith C. Pelham	2002 Sales: $4,800.0 million
Novi, MI 48377	CFO: James H. Combes	1-Yr. Sales Change: 6.7%
Phone: 248-489-5004	HR: William Anderson	Employees: 44,500
Fax: 248-489-6039	Type: Not-for-profit	FYE: June 30
Web: www.trinity-health.org		

Trinity Health is really more of a duo than a trio; the not-for-profit company is the result of a coupling between Mercy Health Services and Holy Cross Health System. Trinity Health runs nearly 50 hospitals and more than 360 outpatient facilities, as well as long-term care facilities, home health agencies, and hospice programs, in seven states. Its subsidiary, Trinity Health Plans, operates the Care Choices HMO in some 10 Michigan counties. Trinity Health sold its majority stake in GNA, formerly its rehabilitation therapy subsidiary. Catholic Health Ministries sponsors the organization.

KEY COMPETITORS
Ascension
Detroit Medical Center
HCA

TRI-STATE GENERATION AND TRANSMISSION ASSOCIATION, INC.

1100 W. 116th Ave.	CEO: Harold Thompson	2001 Sales: $632.5 million
Westminister, CO 80234	CFO: Chuck Yetzbacher	1-Yr. Sales Change: 12.3%
Phone: 303-452-6111	HR: Sara Rivenburgh	Employees: 985
Fax: 303-254-6007	Type: Cooperative	FYE: December 31
Web: www.tristategt.org		

Tri-State Generation and Transmission Association supplies wholesale electricity to 44 rural distribution utilities that serve nearly 500,000 customers in Colorado, Nebraska, New Mexico, and Wyoming. The member-owned cooperative generates about 1,500 MW of electricity, primarily from interests in coal-fired power plants, and it owns or operates 5,300 miles of transmission lines. Tri-State also purchases power and sells its excess supply to other utilities. Formed in 1952, Tri-State entered New Mexico through its 2000 acquisition of Plains Electric Generation and Transmission Cooperative.

KEY COMPETITORS
Basin Electric Power
Nebraska Public Power
PNM Resources

TRT HOLDINGS

420 Decker Dr., Ste. 100	CEO: Robert B. Rowling	2000 Est. Sales: $685.0 mil.
Irving, TX 75062	CFO: Terry Philen	1-Yr. Sales Change: 14.2%
Phone: 972-730-6664	HR: Joy Rothschild	Employees: 10,000
Fax: 972-871-9240	Type: Private	FYE: December 31
Web: www.omnihotels.com		

No one can accuse TRT Holdings of failing to put its energies into the lodging business. After making a fortune from Texas oil and gas holdings, the members of the Rowling family, whose investments are controlled by TRT Holdings, sold their Teco Pipeline and the production arm of their Tana Oil & Gas subsidiary, then focused on the hotel empire they started building in 1990. The jewel in TRT Holdings' crown is the Omni Hotels chain, a string of about 40 luxury hotels (about one-fifth are franchised) in the US, Canada, and Mexico. The company cut its ties to its past in 2000 when it sold essentially all the remaining assets of its Tana Oil & Gas exploration operations to Unocal.

KEY COMPETITORS
Fairmont Hotels
Marriott International
Starwood Hotels & Resorts

In-depth profiles of an additional 200 key private companies are found on pages 36–435.

TRUSTMARK INSURANCE COMPANY

400 Field Dr.	CEO: J. Grover Thomas Jr.	2001 Sales: $1,393.1 million
Lake Forest, IL 60045	CFO: Richard D. Batten	1-Yr. Sales Change: 5.4%
Phone: 847-615-1500	HR: Robert R. Worobow	Employees: 3,400
Fax: 847-615-3910	Type: Mutual company	FYE: December 31
Web: www.trustmarkinsurance.com		

Trustmark Insurance was established in 1913 as the Brotherhood of All Railway Employees to provide disability coverage to railroad workers. Trustmark is licensed in all 50 states and covers more than 2.5 million people from all walks of life. Operations include group and individual health coverage (medical, dental, disability, and life insurance) and voluntary insurance products (specialty products through voluntary payroll deductions). Subsidiary Starmark markets health plans to small businesses. Other subsidiaries offer third-party administration and cost management of health care plans and combat health care fraud. A mutual company, Trustmark's policyholders own the company.

KEY COMPETITORS
Aetna
Blue Cross
CIGNA

TTI, INC.

2441 Northeast Pkwy.	CEO: Paul E. Andrews Jr.	2001 Sales: $750.0 million
Fort Worth, TX 76106	CFO: Nick M. Kypreos	1-Yr. Sales Change: (21.5%)
Phone: 817-740-9000	HR: Myran Dill	Employees: 1,550
Fax: 817-740-9898	Type: Private	FYE: December 31
Web: www.ttiinc.com		

TTI is passionate about passives. Each year the company distributes more than 1.7 million electronic components, including passive components such as resistors and capacitors, and interconnects such as cables, sockets, and filter connectors. Suppliers of its 160,000 line items include 3M, Spectrum Control, Philips, and Vishay Intertechnology. TTI also offers services such as component packaging and supply chain management. TTI, which owner and CEO Paul Andrews founded in 1971 as a supplier to the military, serves manufacturers of aerospace and defense systems, computers, telecom equipment, medical devices, and industrial products. The company is expanding its presence in Europe.

KEY COMPETITORS
All American Semiconductor
Arrow Electronics
Smith & Associates

TTX COMPANY

101 N. Wacker Dr.	CEO: Andrew F. Reardon	2001 Sales: $983.1 million
Chicago, IL 60606	CFO: Thomas D. Marion	1-Yr. Sales Change: (3.7%)
Phone: 312-853-3223	HR: Michelle Pomeroy	Employees: 1,400
Fax: 312-984-3790	Type: Private	FYE: December 31
Web: www.ttx.com		

TTX keeps the railroad industry chugging by leasing railcars to railroad companies in the US and Canada. Rail companies generally prefer to rent railcars as needed rather than buy them because the cars are often switched and traded along the tracks. With 127,000 railcars, TTX's fleet includes three types of railcars (intermodal, autorack, and general use) designed to carry containers, autos, farm and construction equipment, and lumber and steel products. TTX has distribution centers in Illinois and Washington and maintains its fleet through three repair centers (in California, Florida, and South Carolina) and 31 inspection centers across the US. TTX is owned by the largest railroads in the US and Canada.

KEY COMPETITORS
GATX
Greenbrier
Pacer International

In-depth profiles of an additional 200 key private companies are found on pages 36–435.

TUFTS ASSOCIATED HEALTH PLANS, INC.

333 Wyman St.
Waltham, MA 02454
Phone: 781-466-9400
Fax: 781-466-8583
Web: www.tufts-healthplan.com

CEO: Harris A. Berman
CFO: Richard Hallworth
HR: Sally Morrissey
Type: Not-for-profit

2001 Sales: $2,000.0 million
1-Yr. Sales Change: 0.0%
Employees: 2,500
FYE: December 31

Managed health care headaches in the New England states have made times tough for Tufts Associated Health Plans. The not-for-profit company provides management, administrative, and marketing services for its affiliates and subsidiaries, including Tufts Associated Health Maintenance Organization (TAHMO), Total Health Plan, and Tufts Benefit Administrators. Its provider network serves more than 900,000 members. Tufts Associated Health Plans offers HMO, health maintenance organization, PPO, point-of-service, and other health care plans to its customers.

KEY COMPETITORS
Blue Cross (MA)
ConnectiCare
Harvard Pilgrim

TURNER INDUSTRIES, LTD.

8687 United Plaza Blvd., Ste. 500
Baton Rouge, LA 70809
Phone: 225-922-5050
Fax: 225-922-5055
Web: www.turner-industries.com

CEO: Roland Toups
CFO: Lester J. Griffin Jr.
HR: Russell Gauthreaux
Type: Private

2002 Sales: $800.0 million
1-Yr. Sales Change: 1.3%
Employees: 12,000
FYE: October 31

Turner Industries turns out industrial services. Founded in 1961, the company is a top US player in industrial construction, contract maintenance, and outsourcing. Its customers include oil refiners, petrochemical companies, power generators, and pulp and paper mills. Through 16 subsidiaries, Turner Industries provides such services as equipment rental, environmental remediation, heavy hauling and rigging, pipe fabrication, and tank cleaning. Turner Industries also provides maintenance and materials management and training workshops and staffing services. Founder and chairman emeritus Bert Turner is principal shareholder of the company.

KEY COMPETITORS
Halliburton
Shaw Group
Zachry

TUTTLE-CLICK AUTOMOTIVE GROUP

14 Auto Center Dr.
Irvine, CA 92618
Phone: 949-598-4800
Fax: 949-830-0980
Web: www.tuttleclick.com

CEO: Robert H. "Bob" Tuttle
CFO: Chris Cotter
HR: Angie Mejia
Type: Private

2001 Sales: $687.3 million
1-Yr. Sales Change: (4.3%)
Employees: 1,350
FYE: December 31

Despite what you might think, Tuttle-Click Automotive Group does sell cars to Democrats. The firm operates about 10 new- and used-car dealerships throughout Orange County, California, and in Tucson, Arizona. The firm's dealerships sell Ford, DaimlerChrysler, Mitsubishi, Nissan, Hyundai, and Suzuki cars and trucks. It also operates Ford and Chrysler auto service centers. The company was founded by Holmes Tuttle, who sold Ronald Reagan a car in 1946 and ended up a prominent GOP fundraiser; he even persuaded Reagan to run for governor of California in 1966. Tuttle's son, co-CEO Robert Tuttle (a White House aide under Reagan), and Arizona-based co-CEO James Click own the company.

KEY COMPETITORS
AutoNation
David Wilson's
Sonic Automotive

📖 In-depth profiles of an additional 200
key private companies are found on pages 36–435.

UIS, INC.

15 Exchange Place, Ste. 1120	CEO: Andrew E. Pietrini	2001 Est. Sales: $1,000.0 mil.
Jersey City, NJ 07302	CFO: Joseph F. Arrigo	1-Yr. Sales Change: (8.0%)
Phone: 201-946-2600	HR: Andrew E. Pietrini	Employees: 8,900
Fax: 201-946-9325	Type: Private	FYE: December 31

As the maker of those little heart-shaped candies with tiny messages of love, UIS is probably better known for its somewhat tougher products, namely its car parts. UIS' subsidiaries include Champion Laboratories (oil and fuel filters), Neapco (transmission parts), Wells Manufacturing (ignition and electrical components), Pioneer (auto specialty supplier). Other operations include New England Confectionery (Sweethearts, Necco wafers, Clark Bar) and Hurd Millwork (window and patio doors). Founder Harry Lebensfeld started the company in 1945 with the purchase of an Indiana desk maker. UIS is owned by a trust for Lebensfeld's only child (who is married to EVP Richard Pasculano) and her children.

KEY COMPETITORS
Dana
Delphi
Federal-Mogul

UKROP'S SUPER MARKETS, INC.

600 Southlake Blvd.	CEO: Robert S. Ukrop	2001 Sales: $650.0 million
Richmond, VA 23236	CFO: David J. Naquin	1-Yr. Sales Change: 13.0%
Phone: 804-379-7300	HR: Jacquelin Ukrop	Employees: 5,500
Fax: 804-794-7557	Type: Private	FYE: July 31
Web: www.ukrops.com		

Central Virginia shoppers head to Ukrop's Super Markets for baked goods, prescriptions, to-go meals, even banking services. But they don't go for beer or wine, and they don't go on Sundays. Family-owned Ukrop's is Richmond's #1 supermarket chain, operating 27 Ukrop's Super Markets, a Central Bakery and Kitchen, and a distribution center. Ukrop's owns 51% of First Market Bank (branches in 19 Ukrop's stores and six free-standing locales); National Commerce Bancorporation owns the rest. Joe's Market, a new format featuring gourmet and specialty foods opened in mid-2001. Joe and Jacquelin Ukrop started the chain in 1937; their sons run it, adhering to Mom's wishes by not stocking alcohol and closing on Sundays.

KEY COMPETITORS
Delhaize America
Kroger
Winn-Dixie

ULLICO INC.

111 Massachusetts Ave. NW	CEO: Robert A. Georgine	2000 Sales: $885.7 million
Washington, DC 20001	CFO: John K. Grelle	1-Yr. Sales Change: 16.8%
Phone: 202-682-0900	HR: Richard A. Silas	Employees: —
Fax: 202-682-7932	Type: Private	FYE: December 31
Web: www.ullico.com		

This union is for life. Founded in 1925 by the American Federation of Labor to provide life insurance to union members, ULLICO has since grown into an insurance and financial services holding company. ULLICO serves organized employers, individual union members, and jointly managed trust funds through its subsidiaries, including The Union Labor Life Insurance Co. The organization offers an array of products, including group life and health, property and casualty insurance, third-party administration, and investment services. ULLICO has been rocked by allegations that directors profited from insider deals relating to the firm's stake in now-bankrupt Global Crossing.

KEY COMPETITORS
MetLife
Nationwide
Prudential

📖 **In-depth profiles of an additional 200 key private companies are found on pages 36–435.**

UNICCO SERVICE COMPANY

275 Grove St.
Newton, MA 02466
Phone: 617-527-5222
Fax: 617-969-2210
Web: www.unicco.com

CEO: Steven C. Kletjian
CFO: —
HR: Victor A. Munger
Type: Private

2001 Sales: $590.4 million
1-Yr. Sales Change: 6.4%
Employees: 20,500
FYE: June 30

UNICCO Service Company does the dirty work, including windows. The company provides an array of facilities management services to 1,000 industrial, commercial, education, government, and retail clients. Not limited to custodial duties, UNICCO's list of services also includes facilities and production maintenance, HVAC maintenance, landscaping, lighting services, trades, administrative/office services, and the aforementioned window cleaning. UNICCO's staff has even been known to plow snow and serve as switchboard operators. Herb Kletjian founded the company in 1949. The Kletjian family (including chairman and CEO Steven Kletjian and vice chairmen Richard and Robert Kletjian) continues to own and operate UNICCO.

KEY COMPETITORS

ABM Industries
ARAMARK
Encompass Services Corp.

UNIGROUP, INC.

One Premier Dr.
Fenton, MO 63026
Phone: 636-326-3100
Fax: 636-326-1106
Web: www.unigroupinc.com

CEO: Richard McClure
CFO: Jim Powers
HR: Sherry Fagin
Type: Private

2001 Sales: $1,896.0 million
1-Yr. Sales Change: (5.6%)
Employees: 1,400
FYE: December 31

Moving household goods has made many of UniGroup's companies household names. The moving service company transports household goods and other items in more than 100 countries through subsidiaries United Van Lines and Mayflower Transit. Its Trans Advantage unit sells and leases trucks and trailers and provides moving supplies, and its Vanliner Group offers property/casualty insurance to movers. Subsidiary UniGroup Worldwide offers relocation management and assistance. The company also provides corporate relocation services through Pinnacle Group Associates. Founded in 1987, UniGroup is owned by a 250-person group that includes senior management and agents of United Van Lines and Mayflower Transit.

KEY COMPETITORS

AMERCO
Atlas World
SIRVA

THE UNION CENTRAL LIFE INSURANCE COMPANY

1876 Waycross Rd.
Cincinnati, OH 45240
Phone: 513-595-2200
Fax: 513-595-5418
Web: www.unioncentral.com

CEO: John H. Jacobs
CFO: Stephen R. Hatcher
HR: Stephen K. Johnston
Type: Mutual company

2001 Sales: $1,241.4 million
1-Yr. Sales Change: 9.8%
Employees: —
FYE: December 31

Next stop for insurance, Union Central. Union Central Life Insurance Company is a mutual life insurance company that operates in all 50 states and the District of Columbia. The company offers a range of individual life and disability insurance, investment products, annuities, group retirement plans, and group insurance. Union Central also offers employee and executive benefit planning, estate planning, and retirement planning. Union Central's investments are mainly in bonds and collateralized mortgage obligations, of which mortgage investments accounted for about 20%. Union Central was founded in 1867.

KEY COMPETITORS

MetLife
New York Life
Prudential

 In-depth profiles of an additional 200 key private companies are found on pages 36–435.

UNITED SPACE ALLIANCE

600 Gemini St.
Houston, TX 77058
Phone: 281-212-6000
Fax: 281-212-6177
Web: www.unitedspacealliance.com

CEO: Russell D. Turner
CFO: Bill Caple
HR: —
Type: Joint venture

2001 Est. Sales: $1,100.0 mil.
1-Yr. Sales Change: (8.3%)
Employees: 10,000
FYE: December 31

USA! USA! United Space Alliance (USA) is a space-race heavyweight (each of the four Space Shuttles — *Columbia, Discovery, Atlantis,* and *Endeavour* — weighs 173,000 pounds). A joint venture between Lockheed Martin and Boeing, USA was established in 1996 to consolidate NASA's various Space Shuttle contracts under a single entity. As prime contractor, the company is involved in astronaut and flight controller training, flight software development, Shuttle payload integration, and vehicle processing, launch, and recovery operations. USA also provides training and operations planning for the International Space Station. Its main operations are at the Johnson Space Center (Texas) and Kennedy Space Center (Florida).

KEY COMPETITORS
Arianespace
EADS
Northrop Grumman

UNITED SUPERMARKETS, LTD.

7830 Orlando Ave.
Lubbock, TX 79423
Phone: 806-791-0220
Fax: 806-791-7491
Web: www.unitedtexas.com

CEO: Kent Moore
CFO: Keith Mann
HR: Phil Pirkle
Type: Private

2002 Est. Sales: $600.0 mil.
1-Yr. Sales Change: 4.3%
Employees: 5,000
FYE: January 31

From Muleshoe up to Dalhart and on over to Pampa, United Supermarkets keeps the Texas Panhandle well fed. The grocer has more than 40 supermarkets, mostly in rural towns. Its stores feature deli, floral, and bakery shops, as well as groceries, pharmacies, and gas at some locales. The company's larger format, Market Street, stocks more specialty foods. United Supermarkets runs its own distribution facility. H. D. Snell founded the firm in Sayre, Oklahoma, in 1916 as United Cash Store. He bucked the norms of the day — when grocers sold on credit — by selling for cash at lower prices. United Supermarkets is owned and run by the Snell family. (President Gantt Bumstead is the great-great-grandson of the founder.)

KEY COMPETITORS
Albertson's
Homeland Stores
Wal-Mart

THE UNIVERSITY OF ALABAMA SYSTEM

401 Queen City Ave.
Tuscaloosa, AL 35401
Phone: 205-348-5122
Fax: 205-348-5915
Web: www.ua.edu

CEO: Thomas C. Meredith Jr.
CFO: JoAnne G. Jackson
HR: Charlotte Harris
Type: School

2001 Sales: $1,847.5 million
1-Yr. Sales Change: 7.5%
Employees: 20,000
FYE: September 30

Students in the Heart of Dixie can choose among three campuses overseen by the University of Alabama System. The flagship Tuscaloosa campus offers 275 degree programs to its more than 14,000 students. The University of Alabama at Birmingham offers about 140 degree programs and has an enrollment of more than 10,000 students; it is also home to the university's school of medicine and a 900-bed hospital. The system's Huntsville campus has more than 7,000 students enrolled in its five colleges and graduate school. Each campus offers bachelor's, master's, and PhD degree programs. The University of Alabama was founded in Tuscaloosa in 1831 as the state's first public university.

📖 **In-depth profiles of an additional 200 key private companies are found on pages 36–435.**

UNIVERSITY OF FLORIDA

226 Tigert Hall
Gainesville, FL 32611
Phone: 352-392-3261
Fax: 352-392-6278
Web: www.ufl.edu

CEO: Charles E. Young
CFO: John E. Poppell
HR: Larry T. Ellis
Type: School

2001 Sales: $2,781.9 million
1-Yr. Sales Change: 130.2%
Employees: 23,500
FYE: June 30

UF students know it's great to be a Florida Gator. Founded in 1853, the University of Florida is the state's oldest and largest university. The school is a major land-grant research university located on 2,000 acres 115 miles north of Orlando. It has some 44,000 students, making it one of the nation's largest universities. Its 23 colleges and schools offer more than 100 undergraduate majors and nearly 200 graduate programs, including law, dentistry, pharmacy, medicine, and veterinary medicine. A founding member of the Southeastern Conference, the university fields athletic teams (the Florida Gators) that are typically nationally ranked.

THE UNIVERSITY OF IOWA

249 IMU
Iowa City, IA 52242
Phone: 319-335-3500
Fax: 319-335-0860
Web: www.uiowa.edu

CEO: Willard L. Boyd
CFO: Douglas K. True
HR: Susan Buckley
Type: School

2002 Sales: $1,721.4 million
1-Yr. Sales Change: 6.9%
Employees: 12,000
FYE: June 30

The University of Iowa Hawkeyes see clearly from their perch as Iowa's largest university. Founded in 1847, the university has nearly 30,000 students (about two-thirds of which are undergraduates) on its Iowa City campus. The university is home to 11 colleges spanning a variety of majors and disciplines, including distinguished programs in audiology, print making, creative writing, speech pathology, and nursing. Among the University of Iowa's distinguished alumni are Al Jarreau, John Irving, Flannery O'Connor, Gene Wilder, and Tennessee Williams.

THE UNIVERSITY OF MICHIGAN

3074 Fleming Administration Bldg.
Ann Arbor, MI 48109
Phone: 734-764-1817
Fax: 734-764-4546
Web: www.umich.edu

CEO: Mary Sue Coleman
CFO: Robert A. Kasdin
HR: Barbara S. Butterfield
Type: School

2002 Sales: $2,943.8 million
1-Yr. Sales Change: 9.2%
Employees: —
FYE: June 30

Michigan — it's shaped like a mitten, and higher education fits the state like a glove. The University of Michigan has been a leader in the state's education effort since its founding in 1817. With about 53,000 students and more than 5,000 faculty members scattered across three campuses (Ann Arbor, with about 38,000 students; Dearborn; and Flint), the university's diverse academic units span such areas of study as architecture, dentistry, education, law, medicine, music, and social work. Notable alumni include Gerald Ford (the university is home to the Gerald R. Ford Library and the Ford School of Public Policy) and playwright Arthur Miller.

In-depth profiles of an additional 200 key private companies are found on pages 36–435.

UNIVERSITY OF MINNESOTA

234 Morrill Hall, 100 Church St. SE
Minneapolis, MN 55455
Phone: 612-625-5000
Fax: 612-626-1693
Web: www.umn.edu

CEO: Robert Bruininks
CFO: Richard H. Pfutzenreuter
HR: Carol Carrier
Type: School

2001 Sales: $2,301.1 million
1-Yr. Sales Change: (28.6%)
Employees: 30,823
FYE: June 30

The University of Minnesota — this place is a zoo! Gophers scurry about the university's Minneapolis-St. Paul campus, Bulldogs roam its campus in Duluth, Cougars prowl its Morris campus, and Golden Eagles soar across its campus in Crookston. Feeble mascot jokes aside, the land grant institution has been educating students since 1869. Its more than 60,000 students can choose from 370 academic fields ranging from education to engineering to public health. Sources such as *US News & World Report* often list the University of Minnesota as one of the top 20 public schools in the country.

UNIVERSITY OF MISSOURI SYSTEM

321 University Hall
Columbia, MO 65211
Phone: 573-882-2121
Fax: 573-882-2721
Web: www.system.missouri.edu

CEO: Manuel T. Pacheco
CFO: Natalie R. Krawitz
HR: R. Kenneth Hutchinson
Type: School

2002 Sales: $1,720.1 million
1-Yr. Sales Change: 19.0%
Employees: 26,316
FYE: June 30

"Show-Me" the education! The University of Missouri, founded in 1839 (it was the first publicly supported institution of higher education created in the Louisiana Territory), educates more than 56,500 students at four campuses and through a statewide extension program; some 24% of the students are in graduate or professional programs. Nicknamed "Mizzou," the university's cadre of campuses includes flagship UM-Columbia (home to some 23,700 students, 20 schools and colleges, and the University of Missouri Health Sciences Center), UM-Kansas City, UM-Rolla, and UM-St. Louis. Offering fields of study ranging from journalism to law to fine arts, the university has a nearly 9,800-member faculty and research staff.

THE UNIVERSITY OF NEBRASKA

3835 Holdrege St.
Lincoln, NE 68583
Phone: 402-472-2111
Fax: 402-472-1237
Web: www.uneb.edu

CEO: L. Dennis Smith
CFO: David E. Lechner
HR: Ed Wimes
Type: School

2001 Sales: $1,156.5 million
1-Yr. Sales Change: 8.0%
Employees: —
FYE: June 30

The University of Nebraska has sprouted four campuses out in the fields of the Cornhusker State. Founded in 1869, the state university system offers bachelor's, master's, and doctoral degrees in such programs as agriculture, business, education, and engineering at its campuses in Kearney, Lincoln, and Omaha. The university's Medical Center in Omaha trains doctors, performs research, and is affiliated with a 700-bed teaching hospital. The University of Nebraska also operates research and extension services across the state. Nearly 47,000 students attend classes in the university system, which is recovering from a severe 1997 enrollment drop caused by tighter admissions standards.

📖 In-depth profiles of an additional 200
   key private companies are found on pages 36–435.

THE UNIVERSITY OF NORTH CAROLINA AT CHAPEL HILL

103 South Bldg.	CEO: James C. Moeser	2001 Sales: $1,456.7 million
Chapel Hill, NC 27599	CFO: Nancy Suttenfield	1-Yr. Sales Change: —
Phone: 919-962-2211	HR: Laurie T. Charest	Employees: 10,111
Fax: 919-962-1647	Type: School	FYE: June 30
Web: www.unc.edu		

George Washington could have given a commencement address at The University of North Carolina (UNC) at Chapel Hill. Chartered in 1789 as the first state university in the nation, UNC-Chapel Hill has some 24,000 students (including about 7,700 graduate students) at 17 schools and colleges. The highly respected university provides academic programs in areas such as medicine, law, psychology, art, and journalism. It also has study abroad, honors, and ROTC programs, as well as 28 varsity sports teams. About 95% of the some 2,400 faculty members hold PhDs or top degrees in their field. Notable alumni include writer Thomas Wolfe, basketball star Michael Jordan, and former President James Polk.

THE UNIVERSITY OF PENNSYLVANIA

3451 Walnut St.	CEO: Judith Rodin	2001 Sales: $3,190.7 million
Philadelphia, PA 19104	CFO: Craig Carnaroli	1-Yr. Sales Change: 6.1%
Phone: 215-898-5000	HR: John J. Heuer	Employees: 12,290
Fax: 215-898-9659	Type: School	FYE: June 30
Web: www.upenn.edu		

When he wasn't founding our country or experimenting with lightning, Benjamin Franklin established the University of Pennsylvania, the first university in the US. Since opening its doors to students in 1751, the Ivy League university has accumulated a notable list of accomplishments, including the creation of the first medical school in the US and the invention of the ENIAC computer. The university's more than 22,300 students pursue their studies in four undergraduate schools and a dozen graduate and professional schools, including the renowned Wharton School and the Annenburg School for Communications. University president Judith Rodin became the first female to head an Ivy League university in 1994.

UNIVERSITY OF PITTSBURGH OF THE COMMONWEALTH SYSTEM OF HIGHER EDUCATION

4200 5th Ave.	CEO: Mark A. Nordenberg	2001 Sales: $1,096.5 million
Pittsburgh, PA 15260	CFO: Arthur Ramicone	1-Yr. Sales Change: 6.1%
Phone: 412-624-4141	HR: Ronald W. Frisch	Employees: 10,000
Fax: 412-624-7282	Type: School	FYE: June 30
Web: www.pitt.edu		

Now this is a school that really needs a nickname. The University of Pittsburgh of the Commonwealth System of Higher Education (whew! — Pitt for short) has some 32,000 students spread across its five campuses. Its flagship Pittsburgh campus has more than 23,000 students. The Pitt Panthers pursue their studies in 18 schools and colleges, including arts and sciences, engineering, and business. Pitt also is affiliated with the UPMC Health System, which operates a network of hospitals and an insurance company, manages physicians' offices, and offers long-term care and in-home services. The university was founded in 1787 and has an endowment exceeding $1 billion.

📖 In-depth profiles of an additional 200
key private companies are found on pages 36–435.

UNIVERSITY OF ROCHESTER

Administration Bldg.	CEO: Thomas H. Jackson	2002 Sales: —
Rochester, NY 14627	CFO: Ronald J. Paprocki	1-Yr. Sales Change: —
Phone: 585-275-2121	HR: —	Employees: 11,200
Fax: 585-275-0359	Type: School	FYE: June 30
Web: www.rochester.edu		

The buzz about the University of Rochester is music to some ears. The private, upstate New York institution is nationally recognized for its programs in medicine, engineering, and business, and its Eastman School of Music (founded by Eastman Kodak creator George Eastman) is one of the top music schools in the US. The university, which has an endowment of more than $1.1 billion, offers about 175 bachelor's, master's, and doctoral degrees to its more than 8,200 full- and part-time students. Undergraduate tuition runs more than $25,000. Founded as a Baptist-sponsored institution in 1850, the university is nonsectarian today.

THE UNIVERSITY OF SOUTHERN CALIFORNIA

University Park	CEO: Steven B. Sample	2002 Sales: $1,480.4 million
Los Angeles, CA 90089	CFO: Dennis F. Dougherty	1-Yr. Sales Change: 5.8%
Phone: 213-740-2311	HR: —	Employees: 17,000
Fax: 213-740-5229	Type: School	FYE: June 30
Web: www.usc.edu		

This Trojan horse, filled with more than 28,000 students, is more than welcome at the University of Southern California (USC). Founded in 1880, the private university (home of the Trojans) grew up with the city of Los Angeles. It offers 77 undergraduate majors and 139 postgraduate degrees. Recognized for distinguished programs in business, engineering, film, law, medicine, public administration, and science, USC boasts two Los Angeles campuses and a string of research centers and health care facilities. The university also supports medical staffs at five Los Angeles hospitals. USC is the largest private employer in Los Angeles.

UNIVERSITY OF WASHINGTON

301 Gerberding Hall, Ste. 400	CEO: Richard L. McCormick	2001 Sales: $2,646.8 million
Seattle, WA 98195	CFO: V'Ella Warren	1-Yr. Sales Change: (1.8%)
Phone: 206-543-2560	HR: Elizabeth Coveney	Employees: 23,462
Fax: 206-543-5651	Type: School	FYE: June 30
Web: www.washington.edu		

The University of Washington (UW) is Husky indeed, with more than 37,400 students enrolled at its main Seattle campus. Founded in 1861 as the Territorial University of Washington, UW (pronounced "U-dub" by those on campus) also has smaller branches in Tacoma and Bothell. The university maintains 17 schools and colleges for both undergraduate and graduate students (more than 70% of students on the main campus are undergrads). It also operates a health sciences center and an academic medical center, which includes the University of Washington Medical Center and Harborview Medical Center.

In-depth profiles of an additional 200 key private companies are found on pages 36–435.

UNIVERSITY SYSTEM OF MARYLAND

3300 Metzerott Rd.	CEO: William E. Kirwan	2001 Sales: $2,564.9 million
Adelphi, MD 20783	CFO: Joseph F. Vivona	1-Yr. Sales Change: 11.9%
Phone: 301-445-2740	HR: James Sansbury	Employees: 30,901
Fax: 301-445-2761	Type: School	FYE: June 30
Web: www.usmh.usmd.edu		

Maryland's nickname, "The Free State," doesn't apply to its system of higher education. The University System of Maryland (USM) has 11 public campuses and two research institutes that serve nearly 130,000 undergraduate and graduate students. The university system, formed in 1988, combined the former University of Maryland (dating to 1807 and including five campuses) with six other institutions. USM offers more than 600 academic programs, including bachelor's, master's, doctoral, and professional degrees. Its flagship campus at College Park was founded in 1856 and became a public land-grant university in 1865.

U.S. CAN CORPORATION

700 E. Butterfield Rd., Ste. 250	CEO: Paul W. Jones	2001 Sales: $772.2 million
Lombard, IL 60148	CFO: John L. Workman	1-Yr. Sales Change: (4.6%)
Phone: 630-678-8000	HR: Roger B. Farley	Employees: 2,600
Fax: 630-678-8131	Type: Private	FYE: December 31
Web: www.uscanco.com		

U.S. Can doesn't want to stop the flow of new products into the marketplace — it only hopes to contain them. The company makes steel and plastic non-beverage containers in the US and Europe that hold everything from food to paint. Its aerosol containers, which account for the largest portion of sales, are used to package household, automotive, paint, hygiene, and industrial products. Besides standard containers the company offers custom and specialty products such as decorative tins, stampings, and collectible items like metal signs, as well as containers used to store chemicals. Private investment firm Berkshire Partners owns 77% of U.S. Can.

KEY COMPETITORS
Ball Corporation
Crown Cork & Seal
Silgan

U.S. CENTRAL CREDIT UNION

7300 College Blvd., Ste. 600	CEO: Dan Kampen	2001 Sales: $1,279.3 million
Overland Park, KS 66210	CFO: Kathryn Brick	1-Yr. Sales Change: (11.8%)
Phone: 913-661-3800	HR: Linda Pfingsten	Employees: —
Fax: 913-345-2628	Type: Cooperative	FYE: December 31
Web: www.uscentral.org		

Credit unions stand united in U.S. Central Credit Union, a cooperative "central bank" for a network of nearly 35 corporate (or regional) credit unions. These, in turn, represent more than 10,000 consumer credit unions nationwide. The cooperative performs a variety of liquidity and cash management functions, such as funds transfer, settlement services, risk management, and custody services. Subsidiary U.S. Central Capital Markets provides investment advisory services to the corporate credit unions, while majority-owned Corporate Network eCom offers bill payment and technology services to the network and its members.

KEY COMPETITORS
Concord EFS
EDS
Jack Henry

📖 In-depth profiles of an additional 200
key private companies are found on pages 36–435.

U.S. OIL CO., INC.

425 S. Washington St.	CEO: Thomas A. Schmidt	2002 Sales: $753.0 million
Combined Locks, WI 54113	CFO: Paul Bachman	1-Yr. Sales Change: (1.6%)
Phone: 920-739-6101	HR: Diane Hertel	Employees: 730
Fax: 920-788-0531	Type: Private	FYE: July 31
Web: www.usoil.com		

U.S. Oil Co. supplies refined oil products to US residents in the Midwest, and does a lot more. In addition to the wholesale distribution of oil products (its largest revenue generator), the company operates gas stations, and installs gas pumps, tanks, and other petroleum-related equipment. It also provides plumbing and heating services, operates a laboratory for environmental analysis, and collects used waste oil to be processed into burner fuel. Founded in the 1950s as Schmidt Oil by the sons of local fuel distributor Albert Schmidt, U.S. Oil Co. is still controlled by the Schmidt family.

KEY COMPETITORS
Motiva Enterprises
Premcor
Sunoco

UTILITY TRAILER MANUFACTURING CO.

17295 E. Railroad St.	CEO: Paul Bennett	2001 Est. Sales: $700.0 mil.
City of Industry, CA 91748	CFO: Arthur Goolsbee	1-Yr. Sales Change: 2.9%
Phone: 626-965-1541	HR: John Stanton	Employees: 3,400
Fax: 626-965-2790	Type: Private	FYE: December 31
Web: www.utilitytrailer.com		

Utility Trailer Manufacturing is spreading reefer madness. Utility Trailer is one of the US's largest manufacturers of refrigerated trailers, or reefers, as they are known in the business. The company also produces dry freight trailers, flatbeds, and curtain-sided trailers at five plants in the US. Its refrigerated trucks include special designs for the whole food distribution and fast-food markets, such as a truck with separate chambers for frozen and dry goods. The company's trailers are distributed throughout Canada, Mexico, the US, and to a lesser extent in Argentina. Two brothers founded the company in 1914 and their descendants still own it.

KEY COMPETITORS
Great Dane
Lufkin Industries
Wabash National

VANDERBILT UNIVERSITY

2201 West End Ave.	CEO: E. Gordon Gee	2002 Sales: $1,590.4 million
Nashville, TN 37235	CFO: Lauren J. Brisky	1-Yr. Sales Change: 12.1%
Phone: 615-322-7311	HR: Jerry Fife	Employees: 16,679
Fax: —	Type: School	FYE: June 30
Web: www.vanderbilt.edu		

The house that Cornelius built, private Vanderbilt University was founded in 1873 with a $1 million grant from industrialist Cornelius Vanderbilt. The university's endowment has grown to about $2 billion, and the campus today is a haven for nearly 10,500 students and 1,900 full-time faculty. Vanderbilt has 10 schools and colleges; its Owen Graduate School of Management and its medical school rank near the top of national surveys. A major research university, Vanderbilt receives millions a year in sponsored awards to fund its facilities. Vanderbilt offers graduate and professional degrees, as well as undergraduate programs in areas such as education and human development, engineering, and the arts and sciences.

In-depth profiles of an additional 200 key private companies are found on pages 36–435.

THE VANGUARD GROUP, INC.

100 Vanguard Blvd.
Malvern, PA 19355
Phone: 610-648-6000
Fax: 610-669-6605
Web: www.vanguard.com

CEO: John J. Brennan
CFO: Ralph K. Packard
HR: Kathleen C. Gubanich
Type: Private

2001 Est. Sales: $1,700.0 mil.
1-Yr. Sales Change: 6.3%
Employees: 11,000
FYE: December 31

If you buy low and sell high, invest for the long term, don't panic, and generally disapprove of those whippersnappers at Fidelity, then you may end up in the Vanguard of the financial market. The Vanguard Group offers individual and institutional investors a line of highly sought-after mutual funds and brokerage services; it is the #2 fund manager after FMR (aka Fidelity), but is closing the gap, claiming more than $590 billion of assets under management. Vanguard's fund options include more than 140 stock, bond, mixed, and international offerings, as well as variable annuity portfolios; its Vanguard 500 Index Fund now vies with the longtime king, Fidelity's Magellan, as the largest US fund.

KEY COMPETITORS
AMVESCAP
FMR
Putnam Investments

VANGUARD HEALTH SYSTEMS, INC.

20 Burton Hills Blvd., Ste. 100
Nashville, TN 37215
Phone: 615-665-6000
Fax: 615-665-6099
Web: www.vanguardhealth.com

CEO: Charles N. Martin Jr.
CFO: Joseph D. Moore
HR: James Johnston
Type: Private

2002 Sales: $910.6 million
1-Yr. Sales Change: 36.4%
Employees: 8,000
FYE: June 30

Hospitals shouldn't let their guard down with Vanguard Health Systems hanging around the block. The company buys up acute care hospitals and other health care facilities primarily in urban areas. Vanguard acquires hospitals with capital provided by company management as well as various funds controlled by Morgan Stanley Capital Partners. Vanguard seeks to partner with, develop, or convert non-profit hospital systems to investor-owned entities as independent hospitals seek to capitalize on the benefits of becoming part of a larger hospital company. Vanguard also operates a prepaid Medicaid managed health plan called Phoenix Health Plan, serving more than 55,000 members in Arizona.

KEY COMPETITORS
HCA
Rush System for Health
Tenet Healthcare

VARIETY WHOLESALERS, INC.

3401 Gresham Lake Rd.
Raleigh, NC 27615
Phone: 919-876-6000
Fax: 919-790-9526

CEO: John W. Pope Sr.
CFO: Art Pope
HR: Frances Burger
Type: Private

2001 Est. Sales: $800.0 mil.
1-Yr. Sales Change: 15.8%
Employees: 8,300
FYE: December 31

Variety is not only the spice of life — it's also a major purveyor of discount retail goods. With about 500 stores in 14 states from Louisiana to Delaware, Variety Wholesalers has survived even Wal-Mart's march through rural America. The company, which has aggressively bought other chains while closing poorly performing stores, tends to set up shop in small towns where the retail giants fear to tread. The company's retail outlets include Bargain Town, Maxway, Rose's, Super 10 (which prices all items at or below $10), Super Dollar, Super Saver, and Value-Mart. Variety Wholesalers was founded in 1932 by James Pope; the Pope family, including chairman and CEO John Pope, owns and leads the company.

KEY COMPETITORS
Dollar General
Family Dollar Stores
Fred's

📖 In-depth profiles of an additional 200
key private companies are found on pages 36–435.

VARTEC TELECOM, INC.

1600 Viceroy Dr.	CEO: A. Joe Mitchell Jr.	2001 Sales: $1,040.0 million
Dallas, TX 75235	CFO: Gary Egger	1-Yr. Sales Change: 4.5%
Phone: 214-424-1000	HR: —	Employees: 1,793
Fax: 214-424-1555	Type: Private	FYE: December 31
Web: www.vartec.com		

Actors and comedians employed promoting 10-10 calling plans can thank VarTec Telecom, a pioneering provider of "dial-around" long-distance service. VarTec provides residential and business calling plans, as well as Internet access and 800-number service. The company was founded in 1989 by president Joe Mitchell and his wife, chief administrative officer Connie Mitchell, along with Ray Atkinson, president of international operations. Holding company Telephone Electronics Corp. owns a majority stake in VarTec, which acquired Dallas-based long-distance retailer Excel Communications in 2002. VarTec has dropped plans to merge with business telecom services reseller Lightyear Communications.

KEY COMPETITORS
AT&T
Sprint FON
WorldCom

VENTURE INDUSTRIES

33662 James J. Pompo Dr.	CEO: Larry J. Winget Sr.	2001 Sales: $1,860.0 million
Fraser, MI 48026	CFO: Michael D. Alexander	1-Yr. Sales Change: (22.5%)
Phone: 586-294-1500	HR: Debra Wangurd	Employees: 18,000
Fax: 586-296-8863	Type: Private	FYE: December 31
Web: www.ventureindustries.com		

When it comes to plastic automotive components, Venture Industries is ready for uncharted territory. The company is a leading maker of injection-molded plastic components for automotive OEMs. Products include interior systems, cockpit modules, front-end systems, exterior trim, and closures and panels. Venture Industries also offers design, preproduction, engineering, assembly, tooling, and logistics services to most of the world's automakers. Customers include GM, Ford, DaimlerChrysler, BMW, and Volkswagen. The company offers engineering and technology services in Asia, Australia, Europe, and North America and continues to expand into new regions. CEO Larry Winget owns Venture Industries.

KEY COMPETITORS
Johnson Controls
Lear
Visteon

VERIZON WIRELESS INC.

180 Washington Valley Rd.	CEO: Dennis F. Strigl	2001 Sales: $17,393.0 million
Bedminster, NJ 07921	CFO: Andrew Halford	1-Yr. Sales Change: 22.2%
Phone: 908-306-7000	HR: Marc C. Reed	Employees: 40,000
Fax: 908-306-6927	Type: Joint venture	FYE: December 31
Web: www.verizonwireless.com		

Ahead on the horizon, Verizon Wireless is the #1 US mobile phone operator, serving 31.5 million customers nationwide. It is developing third-generation wireless services based on CDMA (code division multiple access) technology. Verizon Wireless began operations in 2000 when Bell Atlantic and Vodafone combined their US wireless assets, including their PrimeCo partnership. Verizon Wireless gained GTE's US wireless operations when Bell Atlantic bought GTE to form Verizon Communications, which owns 55% of the company; Vodafone owns 45%. Plans for an IPO, postponed in 2001, have been revived, but no timetable has been mentioned. The company has teamed up with Microsoft to develop and market wireless data services.

KEY COMPETITORS
AT&T Wireless
Cingular Wireless
Sprint PCS

In-depth profiles of an additional 200 key private companies are found on pages 36–435.

VERTIS INC.

250 W. Pratt St.
Baltimore, MD 21201
Phone: 410-528-9800
Fax: 410-528-9287
Web: www.vertisinc.com

CEO: Donald E. Roland
CFO: Dean D. Durbin
HR: Catherine S. Leggett
Type: Private

2001 Est. Sales: $1,900.0 mil.
1-Yr. Sales Change: (5.0%)
Employees: 10,000
FYE: December 31

Although it has changed its name, Vertis still hopes its advertising business will blossom. The company (formerly Big Flower Holdings) provides integrated marketing and advertising services to more than 3,000 clients. In 2002 the company unified its three operating units under the Vertis name. The company's services include advertising production, direct marketing, digital production, and media planning. Vertis operates the largest digital photography network dedicated to the ad industry and produces newspaper inserts such as color comics, TV magazines, and supplements. An investor group led by Thomas H. Lee Company and Evercore Partners owns Vertis.

KEY COMPETITORS
ACG Holdings
Harte-Hanks
Valassis

VIEWSONIC CORPORATION

381 Brea Canyon Rd.
Walnut, CA 91789
Phone: 909-444-8888
Fax: 909-869-7958
Web: www.viewsonic.com

CEO: James Chu
CFO: James Morlan
HR: Joanne Thielen
Type: Private

2001 Sales: $1,000.0 million
1-Yr. Sales Change: (27.1%)
Employees: 600
FYE: December 31

ViewSonic has a display for every occasion. The company makes CRT, LCD, and plasma computer displays, including the Professional Series for high-end computer-aided design, desktop publishing, and graphic design; the Graphics and E2 lines for homes and small offices; and the A Series for replacing monitors included in bundled systems. ViewSonic also makes LCD projectors, handheld computers, tablet PCs, and devices for connecting TVs to CRT or LCD displays. CEO James Chu, who founded ViewSonic in 1987, is the company's majority owner. ViewSonic has also received financing from the venture capital arm of chip giant Intel, which has partnered with the company to develop inexpensive chipsets for high-definition TV.

KEY COMPETITORS
NEC
Samsung Electronics
Sony

VIRGINIA LOTTERY

900 E. Main St.
Richmond, VA 23219
Phone: 804-692-7000
Fax: 804-692-7102
Web: www.valottery.com

CEO: Penelope W. Kyle
CFO: Donna Van Cleave
HR: —
Type: Government-owned

2001 Sales: $1,002.8 million
1-Yr. Sales Change: 3.1%
Employees: 300
FYE: June 30

For some Virginians taking a chance at the corner store involves more than choosing the least overcooked hot dog. The Virginia State Lottery operates several instant-win scratch-off games, as well as popular number games (Pick 3, Pick 4, and a six-number Lotto game). More than half of the money raised from ticket sales is paid out in prizes; about 35% goes to the state's general fund earmarked for public education. Unclaimed prize money, about $7 million a year, is used specifically to build or renovate schools. Virginia also participates in the seven-state Big Game lottery. Created in 1987, the Virginia State Lottery has collected more than $4 billion for the state.

KEY COMPETITORS
Kentucky Lottery
Maryland State Lottery
Multi-State Lottery

In-depth profiles of an additional 200 key private companies are found on pages 36–435.

VISION SERVICE PLAN

3333 Quality Dr.
Rancho Cordova, CA 95670
Phone: 916-851-5000
Fax: 916-851-4858
Web: www.vsp.com

CEO: Roger Valine
CFO: Patricia Cochran
HR: Walter Grubbs
Type: Private

2001 Sales: $1,770.0 million
1-Yr. Sales Change: 18.0%
Employees: 2,300
FYE: December 31

Thanks to Vision Service Plan (VSP), you can see clearly now. One of the top eye care benefits providers in the US (with 35 million members, more than one in 10 people in the US use the company's services), VSP offers vision coverage ranging from general plans to laser vision correction procedures. The company's Sight for Students program provides uninsured children with vision exams and glasses. Subsidiary Altair Eyewear sells private label frames to VSP doctors. VSP has also set up Eyefinity, providing claims submission services, Web site development, and an optical products marketplace for the eye care industry.

KEY COMPETITORS

Aetna
Blue Cross
UnitedHealth Group

VITALITY BEVERAGES, INC.

400 N. Tampa St., 17th Fl.
Tampa, FL 33602
Phone: 813-301-4600
Fax: 813-301-4670

CEO: Gregory Murray
CFO: Gary Viljoen
HR: —
Type: Private

2001 Sales: $700.0 million
1-Yr. Sales Change: 0.0%
Employees: 1,800
FYE: December 31

Aren't you glad you bought that cheaper, private-label can of orange juice? Vitality Beverages might be. The #1 US seller of private-label juices to grocery store chains, Vitality also packages and sells fruit juice to institutional users and markets juice under the Ocean Spray label. Vitality was formed when Caxton-Iseman Capital and Engles, Urso, Follmer Capital bought the juice operations of Lykes Bros. in 1999. The company then began a spate of acquisitions that included Canada's Pride Beverages, McCain Foods, and distributor Peerless Foods, among others. Vitality Beverages is exiting the juice processing business and shedding noncore operations, including trucking firm Pasco Transport.

KEY COMPETITORS

Minute Maid
SYSCO
Tropicana Products

VOUGHT AIRCRAFT INDUSTRIES, INC.

9314 W. Jefferson Blvd.
Dallas, TX 75211
Phone: 972-946-2011
Fax: 972-946-3465
Web: www.voughtaircraft.com

CEO: Tom Risley
CFO: William J. McMillan
HR: Judith W. Northup
Type: Private

2001 Est. Sales: $1,000.0 mil.
1-Yr. Sales Change: 0.0%
Employees: 5,000
FYE: December 31

The skies are fraught with Vought. Vought Aircraft Industries is one of the world's largest aerostructures subcontractors. The company makes fuselage subassemblies (doors and fuselage panels), nacelles, thrust reversers, empennage structures, wings, and other components for military and commercial aircraft. It makes parts for almost all of Boeing's commercial fleet (ranging from the 737 to the 777), Dassault Aviation, GE, Gulfstream, Lockheed Martin, NASA, and Raytheon. Vought also does subcontract work for military cargo planes (C-17), bombers (B-2), and fighters (F-14 and F/A-18). The Carlyle Group owns about 90% of Vought, which also provides spare parts, maintenance, repair, and overhaul services.

KEY COMPETITORS

CPI Aerostructures
Goodrich
LMI Aerospace

📖 **In-depth profiles of an additional 200 key private companies are found on pages 36–435.**

VT INC.

8500 Shawnee Mission Pkwy., Ste. 200
Shawnee Mission, KS 66202
Phone: 913-895-0200
Fax: 913-789-1039
Web: www.vanenterprises.com

CEO: Cecil Van Tuyl
CFO: Robert J. Holcomb
HR: John A. Morford
Type: Private

2001 Sales: $5,298.8 million
1-Yr. Sales Change: 23.2%
Employees: 7,000
FYE: December 31

VT is in pursuit of the pole-position as one of the top three US car dealers. The company operates about 50 dealerships in 10 states, primarily Texas and Missouri; it sells more than 120,000 new cars per year. It offers nearly 60 brands of new and used cars (and RVs) made by General Motors, Ford, Honda, Isuzu, and Nissan, among others. VT also engages in fleet sales and receives a significant portion of its revenue from back-shop operations such as parts and service and body shop sales. Founder and co-CEO Cecil Van Tuyl began his automotive empire in 1955. He owns the company with son and co-CEO Larry Van Tuyl.

KEY COMPETITORS
AutoNation
Hendrick Automotive
Jordan Automotive

WAFFLE HOUSE INC.

5986 Financial Dr.
Norcross, GA 30071
Phone: 770-729-5700
Fax: 770-729-5999
Web: www.wafflehouse.com

CEO: Joe W. Rogers Jr.
CFO: T.J. Turner
HR: Ann Parker
Type: Private

2001 Est. Sales: $625.0 mil.
1-Yr. Sales Change: 7.8%
Employees: 6,000
FYE: June 30

The pancake's crunchier cousin gets top billing at the Waffle House. The company owns or franchises nearly 1,400 restaurants in 25 states, but the Southeast accounts for most locations. If you need your waffle fix at 3 a.m., Waffle House is open 24 hours a day. The first roadside restaurant opened on Labor Day, 1955, and the menu has changed little since. In addition to their namesake golden grids, the stores offer traditional coffee shop fare with a southern twang, including cheeseburgers, T-bone steaks, sandwiches, grits, omelets, and hash browns. The company has shied away from the media since a 1983 lawsuit alleged it was paying excessively low wages.

KEY COMPETITORS
Denny's
IHOP
Shoney's

WALBRIDGE ALDINGER COMPANY

613 Abbott St.
Detroit, MI 48226
Phone: 313-963-8000
Fax: 313-963-8150
Web: www.walbridge.com

CEO: John Rakolta Jr.
CFO: Vince D'Angelis
HR: Terry Merritt
Type: Private

2000 Sales: $750.0 million
1-Yr. Sales Change: (3.2%)
Employees: 1,000
FYE: December 31

The Motor City has been home to Motown Records, Madonna, and . . . Walbridge Aldinger? Builder Walbridge Aldinger handles design, engineering, and construction management. Much of its business is tied to Michigan's automotive industry, but the company serves all market segments, including commercial, correctional, education, health care, public works, research and development, and retail. Units include rigging and equipment installer Belding Walbridge and engineering and construction firms. The company has expanded with the 2002 acquisition of Canadian electrical and mechanical giant State Group (now Walbridge State). In 1975 the father of CEO John Rakolta bought Walbridge Aldinger, which was founded in 1916.

KEY COMPETITORS
Alberici
Barton Malow
Turner Corporation

📖 **In-depth profiles of an additional 200 key private companies are found on pages 36–435.**

THE WALSH GROUP

929 W. Adams St.
Chicago, IL 60607
Phone: 312-563-5400
Fax: 312-563-5466
Web: www.walshgroup.com

CEO: Matthew M. Walsh
CFO: Larry Kibbon
HR: Rhonda Hardwick
Type: Private

2001 Sales: $1,450.0 million
1-Yr. Sales Change: 11.2%
Employees: 3,000
FYE: December 31

The Walsh Group erects walls, halls, malls, and more. Walsh provides design/build and construction services for industrial, public, and commercial projects throughout the US. Its projects range from prisons to skyscrapers to shopping malls. The group consists of Walsh Construction of Chicago and Archer Western Contractors of Fort Lauderdale, Florida. Operating from 14 regional offices, Walsh provides complete project management services, from planning and demolition to general contracting and finance. It is a major player in bridge and highway construction and also renovates and restores buildings and provides interior construction and design services. The Walsh family still owns the firm, founded in 1898.

KEY COMPETITORS
Bechtel
Granite Construction
Peter Kiewit Sons'

WARREN EQUITIES, INC.

27 Warren Way
Providence, RI 02905
Phone: 401-781-9900
Fax: 401-461-7160
Web: www.warreneq.com

CEO: Herbert Kaplan
CFO: John Dziedzic
HR: Thomas Palumbo
Type: Private

2002 Sales: $1,000.0 million
1-Yr. Sales Change: 1.6%
Employees: 2,200
FYE: May 31

Warren Equities fills car tanks and stomachs in the US Northeast. The holding company sells fuel and groceries from over 400 service stations and convenience stores from Maine to Virginia operating under the Xtra Mart brand. Warren's distribution companies supply those stores, as well as independent outlets, with gasoline, grocery, and tobacco products. Other Warren companies trade and store petroleum, provide environmental testing services, and make promotional signs and clothing. Chairman and owner Warren Alpert founded the company in 1950 after Standard Oil awarded him a distributorship. His foundation gives annual grants to medical researchers; he has donated more than $20 million to Harvard Medical School.

KEY COMPETITORS
7-Eleven
Getty Petroleum Marketing
Wawa

THE WASHINGTON COMPANIES

101 International Way
Missoula, MT 59807
Phone: 406-523-1300
Fax: 406-523-1398
Web: www.washcorp.com

CEO: Michael Haight
CFO: Earl McCall
HR: Jon Barlow
Type: Private

2000 Sales: $734.0 million
1-Yr. Sales Change: (2.1%)
Employees: 4,147
FYE: December 31

Crossing the Delaware was the feat of one Washington, but traversing several industries is Washington Companies' accomplishment. It owns construction, mining, and transportation companies (including marine and rail operations) around the globe. The biggest construction interest is engineering and construction giant Washington Group International, formerly known as Morrison Knudson; its past projects have included the Hoover Dam and the San Francisco Bay Bridge. The group's Montana Resources mines and mills copper and other minerals. Washington Corporation supplies administrative services to other Washington companies. Founder Dennis Washington owns a significant portion of the group.

KEY COMPETITORS
Bechtel
Fluor
Turner Corporation

In-depth profiles of an additional 200 key private companies are found on pages 36–435.

WASHINGTON UNIVERSITY IN ST. LOUIS

1 Brookings Dr.	CEO: Mark Stephen Wrighton	2002 Sales: $1,342.0 million
St. Louis, MO 63130	CFO: Barbara Feiner	1-Yr. Sales Change: 5.0%
Phone: 314-935-5000	HR: —	Employees: 8,000
Fax: 314-935-7088	Type: School	FYE: June 30
Web: www.wustl.edu		

Washington University in St. Louis is the gateway to higher education for more than 12,000 students. Founded in 1853, the private university is renowned for its academic programs in business, law, medical research, occupational therapy, physical therapy, and social work. Students can also explore fields of study such as architecture, art, and engineering. Faculty members include a US poet laureate, a Nobel prize winner, and five recipients of the National Medal of Science. A leader in research, the university receives substantial research funding from the National Science Foundation and the National Institutes of Health.

WATKINS ASSOCIATED INDUSTRIES

1958 Monroe Dr. NE	CEO: John Watkins	2000 Sales: $1,076.0 million
Atlanta, GA 30324	CFO: Richard Wuori	1-Yr. Sales Change: 9.6%
Phone: 404-872-3841	HR: Milton Eades	Employees: 10,000
Fax: 404-872-2812	Type: Private	FYE: December 31

A family business involved in trucking, seafood, and concrete may sound fishy, but the highly diversified Watkins Associated is on the up and up. Its Watkins Motor Lines subsidiary is a long-haul, less-than-truckload (LTL) carrier serving customers in the US, Canada, and Mexico. The trucking company operates more than 4,000 tractors, 11,500 trailers, and 132 terminals. Its services include online tracking and expedited delivery. Watkins Associated's other activities include shrimp processing, real estate development (primarily apartment complexes and shopping centers), bridge building, and citrus growing. Bill Watkins founded the family-owned company in 1932 with a $300 pickup truck.

KEY COMPETITORS
CNF
Old Dominion
Roadway

WAWA, INC.

260 W. Baltimore Pike	CEO: Richard D. Wood Jr.	2001 Sales: $2,010.0 million
Wawa, PA 19063	CFO: Edward Chambers	1-Yr. Sales Change: 34.0%
Phone: 610-358-8000	HR: Karen Casale	Employees: 13,000
Fax: 610-358-8878	Type: Private	FYE: December 31
Web: www.wawa.com		

It's not baby talk — when folks say they need to go to the Wawa, they need groceries. Wawa runs more than 540 Wawa Food Markets in Delaware, Maryland, New Jersey, Pennsylvania, and Virginia. Wawa stores are noted for their coffee and their salad and deli offerings, including hoagie sandwiches; about 100 stores sell gas. Unlike many convenience store chains, Wawa has its own dairy, supplying Wawa stores and about 1,000 hospitals, schools, and other institutions. The company opened its first store in 1964, but its roots go back to an iron foundry begun in 1803 by the Wood family; food operations began in 1902 when George Wood started a dairy in Wawa, Pennsylvania. The Wood family owns 52% of the company.

KEY COMPETITORS
7-Eleven
Sheetz
Uni-Marts

In-depth profiles of an additional 200 key private companies are found on pages 36–435.

WEBCOR BUILDERS

2755 Campus Dr., Ste. 175	CEO: Andrew J. Ball	2001 Sales: $1,154.7 million
San Mateo, CA 94403	CFO: Dave Fisher	1-Yr. Sales Change: 51.9%
Phone: 650-349-2727	HR: Kaela Hanrahan	Employees: —
Fax: 650-577-9444	Type: Private	FYE: December 31
Web: www.webcor.com		

Webcor Builders is a general contractor for mid- and high-rise office buildings, residential and medical facilities, and parking structures, mostly in the San Francisco Bay area. Projects have included headquarters for Oracle, Adobe Systems, and Lucas Companies. Webcor manages projects from design to construction and provides its clients with 24-hour Internet access to updated blueprints and progress reports. Its Interior Construction Group handles renovation for tenants of retail and industrial properties, as well as for clients wishing to upgrade their properties' resistance to earthquakes. The surviving entity of a 1994 merger with A.J. Ball Construction, Webcor is owned by president Andrew Ball.

KEY COMPETITORS
Charles Pankow Builders
Hathaway Dinwiddie Construction
Turner Corporation

WEGMANS FOOD MARKETS, INC.

1500 Brooks Ave.	CEO: Robert B. Wegman	2001 Sales: $2,920.0 million
Rochester, NY 14624	CFO: Jim Leo	1-Yr. Sales Change: 4.3%
Phone: 585-328-2550	HR: Gerald Pierce	Employees: 29,072
Fax: 585-464-4664	Type: Private	FYE: December 31
Web: www.wegmans.com		

One name strikes fear in the hearts of supermarket owners in New York, Pennsylvania, and New Jersey: Wegmans. The supermarket chain owns about 60 stores, but the stores are hardly typical — they're much larger than most supermarkets (up to 120,000 sq. ft.), and they offer specialty shops such as huge in-store cafes, cheese shops with some 400 different varieties, and French-style pastry shops with exotic desserts. The company is known for its gourmet cooking classes and an extensive employee-training program. Wegmans also runs about 15 Chase-Pitkin Home & Garden home-improvement stores. Founded in 1916, the company is still owned by the family of founder John Wegman. His nephew, Robert Wegman, is CEO.

KEY COMPETITORS
Ahold USA
Penn Traffic
Safeway

THE WEITZ GROUP, LLC

Capital Square, 400 Locust, Ste. 300	CEO: Glenn H. De Stigter	2001 Sales: $810.0 million
Des Moines, IA 50309	CFO: Craig Damos	1-Yr. Sales Change: 24.6%
Phone: 515-698-4260	HR: Kris Jensen	Employees: 1,104
Fax: 515-698-4299	Type: Private	FYE: December 31
Web: www.weitz.com		

It took wits for The Weitz Company to become a top US general building contractor. Founded in 1855 by carpenter Charles H. Weitz, the company was run by the Weitz family for four generations before becoming employee-owned. It provides general contracting, construction management, and design/build services, primarily in the western US, building everything from office buildings, industrial plants, senior communities, and schools to hotels, golf courses, supermarkets, and malls. Weitz entered the homebuilding market with its 2001 purchase of Norris Associates, a Colorado-based firm that constructs multimillion-dollar homes in well-heeled resort areas in that state, such as Aspen, Breckenridge, and Vail.

KEY COMPETITORS
Hunt Construction
Turner Corporation
Whiting-Turner

In-depth profiles of an additional 200
key private companies are found on pages 36–435.

WELLS' DAIRY, INC.

1 Blue Bunny Dr.
Le Mars, IA 51031
Phone: 712-546-4000
Fax: 712-546-1782
Web: www.wellsdairy.com

CEO: Gary M. Wells
CFO: Larry Heemstra
HR: Mac Rothenbuhler
Type: Private

2001 Est. Sales: $800.0 mil.
1-Yr. Sales Change: 14.3%
Employees: 2,450
FYE: December 31

From the five-quart tub of Cherry Nut ice cream to red, white, and blue Bomb Pops, Wells' Dairy spans the frozen treat spectrum. Best known for its Blue Bunny ice cream, frozen novelties, and frozen yogurt, Wells' Dairy has a presence in every state and 30 countries. Its products can be found in convenience stores, restaurants, supermarkets, schools, and vending machines. Its Food Service division also produces ice cream cakes and sorbets; its Contract Manufacturing Division produces fluid, cultured, and frozen dairy products for third parties. New products include tropical water ices aimed at Hispanic consumers. Founded in 1913 by the late Fred Wells, the company is still owned by the Wells family.

KEY COMPETITORS
Dreyer's
Nestlé
Unilever

WESTCON GROUP, INC.

520 White Plains Rd., Ste. 100
Tarrytown, NY 10591
Phone: 914-829-7000
Fax: 914-829-7137
Web: www.westcongroup.com

CEO: Alan Marc Smith
CFO: John P. O'Malley III
HR: David Deluke
Type: Private

2002 Sales: $1,670.0 million
1-Yr. Sales Change: (13.9%)
Employees: —
FYE: February 28

Westcon Group is no con — it's pro-global. The company's three divisions, Comstor, Westcon, and Voda One, resell networking equipment made by Cisco Systems (about 55% of sales), Avaya, Nortel Networks, and other top manufacturers. Networking servers, switches, and routers; network security systems; and virtual private network systems top Westcon's product list. The company also provides a variety of support services, including training, network design, logistical support, and others. Chairman Thomas Dolan and EVP Philip Raffiani founded Westcon in 1985. South Africa-based networking company Datatec Ltd. owns 90% of the company, which has acquired Dutch networking products distributor Landis Group.

KEY COMPETITORS
Ingram Micro
ScanSource
Tech Data

W.G. YATES & SONS CONSTRUCTION COMPANY

1 Gully Ave.
Philadelphia, MS 39350
Phone: 601-656-5411
Fax: 601-656-8958
Web: www.wgyates.com

CEO: William G. Yates Jr.
CFO: Marvin Blanks
HR: Kenny Bush
Type: Private

2001 Est. Sales: $750.0 mil.
1-Yr. Sales Change: 1.4%
Employees: 3,000
FYE: December 31

Founded in 1964 by the late William Gully Yates, W.G. Yates & Sons is cashing in on casinos and other big commercial construction projects. With in-house capabilities ranging from steel fabrication and erection to concrete, asphalt, drywall, electrical, and instrumentation, the company is a general contractor for commercial and municipal projects in 20 states, mostly in the Southeast and along the East Coast. Notable projects include the casinos Beau Rivage in Biloxi, Mississippi, and Borgata in Atlantic City (scheduled to open in 2003). The company is owned and run by the Yates family, including co-founder, president, and CEO William Yates Jr.

KEY COMPETITORS
Fluor
Jacobs Engineering
Turner Corporation

In-depth profiles of an additional 200 key private companies are found on pages 36–435.

WHEREHOUSE ENTERTAINMENT, INC.

19701 Hamilton Ave.	CEO: Jerry Comstock	2002 Sales: $604.3 million
Torrance, CA 90502	CFO: Mark A. Velarde	1-Yr. Sales Change: (14.5%)
Phone: 310-965-8300	HR: Toni Caputo	Employees: 5,260
Fax: 310-538-8798	Type: Private	FYE: January 31
Web: www.wherehousemusic.com		

Wherehouse Entertainment wants to be where it's at for music and video lovers. The company operates about 370 stores in 23 states, mostly under the Wherehouse Music, Tu Musica, and XChange names. The stores sell pre-recorded music, videocassettes, DVDs, video games, and accessories. Many of its stores also rent videos and games and buy and sell used CDs. Wherehouse became one of the largest US music retailers after its 1998 purchase of 378-store Blockbuster Music from Viacom. Recent declining sales resulting from discount retailer competition and increases in music downloading have led the company to close some of its stores and file for Chapter 11 bankruptcy protection for the second time in less than 10 years.

KEY COMPETITORS
Best Buy
MTS
Trans World Entertainment

WHITE & CASE LLP

1155 Avenue of the Americas	CEO: Duane D. Wall	2001 Sales: $603.0 million
New York, NY 10036	CFO: James Lotchford	1-Yr. Sales Change: 22.8%
Phone: 212-819-8200	HR: Jill Connors	Employees: —
Fax: 212-354-8113	Type: Partnership	FYE: December 31
Web: www.whitecase.com		

What do you call a law firm with some 1,500 lawyers? Well, the safe answer would be White & Case. One of the world's largest law firms, White & Case has buoyed its global reputation by establishing 34 international offices in locations such as Bangkok; Budapest, Hungary; Istanbul, Turkey; London; Paris; Riyadh, Saudi Arabia; and Warsaw, Poland (the firm also maintains five US offices, including its New York City headquarters). Among White & Case's practice areas are bankruptcy, corporate, intellectual property, litigation, project finance, and tax. The firm's client list has included Deutsche Bank and Royal Ahold. White & Case was founded in 1901.

KEY COMPETITORS
Baker & McKenzie
Clifford Chance
Skadden, Arps

THE WHITING-TURNER CONTRACTING COMPANY

300 E. Joppa Rd.	CEO: Willard Hackerman	2001 Sales: $2,400.0 million
Baltimore, MD 21286	CFO: Charles Irish	1-Yr. Sales Change: 45.8%
Phone: 410-821-1100	HR: Edward Spaulding	Employees: 2,100
Fax: 410-337-5770	Type: Private	FYE: December 31
Web: www.whiting-turner.com		

Whiting-Turner Contracting is a big fish in an ocean of builders. The employee-owned firm provides construction management, general contracting, and design/build services, primarily for large commercial, institutional, and infrastructure projects in the US. Although the general builder subcontracts about 85% of its volume, in-house activities include mechanical and electrical work, concrete forming, and foundation services. A key player in retail construction, the company's diverse projects also include biotech clean rooms, schools, stadiums, and corporate headquarters for such clients as AT&T, General Motors, and the US Army. G. W. C. Whiting and LeBaron Turner founded the company in 1909 to build sewer lines.

KEY COMPETITORS
Clark Enterprises
Skanska
Turner Corporation

In-depth profiles of an additional 200 key private companies are found on pages 36–435.

WILBUR-ELLIS COMPANY

345 California St., 27th Fl.
San Francisco, CA 94104
Phone: 415-772-4000
Fax: 415-772-4005
Web: www.wilbur-ellis.com

CEO: Herbert B. Tully
CFO: Jim Crawford
HR: Ofelia Lee
Type: Private

2001 Sales: $1,185.0 million
1-Yr. Sales Change: 4.8%
Employees: 2,500
FYE: December 31

Helpful hint: Don't stand downwind of the Wilbur-Ellis Company. A distributor for major chemical companies, Wilbur-Ellis sells animal feed, fertilizer, insecticides, seed, and machinery through outlets in North America. Subsidiary Connell Brothers exports and distributes chemicals and feed throughout the Pacific Rim. Additionally, Wilbur-Ellis provides consulting, pesticide spraying, and other agriculture-related services. It also owns Knox McDaniels, a supplier of vitamin and mineral premix products in the western US. Brayton Wilbur Sr. and Floyd Ellis founded the company in 1921 as a fish-oil supplier; it is still owned by the Wilbur family.

KEY COMPETITORS
Agrium
CF Industries
ConAgra

WILLIAM BEAUMONT HOSPITAL

3601 W. 13 Mile Rd.
Royal Oak, MI 48073
Phone: 248-551-5000
Fax: 248-551-1555
Web: www.beaumont.edu

CEO: Ted Wasson
CFO: Dennis R. Herrick
HR: Wesley Kokko
Type: Private

2000 Sales: $1,000.0 million
1-Yr. Sales Change: 14.3%
Employees: 11,500
FYE: December 31

Dr. William Beaumont was an army doctor on Mackinac Island, Michigan, in the 1820s when a French fur trapper stumbled in with a gunshot wound to the gut. The wound left a permanent hole, and Beaumont used the unique insight to undertake groundbreaking studies of the digestive system. Some 200 years later the frontier doctor's name graces William Beaumont Hospital, which includes two teaching hospitals (more than 1,000 beds) in suburban Detroit, a rehab center, five nursing homes, a home health care service, a research institute, and primary and specialty care clinics. The hospitals are affiliated with the University of Michigan Medical School, Wayne State University School of Medicine, and Oakland University.

KEY COMPETITORS
Detroit Medical Center
Henry Ford Health System
Trinity Health

WILLIAMSON-DICKIE MANUFACTURING COMPANY

509 W. Vickery Blvd.
Fort Worth, TX 76104
Phone: 800-336-7201
Fax: 817-877-5027
Web: www.dickies.com

CEO: Philip C. Williamson
CFO: Britt Ingebritson
HR: Marett Cobb
Type: Private

2001 Sales: $844.6 million
1-Yr. Sales Change: 3.0%
Employees: 6,300
FYE: December 31

Appreciated by the working class and the sophomore class alike, Williamson-Dickie Manufacturing Company makes Dickies-brand khaki pants, bib overalls, jeans, and women's and children's apparel. It also produces Workrite safety uniforms. Founded in 1922, the company's work clothes were originally tailored with the blue-collar set in mind, but in recent years the Dickies look has also fallen into favor with fashionable teens. Williamson-Dickie's work clothes portfolio includes Dickies T-shirts, which are made extra long to prevent the display of "plumber's crack" by squatting workmen. Dickies products are sold worldwide through retailers and directly to businesses. The founding Williamson family owns the company.

KEY COMPETITORS
Carhartt
Levi Strauss
VF

📖 **In-depth profiles of an additional 200
key private companies are found on pages 36–435.**

WINCO FOODS, INC.

650 N. Armstrong Place
Boise, ID 83704
Phone: 208-377-0110
Fax: 208-377-0474
Web: www.wincofoods.com

CEO: William D. Long
CFO: Gary R. Piva
HR: Roger Cochell
Type: Private

2002 Sales: $1,540.0 million
1-Yr. Sales Change: 18.5%
Employees: 6,500
FYE: March 31

WinCo Foods isn't just big on self-service — it's giant. Inside the immense stores (most of which are 82,000 sq. ft.) of this mostly employee-owned supermarket chain, customers are asked to shop for food in bulk and bag their own groceries. The company's 30-plus stores also feature pizza shops, bakeries, health and beauty products, and organic foods. WinCo Foods, formerly known as Waremart Foods, was renamed as a shortened version of "winning company." The name is also an acronym for its states of operation, which include Washington, Idaho, Nevada, California, and Oregon. Founded in 1968, WinCo Foods formerly operated stores under the Cub Foods and Waremart names. Employees own about 80% of the company.

KEY COMPETITORS
Albertson's
Raley's
Safeway

WINTEC INDUSTRIES, INC.

4280 Technology Dr.
Fremont, CA 94538
Phone: 510-770-9239
Fax: 510-770-9338
Web: www.wintecindustries.com

CEO: Chu-Hui Jeng
CFO: Lisa Chan
HR: Michael Jeng
Type: Private

2000 Sales: $745.0 million
1-Yr. Sales Change: (6.9%)
Employees: 250
FYE: December 31

If you can't remember to bring the dip, Wintec Industries will provide the memory chips. The company (which was founded in 1998) is a contract manufacturer of integrated circuits, specializing in memory and storage chips for original equipment manufacturers, including customized products for server, storage, and telecommunications applications. Wintec also provides memory modules and third-party products to resellers and systems integrators. In addition to components, the company makes a variety of computer systems, servers, and peripherals for corporate and government end-users, and sells many of its products on its Web site.

KEY COMPETITORS
Kingston Technology
MA Laboratories
Viking Components

WIRTZ CORPORATION

680 N. Lakeshore Dr., 19th Fl.
Chicago, IL 60611
Phone: 312-943-7000
Fax: 312-943-9017

CEO: William W. Wirtz
CFO: Max Mohler
HR: Cindy Krch
Type: Private

2001 Est. Sales: $850.0 mil.
1-Yr. Sales Change: (3.4%)
Employees: 2,000
FYE: June 30

Wirtz does best on ice. It owns the Chicago Blackhawks hockey team and is partnered with Jerry Reinsdorf, majority owner of the Chicago Bulls basketball team, for ownership of the United Center, where the teams play. Wirtz owns liquor distributorships, including Judge & Dolph, the largest in Illinois, and Edison Liquor Co. The Wirtz family gave thousands of dollars to state lawmakers in 1999 to pass a law protecting liquor distributors by making it difficult for liquor producers to switch distributors. (The law later was declared unconstitutional.) The firm owns property in Wisconsin, Mississippi, Texas, Nevada and Florida. Arthur Wirtz (father of CEO William Wirtz) founded the family-controlled empire in 1922.

KEY COMPETITORS
Detroit Red Wings
Johnson Brothers
Southern Wine & Spirits

📖 **In-depth profiles of an additional 200 key private companies are found on pages 36–435.**

WKI HOLDING COMPANY, INC.

One Pyrex Pl.
Elmira, NY 14902
Phone: 607-377-8000
Fax: 607-377-8946
Web: www.worldkitchen.com

CEO: James A. Sharman
CFO: Joseph W. McGarr
HR: Joseph Galligher
Type: Private

2001 Sales: $745.9 million
1-Yr. Sales Change: (9.9%)
Employees: 4,200
FYE: December 31

WKI Holding has cooked up a kitchen kingpin. The holding company's World Kitchen subsidiary (formerly Corning Consumer Products) makes some of the most popular kitchenware and tableware in the US. Its brands include Corelle, CorningWare, Pyrex, Revere, and Visions. The company doubled its size with its 1999 purchases of houseware firms EKCO Group (Farberware, Baker's Secret) and General Housewares (Chicago Cutlery, OXO); it adopted the WKI Holding name in 2000. Buyout firm Kohlberg Kravis Roberts bought most of the company in 1998 from optical fiber and high-performance glass maker Corning. Plans to reduce debt led WKI Holding to file for chapter 11 bankruptcy protection in May 2002.

KEY COMPETITORS
Newell Rubbermaid
SEB
Tupperware

W. L. GORE & ASSOCIATES, INC.

555 Paper Mill Rd.
Newark, DE 19711
Phone: 302-738-4880
Fax: 302-738-7710
Web: www.gore.com

CEO: Robert W. Gore
CFO: Charles Carroll
HR: Sally Gore
Type: Private

2002 Sales: $1,230.0 million
1-Yr. Sales Change: (12.1%)
Employees: 6,000
FYE: March 31

W. L. Gore & Associates would like your clothing to take a deep breath. The company makes a variety of fluoropolymer products; best known is its breathable, waterproof, and windproof GORE-TEX fabric. Product uses range from clothing and shoes to guitar strings, dental floss, space suits, and sutures. In addition to its apparel (popular among hikers and hunters), W. L. Gore makes insulated wire and cables, filtration products, and sealants. Fabrics are offered under such brands as CROSSTECH, DRYLOFT, and WINDSTOPPER. The Gore family owns about 75% of the company; Gore associates own the rest.

KEY COMPETITORS
Belden
Burlington Industries
Malden Mills

WL HOMES LLC

895 Dove St., Ste. 200
Newport Beach, CA 92660
Phone: 949-265-2400
Fax: 949-265-2500
Web: www.wlhomes.com

CEO: H. Lawrence Webb
CFO: Wayne J. Stelmar
HR: —
Type: Private

2001 Est. Sales: $600.0 mil.
1-Yr. Sales Change: (0.5%)
Employees: —
FYE:

Dear John: I am going it alone — at least in spirit if not in name. So goes the story of WL Homes, which was created in 1998 from the merger of UK-based John Laing Homes and US-based Watt Homes. The company is one of the largest homebuilders in Southern California (it gets about two-thirds of its sales from that state) and also has operations in three eastern and three other western states in the US. WL Homes sells homes under the John Laing and Watts Homes names. In 2001 UK-based John Laing Homes sold more than half of its stake in the company (the UK firm still retains 22%) to an investor group led by chairman Ray Watt and CEO Lawrence Webb.

KEY COMPETITORS
D.R. Horton
Lennar
Pulte Homes

In-depth profiles of an additional 200 key private companies are found on pages 36–435.

WOODBRIDGE GROUP

2500 Meijer Dr.
Troy, MI 48084
Phone: 248-288-0100
Fax: 248-288-1640
Web: www.woodbridgegroup.com

CEO: T. Robert Beamish
CFO: Rick Jocsak
HR: Grant Oliver
Type: Private

2001 Est. Sales: $800.0 mil.
1-Yr. Sales Change: (9.1%)
Employees: 4,500
FYE: December 31

Foam is where the heart is for Woodbridge Group. The company is a Tier II supplier of structural, seating, energy absorbing, and mechanical automotive foams. Products include foams for interior components that provide knee and lower-limb protection in the event of a collision. Additional foam applications include head restraints, armrests, rear seat bolsters, carpet padding, and acoustical foams. Woodbridge also offers assembly services and can assist its customers with product design and engineering. Co-founder and chairman T. Robert Beamish controls more than 75% of the company.

KEY COMPETITORS
Carpenter
Foamex
Lear

WORKPLACEUSA, INC.

8150 N. Central Expwy., Ste. 1100
Dallas, TX 75206
Phone: 214-696-6900
Fax: 214-696-0037
Web: wpcompanies.com

CEO: John T. Amend
CFO: —
HR: —
Type: Private

2001 Est. Sales: $640.0 mil.
1-Yr. Sales Change: —
Employees: 120
FYE: December 31

Striving to be the "Wal-Mart of real estate," WorkPlaceUSA offers end-to-end services for commercial real estate projects. Founded in 1989 by CEO and owner John Amend as The Amend Group, the company has evolved from a tenant brokerage firm into a one-stop shop for real estate, design, construction, and technology consulting services. Organized into 16 divisions, the group offers services such as architecture and engineering, construction and project management, interior design, real estate finance information systems, and tenant brokerage. The company provides an Internet-based project management system. Its engineering group designs mechanical, electrical, plumbing, and fire protection systems.

KEY COMPETITORS
Hellmuth, Obata + Kassabaum
Hensel Phelps Construction
Turner Corporation

WORLDTRAVEL BTI

1055 Lenox Park Blvd., Ste. 420
Atlanta, GA 30319
Phone: 404-841-6600
Fax: 404-814-2983
Web: www.worldtravel.com

CEO: Michael A. Buckman
CFO: Thomas Barham
HR: Nancy Pavey
Type: Private

2001 Sales: $3,800.0 million
1-Yr. Sales Change: 0.0%
Employees: 5,175
FYE: December 31

Instead of phoning home, E.T. could have called WorldTravel BTI. WorldTravel has grown from a small travel agency to #3 in the US (behind American Express and Carlson Wagonlit). Clients include many large US corporations such as PepsiCo, Deloitte Touche, and De Beers. WorldTravel has more than 1,600 ticketing locations and 45 affiliates across the US; through Business Travel International (BTI) it offers another 3,000 locations in more than 70 countries. Its WorldTravelNet offers personalized travel information and services, including real-time flight status, hotel rates, weather, and maps. Chairman John Fentener van Vlissingen owns a majority stake in the company through BCD Holdings.

KEY COMPETITORS
American Express
Carlson Wagonlit
Rosenbluth International

📖 In-depth profiles of an additional 200 key private companies are found on pages 36–435.

YALE UNIVERSITY

246 Church St.	CEO: Richard C. Levin	2001 Sales: $1,352.9 million
New Haven, CT 06520	CFO: Robert L. Culver	1-Yr. Sales Change: 7.1%
Phone: 203-432-2331	HR: Katherine F. Matzkin	Employees: 7,398
Fax: 203-432-2334	Type: School	FYE: June 30
Web: www.yale.edu		

What do President George W. Bush, writer William F. Buckley Jr., and actress Meryl Streep have in common? They are all Yalies. Yale University is one of the nation's most prestigious private liberal arts institutions, as well as one of its oldest (founded in 1701). Its $10.7 billion endowment ranks second only to Harvard's in the US. Yale comprises an undergraduate college, a graduate school, and 10 professional schools. Programs of study include architecture, law, medicine, and drama. Its 12 residential colleges (a system borrowed from Oxford) serve as dormitory, dining hall, and social center. The school has more than 11,100 students and some 3,000 faculty members.

YMCA OF THE USA

101 N. Wacker Dr.	CEO: Kenneth L. Gladish	2001 Est. Sales: $4,000.0 mil.
Chicago, IL 60606	CFO: Kate Spencer	1-Yr. Sales Change: 2.4%
Phone: 312-977-0031	HR: —	Employees: 25,000
Fax: 312-977-9063	Type: Not-for-profit	FYE: December 31
Web: www.ymca.net		

If the Village People can be believed, it's fun to stay at the YMCA. One of the nation's largest not-for-profit community service organizations, YMCA of the USA assists the more than 2,400 individual YMCAs across the country and represents them on both national and international levels. YMCAs serve some 18 million people across the US. One of the largest child-care providers in the US, YMCAs also offer programs in areas such as aquatics, arts and humanities, health and fitness, and teen leadership. The first YMCA in the US was established in 1851 as an outgrowth of the YMCA movement launched by George Williams in the UK in 1844.

YOUNG'S MARKET COMPANY, LLC

2164 N. Batavia St.	CEO: Charles Andrews	2002 Est. Sales: $1,490.0 mil.
Orange, CA 92865	CFO: Dennis J. Hamann	1-Yr. Sales Change: 14.6%
Phone: 714-283-4933	HR: Naomi Buenaslor	Employees: 1,700
Fax: 714-283-6175	Type: Private	FYE: February 28
Web: www.youngsmkt.com		

Although no longer young, Young's Market Company is in high spirits. Young's Market is one of the largest distributors of beer, wine, and distilled spirits in the US. The company is a major supplier along the Pacific coast. It also operates in Hawaii through its Better Brands subsidiary. Young's Market distributes products for Bacardi, Brown-Forman, and other distillers and winemakers. John Young founded the company in 1888, which at one time included grocery retailing, and specialty food distribution. The Underwood family, relatives of the Young's, bought Young's Market in 1990.

KEY COMPETITORS
Glazer's Wholesale Drug
Southern Wine & Spirits
Topa Equities

In-depth profiles of an additional 200 key private companies are found on pages 36–435.

ZACHRY CONSTRUCTION CORPORATION

527 Logwood
San Antonio, TX 78221
Phone: 210-475-8000
Fax: 210-475-8060
Web: www.zachry.com

CEO: Henry Bartell Zachry Jr.
CFO: Joe J. Lozano
HR: Steve Hoech
Type: Private

2001 Est. Sales: $1,940.0 mil.
1-Yr. Sales Change: 38.6%
Employees: 14,000
FYE: December 31

H. B. Zachry began building roads and bridges in 1924, and now his son and grandsons are running the show. Zachry Construction builds and maintains power and chemical plants, steel and paper mills, refineries, roadways, dams, airfields, and pipelines. Operating mostly in the southern US, Zachry has built facilities for companies such as DuPont, Samsung, Alcoa, and Shell. It also works internationally and reconstructed the US Embassy in Moscow. In addition, Zachry owns interests in ranches and in oil exploration, cement, hospitality, realty, and entertainment companies, as well as in the San Antonio Spurs basketball team.

KEY COMPETITORS
Bechtel
Fluor
Peter Kiewit Sons'

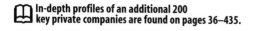
In-depth profiles of an additional 200
key private companies are found on pages 36–435.

Hoover's Handbook of Private Companies

THE INDEXES

AEROSPACE & DEFENSE

Maintenance & Service

United Space Alliance 649

Products

CFM International, Inc. 478
CIC International Ltd. 481
Vought Aircraft Industries, Inc. 659

AUTOMOTIVE & TRANSPORT EQUIPMENT

Auto Manufacturers

New United Motor Manufacturing, Inc. 312

Auto Parts

BREED Technologies, Inc. 468
Delco Remy International, Inc. 494
Eagle-Picher Industries, Inc. 504
Everett Smith Group 508
Findlay Industries, Inc. 511
Mark IV Industries, Inc. 566
Meridian Automotive Systems, Inc. 571
Metaldyne Corporation 572
Oxford Automotive, Inc. 592
Penske Corporation 336
UIS, Inc. 647
Venture Industries 657

Pleasure Boats

Genmar Holdings, Inc. 518

Rail & Trucking Equipment

ACF Industries, Inc. 439
Boler Co. 465
Duchossois Industries, Inc. 502
Great Dane Limited Partnership 525
Utility Trailer Manufacturing Co. 655

Trucks, Buses & Other Vehicles

Motor Coach Industries International, Inc. 577

BANKING

Money Center Banks

Federal Reserve System 156

US West

Navy Federal Credit Union 582

CHEMICALS

Agricultural Chemicals

CF Industries, Inc. 477
Royster-Clark, Inc. 614

Basic & Intermediate Chemicals & Petrochemicals

Chevron Phillips Chemical Company LP 480
Koppers Industries, Inc. 556
Texas Petrochemicals LP 639

Diversified

Huntsman Corporation 204
ICC Industries Inc. 542
Noveon International, Inc. 587

Paints, Coatings & Other Finishing Products

Contran Corporation 487
Schenectady International, Inc. 618

Plastics & Fibers

Carpenter Co. 474
Equistar Chemicals, LP 507
PMC Global, Inc. 600
Resolution Performance Products LLC 609

Specialty Chemicals

Borden Chemical, Inc. 466
Dow Corning Corporation 140
Flint Ink Corporation 512
J. M. Huber Corporation 548
JohnsonDiversey, Inc. 618
NCH Corporation 583

COMPUTER HARDWARE

Computer Peripherals

ViewSonic Corporation 658

Data Storage Devices

Seagate Technology Holdings 368

Personal Computers

eMachines, Inc. 506
MicronPC, LLC 575

COMPUTER SOFTWARE & SERVICES

Computer Products Distribution & Support

ASI Corp. 454
D&H Distributing Co., Inc. 491
MA Laboratories, Inc. 564
Software House International, Inc. 628
Westcon Group, Inc. 664

Corporate, Professional & Financial Software

SAS Institute Inc. 617

Information Technology Consulting Services

DynCorp 503
Forsythe Technology, Inc. 515
Global eXchange Services, Inc. 521
Science Applications International Corporation 366

Multimedia Production, Graphics & Publishing Software

Quark, Inc. 605

The Yucaipa Companies LLC 434

Leasing

TTX Company 645

Miscellaneous Financial Services

A-Mark Financial Corporation 447

NASD 298

New York Stock Exchange, Inc. 320

Services to Financial Companies

CUNA Mutual Group 490

The Depository Trust & Clearing Corporation 495

U.S. Central Credit Union 654

FOOD, BEVERAGE & TOBACCO

Beverages — Bottlers & Wholesale Distributors

Charmer Industries, Inc. 479

Dr Pepper/Seven Up Bottling Group, Inc. 500

Georgia Crown Distributing Company 519

Glazer's Wholesale Drug Company Inc. 521

Honickman Affiliates 537

National Distributing Company, Inc. 579

National Wine & Spirits, Inc 582

Peerless Importers, Inc. 595

Southern Wine & Spirits of America, Inc. 630

Sunbelt Beverage Corporation 634

Topa Equities, Ltd. 641

Wirtz Corporation 667

Young's Market Company, LLC 670

Beverages — Brewers

S&P Company 616

Beverages — Soft Drinks

Ocean Spray Cranberries, Inc. 326

Vitality Beverages, Inc. 659

Beverages — Wineries

E. & J. Gallo Winery 144

Food — Agricultural Operations & Products

Bartlett and Company 459

Cactus Feeders, Inc. 471

ContiGroup Companies, Inc. 118

Farmland Industries, Inc. 154

Florida's Natural Growers 512

J.R. Simplot Company 226

King Ranch, Inc. 232

Michael Foods, Inc. 573

National Grape Cooperative Association, Inc. 580

Southern States Cooperative, Incorporated 629

Sunkist Growers, Inc. 388

Food — Agricultural Services

Ag Processing Inc 44

Agway Inc. 443

Cargill, Incorporated 92

Cenex Harvest States Cooperatives 106

The Connell Company 486

DeBruce Grain, Inc. 494

Dunavant Enterprises, Inc. 502

GROWMARK, Inc. 527

MFA Incorporated 573

The Scoular Company 620

Staple Cotton Cooperative Association 631

Wilbur-Ellis Company 666

Food — Canned & Frozen Foods

Agrilink Foods, Inc. 443

Pinnacle Foods Corporation 598

The Schwan Food Company 364

Food — Dairy Products

Associated Milk Producers Incorporated 456

California Dairies Inc. 472

Dairy Farmers of America 126

Dairylea Cooperative Inc. 491

Foremost Farms USA, Cooperative 514

Great Lakes Cheese Company, Inc. 525

H.P. Hood Inc. 539

Land O'Lakes, Inc. 246

Leprino Foods Company 559

Marathon Cheese Corporation 565

Prairie Farms Dairy Inc. 601

Quality Chekd Dairies, Inc. 605

Schreiber Foods, Inc. 620

Wells' Dairy, Inc. 664

Food — Diversified Foods — Other

Goya Foods, Inc. 170

Rich Products Corporation 611

Food — Food Wholesale — to Grocers

Advantage/ESM Ferolie 440

Affiliated Foods Incorporated 441

Alex Lee, Inc. 445

Associated Food Stores, Inc. 455

Associated Grocers, Inc. 455

Associated Wholesale Grocers, Inc. 60

Associated Wholesalers, Inc. 456

Bozzuto's Inc. 467

C&S Wholesale Grocers, Inc. 90

Central Grocers Cooperative, Inc. 476

Certified Grocers Midwest, Inc. 477

Di Giorgio Corporation 498

Eby-Brown Company 505

The Grocers Supply Co., Inc. 527

GSC Enterprises, Inc. 528

H.T. Hackney Co. 539

Purity Wholesale Grocers, Inc. 604

Roundy's, Inc. 356

S. Abraham & Sons, Inc. 615

Shamrock Foods Company 623

Topco Associates LLC 400

Unified Western Grocers, Inc. 408

Wakefern Food Corporation 428

Food — Food Wholesale — to Restaurants

Ben E. Keith Company 462

Dot Foods, Inc. 500

Golden State Foods 168

Gordon Food Service 523

Keystone Foods LLC 552

The Martin-Brower Company, L.L.C. 566

MBM Corporation 568

Reyes Holdings LLC 610

Services Group of America 623

Food — Grains, Breads & Cereals

McKee Foods Corporation 569

Food — Meat Products

American Foods Group, Inc. 448

Colorado Boxed Beef Company 484

Empire Beef Company, Inc. 506

Foster Poultry Farms 515

Gold Kist Inc. 521

Perdue Farms Incorporated 338

PSF Group Holdings, Inc. 601

Rosen's Diversified, Inc. 613

Swift & Company 636

Food — Miscellaneous Food Products

Dawn Food Products, Inc. 493

R.A.B. Holdings, Inc. 606

Red Chamber Group 608

Trident Seafoods Corporation 643

Food — Other Processed & Packaged Goods

Gilster-Mary Lee Corporation 520

Food — Sugar & Confectionery

American Crystal Sugar Company 448

Mars, Incorporated 264

Tobacco Products

Harold Levinson Associates 531

HEALTH PRODUCTS & SERVICES

Health Care Plans

Blue Cross and Blue Shield Association 74

DHL Worldwide Express, Inc. 497
Fisher Development, Inc. 512
Levi Strauss & Co. 250
Shorenstein Company, L.P. 625
Swinerton Incorporated 636
Wilbur-Ellis Company 666

San Jose
Fry's Electronics, Inc. 164
MA Laboratories, Inc. 564

San Mateo
Webcor Builders 663

San Rafael
Lucasfilm, Ltd. 256

Santa Ana
GeoLogistics Corporation 519

Santa Monica
A-Mark Financial
  Corporation 447
American Golf Corporation 449
Santa Monica Ford
  Corporation 617

Scotts Valley
Seagate Technology Holdings 368

Sherman Oaks
Sunkist Growers, Inc. 388

Stanford
Stanford University 380

Stockton
A. G. Spanos Companies 442

Sun Valley
PMC Global, Inc. 600

Torrance
Wherehouse Entertainment,
  Inc. 665

Vernon
Red Chamber Group 608

Walnut
J.F. Shea Co., Inc. 547
ViewSonic Corporation 658

Watsonville
Marty Franich Auto Center 566

West Sacramento
MTS, Incorporated 292
Raley's Inc. 607

Westlake Village
Consolidated Electrical
  Distributors Inc. 487

COLORADO
Colorado Springs
Phil Long Dealerships, Inc. 597

Denver
Catholic Health Initiatives 102
Duke Energy Field Services
  Corporation 502
Leprino Foods Company 559
MediaNews Group, Inc. 569
Quark, Inc. 605

Englewood
Burt Automotive Network 471

Greeley
Hensel Phelps Construction
  Co. 534
Swift & Company 636

Greenwood Village
CH2M HILL Companies, Ltd. 478

Steamboat Springs
TIC Holdings Inc. 640

Westminister
Tri-State Generation and
  Transmission Association,
  Inc. 644

CONNECTICUT
Cheshire
Bozzuto's Inc. 467

Enfield
Retail Brand Alliance, Inc. 610

Farmington
ConnectiCare Inc. 486

Greenwich
Interactive Brokers Group
  LLC 545

Mashantucket
Mashantucket Pequot Gaming
  Enterprise Inc. 268

Middlebury
Timex Corporation 640

Milford
Doctor's Associates Inc. 136

New Haven
Yale University 670

Norwalk
Micro Warehouse, Inc. 574

Stamford
Conair Corporation 485
Purdue Pharma L.P. 604
Towers Perrin 642

Uncasville
Mohegan Tribal Gaming
  Authority 576

West Hartford
Colt's Manufacturing Company,
  Inc. 112

DELAWARE
Newark
W. L. Gore & Associates, Inc. 668

DISTRICT OF COLUMBIA
Washington
AARP 36
AFL-CIO 42
The American Red Cross 50
The Carlyle Group 98

Corporation for Public
  Broadcasting 122
Federal Reserve System 156
Intelsat, Ltd. 545
International Brotherhood of
  Teamsters 212
NASD 298
National Geographic Society 304
National Railroad Passenger
  Corporation 308
Pension Benefit Guaranty
  Corporation 334
Smithsonian Institution 374
ULLICO Inc. 647
United States Postal Service 410

FLORIDA
Auburndale
Colorado Boxed Beef
  Company 484

Boca Raton
Purity Wholesale Grocers,
  Inc. 604

Bonita Springs
Abbey Carpet Company, Inc. 439

Coral Gables
Planet Automotive Group,
  Inc. 599

Daytona Beach
National Association for Stock
  Car Auto Racing 579

Deerfield Beach
JM Family Enterprises, Inc. 220

Fort Lauderdale
North Broward Hospital
  District 585

Gainesville
University of Florida 650

Jacksonville
Gate Petroleum Company 517
The Haskell Company 532
JEA 547

Lake Wales
Florida's Natural Growers 512

Lakeland
BREED Technologies, Inc. 468
Publix Super Markets, Inc. 346

Miami
Southern Wine & Spirits of
  America, Inc. 630

Seffner
Rooms To Go 612

Tallahassee
State of Florida Department of
  the Lottery 632

Tampa
EPIX Holdings Corporation 507
Seminole Electric Cooperative,
  Inc. 622
Vitality Beverages, Inc. 659

Vero Beach
George E. Warren
  Corporation 519
West Palm Beach
Orius Corp. 591

GEORGIA
Atlanta
American Cancer Society, Inc. 46
Chick-fil-A Inc. 481
Cingular Wireless 482
Cox Enterprises, Inc. 124
Emory University 506
Gold Kist Inc. 521
National Distributing Company,
  Inc. 579
Printpack, Inc. 602
Riverwood Holding, Inc. 611
RTM Restaurant Group 614
Simmons Company 626
Trammell Crow Residential 642
Watkins Associated
  Industries 662
WorldTravel BTI 669
Carrollton
Southwire Company 630
Columbus
Bill Heard Enterprises 463
Georgia Crown Distributing
  Company 519
Dalton
Beaulieu of America, LLC 461
Monroe
Avondale Incorporated 458
Norcross
American Retail Group Inc. 449
Waffle House Inc. 660
Savannah
Great Dane Limited
  Partnership 525
Smyrna
RaceTrac Petroleum, Inc. 607
Tucker
Oglethorpe Power
  Corporation 588

IDAHO
Boise
J.R. Simplot Company 226
WinCo Foods, Inc. 667
Nampa
MicronPC, LLC 575

ILLINOIS
Addison
The Pampered Chef, Ltd. 593
Bedford Park
CHEMCENTRAL
  Corporation 480

Bloomington
GROWMARK, Inc. 527
State Farm Insurance
  Companies 382
Carlinville
Prairie Farms Dairy Inc. 601
Chester
Gilster-Mary Lee Corporation 520
Chicago
AMSTED Industries
  Incorporated 451
Baker & McKenzie 62
Blue Cross and Blue Shield
  Association 74
Chas. Levy Company LLC 479
Encyclopaedia Britannica,
  Inc. 146
Equity Group Investments,
  L.L.C. 150
Grant Thornton
  International 172
Harpo, Inc. 184
Health Care Service
  Corporation 192
Hyatt Corporation 206
IGA, INC. 208
JMB Realty Corporation 548
Johnson Publishing Company,
  Inc. 222
The Marmon Group, Inc. 262
Pepper Construction Group,
  LLC 597
Sidley Austin Brown & Wood
  LLP 625
Strategic Hotel Capital LLC 633
TruServ Corporation 404
TTX Company 645
The University of Chicago 416
The Walsh Group 661
Wirtz Corporation 667
YMCA of the USA 670
Deerfield
Dade Behring Inc. 490
Jordan Industries, Inc. 550
Des Plaines
Frank Consolidated
  Enterprises 515
East Dubuque
Crescent Electric Supply
  Company 488
Elmhurst
Duchossois Industries, Inc. 502
Evanston
Northwestern University 324
Rotary International 354
Frankfort
Provena Health 603
Franklin Park
Central Grocers Cooperative,
  Inc. 476

Highland Park
Solo Cup Company 629
Hodgkins
Certified Grocers Midwest,
  Inc. 477
Itasca
Boler Co. 465
Fellowes, Inc. 511
Serta, Inc. 622
Lake Forest
TAP Pharmaceutical Products
  Inc. 637
Trustmark Insurance
  Company 645
Lawrenceville
Golden Rule Insurance
  Company 522
Lombard
U.S. Can Corporation 654
Long Grove
CF Industries, Inc. 477
Kemper Insurance
  Companies 230
Mount Sterling
Dot Foods, Inc. 500
Mundelein
Medline Industries, Inc. 570
Naperville
Eby-Brown Company 505
Quality Chekd Dairies, Inc. 605
Northbrook
Lane Industries, Inc. 557
Oak Brook
Ace Hardware Corporation 38
Advocate Health Care 441
Clark Retail Group, Inc. 483
The Inland Group, Inc. 544
River Grove
Follett Corporation 513
Rockford
Ingersoll International Inc. 543
Rolling Meadows
Kimball Hill Homes 553
Rosemont
The Martin-Brower Company,
  L.L.C. 566
Reyes Holdings LLC 610
Schaumburg
Motor Coach Industries
  International, Inc. 577
Pliant Corporation 600
Skokie
Forsythe Technology, Inc. 515
Rand McNally & Company 348
Topco Associates LLC 400
Tinley Park
Horseshoe Gaming Holding
  Corp. 538

Tewksbury
Demoulas Super Markets
Inc. 495

Waltham
Tufts Associated Health Plans,
Inc. 646

Wellesley
Harvard Pilgrim Health Care,
Inc. 531

Westwood
Modus Media, Inc. 576

MICHIGAN
Ada
Alticor Inc. 446

Ann Arbor
Domino's, Inc. 138
Flint Ink Corporation 512
The University of Michigan 650

Auburn Hills
Guardian Industries Corp. 178
RGIS Inventory Specialists 610

Battle Creek
W.K. Kellogg Foundation 432

Dearborn
Meridian Automotive Systems,
Inc. 571

Detroit
Blue Cross Blue Shield of
Michigan 78
Detroit Medical Center 496
Henry Ford Health System 534
Penske Corporation 336
Soave Enterprises L.L.C. 628
Walbridge Aldinger Company 660

Fraser
Venture Industries 657

Grand Rapids
Gordon Food Service 523
Meijer, Inc. 278
S. Abraham & Sons, Inc. 615

Holland
Haworth Inc. 188

Jackson
Dawn Food Products, Inc. 493

Lansing
Michigan Lottery 574

Mason
Dart Container Corporation 128

Midland
Dow Corning Corporation 140

Novi
Trinity Health 644

Plymouth
Metaldyne Corporation 572
Plastipak Packaging, Inc. 599

Royal Oak
William Beaumont Hospital 666

Southfield
Barton Malow Company 460
MSX International, Inc. 577

Troy
Oxford Automotive, Inc. 592
Woodbridge Group 669

Warren
The Angelo Iafrate
Companies 452
CenTra, Inc. 476

MINNESOTA
Arden Hills
Land O'Lakes, Inc. 246

Bayport
Andersen Corporation 52

Bloomington
Holiday Companies 536

Burnsville
Northern Tool & Equipment
Co. 586

Eagan
Buffets, Inc. 470

Eden Prairie
Lifetouch Inc. 561

Fairmont
Rosen's Diversified, Inc. 613

Inver Grove Heights
Cenex Harvest States
Cooperatives 106

Marshall
The Schwan Food Company 364

Minneapolis
Aid Association for
Lutherans/Lutheran
Brotherhood 444
Allina Health System 446
Carlson Companies, Inc. 94
Genmar Holdings, Inc. 518
Jostens, Inc. 550
Kraus-Anderson,
Incorporated 556
M. A. Mortenson Company 564
Michael Foods, Inc. 573
University of Minnesota 651

Minnetonka
Opus Corporation 591

Moorhead
American Crystal Sugar
Company 448

New Ulm
Associated Milk Producers
Incorporated 456

North Mankato
Taylor Corporation 638

Owatonna
Federated Insurance
Companies 510

Plymouth
Carlson Wagonlit Travel 96

Rochester
Mayo Foundation 274

St. Paul
AgAmerica, FCB 442
AgriBank, FCB 443
APi Group, Inc. 452
Hubbard Broadcasting Inc. 540
Merrill Corporation 572
Minnesota Mutual Companies,
Inc. 575

Wayzata
Cargill, Incorporated 92

MISSISSIPPI
Greenwood
Staple Cotton Cooperative
Association 631

Jackson
Ergon, Inc. 508

Philadelphia
W.G. Yates & Sons Construction
Company 664

MISSOURI
Chesterfield
Outsourcing Solutions Inc. 592

Clayton
Apex Oil Company, Inc. 452
Graybar Electric Company,
Inc. 174

Columbia
MFA Incorporated 573
University of Missouri
System 651

Des Peres
The Jones Financial Companies,
L.L.L.P. 224

Earth City
CCA Global Partners 476

Fenton
Maritz Inc. 565
UniGroup, Inc. 648

Kansas City
American Century Companies,
Inc. 448
Bartlett and Company 459
Black & Veatch 464
Dairy Farmers of America 126
DeBruce Grain, Inc. 494
Dunn Industries, Inc. 503
Farmland Industries, Inc. 154
Hallmark Cards, Inc. 182
Health Midwest 533
PSF Group Holdings, Inc. 601
Sutherland Lumber Company,
L.P. 635

Springfield
Bass Pro Shops, Inc. 460

St. Charles
ACF Industries, Inc. 439
St. Louis
Alberici Constructors, Inc. 444
Ascension Health 56
BJC Health System 464
Carondelet Health System 473
Enterprise Rent-A-Car 148
Harbour Group Industries,
  Inc. 530
HBE Corporation 532
McCarthy Building Companies,
  Inc. 568
Schnuck Markets, Inc. 619
SSM Health Care System
  Inc. 631
telcobuy.com LLC 639
Washington University in St.
  Louis 662

MONTANA
Missoula
The Washington Companies 661

NEBRASKA
Lincoln
The University of Nebraska 651
Omaha
Ag Processing Inc 44
The Mutual of Omaha
  Companies 294
Peter Kiewit Sons', Inc. 340
The Scoular Company 620
Sidney
Cabela's Inc. 471

NEVADA
Las Vegas
Tang Industries, Inc. 637

NEW JERSEY
Avenel
Bradco Supply Corp. 468
Bedminster
Verizon Wireless Inc. 657
Berkeley Heights
The Connell Company 486
Carteret
Di Giorgio Corporation 498
Cherry Hill
Pinnacle Foods Corporation 598
Cranford
The Newark Group, Inc. 584
East Rutherford
Metromedia Company 282
Edison
J. M. Huber Corporation 548
Elizabeth
Wakefern Food Corporation 428

Florham Park
The Gale Company 516
Hoboken
CIC International Ltd. 481
Jersey City
UIS, Inc. 647
Lyndhurst
Sigma Plastics Group 626
Mahwah
Inserra Supermarkets, Inc. 544
Montvale
Advantage/ESM Ferolie 440
Moorestown
Interline Brands, Inc. 545
North Bergen
Hudson News Company 540
Parsippany
NRT Incorporated 587
Pennsauken
Holman Enterprises 537
Honickman Affiliates 537
Princeton
Educational Testing Service 505
Princeton University 602
Ramsey
Liberty Travel, Inc. 560
Rancocas
Inductotherm Industries,
  Inc. 543
Secaucus
Goya Foods, Inc. 170
The Hartz Mountain
  Corporation 531
Somerset
Software House International,
  Inc. 628
Totowa
Pitman Company 598
Wayne
G-I Holdings Inc. 520

NEW MEXICO
Albuquerque
Presbyterian Healthcare
  Services 601

NEW YORK
Albany
State University of New York 384
Amherst
Mark IV Industries, Inc. 566
Astoria
Charmer Industries, Inc. 479
Bethpage
King Kullen Grocery Company
  Inc. 554

Bronx
Montefiore Medical Center 577
Brooklyn
Peerless Importers, Inc. 595
Buffalo
Delaware North Companies
  Inc. 494
Rich Products Corporation 611
DeWitt
Agway Inc. 443
East Syracuse
Dairylea Cooperative Inc. 491
Elmira
WKI Holding Company, Inc. 668
Farmingdale
P.C. Richard & Son 594
Great Neck
North Shore-Long Island Jewish
  Health System 586
Hicksville
Harold Levinson Associates 531
Ithaca
Cornell University 488
Jamaica
Saint Vincent Catholic Medical
  Centers of New York 616
Jericho
Schonfeld Securities, LLC 619
Long Island City
National Envelope
  Corporation 580
Malta
Stewart's Shops Corp. 633
N. Amityville
Bellco Health Corp. 462
New York
A&E Television Networks 438
Alliance Capital Management
  L.P. 446
American Society of Composers,
  Authors and Publishers 450
The Associated Press 58
Atlantic Mutual Companies 457
Barnes & Noble College
  Bookstores, Inc. 459
Bill Blass Ltd. 463
Bloomberg L.P. 72
Calvin Klein, Inc. 88
Cantor Fitzgerald, L.P. 473
The City University of New
  York 108
Columbia House Company 485
Columbia University 114
ContiGroup Companies, Inc. 118
Cushman & Wakefield Inc. 490
Deloitte Touche Tohmatsu 132
The Depository Trust & Clearing
  Corporation 495
The Dyson-Kissner-Moran
  Corporation 503

Ernst & Young International 152
The Ford Foundation 162
GoodTimes Entertainment Limited 523
Gould Paper Corporation 524
The Guardian Life Insurance Company of America 180
Health Insurance Plan of Greater New York 533
The Hearst Corporation 194
Helmsley Enterprises, Inc. 196
Horsehead Industries Inc. 538
ICC Industries Inc. 542
J. Crew Group, Inc. 546
Kohlberg Kravis Roberts & Co. 240
KPMG International 244
Lifetime Entertainment Services 560
Loews Cineplex Entertainment Corporation 562
M. Fabrikant & Sons, Inc. 563
MacAndrews & Forbes Holdings Inc. 258
Major League Baseball 260
McKinsey & Company 276
Memorial Sloan-Kettering Cancer Center 570
Metropolitan Transportation Authority 284
National Basketball Association 300
National Football League 302
National Hockey League 306
New York City Health and Hospitals Corporation 314
New York Life Insurance Company 316
New York Stock Exchange, Inc. 320
New York University 584
Parsons Brinckerhoff Inc. 594
The Port Authority of New York and New Jersey 342
PricewaterhouseCoopers 344
R.A.B. Holdings, Inc. 606
Red Apple Group, Inc. 608
Renco Group Inc. 609
The Rockefeller Foundation 350
Royster-Clark, Inc. 614
The SF Holdings Group, Inc. 623
Shearman & Sterling 624
Sithe Energies, Inc. 628
Skadden, Arps, Slate, Meagher & Flom LLP 372
The Structure Tone Organization 633
Sunbelt Beverage Corporation 634
Teachers Insurance and Annuity Association - College Retirement Equities Fund 390
Time Warner Entertainment Company, L.P. 640
Tishman Realty & Construction Co. Inc. 641

Transammonia, Inc. 643
The Trump Organization 402
White & Case LLP 665

Purchase
Central National-Gottesman Inc. 477
MasterCard Incorporated 272

Rego Park
The Lefrak Organization 248

Rochester
Agrilink Foods, Inc. 443
Empire Beef Company, Inc. 506
University of Rochester 653
Wegmans Food Markets, Inc. 663

Ronkonkoma
Quality King Distributors Inc. 605

Rye Brook
Parsons & Whittemore, Incorporated 594

Schenectady
The Golub Corporation 522
New York State Lottery 318
Schenectady International, Inc. 618

Staten Island
Advance Publications, Inc. 40

Syracuse
Carrols Corporation 474

Tarrytown
Westcon Group, Inc. 664

Uniondale
Arbor Commercial Mortgage, LLC 453

Westbury
Darby Group Companies, Inc. 491

Westfield
National Grape Cooperative Association, Inc. 580

White Plains
Power Authority of the State of New York 600

Whitestone
Kinray Inc. 554

Woodbury
Levitz Home Furnishings, Inc. 559

Yonkers
Consumers Union of United States, Inc. 116

NORTH CAROLINA
Asheboro
Klaussner Furniture Industries, Inc. 555

Cary
SAS Institute Inc. 617

Chapel Hill
The University of North Carolina at Chapel Hill 652

Charlotte
Baker & Taylor Corporation 458
Belk, Inc. 68
GS Industries, Inc. 528
Hendrick Automotive Group 533
National Gypsum Company 580

Durham
Kerr Drug, Inc. 552

Gastonia
Parkdale Mills, Inc. 593

Hickory
Alex Lee, Inc. 445

Huntersville
Heafner Tire Group, Inc. 532

Raleigh
CARQUEST Corporation 474
General Parts, Inc. 518
Investors Management Corp. 546
North Carolina Electric Membership Corporation 585
Variety Wholesalers, Inc. 656

Rocky Mount
MBM Corporation 568

Trinity
Sealy Corporation 621

Winston-Salem
National Textiles, L.L.C. 581
Novant Health, Inc. 587

OHIO
Akron
Republic Engineered Products LLC 609

Archbold
Sauder Woodworking Co. 617

Cincinnati
Catholic Healthcare Partners 475
CFM International, Inc. 478
Eagle-Picher Industries, Inc. 504
Formica Corporation 514
Ohio National Financial Services 589
The Union Central Life Insurance Company 648

Cleveland
International Management Group 216
Jones, Day, Reavis & Pogue 549
Noveon International, Inc. 587
Ohio Lottery Commission 589

Columbus
Battelle Memorial Institute 64
Borden Chemical, Inc. 466
Nationwide 310
The Ohio State University 328
OhioHealth 589

Safelite Glass Corp. 615
Schottenstein Stores
  Corporation 619
Dayton
Primus, Inc. 602
Elyria
Spitzer Management, Inc. 630
Findlay
Findlay Industries, Inc. 511
Marathon Ashland Petroleum
  LLC 564
Hilliard
Micro Electronics, Inc. 574
Hiram
Great Lakes Cheese Company,
  Inc. 525
Kent
Carter Lumber Company 475
Mayfield Heights
NESCO, Inc. 583
New Bremen
Crown Equipment
  Corporation 489
Newark
The Longaberger Company 562
Parma
Marc Glassman Inc. 565
Solon
Swagelok Company 635
Valley City
MTD Products Inc. 578
Westfield Center
Ohio Farmers Insurance
  Company 588
Westlake
TravelCenters of America,
  Inc. 643
Youngstown
The DeBartolo Corporation 130

OKLAHOMA
Oklahoma City
Express Personnel Services 509
Hobby Lobby Stores, Inc. 535
Tulsa
Hale-Halsell Co. 530
QuikTrip Corporation 606
Rooney Brothers Company 612

OREGON
Dillard
Roseburg Forest Products
  Co. 613
Klamath Falls
JELD-WEN, inc. 547
Portland
Bonneville Power
  Administration 465

Columbia Forest Products
  Inc. 484
Hampton Affiliates 530
Hoffman Corporation 536
KinderCare Learning Centers,
  Inc. 553
North Pacific Group, Inc. 586
R. B. Pamplin Corp. 607
Prineville
Les Schwab Tire Centers 559
Salem
Colson & Colson Construction
  Company 484
Holiday Retirement Corp. 536

PENNSYLVANIA
Altoona
Sheetz, Inc. 624
Blue Bell
Henkels & McCoy, Inc. 534
Danville
Geisinger Health System 517
East Greenville
Knoll, Inc. 555
Eighty Four
84 Lumber Company 438
Harrisburg
D&H Distributing Co., Inc. 491
Horsham
Penn Mutual Life Insurance
  Co. 595
Malvern
The Vanguard Group, Inc. 656
Middletown
The Pennsylvania Lottery 596
Newtown Square
Catholic Health East 100
Philadelphia
Berwind Group 462
Conrail Inc. 487
The Day & Zimmermann Group,
  Inc. 493
Rosenbluth International 352
The University of
  Pennsylvania 652
Pittsburgh
Dick Corporation 498
Giant Eagle Inc. 166
Highmark Inc. 202
Koppers Industries, Inc. 556
University of Pittsburgh of the
  Commonwealth System of
  Higher Education 652
Radnor
Superior Group, Inc. 634
Reading
Boscov's Department Stores 466
EnerSys Inc. 507
Penske Truck Leasing 596

Robesonia
Associated Wholesalers, Inc. 456
Trevose
The Faulkner Organization 510
University Park
The Pennsylvania State
  University 596
Wawa
Wawa, Inc. 662
Wayne
Lumbermens Merchandising
  Corporation 563
West Conshohocken
Keystone Foods LLC 552
Willow Grove
Asplundh Tree Expert Co. 455
York
Graham Packaging Holdings
  Company 525

PUERTO RICO
San Turce
Puerto Rico Electric Power
  Authority 603

RHODE ISLAND
Johnston
FM Global 513
Lincoln
Amica Mutual Insurance
  Company 450
Providence
Gilbane, Inc. 520
Warren Equities, Inc. 661

SOUTH CAROLINA
Columbia
AgFirst Farm Credit Bank 442
Fort Mill
Muzak LLC 296
Springs Industries, Inc. 376
Greenville
Builder Marts of America,
  Inc. 470
Greenville Hospital System 526
Moncks Corner
South Carolina Public Service
  Authority 629
Spartanburg
Milliken & Company Inc. 288

TENNESSEE
Brentwood
Doane Pet Care Company 499
Cleveland
Life Care Centers of America 560
Collegedale
McKee Foods Corporation 569

Belk, John M. 68, 69
Belk, John R. 68, 69
Belk National Bank 68
Belk, Sarah 68
Belk, Thomas M., Jr. 69
Belk, Tim 68
Belk, Tom 68
Belk, William Henry 68
Belk, William Henry, Jr. 68
Bell, Alan J. 516
Bell, Alexander Graham 174, 304
Bell, Andrew 146
Bell Atlantic 657
Bell, Bonnie 639
Bell Canada Enterprises. *See* BCE
Inc.
Bell, Ernie 429
Bell Markets 434
Bell, Michael A. 331
Bellco Health Corporation 462
Bellcore research consortium 366
Bellevue Hospital Center 314, 315
Bellow, Saul 416, 467
BellSouth Corporation 445, 482
Belmont Industries 258
Belmont Plaza shopping center
(Youngstown, OH) 130
Beloved (movie) 184, 185
Bemburg fabrics 289
Bemis, Dennis 592
Ben Arnold-Sunbelt Beverage 634
Ben E. Keith Company 462
Benac, William P. 235
Benanav, Gary G. 316
Benchmark Insurance Company 61
Bendix Corporation 240
Benedict, Vincent 534
Benedictine Sisters of Mother of
God Monastery (Watertown,
SD) 103
Benjamin, Harvey E. 301
Benn, Nathan 484
Bennack, Frank A., Jr. 194, 195
Benne, Paul 601
Bennett, Clive 173
Bennett, Edgar 177
Bennett, Lerone, Jr. 223
Bennett, Paul B. (New York Stock
Exchange) 321
Bennett, Paul (Utility Trailer
Manufacturing) 655
Bennett, Tim 185
Bennett, William 236
Bennigan's restaurants 282, 283
Benson, Donald T. 572
Bensonhurst Co-op (Brooklyn
NY) 249
Bentas, Lily Haseotes 489
Bentley Health Care 577
Benton & Bowles Advertising 146
Benton, William (Benton & Bowles
Advertising) 146
Benton, William (Muzak) 296
Benzel, Craig 177
Benzer, Jody 155
Benzing, William 208
Berardy, Ricky 617
Berberian Enterprises, Inc. 409

Berden, Robert J. 323
Berg, Don 247
Berg Electronics 200
Berg, Thomas G. 451
Bergdorf Goodman department
stores 88
Bergen Brunswig Drug Company.
See AmerisourceBergen
Corporation
Bergen, David G. 251
Berger, Jeff H. 67
Beringer Blas Wine Estates 582
Beringer Wine Estates
Holdings 398
Berkeley building (New York
City) 196
Berkeley, Edmund 214
Berkshire Hathaway Inc. 230, 286,
593
Berkshire Life Insurance Company
of America 180, 181
Berkshire Partners 516, 537, 654
Berlin, Richard 194
Berman, Harris A. 646
Bermingham, Robert P. 435
Bernanke, Ben S. 157
Bernard M. Baruch College 109
Bernard, Richard P. 321
Bernhard, Alexander 83
Bernstein, Alison R. 163
Bernstein, Dale B. 321
Bernstein, Richard A. 606
Berresford, Susan V. 162, 163
Berro, Edward 531
Berry, G. Dennis 125
Berry, L. Wilson 290
Berry, William E. 532
Bertelsmann AG 40, 195
Berube, S. Neal 455
Berwind Group 462
Besnier Group 226
Bessler, Joni 81
Best Buy stores 479, 506
Best Buys for Your Home
(book) 117
Best Choice brands 60, 61
Betadine antiseptic 604
Bethlehem Steel Corporation 352
Betrix 258
Betsch, Philip 548
Better Baked Pizza 364
Better Brands (liquors) 670
Better Business Bureau 164
Bettman, Gary B. 306
Betty Boop lottery game 567
Bevans, Patty 479
Beverage Mart liquor stores 511
Beverly Hills Hotel 461
Beverly, W. Michael 55
Beyda, Daniel 321
Beyster, J. Robert 366
The BFGoodrich Company. *See*
Goodrich Corporation
B.G. Sulzle, Inc. 263
BG Wholesale. *See* Houchens
Industries Inc.
Bhatia, Donna 423
Bianchi, Renee 589

BIB Holdings 474
Bible, Michael 519
Bichel, Susan 526
Bienen, Henry S. 324
Bies, Susan Schmidt 157
Big 4 lottery game 596
Big Bear Farm Stores 400
"Big Blue". *See* International
Business Machines Corporation
Big Bonus Bucks lottery game 397
The Big Bopper (performer) 158
Big Brothers/Big Sisters of
America 412, 413
The Big Dig. *See* Central Artery
Tunnel (Boston)
Big Flower Holdings. *See* Vertis Inc.
Big Game Lottery 318, 567, 574,
658
BIG Internet search engine 146
Big Mac sauce 168
Big Sister (pudding) 226
Big Spin (TV show) 472
Big V Supermarkets, Inc. 428
Big Y Foods, Inc. 91, 401, 463
Biggs, John H. 390
Bigheart Pipe Line 238
Bignon, Patrick 153
Bill & Melinda Gates Children's
Vaccine Program 70
Bill & Melinda Gates
Foundation **70-71**
Bill Blass Ltd. 463
Bill Heard Enterprises 463
Bilous, O. B. 370
bin Laden family 98, 99
Bingham, Hiram 304
Binion, Jack B. 538
Binney & Smith, Inc.
(crayons) 182, 183
Bins Transfer & Storage 362
Biography Channel 438
Biography (TV show) 438
Bionaire air purifiers 537
Biondolillo, Michael A. 595
Biosphere 2 114
Birch Telecom Inc. 240, 241
Bird, Larry 300
Birds Eye frozen foods 443
Birky, Timothy D. 175
The Birmingham (Alabama)
News 41
Bisciotti, Steve 445
Bisco Products 140
Bishop, Philip 643
Bizer, Brian 616
biztravel.com 352
Bizzotto, Anita J. 411
BJC Health System 464
BJ's Wholesale Club, Inc. 91
Black & Veatch 464
Black Angus Beef 155, 623
Black Bear deli items 429
Black Book (business
publication) 195
Black, Carole 560
Black, Cathleen P. 195
Black Entertainment Television 300
Black, Leo F. 275

Black, Leon 120
Black, William 244
Black World (magazine) 222
Blackburn, Gene 441
Blackburn, Larry 522
Blackstone Group L.P. 485, 525
Blackwell, Ron 43
Blackwolf Run golf course (Kohler, WI) 243
Blackwood, Len 97
Blagg, Joe W. 405
Blair, Brett 445
Blair, Cary 588
Blake, Ronald L. 591
Blandin, Edwin 549
Blanes, Ana 603
Blanks, Judith Jones 493
Blanks, Marvin 664
Blass, Bill 376
Blaszyk, Michael 104
Bledsoe, Oscar 631
Blickman, Fred 533
Blinn, Mark A. 235
Block, Roger E. 96
Blockbuster Inc. 424, 529, 543
Blockbuster Music 665
Blom, David P. 589
Blom, Roy 59
Bloom, Steven E. 149
Bloomberg L.P. **72-73**
Bloomberg, Michael R. 72, 73
Bloomberg Money (magazine) 72
Bloomberg Personal Finance (magazine) 72
Bloomberg Wealth Manager (magazine) 72
Bloomberg.com 73
Bloomingdale Insane Asylum 114
Bloomingdale's stores 604
Blount, Daniel J. 611
Blue Bunny ice cream 664
Blue Care Elect-Preferred (managed care plan) 77
Blue Care Network (HMO) 78, 79
Blue Choice New England 76, 77
Blue Choice (point of service) 79
Blue Cross and Blue Shield Association **74-75**, 76, 78, 192
Blue Cross and Blue Shield of Massachusetts, Inc. **76-77**
Blue Cross and Blue Shield of Minnesota 74
Blue Cross and Blue Shield of Texas Inc. 192
Blue Cross Blue Shield of Illinois. *See* Health Care Service Corporation
Blue Cross Blue Shield of Michigan **78-79**
Blue Cross Blue Shield of New Mexico 192
Blue Cross of Connecticut 74
Blue Cross of Western Pennsylvania 202
Blue MedSave 79
Blue Ribbon potatoes 227
Blue Shield Association 76
Blue Square-Israel Ltd. 401

Blue Stamps 166
Bluebird juices 512
BlueCard Worldwide (health insurance) 75
BluesCONNECT (health insurance) 74, 75
Bluhm, Neil 548
Bluhm, Nick 97
Blum Capital Partners 398
Blumb, Jeff 177
Blyth, Robert 479
BMS. *See* Bristol-Myers Squibb Company
BMW. *See* Bayerische Motoren Werke
BNY. *See* The Bank of New York Company
Bo-Linn, George 104
Boan, Joseph E. 556
Boater's World Marine Centers 611
Bob Rohrman Auto Group 464
Bobrow, Richard S. 153
Boccardi, Louis D. 58, 59
Bodinger, Bill 554
Bodnar, Anne Donovan 642
Bodzewski, Michael C. 39
Boeckmann, Herbert F., II 517
Boehlert, Thomas 628
The Boeing Company 98, 366, 478, 628, 649, 659
Boggs, Brucie 473
Bohan, Gloria 590
Bohn, Robert D. 55
Bokser, Stephen 498
Bolch, Carl E., Jr. 607
Bold Venture (racehorse) 232
Bolen, Michael D. 568
Boler Company 465
Boler, John M. 465
Boles, John 291
Boll, Maureen E. 285
Bollinger, Lee C. 115
Bolvig, Peter 461
Bomb Pops frozen treats 664
Bon Appetit (magazine) 41
Bon Secours Health System, Inc. 465
Bonaiuto, Paul M. 551
Bonanza Steakhouse 282, 283
Bond, Alex 585
Bond, Ed 626
Bonderman, David "Bondo" 398, 399
Bonds, Barry 260
Bonewell, Linda 597
Bonneville Power Administration 465, 621
Bonno, Anthony J. 331
Bonsall, Mark B. 631
Bonwit Teller department stores 88
Book of Virtues 236
Bookmyer, Joseph R. 351
Books-A-Million, Inc. (bookstores) 451
Booma, Stephen R. 77, 295
Boon, Jonathan 523
Boone National Bank 224
Boone Valley Cooperative 44

Boone's Farm wines 144, 145
Booth Creek Management Inc. 200, 636
Booth Newspapers 40
Booth, Newton 330
Booth, Robert L. 305
Booth, William 358
Booz-Allen & Hamilton Inc. **80-81**
Booz, Allen Applied Research, Inc. 80
Booz, Edwin 80
Boozer, Renea 481
Borden Chemical, Inc. 466
Borden Inc. 126, 127, 240, 241, 466
Borders Group, Inc. 210
Borg-Warner Security 430
Borgardt, Joel 231
Borgata casino (Atlantic City, NJ) 664
Borman, Laurie 349
Borough of Manhattan Community College 109
Boruch, Daniel M. 59
Bos, Jerry 126
Bosch. *See* Robert Bosch GmbH
Boscov, Albert 466
Boscov, Solomon 466
Boscov's Department Stores 466
Bose, Amar G. 82, 83
Bose Corporation **82-83**
Bossman, Lori L. 39
Boston Bruins (hockey team) 306, 307, 494
Boston Capital Corporation 466
Boston Celtics (basketball team) 301
The Boston Consulting Group 467
Boston Marathon (race) 584
Boston Red Sox (baseball team) 261
Boston Roman Catholic archdiocese 56
Boston, Terry 393
Boston University 467
BostonCoach 160
Boswell, John 589
Botch, Jim 633
Bouckaert, Carl M. 461
Bouckaert, Mieke 461
Boudreau, Donald L. 273
Boudreaux, Gail 193
Boulding, Karen 632
Boult, Michael 353
Bounce (magazine) 293
Bounce pet food 265
Bounty candy 265
Bourbeau, Steven 175
Bourland, Ron 639
Bouvier, Robert 213
Bovaird, Orlene 519
Bowdoin, Ann 466
Bowe, William J. 147
Bowen, Charlie 80
Bower, Curtis A. 333
Bower, Marvin 276
Bowles, Crandall Close 376, 377
Bowman Dam 66
Bowyer, Chris 141
Boxall, Lyn 425

Boy Scouts of America 412, 413
Boyd, Bert 401
Boyd, Christopher A. 367
Boyd, Robert 296
Boyd, Willard L. 650
Boyd, William A. 296
Boyden, Brian V. 383
Boyds Bears 183
The Boyds Collection, Ltd. 241
Boyer, Paul 279
Boylan, Christopher P. 285
Boyle, Marsilia 249
Boyle, R. Emmett 591
Boyle, Robert E. 342
Boys, Jack 120, 121
Boys Markets 408
Bozzelli, Richard L. 505
Bozzuto, Adam 467
Bozzuto, Michael A. 467
Bozzuto's Inc. 209, 467
BP Amoco p.l.c. See BP p.l.c.
BP p.l.c. 154, 366, 549
BRACC. See Budget Rent-a-Car
  Corporation
Brackenridge Hospital (Austin,
  TX) 57
Bradco Supply Corporation 468
Braddock, David L. 543
Bradley, Karen 584
Bradley, Rickford D. 482
Brady, Patricia 421
Brady, Rodney H. 496
Bragg, Suzanne 516
Brake Supply Company 555
Brakken, William 557
Brammen, Howie 619
Brancaccio, Marian 201
Brand, Myles 542
Brandon, David A. 138, 139
Brandt, Andrew 176
Brandt, Kate 57
Brandt, Sandy 39
Braniff Airlines 206, 262
Brasfield & Gorrie, LLC 468
Brasfield, Thomas C. 468
Brasher, Paul V. 345
Brass Bell Bakery 546
Brasuell, Tom 261
Bravman, John 381
Bravo, Charles E. 411
Braxton 132
Breakstone's butter 127
Breco Holding 434
BREED Technologies, Inc. (air
  bags) 468
Brehm, Leonard 173
Breit, Martha 233
Brekkies pet food 265
Bremer, John M. 322
Bren, Donald L. 218, 219
Brenk, Jim 556
Brennan, Edward J. 497
Brennan, John J. 656
Brennan, Kevin 517
Brenneman, Bradley F. 431
Brennen, Susan 560
Brenninkmeyer, Hans 449
Breslin, Brian 279

Bress, Joseph M. 309
Bretthauer, Vicki 497
Brettingen, Tom 59
Brewington, Edward L. 553
Brezenoff, Stanley 314
Briar Hall Country Club (NY) 403
Brick, Kathryn 654
Bride's (magazine) 41
Bridge Information Systems,
  Inc. 72
Bridgestone Corporation 532, 549
Bridgewater Farms frozen
  foods 484
Bridgnell, Chris 531
Bridport plc 262, 263
Briggs, Bob (Carlson Wagonlit) 96
Briggs, John 541
Briggs, Paul 473
Briggs, Robert E. (Kaiser
  Foundation Health) 229
Briggs-Weaver (industrial
  equipment) 616
Brinckerhoff, A. C. 408
Brinkerhoff, Leigh 227
Briones Alonso y Martin
  (attorneys) 62
Brisky, Lauren J. 655
Bristol Farms Markets, Inc. 409
Bristol-Myers Squibb Company 140
Bristol West Insurance Group 241
Britannica Book of the Year 146
Britannica First Edition Replica Set
  (encyclopedia) 147
Britannica.com 146
British Broadcasting
  Corporation 134, 135
British Library 114
British Petroleum. See BP p.l.c.
British Telecommunications 201
Britz, Robert G. 321
Broadband Office 150
Broadband Partners 426
Broaddus, J. Alfred 157
Broadnax, Hazel 335
Broadway Stores, Inc. 150
Broadway Television Network 523
Broatch, Robert E. 180
Bröcker, Willem L. J. 345
Brockton Public Market 400
Brodie, Nancy S. 595
Brodish, Jay D. 345
Brodsky, Howard 476
Brodsky, Peter 201
Brody, Paul 545
Brody, William R. 549
Brokke, Gregory D. 341
Bronfin, Kenneth A. 195
Bronx Community College 108, 109
Bronzelite lighting 518
Brooke, Beth A. 153
Brookhaven Country Club
  (Dallas) 110
Brookhaven National
  Laboratories 366
Brookhaven Science Associates 64
Brooklyn College of the City of New
  York 108, 109
Brooklyn Collegiate Center 108

Brooklyn-Port Authority Marine
  Terminal 343
Brooklyn Rapid Transit 284
Brooklyn Staten Island Family
  Health Network 315
Brooks, George H. 421
Brooks, Pammy 41
Brooks, Robert 176
Brookshire Brothers, Ltd. 469
Brookshire, Bruce G. 469
Brookshire Grocery Company 469
Brookshire, Tim 469
Broome, Anne C. 415
Broomell, John 563
Brose, Bryan 510
Brosnan, Timothy J. 261
Brotherhood of All Railway
  Employees 645
Brouillard, Jack C. 191
Broun, Elizabeth 375
Brouse, John S. 203
Brover, Barry 459
Broward General Hospital (Fort
  Lauderdale, FL) 585
Brown & Wood (law firm) 625
Brown Automotive Group Ltd. 469
Brown, Buster 427
Brown, Collin 221
Brown, Dale 574
Brown, Dennis 175
Brown Fintube Company 239
Brown, Fleming & Murray
  (accounting) 152
Brown-Forman Corporation 270,
  479, 521, 670
Brown, G. Michael "Mickey" 268
Brown, George 351
Brown, Gifford E. 141
Brown, Harris, Stevens (real
  estate) 196
Brown, Jack H. (Stater Brothers
  Holdings) 386, 387
Brown, John (Mutual of
  Omaha) 295
Brown, LaRay 314
Brown, Loren 96
Brown, Michael J. 53
Brown, Michele 265
Brown, Paul F. 513
Brown, Richard 533
Brown, Robert T. 384
Brown, Ronald 332
Brown, Sandy J. 309
Brown, Stephen 94
Brown, Tina 40, 194
Brown, Tonya 419
Brown University 328
Brown, Vincent P. 85
Brown, William J. 411
Browne, Joe 302
Browne, Michael 570
Browning, John 112
Bruce, Peter W. 322
Bruce, Tom 605
Bruckmann, Rosser, Sherill &
  Company 499
Bruininks, Robert 651
Brune Reiseburo (travel agency) 96

Charter School USA 237
Chase Capital Partners 216
Chase Manhattan Corporation. See also J.P. Morgan Chase & Company
Chase, Mike 145
Chase-Pitkin Home & Garden Centers 663
The Chauncey Group International 505
Chavez, Lloyd G. 471
Chavez-Thompson, Linda 43
The Cheapest Store on Earth 68
Checker, Chubby 158
Checkerboard animal feeds 92
CheckOut Entertainment Network 434
Cheetah disk drive 369
Chef Boyardee Quality Foods 200
Chef's Choice brands 339
Chef's Express food 428, 429
CHEMCENTRAL Corporation 480
Chemoil Corporation 480
Chemplex Australia Limited 204
Chen, Jerry 371
Chen, Lincoln C. 350
Cheney, Jeffery P. 242
Cheney, Richard 374
Cheong, Thian C. 600
Chernobyl nuclear plant 66
Cherrier, Tita 339
Cherry, Steve 438
Chester Fried Chicken 528
Chevrolet 82, 312, 336, 451, 463, 510, 558, 592, 613, 630
Chevron Corporation. See ChevronTexaco
Chevron Phillips Chemical Company LP 480
ChevronTexaco 204, 290, 352, 480, 534. See also Texaco Inc.
Chevy Nova 312
CHI. See Catholic Health Initiatives
Chi-Chi's Mexican Food 98
Chiasson, William B. 251
Chicago Bears (football team) 302, 303
Chicago Beverage Systems 610
Chicago Blackhawks (hockey team) 307, 667
Chicago Brothers Frozen Pizza 364
Chicago Bulls (basketball team) 301, 667
Chicago Cubs (baseball team) 261
Chicago Cutlery 668
Chicago Medical College 324
Chicago Style Pizza 528
Chicago Sun-Times 402
Chicago Town pizza 364, 365
Chicago Tribune 80, 324, 348
Chicago White Sox (baseball team) 260, 261
Chick-fil-A Inc. 481, 568
Chicken Run (movie) 142, 143
Chicotel, Richard A. 625
Chieftain International 540
Children's Discovery Centers 236
Children's Health Matters 101

Children's Hospital of Austin (TX) 57
China Comfort (travel agency) 352
China Computer Reseller World (magazine) 214
Chippewa Logging 210
Chirico, James M., Jr. 369
Chlada, John 339
Choice Mall Internet 529
Choice Ride insurance program 422
Choquette, Paul J., Jr. 520
Chorengel, Bernd 206
Chou, Rebecca 636
Chow, Dean 617
Chow, Ricky 564
CHR. See C.H. Robinson Worldwide, Inc.
Chris Evert Women and Children's Center (Fort Lauderdale, FL) 585
Christ Medical Center (Chicago) 441
Christenson, Gary 595
Christian Health Systems 464
Christian Science 208
Christians, Raimundo L. M. 345
Christianson, Robert A. 449
Christopher, Doris K. 593
Christus Health 481
Chronicle Publishing 194
Chrysler Corporation 78, 80, 222, 451, 504, 566, 597, 630. See also DaimlerChrysler AG
CHS. See Cenex Harvest States Cooperatives
CHS Cooperatives 154
Chu, Benjamin K. 314
Chu, James 658
Chuck Taylor All Star basketball sneaker 120
The Chunnel 66
Church of Jesus Christ of Latter-Day Saints 204, 496, 546
Church of Scientology 62
Churchfield, John W. 140
Churchill Downs Inc. (race course) 502
Chvala, Vicki L. 49
CHW. See Catholic Healthcare West
CHW Business Services Center 105
C.I. Foods Systems Company, Ltd. 209
Cialone, Henry J. 65
CIBC World Markets 641
CIC International Ltd. 481
Cieza, Pedro 361
Cigarettes Cheaper 482
CIGNA Corporation 248
Cimini, Louis F. 537
Cimino, Jay 597
Cinader, Arthur 546
Cincinnati Bengals (football team) 303
Cincinnati Red Stockings (baseball team) 260
Cincinnati Reds (baseball team) 261
Cinemark, Inc. 482
Cineplex Odeon 562
Cingular Wireless 482

cinven (buyout specialist) 98
CIO (magazine) 214, 215
Ciple, Tim 131
Cipriani, Jack 213
Circuit City Group 506, 594
Circus Circus hotel and casino (Las Vegas) 206
Cirillo, Frank J. 314
Cirrus (ATM network) 272, 273
Cisco Systems, Inc. 216, 217, 244, 378, 496, 515, 664
Cisneros, Sandy 241
Citadel military academy 624
Citicorp Inc. 98, 224
Citicorp Venture Capital, Ltd. 494, 514
Citigroup Inc. 258, 272, 330, 577, 614, 625
Citizen Kane (movie) 194
Citrus World 512
City and Village Mutual Automobile Insurance 382
City College 109
City University Governance and Financing Act (1979) 108
The City University of New York 108-109
Citystate Holdings 252
Civello, Anthony N. 552
Civil War (TV documentary) 122
Civilian Health and Medical Program for the Uniformed. See CHAMPUS
CK Calvin Klein Jeans 88, 89
cK One fragrance 84-85, 88, 89
Clamato juice 630
Clarent Hospital Corporation 541
Clarity Vision, Inc. 203
Clark, A. James 483
Clark Bar candy 647
Clark Enterprises, Inc. 483
Clark, Gregory J. 237
Clark, Heather 235
Clark, J. Lance 223
Clark, James (Netscape) 380
Clark, Jim (Hunt Consolidated) 540
Clark, Joan 547
Clark Retail Group, Inc. 483
Clark-Schwebel Fiber Glass 376
Clark, Stuart 370
Clark USA (oil refiner) 483
Clarke, James C. 444
Classic Residence by Hyatt (retirement communities) 206, 207
Claus, Christopher W. 423
Clauson, Joe 295
Clay, Don 239
Claypool, Jeffrey C. 621
Clayton, Dubilier & Rice, Inc. (investments) 234, 611, 627
Clean Air Act (1990) 392
Clear Channel Communications, Inc. 150, 200, 296
Clearfield cheese 620
ClearTint dye 289
Cleberg, H. D. "Harry" 154
Clegg, Christopher R. 587

Dahlin, Ross A. 53
The Daiei (retailer) 98
Dailey, John 375
Daily Racing Form
(publication) 122
The Daily Reflector (Greenville,
NC) 125
The Daily Sentinel (Nacogdoches,
TX) 125
Daimler-Benz. *See also*
DaimlerChrysler AG
DaimlerChrysler AG 336, 444, 464,
469, 471, 478, 492, 548, 571, 577,
592, 609, 646, 657. *See also*
Chrysler Corporation
Dairy Farmers of America **126-127**,
246, 491
Dairy Queen 598
Dairylea Cooperative Inc. 491
Dairyman's Cooperative Creamery
Association 246
Daisy Kingdom home
furnishings 377
Dake, William 633
Dakin stuffed animals 406
Dallas Area Rapid Transit 333
Dallas Cowboys (football team) 302,
303
Dallas Mavericks (basketball
team) 301
Dallas Stars (hockey team) 307
Dallas (TV show) 514
Daly, Ann 143
Daly, William 306
Damos, Craig 663
D'Amour, Donald H. 463
D'Amour, Gerald 463
Dana auto parts 474
D&H Distributing Company,
Inc. 491
D'Angelis, Vince 660
D'Angelo Law Library 417
Dangerfield, Dennis 401
Daniel, D. Ronald (Harvard
University) 187
Daniel, Karen 464
Daniel, Ronald (McKinsey &
Company) 276
Daniel, William D. 543
D'Aniello, Daniel A. 98, 99
Danish Creamery Association 472
Danish, Tom 53
Danly Die Set 486
Dan's Supreme Supermarkets,
Inc. 455
Dapsco 602
Darby Drug 491
Darby Group Companies, Inc. 491
Darby-Spencer-Mead Dental
Supply 491
Darcars 492
Darcy, Thomas E. 366
Darden Restaurants, Inc. 568
Darling, Bruce B. 415
Darman, Richard 98
Darnell, Lindsey G. 175
Dart Container
Corporation **128-129**

Dart Energy 128
Dart, Hilary 89
Dart, Kenneth B. 128, 129
Dart, Robert C. 128, 129
Dart, Tom 128
Dart, William A. 128
Dart, William F. 128
Darvish, John R. 492
Darwin Magazine 215
Dassault Aviation 659
Data Broadcasting Corporation 296
Datatec Ltd. 664
DataThing office furniture 189
D'Atri, Justin W. 609
Datz, Linda 557
Daugherty, Arthur 202
Daugherty, Bob 345
Daugherty, Susan 619
Daugherty, Tim R. 155
Daughters of Charity Health Center
(New Orleans) 57
Daughters of Charity National
Health System 56, 102
Daughters of Charity, Province of
the West 104, 105
Dauk, Regis A. 578
Davatzes, Nickolas 438
Davco, Inc. (engine accessories) 337
Davel Communications Group,
Inc. 151
Davenport, Margaret 522
Daverse, Chris 371
David and Lisa (movie) 185
David, Doug 586
David L. Babson & Company,
Inc. 270, 271
The David Leadbetter Golf
Academy 217
David McDavid Auto Group 492
David Sarnoff Research Center 378
David Weekley Homes 492
David Wilson's Automotive
Group 493
Davidowski, Ronald 500
Davids Ltd. 209
Davidson, Sheila K. 317
Davidson, William 178
Davies, David 634
Davis, Alfred 579
Davis, D. James 178
Davis, Donald E. 556
Davis, J. B. 555
Davis, Jacob 250
Davis, James S. (New Balance
Athletic Shoe) 584
Davis, Jay M. 579
Davis, Jim (Allegis) 445
Davis, Joseph D. 219
Davis, Leonard 36
Davis, Melissa D. 641
Davis, Nancy 561
Davis, Richard 348
Davis, Robert G. 422
Davis, Stan 51
Davis Vision, Inc. 203
Davis, W. Stewart 526
Davisson, Bill 527
Dawn Food Products, Inc. 493

Dawson Home Fashions 376
The Day & Zimmermann Group,
Inc. 493
Day, Randy 339
Day, Thomas G. 411
DaySpring (greeting cards) 182,
183
Daytime cable network 560
Dayton (Ohio) *Daily News* 124, 125
DB Capital Partners 587
DDB Needham Worldwide
(advertising) 318
De Beers (diamonds) 669
de Goya y Lucientes, Francisco
José 170
De Luca (entree maker) 338
de Marillac, Louise (Saint) 56
de Munnik, Hans 244
De Paul, Vincent (Saint) 56
De Santi, Dan 213
De Stigter, Glen H. 663
Deal Me In lottery game 397
Dean, Donna J. 350
Dean Foods Company 126, 246
Dean, Lloyd H. 104
The DeBartolo
Corporation **130-131**
DeBartolo, Edward J., Jr. 130
DeBartolo, Edward J., Sr. 130
DeBartolo Entertainment 130
DeBartolo Realty 130
Deberry, Herb 579
DeBiasi, Glenn 445
DeBruce Grain, Inc. 494
DeBruce, Paul 494
DeBruce Transportation 494
DeCarlo, Anthony J. 563
Dechant, Tim 433
Decker, Harold 51
Decker, Michael B. 431
DeCotiis, Michael R. 343
Dedman, Robert H., Jr. 110, 111
Dedman, Robert H., Sr. 110
Deep-Er Discount stores 565
Deep Impact (movie) 142, 143
Deep Sleep mattresses 626
Deep Woods OFF repellents 361
Deering Harvester 288
Deering, William 288
DeFabis, Mike 60
Defender handgun 112
Defense Advanced Research Projects
Agency 370
DeFrancesco, Andrew P. 531
DeFrancisco, Margaret R. 318
Defratus, Kellie 500
DEG Acquisitions 501
DeGiovanni, Frank F. 163
DeGregorio, Bob 247
DeJoria, John Paul 549
Del Monte Foods Company 398,
399
Del Taco restaurants 614
Del Vecchio, Claudio 610
Delaney, Dennis 211
Delark, Robert 534
Delaware North Companies
Inc. 494

GQ (magazine) 41
Grab-It cleaning cloths 360, 361
Graber Industries (window
   furnishings) 376, 377
Grabow, Karen 247
Grady, Daniel A. 83
Graff-Riccio, Rhona 403
Graham Packaging Company,
   L.P. 525
Graham School of General
   Studies 417
Graham, Wallace A. 618
Grain Charitable Foundation 459
Grain Terminal Association 106
Gramlich, Edward M. 157
Granaria Holdings 504
Grand America Hotel 627
Grand Central Terminal 284
Grand Coulee Dam 228
Grand Hyatt Hotel (New York
   City) 402
Grand Metropolitan. *See* Diageo plc
Grand Pequot Tower hotel
   (Connecticut) 268, 269
Grand Rental Station 404, 405
The Grand Union Company 90
Grand Victoria (riverboat
   casino) 206
GrandMet. *See* Diageo plc
Granik, Russell T. 301
Granny's Buffet 470
Granoff, Marty 581
Granoff, Michael 581
Grant, Alexander 172
Grant, Jodi 634
Grant, Joseph 335
Grant Thornton
   International **172-173**, 344
Granville, Irwin 249
Grassilli, Diane 104
Grasso, Richard A. 320, 321
Grauer, Peter T. 73
Graves, Howard D. 394, 395
Gray, Elisha 174
Gray-Felder, Denise 350
Gray, Hanna Holborn 416
Gray, Herb 439
Gray, Robert C. 203
Graybar Electric Company,
   Inc. **174-175**
Gray's Anatomy (book) 147
Greaney, Dennis 266
Great American Foods 106
Great American Management
   Investment Inc. 150
Great American Smokeout 46, 47
*Great Books of the Western
   World* 146, 147, 416
Great Cedar Hotel
   (Connecticut) 268, 269
Great Dane Limited
   Partnership 525
Great Lakes Cheese Company,
   Inc. 491, 525
Great Lakes Chemical
   Corporation 204
Great North Foods 209
Great Starts frozen foods 598

Great Western Railway 132
GreatLand Insurance 231
Grebe, Michael J. 545
Grede Foundries, Inc. 526
Grede, William 526
Green, Barbara 535
Green Bay Machinery 620
Green Bay Packaging Inc. 526
The Green Bay Packers, Inc.
   (football team) **176-177**, 302, 303
Green Bay (Wisconsin) *Press-
   Gazette* 176
Green, David 535
Green, Jeffrey S. 343
Green, Lorraine A. 309
Green Revolution 350
Green Stamps 166, 346
Greenberg, Alan 476
Greenberg, Andrew 523
Greenberg, Shel 349
Greenblatt, Sherwin 82
Greene, James H., Jr. 241
Greenough, William 390
Greenspan, Alan 156, 157, 584
Greenville Hospital System 526
Greenwich Marine 93
Greer, Ray E. 377
Gregg, Donna 123
Gregg, Elaine 449
Gregg Foods 106
Gregg, Gary R. 253
Gregory, Stephen 451
Greig, Andy 67
Grela, Peter 576
Grelle, John K. 647
Grenex (magnetic media) 368
Gresh, Marlene 605
Gretzky, Wayne 216, 217, 306
Grewcock, Bruce E. 341
Grey Advertising 318
Grief, Gary 396
Grier, Roosevelt "Rosie" 596
Griffin, David 632
Griffin, John 304
Griffin, Lester J., Jr. 646
Griffin, Merv 402
Griffin Pipe Products 451
Griffith, Elizabeth A. 123
Griffith, Ray A. 39
Griffiths, John 132
Griffiths-Kerr 376
Griffy, Timothy T. 153
Grigaliunas, Ben 441
Grimes, Don 208
Grimes, Frank 208
Grimmer, Ralph 291
Grimshaw, James A. 175
Grindle, J. William 175
Gristede's Foods, Inc. 608
Groce, Greg 59
Groceries On The Go service 460
The Grocers Supply Company,
   Inc. 527, 528
Grocery Supply Company Inc. *See*
   GSC Enterprises, Inc.
Grode, George F. 203
Groebe, Louis 208
Grolsch beer 630

Grooms, Sharon 539
Gross, Mark 91
Grossberg, Andy 543
Grossman, Ian 401
Grossman, Lawrence S. 498
Grossman, Steven M. 606
Grosvenor, Gilbert M. 304
Grosvenor, Gilbert Melville 304
Grosvenor, Melville Bell 304
Grottke, Robert 208
Ground Zero 342
Group Health Cooperative of Puget
   Sound 228, 527
Groupe, Grupo, Gruppo. *See entry
   under primary company name*
The Grove Park Inn Resort
   (Asheville, NC) 616
Groveman, Michael 463
Grower's Pride juices 512
GROWMARK, Inc. 477, 527
GrowMaster Crop Services 629
Grubb, David H., Sr. 636
Grubbs, Walter 659
Gruber, Thomas 101
Gruen, Frank 529
Gruner + Jahr AG & Company
   (publisher) 195
Gruosso, Gerard 438
Grupe, Steve 235
GS Industries, Inc. 528
GSC Enterprises, Inc. 528
Gsell, Starr 579
GTE Corporation 657
GTECH Holdings Corporation 318,
   396
GU Markets 90
Guardia, Luis 123
Guardian Baillie Gifford, Ltd. 181
Guardian Industries
   Corporation **178-179**, 470
The Guardian Life Insurance
   Company of America **180-181**
Guardian Royal Exchange plc 252
Gubanich, Kathleen C. 656
Guckian, James C. 418
Guerra, Frank F. 361
Guess? 640
Guest, James 116
Guge, Brett 472
Guggenheim Museum (New York
   City) 248
Guide to Baby Products (book) 117
Guide to Health Care for Seniors
   (book) 117
Guido, Bob 39
Guido, Nick 40
Guinness PLC 641
Gulf Oil Limited Partnership 528
Gulf Oil, L.P. 366, 489
Gulf + Western Industries 538
Gulf States Toyota, Inc. 529
Gulfstream Aerospace
   Corporation 659
Gunn, David L. 309
Gunton, Howard E. 271
Gupta, Rajat 276, 277
Gurtner, William H. 415
Guth, Bill 529

Horner, Matina S. 391
Hornsby, John 111
Hornsby's Pub Draft Cider 145
Horsehead Industries Inc. 538
Horseless Carriage restaurant 517
Horseshoe Gaming Holding
 Corporation 538
Horton, Daniel E. 361
Horvath, James J. 448
Horvath, Peter 605
Hosokawa, Koichi 554
Hospital Building & Equipment 532
Hospital Corporation of America.
 See HCA, Inc.
Hospital Services Corporation 192
Host Marriott Corporation 342
Hostos Community College 109
Hot Cherries lottery game 567
Hot Shots lottery game 319
Hotel Bar butter 127
HOTZ sandwiches 606
Hotze, Jim 95
Houchens, Ervin 539
Houchens Industries Inc. 539
Houdaille Industries 240
Houghton, Amory 140
Houghton Mifflin (publisher) 348
Hourigan, Michael P. 299
House & Garden (magazine) 41
House Beautiful (magazine) 195
HouseCalls grocery service 522
Household Finance 503
Housemart.com 635
Houston Astros (baseball team) 261
Houston Chronicle 194, 195
Houston Comets (basketball
 team) 301
Houston, Marc 448
Houston Oilers (football team) 302
Houston Rockets (basketball
 team) 301
Houston Texans (football
 team) 302, 303
Hovde, Rob 613
*How to Plan for a Secure
 Retirement* (book) 117
Howard, Norm 433
Howard the Duck (movie) 257
Howard's On Scholls 409
Howdy Doody (TV show) 264
Howe, Douglas T. 111
Howe, John 404
Howe, Michael W. 446
Howenstine, James D. 405
Howie, Ed 191
Howland Hook Marine
 Terminal 343
Howmet International (aerospace
 castings) 98
Howroyd, Bernard 453
Hoye, Donald J. 404
Hoyle, Mike 453
Hoyler, Geraldine M. 102
HP. *See* Hewlett-Packard Company
H.P. Hood Inc. (dairy) 539
HPHConnect (benefits
 administration) 531
Hsu, Daniel 554

Hsu, Robert C. 331
HT Electric 536
H.T. Hackney Company 539
Huang, Robert 636
Hubbard Broadcasting Inc. 540
Hubbard, Clint 461
Hubbard, Gardiner 304
Hubbard, Sonja Y. 509
Hubbard, Stanley E. 540
Hubbard, Stanley S. 540
Hubbell (electrical supplier) 488
Huber, Hunt & Nichols 541
Huber, Joseph Maria 548
Huber, Raymond A. 167
Huber, Walt 510
HUD. *See* US Department of
 Housing and Urban Development
Hudson-Belk stores 68
Hudson, Betty 305
Hudson cars 220
Hudson County News 540
Hudson, Luanne 561
Hudson News Company 540
Hudson, William L. 369
Huerta, John E. 375
Huerter, M. Jane 294
Hueter, John 100
Huge, Arthur 571
Hughes Aircraft Pension Fund 430
Hughes Electronics 540
Hughes, Mark 198
Hughes Markets 386
Hughes, Marvalene 87
Hughes, Robert S., II 445
Hughes, Timothy W. 125
Hui, Lap Shun (John) 506
Huidekoper, Elizabeth 186
Huizenga, H. Wayne 220
Hullibarger, Gail R. 615
Hulme, Howard 547
Hulseman, Leo J. 629
Hulseman, Robert L. 629
Hulsen, Mike 500
Human Genome Center 381
Humana Inc. 224
Humble Oil of Texas 232
Humboldt State University 86, 87
Hummel, Joseph W. 229
HUMMER vehicle 609
Humphrey, James E. 52
Humphrey, Stephen M. 611
HUMVEE vehicle 609
Hungerford, Henry James 374
Hungry Man frozen dinners 598
Hungry Minds (publishing) 214
Hunt Consolidated Inc. (holding
 company) 540
Hunt Construction Group 541
Hunt Corporation (office
 supply) 462
Hunt, Derald 549
Hunt, H. L. 540
Hunt Investment Group L.P. 609
Hunt, Jack 232, 233
Hunt, Ray L. 540
Hunt Realty Corporation 551
Hunt, Robert G. 541
Hunt, Woody L. 418

Hunter College 108, 109
Hunter, W. K. 208
Huntington, Susan L. 328
Huntsman, Blaine 204
Huntsman Cancer Institute 204
Huntsman Chemical Company 204
Huntsman Corporation **204-205**
Huntsman, Jon Meade, Jr. 205
Huntsman, Jon Meade, Sr. 204, 205
Huntsman, Peter R. 204, 205
Hurd Millwork (windows) 647
Hurdman Cranstoun
 (accounting) 244
Huskins, Keith G. 581
Husky Injection Molding Systems
 Ltd. 599
Hussein, King of Jordan 274
Hutchings, Richard S. 361
Hutchins, Robert Maynard 162, 416
Hutchinson, R. Kenneth 651
Huth, Johannes 241
Hutterly, Jane M. 361
Hutton, Richard E. 427
Huxley, Thomas Henry 146
Huzl, James F. 533
H.Y. Louie (company) 209
Hy-Vee, Inc. 401, 541
Hyatt Corporation **206-207**, 262
Hyatt Regency hotel 182, 633
Hyde, Charles 541
Hylbert, Paul 557
Hyman, Steven 187
Hynes, Toby 529
Hynix Semiconductor Inc. 370, 371
Hypnotic (animation) 236
Hytec plumbing products 242
Hyundai Electronics Industries
 Company, Ltd. *See* Hynix
 Semiconductor
Hyundai Motor Company 464, 504,
 535, 597, 646

I

I. & J. Foods Australia 226
I Can Cope cancer support 47
Iafrate, Angelo E., Sr. 452
The Iams Company (pet foods) 116
Iapalucci, Samuel H. 478
IASIS Healthcare Corporation 541
IB Trader Workstation software 545
IBANCO 424
Ibero-American Media Partners 201
IBM. *See* International Business
 Machines Corporation
IBP, Inc. 506, 636
Ibsen, Greg 227
Icahn, Carl 439
ICC Industries Inc. 542
Ice Capades 282
Ice Follies 158
ICI. *See* Imperial Chemical
 Industries
iColt (smart guns) 112
ICON Health & Fitness, Inc. 542
ICX (trucking) 262
IDC Research Group 214, 215
Ideas Publishing Group, Inc. 40
IDEX Corporation (pumps) 241

International Harvester. *See*
Navistar International Corporation
International Hockey League 307
International Home Foods 200, 201
International Labor Organization
Conference 312
International Management
Group **216-217**
International Multifoods
Corporation 44
International Olympics
Committee 217
International Organization of
Consumers Unions 116
International Outdoor
Advertising 201
International Paper Company 461,
477
International Performance
Institute 217
International Planned Parenthood
Federation 70, 71
International Red Cross and Red
Crescent Movement 50
International Rock and Roll Hall of
Fame and Museum
(Cleveland) 216
International Specialty Products
Inc. 520
International Speedway 336
International Telecommunications
Satellite Organization. *See* Intelsat,
Ltd.
International Telephone and
Telegraph. *See* ITT Industries
International Tuberculosis
Foundation 71
International Vaccine Institute 70,
71
International Wire Holdings
Corporation 201
International YMCA Training
School 300
Internet Commerce Expo
(ICE) 214, 215
Intertrade (feed broker) 338
Interval Research 426
Intracoastal Health System (West
Palm Beach, FL) 101
Intuitive Surgical, Inc. (non-invasive
surgery) 378, 379
Inverrary Country Club
(Florida) 111
Investcorp 626
Investors Management
Corporation 546
Iowa Beef Processors. *See* IBP, Inc.
Ippolito, Gary 145
iPrint.com 234
Ira Higdon Grocery Company 209
Iris Power Engineering, Inc. 239
Irish, Charles 665
Irish, George B. 195
Iron Skillet restaurants 597
Ironman watches 640
Irresistible Ink (handwriting
service) 183

IRS. *See* US Internal Revenue
Service
Irvine Apartment
Communities 218, 219
Irvine, Athalie 218
The Irvine Company Inc. **218-219**
Irvine Foundation 218
Irvine, James 218
Irvine, James, II 218
Irvine, James, III 218
Irvine, Joan 218
Irvine, Myford 218
Irving, John 650
Isakow, Selwyn 592
ISD/Shaw (consulting) 152
Ishii, Kanji 313
The Island ECN 298, 320
Island of Misfit Toys (video) 523
ISTV prison buses 577
Isuzu Motors Limited 116, 464,
478, 624, 660
Italianni's restaurants 94, 95, 96
ITcareers.com 214
ITCO Tire (distributor) 430
Itel 150
ITOCHU Corporation 208, 480
ITT Industries, Inc. 282
ITW. *See* Illinois Tool Works Inc.
iVAST, Inc. (broadband) 427
Iverson, Mark 539
Ives, Nancy J. 421
iVillage Inc. 124, 194, 195
Ivy League 114, 186, 488, 602, 652

J

J. Crew Group, Inc. 398, 399, 546
J. Sosnick and Son 408
Jablonowski, Bill 39
Jack Daniel's whiskey 270, 479
Jack Purcell shoes 120
Jackson, Andrew 410
Jackson, Danny 411
Jackson, Gregory A. 417
Jackson, Jesse 434
Jackson, JoAnne G. 649
Jackson, Kathryn J. 393
Jackson, Mike 370
Jackson, Robert T. 448
Jackson, Stu 301
Jackson, Tammy 485
Jackson, Thomas H. 653
Jackson, Walter 146
Jacksonville Jaguars (football
team) 302, 303
Jacob Delafon plumbing
products 242, 243
Jacobellis, Luke 549
Jacobi Medical Center 315
Jacobs, Bruce E. 526
Jacobs, Burleigh 526
Jacobs, Charles 494
Jacobs, Ilene B. 161
Jacobs, Irwin 518
Jacobs, Jeffrey 184, 185
Jacobs, Jeremy M. 494
Jacobs, John H. 647
Jacobs, Louis 494
Jacobs, Marvin 494

Jacor Communications 150
Jaffe, Kineret S. 417
Jaffer, Azeezaly S. 411
Jagtiani, Anil 182
Jaguar Cars Limited 469, 517, 537,
613
Jain, Terri 281
Jakes, John 328
James, Donna A. 311
James Franck Institute 417
James, Lark S. 585
James Monroe apartments (Jersey
City, NJ) 249
James, Reggie 116
James, Sharon L. 421
James Tower (New York City) 249
J&B scotch 595
J&J. *See* Johnson & Johnson
Jane (magazine) 41
The Janet Weis Children's and
Women's Hospital 517
Janeway, Dean 428, 429
Janik, Douglas J. 271
Janitrol air conditioners 522
Janney Montgomery Scott and
Hornor (brokerage) 595
Jannotta, Edgar D. 417
Japan Travel Bureau. *See* JTB
Corporation
Jarreau, Al 650
Jarrett, Dale 579
Jarvis (facilities management) 67
Jarvis, Roger 232
Jasinkiewicz, Ken 429
Jault, Jean-Yves 313
Javaworks brands 455
Jaws (movie) 142
Jay, John 114
J. C. Penney Corporation, Inc. 552,
561
JCPenney stores. *See* J. C. Penney
Corporation, Inc.
JDI office furniture 555
J. E. Dunn Construction 503
JEA 547
Jean, Roger L. 253
Jedelhauser, Lilo 59
Jeep vehicles 451, 504, 566, 630
Jefferson, John 291
Jefferson-Pilot Corporation 270
Jefferson Properties, Inc. *See* JPI
(apartment management)
JELD-WEN, Inc. (building
products) 547
Jeng, Chu-Hui 667
Jeng, Michael 667
Jenifer, Franklyn G. 419
Jenkens, Alison 523
Jenkins, Alan 163
Jenkins, Carlton J. 435
Jenkins, Charles H., Jr. 346, 347
Jenkins, Decosta E. 579
Jenkins, Francis P., Jr. 614
Jenkins, George 346
Jenkins, Howard M. 346, 347
Jennifer Convertibles, Inc.
(furniture stores) 555
Jennings, Brian J. 307

Walton, R. Keith 115
Walton, Robert D. 85
Walton, Sam 166, 224
WAMD (Minneapolis) 540
Wamsutta home furnishings 376,
  377
Wanek, Ron 454
Wanek, Todd 454
Wangurd, Debra 657
WAPE-FM (Jacksonville, FL) 125
Ward, Jim 257
Warden, Gail L. 534
Warden, Michael L. 419
Warden, William G., IV 634
Waremart Foods 667
Warga, Thomas J. 317
Wargo, John R. 411
Waring, Susan D. 383
Warlick, Anderson D. 593
Warlick-Jarvie, Lois 443
Warm, Ira 616
Warm Wishes greeting cards 182
The Warnaco Group, Inc. 88
Warner Brothers 236, 296, 640
Warner Communications. See AOL
  Time Warner Inc.
Warner, H. Ty 407
Warner, John H., Jr. 366
Warner, Ty 406
Warning: Dieting May Be
  Hazardous To Your Health
  (educational video) 117
Waronker, Lenny 143
Warren Equities, Inc. 661
Warren, George E. 519
Warren, V'Ella 653
Warrin, Catherine 462
Warrington, George D. 308, 309
Warwick, Bruce 177
Washington Capitals (hockey
  team) 307
The Washington Companies. See
  Washington Group International,
  Inc.
Washington (DC) Wholesale
  Liquors 479
Washington, Dennis 661
Washington Group International,
  Inc. 661
Washington Mystics (basketball
  team) 301
Washington Redskins (football
  team) 303
Washington University Medical
  Center 464
Washington Wizards (basketball
  team) 300, 301
Wasilov, Alex 353
Wasp II car 262
Wassall PLC 241
Wasson, Ted 666
Waste Control Specialties 487
Watanabe, Toshizo 585
Waterbury Clock 640
Waterhouse, Edwin 344
WaterPik 65
Watkins, H. Thomas 637
Watkins, Lewis 419

Watkins, Paul 558
Watkins, William D. 369
Watsmann, Judy 249
Watson, Anthony L. 533
Watson, Raymond L. 219
Watt Homes 668
Watt, Ray 668
Watterson, Scott R. 542
Watts, Douglas D. 468
Watts, Howard 100
Watts, W. David 419
Waugh, Ed 548
Waukesha brand 501
Wausau 310
Wausau Commercial Insurance
  Market 253
Wave radio 82, 83
Wavtrace (wireless access
  equipment) 427
Wax, Charles J. 54
WAXN-TV (Charlotte, NC) 125
Waycaster, Bill W. 639
Wayne Farms, LLC 119
Wayne Foods 118
Wayne State University School of
  Medicine 496, 666
W.B. Place (leather clothing) 508
WBAB-FM (Long Island, NY) 125
WBAL-TV (Baltimore) 194
WBHJ-FM (Birmingham, AL) 125
WBHK-FM (Birmingham, AL) 125
WBLI-FM (Long Island, NY) 125
WBTS-FM (Atlanta) 125
WCI Steel, Inc. 609
WDUV-FM (Tampa, FL) 125
We Care Hair Salons 136
WealthBuilder annuities 522
The Weather Channel 557
Weaver, Lance L. 273
Webb, Del 547
Webb, H. Lawrence 668
Webb, Robert W. 263
Webber, Henry 417
Webcor Builders 663
Weber, Arnold R. 324
Weber, Gregory R. 487
Weber, John H. 504
Weber, Paul 546
Weber, Stephen L. 87
Weber, Tom 601
Webster, Bill 459
Webster, Nancy W. 377
Webster, Steve 617
Webvan 66, 228
The Wedding (movie) 185
WeddingChannel.com 258, 259
WEDR-FM (Miami) 125
Weekley, David 492
Weekly, John W. 294
Weekly, Thomas P. 295
Wegman, John 663
Wegman, Robert B. 663
Wegmans Food Markets, Inc. 663
Wehrle, H. Barnard, III 568
Wehrle, Michael H. 568
Weider Health & Fitness 542
Weiler, Tim 632
Weimer, Linda 421

Weinberg College of Arts and
  Sciences 325
Weinberger, Carlyle 454
Weiner, Beth 565
Weiner, Edward G. 643
Weiner, Steven 379
Weinshilboum, Richard M. 275
Weinstein, David C. 161
Weis Markets, Inc. 401, 455
Weiss, Albert 515
Weiss, Douglas A. 123
Weiss, Hal B. 606
Weiss, Jen 182
Weiss, Louis 428
Weiss, Peck & Greer 634
Weisselberg, Allen 403
Weitz, Charles H. 663
The Weitz Group, LLC 663
Weitzman, Betsy 370
Weizenbaum, Morris 166
Welborn Hospital (Evansville,
  IN) 57
Welch Foods 580
Weldment Fabrication Division 590
Welge, Donald 520
Welge, Michael 520
Welge, Robert 520
Wellcraft boats 518
Weller, Gary L. 592
Weller, H. S. 294
Wellmark Health Networks 192
WellPoint Health Networks Inc. 74
Wells' Dairy, Inc. 664
Wells Fargo & Company 98, 430,
  617
Wells, Fred 664
Wells, Gary M. 664
Wells Lamont Corporation 262, 263
Wells Manufacturing Corporation
  (automotive products) 647
Wells, Norman E., Jr. 348, 349
Welsh, Carson, Anderson &
  Stowe 98
Welsh, George A. 203
Welty, John D. 87
Wendel Investissement 240
Wendell, Beth 525
Wendlandt, Gary E. 316
Wendt, Richard 547
Wendt, Roderick C. 547
Wendy's International, Inc. 598
Wentworth art galleries 160
Wentworth, Gerry 237
Werner, Kevin 367
Werner, Mary Ann 391
Wesendonck, Hugo 180
Wesley, James 560
Weslo fitness equipment 542
West, Bob 629
West Coast Hockey League 307
West Coast Life Insurance 310
West, Henry J. 263
West, Richard P. 87
West, Stephen O. 521
West Texas A&M University 394
West Texas Health Plans, L.C. 193
Westbrock, Leon 107
Westcon Group, Inc. 664

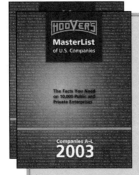